ENCARTA®
ESSENTIAL
THESAURUS

ENCARTA®
ESSENTIAL
THESAURUS

BLOOMSBURY

A BLOOMSBURY REFERENCE BOOK
Created from the Bloomsbury Database of World English

© Bloomsbury Publishing Plc 2002

First published in 2002 by
Bloomsbury Publishing Plc
38 Soho Square
London
W1D 3HB

www.bloomsburymagazine.com

British cataloguing in Publication Data
A CIP record for this book is available from the British Library

ISBN 0 7475 5923 6

10 9 8 7 6 5 4 3 2 1

Typeset by Selwood Systems, Midsomer Norton, Bath, United Kingdom
Printed in Great Britain by Clays Ltd, St Ives plc

Contents

General Editor
Susan Jellis

Editors
David Barnett
Korey Egge
Ros Fergusson
Jennifer Goss Duby
Barbara Kelly
Howard Sargeant

Project Coordinator
David Barnett

Project Assistants
Charlotte Regan
Joel Adams

Proofreaders
Sandra Anderson
Josephine M. P. Curtis
Ruth Hillmore
Susan Turner

Project Manager
Katy McAdam

Production Editor
Nicky Thompson

Database Manager
Edmund Wright

Keyboarders
Simon Arnold
Bernadette Crowley

Design
Nigel Partridge
Nathan Burton

BLOOMSBURY REFERENCE

Editor-in-Chief
Dr Kathy Rooney

Publisher
Nigel Newton

Dictionaries Publisher
Faye Carney

Production Director
Penny Edwards

US General Editor
*Encarta® World
English Dictionary*
Anne H. Soukhanov

How to Use the Thesaurus

The Thesaurus is arranged like a dictionary: you look up an entry word and immediately find alternatives for its common meanings. When there is more than one meaning of a word, each meaning is numbered. The first alternative, printed in **bold**, tells you exactly which meaning is being illustrated. The lists of alternatives are arranged for ease of use, with the more general alternatives towards the beginning of the list.

Alternatives that can be used only in more specific contexts are shown towards the end, often with a label, e.g. *informal* or *literary*, to indicate the type of language they belong to. Words used in informal contexts are labelled *infml* and those used in formal contexts are labelled *fml*.

You will sometimes also be offered words with opposite or contrasting meaning, introduced by the term *Opposite:*

Entry word
for which
alternatives
are given

Part of speech
of entry word

First alternative
indicating the
meaning

Word with
opposite meaning
to entry word

masses *n* **1 common people**, crowd, multitude, commonality, hoi polloi *Opposite*: elite **2** *(infml)* **lots**, loads *(infml)*, tons *(infml)*, heaps *(infml)*, oodles *(infml)*

massif *n* **mountain range**, chain, sierra, ridge, line

massive *adj* **1 bulky**, heavy, solid, weighty, hulking *Opposite*: slight **2 huge**, enormous, gigantic, immense, colossal *Opposite*: tiny

Each meaning
distinguished by
number

Phrases entered
in their alphabetical
place

Label indicating
that entry word
belongs to
informal usage

make a hash of *(infml)* *v* **muddle**, confuse, jumble, spoil, mix up

make allowances *v* **take into account**, bear in mind, consider, take into consideration, allow for

make amends *v* **compensate**, make reparations, make up for, pay back, recompense

At some entries there are also panels listing words that are not alternatives but *types of* the same thing, e.g. types of birds, or names for male or female animals.

---

gender *n* **sex**, sexual category, sexual characteristics, masculinity, femininity

WORD BANK
❏ **types of female animal** bitch, cow, dam, doe, ewe, filly, heifer, hind, jenny, lioness, mare, nanny goat, sow, tigress, vixen
❏ **types of male animal** billy goat, boar, buck, bull, bullock, colt, hart, jackass, ram, stag, stallion, steer, tom, tomcat, wether
❏ **types of male bird or female bird** capon, cob, cock, cockerel, drake, duck, gander, goose, hen, pen, rooster

---

Parts of objects, e.g. parts of an aircraft or the human body, are shown in the same way.

---

alimentary canal *n* **bowels**, guts, innards, insides, intestines

WORD BANK
❏ **parts of an alimentary canal** anus, appendix, bile duct, bladder, bowel, caecum, colon, duodenum, gallbladder, gullet, gut, intestine, kidney, large intestine, liver, oesophagus, pancreas, rectum, small intestine, spleen, stomach, throat

---

The notes shown after some entries help to discriminate between the meanings of closely related words by giving brief definitions for them.

---

accomplish *v* **achieve**, attain, realize, carry out, pull off *(infml)*

COMPARE AND CONTRAST CORE MEANING: bring something to a successful conclusion
accomplish succeed in doing something; **achieve** succeed in something, usually with effort; **attain** reach a specific objective; **realize** fulfil a specific vision or plan; **carry out** perform or accomplish a task or activity; **pull off** *(infml)* accomplish something, despite difficulties.

Test Your Word Power

Once – as a child – you were an expert, an accomplished virtuoso, at learning new words. Today, by comparison, you are a mere amateur.

Does this statement sound insulting? It may be – but if you are the average adult, it is a statement that is, unfortunately, only too true.

Educational testing indicates that children of ten who have grown up in families in which English is the mother tongue have recognition vocabularies of over twenty thousand words – *and that these same ten-year-olds have been learning new words at a rate of many hundreds a year since the age of four.* In astonishing contrast, studies show that adults who are no longer at school increase their vocabularies at a pace slower than twenty-five to fifty words annually.

So how do you assess your own vocabulary?

A Test of Vocabulary Range

Here are some brief phrases, each containing one word in *italics*; your task is to find the closest alternative definition for each italic word. To keep your score valid, avoid making wild guesses. The key to the correct answers will be found at the end of the test.

1. to *parry* a blow is to...
   (a) fend it off
   (b) fear it
   (c) expect it
   (d) invite it
   (e) ignore it

2. a *prevalent* disease is...
   (a) dangerous
   (b) catching
   (c) childhood
   (d) fatal
   (e) widespread

3. an *erudite* person is...
   (a) very wise
   (b) very knowledgeable
   (c) impolite
   (d) serious
   (e) wrong

4. to *supersede* something is to...
   (a) enforce it
   (b) specify penalties for it
   (c) replace it
   (d) repeal it
   (e) continue it

5. an *indefatigable* worker is...
   (a) well-paid
   (b) tired
   (c) skilful
   (d) untiring
   (e) pleasant

6. a *loquacious* person is...
   (a) miserable
   (b) easily annoyed
   (c) indecisive
   (d) good at public speaking
   (e) talkative

7. an *incorrigible* optimist is...
   (a) happy
   (b) impossible to change or reform
   (c) foolish
   (d) hopeful
   (e) unreasonable

8. a notorious *demagogue* is a...
   (a) believer in democracy
   (b) firebrand
   (c) someone who commits fraud
   (d) liar
   (e) spendthrift

9. living in *affluence* involves...
   (a) difficult circumstances
   (b) countrified surroundings
   (c) fear
   (d) wealth
   (e) poverty

10. a *gourmet* is a...
   (a) seasoned traveller
   (b) greedy eater
   (c) vegetarian
   (d) connoisseur of good food
   (e) skilful chef

11. to *simulate* interest is to...
   (a) fake it
   (b) feel it
   (c) lose it
   (d) stir it up
   (e) ask for it

12. a *magnanimous* action is...
   (a) puzzling
   (b) generous
   (c) foolish
   (d) unnecessary
   (e) wise

13. a *clandestine* meeting is...
   (a) prearranged
   (b) hurried
   (c) important
   (d) secret
   (e) public

14. to *vacillate* is to...
   (a) avoid something
   (b) act indecisively
   (c) administer an injection
   (d) treat somebody
   (e) scold somebody

15. a *circumspect* person is...
   (a) restrained
   (b) confident
   (c) cautious
   (d) honest
   (e) intelligent

16. *diaphanous* material is...
   (a) strong
   (b) sheer and gauzy
   (c) colourful
   (d) expensive
   (e) synthetic

17. a *taciturn* host is...
   (a) stingy
   (b) generous
   (c) disinclined to conversation
   (d) charming
   (e) gloomy

18. to *malign* somebody is to...
   (a) accuse somebody
   (b) help somebody
   (c) disbelieve somebody
   (d) denigrate somebody
   (e) introduce somebody

19. a *tendentious* statement is...
   (a) pompous
   (b) biased
   (c) misleading
   (d) formal
   (e) emotional

20. *vicarious* enjoyment is...
   (a) complete
   (b) unspoiled
   (c) experienced by identifying with another person
   (d) long-lasting
   (e) short-lived

21. a *placebo* is...
   (a) a calming drug
   (b) a substance that counteracts a poison
   (c) a drug that has no real effect
   (d) a sleeping pill
   (e) an anti-inflammatory drug

22. an *iconoclastic* attitude is...
   (a) adoring
   (b) sneering at tradition
   (c) troubled
   (d) difficult
   (e) religious

23. a *tyro* is a...
   (a) dominating personality
   (b) beginner
   (c) accomplished musician
   (d) dabbler
   (e) serious student

24. a *laconic* reply is...
   (a) immediate
   (b) assured
   (c) brief
   (d) unintelligible
   (e) angry

25. an *anomalous* situation is...
   (a) dangerous
   (b) intriguing
   (c) uncharacteristic
   (d) pleasant
   (e) unhappy

26. *perspicacity* is...
   (a) sincerity
   (b) astuteness
   (c) love
   (d) faithfulness
   (e) longing

27. an unpopular *martinet* is a...
   (a) candidate
   (b) supervisor
   (c) strict disciplinarian
   (d) military leader
   (e) discourteous snob

28. a *gregarious* person is...
   (a) outwardly calm
   (b) very sociable
   (c) completely untrustworthy
   (d) vicious
   (e) self-effacing and timid

29. an *inveterate* gambler is...
   (a) impoverished
   (b) successful
   (c) hardened
   (d) occasional
   (e) superstitious

30. a *surreptitious* glance is...
   (a) mysterious
   (b) staring
   (c) furtive
   (d) suspicious
   (e) sideways

Key: 1. parry = fend off
      2. prevalent = widespread
      3. erudite = very knowledgeable
      4. supersede = replace
      5. indefatigable = untiring
      6. loquacious = talkative
      7. incorrigible = impossible to change or reform
      8. demagogue = firebrand
      9. affluence = wealth
     10. gourmet = connoisseur of good food
     11. simulate = fake
     12. magnanimous = generous
     13. clandestine = secret
     14. vacillate = act indecisively
     15. circumspect = cautious
     16. diaphanous = sheer and gauzy
     17. taciturn = disinclined to conversation
     18. malign = denigrate
     19. tendentious = biased
     20. vicarious = experienced by identifying with another person
     21. placebo = drug with no real effect
     22. iconoclastic = sneering at tradition
     23. tyro = beginner
     24. laconic = brief
     25. anomalous = uncharacteristic
     26. perspicacity = astuteness
     27. martinet = strict disciplinarian
     28. gregarious = very sociable
     29. inveterate = hardened
     30. surreptitious = furtive

Scoring:
Your **score** (one point for each correct choice): _____

The meaning of your score:
0–5:   below average
6–15:   average
16–24:   above average
25–30   excellent

A Test of Verbal Speed

Part 1

In no more than two minutes (time yourself, or have someone time you), decide whether the word in column B has the *same* (or *approximately the same*) meaning as the word in column A; the *opposite* (or *approximately opposite*) meaning; or whether the two words are merely *different*.

Circle **S** for *same*, **O** for *opposite*, and **D** for *different*.

Column A	Column B			
1. sweet	bitter	S	O	D
2. big	threatening	S	O	D
3. danger	peril	S	O	D
4. love	hate	S	O	D
5. stand	rise	S	O	D
6. tree	branch	S	O	D
7. doubtful	certain	S	O	D
8. begin	start	S	O	D
9. strange	familiar	S	O	D
10. male	female	S	O	D
11. powerful	weak	S	O	D
12. beyond	under	S	O	D
13. go	get	S	O	D
14. growl	cry	S	O	D
15. open	close	S	O	D
16. chair	table	S	O	D
17. want	desire	S	O	D
18. idle	working	S	O	D
19. rich	luxuriant	S	O	D
20. building	structure	S	O	D

Part 2

In no more than three minutes (again, time yourself or have someone time you), write down as many *different* words as you can think of starting with the letter D.

Do not use various forms of a word, such as *do, doing, does, done, doer, etc.*

Key: *Part 1:* 1 – O, 2 – D, 3 – S, 4 – O, 5 – S, 6 – D, 7 – O, 8 – S, 9 – O, 10 – O, 11 – O, 12 – D, 13 – D, 14 – D, 15 – O, 16 – D, 17 – S, 18 – O, 19 – S, 20 – S

Part 2: Any English word starting with D is correct unless it is merely another form of a previous word on the list.

Scoring:

Part 1
Score 5 points for each correct answer. Maximum score: 100 points.
Your score on Part 1: _____

Part 2
Score 1 point for each word.
Your score on Part 2: _____

Total score on verbal speed: _____

The meaning of your verbal speed score:
0–50:   below average
51–99:   average
100–149:   above average
150–200:   excellent

A Test of Verbal Responsiveness

Part 1
Write in the blank column B a word starting with the letter P that has the *same*, or *approximately the same*, meaning as the word given in column A:

Example:
look   peer

Remember: Every answer *must* start with the letter P.

Column A	Column B
1. fragrance	_____
2. faultless	_____
3. maybe	_____
4. forgive	_____
5. own	_____
6. likely	_____
7. annoy	_____
8. good-looking	_____
9. suggest	_____
10. choose	_____

Part 2
Write in the blank column B a word starting with the letter G that is *opposite*, or *approximately opposite*, or in *contrast to* the word given in column A.

Example:
stop   go

Remember: Every answer *must* start with the letter G.

Column A	Column B
1. lose	_____
2. innocent	_____
3. specific	_____
4. rough	_____
5. take	_____
6. host	_____

7. cheerful _____
8. clean _____
9. stingy _____
10. clumsy _____

Key:
Part 1: If more than one answer is given, count as correct any word you have written that is the same as any one of the answers.
  1. fragrance = perfume
  2. faultless = perfect
  3. maybe = perhaps, possibly
  4. forgive = pardon
  5. own = possess
  6. likely = probable, possible
  7. annoy = pester
  8. good-looking = pretty
  9. suggest = propose
  10. choose = pick

Part 2: If more than one answer is given, count as correct any word you have written that is the same as any one of the answers.
  1. lose   *Opposite* gain, get
  2. innocent   *Opposite* guilty
  3. specific   *Opposite* general
  4. rough   *Opposite* gentle
  5. take   *Opposite* give
  6. host   *Opposite* guest
  7. cheerful   *Opposite* gloomy, glum
  8. clean   *Opposite* grubby, grimy
  9. stingy   *Opposite* generous
  10. clumsy   *Opposite* graceful

Scoring:
Score Parts 1 and 2 together. Write in the blank the total number of correct responses you gave: ____

The meaning of your verbal responsiveness score:
0–5:   below average
6–10:   average
11–15:   above average
16–20:   excellent

Vocabulary and Success

Now you know where you stand. If you are in the below average or average groups, you must consider, seriously, whether an inadequate vocabulary may be holding you back. If you scored above average or excellent, you have doubtless already discovered the unique and far-reaching value of a rich vocabulary, and you are eager to add still further to your knowledge of words. In either case, using this Thesaurus regularly will help you to build up a mental library of alternative and opposite terms and vary the words you use to express yourself, whether in speech or writing.

A

A1 (infml) adj **excellent**, first-rate, first-class, perfect, flawless Opposite: inferior

abandon v 1 **dump**, discard, dispose of, throw out, throw away Opposite: keep 2 **desert**, leave, forsake, leave behind, walk out on (infml) 3 **end**, call off, cancel, give up, stop Opposite: continue ■ n **recklessness**, wildness, licence, intemperance, unrestraint Opposite: restraint

abandoned adj 1 **discarded**, forsaken, dumped, neglected, cast off 2 **empty**, deserted, derelict, vacant 3 **wild**, uncontrolled, unrestricted, uninhibited, unrestrained Opposite: restrained

abandonment n **desertion**, leaving behind, leaving, rejection, neglect

abase (literary) v **lower**, demean, degrade, belittle, humiliate Opposite: respect

abase yourself (literary) v **grovel**, humble yourself, demean yourself, debase yourself, degrade yourself

abashed adj **embarrassed**, ashamed, mortified, disconcerted, dismayed Opposite: unabashed

abate (fml) v **decrease**, subside, grow less, decline, fade Opposite: rise

abatement (fml) n 1 **reduction**, decline, lessening, diminution, decrease Opposite: increase 2 **deduction**, discount, cut, reduction, decrease Opposite: increment

abbey n **religious foundation**, religious house, cloister, monastery, convent

abbreviate v **shorten**, cut, cut short, condense, abridge Opposite: lengthen

abbreviated adj **shortened**, condensed, abridged, truncated, curtailed Opposite: full-length

abbreviation n **short form**, contraction, ellipsis, acronym, shortening

ABC n 1 **alphabet**, Roman alphabet, spelling system 2 **basics**, fundamentals, essentials, rudiments, nitty-gritty (infml)

abdicate v **renounce**, relinquish, resign, step down, hand over Opposite: accept

abdication n **resignation**, handing over, renunciation, abandonment, relinquishment

abdominal adj **stomach**, belly, front, intestinal, gut

abduct v **kidnap**, make off with, seize, hold somebody against his or her will, capture

abduction n **kidnap**, seizure, kidnapping, carrying off, capture

abductor n **kidnapper**, hostage taker, captor, hijacker, snatcher (US infml)

aberrant adj **abnormal**, unusual, deviant, anomalous, peculiar Opposite: normal

aberration n **deviation**, abnormality, anomaly, irregularity, peculiarity

abet v 1 **assist**, help, support, aid, back Opposite: hinder 2 **encourage**, urge, connive, put up to, incite Opposite: deter

abhor v **detest**, hate, loathe, dislike, despise Opposite: adore

abhorrence n **hatred**, loathing, detestation, disgust, repugnance Opposite: adoration. See COMPARE AND CONTRAST at **dislike**.

abhorrent adj **repugnant**, objectionable, repulsive, detestable, hateful Opposite: desirable

abide v 1 **put up with**, stand for, stand, bear, stomach 2 (archaic) **withstand**, endure, survive, resist, bear 3 (archaic) **live**, have your home, stay, dwell (literary), lodge (dated)

abide by v **obey**, follow, keep to, conform to, stick to Opposite: defy

abiding adj **enduring**, remaining, surviving, long-lasting, unshakable Opposite: transient

ability n **aptitude**, skill, talent, competence, capacity

COMPARE AND CONTRAST CORE MEANING: the necessary skill, knowledge, or experience to do something

ability natural and acquired skills or knowledge; **skill** the ability to do something well gained through training or experience; **competence** ability measured against a standard; **aptitude** a natural tendency to do something well; **talent** an unusual natural ability to do something well; **capacity** mental or physical ability for something or to do something; **capability** the ability or potential to do something.

---

abject adj 1 **extreme**, utter, absolute, wretched, dismal 2 **humble**, servile, meek, submissive, subservient Opposite: confident

abjection n 1 **wretchedness**, misery, desolation, despair, despondence Opposite: cheerfulness 2 **humility**, humbleness, subservience, deference, servility Opposite: confidence

abjuration n **renunciation**, rejection, denial, repudiation, refrainment Opposite: affirmation

abjure v **renounce**, reject, repudiate, deny, disavow

ablaze adj **on fire**, blazing, burning, in flames, alight

able *adj* **1 capable**, competent, proficient, adept, skilled *Opposite*: incompetent **2 clever**, talented, intelligent, bright, gifted *Opposite*: incapable. *See* COMPARE AND CONTRAST *at* **intelligent**.

able-bodied *adj* **healthy**, fit, well, active, strong *Opposite*: weak

ablutions *(fml) n* **washing**, bathing, wash, cleanup, toilette

ably *adv* **capably**, well, skilfully, competently, with ease *Opposite*: incompetently

abnegate *(fml) v* **renounce**, reject, deny, repudiate, abjure *Opposite*: accept

abnegation *(fml) n* **rejection**, renunciation, repudiation, denial, abstention *Opposite*: acceptance

abnormal *adj* **irregular**, nonstandard, uncharacteristic, atypical, anomalous *Opposite*: normal

abnormality *n* **1 defect**, deformity, irregularity, malformation, malfunction **2 irregularity**, aberration, anomaly, deviation, oddity

aboard *adv* **1 on board**, on the ship, on the bus, on the train, on the plane **2** *(infml)* **involved**, participating, on the team, with us, on our side ■ *prep* **onto**, on, into, inside

abode *(literary) n* **house**, home, residence, place, dwelling *(fml)*

abolish *v* **put an end to**, eliminate, close down, bring to an end, stop *Opposite*: establish

abolition *n* **elimination**, ending, closing down, eradication, closure *Opposite*: establishment

abolitionist *n* **opponent**, objector, protester, eradicator, adversary *Opposite*: supporter

abominable *adj* **dreadful**, repulsive, offensive, detestable, monstrous

abominate *(fml) v* **hate**, loathe, detest, despise, dislike *Opposite*: love

abomination *n* **1 outrage**, disgrace, scandal, eyesore, atrocity **2** *(literary)* **hatred**, dislike, repugnance, loathing, revulsion *Opposite*: love

aboriginal *adj* **indigenous**, original, native, local, autochthonous *Opposite*: foreign. *See* COMPARE AND CONTRAST *at* **native**.

abort *v* **end**, abandon, call off, call a halt, cancel *Opposite*: continue

abortive *adj* **unsuccessful**, failed, fruitless, unproductive, futile *Opposite*: successful

abound *v* **1 thrive**, flourish, prosper, proliferate, be plentiful **2 brim**, overflow, throng, teem, swarm

abounding *adj* **many**, varied, multifarious, plentiful, abundant *Opposite*: scarce

about *prep* **concerning**, regarding, in relation to, on the subject of, on ■ *adv* **1 approximately**, roughly, in the region of, around, almost **2 around**, close, nearby, near, in the vicinity

about to *prep* **ready to**, on the verge of, on the point of, just going to, set to

about-turn *n* **1 turnaround**, reversal, shift, transformation, sea change **2 turn**, U-turn, 180° turn, revolution

above *prep* **1 more than**, greater than, higher than, beyond, exceeding *Opposite*: below **2 on top of**, over, higher than, atop *Opposite*: below

above all *adv* **especially**, in particular, primarily, principally, most of all

aboveboard *adj* **open**, fair, honest, forthright, straightforward *Opposite*: shady ■ *adv* **openly**, fairly, honestly, legally, lawfully *Opposite*: illegally

above-mentioned *adj* **said**, aforementioned *(fml)*, aforesaid *(fml)*

abrade *v* **graze**, scrape, roughen, chafe, grind down *Opposite*: smooth

abrasion *n* **scrape**, scratch, scuff, graze

abrasive *adj* **1 rough**, coarse, harsh, rasping, scratchy *Opposite*: smooth **2 rude**, sharp, harsh, brusque, argumentative *Opposite*: gentle

abreast *adv* **side by side**, alongside, shoulder to shoulder, beside, level ■ *adj* **well-informed**, in touch, up-to-date, up on, up with *Opposite*: ignorant

abridge *v* **shorten**, edit, condense, abbreviate, reduce *Opposite*: expand

abridged *adj* **shortened**, edited, condensed, reduced, abbreviated *Opposite*: complete

abridgement *see* **abridgment**

abridgment *n* **synopsis**, digest, condensation, précis, abstract

abroad *adv* **overseas**, away, out of the country

abrogate *(fml) v* **repeal**, revoke, rescind, retract, nullify. *See* COMPARE AND CONTRAST *at* **nullify**.

abrogation *(fml) n* **retraction**, repeal, annulment, abolition, rescindment

abrupt *adj* **1 sudden**, unexpected, unforeseen, rapid, hasty *Opposite*: gradual **2 curt**, short, brusque, terse, rude *Opposite*: polite

abscess *n* **boil**, pustule, swelling, eruption, blister

abscond *v* **run away**, escape, break out, make off, elope

absconder *n* **deserter**, runaway, escapee, fugitive, truant

absence *n* **1 nonappearance**, absenteeism, time off *Opposite*: presence **2 lack**, deficiency, want, dearth, privation *Opposite*: surplus

absent *adj* **1 missing**, gone, out, away *Opposite*: present **2 inattentive**, absent-minded, far away, preoccupied, vague *Opposite*: alert **3 lacking**, deficient, nonexistent, in short supply *Opposite*: present

absentee *n* **truant**, defaulter, runaway, absconder

absenteeism *n* **absence**, nonattendance, nonappearance, truancy, skiving *(infml)*

absently adv **inattentively**, vaguely, dreamily, distractedly, abstractedly Opposite: attentively

absent-minded adj **forgetful**, distracted, scatterbrained, preoccupied, vague Opposite: attentive

absent yourself v **excuse yourself**, send your apologies, stay away Opposite: attend

absolute adj 1 **total**, complete, utter, unqualified, out-and-out 2 **unconditional**, unlimited, supreme, unmodified, unadulterated Opposite: provisional 3 **conclusive**, resolved, firm, fixed, definite Opposite: unconfirmed ■ n **given**, rule, principle, truth, fundamental

absolution n **forgiveness**, pardon, release, freedom, liberty Opposite: condemnation

absolutism n **totalitarianism**, despotism, dictatorship, tyranny, autocracy

absolve v **pardon**, forgive, clear, release, free Opposite: punish

absorb v 1 **soak up**, attract, take in, take up, suck up Opposite: exude 2 **understand**, learn, grasp, admit, take in 3 **engross**, fascinate, engage, captivate, grip Opposite: bore

absorbed adj **engrossed**, wrapped up, fascinated, captivated, immersed Opposite: detached

absorbency n **porosity**, sponginess, permeability, penetrability, perviousness

absorbent adj **porous**, spongy, permeable, penetrable, pervious

absorbing adj **fascinating**, engrossing, captivating, gripping, enthralling Opposite: boring

absorption n 1 **preoccupation**, fascination, interest, captivation, engagement 2 **amalgamation**, incorporation, assimilation, combination, inclusion Opposite: rejection

abstain v 1 **desist**, refrain, withdraw, withhold, go without Opposite: indulge 2 **sit on the fence**, stay neutral, not take sides, hedge Opposite: vote

abstainer n 1 **avoider**, shunner, teetotaller, withholder, refrainer 2 **nonvoter**, hedger, fence sitter

abstemious adj **self-denying**, self-disciplined, moderate, ascetic, sober Opposite: unrestrained

abstemiousness n **sobriety**, self-denial, moderation, temperance, self-discipline Opposite: excess

abstention n **nonparticipation**, abstaining, refraining, holding back

abstinence n **self-denial**, self-restraint, self-discipline, moderation, asceticism Opposite: indulgence

abstinent adj **ascetic**, abstemious, sober, temperate, teetotal Opposite: indulgent

abstract adj 1 **nonconcrete**, intellectual, mental, immaterial, intangible Opposite: concrete 2 **theoretical**, conceptual, conjectural, hypothetical, speculative Opposite: practical ■ n **summary**, extract, précis, synopsis, abridgment ■ v 1 **conceptualize**, theorize, hypothesize, intellectualize 2 **summarize**, condense, shorten, précis, abridge Opposite: expand 3 **extract**, take out, select, remove, separate

abstracted adj **inattentive**, preoccupied, vague, distant, distracted Opposite: alert

abstractedness n **preoccupation**, inattentiveness, inattention, pensiveness, distractedness Opposite: alertness

abstraction n 1 **pensiveness**, preoccupation, dreaminess, vagueness, daydreaming Opposite: concentration 2 **concept**, idea, thought, notion, construct Opposite: fact 3 **removal**, extraction, withdrawal, deduction Opposite: inclusion

abstractly adv **theoretically**, conceptually, hypothetically, in theory Opposite: practically

abstruse adj **obscure**, perplexing, puzzling, complex, profound Opposite: simple. See COMPARE AND CONTRAST at obscure.

abstruseness n **complexity**, obscurity, difficulty, profundity, mysteriousness Opposite: simplicity

absurd adj 1 **ridiculous**, ludicrous, farcical, nonsensical, illogical Opposite: reasonable 2 **meaningless**, pointless, futile, empty, purposeless Opposite: meaningful

absurdity n 1 **illogicality**, irrationality, silliness, ludicrousness, ridiculousness Opposite: logic 2 **farce**, joke, nonsense, incongruity

absurdly adv **ridiculously**, ludicrously, farcically, nonsensically, preposterously Opposite: reasonably

absurdness see absurdity

abundance n **profusion**, plenty, richness, wealth, copiousness Opposite: scarcity

abundant adj **plentiful**, copious, rich, profuse, ample Opposite: scarce

a bundle of laughs n **good fun**, a barrel of monkeys, a barrel of laughs, a lot of fun, laugh (infml)

abuse n 1 **mistreatment**, cruelty, ill-treatment, violence, maltreatment 2 **misuse**, exploitation, manipulation, taking advantage, mishandling 3 **insults**, verbal abuse, swearing, name-calling, foul language ■ v 1 **exploit**, take advantage, misuse, manipulate 2 **treat badly**, ill-treat, mistreat, maltreat, molest Opposite: look after 3 **insult**, swear, shout abuse, hurl abuse, shout insults Opposite: compliment. See COMPARE AND CONTRAST at misuse.

abused adj **ill-treated**, physically abused, battered, badly treated, injured Opposite: looked after

abusive adj 1 **rude**, insulting, unmannerly, foul, offensive Opposite: polite 2 **violent**, cruel, vicious, sadistic, rough Opposite: gentle

abusiveness n **rudeness**, unpleasantness, impoliteness, nastiness, vulgarity

abut v **be next to**, adjoin, border, be adjacent to, touch

abutment n **support**, buttress, prop, strut, brace

abutting adj **adjoining**, next to, bordering, adjacent to, against

abuzz adj **alive**, throbbing, humming, pulsating, busy Opposite: still

abysmal adj **terrible**, awful, dreadful, horrible, appalling Opposite: superb

abyss n **gulf**, chasm, gorge, hole, void

academia n **academic world**, academic circles, university, university circles, academe (fml)

academic adj 1 **educational**, school, college, university, scholastic 2 **studious**, intellectual, scholarly, bookish, literary 3 **theoretical**, speculative, abstract, moot, hypothetical Opposite: practical ■ n **researcher**, professor, college lecturer, don, scholar

academy n **school**, college, conservatory, conservatoire, arts school

a case in point n **working example**, instance, case, paradigm, illustration

accede v 1 **agree**, assent, consent, comply, grant Opposite: reject 2 **come into**, inherit, succeed, take over, enter upon

accelerate v **go faster**, speed up, increase speed, gather speed, pick up the pace Opposite: slow down

accelerated adj **speeded up**, faster, quicker, speedier, advanced Opposite: slower

acceleration n 1 **increase of rate**, increase of velocity, spurt, burst of speed Opposite: deceleration 2 **speeding up**, stepping up, hastening, hurrying, quickening Opposite: deceleration

accent n 1 **pronunciation**, inflection, intonation, tone of voice, enunciation 2 **emphasis**, stress, beat, accentuation, inflection ■ v **emphasize**, stress, accentuate, put stress on, give weight to

accentuate v **emphasize**, highlight, put emphasis on, stress, draw attention to Opposite: play down

accentuation n 1 **prominence**, highlighting, attention, notice, emphasis 2 **accent**, rhythm, stress, inflection, beat

accept v 1 **receive**, take, agree to take, admit Opposite: refuse 2 **consent**, agree, say yes, say you will, give a positive response Opposite: turn down 3 **put up with**, endure, tolerate, bow, take 4 **believe**, recognize, agree, admit, acknowledge Opposite: deny 5 **take on**, undertake, acknowledge, assume, bear Opposite: reject

acceptability n **suitability**, adequacy, appropriateness, tolerability

acceptable adj 1 **satisfactory**, suitable, good enough, adequate, up to standard Opposite: unacceptable 2 **welcome**, pleasing, gratifying, agreeable, enjoyable Opposite: annoying

acceptably adv **well enough**, adequately, sufficiently well, suitably, tolerably Opposite: unreasonably

acceptance n 1 **agreement**, assent, acquiescence, concurrence, accession Opposite: refusal 2 **receipt**, taking, getting, reception, receiving Opposite: rejection 3 **belief**, acknowledgment, credence, currency, agreement 4 **recognition**, approval, tolerance, acknowledgment, toleration Opposite: disapproval

accepted adj **conventional**, established, customary, acknowledged, usual Opposite: unconventional

accepting adj **tolerant**, compliant, patient, long-suffering, uncomplaining Opposite: intolerant

access n 1 **way in**, entrance, entry, approach, gate Opposite: exit 2 **right of entry**, admission, right to use, admittance, entrée ■ v **get into**, gain access to, retrieve, call up, log on

accessibility n **convenience**, user-friendliness, openness, availability, approachability

accessible adj 1 **nearby**, available, reachable, easily reached, handy Opposite: inaccessible 2 **comprehensible**, understandable, user-friendly, easy to use, clear Opposite: obscure 3 **approachable**, affable, genial, friendly, welcoming Opposite: unapproachable

accessibly adv 1 **conveniently**, handily, suitably, helpfully, usefully Opposite: inconveniently 2 **clearly**, simply, understandably, comprehensibly, straightforwardly Opposite: obscurely

accession n 1 **attainment**, succession, taking over, taking office, appointment 2 **agreement**, consent, concurrence, accord, assent

accessorize v **ornament**, decorate, beautify, trim, embellish

accessory n 1 **addition**, decoration, fixture, fitment, attachment 2 **accomplice**, partner, partner in crime, assistant, abettor

WORD BANK
❑ types of accessory ascot, bandanna, belt, bootlace, bow tie, braces, cravat, cummerbund, earmuffs, glove, handkerchief, hat, jewellery, mitt, mitten, muff, muffler, pashmina, sash, scarf, shawl, stole, tie, veil, wrap

accident n 1 **chance**, coincidence, fortune, fate Opposite: design 2 **crash**, collision, bump, smash, smash-up 3 **mishap**, misfortune, calamity, catastrophe, disaster

accidental adj **unintentional**, unintended, inadvertent, chance, unplanned Opposite: deliberate

accidentally adv **by chance**, by accident, by mistake, unintentionally, inadvertently Opposite: purposely

accident-prone *adj* ill-fated, unfortunate, unlucky, ill-starred, doomed

acclaim *v* praise, sing the praises of, give approval, hail, commend *Opposite*: criticize ■ *n* approval, praise, commendation, acclamation, approbation *Opposite*: disapproval

acclaimed *adj* praised, admired, commended, celebrated, applauded

acclamation *n* 1 acclaim, praise, commendation, approbation, approval 2 applause, clapping, cheering, ovation, roar *Opposite*: jeering

acclimate *see* acclimatize

acclimatization *n* adaptation, becoming accustomed, getting used to, adjustment, accommodation

acclimatize *v* get used to, become accustomed, accustom, adapt, adjust

accolade *n* tribute, honour, compliment, award, praise

accommodate *v* 1 house, lodge, put up, billet, quarter 2 contain, have room for, hold, seat, have capacity for 3 get used to, adapt, adjust, become accustomed to, familiarize 4 assist, help, oblige, be of service, find ways to help

accommodating *adj* helpful, willing, obliging, compliant, cooperative *Opposite*: uncooperative

accommodation *n* 1 lodging, housing, room, space, place 2 adjustment, adaptation, alteration, change, modification

accompaniment *n* supplement, accessory, garnish, adjunct, complement

accompanist *n* pianist, instrumentalist, musician, player

accompany *v* 1 escort, go with, go together with, go along with, attend 2 go together with, come with, be an adjunct to, supplement, complement

accompanying *adj* supplementary, associated, complementary, additional, add-on

accomplice *n* partner in crime, assistant, accessory, collaborator, co-conspirator

accomplish *v* achieve, attain, realize, carry out, pull off (*infml*)

COMPARE AND CONTRAST CORE MEANING: bring something to a successful conclusion
accomplish succeed in doing something; **achieve** succeed in something, usually with effort; **attain** reach a specific objective; **realize** fulfil a specific vision or plan; **carry out** perform or accomplish a task or activity; **pull off** (*infml*) to accomplish something, despite difficulties.

---

accomplished *adj* talented, skilful, gifted, skilled, proficient

accomplishment *n* 1 completion, execution, carrying out, finishing, realization 2 feat, achievement, triumph, success, deed 3 talent, skill, ability, expertise, capability

accord *v* 1 give, allow, permit, render (*fml*), confer (*fml*) 2 agree, concur, fit, match, correspond *Opposite*: clash ■ *n* 1 agreement, treaty, settlement, pact, deal 2 consensus, harmony, concurrence, unity, agreement *Opposite*: disagreement

accordance *n* consensus, agreement, accord, harmony, concord *Opposite*: disagreement

accordingly *adv* 1 appropriately, suitably, correspondingly, fittingly *Opposite*: inappropriately 2 so, for that reason, therefore, as a result, consequently

according to *prep* 1 as said by, as stated by, on the word of 2 consistent with, along with, in line with, in keeping with, in relation to *Opposite*: counter to

accost *v* approach, stop, confront, detain, hound

account *n* 1 report, description, story, relation, narrative 2 explanation, version, interpretation, justification, reason 3 bank account, cheque account, current account, deposit account, savings account 4 arrangement, credit, tally, balance, bill

accountability *n* answerability, responsibility, liability, culpability

accountable *adj* answerable, responsible, liable, held responsible, blamed

accountant *n* bookkeeper, auditor, chartered accountant, certified accountant, cost accountant

account for *v* 1 explain, justify, give an explanation for, give a reason for, answer for 2 comprise, make up, total, represent, constitute

accounts *n* books, balance sheet, financial statement

accoutrement *n* accessory, trapping, trimming, tool of the trade, equipment

accredit *v* recognize, sanction, endorse, authorize, certify

accreditation *n* authorization, endorsement, approval, certification, sanction

accredited *adj* credited, attributed, qualified, endorsed, official *Opposite*: unofficial

accretion *n* 1 accumulation, buildup, increase, enlargement, addition *Opposite*: erosion 2 deposit, layer, mass, lump, bump

accrual *n* accumulation, increase, buildup, accretion, addition *Opposite*: loss

accrue *v* accumulate, grow, mount up, build up, amass *Opposite*: dwindle

accumulate *v* build up, mount up, accrue, amass, collect *Opposite*: disperse. *See* COMPARE AND CONTRAST *at* collect.

accumulation *n* 1 buildup, accretion, accrual, gathering, growth 2 collection, stock, store, hoard, deposit

accumulative *adj* 1 acquisitive, hoarding, materialistic, covetous, grasping 2 incremental, increasing, rising, growing, mounting

accumulator *n* collector, saver, amasser, magpie (*infml*), squirrel (*infml*)

accuracy n **correctness**, accurateness, exactness, precision, truth *Opposite*: inaccuracy

accurate adj **precise**, correct, exact, true, truthful *Opposite*: inaccurate

accusation n **allegation**, indictment, claim, complaint, charge

accusatorial *(fml)* adj **1 critical**, judgmental, condemnatory, accusing, reproachful *Opposite*: complimentary **2 adversarial**, confrontational, argumentative, combative, antagonistic *Opposite*: amicable

accuse v **blame**, lay blame on, indict, point the finger, allege

accuser n **1 challenger**, confronter, criticizer, opponent, faultfinder **2 indicter**, litigant, petitioner, appellant, complainant **3 informer**, telltale, talebearer, whistleblower, sneak

accusing adj **reproachful**, condemning, reproving, critical, condemnatory

accustom v **get used to**, get used to, acclimatize, acclimate, become accustomed to

accustomed adj **1 familiarized**, inured, adapted, comfortable, habituated *(fml)* *Opposite*: unaccustomed **2 usual**, habitual, regular, familiar, customary *Opposite*: unusual

ace n **champion**, star, expert, winner, victor ■ adj *(infml)* **first-rate**, top, world-class, wonderful, excellent *Opposite*: lousy *(infml)*

acerbic adj **cutting**, bitter, caustic, acid, sour *Opposite*: mild

acerbity n **sharpness**, bitterness, sourness, acidity, acrimony

ache n **pain**, throbbing, aching, twinge, headache ■ v **1 hurt**, throb, be painful, sting, smart **2** *(fml)* **long**, desire, yearn, want, wish

achievable adj **attainable**, realizable, possible, reachable, doable *Opposite*: unrealistic

achieve v **attain**, realize, accomplish, reach, complete *Opposite*: fail. *See* COMPARE AND CONTRAST at **accomplish**.

achievement n **attainment**, accomplishment, success, feat, triumph *Opposite*: failure

achiever n **high-flier**, doer, self-starter, success, go-getter *(infml)* *Opposite*: loser

Achilles heel n **weakness**, flaw, failing, weak point, chink in somebody's armour

aching adj **painful**, achy, sore, tender, throbbing ■ n **1 ache**, pain, painful feeling, throbbing, throb **2** *(fml)* **longing**, desire, yearning, pining, itch

achy adj **painful**, aching, sore, tender, throbbing

acid adj **1 acidic**, tart, sour, bitter, sharp *Opposite*: sweet **2 cutting**, biting, caustic, acerbic, mordant *Opposite*: mild

acidic adj **acid**, tart, sour, bitter, sharp *Opposite*: sweet

acidity n **sourness**, sharpness, tartness, bitterness *Opposite*: sweetness

acidly adv **sharply**, cuttingly, tartly, sourly, acerbically *Opposite*: sweetly

acid test n **litmus test**, touchstone, trial, indicator

acknowledge v **1 admit**, recognize, accept, concede, grant *Opposite*: deny **2 greet**, salute, wave, nod, hail *Opposite*: ignore **3 reply**, answer, respond, react, return *Opposite*: ignore

acknowledged adj **recognized**, approved, known, accredited, accepted *Opposite*: denied

acknowledgment n **1 greeting**, salutation, nod, wave, salute **2 response**, reply, reaction, answer, retort **3 recognition**, acceptance, admission, confession, appreciation

acme n **peak**, summit, top, zenith, pinnacle *Opposite*: nadir

acolyte n **1 attendant**, assistant, aide, helper **2 follower**, devotee, disciple, adherent, supporter

acoustic adj **audio**, aural, auditory, audile, sound

acoustics n **audibility**, auditory range, sound quality

acquaint v **make aware**, inform, let know, let in on, make familiar with *Opposite*: keep from

acquaintance n **1 associate**, friend, contact, colleague, consociate *(fml)* *Opposite*: stranger **2 knowledge**, familiarity, understanding, awareness, conversance *Opposite*: ignorance **3 relationship**, contact, association, friendship, relations

acquiesce v **agree**, comply, accept, consent, assent *Opposite*: resist. *See* COMPARE AND CONTRAST at **agree**.

acquiescence n **agreement**, consent, compliance, submission, acceptance *Opposite*: resistance

acquiescent adj **agreeable**, compliant, yielding, accepting, submissive *Opposite*: resistant

acquire v **1 obtain**, get, get hold of, get your hands on, gain *Opposite*: lose **2 develop**, learn, pick up, take up, assimilate *Opposite*: drop. *See* COMPARE AND CONTRAST at **get**.

acquisition n **1 gaining**, attainment, achievement, getting hold of, procurement *Opposite*: loss **2 purchase**, possession, asset, gain

acquisitive adj **greedy**, covetous, grasping, avaricious, materialistic *Opposite*: generous

acquisitiveness n **greed**, hoarding, avarice, covetousness, materialism *Opposite*: generosity

acquit v **find not guilty**, clear, set free, free, release *Opposite*: convict

acquittal n **release**, discharge, freeing, clearing, exoneration *Opposite*: conviction

acquit yourself v **conduct yourself**, act, behave, perform, work

acreage *n* **land**, estate, property, domain, acres

acres *n* **1 land**, estate, domain, property, acreage **2** (*infml*) **expanse**, stretch, tracts, swathes, lots

acrid *adj* **1 pungent**, harsh, unpleasant, choking, bitter *Opposite*: pleasant **2 sharp**, cutting, caustic, bitter, vitriolic *Opposite*: mild

acrimonious *adj* **spiteful**, rancorous, discordant, hostile, unfriendly *Opposite*: amicable

acrimony *n* **bitterness**, spite, rancour, animosity, hostility *Opposite*: harmony

acrobat *n* **tumbler**, trapeze artist, circus performer, gymnast, funambulist

acrobatic *adj* **gymnastic**, athletic, lithe, supple, flexible

acrobatics *n* **1 gymnastics**, aerobics, physical exercises, callisthenics **2 agility**, skill, dexterity, nimbleness, quickness

acronym *n* **abbreviation**, short form, shortening, contraction, condensation

across *adv* **crossways**, crosswise, transversely, diagonally, from corner to corner

across-the-board *adj* **comprehensive**, sweeping, all-embracing, wide-ranging, far-reaching

act *n* **1 action**, deed, doing, undertaking, exploit **2 performance**, entertainment, turn, piece, item **3 pretence**, show, sham, con, feint **4 law**, piece of legislation, statute, decree, enactment ■ *v* **1 take action**, take steps, proceed, be active, perform **2 behave**, conduct yourself, acquit yourself, comport yourself (*fml*) **3 pretend**, put on an act, put it on, play, fake **4 replace**, represent, act on behalf of, appear on behalf of, speak for **5 function**, work, take effect, produce a result, produce an effect **6 perform**, act out, be in, appear, play

acting *n* **drama**, the theatre, amateur dramatics, performing, the stage ■ *adj* **temporary**, substitute, stand-in, interim *Opposite*: permanent

action *n* **1 act**, deed, exploit, achievement, accomplishment *Opposite*: inaction **2 lawsuit**, suit, proceedings, charge, case **3 battle**, fighting, combat, conflict, engagement

actionable *adj* **indictable**, litigious, suable, chargeable, imputable *Opposite*: legal

action-packed *adj* **exciting**, thrilling, gripping, enthralling, suspenseful *Opposite*: dull

activate *v* **make active**, set in motion, set off, turn on, trigger *Opposite*: stop

activation *n* **start**, beginning, initiation, instigation, stimulation

active *adj* **1 lively**, vigorous, energetic, full of life, on the go *Opposite*: inactive **2 in force**, functioning, effective, in action, operating *Opposite*: defunct **3 working**, practising,

involved, committed, enthusiastic *Opposite*: half-hearted

actively *adv* **vigorously**, aggressively, energetically, enthusiastically, dynamically *Opposite*: half-heartedly

activeness *n* **liveliness**, animation, energy, vitality, vigour *Opposite*: passivity

activism *n* **direct action**, political action, social action, involvement, engagement

activist *n* **campaigner**, protester, objector, militant, advocate

activity *n* **1 pursuit**, interest, hobby, occupation, leisure interest **2 action**, movement, motion, bustle, commotion *Opposite*: inactivity

act on *v* **1 follow up on**, tackle, start in on, take action **2 have an effect on**, work, affect, perform

actor *n* **performer**, artist, thespian, artiste, player

act out *v* **1 enact**, perform, portray, act, play **2 work out**, work through, exorcize, express, purge

actress *n* **performer**, artist, thespian, artiste, player

actual *adj* **real**, genuine, authentic, concrete, tangible *Opposite*: imaginary

actuality *n* **1 fact**, certainty, reality, practicality, actual fact **2 real life**, the real world, here and now, reality

actually *adv* **in fact**, really, in point of fact, in reality, truly

actuate (*fml*) *v* **activate**, put into action, set in motion, trigger, start

act up *v* **cause trouble**, play up, be difficult, misbehave, malfunction *Opposite*: behave

acuity *n* **keenness**, acuteness, sharpness, alertness, awareness

acumen *n* **insight**, shrewdness, penetration, judgment, wisdom

acute *adj* **1 severe**, serious, critical, grave, important *Opposite*: moderate **2 perceptive**, shrewd, intelligent, canny, bright *Opposite*: obtuse **3 sensitive**, sharp, keen, heightened, finely tuned *Opposite*: dull **4 intense**, violent, strong, excruciating, piercing *Opposite*: mild

acutely *adv* **very**, intensely, highly, deeply, extremely *Opposite*: slightly

acuteness *n* **1 intensity**, severity, gravity, seriousness **2 sharpness**, keenness, sensitivity, perceptiveness *Opposite*: dullness

ad (*infml*) *n* **advertisement**, public notice, commercial, poster, billboard

adage *n* **saying**, saw, proverb, maxim, axiom

adamant *adj* **obstinate**, obdurate, unyielding, unbending, inflexible *Opposite*: amenable

adapt *v* **1 change**, alter, modify, adjust, vary *Opposite*: leave **2 become accustomed**, familiarize, get a feel for, get used to, acclimatize

adaptability n flexibility, adaptableness, malleability, compliance *Opposite*: inflexibility

adaptable adj flexible, malleable, pliable, adjustable, compliant *Opposite*: inflexible

adaptation n 1 alteration, adjustment, acclimatization, modification, change 2 version, edition, revision, reworking, variation

adapter n electric plug, connector, converter, device

add v 1 put in, insert, adjoin, append, affix *Opposite*: delete 2 add up, add together, tot up, total, combine *Opposite*: subtract 3 enhance, complement, improve, increase, supplement *Opposite*: detract

added adj additional, extra, supplementary, further, other

addendum n addition, supplement, appendix, postscript, PS

addict n devotee, fan, aficionado, fanatic, buff

addiction n habit, compulsion, dependence, need, obsession

addition n 1 adding, adding up, adding together, totalling, totting up *Opposite*: subtraction 2 supplement, add-on, appendage, addendum, adjunct

additional adj extra, added, supplementary, other, further

additionally adv as well, in addition, moreover, furthermore, also

additive n preservative, stabilizer, improver, chemical, colourant

addle v confuse, befuddle, muddle, distract, bewilder

addled adj 1 confused, muddled, bewildered, befuddled, perplexed *Opposite*: clear 2 spoiled, rotten, decayed, off, putrid *Opposite*: fresh

addlepated (archaic) adj confused, muddled, bewildered, befuddled, perplexed *Opposite*: clear

add-on n attachment, addendum, adjunct, appendage, supplement ■ adj supplementary, accompanying, additional, extra, optional *Opposite*: essential

address n speech, talk, discourse, lecture, report ■ v 1 direct, deliver, dispatch, refer, forward 2 speak, lecture, talk, give a lecture, give a talk 3 tackle, deal with, take in hand, attend, concentrate *Opposite*: ignore

adduce (fml) v offer, present, put forward, bring forward, give

add up v 1 add, add together, total, combine, tally up *Opposite*: subtract 2 make sense, hang together, be consistent, ring true, come together

add up to v come to, number, total, amount to, mount up to

adenoidal adj nasal, thick, muffled, indistinct

adept adj skilful, skilled, expert, proficient, adroit *Opposite*: inept

aptness n expertise, proficiency, skill, adro-

itness, aptitude *Opposite*: ineptitude

adequacy n 1 sufficiency, ampleness, abundance *Opposite*: insufficiency 2 competence, capability, suitability, tolerability, appropriateness *Opposite*: inadequacy

adequate adj 1 sufficient, ample, enough, plenty *Opposite*: insufficient 2 passable, satisfactory, tolerable, acceptable, suitable *Opposite*: inadequate

adequately adv sufficiently, passably, tolerably, effectively, satisfactorily *Opposite*: inadequately

adhere v 1 stick to, follow, keep to, stand by, abide by *Opposite*: abandon 2 stick, stick on, hold fast, hold, hold on

adherence n devotion, obedience, observance, loyalty, faithfulness *Opposite*: disobedience

adherent n supporter, believer, devotee, advocate, fanatic *Opposite*: opponent

adhesion n union, sticking power, hold, grip, linkage *Opposite*: separation

adhesive n glue, paste, gum, epoxy resin

ad hoc adj unplanned, informal, impromptu, improvised, off-the-cuff *Opposite*: planned

ad infinitum adv endlessly, for ever, ceaselessly, repeatedly, infinitely

adjacent adj neighbouring, nearby, bordering, next, next door *Opposite*: distant

adjoin v connect, link up, attach, affix, be close to

adjoining adj touching, attached, connecting, abutting, contiguous (fml) *Opposite*: detached

adjourn v 1 suspend, defer, delay, postpone, put off 2 (infml) stop, end, finish, break off, call it a day

adjournment n suspension, postponement, deferment, recess, break

adjudge v 1 judge, find, regard as, consider, decide 2 pronounce, rule, announce, declare, adjudicate

adjudicate v arbitrate, sit in judgment, pass judgment, referee, umpire

adjudication n 1 judgment, arbitration, mediation, negotiation, intercession 2 settlement, decision, judgment, decree, resolution

adjudicator n judge, arbitrator, referee, umpire, mediator

adjunct n 1 addition, attachment, add-on, appendage, accessory 2 assistant, aide, aide-de-camp, secretary, helper

adjure v 1 command, order, instruct, charge, demand 2 appeal, plead, beg, request, petition

adjust v regulate, alter, fiddle with, correct, fine-tune

adjustable adj adaptable, modifiable, changeable, variable, regulating *Opposite*: fixed

adjustment n change, alteration, modification, tuning, fine-tuning

adjutant n **assistant**, aide, aide-de-camp, secretary, personal assistant

ad-lib v **improvise**, do off the cuff, extemporize, make up on the spot, do cold ■ adj **off-the-cuff**, unplanned, informal, impromptu, improvised Opposite: rehearsed

administer v **1 manage**, direct, run, order, control **2 dispense**, give out, hand out, deal out, mete out

administrate v **control**, run, manage, direct, rule

administration n **1 management**, direction, running, supervision, paperwork **2 government**, executive, management, organization, presidency **3 dispensation**, meting out, giving out, handing out, dealing out

administrative adj **managerial**, directorial, organizational, clerical, secretarial

administrator n **manager**, superintendent, commissioner, overseer, officer

admirable adj **estimable**, commendable, venerable, good, splendid Opposite: unworthy

admiration n **respect**, esteem, approbation, regard, approval Opposite: disapproval. See COMPARE AND CONTRAST at **regard**.

admire v **regard**, esteem, approve, think highly of, respect Opposite: disapprove

admired adj **respected**, venerated, esteemed, well-regarded, revered Opposite: despised

admirer n **fan**, devotee, follower, lover, aficionado

admiring adj **appreciative**, approving, complimentary, flattering, favourable Opposite: disapproving

admissibility n **acceptability**, tolerability, permissibility

admissible adj **allowable**, permissible, acceptable, tolerable Opposite: inadmissible

admission n **1 admittance**, entrance, right of entry, access, permission Opposite: exclusion **2 entrance fee**, entry fee, fee, charge, price **3 confession**, declaration, profession, divulgence, disclosure Opposite: denial

admit v **1 confess**, make a clean breast, acknowledge, own up, disclose Opposite: deny **2 let in**, allow in, give access, permit, let pass Opposite: bar

admit defeat v **pull out**, withdraw, stop, call it a day, back out Opposite: persevere

admittance n **admission**, entry, access, right of entry, entrance Opposite: exclusion

admittedly adv **certainly**, definitely, indeed, undeniably, undoubtedly

admonish v **reprove**, caution, warn, reprimand, rebuke Opposite: praise

admonishment n **reprimand**, rebuke, reproach, caution, dressing-down Opposite: approval

admonition n **caution**, warning, reprimand, rebuke, reproach Opposite: approval

admonitory adj **1 reproving**, reproachful, rebuking, condemnatory, critical Opposite: approving **2 advisory**, cautionary, warning, deterrent, instructive

ad nauseam adv **on and on**, for ever, endlessly, interminably, ad infinitum

ado n **bustle**, activity, commotion, bother, excitement

adolescence n **teens**, youth, puberty, teenage years

adolescent n **teenager**, youth, youngster, juvenile, minor ■ adj **teenage**, young, youthful, juvenile, pubescent

adopt v **take on**, accept, assume, approve, take up Opposite: reject

adoption n **acceptance**, implementation, espousal, taking on, embracing Opposite: rejection

adoptive adj **legal**, step Opposite: natural

adorable adj **lovely**, gorgeous, delightful, lovable, delectable Opposite: detestable

adoration n **1 esteem**, high regard, respect, admiration, adulation Opposite: hatred **2 worship**, reverence, idolization, glorification, veneration

adore v **1 love**, esteem, respect, admire, adulate Opposite: hate **2 worship**, revere, idolize, glorify, venerate Opposite: revile **3** (infml) **like**, enjoy, love, be keen on, be partial to Opposite: dislike

adored adj **revered**, venerated, worshipped, idolized, cherished Opposite: hated

adoring adj **affectionate**, loving, doting, admiring, indulgent Opposite: cold

adorn v **decorate**, embellish, ornament, beautify, prettify Opposite: strip

adornment n **decoration**, embellishment, ornamentation, beautification, prettification

adrift adj **drifting**, floating, loose, free Opposite: fixed ■ adv **aimless**, wandering, drifting, at a loose end, lost Opposite: focused

adroit adj **skilful**, nimble, practised, able, dexterous Opposite: clumsy

adroitness n **skilfulness**, nimbleness, ability, dexterity, cleverness Opposite: clumsiness

adulate v **flatter**, put on a pedestal, elevate, praise, adore Opposite: disparage

adulation n **adoration**, praise, worship, hero worship, respect Opposite: disparagement

adulatory adj **praising**, flattering, fawning, sycophantic, obsequious Opposite: disparaging

adult adj **mature**, fully developed, grown-up, grown, fully-grown Opposite: immature

adulterate v **contaminate**, taint, make impure, spoil, pollute Opposite: purify

adulteration n **contamination**, debasement, pollution, tarnishing, corruption Opposite: purification

adulthood n **maturity**, parenthood, middle age, old age, later life Opposite: childhood

advance v **1 go forward**, move forward, move

ahead, press forward, move on *Opposite*: retreat **2 improve**, enhance, take forward, increase, expand *Opposite*: regress ■ *n* **1 development**, improvement, spread, progress, expansion *Opposite*: decline **2 loan**, early payment, down payment, fee, money up front

advanced *adj* **1 higher**, developed, sophisticated, complex, difficult *Opposite*: basic **2 later**, far along, well along, far ahead, well ahead *Opposite*: earlier **3 progressive**, forward-thinking, unconventional, cutting-edge, innovative *Opposite*: traditional

advancement *n* **progression**, progress, development, improvement, spread *Opposite*: decline

advantage *n* **benefit**, gain, lead, pro, improvement *Opposite*: disadvantage

advantageous *adj* **beneficial**, helpful, useful, to your advantage, valuable *Opposite*: disadvantageous

advent *n* **arrival**, start, beginning, coming on, dawn *Opposite*: departure

adventure *n* **escapade**, exploit, quest, venture, exploration

adventurer *n* **1 explorer**, traveller, voyager, buccaneer, swashbuckler **2 entrepreneur**, investor, speculator, trailblazer, pioneer

adventuresome *adj* **risk-taking**, carefree, daring, thrill-seeking, adventurous *Opposite*: unadventurous

adventurous *adj* **daring**, bold, audacious, brave, courageous *Opposite*: unadventurous

adversarial *adj* **confrontational**, argumentative, combative, antagonistic, oppositional *Opposite*: cooperative

adversary *n* **opponent**, challenger, rival, enemy, antagonist *Opposite*: supporter

adverse *adj* **1 opposing**, contrary, hostile, adversative, antagonistic *Opposite*: cooperative **2 unfavourable**, unpleasant, poor, difficult, unhelpful *Opposite*: favourable

adversity *n* **hardship**, difficulty, danger, misfortune, harsh conditions *Opposite*: privilege

advert *(infml)* *n* **advertisement**, public notice, commercial, poster, billboard

advertise *v* **1 promote**, publicize, market, present, push **2 announce**, broadcast, make known, make public, spread about *Opposite*: keep under wraps

advertisement *n* **commercial**, public notice, poster, billboard, announcement

advertiser *n* **publicist**, promoter, backer, supporter, advocate

advertising *n* **publicity**, promotion, marketing, publicizing, public relations

advice *n* **1 recommendation**, suggestion, guidance, opinion, counsel *(fml)* *Opposite*: warning **2 information**, guidance, instruction, assistance, intelligence

advisability *n* **wisdom**, prudence, sense, desirability, suitability *Opposite*: foolishness

advisable *adj* **sensible**, wise, prudent, worthwhile, desirable *Opposite*: unwise

advise *v* **1 recommend**, direct, guide, instruct, warn **2 inform**, let know, make aware, notify, instruct. *See* COMPARE AND CONTRAST *at* recommend.

advisedly *adv* **deliberately**, carefully, purposefully, on purpose, with intent *Opposite*: carelessly

adviser *n* **consultant**, counsellor, advice-giver, guru

advisory *adj* **advice-giving**, consultative, counselling, review

advocacy *n* **support**, encouragement, backing, sponsorship, promotion *Opposite*: opposition

advocate *n* **supporter**, backer, promoter, believer, activist *Opposite*: opponent ■ *v* **support**, encourage, back, promote, recommend *Opposite*: discourage. *See* COMPARE AND CONTRAST *at* recommend.

aegis *n* **auspices**, sponsorship, guidance, protection, support

aeons *n* **a long time**, years, ages *(infml)*, donkey's years *(infml)*, eternity *(infml)*

aerate *v* **ventilate**, let breathe, expose, freshen *Opposite*: close up

aeration *n* **ventilation**, airing, freshening

aerial *adj* **midair**, airborne, above ground, in-flight, floating *Opposite*: terrestrial

aerobatics *n* **stunts**, manoeuvres, aerial tricks

aerobics *n* **exercises**, keep fit, callisthenics, workout

aerodrome *n* **airfield**, airport, landing strip, landing field, airstrip

aerodynamic *adj* **sleek**, smooth, slick, swept-back, clean

aerogram *n* **air letter**, airmail letter, aerogramme

aerogramme *see* aerogram

aeroplane *n* **aircraft**, plane, flying machine, crate *(dated infml)*

aerosol *n* **spray can**, spray, atomizer, mister

aerospace *n* **atmosphere**, upper atmosphere, space, troposphere, stratosphere

aesthete *n* **art lover**, aesthetician, connoisseur, cognoscente

aesthetic *adj* **artistic**, visual, appealing, beautiful

a few *pron* **a small number**, some, one or two, not many, handful *Opposite*: many

affability *n* **friendliness**, sociability, cordiality, joviality, gregariousness *Opposite*: unfriendliness

affable *adj* **genial**, pleasant, friendly, sociable, jovial *Opposite*: unfriendly

affair *n* **matter**, issue, concern, business, situation

affairs *n* **business**, matters, dealings, activities, concerns

affect *v* **1 influence**, involve, shape, concern, change **2 touch**, move, disturb, mark, distress **3 assume**, put on, imitate, fake, adopt

affectation *n* **1 showing off**, pretension, exaggeration, artificiality, affectedness *Opposite*: naturalness **2 mannerism**, way, quirk, show, trait

affected *adj* **pretentious**, artificial, exaggerated, unnatural, precious *Opposite*: natural

affectedness *n* **exaggeration**, pretension, artificiality, affectation, showing off *Opposite*: naturalness

affecting *adj* **moving**, touching, upsetting, distressing, disturbing

affection *n* **liking**, fondness, regard, warmth, attachment *Opposite*: dislike. *See* COMPARE AND CONTRAST *at* **love**.

affectionate *adj* **loving**, demonstrative, warm, friendly, kind *Opposite*: cold

affective *adj* **emotional**, sentimental, moving, touching, affecting

affianced *(fml) adj* **engaged**, attached, promised, spoken for, involved *Opposite*: unattached

affidavit *n* **sworn statement**, official declaration, affirmation, confirmation, proclamation

affiliate *v* **link**, connect, join, associate, belong to ■ *n* **associate**, partner, colleague, member

affiliation *n* **association**, relationship, connection, attachment, membership

affinity *n* **1 empathy**, sympathy, fellow feeling, attraction, kinship *Opposite*: indifference **2 similarity**, resemblance, likeness, correspondence *Opposite*: difference

affirm *v* **1 support**, confirm, encourage, sustain, uphold **2 assert**, insist, establish, state, verify

affirmation *n* **assertion**, confirmation, pronouncement, declaration, announcement *Opposite*: denial

affirmative *adj* **assenting**, positive, confirmatory, agreeing, favourable *Opposite*: negative

affix *v* **attach**, fix, fasten, stick, pin *Opposite*: remove

afflict *v* **trouble**, bother, affect, worry, distress

afflicted *adj* **distressed**, aggrieved, stricken, plagued, tormented

affliction *n* **1 suffering**, difficulty, burden, problem, hardship **2 illness**, sickness, disease, condition, disorder

affluence *n* **riches**, prosperity, comfortable circumstances, material comfort, privileged circumstances *Opposite*: poverty

affluent *adj* **rich**, wealthy, well-off, well-to-do, prosperous *Opposite*: poor

afford *v* **1 pay for**, have the funds for, manage to pay for, find the money for, come up with the money for **2** *(fml)* **give**, offer, present, allow, provide

affordable *adj* **reasonable**, within your means, inexpensive, cheap *Opposite*: expensive

afforest *v* **reforest**, plant *Opposite*: deforest

affray *n* **scuffle**, fight, brawl, disturbance, commotion *Opposite*: agreement

affront *n* **insult**, injury, slur, slight, outrage *Opposite*: compliment ■ *v* **offend**, insult, upset, outrage, slight *Opposite*: compliment

affronted *adj* **insulted**, injured, slighted, disrespected, upset *Opposite*: pleased

aficionada *n* **devotee**, enthusiast, adherent, fanatic, fan

aficionado *n* **devotee**, enthusiast, adherent, fanatic, fan

afire *see* aflame

aflame *adj* **1 on fire**, burning, in flames, ablaze, afire *Opposite*: extinguished **2 fired up**, enthusiastic, passionate, fired, excited *Opposite*: apathetic

afloat *adj* **flooded**, awash, inundated, under water, submerged *Opposite*: dry

aflutter *adv* **agitated**, excited, trembling, aquiver, nervous *Opposite*: calm

afoot *adj* **happening**, going on, occurring, taking place, up

aforementioned *(fml) adj* **above-mentioned**, said, aforesaid *(fml)*

aforesaid *(fml) see* aforementioned

afraid *adj* **frightened**, fearful, terrified, petrified, scared *Opposite*: unafraid

afresh *adv* **anew**, again, once again, once more, over

after *prep* **1 later than**, past, gone *Opposite*: before **2 behind**, following, to the rear of, next to *Opposite*: ahead of **3 in pursuit of**, in search of, in quest of, following, on the trail of **4 regarding**, considering, taking into account, with, bearing in mind **5 following**, subsequent to, later than *Opposite*: before **6 in the manner of**, in imitation of, in the style of, similar to, like ■ *adv* **afterwards**, subsequently, later, next *Opposite*: before ■ *conj* **when**, once, as soon as *Opposite*: before

after all *adv* **on balance**, finally, in the end, in spite of everything, nevertheless

aftercare *n* **1 post-operative care**, post-hospital care, home care, rehabilitation, recovery programme **2 support**, assistance, help, upkeep, maintenance

aftereffect *n* **repercussion**, reverberation, aftermath, aftershock, final outcome *Opposite*: precursor

afterglow *n* **warmth**, glow, serenity, exhilaration, feel-good factor

afterlife *n* **afterworld**, next world, life after death, eternal life, spirit world

aftermath *n* **result**, consequences, outcome, upshot, repercussion

afternoon *n* **after lunch**, p.m., early afternoon, midafternoon, late afternoon *Opposite*: morning

afters (infml) n **dessert**, pudding, sweet, sweet course, dessert course

afterthought n **addition**, postscript, extra, addendum, reflection Opposite: forethought

afterwards adv **later**, after that, subsequently, then, next Opposite: before

afterworld n **afterlife**, next world, life after death, eternal life, spirit world

again adv **once more**, another time, yet again, over, over again

against prep **1 in opposition to**, not in favour, hostile, critical, opposed **2 next to**, alongside, beside, touching, adjacent to **3 in contradiction of**, contrary to, counter to, in contrast to, compared to

age n **1 time of life**, stage, phase, stage of development **2 era**, period, time, times, epoch ■ v **mature**, grow older, grow up, get on, advance in years

aged adj **old**, elderly, matured, ripened, hoary Opposite: young

age group n **generation**, cohort, age range, age bracket, contemporaries

ageless adj **1 youthful**, fresh, unfading, unspoiled **2 timeless**, endless, perpetual, everlasting, infinite

agency n **1 organization**, bureau, society, charity, group **2 activity**, action, work, intervention, help

agenda n **programme**, schedule, plan, outline, memo

agent n **1 go-between**, manager, negotiator, mediator, representative **2 cause**, means, driving force, instrument, vehicle

age-old adj **ancient**, old, long-standing, venerable, hoary Opposite: recent

ages (infml) n **aeons**, forever (infml), eternity (infml), centuries (infml), donkey's years (infml) Opposite: moment

agglomeration n **accumulation**, mass, collection, cluster, group

agglutinate v **adhere**, stick, clump, join, cling Opposite: separate

agglutination n **accretion**, cohesion, adhesion, clumping, joining

aggrandize v **1 increase**, upgrade, expand, enlarge, develop Opposite: downgrade **2** (fml) **exaggerate**, overstate, puff up, build up, magnify Opposite: belittle

aggrandizement n **1 enhancement**, enlargement, expansion, amelioration, improvement Opposite: deterioration **2 empowerment**, enrichment, promotion, magnification, inflation Opposite: deflation **3** (fml) **exaggeration**, overstatement, braggadocio, glorification, embellishment Opposite: understatement

aggravate v **1** (infml) **annoy**, irritate, exasperate, provoke, make angry Opposite: soothe **2 worsen**, exacerbate, exaggerate, heighten, intensify Opposite: alleviate

aggravated adj **1 serious**, worse, intensified, heightened Opposite: alleviated **2** (infml) **annoyed**, angry, upset, put out, irritated Opposite: peaceful

aggravating (infml) adj **annoying**, irritating, infuriating, maddening, exasperating Opposite: pleasing

aggravation n **1** (infml) **bother**, trouble, difficulty, irritation, hassle (infml) **2 worsening**, exacerbation, intensification, magnification, augmentation Opposite: alleviation

aggregate adj (fml) **collective**, total, combined, cumulative, amassed ■ n (fml) **total**, collection, mass, sum, whole ■ v **combine**, amass, gather, collect, accumulate Opposite: separate

aggregation n **combination**, accumulation, collection, accretion, mass

aggression n **1 attack**, assault, invasion, onslaught, offensive Opposite: defence **2 violence**, hostility, anger, belligerence, antagonism Opposite: friendliness

aggressive adj **1 violent**, hostile, destructive, belligerent, antagonistic Opposite: peaceful **2 forceful**, insistent, assertive, hard-hitting, uncompromising Opposite: mild

aggressiveness n **1 violence**, belligerence, bellicosity, ferociousness, antagonism Opposite: friendliness **2 fierceness**, insistence, forcefulness, determination, assertiveness Opposite: mildness

aggressor n **attacker**, invader, assailant, provoker, antagonist Opposite: defender

aggrieve (fml) v **distress**, upset, hurt, injure, pain

aggrieved adj **1 hurt**, angry, upset, distressed, put out **2 wronged**, mistreated, persecuted, maltreated, victimized

aghast adj **horrified**, amazed, shocked, horror-struck, astonished Opposite: unaffected

agile adj **1 nimble**, supple, lithe, sprightly, alert Opposite: clumsy **2 quick-thinking**, alert, clear-headed, bright Opposite: dull

agility n **nimbleness**, suppleness, quickness, dexterity, liveliness Opposite: clumsiness

agitate v **1 disturb**, stir up, trouble, excite, rouse Opposite: calm **2 campaign**, stir up opinion, protest, advocate, raise a fuss **3 stir**, whisk, toss, shake up, disturb

agitated adj **restless**, disturbed, disconcerted, frantic, tense Opposite: calm

agitation n **1 anxiety**, worry, nervousness, tension, distress Opposite: calm **2 campaigning**, activism, demonstration, protest, stir

agitator n **campaigner**, protester, dissenter, activist

aglow adj **glowing**, shining, radiant, rosy, warm Opposite: pale

AGM n **annual general meeting**, annual meeting, open meeting, public meeting, meeting

agnostic n **doubter**, sceptic, doubting Thomas, questioner, nonbeliever Opposite: believer ■ adj **doubting**, sceptical, uncertain, unsure, unconvinced Opposite: believing

agnosticism n **doubt**, reservation, uncertainty, dissent, distrust Opposite: certainty

ago adv **before**, previously, back, past, since Opposite: ahead

agog adj **eager**, excited, impatient, keen, avid Opposite: uninterested

agonize v **worry**, struggle, strive, vacillate, wrestle

agonized adj **anguished**, tormented, suffering, tortured, in pain

agonizing adj **excruciating**, unbearable, painful, distressing, worrying

agony n **anguish**, pain, torture, suffering, distress Opposite: ecstasy

agrarian adj **agricultural**, farm, farming, land, rural Opposite: urban

agree v 1 **be in agreement**, be in accord, concur, see eye to eye, coincide Opposite: differ 2 **consent**, say yes, assent, acquiesce, accede Opposite: refuse 3 **decide**, reach agreement, come to an agreement, come to an understanding, settle Opposite: disagree 4 **correspond**, match, be the same, tie in, harmonize Opposite: differ

---

COMPARE AND CONTRAST CORE MEANING: accept an idea, plan, or course of action that has been put forward
agree be in agreement with somebody else about a course of action; **concur** agree or reach agreement independently on a specified point; **acquiesce** agree to or comply with something passively; **consent** give formal permission for something to happen; **assent** agree to something formally.

---

agreeable adj 1 **pleasant**, pleasing, pleasurable, enjoyable, delightful Opposite: unpleasant 2 **friendly**, affable, pleasant, courteous, delightful Opposite: disagreeable 3 **amenable**, willing, in accord, compliant, happy Opposite: unwilling

agreeably adv **pleasantly**, enjoyably, delightfully, pleasingly, pleasurably Opposite: unpleasantly

agreed adj **decided**, settled, arranged, approved, fixed

agreement n 1 **contract**, arrangement, covenant, treaty, promise 2 **accord**, concord, conformity, harmony, union Opposite: disagreement

agribusiness n **farming industry**, farming, agro-industry, agricultural business, business

agricultural adj 1 **agrarian**, farming, agronomic, farmed, cultivated 2 **unindustrialized**, pastoral, rural, bucolic, undeveloped Opposite: urban

agriculture n **cultivation**, husbandry, crop growing, food production, agronomy

aground adj **beached**, ashore, stranded, stuck, grounded Opposite: afloat

ahead adv 1 **in front**, to the front, in the lead, in advance, further on Opposite: behind 2 **into the future**, in the future, to come, yet to be, forward Opposite: ago 3 **early**, in advance, prematurely, up front, ahead of Opposite: late

ahead of prep 1 **in front of**, before, beyond, up ahead of, in advance of Opposite: behind 2 **before**, in advance of, earlier than, in front of, just before Opposite: after

aid v **help**, assist, support, abet, give support to Opposite: thwart ■ n **assistance**, help, support, relief, encouragement

aid and abet v **conspire**, collaborate, collude, connive, be in league with

aide n **assistant**, adviser, helper, supporter, personal assistant. See COMPARE AND CONTRAST at assistant.

aide-de-camp see aide

aide-mémoire (fml) n 1 **summary**, outline, résumé, synopsis, digest 2 **memory aid**, mnemonic, note, reminder, memorandum

ailing adj 1 **underperforming**, failing, deteriorating, inadequate Opposite: thriving 2 (dated) **unwell**, ill, sick, unfit, laid up Opposite: well

ailment n **illness**, sickness, disease, disorder, complaint

aim v 1 **aspire**, plan, intend, try, mean 2 **point towards**, point, take aim, direct, mark ■ n **goal**, purpose, intention, object, objective

aimless adj **pointless**, meaningless, useless, worthless, purposeless Opposite: purposeful

aimlessness n **pointlessness**, purposelessness, senselessness Opposite: purposefulness

air n 1 **atmosphere**, space, sky, heaven 2 **appearance**, look, manner, tone, way of being 3 **tune**, melody, song ■ v 1 **declare**, express, vent, make public, proclaim Opposite: suppress 2 **ventilate**, aerate, expose

airborne adj **flying**, aerial, floating, midair, in-flight

airbrush v **blend in**, touch up, cover up, colour, blend

air conditioner n **air cooler**, air exchanger, ventilator, dehumidifier, extractor Opposite: heater

air conditioning n **air-cooling system**, ventilation system, air-circulation system, air exchange system, climate control Opposite: heating

aircraft n **aeroplane**, plane, flying machine, airplane (US)

WORD BANK
❏ **types of civil aircraft** airliner, airship, autogiro, biplane, blimp, dirigible, convertible jet, glider, hang glider, helicopter, jet, light aircraft, microlight, monoplane, paraglider, seaplane, skiplane, STOL, zeppelin
❏ **types of military aircraft** bomber, convertiplane,

fighter, fighter-bomber, helicopter gunship, stealth bomber, transport, VTOL
❑ **parts of an aircraft** aileron, air brake, autopilot, cabin, cockpit, ejector seat, fin, flight deck, flight recorder, fuselage, jet engine, joystick, landing gear, nose cone, nose wheel, propeller, rotor, rudder, tail, tailplane, tail rotor, turbofan, turbojet, turboprop, undercarriage, wing

airdrop v parachute in, airlift, send in, parachute, drop

airfare n fare, tariff, charge, ticket price, seat rate

airfield n airstrip, landing field, landing strip, aerodrome, airport

airily adv lightheartedly, lightly, carelessly, casually, easily Opposite: seriously

airiness n 1 lightheartedness, buoyancy, animation, vivacity, cheerfulness Opposite: seriousness 2 spaciousness, openness, freshness, lightness Opposite: closeness

airing n 1 ventilation, aeration, exposure to air, drying, freshening 2 outing, trip, excursion 3 exposure, expression, disclosure, divulgence, ventilation

airless adj stuffy, close, muggy, unventilated, oppressive Opposite: airy

airlift v fly, transfer, winch, lift

airline n air company, commercial airline, scheduled carrier, carrier

airlock n 1 blockage, obstruction, air bubble, occlusion, block 2 compartment, cubicle, cell, chamber

airmail v post, send, dispatch, mail (US)

airplay n airtime, playing time, exposure, promotion, publicity

airport n airfield, aerodrome, airstrip, landing field, landing strip

airpower n air strength, airborne army, air force, air defence

air raid n aerial attack, aerial bombardment, air attack, bombing, air strike

airship n dirigible, zeppelin, blimp, aircraft

airshow n aerobatics, stunts, show, exhibition, fly-past

airsick adj travel sick, nauseous, queasy, sick, ill

airsickness n travel sickness, nausea, queasiness, sickness

airspace n territory, skies, boundaries, limits, flight exclusion zone

air strike n aerial attack, aerial bombardment, bombing, air raid, air offensive

airstrip n runway, landing strip, strip, landing field, airfield

airtight adj 1 sealed, hermetically sealed, hermetic, impermeable 2 sound, strong, unquestionable, unassailable, watertight Opposite: vulnerable

airwaves n radio waves, frequencies, frequency bands, radio frequencies, broadcasting frequencies

airway n 1 air route, air corridor, flight lane, air lane, route 2 airline, air transport company, air network

airworthiness n safety, soundness, reliability, working order

airworthy adj flyable, flightworthy, in working order, in good order, safe

airy adj 1 roomy, ventilated, fresh, light, open Opposite: stuffy 2 unconcerned, nonchalant, casual, light, carefree Opposite: serious

airy-fairy (infml) adj vague, unfocused, fanciful, unrealistic, impractical Opposite: practical

aisle n passageway, gangway, walkway, passage, corridor

ajar adj half closed, open, agape (literary)

a.k.a. adj also known as, better known as, otherwise known as, known to you and me as, alias

akin adj similar, of the same kind, parallel, like, analogous Opposite: unlike

alacrity n promptness, quickness, rapidity, speed, readiness Opposite: sluggishness

alarm n 1 fear, apprehension, terror, fright, panic 2 alarm bell, bell, warning, distress signal, siren ■ v frighten, terrify, panic, distress, startle Opposite: calm

alarmed adj worried, upset, distressed, shocked, frightened Opposite: untroubled

alarming adj disturbing, upsetting, frightening, distressing, shocking Opposite: soothing

alarmist n pessimist, doom merchant, doomsayer, doomster (infml) ■ adj pessimistic, gloomy, panicky, exaggerated, hysterical Opposite: down-to-earth

alas adv unfortunately, sadly, regrettably, unhappily, unluckily

albatross n millstone, shackle, encumbrance, burden, impediment

albeit conj although, though, even though, even if, notwithstanding (fml)

album n 1 book, folder, photograph album, photo album, autograph album 2 record, LP, CD, tape, cassette

albumen n egg white, white, white of egg

alchemy n pseudoscience, experimentation, transformation

alcoholic adj intoxicating, inebriating, fermented, distilled, strong Opposite: nonalcoholic

alcove n recess, niche, bay, cubicle, nook

alert adj attentive, watchful, prepared, aware, vigilant Opposite: unprepared ■ n warning, signal, alarm, siren, red alert ■ v warn, forewarn, notify, draw somebody's attention to, tell

alertness n attentiveness, watchfulness, awareness, preparedness, vigilance Opposite: inattentiveness

alfresco *adv* **out of doors**, outdoors, outside, in the open air, on the lawn *Opposite*: indoors ■ *adj* **outdoor**, open-air, outside, patio, picnic *Opposite*: indoor

algorithm *n* **procedure**, process, system, set of rules

alias *adj* **also known as**, also called, otherwise known as, under the name of, a.k.a. ■ *n* **assumed name**, pseudonym, pen name, nom de plume, stage name

alibi *(infml)* *n* **explanation**, excuse, reason, defence, account

alien *n* **1 extraterrestrial**, creature from outer space, space invader, Martian, intelligent life form **2 foreigner**, stranger, immigrant, resident alien ■ *adj* **unfamiliar**, unknown, strange, outlandish, unusual *Opposite*: familiar

alienate *v* **estrange**, make unfriendly, disaffect, set against, distance *Opposite*: involve

alienated *adj* **estranged**, disaffected, isolated, withdrawn, separate *Opposite*: involved

alienation *n* **estrangement**, disaffection, unfriendliness, hostility, isolation *Opposite*: closeness

alight *v* **1 get off**, get out, descend, dismount **2 land**, perch, rest, stop, settle ■ *adj* **burning**, on fire, in flames, blazing, ablaze

align *v* **1 bring into line**, line up, make straight, make parallel, make even *Opposite*: disarrange **2 side with**, support, ally, affiliate, associate *Opposite*: distance

aligned *adj* **allied**, united, associated, affiliated, ranged

alignment *n* **1 position**, arrangement, placement, configuration, orientation *Opposite*: disorder **2 alliance**, association, coalition, grouping, affiliation

alike *adj* **similar**, comparable, the same, identical, like *Opposite*: different

alimentary canal *n* **bowels**, guts, innards, insides, intestines

---

WORD BANK
❑ **parts of an alimentary canal** anus, appendix, bile duct, bladder, bowel, caecum, colon, duodenum, gallbladder, gullet, gut, intestine, kidney, large intestine, liver, oesophagus, pancreas, rectum, small intestine, spleen, stomach, throat

---

alimony *n* **allowance**, maintenance, support, financial support, funding

alive *adj* **1 living**, animate, breathing *Opposite*: dead **2 energetic**, busy, active, perky, vibrant *Opposite*: inactive **3 thriving**, active, flourishing, successful, blooming *Opposite*: quiet **4 full**, packed, teeming, awash, swarming *Opposite*: dead **5 aware**, sensitive, tuned in, alert, interested *Opposite*: unaware. *See* COMPARE AND CONTRAST *at* living.

all *adv* *(infml)* **altogether**, completely, entirely, very, wholly ■ *pron* **1 every one**, each and

every one, every single one, each *Opposite*: none **2 every bit**, the entire, the complete, the whole *Opposite*: none

all along *adv* **from the start**, right from the start, from the very beginning, from the word go, from the beginning

all and sundry *pron* **everyone**, everybody, one and all, every person, the whole world *Opposite*: nobody

allay *v* **dispel**, alleviate, calm, assuage, relieve *Opposite*: stimulate

all clear *n* **green light**, all-clear signal, nod, signal, permission *Opposite*: thumbs-down *(infml)*

all-comers *n* **everyone**, everybody, one and all, all, the general public

allegation *n* **claim**, accusation, assertion, contention, charge

allege *v* **claim**, assert, contend, charge, declare

alleged *adj* **supposed**, unproven, suspected, so-called, assumed *Opposite*: confirmed

allegiance *n* **loyalty**, commitment, adherence, faithfulness, duty *Opposite*: disloyalty

allegorical *adj* **metaphorical**, symbolic, emblematic, figurative, allegoric *Opposite*: literal

allegory *n* **parable**, fable, metaphor, symbol, extended metaphor

all-embracing *adj* **comprehensive**, complete, extensive, catholic, wide-ranging *Opposite*: narrow

all-encompassing *see* **all-embracing**

allergic *adj* **sensitive**, affected, sensitized, hypersensitive, averse *(fml)*

allergy *n* **1 reaction**, allergic reaction, sensitivity, hypersensitivity **2** *(infml)* **aversion**, dislike, antipathy, distaste, hate *Opposite*: liking

alleviate *v* **ease**, lessen, assuage, improve, lighten *Opposite*: aggravate

alleviation *n* **mitigation**, lessening, improvement, easing, assuagement *Opposite*: aggravation

all for *prep* **in favour of**, pro, for, in support of *Opposite*: against

alliance *n* **1 coalition**, grouping, association, union, cooperation **2 relationship**, partnership, bond, link, tie

allied *adj* **1 joined**, united, combined, amalgamated, aligned *Opposite*: unilateral **2 related**, associated, connected, akin, linked *Opposite*: unrelated

all in *adj* **1 total**, inclusive, overall, global, all-inclusive **2 exhausted**, weary, tired, tired out, worn out *Opposite*: fresh

all in all *adv* **all things considered**, on the whole, in general, generally speaking, when all is said and done

all-inclusive *adj* **comprehensive**, grand, complete, broad, all-embracing *Opposite*: incomplete

alliteration *n* **assonance**, consonance, sound repetition, sound pattern, resonance

alliterative *adj* **repetitive**, echoing, assonant, poetic

allocate *v* **assign**, allot, apportion, distribute, deal

allocation *n* **1 distribution**, provision, sharing out, apportionment, division **2 share**, portion, allotment, allowance

all-or-nothing *adj* **win-or-lose**, uncompromising, winner-take-all, rigid, zero-sum *Opposite*: flexible

allot *v* **assign**, designate, allocate, earmark, apportion

allotment *n* **1 vegetable garden**, vegetable patch, plot **2 share**, portion, part, allocation, allowance

all-out *adj* **maximum**, supreme, extreme, thoroughgoing, determined *Opposite*: halfhearted

allow *v* **1 let**, permit, agree, consent, tolerate *Opposite*: forbid **2 allocate**, set aside, make available, set a limit, allot **3** *(fml)* **accept**, admit, acknowledge, admit as true, grant *Opposite*: disallow

allowable *adj* **permissible**, acceptable, tolerable, admissible, suitable *Opposite*: unacceptable

allowance *n* **payment**, grant, stipend, pocket money, pin money

allowed *adj* **permitted**, allotted, authorized, approved, legitimate *Opposite*: prohibited

allow for *v* **take into account**, take into consideration, make allowance for, make allowances for, bear in mind

alloy *n* **1 blend**, amalgam, compound, mixture, composite **2 additive**, contaminant, adulterant, pollutant, ingredient. *See* COMPARE AND CONTRAST *at* mixture.

all-powerful *adj* **omnipotent**, invincible, supreme, almighty *Opposite*: weak

all-purpose *adj* **general purpose**, multipurpose, universal, overall, versatile *Opposite*: specialized

all-round *adj* **1 versatile**, multifaceted, exceptional, outstanding, talented **2 all-inclusive**, grand, inclusive, sweeping, large-scale *Opposite*: restricted **3 on all sides**, in every direction, everywhere, in all directions

all-star *adj* **star-studded**, celebrity, famous, prestigious, well-known *Opposite*: unknown

all-time *adj* **unsurpassed**, record, unprecedented, unparalleled, best *Opposite*: insignificant

allude *v* **refer**, make reference, make allusion, mention, indicate

allure *n* **attraction**, appeal, draw, magnetism, charm

alluring *adj* **appealing**, attractive, tempting, interesting, fascinating *Opposite*: repulsive

allusion *n* **reference**, mention, hint, suggestion, insinuation

allusive *adj* **indirect**, oblique, hinting, referential, suggestive *Opposite*: direct

alluvial *adj* **sedimentary**, silty, deposited, muddy, sandy

all-weather *adj* **year-round**, all-season, rain-or-shine, all-purpose, four-season

ally *v* **associate**, join, affiliate, align, connect ■ *n* **friend**, helper, supporter, assistant, partner *Opposite*: enemy

alma mater *n* **old school**, college, university, school, institution

almanac *n* **directory**, calendar, yearbook, handbook, manual

almighty *adj* **1 omnipotent**, invincible, allpowerful, supreme, omnipresent **2** *(infml)* **enormous**, massive, huge, immense, gigantic

almost *adv* **nearly**, not quite, just about, virtually, practically *Opposite*: exactly

alms *n* **charity**, donation, contribution, gift, offering

aloft *adv* **in the air**, in flight, airborne, on the wing, high up *Opposite*: below

alone *adv* **unaccompanied**, by yourself, on your own, single-handedly, unaided *Opposite*: accompanied ■ *adj* **lonely**, abandoned, deserted, isolated, forlorn

along *prep* **next to**, beside, by the side of, by, adjacent to

alongside *prep* **next to**, beside, at the side of, flanking, near ■ *adv* **abreast**, nearby, cheek by jowl, shoulder to shoulder, at close quarters

along with *prep* **with**, together with, in company with, in conjunction with, as well as *Opposite*: without

aloof *adj* **1 remote**, standoffish, proud, reserved, indifferent *Opposite*: friendly **2 separate**, remote, distant, set apart, away *Opposite*: close

aloofness *n* **1 unfriendliness**, coldness, detachment, remoteness, reserve *Opposite*: friendliness **2 distance**, remoteness, separateness, independence *Opposite*: closeness

aloud *adv* **1 audibly**, out loud, distinctly, noticeably, clearly *Opposite*: silently **2 loudly**, noisily, riotously, blusteringly, boisterously *Opposite*: quietly

alpha *adj* **important**, dominant, chief, primary, leading

alphabet *n* **writing system**, script, character set, letters, symbols

WORD BANK
❏ types of alphabet Arabic, Braille, cuneiform, Cyrillic, Greek, Hebrew, hieroglyphics, hiragana, ideogram, kanji, katakana, phonetic, pictogram, Roman, runic

alphabetic *see* alphabetical

alphabetical *adj* **arranged**, in order, listed, in a list, sequential

alpine *adj* **mountainous**, mountain, high-altitude, hilly, high

already *adv* **by now**, previously, before now, even now, by this time

also *adv* **1 in addition**, and, what's more, moreover, furthermore **2 too**, as well, likewise, similarly, correspondingly

also-ran *n* **loser**, failure, no-hoper *(infml)*, flop *(infml)*, dud *(infml)* *Opposite*: winner

altar *n* **table**, bench, slab, stand, platform

alter *v* **change**, modify, adjust, vary, amend *Opposite*: maintain. *See* COMPARE AND CONTRAST *at* **change**.

alteration *n* **modification**, adjustment, change, variation, amendment

altercate *v* **argue**, quarrel, disagree, dispute, squabble

altercation *n* **argument**, quarrel, disagreement, dispute, exchange

alter ego *n* **double**, shadow, doppelgänger, twin, clone

alternate *v* **1 interchange**, rotate, exchange, intersperse, substitute **2 fluctuate**, vary, swing, oscillate, vacillate ■ *adj* **1 every other**, alternating, every second **2 alternative**, substitute, different, another, other *Opposite*: same

alternately *adv* **off and on**, in turn, by turns, one after the other, interchangeably *Opposite*: consecutively

alternation *n* **change**, interchange, repetition, rotation, fluctuation

alternative *n* **1 replacement**, substitute, substitution, change, another possibility **2 option**, choice, freedom of choice, discretion ■ *adj* **1 other**, another, substitute, alternate, different **2 unconventional**, unorthodox, nonstandard, complementary, unusual *Opposite*: conventional

alternatively *adv* **on the other hand**, otherwise, instead, then again

although *conj* **though**, even though, even if, while, granting

altitude *n* **height**, elevation, height above sea level, loftiness, highness

altogether *adv* **1 in total**, all in all, all told, overall, in sum **2 totally**, completely, wholly, thoroughly, entirely **3 on the whole**, when all's said and done, overall, in general, mostly

altruism *n* **unselfishness**, self-sacrifice, humanity, selflessness, philanthropy *Opposite*: selfishness

altruistic *adj* **unselfish**, humane, selfless, philanthropic, noble *Opposite*: selfish

alumna *n* **graduate**, former student, ex-student, alum *(infml)*

alumnus *n* **graduate**, former student, ex-student, alum *(infml)*

always *adv* **1 at all times**, continuously, all the time, continually, constantly *Opposite*:

never **2 forever**, for all time, for eternity, until the end of time, for ever and a day *Opposite*: temporarily

a.m. *adj* **morning**, before noon, before lunch, pre-lunch *Opposite*: p.m.

amalgam *n* **mixture**, mix, combination, blend, fusion. *See* COMPARE AND CONTRAST *at* **mixture**.

amalgamate *v* **merge**, join, combine, unite, integrate *Opposite*: separate

amalgamated *adj* **combined**, merged, joined, incorporated, united *Opposite*: separated

amalgamation *n* **1 combination**, mixture, mix, blend, fusion **2 merger**, union, incorporation, consolidation, unification

amanuensis *n* **secretary**, scribe, writer, copier, copyist

amass *v* **accumulate**, collect, gather, stockpile, hoard *Opposite*: distribute. *See* COMPARE AND CONTRAST *at* **collect**.

amateur *adj* **1 part-time**, unpaid, non-professional, leisure, recreational *Opposite*: full-time **2 unprofessional**, shoddy, slapdash, substandard, incompetent *Opposite*: skilful ■ *n* **layperson**, nonprofessional, dilettante, dabbler *Opposite*: professional

amateurish *adj* **unprofessional**, shoddy, slapdash, clumsy, crude *Opposite*: skilful

amateurishness *n* **clumsiness**, ineptness, incompetence, unprofessionalism, shoddiness *Opposite*: professionalism

amaze *v* **astonish**, astound, shock, stun, startle

amazed *adj* **astonished**, astounded, shocked, stunned, startled

amazement *n* **astonishment**, wonder, admiration, shock, incredulity

amazing *adj* **astonishing**, astounding, remarkable, wonderful, incredible *Opposite*: unremarkable

ambassador *n* **diplomat**, envoy, representative, emissary, legate

ambience *n* **atmosphere**, feel, setting, environment, mood

ambient *adj* **surrounding**, background, local, neighbouring

ambiguity *n* **vagueness**, uncertainty, haziness, doubt, indistinctness *Opposite*: clarity

ambiguous *adj* **vague**, unclear, abstruse, equivocal, uncertain *Opposite*: clear

ambiguousness *n* **abstruseness**, opacity, obscurity, vagueness, uncertainty *Opposite*: clarity

ambit *n* **scope**, extent, range, realm, area

ambition *n* **1 drive**, determination, motivation, desire, spirit *Opposite*: apathy **2 goal**, aim, objective, aspiration, dream

ambitious *adj* **1 determined**, ruthless, striving, motivated, aspiring *Opposite*: unmotivated **2 grand**, impressive, bold, large-scale, elaborate *Opposite*: small-scale

ambitiously *adv* **1 determinedly**, ruthlessly, single-mindedly, energetically, pushily *(infml) Opposite*: unambitiously **2 optimistically**, overconfidently, unrealistically, idealistically, impractically *Opposite*: realistically

ambivalence *n* **uncertainty**, contradiction, unsureness, doubt, inconsistency *Opposite*: certainty

ambivalent *adj* **unsure**, undecided, in two minds, hesitant, uncertain *Opposite*: decisive

amble *v* **stroll**, saunter, wander, walk, mosey *(infml) Opposite*: dash

ambush *n* **trap**, surprise attack, ensnarement, ambuscade *(literary)* ▪ *v* **trap**, ensnare, lie in wait, take by surprise, waylay

ameliorate *(fml) v* **better**, perfect, amend, upgrade, enrich *Opposite*: deteriorate

amelioration *n* **improvement**, enhancement, enrichment, upgrading, amendment *Opposite*: deterioration

amenability *n* **acquiescence**, docility, willingness, responsiveness, pliability *Opposite*: stubbornness

amenable *adj* **agreeable**, open, acquiescent, willing, docile *Opposite*: stubborn

amend *v* **alter**, adjust, modify, revise, change *Opposite*: maintain

amendment *n* **alteration**, adjustment, modification, revision, change

amends *n* **compensation**, recompense, replacement, restitution, return

amenity *n* **1 facility**, convenience, comfort, service, feature **2 pleasantness**, attractiveness, niceness, agreeableness, affability *Opposite*: discomfort

amiability *n* **friendliness**, amicability, sociability, cordiality, agreeableness *Opposite*: unfriendliness

amiable *adj* **friendly**, sociable, agreeable, affable, kind *Opposite*: unfriendly

amicable *adj* **friendly**, good-natured, harmonious, agreeable, good-humoured *Opposite*: hostile

amid *prep* **1 in the middle of**, among, in the midst of, within, in **2 accompanied by**, along with, in the course of, during, at the same time as

amidst *see* **amid**

amiss *adv* **incorrectly**, inappropriately, mistakenly, wrongly, erroneously *Opposite*: correctly ▪ *adj* **incorrect**, inappropriate, mistaken, wrong, erroneous *Opposite*: correct

amity *(fml) n* **friendship**, peace, good relations, goodwill, harmony *Opposite*: hostility

ammo *(infml) see* **ammunition**

ammunition *n* **bullets**, shells, missiles, bombs, grenades

amnesia *n* **loss of memory**, memory loss, forgetfulness, obliviousness, oblivion *Opposite*: recall

amnesty *n* **pardon**, reprieve, forgiveness, absolution, exoneration

among *prep* **1 in the middle of**, in the midst of, amid, amidst, surrounded by **2 with**, along with, amid, together with, in the company of **3 as well as**, including, in addition to

amongst *see* **among**

amoral *adj* **unprincipled**, unethical, dishonourable, unscrupulous, immoral *Opposite*: principled

amorality *n* **wickedness**, sinfulness, unscrupulousness, immorality *Opposite*: morality

amorous *adj* **ardent**, passionate, affectionate, loving, romantic *Opposite*: dispassionate

amorphous *adj* **formless**, shapeless, nebulous, vague, unstructured *Opposite*: defined

amortization *n* **repayment**, paying back, payback, paying off, remuneration

amortize *v* **pay back**, repay, pay off, remunerate

amount *n* **quantity**, sum, total, volume, expanse

amount to *v* **add up to**, total, come to, make, be equal to

ampersand *n* **and sign**, and, symbol, character

amphitheatre *n* **1 stadium**, arena, bowl, ring, dome **2 lecture theatre**, auditorium, lecture hall, lecture room

ample *adj* **enough**, sufficient, adequate, plenty, plentiful *Opposite*: insufficient

amplification *n* **1 intensification**, strengthening, magnification, augmentation, extension *Opposite*: reduction **2 elaboration**, clarification, development, expansion *Opposite*: obfuscation

amplify *v* **1 intensify**, increase, strengthen, magnify, enlarge *Opposite*: reduce **2 enlarge on**, go into detail, elaborate, add to, expand *Opposite*: abbreviate. *See* COMPARE AND CONTRAST *at* increase.

amplitude *n* **largeness**, scale, fullness, breadth, generosity

amply *adv* **sufficiently**, adequately, abundantly, thoroughly, fully *Opposite*: insufficiently

ampoule *n* **container**, vessel, bottle, flask

ampule *see* **ampoule**

amputate *v* **cut off**, chop off, remove, sever, separate

amulet *n* **charm**, good luck charm, talisman, lucky charm, juju

amuse *v* **1 make laugh**, make smile, charm, please, divert *Opposite*: depress **2 entertain**, keep busy, interest, absorb, engross *Opposite*: bore

amused *adj* **smiling**, laughing, pleased, tickled, entertained *Opposite*: annoyed

amusement *n* **1 laughter**, enjoyment, delight, fun, pleasure *Opposite*: sadness **2 entertainment**, pastime, hobby, distraction, diversion

amusement park *n* **funfair**, fair, theme park, amusements

amusements *n* **fun fair**, amusement arcade, amusement park, pier

amusing adj **funny**, humorous, entertaining, comical, witty Opposite: turgid

anachronism n **relic**, leftover, archaism, holdover, survival

anachronistic adj **out-of-date**, dated, old-fashioned, old, obsolete Opposite: contemporary

anaemic adj **weak**, feeble, lacklustre, insipid, pale Opposite: strong

anaesthetic n **painkiller**, local anaesthetic, general anaesthetic, sedative, analgesic ■ adj **painkilling**, numbing, deadening, sedating

anaesthetize v **deaden**, numb, freeze, sedate, put under

anaesthetized adj **knocked out**, out cold, under, asleep, sedated

analgesia n 1 **numbness**, painlessness, insensibility, insensitivity, unawareness Opposite: pain 2 **pain control**, pain relief, pain management, pain killing, numbing

analgesic adj **painkilling**, palliative, pain-relieving, deadening, anodyne ■ n **painkiller**, palliative, pain reliever, anodyne, anaesthetic

analogous adj **similar**, equivalent, parallel, corresponding, comparable Opposite: different

analogue n **equivalent**, similarity, referent, correspondent (fml)

analogy n **similarity**, likeness, equivalence, parallel, correspondence Opposite: contrast

analyse v **examine**, study, investigate, scrutinize, evaluate

analysis n 1 **testing**, examination, assay, assessment 2 **examination**, study, investigation, scrutiny, breakdown 3 **psychoanalysis**, psychotherapy, psychiatry

analyst n 1 **forecaster**, predictor, market analyst, city analyst, expert 2 **psychoanalyst**, psychotherapist, psychiatrist

analytic adj **logical**, investigative, diagnostic, systematic, critical Opposite: illogical

analytical see analytic

anarchic adj 1 **revolutionary**, radical, anarchistic, rebellious, anarchical 2 **lawless**, chaotic, disordered, disorderly, out of control Opposite: orderly

anarchical see anarchic

anarchist n **revolutionary**, rebel, nihilist, radical

anarchistic adj **revolutionary**, antigovernment, anarchic, anarchical, rebellious

anarchy n **disorder**, chaos, lawlessness, revolution, mob rule Opposite: order

an arm and a leg (infml) n **king's ransom**, small fortune, fortune, packet (infml), bomb (infml) Opposite: pittance

anathema n **bane**, scourge, canker, thorn in somebody's side, irritant

anatomical adj **functional**, structural, material, bodily, body

anatomy n 1 **structure**, composition, makeup, framework, frame 2 **analysis**, examination, investigation, review, study

ancestor n 1 **forebear**, antecedent, forefather, predecessor, progenitor Opposite: descendant 2 **forerunner**, precursor, antecedent, prototype, progenitor Opposite: successor

ancestral adj **family**, familial, inherited

ancestry n **lineage**, descent, origin, heritage, extraction

anchor n **newsreader**, commentator, presenter, announcer, broadcaster ■ v **fasten**, attach, fix, affix, secure Opposite: unfasten

anchorage n **port**, harbour, marina, dock, quay

anchorite n **hermit**, recluse, solitary

anchorman see anchorperson

anchorperson n **newsreader**, presenter, broadcaster, anchor, journalist

anchorwoman see anchorperson

ancient adj 1 **antique**, early, earliest, prehistoric, primeval Opposite: modern 2 **old-fashioned**, archaic, obsolete, outdated, antiquated Opposite: up-to-date

ancillary adj **auxiliary**, subsidiary, supplementary, additional, secondary Opposite: main

and conj 1 **then**, after that, next, as a consequence, afterwards 2 **in addition to**, as well as, with, along with, coupled with 3 **furthermore**, moreover, also, what is more, in addition

and/or conj **either/or**, one or both, either or both

android n **robot**, automaton, bionic person, machine, humanoid

anecdotal adj **subjective**, circumstantial, hearsay, unreliable, untrustworthy Opposite: objective

anecdote n **story**, tale, sketch, narrative, narration

anew adv **again**, afresh, once again, once more, over

angel n 1 **seraph**, archangel, cherub, messenger, spirit Opposite: demon 2 **backer**, sponsor, guarantor, patron, benefactor. See COMPARE AND CONTRAST at backer.

angelic adj **innocent**, good, saintly, adorable, virtuous Opposite: wicked

anger n **annoyance**, irritation, fury, rage, wrath Opposite: calmness ■ v **annoy**, irritate, infuriate, incense, enrage Opposite: pacify

COMPARE AND CONTRAST CORE MEANING: a feeling of strong displeasure in response to an assumed injury

anger a strong feeling of grievance; **annoyance** mild anger and impatience; **irritation** impatience and exasperation; **resentment** aggrieved feelings caused by a sense of unfair treatment; **indignation** anger because something seems unfair or unreasonable; **fury** violent anger; **rage** sudden and extreme anger; **wrath** strong anger, often with a desire for revenge; **ire** (literary) strong anger.

angle n point of view, viewpoint, approach, position, slant ■ v slant, tilt, turn, twist, slope *Opposite*: level

angle for v fish for, seek, solicit, try for, try to get

angry adj annoyed, irritated, fuming, livid, irate *Opposite*: calm

angst n anguish, torment, anxiety, trouble, worry *Opposite*: happiness. *See* COMPARE AND CONTRAST *at* worry.

angst-ridden adj anguished, tormented, fearful, troubled, worried *Opposite*: content

anguish n suffering, torment, agony, torture, pain *Opposite*: contentment

anguished adj tormented, suffering, agonized, tortured, pained *Opposite*: content

angular adj bony, rawboned, rangy, lanky, gaunt *Opposite*: rounded

angularity n boniness, thinness, ranginess, lankiness, sharpness *Opposite*: roundness

animal n 1 creature, being, beast, mammal, organism 2 monster, beast, brute, swine ■ adj physical, bodily, visceral, instinctive, innate *Opposite*: spiritual

animate v liven up, enliven, rouse, bring to life, stir *Opposite*: put a damper on ■ adj living, alive, live, breathing, flesh-and-blood *Opposite*: inanimate. *See* COMPARE AND CONTRAST *at* living.

animated adj energetic, active, vibrant, vivacious, dynamic *Opposite*: lifeless

animation n 1 liveliness, energy, vibrancy, life, vigour *Opposite*: apathy 2 cartoon, moving picture, animatronics, computer graphics, simulation

animosity n hostility, hatred, loathing, ill feeling, ill will *Opposite*: goodwill. *See* COMPARE AND CONTRAST *at* dislike.

animus n 1 hostility, animosity, hatred, ill will, detestation *Opposite*: friendliness 2 temperament, personality, disposition, spirit, attitude

anklet n chain, bangle, band

annals n records, archives, chronicles, history, accounts

anneal v harden, strengthen, toughen, galvanize, forge

annex v take possession of, seize, take over, capture, invade *Opposite*: cede

annexation n capture, seizure, takeover, occupation, invasion *Opposite*: surrender

annexe n extension, new building, addition, wing, ancillary building

annihilate v 1 destroy, obliterate, extinguish, eradicate, exterminate *Opposite*: protect 2 defeat, rout, thrash, overwhelm, crush *Opposite*: lose

annihilation n total destruction, obliteration, extinction, eradication, extermination *Opposite*: protection

anniversary n birthday, centenary, bicentenary, wedding anniversary, centennial *(US)*

annotate v gloss, add footnotes, interpret, explain, make notes on

annotated adj glossed, marked, marked up

annotation n footnote, gloss, marginal note, explanation, note

announce v proclaim, make known, publicize, broadcast, declare *Opposite*: keep secret

announcement n statement, declaration, message, notice, proclamation

announcer n presenter, broadcaster, telecaster, reporter, newsreader

annoy v irritate, exasperate, vex, irk, get on your nerves, bother *Opposite*: please

COMPARE AND CONTRAST CORE MEANING: cause a mild degree of anger in somebody
annoy cause impatience or anger in somebody; **irritate** annoy somebody slightly; **exasperate** arouse anger or frustration in somebody; **vex** annoy somebody, especially causing upset or distress; **irk** annoy somebody by being tiresome or tedious.

annoyance n irritation, displeasure, exasperation, anger, infuriation *Opposite*: pleasure. *See* COMPARE AND CONTRAST *at* anger.

annoyed adj angry, irritated, infuriated, exasperated, aggravated *Opposite*: pleased

annoying adj maddening, irritating, infuriating, bothersome, exasperating *Opposite*: pleasing

annual adj yearly, twelve-monthly, once a year, once yearly, every twelve months

annuity n pension, allowance, income, grant, stipend

annul v cancel, call off, withdraw, end, dissolve *Opposite*: prolong. *See* COMPARE AND CONTRAST *at* nullify.

annulment n cancellation, withdrawal, dissolution, invalidation, deletion

anode n terminal, connection, contact

anodyne adj painkilling, palliative, pain-relieving, deadening, analgesic

anoint v smear, daub, rub, smooth, massage

anomalous adj irregular, uncharacteristic, strange, abnormal, inconsistent *Opposite*: usual

anomaly n irregularity, incongruity, difference, variance, abnormality

anonymity n 1 secrecy, obscurity, concealment, inconspicuousness, namelessness 2 indistinctness, blandness, insignificance, ordinariness, dullness *Opposite*: distinctiveness

anonymous adj 1 nameless, unidentified, unnamed, unsigned, unspecified *Opposite*: named 2 undistinguished, indistinctive, ordinary, everyday, run of the mill *Opposite*: distinctive

anonymously adv incognito, namelessly, in secret, secretly, in disguise

another adj **one more**, additional, a new, a different, a further

answer n **1 response**, reply, riposte, retort, rejoinder (fml) Opposite: question **2 solution**, key, way out, resolution, remedy Opposite: problem ■ v **1 reply**, respond, react, come back with, counter Opposite: challenge **2 solve**, satisfy, resolve, fulfil, lay to rest

---

COMPARE AND CONTRAST CORE MEANING: something said, written, or done in acknowledgment of a question or remark, or in reaction to a situation **answer** an acknowledgment of a question, letter, or situation; **reply** or **response** a spoken or written answer, or a reaction to a situation; **rejoinder** (fml) a sharp, critical, angry, or clever reply, usually spoken; **retort** a sharp spoken reply, often to criticism; **riposte** a quick or witty reply, usually spoken.

---

answerable adj **responsible**, accountable, liable, chargeable, subject to blame Opposite: unaccountable

answer back v **retort**, argue, counter, respond, riposte

answer for v **1 pay for**, suffer for, be punished for, make amends for, take the rap (slang) Opposite: get away with **2 be responsible for**, be accountable for, vouch for, take the responsibility for, be to blame for

antagonism n **1 resentment**, dislike, bitterness, hatred, antipathy Opposite: friendliness **2 rivalry**, opposition, aggression, hostility, enmity Opposite: cooperation

antagonist n **rival**, adversary, opponent, enemy, contender Opposite: friend

antagonistic adj **aggressive**, hostile, argumentative, unfriendly, incompatible Opposite: friendly

antagonize v **provoke**, irritate, annoy, upset, get your back up Opposite: mollify

ante n **bet**, wager, stake, payment, raise

antebellum adj **early nineteenth-century**, eighteenth-century, colonial, historical, Federalist

antecedent n **precursor**, forerunner, ancestor, predecessor, forebear

antecedents n **past history**, background, record, previous circumstances, qualifications

antedate v **predate**, go before, be earlier than, date from before, occur before

antediluvian adj **1 prehistoric**, ancient, old, primitive, primeval Opposite: modern **2** (infml) **antiquated**, out-of-date, obsolete, old-fashioned, archaic Opposite: up-to-date

antenatal adj **pre-birth**, pregnancy, prenatal (US) Opposite: postnatal

antenna n **feeler**, projection, tentacle, probe, protuberance

anterior adj **1 fore**, front, leading, foremost Opposite: anterior **2** (fml) **before**, earlier, sooner Opposite: posterior (fml)

anthem n **song of praise**, national hymn, sacred song, psalm, hymn

anthology n **collection**, compilation, album, omnibus, compendium

anthropomorphize v **humanize**, personify, make human, give a human face to, sentimentalize

anti (infml) adj **opposed**, against, antagonistic, ill-disposed, hostile Opposite: pro

anticipate v **1 expect**, foresee, await, wait for, predict **2 do in advance**, think ahead, look forward, jump the gun

anticipated adj **expected**, predicted, projected, estimated, awaited Opposite: unexpected

anticipation n **expectation**, expectancy, hope, eagerness, keenness

anticlimax n **letdown**, disappointment, deflation, comedown (infml), damp squib (infml) Opposite: climax

antics n **clowning**, tricks, pranks, larks, frolics

antidote n **cure**, remedy, solution, answer, corrective Opposite: poison

antipathetic adj **opposed**, hostile, antagonistic, conflicting, anti (infml) Opposite: sympathetic

antipathy n **opposition**, aversion, hostility, antagonism, hatred Opposite: support. See COMPARE AND CONTRAST at **dislike**.

antiquated adj **out-of-date**, old-fashioned, old, obsolete, archaic Opposite: modern. See COMPARE AND CONTRAST at **old-fashioned**.

antique adj **old**, traditional, aged, historic, old-fashioned Opposite: new

antiquity n **1 ancient times**, the distant past, olden days, olden times, time immemorial **2 relic**, remains, archaeological find, antique, artefact

antiseptic adj **1 sterile**, antibacterial, uncontaminated, clean, pure Opposite: infected **2 bland**, insipid, tame, uninteresting, colourless Opposite: colourful

antisocial adj **1 disruptive**, rebellious, harmful, inconsiderate, belligerent Opposite: constructive **2 unsociable**, unfriendly, disagreeable, shy, reserved Opposite: sociable

antithesis n **opposite**, direct opposite, exact opposite, contrast, converse Opposite: epitome

antithetic see **antithetical**

antithetical (fml) adj **opposite**, differing, contradictory, opposed, contrary

anxiety n **nervousness**, worry, concern, unease, apprehension Opposite: calmness. See COMPARE AND CONTRAST at **worry**.

anxious adj **1 worried**, concerned, uneasy, apprehensive, restless Opposite: calm **2 eager**, keen, enthusiastic, impatient, itching Opposite: indifferent

any adj **1 some**, one, several, a few Opposite: none **2 every**, each, whichever, whatever ■ adv **at all**, in the least, slightly, a little, somewhat

anybody *pron* **anyone**, any person, somebody, someone, everybody *Opposite*: nobody

anyhow *adv* **anyway**, in any case, at any rate, nevertheless, nonetheless

anyone *pron* **anybody**, any person, someone, somebody, everyone *Opposite*: no one

anyway *adv* **anyhow**, at any rate, in any case, nevertheless, nonetheless

anywhere *adv* **wherever**, where, somewhere, everywhere, someplace *(US infml)*

A-OK *(infml)* *adv* **excellent**, perfect, all right, just right, good

apace *adv* **quickly**, rapidly, swiftly, briskly, at a rate of knots *Opposite*: slowly

apart *adv* **separately**, not together, at a distance, to one side, away from each other *Opposite*: together

apart from *prep* **1 aside from**, except for, with the exception of, not counting, excluding *Opposite*: including **2 as well as**, in addition to, on top of, besides

apathetic *adj* **indifferent**, uninterested, listless, dispirited, lethargic *Opposite*: enthusiastic. *See* COMPARE AND CONTRAST *at* **impassive**.

apathy *n* **indifference**, unconcern, lethargy, laziness, boredom *Opposite*: interest

ape *v* **imitate**, mimic, copy, reproduce, simulate. *See* COMPARE AND CONTRAST *at* **imitate**.

aperture *n* **opening**, hole, space, crack, slit

apex *n* **top**, peak, summit, climax, zenith *Opposite*: base

aphorism *n* **saying**, maxim, adage, cliché, saw

apiece *adv* **each**, respectively, to each, for each, individually *Opposite*: collectively

aplomb *n* **assurance**, self-confidence, self-possession, composure, style *Opposite*: awkwardness

apocalypse *n* **catastrophe**, disaster, destruction, cataclysm, Armageddon

Apocalypse *n* **end of the world**, day of reckoning, Judgment Day, Armageddon

apocryphal *adj* **mythical**, fictional, untrue, legendary, invented *Opposite*: true

apologetic *adj* **sorry**, remorseful, contrite, repentant, rueful *Opposite*: unrepentant

apologist *n* **defender**, supporter, ally, protector, champion

apologize *v* **say sorry**, make an apology, ask for forgiveness, beg forgiveness, express regret

apology *n* **1 admission of guilt**, request for forgiveness, expression of regret, confession, act of contrition **2 poor substitute**, pathetic excuse, poor example, pretence, stopgap **3 defence**, excuse, explanation, justification

apostate *n* **renouncer**, defector, deserter, renegade

apostle *n* **1 advocate**, supporter, promoter, champion, proponent *Opposite*: detractor **2 disciple**, follower, missionary, messenger, devotee *Opposite*: leader

apotheosis *n* **high point**, acme, apogee, climax, limit *Opposite*: nadir

appal *v* **horrify**, shock, disgust, repel, sicken *Opposite*: please

appalled *adj* **horrified**, shocked, outraged, disgusted, repelled *Opposite*: delighted

appalling *adj* **1 horrifying**, shocking, disgusting, sickening, outrageous *Opposite*: appealing **2 awful**, terrible, dreadful, horrendous, inexcusable *Opposite*: wonderful

appallingly *adv* **extremely**, very, utterly, awfully, terribly *Opposite*: wonderfully

apparatus *n* **1 device**, gadget, gear, tackle, kit **2 system**, method, mechanism, arrangement, operation

apparel *n* **clothing**, clothes, garb, wear, kit

apparent *adj* **1 obvious**, clear, evident, plain, noticeable *Opposite*: unclear **2 seeming**, ostensible, deceptive, superficial, specious *Opposite*: actual

apparently *adv* **1 it seems that**, it appears that, in fact, rumour has it that, evidently **2 seemingly**, deceptively, speciously, ostensibly, outwardly *Opposite*: actually

apparition *n* **ghost**, spirit, spectre, phantom, ghoul

appeal *n* **1 plea**, petition, application, request, call **2 charm**, attractiveness, attraction, allure, influence *Opposite*: repulsion ■ *v* **1 request**, ask, plead, urge, petition **2 attract**, interest, fascinate, charm, tempt *Opposite*: repel

appealing *adj* **attractive**, tempting, interesting, pleasing, alluring *Opposite*: repulsive

appear *v* **1 come into view**, come into sight, become visible, emerge, come out *Opposite*: disappear **2 happen**, occur, be found, exist, surface **3 seem**, look, look as if, give the impression, give the idea **4 perform**, be seen, act, play, take part in **5 turn up**, show, be seen, arrive, roll up

appearance *n* **1 emergence**, development, arrival, growth, beginning *Opposite*: disappearance **2 look**, form, exterior, manifestation, outer shell **3 arrival**, entrance, advent, attendance, presence

appease *v* **1 mollify**, conciliate, pacify, placate, soothe *Opposite*: provoke **2 satisfy**, assuage, attenuate, calm, soothe *Opposite*: intensify

appeasement *n* **conciliation**, pacification, accession, mollification, placation *Opposite*: provocation

appeaser *n* **conciliator**, pacifier, gratifier, mollifier

appellation *(fml)* *n* **name**, designation, title, style, tag

append *v* **add**, add on, tag on, attach, affix *Opposite*: detach

appendage *n* **1 addition**, attachment, adjunct, add-on, accessory **2 extremity**, feeler, limb, member, projection

appendix *n* **adjunct**, add-on, supplement, PS, appendage

appertain *(fml)* *v* **relate**, belong, be associated with, be relevant to, have a bearing on

appetite *n* **1 hunger**, craving, taste, need to eat, desire for food **2 desire**, taste, enthusiasm, eagerness, keenness *Opposite*: aversion

appetizer *n* **taster**, sample, introduction, sneak preview, taste

appetizing *adj* **1 delicious**, tasty, mouthwatering, enticing, tempting *Opposite*: revolting **2 appealing**, inviting, attractive, desirable, enticing *Opposite*: unappealing

applaud *v* **1 clap**, give a round of applause, give a standing ovation, show your appreciation, congratulate *Opposite*: boo **2 approve**, support, admire, celebrate, congratulate *Opposite*: condemn

applause *n* **1 clapping**, round of applause, ovation, hand, handclapping *Opposite*: jeering **2 praise**, appreciation, approval, approbation, support *Opposite*: condemnation

appliance *n* **1 domestic appliance**, laboursaving device, electrical equipment, machine, device **2 application**, use, employment, utilization, purpose

---

WORD BANK
❏ **types of appliance** blender, coffeemaker, cooker, dishwasher, dryer, food processor, grill, hob, iron, juicer, microwave, microwave oven, minibar, mixer, percolator, range, rotisserie, smoke alarm, smoke detector, spin-dryer, stove, television, toaster, tumble dryer, washing machine, waste disposal

---

applicable *adj* **appropriate**, valid, related, pertinent, relevant *Opposite*: unrelated

applicant *n* **candidate**, interviewee, claimant, hopeful, aspirant. *See* COMPARE AND CONTRAST *at* **candidate**.

application *n* **1 request**, claim, submission, bid, tender **2 use**, function, purpose, relevance, appliance **3 diligence**, concentration, hard work, effort, attention *Opposite*: negligence

applied *adj* **practical**, functional, useful, everyday, pragmatic *Opposite*: theoretical

apply *v* **1 submit an application**, request, ask, go in, put in **2 use**, operate, put into operation, employ, utilize **3 be relevant**, relate, pertain, affect, concern **4 put on**, rub on, spread over, smear, spread on *Opposite*: remove

apply yourself *v* **devote yourself**, work hard, concentrate, direct your efforts towards, attend to *Opposite*: neglect

appoint *v* **1 employ**, sign up, hire, assign, take on *Opposite*: dismiss **2** *(fml)* **select**, choose, settle on, agree, pick *Opposite*: reject

appointed *adj* **chosen**, selected, agreed, fixed, prearranged

appointment *n* **1 meeting**, date, scheduled time, engagement, rendezvous **2 selection**, choice, choosing, nomination *Opposite*: dismissal **3 job**, position, opening, office, post

apportion *v* **allocate**, allot, assign, divide up, distribute

apposite *adj* **appropriate**, apt, pertinent, relevant, suitable *Opposite*: inappropriate

appraisal *n* **assessment**, evaluation, judgment, review, consideration

appraise *v* **assess**, evaluate, judge, review, consider

appreciable *adj* **considerable**, substantial, significant, noticeable, palpable *Opposite*: insignificant

appreciate *v* **1 be grateful for**, be thankful for, be glad about, be pleased about, value **2 understand**, realize, be aware, recognize the value of, grasp **3 increase in value**, go up in price, rise, escalate, soar *Opposite*: depreciate

appreciation *n* **1 thanks**, gratitude, indebtedness, gratefulness, obligation *Opposite*: ingratitude **2 approval**, admiration, positive reception, enjoyment, pleasure *Opposite*: disapproval **3 understanding**, grasp, comprehension, perception, sense **4 rise**, increase, escalation, growth, inflation *Opposite*: depreciation

appreciative *adj* **1 grateful**, thankful, indebted, obliged, beholden *Opposite*: ungrateful **2 approving**, enthusiastic, admiring, positive, favourable *Opposite*: disapproving

apprehend *v* **catch**, arrest, detain, take in for questioning, take into custody *Opposite*: release

apprehension *n* **1 anxiety**, uneasiness, worry, trepidation, nervousness *Opposite*: confidence **2 capture**, arrest, detention, seizure, taking *Opposite*: discharge

apprehensive *adj* **uneasy**, worried, nervous, fearful, hesitant *Opposite*: confident

apprehensiveness *see* **apprehension**

apprentice *n* **trainee**, learner, beginner, novice, student *Opposite*: expert. *See* COMPARE AND CONTRAST *at* **beginner**.

apprenticeship *n* **traineeship**, training, education, preparation, internship *(US)*

approach *v* **1 move towards**, come up to, come near, draw near, come within reach of *Opposite*: retreat **2 speak to**, talk to, get in touch with, contact, make contact with **3 set about**, tackle, deal with, handle, manage **4 approximate**, come close to, be similar to, come near to, move towards ■ *n* **method**, line of attack, tactic, line, slant

approachability *n* **1 friendliness**, accessibility, openness, affability, cordiality *Opposite*: aloofness **2 user-friendliness**, accessibility, availability, ease of use, usability *Opposite*: inaccessibility

approachable adj 1 **friendly**, amicable, sociable, open, open-minded *Opposite*: forbidding 2 **user-friendly**, accessible, usable, useful, helpful *Opposite*: inaccessible

approaching adj **imminent**, impending, pending, future, forthcoming

approbation n **approval**, consent, praise, admiration, esteem *Opposite*: disapproval

appropriate adj **suitable**, fitting, apt, apposite, right *Opposite*: inappropriate ■ v **take**, take over, misappropriate, seize, assume

appropriateness n **suitability**, correctness, aptness, appositeness, relevance

appropriation n **seizure**, assumption, annexation, adoption, arrogation *(fml)*

approval n 1 **appreciation**, admiration, liking, praise, esteem *Opposite*: disdain 2 **endorsement**, support, sanction, consent, agreement

approve v 1 **favour**, like, support, agree, accept *Opposite*: disapprove 2 **grant**, consent, sanction, allow, pass *Opposite*: reject

approved adj **accepted**, permitted, official, agreed, sanctioned

approving adj **positive**, favourable, appreciative, sympathetic, complimentary *Opposite*: disapproving

approximate adj **estimated**, rough, loose, near, inexact *Opposite*: exact

approximation n **estimate**, guess, calculation, guesstimate *(infml)*

apron n **bib**, pinafore, overall, pinny *(infml)*

apropos *(fml)* prep **regarding**, concerning, about, on the subject of, in relation to ■ adj **appropriate**, suitable, fitting, apt, apposite *Opposite*: inappropriate

apt adj 1 **appropriate**, suitable, fitting, apposite, pertinent *Opposite*: inappropriate 2 **prone**, likely, given to, inclined, tending 3 **quick**, capable, competent, able, skilled *Opposite*: inept

aptitude n **ability**, skill, talent, gift, capacity *Opposite*: inability. *See* COMPARE AND CONTRAST *at* **ability, talent**.

aptly adv **appropriately**, fittingly, suitably, rightly, pertinently *Opposite*: inappropriately

aquatic adj **water**, marine, sea, river

aqueduct n **channel**, conduit, canal, watercourse, culvert

arbiter n 1 **arbitrator**, mediator, intermediary, negotiator, go-between 2 **authority**, influence, role model, leader, example

arbitrary adj **random**, chance, subjective, uninformed, illogical *Opposite*: systematic

arbitrate v **judge**, adjudicate, pass judgment, decide, settle

arbitration n **adjudication**, negotiation, mediation, settlement, intercession

arbitrator n **judge**, arbiter, mediator, go-between, intermediary

arbour n **bower**, retreat, nook, dell *(literary)*

arc n **curve**, arch, semicircle, sweep, bow

arcade n 1 **colonnade**, cloister, loggia, gallery, walkway 2 **precinct**, shopping centre, shopping arcade, shopping mall *(US)* 3 **video arcade**, amusement arcade, game parlor *(US)*

arcane adj **mysterious**, secret, esoteric, deep, hidden. *See* COMPARE AND CONTRAST *at* **obscure**.

arch n 1 **arc**, curve, semicircle, bend, bow 2 **archway**, doorway, portico ■ v **curve**, bend, bow, arc *Opposite*: straighten ■ adj **playful**, mischievous, roguish, knowing, cunning

archaic adj **old**, ancient, dated, outdated, out-of-date *Opposite*: modern

arched adj **curved**, rounded, round, high, bowed

archenemy n **opponent**, enemy, rival, challenger, foe *(fml) Opposite*: ally

archetypal adj **typical**, model, representative, standard, archetypical *Opposite*: unconventional

archetype n **model**, epitome, prototype, original, classic

archetypical *see* **archetype**

architect n 1 **designer**, draughtsman, draughtswoman, draughtsperson, planner 2 **originator**, inventor, founder, creator, engineer

architecture n **design**, planning, building, construction

archive n **record**, file, documentation, document, library

archly adv **playfully**, mischievously, roguishly, knowingly, cunningly

archness n **playfulness**, mischievousness, roguishness, cunning, coyness

archway n **arch**, arcade, pergola, portico, doorway

arctic *(infml)* adj **freezing**, cold, chilly, wintry, frozen *Opposite*: tropical

ardent adj **passionate**, enthusiastic, keen, fervent, zealous *Opposite*: dispassionate

ardour n **passion**, love, enthusiasm, zeal, fervour *Opposite*: indifference

arduous adj **difficult**, hard, laborious, gruelling, demanding *Opposite*: easy. *See* COMPARE AND CONTRAST *at* **hard**.

arduousness n **difficulty**, laboriousness, strenuousness, onerousness, rigorousness *Opposite*: ease

area n 1 **part**, zone, extent, expanse, range 2 **neighbourhood**, locale, vicinity, part, quarter 3 **subject**, topic, field, question, matter

arena n **stadium**, ground, showground, sports ground, pitch

argot n **jargon**, slang, idiom, speech, dialect

arguable adj **debatable**, open to question, questionable, doubtful, dubious *Opposite*: certain

arguably *adv* debatably, questionably, perhaps, possibly, maybe *Opposite*: certainly

argue *v* **1 quarrel**, dispute, fight, disagree, bicker *Opposite*: agree **2 make a case**, contend, claim, say, maintain **3 debate**, dispute, discuss, go over, explore. *See* COMPARE AND CONTRAST *at* disagree.

argument *n* **1 quarrel**, fight, disagreement, dispute, row **2 case**, line of reasoning, reason, contention, claim

argumentative *adj* **quarrelsome**, confrontational, contrary, belligerent, aggressive *Opposite*: peaceable

arid *adj* **1 dry**, parched, bone dry, baked, waterless *Opposite*: humid **2 boring**, dull, uninteresting, uninspiring, dry *Opposite*: exciting. *See* COMPARE AND CONTRAST *at* dry.

aridity *n* dryness, drought, desiccation, parchedness, aridness *Opposite*: humidity

aridness *see* aridity

arise *v* **1 happen**, occur, take place, come up, begin **2 result from**, be the result of, arise from, arise out of, be caused by

aristocracy *n* nobility, upper classes, peers of the realm, landed gentry, lords and ladies *Opposite*: lower class

aristocrat *n* noble, lord, lady, peer, grandee

WORD BANK

❏ **types of aristocrat** baron, baroness, baronet, count, countess, crown prince, duchess, duke, earl, knight, marchioness, marquess, prince, princess, viscount, viscountess

---

aristocratic *adj* **1 noble**, titled, patrician, upper-class, blue-blooded *Opposite*: lower-class **2 refined**, well-bred, patrician, noble *Opposite*: lowly

arm *n* **1 limb**, appendage, member **2 support**, armrest, rest **3 division**, wing, branch, subdivision, offshoot ■ *v* **equip**, provide, supply, prepare, ready *Opposite*: disarm

---

WORD BANK

❏ **parts of an arm or hand** ball, cuticle, elbow, finger, fingernail, fingerprint, fingertip, fist, forearm, forefinger, funny bone *(infml)*, hand, hangnail, heel, index finger, knuckle, little finger, middle finger, palm, pinkie *(infml)*, ring finger, thumb, thumbnail, wrist

---

armada *n* fleet, flotilla, navy, squadron, task force

Armageddon *n* **1 end of the world**, day of reckoning, Judgment Day, Apocalypse **2 disaster**, destruction, catastrophe, cataclysm, apocalypse

armament *n* arming, mobilization, rearmament, deployment, buildup *Opposite*: disarmament

armaments *n* arms, weapons, weaponry, guns, missiles

armed *adj* equipped, fortified, prepared *Opposite*: unarmed

armed forces *n* military, services, forces, defence force, militia

armhole *n* opening, slit, hole

armistice *n* truce, peace agreement, settlement, ceasefire, resolution

armour *n* **1 body armour**, bulletproof vest, flak jacket, breastplate, panoply **2 protection**, reinforcement, defence, covering, cover

armoured *adj* reinforced, steel-clad, armour-plated, strengthened, bulletproof *Opposite*: unprotected

armour-plated *adj* reinforced, steel-clad, armoured, strengthened, bulletproof *Opposite*: unprotected

armoury *n* **1 arsenal**, arms depot, magazine, ordnance depot, munitions store **2 stock**, source, supply, resource

armrest *n* support, arm, rest

arms *n* weapons, weaponry, armaments, guns, missiles

army *n* **1 military**, armed forces, defence force, militia, troops **2 crowd**, throng, mass, host, multitude

aroma *n* smell, perfume, fragrance, scent, odour. *See* COMPARE AND CONTRAST *at* smell.

aromatic *adj* perfumed, fragrant, sweet-smelling, scented, pungent *Opposite*: odourless

around *prep* **1 about**, all round, surrounding, covering, over **2 close to**, near, in the vicinity, in the neighbourhood, in the environs **3 all over**, throughout, here and there, about, round **4 approximately**, about, in the region of, just about, roughly ■ *adv* **1 in**, here, round, about, present **2 from one place to another**, from place to place, about, everywhere, all over the place *(infml)* **3 round here**, near here, nearby, about, round

arousal *n* stimulation, provocation, awakening, encouragement, excitement

arouse *v* stimulate, provoke, awaken, produce, stir *Opposite*: dampen

arraign *v* accuse, impeach, prosecute, bring before the court, have up *(infml)*

arraignment *n* charge, prosecution, legal process, legal action, indictment *Opposite*: exculpation *(fml)*

arrange *v* **1 organize**, set up, coordinate, fix, fix up *Opposite*: cancel **2 position**, put in order, place, assemble, put together *Opposite*: disarrange

arranged *adj* decided, agreed, set, settled, organized

arrangement *n* **1 preparation**, plan, procedure, prearrangement, provision **2 agreement**, understanding, bargain, pact, deal **3 display**, array, composition, layout, assembly

arrant *adj* complete, total, outright, unmitigated, utter

array *n* **1 collection**, selection, display, range,

arrangement **2 dress**, clothing, regalia, finery, garb ■ *v* **1** *(fml)* **arrange**, display, organize, set out, exhibit **2** *(literary)* **clothe**, dress, deck out, drape, attire *(fml)*

arrears *n* **amount overdue**, amount outstanding, debts, sum unpaid *Opposite*: credit

arrest *v* **1 take into custody**, seize, capture, detain, catch *Opposite*: release **2** *(fml)* **halt**, stop, block, prevent, obstruct **3** *(fml)* **attract**, engage, catch, hold, fix ■ *n* **capture**, seizure, detention, apprehension *Opposite*: release

arresting *adj* **impressive**, eye-catching, stunning, striking, interesting *Opposite*: uninteresting

arrival *n* **1 entrance**, entry, coming, appearance *Opposite*: departure **2 onset**, advent, occurrence, influx, coming *Opposite*: disappearance **3 newcomer**, visitor, guest, incomer, caller

arrive *v* **1 reach**, turn up, get there, land, disembark *Opposite*: depart **2 work out**, reach, come to, come up with, attain **3 succeed**, be successful, gain recognition, make your mark, make it *(infml)*

arrogance *n* **conceit**, haughtiness, egotism, pride, overconfidence *Opposite*: humility

arrogant *adj* **conceited**, haughty, egotistic, superior, proud *Opposite*: humble. *See* COMPARE AND CONTRAST *at* **proud**.

arrogate *(fml) v* **claim**, lay claim to, appropriate, misappropriate, assume *Opposite*: cede *(fml)*

arrogation *(fml)* *n* **appropriation**, misappropriation, assumption, takeover, annexation

arrow *n* **1 projectile**, missile, dart, barb, shaft **2 symbol**, sign, pointer, marker, indicator

arrowhead *n* **point**, tip, barb

arsenal *n* **1 weapon store**, munitions store, magazine, armoury **2 store**, battery, fund, cache, collection

arson *n* **fire raising**, pyromania, burning, incineration, ignition

arsonist *n* **fire raiser**, pyromaniac, burner, firebomber, incendiary

art *n* **1 painting**, drawing, fine art, graphic arts, sculpture **2 skill**, talent, knack, ability, virtuosity

artefact *n* **object**, objet d'art, manufactured object, article, manufactured article

arterial *adj* **major**, main, trunk, principal, through *Opposite*: subsidiary

artery *n* **route**, road, line, channel, pathway

artful *adj* **crafty**, devious, sly, deceitful, cunning *Opposite*: open

artfulness *n* **craftiness**, deviousness, slyness, cleverness, deceitfulness *Opposite*: straightforwardness

art-house *adj* **highbrow**, intellectual, sophisticated, esoteric, avant-garde *Opposite*: lowbrow

arthritic *adj* **stiff**, swollen, aching, sore, painful

article *n* **1 piece of writing**, editorial, piece, item, commentary **2 object**, item, piece, thing, artefact **3 clause**, term, stipulation, condition, regulation

articles *n* **training**, traineeship, apprenticeship, tutelage, course

articulacy *n* **self-expression**, expressiveness, eloquence, fluency, articulateness

articulate *adj* **eloquent**, clear, coherent, fluent, lucid *Opposite*: inarticulate ■ *v* **1 speak about**, express, state, put into words, convey *Opposite*: suppress **2 enunciate**, pronounce, speak clearly, speak, say *Opposite*: mumble

articulated *adj* **1 modular**, jointed, coupled, linked, connected *Opposite*: rigid **2 spoken**, voiced, uttered, expressed, pronounced *Opposite*: unspoken

articulateness *n* **eloquence**, expressiveness, fluency, self-expression, coherence

articulation *n* **1 enunciation**, pronunciation, speech, diction, delivery **2 expression**, verbalization, communication, formulation

artifact *see* **artefact**

artifice *(fml)* *n* **1 pretence**, ploy, trick, lie, sleight of hand **2 deception**, deceit, cunning, trickery, artfulness

artificial *adj* **1 false**, fake, mock, reproduction, synthetic *Opposite*: natural **2 insincere**, false, put-on, pretend, fake *Opposite*: sincere

artificiality *n* **insincerity**, disingenuousness, affectedness, affectation, phoniness *Opposite*: sincerity

artillery *n* **weaponry**, arms, guns, armaments, weapons

artisan *n* **craftsperson**, skilled worker, craftworker, artist, artificer *(dated)*

artist *n* **1 painter**, illustrator, drawer, sketcher, cartoonist **2 performer**, entertainer, artiste

artiste *n* **performer**, entertainer, artist

artistic *adj* **creative**, imaginative, inventive, arty *(infml)*

artistry *n* **creativity**, originality, artistic ability, imagination, invention

artless *adj* **simple**, guileless, natural, unworldly, ingenuous *Opposite*: disingenuous

artlessness *n* **guilelessness**, naturalness, innocence, unaffectedness, inexperience *Opposite*: disingenuousness

artwork *n* **1 work of art**, creation, representation, reproduction, painting **2 illustrations**, pictures, photographs, diagrams, plates

arty *(infml) adj* **creative**, imaginative, inventive, artistic

arty-crafty *(infml) adj* **1 overdecorative**, fanciful, pretentious, artistic **2 rustic**, homespun, homemade, traditional, artistic *Opposite*: sophisticated

as *conj* **1 while**, when, during, whilst **2 because**, since, seeing that, being as, considering that

as a result of *prep* **because of**, by, through, by means of, on account of

ascend *v* **1 rise**, climb, soar, go up, come up *Opposite*: descend **2 climb**, go up, come up, mount, scale *Opposite*: descend

ascendancy *n* **dominance**, domination, predominance, pre-eminence, power *Opposite*: subordination

ascendant *adj* **1 rising**, dominant, ascending, prevailing, mounting *Opposite*: descendent **2 dominant**, controlling, governing, ruling, influential *Opposite*: subordinate

ascendency *see* **ascendancy**

ascension *(fml) n* **rise**, ascent, climb, mounting, scaling *Opposite*: descent

ascent *n* **1 climb**, rise, mounting, scaling, ascension *(fml) Opposite*: descent **2 gradient**, slope, incline, rake, angle

ascertain *v* **determine**, discover, find out, learn, make certain

ascetic *n* **abstainer**, celibate, puritan, penitent *Opposite*: hedonist ■ *adj* **austere**, abstinent, frugal, abstemious, spartan *Opposite*: hedonistic

asceticism *n* **austerity**, self-discipline, abstemiousness, self-denial, self-restraint *Opposite*: hedonism

ascribe *(fml) v* **1 assign**, credit, attribute, accredit, chalk up **2 put down to**, attribute, blame on, lay at the door of, charge

aseptic *adj* **clean**, sterile, pure, sterilized, uninfected *Opposite*: septic

asexual *adj* **1 genderless**, androgynous, neutral, sexless **2 vegetative**, somatic, parthenogenetic, nonsexual

as far as *conj* **to the extent that**, to the degree that, so far as, insofar as, as much as

ash *n* **residue**, cinders, slag, embers, powder

ashamed *adj* **1 embarrassed**, mortified, humiliated, abashed, humbled *Opposite*: proud **2 unwilling**, reluctant, hesitant, unhappy, sorry *Opposite*: pleased

ashen *adj* **pallid**, wan, pasty, white as a sheet, drained of colour *Opposite*: rosy

ashes *n* **ruins**, remains, vestiges, remnants, fragments

ashore *adv* **aground**, onto land, onto dry land, on shore

ashy *see* **ashen**

aside *adv* **1 sideways**, away, to the side, sidewise, to one side **2 disregarded**, ignored, excluded, set aside, apart **3 in reserve**, separately, away, to one side, up your sleeve ■ *n* **1 digression**, departure, tangent, interposition, parenthesis **2 whisper**, mumbled comment, remark, undertone, by-play

aside from *prep* **1 as well as**, in addition to, on top of, besides, over and beyond **2 barring**, excluding, ignoring, except, except for *Opposite*: including

asinine *adj* **silly**, foolish, unintelligent *Opposite*: intelligent

ask *v* **1 request**, inquire, solicit, question, query *Opposite*: answer **2 invite**, ask over, have over, summon, request **3 count on**, expect, demand, look for, require

askance *adv* **doubtfully**, suspiciously, sideways, dubiously, distrustfully

askew *adv* **crookedly**, awry, out of kilter, off centre, cockeyed *Opposite*: straight

ask for *v* **request**, provoke, solicit, inspire, demand *Opposite*: refuse

asking price *n* **price**, selling price, starting price, marked price, cost

aslant *adv* **obliquely**, at an angle, on a slope, diagonally, slantingly *Opposite*: straight ■ *adj* **slanting**, slant, slantwise, oblique, diagonal

asleep *adj* **1 sleeping**, slumbering, dead to the world, napping, sound asleep *Opposite*: awake **2 numb**, dead, benumbed, without feeling, lifeless

as long as *conj* **providing**, on condition that, given that, provided that, if

as of *(fml) prep* **from**, after, on or after, beginning, starting

aspect *n* **1 feature**, facet, characteristic, part, piece **2 position**, outlook, side, standpoint, viewpoint **3 appearance**, look, quality, bearing, air

as per *prep* **according to**, in accordance with, following, consistent with, in keeping with *Opposite*: counter

asperity *(fml) n* **severity**, brusqueness, gruffness, harshness, sharpness *Opposite*: affability

aspersion *n* **slander**, slur, slight, smear, accusation *Opposite*: praise

asphalt *n* **tar**, Tarmac, bitumen, blacktop *(US)*

asphyxia *n* **suffocation**, choking, lack of oxygen, oxygen deprivation, unconsciousness

asphyxiate *v* **suffocate**, smother, choke, stifle, strangle *Opposite*: resuscitate

asphyxiation *n* **suffocation**, choking, smothering, stifling, throttling

aspic *n* **jelly**, gel, mousseline

aspirant *n* **contender**, candidate, applicant, hopeful, seeker ■ *adj* **hopeful**, would-be, aspiring, wannabe *(infml)*. *See* COMPARE AND CONTRAST *at* **candidate**.

aspirate *v* **1 pronounce**, enunciate, articulate, sound, voice **2 remove**, extract, suck out, draw out, take out *Opposite*: inject

aspiration *n* **ambition**, goal, objective, aim, end

aspirational *adj* **ambitious**, self-improving, aspiring, hopeful, eager *Opposite*: unambitious

aspire _v_ **seek**, aim, hope, desire, want

aspiring _adj_ **hopeful**, would-be, ambitious, aspirant, wannabe _(infml)_

as regards _prep_ **with regard to**, regarding, concerning, with reference to, as to

assail _v_ **1 attack**, assault, set about, lay into, beset _Opposite_: defend **2 criticize**, attack, lay into, berate, revile _Opposite_: praise

assailant _n_ **attacker**, mugger, accoster, assaulter, aggressor

assassin _n_ **killer**, murderer, cutthroat, dispatcher, hired gun _(slang)_

assassinate _v_ **kill**, murder, shoot, kill in cold blood, eliminate. _See_ COMPARE AND CONTRAST _at_ **kill**.

assassination _n_ **foul play**, murder, killing, shooting, elimination

assault _n_ **1 attack**, beating, stabbing, mugging, battering **2 offensive**, attack, onslaught, incursion, storming _Opposite_: retreat ■ _v_ **attack**, mug, set about, assail, lay into _Opposite_: defend

assay _v_ **examine**, assess, analyse, evaluate, test

assemblage _n_ **1 accumulation**, grouping, assembly, collection, meeting **2 crowd**, throng, assembly, group, mass

assemble _v_ **1 bring together**, collect, pull together, draw together, accumulate _Opposite_: disband **2 muster**, collect, meet, come together, convene _Opposite_: disperse **3 put together**, build, fit together, make, compile _Opposite_: take apart. _See_ COMPARE AND CONTRAST _at_ **collect**.

assembly _n_ **1 gathering**, coming together, meeting, association, assemblage **2 meeting**, congress, assemblage, gathering, muster **3 legislative body**, legislature, council, government, representatives **4 construction**, building, compilation, putting together, fabrication _Opposite_: destruction

assembly point _n_ **meeting point**, meeting place, rendezvous, rallying point, muster station

assent _v_ **agree**, acquiesce, concur, go along with, subscribe to _Opposite_: disagree ■ _n_ **agreement**, acquiescence, concurrence, acceptance, approval _Opposite_: disagreement. _See_ COMPARE AND CONTRAST _at_ **agree**.

assert _v_ **1 declare**, state, insist on, proclaim, emphasize _Opposite_: deny **2 stand up for**, profess, defend, maintain, uphold _Opposite_: renounce

assertion _n_ **declaration**, statement, proclamation, claim, allegation _Opposite_: denial

assertive _adj_ **self-confident**, self-assured, confident, firm, forceful _Opposite_: shy

assertiveness _n_ **confidence**, forcefulness, insistence, decisiveness, boldness _Opposite_: shyness

assess _v_ **1 review**, consider, appraise, evaluate, judge **2 calculate**, evaluate, value, rate, estimate

assessment _n_ **1 evaluation**, appraisal, judgment, review, consideration **2 calculation**, estimation, valuation **3 duty**, charge, impost, debt, bill

assessor _n_ **evaluator**, appraiser, judge, inspector

asset _n_ **1 advantage**, strength, benefit, plus point, positive feature _Opposite_: drawback **2 possession**, property, resource, holding

assets _n_ **possessions**, property, resources, material goods, worldly goods

asset-stripping _n_ **profit taking**, profitmaking, selling off, buying and selling, trading

assiduity _n_ **diligence**, care, attention, application, industriousness _Opposite_: carelessness

assiduous _adj_ **diligent**, persevering, industrious, painstaking, careful _Opposite_: lazy. _See_ COMPARE AND CONTRAST _at_ **careful**.

assiduousness _n_ **diligence**, persistence, industriousness, attentiveness, tirelessness _Opposite_: laziness

assign _v_ **1 allocate**, allot, give, dispense, disperse **2 appoint**, designate, delegate, send, transfer

assignation _n_ **meeting**, tryst, rendezvous, appointment, date

assignment _n_ **1 task**, job, project, duty, obligation **2 appointment**, duty, position, role, job **3 transfer**, handing over, consignment, allocation, delegation

assimilate _v_ **1 integrate**, adapt, adjust, blend in, fit in **2 incorporate**, take in, digest, absorb, understand _Opposite_: reject

assimilation _n_ **1 integration**, adjustment, acclimatization, accommodation, adaptation **2 absorption**, incorporation, digestion, ingestion, inculcation

assist _v_ **help**, aid, help out, lend a hand, give a hand _Opposite_: hinder

assistance _n_ **help**, aid, support, backing, cooperation _Opposite_: hindrance

assistant _n_ **helper**, aide, deputy, personal assistant, subordinate ■ _adj_ **associate**, subordinate, secondary, junior

COMPARE AND CONTRAST CORE MEANING: somebody who helps another person in carrying out a task

assistant somebody who works to somebody else's instructions, often in a paid capacity; **helper** somebody who takes on an informal, often voluntary, role; **deputy** an officially designated chief assistant authorized to act on a superior's behalf; **aide** an assistant in military, political, or commercial contexts.

assisted _adj_ **aided**, helped, abetted, supported, sponsored _Opposite_: unassisted

assizes _n_ **court session**, judicial proceedings, court sitting, circuit court

associate _v_ **1 connect**, relate, link, correlate, bracket _Opposite_: separate **2 mix**, socialize, spend time with, go around with, see *Opposite*: avoid **3 unite**, combine, join together, group together, join *Opposite*: disband ■ *n* **1 partner**, colleague, business partner, fellow worker, coworker **2 companion**, comrade, acquaintance, friend, ally ■ *adj* **subordinate**, secondary, junior, assistant

associated *adj* **related**, allied, linked, connected, accompanying

association *n* **1 organization**, union, alliance, society, company **2 friendship**, relationship, connection, fellowship, involvement **3 connotation**, overtone, suggestion, memory, reminder

assonance *n* **repetition**, recurrence, duplication, iteration, alliteration

as soon as *conj* **once**, the moment, the instant, the minute, immediately

assort *v* **classify**, separate, sort out, group, divide *Opposite*: disarrange

assorted *adj* **mixed**, various, miscellaneous, varied, multifarious *Opposite*: uniform

assortment *n* **variety**, collection, range, mixture, mixed bag

assort with *v* **associate**, mix with, socialize with, see, spend time with

assuage *v* **moderate**, ease, soften, lessen, appease *Opposite*: inflame

assume *v* **1 take for granted**, suppose, presume, presuppose, deduce **2 take up**, take responsibility, take on, take upon yourself, shoulder **3 feign**, affect, fake, simulate, put on. See COMPARE AND CONTRAST at deduce.

assumed *adj* **1 expected**, presumed, supposed, rumoured, implicit **2 false**, artificial, fake, phoney, bogus

assumed name *n* **alias**, pseudonym, pen name, nom de plume, stage name

assuming *adj* **presumptuous**, pretentious, arrogant, haughty, high and mighty *Opposite*: humble

assumption *n* **supposition**, statement, postulation, hypothesis, guess

assurance *n* **1 pledge**, declaration, word, guarantee, oath **2 self-confidence**, self-possession, self-reliance, confidence, poise *Opposite*: timidity

assure *v* **1 promise**, guarantee, give surety, pledge, swear **2 make certain**, ensure, guarantee, nail down, know for certain

assured *adj* **1 certain**, guaranteed, sure, confident, solid *Opposite*: uncertain **2 confident**, self-confident, self-assured, self-possessed, poised *Opposite*: diffident

asterisk *n* **symbol**, sign, mark, character, star ■ *v* **mark**, identify, label, specify

astern *adv* **1 behind**, aft, at the back, at the rear *Opposite*: forward **2 to the rear**, backwards, in reverse *Opposite*: ahead

astir *adj* **1 awake**, out of bed, up, up and about, aroused *Opposite*: asleep **2 active**, alive,

moving, stirring, live *Opposite*: inactive

as to *prep* **with regard to**, as regards, regarding, concerning, in respect of

astonish *v* **surprise**, amaze, astound, dumbfound, overwhelm

astonished *adj* **surprised**, amazed, astounded, dumbfounded, incredulous

astonishing *adj* **amazing**, surprising, astounding, shocking, bewildering *Opposite*: predictable

astonishment *n* **surprise**, amazement, wonder, bewilderment, shock

astound *v* **amaze**, astonish, surprise, shock, dumbfound

astounded *adj* **astonished**, surprised, amazed, stunned, dazed

astounding *adj* **amazing**, astonishing, surprising, shocking, beyond belief *Opposite*: unsurprising

astral *adj* **1 stellar**, astronomical, astrophysical, cosmological, celestial **2 immaterial**, spiritual, psychical, otherworldly, transcendent *Opposite*: material

astray *adv* **off course**, lost, off track, off target, off beam

astride *prep* **on both sides of**, spanning, straddling, across

astringency *n* **acerbity**, acidity, causticity, mordancy, sharpness *Opposite*: blandness

astringent *adj* **harsh**, severe, biting, caustic, acerbic *Opposite*: bland

astrologer *n* **fortune-teller**, seer, soothsayer, prophet, forecaster

astrological *adj* **zodiacal**, horoscopic, fortune-telling, prophetic, forecasting

astrology *n* **fortune-telling**, clairvoyance, soothsaying, forecasting, prediction

astronaut *n* **space traveller**, space pilot, cosmonaut, rocket pilot, spaceman

astronomical *adj* **1 astral**, planetary, cosmological, astrophysical, lunar **2** *(infml)* **exorbitant**, excessive, sky-high, through the roof, huge *Opposite*: affordable

astronomically *(infml)* *adv* **exorbitantly**, exceedingly, excessively, inordinately, extremely

astute *adj* **shrewd**, smart, perceptive, judicious, incisive *Opposite*: credulous

astuteness *n* **shrewdness**, good judgment, smartness, intelligence, wisdom *Opposite*: credulity

asunder *(fml)* *adv* **apart**, open, in pieces, in bits, in halves *Opposite*: together

as well *adv* **too**, also, additionally, in addition, on top

as well as *conj* **in addition to**, on top of, over and above, with, and

asylum *n* **1 place of safety**, refuge, haven, safe haven, sanctuary **2 protection**, security, refuge, sanctuary, shelter

asymmetric *adj* **unequal**, uneven, lopsided,

irregular, disproportionate *Opposite*: symmetrical

asymmetrical *see* **asymmetric**

asymmetry *n* **irregularity**, lopsidedness, unevenness, disproportionateness *Opposite*: symmetry

atavistic *adj* **primitive**, primeval, primal, ancient, ancestral

atheism *n* **unbelief**, doubt, freethinking, humanism, nonbelief *Opposite*: belief

atheist *n* **unbeliever**, doubter, sceptic, nonbeliever, agnostic *Opposite*: believer

atheistic *adj* **unbelieving**, nonbelieving, disbelieving, incredulous, irreligious *Opposite*: believing

athlete *n* **sportsperson**, contestant, participant, competitor, team member

athletic *adj* **fit**, sporty, healthy, in good shape, physical *Opposite*: unfit

athleticism *n* **fitness**, sportiness, litheness, agility, suppleness

atmosphere *n* **1 air**, sky, heavens, ether *(literary)* **2 ambience**, impression, feeling, feel, mood

WORD BANK
❑ **parts of the atmosphere** exosphere, ionosphere, mesosphere, ozone layer, stratosphere, thermosphere, tropopause, troposphere

atmospheric *adj* **impressive**, distinctive, moody, special, full of character

atmospherics *n* **interference**, disturbance, static, snow, hissing

atoll *n* **island**, isle, islet, coral reef, coral island

atom *n* **particle**, bit, tiny part, iota, jot

atomic *adj* **1 nuclear**, thermonuclear, fissionable **2 microscopic**, submicroscopic, minute, infinitesimal, minuscule *Opposite*: gigantic

atomizer *n* **spray**, spray can, vaporizer, aerosol

atonal *adj* **twelve-note**, twelve-tone, discordant, dissonant, inharmonious

atonality *n* **twelve-note scale**, twelve-tone scale, serialism, discordance, dissonance *Opposite*: tonality

atone *(fml)* *v* **compensate**, make up, make amends, redress, apologize

atonement *n* **compensation**, amends, penitence, penance, punishment

atrium *n* **hall**, foyer, entrance hall, entrance, vestibule

atrocious *adj* **1 bad**, terrible, dreadful, appalling, awful **2 brutal**, vicious, wicked, evil, cruel

atrociously *adv* **1 badly**, terribly, appallingly, fearfully, dreadfully *Opposite*: wonderfully **2 brutally**, viciously, wickedly, evilly, cruelly

atrociousness *n* **fearfulness**, dreadfulness, viciousness, wickedness, frightfulness

atrocity *n* **1 act of violence**, massacre, killing, outrage, brutality **2 violence**, cruelty, viciousness, barbarity

atrophy *v* **waste away**, waste, wither, weaken, shrivel

attach *v* **1 fasten**, join, connect, fix, put together *Opposite*: detach **2 assign**, award, attribute, accord, ascribe *(fml)*

attaché *n* **diplomat**, public servant, civil servant, representative, envoy

attached *adj* **1 enclosed**, accompanying, supporting, supplementary **2** *(infml)* **emotionally involved**, devoted, fond of, close, friendly *Opposite*: uninvolved

attachment *n* **1 add-on**, accessory, extra, addition, supplement **2 bond**, affection, connection, regard, friendship

attack *v* **1 harm**, assault, harass, bother, molest *Opposite*: defend **2 criticize**, argue, confront, pounce on, disagree *Opposite*: support **3 infect**, occur, strike, hit, strike down **4 begin**, set to, deal with, tackle, pile in ■ *n* **1 bout**, dose, spell, occurrence, outbreak **2 violence**, assault, confrontation, act of violence, incident *Opposite*: defence **3 criticism**, condemnation, argument, disagreement *Opposite*: praise

attacker *n* **assailant**, aggressor, invader, enemy, foe *(fml)* *Opposite*: defender

attack the dignity of *v* **insult**, call names, abuse, give offence, offend

attain *v* **reach**, achieve, accomplish, conquer, manage *Opposite*: fall short. *See* COMPARE AND CONTRAST *at* **accomplish**.

attainable *adj* **within reach**, possible, achievable, realistic, reasonable *Opposite*: unattainable

attainment *n* **1 achievement**, accomplishment, realization, fulfilment, completion *Opposite*: failure **2 skill**, ability, talent, achievement, accomplishment

attar *n* **essence**, extract, essential oil, distillate, perfume

attempt *v* **endeavour**, make an effort, try, bid, make an attempt ■ *n* **effort**, try, go, shot, bid. *See* COMPARE AND CONTRAST *at* **try**.

attend *v* **1 be present**, go to, be there, grace with your presence, appear *Opposite*: miss **2 listen**, concentrate, focus, keep your mind on, pay attention *Opposite*: ignore

attendance *n* **1 presence**, attending, appearance, being present *Opposite*: non-attendance **2 turnout**, audience, number present, gate, crowd

attendant *adj* **associated**, linked, related, connected, consequent ■ *n* **1 assistant**, helper, aide, guide, employee **2 escort**, usher, bridesmaid, groomsman, pageboy

attend to *v* **deal with**, see to, tackle, turn your attention to, address *Opposite*: ignore

attention *n* **1 notice**, concentration, thought, awareness, consideration *Opposite*: inattention **2 care**, courtesy, consideration, kindness, devotion *Opposite*: neglect

attention-grabbing adj eye-catching, conspicuous, arresting, noticeable, striking Opposite: understated

attention to detail n meticulousness, thoroughness, care, carefulness, exactness Opposite: carelessness

attentive adj 1 considerate, responsive, helpful, caring, thoughtful Opposite: inconsiderate 2 paying attention, listening carefully, concentrating, observant, focused Opposite: inattentive

attentiveness n 1 care, courtesy, thoughtfulness, consideration, kindness Opposite: neglect 2 concentration, attention, focus, alertness Opposite: inattention

attenuate v reduce, decrease, lessen, diminish, dilute Opposite: intensify

attenuation n reduction, decrease, lessening, diminution, dilution Opposite: intensification

attest v show, bear out, prove, confirm, corroborate Opposite: refute

attestation n confirmation, corroboration, substantiation, verification, testimony Opposite: refutation

at the side of prep beside, next to, alongside, with, adjacent to

attic n loft, garret, roof space, upper floor Opposite: basement

attire (fml) n clothing, dress, clothes, outfit, garments

attitude n 1 view, opinion, viewpoint, point of view, feeling 2 posture, pose, position, bearing, stance 3 (infml) boldness, brashness, arrogance, insolence, defiance

attract v 1 draw, bring together, pull, exert a pull on Opposite: repel 2 entice, appeal, fascinate, charm, interest Opposite: put off

attraction n magnetism, lure, desirability, hold, charm Opposite: repulsion

attractive adj 1 appealing, alluring, charming, pleasing, inviting Opposite: unattractive 2 good-looking, beautiful, handsome, lovely, pretty Opposite: ugly. See COMPARE AND CONTRAST at good-looking.

attractively adv nicely, delightfully, charmingly, appealingly, prettily Opposite: unattractively

attractiveness n 1 good looks, pleasant appearance, beauty, prettiness, charm Opposite: ugliness 2 magnetism, charisma, draw, appeal, lure Opposite: repulsiveness

attribute v ascribe, put down to, lay at the door of, impute, blame on ■ n quality, characteristic, trait, property, feature

attribution n credit, acknowledgment, designation, ascription (fml)

attributive adj prenominal, preceding, modifying, qualifying

attrition n abrasion, erosion, slow destruction

attune v adjust, accustom, adapt, accommodate, acclimatize

atypical adj different, unusual, uncommon, strange, odd Opposite: typical

auction n sale, mart, Dutch auction, silent auction

audacious adj 1 daring, bold, brave, fearless, courageous Opposite: cowardly (fml) 2 impudent, bold, disrespectful, overconfident, cheeky Opposite: courteous

audaciousness see audacity

audacity n 1 boldness, daring, courage, bravery, fearlessness Opposite: cowardice 2 impudence, disrespect, boldness, rudeness, discourtesy Opposite: courtesy

audibility n loudness, noise, distinctness, discernibility, perceptibility Opposite: inaudibility

audible adj perceptible, clear, distinct, noticeable, loud Opposite: inaudible

audience n 1 spectators, viewers, addressees, listeners, onlookers 2 meeting, interview, consultation, appointment, hearing

audio adj acoustic, auditory, aural, audial

audiovisual adj video, filmed, film, cinematic, cinematographic

audit n review, check, inspection, examination, assessment ■ v review, inspect, examine, assess, appraise

audition n test, tryout, trial, interview ■ v try out, test, hear, interview

auditor n 1 examiner, accountant, assessor, checker 2 (fml) listener, hearer, eavesdropper

auditorium n hall, theatre, amphitheatre, lecture hall

auditory adj aural, hearing, audio, acoustic

au fait adj familiar, at home with, at ease with, used to, accustomed Opposite: unaccustomed

augment (fml) v increase, enlarge, expand, extend, amplify Opposite: diminish. See COMPARE AND CONTRAST at increase.

augmentation n increase, growth, rise, expansion, intensification Opposite: decrease

augur v foretell, predict, portend, promise, prophesy

augury n 1 divination, prediction, prophecy, forecasting, prognostication 2 portent, omen, auspice, indication, prediction

august (fml) adj imposing, impressive, grand, majestic, dignified Opposite: humble

aura n air, atmosphere, force, appearance, quality

aural adj auditory, hearing, acoustic, audio

auspice n omen, portent, augury, sign, indication

auspices n sponsorship, patronage, backing, support, help

auspicious adj favourable, fortunate, promising, propitious, lucky Opposite: inauspicious

austere adj 1 stark, severe, simple, basic,

sparse *Opposite*: comfortable **2 serious**, grim, severe, unsmiling, harsh *Opposite*: gentle **3 plain**, bare, simple, clean, undecorated *Opposite*: ornate

austerity *n* **1 severity**, strictness, sternness, gravity, soberness *Opposite*: levity **2 self-denial**, shortage, scarcity, economy *Opposite*: abundance **3 plainness**, starkness, bareness, simplicity, cleanness *Opposite*: opulence

autarchy *n* **autocracy**, absolute power, absolutism, despotism, tyranny *Opposite*: democracy

authentic *adj* **1 genuine**, original, authenticated, valid *Opposite*: fake **2 true**, reliable, dependable, trustworthy, faithful *Opposite*: false

authenticate *v* **validate**, confirm, verify, substantiate, endorse

authentication *n* **verification**, confirmation, substantiation, validation, certification

authenticity *n* **genuineness**, legitimacy, validity, reality, truth

author *n* **1 writer**, novelist, playwright, dramatist, poet **2 creator**, originator, inventor, source

authoritarian *adj* **strict**, demanding, totalitarian, despotic, absolute *Opposite*: liberal

authoritarianism *n* **totalitarianism**, dictatorship, oppression, absolutism, tyranny *Opposite*: democracy

authoritative *adj* **1 reliable**, trustworthy, dependable, respected, convincing *Opposite*: unreliable **2 commanding**, imposing, firm, confident, convincing *Opposite*: weak

authoritatively *adv* **with authority**, confidently, firmly, commandingly, convincingly

authoritativeness *n* **1 reliability**, trustworthiness, dependability, validity, credibility *Opposite*: unreliability **2 authority**, command, standing, position, weight

authority *n* **1 power**, right, ability, influence, weight **2 agency**, group, government department, board, corporation **3 confidence**, conviction, knowledge, experience **4 citation**, source, evidence **5 expert**, specialist, consultant, buff, expert witness

authority figure *n* **mentor**, person of influence, leader, role model, example

authorization *n* **approval**, consent, endorsement, sanction, agreement

authorize *v* **approve**, allow, sanction, permit, give permission *Opposite*: forbid

authorized *adj* **official**, lawful, legal, sanctioned, approved *Opposite*: unauthorized

authorship *n* **1 writing**, composition, invention, production, output **2 origin**, source, provenance, derivation, genesis

autobiographical *adj* **nonfictional**, factual, first-person, real-life, true to life *Opposite*: fictional

autobiography *n* **memoirs**, life story, life history

autochthonous *adj* **original**, native, indigenous, aboriginal. *See* COMPARE AND CONTRAST *at* **native**.

autocracy *n* **dictatorship**, monocracy, despotism, tyranny, absolutism *Opposite*: democracy

autocrat *n* **dictator**, absolute ruler, tyrant, despot

autocratic *adj* **1 despotic**, tyrannical, repressive, oppressive, monocratic *Opposite*: democratic **2 dictatorial**, domineering, bossy, overbearing, imperious

autograph *n* **signature**, name, inscription, dedication

automated *adj* **automatic**, mechanical, programmed, preset, mechanized *Opposite*: manual

automatic *adj* **1 mechanized**, automated, mechanical, programmed, preset *Opposite*: manual **2 involuntary**, reflex, unconscious, instinctive, programmed *Opposite*: voluntary **3 routine**, habitual, mechanical, regular, repeated *Opposite*: spontaneous

automation *n* **mechanization**, computerization, robotics

automaton *n* **robot**, android, machine

autonomous *adj* **self-governing**, sovereign, free, independent, separate *Opposite*: dependent

autonomy *n* **independence**, self-government, self-rule, sovereignty *Opposite*: dependence

autopsy *n* **postmortem**, dissection, analysis, debriefing, examination

autosuggestion *n* **self-suggestion**, self-hypnosis, autohypnosis, power of suggestion, self-deception

autumn *n* **1 season**, harvest time, equinox, Indian summer, fall *(US)* **2 end**, conclusion, close, culmination, decline

autumnal *adj* **seasonal**, equinoctial, fall *(US)* *Opposite*: spring

auxiliary *adj* **supplementary**, secondary, support, supporting, assisting *Opposite*: main

avail *n* **benefit**, advantage, reward, gain, purpose

availability *n* **obtainability**, handiness, convenience, readiness, accessibility *Opposite*: unavailability

available *adj* **obtainable**, accessible, on hand, to be had, existing *Opposite*: unavailable

avail yourself *v* **make use of**, use, benefit from, take, help yourself to

avalanche *n* **1 snow slip**, fall, slide **2 quantity**, increase, mass, flood, shower

avant-garde *adj* **new**, modern, experimental, unconventional, innovative *Opposite*: traditional

avarice n **greed**, greediness, materialism, covetousness, acquisitiveness Opposite: generosity

avaricious adj **greedy**, rapacious, grasping, acquisitive, covetous Opposite: generous

avariciousness see avarice

avenge v **retaliate**, punish, even the score, take vengeance, get even

avenger n **punisher**, retaliator, nemesis (literary)

avenue n **opportunity**, possibility, way, chance, opening

aver (fml) v **affirm**, state, claim, declare, assert Opposite: refute

average n **mean**, arithmetic mean, mode, median, norm ■ adj **regular**, normal, usual, typical, middling Opposite: extraordinary ■ v **be around**, be in the region of, be more or less, be close to

average down v round down, level down, bring down, lower, decrease

averagely adv **1 on average**, normally, typically, standardly, commonly Opposite: exceptionally **2 passably**, tolerably, adequately, unspectacularly, indifferently Opposite: exceptionally

average out v equalize, level out, balance out, even out

average up v round up, level up, bring up, raise, increase

averse (fml) adj **opposed**, antagonistic, loath, unenthusiastic, ill-disposed Opposite: favourable

aversion n **dislike**, hatred, loathing, repugnance, distaste At dislike. See COMPARE AND CONTRAST at dislike.

avert v **1 prevent**, stop, ward off, avoid, forestall **2 turn away**, turn from, turn aside, divert, deflect

aviary n birdcage, coop, chicken coop, chicken run, hen house

aviation n flying, flight, aeronautics, air travel

aviator n pilot, flier, aeronaut, copilot

avid adj keen, enthusiastic, passionate, eager, devoted Opposite: indifferent

avidity n greed, eagerness, voracity, covetousness, greediness Opposite: indifference

avidly adv **keenly**, enthusiastically, passionately, eagerly, devotedly Opposite: indifferently

avocation (fml) n **1 occupation**, job, vocation, calling, profession **2 hobby**, pastime, diversion, amusement, sport

avoid v **1 keep away**, stay away from, shun, steer clear, let alone **2 evade**, circumvent, get round, get out of, dodge Opposite: face **3 prevent**, forestall, avert, preclude (fml) Opposite: promote

avoidable adj preventable, unnecessary, needless, stoppable Opposite: inevitable

avoidance n **1 evasion**, escaping, evading, dodging, circumvention **2 prevention**, antici-

pation, averting, forestalling, annulment Opposite: promotion **3 abstention**, refraining, refrainment, holding off, eschewal Opposite: indulgence

avow (fml) v **affirm**, state, declare, acknowledge, admit Opposite: deny

avowal (fml) n **affirmation**, statement, confirmation, declaration, acknowledgment Opposite: denial

avowed (fml) adj **affirmed**, stated, confirmed, declared, acknowledged Opposite: unspoken

avowedly (fml) adv **admittedly**, by your own admission, openly, self-confessedly, frankly

avuncular adj **kindly**, kind, kind-hearted, benign, friendly Opposite: unkindly

await v **1 lie in wait for**, wait on, expect, look forward to, look out for **2 lie ahead**, be in store, be to come, loom, near

awaited adj **anticipated**, expected, presumed, waited for Opposite: unexpected

awake adj **wide-awake**, conscious, wakeful, up, up and about Opposite: asleep

awaken v **1 wake**, wake up, rouse, get up, stir **2 rouse**, arouse, set off, stir, promote Opposite: suppress

awakening adj **developing**, growing, emerging, emergent, new ■ n **1 arousal**, wakening, emergence, stirring **2 awareness**, attention, recognition, realization, revival

award n **1 prize**, honour, reward, gift, grant **2 verdict**, decision, determination, judgment, settlement ■ v **give**, present, grant, endow, bestow (fml)

aware adj **1 conscious**, mindful, alert, attentive, responsive Opposite: oblivious **2 knowledgeable**, interested, concerned, informed, experienced Opposite: ignorant

COMPARE AND CONTRAST CORE MEANING: having knowledge of the existence of something
aware knowing something either intellectually or intuitively; **conscious** keenly aware of something and regarding it as important; **mindful** actively attentive, or deliberately keeping something in mind; **cognizant** (fml) having special knowledge about something; **sensible** (fml) keenly aware of something.

awareness n **1 consciousness**, mindfulness, alertness, responsiveness, attentiveness Opposite: oblivion **2 knowledge**, understanding, grasp, appreciation, familiarity Opposite: ignorance

awash adj **1 soaked**, flooded, drenched, waterlogged, saturated Opposite: dry **2 oversupplied**, full of, overflowing, packed, crammed Opposite: lacking

away adj absent, gone, left, missing, not here Opposite: present

awe n **1 wonder**, admiration, respect, amazement, surprise **2 fear**, terror, dread, fright, trepidation

awe-inspiring *adj* **overwhelming**, grand, breathtaking, splendid, tremendous

awesome *see* awe-inspiring

awestricken *see* awestruck

awestruck *adj* **impressed**, overwhelmed, stunned, enthralled, rapt *Opposite*: unimpressed

awful *adj* **dreadful**, terrible, appalling, unpleasant, horrible *Opposite*: wonderful

awfully *adv* **1 extremely**, very, really, terrifically, terribly **2 badly**, unpleasantly, dreadfully, terribly, appallingly *Opposite*: well

awfulness *n* **dreadfulness**, horror, misery, unpleasantness, terribleness

awkward *adj* **1 embarrassing**, tricky, problematic, difficult, thorny *Opposite*: straightforward **2 uncooperative**, difficult, stubborn, obstinate, obdurate *Opposite*: cooperative **3 unwieldy**, cumbersome, bulky *Opposite*: compact **4 clumsy**, inelegant, graceless, uncoordinated, ungainly *Opposite*: graceful **5 uncomfortable**, embarrassed, out of your depth, tongue-tied, self-conscious *Opposite*: comfortable

awkwardly *adv* **1 uncomfortably**, uneasily, with embarrassment, self-consciously, gauchely *Opposite*: comfortably **2 clumsily**, inelegantly, gracelessly, cumbersomely, gawkily *(infml) Opposite*: easily

awkwardness *n* **1 discomfort**, unease, embarrassment, uneasiness, self-consciousness *Opposite*: ease **2 clumsiness**, ineptness, inelegance, gracelessness, ungainliness *Opposite*: ease

awning *n* **canopy**, sunshade, sun shelter, blind

AWOL *adj* **absent without leave**, absent, missing, deserting, wanted *Opposite*: present

awry *adj* **1 crooked**, askew, skewed, off beam, out of kilter *Opposite*: straight **2 amiss**, wrong, muddled, incorrect, astray *Opposite*: right

axe *v* **1** *(infml)* **dismiss**, make redundant, let go, lay off, fire *(infml) Opposite*: employ **2 cut**, cut back, scale down, slim down, downsize

axiom *n* **maxim**, adage, saying, saw, proverb

axiomatic *adj* **self-evident**, goes without saying, obvious, manifest, clear

axis *n* **alliance**, partnership, bloc, league, federation

B

babble *v* **gabble**, mutter, prattle, chatter, blather *(infml)* ■ *n* **hum**, buzz, hubbub, drone, murmur

baby *n* **infant**, child, newborn, babe in arms, little one ■ *v* **pamper**, coddle, mollycoddle, cosset, overprotect

baby-faced *adj* **youthful**, boyish, girlish, childlike, wide-eyed *Opposite*: wizened

babyhood *n* **infancy**, childhood, early years, youth

babyish *adj* **childish**, infantile, immature, puerile, adolescent *Opposite*: mature

babysit *v* **look after**, child mind, protect, watch, mind

babysitter *n* **child minder**, minder, carer, sitter, childcare provider

bachelor *n* **unmarried man**, single man, eligible male, unattached man, confirmed bachelor

back *n* **backbone**, spine, spinal column, vertebral column, vertebrae ■ *adv* **behind**, to the rear, backwards, rearward *Opposite*: forwards ■ *v* **1 support**, provide for, finance, fund, help **2 go backwards**, reverse, move backwards, recede, back up *Opposite*: proceed

backache *n* **back pain**, back trouble, bad back, lumbago, sciatica

back away *v* **recoil**, shrink, draw back, shy away, back off *Opposite*: stay

backbiting *n* **spitefulness**, backstabbing, scandalmongering, cattiness, maliciousness

backbone *n* **1 spine**, spinal column, vertebral column, back, vertebrae **2 mainstay**, support, prop, spine, pillar **3 moral fibre**, strength of character, stamina, fortitude, courage

backbreaking *adj* **strenuous**, arduous, gruelling, exhausting, taxing *Opposite*: easy

backchat *(infml) n* **rudeness**, impudence, impertinence, disrespect, cheekiness *Opposite*: respect

backcloth *n* **backdrop**, scenery, set, stage set, background

backcomb *v* **brush**, comb, style, coif *(fml)*, tease *(US)*

back down *v* **withdraw**, concede defeat, accept defeat, yield, admit defeat *Opposite*: stand your ground

backdrop *n* **1 backcloth**, scenery, set, stage set, scene **2 background**, setting, milieu, environment, framework

backer *n* **1 sponsor**, patron, guarantor, benefactor, angel **2 supporter**, promoter, champion, advocate, ally

COMPARE AND CONTRAST CORE MEANING: somebody who provides financial support
backer a person who gives moral or financial support; **angel** a person who provides financial support for an enterprise, e.g. a theatrical venture; **guarantor** a person who gives a legal undertaking to be responsible for somebody else's debts or obligations; **patron** a person who gives financial or

moral support to a person, institution, or charity, especially in the arts; **sponsor** a person or organization that contributes money to help fund an event, usually in return for publicity, or gives money to a person taking part in a fundraising activity.

backfire *v* **go wrong**, boomerang, miscarry, fail, not go as planned

background *n* **1 upbringing**, circumstances, personal history, family, experience **2 backdrop**, setting, milieu, environment, surroundings *Opposite*: foreground

backhanded *adj* **indirect**, doubtful, oblique, insincere, snide

backhander *(infml)* *n* **bribe**, kickback, incentive, sweetener *(infml)*, rake-off *(infml)*

backing *n* **support**, help, assistance, sponsorship, patronage

backlash *n* **reaction**, repercussion, counterattack, criticism, hostile response

backlog *n* **accumulation**, buildup, excess, surfeit, logjam

back off *v* **1 retreat**, pull back, move away, go backwards, recoil *Opposite*: advance **2 yield**, withdraw, admit you were wrong, backpedal, take back *Opposite*: insist

back out *v* **pull out**, withdraw, renege, go back on, cancel *Opposite*: continue

backpack *n* **rucksack**, knapsack, pack, bag, haversack

backpacker *n* **traveller**, hiker, walker, tourist, hitchhiker

back pain *n* **backache**, lumbago, back trouble, bad back, sciatica

backpedal *v* **backtrack**, back down, shift ground, go back on your word, recant

backroom *adj* **unobtrusive**, clandestine, secret, private, secretive *Opposite*: public

backside *(infml)* *n* **buttocks**, rump, behind, bottom, rear *(infml)*

backslide *v* **relapse**, go back to your old ways, lapse, revert, regress

backslider *n* **recidivist**, defaulter, transgressor, apostate, deserter

backstage *adv* **offstage**, behind the scenes, in the wings, in private, in secret

backstreet *n* **alley**, back alley, lane, side street *Opposite*: thoroughfare

back-to-back *adj* **consecutive**, end-to-end, nonstop, continuous, uninterrupted

backtrack *v* **1 retrace your steps**, go back over the same ground, turn back, begin again *Opposite*: move on **2 backpedal**, go into reverse, do a volte-face, do an about-turn, do a U-turn

back up *v* **1 corroborate**, substantiate, authenticate, vouch for, reinforce *Opposite*: contradict **2 copy**, duplicate, make a backup, keep a backup, keep a copy **3 move backwards**, reverse, go backwards, recede *Opposite*: advance

backup *n* **1 support**, encouragement, help, moral support, assistance **2 stand-by**, reserve, substitute, replacement, reinforcement **3 copy**, duplicate, replica, substitute, fill-in

backward *adj* **1 rearward**, to the rear, towards the back *Opposite*: forward **2 retrograde**, regressive, recessive *Opposite*: progressive **3 shy**, diffident, hesitant, reluctant, timid *Opposite*: confident

backward-looking *adj* **retrospective**, nostalgic, retrograde, traditional, conservative *Opposite*: forward-looking

backwards *adv* **1 towards the back**, back, rearward, towards the rear *Opposite*: forwards **2 the wrong way**, in reverse, back to front, the wrong way round

backwater *n* **backwoods**, the back of beyond, the middle of nowhere, sticks *(infml)*, boondocks *(US infml)*

backwoods *n* **1 wilderness**, wilds, rough country, back country *(US)* **2 the middle of nowhere**, backwater, the back of beyond, sticks *(infml)*, boondocks *(US infml)*

back yard *n* **courtyard**, patio, yard, terrace, porch

bacterial *adj* **microbial**, bacteriological, infective, infectious, contagious

bacteriological *adj* **microbiological**, biological, bacterial, pathological

bad *adj* **1 poor**, inferior, deficient, flawed, faulty *Opposite*: good **2 evil**, wicked, corrupt, immoral, depraved *Opposite*: good **3 naughty**, disobedient, troublesome, wayward, mischievous *Opposite*: good **4 harmful**, damaging, injurious, ruinous, dangerous *Opposite*: good **5 rotten**, off, decayed, decaying, decomposing *Opposite*: fresh **6 regretful**, penitent, remorseful, ashamed, apologetic *Opposite*: good **7 awful**, terrible, dreadful, appalling, shocking *Opposite*: good **8 adverse**, difficult, unhappy, testing, unpleasant *Opposite*: good **9 serious**, severe, grave, critical, life-threatening *Opposite*: slight

COMPARE AND CONTRAST CORE MEANING: indicating wrongdoing

bad applies to a whole range of wrongdoing from the most trivial to the most immoral or evil; **criminal** punishable as a crime under the law; **delinquent** antisocial or unlawful, or *(fml)* neglecting a duty, commitment, or responsibility; **mischievous** playfully naughty or troublesome, or *(fml)* causing or meant to cause serious trouble, damage, or hurt; **naughty** badly behaved or disobedient, or *(infml)* mildly indecent or sinful.

bad blood *n* **bad feeling**, ill feeling, bitterness, acrimony, antagonism *Opposite*: affection

baddie *(infml)* *n* **bad character**, rogue, villain, scoundrel, outlaw *Opposite*: hero

bad feeling *n* **spite**, rancour, spitefulness, bad blood, bitterness *Opposite*: affection

badge *n* **1 brooch**, pin, clasp **2 insignia**, emblem, symbol, mark, device

badger v **pester**, press, harass, plague, harry

bad habit n **weakness**, failing, flaw, character defect, vice *Opposite*: virtue

badinage n **banter**, repartee, teasing, joking, mockery

bad language n **swearing**, swearwords, vulgar language, profanities, coarse language

bad luck n **misfortune**, hard luck, ill luck, unluckiness, ill fortune *Opposite*: luck

badly adv **1 poorly**, deficiently, faultily, defectively, imperfectly *Opposite*: well **2 seriously**, severely, gravely, critically, desperately *Opposite*: slightly **3 naughtily**, disobediently, troublesomely, waywardly, mischievously

bad-mannered adj **rude**, ill-mannered, impolite, charmless, discourteous *Opposite*: well-mannered

bad manners n **rudeness**, impoliteness, incivility, discourtesy, discourteousness *Opposite*: courtesy

bad mood n **bad humour**, sulk, huff, bad temper, temper

badness n **evilness**, wickedness, immorality, evil, depravity *Opposite*: goodness

bad taste n **tastelessness**, vulgarity, showiness, crassness, crudeness *Opposite*: good taste

bad temper n **irritability**, petulance, sulkiness, ill temper, bad mood

bad-tempered adj **cross**, ill-tempered, ill-humoured, irascible, short-tempered *Opposite*: good-tempered

baffle v **confuse**, perplex, puzzle, stump, nonplus

baffled adj **puzzled**, perplexed, mystified, lost, stumped

bafflement n **bewilderment**, perplexity, confusion, puzzlement, bemusement *Opposite*: understanding

baffling adj **puzzling**, perplexing, mystifying, confusing, bewildering *Opposite*: obvious

bag n **container**, receptacle, sack, paper bag, plastic bag ■ v **1 take possession of**, grab, occupy, reserve, keep **2 catch**, shoot, snare, take, capture

WORD BANK

❏ **types of bag** bum bag, carrier, carrier bag, clutch bag, handbag, mailbag, nosebag, pocketbook, postbag, pouch, purse, reticule, satchel, shopper, shopping bag, shopping basket, shoulder bag, sporran, tote bag

bagatelle (fml) n **trifle**, trifling sum, nothing, a drop in the ocean, thing of no importance

baggage n **luggage**, bags, suitcases, cases, belongings

WORD BANK

❏ **types of baggage** attaché case, backpack, briefcase, carrycase, case, duffel bag, flight bag, haversack, holdall, kitbag, knapsack, luggage, overnight bag, pack, portmanteau, rucksack, suitcase, travel case, valise, vanity case, weekend bag

bagginess n **looseness**, formlessness, shapelessness, roominess, floppiness *Opposite*: tightness

baggy adj **loose**, loose-fitting, slack, shapeless, saggy *Opposite*: tight

bags n **luggage**, baggage, belongings, personal belongings, gear (infml)

bags of (infml) n **lots**, plenty, masses (infml), loads (infml), heaps (infml)

bail n **security**, surety, payment, financial guarantee, bond

bailiff n **1 steward**, agent, factor, estate manager, overseer **2 sheriff's officer**, law officer, legal officer, dispossessor, evictor

bail out v **1 stand surety**, obtain somebody's release, put up bail **2 escape**, run away, desert, flee, evacuate *Opposite*: stick out **3 help**, rescue, save, assist, aid

bait n **lure**, attraction, enticement, temptation, inducement ■ v **1 entice**, lure, tempt, attract, draw **2 taunt**, tease, torment, harass, provoke

bake v **1 cook**, heat, harden, dry out **2** (infml) **swelter**, overheat, scorch, burn, roast *Opposite*: freeze

baking adj **sweltering**, boiling, blazing, burning, blistering *Opposite*: freezing

baksheesh n **bribe**, handout, tip, gift, token

balance n **1 equilibrium**, poise, sense of balance, stability, steadiness *Opposite*: unsteadiness **2 weighing machine**, weighing scales, set of scales **3 remainder**, surplus, rest, what's left, residue ■ v **1 maintain equilibrium**, stay poised, keep upright, keep steady, poise *Opposite*: wobble **2 assess**, weigh up, weigh, consider, compare **3 equalize**, square, settle, even out, offset *Opposite*: weight

balanced adj **1 fair**, impartial, unbiased, unprejudiced, disinterested *Opposite*: biased **2 stable**, composed, well-adjusted, sensible, sane *Opposite*: unbalanced

balance out v **even out**, offset, compensate, make up, redress the balance *Opposite*: weight

balcony n **1 veranda**, terrace, loggia, lanai, gallery **2 circle**, upper circle, gallery, upper tier, the gods (infml)

bald adj **1 hairless**, balding, receding, thin on top, baldheaded *Opposite*: hirsute **2 bare**, worn, threadbare, smooth, patchy **3 plain**, blunt, frank, direct, straightforward *Opposite*: florid

balderdash n **rubbish**, nonsense, garbage, drivel, baloney (infml)

baldheaded adj **bald**, hairless, balding, receding, thin on top *Opposite*: hirsute

balding adj **bald**, baldheaded, hairless, receding, thin on top *Opposite*: hirsute

baldly adv **bluntly**, plainly, flatly, frankly, directly

baldness *n* **1 hairlessness**, hair loss, bald-headedness, lack of hair *Opposite*: hairiness **2 bluntness**, plainness, frankness, directness, straightforwardness *Opposite*: deviousness

bale *n* **bundle**, package, pack, roll, block

baleful *adj* **threatening**, menacing, malevolent, sinister, malignant *Opposite*: benevolent

balk *see* **baulk**

ball *n* **sphere**, orb, globe, globule, blob

ballad *n* **poem**, song, narrative, folk song, traditional song

ballast *n* **weight**, bulk, makeweight, stabilizer, balance

ball cock *n* **regulator**, controller, control, device

ballistic *adj* **airborne**, air-to-air, surface-to-air, flying

balloon *n* **hot-air balloon**, helium balloon, inflatable, dirigible ■ *v* **swell**, distend, inflate, expand, puff out *Opposite*: deflate

ballot *n* **vote**, secret ballot, poll, election, survey ■ *v* **canvass**, consult, survey, poll, assess opinion

ballyhoo *n* **uproar**, hullabaloo, commotion, ruckus, to-do *(infml)*

balm *n* **1 ointment**, unguent, salve, oil, cream *Opposite*: irritant **2 comfort**, relief, solace, consolation, palliative

balmy *adj* **mild**, clement, pleasant, temperate, gentle *Opposite*: wintry

baloney *(infml) n* **drivel**, balderdash, nonsense, rubbish, garbage

baluster *n* **post**, support, leg, upright, pole

balustrade *n* **railing**, handrail, guardrail, rail, banister

bamboozle *(infml) v* **1 cheat**, deceive, con, trick, hoodwink **2 confuse**, bewilder, puzzle, bemuse, perplex

ban *v* **forbid**, outlaw, prohibit, veto, bar *Opposite*: allow ■ *n* **prohibition**, veto, bar, injunction, embargo

banal *adj* **commonplace**, hackneyed, prosaic, predictable, ordinary *Opposite*: original

banality *n* **triteness**, predictability, ordinariness, dullness, triviality *Opposite*: originality

band *n* **1 group**, combo, ensemble **2 gang**, crowd, mob, group, crew *(infml)* **3 stripe**, strip, belt, stretch, range

WORD BANK
❑ **types of band** big band, brass band, chamber orchestra, choir, dance band, duo, ensemble, jazz band, mariachi, octet, orchestra, pipe band, pop group, quartet, quintet, septet, sextet, sinfonietta, steel band, string band, string quartet, symphony orchestra, trio

bandage *n* **dressing**, binding, strapping, compress ■ *v* **dress**, bind, tie up, cover, bind up

bandanna *n* **scarf**, neckerchief, headscarf, headsquare, kerchief

bandit *n* **outlaw**, robber, thief, thug, gangster

banditry *n* **robbery**, theft, thieving, raiding, armed robbery

bandstand *n* **platform**, pavilion, stand, shelter, podium

band together *v* **join up**, unite, associate, get together, combine

bandwagon *n* **movement**, cause, trend, craze, fashion

bandy *v* **exchange**, toss around, throw around, mention, debate ■ *adj* **outward-curving**, bowed, bent, warped, convex *Opposite*: straight

bandy-legged *adj* **bowlegged**, bent, bowed, bandy

bandy words with *v* **argue**, dispute, bicker, wrangle, spar

bane *n* **nuisance**, curse, blight, bother, irritation *Opposite*: blessing

bang *n* **1 explosion**, boom, crash, knock, thud **2 knock**, hit, bump, blow, thump ■ *v* **1 hit**, knock, thump, hammer, pound **2 bump**, collide, crash, jolt, knock

banger *(infml)* *n* **wreck**, rattletrap *(infml)*, heap *(slang)*, jalopy *(dated infml)*

banish *v* **1 expel**, send away, exile, deport, evict **2 get rid of**, remove, dismiss, eliminate, discard

banishment *n* **expulsion**, exile, deportation, eviction, exclusion

banister *n* **handrail**, balustrade, guardrail, bar, rail

bank *n* **1 set**, row, tier, series, group **2 store**, depository, reservoir, stock, collection **3 side**, edge, margin, embankment, border **4 pile**, heap, mound, stack, mass ■ *v* **1 deposit**, pay in, cash in, put in *Opposite*: withdraw **2 have an account**, save, deposit, invest **3 heap**, pile, mound, stack, mass *Opposite*: disperse **4 tilt**, pitch, turn, lean, veer *Opposite*: level off

bank account *n* **account**, current account, deposit account, loan account, joint account

banker *n* **banking executive**, investment banker, merchant banker, financier

banking *n* **investment**, lending, funding, financial transactions, online banking

banknote *n* **note**, paper money, folding money *(infml)*, bill *(US)*, dollar bill *(US)* *Opposite*: coin

bank on *v* **count on**, depend on, rely on, trust, have confidence in *Opposite*: doubt

bankroll *(infml) v* **finance**, fund, back, pay, sponsor

bankrupt *adj* **insolvent**, penniless, ruined, broke *(infml)*, bust *(infml) Opposite*: solvent ■ *v* **ruin**, destroy, liquidate, impoverish, make destitute

bankruptcy *n* **insolvency**, ruin, liquidation, economic failure, impoverishment

banned *adj* **1 barred**, disqualified, debarred,

excluded, expelled *Opposite*: admitted **2 forbidden**, proscribed, prohibited, illegal, illicit *Opposite*: permitted

banner *n* sign, poster, flag, placard, streamer

banquet *n* feast, dinner, meal, formal meal, ceremonial meal

banshee *n* spirit, supernatural being, ghost, ghoul, spectre

banter *n* teasing, mockery, joking, repartee, wit ■ *v* tease, mock, joke, poke fun at, make fun of

baptism *n* initiation, introduction, debut, beginning, induction

baptize *v* christen, bless, immerse, sprinkle, initiate

bar *n* **1** rod, pole, stick, staff, shaft **2** block, slab, piece, ingot **3** obstruction, hindrance, block, barrier, impediment **4** hostelry, drinking place, watering hole *(infml)* ■ *v* **1** secure, fasten, bolt, lock, barricade **2** obstruct, close off, hinder, get in the way, block **3** ban, exclude, keep out, debar, prohibit *Opposite*: admit ■ *prep* excluding, save, except, with the exception of, apart from

WORD BANK
❏ **types of bar or club** bodega, casino, country club, joint *(slang)*, local *(infml)*, nightclub, nightspot, pub, roadhouse *(dated)*, saloon, shebeen, speakeasy, tavern *(archaic)*, wine bar

barb *n* **1** point, hook, tip, spur, spike **2** gibe, insult, dig, taunt, cutting remark

barbaric *adj* cruel, brutal, vicious, ferocious, fierce *Opposite*: gentle

barbarism *n* cruelty, brutality, savagery, viciousness, ferociousness *Opposite*: gentleness

barbarity *n* **1** cruelty, brutality, savagery, viciousness, ferociousness *Opposite*: gentleness **2** atrocity, cruelty, outrage, assault, abuse

barbarous *adj* cruel, brutal, vicious, ferocious, fierce *Opposite*: gentle

barbecue *v* grill, flame, chargrill, sear, cook on a spit

barbed *adj* **1** pointed, hooked, spiky, spiny, thorny **2** snide, pointed, cutting, unkind, hurtful

barber *n* gents' hairdresser, gents' hair stylist, hairdresser, hair stylist, coiffeur *(fml)*

barbican *n* tower, keep, stronghold, turret, fortification

bard *(literary)* *n* poet, versifier, composer, wordsmith, songster

bare *adj* **1** naked, nude, exposed, uncovered, undressed *Opposite*: covered **2** empty, vacant, blank, clean, clear *Opposite*: full **3** stark, barren, austere, severe, hard *Opposite*: lush **4** simple, unadorned, plain, basic, unembellished *Opposite*: ornate **5** mere, scant, meagre, measly *(infml)* ■ *v* expose, reveal, display, show, uncover *Opposite*:

cover. *See* COMPARE AND CONTRAST *at* naked.

barefaced *adj* brazen, blatant, unashamed, obvious, unabashed

barefoot *adj* unshod, shoeless, barefooted

barely *adv* hardly, scarcely, only just, just about *Opposite*: easily

bareness *n* emptiness, nakedness, starkness, austerity, plainness

bargain *n* **1** good deal, good buy, steal *(infml)*, snip *(infml)*, giveaway *(infml)* **2** deal, agreement, accord, arrangement, pact ■ *v* haggle, barter, negotiate, make a deal, trade ■ *adj* cheap, low, reduced, inexpensive, rock-bottom

bargain-basement *adj* cheap, cut-price, low-priced, reduced-price, bargain

bargain for *v* expect, count on, take into account, depend on, reckon with

bargain on *see* bargain for

barge *v* rush, push, elbow, burst, surge

barge in *v* **1** walk in, storm in, push in, rush in, breeze in **2** interrupt, butt in, cut in, break in, interject

barge into *v* bump into, collide with, clash with, smash into, knock into

bark *v* howl, yap, growl, yowl, snarl

barmy *(infml)* *adj* irrational, crazy *(infml)*, silly, batty *(infml)*, crackers *(infml)* *Opposite*: rational

barn *n* outbuilding, outhouse, shed, cowshed, byre

barney *(infml)* *n* argument, spat, row, quarrel, tiff

barnyard *n* farmyard, yard, court, forecourt

barometer *n* weatherglass, indicator, gauge, aneroid barometer, barograph

barometric *adj* atmospheric, air, meteorological

baron *n* tycoon, magnate, mogul, industrialist, captain of industry

baronial *adj* grand, impressive, opulent, stately, imposing *Opposite*: humble

baroque *adj* **1** ornate, ornamental, decorative, elaborate, exaggerated *Opposite*: plain **2** flamboyant, exaggerated, overdone, over-the-top *(infml)* *Opposite*: restrained

barrack *(infml)* *v* heckle, shout, interrupt, jeer

barracks *n* quarters, garrison, station, billet

barrage *n* **1** bombardment, salvo, volley, fusillade **2** onslaught, outpouring, hail, storm, flood *Opposite*: trickle **3** dam, dike, bank, embankment

barred *adj* **1** striped, banded, lined, stripy, streaked **2** grilled, meshed, fenced, secure, solid **3** banned, excluded, disqualified, debarred, not allowed *Opposite*: admitted

barrel *n* tub, cask, vat, butt, water butt

barren *adj* **1** desolate, bleak, inhospitable, stark, harsh **2** infertile, unproductive, sterile, unfruitful *Opposite*: fertile

barrenness n 1 **emptiness**, bleakness, bareness, loneliness, inhospitableness 2 **infertility**, sterility, unfruitfulness, unproductiveness *Opposite*: fertility

barricade n **blockade**, barrier, cordon, obstruction, fortification ■ v **secure**, obstruct, bar, fortify, block

barrier n 1 **obstacle**, difficulty, stumbling block, sticking point, impediment 2 **fence**, wall, barricade, blockade, block

barring prep **except for**, without, excluding, apart from

barrister n **lawyer**, attorney, counsellor, advocate, defender

barrow n 1 **cart**, handcart, stall, fruit stall, pushcart (US) 2 **wheelbarrow**, trolley, transporter, trailer, truck 3 **burial mound**, mound, tumulus, long barrow, tomb

barter v **exchange**, trade, switch, negotiate, bargain

base n 1 **foundation**, support, stand, pedestal, rest 2 **source**, origin, heart, starting point, root 3 **headquarters**, centre, main office, seat, station ■ v **found**, ground, build, create, construct ■ adj **dishonourable**, sordid, disreputable, squalid, immoral *Opposite*: honourable

baseless adj **unfounded**, untrue, unjustified, unsubstantiated, groundless *Opposite*: well-founded

baseline n 1 **starting point**, point of departure, reference point, reference line, starting position 2 **standard**, model, criterion, starting point, quality check 3 **reference**, control, check, set of data, set of values 4 **boundary**, boundary line, line, periphery, white line

basement n **cellar**, vault, crypt, lower ground floor *Opposite*: attic

baseness n **wickedness**, sordidness, vileness, immorality, ignobility *Opposite*: nobility

bash v 1 **thump**, punch, smash, whack, clout 2 **criticize**, condemn, find fault with, attack, knock ■ n 1 **punch**, hit, blow, thump, knock 2 **dent**, bump, smash, knock, prang (infml) 3 (infml) **attempt**, try, go, stab (infml), whirl (infml) 4 (infml) **party**, celebration, dance, ball, gala

bashful adj **shy**, timid, reserved, retiring, self-conscious *Opposite*: bold

bashfulness n **shyness**, modesty, self-consciousness, quietness, coyness *Opposite*: boldness

basic adj 1 **essential**, central, key, principal, main *Opposite*: trivial 2 **rudimentary**, straightforward, elementary, undeveloped, uncomplicated *Opposite*: complex

basics n **fundamentals**, essentials, necessities, nitty-gritty (infml), nuts and bolts (infml)

basin n 1 **sink**, hand basin, washbasin, washbowl 2 **bowl**, mixing bowl, dish

basis n **foundation**, base, root, source, starting point

bask v 1 **laze around**, lie, recline, lounge, stretch out 2 **enjoy**, savour, relish, soak up, luxuriate

basket n **carrier**, bag, hamper, picnic basket, linen basket

---

WORD BANK
❑ **types of basket** breadbasket, creel, hamper, laundry basket, linen basket, Moses basket, picnic basket, shopping basket, wicker basket

---

bas-relief n **moulding**, relief, basso-relievo, panelling, carving

bass adj **deep**, deep-toned, deep-voiced, low-pitched *Opposite*: high

baste v 1 **moisten**, drizzle, grease, cover, saturate 2 **thrash**, thump, clobber (infml), bash (infml), beat up (infml) 3 **sew**, stitch, tack, hem, seam

bastion n 1 **stronghold**, fortification, rampart, defence, bulwark 2 **mainstay**, support, defender, upholder, supporter

bat n 1 **racket**, paddle, willow, club 2 **batter**, player, batsman, batswoman, cricketer ■ v **flutter**, wink, flicker, flap, blink

batch n **lot**, consignment, group, set, bunch

bath n 1 **bathtub**, tub, hip bath 2 **immersion**, soak, steam bath, bubble bath, bed bath 3 **tank**, basin, reservoir, container ■ v **soak**, immerse yourself, have a bath, take a bath, wash

bathe v 1 **swim**, go for a dip, paddle 2 **immerse**, dip, soak, rinse, dunk

bather n **swimmer**, diver, snorkeller, paddler, skinny-dipper (infml)

bathetic adj 1 **anticlimactic**, disappointing, unsatisfying 2 **trite**, sentimental, unsatisfying, commonplace

bathos n **anticlimax**, letdown, comedown (infml)

baths n 1 **bathhouse**, Turkish bath, steam bath, sauna 2 **swimming pool**, pool, swimming baths

baton n **stick**, rod, wand, cane, pointer

batsman see **batter**

batswoman see **batter**

battalion n **throng**, crowd, mass, multitude, horde

batten v **fasten**, fix, close, secure, batten down *Opposite*: open

batter v 1 **pound**, bang, thump, thrash, hit 2 **assault**, maim, brutalize, attack, abuse ■ n **player**, bat, cricketer, batsman, batswoman

battered adj 1 **maltreated**, assaulted, abused, beaten, injured 2 **tattered**, tatty, decrepit, worn out, weather-beaten *Opposite*: pristine

battering n **pounding**, buffeting, hammering, beating, lashing

battery n **series**, set, sequence, succession, run

battle n 1 **fight**, clash, encounter, skirmish, engagement 2 **struggle**, crusade, fight, war, campaign ■ v 1 **fight**, go to war, attack, come to blows, engage **2 struggle**, wrestle, contend, fight, strive. *See* COMPARE AND CONTRAST *at* **fight**.

battleaxe *n* axe, hatchet, tomahawk, halberd

battle cry *n* whoop, war cry, yell, shout, cry

battlefield *n* battleground, combat zone, arena, theatre of war, front line

battleground *see* **battlefield**

battlements *n* ramparts, fortifications, walls, parapet, bulwark

batty *(infml)* *adj* irrational, eccentric, crazy *(infml)*, potty *(infml)*, barmy *(infml)* *Opposite*: rational

bauble *n* trinket, trifle, gewgaw, decoration, ornament

baulk *v* **1** recoil, draw back, hesitate, pull back *Opposite*: leap at **2 stop short**, pull up short, rein in

bawdy *adj* ribald, earthy, risqué, suggestive, indecent

bawl *v* **1** shout, yell, roar, shriek, screech *Opposite*: whisper **2** *(infml)* cry, howl, wail, sob, weep

bawl out *(infml)* *v* tell off *(infml)*, haul over the coals, read the riot act to, take to task, give a talking-to *(infml)*

bay *n* **1** inlet, cove, natural harbour, haven *(literary)*, anchorage **2 compartment**, alcove, cubicle, recess, loading bay ▪ *v* woof, bark, yap, yelp, howl

bay for *v* demand, insist on, be out for, cry for, shout for

bayonet *n* blade, knife, dagger, lance, spike ▪ *v* stab, spear, impale, spike, knife

bazaar *n* market, marketplace, souk, open market, flea market

be *v* **1** exist, live, have being, be present, coexist **2 take place**, happen, occur, transpire, come about **3 be situated**, be located, remain, be there, be present

beach *n* seashore, seaside, coast, shore, coastline

beachcomber *n* scavenger, forager, explorer, collector, hoarder

beached *adj* stranded, aground, stuck, high and dry, run aground *Opposite*: afloat

beachhead *n* strategic position, foothold, base, position, foot in the door

beachwear *n* swimwear, leisurewear, sportswear

WORD BANK
❑ **types of beachwear** bathing costume *(dated)*, bathing trunks, bikini, cover-up, one-piece, swimming costume, swimming trunks, swimsuit, tankini, trunks, two-piece

beacon *n* **1** signal, sign, alarm, warning, flare **2 bonfire**, fire, flare **3** *(literary)* inspiration, guiding light, encouragement, example, shining example

bead *n* drop, droplet, drip, blob, globule

beaded *adj* **1** decorated, ornate, bead-trimmed, encrusted, sequinned **2 wet**, moist, dripping, soaked, drenched

beading *n* edging, border, trim, detail, moulding

beady *adj* **1** small, round, shiny, bright, shining **2 beaded**, decorated, ornate, bead-trimmed, sequinned **3** *(infml)* watchful, unblinking, piercing, attentive, bright

beaked *adj* hooked, aquiline, Roman

beaker *n* cup, glass, mug, paper cup, plastic cup

beam *n* **1** girder, rafter, joist, RSJ, timber **2 ray**, shaft of light, sunbeam, stream of light **3 smile**, grin, wide smile, big smile *Opposite*: scowl ▪ *v* **1 smile**, grin, look happy *Opposite*: scowl **2 shine**, radiate, emit, send out, glow

beaming *adj* smiling, cheery, cheerful, sunny, genial *Opposite*: scowling

beanpole *n* support, stick, pole, post, cane

bear *v* **1** tolerate, stand, put up with, stomach, accept **2 support**, take, stand, sustain, hold **3 assume**, accept, shoulder, carry, take **4 show**, display, exhibit, present, evince **5 carry**, convey, bring, take, transport **6 produce**, develop, yield, give birth to, bring forth

bearable *adj* manageable, tolerable, endurable, acceptable, sufferable *Opposite*: unbearable

bear a grudge *v* resent, begrudge, feel bitter about, have hard feelings about, feel aggrieved

beard *n* facial hair, whiskers, goatee, bush, stubble ▪ *v* challenge, confront, accost, stand up to, face up to

bearded *adj* unshaven, hirsute, hairy, whiskery, bewhiskered *Opposite*: clean-shaven

bear down on *v* **1** advance on, close in on, converge on, march on, charge *Opposite*: retreat **2 push down**, press down, thrust, press, lean on

bearer *n* **1** carrier, bringer, deliverer, conveyor, transporter **2 holder**, possessor, owner, keeper, custodian

bear false witness *v* commit perjury, lie, equivocate, stretch the truth

bear fruit *v* succeed, be successful, show results, produce results, pay off *Opposite*: fail

bear hug *n* embrace, hug, cuddle, clinch, squeeze

bearing *n* **1** influence, effect, impact, connection, relevance **2 manner**, behaviour, attitude, deportment, demeanour **3 compass reading**, direction, course, orientation, point of reference

bear in mind *v* remember, keep in mind, think of, consider, take into consideration *Opposite*: forget

41   **bedrock**

bear out *v* **support**, verify, prove, substantiate, corroborate *Opposite*: undermine

bear the brunt *v* **receive the impact**, take the strain, receive the full force, bear the burden, bear the responsibility

bear up *v* **hold up**, hold out, cope, manage, get along *Opposite*: give in

bear with *v* **be patient with**, put up with, make allowance for, show forbearance, bear

beast *n* **1 creature**, animal, being, living thing, quadruped **2 monster**, fiend, ogre, animal, brute *(literary)*

beat *v* **1 defeat**, overcome, overwhelm, thrash, trounce **2 hit**, strike, bang, hammer, thump **3 throb**, palpitate, thump, pound, pulsate **4 whisk**, whip, blend, mix, combine **5 surpass**, break, smash, do better than, go one better than ■ *n* **1 stroke**, blow, hit, bang, thump **2 rhythm**, pulse, pulsation, throb, thump ■ *adj (infml)* **tired**, tired out, worn out, weary, exhausted *Opposite*: fresh. *See* COMPARE AND CONTRAST *at defeat.*

beat a hasty retreat *v* **depart**, leave, make off, run away, make a run for it

beat around the bush *v* **digress**, ramble, waffle, rabbit, bumble

beaten *adj* **1 compressed**, packed down, trodden, flattened, crushed **2 defeated**, conquered, crushed, vanquished

beaten-up *adj* **scruffy**, battered, tatty, tattered, worn out *Opposite*: pristine

beater *n* **whisk**, blade, attachment, paddle, stick

beatification *n* **sanctification**, canonization, sainting, elevation, blessing

beatify *v* **sanctify**, bless, consecrate, canonize, saint

beating *n* **1 thrashing**, whipping, thumping, pounding, hiding *(infml)* **2 defeat**, setback, thrashing, trouncing, pasting *(infml)*

beat it *(infml) v* **go away**, leave, be off, head off, clear off *(infml) Opposite*: stay

beat up *(infml) v* **attack**, assault, batter, mug, injure

beat-up *(infml) adj* **battered**, tattered, tatty, dilapidated, decrepit *Opposite*: pristine

beau *n* **1** *(dated)* **boyfriend**, admirer, steady *(infml)*, suitor *(fml)*, squire *(dated)* **2** *(archaic)* **fop**, peacock, poseur, dandy *(infml)*, swell *(dated infml)*

beautification *n* **enhancement**, sprucing up, prettification, embellishment, improvement

beautiful *adj* **1 good-looking**, lovely, gorgeous, stunning, striking *Opposite*: ugly **2 lovely**, picturesque, scenic, delightful, charming *Opposite*: unattractive. *See* COMPARE AND CONTRAST *at good-looking.*

beautifully *adv* **1 attractively**, gorgeously, stunningly, handsomely, prettily *Opposite*: unattractively **2 well**, excellently, superbly, brilliantly, magnificently *Opposite*: poorly

beautify *v* **prettify**, smarten, enhance, remodel, spruce up

beauty *n* **1 loveliness**, attractiveness, good looks, prettiness, exquisiteness *Opposite*: unattractiveness **2 advantage**, attraction, benefit, upside, plus *(infml) Opposite*: drawback

beauty salon *n* **salon**, hair salon, beautician's

beaver *(infml) v* **work**, labour, toil, exert yourself, keep at *Opposite*: idle

becalmed *adj* **stuck**, at a standstill, stationary, at a halt, marooned *Opposite*: moving

because *conj* **since**, as, for

because of *prep* **owing to**, on account of, as a consequence of, due to, as a result of *Opposite*: despite

beck *n* **stream**, rivulet, burn, brook *(literary)*

beckon *v* **signal**, sign, summon, gesture, indicate *Opposite*: dismiss

become *v* **1 turn out to be**, turn into, develop, convert, grow into **2 suit**, befit, flatter, enhance, show off

become acquainted *v* **meet**, meet for the first time, be introduced to, make the acquaintance of, get to know

become aware of *v* **notice**, detect, discern, make out, sense *Opposite*: miss

become of *v* **happen to**, occur, be the outcome of, befall *(literary)*

becoming *adj* **1 flattering**, attractive, fetching, charming, pretty *Opposite*: unattractive **2 suitable**, appropriate, apt, fitting, befitting *Opposite*: inappropriate

bed *n* **1 plot**, flowerbed, patch, border **2 layer**, band, base, strip, seam **3 bottom**, floor, base, seabed, riverbed

WORD BANK
❏ **types of bed** bassinet, berth, bunk, bunk bed, camp bed, carrycot, cot, couchette, cradle, day bed, divan, double bed, four-poster, futon, hammock, king-size bed, Moses basket, queen-size bed, single bed, sofa bed, studio couch, trundle bed, twin bed, water bed

bedazzle *(literary) v* **amaze**, stun, impress, bewilder, daze

bedding *n* **bedclothes**, bedcovers, bed linen, covers

bedevil *v* **beset**, assail, torment, harass, trouble

bedlam *n* **chaos**, pandemonium, confusion, anarchy, disorder *Opposite*: order

bed linen *see* **bedding**

bedpan *n* **chamber pot**, pot, potty, commode

bedraggled *adj* **unkempt**, dishevelled, untidy, messy, scruffy *Opposite*: neat

bedridden *adj* **confined to bed**, flat on your back, laid up, incapacitated, disabled *Opposite*: active

bedrock *n* **1 rock layer**, substratum, solid rock,

base, foundation **2 basis**, base, core, heart, root

bedroom *n* **dormitory**, sleeping quarters, boudoir, room, dorm *(infml)*

bedside manner *n* **rapport**, style, approach, relationship, conduct

bedsit *n* **flat**, studio flat, bedsitter, studio apartment, studio

bedsore *n* **ulcer**, pressure sore, ulceration, sore, bruise

bedspread *n* **coverlet**, cover, quilt, throw, eiderdown

bedstead *n* **bed**, frame, base

bedtime *n* **time for bed**, sleep time, time to turn in *(infml)*, time to hit the hay *(infml)*, time to hit the sack *(infml)*

beefiness *n* **muscularity**, sturdiness, burliness, brawniness, stockiness

beef up *(infml)* *v* **strengthen**, improve, enhance, boost, reinforce *Opposite*: weaken

beefy *adj* **muscular**, brawny, heavy, hefty, burly *Opposite*: puny

beehive *n* **apiary**, hive, skep

beep *v* **toot**, peep, parp, bleep, beep-beep

beeper *(infml)* *n* **pager**, bleeper, monitor

beermat *n* **coaster**, mat, rest, bar cloth

beet *n* **sugar beet**, beetroot, chard, Swiss chard

beetle 1 *n* **insect**, bug, creepy-crawly *(infml)* **2** *v* *(infml)* **hurry**, scurry, scuttle, scud, dart

WORD BANK
❏ **types of beetle** cockroach, Colorado beetle, deathwatch beetle, dung beetle, flea beetle, Japanese beetle, ladybird, rhinoceros beetle, roach *(infml)*, scarab, stag beetle, water beetle, weevil

befit *v* **suit**, become, be fitting, be suitable for, be appropriate

befitting *adj* **becoming**, suitable, appropriate, apt, fitting *Opposite*: unsuitable

before *prep* **1 in front of**, facing, ahead of *Opposite*: behind **2 previous to**, earlier than, sooner than, prior to, ahead of *Opposite*: after ■ *adv* **beforehand**, previously, earlier, in advance, in the past *Opposite*: afterwards

beforehand *adv* **earlier**, in advance, before, early, ahead of time *Opposite*: late

befriend *v* **make friends with**, take care of, look after, help, assist *Opposite*: shun

befuddle *v* **confuse**, muddle, mix up, bewilder, baffle *Opposite*: enlighten

befuddled *adj* **confused**, muddled, baffled, puzzled, perplexed *Opposite*: clear-headed

befuddlement *n* **confusion**, perplexity, bewilderment, bafflement, puzzlement *Opposite*: clarity

beg *v* **ask for**, request, plead, solicit, entreat

beget *v* **cause**, bring about, precipitate, create, bring

beg forgiveness *v* **apologize**, make an apology, express regret, say sorry

beggar *n* **vagrant**, tramp, homeless person, rough sleeper, street dweller ■ *v* **defy**, be beyond, confound, surpass, exceed

begin *v* **1 start**, start on, commence, start in on, set in motion *Opposite*: finish **2 bring into being**, instigate, initiate, inaugurate, activate **3 start the ball rolling**, get down to, get to, get under way, set off *Opposite*: end

beginner *n* **novice**, learner, trainee, apprentice, student *Opposite*: old hand

COMPARE AND CONTRAST CORE MEANING: a person who has not acquired the necessary experience or skills to do something
beginner somebody who has just started to learn or do something; **apprentice** somebody who is being taught the skills of a trade over an agreed period of time by somebody fully trained; **greenhorn** somebody who lacks experience and may be naive or gullible; **novice** somebody with no previous experience or skill in the activity undertaken; **tyro** somebody who is raw and inexperienced.

beginning *n* **start**, opening, launch, establishment, creation *Opposite*: end

beg off *v* **back out**, bow out, duck out, cry off *(infml)*

begrudge *v* **resent**, envy, be envious, be jealous, be resentful

beg to differ *v* **disagree**, take issue with, demur, dissent, object *Opposite*: agree

beguile *v* **entice**, lure, charm, captivate, mesmerize

beguiling *adj* **enticing**, charming, mesmeric, fascinating, captivating

behave *v* **1 act**, perform, conduct yourself, deport yourself, work **2 be good**, obey the rules, do the right thing, toe the line, keep out of mischief *Opposite*: misbehave

behaviour *n* **performance**, actions, deeds, activities, manners

behavioural *adj* **social**, interactive, communicative, negotiating, developmental

behead *v* **decapitate**, cut off somebody's head, guillotine, execute, put to death

behind *prep* **following**, after, in the wake of, at the back of, at the rear of ■ *adv* **at the back**, at the rear, after, following, last *Opposite*: in front ■ *adj* **behindhand**, late, overdue, behind schedule, in arrears *Opposite*: early

behindhand *adj* **late**, behind, behind schedule, overdue, slow *Opposite*: early

beholden *adj* **obliged**, grateful, in somebody's debt, indebted, obligated

behove *(fml)* *v* **be the duty of**, be the bounden duty of, fall to, befit, be incumbent upon *(fml)*

being *n* **1 existence**, life, actuality, presence, animation *Opposite*: nothingness **2 self**, soul, mind, essence, spirit **3 life form**, organism, creature, living being, human being

belabour *v* **overemphasize**, overdo, overstate, labour, stress

belated *adj* **late**, delayed, postponed, deferred, tardy *Opposite*: timely

belch *v* **bring up wind**, burp, hiccup, gulp, posset ∎ *n* burp, hiccup, eructation

beleaguer *v* 1 **harass**, annoy, pester, plague, badger 2 **besiege**, surround, lay siege to, threaten, menace

beleaguered *adj* **under pressure**, harassed, fraught, careworn, stressed *Opposite*: care-free

belfry *n* **bell tower**, campanile, tower, spire, steeple

belie *v* **contradict**, disprove, give the lie to, call into question, deny *Opposite*: confirm

belief *n* 1 **faith**, conviction, principle, creed, idea 2 **confidence**, trust, certainty, credence, acceptance *Opposite*: distrust

believability *n* **credibility**, plausibility, acceptability, trustworthiness, authenticity

believable *adj* **credible**, authentic, realistic, plausible, convincing *Opposite*: unbelievable

believe *v* 1 **trust**, have faith in, be certain of, have confidence in, accept as true *Opposite*: disbelieve 2 **consider**, think, suppose, judge, imagine *Opposite*: doubt

believer *n* **supporter**, advocate, fan, devotee, follower *Opposite*: sceptic

belittle *v* **disparage**, demean, decry, deride, depreciate *Opposite*: praise

belittlement *n* **depreciation**, disparagement, derision, disdain *Opposite*: praise

belittling *adj* **demeaning**, disparaging, depreciating, condescending, patronizing *Opposite*: supportive

bell *n* 1 **hand bell**, church bell, ship's bell, sleigh bell, school bell 2 **buzzer**, doorbell, chime, alarm, alarm bell 3 *(infml)* **call**, ring, phone call, buzz *(infml)*, tinkle *(infml)*

bellicose *adj* **belligerent**, aggressive, warlike, pugnacious, combative *Opposite*: compliant

belligerence *n* **hostility**, pugnaciousness, bellicosity, pugnacity, aggression

belligerency *see* **belligerence**

belligerent *adj* **aggressive**, argumentative, quarrelsome, confrontational, pugnacious *Opposite*: cooperative

bellow *n* **roar**, shout, yell, bawl, holler *(US infml)* *Opposite*: whisper ∎ *v* **shout**, roar, yell, bawl, thunder *Opposite*: whisper

belly *(infml)* *n* **stomach**, abdomen, middle, tummy *(infml)*, gut *(slang)*

bellyache *(infml)* *n* 1 **upset stomach**, stomach ache, stomach pains, tummy ache *(infml)* 2 **complaint**, grumble, moan *(infml)*, grouse *(infml)*, gripe *(infml)* ∎ *v* **complain**, grumble, carp, whine, moan *(infml)*

bellybutton *(infml)* *n* **navel**, umbilicus, tummy button *(infml)*

belly flop *n* **fall**, flop, crash, dive

belly laugh *n* **guffaw**, laugh, chortle, horse-laugh, hoot

belong *v* **fit in**, fit, go, have its place, be in the right place

belongings *n* **possessions**, property, things, stuff, luggage

beloved *adj* **much-loved**, dearly loved, adored, favourite, darling *Opposite*: despised

below *prep* **less than**, under, not more than, beneath *(fml)* ∎ *adv* 1 **underneath**, under, lower, beneath *(fml)* *Opposite*: above 2 **under**, underneath, lower than, further down, beneath *(fml)* *Opposite*: above

belt *n* 1 **girdle**, tie, sash, cummerbund, strap 2 **band**, ring, strip, ribbon, line ∎ *v* 1 **fasten**, buckle, secure, attach, belt up *Opposite*: undo 2 *(infml)* **hit**, thump, thrash, beat, strike 3 *(infml)* **dash**, rush, speed, hurry, race *Opposite*: dawdle

belt up *v* **fasten your belt**, secure your belt, put on your belt, buckle up

bemoan *v* **lament**, regret, mourn, complain, grumble *Opposite*: applaud

bemuse *v* **confuse**, daze, puzzle, perplex, stun

bemused *adj* **confused**, dazed, puzzled, perplexed, mystified *Opposite*: clear-headed

bench *n* 1 **seat**, pew, stall, form, bleacher *(US)* 2 **worktable**, counter, work surface, worktop, workbench

benchmark *n* **standard**, yardstick, level, target, point of reference

bend *n* **curve**, turn, crook, twist, curvature ∎ *v* 1 **turn**, bow, twist, crook, change direction *Opposite*: straighten 2 **stoop**, bow, bend over, lean down, lean over *Opposite*: straighten up

bendable *adj* **bendy**, flexible, pliant, pliable, malleable *Opposite*: inflexible

bend over backwards *v* **do all you can**, put yourself out, pull out all the stops, do your utmost, go all out

bendy *adj* **flexible**, malleable, plastic, supple, bendable *Opposite*: stiff

beneath *(fml)* *prep* **under**, underneath, below, lower than, less than *Opposite*: over ∎ *adv* **underneath**, under, below, lower *Opposite*: above

benediction *n* **approval**, sanction, blessing *Opposite*: malediction *(fml)*

benefactor *n* **sponsor**, patron, supporter, backer

beneficence *n* **generosity**, charity, benevolence, big-heartedness, magnanimity *Opposite*: parsimony

beneficent *adj* 1 **charitable**, altruistic, generous, benevolent, humanitarian *Opposite*: self-seeking 2 **beneficial**, helpful, useful, advantageous, valuable *Opposite*: deleterious

beneficial *adj* **helpful**, useful, valuable, advantageous, positive *Opposite*: detrimental

beneficiary n recipient, receiver, heir, payee, legatee *Opposite*: benefactor

benefit n **1** advantage, profit, help, assistance, use *Opposite*: detriment **2** subsidy, allowance, payment, grant **3** fundraiser, charity performance, charity event ■ v help, promote, profit, do good to, advance *Opposite*: harm

benefit from v profit from, enjoy, use, gain from, take advantage of

benevolence n kindness, compassion, generosity, munificence, goodwill *Opposite*: malevolence

benevolent adj kind, caring, compassionate, generous, giving *Opposite*: malevolent

benighted adj ignorant, unenlightened, unfortunate, disadvantaged *Opposite*: enlightened

benign adj kind, benevolent, caring, kindly, gentle *Opposite*: malignant

benignity n kindliness, gentleness, benevolence, compassion, warm-heartedness *Opposite*: malice

bent adj **1** twisted, curved, bowed, crooked, turned *Opposite*: straight **2** determined, set, fixed, resolved, decided ■ n inclination, gift, talent, flair. *See* COMPARE AND CONTRAST at **talent**.

bequeath v leave, give, donate, hand down, will *Opposite*: inherit

bequest n inheritance, legacy, gift, donation, settlement

berate v rebuke, shout at, harangue, criticize, scold *Opposite*: praise

bereaved adj mourning, bereft, in mourning, grieving, orphaned

bereavement n loss, grief, sorrow, mourning

bereft adj **1** bereaved, mourning, in mourning, grieving, orphaned **2** empty, starved, devoid, deprived, stripped

berserk adj irrational, mad, out of control, wild, off the deep end *Opposite*: rational

berth n mooring, dock, landing place, mooring place, wharf ■ v dock, moor, tie up, come in, land *Opposite*: put out

beset adj plagued, tormented, overwhelmed, overcome, harassed *Opposite*: free ■ v **1** harass, annoy, hamper, trouble, overwhelm *Opposite*: leave alone **2** (fml) surround, attack, overcome, overwhelm, assail

beside prep next to, at the side of, alongside, by, near

besides adv **1** as well, in addition, also, above and beyond, too **2** moreover, what's more, further, more to the point, anyway

besiege v surround, siege, lay siege to, encircle, blockade *Opposite*: defend

besieged adj overwhelmed, inundated, beleaguered, weighed down, plagued

besmirch v sully, defame, tarnish, damage, slander *Opposite*: praise

besotted adj infatuated, love-struck, head over

heels in love, fanatical, obsessed *Opposite*: repelled

bespeak v signify, signal, indicate, convey, reveal

bespoke adj custom-made, tailor-made, made to measure, customized, custom-built *Opposite*: off-the-shelf

best adj top, finest, greatest, unsurpassed, paramount *Opposite*: worst ■ v outdo, overcome, top, surpass, defeat

bestial adj inhuman, foul, degrading, cruel, brutish *Opposite*: humane

bestiality n cruelty, inhumanity, savagery, brutality, depravity *Opposite*: humanity

bestir yourself (fml) v motivate yourself, stir yourself, busy yourself, rouse yourself, get going

bestow (fml) v give, bequeath, donate, grant, present *Opposite*: withdraw. *See* COMPARE AND CONTRAST at **give**.

bestride v straddle, span, sit astride, stand astride, be astride

bestseller n hit, smash, success, winner, moneymaker *Opposite*: flop (infml)

bestselling adj successful, popular, blockbusting, hit, chart-topping

bet v **1** gamble, stake, wager, put money on, lay a wager **2** (infml) think, expect, anticipate, consider, believe ■ n **1** wager, gamble, stake, play, ante **2** option, alternative, candidate, choice, plan

betray v **1** be disloyal, give up, hand over, inform on, double cross *Opposite*: stand by **2** disclose, leak, tell, give away, reveal

betrayal n disloyalty, unfaithfulness, bad faith, duplicity, infidelity *Opposite*: loyalty

betrothal (fml) n engagement, promise, pact, compact, troth (archaic)

betrothed (fml) n fiancé, fiancée, husband-to-be, wife-to-be, girlfriend

better adj **1** improved, enhanced, superior *Opposite*: worse **2** healthier, improved, well, recovering, in good health *Opposite*: worse ■ v **1** (fml) improve on, top, outdo, outstrip, outshine **2** (fml) enhance, improve, change for the better, advance, ameliorate (fml) *Opposite*: worsen

betterment (fml) n furtherance, improvement, advancement, benefit, progress *Opposite*: deterioration

better-off adj rich, wealthy, affluent, comfortable, prosperous *Opposite*: poor

between prep **1** flanked by, sandwiched between, stuck between, amid, among **2** connecting, linking, joining, involving, concerning

bevelled adj oblique, slanting, sloping, chamfered, bias-cut

beverage (fml) n drink, hot drink, cold drink, liquid refreshment, brew (infml)

bewail (fml) v lament, bemoan, complain,

regret, grumble Opposite: applaud

beware v be careful, be cautious, be wary, look out, watch out

bewilder v confuse, puzzle, baffle, perplex, confound

bewildered adj confused, puzzled, dazed, bemused, befuddled Opposite: clear-headed

bewildering adj confusing, puzzling, baffling, mystifying, incomprehensible Opposite: clear

bewilderment n confusion, incomprehension, bafflement, puzzlement, perplexity Opposite: clarity

bewitch v enchant, fascinate, captivate, charm, mesmerize, intrigue Opposite: repel

beyond prep further than, past, away from, clear of, ahead of

biannual adj 1 twice-yearly, twice-a-year, six-monthly, semiannual 2 every other year, biennial, two-yearly, regular, periodic

bias n prejudice, partiality, preference, unfairness, predisposition Opposite: impartiality

biased adj prejudiced, unfair, partial, influenced, predisposed Opposite: unbiased

biblical adj scriptural, holy, bible, sacred, theological

bibliography n list, index, appendix, checklist, catalogue

bicameral adj two-tier, two-house, dual, bilateral, bipartite

bicentenary n 200th anniversary, 200th birthday, anniversary, bicentennial (US)

bicker v argue, dispute, quarrel, debate, squabble Opposite: agree

bicycle n cycle, two-wheeler, bike (infml), push-bike (infml)

bid v 1 tender, offer, propose, submit, proffer 2 try, attempt, undertake, endeavour, seek 3 (archaic) order, call on, command, direct, tell ■ n 1 offer, proposal, proposition, tender, submission 2 attempt, try, effort, undertaking, endeavour

biddable adj compliant, acquiescent, docile, obedient, amenable Opposite: intractable (fml)

bidder n buyer, collector, dealer, purchaser, customer

bidding n request, command, order, will, call

bide your time v wait, be patient, wait and see, play the waiting game, hold back

biennial adj two-yearly, biannual, regular, periodic

bier n stand, rest, base, pedestal, table

biff (infml) v hit, punch, thump, knock, clout

bifurcate v divide, branch, split, fork, diverge Opposite: converge

bifurcation n fork, junction, split, divergence, branching Opposite: convergence

big adj 1 large, giant, immense, vast, great Opposite: small 2 spacious, capacious, roomy, large, deep Opposite: cramped 3 significant, considerable, substantial, sizable, large Opposite: insignificant 4 extensive, vast, immense, wide, great Opposite: narrow 5 older, elder, grown-up, adult, mature Opposite: little 6 bulky, large, cumbersome, massive, outsize Opposite: petite 7 tall, high, lofty, towering, soaring Opposite: short

bigamous adj polygamous, adulterous, two-timing (infml) Opposite: monogamous

bigamy n polygamy, adultery, two-timing (infml) Opposite: monogamy

big business n trade, commerce, industry, business sector, business world

big deal (infml) n major concern, serious issue, matter of life and death, federal case (US)

biggie (infml) n 1 big one, giant, colossus, monster, whopper (infml) 2 key player, major player, VIP, big gun, big shot (infml) Opposite: nobody

bighead (infml) n boaster, bragger, show-off (infml), smart aleck (infml), clever clogs (infml)

bigheaded (infml) adj conceited, egotistical, arrogant, vain, self-centred Opposite: modest

big-hearted adj kind, good-natured, supportive, helpful, kindly Opposite: mean-spirited

bigmouth (infml) n 1 gossip, gossipmonger, telltale, tattler, blabbermouth (infml) 2 boaster, bragger, braggart, know-all (infml), bighead (infml)

big name n famous name, celebrity, star, superstar, VIP Opposite: unknown

bigot n chauvinist, extremist, dogmatist, fanatic, diehard

bigoted adj prejudiced, intolerant, chauvinistic, dogmatic, opinionated Opposite: open-minded

bigotry n prejudice, intolerance, chauvinism, narrow-mindedness, fanaticism Opposite: open-mindedness

big shot (infml) n key player, major player, VIP, big gun (infml), bigwig (infml) Opposite: nobody

bigwig (infml) see big shot

bijou adj compact, tiny, cramped, small, poky (infml) Opposite: spacious

bike (infml) n bicycle, cycle, motorbike, motorcycle, push-bike (infml)

WORD BANK
❑ **types of bike** boneshaker, dirt bike, exercise bike, moped, motor scooter, mountain bike, penny-farthing, racing bike, rickshaw, scooter, scrambler, tandem, ten-speed, three-wheeler, trail bike, tricycle, two-wheeler, unicycle
❑ **parts of a bike** brake, chain, crossbar, derailleur, fork, frame, handlebars, mudguard, pedal, reflector, seat, spoke, tyre, wheel

biker n motorcyclist, scrambler, racer, rider, cyclist

bikini n swimsuit, two-piece, swimming costume, bathing costume *(dated)*, bathing suit *(US)*

bilateral adj **two-sided**, two-pronged, joint, mutual, consensual *Opposite*: unilateral

bilge n 1 **hull**, keel, base, bottom 2 **hold**, tank, interior, recesses, bowels 3 **sludge**, mud, bilge water, silt, effluent 4 *(infml)* **nonsense**, rubbish, garbage, trash, drivel

bilingual adj **fluent**, multilingual, polyglot

bilious adj **nauseous**, sickly, queasy, sick, ill

bilk *(infml)* v **cheat**, trick, deceive, con, swindle

bill n 1 **invoice**, statement, demand, receipt, damage *(infml)* 2 **amount**, total, sum, fee, price 3 **proposal**, measure, document, petition, proposition 4 **beak**, mouth, mandible ■ v **charge**, invoice, debit, send the bill to

billboard n **sign**, hoarding, poster, advertisement, panel

billet n **accommodation**, quarters, boarding house, guest house, lodgings *(dated)* ■ v **accommodate**, quarter, house, station, shelter

billionaire n **multimillionaire**, magnate, tycoon, moneybags *(infml)*, fat cat *(slang)*

billionth n **tiny part**, morsel, particle, modicum, touch

billow v 1 **catch the wind**, swell, bulge, balloon, fill *Opposite*: sag 2 **roll upwards**, waft, rise, curl, flow *Opposite*: fall ■ n **puff**, cloud, swell, swirl, rush

billycan n **cooking pot**, pail, pan, pot, tin

bin n 1 **rubbish bin**, wastepaper basket, waste bin, dustbin, litter bin 2 **storage bin**, basket, container, silo, holder ■ v **throw away**, throw out, toss, discard, dispose of *Opposite*: keep

binary adj **two-part**, dual, double, twin, twofold

bind v 1 **attach**, connect, join, combine, unite *Opposite*: undo 2 **oblige**, force, require, compel, coerce ■ n 1 **quandary**, tight situation, predicament, dilemma, muddle 2 **nuisance**, drag, bore, annoyance, pain *(infml)*

binder n **folder**, file, ring binder, looseleaf folder

binding n 1 **tie**, band, attachment, fastening, truss 2 **edging**, cover, trim, stitching, strip ■ adj **compulsory**, obligatory, required, necessary, mandatory *Opposite*: voluntary

binge n **spree**, orgy, rampage, splurge *(infml)*, bender *(slang)* ■ v **overdo**, indulge, overindulge, gorge, pig out *(infml)* *Opposite*: diet

binoculars n **field glasses**, opera glasses, eyeglasses *(US fml)*

biochemical adj **chemical**, biological, living, organic, natural

biodegradable adj **recyclable**, decomposable, ecological, environmental, green

biographer n **writer**, author, autobiographer, historian, profiler

biographical adj **factual**, nonfiction, true, fact-based, realistic *Opposite*: fictional

biography n **life story**, life history, profile, memoir, life

biological adj 1 **organic**, life, living, natural, biotic 2 **natal**, birth, natural, genetic, true *Opposite*: adoptive

bionic adj **electronic**, automatic, robotic, electromechanical

biopic n **film**, movie, biography, documentary, life story

biopsy n **cell removal**, operation, surgery, culture, tissue removal

biorhythm n **cycle**, change, cyclical change, rhythm

biosphere n **environment**, planet, earth, land, sea

bipartisan adj **two-party**, dual-party, cross-party, joint, combined

bipartite adj **two-party**, two-part, mutual, shared, in common

biped n **two-legged animal**, human, primate, humanoid

birch n **cane**, rod, stick, switch, whip ■ v **whip**, flog, thrash, lash, strike

birdbath n **basin**, bowl, receptacle

birdbrained *(infml)* adj **silly**, foolish, stupid, asinine, witless *Opposite*: sensible

birdcage n **cage**, coop, pen, aviary, enclosure

birdlike adj **dainty**, petite, small-boned, delicate, slight *Opposite*: heavyset

birdseed n **seed**, grain, mixture, feed, chicken feed

birdsong n **call**, cry, song, trill, whistle

birdwatcher n **ornithologist**, bird lover, twitcher, birder

birth n 1 **delivery**, labour, childbirth, nativity, parturition *(fml)* *Opposite*: death 2 **beginning**, origin, dawn, start, onset *Opposite*: end ■ adj **natal**, natural, true, biological, genetic *Opposite*: adoptive

birthdate *see* **birthday**

birthday n **date of birth**, birthdate, anniversary

birthmark n **mark**, stain, discoloration, blemish, strawberry mark

birthplace n **origin**, source, home, home town, place of birth

birthright n **inheritance**, legacy, bequest, heritage, patrimony

birth sign n **sign of the Zodiac**, astrological sign, star sign

bisect v **cut in half**, intersect, divide, cut across, sever *Opposite*: join

bisection n **halving**, splitting, dissection, division, parting *Opposite*: union

bit n 1 **piece**, morsel, crumb, fragment, speck 2 **minute**, while, moment, second, a little while

bite *v* **1 sink your teeth into**, nibble, gnaw, bite off, bite into **2 wound**, nip, snap, attack, maul **3 hurt**, sting, feel painful, nip, prick ■ *n* **1 taste**, mouthful, nibble, chew, piece **2 wound**, sting, puncture, bite mark **3 sharp taste**, spiciness, tartness, piquancy, tang

bite-sized *adj* **small**, little, minute, tiny, petite *Opposite*: big

bite the bullet *v* **grasp the nettle**, take the bull by the horns, do it, face up to, go for it *(slang)* *Opposite*: avoid

bite the dust *(infml)* *v* **1 fall down**, fall flat, take a fall, tumble, tumble down **2 die**, pass away, kick the bucket *(infml)*, croak *(infml)*, expire *(fml)* **3 fail**, go under, die a death, be unsuccessful, go bankrupt *Opposite*: succeed

biting *adj* **1 cold**, freezing, piercing, cutting, stinging *Opposite*: hot **2 sarcastic**, scathing, acerbic, mordant, satirical *Opposite*: sympathetic

bitingly *adv* **acidly**, acerbically, tartly, woundingly, cruelly *Opposite*: sympathetically

bits and bobs *(infml)* *see* **bits and pieces**

bits and pieces *(infml)* *n* **1 belongings**, things, odds and ends, stuff, personal possessions **2 knick-knacks**, leftovers, scraps, odds and ends, stuff

bitter *adj* **1 sour**, acid, acidic, tart, astringent *Opposite*: sweet **2 resentful**, embittered, sulky, cheated, angry *Opposite*: glad **3 unpleasant**, acrimonious, antagonistic, nasty, hostile *Opposite*: amicable **4 vicious**, rancorous, virulent, vehement *Opposite*: mild **5 cold**, freezing, icy, biting, raw *Opposite*: hot

bitterly *adv* **1 resentfully**, acrimoniously, sulkily, sullenly, cynically *Opposite*: gladly **2 severely**, excessively, intensely, inordinately, desperately *Opposite*: slightly

bitterness *n* **1 resentment**, acrimony, unpleasantness, sullenness, anger *Opposite*: friendliness **2 sourness**, acidity, sour taste, astringency, bitter taste *Opposite*: sweetness

bittersweet *adj* **poignant**, nostalgic, affecting, touching, sentimental

bitty *adj* **disjointed**, fragmented, scrappy, fragmentary *Opposite*: cohesive

bitumen *n* **tar**, asphalt, Tarmac, pitch, blacktop (US)

bivouac *n* **1 camp**, encampment, temporary camp, mountaineering camp, military camp **2 shelter**, awning, tent, pup tent, lean to (US) ■ *v* **camp**, set up camp, pitch a tent

biweekly *adv* **1 once every two weeks**, every other week, twice a month, every fortnight, once a fortnight **2 twice a week**, semiweekly, every few days

bizarre *adj* **strange**, curious, inexplicable, out of the ordinary, unusual *Opposite*: ordinary

blab *(infml)* *v* **tell tales**, gossip, tattle, leak, tell

blabber *v* **chatter**, babble, go on, drivel, jabber

blabbermouth *(infml)* *n* **gossip**, telltale, chatterer, sneak, bigmouth *(infml)*

black *adj* **dark**, gloomy, obscure, dusky, murky *Opposite*: light

---

WORD BANK

❑ **types of black** blue-black, coal black, ebony, inky, jet black, pitch-black, raven, sable

---

black-and-blue *adj* **bruised**, aching, hurt, injured, battered

black-and-white *adj* **clear-cut**, straightforward, unambiguous, categorical, explicit *Opposite*: ambiguous

blackball *v* **exclude**, ban, keep out, reject, bar *Opposite*: invite

blackboard *n* **board**, slate, whiteboard, chalkboard (US)

blacken *v* **1 darken**, make black, dirty, turn black, besmirch *Opposite*: lighten **2 slander**, libel, defame, vilify, malign *Opposite*: praise

blackguard *n* **scoundrel**, rascal, rogue, villain, wretch *(fml)*

blackhead *n* **blocked pore**, spot, pimple, blemish, zit *(slang)*

blacklist *v* **ban**, debar, bar, exclude, shut out

blackly *adv* **1 angrily**, menacingly, threateningly, belligerently, aggressively *Opposite*: optimistically **2 hopelessly**, gloomily, lugubriously, dismally, dolefully *Opposite*: sunnily

blackmail *n* **extortion**, intimidation, bribery, corruption, extraction ■ *v* **extort**, extract, exact, hold to ransom, bribe

blackmailer *n* **extortionist**, coercer, criminal, crook *(infml)*

blackness *n* **1 darkness**, duskiness, dimness, shadow, gloom *Opposite*: light **2 hopelessness**, despondency, gloominess, depression, dolefulness *Opposite*: optimism **3 anger**, fury, temper, aggression, belligerence *Opposite*: cheerfulness

black out *v* **faint**, pass out, lose consciousness, collapse, become unconscious *Opposite*: come to

blackout *n* **1 fainting fit**, seizure, loss of consciousness, collapse **2 power cut**, shutdown, power failure, power outage (US) **3 embargo**, veto, clampdown, suppression, censorship

black-tie *adj* **formal**, dressy, ceremonial, posh *(infml)* *Opposite*: casual

blade *n* **1 cutting edge**, knife-edge, edge, razor blade, knife blade **2 vane**, fin, propeller, sail, oar

blame *v* **1 hold responsible**, censure, accuse, point the finger at, hold accountable *Opposite*: exculpate *(fml)* **2 criticize**, reproach, find fault with, condemn, think badly of *Opposite*: commend ■ *n* **responsibility**, guilt, culpability, fault, blameworthiness *Opposite*: commendation

blameless *adj* **innocent**, virtuous, righteous, faultless, irreproachable *Opposite*: guilty

blameworthy *adj* **responsible**, guilty, culpable, at fault, chargeable *Opposite*: innocent

blanch *v* **go pale**, grow pale, turn white, lighten, blench *Opposite*: redden

bland *adj* **1 insipid**, weak, tasteless, mild, plain *Opposite*: tasty **2 featureless**, ordinary, dull, lacklustre, humdrum *Opposite*: exciting

blandishment *n* **flattery**, cajolery, praise, fawning, soft words

blandness *n* **1 tastelessness**, weakness, insipidness, mildness, plainness *Opposite*: tastiness **2 dullness**, banality, flatness, triteness, insipidness *Opposite*: interest

blank *adj* **1 empty**, vacant, bare, clean, clear *Opposite*: full **2 outright**, complete, total, absolute, unqualified *Opposite*: partial **3 uncomprehending**, impassive, vacant, empty, bemused *Opposite*: expressive ■ *n* **space**, void, gap, empty space, break

blanket *n* **coverlet**, cover, covering, throw, spread ■ *adj* **comprehensive**, extensive, complete, total, wholesale *Opposite*: partial ■ *v* **cover**, obscure, encase, drape, carpet *Opposite*: uncover

blankness *n* **1 emptiness**, void, vacancy, bareness, barrenness **2 lack of expression**, vacancy, indifference, emotionlessness, vacuousness *Opposite*: animation **3 bewilderment**, confusion, obliviousness, incomprehension, lack of understanding *Opposite*: acuity

blank out *v* **block out**, blot out, suppress, wipe out, erase *Opposite*: acknowledge

blare *v* **ring out**, make a racket, boom, blast out, blare out

blare out *see* **blare**

blaring *adj* **deafening**, earsplitting, cacophonous, raucous, booming *Opposite*: quiet

blarney *(infml)* *n* **nonsense**, smooth talk, charm, drivel, flattery

blasé *adj* **nonchalant**, laid back, cool, relaxed, unmoved *Opposite*: concerned

blaspheme *v* **curse**, swear, issue oaths, use profanities, use foul language

blasphemer *n* **swearer**, curser, profaner, foul mouth, profaner

blasphemous *adj* **profane**, sacrilegious, irreligious, offensive, improper *Opposite*: pious

blasphemy *n* **1 profanity**, sacrilege, wickedness, irreverence, violation *Opposite*: piety **2 oath**, curse, profanity, swearword, imprecation *(fml)*

blast *n* **explosion**, detonation, flash, flare, gust ■ *v* **1 blow up**, explode, detonate, demolish, blow away *(US slang)* **2** *(infml)* **blare**, resound, boom, make a racket, ring out **3** *(infml)* **criticize**, attack, lambaste, vilify, censure **4 damage**, blight, disfigure, burn, blister. *See* COMPARE AND CONTRAST *at* **criticize**.

blast off *v* **take off**, lift off, launch *Opposite*: touch down

blastoff *n* **launch**, takeoff, liftoff *Opposite*: touchdown

blast out *v* **blare out**, ring out, make a racket, blare, boom

blatancy *n* **obviousness**, conspicuousness, ostentation, flagrancy, overtness *Opposite*: subtlety

blatant *adj* **obvious**, unconcealed, barefaced, unashamed, deliberate *Opposite*: furtive

blather *(infml)* *v* **chatter**, go on, babble, blabber, jabber ■ *n* **drivel**, prattle, chatter, babble, blabber

blaze *v* **burn**, be on fire, burst into flames, rage, glow ■ *n* **1 fire**, inferno, conflagration, combustion **2 glare**, glow, flash, brightness, intensity

blazing *adj* **1 intense**, raging, mighty, heated, furious **2 burning**, glowing, shining, radiating, blistering

blazon *v* **splash**, embellish, emblazon, display, show

bleach *v* **lighten**, peroxide, blanch, blench, whiten *Opposite*: colour

bleached *adj* **lightened**, faded, sun-bleached, washed-out, blanched

bleak *adj* **1 hopeless**, unpromising, gloomy, doubtful, futile *Opposite*: promising **2 unwelcoming**, austere, miserable, bare, drab *Opposite*: welcoming **3 cold**, harsh, wintry, cheerless, miserable *Opposite*: warm **4 forlorn**, miserable, dejected, disheartened, downhearted *Opposite*: cheerful

bleakly *adv* **forlornly**, dismally, hopelessly, drearily, despondently *Opposite*: cheerfully

bleakness *n* **1 hopelessness**, despondency, sorrow, misery, sadness *Opposite*: hopefulness **2 cheerlessness**, drabness, austerity, harshness, bareness *Opposite*: comfort

bleary *adj* **hazy**, watery, unfocused, fuzzy, blurry *Opposite*: clear

bleary-eyed *adj* **sleepy**, tired, half-awake, dozy, groggy *Opposite*: alert

bleat *v* **whine**, complain, nag, fuss, whinge *(infml)*

bleed *v* **1 lose blood**, haemorrhage, shed blood **2** *(infml)* **extort**, exploit, drain, wring, deplete ■ *n* **blood loss**, haemorrhage, nosebleed

bleed dry *(infml)* *v* **drain**, suck dry, deplete, bring to its knees, exploit *Opposite*: replenish

bleeding *n* **blood loss**, haemorrhage, flow of blood, flow

bleep *n* **beep**, tone, sound, noise ■ *v* **call**, page, alert, signal, contact

bleeper *n* **pager**, monitor, beeper *(infml)*

blemish *n* **mark**, defect, imperfection, flaw, fault ■ *v* **damage**, tarnish, spoil, ruin, stain *Opposite*: restore. *See* COMPARE AND CONTRAST *at* **flaw**.

blemished *adj* **marked**, stained, imperfect, flawed, tarnished *Opposite*: unblemished

blench *v* 1 **go pale**, grow pale, lighten, blanch, whiten *Opposite*: redden 2 **draw back**, hesitate, falter, recoil, flinch

blend *v* **mix**, merge, combine, bring together, unify *Opposite*: separate ■ *n* **mixture**, merger, combination, assortment, amalgam. *See* COMPARE AND CONTRAST *at* **mixture**.

blender *n* **mixer**, food processor, chopper, liquidizer

bless *v* 1 **sanctify**, consecrate, hallow, extol, laud *Opposite*: curse 2 **approve**, sanction, support, endorse, back *Opposite*: decry

blessed *adj* 1 **holy**, sacred, sanctified, hallowed, consecrated *Opposite*: profane 2 **welcome**, providential, lucky, fortunate, pleasant *Opposite*: unfortunate

blessing *n* 1 **consecration**, sanctification, benediction, dedication 2 **approval**, sanction, permission, consent, approbation *Opposite*: veto 3 **lucky thing**, good thing, miracle, piece of good fortune, stroke of luck *Opposite*: disaster

blether *(infml)* *v* **chatter**, go on, babble, jabber, ramble ■ *n* **drivel**, prattle, chatter, gibberish, gossip

blight *n* **disfigurement**, stain, scar, blot, affliction ■ *v* **ruin**, disfigure, stain, scar, impair

blimpish *adj* **bigoted**, narrow-minded, prejudiced, intolerant, dogmatic *Opposite*: tolerant

blind *adj* **sightless**, unsighted, vision-impaired *Opposite*: sighted ■ *n* **screen**, window shade, canopy, awning, visor

blind alley *n* **dead end**, cul-de-sac, impasse

blind date *n* **rendezvous**, date, meeting, assignation, appointment

blindfold *n* **bandage**, cloth, covering, scarf, band

blinding *adj* 1 **glaring**, dazzling, bright, bedazzling, strong *Opposite*: soft 2 *(infml)* **striking**, extraordinary, outstanding, arresting, amazing *Opposite*: ordinary

blindness *n* 1 **sightlessness**, loss of sight, impaired vision *Opposite*: sight 2 **thoughtlessness**, carelessness, obliviousness, recklessness, rashness *Opposite*: thoughtfulness

blind spot *n* **weakness**, failing, failure, fault, flaw *Opposite*: strength

blink *v* 1 **wink**, bat an eyelid, flutter an eyelid, flicker an eyelid 2 **flash**, wink, flicker, twinkle, signal

blinkered *adj* **inward-looking**, insular, narrow-minded, narrow, limited

blip *n* **problem**, glitch, error, failure, breakdown

bliss *n* **ecstasy**, heaven, paradise, enjoyment, happiness *Opposite*: misery

blissful *adj* **heavenly**, wonderful, delightful, idyllic, perfect *Opposite*: miserable

blissfully *adv* **supremely**, wonderfully, ecstatically, delightfully, happily *Opposite*: miserably

blister *n* **sore**, swelling, eruption, burn, blood blister ■ *v* **swell up**, erupt, bubble, bulge, break out

blistering *adj* **sweltering**, baking, blazing, burning, searing *Opposite*: freezing

blithe *adj* **casual**, unconcerned, indifferent, unthinking, uncaring *Opposite*: thoughtful

blitz *n* 1 **bombardment**, blitzkrieg, saturation bombing, onslaught, attack, crackdown, concerted effort, clear-out ■ *v* 1 *(infml)* **crack down on**, concentrate on, focus on, come down on, fall on 2 **bombard**, bomb, blast, barrage, hit 3 *(infml)* **clean**, clean up, tidy, whip round, clear away

blizzard *n* **snowstorm**, whiteout, storm, winter storm *(US)*

bloat *v* **swell**, inflate, blow up, expand, distend *Opposite*: contract

bloated *adj* **swollen**, distended, overstuffed, full, overfed

blob *n* **splotch**, globule, spot, splash, dash ■ *v* **splotch**, dot, dab, daub, smudge

bloc *n* **alliance**, coalition, union, federation, league

block *n* 1 **chunk**, hunk, lump, slab, wedge 2 **building**, apartment block, block of flats 3 **wing**, extension, unit, module, part 4 **cellblock**, toilet block, shower block, tower block 5 **expanse**, section, sector, zone, band ■ *v* **obstruct**, impede, hinder, jam, prevent *Opposite*: encourage. *See* COMPARE AND CONTRAST *at* **hinder**.

blockade *n* **barrier**, barricade, obstruction, line of defence, cordon ■ *v* **deny access to**, lay siege to, obstruct, defend, block

blockage *n* **obstruction**, impasse, jam, bottleneck, snarl-up

blockbuster *(infml)* *n* **runaway success**, hit, smash hit, chartbuster, bestseller *Opposite*: flop *(infml)*

blockbusting *adj* **successful**, sensational, outstanding, popular, record-breaking

blocked *adj* **congested**, impassable, choked up, jammed, gridlocked *Opposite*: clear

blocking *adj* **obstructive**, delaying, stalling, hindering, spoiling *Opposite*: cooperative

block off *v* 1 **close off**, block, close, cordon off, isolate *Opposite*: free 2 **obstruct**, obscure, hide, mask, cover *Opposite*: reveal

block out *v* **blank out**, blot out, suppress, wipe out, erase *Opposite*: acknowledge

block up *v* **jam**, fill, stop, obstruct, choke *Opposite*: free

bloke *(infml)* *n* **man**, fella *(infml)*, guy *(infml)*, lad *(infml)*, fellow *(dated)*

blond *adj* **fair-haired**, towheaded, light-coloured, pale, flaxen *Opposite*: dark

blonde *see* **blond**

blood *n* **1 gore**, body fluid, plasma, lifeblood **2 family**, relations, kin, relatives, kinfolks **3 lineage**, ancestry, extraction, heritage, stock

bloodbath *n* **massacre**, slaughter, atrocity, scene of carnage

blood brother *n* **best friend**, friend, mate, ally, supporter *Opposite*: enemy

bloodcurdling *adj* **terrifying**, frightening, hair-raising, chilling, spine-tingling *Opposite*: comforting

bloodless *adj* **1 nonviolent**, peaceful, non-aggressive, orderly, controlled *Opposite*: violent **2 pale**, anaemic, white, pallid, wan *Opposite*: ruddy

bloodletting *n* **quarrel**, fight, dispute, argument, fracas

bloodline *n* **descent**, heritage, lineage, ancestry, background

blood lust *n* **bloodthirstiness**, hatred, cruelty, inhumanity, revenge

blood money *n* **compensation**, money, recompense, retribution, atonement

bloodshed *n* **carnage**, killing, violence, slaughter, murder

bloodshot *adj* **red**, inflamed, sore, pink *Opposite*: clear

bloodstream *n* **flow**, circulation, blood, arteries, veins

bloodsucker *n* **parasite**, leech, tick, mosquito, vampire

bloodsucking *adj* **parasitical**, leechlike, vampiric, vampirish

bloodthirstiness *n* **ferociousness**, viciousness, cruelty, barbarism, brutality

bloodthirsty *adj* **cruel**, gory, murderous, ferocious, vicious

bloody *adj* **gory**, blood-spattered, bleeding, wounded, injured

bloody-minded *(infml)* *adj* **uncooperative**, obstructive, stubborn, pigheaded, contrary *Opposite*: cooperative

bloody-mindedness *(infml)* *n* **lack of cooperation**, obstructiveness, stubbornness, obstinacy, pigheadedness *Opposite*: cooperation

bloom *n* **coloration**, tinge, tint, shadow, flush *Opposite*: pallor ■ *v* **blossom**, flower, come into flower, come into bud *Opposite*: wither

bloomer *(infml)* *n* **error**, blunder, mistake, gaffe, slip

blooming *adj* **1 flourishing**, thriving, budding, up-and-coming, promising *Opposite*: struggling **2 blossoming**, flowering, budding, in flower, in bloom

blossom *n* **flower**, flower head, bloom, bud ■ *v* **1 bloom**, flower, bud, come into flower, come into bud *Opposite*: wither **2 flourish**, thrive, grow, bloom, prosper *Opposite*: struggle **3 develop**, grow, come out of your shell, mature, come out of yourself

blossoming *adj* **developing**, growing, prospering, maturing, thriving

blossom out *v* **develop**, grow, come out of your shell, come out of yourself, blossom

blot *n* **spot**, blemish, stain, mark, imperfection ■ *v* **stain**, tarnish, spoil, ruin, disfigure

blotch *n* **blot**, mark, blemish, spot, splodge

blotchy *adj* **mottled**, blemished, marked, spotty, spotted *Opposite*: plain

blot on the landscape *n* **eyesore**, scar, blemish, disfigurement, monstrosity

blot out *v* **1 conceal**, hide, cover, eclipse, block *Opposite*: reveal **2 blank out**, block out, forget, erase, put out of your mind *Opposite*: recall

blow *v* **1 whoosh**, gust, waft, puff, bluster **2 move**, propel, drive, carry, waft ■ *n* **1 knock**, crack, jolt, swipe, strike **2 setback**, upset, disappointment, shock, misfortune *Opposite*: boost

blow away *v* **distribute**, disperse, scatter, dispel, spread

blowback *(infml)* *n* **reaction**, response, repercussion, feedback

blow-by-blow *adj* **thorough**, step by step, detailed, full, complete *Opposite*: sketchy

blower *(dated infml)* *n* **phone**, telephone, mobile, line, dog and bone *(slang)*

blown-up *adj* **1 inflated**, air-filled, hard, rigid, pumped-up *Opposite*: deflated **2 distended**, swollen, bloated, enlarged, puffed-up *Opposite*: sunken **3 overdone**, exaggerated, attention-grabbing, hyped, puffed-up *Opposite*: understated **4 bombed**, wrecked, burned-out, ruined, demolished

blow out *v* **extinguish**, put out, snuff out, douse, dampen *Opposite*: ignite

blow somebody's cover *v* **unmask**, expose, uncover, make known, bring to light

blow the whistle *v* **inform**, report, turn in, expose, sneak

blow up *v* **1 destroy**, explode, detonate, blast, demolish **2 inflate**, pump up, fill, puff up, swell *Opposite*: deflate **3 enlarge**, magnify, expand, increase, make larger *Opposite*: reduce **4** *(infml)* **lose your temper**, explode, be furious, flare up, hit the roof **5** *(infml)* **exaggerate**, overstress, embellish, embroider, make a mountain out of a molehill *Opposite*: play down

blowup *n* **enlargement**, magnification *Opposite*: reduction

blowy *(infml)* *adj* **windy**, breezy, blustery, gusty, squally *Opposite*: calm

blow your own trumpet *(infml)* *v* **brag**, boast, crow, show off, sing your own praises *Opposite*: deprecate

blow your top *(infml)* *v* **flare up**, lose your temper, fly into a rage, explode, hit the roof *(infml)* *Opposite*: calm down

blowzy *adj* **1 ruddy**, red-faced, rubicund, coarse

complexioned **2 unkempt**, bedraggled, messy, tousled, dishevelled *Opposite:* smart

blub *(infml) see* **blubber**

blubber *(infml)* v **sob**, weep, cry, snivel, whimper

bludgeon v **1 beat**, hit, slam, strike, batter **2 coerce**, compel, bully, bulldoze, steamroller

blue *(infml)* adj **depressed**, down, sad, low, dejected *Opposite:* happy

---

WORD BANK

❑ **types of blue** azure, baby blue, cobalt blue, cornflower blue, cyan, electric blue, ice blue, indigo, lapis lazuli, midnight blue, navy blue, peacock blue, powder blue, Prussian blue, royal blue, sapphire, saxe blue, sky blue, slate blue, steel blue, turquoise, ultramarine

---

blue-blooded adj **aristocratic**, noble, high-class, well-bred, refined *Opposite:* common

blue-chip adj **top-class**, first-class, first-rate, top-grade, topnotch *(infml)* *Opposite:* second-rate

blue-collar adj **labouring**, manual, proletarian, working class *Opposite:* white-collar

blueprint n **plan**, drawing, design, proposal, outline

blues *(infml)* n **sadness**, melancholy, dejection, depression, despair *Opposite:* happiness

bluff v **trick**, con, fake, lie, pretend ■ n **1 sham**, trick, con, pretence, fake **2 cliff**, headland, hillside, hill, mound ■ adj **plain-spoken**, cheery, loud, hearty, forthright

bluffness n **cheeriness**, heartiness, directness, bluntness, plain-spokenness

blunder n **mistake**, gaffe, error, mix-up, misstep ■ v **1 make a mistake**, get it wrong, slip up *(infml)*, foul up *(infml)*, mess up *(infml)* **2 stumble**, stagger, lurch, flounder, trip. *See* COMPARE AND CONTRAST *at* **mistake**.

blundering adj **clumsy**, careless, awkward, lumbering, ungainly *Opposite:* dexterous

blunt adj **1 dull**, rounded, dulled, blunted *Opposite:* sharp **2 uncompromising**, straightforward, direct, frank, honest *Opposite:* indirect ■ v **dampen**, dull, put a damper on, take the edge off, diminish *Opposite:* heighten

bluntly adv **frankly**, straightforwardly, honestly, directly, candidly *Opposite:* indirectly

bluntness n **candour**, frankness, directness, straightforwardness, honesty *Opposite:* mendacity

blur v **obscure**, cloud, make indistinct, hide, conceal *Opposite:* clarify ■ n **1 blob**, smudge, smear, blot, blotch **2 distortion**, fuzziness, haze, impression, shape ■ v **smudge**, smear, distort, confuse, shade *Opposite:* clear

blurred adj **blurry**, indistinct, unclear, hazy, distorted *Opposite:* distinct

blurry *see* **blurred**

blurt v **exclaim**, cry, utter, come out with, announce

blush v **go red**, flush, colour, go red in the face, redden *Opposite:* blanch

blusher n **makeup**, cosmetic, rouge *(dated)*

blushing adj **embarrassed**, self-conscious, red-faced, flushed, coy *Opposite:* bold

bluster v **1 harangue**, threaten, bully, protest, rant **2 blow**, gust, rage, puff, waft

blustery adj **windy**, gusty, stormy, squally, breezy *Opposite:* still

B movie n **supporting film**, short, B picture, B film, support

BO *(infml)* n **body odour**, smell, sweatiness, rankness, reek

board n **1 plank**, slat, floorboard, timber, beam **2 panel**, sheet, boarding **3 committee**, panel, commission, management team, advisory group **4 food**, meal, sustenance, nourishment, rations ■ v **1 embark**, enter, go on board, go aboard, go into *Opposite:* disembark **2 live**, room, be accommodated, stay, lodge *(dated)*

boarder n **lodger**, paying guest, resident, tenant, occupant

board up v **close**, shutter, secure, cover up

boardwalk n **walkway**, footpath, path, causeway

boast v **1 brag**, show off, crow, swank *(infml)*, fly your own kite *(infml)* **2 have**, possess, pride yourself on, lay claim to, feature ■ n **claim**, assertion, brag, vaunt, pretension

boastful adj **arrogant**, proud, conceited, full of yourself, bragging *Opposite:* modest

boastfulness n **immodesty**, arrogance, conceit, self-importance, showing off *Opposite:* modesty

boasting n **boastfulness**, bragging, showing off, arrogance, self-aggrandizement *Opposite:* modesty ■ adj **boastful**, swaggering, arrogant, self-important, conceited *Opposite:* modest

boat n **craft**, ship, vessel

bob v **1 move up and down**, nod, dip, bobble, jog **2 curtsy**, bow, nod, duck, genuflect

bobbin n **reel**, spindle, spool, cylinder, roll

bobble n **ball**, pompom, tassel ■ v **move up and down**, nod, bob, jog, dip

bobbly adj **bumpy**, lumpy, rough, knobbly, textured *Opposite:* smooth

bobby *(dated infml)* n **police officer**, constable, cop *(slang)*

bobsleigh n **toboggan**, sledge, sled *(US)*, bobsled *(US)*

bode v **augur**, portend, promise, predict, divine

bodge *(infml)* v **spoil**, damage, do badly, ruin, botch *(infml)*

bodily adj **physical**, corporal, corporeal,

fleshly, material *Opposite*: spiritual

body *n* **1 form**, figure, frame, physique, build **2 corpse**, dead body, cadaver, remains, carcass **3 organization**, group, association, federation, society **4 quantity**, corpus, amount, mass, area **5 bulk**, main part, essence, majority, mass

body blow *n* **setback**, blow, disappointment, upset, shock

body builder *n* **athlete**, weightlifter, muscle builder

body fluid *n* **saliva**, blood, urine, sweat, semen

bodyguard *n* **guard**, escort, attendant, guardian, protection officer

body language *n* **mannerisms**, stance, facial expression, movements, motion

boffin *(infml)* *n* **scientist**, expert, genius, researcher, inventor

bog *n* **swamp**, quagmire, mire, fen, fenland

bogey *n* **1 worry**, problem, concern, bother, annoyance **2 monster**, creature, beast, monstrosity, bogeyman

bogeyman *n* **monster**, creature, beast, monstrosity, bogey

boggle *(infml)* *v* **confuse**, baffle, perplex, astonish, overwhelm

boggy *adj* **marshy**, swampy, muddy, watery, wet *Opposite*: parched

bog-standard *(infml)* *adj* **basic**, standard, ordinary, simple, unadorned *Opposite*: superior

bogus *adj* **false**, fake, counterfeit, phoney, trick *Opposite*: genuine

bohemian *n* **free spirit**, freethinker, nonconformist, hippie, New Age traveller ■ *adj* **unconventional**, nonconformist, offbeat, alternative, carefree *Opposite*: conformist

boil *v* **1 simmer**, bubble, poach, cook, stew **2 rage**, fume, seethe, be angry, be irate **3** *(infml)* **overheat**, swelter, stew, bake, burn *Opposite*: freeze ■ *n* **ulcer**, sore, spot, swelling, abscess

boil down to *(infml)* *v* **amount to**, come down to, end up as, add up to, wind up as

boiler suit *n* **overalls**, coveralls, protective clothing, dungarees

boiling *adj* **hot**, sweltering, baking, steaming, torrid *Opposite*: freezing

boiling point *n* **crisis point**, danger level, flashpoint, high point, peak

boil over *v* **overflow**, bubble up, overheat, spill over, blow

boisterous *adj* **1 exuberant**, animated, spirited, rowdy, rambunctious *Opposite*: placid **2 wild**, turbulent, rough, stormy *Opposite*: calm

boisterousness *n* **1 exuberance**, high spirits, unruliness, roughness, riotousness *Opposite*: placidity **2 wildness**, turbulence, roughness, storminess *Opposite*: calmness

bold *adj* **1 brave**, daring, courageous, audacious, valiant *Opposite*: cowardly **2 confident**, forward, brash, brazen, self-assured *Opposite*: timid **3 conspicuous**, bright, vivid, flashy, showy *Opposite*: muted **4 black**, heavy, boldface *Opposite*: light

boldface *adj* **black**, heavy, bold *Opposite*: lightface

bold-faced *adj* **impudent**, brash, brazen, unconcerned, shameless *Opposite*: unassuming

boldness *n* **1 courage**, daring, bravery, bravado, valour *Opposite*: cowardice **2 confidence**, self-assurance, brashness, nerve, impudence *Opposite*: timidity

bole *n* **trunk**, stem, stalk

bollard *n* **post**, marker, pillar, stake, pole

bolster *v* **boost**, strengthen, reinforce, encourage, shore up *Opposite*: undermine

bolt *n* **bar**, pin, rod, catch, latch ■ *v* **1 fasten**, secure, lock, lock up, attach *Opposite*: unlock **2 run off**, make a dash for it, run, make a run for it, disappear **3 gulp**, wolf, gobble, devour, down *Opposite*: nibble

bolt from the blue *n* **surprise**, shock, upset, jolt, blow

bolthole *n* **hideaway**, refuge, sanctuary, den, place of safety

bomb *v* **1 bombard**, shell, blast, barrage, blitz **2** *(infml)* **fail**, flop, fall flat, sink without trace, disappoint *Opposite*: succeed

bombard *v* **1 bomb**, shell, open fire on, blast, barrage **2 assail**, shower, flood, inundate, overrun

bombardment *n* **1 attack**, offensive, assault, salvo, bombing **2 barrage**, flood, onslaught, blitz, volley

bombast *n* **pomposity**, pretentiousness, verboseness, affectation, grandiloquence *Opposite*: directness

bombastic *adj* **pompous**, pretentious, verbose, long-winded, grandiloquent *Opposite*: direct

bombshell *(infml)* *n* **shock**, surprise, bolt from the blue, blow, upset

bomb site *n* **area of devastation**, crater, ruins, battlefield, wasteland

bona fide *adj* **genuine**, authentic, true, real, valid *Opposite*: bogus

bonanza *n* **jackpot**, pot of gold, gold mine, stroke of luck, bonus

bonce *(infml)* *n* **head**, skull, cranium, nut *(infml)*, noddle *(dated infml)*

bond *n* **1 tie**, link, connection, union, attachment **2 promise**, pledge, oath, word ■ *v* **1 adhere**, stick, glue, fix, join **2 connect**, get on, become attached, relate, hit it off *(infml)* *Opposite*: clash

bondage *n* **slavery**, enslavement, captivity, oppression, servitude *Opposite*: freedom

bonded *adj* **fused together**, fused, stuck, glued, attached *Opposite*: split

borderline

bonding *n* **attachment**, closeness, tie, connection, love

bone of contention *n* **disagreement**, sticking point, difficulty, problem, obstacle

boner *(infml)* *n* **mistake**, blunder, error, gaffe, misstep

boneshaker *(infml)* *n* **wreck**, banger *(infml)*, rattletrap *(infml)*, jalopy *(dated infml)*, heap *(slang)*

bone up *(infml)* *v* **find out about**, research, look into, gen up *(infml)*, swot up *(infml)*

bonfire *n* **fire**, conflagration, blaze, beacon

bong *n* **bang**, blow, thud, crash, knock

bonhomie *n* **friendliness**, sociability, affability, geniality, amenability

bonk *(infml)* *v* **hit**, bang, knock, tap, slap ■ *n* **knock**, blow, slap, bang, tap

bonkers *(infml)* *adj* **irrational**, silly, crazy *(infml)*, daft *(infml)*, off the deep end *(infml)* *Opposite*: rational

bon mot *n* **witticism**, quip, joke, epigram, clever remark

bonny *adj* **good-looking**, lovely, pretty, handsome, attractive *Opposite*: unattractive

bonus *n* **1 extra**, addition, advantage, windfall, benefit **2 gratuity**, handout, pay supplement, reward

bon vivant *n* **pleasure-seeker**, lotus-eater, gourmet, epicure, gourmand *Opposite*: ascetic

bony *adj* **skinny**, scrawny, lanky, lean, thin *Opposite*: plump

boo *n* **catcall**, jeer, hoot, raspberry *Opposite*: cheer ■ *v* **jeer**, hoot, catcall, hiss, barrack *(infml)* *Opposite*: applaud

boob *(infml)* *n* **1 blunder**, mistake, error, gaffe, slip-up *(infml)* **2 fool**, dupe, sucker *(infml)*, mug *(slang)*, fall guy *(slang)* ■ *v* **make a mistake**, get it wrong, slip up *(infml)*, foul up *(infml)*, mess up *(infml)*

boo-boo *(infml)* *n* **blunder**, mistake, error, gaffe, slip-up *(infml)*

booby trap *n* **1 snare**, trap, trick, ruse, con **2 bomb**, tripwire, mine, explosive device

boogie *v* *(infml)* **dance**, jig, jive, bop *(infml)*, party *(infml)* ■ *n* **jig**, jive, bop *(infml)*, party *(infml)*

book *n* **volume**, tome, manuscript, paperback, hardback ■ *v* **reserve**, order, engage, put your name down for, sign up for

book in *v* **check in**, register, sign in, enlist, enrol *Opposite*: leave

booking *n* **reservation**, hold, option, deposit

bookish *adj* **studious**, serious, academic, scholarly, brainy

bookishness *n* **studiousness**, erudition, scholarliness, learning, learnedness

booklet *n* **brochure**, pamphlet, leaflet, flier

books *n* **records**, accounts, financial statements, balance sheet, profit and loss

bookworm *(infml)* *n* **avid reader**, book lover, bibliophile

boom *v* **1 roar**, rumble, thunder, bellow, resound **2 grow**, soar, rocket, increase, rise *Opposite*: collapse ■ *n* **1 growth**, increase, rise, upsurge, expansion *Opposite*: collapse **2 pole**, arm, bracket, beam ■ *adj* **prosperous**, flourishing, affluent, successful, thriving

boomerang *v* **rebound**, bounce back, return, ricochet, come back

booming *adj* **1 thriving**, prosperous, wealthy, flourishing, successful *Opposite*: failing **2 thunderous**, roaring, resounding, resonant, sonorous *Opposite*: quiet

boon *n* **advantage**, benefit, bonus, help, godsend *Opposite*: disadvantage

boor *n* **lout**, oaf, yob *(infml)*, yobbo *(infml)*, loudmouth *(infml)*

boorish *adj* **rude**, ill-mannered, impolite, coarse, rough *Opposite*: well-mannered

boorishness *n* **crudeness**, loutishness, uncouthness, incivility, rudeness *Opposite*: courteousness

boost *v* **1 increase**, improve, enhance, make better, further *Opposite*: reduce **2 encourage**, support, lift, uplift, give a boost to *Opposite*: discourage ■ *n* **improvement**, increase, enhancement, lift, helping hand *Opposite*: blow

booster *n* **injection**, inoculation, vaccination, immunization, shot *(infml)*

boost up *v* **1 increase**, improve, enhance, boost, add to *Opposite*: reduce **2 encourage**, support, lift, uplift, give a boost to *Opposite*: discourage

booth *n* **cubicle**, stand, closet, compartment, sukkah

bootlace *n* **shoelace**, cord, lace, strap, tie

bootleg *adj* **illegal**, pirated, stolen, illicit, unlicensed *Opposite*: legal

bootless *adj* **useless**, scant, feeble, inadequate, unsuccessful *Opposite*: successful

boot out *(infml)* *v* **dismiss**, get rid of, eject, evict, bounce *Opposite*: appoint

booty *n* **loot**, spoils, plunder, ill-gotten gains, valuables

bop *(infml)* *v* **1 dance**, jig, jive, boogie *(infml)* **2 hit**, bang, knock, tap, thump ■ *n* **1 jig**, dance, jive, boogie *(infml)* **2 disco**, dance, party, ball, rave *(slang)*

border *n* **1 frontier**, borderline, boundary **2 edge**, limit, boundary, margin, verge *Opposite*: centre **3 flowerbed**, bed, shrub border, herbaceous border ■ *v* **be next to**, touch, be bounded by, border on, run alongside

bordering *adj* **adjoining**, neighbouring, adjacent, next door, nearby

borderland *n* **boundary**, edge, frontier, limits, border *Opposite*: heartland

borderline *adj* **marginal**, disputed, uncertain, doubtful, unclear *Opposite*: clear-cut ■ *n* **frontier**, boundary, border

border on v 1 **approach**, be close to, resemble, be similar to, verge on 2 **be next to**, touch, be bounded by, border, adjoin

bore v 1 **turn off** (infml), weary, send to sleep, bore to death, bore to tears Opposite: interest 2 **drill**, perforate, penetrate, pierce, tunnel

bored adj **uninterested**, tired, bored rigid, bored stiff, bored to death Opposite: fascinated

boredom n **tedium**, monotony, dullness, tediousness, ennui Opposite: interest

borehole n **well**, hole, shaft

boring adj **uninteresting**, tedious, dull, dreary, mind-numbing Opposite: exciting

born adj **instinctive**, congenital, innate, intuitive, natural Opposite: trained

born-again adj **reinvigorated**, reborn, enthusiastic, avid, fervid

borough n **area**, district, municipality, division, township (US)

borrow v 1 **use**, make use of, have access to, scrounge (infml), sponge (infml) Opposite: lend 2 **copy**, plagiarize, derive, pirate, steal

borstal n **detention centre**, youth custody centre, prison, reformatory, jail

bosom (infml) adj **close**, best, dearest, special, firm Opposite: distant

boss n **manager**, supervisor, chief, head, person in charge Opposite: subordinate ■ v **give orders**, tell what to do, boss about, boss around, order around Opposite: obey

boss about see boss around

boss around v **give orders**, tell what to do, order about, order around, boss Opposite: obey

bossiness n **imperiousness**, officiousness, high-handedness, authoritarianism, overbearingness Opposite: meekness

bossy adj **domineering**, officious, dominant, high-handed, dictatorial Opposite: meek

botanic see botanical

botanical adj **vegetal**, plant, botanic

botch v **spoil**, damage, ruin, do badly, make a mess of ■ n (infml) **fiasco**, failure, disaster, flop (infml), cockup (infml)

botched adj **failed**, substandard, poor, ruined, inferior Opposite: first-rate

bother v 1 **make an effort**, take the trouble, put yourself out, go to the trouble of, extend yourself 2 **worry**, trouble, disturb, upset, unsettle 3 **interrupt**, disturb, distract, trouble, pester ■ n **trouble**, difficulty, problem, nuisance, inconvenience

COMPARE AND CONTRAST CORE MEANING: interfere with somebody's composure
bother cause to feel worried, anxious, or upset, or disturb or interrupt; **annoy** irritate or harass; **bug** (infml) persistently cause trouble and annoy; **disturb** interrupt or distract in the process of doing something, or to upset the peace of mind of; **trouble** cause distress or inconvenience to; **worry** cause to be anxious.

bothered adj **worried**, concerned, troubled, anxious, apprehensive Opposite: untroubled

bothersome adj **troublesome**, inconvenient, worrisome, niggling, difficult

bothy n **hut**, cottage, cabin, house, shelter

bottle n 1 **flask**, jug, carafe, flagon, decanter 2 (infml) **courage**, bravery, nerve, spirit, spine

bottleneck n **block**, blockage, restricted access, holdup, traffic jam

bottle out (infml) v **withdraw**, fail, refuse to do, lose courage, chicken out (infml)

bottle up v **contain**, repress, suppress, keep in check, keep inside

bottom n 1 **base**, bed, foot, floor, substructure Opposite: top 2 **end**, far end, foot, extremity, limit Opposite: top 3 **underside**, underneath, bottom side, underbelly Opposite: top ■ adj **lowest**, bottommost, lowermost, nethermost (fml) Opposite: top

bottomless adj **unlimited**, unrestricted, endless, limitless, unending Opposite: restricted

bottom line n 1 **fundamental issue**, key issue, fact of the matter, thing to bear in mind, crucial thing 2 **lower limit**, threshold, floor, cutoff point, limit

bottommost adj **lowest**, last, bottom, final Opposite: topmost

boudoir n **bedroom**, dressing room, chamber (literary), bedchamber (literary)

bouffant adj **backcombed**, fluffy, full, puffed up, voluminous

bough n **branch**, limb, spur

boulder n **rock**, stone, sarsen

bounce v 1 **rebound**, spring back, bound, spring up, recoil 2 **spring**, jump, bound, bob, bobble 3 **eject**, evict, throw out, remove, expel

bounce back v **recover**, improve, get better, pull through, perk up

bounciness n 1 **liveliness**, spirit, vivacity, friskiness, playfulness Opposite: lethargy 2 **elasticity**, springiness, resistance, resilience, pliability Opposite: firmness

bouncy adj 1 **effervescent**, energetic, playful, lively, vivacious Opposite: lethargic 2 **springy**, elastic, pliable Opposite: firm

bound adj 1 **certain**, sure, guaranteed, destined, assured Opposite: unlikely 2 **obliged**, compelled, forced, obligated, duty-bound Opposite: free ■ v **border**, border on, be next to, touch, be adjacent to ■ n **jump**, leap, spring, bounce, hop

boundary n **border**, frontier, borderline, edge, dividing line

bounded adj 1 **surrounded**, bordered, enclosed, encircled, delimited 2 **restricted**, hemmed in, limited, constrained, confined Opposite: free

boundless adj **unlimited**, endless, limitless, infinite, ceaseless Opposite: restricted

bounds n **limits**, boundaries, confines, restrictions, constraints

bounteous *(literary) see* **bountiful**

bountiful *(literary)* adj **1 generous**, giving, munificent, openhanded, liberal *Opposite*: parsimonious **2 plentiful**, generous, abundant, copious, profuse *Opposite*: scarce. *See* COMPARE AND CONTRAST *at* **generous**.

bounty n **reward**, price, prize, payment, gift

bouquet n **1 bunch**, spray, posy, arrangement, nosegay **2 smell**, aroma, scent, fragrance, perfume. *See* COMPARE AND CONTRAST *at* **smell**.

bourgeois adj **middle-class**, conventional, conformist, unadventurous, staid ■ n **conservative**, traditionalist, conformist, reactionary, conventional person

bout n **short period**, short time, session, spell, attack

bow n **1 arc**, curve, arch, sweep, bend **2 bob**, bend, curtsy, obeisance *(fml)* ■ v **1 bend**, bend over, lower, stoop, lean *Opposite*: straighten up **2 distort**, deform, arch, droop, sag *Opposite*: straighten

---

WORD BANK

❏ **types of bow** crossbow, Cupid's bow, longbow

---

bowdlerize v **censor**, edit, abridge, clean up, expurgate

bowed adj **curved**, bent, deformed, convex, hooked *Opposite*: straight

bowels n **guts**, entrails, viscera, innards *(infml)*, insides *(infml)*

bower n **arbour**, retreat, grove, copse, den

bowl n **1 container**, vessel, dish, basin, mixing bowl **2 hollow**, depression, crater, basin, valley **3 ball**, wood, boule ■ v **1 career**, career, roll along, travel, speed **2 roll**, pitch, throw, lob, hurl

bowlegged adj **bandy-legged**, bandy, bent, bowed

bowl over v **1 astonish**, amaze, delight, overwhelm, take by surprise **2 knock down**, knock over, scatter, upturn, overturn

bow out v **back out**, beg off, duck out, cry off *(infml)*

bow tie n **tie**, cravat, dicky bow *(infml)*, dicky *(infml)*, necktie *(US)*

bow to v **accept**, yield, resign yourself to, recognize, acknowledge *Opposite*: reject

box n **1 container**, case, chest, packet, carton **2 rectangle**, square, frame, tick box, check box **3 cubicle**, stall, booth, compartment, enclosure ■ v **fight**, spar, punch, hit, thump

box in v **enclose**, surround, contain, shut in, trap

boxroom n **cubbyhole**, spare room, storeroom, glory hole *(infml)*, closet *(US)*

boy n **young man**, lad, schoolboy, son, youngster

boycott v **refuse**, stay away from, impose sanctions, embargo, shun

boyfriend n **male friend**, date, escort, fiancé, partner *Opposite*: girlfriend

boyhood n **childhood**, youth, early years

boyish adj **youthful**, adolescent, childlike, fresh-faced, young

brace n **support**, strut, prop, stay, bracket

brace yourself v **prepare yourself**, ready yourself, make preparations, get ready for, prime yourself

bracing adj **invigorating**, stimulating, brisk, healthy, cold *Opposite*: soporific

bracket n **1 support**, strut, prop, stay, brace **2 group**, set, range, cohort, band ■ v **connect**, link, join, relate, associate *Opposite*: separate

brackish adj **salty**, saline, salted, briny, salt *Opposite*: fresh

brag v **boast**, crow, show off, swagger, talk big *Opposite*: underplay

braggart n **boaster**, egotist, show-off *(infml)*, bigmouth *(infml)*, loudmouth *(infml)*

bragging n **boasting**, boastfulness, showing off, arrogance, self-aggrandizement *Opposite*: modesty ■ adj **boastful**, arrogant, self-important, conceited, swaggering *Opposite*: modest

braid v **1 plait**, interweave, interlace, intertwine, weave *Opposite*: unravel **2 decorate**, trim, edge, fringe, bind *Opposite*: strip

brain n **1 intelligence**, mind, intellect, head, wits **2** *(infml)* **intellectual**, genius, intellect, prodigy, brainbox

brainchild n **idea**, invention, creation, innovation, breakthrough

brainless adj **foolish**, stupid, mindless, unintelligent, silly *Opposite*: sensible

brainpower n **intellect**, brains, capacity, ability, intellectual capacity

brains n **intelligence**, common sense, wits, intellect, brainpower *Opposite*: ignorance

brainstorm n **aberration**, fit, turn, disturbance, upset ■ v **think**, suggest, come up with, devise, dream up

brainteaser n **problem**, puzzle, riddle, challenge, conundrum

brainwash v **persuade**, indoctrinate, condition, convince, programme

brain wave *(infml)* n **bright idea**, inspiration, idea, breakthrough, innovation

brainy *(infml)* adj **intelligent**, clever, bright, quick, academic *Opposite*: unintelligent

braise v **cook**, stew, casserole, steam, simmer

brake v **decelerate**, slow down, reduce speed, put on the brakes, lose speed *Opposite*: accelerate ■ n **restraint**, constraint, curb, control, limitation *Opposite*: incentive

bran n **fibre**, dietary fibre, cellulose, roughage, bulk

branch n **1 bough**, limb, spur, twig **2 local office**, division, area office, subdivision, outlet *Opposite*: headquarters **3 division**, department, offshoot, wing, arm **4 area**, field, topic, domain, sphere **5 turning**, turn-off, arm, tributary, fork ■ v **split**, fork, divide, diverge, separate *Opposite*: converge

branch off v **split**, fork, divide, turn off, leave *Opposite*: merge

branch out v **diversify**, diverge, take a new direction, broaden, expand *Opposite*: consolidate

brand n 1 **make**, product, brand name, trade name, trademark 2 **type**, kind, sort, style, variety 3 **identifying mark**, mark, marker, identification, label ■ v 1 **mark**, imprint, stamp, label 2 **call**, classify, label, name, describe

brandish v **wield**, wave, flourish, handle, flaunt

brand name n **trade name**, brand, label, make, trademark

brand-new adj **new**, unused, pristine, fresh, mint *Opposite*: old

brash adj 1 **aggressive**, arrogant, self-confident, brazen, presumptuous *Opposite*: self-effacing 2 **loud**, garish, vulgar, gaudy, bright *Opposite*: muted

brashness n **boldness**, brazenness, forcefulness, insolence, assertiveness *Opposite*: shyness

brass (*infml*) n **nerve**, impudence, self-assurance, self-confidence, cheek (*infml*) *Opposite*: bashfulness

brass tacks n **basics**, essentials, fundamentals, bare essentials, nuts and bolts (*infml*)

brassy adj 1 **harsh**, loud, metallic, strident, grating *Opposite*: soft 2 **brazen**, strident, overbearing, brash, arrogant *Opposite*: self-effacing

brat n **little monster**, imp, spoiled brat, terror (*infml*), holy terror (*infml*) *Opposite*: cherub

bratty adj **obnoxious**, spoiled, demanding, overindulged, selfish *Opposite*: well-behaved

bravado n **audacity**, boldness, daring, bluster, boasting *Opposite*: cowardice

brave adj **courageous**, valiant, heroic, bold, daring *Opposite*: cowardly ■ v **defy**, face, stand up to, confront, take on *Opposite*: shrink

brave out v **suffer**, face, bear, endure, stay the course *Opposite*: give up

bravery n **courage**, courageousness, valour, gallantry, daring *Opposite*: cowardice. *See* COMPARE AND CONTRAST *at* **courage**.

bravura n **boldness**, daring, spirit, nerve, guts (*slang*) *Opposite*: timidity ■ adj **brilliant**, magnificent, exceptional, dazzling, outstanding *Opposite*: nondescript

brawl n **scuffle**, fight, punch-up, clash, affray ■ v **fight**, scuffle, tussle, wrestle, clash

brawn n **strength**, muscle, brute force, power, burliness *Opposite*: weakness

brawny adj **muscular**, strong, powerfully built, hefty, burly *Opposite*: scrawny

bray v 1 **whinny**, neigh, cry, call 2 **grate**, rasp, bark, bellow, snort *Opposite*: murmur

braying adj **harsh**, loud, strident, jarring, grating *Opposite*: soft

brazen adj **bold**, barefaced, shameless, brash, unabashed *Opposite*: discreet

brazenness n **shamelessness**, boldness, barefacedness, flagrancy, impudence *Opposite*: discretion

brazen out v **face down**, stand your ground, face out, hold your own, stay the course *Opposite*: cave in

brazier n **stove**, barbecue, grill, hibachi, fire

breach v 1 **get through**, break through, break, rupture, penetrate *Opposite*: block 2 **break**, violate, contravene, infringe, flout *Opposite*: honour ■ n 1 **opening**, break, hole, crack, fissure 2 **violation**, contravention, infringement, defiance, betrayal *Opposite*: compliance 3 **rift**, separation, division, rupture, estrangement *Opposite*: reconciliation

breach of the peace n **public disturbance**, public nuisance, nuisance, riot, fracas *Opposite*: order

bread n **food**, daily bread, sustenance, nourishment, rations

WORD BANK
❏ **types of bread** baguette, black bread, bloomer, brown bread, challah, chapati, ciabatta, cob, cottage loaf, crouton, flat bread, focaccia, matzo, nan, pitta, poppadom, pumpernickel, puri, roti, rye bread, soda bread, sourdough, toast, tortilla, wheat bread, white bread, wholemeal
❏ **types of roll or bun** bagel, bap, brioche, bun, croissant, crumpet, muffin, roll

bread and butter n 1 **livelihood**, living, income, maintenance, upkeep 2 **mainstay**, lifeblood, backbone, basis, core

bread-and-butter adj **basic**, primary, fundamental, essential, important *Opposite*: superfluous

breadth n 1 **width**, span, wideness, extent, size *Opposite*: depth 2 **extensiveness**, extent, range, scope, span *Opposite*: narrowness 3 **latitude**, room, freedom, space, leeway *Opposite*: restriction

breadthways adj **sideways**, side-to-side, widthways, breadthwise (*US*) ■ adv **across**, from side to side, breadthwise (*US*)

breadwinner n **wage earner**, worker, employee *Opposite*: dependant

break v 1 **smash**, fracture, rupture, shatter, split *Opposite*: mend 2 **break down**, stop working, fail, collapse, crash 3 **infringe**, violate, contravene, breach, disobey *Opposite*: uphold 4 **stop**, end, interrupt, disturb, break into 5 **take a break**, break into, have a break, rest, stop 6 **beat**, surpass, exceed, top, better 7 **destroy**, shatter, crush, overwhelm, defeat **8 become known**, make public, become public, disclose, get round **9 decipher**, crack, decode, solve, unravel ■ *n* **1 disruption**, breakdown, discontinuity, interruption, pause **2 rest**, respite, coffee break, pause, lunch break **3 holiday**, time off, weekend break, trip, vacation **4 interruption**, pause, space, disruption, halt **5** (*infml*) **chance**, opportunity, opening, occasion, leg up

breakable *adj* **fragile**, delicate, brittle, frail, flimsy *Opposite*: sturdy

breakage *n* **breaking**, smashing, cracking, rupture, splintering *Opposite*: mending

break away *v* **secede**, separate, become independent, split, disaffiliate *Opposite*: join

breakaway *n* **separation**, rupture, severance, splitting up, breakup *Opposite*: fusion ■ *adj* **separate**, splinter, independent, autonomous, alternative *Opposite*: mainstream

break down *v* **1 stop working**, break, fail, go down, crash **2 lose control**, cry, be overcome, collapse, burst into tears **3 overcome**, defeat, destroy, knock down, smash down *Opposite*: build **4 analyse**, separate, dissect, break up, split **5 divide**, classify, categorize, split, separate *Opposite*: lump **6 decompose**, decay, putrefy, disintegrate, moulder

breakdown *n* **1 failure**, collapse, cessation, halt, interruption **2 analysis**, rundown, classification, dissection, summary

breaker *n* **wave**, roller, whitecap, white horse

break free *v* **escape**, break away, break with, separate, get away

break in *v* **1 tame**, train, discipline, domesticate, housetrain **2 force an entry**, break into, burgle, break and enter, force the lock **3 interrupt**, butt in, interject, interpose, cut in

break-in *n* **forced entry**, burglary, robbery, crime, felony

breaking *n* **contravention**, infringement, violation, breach, transgression *Opposite*: observance

breaking point *n* **verge of collapse**, limit, threshold, snapping point, crisis

break into *v* **1 break in**, force an entry, burgle, break and enter, break down the door **2 begin**, burst into, launch into, embark on, burst out *Opposite*: break off

breakneck *adj* **quick**, speedy, hurried, hasty, rapid *Opposite*: slow

break new ground *v* **be the first**, blaze a trail, lead the way, be in the vanguard, set a trend

break of day *n* **daybreak**, sunrise, daylight, first light, dawn *Opposite*: sundown

break off *v* **1 detach**, come off, snap off, come away, separate *Opposite*: attach **2 end**, terminate, stop, cease, finish *Opposite*: begin

breakoff *n* **discontinuation**, ending, interruption, suspension, stopping *Opposite*: continuation

break open *v* **open**, divide, come apart, burst, shatter

break out *v* **1 begin**, start, erupt, burst into, embark on *Opposite*: end **2 escape**, break loose, burst out, break free, emerge

breakout *n* **escape**, getaway, flight, running away, running off

break the ice *v* **get to know**, make friends, get acquainted, introduce yourself, set the ball rolling

break through *v* **burst through**, penetrate, come through, breach, wear down

breakthrough *n* **advance**, step forward, leap forward, new idea, innovation

break up *v* **1 divide**, fragment, disintegrate, crumble, fall apart *Opposite*: fuse **2 disperse**, separate, split up, keep apart, divide up *Opposite*: unite **3 separate**, tell somebody it's over, split up, end, finish

breakup *n* **1 disintegration**, fragmentation, division, crumbling, destruction *Opposite*: merger **2 ending**, end, splitting up, finish, separation

breakwater *n* **offshore barrier**, sea wall, harbour wall, causeway, pier

break with *v* **separate**, split, leave, part company, escape *Opposite*: associate

breath *n* **1 gasp**, sigh, pant, inhalation, exhalation **2 puff**, waft, current, draught, gush

breathe *v* **respire**, take breaths, inhale, exhale, suck in air

breathe new life into *v* **revitalize**, reinvigorate, revive, resurrect, rejuvenate

breather (*infml*) *n* **rest**, break, respite, sit-down (*infml*), time out (*US*)

breathing *n* **inhalation**, exhalation, panting, gasping, puffing ■ *adj* **living**, alive, conscious, sentient, aware

breathing space *n* **respite**, relief, space, recovery time, time

breathless *adj* **out of breath**, panting, gasping, puffing, winded

breathlessly *adv* **eagerly**, excitedly, with bated breath, on tenterhooks, anxiously *Opposite*: nonchalantly

breathtaking *adj* **out of this world**, wonderful, magnificent, spectacular, incredible *Opposite*: banal

breathy *adj* **wheezy**, hissing, gasping, panting, husky

breed *n* **type**, strain, class, kind, variety ■ *v* **1 reproduce**, have babies, propagate, procreate, multiply **2 raise**, rear, bring up, farm, produce **3 cause**, create, generate, bring about, produce

breeding *n* **upbringing**, education, background, social standing, refinement

breeding ground *n* **environment**, conditions, source, medium, place

breeze *n* **1 wind**, gust, gentle wind, light wind, waft *Opposite*: gale **2** (*infml*) **child's play**, cinch (*infml*), piece of cake (*infml*), doddle (*infml*), walkover (*infml*)

breezily adv **brightly**, cheerfully, cheerily, happily, merrily Opposite: seriously

breezy adj 1 **blustery**, gusty, windy, brisk, windswept Opposite: still 2 **cheerful**, cheery, jolly, lighthearted, flippant Opposite: serious

breviary n **missal**, prayer book, hymnal, book of psalms

brevity n 1 **shortness**, briefness, quickness, swiftness, transience Opposite: length 2 **conciseness**, succinctness, concision, pithiness, terseness Opposite: verbosity

brew n 1 (infml) **drink**, potion, infusion, cocktail, beverage (fml) 2 **mixture**, mix, blend, combination, concoction ■ v 1 **prepare**, make, infuse, steep, ferment 2 **develop**, loom, threaten, grow, blow up

bribe n **inducement**, enticement, carrot, kickback, slush fund ■ v **induce**, corrupt, entice, suborn, persuade

bribery n **corruption**, inducement, enticement, subornation

bric-a-brac n **curios**, ornaments, stuff, jumble, knick-knacks

brick n **block**, slab, ingot, lump, piece

brickbat n **insult**, criticism, insinuation, suggestion, comment

brickwork n **fabric**, structure, bricks and mortar, masonry, stonework

bridal adj **wedding**, nuptial, marriage, honeymoon

bride n **wife**, wife-to-be, newlywed, spouse, partner

bridegroom n **husband**, husband-to-be, newlywed, spouse, partner

bridesmaid n **maid of honour**, attendant, matron of honour, flower girl

bridge n **bond**, tie, link, connection, conduit ■ v **link**, connect, join, span, tie together

---

WORD BANK

❏ **types of bridge** aqueduct, arch bridge, Bailey bridge, bascule bridge, beam bridge, cable-stayed bridge, cantilever bridge, drawbridge, flyover, footbridge, gangplank, humpback bridge, pontoon bridge, suspension bridge, swing bridge, viaduct, walkway

---

bridgehead n **foothold**, position, stepping stone, jumping-off point, vantage point

bridle v 1 **bristle**, get angry, become annoyed, become indignant, prickle 2 **curb**, restrain, control, rein in, keep in check Opposite: let loose

bridle path n **bridleway**, ride, path, track, trail

brief adj 1 **short-lived**, transitory, fleeting, ephemeral, short-term Opposite: lasting 2 **short**, concise, succinct, to the point, pithy Opposite: lengthy ■ n 1 **synopsis**, summary, digest, abstract, outline 2 **briefing**, instructions, guidelines, preparation, orders 3 **task**, remit, mission, mandate, assignment

4 (infml) **legal representative**, lawyer, barrister, QC, attorney ■ v **inform**, tell, give instructions, prepare, instruct

briefcase n **document case**, attaché case, case, portfolio, music case

briefing n **meeting**, conference, seminar, press conference, updating session

brigade n **group**, team, crew, contingent, gang

bright adj 1 **brilliant**, vivid, intense, dazzling, light Opposite: dark 2 **intelligent**, quick, sharp-witted, clever, smart Opposite: unintelligent 3 **cheerful**, happy, lively, optimistic, positive Opposite: gloomy. See COMPARE AND CONTRAST at **intelligent**.

brighten v 1 **feel better**, brighten up, look up, perk up, cheer up 2 **make brighter**, lighten, make lighter, brighten up, illuminate Opposite: darken 3 **improve**, make better, enhance, animate, revivify

brighten up v **raise the spirits**, make brighter, brighten, lighten, make lighter Opposite: cast down

brightly adv 1 **luminously**, lustrously, radiantly, glossily, glowingly Opposite: dully 2 **sunnily**, perkily, cheerfully, cheerily, optimistically Opposite: gloomily

brightness n 1 **illumination**, glare, intensity, brilliance, vividness Opposite: dullness 2 **sunniness**, high spirits, cheerfulness, optimism, cheeriness Opposite: gloominess

brilliance n 1 **brightness**, intensity, vividness, luminosity, radiance Opposite: dullness 2 **cleverness**, wisdom, smartness, genius, talent Opposite: stupidity

brilliancy see **brilliance**

brilliant adj 1 **luminous**, radiant, dazzling, sparkling, gleaming Opposite: dull 2 **vivid**, bright, clear, intense, dazzling Opposite: faded 3 **talented**, virtuoso, inspired, skilful, gifted Opposite: mediocre 4 (infml) **wonderful**, marvellous, superb, excellent, magnificent Opposite: awful

brim n **ridge**, edge, top, rim, lip

brimful adj **full to the top**, full, filled up, filled to the brim, overfull Opposite: empty

brimming adj **bursting**, teeming, overflowing, packed, filled

brine n **saline**, salt water, sea water

bring v 1 **take along**, carry, fetch, convey, transport Opposite: take away 2 **cause**, bring about, produce, lead to, result in 3 **command**, earn, produce, make, bring in

bring about v **generate**, cause, produce, result in, end in Opposite: prevent

bring alive v **awaken**, bring to life, make real, animate, enliven

bring back v 1 **evoke**, recall, bring to mind, summon up, reawaken 2 **return**, replace, restore, reinstate, recapture Opposite: carry off

bring down v 1 **overthrow**, topple, depose,

defeat, dethrone *Opposite*: elect **2 fell**, floor, topple, demolish, knock over *Opposite*: raise

bring down a peg *v* **humble**, chasten, force to eat humble pie, cut down to size, put in their place

bring down to earth *v* **disillusion**, disappoint, disenchant, enlighten, disabuse

bring forth *v* **deliver**, bear, give birth to, produce, yield

bring forward *v* **1 speed**, advance, reschedule, move forward, change *Opposite*: delay **2 put on the table**, produce, present, offer, bring out *Opposite*: withdraw

bring home *v* **make clear**, clarify, illustrate, illuminate, underline

bring home the bacon *(infml)* *v* **1 be successful**, bring off, come up with the goods, come through, keep your end of the bargain *Opposite*: fail **2 provide**, keep a roof over your head, put food on the table, keep the wolf from the door, keep clothes on your back

bring in *v* **1 introduce**, set up, establish, launch, start *Opposite*: end **2 recoup**, acquire, earn, make, take home *Opposite*: lose

bring into being *v* **create**, establish, found, institute, set up *Opposite*: destroy

bring into disrepute *v* **discredit**, dishonour, disgrace, shame, smear *Opposite*: honour

bring into line *v* **standardize**, coordinate, synchronize, make uniform, harmonize

bring off *v* **succeed**, carry off, achieve, accomplish, engineer *Opposite*: fail

bring on *v* **cause**, create, produce, make, start

bring out *v* **1 highlight**, spotlight, show up, reveal, bring to the surface *Opposite*: suppress **2 introduce**, produce, release, put on sale, launch *Opposite*: withdraw

bring round *v* **1 sway**, reason, get round, convince, persuade *Opposite*: deter **2 bring to**, rouse, awaken, wake up, revive *Opposite*: knock out

bring shame on *v* **discredit**, sully, tarnish, smear, stain *Opposite*: honour

bring to *v* **bring round**, rouse, awaken, wake up, revive *Opposite*: knock out

bring to a close *see* bring to an end

bring to an end *v* **conclude**, bring to a close, put a stop to, end, stop *Opposite*: start

bring together *v* **1 combine**, mix, mix together, blend, pool *Opposite*: separate **2 gather**, amass, rally, compile, glean *Opposite*: distribute **3 reconcile**, integrate, unite, unify, link

bring to life *v* **make real**, animate, bring alive, anthropomorphize, give life to

bring to light *v* **expose**, unearth, disclose, uncover, publicize *Opposite*: hide

bring to mind *v* **summon up**, reawaken, rekindle, stir up, bring back

bring up *v* **1 mention**, broach, raise, suggest, introduce *Opposite*: gloss over **2 raise**, rear, care for, nurture, look after **3 vomit**, expel, spew, regurgitate, disgorge

bring up-to-date *v* **inform**, give the lowdown, look after, put in the picture, update *Opposite*: keep in the dark

brink *n* **1 verge**, threshold, edge, point, precipice **2 edge**, rim, lip, brim, border *Opposite*: centre

brinkmanship *n* **strategy**, tactics, politics, bluff, bluffing

briny *adj* **salty**, salt, saline, salted, brackish ■ *n* **sea**, ocean, deep, drink *(infml)*

briquette *n* **block**, lump, brick, piece, cake

brisk *adj* **1 energetic**, fast, quick, rapid, hurried *Opposite*: slow **2 abrupt**, curt, impatient, brusque, hurried *Opposite*: measured **3 refreshing**, cool, cold, invigorating, stimulating *Opposite*: warm

briskness *n* **1 speed**, rapidity, vigour, efficiency, urgency *Opposite*: tardiness **2 abruptness**, coldness, reserve, brusqueness, curtness *Opposite*: patience

bristle *n* **stubble**, hackle, hair, spine, spike ■ *v* **1 stiffen**, become erect, stand up, rise, prickle **2 bridle**, be resentful, get your hackles up, object, get angry **3 brim**, be full, teem, overflow, be thick with

bristly *adj* **spiky**, coarse, wiry, stubbly, sharp *Opposite*: smooth

brittle *adj* **hard**, stiff, inelastic, fragile, breakable *Opposite*: robust

brittleness *n* **hardness**, stiffness, fragility, weakness, frailty *Opposite*: robustness

broach *v* **propose**, present, submit, mention, raise

broad *adj* **1 spacious**, wide, large, big, extensive *Opposite*: narrow **2 comprehensive**, extensive, wide, far-reaching, wide-ranging *Opposite*: restricted **3 inexact**, rough, general, approximate, sketchy *Opposite*: precise **4 visible**, obvious, plain, clear, patent *Opposite*: subtle **5 distinctive**, distinct, thick, heavy, strong *Opposite*: slight ■ *n* **lake**, expanse of water, stretch of water, body of water, mere *(literary)*

broad-brush *adj* **inclusive**, comprehensive, broad, across-the-board, all-embracing *Opposite*: narrow

broadcast *v* **1 transmit**, air, show, televise, screen **2 air**, spread, disseminate, publicize, make known **3 scatter**, sow, distribute, disseminate, strew ■ *n* **transmission**, programme, show, airing, newscast

WORD BANK
❏ **types of broadcast** chat show, commercial, concert, current affairs, distance learning, docudrama, documentary, drama, game show, infomercial, infotainment, makeover programme, miniseries, news, newscast, news flash, newsreel, phone-in, play, quiz show, reality show, sitcom *(infml)*, soap *(infml)*, soap opera, sports, sportscast, telethon, travelogue

broadcaster *n* **presenter**, anchor, announcer, reporter, journalist

broaden *v* **widen**, extend, increase, make wider, become wider *Opposite*: narrow

broadly *adv* **approximately**, sketchily, generally, largely, roughly

broadly-based *adj* **wide**, broad, wide-ranging, extensive, sweeping

broad-minded *adj* **tolerant**, progressive, liberal, permissive, open-minded *Opposite*: narrow-minded

broad-mindedness *n* **liberality**, open-mindedness, tolerance, progressiveness, permissiveness *Opposite*: narrow-mindedness

broadness *n* **1 width**, breadth, wideness **2 scope**, breadth, span, range, extensiveness

broadsheet *n* **paper**, newspaper, quality newspaper, serious newspaper, heavyweight

broadside *n* **attack**, diatribe, tirade, onslaught, volley

brochure *n* **booklet**, catalogue, leaflet, pamphlet, information sheet

brogue *n* **accent**, burr, drawl

broil *v* **swelter**, burn, roast, bake, boil *Opposite*: freeze

broke *(infml) adj* **bankrupt**, penniless, poor, in the red, overdrawn *Opposite*: wealthy

broken *adj* **1 wrecked**, imperfect, fragmented, fractured, shattered *Opposite*: intact **2 inoperative**, malfunctioning, faulty, defective, out of order *Opposite*: working **3 beaten**, licked, defeated, dejected, crushed *Opposite*: triumphant

broken-down *adj* **1 inoperative**, malfunctioning, not working, broken, out of order *Opposite*: working **2 in poor condition**, dilapidated, run-down, falling apart, ramshackle

brokenhearted *adj* **sad**, grief-stricken, disappointed, desolate, despairing *Opposite*: overjoyed

broker *n* **trader**, agent, dealer, negotiator, stockbroker

bronze *n* **sculpture**, figure, statue, statuette, effigy

bronzed *adj* **tanned**, brown, suntanned, golden-brown, coppery

brooch *n* **pin**, badge, ornament, trinket, accessory

brood *n* **1 young**, clutch, litter, issue, family **2 children**, offspring, family, progeny, kids *(infml)* ■ *v* **ruminate**, worry, mope, dwell on, fret

broodily *adv* **thoughtfully**, pensively, meditatively, fretfully, sullenly *Opposite*: cheerfully

broodiness *n* **pensiveness**, glumness, fretfulness, sullenness, moroseness

brooding *adj* **ominous**, menacing, threatening, gloomy, dark

broodingly *adv* **glumly**, fretfully, sullenly, morosely, moodily *Opposite*: cheerfully

broody *adj* **1 sullen**, thoughtful, pensive, moody, glum *Opposite*: cheerful **2 maternal**, motherly, tender, caring

brook *n* **stream**, beck, rivulet, river, burn

broom *n* **brush**, sweeper, besom

broomstick *n* **handle**, broom handle, pole, stick, stave

brother *n* **comrade**, member, colleague, associate

brotherhood *n* **1 comradeship**, friendship, companionship, unity, loyalty **2 association**, society, union, guild, organization

brotherly *adj* **companionable**, fraternal, affectionate, kind, friendly

brouhaha *n* **commotion**, ruckus, brawl, rumpus, melee

brow *n* **summit**, top, crest, ridge, peak

browbeat *v* **intimidate**, badger, bully, dragoon, nag *Opposite*: coax

browbeaten *adj* **downtrodden**, oppressed, intimidated, bullied, subjugated *Opposite*: defiant

brown *adj* **tanned**, sunburnt, bronzed ■ *v* **fry**, grill, sear, toast, char

---

WORD BANK

❏ **types of brown** auburn, bay, bronze, burnt sienna, burnt umber, caramel, chestnut, chocolate, copper, hazel, henna, khaki, liver, mahogany, mocha, mousy, nut-brown, roan, russet, sorrel, tan, tawny, umber, walnut

❏ **types of light brown** beige, biscuit, buff, butterscotch, café au lait, camel, coffee, dun, ecru, fawn, flesh colour, honey, oatmeal

---

browse *v* **glance**, cruise, look, peruse, surf

bruise *n* **discoloration**, black eye, welt, bump, shiner *(infml)* ■ *v* **hurt**, damage, mark, injure, discolour

bruised *adj* **1 injured**, hurt, sore, black-and-blue, damaged *Opposite*: unhurt **2 wounded**, upset, hurt, offended, affected *Opposite*: unaffected

bruiser *(infml) n* **muscleman**, bodyguard, bouncer, tough, heavyweight

brunette *adj* **dark**, brown, raven *(literary) Opposite*: blond

brunt *n* **effect**, force, full force, impact, full impact

brush *n* **1 broom**, sweeper, besom **2 contact**, touch, stroke, graze, sweep **3 encounter**, meeting, confrontation, skirmish, disagreement ■ *v* **1 scrub**, clear, coat, groom, sweep **2 touch**, graze, scrape, sweep, stroke

brushed *adj* **fleecy**, fluffy, downy, furry, soft

brush off *v* **dismiss**, rebuff, snub, reject, give the cold shoulder to

brushoff *(infml) n* **turndown**, rebuff, snub, rejection, cold shoulder

brush up *v* reread, refresh, renew, revise, review

brushwood *n* firewood, twigs, branches, undergrowth, kindling

brusque *adj* abrupt, curt, offhand, rough, brisk *Opposite*: friendly

brusqueness *n* roughness, terseness, abruptness, offhandedness, lack of warmth *Opposite*: friendliness

brutal *adj* 1 ruthless, cruel, vicious, fierce, pitiless *Opposite*: humane 2 harsh, severe, rough, callous, insensitive *Opposite*: kind

brutality *n* cruelty, viciousness, violence, rough treatment, harshness *Opposite*: gentleness

brutalize *v* 1 coarsen, harden, dehumanize, desensitize *Opposite*: humanize 2 abuse, assault, maltreat, ill-treat

brute *n* 1 bully, thug, beast, swine, monster 2 (*literary*) animal, beast, creature, monster

brutish *adj* 1 animal, wild, violent, bestial 2 cruel, ruthless, insensitive, pitiless, harsh *Opposite*: humane 3 loutish, boorish, rough, unrefined, uncivilized *Opposite*: civilized

brutishly *adv* cruelly, harshly, unfeelingly, insensitively, callously *Opposite*: humanely

brutishness *n* cruelty, harshness, unkindness, unfeelingness, insensitivity *Opposite*: humanity

bubble *v* fizz, effervesce, boil, simmer

bubbly *adj* 1 effervescent, foamy, sparkling, fizzy, fizzing *Opposite*: still 2 cheerful, lively, sparkling, vivacious, bouncy *Opposite*: sad

buccaneer *n* pirate, adventurer, swashbuckler

buck *n* (*infml*) responsibility, blame, liability, culpability, fault ■ *v* 1 jump, rear, kick, kick out, bound 2 resist, oppose, fly in the face of, go against, challenge

bucket *n* pail, container, vessel ■ *v* (*infml*) pour, pour with rain, pour down, teem, come down in torrents

buckets (*infml*) *n* lots, scores, loads (*infml*), tons (*infml*), heaps (*infml*)

buckle *n* clasp, clip, fastener, catch, fastening ■ *v* 1 fasten, clip, clasp, secure, close *Opposite*: undo 2 collapse, crumple, cave in, bulge, fold *Opposite*: straighten

buckle down (*infml*) *v* get on with, put your shoulder to the wheel, set to, get down to, knuckle down (*infml*)

buckshee (*infml*) *adj* free, complimentary, gratis, on the house ■ *adv* free of charge, free, gratis, for nothing, without paying

buck up *v* 1 (*infml*) raise the morale of, cheer up, raise the spirits of, hearten 2 improve, get better, look up, liven up, pick up *Opposite*: take a turn for the worse 3 (*infml dated*) hurry up, get going, look lively, get a move on (*infml*), get your skates on (*infml*)

bucolic *adj* rural, pastoral, rustic, country, countrified *Opposite*: urban

bud *n* sprout, blossom, shoot, outgrowth ■ *v* blossom, flower, grow, bloom, open out

budding *adj* promising, potential, up-and-coming, nascent, burgeoning

budge *v* move, shift, dislodge, nudge, push

budget *n* financial plan, financial statement, accounts, finances, funds ■ *adj* cheap, economical, inexpensive, reasonable, low-priced *Opposite*: expensive ■ *v* plan, account, make financial arrangements, make provisions, cost

budgetary *adj* financial, economic, fiscal, commercial, monetary

buff *n* fan, enthusiast, expert, connoisseur, aficionado ■ *v* polish, rub, rub up, burnish, shine

buffalo (*infml*) *v* intimidate, coerce, threaten, inhibit, bully

buffer *n* shock absorber, bumper, cushion, barrier, shield ■ *v* cushion, shield, safeguard, defend, protect

buffet *v* rock, pound, batter, bang, knock

buffeting *n* battering, pounding, knocking, beating, pummelling

buffoon *n* clown, joker, comedian, fool, wag (*dated*)

buffoonery *n* horseplay, clowning, fooling around, frivolity, tomfoolery (*infml*)

bug *n* 1 insect, fly, pest, creature, creepy-crawly (*infml*) 2 (*infml*) germ, microbe, virus, bacterium, infection 3 (*infml*) fault, error, mistake, problem, gremlin (*infml*) 4 (*infml*) listening device, hidden microphone, surveillance device, wiretap ■ *v* 1 (*infml*) annoy, irritate, infuriate, bother, madden 2 tap, listen in on, keep under surveillance, spy on. *See* COMPARE AND CONTRAST *at* bother.

bugaboo *see* bugbear

bugbear *n* worry, problem, concern, bother, annoyance

bug-eyed (*infml*) *adj* popeyed, staring, big-eyed, wide-eyed, agog

buggy *n* 1 cart, vehicle, truck, transporter 2 pushchair, pram, perambulator (*fml*), stroller (*US*)

bugle *v* announce, herald, trumpet

build *v* 1 construct, put up, erect, make, put together *Opposite*: destroy 2 put together, create, make, join, assemble ■ *n* shape, size, figure, body, physique

build in *v* incorporate, include, integrate, add in *Opposite*: exclude

building *n* structure, construction, edifice, erection (*fml*)

WORD BANK
❑ **parts of a building** balcony, buttress, chimney, colonnade, doorway, elevation, escalator, exterior, façade, fire escape, frame, frontage, gable, guttering, landing, lift, porch, roof, smokestack, soffit, stairwell, veranda, vestibule, wall, window, wing

build up v 1 **increase**, rise, develop, expand, enlarge Opposite: fall off 2 **boost**, bolster, pump up, inspire, encourage Opposite: discourage

buildup n 1 **accumulation**, backlog, accrual, collection, stockpile 2 **hype**, publicity, puff, praise, flattery

built-in adj 1 **integral**, fitted, fixed, en suite, in-built 2 **natural**, inherent, innate, intrinsic, ingrained Opposite: acquired

built-up adj **urbanized**, urban, developed, residential, industrial

bulb n **corm**, rhizome, tuber, storage organ, underground part

---

WORD BANK
❑ **types of flower grown from a bulb** anemone, bluebell, crocus, cyclamen, daffodil, dahlia, freesia, gladiolus, hyacinth, iris, jonquil, lily, narcissus, snowdrop, tulip

---

bulbous adj **rounded**, spherical, bulging, globular, swollen

bulge v **stick out**, protrude, expand, be full to bursting, swell ■ n **protuberance**, swell, swelling, knot, lump

bulging adj 1 **protruding**, protuberant, distended, swollen, swelling Opposite: flat 2 **full**, overfull, overfilled, overstuffed, crammed Opposite: empty

bulk n 1 **size**, mass, volume, immensity, vastness 2 **form**, body, weight, mass, hulk 3 **greater part**, main part, largest part, majority, substance

bulkhead n **partition**, wall, dividing wall, screen, divider

bulkiness n 1 **unwieldiness**, awkwardness, ungainliness, cumbersomeness, ponderousness 2 **large size**, largeness, weight, bulk, mass Opposite: compactness

bulk large v **be prominent**, figure prominently, loom large, dominate, be important

bulk up (infml) v **build up**, increase, pad out, gain weight, gain muscle

bulky adj 1 **unwieldy**, cumbersome, awkward, ungainly, ponderous Opposite: manageable 2 **large**, huge, immense, massive, colossal Opposite: compact

bull n **papal decree**, decree, official statement, encyclical, instruction

bulldoze v 1 **flatten**, raze, level, demolish, clear 2 (infml) **coerce**, bully, bludgeon, browbeat, steamroller

bulletin n 1 **news report**, update, news item, news summary, press release 2 **official statement**, communiqué, statement, announcement, press release 3 **periodical**, journal, newsletter, newspaper, publication

bulletproof adj 1 **toughened**, armoured, protective, reinforced, shatterproof 2 (infml) **invulnerable**, secure, invincible, unassailable, untouchable Opposite: vulnerable

bullheaded (infml) adj **obstinate**, headstrong, stubborn, wilful, intransigent

bullheadedness (infml) n **obstinacy**, stubbornness, wilfulness, intransigence, self-will

bullion n **gold**, gold bars, gold ingots

bullish adj 1 **muscular**, strong, hulking, brawny 2 (infml) **optimistic**, confident, buoyant, cheerful, enthusiastic Opposite: pessimistic

bullishness (infml) n **confidence**, optimism, buoyancy, hopefulness, self-confidence Opposite: diffidence

bullnecked adj **stocky**, bullish, brawny, beefy, muscular

bullring n **arena**, ring, stadium, amphitheatre, sports stadium

bull's eye n **target**, centre, mark, middle, middle point

bully n **tormentor**, aggressor, persecutor, tyrant, oppressor ■ v **intimidate**, terrorize, persecute, torment, frighten

bullyboy n **thug**, bully, yob (infml), hooligan (infml), heavy (slang) ■ adj **aggressive**, intimidating, bullying, rough, threatening

bullying n **intimidation**, mistreatment, oppression, harassment, victimization

bully-off n **start of play**, start, kickoff, beginning, commencement (fml)

bulwark n 1 **fortification**, embankment, earthwork, barricade, rampart 2 **safeguard**, protection, defence, buttress, buffer

bumble v 1 **mumble**, murmur, hesitate, mutter, stutter 2 **stumble**, lumber, blunder, stagger, lurch

bumbling (infml) adj **awkward**, clumsy, blundering, lumbering, ungainly Opposite: graceful

bumf (infml) n **documents**, leaflets, pamphlets, brochures, papers

bump v 1 **hit**, knock, bang, strike, wallop (infml) 2 **jolt**, bounce, jounce, jar, jerk 3 **collide**, slam into, crash into, knock, smash into ■ n 1 **knock**, collision, smash, accident, crash 2 **swelling**, lump, bruise, bulge, contusion (fml) 3 **thud**, thump, bang, crash, blow

bumper adj **plentiful**, profuse, copious, extra-large, jumbo Opposite: meagre

bumpiness n **unevenness**, roughness, lumpiness Opposite: smoothness

bump into v 1 **collide**, slam into, crash into, knock into, smash into 2 **meet by chance**, run into, happen upon, happen on, meet

bumptious adj **full of yourself**, pleased with yourself, self-satisfied, self-important, smug Opposite: modest

bumptiousness n **self-importance**, conceitedness, arrogance, pompousness, brashness Opposite: modesty

bump up (infml) v **increase**, put up, boost, enhance, add to Opposite: decrease

bumpy adj 1 **uneven**, rough, rutted, potholed Opposite: smooth 2 **uncomfortable**, rough, bouncy, jarring, jerky *Opposite*: smooth

bunch n **1 group**, set, lot, mixture, collection **2 bouquet**, posy, spray, corsage **3** (*infml*) **gang**, gathering, team, set, group ■ v **crowd together**, huddle, form a group, gather, cluster *Opposite*: disperse

bundle n **package**, pack, parcel, packet, bale ■ v (*infml*) **hurry**, rush, push, shove

bundle up v **1 package**, pack, wrap, parcel, parcel up **2** (*infml*) **dress warmly**, wrap up, wrap up warmly

bung n **stopper**, plug, cork ■ v (*infml*) **throw**, toss, fling, lob, pass

bungle (*infml*) v **do badly**, make a mess of, make a dog's dinner of, mismanage, ruin *Opposite*: succeed

bungler (*infml*) n **blunderer**, incompetent, bumbler, botcher, muddler

bungling (*infml*) adj **clumsy**, incompetent, inept, blundering, maladroit *Opposite*: competent

bung up (*infml*) v **stop up**, block, close, clog, caulk *Opposite*: open

bunion n **swelling**, lump, enlargement, distension, bulge

bunk n **bed**, single bed, berth, couchette, bunk bed

bunker n **1 bin**, chest, container, box, store **2 underground shelter**, shelter, dugout, foxhole, ditch

bunkum (*infml*) n **nonsense**, humbug, drivel, gibberish, rubbish

bunting n **streamers**, decorations, flags, paper chains, ticker tape

buoy n **marker**, float, navigational aid ■ v **keep afloat**, hold up, sustain, maintain, prop up

buoyancy n **1 lightness**, weightlessness *Opposite*: heaviness **2 resilience**, resistance, flexibility, toughness **3 optimism**, cheerfulness, good spirits, enthusiasm, jauntiness *Opposite*: pessimism

buoyant adj **1 floating**, afloat, light **2 resilient**, resistant, flexible, tough **3 cheerful**, optimistic, happy, jaunty, carefree *Opposite*: morose

buoy up v **cheer**, uplift, encourage, boost, lift *Opposite*: depress

burble v **1 bubble**, ripple, babble, splash, murmur **2** (*infml*) **gush**, babble, ramble, go on about, blather

burden n **1 load**, weight, cargo **2 problem**, drain, encumbrance, affliction, liability **3** (*literary*) **theme**, topic, subject, subject matter ■ v **lumber** (*infml*), weigh down, saddle, encumber, trouble. *See* COMPARE AND CONTRAST *at* **subject**.

burdened adj **loaded**, fraught, weighed down, laden, held back

burdensome adj **onerous**, heavy, taxing, troublesome, arduous

bureau n **1 government department**, agency,

office, department, unit **2 writing desk**, desk, writing table, escritoire

bureaucracy n **1 system of government**, government, administration, civil service, establishment **2 official procedure**, rules and regulations, formalities, paperwork, red tape (*infml*)

bureaucrat n **official**, public servant, civil servant, administrator, office holder

bureaucratic adj **1 administrative**, official, governmental, civil service, organizational **2 rigid**, inflexible, unbending, officious, involved

burgeoning adj **1 growing**, mushrooming, increasing, escalating, expanding *Opposite*: dwindling **2 budding**, promising, up-and-coming, nascent *Opposite*: fading

burgher n **citizen**, resident, inhabitant, denizen, voter

burglar n **thief**, robber, intruder, cat burglar, criminal

burglary n **1 breaking and entering**, theft, robbery, aggravated burglary, stealing **2 break-in**, theft, robbery, crime, housebreak (*US*)

burgle v **rob**, thieve, break in, loot, steal from

burial n **interment**, committal, entombment, funeral

burial chamber n **sepulchre**, tomb, mausoleum, vault, crypt

burial ground n **cemetery**, graveyard, churchyard, necropolis, garden of remembrance

burial place n **last resting place**, grave, tomb, crypt, mausoleum

buried adj **1 underground**, concealed, hidden, covered, dug in *Opposite*: dug up **2 suppressed**, hidden, covered up, repressed, forgotten *Opposite*: exposed

burlesque n **parody**, caricature, travesty, lampoon, skit ■ v **spoof**, mock, make fun of, lampoon, caricature

burliness n **brawniness**, heftiness, broad shoulders, muscularity, robustness *Opposite*: slimness

burly adj **brawny**, hefty, broad-shouldered, husky, muscular *Opposite*: slim

burn v **1 blaze**, be ablaze, flame, smoulder, glow **2 burn up**, burn down, burn away, gut, reduce to ashes **3 scorch**, singe, sear, char, scald **4 use up**, use, expend, consume **5 go red**, flush, blush, redden, colour **6 tingle**, sting, hurt, prickle, be on fire **7 corrode**, eat away, eat into **8 glow**, shine, twinkle, flare, glimmer **9** (*infml*) **race**, hurtle, tear, speed, scorch *Opposite*: dawdle ■ n **1 injury**, blister, scald, scorch **2 stream**, rivulet, beck, brook (*literary*)

burn down v **incinerate**, go up in flames, burn to the ground, burn to a crisp, reduce to ashes

burned-out adj **1 gutted**, destroyed, reduced to ashes, burnt down, burnt up **2 exhausted**, worn out, tired out, drained, unwell

burner n gas ring, ring, heat, flame, gas jet

burning adj 1 red-hot, piping hot, boiling hot, fiery hot, sweltering Opposite: cold 2 on fire, ablaze, blazing, flaming, smouldering Opposite: extinguished 3 strong, ardent, fervent, all-consuming, passionate Opposite: weak 4 important, vital, crucial, urgent, significant Opposite: insignificant 5 smarting, stinging, tingly, prickly, painful 6 feverish, febrile, flushed, hot, red Opposite: cool

burnish v polish, shine, buff, rub up, rub

burn out (infml) v exhaust, break down, wear out, tire, fatigue

burnout n exhaustion, stress, tension, weariness, poor health

burnt adj overcooked, well-done, cooked, seared, singed Opposite: rare

burn the candle at both ends v overdo things, wear yourself out, do too much, exhaust yourself, burn the midnight oil

burn the midnight oil v work late, stay up, work day and night, work overtime, burn the candle at both ends Opposite: slack

burnt-out see burned-out

burn up v incinerate, burn, burn down, reduce to ashes, burn to a crisp

burn your boats see burn your bridges

burn your bridges v pass the point of no return, cross the Rubicon, nail your colours to the mast, burn your boats

burr n 1 seed husk, pod, pericarp, seed pod 2 accent, twang, drawl, brogue, intonation

burrow n hole, warren, den, lair, hideaway ■ v 1 dig, tunnel, excavate, channel, dig out 2 search, dig, investigate, delve, scrabble 3 nestle, snuggle, cuddle, nuzzle, cosy up

bursary n scholarship, grant, award, fund, exhibition

burst v 1 rupture, split open, disintegrate, break open, fracture 2 erupt, spout, gush, rush, break out Opposite: trickle ■ n spurt, eruption, gust, torrent, rupture Opposite: trickle

bursting adj 1 full, overflowing, teeming, full to bursting, packed Opposite: empty 2 (infml) eager, desperate, keen, dying, longing Opposite: unwilling

burst in on v 1 interrupt, intrude upon, intrude on, come upon, disturb 2 surprise, take by surprise, catch unawares, take unawares, catch in the act

burst into tears v break down, dissolve in tears, break down and cry, burst out crying, lose control Opposite: laugh

burst out v 1 start, begin, commence, burst into, break into 2 exclaim, shout, cry, call out, say Opposite: whisper

bury v 1 inter, put in the ground, lay to rest, entomb, put six feet under Opposite: exhume 2 hide, conceal, cover, put out of sight, submerge Opposite: expose

bury the hatchet v make up, make peace, be reconciled, kiss and make up, resolve differences Opposite: fight

bus v transport, carry, take, convey, move

bush n 1 shrub, plant, flowering shrub, hedging plant 2 scrubland, wilds, outback, savanna, scrub

bushed (infml) adj exhausted, tired, worn-out, dead on your feet, all in Opposite: refreshed

bushes n undergrowth, scrub, shrubbery, greenery, underbrush (US)

bushy adj luxuriant, abundant, profuse, shaggy, thick Opposite: sparse

busily adv actively, energetically, briskly, industriously, vigorously Opposite: lazily

business n 1 commerce, trade, industry, selling, production 2 company, corporation, conglomerate, establishment, partnership 3 custom, trade, dealings, transactions, sales 4 concern, affair, problem, responsibility, interest 5 matter, affair, issue, situation, event ■ adj commercial, occupational, corporate, professional Opposite: private

businesslike adj 1 efficient, practical, professional, competent, systematic Opposite: unprofessional 2 unemotional, objective, professional, detached, uninvolved Opposite: emotional

businessperson n business executive, executive, executive director, director, manager

busk v entertain, perform, sing, play

busker n street entertainer, street musician, entertainer, performer, musician

bust n sculpture, torso, statue, figure, model ■ v (infml) break, smash, shatter, burst, fracture Opposite: mend ■ adj (infml) not working, out of order, broken, ruined, had it (infml)

bustle v busy yourself, be on the go, be busy, hurry, rush around ■ n activity, movement, stir, hustle and bustle, commotion Opposite: calm

bustling adj busy, active, full of go, full of life, hurried Opposite: still

bust up (infml) v split up, break up, separate, part, break apart Opposite: make up

bust-up (infml) n argument, disagreement, fight, split

busy adj 1 active, on the go, hard-working, hard at it, diligent Opposite: idle 2 full, full of activity, demanding, hard, tiring Opposite: empty 3 engaged, occupied, unavailable, taken Opposite: free

busybody (infml) n interferer, meddler, nuisance, gossip, scandalmonger

but prep 1 however, although, nevertheless, on the contrary 2 other than, except, excluding, bar, save for ■ n (infml) objection, proviso, provision, rider, condition

butch adj masculine, tough, strong, muscular, beefy

butcher n killer, murderer, slaughterer, exterminator, slayer *(fml or literary)* ▪ v **1 slaughter**, murder, kill, exterminate, massacre **2** *(infml)* **make a mess of**, ruin, spoil, botch *(infml)*, make a hash of *(infml)*

butchery n **slaughter**, carnage, bloodshed, killing

butt v **ram**, hit, bump, strike, run into ▪ n **1 object**, target, victim, scapegoat, stooge **2 handle**, stock, grip **3 end**, stub, stump, base, nub end **4 barrel**, tub, drum, cask, container

butte n **hill**, foothill, rise, mount, bluff

butterflies *(infml)* n **nervousness**, excitement, anxiety, tenseness, apprehension *Opposite*: confidence

butter up *(infml)* v **flatter**, curry favour, get on the right side of, sweet-talk *(infml)*, suck up to *(infml) Opposite*: insult

butt in v **1 interrupt**, break in, cut in, interfere, interject *Opposite*: mind your own business **2 squeeze in**, barge in, shove in, jump the queue, queue-jump

button n **push button**, switch, knob, key ▪ v **fasten**, do up, close *Opposite*: undo

buttonhole n **flower**, spray, corsage ▪ v *(infml)* **accost**, waylay, corner, grab, confront

button up *(infml)* v **be quiet**, keep quiet, be silent, say nothing, stop talking *Opposite*: blather *(infml)*

buttress n **support**, prop, reinforcement, flying buttress, structure ▪ v **strengthen**, support, prop, prop up, reinforce

butty *(infml)* n **sandwich**, baguette, roll, bagel, wrap

buxom adj **plump**, rounded, ample, curvaceous, curvy

buy v **pay for**, purchase, acquire, procure, obtain *Opposite*: sell ▪ n **purchase**, acquisition, bargain, deal

buyer n **purchaser**, consumer, shopper, bargain hunter, customer *Opposite*: seller

buy off v **bribe**, induce, corrupt, suborn, pay off *(infml)*

buy out v **acquire**, take over, purchase, take control of

buyout n **takeover**, merger, acquisition, purchase

buzz n **1** *(infml)* **telephone call**, call, ring, phone call, bell *(infml)* **2** *(infml)* **thrill**, high, kick, lift, jolt *Opposite*: downer *(infml)* **3** *(infml)* **gossip**, talk, word, rumour, whisper ▪ v **hum**, drone, murmur, whine, whirr

buzzer n **signal**, bell, beeper *(infml)*, bleeper

buzzing adj **busy**, bustling, vibrant, full of life, lively *Opposite*: still

buzzword *(infml)* n **slogan**, catchword, saying, byword, catch phrase

by prep **1 with**, near, next to, beside **2 through**, via, in, by means of, as a result of **3 not later than**, before, sooner than

bye-byes *(infml)* n **sleep**, bed, land of nod *(infml)*, beddy-bye *(infml)*

bygone adj **past**, former, previous, long-gone, departed *(literary) Opposite*: future

bylaw n **regulation**, rule, ruling, statute, guideline

byline n **acknowledgement**, credit, heading, strap line

bypass v **go around**, avoid, get round, find a way round, sidestep

by-product n **side effect**, spin-off, consequence, result, derivative

byre n **cowshed**, shed, barn, milking parlour, stable

bystander n **onlooker**, passer-by, witness, eyewitness, spectator *Opposite*: participant

byword n **1 embodiment**, perfect example, epitome, shining example **2 catch phrase**, proverb, axiom, slogan, saying

byzantine adj **1 complex**, intricate, tortuous, convoluted, complicated *Opposite*: straightforward **2 devious**, scheming, underhand, deceitful, secretive *Opposite*: honest

C

cab n **1 taxi**, taxicab, black cab, hackney cab, hackney carriage **2 cabin**, compartment, cockpit

cabal n **1 faction**, section, unit, group, sect **2 plot**, scheme, conspiracy, connivance, collusion

cabaret n **1 show**, floor show, live entertainment, burlesque **2 nightclub**, club, bar, nightspot

caber n **log**, beam, pole, stick

cabin n **1 hut**, log cabin, cottage, bungalow, chalet **2 compartment**, cubicle, stateroom, room, berth

caboodle *(infml)* n **lot**, whole lot, entirety, totality, integrality

cache n **hoard**, store, accumulation, reserve, collection ▪ v **hide**, hoard, store, secrete, reserve *Opposite*: discard

cachet n **status**, prestige, distinction, respect, reputation

cack-handed (infml) adj **clumsy**, awkward, gauche, maladroit, ham-handed (infml) Opposite: dexterous

cackle v **laugh**, hoot, screech, crow, guffaw

cacophonous adj **discordant**, unmusical, unmelodious, dissonant, inharmonious Opposite: melodious

cacophony n **discord**, discordance, dissonance, disharmony, unmusicality Opposite: melodiousness

cad (dated) n **rogue**, scoundrel, rake, rascal, blackguard Opposite: gentleman

CAD n **computer-aided design**, computer graphics, graphics, product design, drafting

cadaver n **corpse**, dead body, remains, body

cadaverous adj **bony**, skeletal, emaciated, wasted, gaunt Opposite: healthy

caddie n **assistant**, porter, carrier, transporter ■ v **transport**, assist, carry

caddish (dated) adj **dishonourable**, ungallant, rascally, rakish, ungentlemanly Opposite: gallant

caddy n **container**, tin, box, receptacle, carton

cadence n **1 tempo**, rhythm, pace, pulse, stroke **2 lilt**, intonation, accent, modulation, inflection

cadenza n **solo passage**, improvisation, solo, unaccompanied passage, showpiece

cadet n **trainee**, police cadet, army cadet, sea cadet

cadger (infml) n **scrounger** (infml), borrower, moocher (infml), sponger (infml), ligger (infml)

cadre n **1 squad**, corps, unit, team, band **2 faction**, group, core, hard core, band

cage n **enclosure**, coop, pen, birdcage, crate ■ v **confine**, enclose, pen, coop up, impound Opposite: release

WORD BANK
❑ **types of pen or cage** apiary, aquarium, aviary, beehive, birdcage, chicken coop, chicken run, coop, cowshed, dovecote, henhouse, hutch, kennel, piggery, pigsty, pound, stable, stall, sty

caged adj **captive**, detained, confined, imprisoned, jailed Opposite: free

cagey (infml) adj **wary**, guarded, cautious, careful, reticent Opposite: reckless

caginess (infml) n **wariness**, caution, reticence, evasiveness, chariness Opposite: carelessness

cagoule n **waterproof jacket**, anorak, windcheater, parka, raincoat

cairn n **1 landmark**, marker, signpost, direction post, milestone **2 memorial**, monument, barrow, tomb, tombstone

cajole v **coax**, persuade, wheedle, entice, inveigle Opposite: compel

cake n **1 gateau**, pastry, fancy **2 bar**, block, slab, lump, tablet ■ v **cover**, coat, encrust, congeal, coagulate

WORD BANK
❑ **types of cake** angel food cake, barm brack, birthday cake, Black Forest gateau, brownie, carrot cake, cheesecake, Christmas cake, coffee cake, cruller, cupcake, Danish pastry, devil's food cake, doughnut, éclair, flapjack, fruitcake, gateau, gingerbread, key lime pie, macaroon, Madeira cake, madeleine, mince pie, muffin, pain au chocolat, petit four, seedcake, sponge cake, strudel, Swiss roll, torte, turnover, wedding cake

caked adj **covered**, coated, encrusted, layered

cakewalk (infml) n **child's play**, kid's stuff, easy victory, runaway victory, cinch (infml)

calamitous adj **disastrous**, dreadful, catastrophic, ruinous, tragic Opposite: beneficial

calamity n **disaster**, catastrophe, mishap, misfortune, tragedy

calcify v **harden**, set, solidify, fossilize, turn into stone Opposite: soften

calculable adj **1 quantifiable**, countable, finite, assessable, measurable Opposite: incalculable **2 predictable**, anticipated, expected, foreseeable, likely Opposite: unpredictable

calculate v **work out**, compute, estimate, weigh up, gauge

calculated adj **intended**, designed, planned, considered, premeditated Opposite: spontaneous

calculating adj **scheming**, manipulative, devious, shrewd, conniving Opposite: candid

calculation n **1 computation**, estimate, reckoning, sum, result **2 control**, cunning, scheming, intention, design Opposite: candidness

calendar n **diary**, schedule, year planner, timetable

calibrate v **standardize**, adjust, regulate, tune, bring into line

calibration n **1 standardization**, correction, adjustment, tuning, setting **2 graduation**, gradation, mark, measurement, degree

calibre n **1 quality**, ability, capacity, talent, competence **2 size**, bore, diameter, gauge, measure

call v **1 name**, describe, identify, entitle, label **2 shout**, cry out, scream, yell, call out **3 request**, summon, call on, invite, beckon **4 phone**, telephone, give a call, call up, phone up **5 visit**, call on, pay a visit, drop in, stop off **6 arrange**, convene, set up, organize, assemble ■ n **1 noise**, shout, cry, sound **2 song**, cry, birdsong **3 phone call**, telephone call, ring, buzz (infml), bell (infml) **4 visit**, stop, halt **5 demand**, request, plea, appeal, bid **6 judgment**, verdict, decision, assessment, ruling

call a halt v **end**, stop, halt, bring to an end, close Opposite: start up

call a spade a spade v **be direct**, speak plainly, be blunt, speak your mind, lay it on the line (infml) Opposite: prevaricate

call attention to v make known, draw attention to, expose, publicize, highlight Opposite: conceal

call by v visit, stop by, come round, drop in, call in

call down v invoke, invite, request, appeal, pray

caller n visitor, guest, friend

call for v 1 order, demand, claim, clamour, request 2 need, require, justify, necessitate, cry out for

call forth v produce, cause, inspire, provoke, stimulate

calligraphy n handwriting, hand, writing, script, print

call in v 1 visit, drop in, drop by, come by, come round 2 phone, call, ring, telephone, give a call 3 recall, call back, pull in, take off the market 4 summon, invite in, call for, send for, bring in

calling n vocation, profession, occupation, business, line

call into question v query, question, dispute, challenge, doubt Opposite: accept

callisthenics n exercise system, keep fit, exercises, aerobics, step aerobics

call it a day v stop, finish, end, give up, break off Opposite: start up

call names v insult, abuse, hurl insults at, taunt, bait Opposite: compliment

call off v cancel, stop, abandon, suspend, shelve

call on v 1 ask, request, appeal to, urge, entreat 2 visit, drop in on, go to see, look up, look in on

callous adj heartless, unfeeling, cold-hearted, hardhearted, uncaring Opposite: warm-hearted

calloused adj hard, hardened, hard-skinned, rough, rough-skinned Opposite: soft

callousness n heartlessness, insensitivity, cruelty, coldness, cold-heartedness Opposite: warm-heartedness

call out v 1 summon, send for, call for, get, page 2 shout out, exclaim, call, yell, make a noise

call out for v demand, clamour, be in dire need of, require, request

callow adj inexperienced, immature, naive, adolescent, green Opposite: mature

call together v summon, convene, gather, collect, round up Opposite: disperse

call to mind v evoke, recall, recollect, suggest, call up Opposite: forget

call up v phone, call, telephone, give a call, give a ring

call-up n conscription, mobilization, recruitment, enlistment, muster Opposite: demobilization

call upon v 1 ask, request, appeal to, urge, entreat 2 make demands on, demand, require, use, call for

callus n hard skin, corn, bump, lump, nodule

calm adj tranquil, peaceful, still, cool, composed Opposite: agitated ■ n peace, tranquillity, quietness, stillness, calmness Opposite: turbulence ■ v pacify, calm down, quieten, quieten down, soothe Opposite: excite

calmative adj calming, soothing, pacifying, quietening, relaxing Opposite: disturbing

calm down v settle down, relax, soothe, quieten, quieten down Opposite: agitate

calming adj soothing, reassuring, comforting, restful, sedative Opposite: disturbing

calmness n serenity, tranquillity, quietness, stillness, peace Opposite: restlessness

calumny (fml) n slander, defamation, denigration, libel, lies

calve v give birth, drop, reproduce, produce

camaraderie n friendship, companionship, solidarity, company, comradeship Opposite: enmity

cameo n character part, cameo role, appearance, role, part

camera-shy adj reclusive, retiring, reserved, private, aloof Opposite: extrovert

camouflage n concealment, disguise, smoke screen, cover-up, façade ■ v disguise, mask, hide, conceal, obscure

camp n 1 site, campsite, encampment, base camp, holiday camp 2 group, faction, followers, clique, supporters ■ v go camping, camp out, sleep out

campaign n movement, crusade, operation, drive, fight ■ v 1 fight, work, push, struggle, battle 2 electioneer, canvass, drum up support, solicit votes, stump

campaigner n activist, crusader, fighter, supporter, champion

campsite n encampment, camping area, campground (US)

campus n grounds, precincts, site, property, estate

canal n 1 waterway, channel, seaway 2 duct, tube, passage, vessel

canalize (fml) v direct, channel, funnel, guide, convey Opposite: diffuse

cancel v 1 call off, stop, abandon, withdraw, scratch Opposite: arrange 2 annul, revoke, stop, rescind, repeal Opposite: reinstate

cancel out v nullify, efface, undo, contradict, neutralize

cancer n 1 growth, tumour, malignancy, disease, melanoma 2 evil, blight, scourge, canker, plague

cancerous adj 1 tumorous, malignant, carcinomatous, carcinogenic, oncogenic Opposite: benign 2 harmful, pernicious, malign, malignant, noxious Opposite: beneficent

candelabrum *n* **candleholder**, candlestick, chandelier, lamp holder, lamp

candid *adj* **honest**, frank, open, truthful, sincere *Opposite*: guarded

candidacy *n* **application**, contention, entry, submission, candidature

candidate *n* **applicant**, contender, entrant, runner, aspirant

---

COMPARE AND CONTRAST CORE MEANING: somebody who is seeking to be chosen for something or to win something
candidate somebody who is being considered for a job, grant, or prize, standing for election, or taking part in an examination; **contender** a competitor, especially somebody who has a good chance of winning; **contestant** somebody who takes part in a contest or competitive event; **aspirant** somebody aspiring to distinction or advancement; **applicant** somebody who has formally applied to be a candidate for something; **entrant** somebody who enters a competition or examination.

---

candidness *n* **honesty**, frankness, openness, truthfulness, bluntness

candied *adj* **crystallized**, glacé, preserved, sugar-coated, sugared

candle *n* **taper**, nightlight, rush light, rush candle, rush

candlelight *n* **dim light**, soft light, low light, glow, glimmer

candlestick *n* **candleholder**, candelabra, chandelier, sconce

can-do *(infml) adj* **positive**, willing, confident, ambitious, eager *Opposite*: diffident

candour *n* **frankness**, forthrightness, directness, candidness, outspokenness

candy-striped *adj* **striped**, stripy, pink-and-white striped

cane *n* **1 bamboo**, wicker, rattan **2 stick**, walking stick, staff ■ *v* **beat**, thrash, strike, hit, punish

canine *adj* **doggy**, dog-like, doggish ■ *n* **dog**, mongrel, cur, hound, pooch *(infml)*

WORD BANK
❑ **types of canine** coyote, dingo, dog, fox, jackal, wolf

---

canister *n* **container**, can, tin, flask, cylinder

canker *n* **evil**, cancer, scourge, blight, plague

canned *adj* **1 tinned**, preserved, conserved *Opposite*: fresh **2 prerecorded**, recorded, taped, reproduced, artificial *Opposite*: live

canniness *n* **shrewdness**, astuteness, sharpness, smartness, cleverness

cannonade *n* **barrage**, bombardment, hail, onslaught, pounding

cannonball *n* **projectile**, missile, ball, stone, grapeshot

canny *adj* **shrewd**, astute, sharp, smart, clever

canonical *adj* **official**, recognized, acknowledged, established, undisputed *Opposite*: apocryphal

canonization *n* **1 making into a saint**, beatification, sanctification, consecration, hallowing **2 idolization**, glorification, adoration, worship, adulation

canonize *v* **1 make into a saint**, beatify, sanctify, consecrate, hallow **2 idolize**, glorify, adore, worship, venerate

canoodle *(infml) v* **carry on**, kiss and cuddle, pet, smooch *(infml)*, snog *(slang)*

canopy *n* **1 awning**, cover, covering, shelter, blind **2 top**, crown, roof, covering, cover

cant *n* **1 clichés**, platitudes, banalities, commonplaces, triteness **2 hypocrisy**, insincerity, false piety, humbug, lip service *Opposite*: sincerity **3 jargon**, slang, argot, patois, vernacular

cantankerous *adj* **grumpy**, irascible, irritable, crusty, quarrelsome

canter *n* **trot**, run, gallop, jog, sprint ■ *v* **run**, gallop, trot, jog, sprint

cantilever *n* **beam**, plank, girder

canto *n* **stanza**, verse, strophe, section, division

canton *n* **region**, district, area, borough, constituency

canvas *n* **1 painting**, oil painting, picture, old master, work of art **2 background**, backdrop, setting, context, scene

canvass *v* **1 campaign**, electioneer, drum up support, solicit votes, stump **2 test**, research, investigate, survey, poll

canvasser *n* **1 campaigner**, supporter, party worker **2 researcher**, investigator, examiner, pollster

canyon *n* **ravine**, gully, gorge, chasm, rift

cap *n* **1 cover**, lid, top, stopper, plug **2 restraint**, limit, control, restriction, check ■ *v* **1 cover**, top, stop, plug, stopper **2 surpass**, top, improve, better, outdo **3 limit**, regulate, control, restrain, restrict

capability *n* **ability**, capacity, competence, skill, resources. *See* COMPARE AND CONTRAST *at* **ability**.

capable *adj* **1 accomplished**, talented, skilled, gifted, clever *Opposite*: inept **2 able**, competent, proficient, efficient, qualified *Opposite*: incapable

capacious *adj* **roomy**, spacious, large, ample, big *Opposite*: cramped

capacity *n* **1 ability**, capability, skill, talent, aptitude **2 volume**, space, room, size, dimensions **3 role**, position, responsibility, function, office. *See* COMPARE AND CONTRAST *at* **ability**.

cape *n* **promontory**, peninsula, headland, outcrop, point

caper *n* **escapade**, adventure, jaunt, lark, antics ■ *v* **frolic**, cavort, jump, leap, dance

capital *n* **1 assets**, resources, funds, wealth, money **2 centre**, headquarters, hub

capitalist n entrepreneur, financier, industrialist, businessperson, investor ▪ adj **entrepreneurial**, industrial, consumerist, consumer, commercial

capitalize v fund, finance, raise funding for, provide backing for

capitalize on v make the most of, maximize, take advantage of, use, utilize

capitation n 1 tax, poll tax, levy, toll, duty 2 fee, charge, payment, amount

capitulate v surrender, submit, yield, succumb, give way Opposite: resist. See COMPARE AND CONTRAST at yield.

capitulation n surrender, submission, defeat, retreat Opposite: resistance

caprice n whim, impulse, quirk, fancy, fad

capricious adj unpredictable, changeable, variable, impulsive, whimsical Opposite: predictable

capsize v overturn, turn over, roll over, keel over, turn turtle Opposite: right

capsule n 1 pod, container, case, casing, shell 2 pill, tablet, lozenge

captain n head, skipper, leader, chief, boss ▪ v lead, skipper, manage, take charge, head

caption n slogan, subtitle, title, description, legend

captious adj 1 critical, pedantic, trivial, petty, nitpicking 2 confusing, misleading, devious, bewildering, disingenuous Opposite: clear

captivate v attract, charm, enchant, fascinate, entrance Opposite: repel

captivated adj enchanted, fascinated, charmed, entranced, spellbound Opposite: repulsed

captivating adj charming, attractive, appealing, fascinating, charismatic

captive n prisoner, detainee, internee, prisoner of war, hostage Opposite: escapee ▪ adj 1 imprisoned, in prison, locked up, enslaved, confined Opposite: free 2 attentive, intent, fascinated, spellbound, rapt

captivity n imprisonment, custody, detention, confinement, internment Opposite: freedom

captor n abductor, imprisoner, kidnapper, hostage taker, jailer Opposite: liberator

capture v 1 take, seize, apprehend, arrest, pick up Opposite: release 2 imprison, detain, arrest, confine, take into custody Opposite: liberate 3 encapsulate, summarize, sum up, portray, describe 4 secure, attain, gain, acquire, obtain Opposite: lose 5 catch, seize, grab hold of, trap, ensnare ▪ n imprisonment, detention, arrest, seizure, apprehension Opposite: release

capture your imagination v fascinate, excite, inspire, interest, enchant

car n 1 automobile, motor (slang), wheels (slang), auto (US) 2 railway carriage, cabin, carriage, coach, compartment

WORD BANK
❑ **types of car** all-terrain vehicle, compact, convertible, coupé, dragster, estate car, four-by-four, hatchback, hot rod (slang), limo, limousine, minivan, off-roader (infml), people carrier, racing car, runabout, saloon, sports car, stock car, stretch limo, three-wheeler

carafe n flask, decanter, bottle

caramelize v burn, heat, scorch, brown, broil (US)

carapace n case, shell, covering, sheath, outside

caravan n convoy, group, procession, parade, motorcade

carbohydrate n biological compound, simple carbohydrate, complex carbohydrate, starch, sugar

carbon copy n replica, duplicate, copy, facsimile, exact likeness Opposite: original

carbuncle n spot, blemish, boil, pustule, abscess

carcass n corpse, remains, cadaver, body, skeleton

carcinogenic adj cancer-causing, oncogenic, hazardous, toxic, poisonous

card n 1 greetings card, birthday card, anniversary card, postcard, picture postcard 2 pass, identification card, membership card, business card, calling card

cardboard n board, paper, card, packaging, packing ▪ adj insubstantial, unconvincing, phoney, plastic, wooden Opposite: substantial

card-carrying adj official, paid-up, bona fide, listed, genuine

cardinal adj basic, fundamental, key, prime, serious Opposite: secondary

cardiovascular adj circulatory, cardiac, vascular, heart, blood

cardsharp n cheat, gambler, hustler, swindler, pro (infml)

care v be concerned, be interested, feel a concern, take an interest Opposite: disregard ▪ n 1 upkeep, maintenance, repair, overhaul Opposite: neglect 2 attention, caution, precaution, carefulness, watchfulness 3 worry, concern, anxiety, trouble, unease Opposite: nonchalance 4 treatment, provision, support, attention Opposite: ill-treatment 5 supervision, guardianship, protection, custody, oversight (fml). See COMPARE AND CONTRAST at worry.

careen v swerve, sway, weave, lurch, swing

career n vocation, job, occupation, profession, calling ▪ v rush, race, hurry, dash, speed

careerism n determination, single-mindedness, motivation, commitment, drive

careerist n professional, achiever, high flier, go-getter (infml) ▪ adj single-minded, determined, motivated, focused, professional

care for v 1 **like**, feel affection for, love, have a soft spot for, cherish Opposite: dislike 2 **look after**, take care of, tend, supervise, oversee Opposite: ignore 3 (fml) **want**, desire, like to have, fancy, appreciate

carefree adj **untroubled**, happy-go-lucky, cheery, relaxed, cheerful Opposite: troubled

carefreeness n **lightheartedness**, cheerfulness, cheeriness, happiness, jollity Opposite: anxiety

careful adj 1 **cautious**, wary, vigilant, watchful, alert Opposite: reckless 2 **thorough**, meticulous, painstaking, particular, conscientious Opposite: careless 3 **prudent**, sensible, judicious, cautious, well thought-out Opposite: foolish 4 **protective**, sympathetic, sensitive, gentle, tender Opposite: rough

COMPARE AND CONTRAST CORE MEANING: exercising care and attention in doing something **careful** a wide-ranging term, suggesting attention to detail and implying cautiousness in avoiding errors or inaccuracies; **conscientious** showing great care, attention, and industriousness in carrying out a task; **scrupulous** having or showing careful regard for what is morally right; **thorough** extremely careful and accurate; **meticulous** extremely careful and precise; **painstaking** involving or showing great care and attention to detail; **assiduous** undeviating in effort and care; **punctilious** very careful about the conventions of correct behaviour and etiquette; **finicky** concentrating too much on unimportant details; **fussy** tending to worry over details or trivial things.

carefulness n 1 **caution**, care, wariness, watchfulness, alertness Opposite: rashness 2 **attention to detail**, thoroughness, precision, care, meticulousness Opposite: carelessness 3 **prudence**, caution, judiciousness, wisdom, judgment Opposite: foolishness

careless adj 1 **slapdash**, happy-go-lucky, devil-may-care, casual, slipshod Opposite: careful 2 **uncaring**, thoughtless, offhand, inconsiderate, unthinking Opposite: considerate

carelessness n **sloppiness**, inattentiveness, inaccuracy, imprecision, negligence Opposite: care

caress v **stroke**, touch, pat, embrace, cuddle ■ n **touch**, stroke, pat, embrace, hug

caretaker n **concierge**, warden, porter, custodian, janitor

careworn adj **haggard**, drawn, beleaguered, worried, burdened Opposite: carefree

cargo n **load**, freight, consignment, shipment, goods

caricature n 1 **cartoon**, picture, drawing, sketch 2 **travesty**, misrepresentation, false impression, distortion, falsification

caricaturist n **artist**, cartoonist, humorist, satirist

caring adj **kind**, thoughtful, gentle, helpful, considerate Opposite: uncaring

carnage n **killing**, bloodshed, slaughter, massacre, bloodbath

carnal (fml) adj **physical**, fleshy, sensual, sexual Opposite: spiritual

carnival n **festival**, celebration, street party, fair, fete

carnivore n **flesh-eater**, meat-eater, predator, scavenger, insectivore

carnivorous adj **flesh-eating**, meat-eating, predatory, scavenging, insectivorous

carol n **song**, hymn, chant, chorus

carouse (literary) v **revel**, celebrate, drink, get drunk, raise the roof

carousel n 1 **merry-go-round**, roundabout, ride 2 **container**, cassette, cartridge, drum, magazine

carp v **complain**, grumble, find fault, nag, go on. See COMPARE AND CONTRAST at **complain**.

carpentry n **joinery**, woodwork, turning, carving, cabinetmaking

carpet n 1 **rug**, mat, runner, fitted carpet, carpet tiles 2 **covering**, layer, blanket, mass, spread ■ v (infml) **reprimand**, tell off, rebuke, criticize, blast (infml)

carpeting n **floor covering**, flooring, matting, carpet tiles

carping adj **critical**, nitpicking, complaining, dissatisfied, discontented ■ n **complaining**, nitpicking, faultfinding, dissatisfaction, whining

carport n **garage**, lean-to, shelter, porch, parking space

carriage n 1 **horse-drawn carriage**, coach, horse and carriage 2 (fml) **bearing**, posture, deportment, air, presence 3 **transportation**, delivery, carrying, haulage, conveyance

carriageway n **lane**, lane of traffic, roadway, road, thoroughfare

carried adj **approved**, accepted, passed, agreed, supported Opposite: rejected

carrier n 1 **transporter**, haulier, delivery service, carter, shipper 2 **shopping bag**, carrier bag, shopper

carrion n **flesh**, meat, tissue

carrot n **incentive**, inducement, bribe, bait, lure

carroty adj **orange**, red, auburn, ginger

carry v 1 **take**, bear, hold, support, clutch 2 **transmit**, transport, convey, transfer, bring 3 **contain**, include, involve, incorporate, hold 4 **have in stock**, stock, store, keep, supply 5 **approve**, accept, pass, agree, vote for

carrying adj **loud**, resonant, resounding, booming, ringing Opposite: quiet

carrying-on (infml) n **pranks**, goings-on (infml), doings (infml), high jinks (infml)

carry off v 1 **take away**, take off, remove, steal, abduct Opposite: bring back 2 **succeed**, manage, accomplish, achieve, do Opposite: fail

carry on v 1 **continue**, keep, keep on, keep at, go on *Opposite*: stop 2 **complain**, grumble, carp, nag, go on

carry-on *(infml)* n **fuss**, commotion, hullabaloo, palaver, to-do *(infml)*

carry out v **do**, perform, complete, achieve, succeed *Opposite*: neglect. *See* COMPARE AND CONTRAST *at* **accomplish, perform**.

carryout n **takeaway**, fast food, takeout *(US)*

carry over v **postpone**, defer, leave, reschedule, put back *Opposite*: expedite *(fml)*

carryover n **leftover**, legacy, inheritance, residue, remnant

carry the can *(infml)* v **take the blame**, accept responsibility, accept the blame, shoulder the blame, be the scapegoat

carsick adj **sick**, nauseous, ill, unwell, poorly *(infml)*

cart n 1 **farm cart**, wagon, dray, tumbrel, wain *(literary)* 2 **handcart**, barrow, wheelbarrow, trolley, pushcart *(US)* ■ v **carry**, lug, heave, haul, drag

carte blanche n **free hand**, free rein, blank cheque, complete freedom, full authority

cartel n **interest group**, lobby, alliance, association, union

cart off v **remove**, drag off, take away, haul off, carry off

carton n **box**, cardboard box, container, pack, sachet

cartoon n 1 **animation**, animated film, animated movie 2 **drawing**, caricature, picture, comic strip

cartoonist n **artist**, animator, caricaturist, satirist, humorist

cartridge n **container**, holder, casing, unit, cassette

cartwheel v **turn**, somersault, go head over heels, roll, flip

carve v 1 **engrave**, inscribe, etch, cut, notch 2 **slice**, pare, cut in slices, whittle, cut up

carve out v **create**, make, establish, build, set up

carve up *(infml)* v **divide**, allocate, share out, apportion, distribute

carve-up *(infml)* n **division**, allocation, distribution, partitioning, share-out

carving n 1 **artefact**, model, statue, statuette, figure 2 **cutting**, engraving, etching, sculpting, fashioning

Casanova n **libertine**, Don Juan, gigolo, Romeo, ladies' man

cascade n **waterfall**, chute, cataract, force, falls ■ v **flow**, pour, fall, drop, gush

case n 1 **circumstance**, situation, instance, event, occasion 2 **instance**, item, example, illustration, paradigm 3 **job**, project, commission, assignment, task 4 **court case**, legal action, lawsuit, suit, indictment 5 **argument**, reason, defence, justification, rationale 6 **container**, holder, box, casing, cover 7 **suit**case, overnight case, weekend case, briefcase, attaché case

casebook n **record**, log, diary, journal, notebook

case-hardened adj **unsympathetic**, unfeeling, hard, hardened, toughened *Opposite*: sensitive

cash n **money**, hard cash, ready money, coins, currency

cashier n 1 **treasurer**, banker, bursar 2 **bank clerk**, clerk, teller, official, assistant ■ v **dismiss**, expel, drum out, court martial, boot out *(infml)*

cash in v **redeem**, trade in, sell, realize, bank

cash-in-hand adj **in cash**, cash, no questions asked, unofficially, off the record

cash in on v **take advantage of**, benefit from, do well from, exploit, make the most of

cashpoint n **cash dispenser**, cash machine, till, ATM, hole-in-the-wall *(infml)*

casing n **covering**, case, outside, exterior, skin

casino n **gaming club**, gambling den, nightclub, gaming house

cask n **barrel**, tub, drum, butt, vat

casserole n **cooking pot**, deep dish, covered dish, oven dish

cassette n 1 **cartridge**, tape, videotape 2 **case**, cartridge, holder, container, cover

cast v 1 **throw**, hurl, fling, toss, pitch 2 **produce**, generate, create, give rise to, engender 3 **mould**, form, shape, model ■ n **company**, troupe, dramatis personae, actors, players. *See* COMPARE AND CONTRAST *at* **throw**.

cast about *see* **cast around**

cast an eye over v **scan**, skim, skim through, dip into, pick through *Opposite*: study

cast around v **search**, look for, seek, seek out, hunt out

cast a shadow over v **spoil**, hang over, darken, loom over, eclipse *Opposite*: brighten

cast aside v **get rid of**, put aside, throw away, toss aside, forget *Opposite*: keep

cast away v **give up**, throw away, cast off, discard, jettison *Opposite*: keep

castaway n **shipwrecked person**, survivor, exile

cast down v **discourage**, dishearten, depress, demoralize, disparage *Opposite*: cheer up

caste n **class**, social group, standing, background, social order

castigate *(fml)* v **criticize**, reprimand, chastise, scold, rebuke *Opposite*: praise. *See* COMPARE AND CONTRAST *at* **criticize**.

castigation *(fml)* n **criticism**, rebuke, reprimand, scolding, telling-off *(infml)* *Opposite*: praise

casting n 1 **forming**, manufacture, moulding 2 **object**, artefact, cast, moulding 3 **audition**, selection, screen test, interview, test

cast-iron adj 1 **inflexible**, rigid, unchangeable, immutable, fixed *Opposite*: flexible

2 guaranteed, definite, firm, sure, watertight

castle n **fortress**, fort, citadel, stronghold, bastion

castles in Spain see castles in the air

castles in the air n **flight of fancy**, fancy, dream, fantasy, notion Opposite: reality

cast off v **discard**, get rid of, reject, dispose of, abandon

castoff n **reject**, discard, hand-me-down, throwaway Opposite: purchase ■ adj **discarded**, rejected, unwanted, old, secondhand Opposite: new

cast out v **throw out**, evict, oust, eject, reject Opposite: install

castrate v **neuter**, sterilize, geld, spay

casual adj **1 unpremeditated**, unplanned, chance, unintentional, unintended Opposite: premeditated **2 seasonal**, informal, temporary, occasional, periodic Opposite: permanent **3 informal**, nonchalant, relaxed, calm, cool Opposite: formal **4 indifferent**, careless, offhand, blasé, cavalier Opposite: careful

casualness n **1 informality**, nonchalance, calmness, coolness, insouciance Opposite: formality **2 indifference**, carelessness, negligence, disregard, heedlessness Opposite: care

casualty n **injured person**, wounded person, dead person, fatality, loss

casuistry n **sophistry**, unsound reasoning, rationalization, excuse, twisting the facts

cat n **feline**, mouser, tom, big cat

WORD BANK
❑ **types of cat** Abyssinian, American shorthair, Birman, bobcat, British shorthair, Burmese cat, cheetah, Egyptian mau, jaguar, leopard, lion, lynx, Manx cat, Norwegian forest cat, ocelot, panther, Persian cat, puma, Siamese cat, tabby, tiger, tortoiseshell, wildcat

cataclysm n **catastrophe**, disaster, upheaval, calamity, debacle

cataclysmic adj **catastrophic**, disastrous, calamitous, dreadful, tragic

catacomb n **1 underground cemetery**, crypt, vault, tomb, mausoleum **2 tunnel network**, underground passage, labyrinth, warren, maze

catalogue n **1 list**, directory, index, file, register **2 set**, collection, list, litany, series ■ v **1 classify**, assemble, compile, arrange, categorize **2 enter**, record, insert, include, document **3 itemize**, list, enumerate, document, detail

cataloguing n **classification**, categorization, logging, sorting, taking down

catalyst n **promoter**, facilitator, stimulus, spur, incentive

cat-and-mouse adj **cruel**, sadistic, heartless, merciless, callous

catapult v **hurtle**, shoot, throw, project, propel

cataract n **waterfall**, cascade, falls, chute, torrent

catarrh n **mucus**, phlegm, discharge

catastrophe n **disaster**, calamity, upheaval, devastation, ruin Opposite: good fortune

catastrophic adj **disastrous**, shattering, calamitous, appalling, terrible Opposite: fortunate

catatonic adj **1 inert**, rigid, unresponsive, withdrawn, impassive **2** (infml) **unconscious**, asleep, comatose, inert, stupefied

catcall n **jeer**, hiss, boo, whistle, shout ■ v **taunt**, jeer, hiss, boo, shout

catch v **1 hold**, hold on to, gather, grasp, receive **2 grasp**, grab, hold, take, clutch Opposite: drop **3 snare**, ensnare, entrap, hook, net **4 capture**, arrest, apprehend, take prisoner, detain Opposite: release **5 contract**, become infected with, fall victim to, pick up, go down with **6 find**, discover, surprise, spot, notice **7 hear**, perceive, notice, become aware of, grasp **8 hit**, strike, knock, bump, bump into **9 stick**, get trapped in, snag, cling, entangle Opposite: free ■ n **1 fastening**, fastener, clasp, hook, latch **2** (infml) **snag**, drawback, problem, difficulty, hitch

catch-22 n **predicament**, no-win situation, dilemma, quandary, impossibility

catch a glimpse of v **spot**, notice, spy, glimpse, catch sight of

catchall adj **general**, universal, all-encompassing, wide-ranging, blanket

catch hold of v **take**, grab, clutch, seize, grasp

catching adj **infectious**, contagious, communicable, transmittable, easily spread

catch napping v **surprise**, take by surprise, catch out, catch on the hop, catch in the act

catch on (infml) v **1 become popular**, rise in popularity, become fashionable, be in fashion, take off (infml) Opposite: flop (infml) **2 understand**, be with you, follow you, comprehend, grasp Opposite: misunderstand

catch out (infml) v **expose**, trip up, wrong-foot, discover, catch

catch phrase n **catchword**, motto, slogan, tag

catch sight of v **spot**, notice, spy, glimpse, catch a glimpse of Opposite: miss

catch unawares v **surprise**, startle, creep up on, give somebody a shock, ambush

catch up v **draw near**, draw level, get closer to, become equal, pull alongside Opposite: fall behind

catchword n **catch phrase**, byword, motto, watchword, slogan

catchy adj **memorable**, attractive, likable, beguiling, haunting Opposite: forgettable

catechesis see catechism

catechism n **1 religious instruction**, religious education, religious teaching **2 dogma**, party line, mantra, article of faith, tenet **3 exam-**

ination, questioning, interrogation, dialectic

categorical *adj* **definite**, clear-cut, uncompromising, unconditional, unqualified *Opposite*: tentative

categorization *n* **1 classification**, cataloguing, labelling, tagging, grouping **2 category**, class, group, set, grouping

categorize *v* **classify**, sort out, catalogue, label, tag

category *n* **class**, sort, grouping, type, kind. *See* COMPARE AND CONTRAST *at* **type**.

cater *v* **provide**, supply, outfit, accommodate, gratify

caterwaul *v* **howl**, yowl, wail, squall, squeal

catgut *n* **cord**, line, thread, string, filament

catharsis *n* **release**, liberation, freeing up, cleansing, purification

cathartic *adj* **1 therapeutic**, liberating, releasing, emotional, intense **2 purifying**, cleansing, excretory, expulsive, purgative *(fml)*

catheter *n* **tube**, line, drip, drain, feed

catholic *adj* **wide-ranging**, broad, wide-reaching, all-embracing, extensive *Opposite*: narrow

catkin *n* **flower**, tassel, ament

catnap *n* **nap**, doze, rest, siesta, power nap ■ *v* **nap**, nod off, doze, sleep, catch some z's *(infml)*

cat-o'-nine-tails *n* **whip**, scourge, lash, birch

cattiness *n* **spitefulness**, nastiness, meanness, maliciousness, malevolence *Opposite*: kindness

cattle *n* **cows**, oxen, bulls, bullocks, steers

catty *adj* **spiteful**, nasty, venomous, mean, malicious *Opposite*: kind

catwalk *n* **1 stage**, walkway, runway, ramp, gangplank **2 bridge**, footbridge, walkway

caucus *n* **1 conclave**, assembly, committee, conference, convention **2 faction**, bloc, alliance, league, union

cauldron *n* **pan**, container, cooking pot, pot, vat

caulk *v* **seal**, waterproof, fill, block, plug

causal *adj* **fundamental**, underlying, contributory, contributing, connecting

causality *n* **cause and effect**, connection, interconnection, connectedness, causation

causation *n* **action**, connection, interconnection, relationship, causality

causative *adj* **causal**, instrumental, contributing, contributory, connective

cause *n* **reason**, grounds, source, root, origin *Opposite*: effect ■ *v* **make happen**, bring about, produce, set off, instigate *Opposite*: impede

cause offence *v* **be offensive**, shock, hurt somebody's feelings, offend, put somebody's nose out of joint

causeway *n* **walkway**, ramp, boardwalk, road, dike

caustic *adj* **1 corrosive**, acid, acidic, corroding, burning **2 sarcastic**, scathing, mordant, astringent, cutting *Opposite*: gentle. *See* COMPARE AND CONTRAST *at* **sarcastic**.

cauterize *v* **seal**, close, burn, sear, treat

caution *n* **1 carefulness**, thoughtfulness, attentiveness, attention, risk avoidance *Opposite*: carelessness **2 warning**, alert, notification, ultimatum, caveat ■ *v* **warn**, alert, notify, signal, give notice

cautionary *adj* **warning**, deterrent, admonitory, advisory, instructive

cautious *adj* **careful**, vigilant, guarded, wary, circumspect *Opposite*: reckless

---

COMPARE AND CONTRAST CORE MEANING: attentive to risk or danger

cautious aware of potential risk and behaving accordingly; **careful** taking reasonable care to avoid risks; **chary** cautiously reluctant to act; **circumspect** taking into consideration all possible circumstances and consequences before acting; **prudent** showing good judgment or shrewdness; **vigilant** alert and conscious of possible dangers; **wary** showing watchfulness or suspicion; **guarded** reluctant to share information with others; **cagey** *(infml)* secretive and guarded.

---

cautiousness *n* **caution**, carefulness, thoughtfulness, attentiveness, wariness *Opposite*: carelessness

cavalcade *n* **procession**, parade, column, line, convoy

cavalier *adj* **careless**, offhand, inconsiderate, high-handed, arrogant *Opposite*: polite

cavalry *n* **mounted troops**, horse regiment, horse soldiers

cave *n* **cavern**, grotto, hollow, pothole, fissure

caveat *n* **warning**, caution, admonition, qualification, stipulation

cave in *v* **1 collapse**, subside, fall in, fall down, topple **2 yield**, give in, surrender, give way, admit defeat *Opposite*: withstand

cave-in *n* **1 collapse**, fall, drop, slide, demolition **2 capitulation**, yielding, collapse, surrender, concession

cavern *n* **cave**, grotto, pothole, hollow, cavity

cavernous *adj* **1 vast**, spacious, deep, yawning, gaping *Opposite*: cramped **2 hollow**, echoing, resounding, sounding, resonant

caviar *n* **roe**, eggs, spawn

cavil *v* **quibble**, split hairs, be picky, complain, carp *Opposite*: accept

cavity *n* **hole**, space, hollow, crater, void

cavort *v* **frolic**, prance, caper, gambol, romp

caw *v* **call**, cry, croak, squawk

CB *n* **radio**, shortwave radio, citizens' band, telecommunication, walkie-talkie

CD player *n* **stereo**, personal stereo, hi-fi, CD, sound system

cease *v* **stop**, finish, end, come to an end, come to a close *Opposite*: start

ceasefire n truce, armistice, cessation of hostilities, end of hostilities, break in fighting

ceaseless adj unending, continual, constant, incessant, perpetual Opposite: sporadic

cease trading v go out of business, shut down, go bankrupt, close, fold

cede (fml) v yield, concede, give up, give, let go Opposite: resist

ceilidh n dance, barn dance, singsong, party, celebration

ceiling n limit, threshold, cutoff point, cap, check

celebrate v 1 enjoy yourself, have fun, have a good time, make merry, revel Opposite: lament 2 commemorate, observe, mark, keep, remember 3 praise, acclaim, commend, applaud, hail

celebrated adj famous, renowned, eminent, distinguished, illustrious Opposite: unknown

celebration n 1 festivity, party, festival, gala, fete Opposite: lamentation 2 commemoration, remembrance, observance, salutation, memorial

celebratory adj festive, triumphant, special, congratulatory, commemorative

celebrity n 1 superstar, star, personality, name, figure Opposite: nobody 2 fame, renown, notoriety, superstardom, prominence Opposite: obscurity

celestial adj 1 heavenly, holy, spiritual, godly, otherworldly 2 cosmic, astronomical, planetary, galactic, solar

celibate adj chaste, abstinent, self-restrained

cell n 1 lockup, prison cell, jail cell 2 group, sect, faction, cabal, caucus

cellulite n fat, fatty deposits, orange-peel skin, lumpiness, dimpling

cement n glue, adhesive, paste, epoxy resin ■ v 1 join, stick, fix, glue, fasten together Opposite: separate 2 strengthen, reinforce, make stronger, prop up, fortify Opposite: undermine

cemetery n graveyard, burial ground, churchyard, garden of remembrance, mausoleum

cenotaph n war memorial, monument, memorial

censor v 1 edit, cut, remove, expurgate, bowdlerize 2 stifle, gag, repress, suppress, control

censored adj cut, expurgated, bowdlerized, changed, amended Opposite: complete

censorious adj disapproving, critical, severe, stern, hypercritical Opposite: approving

censorship n restriction, control, cutting, editing, bowdlerization

censure n criticism, disapproval, condemnation, denunciation, deprecation Opposite: approval ■ v criticize, fault, reprimand, condemn, reproach Opposite: praise. See COMPARE AND CONTRAST at criticize, disapprove.

census n count, survey, poll, registration, tally

centenary n anniversary, birthday, centennial (US)

central adj 1 middle, mid, inner, innermost Opposite: outer 2 vital, dominant, essential, fundamental, chief Opposite: unimportant

centralism n control, concentration, monopolism, authoritarianism, centralization

centrality n importance, significance, criticality, supremacy, uniqueness Opposite: irrelevance

centralization n unification, integration, concentration, control, domination Opposite: decentralization

centralize v unify, consolidate, integrate, compact, concentrate Opposite: decentralize

centre n 1 midpoint, middle, halfway point, focus, focal point Opposite: edge 2 filling, inside, middle, core, layer Opposite: coating 3 heart, city centre, downtown (US) 4 complex, facility, development, building 5 focus, heart, core, bottom, root Opposite: periphery 6 cluster, concentration, focus, magnet, hotbed 7 middle ground, consensus, majority, middle course, happy medium Opposite: extreme 8 axis, pivot, pivotal point, fulcrum ■ v 1 align, position, arrange, balance, adjust 2 focus on, turn on, concentrate on, home in on, target Opposite: ignore

centrepiece n centre of attention, focus, key feature, flagship, jewel in the crown

centrist adj middle-of-the-road, moderate, mainstream, reasonable, uncontroversial Opposite: extreme

century n period, era, time, span, epoch

CEO n chief executive officer, boss, chief, head, manager

ceramic adj earthenware, clay, pottery, terracotta, ironstone china

cereal n breakfast cereal, porridge, grits (US)

WORD BANK

❑ **types of cereal** barley, maize, millet, oat, rice, rye, sorghum, wheat

---

cerebral adj intellectual, rational, highbrow, logical, analytical Opposite: intuitive

ceremonial adj ritual, traditional, ritualistic, formal, official Opposite: informal ■ n rite, ritual, ceremony, pomp, pageantry

ceremonious adj formal, solemn, dignified, grand, majestic Opposite: informal

ceremony n rite, ritual, formality, formal procedure, service

cert (infml) n certainty, foregone conclusion, cast-iron certainty, fait accompli, dead cert (infml)

certain adj 1 sure, convinced, positive, confident, firm Opposite: unsure 2 some, a number of, a few, several, selected Opposite: all

3 reliable, dependable, undeniable, guaranteed, clear *Opposite*: uncertain **4 particular**, specific, individual, precise, specified

certainly *adv* **1 surely**, positively, definitely, without doubt, undoubtedly *Opposite*: possibly **2 indeed**, absolutely, definitely, of course, emphatically

certainty *n* **1 foregone conclusion**, safe bet, cast-iron certainty, inevitability, cert *(infml)* **2 confidence**, conviction, faith, belief, assurance *Opposite*: uncertainty

certificate *n* **document**, licence, diploma, credential, documentation

certification *n* **guarantee**, warranty, documentation, authorization, accreditation

certified *adj* **official**, licensed, approved, authorized, accredited

certify *v* **confirm**, state, verify, endorse, attest

certitude *n* **conviction**, certainty, sureness, assurance, confidence *Opposite*: uncertainty

cessation *n* **end**, termination, close, stop, ending *Opposite*: start

cesspit *n* **tank**, pit, sewer, drain, gutter

chafe *v* **1 rub**, scrape, irritate, scratch, abrade **2 annoy**, bother, provoke, vex, irritate

chaff *v* **tease**, mock, make fun of, josh *(infml)*, pull somebody's leg *(infml)* ■ *n* **joking**, banter, repartee, teasing

chagrin *n* **humiliation**, mortification, vexation, irritation, disappointment

chain *n* **1 cable**, hawser, line **2 restraint**, shackle, manacle, fetter **3 group**, string, franchise, series **4 sequence**, series, string, succession, procession ■ *v* **bind**, manacle, shackle, lock up, restrain *Opposite*: unchain

chain reaction *n* **series of events**, train of events, knock-on effect, domino effect

chair *n* **chairperson**, presiding officer, president, head, leader ■ *v* **preside**, take the chair, lead, direct, oversee

chairperson *n* **presiding officer**, president, chair, head, leader

chalk *v* **write**, draw, mark, doodle, scribble

chalk up *v* **score**, mark up, gain, win, obtain

chalky *adj* **1 crumbly**, dry, powdery, fine, dusty **2 white**, pale, pallid, ghostly, deathly

challenge *v* **1 dare**, defy, throw down the gauntlet to, test **2 confront**, defy, brave, face up to *Opposite*: shirk **3 dispute**, contest, object to, question, argue *Opposite*: agree ■ *n* **test**, trial, task, contest, encounter

challenger *n* **contestant**, contender, competitor, opponent, pretender

challenging *adj* **1 demanding**, taxing, testing, difficult, tough *Opposite*: easy **2 stimulating**, thought-provoking, interesting, inspiring, exciting *Opposite*: routine **3 defiant**, disobedient, rebellious, insolent, impudent *Opposite*: compliant

chamber *n* **1 hall**, assembly room, meeting room, boardroom, legislative chamber **2 cavity**, hollow, compartment, space, slot

chamberlain *n* **official**, attendant, courtier, servant, manager

chameleon *n* **changeable person**, butterfly, trimmer, dilettante

champ *v* **chew**, munch, grind, masticate, chomp *(infml)* ■ *n (infml)* **champion**, winner, victor, title holder

champion *n* **1 winner**, victor, title holder, champ *(infml)* **2 defender**, supporter, backer, campaigner, advocate ■ *v* **defend**, support, back, campaign for, fight for

championship *n* **finals**, contest, challenge, title fight, battle

chance *n* **1 possibility**, probability, likelihood, prospect, risk **2 opening**, opportunity, option, occasion **3 gamble**, risk, hazard, venture, stake **4 luck**, fate, fortune, destiny, good fortune ■ *v* **risk**, hazard, gamble, try, attempt ■ *adj* **accidental**, coincidental, casual, fortuitous, unintended *Opposite*: planned

chancellor *n* **president**, leader, head of state, premier, prime minister

chance occurrence *n* **coincidence**, accident, twist of fate, quirk, happenstance

chance on *v* **stumble on**, happen on, strike on, hit on, come across

chancy *adj* **risky**, hazardous, dangerous, perilous, uncertain *Opposite*: safe

change *n* **1 alteration**, modification, variation, transformation, conversion **2 coins**, cash, loose change ■ *v* **1 alter**, modify, vary, adjust, amend **2 exchange**, replace, convert, substitute, transform

---

COMPARE AND CONTRAST CORE MEANING: make or become different

change make or become different in any way; **alter** change, especially to change an aspect of something; **modify** make minor changes or alterations, especially in order to improve something; **convert** change something from one form or function to another; **vary** change within a range of possibilities, or in connection with something else, with a suggestion of instability; **shift** change from one position or direction to another; **transform** make a radical change into a different form; **transmute** change into another form.

---

changeability *n* **1 unpredictability**, unsettledness, variableness, variability, irregularity *Opposite*: constancy **2 indecisiveness**, fickleness, unpredictability, flightiness, volatility *Opposite*: steadiness

changeable *adj* **variable**, unsettled, unpredictable, unreliable, unstable *Opposite*: constant

changed *adj* **altered**, different, transformed, reformed, rehabilitated *Opposite*: unchanged

change direction *v* **1 veer off**, swerve, turn,

bend, curve round **2 start afresh**, change course, change tack, pick up *(infml) Opposite*: deteriorate ■ *n* **improvement**, progress, development, upswing, upturn *Opposite*: deterioration

change for the better *v* **improve**, get better, look up, progress, pick up *(infml) Opposite*: deteriorate ■ *n* **improvement**, progress, development, upswing, upturn *Opposite*: deterioration

changeless *adj* **unchanging**, consistent, fixed, immutable, permanent *Opposite*: changing

changelessness *n* **permanence**, consistency, immutability, unalterability, invariability

change of heart *n* **about-turn**, volte-face, second thoughts, rethink, change of attitude

change over *v* **switch**, substitute, convert, transfer, change round

changeover *n* **move**, reversal, conversion, alteration, substitution

change round *v* **1 alter**, modify, amend, adjust, juggle *Opposite*: leave alone **2 exchange**, substitute, change, change over, reverse

change your mind *v* **have second thoughts**, come round, relent, back out, pull out

changing *adj* **altering**, varying, shifting, moving, fluctuating *Opposite*: changeless

channel *n* **1 canal**, conduit, waterway, strait, passage **2 ditch**, dike, groove, drain, trench **3 means**, outlet, conduit, path, way **4 station**, network, frequency ■ *v* **direct**, control, feed, conduct, route

chant *n* **song**, hymn, mantra, tune, carol ■ *v* **sing**, recite, repeat, vocalize, intone *(fml)*

chaos *n* **disorder**, confusion, bedlam, anarchy, pandemonium *Opposite*: order

chaotic *adj* **disordered**, muddled, confused, messy, untidy *Opposite*: orderly

chap *(infml)* *n* **guy** *(infml)*, bloke, gentleman, man, fella *(infml)*

chapel *n* **sanctuary**, oratory, chantry, side chapel, side altar

chaperon *n* **supervisor**, attendant, overseer, governess, escort ■ *v* **supervise**, oversee, escort, watch, look after

chaperone *see* **chaperon**

chaplain *n* **minister**, vicar, priest, pastor, rabbi

chapter *n* **1 section**, part, subdivision, division, segment **2 period**, episode, stage, phase, interval

char *v* **burn**, singe, scorch, carbonize, sear ■ *n* **domestic**, help, cleaner

character *n* **1 nature**, quality, temperament, personality, disposition **2 charm**, appeal, atmosphere, attractiveness, charisma **3 integrity**, strength, uprightness, rectitude, honour **4 eccentric**, personality, oddity, original **5 person**, individual, creature, sort, type

character assassination *n* **defamation**, slander, libel, affront, verbal abuse

character-building *adj* **challenging**, demanding, instructive, educative, empowering

characterful *adj* **individual**, distinctive, strong, upright, inspiring

characteristic *n* **trait**, feature, quality, attribute, point ■ *adj* **typical**, distinguishing, distinctive, individual, representative *Opposite*: uncharacteristic

characteristically *adv* **typically**, usually, normally, naturally, routinely *Opposite*: unusually

characterization *n* **description**, classification, account, portrayal, depiction

characterize *v* **1 describe**, portray, illustrate, depict, brand **2 typify**, set apart, distinguish, differentiate, exemplify

characterless *adj* **bland**, dull, soulless, uninteresting, insipid *Opposite*: interesting

characterlessness *n* **dullness**, soullessness, insipidness

charade *n* **pretence**, farce, sham, fake, travesty

charge *v* **1 accuse**, indict, allege, arraign, incriminate *Opposite*: absolve **2 attack**, rush, storm, assault, assail *Opposite*: retreat **3 rush**, dash, hurtle, stampede, hurry ■ *n* **1 cost**, price, expense, rate, amount **2 custody**, care, responsibility, control, trust **3 accusation**, indictment, allegation, arraignment, imputation **4 assault**, attack, advance, offensive, onslaught **5 order**, command, direction, instruction, injunction

chargeable *adj* **1 punishable**, criminal, indictable, imputable, actionable **2 taxable**, liable to tax, declarable, dutiable

charged *adj* **emotional**, exciting, electric, thrilling, stimulating *Opposite*: calm

chariness *n* **wariness**, caution, circumspection

charisma *n* **charm**, personality, appeal, magnetism, allure

charismatic *adj* **magnetic**, compelling, alluring, fascinating, captivating

charitable *adj* **1 generous**, giving, benevolent, altruistic, helpful *Opposite*: uncharitable **2 considerate**, understanding, accepting, sympathetic, tolerant *Opposite*: unforgiving

charity *n* **1 aid**, contributions, gifts, donations, help **2 aid organization**, charitable trust, charitable foundation, aid agency **3 kindness**, tolerance, humanity, compassion, generosity *Opposite*: unkindness

charlatan *n* **fake**, fraud, swindler, quack, counterfeit

charlatanism *n* **quackery**, trickery, pretence

charm *n* **1 attraction**, appeal, allure, charisma, magic **2 ornament**, keepsake, trinket, talisman, amulet ■ *v* **captivate**, enchant, beguile, hypnotize, mesmerize

charmed *adj* **1 lucky**, fortunate, enchanted, magical, fairy-tale *Opposite*: unlucky **2 delighted**, pleased, enchanted, thrilled, glad

charmer *n* **smooth talker**, enchanter, fascinator, smooth operator, ladies' man

charming adj **delightful**, amiable, attractive, appealing, charismatic Opposite: unattractive

charmless adj **unattractive**, unappealing, uninteresting, unsympathetic, unprepossessing Opposite: charming

chart n **diagram**, plan, graph, table, graphic representation ■ v **register**, record, project, plot, chronicle

charter n **contract**, deed, agreement, licence, grant ■ v **rent**, lease, hire, take on, commission

chary adj **wary**, cautious, suspicious, guarded, careful Opposite: reckless. See COMPARE AND CONTRAST at **cautious**.

chase v 1 **pursue**, run after, hunt, hound, follow 2 **race**, dash, rush, career, hurtle ■ n **pursuit**, hunt, hunting. See COMPARE AND CONTRAST at **follow**.

chaser n **pursuer**, follower, hunter, shadow, tail

chasm n **crater**, gulf, gap, abyss, gorge

chaste adj **innocent**, uncorrupted, virtuous, unblemished, unsullied Opposite: impure

chasten v 1 **subdue**, suppress, restrain, tame, humble 2 **punish**, reprimand, discipline, censure, chastise

chasteness n **pureness**, innocence, purity, virtuousness, faithfulness Opposite: immorality

chastise v **reprimand**, discipline, censure, punish, rebuke Opposite: praise

chastisement (fml) n **reprimand**, discipline, punishment, rebuke, scolding Opposite: praise

chastity n **purity**, innocence, virtue

chat v **talk**, converse, gossip, gab (infml), natter (infml) ■ n **conversation**, one-to-one, heart-to-heart, tête-à-tête, talk

chattels n **possessions**, belongings, things, stuff, personal property

chatter v **babble**, rattle on, prattle, rant, gossip Opposite: shut up ■ n **talk**, gossip, chat, conversation Opposite: silence

chatterbox (infml) n **talker**, gossip, chatterer, tattler, blabbermouth (infml)

chatterer see **chatterbox**

chattily adv **conversationally**, informally, casually, easily

chattiness n **garrulity**, loquacity, communicativeness, informality

chatty adj 1 **talkative**, garrulous, loquacious, forthcoming, gossipy Opposite: quiet 2 **informal**, friendly, personal, casual, relaxed Opposite: formal. See COMPARE AND CONTRAST at **talkative**.

chat up (infml) v **flirt**, lead on, pick up (infml), hit on (US slang)

chauffeur n **driver**, motorist, valet

chauvinism n **bigotry**, sexism, prejudice, narrow-mindedness, dogmatism

chauvinist n **bigot**, sexist, racist, homophobe, jingoist

chauvinistic adj **bigoted**, prejudiced, opinionated, dogmatic, narrow-minded

cheap adj 1 **inexpensive**, economy, low-priced, economical, discounted Opposite: expensive 2 **shoddy**, inferior, second-rate, substandard, common Opposite: superior 3 **contemptible**, despicable, shameful, low, base Opposite: admirable 4 **tightfisted**, miserly, mean, parsimonious, stingy (infml) Opposite: generous

cheapen v **denigrate**, demean, belittle, lower, degrade Opposite: elevate

cheaply adv **inexpensively**, economically, reasonably, modestly, competitively Opposite: expensively

cheapness n 1 **tawdriness**, inferiority, shoddiness, tackiness (infml) Opposite: tastefulness 2 **tightfistedness**, miserliness, meanness, parsimony, stinginess (infml) Opposite: generosity

cheapskate (infml) n **miser**, skinflint, killjoy, scrooge (infml), meanie (infml)

cheat v **deceive**, trick, con, swindle, defraud ■ n **double-dealer**, rogue, cheater, charlatan, trickster

cheating adj **duplicitous**, double-dealing, dishonest, unprincipled, deceitful Opposite: honest ■ n **dishonesty**, deceit, deception, duplicity, chicanery

check v 1 **test**, test out, prove, try, try out 2 **make sure**, ensure, verify, confirm, certify 3 **limit**, hold in, stop, impede, hold up Opposite: expedite (fml) ■ n 1 **inspection**, examination, test, assessment, trial 2 **safeguard**, curb, restraint, buttress, catch

checked adj **check**, patterned, crisscross, plaid, squared

checker n **inspector**, examiner, assessor, regulator, overseer

check in v **register**, sign in, sign up, sign on, enrol

check-in n **registration desk**, registration, reception desk, reception area, reception

checklist n **list**, specification, agenda, worksheet, spec (infml)

checkmate n **check**, mate, end, ending, victory Opposite: stalemate

check out v 1 **leave**, depart, vacate, sign out, exit 2 **inspect**, investigate, look into, explore, examine

check over v **look over**, reread, go through, go over, examine

checkpoint n **barrier**, turnpike, frontier, border, spot check

checkup n **examination**, medical, inspection, health check, once-over (infml)

check up on v **keep an eye on**, check on, spy on, watch, monitor Opposite: ignore

cheek (infml) n **nerve**, gall, impertinence, effrontery, audacity Opposite: humility

cheek by jowl *adv* **side by side**, on top of one another, close together, together, close

cheekiness *(infml)* *n* **impudence**, disrespect, effrontery, insolence, irreverence *Opposite*: respect

cheek-to-cheek *adv* **close**, close up, close together, together, intimately

cheeky *adj* **impudent**, audacious, bold, defiant, insolent *Opposite*: respectful

cheep *v* **chirp**, peep, tweet, twitter, sing

cheeping *n* **chirping**, tweeting, peeping, twittering, singing

cheer *n* **cheerfulness**, optimism, merriment, joyfulness, liveliness *Opposite*: gloom ■ *v* **applaud**, shout, root for, hail, praise *Opposite*: boo

cheerful *adj* **happy**, cheery, bright, smiling, joyful *Opposite*: sad

cheerfully *adv* **1 happily**, optimistically, merrily, joyfully, gleefully *Opposite*: sadly **2 gladly**, willingly, readily, with pleasure *Opposite*: grudgingly

cheerfulness *n* **happiness**, joyfulness, cheer, cheeriness, merriment *Opposite*: sadness

cheeriness *n* **cheerfulness**, happiness, joyfulness, liveliness, joviality *Opposite*: gloominess

cheering *adj* **heartening**, encouraging, positive, uplifting, promising *Opposite*: discouraging

cheerless *adj* **gloomy**, depressing, dismal, miserable, sad *Opposite*: bright

cheerlessness *n* **bleakness**, dreariness, gloominess, soullessness, wintriness *Opposite*: brightness

cheer on *v* **encourage**, root for, support, laud, egg on *Opposite*: discourage

cheer up *v* **perk up**, brighten, brighten up, liven, enliven *Opposite*: depress

cheery *adj* **happy**, joyful, smiling, cheerful, merry *Opposite*: gloomy

cheeseparing *adj* **mean**, miserly, mean-spirited, avaricious, tightfisted *Opposite*: generous ■ *n* **meanness**, miserliness, stinginess, mean-spiritedness, avarice *Opposite*: generosity

cheesy *(infml)* *adj* **tasteless**, cheap, tawdry, unpleasant, tacky *(infml)* *Opposite*: stylish

chemical *n* **substance**, element, compound

chemistry *n* **interaction**, attraction, understanding, empathy, sympathy

cheque *n* **payment**, form, order, draft, authorization

chequered *adj* **1 check**, checked, squared, patterned, crisscross **2 uneven**, inconsistent, up-and-down, variable, changeable *Opposite*: even

cherish *v* **treasure**, appreciate, relish, esteem, revere *Opposite*: neglect

cherished *adj* **valued**, precious, beloved, esteemed, appreciated *Opposite*: neglected

cherry-pick *v* **select**, choose, pick, handpick, pick and choose

cherub *n* **angel**, cupid, amoretto, putto

cherubic *adj* **1 holy**, divine, spiritual, saintly, blessed **2 angelic**, cute, innocent, attractive, lovable

chest *n* **upper body**, torso, rib cage, ribs, trunk

chestnut *(infml)* *n* **joke**, tired joke, anecdote, cliché, old favourite *(infml)*

chesty *adj* **wheezy**, rasping, phlegmy, congested

chevron *n* **V-shape**, V, stripe, badge, insignia

chew *v* **masticate**, chew up, gnaw, grind, crush

chew over *v* **meditate**, ponder, think about, ruminate on, consider

chew up *v* **1 damage**, crush, rip up, injure, destroy **2 chew**, grind, masticate, champ, munch

chewy *adj* **rubbery**, stringy, fibrous, gristly, leathery *Opposite*: tender

chic *adj* **stylish**, fashionable, well-dressed, attractive, smart *Opposite*: unfashionable ■ *n* **style**, elegance, panache, stylishness, modishness

chicanery *n* **deception**, trickery, verbiage, nonsense, underhandedness

chichi *adj* **contrived**, recherché, self-conscious, pretentious, affected

chicken *(infml)* *adj* **cowardly**, frightened, scared, reluctant, fearful *Opposite*: brave. *See* COMPARE AND CONTRAST *at* cowardly.

chicken feed *(infml)* *n* **small change**, next to nothing, small beer *(infml)*, small potatoes *(infml)*

chief *n* **ruler**, head, boss, captain, commander ■ *adj* **principal**, main, topmost, leading, foremost

chief executive *n* **CEO**, boss, leader, president

chiefly *adv* **primarily**, mainly, essentially, mostly, predominantly

chieftain *n* **tribal chief**, ruler, chief, overlord, lord

chieftainship *n* **leadership**, command, authority, rank, status

chilblain *n* **swelling**, inflammation, blister

child *n* **1 youngster**, young person, adolescent, youth, juvenile **2 offspring**, descendant, spawn, scion, son **3 baby**, infant, newborn, toddler, nursling **4 result**, product, outcome, creation. *See* COMPARE AND CONTRAST *at* youth.

childbearing *n* **reproduction**, pregnancy, gestation, childbirth, motherhood

childbirth *n* **giving birth**, delivery, labour, contractions, childbearing

childhood *n* **babyhood**, infancy, youth, upbringing, infanthood *Opposite*: adulthood

childish *adj* **1 immature**, irresponsible, silly, foolish, infantile *Opposite*: mature **2 child-like**, juvenile, innocent, ingenuous

childishness n **immaturity**, silliness, irresponsibility, pettiness *Opposite*: maturity

childlike adj **innocent**, naive, candid, unsophisticated, trusting *Opposite*: jaded

childproof adj **safe**, tamper-proof, secure

child's play n **piece of cake** (infml), picnic (infml), doddle (infml), walkover (infml), pushover (infml)

chill n **1 coldness**, coolness, low temperature, chilliness, nippiness *Opposite*: warmth **2 sudden fear**, anxiety, apprehension, wariness, shudder **3 gloom**, depression, pall, shadow **4 unfriendliness**, aloofness, detachment, coolness, coldness *Opposite*: warmth ■ adj **1 biting**, freezing, wintry, nippy, chilly **2 remote**, uninvolved, aloof, indifferent, chilly *Opposite*: warm ■ v **1 cool**, freeze, make colder, put on ice, refrigerate *Opposite*: warm **2 discourage**, depress, deter, dispirit, cast a shadow over *Opposite*: encourage

chilled adj **ice-cold**, freezing, frozen, refrigerated, cooled *Opposite*: hot

chilliness n **1 coolness**, coldness, frostiness, nippiness, low temperature *Opposite*: warmth **2 unfriendliness**, aloofness, stiffness, detachment, formality *Opposite*: friendliness

chilling adj **frightening**, alarming, unsettling, distressing, terrifying *Opposite*: reassuring

chill out (infml) v **1 calm down**, take it easy, stop worrying, lighten up (infml) **2 relax**, loosen up, rest, unwind, kick back (infml)

chilly adj **1 cold**, cool, nippy, chill, frosty *Opposite*: warm **2 frigid**, formal, supercilious, aloof, detached *Opposite*: welcoming

chime n **clang**, ding, ding-dong, sound, peal ■ v **strike**, peal, ring, sound, ring out

chime in v **butt in**, interrupt, interject, voice your opinion, speak up **2 agree**, be compatible, be consistent, be in line, be in agreement *Opposite*: contradict

chimera n **fantasy**, fancy, whimsy, illusion, mirage

chimerical adj **imaginary**, fantastical, illusory, unreal

chimes n **bells**, glockenspiel, carillon

china n **1 tableware**, crockery, porcelain **2 collectibles**, ornaments, figurines

chink n **narrow opening**, crack, crevice, slit, opening

chink in somebody's armour n **weak spot**, weakness, Achilles heel, flaw, failing

chinless adj **weak**, ineffectual, irresolute, inept, spineless *Opposite*: bold

chintzy (infml) adj **fussy**, quaint, cottagey, over-elaborate, busy

chinwag (infml) n **chat**, gossip, talk, conversation, natter (infml) ■ v **chatter**, talk, chat, gossip, converse

chip n **1 piece**, bit, crumb, flake, chunk **2 mark**, damage, imperfection, flaw, blemish

3 token, counter, marker, playing piece, poker chip ■ v **1 break off**, fragment, hew, flake, pare **2 damage**, disfigure, mark, blemish, notch

chip away at v **weaken**, wear away, eat into, erode, diminish

chip in (infml) v **1 contribute**, help, participate, collaborate, take part **2 chime in**, butt in, interject, voice your opinion, say what you think

chip off the old block (infml) n **younger version**, mirror image, clone, living image, replica

chipper (infml) adj **1 cheerful**, high-spirited, lively, exuberant, good-humoured *Opposite*: glum **2 smartly dressed**, well-dressed, neat, trim, smart *Opposite*: scruffy

chipping n **chip**, piece, fragment, bit, shaving

chippings n **stones**, pebbles, gravel, shingle

chirpy (infml) adj **lively**, vivacious, alert, bright, effervescent *Opposite*: gloomy

chiselled adj **regular**, clean-cut, strong, delicate, fine-boned

chit (dated) n **receipt**, bill, tally, account, tab (US infml)

chitchat (infml) v **talk**, discuss, have a chat, gossip, babble ■ n **chatter**, gossip, chat, conversation, talk

chivalrous adj **1 courteous**, mannerly, gracious, polite, civil *Opposite*: discourteous **2 gallant**, courtly, brave, valiant, loyal *Opposite*: cowardly

chivalry n **1 courtesy**, courteousness, politeness, attentiveness, gentility *Opposite*: discourteousness **2 gallantry**, courtliness, loyalty, courage, bravery *Opposite*: cowardice

chivvy v **urge**, pester, harass, badger, pressure *Opposite*: discourage

chock n **wedge**, block, doorstop, chuck ■ v **brace**, steady, fix, block, stop *Opposite*: release

chock-a-block (infml) see **chock-full**

chock-full (infml) adj **packed**, jammed, crammed, full, crowded *Opposite*: empty

chocolate-box adj **pretty**, romanticized, twee, picturesque, soft-focus

choice n **1 selection**, choosing, pick, election, adoption **2 range**, selection, variety, set, group ■ adj **excellent**, high-quality, superior, special, prime

choke v **1 strangle**, throttle, stifle, suffocate, asphyxiate **2 obstruct**, clog, block, stop up, congest *Opposite*: free up (infml) **3 fill with emotion**, freeze up, weep, well up

choke back v **suppress**, hold back, fight back, stifle, repress *Opposite*: let out

choked (infml) adj **upset**, emotional, overcome, dismayed, disappointed

cholesterol n **fat**, saturated fat, saturated fatty acid, fatty acid, lipid

chomp (infml) v chew, munch, crunch, eat, masticate Opposite: nibble

choose v 1 select, pick, take, pick out, single out Opposite: reject 2 decide, want, prefer, desire, wish

choosy (infml) adj particular, hard to please, fussy, picky, fastidious Opposite: indifferent

chop v cut, slice, hack, axe, lop

chop down v shorten, decrease, cut back, cut down, lop off

choppy adj rough, stormy, wild, tempestuous Opposite: calm

chops (infml) n jaw, mouth, gob (slang)

chop up v cut up, chop, cut into pieces, slice, cube

choral adj vocal, harmonic, sung

chord n harmony, triad, arpeggio, major chord, minor chord

chore n 1 task, job, errand, odd job, assignment 2 routine, bore, hard work, imposition, inconvenience

choreograph v 1 create, compose, design, arrange, put together 2 manoeuvre, plan, direct, strategize, manage

choreography n 1 composition, dance routine, step design, step sequence, step arrangement 2 manoeuvring, direction, management, manipulation, strategy

chorister n singer, musician, treble

chortle n laugh, chuckle, gurgle, giggle, snigger ■ v chuckle, laugh, gurgle, giggle, snigger

chorus n refrain, chorus line, response, repeat, repetition ■ v speak at once, speak together, speak in unison

chosen adj selected, select, elect, preferred, special

christen v 1 baptize, name, bless, sanctify 2 name, nickname, call, dub, label 3 (infml) launch, inaugurate, debut

christening n 1 baptism, ceremony, rite, naming 2 (infml) launch, first use, inauguration, debut

Christian name n first name, given name, forename, personal name, praenomen

chronic adj 1 long-lasting, lingering, persistent, continuing, enduring Opposite: fleeting 2 habitual, persistent, ingrained, inveterate, established Opposite: occasional

chronicle n record, history, account, annals, journal ■ v report, record, recount, relate, narrate

chronological adj sequential, consecutive, linear

chronology n 1 sequence of events, order of events, time line, timetable, train of events 2 account, record, chronicle, narrative, history

chubbiness n plumpness, roundness, fleshiness, stoutness, fatness Opposite: slenderness

chubby adj plump, rotund, round, fleshy, stout Opposite: slender

chuck v 1 (infml) throw, hurl, toss, fling, pitch 2 (infml) get rid of, throw out, throw away, dispose of, discard Opposite: keep 3 (infml) quit, resign, walk off, leave, walk out 4 tap, pat lightly, pat, tickle ■ n chock, wedge, block, clamp. See COMPARE AND CONTRAST at throw.

chuck down (infml) v rain hard, teem, pour, rain cats and dogs (infml), bucket (infml) Opposite: drizzle

chuck in (infml) v give up, pack it in, throw in the towel (infml), call it quits (infml)

chuckle v laugh, laugh to yourself, chortle, laugh inwardly, giggle ■ n laughter, chortle, inward laughter, giggle, snigger

chuck out (infml) v get rid of, throw out, throw away, dispose of, discard

chuffed (infml) adj pleased, content, satisfied, happy, delighted

chug (infml) v continue, keep going, keep at it, persist, plug away (infml) Opposite: stop

chum (infml) n friend, associate, acquaintance, mate, pal (infml) Opposite: stranger

chumminess (infml) n friendliness, sociability, closeness, intimacy, matiness

chummy (infml) adj friendly, sociable, congenial, matey, close

chunk n piece, hunk, mass, lump, portion

chunky adj 1 lumpy, bumpy, coarse, rough Opposite: smooth 2 solid, heavy, hefty, weighty, substantial Opposite: lightweight 3 (infml) stocky, stout, fat, chubby, plump Opposite: slender

churchgoer n worshipper, congregant, communicant

churchyard n graveyard, burial ground, cemetery, necropolis, boneyard (infml)

churlish adj 1 rude, boorish, coarse, truculent, crass Opposite: polite 2 ill-natured, irritable, unpleasant, grumpy, sullen Opposite: pleasant

churn v mix, roil, agitate, shake, whip

churn out v mass-produce, manufacture, turn out, roll out, issue

chute n 1 shaft, slide, channel, sluice, raceway 2 waterfall, cascade, force, cataract, descent

chutzpah (infml) n 1 boldness, self-confidence, self-assurance, assertiveness, bravado 2 gall, boldness, nerve, impudence, cheek (infml)

C in C n commander in chief, field marshal, generalissimo, commander, leader

cinch n 1 (infml) child's play, piece of cake (infml), breeze (infml), walk in the park (infml), doddle (infml) 2 (infml) sure bet, certainty, dead certainty, sure thing (infml) 3 girth, restraint, belt, strap ■ v 1 bind, restrain, fix, tighten, gird (literary) 2 (dated infml) guarantee, assure, insure, settle, make certain

cinders n embers, ashes, residue, coals

cinema n films, movies, motion pictures, film, pictures (infml dated)

cinematic adj filmic, photographic, movie-like, filmmaking, moviemaking

cinematography n photography, shooting, film making, picture making, movie making

cipher n 1 code, secret message, symbols, cryptograph, encryption 2 nobody, non-entity, nothing, zero

circa prep approximately, about, around, roughly, round about Opposite: exactly

circadian adj daily, 24-hour, 24-hourly, diurnal, day by day

circle n 1 ring, loop, round, sphere, disc 2 group, gang, set, clique, crowd ■ v 1 go around, orbit, fly round, fly in a circle, circumnavigate 2 encircle, surround, ring, enclose, bound

circlet n band, coronet, tiara, diadem, crown

circuit n 1 route, track, trail, path 2 tour, trip, journey, route, round

circuitous adj 1 indirect, winding, meandering, roundabout, twisting Opposite: direct 2 complicated, convoluted, discursive, tangential, long-winded Opposite: straightforward

circuitry n electrical system, electric circuit, circuit board, motherboard, printed circuit

circular adj spherical, rounded, globular, round ■ n leaflet, flier, pamphlet, advertisement, handbill

circularity n indirectness, circuitousness, obliqueness, roundaboutness, convolutedness Opposite: directness

circulate v 1 flow, move, travel, pass 2 pass around, distribute, hand out, give out, send out Opposite: withhold 3 (infml) mingle, socialize, mix, meet people, be sociable

circulation n 1 flow, movement, passage, motion, rotation 2 exchange, flow, transmission, spread, dissemination 3 distribution, readership, sales

circumference n perimeter, boundary, bounds, limits, edge Opposite: middle

circumlocution n periphrasis, indirectness, roundaboutness, long-windedness, convolutedness Opposite: directness

circumlocutory adj periphrastic, indirect, meandering, roundabout, long-winded Opposite: direct

circumnavigate v sail round, orbit, circle, travel round, go around

circumscribe (fml) v limit, restrict, define, demarcate, mark out

circumscription (fml) n restriction, limit, limitation, constraint, restraint Opposite: freedom

circumspect adj cautious, prudent, careful, guarded, wary Opposite: reckless. See COMPARE AND CONTRAST at cautious.

circumspection n care, carefulness, caution, cautiousness, judiciousness Opposite: rashness

circumstance n 1 condition, situation, state of affairs, status quo, context 2 (fml) event, occurrence, incident, instance, happening

circumstantial adj incidental, contingent, indirect, inferred, conditional Opposite: concrete

circumvent v avoid, get round, evade, skirt, dodge

circumvention n avoidance, evasion, escape, sidestepping, dodging

circus (infml) n show, festival, spectacle, extravaganza, event

cirque n corrie, cwm, combe, hollow, valley

cistern n water tank, storage tank, tank, reservoir, container

citadel n fortress, stronghold, bastion, fort, castle

citation n quote, quotation, mention, reference, excerpt

cite (fml) v quote, mention, refer to, allude to

citified adj oversophisticated, sophisticated, cosmopolitan, slick, suave Opposite: countrified

citizen n inhabitant, national, resident, legal resident, voter

citizenry (fml) n people, population, community, public, electorate

citizenship n 1 nationality, residency, right of abode 2 social responsibility, public spirit, social conscience, civic duty

city n metropolis, municipality, conurbation, capital, town Opposite: hamlet ■ adj urban, metropolitan, town, municipal

COMPARE AND CONTRAST CORE MEANING: an urban area where a large number of people live **city** originally a town having a cathedral or having such a status conferred on it by the Crown; in the United States, a large municipal centre governed under a charter granted by the state; in Canada, a large municipal unit incorporated by the provincial government, but now used generally for any large urban area; **conurbation** an urban region formed or enlarged by the merging of adjacent cities and towns through expansion or development; **metropolis** a large or important city, sometimes the capital of a country, state, or region; **town** a populated area smaller than a city and larger than a village; **municipality** a city, town, or area with some degree of self-government.

city dweller n urbanite, citizen, burgher, townie (infml)

civic adj public, municipal, local, community, town Opposite: private

civil adj 1 public, political, municipal, civic, civilian 2 courteous, polite, respectful, well-mannered, accommodating Opposite: rude

civilian n noncombatant, private citizen, citizen, member of the public, neutral Opposite: martial

civility n **politeness**, courtesy, good manners, courteousness, respect *Opposite*: rudeness

civilization n **1 society**, nation, culture, empire, polity **2 development**, evolution, progress, cultivation, refinement

civilize v **enlighten**, educate, cultivate, improve, advance

civilized adj **cultured**, educated, refined, enlightened, polite *Opposite*: barbarous

civilizing adj **humanizing**, taming, educating, cultivating, refining

civil liberties *see* civil rights

civilly adv **politely**, respectfully, courteously, amicably, considerately *Opposite*: rudely

civil rights n **human rights**, rights, constitutional rights, privileges, civil liberties

civil servant n **public servant**, government employee, bureaucrat, official, administrator

clack v **snap**, click, clap, bang, rap

clad adj **dressed**, clothed, covered, attired *(fml)*, arrayed *(literary)*

cladding n **covering**, layer, facing, casing, shell

claim v **1 maintain**, assert, say, state, declare **2 ask for**, call for, demand, apply for, request *Opposite*: deny **3 receive**, obtain, take, pick up, retrieve ■ n **1 assertion**, statement, accusation, declaration, allegation **2 demand**, request, application, petition, call **3 right**, entitlement, prerogative, privilege, due

claimant n **applicant**, plaintiff, pretender, petitioner, appellant

clairvoyance n **psychic power**, telepathy, prophecy, fortune-telling, palm reading

clairvoyant n **psychic**, mystic, spiritualist, telepathist, diviner ■ adj **intuitive**, psychic, telepathic, second-sighted, perceptive

clamber v **climb**, scramble, crawl, scale

clamminess n **1 dampness**, wetness, moistness, dankness, sliminess *Opposite*: dryness **2 humidity**, mugginess, closeness, heat, airlessness *Opposite*: freshness

clammy adj **1 damp**, wet, moist, dank, slimy *Opposite*: dry **2 humid**, muggy, close, sticky, sweaty *Opposite*: fresh

clamorous adj **noisy**, vociferous, loud, rowdy, boisterous *Opposite*: tranquil

clamour v **1 shout**, scream, yell, cry, screech *Opposite*: whisper **2 demand**, insist, appeal, cry out, bay ■ n **1 appeal**, demand, call, request, cry **2 uproar**, hullabaloo, din, commotion, noise

clamp v **fasten**, hold, compress, fix, brace

clamp down v **shut down**, take tough action, come down hard, restrict, limit *Opposite*: relent

clampdown n **crackdown**, restriction, curb, suppression, embargo

clam up *(infml)* v **stop talking**, choke, refuse to speak, remain silent, be unforthcoming *Opposite*: rattle on

clan n **1 tribe**, family, relations, relatives, kinsfolk **2** *(infml)* **clique**, fraternity, band, coterie, set

clandestine adj **secret**, underground, covert, concealed, stealthy *Opposite*: open. *See* COMPARE AND CONTRAST *at* secret.

clang v **clank**, sound, toll, ring, reverberate

clanger *(infml)* n **blunder**, mistake, error, slip-up *(infml)*, boob *(infml)*

clank n **clang**, clink, clatter, clash, bang

clannish adj **cliquey**, cliquish, unfriendly, unsociable, aloof *Opposite*: open

clap v **applaud**, give a standing ovation, put your hands together, give a round of applause, acclaim *Opposite*: boo ■ n **slap**, pat, tap, thrust, thwack

clapped-out *(infml)* adj **worn out**, dilapidated, rundown, decrepit, falling apart

clapping n **applause**, appreciation, ovation, acclamation, acclaim *Opposite*: jeering

claptrap *(infml)* n **nonsense**, rubbish, humbug, drivel, hogwash *(infml)* *Opposite*: sense

clarification n **explanation**, amplification, illumination, clearing up, explaining *Opposite*: obfuscation

clarify v **1 elucidate**, make clear, explain, clear up, illuminate *Opposite*: confuse **2 refine**, purify, cleanse, filter, process *Opposite*: cloud

clarity n **clearness**, lucidity, simplicity, precision, intelligibility *Opposite*: ambiguity

clash v **1 fight**, conflict, disagree, quarrel, collide *Opposite*: agree **2 clatter**, clank, clang, crash, bang **3 conflict**, mismatch, jar, contravene *Opposite*: match ■ n **1 clank**, clatter, clang, crash, bang **2 battle**, encounter, brush, fight, skirmish **3 disagreement**, quarrel, argument, row, fight. *See* COMPARE AND CONTRAST *at* fight.

clashing adj **inharmonious**, conflicting, jarring, incompatible, nonmatching *Opposite*: compatible

clasp v **grasp**, hold, clutch, embrace, hug *Opposite*: release ■ n **fastener**, hook, catch, hook and eye, popper

class n **1 group**, set, tutorial group, tutor group, course group **2 lesson**, period, session, lecture, seminar **3 category**, type, sort, kind, genre **4 refinement**, sophistication, elegance, style, flair *Opposite*: tackiness *(infml)* ■ v **categorize**, classify, rank, assign, group. *See* COMPARE AND CONTRAST *at* type.

class-conscious adj **snobbish**, classist, elitist, toffee-nosed *(infml)*, stuck-up *(infml)* *Opposite*: egalitarian

classic adj **1 timeless**, immortal, unforgettable, memorable, abiding **2 definitive**, typical, characteristic, standard, model *Opposite*: atypical **3 simple**, stylish, elegant, chic, understated ■ n **masterpiece**, landmark, benchmark, model, masterwork

classical adj **traditional**, conventional, orthodox, usual, typical *Opposite*: modern

classification n 1 **organization**, cataloguing, arrangement, sorting, ordering 2 **category**, class, group, grouping, set

classified adj **secret**, confidential, top secret, off the record, hush-hush *(infml)* *Opposite*: open

classify v **categorize**, order, organize, pigeonhole, catalogue

classiness *(infml)* n **refinement**, sophistication, elegance, stylishness, class *Opposite*: tackiness *(infml)*

classless adj **egalitarian**, meritocratic, equal, open, free *Opposite*: class-conscious

classmate n **fellow student**, fellow pupil, contemporary, peer

classroom n **schoolroom**, teaching space, seminar room, tutorial room, lecture theatre

classy *(infml)* adj **refined**, sophisticated, elegant, stylish, chic *Opposite*: tacky *(infml)*

clatter v **rattle**, bang, clang, smash, clank

clause n **section**, article, part, division, passage

claustrophobic adj **enclosed**, confining, oppressive, suffocating, stifling

claw v **scrape**, scratch, scrabble, tear, graze ■ n **talon**, nail, hook

claw back v **recover**, regain, recoup, retrieve *Opposite*: lose

clay n **soil**, earth, dirt, mud

clean adj 1 **spotless**, dirt-free, unsoiled, fresh, sparkling *Opposite*: dirty 2 **pure**, wholesome, untainted, unadulterated, unpolluted *Opposite*: impure 3 **tidy**, neat, orderly, shipshape, immaculate *Opposite*: slovenly ■ v **scrub**, scour, wipe, cleanse, dust *Opposite*: soil

clean-cut adj **neat**, well-groomed, tidy, smart, well turned-out *Opposite*: untidy

cleaner n 1 **domestic**, home help, help, char, domestic worker *(US)* 2 **cleaning product**, detergent, stain remover, cleanser, soap

cleaning n **housework**, spring-cleaning, scrubbing, dusting, washing

cleanliness n **hygiene**, sanitation, purity, spotlessness *Opposite*: dirtiness

clean-living adj **abstemious**, teetotal, moderate, wholesome

cleanly adv **easily**, efficiently, effectively, neatly, simply

cleanness n **purity**, freshness, simplicity, clearness *Opposite*: filthiness

clean out v 1 *(infml)* **bankrupt**, impoverish, reduce, drain, make somebody broke 2 **unclog**, flush, clear, clean, wash out *Opposite*: block up

cleanse v **rinse**, clean, rinse out, bathe, purify *Opposite*: soil

cleanser n 1 **cleaner**, cleaning product, detergent, stain remover, soap 2 **makeup remover**, cleansing cream, lotion, cream, cold cream

clean-shaven adj **shaved**, smooth, smooth-shaven, hairless *Opposite*: bearded

cleansing n **cleaning**, washing, scrubbing, bathing, rinsing

clean up v 1 **smarten**, spruce up, tidy up, sanitize, clear up 2 **wipe out**, eradicate, eliminate, get rid of, do away with

cleanup n **crackdown**, clampdown, elimination, onslaught, attack

clear adj 1 **transparent**, translucent, see-through, sheer, filmy *Opposite*: opaque 2 **strong**, rich, pure, vibrant *Opposite*: indistinct 3 **unblemished**, perfect, pure, flawless, faultless 4 **well-defined**, sharp, distinct, clear-cut *Opposite*: indistinct 5 **ringing**, pure, bell-like, resounding *Opposite*: muffled 6 **obvious**, evident, patent, incontrovertible, out-and-out *Opposite*: unclear 7 **unambiguous**, understandable, comprehensible, lucid, self-evident *Opposite*: unclear 8 **unobstructed**, empty, free, free-flowing, open *Opposite*: blocked 9 **cloudless**, bright, sunny, fine, fair *Opposite*: cloudy ■ v 1 **evaporate**, dissipate, sheer, disperse, disappear, settle *Opposite*: form 2 **unblock**, free, unclog, empty *Opposite*: block 3 **tidy**, clear out, empty, straighten, clean up 4 **free**, vindicate, exonerate, absolve, acquit 5 *(infml)* **net**, earn, gain, take home, make *Opposite*: gross

clearance n **permission**, authorization, consent, approval, sanction *Opposite*: prohibition

clear-cut adj **precise**, distinct, definite, sharp, clear *Opposite*: ambiguous

clear-headed adj **lucid**, alert, coherent, perceptive, decisive *Opposite*: muddled

clearing n **glade**, clearance, dell *(literary)* *Opposite*: thicket

clearly adv **obviously**, evidently, undoubtedly, plainly, visibly *Opposite*: ambiguously

clearness n 1 **translucency**, transparency, flawlessness, luminousness, limpidity *Opposite*: opacity 2 **directness**, clarity, lucidity, comprehensibility, plainness *Opposite*: vagueness

clear off *(infml)* v **go away**, leave, depart, get going, head off *Opposite*: stay

clear out v 1 **leave**, depart, get going, head off, be off 2 **empty**, clear, clean up, turn out, throw out

clear-out n **clean-out**, throw-out, tidy, spring clean, tidy-up

clear-sighted adj **perceptive**, insightful, percipient, realistic, sensible *Opposite*: confused

clear up v 1 **tidy up**, straighten, clear, clean up, tidy 2 **resolve**, solve, clarify, explain, settle *Opposite*: complicate

cleave v **slice**, cut, slash, hew, chop *Opposite*: join

cleft n **fissure**, crevice, crack, gap, split

clemency n **mercy**, leniency, forgiveness, pity, compassion *Opposite*: heartlessness

clement adj **mild**, moderate, temperate, balmy, pleasant *Opposite*: inclement

clench v **compress**, grit, tighten, clasp, scrunch *Opposite*: relax

clergy n **priesthood**, ministry, ordained priests, clerics *Opposite*: laity

cleric n **priest**, minister, ecclesiastic

clerical adj **1 secretarial**, office, bookkeeping, accounting **2 religious**, ecclesiastical, church, priestly *(literary)*

clerk n **1 office worker**, counter clerk, bank clerk, accounts clerk, filing clerk **2 administrator**, official, recorder, clerk to the council, clerk to the governors

clever adj **1 bright**, intelligent, smart, knowledgeable, intellectual *Opposite*: foolish **2 ingenious**, shrewd, astute, adroit, crafty *Opposite*: inept **3 glib**, smart, slick, pert, flippant **4 skilful**, talented, quick, adroit, gifted *Opposite*: clumsy **5 useful**, handy, convenient, effective, ingenious *Opposite*: useless. *See* COMPARE AND CONTRAST *at* **intelligent**.

cleverness n **skill**, ingenuity, quickness, shrewdness, smartness *Opposite*: ineptness

cliché n **truism**, formula, line, platitude, prosaism

clichéd adj **corny**, hackneyed, trite, old, unoriginal *Opposite*: original

click n **clack**, tick, snap, clunk ■ v **1** *(infml)* **make sense**, shrewd, sink in, become clear, fall into place **2** *(infml)* **get on**, be on the same wavelength, connect, relate to, hit it off *(infml)* *Opposite*: clash

client n **customer**, shopper, consumer, user, end user

clientele n **customers**, clients, regulars, patrons, custom

cliff n **precipice**, rock face, face, crag, overhang

cliffhanger n **crisis**, tiebreaker, knife-edge, nail-biter *(infml)*

climate n **1 weather**, temperature, environment, microclimate, macroclimate **2 atmosphere**, situation, ambience, surroundings, environment

climax n **peak**, high point, pinnacle, culmination, height *Opposite*: low point

climb v **1 scale**, go up, move up, mount, ascend *Opposite*: fall **2 rise**, soar, go up, rocket, escalate *Opposite*: descend ■ n **1 ascent**, scramble *Opposite*: descent **2 increase**, rise, upswing, hike *Opposite*: fall

climb down v **1 descend**, go down, get down, come down, dismount *Opposite*: ascend **2 back down**, retreat, make concessions, give way, backpedal *Opposite*: stand your ground

climbdown n **change of mind**, concession, U-turn, shift, retreat

climber n **1 mountaineer**, rock climber, alpinist **2 climbing plant**, trailer, creeper, vine

---

WORD BANK

❑ **types of climber** bougainvillea, bryony, clematis, convolvulus, grapevine, honeysuckle, ivy, jasmine, kudzu, liana, morning glory, passionflower, rattan, sarsaparilla, Virginia creeper, wisteria, woodbine

---

climbing n **mountaineering**, hiking, hill-walking, alpinism, rock climbing

clinch v **settle**, seal, close, tie up, decide ■ n **embrace**, hug, hold, bear hug, cuddle

cling v **1 clutch**, grasp, hug, hang on to, hold *Opposite*: let go **2 adhere**, grip, stick, hug, fit tightly **3 retain**, maintain, hold to, keep to *Opposite*: give up **4 latch onto**, be dependent on, depend on, hang on, attach

clingy adj **1** *(infml)* **clinging**, figure-hugging, tight-fitting, snug, close-fitting *Opposite*: baggy **2 dependent**, insecure, anxious, clinging *Opposite*: independent

clinic n **1 hospital**, health centre, surgery, consulting room, private clinic **2 workshop**, seminar, class, meeting

clinical adj **1 scientific**, medical, experimental, quantifiable, proven **2 detached**, disinterested, dispassionate, scientific, cold *Opposite*: personal

clink v **clank**, jingle, tinkle, chink, jangle

clip v **1 cut**, trim, shorten, shear, cut off **2 fasten**, attach, pin, staple, secure *Opposite*: undo ■ n **1 excerpt**, passage, extract, quotation, quote **2 fastener**, pin, staple, paperclip, clasp

clip-on adj **attachable**, fasten-on, hook-on, separable, removable

clipped adj **1 trimmed**, neat, cut back, tidy, cut **2 distinct**, short, brusque, concise, curt

clipping n **cutting**, extract, excerpt, article, feature

clippings n **trimmings**, parings, ends, offcuts, pieces

clique n **group**, in-group, faction, set, gang

cliquey adj **cliquish**, exclusive, clannish, unfriendly, unsociable *Opposite*: open

cloak n *(literary)* **screen**, cover, shroud, veil, façade ■ v **cover**, hide, conceal, shroud, veil *Opposite*: reveal

cloak-and-dagger adj **secret**, clandestine, undercover, covert, mysterious *Opposite*: aboveboard

cloakroom n **lavatory**, toilet, WC, powder room, rest room

clobber *(infml)* v **hit**, thump, beat, strike, punch ■ n **1 stuff**, tackle, things, belongings, gear *(infml)* **2 clothes**, outfit, clothing, kit *(infml)*, threads *(US slang)*

cloche n **cover**, cold frame, protection

clock n **1 timepiece**, timer, chronometer **2 regulator**, timer, device, control, meter

WORD BANK

❑ **types of clock** alarm, alarm clock, carriage clock, clock radio, cuckoo clock, digital clock, grandfather clock, hourglass, longcase clock, pocket watch, quartz clock, stopwatch, sundial, watch, wristwatch

clock up v achieve, reach, score, attain, accomplish

clockwork n 1 **mechanism**, device, machinery 2 **regularity**, preciseness, accuracy, flawlessness, smoothness

clod n **lump**, clump, chunk, wad, hunk

clog v **block**, clog up, stop up, choke, obstruct *Opposite*: unblock

clogged adj **blocked**, obstructed, choked, congested

clog up v **block**, jam, obstruct, congest, stop up *Opposite*: unblock

cloister n 1 **quadrangle**, colonnade, arcade, portico, walkway 2 **monastery**, abbey, friary, convent, nunnery ■ v **seclude**, shelter, retreat, withdraw, closet

cloistered adj **secluded**, sheltered, confined, protected, insulated *Opposite*: accessible

clomp v **clump**, stomp, stamp, thump, bang *Opposite*: tiptoe

clone n **replica**, duplicate, genetic copy, twin, double ■ v **duplicate**, copy, make a replica of, replicate, emulate. *See* COMPARE AND CONTRAST *at* copy.

clonk v **knock**, bump, crash into, thump, bang

close adj 1 **near**, nearby, close by, adjacent, local *Opposite*: distant 2 **intimate**, familiar, dear, devoted, loving *Opposite*: distant 3 **careful**, rigorous, particular, keen, meticulous *Opposite*: lax 4 **compact**, tight, concentrated, dense, packed *Opposite*: loose 5 **similar**, faithful, precise, exact, literal 6 **silent**, secretive, taciturn, uncommunicative, quiet *Opposite*: open 7 **oppressive**, muggy, airless, sultry, heavy *Opposite*: fresh 8 **miserly**, tight, tightfisted, grudging, mean *Opposite*: generous ■ v 1 **shut**, lock, seal, close up, slam *Opposite*: open 2 **come together**, meet, join, unite, gather 3 **shut down**, close down, shut up shop, go out of business, stop trading *Opposite*: open 4 **block**, bar, plug, obstruct, seal off *Opposite*: unblock 5 **conclude**, end, finish, complete, terminate *Opposite*: start ■ n **end**, conclusion, finale, completion, finish *Opposite*: start

close call n **close thing**, close shave, near miss, narrow escape, lucky escape

close-cropped adj **short**, close-cut, trimmed, close-trimmed

closed adj 1 **shut**, locked, bolted, padlocked, fastened *Opposite*: open 2 **impassable**, inaccessible, blocked, obstructed, impenetrable *Opposite*: open 3 **settled**, concluded, terminated, decided, ended *Opposite*:

unfinished 4 **narrow-minded**, closed-minded, prejudiced, bigoted, intolerant *Opposite*: open 5 **exclusive**, restricted, private, limited, cliquish *Opposite*: open

closed book n **mystery**, puzzle, enigma, conundrum, riddle

close down v 1 **end**, shut down, pull the plug on, close, conclude *Opposite*: start 2 **shut**, go out of business, cease trading, come to an end, wind down *Opposite*: open

closedown n **closure**, closing down, shutting, shutting down, closing *Opposite*: inauguration

close-fisted (*infml*) adj **miserly**, tight, niggardly, parsimonious, tightfisted *Opposite*: generous

close-fitting adj **body-hugging**, tight-fitting, figure-hugging, clinging, tight *Opposite*: baggy

close in v **draw near**, bear down, move in, approach, creep up *Opposite*: move away

close-knit adj **close**, supportive, strong, caring, cohesive *Opposite*: loose

close-lipped *see* closemouthed

closemouthed adj **reticent**, tight-lipped, reserved, silent, close-lipped *Opposite*: forthcoming

closeness n 1 **nearness**, proximity, propinquity (*fml*) *Opposite*: remoteness 2 **intimacy**, familiarity, friendship, nearness, understanding *Opposite*: distance 3 **airlessness**, stuffiness, mugginess, sultriness, oppressiveness *Opposite*: freshness

close-run adj **near**, close, closely contested, neck and neck, hard-fought

close shave *see* close call

closet v **cloister**, seclude, confine, shut up, lock up ■ adj **secret**, private, clandestine, undeclared, unprofessed *Opposite*: open

close thing *see* close call

close up v 1 **shut**, close, lock, lock up, secure *Opposite*: open 2 **huddle together**, squeeze up, squash up, bunch up, move up

close-up n **detail**, zoom, camera shot, shot, photo

close your eyes to v **ignore**, overlook, disregard, turn a blind eye to, pay no attention to *Opposite*: notice

closing adj **final**, concluding, last, finishing, ultimate *Opposite*: opening

closing stages n **last part**, final stages, conclusion, end, finale

closure n 1 **end**, conclusion, finish, closing, shutting *Opposite*: opening 2 **finality**, resolution, conclusiveness, definiteness, inevitability

clot n **mass**, lump, accumulation, globule, blob ■ v **coagulate**, coalesce, thicken, congeal, set

cloth n 1 **material**, fabric, textile, stuff, yard goods 2 **rag**, duster, tablecloth, handkerchief, napkin

clothe v dress, fit out, cover, garb, cloak Opposite: undress

clothes n dress, garments, outfit, wardrobe, apparel

clothing see clothes

cloud n mist, fog, haze, bank of cloud, cloud cover ■ v veil, blur, obscure, shadow, make unclear Opposite: clarify

WORD BANK
❏ types of cloud altocumulus, altostratus, cirrocumulus, cirrus, cumulonimbus, cumulus, funnel cloud, mare's-tail, nimbus, rain cloud, storm cloud, stratocumulus, stratus, thundercloud

cloudburst n rainstorm, downpour, deluge, flood, shower

cloud-cuckoo-land n dream world, fantasy world, land of make-believe, dreamland, pipe dream

clouded adj 1 troubled, anxious, concerned, worried, apprehensive Opposite: untroubled 2 opaque, cloudy, murky, misty, hazy Opposite: clear

cloudiness n 1 muddiness, murkiness, dirtiness, mistiness, opacity Opposite: transparency 2 vagueness, confusion, ambiguousness, uncertainness, imprecision Opposite: clarity 3 darkness, gloominess, dullness, greyness Opposite: brightness

cloudless adj clear, blue, sunny, bright, brilliant Opposite: cloudy

cloud nine n seventh heaven, raptures, bliss, nirvana, delight Opposite: despair

cloudy adj 1 overcast, grey, gloomy, dull, hazy Opposite: bright 2 murky, muddy, opaque, milky, churned up Opposite: transparent 3 uncertain, unclear, vague, confused, imprecise Opposite: clear

clout n 1 (infml) influence, power, authority, weight, sway 2 thump, whack, smack, blow, cuff ■ v hit, strike, thump, smack, slap

clove n piece, segment, section, portion, fragment

clover n ease, good life, high life

cloverleaf n junction, intersection, crossroads, crossing, interchange

clown n (infml) joker, tease, fool, buffoon, prankster ■ v clown around, fool around, horse around, play the fool, lark about

clowning n joking, buffoonery, horseplay, playing around, fooling around Opposite: seriousness

cloy v nauseate, sicken, be too much, satiate, pall

cloying adj 1 syrupy, sticky, sickly, sugary, saccharine 2 sentimental, nauseating, sickly-sweet, sickening, heavy

club n 1 association, society, guild, organization, union 2 weapon, blunt instrument, stick, cudgel 3 nightclub, disco, discotheque, casino, private club ■ v batter, hit, bludgeon, bang, strike

WORD BANK
❏ types of club baton, blackjack, bludgeon, cosh, cudgel, mace, shillelagh, truncheon

cluck v 1 cackle, squawk, clack, make a commotion 2 fuss, coo, chuckle, tut, flap (infml)

clue n sign, hint, evidence, inkling, suspicion

clued-up (infml) adj well-informed, knowledgeable, au fait, competent, on the ball (infml) Opposite: clueless (infml)

clueless (infml) adj naive, inexperienced, impractical, incompetent, ignorant Opposite: well-informed

clump n bunch, cluster, mass, tuft, thicket ■ v clomp, plod, stomp, clatter, tramp

clumpy adj ungainly, awkward, cumbersome, unwieldy, chunky Opposite: dainty

clumsiness n awkwardness, ungainliness, ineptness, gaucheness, gaucherie Opposite: gracefulness

clumsy adj awkward, inept, ungainly, maladroit, gauche Opposite: graceful

clunk n clang, clank, clink, thud

clunky adj chunky, heavy, solid, bulky, awkward

cluster n bunch, group, collection, band, gathering ■ v gather, come together, bunch, group, collect Opposite: disperse

clutch v grasp, hold, grab, grip, hang on to

clutter n mess, litter, disorder, confusion, untidiness Opposite: order ■ v encumber, litter, strew, fill, cover Opposite: free

cluttered adj untidy, messy, disordered, muddled, jumbled Opposite: orderly

coach n trainer, teacher, instructor, tutor ■ v teach, train, prepare, instruct, tutor. See COMPARE AND CONTRAST at teach.

coaching n training, education, schooling, teaching, tutoring

coachload n busload, group, party, crowd, horde

coachwork n bodywork, exterior, outside, paintwork

coagulate v clot, congeal, thicken, coalesce, set Opposite: thin

coagulation n 1 clotting, thickening, setting, congealing, gelling 2 clot, lump, ball, mass, cake

coalesce v merge, unite, combine, amalgamate, fuse Opposite: separate

coalescence n union, combination, amalgamation, meld, merger Opposite: separation

coalfield n coalmine, seam, mine, pit, colliery

coalition n alliance, union, partnership, combination, league

coalmine n colliery, mine, pit, coalface, quarry

coarse adj 1 rough, uneven, abrasive, stiff, bristly Opposite: smooth 2 indelicate, tasteless, vulgar, uncouth, crude Opposite: polite

3 **unrefined**, crude, untreated, organic, unprocessed *Opposite*: refined

coarsen v **roughen**, harden, toughen, season, stiffen *Opposite*: soften

coast n **shore**, shoreline, coastline, beach, seashore *Opposite*: interior ■ v **glide**, cruise, drift, sail, freewheel *Opposite*: struggle

coastal adj **seaside**, littoral, sea, ocean, beach

coastline n **shoreline**, seashore, coast, shore, seaboard *Opposite*: interior

coast-to-coast adj **comprehensive**, extensive, complete, umbrella, blanket

coat n 1 **fur**, wool, fleece, hide, skin 2 **covering**, coating, layer, veneer, glaze ■ v **cover**, paint, smother, dip, smear

WORD BANK
❏ **types of jacket** anorak, blazer, blouson, bomber jacket, dinner jacket, DJ, double-breasted jacket, flak jacket, fleece, jacket, Nehru jacket, reefer jacket, safari jacket, single-breasted jacket, smoking jacket, sports jacket, tail coat, tails, waterproof jacket, windcheater
❏ **types of overcoat** cagoule, cape, cloak, duffel coat, frock coat, gabardine, greatcoat, mac *(infml)*, mackintosh *(dated)*, overcoat, parka, pea coat, poncho, raincoat, topcoat, trench coat

coated adj **covered**, caked, frosted, glazed, treated

coating n **covering**, veneer, varnish, glaze, layer

coat of arms n **crest**, emblem, badge, logo, design

coax v **wheedle**, persuade, cajole, charm, entice *Opposite*: browbeat

cobble n **cobblestone**, paving stone, paver, sett, stone ■ v **mend**, repair, patch, patch up, stitch

cobbled adj **paved**, cobblestoned, flagged

cobblestone n **cobble**, paving stone, paver, sett, stone

cobble together v **improvise**, rig, concoct, contrive, devise

cobwebs n **sluggishness**, tiredness, torpor, lethargy, listlessness *Opposite*: liveliness

cochineal n **colouring**, food dye, dye, food additive, additive

cock v **tilt**, lift, slant, angle, incline *Opposite*: lower

cock-a-doodle-doo n **crowing**, crow, cry, call

cock-a-hoop adj **elated**, delighted, thrilled, overjoyed, jubilant *Opposite*: dejected

cockeyed adj 1 *(infml)* **foolish**, absurd, madcap, ridiculous, silly *Opposite*: sensible 2 **misaligned**, crooked, askew, awry, uneven *Opposite*: straight

cockpit n **arena**, battleground, boxing ring, floor, ring

cocksure adj **smug**, arrogant, conceited, confident, overconfident *Opposite*: modest

cocktail n **concoction**, mixture, brew, blend, combination

cockup *(infml)* n **blunder**, mess, mistake, error, mess-up *(infml)*

cocky *(infml)* adj **smug**, arrogant, boastful, brash, self-assured *Opposite*: modest

co-conspirator n **collaborator**, partner in crime, accomplice, partner, associate

cocoon n **sheath**, covering, shell, case, bubble ■ v **wrap**, cover, envelop, insulate, protect *Opposite*: expose

coda n 1 **conclusion**, ending, end, close, finale *Opposite*: introduction 2 **addendum**, postscript, addition, afterthought, adjunct

coddle v **pamper**, mollycoddle, indulge, baby, overprotect

code n 1 **cipher**, cryptogram, encryption, cryptograph, enigma 2 **program**, programming, data, instructions, machine code 3 **system**, policy, convention, regulations, rules

code-named adj **alias**, known as, dubbed, identified, named

code of conduct n **agreement**, rules, guidelines, regulations, protocol

code of practice n **regulations**, rules, guidelines, principles, protocol

codex n **manuscript**, scroll, papyrus, palimpsest, parchment

codicil *(fml)* n **appendix**, supplement, addition, rider, add-on

codification n **systematization**, organization, categorization, classification, collation

codify v **organize**, collect, collate, arrange, order

codswallop *(infml)* n **nonsense**, rubbish, drivel, claptrap *(infml)*, twaddle *(infml)*

coefficient n **number**, constant, factor, amount, quantity

coerce v **force**, press, pressure, compel, bully

coercion n **pressure**, compulsion, force, intimidation, bullying *Opposite*: volition

coercive adj **forced**, forcible, intimidating, bullying, strong *Opposite*: gentle

coexist v 1 **live**, exist, cohabit, live together, coincide 2 **harmonize**, synchronize, collaborate, cooperate, reconcile

coexistence n 1 **cohabitation**, living together, co-occurrence, symbiosis, concomitance 2 **harmony**, accord, cohabitation, coevolution, synchronization

coexistent adj **concurrent**, simultaneous, contemporaneous, coincident, concomitant

coextensive adj **coincident**, equivalent, equal, parallel, corresponding

coffee break n **time off**, break, rest, time out, breather *(infml)*

coffeemaker n **percolator**, espresso machine, coffeepot, filter, cafetière

coffer n **strongbox**, chest, moneybox, cash box, treasure chest

coffers n funds, reserves, assets, capital, resources

coffin n box, sarcophagus, cist, casket (US)

cog n component, part, gear, mechanism, cogwheel

cogency n power, strength, intensity, vigour, coherence

cogent adj forceful, convincing, persuasive, coherent, lucid Opposite: unconvincing. See COMPARE AND CONTRAST at **valid**.

cogitate (fml) v think, consider, reflect, deliberate, ponder

cogitation (fml) n thought, consideration, rumination, musing, reflection

cognate adj similar, alike, related, kindred, equivalent Opposite: different

cognition n thought, reasoning, understanding, perception, reason

cognitive adj reasoning, mental, intellectual, cerebral, perceptive

cognizance (fml) n knowledge, awareness, grasp, perception, understanding Opposite: ignorance

cognizant (fml) adj knowing, aware, conscious, acquainted, familiar Opposite: ignorant. See COMPARE AND CONTRAST at **aware**.

cognoscenti n connoisseurs, experts, specialists, authorities, pundits

cogwheel n cog, wheel, gearwheel, gear, flywheel

cohabit v live together, shack up (infml), live in sin (dated)

cohabitation n living together, sharing, living in sin (dated)

cohabitee n partner, domestic partner, significant other, spousal equivalent (US)

cohere (fml) v 1 adhere, bind, stick, join together, stick together 2 conform, match, tally, correspond, hang together Opposite: disagree

coherence n consistency, unity, rationality, logic, lucidity Opposite: inconsistency

coherent adj 1 consistent, logical, sound, reasoned, reasonable Opposite: inconsistent 2 intelligible, clear, comprehensible, articulate, lucid Opposite: unintelligible

cohesion n sticking together, unity, consistency, solidity, organization Opposite: disintegration

cohesive adj unified, consistent, solid, interconnected, organized Opposite: fragmented

cohort n unit, troop, regiment, legion, army

coiffure (fml) n hairstyle, haircut, hairdo (infml) ■ v style, arrange, dress, cut, coif (fml)

coil n loop, curl, spiral, twist, twirl ■ v wind, convolute, twine, curl, loop

coin n currency, money, coinage, denomination, change ■ v invent, think up, make up, create, devise

coincide v accord, agree, match, correspond, concur Opposite: differ

coincidence n 1 accident, chance, luck, twist of fate, quirk 2 (fml) concurrence, correspondence, correlation, agreement, relationship

coincidental adj 1 accidental, chance, unplanned, spontaneous, unexpected Opposite: intentional 2 concurrent, corresponding, simultaneous, synchronous, correlated Opposite: separate

coincidentally adv accidentally, by accident, by chance, unpredictably, unexpectedly Opposite: intentionally

col n pass, saddle, gap, dip, passage

cold adj 1 chilly, freezing, icy, frosty, bitter Opposite: hot 2 emotionless, unfriendly, unemotional, unsympathetic, unkind Opposite: friendly ■ n 1 coldness, chill, chilliness, frost, iciness Opposite: heat 2 common cold, head cold, flu, influenza, chill

cold-blooded adj pitiless, hardhearted, cold, cold-hearted, callous Opposite: compassionate

cold-bloodedness n pitilessness, coldness, hardheartedness, cold-heartedness, callousness Opposite: compassion

cold-hearted adj cold-blooded, cruel, callous, ruthless, unfeeling Opposite: compassionate

cold-heartedness n cold-bloodedness, cruelty, callousness, ruthlessness, unfeelingness Opposite: compassion

coldness n 1 cold, chilliness, frostiness, iciness, wintriness Opposite: warmth 2 emotionlessness, unkindness, unfriendliness, aloofness, distantness Opposite: friendliness

cold shoulder n rebuff, rejection, snub, slight, brushoff (infml) Opposite: welcome

cold snap n freeze, frost, iciness, wintriness, cold spell

colic n stomachache, cramp, indigestion, irritable bowel syndrome, stitch

collaborate v work together, join forces, team up, work in partnership, pool resources

collaboration n cooperation, teamwork, partnership, association, alliance

collaborative adj cooperative, concerted, collective, joint, combined

collaborator n 1 colleague, coworker, partner, team-mate, associate 2 traitor, turncoat, spy, agent, double agent

collage n collection, combination, assortment, hotchpotch, medley

collapse v 1 fall down, cave in, give way, crumple, subside 2 fail, end, fold, break down, dissolve Opposite: boom 3 fold, disassemble, fold up, put away, minimize Opposite: expand ■ n 1 failure, ruin, downfall, breakdown, flop 2 illness, breakdown, attack, crisis, crack-up (infml)

collapsible adj folding, foldup, stacking, foldaway, portable

collate v order, organize, collect, gather, assemble

collateral n **security**, surety, warranty, guarantee, insurance

collation n 1 **ordering**, organization, collection, gathering, assembling 2 **meal**, snack, buffet, spread (infml), repast (literary)

colleague n **coworker**, associate, assistant, partner, collaborator

collect v 1 **gather**, amass, assemble, accumulate, garner Opposite: disperse 2 **store**, hoard, amass, stockpile, squirrel

COMPARE AND CONTRAST CORE MEANING: bring dispersed things together
collect bring things together, or to make a collection of similar things as a hobby; **accumulate** obtain things over a period of time; **gather** bring together things from various locations; **amass** obtain a large number of things over an extended period; **assemble** bring things together in an orderly way; **stockpile** collect and store things in large amounts for future use; **hoard** collect and store things in large amounts, often secretly.

collected adj **calm**, composed, poised, placid, serene Opposite: flustered

collection n 1 **group**, gathering, assortment, assembly, assemblage 2 **compendium**, compilation, set, corpus, anthology

collective adj **shared**, cooperative, communal, joint, united Opposite: individual ■ n **cooperative**, colony, kibbutz, commune, farm

collectively adv **en masse**, cooperatively, communally, jointly, together Opposite: individually

collectivism n **communism**, socialism, syndicalism, Marxism, Leninism

collectivist adj **communist**, socialist, syndicalist, Marxist, Leninist

collector n **gatherer**, amasser, gleaner, hoarder, accumulator

college n **school**, university, academy, seminary, institution

collegial adj 1 **shared**, reciprocal, mutual, interconnected, communal 2 **collegiate**, scholastic, academic, educational, institutional

collegiate adj **academic**, university, scholastic, educational, institutional

collide v **hit**, strike, crash, bump, bump into

colliery n **coalmine**, shaft, seam, pit, mine

collision n 1 **crash**, smash, accident, impact, pile-up (infml) 2 **clash**, conflict, confrontation, disagreement, difficulty

colloquial adj **informal**, idiomatic, conversational, everyday, spoken Opposite: formal

colloquialism n **idiom**, popular expression, common term, vulgarism

colloquium n **seminar**, symposium, discussion, conference, debate

colloquy (fml) n **discussion**, meeting, conference, seminar, conversation

collude v **conspire**, plot, scheme, plan, connive

collusion n **conspiracy**, complicity, involvement, agreement, knowledge

cologne n **fragrance**, perfume, eau de toilette, scent, aftershave

colonial adj **foreign**, overseas, expatriate ■ n **expatriate**, settler, emigrant, émigré, migrant

colonialism n **expansionism**, colonization, imperialism, interventionism

colonialist adj **expansionist**, imperialist, interventionist, colonial

colonist n **settler**, immigrant, pioneer, migrant, explorer Opposite: native

colonization n **settlement**, establishment, foundation, occupation, annexation

colonize v **settle**, people, inhabit, take over, take possession of

colonizer n **settler**, immigrant, colonist, explorer, conqueror

colonnade n **arcade**, walkway, portico, porch, loggia

colony n 1 **settlement**, outpost, dependency, protectorate, satellite 2 **gathering**, group, collection, cluster, association

coloration n **pattern**, colouring, colour, pigmentation, shade

colossal adj **huge**, massive, immense, gigantic, enormous Opposite: tiny

colossus n **giant**, titan, leviathan, behemoth, juggernaut

colour n **hue**, tint, shade, dye, paint ■ v 1 **tint**, dye, paint, shade, wash Opposite: bleach 2 **blush**, go red, flush, redden Opposite: blanch 3 **affect**, influence, modify, alter, tint

WORD BANK
❑ **types of colour** beige, black, blue, brown, green, grey, orange, pink, purple, red, white, yellow

colourant n **dye**, hair dye, hair colour, pigment, stain

colouration see coloration

coloured adj **tinted**, dyed, painted, highlighted, stained

colourful adj 1 **bright**, multicoloured, rich, vivid, vibrant Opposite: dull 2 **interesting**, vibrant, flamboyant, imaginative, lively Opposite: uninteresting

colouring n **complexion**, skin tone, skin colour, ruddiness, pallor

colourless adj 1 **neutral**, monochrome, pale, pallid, drab Opposite: colourful 2 **dull**, dreary, monotonous, uninteresting, prosaic Opposite: interesting

colours n **flag**, standard, ensign, insignia

column n 1 **pillar**, post, support, pilaster, stake 2 **line**, file, string, procession, queue 3 **article**, feature, editorial, piece, op-ed

columnist n **writer**, journalist, newspaper columnist, magazine columnist, correspondent

coma *n* **unconsciousness**, blackout, stupor, oblivion, persistent vegetative state

comatose *adj* **1 unconscious**, passed out, blacked out, out for the count *(infml)* **2** *(infml)* **exhausted**, tired, spent, used up, all in *Opposite*: energetic

comb *v* **1 untangle**, unsnarl, disentangle, get knots out of, run through **2 search**, examine, scrutinize, explore, rake

combat *n* **battle**, fight, war, contest, struggle ■ *v* **1 fight**, battle, oppose, contest, contend **2 resist**, prevent, check, reduce, stop

combatant *n* **fighter**, soldier, enemy, warrior, participant

combative *adj* **argumentative**, antagonistic, aggressive, belligerent, confrontational *Opposite*: peaceable

combat zone *n* **battleground**, battlefield, front line, theatre of war, war zone

combination *n* **1 mixture**, grouping, blend, amalgamation, recipe **2 arrangement**, permutation, code, pattern, order. *See* COMPARE AND CONTRAST *at* mixture.

combine *v* **1 unite**, join, merge, coalesce, mingle *Opposite*: divide **2 mix**, blend, intermix, amalgamate, bring together *Opposite*: separate ■ *n* **1 syndicate**, cartel, bloc, trust, association **2 harvester**, thresher, reaper

combined *adj* **joint**, mutual, shared, collective, united *Opposite*: individual

combustible *adj* **flammable**, inflammable, explosive, burnable, ignitable *Opposite*: fireproof

combustion *n* **ignition**, fire, burning, incineration

come *v* **1 approach**, move towards, draw closer to, get nearer to, come up to *Opposite*: leave **2 arrive**, appear, turn up, get here, roll up *Opposite*: go **3 happen**, occur, take place, fall, befall *(literary)* **4 reach**, extend, stretch, go, touch **5 originate**, hail from, derive, come from, stem from

come about *v* **happen**, occur, take place, transpire, fall out

come across *v* **1 stumble across**, meet, find, happen upon, encounter **2 look**, appear, seem, strike, impress

come alive *v* **bloom**, thrive, blossom, take off, enliven

come along *v* **1 appear**, arrive, turn up, occur, materialize *Opposite*: disappear **2 progress**, make headway, proceed, advance, unfold **3 accompany**, chaperone, escort, tag along, follow

come apart *v* **tear**, fall apart, break, shatter, collapse

come at *v* **rush**, pounce on, attack, threaten, fly at

come back *v* **return**, reappear, flood back, rush back, revive *Opposite*: go away

comeback *n* **1 retaliation**, reply, retort, response, riposte **2 return**, revival, reappearance, recovery, reinstatement

come between *v* **interfere**, set against, meddle, alienate, disaffect *Opposite*: unite

come by *v* **obtain**, acquire, get, get hold of, get your hands on *Opposite*: lose

come clean *(infml)* *v* **bare**, reveal, confess, own up, tell the truth *Opposite*: keep secret

comedian *n* **humorist**, comic, standup, clown, wit

come down *v* **1 decrease**, drop, go down, dip, plunge *Opposite*: go up **2 lose status**, suffer reverses, know misfortune, have a run of bad luck, have a change of fortune

comedown *(infml)* *n* **disillusionment**, blow, disappointment, letdown, downer *(slang)* *Opposite*: boost

come down in favour of *v* **approve**, back, support, get behind, come down on the side of

come down in sheets *(infml)* *v* **pour**, sheet down, pelt down, come down in torrents

come down in torrents *see* come down in sheets

come down on *v* **take to task**, pick on, be hard on, scold, punish

come down on the side of *v* **support**, come down in favour of, favour, back, endorse *Opposite*: oppose

come down to *v* **signify**, amount to, mean, hinge on, boil down to *(infml)*

come down with *v* **contract**, sicken, incubate, take to your bed, catch *Opposite*: fight off

comedy *n* **funniness**, joking, amusement, entertainment, humour *Opposite*: tragedy

come first *v* **1 head**, top, be at the top, be at the head, be in the lead *Opposite*: lose **2 be your priority**, be your main concern, be the most important thing, be paramount, be the only thing that matters

come forward *v* **volunteer**, offer, put up your hand, step forward, reveal yourself *Opposite*: hold back

come from *v* **1 descend**, derive, issue, emanate, originate **2 originate from**, be from, hail from, live in, grow up in

come in *v* **1 finish**, cross the line, be placed, finish up, end up **2 land**, berth, enter, arrive, pull in *Opposite*: depart

come into *v* **inherit**, receive, be left, be bequeathed, take over

come into being *v* **come about**, begin life, develop, take form, take shape

come into bud *v* **blossom**, flower, bud, come to life, burgeon *(literary)*

come into contact with *v* **1 meet**, encounter, experience, come across, have dealings with **2 touch**, brush against, press against, rub up against, meet

come into flower *v* **blossom**, bloom, come into bloom, flower, come to life

come into sight v **appear**, emerge, come into view, become visible, heave into view *(literary)* Opposite: disappear

come off *(infml)* v **happen**, occur, take place, come about, succeed Opposite: fail

come on v **start**, begin, go on, occur, kick in *(infml)* Opposite: stop

come out v **emerge**, materialize, appear, surface, come to light

come out of v 1 **originate**, grow, develop, arise, have roots in 2 **survive**, live through, escape, endure, come through

come out on top v **succeed**, triumph, win, emerge triumphant

come out with v **utter**, confess, admit, make known, blurt Opposite: conceal

come over v 1 **affect**, engulf, flow over, sweep over 2 **visit**, stop by, drop round, drop in, come round

come round v 1 **visit**, stop by, call, call by, come over 2 **regain consciousness**, come to, revive, wake up, awaken Opposite: black out 3 **agree**, consent, comply, acquiesce, yield

comestible *(fml)* adj **edible**, eatable, digestible

comestibles *(fml)* n **food**, provisions, fare, groceries

come through v **survive**, endure, last, prevail, get through

come to v 1 **regain consciousness**, come round, awaken, wake up, revive Opposite: black out 2 **amount to**, total, add up to, equal, make

come to a close v **end**, finish, conclude, come to an end, stop Opposite: begin

come to a decision v **make up your mind**, reach a verdict, decide, make a choice, reach an agreement Opposite: prevaricate

come to a halt v **stop**, come to rest, come to a stop, stop in your tracks, stop dead Opposite: continue

come to a standstill see **come to a halt**

come to blows v **fight**, exchange blows, start fighting, raise your fists, go for each other

come together v 1 **meet**, rendezvous, converge, gather together, congregate Opposite: disperse 2 **combine**, mingle, meld, unite, take shape Opposite: separate

come to grief v **fall flat**, go up in smoke, come to a bad end, collapse, fail Opposite: succeed

come to grips with v **cope with**, deal with, manage, handle, tackle

come to life v **awaken**, come to, revive, regenerate, breathe Opposite: flag

come to light v **leak out**, surface, emerge, come out, arise

come to naught see **come to nothing**

come to nothing v **end in failure**, fail, end in tears, fall apart, fall through Opposite: succeed

come to rest v **pause**, stop, come to a halt, come to a standstill, halt

come to terms with v **accept**, deal with, cope with, put behind you, get over

come up v **arise**, turn up, happen, occur, come about

come up against v **experience**, encounter, meet, run into, hit

come up for air v **take a break**, relax, break off, rest, take a breather *(infml)* Opposite: continue

come upon v **happen upon**, fall upon, come across, encounter, meet

comeuppance *(infml)* n **due**, punishment, just deserts, poetic justice, nemesis

come up to v **match**, meet, equal, satisfy, reach

come up with v **create**, produce, provide, supply, find

comfort n 1 **wellbeing**, ease, relief, security, relaxation Opposite: discomfort 2 **consolation**, reassurance, relief, cheer, solace Opposite: distress ■ v 1 **cheer**, cheer up, encourage, gladden, hearten Opposite: depress 2 **pacify**, soothe, console, reassure, calm Opposite: upset

comfortable adj 1 **relaxed**, at ease, contented, happy, easy Opposite: nervous 2 **snug**, cosy, relaxing, restful, secure Opposite: uncomfortable 3 **well-off**, well-to-do, rich, wealthy, affluent Opposite: poor

comforted adj **consoled**, supported, reassured, cheered, heartened Opposite: distressed

comforter n **consoler**, reliever, comfort, support, ray of sunshine

comforting adj **heartening**, uplifting, reassuring, cheering, encouraging Opposite: upsetting

comfy *(infml)* adj **comfortable**, secure, snug, cosy, relaxing Opposite: uncomfortable

comic adj **amusing**, funny, humorous, droll, sidesplitting Opposite: tragic ■ n 1 **joker**, jester, comedian, standup, clown 2 **comic book**, magazine, funny book, funny paper, comic strip

comical adj **amusing**, funny, humorous, droll, hilarious Opposite: tragic. See COMPARE AND CONTRAST at **funny**.

comicality n **funniness**, drollness, hilariousness, humour, comicalness

comics n **funnies**, comic books, comic strips, cartoons, cartoon strips

coming adj **forthcoming**, pending, impending, approaching, imminent Opposite: past ■ n **emergence**, launch, arrival, appearance, approach Opposite: departure

comings and goings n **activity**, movements, toing and froing, goings-on *(infml)*

command n 1 **order**, directive, commandment, demand, charge 2 **knowledge**, facility, knack, grasp, expertise 3 **authority**, control, rule, domination, power ■ v 1 **order**, direct, demand, charge, instruct *Opposite*: obey **2 control**, dominate, rule, lead, be in charge

commandant *n* **superior**, chief, commander, chief officer, commanding officer

commandeer *v* **seize**, requisition, hijack, take, appropriate *Opposite*: request

commandeering *n* **appropriation**, acquisition, confiscation, seizure, sequestration

commander *n* **superior**, chief, commandant, chief officer, commanding officer

commanding *adj* **impressive**, forceful, strong, powerful, imposing *Opposite*: weak

commando *n* **SAS**, trooper, paratrooper

commemorate *v* **honour**, remember, celebrate, observe, venerate *Opposite*: ignore

commemoration *n* **memorial**, tribute, honour, remembrance, commemorative *(US)*

commemorative *adj* **memorial**, dedicatory, celebratory, honouring

commence *v* **begin**, start, originate, inaugurate, instigate *Opposite*: terminate

commencement *(fml)* *n* **beginning**, start, origination, inauguration, instigation *Opposite*: end

commend *v* **1 praise**, speak well of, acclaim, extol, laud *Opposite*: denigrate **2 entrust**, convey, hand over, consign, commit *Opposite*: keep

commendable *adj* **praiseworthy**, admirable, worthy, creditable, laudable *Opposite*: lamentable

commendation *n* **1 praise**, approval, recommendation, acclamation, approbation *Opposite*: criticism **2 award**, citation, certificate, honour, special mention

commensurate *(fml)* *adj* **equal**, proportionate, corresponding, appropriate, adequate *Opposite*: disproportionate

comment *n* **1 remark**, observation, statement, aside, reference **2 judgment**, observation, criticism, analysis, critique **3 explanation**, interpretation, clarification, expansion, commentary ■ *v* **observe**, remark, mention, state, note

commentary *n* **1 comment**, explanation, observation, note, annotation **2 review**, essay, report, treatise, thesis

commentate *v* **describe**, explain, report, analyse, review

commentator *n* **critic**, observer, reporter, analyst, reviewer

commerce *n* **trade**, business, market, buying, selling

commercial *adj* **1 business**, business-related, trade, industrial, mercantile *Opposite*: charitable **2 profitable**, saleable, marketable, viable, moneymaking *Opposite*: unprofitable ■ *n* **advertisement**, infomercial, trailer, ad *(infml)*, advert *(infml)*

commiserate *v* **sympathize**, pity, empathize, show compassion, offer condolences

commiseration *n* **sympathy**, condolences, compassion

commission *n* **1 payment**, costs, percentage, cut *(infml)* **2 task**, assignment, duty, job, charge **3 committee**, authority, agency, administration, board **4 formal order**, command, directive, instruction, charge **5 authority**, power, responsibility, position, appointment ■ *v* **assign**, appoint, authorize, contract, order

commissioner *n* **official**, officer, representative, administrator

commit *v* **1 obligate**, pledge, bind, promise, oblige **2 earmark**, designate, dedicate, reserve, devote **3 do**, perform, execute, carry out, perpetrate **4 entrust**, give, consign, place, hand over

commit hara-kiri *see* **commit suicide**

commitment *n* **1 promise**, pledge, vow, obligation, assurance **2 dedication**, loyalty, devotion, steadfastness, allegiance *Opposite*: indifference **3 obligation**, duty, responsibility, liability, charge

commit suicide *v* **kill yourself**, take your own life, end it all, fall on your sword, commit hara-kiri

committed *adj* **devoted**, dedicated, loyal, staunch, steadfast *Opposite*: uncommitted

committee *n* **group**, board, team, commission, working group

commit to memory *v* **learn**, memorize, learn by heart

commodious *adj* **spacious**, roomy, capacious, sizable, ample *Opposite*: cramped

commodity *n* **product**, service, goods, article of trade

common *adj* **1 shared**, mutual, joint, public, communal *Opposite*: individual **2 everyday**, usual, customary, familiar, normal *Opposite*: extraordinary **3 widespread**, frequent, general, universal, familiar *Opposite*: rare **4 vulgar**, coarse, ill-mannered, rough, lowclass *Opposite*: refined ■ *n* **green**, park, open space, playing field, playground

common denominator *n* **shared quality**, shared belief, commonality, common ground, unifying factor

commonly *adv* **usually**, normally, frequently, generally, regularly *Opposite*: unusually

commonness *n* **ordinariness**, normalness, frequency, prevalence, regularity

commonplace *adj* **1 ordinary**, everyday, usual, routine, common *Opposite*: extraordinary **2 dull**, pedestrian, hackneyed, trite, stale *Opposite*: original

common sense *n* **good judgment**, good sense, practicality, realism, judgment

commonsense *adj* **sensible**, practical, downto-earth, realistic, commonsensical

commonsensical *see* **commonsense**

commonwealth n **nation**, people, nationality, state, country

commotion n **ruckus**, tumult, uproar, turmoil, hubbub *Opposite*: peace

communal adj **shared**, public, collective, joint, mutual *Opposite*: individual

commune n **community**, collective, collective farm, kibbutz, cooperative ■ v **communicate**, converse, empathize, connect, be in touch

communicable adj **infectious**, catching, transmissible, contagious, transmittable

communicant n **church member**, churchgoer, worshipper

communicate v **1 converse**, talk, speak, be in contact, be in touch **2 convey**, share, impart, transmit, reveal **3 connect**, interconnect, lead into, link, join

communication n **1 contact**, interaction, consultation, transfer, exchange **2 message**, communiqué, announcement, statement, letter

communications n **1 infrastructure**, public services, transportation, transport network, links **2 telecommunications**, broadcasting, postal system, data lines, network

communicative adj **talkative**, open, forthcoming, outgoing, chatty *Opposite*: reticent

communion n **unity**, spiritual union, empathy, closeness, relationship

communiqué n **announcement**, statement, communication, press release, bulletin

communism n **collectivism**, socialism, communalism, Marxism, Trotskyism

communist n **socialist**, collectivist, communalist, Marxist, Trotskyist *Opposite*: capitalist

community n **1 neighbourhood**, area, village, hamlet, commune **2 kinship**, unity, identity, cooperation, convergence *Opposite*: isolation **3 society**, public, people, population, group

commute v **1 travel**, go back and forth, shuttle **2 convert**, alter, exchange, transform, substitute

compact adj **1 dense**, solid, packed in, packed together, compressed *Opposite*: loose **2 small**, neat, trim, tiny, miniature *Opposite*: large ■ v **compress**, pack, squeeze, squash, tamp *Opposite*: loosen ■ n **contract**, pact, agreement, deal, treaty

compact disc player n **stereo**, personal stereo, hi-fi, CD, boom box

compactness n **1 density**, solidity, compression, firmness *Opposite*: looseness **2 smallness**, neatness, trimness, tininess, miniaturization *Opposite*: largeness

companion n **1 friend**, mate, acquaintance, confidant, colleague **2 escort**, attendant, chaperon, fellow traveller, arm candy *(US slang)*

companionability n **friendliness**, bonhomie, camaraderie, affability

companionable adj **friendly**, sociable, close, intimate, chummy *(infml)* *Opposite*: frosty

companionship n **company**, friendship, camaraderie, comradeship, esprit de corps *Opposite*: enmity

company n **1 business**, corporation, firm, concern, enterprise **2 companionship**, friendship, camaraderie, comradeship, esprit de corps *Opposite*: isolation **3 group**, crowd, circle, set, party *Opposite*: individual **4 visitors**, guests, friends, companions, invitees **5 theatre company**, troupe, theatre group, ballet, touring company

comparable adj **similar**, analogous, akin, equal, equivalent *Opposite*: dissimilar

comparative adj **relative**, reasonable, fair *Opposite*: absolute

compare v **1 evaluate**, contrast, assess, measure up, match up to **2 liken**, associate, link, relate, equate **3 equal**, match, measure up, parallel, compete

compare notes v **exchange information**, tell, relate, share, pass on

comparison n **1 contrast**, judgment, assessment, evaluation, appraisal **2 association**, link, relationship, similarity, likeness

compartment n **cubicle**, booth, partition, box, stall

compass n **scope**, range, area, extent, breadth

compassion n **sympathy**, empathy, concern, kindness, consideration *Opposite*: coldness

compassionate adj **sympathetic**, empathetic, feeling, concerned, kind *Opposite*: unfeeling

compassionless adj **unsympathetic**, unkind, unfeeling, uncaring, cold

compatible adj **1 well-matched**, like-minded, well-suited, companionable, friendly *Opposite*: incompatible **2 matching**, fitting, consistent, corresponding, harmonizing *Opposite*: incompatible

compatriot n **national**, fellow citizen, countryman, countrywoman *Opposite*: foreigner

compel v **force**, induce, require, coerce, oblige *Opposite*: cajole

compelling adj **1 convincing**, persuasive, gripping, captivating, fascinating *Opposite*: unconvincing **2 forceful**, powerful, urgent, undeniable, insistent

compendium n **collection**, anthology, digest

compensate v **1 recompense**, reimburse, pay off, pay compensation, pay damages **2 balance**, counterweigh, counteract, counterbalance, offset

compensation n **1 recompense**, reimbursement, payment, damages, costs **2 advantage**, reward, recompense, return, benefit

compete v **1 contest**, contend, vie, strive, participate **2 compare**, equal, measure up, rival, match

competence n **ability**, capability, skill, apti-

tude, proficiency *Opposite*: ineptitude. *See*
COMPARE AND CONTRAST *at* ability.

competent *adj* **able**, capable, skilled, proficient, adept *Opposite*: inept

competition *n* **1 rivalry**, opposition, antagonism, war, struggle *Opposite*: cooperation **2 contest**, match, race, struggle, battle

competitive *adj* **1 spirited**, aggressive, rivalrous, adversarial, cutthroat *Opposite*: passive **2 reasonable**, modest, good, inexpensive, cheap *Opposite*: expensive

competitor *n* **contestant**, participant, entrant, player, opponent

compilation *n* **1 gathering**, compiling, collecting, assembling, composing *Opposite*: dispersal **2 collection**, set, anthology, assemblage, edition

compile *v* **1 amass**, accumulate, collect, bring together, assemble *Opposite*: disperse **2 list**, draw up, compose, set down, register

complacency *n* **satisfaction**, smugness, self-satisfaction, contentment, gratification *Opposite*: anxiety

complacent *adj* **satisfied**, self-satisfied, smug, gratified, content *Opposite*: anxious

complain *v* **1 grumble**, grouse, carp, whine, moan *(infml)* **2 protest**, object, criticize, find fault, pick holes in *Opposite*: praise

---

COMPARE AND CONTRAST CORE MEANING: indicate dissatisfaction with something
complain express discontent or unhappiness about a situation; **object** be opposed to something, or express opposition to it; **protest** express strong disapproval or disagreement; **grumble** disagree in a discontented way, possibly repeatedly or continually; **grouse** complain regularly and continually, often in a way that is not constructive; **carp** keep complaining or finding fault, especially about unimportant things; **gripe** *(infml)* to complain continually and irritatingly; **whine** complain in an unreasonable, repeated, or irritating way; **nag** find fault with somebody regularly and repeatedly.

---

complainer *n* **whiner**, objector, protester, grumbler, faultfinder

complaint *n* **1 grievance**, criticism, protest, grumble, objection *Opposite*: praise **2 illness**, condition, ailment, disorder

complaisant *adj* **acquiescent**, amenable, tractable, willing

complement *n* **1 accompaniment**, foil, match, balance, counterpart **2 quota**, set, allowance, quantity, number ■ *v* **1 complete**, add, supplement, round out, make up for *Opposite*: detract **2 balance**, set off, harmonize, match, be a foil for *Opposite*: clash

complementary *adj* **balancing**, opposite, matching, corresponding *Opposite*: clashing

complete *adj* **1 whole**, comprehensive, wide-ranging, overall, thorough *Opposite*: partial **2 finished**, completed, concluded, accomplished, fulfilled *Opposite*: unfinished **3 absolute**, utter, downright, perfect, total ■ *v* **1 finish**, finalize, conclude, end, bring to an end *Opposite*: start **2 accomplish**, achieve, fulfil, carry out, realize

completed *adj* **finished**, accomplished, finalized, done, complete *Opposite*: unfinished

completely *adv* **totally**, wholly, entirely, fully, utterly *Opposite*: partially

completeness *n* **wholeness**, fullness, extensiveness, comprehensiveness, inclusiveness

completion *n* **conclusion**, close, achievement, accomplishment, end *Opposite*: start

complex *adj* **1 complicated**, difficult, convoluted, involved, dense *Opposite*: simple **2 multifaceted**, compound, composite, multipart, intricate *Opposite*: simple ■ *n* **1** *(infml)* **fixation**, psychosis, phobia, obsession, neurosis **2 development**, centre, campus, facility, multiplex

complexion *n* **1 skin**, face, colouring, appearance, features **2 nature**, character, cast, tone, aspect

complexity *n* **difficulty**, intricacy, complication, complicatedness, density *Opposite*: simplicity

compliance *n* **1 obedience**, acquiescence, agreement, submission, amenability *Opposite*: defiance **2 conformity**, observance, accordance, fulfilment *Opposite*: noncompliance

compliant *adj* **1 acquiescent**, obedient, biddable, yielding, amenable *Opposite*: defiant **2 conforming**, in compliance, compatible *Opposite*: noncompliant

complicate *v* **make difficulties**, set hurdles, thwart, confound, confuse *Opposite*: simplify

complicated *adj* **complex**, difficult, intricate, byzantine, thorny *Opposite*: simple

complication *n* **difficulty**, snag, problem, impediment, obstacle *Opposite*: solution

complicity *n* **involvement**, collusion, collaboration, connivance, participation *Opposite*: detachment

compliment *n* **praise**, commendation, tribute, accolade, approval *Opposite*: criticism ■ *v* **flatter**, praise, admire, congratulate, approve *Opposite*: criticize

complimentary *adj* **1 flattering**, admiring, kind, gracious, civil *Opposite*: critical **2 free**, gratis, courtesy, on the house, free of charge

comply with *v* **obey**, fulfil, observe, conform, abide by *Opposite*: disobey

component *n* **constituent**, module, section, factor, element *Opposite*: whole

comportment *(fml)* *n* **behaviour**, conduct, bearing, deportment, carriage *(fml)*

compose *v* **1 make up**, comprise, constitute, combine, unite **2 arrange**, order, set out, marshal, organize *Opposite*: disturb **3 create**, invent, make up, make, compile

composed adj **calm**, collected, self-possessed, serene, unruffled Opposite: flustered

composer n **creator**, originator, musician, writer, author

compose yourself v **calm yourself**, control yourself, calm down, get a hold of yourself, settle down Opposite: panic

composite adj **compound**, complex, multiple, multipart, multifactorial Opposite: simple ■ n **amalgam**, mixture, complex, compound, fusion

composition n **1 constitution**, makeup, structure, components, constituents **2 work of art**, creation, work, opus, masterpiece **3 arrangement**, configuration, conformation, structure, alignment

composure n **equanimity**, calm, serenity, self-possession, tranquillity Opposite: agitation

compound n **mix**, mixture, complex, amalgam, composite ■ adj **multiple**, complex, composite, multifaceted, multifarious Opposite: simple. See COMPARE AND CONTRAST at mixture.

comprehend v **1 understand**, know, realize, grasp, figure out **2** (fml) **include**, incorporate, bring in, add in, involve

comprehensible adj **understandable**, clear, logical, plain, coherent Opposite: unintelligible

comprehension n **understanding**, grasp, knowledge, command, conception

comprehensive adj **complete**, inclusive, full, all-inclusive, wide-ranging Opposite: incomplete

comprehensiveness n **inclusiveness**, completeness, all-inclusiveness, exhaustiveness, extensiveness

compress v **squeeze**, condense, pack together, squash, constrict Opposite: expand ■ n **pad**, wad, cold compress, ice pack, wrapping

comprise v **include**, encompass, contain, cover, consist of Opposite: exclude

compromise n **agreement**, settlement, arrangement, bargain, concession ■ v **cooperate**, bargain, negotiate, meet halfway, find the middle ground Opposite: confront

compulsion n **1 urge**, impulse, desire, craving, force **2 coercion**, force, pressure, obligation, duress

compulsive adj **1 obsessive**, neurotic, habitual, uncontrollable, irrational Opposite: rational **2 gripping**, compelling, mesmerizing, attention-grabbing, exciting Opposite: boring

compulsory adj **required**, obligatory, necessary, enforced, essential Opposite: optional

compunction n **regret**, scruple, reluctance, qualm, second thoughts

computation n **calculation**, reckoning, totalling, addition, subtraction Opposite: estimation

compute v **calculate**, work out, total, add, subtract Opposite: estimate

computer-aided design n **CAD**, computer graphics, graphics, product design, drafting

comrade n **friend**, companion, mate, pal (infml), chum (infml) Opposite: enemy

comradely adj **friendly**, companionable, brotherly

comradeship n **camaraderie**, brotherhood, friendship

con v **1 swindle**, defraud, cheat, trick, do (infml) **2** (infml) **deceive**, hoodwink, trick, mislead, dupe ■ n **1 negative**, disadvantage, minus, objection, downside Opposite: pro **2 confidence trick**, fraud, ploy, con trick (infml), rip-off (infml)

concave adj **curved in**, dished, hollow, sunken Opposite: convex

conceal v **1 hide**, cover, secrete, screen, obscure Opposite: reveal **2 suppress**, keep quiet, keep under wraps, sit on, censor Opposite: divulge

concealed adj **1 hidden**, covered, buried, obscured, masked Opposite: visible **2 secret**, cloaked, masked, veiled, disguised Opposite: open

concealment n **cover-up**, disguise, camouflage, suppression Opposite: revelation

concede v **1 acknowledge**, grant, admit, accept, allow (fml) Opposite: deny **2 yield**, give in, give up, admit defeat, compromise Opposite: stand firm

conceit n **self-importance**, pride, vanity, arrogance, superiority Opposite: modesty

conceited adj **self-important**, proud, vain, arrogant, high and mighty Opposite: modest. See COMPARE AND CONTRAST at proud.

conceitedness n **self-importance**, arrogance, narcissism, bigheadedness

conceivable adj **imaginable**, believable, possible, plausible, likely Opposite: implausible

conceive v **1 imagine**, visualize, envision, envisage, think up **2 create**, think up, dream up, make up, invent **3 consider**, regard, think of, look on, perceive

concentrate v **1 think**, focus, ponder, muse, deliberate Opposite: daydream **2 converge**, come together, assemble, collect, cluster Opposite: disperse **3 thicken**, strengthen, reduce, purify, distil Opposite: dilute ■ n **distillate**, essence, quintessence, reduction

concentrated adj **1 strong**, thick, condensed, reduced Opposite: diluted **2 focused**, intense, concerted, rigorous, strenuous Opposite: half-hearted

concentration n **1 attentiveness**, attention, absorption, awareness, focus Opposite: distraction **2 strength**, intensity, potency Opposite: dilution

concept n **idea**, notion, thought, impression, perception

conception n **1 comprehension**, understanding, grasp, command **2 idea**, notion, concept, thought, impression **3 beginning**, start, outset, origin, formation

concern v **1 worry**, trouble, disturb, bother, upset *Opposite*: reassure **2 relate to**, affect, be about, have to do with, be connected with ■ n **1 anxiety**, worry, apprehension, distress, alarm *Opposite*: reassurance **2 interest**, business, point, item, affair **3 company**, firm, business, enterprise, establishment

concerned adj **worried**, anxious, disturbed, alarmed, uneasy *Opposite*: carefree

concerning prep **about**, relating to, regarding, with reference to, as to

concert n **recital**, performance, show, gig (infml)

concerted adj **1 combined**, collaborative, joint, mutual *Opposite*: solitary **2 concentrated**, intensive, rigorous, strenuous, determined *Opposite*: half-hearted

concession n **1 privilege**, allowance, dispensation, indulgence, acknowledgment **2 reduction**, discount, allowance, markdown, decrease **3 yielding**, surrendering, granting, giving way, conceding

concierge n **caretaker**, janitor, doorman, doorkeeper, gatekeeper

conciliate v **reconcile**, appease, placate, pacify, make peace *Opposite*: provoke

conciliation n **reconciliation**, appeasement, pacification, reunion, mollification *Opposite*: provocation

conciliator n **peacemaker**, mediator, intermediary, arbitrator, arbiter *Opposite*: troublemaker

conciliatory adj **appeasing**, peacemaking, placatory, pacifying, assuaging *Opposite*: provocative

concise adj **brief**, short, to the point, succinct, terse *Opposite*: verbose

conciseness see concision

concision n **succinctness**, terseness, brevity, shortness, curtness *Opposite*: wordiness

conclave n **meeting**, assembly, council, congress, gathering

conclude v **1 deduce**, assume, presume, decide, reckon *Opposite*: speculate **2 end**, close, finish, terminate, finish off *Opposite*: start **3 settle**, complete, close, clinch, arrange. *See* COMPARE AND CONTRAST *at* deduce.

concluded adj **decided**, settled, determined, resolved, clinched *Opposite*: unresolved

concluding adj **closing**, final, last, ultimate, ending *Opposite*: opening

conclusion n **1 deduction**, assumption, inference, supposition, decision **2 end**, close, finish, termination, finale *Opposite*: start

conclusive adj **decisive**, beyond question, definite, convincing, irrefutable *Opposite*: inconclusive

concoct v **1 prepare**, cook, make, put together, mix up **2 make up**, create, devise, invent, dream up

concoction n **1 mixture**, brew, blend, potion, drink **2 invention**, creation, fabrication, fantasy, fiction

concomitance n **accompaniment**, coexistence, conjunction, combination, association *Opposite*: independence

concomitant adj **1 simultaneous**, parallel, concurrent, coexistent, contemporaneous *Opposite*: independent **2 attendant**, associated, accompanying, connected, affiliated *Opposite*: unrelated

concord n **1 agreement**, harmony, unity, accord, peace *Opposite*: conflict **2 treaty**, pact, agreement, settlement, compact

concourse n **1 open space**, public space, forecourt, courtyard, square **2 crowd**, throng, horde, multitude, mass **3 gathering**, assembly, meeting, rally, muster

concrete adj **1 tangible**, existing, actual, material, solid *Opposite*: abstract **2 specific**, particular, distinct, certain, definite *Opposite*: indeterminate

concubine n **mistress**, kept woman, hetaera, odalisque

concur v **1 agree**, harmonize, be in accord, correspond, coincide *Opposite*: conflict **2 assent**, go along with, agree to, acquiesce, accept *Opposite*: resist **3 coincide**, synchronize, fall together, coexist *Opposite*: diverge. *See* COMPARE AND CONTRAST *at* agree.

concurrence n **1 agreement**, accord, harmony, consensus, correspondence *Opposite*: conflict **2 simultaneity**, coexistence, concomitance, coincidence, synchronism

concurrent adj **simultaneous**, synchronous, parallel, coexisting, contemporaneous *Opposite*: separate

condemn v **1 censure**, denounce, deprecate, criticize, attack *Opposite*: commend **2 rebuke**, reprove, reprimand, reproach, blame *Opposite*: commend **3 convict**, sentence, find guilty, doom, judge *Opposite*: absolve. *See* COMPARE AND CONTRAST *at* criticize, disapprove.

condemnation n **1 censure**, disapproval, blame, denunciation, criticism *Opposite*: commendation **2 conviction**, sentence, judgment *Opposite*: absolution

condemnatory adj **disapproving**, critical, disparaging, reproving, denouncing *Opposite*: approving

condensation n **1 wetness**, dampness, damp, humidity, water **2 concentration**, compression, reduction **3 abbreviation**, shortening, abridgment, summarization, cutting *Opposite*: expansion

condense v **1 concentrate**, compress, compact, squeeze, pack *Opposite*: expand **2 abbreviate**, shorten, abridge, summarize, reduce *Opposite*: expand

condensed adj **1 shortened**, reduced, summarized, edited, abbreviated *Opposite*: expanded **2 concentrated**, thickened, reduced, evaporated, thick *Opposite*: diluted

condescend v 1 patronize, humiliate, talk down, look down on, disdain *Opposite*: respect 2 deign, lower yourself, stoop, humble yourself, demean yourself

condescending adj patronizing, disdainful, superior, haughty, pompous *Opposite*: deferential

condescension n disdain, superciliousness, aloofness, haughtiness, arrogance *Opposite*: deference

condition n 1 state, form, order, repair, fitness 2 stipulation, clause, proviso, provision, requirement 3 disorder, illness, complaint, ailment ■ v acclimatize, get used to, prepare, train, get ready

conditional adj provisional, restricted, restrictive, qualified, uncertain *Opposite*: unrestricted

conditioned adj trained, broken in, inured, hardened, accustomed *Opposite*: untrained

conditioning n training, breaking in, taming, habituation *(fml)*

conditions n circumstances, situation, surroundings, setting, environment

condolence n sympathy, commiseration, pity, comfort, concern

condolences n commiserations, words of comfort, deepest sympathy

condone v overlook, excuse, disregard, forgive, ignore *Opposite*: oppose

conducive adj favourable, helpful, contributing, encouraging, advantageous

conduct v 1 manage, run, control, direct, organize 2 lead, show, direct, accompany, guide ■ n 1 behaviour, demeanour, way, manner, deportment 2 management, handling, organization, administration, running. *See* COMPARE AND CONTRAST *at* guide.

conduction n transmission, transference, transfer, conveyance, passage

conduct yourself v behave, act, acquit yourself, behave yourself, carry yourself

conduit n channel, canal, duct, tube, pipe

confab *(infml)* n chat, tête-à-tête, heart to heart

confederacy n union, league, association, alliance, confederation

confederate n partner, associate, ally, colleague, accomplice *Opposite*: rival ■ adj allied, united, joined, associated, affiliated *Opposite*: rival ■ v ally, unite, join, affiliate, associate *Opposite*: disconnect

confederation n association, league, union, coalition, confederacy

confer v 1 *(fml)* award, present, grant, give, bestow *(fml) Opposite*: withhold 2 discuss, consider, talk over, go over, thrash out. *See* COMPARE AND CONTRAST *at* give.

conference n 1 session, meeting, consultation, discussion, talks 2 symposium,

seminar, convention, forum, meeting 3 league, association, alliance, union, federation

confess v 1 admit, own up, acknowledge, make a clean breast, come clean *(infml) Opposite*: deny 2 declare, profess, affirm, assert, make known *Opposite*: repress

confession n 1 admission, concession, revelation, acknowledgment *Opposite*: denial 2 declaration, affirmation, profession, assertion, statement

confidant n friend, soul mate, alter ego, sister, brother

confidante n friend, intimate, sister, soul mate

confide v unburden, disclose, reveal, divulge, tell *Opposite*: withhold

confidence n 1 self-assurance, sureness, self-confidence, poise, assurance *Opposite*: timidity 2 certainty, conviction, belief, faith, trust *Opposite*: doubt 3 secret, intimacy, classified information

confidence trick *see* con trick

confident adj 1 self-assured, poised, self-confident, self-possessed, cool *Opposite*: timid 2 definite, sure, certain, positive, convinced *Opposite*: unsure

confidential adj 1 private, secret, classified, off the record, restricted *Opposite*: unrestricted 2 intimate, private, close, personal 3 sound, stable, trusted, trustworthy, reliable *Opposite*: untrustworthy

confidentially adv behind the scenes, privately, in secret, just between you and me, behind closed doors *Opposite*: openly

configuration n shape, outline, formation, conformation, arrangement

configure v arrange, design, set up, construct, align

confine v 1 restrain, restrict, limit, narrow, keep *Opposite*: unleash 2 detain, quarantine, imprison, jail, lock up *Opposite*: release

confined adj 1 limited, restricted, curbed, restrained, hemmed in *Opposite*: free 2 constricted, restricted, small, cramped, enclosed *Opposite*: open

confinement n 1 *(dated)* labour, childbirth, giving birth 2 imprisonment, quarantine, internment, detention, captivity *Opposite*: freedom 3 limitation, scope, restriction, restraint, limit

confines n limits, boundaries, borders, limitations, margins

confirm v 1 corroborate, verify, substantiate, bear out, prove *Opposite*: refute 2 settle, check, authorize, approve, sanction 3 *(fml)* strengthen, firm up, fortify, reinforce, deepen *Opposite*: undermine

confirmation n 1 corroboration, verification, substantiation, authentication, evidence *Opposite*: denial 2 validation, authorization, approval, sanction, endorsement *Opposite*: refusal

confirmed adj **long-established**, established, dyed-in-the-wool, inveterate, deep-rooted

confiscate v **take away**, remove, sequester, seize, impound Opposite: restore

confiscation n **seizure**, repossession, appropriation, removal, sequestration Opposite: return

conflagration n **fire**, blaze, inferno, forest fire, brush fire

conflate v **combine**, amalgamate, consolidate, merge

conflation n **combination**, amalgamation, consolidation, merger

conflict n **1 battle**, fight, war, struggle, encounter Opposite: peace **2 opposition**, disagreement, difference, clash, argument Opposite: concord ■ v **1 disagree**, oppose, clash, differ, be at odds Opposite: concur **2 fight**, quarrel, struggle, argue, scrap Opposite: agree. See COMPARE AND CONTRAST at **fight**.

conflicting adj **contradictory**, incompatible, at odds, inconsistent, differing Opposite: consistent

confluence n **meeting**, convergence, union, joining together, coming together Opposite: divergence

conform v **1 fit in**, imitate, follow, toe the line, obey Opposite: rebel **2 agree**, match, correspond, fit, coincide Opposite: contradict

conformism n **conventionality**, toeing the line, conformity, orthodoxy, traditionalism Opposite: dissidence

conformist n **yes man**, traditionalist, follower, sheep Opposite: rebel ■ adj **conventional**, traditional, orthodox, obedient, unadventurous Opposite: rebellious

conformity n **1 toeing the line**, playing the game, conformism, conventionality, traditionalism Opposite: rebellion **2 agreement**, compliance, consistency, correspondence, accord Opposite: divergence

confound v **1 confuse**, muddle, mix up, mistake, misperceive Opposite: distinguish **2 stun**, amaze, puzzle, mystify, confuse

confounded adj **1** (infml) **annoying**, irritating, wretched, blasted (infml), darned (infml) **2 confused**, perplexed, mystified, baffled, puzzled

confrère (fml) n **colleague**, associate, collaborator, coworker

confront v **1 challenge**, oppose, antagonize, provoke, meet Opposite: appease **2 encounter**, handle, tackle, face up to, meet Opposite: duck

confrontation n **1 opposition**, argument, disagreement, quarrel, altercation Opposite: consensus **2 hostility**, war, battle, fight, clash

confrontational adj **argumentative**, quarrelsome, hostile, challenging, aggressive Opposite: amicable

confuse v **1 puzzle**, perplex, baffle, mystify, bewilder Opposite: enlighten **2 cloud**, muddy the waters, complicate, blur, muddy Opposite: clarify **3 muddle**, mix up, misperceive, mistake, confound Opposite: distinguish

confused adj **1 puzzled**, perplexed, baffled, mystified, bewildered Opposite: enlightened **2 disordered**, disorderly, muddled, mixed up, in disarray Opposite: orderly

confusing adj **unclear**, puzzling, perplexing, baffling, mystifying Opposite: clear

confusion n **1 bewilderment**, perplexity, puzzlement, mystification, uncertainty Opposite: understanding **2 misperception**, misunderstanding, mix-up, muddle, mistake Opposite: clarity **3 disorder**, chaos, turmoil, upheaval, commotion Opposite: order **4 embarrassment**, awkwardness, disorientation, uncertainty, self-consciousness Opposite: confidence

congeal v **set**, clot, coagulate, thicken, solidify Opposite: liquefy

congealed adj **set**, dried, coagulated, clotted

congenial adj **agreeable**, friendly, affable, amiable, pleasant Opposite: hostile

congeniality n **affability**, bonhomie, geniality

congenital adj **1 inherited**, hereditary, inborn, inbred, genetic Opposite: acquired **2 ingrained**, established, long-established, habitual, inveterate

congest v **clog**, overfill, overcrowd, block, jam Opposite: clear

congested adj **1 overfilled**, jammed, choked, clogged, blocked Opposite: empty **2 obstructed**, clogged, mucous, stuffy, filled Opposite: clear

congestion n **1 overcrowding**, bottleneck, cramming, jamming, blocking Opposite: emptiness **2 blockage**, clogging, obstruction

conglomerate n **corporation**, multinational, company, firm, business

conglomeration n **1 composite**, accumulation, mass, collection, assembly **2 assortment**, potpourri, hotchpotch, collection, accumulation

congratulate v **commend**, toast, pat on the back, cheer, applaud Opposite: denigrate

congregate v **gather**, assemble, collect, meet, mass Opposite: disperse

congregation n **1 worshippers**, churchgoers, parishioners, flock **2 gathering**, crowd, throng, host, mass

congress n **assembly**, council, conference, meeting, convention

congressperson n **representative**, senator, legislator, lawmaker, deputy

congruent (fml) adj **corresponding**, consistent, matching, compatible, similar Opposite: disparate

conjectural adj **speculative**, tentative, unsubstantial, unsupported

conjecture n **guesswork**, estimation, guess,

surmise, inference ■ v **estimate**, imagine, guess, speculate, infer

conjoin (fml) v **link**, join, connect, couple

conjugal adj **marital**, matrimonial, married, wedded, spousal Opposite: unmarried

conjunction n **combination**, union, unification, coincidence, concurrence

conjure v **1 raise**, summon, call up, invoke, conjure up **2 mesmerize**, charm, trick, voodoo, spellbind

conjure up v **1 evoke**, create, recall, call up, bring to mind **2 raise**, conjure, summon, call up, invoke

conjuring n **magic**, illusion, sleight of hand, trickery

conked-out (infml) adj **asleep**, dead to the world, crashed-out (slang)

conk out (infml) v **1 fail**, break, wear out, malfunction, stall Opposite: start up **2 collapse**, pass out, doze off, nod off, fall asleep Opposite: wake up

connect v **1 attach**, join, link, fix, fasten Opposite: disconnect **2 associate**, relate, link, tie, link up Opposite: separate **3 get along**, get on, bond, click (infml), hook up (infml)

connected adj **1 joined**, attached, fixed, united, tied Opposite: separate **2 linked**, associated, related, allied, coupled Opposite: unrelated

connection n **1 joining**, fitting together, assembly, linking, piecing together **2 bond**, tie, union, link, join **3 context**, association, relationship, correlation, relation

connections n **1 influence**, network, associates, acquaintances, links **2 relations**, relatives, associations, links, family

connive v **plot**, scheme, conspire, collude, plan

conniver n **manipulator**, schemer, plotter, intriguer, planner

conniving adj **devious**, scheming, conspiratorial, sly, crafty Opposite: ingenuous

connoisseur n **specialist**, expert, enthusiast, aficionado, buff

connotation n **implication**, association, suggestion, meaning, undertone

connote v **mean**, signify, suggest, intimate, imply

conquer v **1 seize**, take, take over, take control of, capture Opposite: surrender **2 defeat**, beat, overpower, overthrow, subjugate Opposite: lose **3 overcome**, surmount, get the better of, triumph over, master Opposite: give in. See COMPARE AND CONTRAST at **defeat**.

conquered adj **defeated**, beaten, vanquished, overpowered

conqueror n **defeater**, vanquisher, subjugator, captor, victor Opposite: vanquished

conquest n **1 defeat**, subjugation, overthrow, takeover, rout Opposite: surrender **2 victory**, success, triumph, win Opposite: defeat

conscience n **scruples**, principles, ethics, integrity, sense of right and wrong

conscience-stricken adj **guilty**, sorry, remorseful, guilt-ridden, contrite

conscientious adj **1 careful**, thorough, meticulous, painstaking, punctilious Opposite: careless **2 dutiful**, responsible, honourable, upright, upstanding Opposite: dishonest. See COMPARE AND CONTRAST at **careful**.

conscientiousness n **scrupulousness**, thoroughness, assiduousness, meticulousness, carefulness Opposite: carelessness

conscious adj **1 awake**, wide awake, sleepless, insomniac Opposite: unconscious **2 aware**, mindful, sentient, sensible, cognizant (fml) Opposite: unaware **3 deliberate**, intentional, premeditated, wilful, determined Opposite: unintentional. See COMPARE AND CONTRAST at **aware**.

consciously adv **deliberately**, intentionally, knowingly, determinedly, wilfully Opposite: unintentionally

consciousness n **awareness**, realization, perception, mindfulness, notice Opposite: unconsciousness

conscript v **call up**, recruit, enlist, enrol, draft (US) ■ n **recruit**, novice, draftee (US), rookie (US infml)

conscription n **recruitment**, call-up, mobilization, enlistment, enrolment

consecrate v **sanctify**, bless, set apart, hallow, dedicate Opposite: desecrate

consecrated adj **hallowed**, sanctified, sacred, holy, blessed Opposite: desecrated

consecration n **sanctification**, dedication, blessing, hallowing Opposite: desecration

consecutive adj **successive**, uninterrupted, following, repeated, serial Opposite: alternate

consensus n **agreement**, accord, harmony, compromise, consent Opposite: disagreement

consent v **1 permit**, allow, approve, accept, sanction Opposite: forbid **2 agree**, comply, assent, acquiesce, accede Opposite: refuse ■ n **1 permission**, approval, assent, blessing, sanction Opposite: refusal **2 agreement**, accord, consensus, harmony. See COMPARE AND CONTRAST at **agree**.

consequence n **1** (fml) **importance**, significance, value, concern, import **2 result**, effect, outcome, end result, corollary

consequent adj **resulting**, resultant, consequential, following, subsequent

consequential adj **1 resulting**, resultant, consequent, following, subsequent **2 important**, significant, momentous, far-reaching, substantial Opposite: inconsequential

consequently adv **as a result**, so, therefore, subsequently, accordingly

conservation n **preservation**, upkeep, maintenance, protection, management Opposite: destruction

conservative adj 1 **traditional**, middle-of-the-road, conventional, conformist, reactionary Opposite: avant-garde 2 **cautious**, moderate, careful Opposite: speculative ■ n **traditionalist**, conformist, reactionary, fundamentalist, purist Opposite: progressive

conservatory n 1 **greenhouse**, glasshouse, hothouse, garden room, porch 2 **school of the arts**, music school, art school, school of dance, conservatoire

conserve v 1 **preserve**, save, keep, protect, safeguard Opposite: destroy 2 **store**, save, keep, eke out, be careful with Opposite: expend ■ n **jam**, marmalade, preserve

consider v 1 **think through**, mull over, reflect, deliberate, contemplate 2 **judge**, believe, think, regard, deem (fml) 3 **respect**, bear in mind, care about, take into consideration, count Opposite: disregard

considerable adj **substantial**, significant, large, extensive, sizable Opposite: insignificant

considerably adv **significantly**, much, noticeably, by far, greatly Opposite: slightly

considerate adj **thoughtful**, kind, understanding, caring, sensitive Opposite: inconsiderate

consideration n 1 **thought**, reflection, contemplation, attention, deliberation (fml) 2 **respect**, concern, thoughtfulness, kindness, selflessness Opposite: thoughtlessness 3 **matter**, factor, point, issue, fact 4 **regard**, esteem, importance, significance, weight

considered adj **careful**, measured, well-thought-out, painstaking Opposite: rash

considering prep **bearing in mind**, allowing for, in view of, given, taking into account Opposite: excluding

consign v 1 **entrust**, commit, hand over, give 2 **relegate**, dispatch, condemn, banish, get rid of 3 **deliver**, transfer, send, dispatch, ship

consignment n **batch**, delivery, shipment, load, package

consist v 1 **reside**, lie, be based on, depend on, be defined by 2 **contain**, be made up of, be made of, entail, involve

consistency n 1 **constancy**, steadiness, reliability, uniformity, evenness Opposite: inconsistency 2 **texture**, thickness, runniness, feel, makeup

consistent adj 1 **reliable**, steady, dependable, constant, unswerving Opposite: inconsistent 2 **coherent**, uniform, harmonious, even Opposite: contradictory

consistently adv 1 **time after time**, time and again, again and again, repeatedly, every time Opposite: erratically 2 **reliably**, steadily, dependably, constantly, unswervingly Opposite: inconsistently

consolation n **comfort**, solace, relief, support Opposite: grief

consolatory adj **comforting**, consoling, cheering, soothing

console v **comfort**, cheer up, soothe, calm, relieve Opposite: depress

consolidate v 1 **combine**, unite, join, fuse, merge Opposite: split up 2 **strengthen**, firm up, establish, confirm, enhance Opposite: weaken

consolidation n 1 **alliance**, merging, union, link, association Opposite: split 2 **strengthening**, firming, establishment, solidification, firming up Opposite: weakening

consoling adj **comforting**, soothing, cheering, calming

consort n 1 (fml) **companion**, partner, associate, spouse, wife 2 **ensemble**, group, orchestra, band

consortium n **group**, grouping, association, conglomerate, syndicate

consort with (fml) v **associate**, accompany, mix, mingle, hang around

conspicuous adj 1 **visible**, noticeable, obvious, exposed, on show Opposite: inconspicuous 2 **eye-catching**, striking, prominent, outstanding, notable Opposite: unremarkable

conspicuously adv **noticeably**, obviously, clearly, evidently, blatantly Opposite: inconspicuously

conspicuousness n **obviousness**, plainness, prominence, overtness

conspiracy n **plot**, scheme, plan, intrigue, collusion

conspirator n **schemer**, plotter, conniver, collaborator, accomplice

conspiratorial adj **private**, shared, confidential, complicit, collusive

conspire v 1 **plot**, connive, plan, scheme, work against 2 **combine**, work together, unite, collaborate, collude

constancy n 1 **faithfulness**, loyalty, fidelity, dependability, reliability Opposite: unfaithfulness 2 **steadiness**, firmness, consistency, steadfastness, endurance Opposite: inconsistency

constant adj 1 **continuous**, endless, relentless, continual, persistent Opposite: intermittent 2 **frequent**, persistent, recurrent, incessant, recurring Opposite: occasional 3 **steady**, stable, even, invariable, unvarying Opposite: irregular 4 **faithful**, loyal, trustworthy, devoted, staunch Opposite: disloyal

constantly adv **continually**, continuously, always, regularly, frequently Opposite: intermittently

constellation n **group**, gathering, collection, assemblage, pattern

consternation n **dismay**, disquiet, alarm, anxiety, worry Opposite: composure

constituency n 1 **area**, borough, ward, region 2 **electorate**, voters, population, public, community

constituent n **1 voter**, citizen, resident **2 ingredient**, element, component, part ■ adj **basic**, essential, integral, component, fundamental

constitute v **1 amount to**, represent, add up to, signify, total Opposite: fall short **2 make up**, form, compose, represent **3** (fml) **set up**, establish, found, create, institute Opposite: disband

constitution n **1 charter**, bill, instrument of government, statute **2 health**, makeup, disposition, nature, condition **3 establishment**, creation, formation, organization, foundation **4 composition**, structure, makeup, components, constituents

constitutional adj **legitimate**, legal, lawful, statutory Opposite: unconstitutional

constrain v **1 oblige**, compel, pressure, make, coerce **2 limit**, restrain, hold back, confine, restrict

constrained adj **forced**, unnatural, inhibited, unspontaneous, embarrassed Opposite: natural

constraint n **restriction**, limitation, restraint, constriction, limit Opposite: freedom

constrict v **1 tighten**, narrow, contract, compress, shrink Opposite: loosen **2 limit**, restrict, constrain, narrow, control Opposite: extend

constricted adj **limited**, restricted, restrained, bound, confined Opposite: free

constriction n **1 tightening**, contraction, narrowing, compression, shrinking Opposite: loosening **2 restriction**, constraint, limitation, limit, condition

construct v **1 build**, make, create, put up, erect Opposite: knock down **2 compose**, put together, create, structure, piece together Opposite: take apart ■ n **concept**, hypothesis, theory, paradigm, idea

construction n **1 creation**, assembly, manufacture, production, erection Opposite: destruction **2 building**, edifice, structure, creation, erection (fml) **3 interpretation**, understanding, comprehension, meaning, explanation

constructive adj **positive**, helpful, productive, useful, beneficial Opposite: unhelpful

construe v **interpret**, take, read, see, understand

consul n **diplomat**, ambassador, representative, emissary, envoy

consult v **1 ask**, check, discuss, talk to, confer **2 refer**, look up, turn to, check, access

consultant n **adviser**, mentor, counsellor, expert, specialist

consultation n **discussion**, dialogue, talk, session, meeting

consume v **1 eat**, drink, devour, munch, feed on **2 use**, use up, expend, spend, utilize Opposite: conserve **3 destroy**, annihilate, burn up, incinerate, burn down

consumer n **buyer**, purchaser, shopper, customer, user

consummate v **complete**, carry out, achieve, accomplish, conclude ■ adj **1 skilled**, skilful, expert, accomplished, talented Opposite: inept **2 perfect**, excellent, complete, ideal, flawless Opposite: imperfect **3 utter**, out-and-out, total, complete, absolute

consumption n **1 depletion**, use, expenditure, utilization, spending Opposite: conservation **2 ingesting**, feasting, feeding, eating, drinking

contact n **1 interaction**, communication, dealings, connection, exchange **2 connection**, acquaintance, friend, link, associate ■ v **get in touch**, make contact, drop a line, communicate, write

contagious adj **transmissible**, transmittable, spreadable, infectious, catching

contain v **1 cover**, take in, comprise, encompass, hold Opposite: exclude **2 check**, control, restrain, hold back, inhibit Opposite: unleash **3 limit**, control, keep in check, delimit, restrict

contained adj **limited**, controlled, checked, confined, restricted Opposite: unbounded

contaminate v **soil**, pollute, foul, taint, infect Opposite: purify

contaminated adj **dirty**, dirtied, filthy, soiled, polluted Opposite: pure

contamination n **pollution**, adulteration, corruption, infection, uncleanness Opposite: decontamination

contemplate v **1 look**, gaze, stare, watch, examine **2 weigh**, muse, deliberate, consider, think **3 anticipate**, expect, plan, think of, consider **4 meditate**, muse, imagine, envisage, envision

contemplation n **1 inspection**, observation, survey, review, scrutiny **2 thought**, meditation, consideration, study, reflection

contemplative adj **thoughtful**, meditative, deep in thought, lost in thought, absorbed Opposite: unthinking

contemporaneity n **concurrence**, simultaneity, coexistence, contemporaneousness

contemporaneous adj **concurrent**, coexistent, concomitant, contemporary, simultaneous

contemporaneousness see **contemporaneity**

contemporaries n **age group**, generation, peers, coevals (fml)

contemporary adj **current**, modern, up-to-date, latest, present-day Opposite: old ■ n **peer**, colleague, classmate, coeval (fml)

contempt n **disdain**, dislike, disrespect, disapproval, scorn Opposite: admiration

contemptibility n **shamefulness**, reprehensibility, vileness, contemptibleness

contemptible adj **despicable**, disgraceful, shameful, detestable, distasteful Opposite: laudable

contemptibleness see **contemptibility**

contemptuous adj **scornful**, derisive, disdainful, disapproving, sneering Opposite: admiring

contemptuousness n **scornfulness**, disrespect, scorn, disdain, derision Opposite: admiration

contend v 1 **argue**, assert, allege, insist, maintain 2 **compete**, vie, challenge, run, put yourself forward 3 **struggle**, resist, oppose, deal with, put up with

contender n **candidate**, nominee, competitor, contestant, challenger. See COMPARE AND CONTRAST at **candidate**.

contend with v **deal with**, cope with, face, experience

content n **substance**, matter, subject matter, theme, gist ■ adj **gratified**, happy, satisfied, contented, pleased Opposite: unhappy ■ v **gladden**, soothe, satisfy, please, make happy Opposite: dissatisfy

contented adj **happy**, satisfied, pleased, content, comfortable Opposite: unhappy

contention n 1 **assertion**, position, argument, opinion, belief 2 **argument**, disagreement, dispute, debate, conflict Opposite: harmony

contentious adj 1 **controversial**, polemical, provocative, divisive, debatable Opposite: uncontroversial 2 **argumentative**, combative, quarrelsome, antagonistic, disputatious Opposite: easygoing

contentment n **serenity**, gladness, satisfaction, happiness, pleasure Opposite: discontent

contest n **competition**, tournament, challenge, race, match ■ v **challenge**, dispute, question, oppose, query Opposite: accept

contestant n **competitor**, contender, participant, participator, challenger Opposite: question master. See COMPARE AND CONTRAST at **candidate**.

context n **setting**, background, circumstances, situation, framework

contextual adj **background**, related, circumstantial, framing

contiguity (fml) n **proximity**, nearness, closeness, adjacency

contiguous (fml) adj **adjoining**, bordering, next to, adjacent, side by side

continent n **landmass**, mainland, land

contingency n **eventuality**, possibility, likelihood, exigency, emergency

contingent adj **depending**, liable, dependent, reliant, conditional ■ n **commission**, legation, committee, party, group

continual adj **repeated**, frequent, recurrent, incessant, constant Opposite: intermittent

continuance n **extension**, protraction, extending, protracting, perpetuation Opposite: halting

continuation n 1 **perpetuation**, progression, extension, drawing out, persistence Opposite: cessation 2 **addition**, sequel, instalment, extension, carryover

continue v 1 **prolong**, maintain, sustain, perpetuate, carry on Opposite: stop 2 **last**, endure, linger, remain, stay Opposite: end 3 **renew**, restart, resume, reprise, revive

continuing adj **ongoing**, current, enduring, remaining, unending Opposite: finished

continuity n **steadiness**, endurance, continuousness, permanence, stability Opposite: interruption

continuous adj **incessant**, unceasing, nonstop, unremitting, constant Opposite: intermittent

continuousness n **continuity**, constancy, permanence

contort v **distort**, twist, screw, warp, deform

contour n **outline**, delineation, silhouette, relief, curve

contract n **agreement**, bond, indenture, pact, convention ■ v 1 **diminish**, grow smaller, shrink, tighten, narrow Opposite: expand 2 **become infected with**, catch, go down with, get, develop Opposite: fight off 3 **sign**, commission, sign up, commit, engage

contraction n 1 **reduction**, shrinkage, tightening, narrowing, retrenchment Opposite: expansion 2 **tightening**, jerking, cramp, spasm, tic 3 **shortening**, merging, combining, abbreviation, ellipsis

contractor n **worker**, independent, outworker, outside worker, freelancer

contract out v **delegate**, offer, subcontract, outsource, farm

contradict v 1 **deny**, oppose, challenge, dispute, refute Opposite: confirm 2 **disprove**, cancel, refute, dispute, undermine Opposite: support. See COMPARE AND CONTRAST at **disagree**.

contradiction n 1 **illogicality**, flaw, inconsistency, incongruity, ambiguity 2 **denial**, disagreement, challenge, negation, opposition Opposite: confirmation

contradictory adj **inconsistent**, contrary, self-contradictory, opposing, clashing Opposite: consistent

contraption n **gadget**, machine, device, apparatus, contrivance

contrarily adv **disobediently**, rebelliously, stubbornly, wilfully, defiantly Opposite: cooperatively

contrariness n **disobedience**, uncooperativeness, perversity, rebelliousness, wilfulness Opposite: cooperation

contrary adj 1 **conflicting**, opposing, different, differing, divergent Opposite: similar 2 **disobedient**, rebellious, obstinate, uncooperative, defiant Opposite: cooperative ■ n **opposite**, inverse, other side of the coin, converse, reverse

contrast n **difference**, dissimilarity, distinction, disparity, gap Opposite: similarity ■ v 1 **compare**, juxtapose, analogize, weigh, distinguish 2 **stand out**, stick out like a sore thumb, differ, diverge, conflict *Opposite*: agree

contrasting *adj* **conflicting**, opposing, complementary, different, distinct *Opposite*: similar

contravene *v* **break**, flout, breach, disobey, disregard *Opposite*: observe

contravention *n* **breaking**, flouting, breach, infringement, disobeying *Opposite*: observance

contribute *v* **1 donate**, pay, underwrite, subsidize, back **2 weigh in**, have a say, add, throw in, say **3 cause**, further, influence, impact, participate

contribution *n* **1 donation**, gift, giving, payment, subsidy **2 influence**, input, role, involvement, say

contributor *n* **donor**, sponsor, backer, giver, supplier

contributory *adj* **related**, influential, causal, causative, contributing

con trick *(infml)* *n* **swindle**, confidence trick, trick, rip-off *(infml)*

contrite *adj* **sorry**, repentant, remorseful, regretful, apologetic *Opposite*: impenitent

contriteness *see* contrition

contrition *n* **remorse**, repentance, penitence, regret, sorrow *Opposite*: shamelessness

contrivance *n* **1 gadget**, device, apparatus, machine, contraption **2 plot**, plan, plot, ruse, scheme

contrive *v* **design**, lay out, engineer, arrange, plan

contrived *adj* **forced**, artificial, unnatural, manufactured, affected *Opposite*: genuine

control *v* **1 operate**, work, run, use, utilize **2 restrain**, limit, restrict, hold back, rein in *Opposite*: release **3 manage**, command, supervise, run, direct **4 rule**, manipulate, influence, dominate, oppress **5 oversee**, monitor, regulate, inspect, watch over ■ *n* **1 switch**, regulator, controller, governor, circuit breaker **2 power**, jurisdiction, rule, domination, hegemony **3 skill**, manipulation, influence, handling, expertise **4 limit**, limitation, constraint, restriction, restraint

controllable *adj* **manageable**, governable, malleable, tractable, easy to deal with *Opposite*: uncontrollable

controlled *adj* **1 contained**, unflappable, under control, self-controlled, self-possessed *Opposite*: panicky **2 skilful**, accurate, measured, precise, meticulous *Opposite*: imprecise **3 regulated**, structured, planned, measured, delimited *Opposite*: free

controller *n* **1 supervisor**, manager, organizer, regulator, director **2 regulator**, switch, control, device, governor

control panel *n* **instrument panel**, console, dashboard, dash, instrumentation

controls *n* **instrument panel**, wheel, helm

controversial *adj* **contentious**, provocative, hotly debated, debatable, divisive *Opposite*: uncontroversial

controversy *n* **disagreement**, argument, debate, storm, hullabaloo *Opposite*: agreement

contumacious *(fml)* *adj* **insubordinate**, rebellious, disobedient, defiant, noncompliant *Opposite*: conformist

conundrum *n* **puzzle**, mystery, challenge, problem, riddle. *See* COMPARE AND CONTRAST *at* **problem**.

conurbation *n* **urban area**, built-up area, urban sprawl, city, metropolis. *See* COMPARE AND CONTRAST *at* **city**.

convalesce *v* **improve**, recover, recuperate, get better, rally *Opposite*: deteriorate

convalescence *n* **recuperation**, recovery, restoration, rehabilitation, R and R *Opposite*: deterioration

convalescent *adj* **convalescing**, recovering, recuperating, improving, getting better *Opposite*: deteriorating

convene *v* **call together**, assemble, summon, set up, organize *Opposite*: disband

convenience *n* **suitability**, expediency, ease, handiness, opportuneness *Opposite*: inconvenience

convenient *adj* **1 suitable**, expedient, opportune, fitting, appropriate *Opposite*: inconvenient **2 handy**, close at hand, adjacent, near, close *Opposite*: out-of-the-way

conveniently *adv* **suitably**, expediently, handily, opportunely, accessibly *Opposite*: inconveniently

convent *n* **nunnery**, religious foundation, religious community, cloister

convention *n* **1 gathering**, meeting, conference, congress, assembly **2 agreement**, pact, resolution, contract, settlement **3 rule**, principle, custom, practice, habit

conventional *adj* **1 conservative**, conformist, predictable, unadventurous, middle-of-the-road *Opposite*: adventurous **2 usual**, established, standard, normal, regular *Opposite*: unusual

conventionality *n* **conformism**, conservatism, orthodoxy, predictability *Opposite*: unconventionality

converge *v* **meet**, join, touch, unite, congregate *Opposite*: diverge

convergence *n* **meeting**, junction, union, coming together, conjunction *Opposite*: divergence

conversance *n* **familiarity**, acquaintance, awareness, knowledge

conversant *adj* **familiar**, up-to-date, au fait, well-informed, acquainted *Opposite*: unfamiliar

conversation *n* **talk**, chat, discussion, tête-à-tête, dialogue *Opposite*: monologue

conversational adj **1 informal**, chatty, relaxed, casual, familiar Opposite: formal **2 colloquial**, spoken, everyday, vernacular, informal

conversationalist n **talker**, communicator, gossip, raconteur, speaker

converse v **talk**, speak, communicate, chat, discuss ■ n **contrary**, opposite, reverse, inverse, antithesis Opposite: same ■ adj **opposite**, contrary, opposing, reverse, inverse Opposite: same

conversely adv **on the other hand**, equally, by the same token, on the contrary, in opposition

conversion n **1 change**, adaptation, alteration, translation, renovation **2 switch**, change, changeover, transfer, move

convert v **1 change**, adapt, alter, renovate, remodel **2 switch**, change, change over, transfer, go over **3 win over**, bring round, talk round, convince, induce Opposite: dissuade ■ n **recruit**, follower, disciple, supporter, proselyte. See COMPARE AND CONTRAST at **change**.

convertible adj **adaptable**, exchangeable, alterable, translatable, changeable

convex adj **curved**, curving, arched, rounded, bowed Opposite: concave

convey v **1 take**, carry, transport, bear, send **2 communicate**, express, suggest, put across, get across

conveyance n **1 means of transport**, transport, vehicle **2 transportation**, transport, carriage, transference, transmission

convict v **find guilty**, sentence, imprison, condemn, detain Opposite: acquit ■ n **criminal**, offender, prisoner, felon, villain (slang)

conviction n **1 certainty**, certitude, confidence, assurance, sincerity Opposite: doubt **2 belief**, opinion, principle, faith, persuasion **3 sentence**, verdict, condemnation, imprisonment Opposite: acquittal

convince v **persuade**, prove, sway, influence, induce Opposite: dissuade

convinced adj **1 persuaded**, influenced, swayed, won over, converted Opposite: doubtful **2 certain**, sure, positive, persuaded, confident Opposite: unsure **3 committed**, strong, firm, staunch, wholehearted Opposite: weak

convincing adj **1 persuasive**, plausible, believable, credible, compelling Opposite: unconvincing **2 authentic**, realistic, believable, credible, lifelike Opposite: implausible **3 undoubted**, substantial, resounding, considerable, conclusive Opposite: dubious. See COMPARE AND CONTRAST at **valid**.

convincingly adv **believably**, credibly, plausibly, persuasively, winningly Opposite: unconvincingly

convivial adj **pleasant**, welcoming, warm, friendly, hospitable Opposite: unfriendly

conviviality n **pleasantness**, welcome, warmth, friendliness, hospitality Opposite: unfriendliness

convoluted adj **intricate**, complex, complicated, long-winded, elaborate Opposite: straightforward

convoy n **1 group**, band, party, company, line **2 motorcade**, cavalcade, cortege, caravan, flotilla

convulse v **shake**, jerk, tremble, shudder, quiver

convulsion n **seizure**, fit, spasm, paroxysm, tremor

convulsive adj **jerky**, sudden, abrupt, violent, uncontrollable

co-occur v **coexist**, coincide, concur

cook v **heat**, boil, prepare, fry, roast ■ n **chef**, caterer, kitchen worker

WORD BANK
❏ **types of cook** baker, celebrity chef, commis chef, cordon-bleu chef, head chef, pastry chef, sous-chef

cooked adj **heated**, baked, prepared, roasted, microwaved Opposite: raw

cookery see **cooking**

cookie (infml) n **person**, character, individual, sort (infml), type (infml)

cooking n **cuisine**, catering, food service, home economics, cookery

cook up v **1 prepare**, concoct, make, throw together (infml), rustle up (infml) **2** (infml) **invent**, think up, concoct, devise, plan

cool adj **1 cold**, chilly, chill, nippy, fresh Opposite: warm **2 calm**, unruffled, nonchalant, casual, imperturbable Opposite: uptight (infml) **3 unfriendly**, unenthusiastic, offhand, icy, distant Opposite: friendly **4** (infml) **fashionable**, sophisticated, stylish, trendy (infml), hip (slang) Opposite: unfashionable ■ v **1 make cold**, freshen, refrigerate, chill, cool off Opposite: warm **2 wane**, dampen down, dampen, cool off, decrease Opposite: increase

cool bag see **cool box**

cool box n **cool bag**, chiller, cooler

cool down v **1 turn cold**, cool, cool off, freshen Opposite: warm up **2 calm down**, compose yourself, settle down, simmer down, back off Opposite: flare up

cooler n **chiller**, cool box, cool bag

WORD BANK
❏ **types of cooling appliance** air conditioner, air cooler, air exchanger, deepfreeze, freezer, fridge, fridge-freezer, refrigerator

coolness n **1 cold**, coldness, chill, chilliness, freshness Opposite: warmth **2 calmness**, level-headedness, detachment, aloofness, distance **3 unfriendliness**, chill, chilliness, reserve, hostility Opposite: friendliness

cool off v **1 turn cold**, cool, freshen, grow

chilly *Opposite*: warm up **2** *(infml)* **calm down**, compose yourself, settle down, simmer down, cool down *Opposite*: flare up

coop *n* **pen**, cage, run, enclosure, hutch

co-op *(infml)* *n* **cooperative**, collective, mutual society, friendly society

cooperate *v* **1 collaborate**, work together, unite, liaise, band *Opposite*: compete **2 oblige**, accommodate, help, aid, assist *Opposite*: hinder

cooperation *n* **collaboration**, assistance, help, support, teamwork *Opposite*: hindrance

cooperative *adj* **1 obliging**, helpful, supportive, accommodating, willing *Opposite*: difficult **2 joint**, two-way, mutual, shared, collaborative *Opposite*: individual ■ *n* **collective**, company, organization, association, enterprise

co-opt *v* **appoint**, designate, choose, bring on board, draft *Opposite*: discharge

coop up *v* **cage**, enclose, pen, house, imprison *Opposite*: let out

coordinate *v* **organize**, direct, manage, synchronize, harmonize

coordination *n* **1 organization**, direction, management, logistics, harmonization *Opposite*: disorganization **2 dexterity**, skill, adroitness, grace, proficiency *Opposite*: clumsiness

cope *v* **manage**, handle, deal with, survive, get through *Opposite*: founder

copied *adj* **imitated**, imitative, counterfeit, mock, imitation *Opposite*: original

copious *adj* **abundant**, plentiful, profuse, many, numerous *Opposite*: scant

coppice *see* **copse**

copse *n* **wood**, coppice, thicket, grove, covert

copy *n* **1 reproduction**, duplicate, replica, facsimile, print *Opposite*: original **2 item**, book, disk, version, publication **3 text**, words, manuscript, typescript, file ■ *v* **1 reproduce**, duplicate, clone, replicate, re-create **2 imitate**, mimic, emulate, ape, simulate *Opposite*: originate

---

COMPARE AND CONTRAST CORE MEANING: make something that resembles something else to a greater or lesser degree
copy make an identical version of something; **reproduce** make a copy of something by technical means; **duplicate** create an identical version of something two or more times; **clone** make a near or exact reproduction, especially of a piece of equipment or an organism; **replicate** create an identical version of something repeatedly and exactly; **re-create** make something that appears to be the same as something that no longer exists, or that exists in a different place.

---

cord *n* **string**, twine, rope, cable, flex

cordial *adj* **pleasant**, affable, genial, friendly, affectionate *Opposite*: unfriendly

cordiality *n* **pleasantness**, geniality, affability, friendliness, affection *Opposite*: unfriendliness

cordless *adj* **battery**, battery-operated, freestyle, hand-held, mobile

cordon *n* **barrier**, barricade, obstruction, obstacle, line

cordon off *v* **close**, bar, isolate, block off, barricade *Opposite*: open

core *n* **1 centre**, heart, hub, nucleus, middle **2 essence**, spirit, soul, heart, gist **3 sample**, plug, extract ■ *adj* **essential**, central, fundamental, main, principal *Opposite*: peripheral

corner *n* **1 angle**, crook, bend **2 turn**, turning, curve, junction, bend *Opposite*: straight **3 place**, spot, area, location, locality ■ *v* **pin down**, surround, trap, restrict, confront

cornerstone *n* **foundation stone**, keystone, foundation, basis

corner the market *v* **dominate**, monopolize, control, command, predominate

cornucopia *n* **abundance**, profusion, wealth, copiousness, plethora *Opposite*: dearth

corny *adj* **unsophisticated**, trite, banal, clichéd, hackneyed *Opposite*: original

corollary *n* **consequence**, result, effect, outcome, upshot

coronet *n* **crown**, tiara, diadem, circlet, wreath

corporate *adj* **1 business**, company, commercial, trade **2 communal**, shared, group, community, mutual *Opposite*: individual

corporation *n* **company**, business, firm, establishment, concern

corps *n* **1 force**, troop, group, company, cadre **2 group**, body, company, organization, league

corpse *n* **dead body**, cadaver, carcass, stiff *(slang)*

corpulence *n* **obesity**, plumpness, fleshiness, middle-age spread, spare tyre

corpulent *adj* **obese**, fat, fleshy, rotund, plump *Opposite*: slim

correct *v* **1 rectify**, fix, put right, sort out, mark **2 modify**, amend, alter, adjust, revise ■ *adj* **1 precise**, right, accurate, exact, truthful *Opposite*: inaccurate **2 appropriate**, suitable, proper, acceptable, approved *Opposite*: unsuitable

correction *n* **alteration**, improvement, rectification, modification, amendment

correctness *n* **1 precision**, rightness, truth, accuracy, exactness *Opposite*: inaccuracy **2 appropriateness**, suitability, acceptability, fittingness, uprightness *Opposite*: unsuitability

correlate *v* **relate**, associate, compare, link, draw a parallel *Opposite*: dissociate

correlation *n* **association**, connection, relationship, link, parallel

correspond *v* **1 agree**, resemble, parallel, match, match up *Opposite*: conflict **2 communicate**, keep in touch, write, drop a line, fax

correspondence *n* **1 letters**, mail, communication, messages, memos **2 agreement**, similarity, resemblance, association, connection *Opposite*: clash

correspondent *n* **1 communicator**, letter-writer, writer, pen friend, pen pal **2 foreign correspondent**, newspaperman, newspaperwoman, columnist, reporter

corresponding *adj* **consistent**, conforming, agreeing, matching, equivalent

corridor *n* **1 passage**, passageway, hall, hallway, walkway **2 strip**, access strip, air corridor, flight path

corroborate *v* **verify**, validate, document, support, agree *Opposite*: contradict

corrode *v* **rust**, disintegrate, destroy, decompose, decay

corroded *adj* **rusty**, rusted, tarnished, blemished, oxidized *Opposite*: pristine

corrosion *n* **erosion**, weathering, decay, rust, deterioration

corrosive *adj* **1 harsh**, scarring, eroding, destructive, acidic *Opposite*: gentle **2 sarcastic**, acerbic, harsh, bitter, biting *Opposite*: kind

corrugated *adj* **crenellated**, ridged, ribbed, grooved, wavy *Opposite*: smooth

corrupt *adj* **immoral**, unethical, dishonest, shady, fraudulent *Opposite*: honest ■ *v* **debase**, degrade, taint, pervert, warp

corrupted *adj* **debased**, degraded, sullied, despoiled, spoiled *Opposite*: pure *(literary)*

corruption *n* **1 dishonesty**, exploitation, bribery, sleaze, fraud *Opposite*: honesty **2 depravity**, perversion, immorality, harm, debasement *Opposite*: purity *(literary)*

corruptness *n* **dishonesty**, immorality, sleaziness, degenerateness

corsage *n* **bouquet**, spray, posy, flowers, arrangement

cosh *v* **hit**, bludgeon, club, strike

cosily *adv* **1 snugly**, warmly, pleasantly, comfortably, invitingly *Opposite*: bleakly **2 familiarly**, intimately, closely, warmly, lovingly *Opposite*: coldly

cosmetic *adj* **1 ornamental**, decorative, aesthetic *Opposite*: substantive **2 superficial**, skin-deep, surface, token, outer *Opposite*: in-depth

---

WORD BANK

❏ **types of cosmetic** blusher, concealer, eye shadow, eyeliner, face powder, foundation, kohl, lip gloss, lip pencil, lipstick, mascara, nail polish, powder, rouge *(dated)*

---

cosmetic surgery *n* **plastic surgery**, laser surgery, tuck, lift

---

WORD BANK

❏ **types of cosmetic surgery** Botox™ injection, breast enhancement, collagen injection, ear

---

pinning, facelift, face peel, lipectomy, liposuction, nose job, rhinoplasty

cosmic *adj* **1 intergalactic**, interplanetary, interstellar, galactic, planetary *Opposite*: terrestrial **2 universal**, vast, enormous, huge, immense *Opposite*: tiny

cosmopolitan *adj* **multicultural**, multiethnic, pluralistic, diverse, international *Opposite*: provincial

cosmos *n* **universe**, space, outer space, ether, heaven

cosset *v* **shelter**, protect, spoil, mollycoddle, indulge *Opposite*: neglect

cost *n* **1 price**, charge, rate, fee, price tag **2 budget**, amount, outlay, expenditure, expense **3 effort**, suffering, detriment, loss, expense

co-star *n* **star**, film star, actor, lead, movie star *(US)* ■ *v* **1 perform**, collaborate, entertain, star, appear **2 feature**, showcase, spotlight, star

cost-cutting *n* **saving**, cutbacks, economizing, cutting back, belt-tightening

cost-effective *adj* **lucrative**, moneymaking, profitable, bankable, gainful *Opposite*: uneconomical

costly *adj* **1 expensive**, overpriced, inflated, highly priced, exorbitant *Opposite*: inexpensive **2 luxurious**, precious, valuable, lavish, rich *Opposite*: basic **3 damaging**, harmful, detrimental, disadvantageous, injurious *Opposite*: beneficial

costs *n* **price**, charges, budget, expenses, outlay

costume *n* **clothes**, clothing, regalia, dress, outfit

costume drama *n* **play**, spectacle, drama, historical drama, period piece

cosy *adj* **1 snug**, warm, pleasant, comfortable, inviting *Opposite*: inhospitable **2 familiar**, friendly, intimate, close, warm *Opposite*: cold **3 expedient**, convenient, self-serving, cliquey, clannish

cosy up *v* **ingratiate yourself**, curry favour with, make overtures, pander, insinuate *Opposite*: distance

coterie *n* **clique**, circle, band

cotton on *(infml)* *v* **comprehend**, understand, follow, grasp, realize

couch *n* **sofa**, settee, divan, chaise lounge, chesterfield ■ *v* **express**, phrase, put, dress up, word

cough up *(infml)* *v* **pay up**, pay, give, fork out *(infml)*, fork up *(infml)*

council *n* **assembly**, meeting, board, congress, body

counsel *n* *(fml or literary)* **advice**, guidance, direction, warning, guidelines ■ *v* **1** *(fml or literary)* **advise**, recommend, advocate, suggest, propose **2 support**, help, guide, aid, encourage

counselling *n* **therapy**, psychotherapy, psychoanalysis, analysis, treatment

counsellor n therapist, psychotherapist, psychoanalyst, analyst, social worker

count v 1 add up, total, calculate, tot up, tally 2 consider, regard, view, hold, esteem 3 make your mark, weigh, amount to something, matter, be important ■ n 1 calculation, computation, reckoning, head count, bottom line 2 total, sum total, sum, amount, tally

countable adj calculable, measurable, assessable, finite, quantifiable Opposite: incalculable

count against v weigh against, detract, diminish, hurt, backfire Opposite: help

countenance n expression, face, features, physiognomy, mien (fml) ■ v (fml) tolerate, stand for, put up with, allow, approve

counter v 1 contradict, dispute, refute, oppose, answer 2 counteract, offset, foil, frustrate, thwart

counteract v counter, offset, respond, frustrate, thwart

counterattack n attack, revenge, counteroffensive, retaliation, defence

counterbalance v tip the scales, offset, balance, correct, compensate ■ n counterweight, makeweight, ballast

counterfeit adj fake, forged, bootleg, phoney, bogus Opposite: genuine ■ v forge, fake, copy, fabricate, imitate ■ n forgery, copy, fake, imitation, reproduction Opposite: original

counterfeiter n forger, criminal, fraudster, imitator, faker

countermand v cancel, revoke, stop, reverse, annul

counterpart n opposite number, equal, equivalent, colleague

counter-revolutionary n rebel, insurgent, insurrectionist, anarchist, radical ■ adj anti-revolutionary, moderate, democratic, pacifist Opposite: revolutionary

counter to prep against, contrary to, in opposition to, at odds with, in conflict with Opposite: according to

countless adj uncountable, innumerable, myriad, limitless, immeasurable Opposite: few

count on v depend on, be sure of, rely on, trust, bank on

count out v exclude, weed out, leave out, omit, disregard Opposite: include

countrified adj 1 rustic, rural, unspoiled Opposite: urban 2 unsophisticated, unpolished, unfashionable, simple, rough Opposite: urbane

country n 1 republic, state, nation, realm, kingdom 2 farmland, woodland, grazing, pastures, wilderness Opposite: town 3 people, inhabitants, residents, nation, population

countryman n compatriot, national, fellow citizen, inhabitant, native

countrywoman n compatriot, national, fellow citizen, inhabitant, native

count up v total, add up, count, calculate, tot up

county n region, section, province, district, shire

coup n 1 coup d'état, overthrow, revolution, rebellion, putsch 2 feather in somebody's cap, achievement, accomplishment, triumph, feat

coup de grâce n deathblow, last nail in the coffin, knockout punch, killer punch

coup d'état n overthrow, coup, revolution, rebellion, putsch

couple n twosome, pair, duo, dyad ■ v combine, link, join, connect, pair Opposite: separate

coupled with prep together with, in addition to, on top of, as well as, besides

couplet n verse, distich, stanza, unit, rhyme

coupling n 1 link, join, connection, connector, coupler 2 combination, juxtaposition, pairing, blend, mixture

coupon n voucher, ticket, token, slip, form

courage n bravery, nerve, pluck, fearlessness, mettle Opposite: cowardice

COMPARE AND CONTRAST CORE MEANING: personal resoluteness in the face of danger or difficulties
courage the ability to show resoluteness and determination, whether physical, mental, or moral, against a wide range of difficulties or dangers; **bravery** extreme lack of fear; **fearlessness** resoluteness in the face of dangers or challenges; **nerve** coolness, steadiness, and self-assurance; **guts** (slang) strength of character and boldness; **pluck** resolution and willingness to continue struggling against the odds; **mettle** spirited determination.

courageous adj brave, daring, bold, spirited, plucky Opposite: cowardly

courageousness see courage

courier n 1 messenger, carrier, biker, dispatch rider 2 holiday rep, rep, agent, guide

course n 1 sequence, progression, development, passage 2 direction, route, path, track, road 3 option, choice, possibility, route, avenue 4 lesson, class, programme, module, curriculum ■ v flow, pour, run, gush, stream Opposite: trickle

course of action n strategy, course, policy, plan, method

coursework n assignments, homework, reading, project, prep (infml)

court n 1 law court, court of law, tribunal 2 courtyard, square, yard, patio, piazza ■ v 1 (dated) date, go out, see, pay court to (dated) 2 woo, curry favour with, cosy up to, pander to, flatter Opposite: shun 3 risk, invite, encourage, incite, attract Opposite: avoid

court case n lawsuit, suit, case, hearing, indictment

courteous adj polite, well-mannered, considerate, chivalrous, civil Opposite: rude

courteousness n politeness, good manners, courtesy, consideration, civility Opposite: rudeness

courtesy n politeness, good manners, courteousness, consideration, civility Opposite: rudeness

courthouse n court, law court, court of law, high court, crown court

courtier n flatterer, sycophant, self-seeker, creature, toady

courtly adj courteous, chivalrous, polite, civil, refined Opposite: rude

court order n legal ruling, order, sanction, interdict, veto

courtship n wooing, dating, relationship

courtyard n patio, yard, square, court, enclosure

cousin n friend, companion, colleague, partner, counterpart

cove n bay, inlet, harbour

covenant n agreement, contract, treaty, promise, pledge

cover v 1 conceal, hide, cover up, obscure, disguise Opposite: expose 2 protect, shield, guard, shelter, defend 3 wrap, coat, cover up, envelop, swathe Opposite: reveal 4 deal with, include, comprise, embrace, take in Opposite: overlook 5 travel, cross, traverse, pass through, go through ■ n 1 covering, wrapping, jacket, shell, case 2 shelter, concealment, protection, hiding place, refuge

coverage n attention, treatment, reporting, exposure, handling

covered adj enclosed, roofed, sheltered, protected, shielded Opposite: exposed

covering n cover, casing, top, lid, layer

coverlet n bedspread, cover, throw, bedcover, counterpane (dated)

covert adj secret, clandestine, underground, concealed, hidden Opposite: open ■ n copse, wood, thicket, coppice, undergrowth. See COMPARE AND CONTRAST at secret.

covertness n secrecy, stealth, concealment, surreptitiousness, underhandedness Opposite: openness

cover up v 1 conceal, hide, obscure, mask, disguise Opposite: expose 2 suppress, keep under wraps, keep secret, paper over, hide Opposite: divulge

cover-up n conspiracy, plot, scheme, smoke screen, fig leaf

covet v want, long for, yearn for, crave, hanker after. See COMPARE AND CONTRAST at want.

coveted adj sought-after, longed for, wanted, fashionable, desired Opposite: scorned

covetous adj envious, jealous, greedy, avaricious, acquisitive Opposite: generous

covetousness n envy, enviousness, jealousy, avarice, avariciousness Opposite: generosity

cow v intimidate, scare, frighten, bully, overawe

coward n sissy, deserter, runaway, weakling, chicken (infml)

cowardice n weakness, fearfulness, spinelessness, fear, timidity Opposite: courage

cowardly adj gutless, spineless, craven, pusillanimous, faint-hearted Opposite: brave

---

COMPARE AND CONTRAST CORE MEANING: lacking in courage

cowardly lacking in courage, or caused by a lack of courage; **faint-hearted** timid and lacking in resolve; **spineless** seriously lacking willpower or strength of character; **gutless** seriously lacking in courage and determination; **pusillanimous** showing a contemptible degree of cowardice; **craven** showing a contemptible degree of cowardice and weakness of will; **chicken** (infml, often used by children and young people) cowardly.

---

cowboy n 1 cowhand, cowman, herdsman, stockman, rancher 2 (infml) fly-by-night, dodgy operator, crook (infml)

cowed adj intimidated, browbeaten, scared, frightened, submissive Opposite: defiant

cower v shrink, cringe, tremble, recoil, shy away Opposite: stand your ground

cowl n hood, cover, cloak, top

coworker n colleague, fellow worker, collaborator, associate, workmate

cowshed n barn, stable, pen, stockyard, byre

cox v steer, direct, pilot, navigate, coxswain

coy adj 1 teasing, playful, engaging, coquettish (literary) 2 shy, bashful, timid, modest, reserved Opposite: brazen

crabbed see crabby

crabbiness n bad-temperedness, bad temper, irritability, grumpiness, cantankerousness Opposite: equanimity

crabby adj grumpy, bad-tempered, short-tempered, irritable, snappy Opposite: easygoing

crack v 1 break, fracture, split, splinter, snap 2 break down, go to pieces, lose control, collapse, crack up (infml) 3 bang, bump, hit, whack, bash (infml) 4 (infml) solve, work out, figure out, fathom, decipher ■ n 1 fissure, flaw, break, fracture, chink 2 weakness, flaw, fault, imperfection, defect 3 (infml) blow, crash, bang, snap, pop 4 (infml) gibe, quip, dig, joke, aside ■ adj expert, top-flight, ace (infml)

crack a joke v make a joke, quip, joke, jest (literary)

crackbrained adj eccentric, irrational, foolish, stupid, crazed Opposite: rational

crack down (infml) v clamp down, tighten up, come down hard, get tough

cracked adj 1 fractured, broken, split, splintered, cleft Opposite: intact 2 (infml)

irrational, eccentric, crazed, crackbrained, foolish *Opposite*: rational

cracking (*infml*) *adj* **1 fast**, furious, rapid, swift, outrageous *Opposite*: slow **2 excellent**, brilliant, great, fantastic, fabulous *Opposite*: terrible ■ *adv* **very**, extremely, especially, terribly, exceedingly

crackle *v* **crunch**, snap, pop, sizzle, crack

crack of dawn *n* **daybreak**, dawn, daylight, sunrise, first light *Opposite*: dusk

crackpot (*infml*) *adj* **impractical**, unrealistic, eccentric, wild, outlandish *Opposite*: realistic

crack up (*infml*) *v* **1 break down**, go to pieces, lose control, collapse, crack (*infml*) **2 break up**, laugh, guffaw, giggle, titter

crack-up (*infml*) *n* **1 breakdown**, collapse, crisis, meltdown, burnout **2 crash**, accident, wreck, smash, collision

cradle *n* **support**, frame, structure, framework, underpinning ■ *v* **hold**, embrace, support, cuddle, clasp *Opposite*: drop

craft *n* **1 skill**, dexterity, expertise, ability, craftsmanship **2 trade**, profession, art, job, calling **3 vehicle**, vessel, boat, aircraft, spacecraft **4 cunning**, deceit, slyness, wiliness, shrewdness *Opposite*: forthrightness ■ *v* **make**, fashion, create, manufacture, construct

craftiness *n* **cunning**, slyness, shrewdness, wiliness, guile *Opposite*: forthrightness

craftsmanship *n* **skill**, artistry, workmanship, expertise, technique

craftsperson *n* **craftworker**, artisan, artist

crafty *adj* **cunning**, sneaky, sly, shrewd, devious *Opposite*: forthright

crag *n* **cliff**, rock face, precipice, peak, scarp

craggy *adj* **1 rocky**, stony, rough, rugged, uneven *Opposite*: even **2 lined**, rugged, wrinkled, wrinkly, weathered *Opposite*: smooth

cram *v* **1 stuff**, pack, fill up, ram, shove *Opposite*: remove **2** (*infml*) **study**, revise, go over, review, memorize *Opposite*: forget

crammed *adj* **full**, packed, filled, crowded, cramped *Opposite*: empty

cramp *n* **spasm**, pain, contraction, shooting pain, twinge ■ *v* **restrict**, hamper, limit, constrict, constrain

cramped *adj* **overcrowded**, confined, restricted, close, poky (*infml*) *Opposite*: spacious

crane *n* **hoist**, derrick, winch, gantry

crank *v* **turn**, reel, wind, activate, move

crankiness (*infml*) *n* **eccentricity**, nonconformity, originality, idiosyncrasy, quirkiness

crank up *v* **start**, turn on, wind up, activate, get going *Opposite*: turn off

cranky (*infml*) *adj* **eccentric**, quirky, idiosyncratic, bizarre, strange *Opposite*: ordinary

cranny *n* **crevice**, crack, fissure, chink, cleft

crash *n* **1 collision**, accident, smash, smash-up, pile-up (*infml*) **2 failure**, breakdown, collapse, shutdown **3 bang**, smash, din, clatter, clang **4 bankruptcy**, failure, collapse, liquidation ■ *v* **1 collide**, run into, smash into, bump into, hurtle **2 break down**, collapse, fizzle, fail **3 boom**, bang, thunder, clash, clatter **4 go under**, go bankrupt, fold, collapse, fail *Opposite*: thrive

crash course *n* **training**, orientation, workshop, induction, immersion

crash-land *v* **collide**, crash, fall, smash, come down

crass *adj* **insensitive**, tactless, thoughtless, vulgar, obnoxious *Opposite*: sensitive

crassness *n* **insensitivity**, vulgarity, tactlessness, obnoxiousness, grossness *Opposite*: sensitivity

crater *n* **pit**, depression, hole, cavity, hollow *Opposite*: mound

crave *v* **1 desire**, long for, need, want, yearn for *Opposite*: dislike **2** (*archaic*) **ask**, beg, pray, request, entreat *Opposite*: reject. *See* COMPARE AND CONTRAST *at* **want**.

craven *adj* **cowardly**, gutless, spineless, weak, timorous *Opposite*: bold. *See* COMPARE AND CONTRAST *at* **cowardly**.

craving *n* **longing**, desire, passion, hunger, thirst *Opposite*: dislike

crawl *v* **1 creep**, edge, inch, wriggle, slither **2 skulk**, scuttle, creep, sneak, slink **3** (*infml*) **grovel**, ingratiate yourself, flatter, fawn, suck up (*infml*) *Opposite*: alienate **4 apologize**, eat humble pie, grovel, humiliate yourself, prostrate yourself

craze *n* **fad**, trend, fashion, enthusiasm, rage

crazed *adj* **irrational**, distraught, overwrought, wild, inflamed *Opposite*: rational

craziness (*infml*) *n* **foolishness**, stupidity, folly, idiocy, madness *Opposite*: reasonableness

crazy (*infml*) *adj* **1 foolish**, unwise, silly, senseless, irrational *Opposite*: sensible **2 fond**, keen, passionate, enthusiastic, devoted *Opposite*: lukewarm

creak *v* **squeak**, screech, scrape, grate, groan

creaky *adj* **1 squeaky**, rusty, grating, rasping **2** (*infml*) **stiff**, rigid, inflexible, tight, arthritic *Opposite*: supple

cream *n* **1 ointment**, salve, balm, unguent, emulsion **2 best**, elite, finest, cream of the crop, pick of the bunch *Opposite*: dregs ■ *v* **blend**, soften, mash, emulsify, combine

cream off *v* **skim off**, handpick, select, choose, pick out *Opposite*: reject

crease *n* **1 pleat**, fold, tuck, gather **2 crinkle**, crumple, wrinkle, rumple, pucker **3 furrow**, wrinkle, line, groove, crow's foot ■ *v* **1 fold**, pleat, tuck, gather **2 crumple**, wrinkle, scrunch, crinkle, rumple *Opposite*: smooth

creased *adj* **wrinkled**, wrinkly, crinkled, crinkly, lined *Opposite*: smooth

crease up (infml) v amuse, break up, have somebody in hysterics, tickle pink, tickle

create v 1 make, produce, generate, fashion, form Opposite: destroy 2 invent, design, originate, initiate, give rise to 3 establish, set up, found, start, get going 4 (infml) make a fuss, kick up a fuss, kick up a rumpus, complain, cry

creation n 1 formation, making, conception, construction, manufacture Opposite: destruction 2 nature, cosmos, universe, life, world 3 invention, handiwork, fabrication, innovation, concept

creative adj original, imaginative, inspired, artistic, inventive Opposite: unimaginative

creativeness see creativity

creativity n originality, imagination, inspiration, ingenuity, inventiveness

creator n maker, inventor, originator, architect, designer Opposite: destroyer

creature n 1 being, living being, person, man, woman 2 animal, beast, organism, insect, critter (slang)

crèche n playgroup, kindergarten, playschool, nursery

credence n credibility, authority, weight, belief, confidence

credential n qualification, diploma, recommendation, testimonial, certificate

credentials n identification, authorization, ID, permit, pass

credibility n trustworthiness, reliability, authority, standing, sincerity

credible adj 1 believable, convincing, plausible, likely, probable Opposite: implausible 2 trustworthy, reliable, sincere, dependable, sound Opposite: unreliable

credit n 1 praise, recognition, thanks, acclaim, glory Opposite: blame 2 standing, position, status, esteem, prestige 3 belief, confidence, trust, faith Opposite: disbelief ■ v 1 believe, accept, trust, have faith in, have confidence in Opposite: disbelieve 2 acknowledge, recognize, acclaim, pay tribute, praise

creditable adj admirable, praiseworthy, good, worthy, laudable Opposite: shameful

credo n creed, doctrine, ideology, principle, view

credulity n gullibility, naivety, innocence, trust, imprudence Opposite: astuteness

credulous adj gullible, naive, trusting, imprudent, unsuspecting Opposite: astute

credulousness see credulity

creed n faith, dogma, doctrine, credo, belief

creek n cove, bay, inlet, gulf

creep v 1 tiptoe, skulk, steal, sneak, slink Opposite: stomp 2 crawl, slither, inch, edge, worm 3 (infml) grovel, crawl, fawn, toady, flatter ■ n (infml) flatterer, toady, sycophant, bootlicker (infml), crawler (infml)

creeper n climber, trailer, vine, liana

creepiness (infml) n eeriness, scariness, weirdness, uncanniness, strangeness

creep up on v sneak up on, surprise, stalk, take by surprise

creepy (infml) adj eerie, disturbing, spine-chilling, uncanny, weird

creepy-crawly (infml) n insect, bug, beastie (infml)

cremate v incinerate, burn, consume, immolate (literary)

cremation n burning, incineration, immolation (fml)

crème de la crème n best, cream, pick, flower, elite

crenellated adj fortified, notched, indented

crescendo n increase, upsurge, swelling, buildup, climax

crescent adj semicircular, hemispherical, curved, arced, falcate

crest n 1 top, peak, summit, crown, apex Opposite: base 2 tuft, topknot, growth, cockscomb, comb 3 coat of arms, blazon, emblem, symbol, heraldry

crestfallen adj downcast, dejected, disappointed, deflated, subdued Opposite: confident

crevasse n fissure, cleft, crack, split, fracture

crevice n crack, fissure, chink, split, cleft

crew n 1 team, squad, staff, troop, company 2 (infml) group, gang, party, circle, crowd

crib (infml) v cheat, copy, plagiarize, steal, borrow

crick n pain, strain, discomfort, cramp, spasm ■ v strain, hurt, pull, cramp, wrench

crime n 1 offence, misdeed, felony, misdemeanour, transgression 2 corruption, wrongdoing, misconduct, lawbreaking, delinquency 3 wrong, sin, fault, transgression

crime novel n detective story, whodunit, thriller

criminal n offender, convict, prisoner, felon, lawbreaker ■ adj 1 illegal, wrong, against the law, illicit, unlawful Opposite: legal 2 scandalous, excessive, iniquitous, senseless, outrageous

criminality n delinquency, misconduct, wrongdoing, corruption, lawbreaking Opposite: honesty

criminalization n 1 outlawing, banning, interdiction, proscription (fml), illegalization (US) Opposite: legalization 2 corruption, delinquency, marginalization, alienation, deterioration Opposite: rehabilitation

criminalize v 1 outlaw, ban, forbid, proscribe, interdict Opposite: legalize 2 corrupt, marginalize, deprave, pervert Opposite: rehabilitate

criminal world n underworld, gangland, underbelly of society

crimp *v* **1 fold**, crumple, crinkle, press, rumple **2 pleat**, gather, fold, concertina, ruche *Opposite*: smooth **3 interfere**, hamper, hinder, constrain, curb

cringe *v* **1 recoil**, wince, flinch, shrink, shy away **2 squirm**, blush, wince, be embarrassed

crinkle *v* **crumple**, crease, rumple, wrinkle, ruffle *Opposite*: straighten out ■ *n* **wrinkle**, fold, crease, line, pucker

crinkled *adj* **creased**, lined, wrinkled, crumpled, rumpled *Opposite*: straight

crinkly *adj* **wrinkled**, creased, furrowed, wavy, puckered *Opposite*: smooth

crippling *adj* **damaging**, debilitating, incapacitating, destabilizing, swingeing

crisis *n* **1 disaster**, catastrophe, emergency, calamity, predicament **2 turning point**, head, watershed, crossroads, defining moment

crisis point *n* **critical stage**, flashpoint, breaking point, crunch time

crisp *adj* **1 crunchy**, brittle, hard, crusty, crispy *Opposite*: soggy **2 snappy**, brusque, terse, curt, sharp **3 cold**, cool, fresh, frosty, chilly *Opposite*: stuffy **4 incisive**, decisive, confident, businesslike, efficient *Opposite*: hesitant

crispy *adj* **crunchy**, brittle, hard, crusty, crisp *Opposite*: soggy

crisscross *n* **lattice**, network, grid ■ *v* **cross**, traverse, intersect, overlap, cross over

criterion *n* **standard**, principle, measure, norm, condition

critic *n* **1 reviewer**, columnist, commentator, reporter, journalist **2 evaluator**, appraiser, judge, commentator **3 detractor**, opponent, enemy, censor, criticizer *Opposite*: supporter

critical *adj* **1 unfavourable**, disparaging, disapproving, nitpicking, judgmental *Opposite*: favourable **2 analytical**, judicious, diagnostic, serious, detailed **3 significant**, decisive, vital, important, essential *Opposite*: insignificant **4 dangerous**, serious, grave, life-threatening, perilous

critically *adv* **seriously**, gravely, dangerously, perilously, precariously *Opposite*: mildly

criticism *n* **1 censure**, disapproval, reproach, disparagement, condemnation *Opposite*: praise **2 analysis**, appreciation, assessment, evaluation, critique

criticize *v* **1 assess**, analyse, dissect, evaluate, appraise **2 disapprove**, censure, condemn, find fault with, castigate *(fml)* *Opposite*: praise

COMPARE AND CONTRAST CORE MEANING: express disapproval or dissatisfaction with somebody or something
criticize point out faults; **censure** make a formal, often public or official, statement of disapproval; **castigate** *(fml)* to criticize or rebuke severely; **blast** *(infml)* to criticize severely; **condemn** give an unfavourable judgment on somebody or some-

thing; **find fault with** criticize, often unfairly; **pick holes in** look for and find mistakes, particularly in an argument; **nitpick** find fault, often unjustifiably, with insignificant details.

critique *n* **analysis**, assessment, evaluation, account, review ■ *v* **assess**, evaluate, criticize, comment, review

croak *n* **cry**, caw, rasp, squawk ■ *v* **1 call**, cry, squawk, caw, rasp **2 grate**, gutturalize, rasp, growl **3** *(infml)* **grumble**, mutter, complain, moan, grouse *(infml)*

croaky *adj* **hoarse**, rasping, guttural

crockery *n* **tableware**, china, earthenware, plates, dishes

crony *n* **associate**, ally, supporter, accomplice, co-conspirator

cronyism *n* **favouritism**, job for the boys *(infml)*, nepotism, patronage

crook *n* **1** *(infml)* **criminal**, offender, felon, robber, lawbreaker **2 staff**, rod, stick, crosier

crooked *adj* **1 bent**, curved, warped, twisted, kinked *Opposite*: straight **2 uneven**, jagged, zigzag, oblique, askew *Opposite*: straight **3** *(infml)* **dishonest**, criminal, corrupt, fraudulent, illegal *Opposite*: honest

crookedness *n* **dishonesty**, shadiness, corruption, illegality, fraudulence *Opposite*: honesty

croon *v* **sing**, serenade, murmur, hum, warble

crop *n* **harvest**, yield, produce, cash crop, catch crop ■ *v* **1 collect**, harvest, gather, pick, bring in **2 cut**, shorten, clip, trim, shear

cropped *adj* **short-haired**, close-cropped, clipped

crop up *(infml)* *v* **appear**, happen, turn up, arise, emerge

crosier *n* **staff**, rod, stick, crook

cross *n* **symbol**, mark, sign ■ *v* **1 traverse**, go across, crisscross, cut across, span **2 thwart**, frustrate, impede, oppose, obstruct *Opposite*: assist ■ *adj* **irritated**, angry, irritable, annoyed, snappy

WORD BANK
❑ **types of cross** Celtic cross, cross of Lorraine, Greek cross, Latin cross, Maltese cross, St. Andrew's cross, St. Anthony's cross, St. George's cross, tau cross

crossbreed *v* **hybridize**, cross, interbreed, mongrelize

crosscheck *v* **validate**, substantiate, check, double-check, verify ■ *n* **validation**, substantiation, double-checking, verification

cross-country *adj* **off-road**, rough, outdoor, all-terrain

cross-cultural *adj* **multicultural**, multiracial, multiethnic, diverse, cosmopolitan

crosscurrent *n* **contrast**, divergence, deviation, rebellion, nonconformity

cross-examination *n* **questioning**, re-examination, interrogation, cross-questioning, probe

cross-examine *v* **question**, cross-question, interrogate, quiz, probe

cross-fertilization *n* **1 pollination**, fertilization, cross-pollination *Opposite*: self-fertilization **2 exchange**, interchange, interaction, synthesis, synergy

cross-fertilize *v* **1 fertilize**, pollinate, cross-pollinate **2 exchange**, interchange, interact, synthesize, share

crossfire *n* **clash**, disagreement, conflict, antagonism, flak

crossing *n* **1 journey**, adventure, trip, voyage, passage **2 intersection**, junction, overpass, flyover, level crossing

cross out *v* **score out**, score through, strike out, strike through, rub out

crossover *n* **1 switch**, change, sea change, conversion, move **2 overlap**, common ground, commonality

crosspatch *(dated infml)* *n* **curmudgeon**, malcontent, grouch *(infml)*, grump *(infml)*, pain *(infml)*

cross-purposes *n* **disagreement**, disparity, variance, contrast, frustration

cross-question *v* **cross-examine**, re-examine, interrogate, question, review

cross-questioning *n* **cross-examination**, re-examination, interrogation, review, double-checking

cross-reference *n* **citation**, reference, documentation, source, note

crossroads *n* **1 junction**, intersection, crossing, roundabout **2 turning point**, landmark, decision, moment of truth, crisis

cross section *n* **1 view**, section, slice, layer, plane **2 sample**, example, range, representation

cross swords *v* **clash**, argue, disagree, do battle, fight *Opposite*: agree

crossways *see* **crosswise**

crosswise *adv* **sideways**, diagonally, across, corner to corner, obliquely

crossword *n* **acrostic**, mind-bender, game, puzzle, cryptic crossword

crotchetiness *(infml)* *n* **grumpiness**, grouchiness, tetchiness

crotchety *(infml)* *adj* **grumpy**, bad-tempered, irritable, difficult, cantankerous *Opposite*: good-humoured

crouch *v* **squat**, bend, hunker, stoop, duck

crow *v* **1 caw**, cry, call, squawk, screech **2 gloat**, boast, brag, show off, swagger

crowd *n* **1 troop**, throng, mass, multitude, swarm **2 group**, set, gang, circle, clique ■ *v* **1 throng**, flock, herd, assemble, gather **2 overcrowd**, pack, cram, squeeze, squash

crowded *adj* **overcrowded**, packed, full, teeming, swarming *Opposite*: deserted

crown *n* **1 circlet**, coronet, tiara, diadem **2 trophy**, prize, garland, laurels, honour **3 top**, peak, summit, pinnacle, head ■ *v* **cap**, top, round off, complete, finish off

crow's foot *n* **wrinkle**, line, laughter line

crucial *adj* **vital**, critical, central, decisive, key *Opposite*: trivial

crucible *n* **1 container**, pot, receptacle, vat, kettle **2 ordeal**, trial, test, baptism of fire **3 hotbed**, hothouse, forcing ground, melting pot, ground zero

crucifixion *n* **1 execution**, killing, punishment **2 ordeal**, victimization, torment, agony, suffering

crucify *v* **1 execute**, kill, hang, punish **2 torment**, victimize, attack, savage, maul

crud *(infml)* *n* **nonsense**, gibberish, malarkey *(infml)*, twaddle *(infml)*

crude *adj* **1 raw**, unrefined, unprocessed *Opposite*: refined **2 approximate**, rough, inaccurate, inexact, loose *Opposite*: precise **3 unpolished**, basic, simple, rudimentary, makeshift *Opposite*: sophisticated **4 vulgar**, indecent, rude, coarse, obscene *Opposite*: delicate

crudeness *n* **1 primitiveness**, roughness, rawness, coarseness, simplicity *Opposite*: sophistication **2 vulgarity**, crudity, coarseness, rudeness, offensiveness *Opposite*: delicacy

crudity *n* **1 rudeness**, crudeness, coarseness, vulgarity, offensiveness *Opposite*: delicacy **2 roughness**, coarseness, rawness, simplicity, rusticity *Opposite*: sophistication

cruel *adj* **1 unkind**, merciless, nasty, pitiless, brutal *Opposite*: kind **2 painful**, punishing, devastating, harsh, hard *Opposite*: pleasant

cruelty *n* **unkindness**, nastiness, brutality, malice, spite *Opposite*: kindness

cruise *v* **1 voyage**, sail, journey, travel, boat **2 coast**, skim, spin, travel, glide ■ *n* **voyage**, vacation, trip, journey, tour

crumb *n* **morsel**, scrap, titbit, bit, speck

crumble *v* **1 smash**, beat, crush, grind, powder **2 disintegrate**, dissolve, deteriorate, fall apart, fall down

crumbling *adj* **disintegrating**, decomposing, decaying, putrefying, caving in *Opposite*: solid

crumbly *adj* **brittle**, powdery, flaky, friable, crumbling *Opposite*: solid

crummy *(infml)* *adj* **1 inferior**, shoddy, shabby, worthless, poor-quality *Opposite*: superior **2 unwell**, sick, ill, sickly, miserable *Opposite*: healthy

crumple *v* **crease**, crinkle, rumple, crush, screw *Opposite*: smooth

crumpled *adj* **creased**, wrinkled, wrinkly, crinkly, lined *Opposite*: smooth

crunch *v* **munch**, chew, champ, chomp *(infml)* ■ *n* **crisis**, moment of truth, crunch time, critical situation, crux

crunchy adj **crispy**, crisp, brittle, crusty Opposite: soggy

crusade n **cause**, campaign, movement, battle, fight ■ v **campaign**, lobby, struggle, battle, apply yourself

crusader n **campaigner**, supporter, advocate, champion, activist

crush v 1 **squash**, squeeze, compress, press, mash 2 **quell**, suppress, put down, quash, subdue 3 **defeat**, rout, massacre, trounce, overwhelm 4 **humiliate**, devastate, mortify, put down, abash ■ n 1 (infml) **infatuation**, passion, affection, fondness, liking Opposite: dislike 2 **press**, squash, squeeze, crowd, throng. See COMPARE AND CONTRAST at love.

crushed adj **crumpled**, creased, wrinkled, crinkly, crinkled Opposite: smooth

crushing adj **devastating**, overwhelming, swingeing, severe, draconian Opposite: mild

crushingly adv **triumphantly**, exultantly, superciliously, haughtily, contemptuously

crust n **coating**, outside, outer layer, shell, top

crusted adj **encrusted**, caked, coated, covered, thick

crusty adj 1 **crispy**, crisp, hard, brittle, crunchy Opposite: soft 2 **grumpy**, bad-tempered, irritable, testy, cantankerous Opposite: good-humoured

crutch n 1 **stick**, support, prop, walking aid, staff 2 **prop**, support, aid, help, buttress

crux n **root**, bottom, heart, core, nub

cry v 1 **weep**, sob, snivel, whimper, shed tears Opposite: laugh 2 **shout**, exclaim, shout out, call, call out Opposite: whisper ■ n **call**, shout, exclamation, yell, scream Opposite: whisper

crying adj 1 **in tears**, tearful, teary, sobbing, weeping 2 **desperate**, deplorable, awful, horrible, terrible

cry out v 1 **shout out**, shout, cry, call, call out Opposite: whisper 2 **need**, be in need of, require, demand, call for

crypt n **vault**, tomb, catacomb, sepulchre, burial chamber

cryptic adj **mysterious**, enigmatic, puzzling, obscure, ambiguous Opposite: obvious. See COMPARE AND CONTRAST at obscure.

crystal n **mineral**, rock crystal, quartz

crystalline adj 1 **crystal-like**, glassy, sparkling 2 **clear**, transparent, crystal clear, limpid, translucent Opposite: opaque

crystallization n **manifestation**, representation, outward expression, illustration, summation

crystallize v **form**, take shape, fall into place, come together, shape up Opposite: disintegrate

cry your eyes out v **weep**, sob, blubber (infml)

cub n **novice**, beginner, learner, apprentice, trainee Opposite: old hand

cubbyhole n **compartment**, nook, cranny, pigeonhole, cupboard

cubicle n **compartment**, booth, partition, stall, workspace

cubist adj **abstract**, geometric, modern

cuckoo (infml) adj **eccentric**, strange, weird, unusual, bizarre Opposite: ordinary

cuddle v **hug**, embrace, clasp, hold, nuzzle ■ n **embrace**, hug, clasp, hold, clinch

cuddle up v **snuggle up**, curl up, cosy up

cuddly adj **soft**, lovable, fluffy, warm, endearing

cudgel v **hit**, bludgeon, whack, pound, batter

cue n **signal**, prompt, sign, indication, reminder ■ v **prompt**, signal, show, indicate, remind

cuff v **buffet**, slap, strike, hit, rap

cuisine n **food**, fare, cooking, gastronomy, cookery

cul-de-sac n **dead end**, no through road, impasse, blind alley

culinary adj **cooking**, gastronomic, cookery, food

cull v 1 **discard**, reject, remove, scrap, get rid of Opposite: retain 2 **pick**, select, choose, gather, harvest ■ n **reject**, scrap, discard, castoff, second

culminate v **end**, conclude, finish, terminate, climax Opposite: start

culmination n **conclusion**, finale, peak, height, zenith Opposite: inception (fml)

culpability n **blameworthiness**, liability, blame, guilt, fault Opposite: innocence

culpable adj **guilty**, in the wrong, to blame, blameworthy, responsible Opposite: innocent

culprit n **offender**, criminal, guilty party, perpetrator, wrongdoer

cult n 1 **sect**, religious group, religious persuasion, movement 2 **fad**, craze, trend, adoration, veneration ■ adj **alternative**, offbeat, out of the ordinary, unusual, trendy (infml) Opposite: mainstream

cultivate v 1 **farm**, grow, plant, plough, tend 2 **promote**, encourage, nurture, work on, foster Opposite: neglect

cultivated adj **refined**, educated, cultured, sophisticated, urbane Opposite: uncouth

cultivation n 1 **farming**, agriculture, husbandry, crop growing, agronomy 2 **development**, promotion, encouragement, nurturing, fostering Opposite: neglect 3 **refinement**, education, culture, sophistication, urbanity Opposite: uncouthness

cultivator n **grower**, farmer, gardener, planter, agronomist

cultural adj 1 **national**, social, ethnic, folk, traditional 2 **artistic**, literary, intellectual, educational, edifying

culture n 1 **civilization**, society, mores, traditions, customs **2 ethos**, philosophy, values, principles, beliefs **3 sophistication**, refinement, urbanity, civilization, cultivation *Opposite*: uncouthness **4 art, music, and literature**, arts, humanities, fine arts, performing arts

cultured *adj* **refined**, well-educated, learned, educated, erudite *Opposite*: uncouth

culvert *n* **duct**, channel, conduit, tunnel, main

cum *(infml)* *prep* **with**, together with, along with, in combination with, also used as

cumbersome *adj* **unwieldy**, awkward, weighty, bulky, clumsy *Opposite*: manageable

cumulative *adj* **increasing**, snowballing, swelling, accumulative, growing *Opposite*: diminishing

cunning *adj* **1 sly**, wily, crafty, sneaky, shrewd *Opposite*: guileless **2 ingenious**, inventive, resourceful, creative, innovative ■ *n* **1 slyness**, wiliness, craftiness, sneakiness, shrewdness *Opposite*: ingenuousness **2 skill**, cleverness, ingenuity, creativity, dexterity

cup *n* **1 mug**, beaker, demitasse, teacup **2 trophy**, chalice, goblet, prize

cupidity *(fml)* *n* **greed**, avarice, covetousness, materialism, conspicuous consumption *Opposite*: generosity

cupola *n* **dome**, vault, roof, ceiling

cur *n* **mongrel**, dog, hound, mutt *(slang)* *Opposite*: purebred

curable *adj* **treatable**, remediable, correctable, mendable, repairable *Opposite*: incurable

curate *n* **priest**, minister, cleric, ecclesiastic ■ *v* **create**, mount, install, stage

curative *adj* **healing**, remedial, restorative, therapeutic, palliative *Opposite*: injurious

curator *n* **warden**, custodian, keeper, steward, guardian

curb *n* **control**, limit, restriction, restraint, check ■ *v* **restrain**, control, limit, hold back, rein in *Opposite*: promote

curdle *v* **1 coagulate**, clot, thicken, congeal, gel *Opposite*: separate **2** *(infml)* **go sour**, go bad, go off, turn, sour

cure *v* **heal**, treat, make well, restore to health, alleviate *Opposite*: exacerbate ■ *n* **treatment**, therapy, medicine, medication, remedy ■ *v* **preserve**, smoke, dry, salt, pickle

cure-all *n* **panacea**, universal remedy, magic potion, magic bullet, antidote

curfew *n* **restriction**, time limit, deadline, guillotine, limitation

curio *n* **trinket**, antique, curiosity, souvenir, knick-knack

curiosity *n* **1 inquisitiveness**, interest, prying, nosiness *(infml)*, snooping *(infml)* *Opposite*: disinterest **2 oddity**, rarity, novelty, curio, strange thing

curious *adj* **1 inquisitive**, inquiring, interested, questioning, probing *Opposite*: uninterested **2 peculiar**, odd, strange, unusual, intriguing *Opposite*: ordinary

curl *v* **1 twist**, coil, bend, wave, crimp **2 swirl**, spiral, twirl, twist, curve ■ *n* **1 coil**, twist, whorl, spiral, eddy **2 ringlet**, wave, lock, kiss curl, spit curl *(US)*

curl up *v* **double up**, crouch, hug your knees, roll into a ball, go into the foetal position *Opposite*: straighten

curly *adj* **wavy**, coiled, twisted, frizzy, crimped *Opposite*: straight

curmudgeon *n* **malcontent**, grouch *(infml)*, grump *(infml)*, pain *(infml)*, misery *(infml)*

curmudgeonly *adj* **bad-tempered**, crabby, cantankerous, grumpy, testy *Opposite*: pleasant

currency *n* **1 money**, legal tender, coinage, coins, exchange **2 prevalence**, frequency, vogue, commonness, popularity

current *adj* **present**, existing, actual, in progress, recent *Opposite*: former ■ *n* **flow**, stream, undercurrent, tide, flux

curriculum *n* **course**, prospectus, programme, syllabus, core curriculum

curry favour *v* **ingratiate yourself**, cosy up, get in with, play up to, smarm *(infml)*

curse *n* **1 swearword**, oath, expletive, epithet, blasphemy **2 jinx**, spell, magic, setback, blow *Opposite*: blessing **3 scourge**, plague, blight, bane, misfortune ■ *v* **1 swear**, blaspheme, damn, use bad language, eff and blind *(slang)* *Opposite*: bless **2 plague**, afflict, trouble, blight, torment

cursed *adj* **1 damned**, afflicted, banned, anathematized, blighted *Opposite*: blessed **2** *(infml)* **annoying**, irritating, bothersome, vexatious, perturbing

cursor *n* **pointer**, arrow, marker, indicator

cursory *adj* **superficial**, hasty, brief, passing, quick *Opposite*: thorough

curt *adj* **abrupt**, brisk, brusque, rude, brief *Opposite*: civil

curtail *v* **limit**, restrain, restrict, hold back, cut back *Opposite*: extend

curtailment *n* **limitation**, restriction, curb, shortening, reduction *Opposite*: extension

curtain *n* **drape**, blind, screen, shutter, shade

curtain raiser *n* **prelude**, overture, prologue, preamble, lead-in

curtness *n* **brusqueness**, abruptness, shortness, briskness, snappiness *Opposite*: civility

curtsy *v* **genuflect**, bow, bob, kneel, stoop ■ *n* **bow**, genuflection, bob, obeisance *(fml)*

curvaceous *adj* **curvy**, rounded, curved, shapely, voluptuous

curvature *n* **curving**, bend, twist, warp, arc

curve *n* **arc**, bend, bow, arch, camber ■ *v* **bend**, bow, curl, coil, twist *Opposite*: straighten

curved *adj* **rounded**, curled, coiled, arched, bent *Opposite*: straight

curvilinear *see* **curved**

curviness *n* **roundedness**, sinuousness, shapeliness, curvaceousness

curving adj 1 **curved**, curvy, bending, sinuous, snaking Opposite: straight 2 **bent**, warped, twisted, bowed, crooked Opposite: straight

curvy adj **undulating**, wavy, rounded, curved, curvilinear Opposite: straight

cushion n **pillow**, bolster, pad, headrest, beanbag ■ v 1 **protect**, shield, guard, support, bolster Opposite: expose 2 **mitigate**, moderate, lessen, stifle, soften Opposite: exacerbate

cushy (infml) adj **easy**, comfortable, undemanding, cosy, jammy (infml) Opposite: difficult

cusp n 1 **point**, tip, nib, end 2 **crossover**, border, limit, edge, verge

cussed (infml) adj **annoying**, irritating, uncooperative, obstinate, stubborn Opposite: cooperative

cussedness (infml) n **pigheadedness**, stubbornness, obstinacy, wilfulness, perversity Opposite: cooperation

custodial adj 1 **prison**, jail, secure, penal, residential 2 **protective**, safeguarding, safekeeping, sheltered, supervisory

custodian n 1 **guardian**, curator, keeper, defender, upholder 2 **caretaker**, janitor, concierge, warden, night watchman

custody n 1 **detention**, arrest, confinement, imprisonment, incarceration (fml) Opposite: liberty 2 **protection**, keeping, safekeeping, care, charge

custom n 1 **tradition**, practice, convention, institution, ritual Opposite: novelty 2 **habit**, practice, routine, pattern, way 3 **trade**, business, patronage, clientele, market. See COMPARE AND CONTRAST at **habit**.

customary adj 1 **usual**, normal, habitual, expected, routine Opposite: exceptional 2 **traditional**, conventional, time-honoured, established, long-established Opposite: unconventional 3 **typical**, characteristic, usual, habitual, normal Opposite: uncharacteristic. See COMPARE AND CONTRAST at **usual**.

custom-built adj **specially made**, commissioned, bespoke, customized, personalized Opposite: off-the-peg

customer n **client**, buyer, shopper, purchaser, patron

customize v **modify**, tailor, adapt, alter, make to order

customized adj **modified**, tailored, adapted, personalized, custom-made Opposite: mass-produced

custom-made see **custom-built**

customs n **tax**, duty, levy, impost, toll

cut v 1 **chop**, slice, carve, saw, hack Opposite: join 2 **pierce**, score, nick, incise, engrave Opposite: seal 3 **reduce**, decrease, limit, curtail, cut down Opposite: increase 4 **edit**, shorten, censor, condense, chop Opposite: restore 5 **stop**, discontinue, bring to an end, bring to a halt, finish Opposite: continue ■

n 1 **scratch**, wound, slash, graze, incision 2 **reduction**, decrease, cutback, decline, drop Opposite: increase 3 (infml) **share**, commission, percentage, kickback, rake-off (infml)

cut-and-dried adj 1 **decided**, finished, settled, fixed, agreed Opposite: undecided 2 **predictable**, obvious, open-and-shut, anticipated, expected Opposite: anomalous

cut back v **reduce**, curtail, curb, decrease, restrain Opposite: develop

cutback n **reduction**, cut, decrease, decline, drop

cut dead v **snub**, cold-shoulder, rebuff

cut down v 1 **reduce**, decrease, cut back, ease up on, rein back Opposite: increase 2 **fell**, chop down, bring down, hack down, lop 3 (infml) **kill**, strike down, slaughter, mow down, assassinate

cute adj 1 **attractive**, pretty, delightful, charming, appealing Opposite: ugly 2 **shrewd**, cunning, smart, sharp, quick

cuteness n 1 **adorability**, lovability, attractiveness, appeal, charm Opposite: ugliness 2 **shrewdness**, cunning, smartness, sharpness, quickwittedness

cutesy adj **mawkish**, saccharine, sugary, twee, chocolate-box Opposite: austere

cut-glass adj **upper-class**, plummy, public-school, posh (infml), county (infml) Opposite: broad

cut in v **interrupt**, break in, butt in, interject, move in

cutlery n **knives and forks**, tableware, silverware, silver, fighting irons

WORD BANK
❏ **types of cutlery** butter knife, cake slice, carving knife, chopstick, dessertspoon, fish knife, fork, knife, pastry fork, pastry slice, serving spoon, soupspoon, spoon, steak knife, tablespoon, teaspoon

cut loose (infml) v **get free**, get away, escape, make a break, break away

cut off v 1 **remove**, sever, amputate, excise, detach Opposite: reconnect 2 **stop**, disconnect, discontinue, bring to an end, halt Opposite: restore 3 **isolate**, separate, keep apart, strand, detach Opposite: connect 4 **interrupt**, break in, cut short, cut in, butt in

cutoff n 1 **limit**, end point, end date, deadline, expiry Opposite: start 2 **stoppage**, end, finish, halt, freeze Opposite: continuation

cut out v 1 **remove**, take away, excise, extract, take out Opposite: put in 2 **give up**, stop, renounce, forgo, do without 3 **exclude**, ignore, overlook, isolate, marginalize Opposite: include

cutout n 1 **shape**, template, stencil, outline, silhouette 2 **safety device**, circuit breaker, safety switch, trip switch

cut-price adj **reduced**, cheap, bargain, budget, discount

cut short v break off, discontinue, call a halt, suspend, stop in full flow *Opposite*: extend

cutthroat adj merciless, pitiless, ruthless, unsparing, fierce *Opposite*: merciful

cutting adj 1 hurtful, wounding, unkind, acerbic, critical *Opposite*: kind 2 cold, biting, icy, sharp, keen *Opposite*: mild ■ n sprig, offshoot, scion

cutting edge n 1 vanguard, van, forefront, edge, leading edge *Opposite*: rearguard 2 sharp edge, razor edge, knife edge, blade, razor blade

cutting-edge adj leading-edge, front-line, pioneering, trailblazing, radical *Opposite*: old-fashioned

cuttingly adv harshly, abrasively, hurtfully, sharply, severely *Opposite*: kindly

cut up v chop, mince, slice, chop up, dice ■ adj (infml) distressed, upset, affected, distraught, heartbroken *Opposite*: happy

CV n curriculum vitae, qualifications, employment record, résumé (US)

cybernetics n artificial intelligence, information technology, AI, IT

cyberspace n Internet, World Wide Web, information superhighway, data superhighway, infobahn

cycle n series, sequence, set, round, rotation

cyclic see cyclical

cyclical adj recurring, returning, repeated, cyclical, recurrent *Opposite*: unique

cyclone n storm, windstorm, hurricane, typhoon, tornado

cylinder n 1 tube, roll, pipe 2 container, drum, canister, tank, bottle

cylindrical adj tubular, tube-shaped, cylinder-shaped, rod-shaped, rodlike

cynic n sceptic, doubter, detractor, disparager, misanthropist

cynical adj 1 sceptical, distrustful, suspicious, disparaging, negative *Opposite*: naive 2 sarcastic, mocking, scornful, sardonic, sneering *Opposite*: respectful

cynicism n scepticism, sarcasm, distrust, doubt, scorn *Opposite*: naivety

cyst n swelling, lump, polyp, nodule, growth

czar see tsar

D

dab v pat, wipe, apply, touch, tap ■ n bit, blob, spot, dash, drop

dabble v 1 experiment, try your hand, dip into, play at, potter 2 dip, paddle, splash, immerse

dab hand (infml) n expert, specialist, authority, whiz (infml), ace (infml)

dad (infml) n father, daddy (infml), pa (infml), papa (dated), pop (US infml)

daddy (infml) see dad

dado n panel, moulding, frieze, feature

daemon n 1 demigod, supernatural being, spirit 2 guardian spirit, inspiration, guiding force, inner spirit, muse

daft (infml) adj silly, foolish, eccentric, dippy (infml), daffy (infml) *Opposite*: sensible

daftness (infml) n silliness, foolishness, thoughtlessness, eccentricity, dimness *Opposite*: good sense

daily adv every day, each day, on a daily basis, day by day, day after day ■ adj everyday, day-to-day, regular, diurnal, circadian

daintiness n delicacy, elegance, gracefulness, refinement, prettiness *Opposite*: clumsiness

dainty adj pretty, delicate, graceful, refined, exquisite *Opposite*: clumsy

dais n platform, podium, pulpit, stage, stand

dale n valley, glen, dene, vale (literary) *Opposite*: hill

dally v linger, hang about, dawdle, loiter, hang around *Opposite*: hurry

dam n barrier, barrage, weir, wall, boom ■ v block, block up, stem, hold back, control

damage n 1 injury, harm, hurt, impairment, destruction *Opposite*: reparation 2 (infml) cost, price, bill, total, amount ■ v injure, harm, spoil, hurt, smash up *Opposite*: repair. See COMPARE AND CONTRAST at harm.

damaged adj injured, hurt, spoiled, dented, scratched *Opposite*: pristine

damages n compensation, costs, reparation, reimbursement, recompense

damaging adj harmful, destructive, negative, detrimental, hurtful *Opposite*: harmless

damn v 1 condemn, sentence, doom, consign, punish 2 criticize, denounce, censure, lambaste, pan (infml)

damning adj critical, negative, disapproving, unfavourable, condemning *Opposite*: complimentary

damp adj 1 dank, moist, humid, soggy, clammy *Opposite*: dry 2 half-hearted, indifferent, insipid, unenthusiastic, weak *Opposite*: enthusiastic ■ n moisture, dampness, humidity, clamminess, wetness *Opposite*: dryness ■ *v* 1 **check**, curb, restrain, hinder, hamper *Opposite*: encourage 2 **dampen**, moisten, humidify, wet *Opposite*: dry out

damp down *v* **dampen**, diminish, check, dull, curb *Opposite*: increase

dampen *v* 1 **damp**, moisten, humidify, wet *Opposite*: dry out 2 **damp down**, reduce, diminish, check, dull *Opposite*: increase

damper *n* 1 **discouragement**, inhibition, hindrance, impediment, obstruction *Opposite*: spur 2 **mute**, silencer, softener, muffler (*US*) 3 **regulator**, stopper, control, controller

dampness *n* **humidity**, moisture, moistness, clamminess, wetness *Opposite*: dryness

dance *v* 1 **twirl**, pirouette, sway, turn, bop (*infml*) 2 **gambol**, prance, skip, caper, frolic ■ *n* **ball**, disco, rave (*slang*), hop (*dated infml*)

WORD BANK
❏ types of dance ballet, barn dance, belly dance, bop (*infml*), bossa nova, breakdance, cancan, cha-cha, Charleston, fandango, flamenco, foxtrot, jig, jitterbug, jive, lambada, limbo, lindy hop, line dancing, macarena, mambo, merengue, minuet, morris dancing, polka, quadrille, quickstep, rumba, salsa, samba, square dance, step dancing, strathspey, tango, tap dance, waltz

dandified (*dated*) *adj* **dressed up**, dressed to kill, overdressed, fashionable, natty *Opposite*: scruffy

dandle *v* 1 **jiggle**, jog, bounce, dance, rock 2 **pet**, stroke, caress, fondle, pamper

dandruff *n* **scurf**, scale, skin flake

dandy (*dated*) *n* **fop**, fashion plate, clotheshorse (*infml*), beau (*archaic*), coxcomb (*archaic*)

danger *n* 1 **hazard**, risk, peril, threat, menace *Opposite*: safety 2 **chance**, possibility, likelihood, risk

dangerous *adj* 1 **unsafe**, hazardous, risky, treacherous, perilous *Opposite*: safe 2 **grave**, serious, critical, grievous, alarming *Opposite*: safe

dangle *v* **hang**, hang down, swing, sway, suspend *Opposite*: stick up

dank *adj* **damp**, moist, chilly, clammy, humid *Opposite*: warm

dankness *n* **wetness**, dampness, moistness, humidity, clamminess *Opposite*: warmth

dapper *adj* **neat**, elegant, smart, trim, well-dressed *Opposite*: scruffy

dappled *adj* **speckled**, spotted, mottled, stippled, piebald

dare *v* 1 **venture**, risk, gamble, face up to, have the courage 2 **challenge**, defy, taunt, provoke, goad 3 **presume**, venture, have the audacity, be so bold, take the liberty ■ *n* **taunt**, challenge, provocation, ultimatum, goad

daredevil *n* **risk-taker**, madcap, hothead, show-off (*infml*) *Opposite*: stick-in-the-mud (*infml*) ■ *adj* **reckless**, rash, madcap, hot-headed, bold *Opposite*: staid

daresay *v* **guess**, suppose, expect, assume, admit *Opposite*: deny

daring *adj* 1 **bold**, brave, audacious, courageous, enterprising *Opposite*: cowardly 2 **dangerous**, risky, unsafe, hazardous, treacherous *Opposite*: safe ■ *n* **bravery**, nerve, boldness, audacity, courage *Opposite*: cowardice

dark *adj* 1 **dim**, shady, shadowy, murky, gloomy *Opposite*: bright 2 **black**, brunette, brown, chestnut, sable *Opposite*: fair 3 **gloomy**, depressing, bleak, sad, unhappy *Opposite*: cheery 4 **sinister**, mysterious, threatening, evil, nefarious *Opposite*: good ■ *n* **darkness**, dusk, gloom, dimness, shadows *Opposite*: light

darken *v* **blacken**, dim, deepen, cast a shadow, grow dim *Opposite*: brighten

dark glasses *n* **sunglasses**, sunspecs (*infml*), shades (*infml*)

darkness *n* **dark**, night, dusk, gloom, dimness *Opposite*: light

darling *n* 1 **sweetheart**, dear, love, dearest, beloved 2 **favourite**, firm favourite, pet, the apple of somebody's eye ■ *adj* **wonderful**, gorgeous, lovely, adorable, dear *Opposite*: horrible

darn *v* **sew**, stitch, repair, mend, sew up *Opposite*: tear ■ *adj* (*infml*) **very**, extremely, exceptionally, extraordinarily

dart *n* **arrow**, barb, shaft, missile, projectile ■ *v* **dash**, scurry, whiz, rush, run *Opposite*: saunter

dash *n* 1 **sprint**, rush, run, race, surge 2 **trace**, splash, drop, pinch, soupçon 3 **verve**, vigour, spirit, flair, panache ■ *v* 1 **rush**, hurry, hasten, tear, race *Opposite*: amble 2 (*fml*) **knock**, throw, hurl, slam, fling 3 (*fml*) **smash**, break, shatter, crash, splinter 4 **shatter**, ruin, crush, blight, destroy *Opposite*: bolster 5 **frustrate**, confound, foil, shatter, discourage *Opposite*: encourage

dashing *adj* 1 (*dated*) **spirited**, confident, jaunty, flamboyant, bold *Opposite*: staid 2 **elegant**, stylish, chic, debonair, fashionable *Opposite*: dowdy

dastardly *adj* **low**, shameful, dishonourable, mean, reprehensible *Opposite*: honourable

data *n* **information**, statistics, facts, figures, numbers

database *n* **data bank**, store, folder, list, archive

data processing *n* **information retrieval**, data handling, number-crunching (*slang*)

date *n* 1 **day**, day of the week, year, time 2 **time**, point in time, period, era, day 3 **meeting**, rendezvous, appointment, blind date, engagement

dated *adj* **old-fashioned**, old, behind the times, unfashionable, passé *Opposite*: up-to-date

dateline *n* **heading**, subheading, subhead, identification

daub v smear, spread, slap, spatter, slop ■ n blot, blotch, spot, splotch, stain

daunt v put off, deter, discourage, intimidate, scare *Opposite*: encourage

daunting adj **intimidating**, unnerving, discouraging, frightening, overwhelming *Opposite*: heartening

dawdle v 1 **loiter**, delay, linger, plod, lag *Opposite*: hurry 2 **waste time**, hang around, hang about, dally, linger *Opposite*: hurry

dawdler n 1 **straggler**, stroller, wanderer, laggard, dallier *Opposite*: leader 2 **idler**, slacker, shirker, timewaster, shilly-shallier

dawdling n **dilly-dallying**, shilly-shallying, delaying, tarrying, loitering *Opposite*: haste ■ adj **slow**, sluggish, measured, leisurely, casual *Opposite*: hasty

dawn n 1 **sunrise**, crack of dawn, daybreak, first light, daylight *Opposite*: dusk 2 **beginning**, start, birth, emergence, dawning *Opposite*: end ■ v 1 **begin**, start, be born, emerge, originate *Opposite*: end 2 **occur**, cross your mind, register with, strike, become clear to

day n 1 **daylight hours**, daylight, daytime, sunlight hours *Opposite*: night 2 **date**, day of the week, calendar day 3 **time**, era, period, generation, epoch

daybreak n **dawn**, crack of dawn, first light, daylight, morning *Opposite*: dusk

daydream n **reverie**, fantasy, musing, contemplation, dream ■ v **dream**, have your head in the clouds, be miles away, be inattentive, fantasize *Opposite*: concentrate

daydreamer n **idealist**, dreamer, fantasist, visionary, woolgatherer

daydreaming n **reverie**, woolgathering, fantasizing, pensiveness, dreaminess *Opposite*: concentration

daylight n 1 **day**, daytime, sunshine, light of day, hours of daylight *Opposite*: nighttime 2 **dawn**, crack of dawn, sunrise, daybreak, first light *Opposite*: dusk

day out n **outing**, away day, trip, spree, jaunt

day room n **lounge**, recreation room, seating area, reception room, sitting room

days gone by n **former times**, earlier times, previous times, days of old, olden days *Opposite*: future

daytime n **day**, daylight, hours of daylight, morning, afternoon *Opposite*: nighttime

day-to-day adj **everyday**, commonplace, daily, routine, usual *Opposite*: unusual

day trip n **excursion**, outing, day out, trip, visit

day tripper n **tourist**, traveller, sightseer, holidaymaker, tripper *(infml)*

daze n **confused state**, stupor, trance, dream, daydream ■ v **stun**, shock, astonish, astound, surprise

dazzle v 1 **blind**, daze, confuse, overwhelm, bedazzle *(literary)* 2 **amaze**, astonish, astound, impress, overwhelm *Opposite*: bore ■ n **glare**, brightness, reflection, blaze, brilliance

dazzling adj 1 **stunning**, amazing, astounding, incredible, alluring *Opposite*: unimpressive 2 **bright**, glaring, glittering, blazing, luminous *Opposite*: dull

deactivate v **neutralize**, disable, switch off, turn off, disengage *Opposite*: activate

dead adj 1 **lifeless**, late, defunct, deceased *(fml)*, departed *(literary)* *Opposite*: alive 2 **numb**, benumbed, stiff, insensitive, frozen *Opposite*: sensitive 3 **boring**, quiet, dull, uninteresting, deadly *Opposite*: exciting 4 **finished**, obsolete, over, ended, empty *Opposite*: current 5 **silent**, blank, quiet, down, inactive *Opposite*: live

---

COMPARE AND CONTRAST CORE MEANING: no longer living, functioning, or in existence

dead describes organisms that are no longer alive, physical objects that no longer function or exist, and abstract entities that are no longer valid or relevant; **deceased** *(fml*, restricted to people, especially in legal or other technical contexts, or as a euphemism) no longer living; **departed** *(literary*, restricted to people) no longer living; **late** (restricted to people) having died recently or within living memory; **lifeless** not living, or apparently not living; **defunct** no longer operative, valid, or functional, or no longer in existence; **extinct** no longer in existence, or no longer active.

---

deaden v **soften**, dull, muffle, dampen, mute *Opposite*: amplify

dead end n 1 **cul-de-sac**, blind alley, impasse, no through road, roadblock 2 **block**, stalemate, standstill, impasse, deadlock

deadened adj **desensitized**, unfeeling, insensitive, insensible, numb *Opposite*: sensitive

deadhead v **take away**, cut off, remove

dead heat n **draw**, tie, photo finish, drawn game, stalemate

deadline n **time limit**, limit, goal, aim, target *Opposite*: extension

deadlock n **impasse**, stalemate, gridlock, standstill, logjam

deadly adj 1 **lethal**, fatal, terminal, mortal, poisonous *Opposite*: harmless 2 *(infml)* **boring**, tedious, tiresome, dull, dead *Opposite*: interesting ■ adv **completely**, absolutely, extremely, very, perfectly *Opposite*: slightly ■ adj **extreme**, implacable, mortal, sworn, absolute

---

COMPARE AND CONTRAST CORE MEANING: causing death

deadly likely or designed to cause death; **fatal** describes accidents or illnesses that result in death; **mortal** causing, continuing until, or relating to death; **lethal** certain to or intended to cause death; **terminal** describes illnesses that result in death.

---

deadpan adj **unsmiling**, straight-faced, poker-faced, expressionless, blank *Opposite*: expressive

dead ringer *(infml)* n **double**, doppelgänger, image, spitting image *(infml)*, lookalike *(infml) Opposite*: opposite

deaf adj **1 hearing-impaired**, deafened, tone-deaf *Opposite*: hearing **2 unresponsive**, indifferent, oblivious, heedless, unmoved *Opposite*: mindful

deafening adj **loud**, earsplitting, ear-piercing, booming, thunderous *Opposite*: noiseless

deal n **transaction**, contract, agreement, arrangement, pact ■ v **1 distribute**, share out, give out, allocate, apportion *Opposite*: receive **2 trade**, do business, exchange, sell, transact business *Opposite*: buy

dealer n **trader**, merchant, seller, broker, supplier

dealership n **1 charter**, authorization, agreement, right, licence **2 premises**, showroom, offices, workplace, workshop

dealings n **transactions**, contact, communication, business, connections

deal out v **give out**, issue, distribute, mete out, administer *Opposite*: collect

deal with v **cope with**, manage, handle, see to, take care of *Opposite*: evade

dear adj **1 beloved**, cherished, prized, valued, precious *Opposite*: hated **2 expensive**, costly, extortionate, valuable, exorbitant *Opposite*: cheap ■ n **darling**, sweetheart, dearest, beloved, pet

dearest n **love**, sweetheart, pet, precious, sugar *(infml)*

dearly adv **greatly**, extremely, exceedingly, profoundly, sincerely

dearth n **lack**, shortage, scarcity, drought, famine *Opposite*: glut. *See* COMPARE AND CONTRAST *at* **lack**.

death n **1 passing**, bereavement, loss, demise *(fml)*, decease *(fml) Opposite*: birth **2 fatality**, casualty, loss of life, killing, murder *Opposite*: birth **3 end**, fall, downfall, ruin, collapse *Opposite*: beginning

deathblow n **body blow**, final blow, last straw, last nail in the coffin, end

death knell n **finish**, last nail in the coffin, end of the road, point of no return, last straw

deathless adj **eternal**, timeless, immortal, everlasting, undying *Opposite*: mortal

deathlike adj **skeletal**, gaunt, ashen, spectral, pallid

deathly adj **deadly**, deathlike, tomblike, deep, stony ■ adv **extremely**, intensely, deadly, intensively, absolutely *Opposite*: slightly

death mask n **effigy**, cast, head, model, sculpture

death rattle n **gurgle**, rattle, rasp, wheeze, croak

death toll n **fatalities**, death rate, mortality rate, fatality rate, loss of life

deathtrap *(infml)* n **safety risk**, hazard, minefield, pitfall, health hazard

death warrant *see* **death knell**

debacle n **disaster**, catastrophe, fiasco, shambles, tragedy *Opposite*: success

debar v **exclude**, expel, bar, ban, prohibit *Opposite*: admit

debark v **disembark**, alight, go ashore, land, get off *Opposite*: embark

debarkation n **disembarkation**, alighting, going ashore, landing, getting off

debase v **1 degrade**, impair, adulterate, sully, corrupt *Opposite*: purify **2 humiliate**, demean, degrade, shame, humble *Opposite*: glorify

debasement n **1 ruination**, adulteration, corruption, defilement, tarnishing *Opposite*: purification **2 humiliation**, degradation, disgrace, shame, disparagement *Opposite*: glorification

debatable adj **arguable**, dubious, controversial, doubtful, contentious *Opposite*: settled

debate v **1 discuss**, argue, dispute, deliberate, contest *Opposite*: conclude **2 ponder**, wonder, deliberate, weigh up, consider *Opposite*: decide ■ n **discussion**, argument, dispute, examination, consideration *Opposite*: conclusion

debater n **speaker**, orator, public speaker, disputant, arguer

debauched adj **decadent**, dissolute, degenerate, dissipated, immoral *Opposite*: moral

debauchery n **decadence**, dissoluteness, immorality, self-indulgence *Opposite*: morality

debilitate v **weaken**, incapacitate, enervate, drain, hamper *Opposite*: fortify

debilitated adj **weakened**, incapacitated, enervated, drained, hampered *Opposite*: fortified. *See* COMPARE AND CONTRAST *at* **weak**.

debilitating adj **weakening**, incapacitating, enervating, draining, devastating *Opposite*: refreshing

debility n **weakness**, incapacity, frailty, ineffectiveness, enfeeblement *Opposite*: strength

debit n **withdrawal**, subtraction, deduction, debt, charge *Opposite*: credit ■ v **deduct**, take out, withdraw, subtract, charge *Opposite*: credit

debonair adj **suave**, elegant, refined, charming, well-groomed *Opposite*: graceless

debouch v **emerge**, move out, spread out, exit, come out *Opposite*: confine

debrief v **question**, interrogate, interview, examine, quiz

debriefing n **interrogation**, questioning, interview, examination, probing *Opposite*: briefing

debris *n* **wreckage**, remains, fragments, rubble, waste

debt *n* **1 arrears**, liability, debit, balance, balance due *Opposite*: credit **2 obligation**, duty, responsibility, dues, liability

debtor *n* **borrower**, mortgagor, insolvent, defaulter, pledger

debug *v* **clear up**, correct, sort out, repair, fix *Opposite*: corrupt

debunk *v* **expose**, show up, deflate, demystify, discredit *Opposite*: perpetuate

debut *n* **entrance**, introduction, unveiling, presentation, inauguration *Opposite*: retirement

decade *n* **period**, era, time, epoch

decadence *n* **corruption**, debauchery, depravity, dissolution, self-indulgence *Opposite*: temperance

decadent *adj* **debauched**, corrupt, depraved, dissolute, degenerate *Opposite*: innocent

decamp *v* **run away**, run off, escape, flee, abscond *Opposite*: turn up

decant *v* **pour**, pour out, transfer, empty, empty out *Opposite*: fill

decanter *n* **carafe**, flask, vessel, bottle, pitcher

decapitate *v* **behead**, guillotine, execute, amputate, truncate

decapitation *n* **beheading**, amputation, killing, guillotining, execution

decay *v* **1 decompose**, rot, fester, perish, crumble **2 decline**, degenerate, deteriorate, fall off, dwindle *Opposite*: flourish ■ *n* **1 deterioration**, decline, degeneration, falling-off, falloff *Opposite*: growth **2 decomposition**, rot, rotting, putrefaction, corrosion

decayed *adj* **decomposed**, rotten, rotting, putrefied, perished *Opposite*: fresh

decaying *adj* **decomposing**, rotting, rotten, putrefying, crumbling *Opposite*: fresh

decease *(fml)* *n* **death**, passing, departure, release, demise *(fml)* *Opposite*: birth

deceased *(fml)* *n* **corpse**, cadaver, body, decedent *(fml)*, departed *(fml or literary)* ■ *adj* **dead**, late, lifeless, defunct, extinct *Opposite*: alive. *See* COMPARE AND CONTRAST *at* **dead**.

deceit *n* **dishonesty**, treachery, deceitfulness, deception, trickery *Opposite*: honesty

deceitful *adj* **dishonest**, deceiving, fraudulent, untrustworthy, cunning *Opposite*: honest

deceitfully *adv* **dishonestly**, cunningly, fraudulently, deviously, treacherously *Opposite*: honestly

deceitfulness *n* **dishonesty**, deceit, treachery, lies, falseness *Opposite*: honesty

deceive *v* **1 mislead**, betray, trick, take in, lie to **2 cheat**, two-time, betray, play away *(infml)*, cuckold *(literary)*

deceiver *n* **liar**, fraud, swindler, cheat, fraudster

deceiving *adj* **misleading**, lying, cheating, devious, deceptive *Opposite*: honest

decelerate *v* **slow down**, slow, slow up, brake, lose speed *Opposite*: accelerate

deceleration *n* **slowing down**, slowing up, slowing, braking, checking *Opposite*: acceleration

decency *n* **1 politeness**, decorum, decorousness, civility, courtesy *Opposite*: incivility **2 modesty**, respectability, uprightness, integrity, wholesomeness *Opposite*: decadence

decent *adj* **1 moral**, honest, virtuous, wholesome, demure *Opposite*: decadent **2 good**, right, proper, correct, suitable *Opposite*: inappropriate **3 reasonable**, respectable, adequate, sizable, generous *Opposite*: inadequate **4** *(infml)* **dressed**, clothed, clad, garbed, covered *Opposite*: undressed **5 respectable**, upright, polite, civilized, well-mannered

decentralization *n* **devolution**, subsidiarity, regionalization, delegation, reorganization *Opposite*: centralization

decentralize *v* **devolve**, regionalize, reorganize, disperse, distribute *Opposite*: centralize

deception *n* **1 dishonesty**, duplicity, deceptiveness, deceit, cheating *Opposite*: truthfulness **2 trick**, ruse, sham, fraud, con

deceptive *adj* **misleading**, illusory, deceiving, dishonest, false *Opposite*: reliable

deceptiveness *n* **falseness**, falsity, disingenuousness, deviousness, spuriousness *Opposite*: reliability

decide *v* **1 make a decision**, choose, come to a decision, make your mind up, settle on *Opposite*: equivocate **2 settle**, determine, conclude, resolve, decree *Opposite*: put off

decided *adj* **1 obvious**, definite, absolute, categorical, unquestionable *Opposite*: unclear **2 determined**, resolute, decisive, firm, sure *Opposite*: hesitant

decidedly *adv* **categorically**, definitely, absolutely, distinctly, particularly *Opposite*: possibly

decider *n* **game**, match, contest, trial, play-off

deciding *adj* **determining**, decisive, conclusive, key, pivotal *Opposite*: insignificant

decimal *n* **number**, fraction, unit

decimate *v* **devastate**, destroy, annihilate, ruin, cut a swath through

decimation *n* **devastation**, destruction, slaughter, annihilation, ruin

decipher *v* **decode**, decrypt, interpret, translate, make out *Opposite*: encode

decipherable *adj* **readable**, legible, intelligible, comprehensible, understandable *Opposite*: unintelligible

decision *n* **1 choice**, result, conclusion, verdict, pronouncement **2 determination**, resolve, firmness, willpower, strength of mind *Opposite*: indecision

decisive adj 1 **conclusive**, pivotal, key, critical, significant Opposite: insignificant 2 **strong-minded**, resolute, determined, certain, clear-sighted Opposite: uncertain

decisiveness n **resoluteness**, determination, conclusiveness, authoritativeness, positiveness Opposite: indecisiveness

deck n **level**, floor, surface, area, sun deck ■ v (infml) **hit**, knock down, knock over, floor, thump

deck hand n **sailor**, rating, seaman

declaim v **hold forth**, pronounce, proclaim, declare, utter Opposite: mutter

declamatory adj **dramatic**, formal, oratorical, rhetorical, theatrical Opposite: low-key

declaration n **statement**, announcement, assertion, speech, pronouncement

declare v **announce**, state, speak out, assert, affirm

declassification n **release**, publication, open access, derestriction, decontrol Opposite: restriction

declassify v **release**, publish, derestrict, open up, bring out Opposite: classify

decline v 1 **refuse**, turn down, reject, pass up, beg off Opposite: accept 2 **weaken**, fail, deteriorate, degenerate, fall off Opposite: improve ■ n **deterioration**, falling-off, falloff, decay, drop Opposite: improvement

declining adj **deteriorating**, decreasing, lessening, falling, diminishing Opposite: improving

decode v **decipher**, make out, make sense of, interpret, translate Opposite: encode

decoder n **cryptographer**, decipherer, interpreter, translator

décolleté adj **low-necked**, low-cut, plunging, low, revealing

decommission v **retire**, mothball, withdraw, take out, neutralize Opposite: introduce

decompose v **rot**, decay, crumble, fester, putrefy

decomposed adj **rotten**, disintegrated, decayed, perished, putrid Opposite: fresh

decomposing adj **rotting**, disintegrating, decaying, putrid, putrefying Opposite: fresh

decomposition n **decay**, rottenness, putrefaction, breakdown, disintegration Opposite: soundness

deconstruct v **critique**, criticize, decompose, review, analyse

decontaminate v **cleanse**, clean up, clean, purify, disinfect Opposite: contaminate

decontrol v **deregulate**, delimit, free, set free, loosen Opposite: control

decor n **decoration**, furnishings, colour scheme, interior decoration, scheme

decorate v 1 **beautify**, adorn, ornament, embellish, trim Opposite: strip 2 **paint**, smarten up, do up, spruce, do over (slang) 3 **honour**, award, garland, recognize, acknowledge

decorated adj **ornamented**, ornate, adorned, festooned, draped Opposite: plain

decoration n 1 **feature**, festoon, beading, border, carving 2 **beautification**, adornment, ornament, ornamentation, embellishment 3 **honour**, medal, award, sash, ribbon

decorative adj **ornamental**, pretty, attractive, pleasing to the eye, enhancing Opposite: ugly

decorous adj **well-mannered**, well-behaved, good, correct, modest Opposite: improper

decorum n **dignity**, propriety, sedateness, good behaviour, modesty Opposite: abandon

decoy n **lure**, trap, snare, trick, distraction ■ v **entice**, lure, lead astray, distract, entrap

decrease v 1 **reduce**, cut, diminish, cut down, contract Opposite: increase 2 **diminish**, decline, dwindle, subside, lessen ■ n **reduction**, cut, diminution, lessening, decline Opposite: increase

decreasing adj **diminishing**, declining, reducing, dwindling, shrinking Opposite: increasing

decree n **ruling**, verdict, announcement, pronouncement, declaration Opposite: request ■ v **command**, rule, pronounce, announce, dictate

decrepit adj 1 **dilapidated**, crumbling, decaying, falling to pieces, falling apart Opposite: pristine 2 (infml) **old**, feeble, frail, weak, infirm Opposite: vigorous. See COMPARE AND CONTRAST at **weak**.

decrepitude n 1 **decay**, dilapidation, ruin, shabbiness Opposite: soundness 2 (infml) **infirmity**, frailty, feebleness, weakness, debility

decriminalization n **legalization**, acceptance, allowance, toleration, sanction Opposite: criminalization

decriminalize v **make legal**, legalize, authorize, sanction, permit Opposite: outlaw

decry v **criticize**, complain, belittle, disparage, deprecate Opposite: praise

dedicate v 1 **give**, commit, devote, consecrate, pledge 2 **reserve**, devote, set aside, earmark, give over to

dedicated adj **committed**, devoted, steadfast, loyal, faithful Opposite: uncommitted

dedication n **devotion**, commitment, enthusiasm, keenness, perseverance

deduce v 1 **conclude**, assume, presume, suppose, gather 2 **infer**, reason, conclude, work out, figure out

COMPARE AND CONTRAST CORE MEANING: reach a logical conclusion on the basis of information **deduce** reach a conclusion using available knowledge; **infer** draw a conclusion from specific circumstances or evidence; **assume** take a premise or information as true without checking or confirming it; **reason** consider information and use it to reach a conclusion in a logical way; **conclude** form an opinion or make a judgment after much consideration; **work out** find a solution or explanation by careful thought or reasoning; **figure out** find a solution or reach a conclusion by careful thought or reasoning.

deduct v **subtract**, take away, take, remove, abstract *Opposite*: add

deduction n **1 inference**, assumption, conclusion, presumption, judgment **2 subtraction**, removal, withdrawal, abstraction, contribution *Opposite*: addition

deductive adj **logical**, inferential, reasonable, empirical, rational *Opposite*: illogical

deed n **1 action**, feat, act, endeavour, exploit **2 document**, title deed, title, charter, record

deem (*fml*) v **think**, believe, consider, estimate, suppose

deep adj **1 bottomless**, profound, unfathomable, subterranean, cavernous *Opposite*: shallow **2 deep-seated**, innate, inherent, entrenched, subconscious *Opposite*: superficial **3 low**, rumbling, booming, sonorous, resonant *Opposite*: shrill **4 intense**, profound, concentrated, potent, powerful *Opposite*: slight **5 profound**, multifaceted, multilayered, mysterious, meaningful *Opposite*: transparent **6 hidden**, secret, arcane, mysterious, silent *Opposite*: open

deepen v **1 intensify**, extend, expand, concentrate, accumulate *Opposite*: weaken **2 dig out**, excavate, hollow out, scoop out, extend *Opposite*: fill in

deeply adv **intensely**, profoundly, seriously, extremely, greatly *Opposite*: mildly

deepness n **1 depth**, profundity, profoundness, bottomlessness, fathomlessness **2 lowness**, resonance, sonority, low pitch

deep-rooted *see* **deep-seated**

deep-sea adj **marine**, oceanic, ocean

deep-seated adj **innate**, inherent, entrenched, subconscious, ingrained *Opposite*: superficial

de-escalate v **scale down**, cut back, reduce, decrease, slow *Opposite*: escalate

de-escalation n **reduction**, stepping down, scaling down, cutback, decrease *Opposite*: escalation

deface v **spoil**, ruin, mar, disfigure, mutilate *Opposite*: renovate

defacement n **disfigurement**, mutilation, vandalism, destruction, damage *Opposite*: restoration

de facto adv **in effect**, to all intents and purposes, in reality, actually, effectively ■ adj **actual**, genuine, effective, existing, real

defamation n **insult**, offence, slander, libel, slur *Opposite*: praise

defamatory adj **insulting**, offensive, slanderous, libellous, derogatory *Opposite*: complimentary

defame v **insult**, slander, libel, denigrate, malign *Opposite*: praise. *See* COMPARE AND CONTRAST *at* malign.

default n **evasion**, avoidance, nonpayment, defaulting, nonattendance ■ v **fail to pay**, evade, dodge, shirk, duck (*infml*) *Opposite*: pay

defaulter n **1 nonpayer**, debtor, cheat, tax dodger (*infml*) **2 shirker**, slacker, absentee, dodger (*infml*)

defeat n **1 overthrow**, conquest, downfall, rout *Opposite*: victory **2 loss**, reverse, setback, thrashing, beating *Opposite*: victory ■ v **1 beat**, overcome, conquer, vanquish, trounce *Opposite*: lose **2 baffle**, confound, foil, frustrate, thwart

COMPARE AND CONTRAST CORE MEANING: win a victory

defeat win a victory over an enemy or competitor, or to cause failure; **beat** defeat somebody in a contest, or to overcome a difficulty; **conquer** defeat decisively in battle, or to overcome a difficulty; **vanquish** defeat decisively in battle or competition; **overcome** win or succeed after a struggle; **triumph over** succeed against an adversary or against difficult odds; **thrash** gain an easy decisive victory in a sporting contest; **trounce** defeat an opponent convincingly.

defeatism n **pessimism**, resignation, despondency, despair, negativity *Opposite*: optimism

defeatist adj **pessimistic**, negative, fatalistic, resigned, despondent *Opposite*: optimistic ■ n **pessimist**, loser, fatalist, doomsayer, doommonger *Opposite*: optimist

defecate (*fml*) v **excrete**, eliminate waste, empty the bowels, have a bowel movement, evacuate

defecation n **excretion**, evacuation, elimination

defect n **flaw**, fault, imperfection, blemish, shortcoming ■ v **desert**, change sides, abscond, go over, turn traitor. *See* COMPARE AND CONTRAST *at* flaw.

defective adj **faulty**, imperfect, flawed, substandard, malfunctioning *Opposite*: perfect

defectiveness n **faultiness**, failure, inadequacy, unreliability, imperfection

defector n **traitor**, turncoat, renegade, convert, rebel *Opposite*: loyalist

defence n **1 protection**, resistance, guard, security, cover *Opposite*: attack **2 justification**, argument, vindication, plea, apology *Opposite*: accusation

defence force n **army**, armed forces, armed services, task force, fighters

defenceless adj **unprotected**, unarmed, exposed, unguarded, vulnerable *Opposite*: protected

defencelessness n **vulnerability**, helplessness, powerlessness, weakness, frailty *Opposite*: strength

defences n **1 resistance**, immunity, protection, shield, safeguard **2 fortifications**, ramparts, battlements, earthworks, emplacements

defend v 1 **protect**, guard, shield, safeguard, preserve *Opposite*: attack 2 **support**, stand up for, stick up for, stand for, represent *Opposite*: oppose. *See* COMPARE AND CONTRAST *at* **safeguard**.

defendant n **accused**, respondent, suspect, corespondent *Opposite*: accuser

defender n 1 **protector**, guard, warden, guardian, escort *Opposite*: attacker 2 **supporter**, champion, advocate, sponsor, upholder *Opposite*: opponent

defensible adj 1 **defendable**, impregnable, unassailable, invulnerable, secure *Opposite*: vulnerable 2 **justifiable**, valid, cast-iron, secure, rock-solid *Opposite*: indefensible

defensibly adv **excusably**, justifiably, explicably, forgivably, understandably *Opposite*: unjustifiably

defensive adj 1 **self-justifying**, self-protective, apologetic, touchy, distrustful *Opposite*: aggressive 2 **protective**, protecting, defending, shielding, fortified

defer v 1 **put off**, reschedule, put back, postpone, delay *Opposite*: bring forward 2 **bow to**, submit, be deferential, accede, comply

deference n **respect**, esteem, regard, reverence, admiration *Opposite*: disrespect

deferential adj **respectful**, admiring, reverent, polite, obsequious *Opposite*: disrespectful

deferment n **adjournment**, postponement, delay, stay, deferral

deferral n **postponement**, adjournment, delay, stay, deferment

defiance n **insubordination**, disobedience, insolence, rebelliousness, boldness *Opposite*: compliance

defiant adj **disobedient**, insolent, insubordinate, rebellious, bold *Opposite*: compliant

deficiency n 1 **lack**, shortage, absence, deficit, dearth *Opposite*: excess 2 **inadequacy**, defect, flaw, fault, imperfection. *See* COMPARE AND CONTRAST *at* **lack**.

deficient adj 1 **lacking**, poor, underprovided, undersupplied, short *Opposite*: abundant 2 **inadequate**, flawed, faulty, unsatisfactory, defective *Opposite*: perfect

deficiently adv **inadequately**, defectively, faultily, incorrectly, wrongly *Opposite*: perfectly

deficit n **shortfall**, shortage, arrears, discrepancy, debit *Opposite*: surplus. *See* COMPARE AND CONTRAST *at* **lack**.

defile v 1 *(fml)* **corrupt**, taint, besmirch, sully, spoil *Opposite*: purify 2 *(fml)* **dishonour**, desecrate, sully, violate, debase *Opposite*: respect ∎ n **pass**, valley, gorge, gap

defiled *(fml)* adj 1 **corrupted**, tainted, besmirched, sullied, tarnished *Opposite*: untarnished 2 **dishonoured**, desecrated, sullied, violated, debased *Opposite*: respected

define v 1 **describe**, outline, express, state, explain 2 **characterize**, classify, identify, distinguish, specify 3 **mark out**, outline, delimit, demarcate, mark

defined adj **clear**, distinct, definite, well-defined, sharp *Opposite*: indistinct

defining moment n **turning point**, landmark, watershed, crossroads, moment of truth

definite adj 1 **exact**, specific, explicit, clear-cut, unambiguous *Opposite*: vague 2 **obvious**, recognized, significant, unquestionable, unmistakable *Opposite*: dubious 3 **fixed**, settled, agreed, final, assured *Opposite*: indefinite 4 **sure**, certain, positive, set on, determined *Opposite*: uncertain

definitely adv **certainly**, absolutely, positively, unquestionably, without doubt *Opposite*: possibly

definiteness n **certainty**, assurance, assuredness, conviction, finality *Opposite*: uncertainty

definition n 1 **meaning**, description, explanation, classification, characterization 2 **clarity**, sharpness, distinctness, focus, clearness *Opposite*: haziness

definitive adj 1 **conclusive**, final, decisive, ultimate, absolute *Opposite*: tentative 2 **authoritative**, conclusive, perfect, best, classic

deflate v 1 **let the air out**, go down, let down, collapse, shrink *Opposite*: inflate 2 **belittle**, disappoint, flatten, squash, quash *Opposite*: boost 3 **devalue**, depress, decrease, reduce, lower

deflated adj 1 **subdued**, humiliated, flattened, humbled, dispirited *Opposite*: exhilarated 2 **emptied**, flattened, shrunk, collapsed, let down *Opposite*: inflated

deflation n **depression**, devaluation, depreciation, reduction, decrease *Opposite*: inflation

deflect v 1 **bounce**, glance, ricochet, rebound, bend 2 **turn aside**, ward off, repel, redirect, sidetrack *Opposite*: attract

deflection n **refraction**, ricochet, rebound, glance, bend

deforest v **log**, denude, strip, clear-cut, desolate

deform v **distort**, bend, warp, buckle, bow

deformation n **distortion**, twist, buckle, bend, warp

deformed adj 1 **misshapen**, distorted, bent, warped, malformed 2 **abnormal**, corrupted, perverted, ruined, damaged

deformity n **disfigurement**, malformation, distortion, abnormality, misshapenness

defraud v **deceive**, swindle, cheat, trick, take advantage of

defray v **pay**, cover, meet, contribute, finance

defrock v **unfrock**, excommunicate, disqualify, drum out, expel

defrost v melt, thaw, thaw out, de-ice, unfreeze Opposite: freeze

deft adj skilful, adroit, neat, nimble, dexterous Opposite: clumsy

deftness n skill, dexterity, precision, handiness, swiftness Opposite: clumsiness

defunct adj **1** obsolete, invalid, redundant, outdated, out-of-date Opposite: current **2 dead**, expired, extinct, gone (infml), deceased (fml) Opposite: alive. See COMPARE AND CONTRAST at dead.

defuse v resolve, calm, soothe, smooth out, neutralize Opposite: aggravate

defy v **challenge**, confront, disobey, rebel, resist Opposite: obey

degeneracy n depravity, wickedness, corruption, dissoluteness, decadence Opposite: morality

degenerate v deteriorate, collapse, relapse, worsen, reduce Opposite: improve ■ adj debased, decadent, immoral, debauched, corrupt Opposite: moral

degeneration n deterioration, collapse, disintegration, falling apart, worsening Opposite: regeneration

degenerative adj wasting, worsening, deteriorating, progressive

degradation n **1** humiliation, disgrace, shame, mortification, misery **2 squalor**, filth, dilapidation, deprivation, poverty

degrade v **1** humiliate, shame, disgrace, mortify, demean Opposite: exalt (fml) **2 damage**, destroy, reduce, cut down, worsen Opposite: upgrade **3 decay**, decompose, disintegrate, break down, rot

degrading adj humiliating, debasing, demeaning, undignified, corrupting Opposite: ennobling

degree n **1 extent**, quantity, intensity, magnitude, level **2 grade**, gradation, mark, notch, step

dehumanize v desensitize, brutalize, degrade, debase Opposite: humanize

dehydrate v dry out, dry up, become dry, desiccate, parch

dehydrated adj dry, dried out, arid, parched, desiccated. See COMPARE AND CONTRAST at dry.

dehydration n dryness, drying out, drying up, desiccation, thirst

de-ice v unfreeze, melt, thaw Opposite: ice up

deification n elevation, veneration, adoration, beatification, exaltation (fml)

deify v idolize, worship, glorify, adore, venerate

deign v condescend, lower yourself, stoop, consent, agree

deity n divinity, god, goddess, godhead, divine being

dejected adj sad, disappointed, unhappy, miserable, depressed Opposite: cheerful

dejection n sadness, unhappiness, misery, gloom, depression Opposite: cheerfulness

dekko (infml) n look, glance, peek, shufti (infml), gander (infml)

delay v **1** postpone, put off, suspend, adjourn, defer Opposite: bring forward **2 procrastinate**, hesitate, linger, dawdle, pause Opposite: hurry up **3 slow down**, slow up, hold up, set back, obstruct Opposite: speed up ■ n **1** postponement, interruption, stay, suspension, adjournment **2 interval**, wait, pause, break, lull

delayed adj late, behind, behind schedule, overdue, tardy Opposite: early

delectable adj **1** delicious, tasty, mouthwatering, appetizing, luscious Opposite: tasteless **2 delightful**, charming, adorable, appealing, heavenly Opposite: unappealing

delectation (fml) n enjoyment, delight, pleasure, appreciation, entertainment

delegate n representative, agent, envoy, ambassador, deputy ■ v **1 hand over**, farm out, pass on, give, assign Opposite: retain **2 designate**, assign, appoint, allocate, deputize

delegation n **1 commission**, deputation, mission, lobby **2 allocation**, assignment, handing over, giving out, passing on Opposite: retention

delete v erase, remove, strike out, cross out, obliterate Opposite: insert

deleterious adj damaging, harmful, injurious, destructive, adverse Opposite: beneficial

deletion n removal, obliteration, erasure, loss, omission Opposite: addition

deliberate adj **1** intentional, purposeful, premeditated, conscious, calculated Opposite: accidental **2 careful**, thoughtful, slow, cautious, unhurried Opposite: hasty ■ v **think**, reflect, consider, mull over, weigh up

deliberation n **1** (fml) reflection, thought, consideration, care, forethought Opposite: impulsiveness **2 discussion**, debate, negotiation, planning, pondering

deliberative (fml) adj considered, premeditated, planned, calculated, thought through Opposite: casual

delicacy n **1 titbit**, treat, luxury, dainty, fancy **2 sensitivity**, tact, diplomacy, consideration, care Opposite: insensitivity **3 refinement**, fastidiousness, subtlety, elegance, fineness Opposite: vulgarity **4 gracefulness**, attractiveness, elegance, charm, grace Opposite: awkwardness **5 fragility**, flimsiness, slenderness, frailty, weakness Opposite: sturdiness **6 precision**, skill, care, deftness, adroitness Opposite: inaccuracy

delicate adj **1** fragile, frail, weak, slight, flimsy Opposite: robust **2 subtle**, faint, slight, gentle, mild Opposite: overpowering **3 fine**, precise, detailed, accurate, skilled Opposite: rough **4 refined**, graceful, elegant, dainty, nice Opposite: inelegant **5 difficult**, tricky, complicated, sensitive, awkward *Opposite*: straightforward **6 sensitive**, refined, thoughtful, considerate, sympathetic *Opposite*: tactless. *See* COMPARE AND CONTRAST *at* **fragile**.

delicateness *n* fragility, fragileness, frailty, vulnerability, feebleness *Opposite*: robustness

delicious *adj* **1 tasty**, appetizing, luscious, delectable, mouthwatering *Opposite*: tasteless **2 delightful**, lovely, wonderful, pleasant, enjoyable *Opposite*: unpleasant

deliciousness *n* **1 delectableness**, lusciousness, sweetness, tastiness, scrumptiousness *(infml) Opposite*: tastelessness **2 delightfulness**, charm, sweetness, attractiveness, pleasantness *Opposite*: unpleasantness

delight *n* joy, enjoyment, pleasure, happiness, glee *Opposite*: displeasure ■ *v* **1 please**, charm, amuse, thrill, gratify *Opposite*: disappoint **2 take pleasure in**, appreciate, revel in, relish, enjoy *Opposite*: dislike

delighted *adj* pleased, happy, charmed, enchanted, thrilled *Opposite*: unhappy

delightful *adj* pleasant, charming, lovely, wonderful, enjoyable *Opposite*: unpleasant

delimit *v* set the limits of, demarcate, define, restrict, mark out

delimitation *(fml) n* demarcation, definition, marking out, limitation, restriction

delineate *v* **1** *(fml)* **define**, describe, explain, portray, present **2 outline**, delimit, mark out, demarcate, define

delineation *n* **1** *(fml)* **description**, definition, explanation, setting down **2 demarcation**, definition, allocation, marking out, outlining

delinquency *n* **1 criminal behaviour**, crime, felony, lawbreaking, misbehaviour *Opposite*: uprightness **2** *(fml)* **negligence**, carelessness, recklessness, failure, irresponsibility *Opposite*: carefulness

delinquent *n* criminal, guilty party, felon, lawbreaker, wrongdoer ■ *adj* **1 criminal**, aberrant, antisocial, offending, felonious *Opposite*: law-abiding **2** *(fml)* **negligent**, careless, reckless, irresponsible, neglectful *Opposite*: dutiful

delirious *adj* **1 feverish**, fevered, hot, hallucinating, rambling *Opposite*: rational **2 elated**, ecstatic, transported, in seventh heaven, beside yourself *Opposite*: dejected

delirium *n* **1 fever**, hallucination, restlessness, confusion, frenzy *Opposite*: clarity **2 ecstasy**, elation, fervour, euphoria, excitement *Opposite*: dejection

deliver *v* **1 carry**, bring, transport, distribute, send *Opposite*: take away **2 produce**, provide, supply, dispense, serve **3** *(literary)* **set free**, release, rescue, save, liberate *Opposite*: capture **4 hand over**, give up, surrender, transfer, relinquish *Opposite*: keep

deliverance *(fml) n* **rescue**, release, liberation, relief, escape *Opposite*: capture

delivery *n* **1 distribution**, transfer, transport, sending, conveyance **2 manner of speaking**, presentation, approach, manner, technique **3 rescue**, release, liberation, relief, escape *Opposite*: capture

delta *n* estuary, outlet, mouth, channel

delude *v* deceive, take in, cheat, mislead, con

deluded *adj* **mistaken**, deceived, misled, duped, conned

deluge *n* **1 torrent**, flood, downpour, cloudburst, rainstorm **2 upsurge**, spate, flood, cascade, avalanche *Opposite*: trickle ■ *v* **1 overwhelm**, overload, overrun, swamp, bury **2 inundate**, flood, swamp, drown, soak *Opposite*: dry up

delusion *n* **1 illusion**, hallucination, vision, mirage, figment of the imagination *Opposite*: reality **2 misunderstanding**, misapprehension, misbelief, false impression, misconception

delusive *adj* **deceptive**, chimerical, misleading, specious, illusory *Opposite*: genuine

deluxe *adj* sumptuous, luxurious, luxury, exclusive, select *Opposite*: cheap

delve *v* **1 look into**, investigate, research, probe, explore **2** *(archaic)* **dig**, burrow, tunnel, scrabble, scratch ■ *n* rummage, hunt, dig, search, dive

demagogic *adj* rabble-rousing, inflammatory, manipulative, declamatory, agitating

demagogical *see* demagogic

demagogue *n* firebrand, agitator, manipulator, crowd pleaser, haranguer

demand *n* **1 request**, call, claim, petition, mandate *Opposite*: response **2 requirement**, need, pressure, exigency, claim ■ *v* **1 insist**, command, order, require, stipulate *Opposite*: request **2 ask**, inquire, question, query, want *Opposite*: answer **3 require**, need, want, call for, necessitate

demanding *adj* **1 difficult**, hard, challenging, tough, severe *Opposite*: easy **2 insistent**, self-centred, persistent, dissatisfied, discontented *Opposite*: satisfied

demarcate *v* **1 define**, mark out, delineate, draw, fix **2 separate**, distinguish, differentiate, isolate, discriminate *Opposite*: unite

demarcation *n* separation, differentiation, distinction, discrimination, segregation

demean *v* degrade, debase, humiliate, disgrace, humble *Opposite*: uplift

demeanour *n* manner, conduct, behaviour, character, deportment

demean yourself *v* lower yourself, swallow your pride, stoop low, go down on your knees, abase yourself *(literary)*

demented *(infml) adj* **irrational**, unreasonable, wild, frenzied, frantic *Opposite*: rational

demerger *n* **separation**, split, break, breakup, divergence *Opposite*: merger

demerit *n* **disadvantage**, failing, shortcoming, drawback, fault *Opposite*: merit

demijohn *n* **bottle**, flagon, magnum, jeroboam, rehoboam

demise *(fml)* *n* **1 death**, passing, departure, decease *(fml)*, expiry *(fml or literary) Opposite*: birth **2 end**, termination, finish, failure, ruin *Opposite*: creation

demo *n* **1** *(infml)* **sample**, showpiece, example, specimen, demonstrator **2** *(infml)* **demonstration**, presentation, display, show, exhibition **3 protest**, demonstration, protest march, march, protest rally

demob *(infml)* *v* **demobilize**, discharge, dismiss, disband, release *Opposite*: mobilize ∎ *n* **demobilization**, disbandment, discharge, release, dismissal

demobilization *n* **discharge**, release, disbandment, dismissal, retirement *Opposite*: mobilization

demobilize *v* **discharge**, dismiss, disband, release, retire *Opposite*: mobilize

democracy *n* **1 social equality**, equality, egalitarianism, classlessness, consensus *Opposite*: inequality **2 democratic system**, democratic state, democratic organization, representative form of government, republic *Opposite*: dictatorship

democrat *n* **egalitarian**, populist, republican, social democrat, constitutionalist *Opposite*: totalitarian

democratic *adj* **1 self-governing**, self-ruled, independent, autonomous, elected *Opposite*: autocratic **2 egalitarian**, free, classless, equal, open *Opposite*: repressive

demolish *v* **1 knock down**, tear down, pull down, bulldoze, blow up *Opposite*: build **2 destroy**, ruin, flatten, smash, wreck *Opposite*: preserve **3** *(infml)* **beat**, annihilate, defeat, rout, thrash **4** *(infml)* **disprove**, tear to pieces, dismantle, undermine, take apart *(infml) Opposite*: support **5** *(infml)* **devour**, wolf, gobble, eat, consume *Opposite*: nibble

demolition *n* **destruction**, pulling down, knocking down, annihilation, devastation *Opposite*: construction

demon *n* **1 fiend**, evil spirit, devil, monster *Opposite*: angel **2 fear**, anxiety, terror, torment, trouble **3** *(infml)* **expert**, genius, fiend, whiz *(infml)*, wizard *(infml)*

demonstrable *adj* **1 obvious**, palpable, patent, evident, noticeable *Opposite*: imperceptible **2 provable**, verifiable, self-evident, confirmable, comprehensible *Opposite*: doubtful

demonstrate *v* **1 explain**, expound, display, operate, instruct **2 prove**, validate, establish, reveal, make evident **3 protest**, march, rally, lobby, support

demonstration *n* **1 presentation**, display, illustration, explanation, exposition **2 proof**, evidence, validation, establishment, revelation

demonstrative *adj* **affectionate**, warm, loving, friendly, emotional *Opposite*: reserved

demonstrator *n* **1 protester**, supporter, activist, campaigner, lobbyist **2 presenter**, instructor, tutor, teacher, trainer

demoralization *n* **discouragement**, deflation, undermining, depression, dejection *Opposite*: encouragement

demoralize *v* **dishearten**, undermine, dispirit, deflate, discourage *Opposite*: encourage

demoralized *adj* **disheartened**, dispirited, downhearted, discouraged, deflated *Opposite*: optimistic

demoralizing *adj* **disheartening**, discouraging, depressing, dispiriting, crushing *Opposite*: encouraging

demote *v* **downgrade**, relegate, move down, devalue, reduce *Opposite*: promote

demotion *n* **relegation**, downgrading, devaluation, reduction, lowering *Opposite*: promotion

demotivate *v* **discourage**, demoralize, dishearten, dispirit, deter *Opposite*: motivate

demotivation *n* **demoralization**, discouragement, disheartenment, deterrence, dissuasion *Opposite*: motivation

demur *v* **object**, protest, raise objections, baulk, express doubts *Opposite*: agree. *See* COMPARE AND CONTRAST *at* object.

demure *adj* **1 modest**, sedate, decorous, reserved, shy *Opposite*: bold **2 prim**, coy, prudish, strait-laced *Opposite*: pert

demystification *n* **clarification**, explanation, interpretation, revelation, decipherment *Opposite*: obfuscation

demystify *v* **clarify**, explain, elucidate, interpret, reveal *Opposite*: obscure

denial *n* **1 disavowal** *(fml)*, refutation, rejection, rebuttal, contradiction *Opposite*: confirmation **2 refusal**, deprivation, withholding, begrudging, turning down

denigrate *v* **1 defame**, slander, libel, abuse, stigmatize *Opposite*: praise **2 disparage**, vilify, pour scorn on, degrade, belittle *Opposite*: glorify

denigration *n* **1 defamation**, slander, libel, abuse, stigmatization *Opposite*: commendation **2 disparagement**, vilification, scorn, depreciation, belittling *Opposite*: glorification

denizen *n* **inhabitant**, resident, citizen, occupant, native

denotation *n* **meaning**, import, sense, signification, significance

denote *v* **1 mean**, signify, stand for, represent, symbolize **2 refer to**, allude to, imply, convey, express

denouement *n* **ending**, end, finale, conclusion, termination *Opposite*: opening

denounce v 1 **criticize**, censure, deplore, deprecate, condemn Opposite: support 2 **accuse**, point the finger at, blame, charge, inform. See COMPARE AND CONTRAST at **disapprove**.

dense adj 1 **crowded**, packed, packed in, full, jam-packed (infml) 2 **thick**, solid, impenetrable, compressed, condensed 3 **complicated**, complex, difficult, obscure, deep

denseness n 1 **crowdedness**, crowding, tightness, impenetrability, closeness 2 **thickness**, opacity, solidity, impenetrability, darkness 3 **complexity**, difficulty, complication, obscurity, opacity

density n **thickness**, compactness, mass, concentration, bulk

dent v 1 **knock**, hit, bump, bang, indent 2 **damage**, hurt, undermine, diminish, lessen ■ n 1 **hollow**, indentation, depression, dimple, cavity Opposite: lump 2 (infml) **blow**, knock, shock, setback, reversal Opposite: boost 3 (infml) **reduction**, hole, cut, dip, decrease

denude v **strip**, uncover, bare, remove, shed Opposite: cover

denunciate (fml) v **condemn**, criticize, accuse, censure, reprove Opposite: commend

denunciation n **condemnation**, criticism, accusation, censure, reproof Opposite: commendation

deny v 1 **repudiate**, refute, reject, contradict, disagree Opposite: agree 2 **refuse**, disallow, block, forbid, prevent Opposite: permit 3 **forgo**, renounce, disavow, reject, disown

deodorant n **roll-on**, deodorizer, spray

deodorize v **freshen**, scent, refresh, perfume, aromatize

depart v 1 **start out**, set out, move off, set off, leave Opposite: return 2 **deviate**, diverge, differ, vary, change Opposite: stick to 3 **pull out**, leave, go away, disappear, be off Opposite: arrive 4 (fml) **die**, pass on, pass away, succumb, expire (fml)

departed (fml or literary) adj **dead**, late, defunct, lamented Opposite: living. See COMPARE AND CONTRAST at **dead**.

departing n **leaving**, going away, withdrawal, departure, retreat Opposite: arriving

department n 1 **subdivision**, division, branch, sector, section 2 (infml) **responsibility**, area, speciality, realm, sphere

departure n 1 **leaving**, going away, parting, exit, exodus Opposite: arrival 2 **change**, deviation, divergence, digression, variation 3 **venture**, project, enterprise, endeavour, undertaking

depend v **be contingent**, hinge on, rest on, be subject to, hang on

dependability n **reliability**, steadiness, trustworthiness, loyalty, fidelity Opposite: unreliability

dependable adj **reliable**, trustworthy, loyal, faithful, steady Opposite: unreliable

dependence n 1 **reliance**, trust, confidence, belief, hope Opposite: independence 2 **need**, requirement, necessity, want 3 **addiction**, dependency, reliance, need, craving

dependency n 1 **territory**, colony, dependent state, dependent territory, adjunct 2 **dependence**, need, reliance, addiction, habit

dependent adj 1 **needy**, reliant, helpless, supported Opposite: independent 2 **reliant on**, in need of, at the mercy of, hooked on (slang) 3 **contingent**, conditional, determined, subject, related Opposite: independent

depend on v 1 **need**, require, rely on, be dependent on, lean on 2 **rely on**, count on, trust, be sure of, be certain of Opposite: mistrust

depict v **portray**, show, represent, describe, illustrate

depiction n **representation**, portrayal, description, illustration, delineation

deplete v **use up**, drain, exhaust, diminish, lessen Opposite: increase

depletion n **reduction**, exhaustion, diminution, lessening, running down Opposite: restoration

deplorable adj 1 **disgraceful**, terrible, awful, appalling, unacceptable Opposite: praiseworthy 2 **pitiful**, lamentable, execrable, woeful, appalling

deplore v 1 **censure**, condemn, criticize, deprecate, disapprove Opposite: praise 2 **lament**, bemoan, regret, be sorry, rue. See COMPARE AND CONTRAST at **disapprove**.

deploy v 1 **position**, arrange, set up, set out, install 2 **use**, employ, implement, utilize, adopt

deployment n 1 **placement**, disposition, positioning, distribution, arrangement 2 **utilization**, employment, implementation

depoliticize v **humanize**, personalize, socialize, neutralize Opposite: politicize

depopulate v **clear**, relocate, remove, clear out, evacuate Opposite: populate

depopulation n **clearance**, relocation, removal, evacuation, abandonment Opposite: settlement

deport v **expel**, extradite, banish, exile, transport

deportation n **exile**, banishment, extradition, repatriation, expulsion

deportee n **exile**, outcast, displaced person, refugee, evacuee

deportment n **manner**, gait, attitude, posture, bearing

depose v **overthrow**, oust, topple, throw out, remove Opposite: install

deposit v 1 **put**, put down, set down, leave, place Opposite: remove 2 **accumulate**, lay down, leave behind, build up, pile up 3 **pay in**, credit, put in, bank, consign Opposite: withdraw ■ n 1 **credit**, payment, sum Oppo-

site: withdrawal **2 security**, guarantee, pledge, surety **3 sediment**, residue, accretion, layer, accumulation

deposition *n* **1 statement**, testimony, admission, sworn testimony, confession **2 removal**, overthrow, unseating, ousting, dethronement **3 accumulation**, accretion, sedimentation, silting, buildup

depositor *n* **saver**, investor, account holder, creditor

depot *n* **yard**, maintenance yard, goods yard, garage, workshop

deprave *v* **lead astray**, corrupt, degrade, ruin, debase

depraved *adj* **debauched**, immoral, corrupt, evil, wicked *Opposite*: righteous

depravity *n* **debauchery**, immorality, corruption, wickedness, evil *Opposite*: righteousness

deprecate *v* **condemn**, censure, denigrate, denounce, deplore *Opposite*: approve

deprecating *adj* **condemnatory**, disapproving, derogatory, deprecatory, pejorative *(fml)* *Opposite*: approving

deprecation *n* **disapproval**, denigration, condemnation, censure, criticism *Opposite*: praise

deprecatory *adj* **1 disapproving**, derogatory, critical, denigrating, condemnatory *Opposite*: approving **2 apologetic**, sorry, repentant, contrite, remorseful *Opposite*: unrepentant

depreciate *v* **1 lessen**, devalue, deflate, decline, downgrade *Opposite*: appreciate **2 denigrate**, belittle, disparage, run down, criticize *Opposite*: commend

depreciation *n* **devaluation**, reduction, decrease, decline, downgrading *Opposite*: rise

depreciatory *adj* **belittling**, deprecatory, critical, denigrating, derogatory *Opposite*: complimentary

depredation *n* **plunder**, destruction, pillage, despoliation, attack

depress *v* **1 sadden**, dishearten, discourage, dispirit, demoralize *Opposite*: cheer up **2 press down**, push down, press, push, lower *Opposite*: release

depressant *n* **tranquillizer**, sedative, drug, narcotic, downer *(slang)* ■ *adj* **sedative**, tranquillizing, sedating, calming, narcotic

depressed *adj* **1 unhappy**, miserable, dejected, low, disheartened *Opposite*: happy **2 rundown**, deprived, poor, underprivileged, neglected *Opposite*: affluent

depressing *adj* **sad**, miserable, disheartening, discouraging, gloomy *Opposite*: cheering

depression *n* **1 downheartedness**, unhappiness, despair, sadness, gloominess *Opposite*: happiness **2 slump**, recession, decline, downturn, slide *Opposite*: boom **3 hollow**,

dip, dent, impression, dimple *Opposite*: hump

depressive *adj* **gloomy**, depressing, cheerless, miserable, bleak *Opposite*: uplifting

deprivation *n* **lack**, deficiency, scarcity, denial, withdrawal *Opposite*: plenty

deprive *v* **divest**, rob, deny, take away, remove *Opposite*: provide

deprived *adj* **disadvantaged**, underprivileged, poor, destitute, depressed *Opposite*: privileged

depth *n* **1 deepness**, profundity, distance **2 intensity**, strength, power, vigour, concentration *Opposite*: weakness **3 complexity**, profundity, seriousness, gravity, wisdom *Opposite*: flippancy

deputation *n* **delegation**, commission, mission, lobby group

depute *v* **delegate**, hand over, relinquish, allot, transfer

deputize *v* **stand in**, represent, fill in, act, replace

deputy *n* **second-in-command**, assistant, agent, delegate, representative. *See* COMPARE AND CONTRAST *at* **assistant**.

derail *v* **disrupt**, upset, wreck, ruin, spoil

derange *v* **1 distress**, unsettle, upset, unhinge, shake **2 disorganize**, disrupt, disturb, dislocate, upset

derangement *n* **1 imbalance**, irrationality, madness, insanity, instability *Opposite*: sanity **2 disorder**, confusion, muddle, disorganization, disturbance *Opposite*: order

derby *n* **contest**, race, match, clash, sporting event

deregulate *v* **free**, relax, liberalize, decontrol, derestrict *Opposite*: regulate

derelict *adj* **dilapidated**, in ruins, rundown, ruined, neglected

dereliction *n* **1 neglect**, negligence, disregard, recklessness, carelessness *Opposite*: assiduousness **2 abandonment**, desertion, neglect, dilapidation, default

deride *v* **ridicule**, scoff, disparage, mock, scorn *Opposite*: admire. *See* COMPARE AND CONTRAST *at* **ridicule**.

derision *n* **disparagement**, scorn, disdain, mockery, ridicule *Opposite*: admiration

derisive *adj* **mocking**, scathing, sarcastic, irreverent, contemptuous *Opposite*: admiring

derisory *adj* **pitiful**, laughable, insulting, ridiculous, contemptible *Opposite*: generous

derivation *n* **origin**, root, source, beginning, seed. *See* COMPARE AND CONTRAST *at* **origin**.

derivative *adj* **unoriginal**, imitative, plagiaristic, copied, derived *Opposite*: original ■ *n* **offshoot**, by-product, result, end product, spin-off

derive *v* **1 get**, gain, obtain, draw, receive **2 originate**, stem, spring, arise, descend

derogatory adj **disparaging**, critical, insulting, offensive, depreciating Opposite: complimentary

derrick n **1 crane**, hoist, winch, elevator, lift **2 wellhead**, rig, gantry, oil platform, frame

desalinate v **purify**, desalt, detoxify, distil, refine

desalination n **purification**, detoxification, distillation, salt removal

descale v **clean out**, scrape, scour, flush, clean

descant n **harmony**, part, line, tune, air

descend v **1 go down**, move down, come down, slide down, fall down Opposite: ascend **2 slope**, decline, fall away, go downhill, drop away Opposite: ascend **3 derive**, originate, come from, stem, spring **4 lower yourself**, stoop, sink, resort, fall Opposite: rise **5 arrive**, drop in, appear, turn up, show up Opposite: leave **6 fall**, fall on, affect, come over, come upon

descendant n **successor**, offspring, progeny, child, heir Opposite: ancestor

descendent adj **descending**, down, downward, plunging, sinking Opposite: ascendant

descent n **1 fall**, drop, dive, tumble, plunge Opposite: ascent **2 decline**, deterioration, depreciation, degeneration, drop Opposite: improvement **3 ancestry**, parentage, lineage, origin, succession

describe v **1 explain**, portray, depict, illustrate, express **2 label**, refer to, define, designate, pronounce

description n **1 account**, report, explanation, portrayal, picture **2 type**, sort, kind, class, variety

descriptive adj **1 explanatory**, illustrative, narrative, informative, factual Opposite: imaginative **2 evocative**, expressive, vivid, graphic, eloquent

desecrate v **defile**, vandalize, insult, violate, outrage Opposite: consecrate

desecration n **violation**, defilement, vandalism, sacrilege, despoliation Opposite: consecration

deseed v **pit**, stone, core

desegregate v **integrate**, unify, unite, bring together, merge Opposite: segregate

desegregation n **integration**, unification, reunion, reconciliation, merging Opposite: segregation

deselect v **reject**, abandon, discard, cast off, remove Opposite: select

desensitize v **numb**, deaden, dull, soothe, pacify Opposite: sensitize

desert n **1 wasteland**, wilderness, barren region, arid region, waste **2 reward**, return, recompense, wages, just reward ■ v **1 abandon**, leave high and dry, leave, forsake, discard Opposite: support **2 abscond**, leave, go missing, go AWOL, run away Opposite: stay

deserted adj **1 empty**, isolated, uninhabited, desolate, solitary Opposite: inhabited **2 abandoned**, discarded, forsaken, cast off, ditched (infml)

deserter n **absconder**, runaway, fugitive, defector, traitor

desertion n **absconding**, abandonment, running away, disappearance, departure

deserve v **merit**, be worthy, earn, warrant, justify

deservedly adv **justly**, rightly, justifiably, reasonably, properly Opposite: unreasonably

deserving adj **worthy**, commendable, admirable, praiseworthy, justified Opposite: unworthy

desiccate v **dry up**, wither, dry out, dehydrate, parch

desiccated adj **dry**, dried, dried out, shrivelled, dehydrated Opposite: moist. See COMPARE AND CONTRAST at **dry**.

desiccation n **dryness**, dehydration, withering, shrivelling, drying

design v **1 create**, invent, conceive, originate, fabricate **2 plan**, intend, aim, devise, propose ■ n **1 project**, scheme, enterprise, plan, strategy **2 drawing**, blueprint, plan, sketch, outline **3 pattern**, motif, figure, shape, device **4 intention**, purpose, scheme, plan, object Opposite: serendipity

designate v **1 call**, label, title, entitle, term **2 assign**, select, choose, delegate, allocate **3 specify**, point out, indicate, choose, select ■ adj **in waiting**, elect, to be

designation n **title**, name, description, term, label

designedly adv **intentionally**, on purpose, purposely, deliberately, purposefully Opposite: accidentally

designer n **creator**, inventor, originator, engineer, stylist ■ adj **fashionable**, stylish, chic, expensive, exclusive Opposite: mass-produced

designing adj **scheming**, conniving, deceitful, wily, manipulative Opposite: ingenuous

desirability n **1 appeal**, attractiveness, attraction, allure, prestige **2 appropriateness**, aptness, rightness, suitability, advantage

desirable adj **1 wanted**, needed, necessary, required, looked-for Opposite: undesirable **2 attractive**, pleasing, enviable, pleasant, popular Opposite: undesirable

desire v **1 want**, wish for, long for, covet, crave **2** (fml) **request**, ask, require, appeal, entreat ■ n **wish**, want, longing, craving, yearning. See COMPARE AND CONTRAST at **want**.

desired adj **wanted**, anticipated, sought after, looked-for, favourite Opposite: unwanted

desirous (fml) adj **eager**, hopeful, wishing for, longing for, hoping for

desist v **cease**, stop, discontinue, give up, end Opposite: continue

desolate adj **1 deserted**, isolated, bleak, abandoned, forsaken *Opposite*: populous **2 unhappy**, forlorn, miserable, depressed, inconsolable *Opposite*: happy **3 depressing**, gloomy, dismal, austere, forbidding *Opposite*: cheerful

desolation n **1 barrenness**, isolation, bleakness, emptiness, dereliction **2 unhappiness**, misery, despair, anguish, sadness *Opposite*: happiness

despair n misery, desolation, hopelessness, anguish, gloom *Opposite*: joy ■ v **lose hope**, give up hope, have no hope, see no light at the end of the tunnel, lose heart *Opposite*: hope

despairing adj hopeless, desolate, miserable, pained, despondent *Opposite*: hopeful

desperado n **criminal**, outlaw, gangster, bandit, villain

desperate adj **1 frantic**, anxious, worried, distressed, distracted *Opposite*: calm **2 reckless**, careless, rash, impulsive, dangerous *Opposite*: safe **3 serious**, grave, extreme, critical, threatening *Opposite*: harmless **4 eager**, dying, raring, bursting, impatient *Opposite*: loath **5 hopeless**, wretched, irredeemable, deplorable, dreadful *Opposite*: hopeful

desperately adv **1 frantically**, anxiously, frenziedly, hastily, distractedly *Opposite*: calmly **2 very much**, badly, to a great extent, dreadfully, urgently *Opposite*: hardly

desperation n **1 anxiety**, worry, fear, distraction, nervousness *Opposite*: calmness **2 hopelessness**, despair, despondency, misery, anguish *Opposite*: hopefulness

despicable adj **appalling**, dreadful, contemptible, wicked, shameful *Opposite*: admirable

despise v **loathe**, scorn, look down on, hate, spurn *Opposite*: admire

despised adj hated, reviled, loathed, shunned, scorned *Opposite*: beloved

despite prep **in spite of**, regardless of, in the face of, even with, notwithstanding *(fml)* *Opposite*: because of

despoil v rob, plunder, sack, pillage, loot

despoilment n **despoliation**, vandalism, defacement, destruction, desecration

despoliation n **plundering**, pillage, sack, theft, robbery

despondency n hopelessness, sadness, misery, dejection, depression *Opposite*: cheerfulness

despondent adj **hopeless**, low, dejected, despairing, downhearted *Opposite*: cheerful

despot n **dictator**, tyrant, autocrat, oppressor, authoritarian

despotic adj **tyrannical**, dictatorial, autocratic, authoritarian, repressive *Opposite*: democratic

despotism n **tyranny**, dictatorship, absolutism, autocracy, authoritarianism *Opposite*: democracy

dessert n **sweet**, pudding, pud *(infml)*, afters *(infml)*

WORD BANK
❏ types of dessert baklava, banoffee pie, blancmange, bombe, cake, cassata, clafoutis, cobbler, crème brûlée, crème caramel, crumble, custard, flan, fruit salad, granita, ice cream, jelly, junket, meringue, mousse, pannacotta, pavlova, peach Melba, pie, profiteroles, pudding, sorbet, soufflé, sundae, syllabub, tart, tiramisu, zabaglione

destabilization n **weakening**, subversion, undermining, disruption, dislocation

destabilize v **undermine**, subvert, weaken, threaten, disrupt *Opposite*: strengthen

destination n **1 journey's end**, terminus, last stop, end point, end of the road *Opposite*: starting point **2 end**, purpose, target, aim, goal

destined adj intended, meant, fated, designed, certain

destiny n **1 fate**, fortune, lot, luck, providence **2 purpose**, vocation, intention, call, calling

destitute adj **poor**, penniless, impoverished, insolvent, needy *Opposite*: solvent

destitution n **poverty**, penury, hardship, need, insolvency *Opposite*: prosperity

destroy v **1 obliterate**, annihilate, demolish, devastate, tear down *Opposite*: build **2 ruin**, damage, break, break up, spoil *Opposite*: conserve **3 abolish**, put an end to, get rid of, end, extinguish *Opposite*: sustain **4 defeat**, crush, subdue, demolish, overcome

destroyed adj demolished, devastated, ruined, wrecked, smashed *Opposite*: intact

destroyer n **destructive force**, natural disaster, cause of death, killer, demolisher *Opposite*: creator

destruction n **obliteration**, annihilation, devastation, demolition, ruin *Opposite*: construction

destructive adj **1 damaging**, devastating, harmful, detrimental, injurious **2 unhelpful**, critical, negative, damaging, disparaging *Opposite*: constructive

destructiveness n **1 harmfulness**, power, force, violence, ferocity **2 criticism**, negativity, harshness, viciousness, hurtfulness *Opposite*: helpfulness

desultory adj **aimless**, casual, random, unfocused, haphazard *Opposite*: methodical

detach v **separate**, remove, disengage, disconnect, isolate *Opposite*: attach

detachable adj removable, separable, clip-on, hook-on, attachable *Opposite*: fixed

detached adj **1 separate**, disconnected, standing apart, apart, removed *Opposite*: connected **2 aloof**, indifferent, unemotional, unbiased, uninvolved *Opposite*: involved

detachment n **1 aloofness**, remoteness, indifference, impassiveness, distance *Opposite*: involvement **2 objectivity**, disinterest, disinterestedness, impartiality, fairness **3 disconnection**, separation, disengagement, disentanglement, extrication *Opposite*: connection **4 group**, unit, task force, detail, party

detail *n* **1 part**, feature, aspect, point, element **2 group**, unit, task force, detachment, party ■ *n* **1 list**, specify, describe, itemize, particularize **2 assign**, delegate, allocate, conscript, designate

detailed *adj* **full**, thorough, comprehensive, complete, exhaustive *Opposite*: sketchy

details *n* particulars, facts, information, minutiae, niceties

detain *v* **1 delay**, hold up, keep, keep back, impede *Opposite*: let go **2 arrest**, hold, keep in custody, capture, confine *Opposite*: release

detained *adj* **in custody**, in detention, under arrest, behind bars, in prison *Opposite*: free

detainee *n* prisoner, captive, internee, hostage, convict

detect *v* **notice**, sense, become aware of, perceive, spot

detectable *adj* **obvious**, visible, noticeable, measurable, demonstrable *Opposite*: undetectable

detection *n* **discovery**, uncovering, finding, recognition, exposure *Opposite*: concealment

detective *n* **investigator**, private detective, plain-clothes officer, private eye *(infml)*, sleuth *(infml)*

detector *n* **sensor**, indicator, gauge, finder

détente *n* **rapprochement**, agreement, cooperation, compromise, accommodation *Opposite*: hostility

detention *n* **custody**, imprisonment, confinement, arrest, locking up *Opposite*: release

deter *v* **discourage**, put off, daunt, dissuade, prevent *Opposite*: encourage

detergent *n* **cleaner**, cleansing agent, cleanser, shampoo, washing-up liquid

deteriorate *v* **get worse**, worsen, decline, depreciate, go downhill *Opposite*: improve

deteriorating *adj* **worsening**, getting worse, falling, fading, waning *Opposite*: improving

deterioration *n* **worsening**, decline, weakening, drop, descent *Opposite*: improvement

determinant *n* **cause**, determining factor, factor, element, basis

determination *n* **strength of mind**, willpower, resolve, purpose, fortitude *Opposite*: weakness

determine *v* **1 decide**, settle, conclude, resolve, agree **2 find out**, verify, clarify, uncover, establish **3 influence**, affect, shape, mould, form **4 control**, regulate, govern, fix, limit

determined *adj* **strong-minded**, resolute, gritty, single-minded, unwavering *Opposite*: irresolute

determining *adj* **decisive**, causal, defining, influential, shaping *Opposite*: irrelevant

deterrence *n* **discouragement**, dissuasion, preemption, prevention, restriction *Opposite*: encouragement

deterrent *adj* **warning**, preventive, restrictive, restraining, limiting *Opposite*: encouraging ■ *n* **restraint**, disincentive, rein, curb, limit *Opposite*: incitement

detest *v* **hate**, loathe, despise, dislike, abhor *Opposite*: love

detestable *adj* **hateful**, despicable, repugnant, vile, revolting *Opposite*: lovable

detestation *n* **hatred**, hate, abhorrence, loathing, dislike *Opposite*: adoration

dethrone *v* **depose**, oust, unseat, overthrow, overwhelm *Opposite*: install

detonate *v* **explode**, blow up, set off, ignite, spark off

detonation *n* **explosion**, blast, ignition, report, bang

detour *n* **deviation**, diversion, roundabout route, alternative route, long way round

detoxication *see* detoxification

detoxification *n* **cleansing**, decontamination, purification, detoxication, reclamation *Opposite*: contamination

detoxify *v* **cleanse**, purify, clear, clean, depollute *Opposite*: contaminate

detract *v* **take away from**, diminish, lessen, reduce, weaken *Opposite*: bolster

detraction *n* **1** *(fml)* **slander**, abuse, disparagement, aspersion, denigration *Opposite*: praise **2 lessening**, reduction, subtraction, taking away, deduction *Opposite*: addition

detractor *n* **critic**, disparager, cynic, heckler, attacker *Opposite*: supporter

detriment *n* **disadvantage**, loss, harm, damage, injury *Opposite*: advantage

detrimental *adj* **harmful**, damaging, disadvantageous, unfavourable, negative *Opposite*: beneficial

detritus *n* **debris**, litter, waste, trash, rubbish

deuce *n* **tie**, draw, level pegging, even-steven *(infml)*

devaluation *n* **deflation**, depreciation, reduction, depression, devaluing *Opposite*: appreciation

devalue *v* **diminish**, lessen, undervalue, bring down, cheapen *Opposite*: overvalue

devastate *v* **1 destroy**, demolish, ravage, wreck, ruin *Opposite*: preserve **2 overwhelm**, overcome, shock, distress, upset *Opposite*: comfort

devastated *adj* **overwhelmed**, overcome, shattered, confounded, shocked *Opposite*: comforted

devastating *adj* **1 destructive**, harmful, damaging, ruinous, injurious **2 overwhelming**, shocking, upsetting, disturbing, distressing *Opposite*: comforting

devastatingly *adv* **terribly**, dreadfully, overwhelmingly, extraordinarily, hugely

devastation *n* **destruction**, damage, ruin, desolation, waste *Opposite*: preservation

develop *v* **1 grow**, mature, progress, advance, change **2 arise**, result, happen, stem, come **3 acquire**, pick up, foster, create, breed **4 expand**, enlarge, extend, increase, widen *Opposite*: contract **5 work out**, flesh out, expound, fill in, explain *Opposite*: outline **6 build on**, exploit, utilize, build **7 improve**, do up, renovate, refurbish, remodel

developed *adj* **technologically advanced**, industrialized, advanced, established, settled *Opposite*: developing

developer *n* **1 designer**, creator, inventor, brains, maker **2 buyer**, property developer, land developer, contractor, speculator

developing *adj* **emerging**, emergent, evolving *Opposite*: developed

development *n* **1 event**, happening, occurrence, change, incident **2 growth**, expansion, progress, advance, change *Opposite*: stasis **3 enhancement**, expansion, advancement, training, education

developmental *adj* **1 developing**, growing, evolving, changing, progressive *Opposite*: static **2 age-related**, age-linked, growth-related, hormonal, child-development

deviance *n* **nonconformity**, unconventionality, eccentricity, unorthodoxy, aberration *Opposite*: conformity

deviant *adj* **different**, divergent, nonstandard, aberrant, irregular *Opposite*: standard

deviate *v* **1 differ**, depart, diverge, stray, digress *Opposite*: conform **2 diverge**, move away, stray, depart, swerve *Opposite*: keep to

deviation *n* **1 difference**, departure, change, divergence, variation *Opposite*: normalization **2 nonconformity**, unconventionality, eccentricity, unorthodoxy, aberration

device *n* **1 machine**, tool, piece of equipment, mechanism, apparatus **2 expedient**, manoeuvre, stratagem, ruse, dodge **3 design**, emblem, logo, badge, crest

devious *adj* **1 deceitful**, tricky, scheming, designing, wily *Opposite*: straightforward **2 circuitous**, oblique, meandering, tortuous, winding *Opposite*: direct

deviousness *n* **guile**, cunning, artfulness, deceitfulness, untrustworthiness *Opposite*: straightforwardness

devise *v* **think up**, plan, figure out, work out, invent

devoid *adj* **empty**, barren, without, bereft, lacking *Opposite*: full

devolution *n* **decentralization**, delegation, transference, transfer *Opposite*: centralization

devolve *v* **transfer**, decentralize, give to, hand to, pass to *Opposite*: centralize

devote *v* **dedicate**, give, offer, apply, assign

devoted *adj* **1 committed**, loving, caring, affectionate, kind *Opposite*: uncaring **2 dedicated**, loyal, dutiful, faithful, staunch *Opposite*: uncommitted **3 keen**, enthusiastic, dedicated, ardent, fervent *Opposite*: unenthusiastic

devotee *n* **1 fan**, follower, supporter, aficionado, aficionada **2 disciple**, follower, believer, votary

devotion *n* **1 commitment**, attachment, love, fondness, affection *Opposite*: dislike **2 dedication**, care, attentiveness, support, loyalty *Opposite*: neglect **3 enthusiasm**, admiration, zeal, keenness, fervour *Opposite*: apathy **4** (*fml*) **piety**, devoutness, religious zeal, religious fervour, religious observance *Opposite*: impiety

devotional *adj* **religious**, worshipful, worshipping, prayerful, holy

devotions *n* **prayers**, holy rites, observances, supplications (*fml*)

devour *v* **1 consume**, demolish, dispose of, gulp, wolf **2** (*literary*) **overwhelm**, overcome, engulf, consume, destroy

devout *adj* **1 religious**, pious, spiritual, devoted, dedicated *Opposite*: uncommitted **2** (*fml*) **sincere**, heartfelt, deep, earnest, fervent *Opposite*: insincere **3 enthusiastic**, keen, ardent, zealous, fanatical *Opposite*: casual

devoutly *adv* **deeply**, keenly, seriously, intensely, profoundly

devoutness *n* **piety**, spirituality, religious fervour, religious zeal, piousness *Opposite*: impiety

dew *n* **droplets**, precipitation, condensation, dewdrops

dewdrop *n* **bead of moisture**, droplet, drop, drip

dewy *adj* **wet**, dew-covered, heavy with dew, damp, moist *Opposite*: dry

dewy-eyed *adj* **innocent**, naive, trusting, unrealistic, idealistic *Opposite*: down-to-earth

dexterity *n* **1 deftness**, skill, adroitness, handiness, legerdemain *Opposite*: clumsiness **2 ingenuity**, acuity, sharpness, quickness, resourcefulness *Opposite*: dullness

dexterous *adj* **1 deft**, adroit, handy, nimble-fingered, nimble *Opposite*: clumsy **2 quick-witted**, sharp, acute, resourceful, clever *Opposite*: dull

dextrous *see* **dexterous**

diadem *n* **crown**, tiara, circlet, coronet, wreath

diagnose *v* **make a diagnosis**, identify, analyse, spot, detect

diagnosis *n* **identification**, analysis, judgment, finding, verdict

diagnostic adj **analytic**, analytical, indicative, investigative, problem-solving

diagonal adj **slanting**, oblique, sloping, crossways, crosswise

diagram n **drawing**, figure, illustration, plan, map

diagrammatic adj **graphic**, illustrative, pictorial, visual, drawn Opposite: verbal

dial n **1 face**, gauge, indicator, disc, control panel **2 knob**, handle, control, button ■ v **call**, telephone, phone, phone up, ring

dialect n **vernacular**, language, parlance, tongue, idiom

dialectic n **1 tension**, conflict, interaction, clash, opposition Opposite: harmony **2 discussion**, debate, investigation, examination, analysis

dialogue n **1 discussion**, exchange of ideas, channel of communication, discourse, interchange Opposite: silence **2** (fml) **conversation**, interview, chat, discussion, discourse Opposite: monologue

diamanté adj **glittery**, sparkly, glittering, sparkling, diamantine Opposite: dull ■ n **rhinestones**, paste, strass

diameter n **width**, thickness, breadth, length, distance

diametrically adv **absolutely**, completely, utterly, totally, entirely Opposite: partially

diamond n **rhombus**, parallelogram, lozenge, equilateral

diaphanous adj **transparent**, delicate, gauzy, see-through, sheer Opposite: opaque

diarist n **memoirist**, writer, autobiographer, author, chronicler

diary n **1 appointment book**, personal organizer, PDA, personal digital assistant, calendar **2 journal**, record, log, chronicle, memoir

diaspora n **dispersion**, scattering, movement, displacement, migration Opposite: concentration

diatribe n **criticism**, attack, tirade, denunciation, harangue

dice v **1 cube**, cut up, chop, cut into cubes **2 gamble**, risk, stake, bet, wager

dice with death v **face danger**, sail close to the wind, play a dangerous game, cut it fine, play Russian roulette

dicey (infml) adj **risky**, dangerous, hazardous, chancy, uncertain Opposite: safe

dichotomy n **contrast**, opposition, irreconcilable difference, contradiction, gulf Opposite: harmony

dicker (infml) v **bargain**, haggle, argue, trade, wrangle

dicky (infml) see **bow tie**

dicky bow (infml) see **bow tie**

dictate v **1 speak**, say, say aloud, read out, read aloud **2 order**, state, command, decree, lay down **3 control**, determine, have a bearing on, influence, shape ■ n **1 principle**, rule, standard, tenet, precept (fml) **2 command**, order, decree, prescription, injunction

dictation n **transcription**, notation, transcript

dictator n **tyrant**, ruler, despot, autocrat, authoritarian Opposite: democrat

dictatorial adj **tyrannical**, despotic, autocratic, authoritarian, overbearing Opposite: democratic

dictatorship n **1 regime**, government, rule, era, reign **2 despotism**, autocracy, totalitarianism, authoritarianism, tyranny Opposite: democracy

diction n **1 pronunciation**, enunciation, articulation, delivery, elocution **2 wording**, language, expression, phraseology, phrasing

dictionary n **lexicon**, vocabulary, glossary, phrase book, word list

dictum (fml) n **pronouncement**, dictate, saying, statement, maxim

didactic adj **educational**, instructive, informative, edifying, teaching

die v **1 pass away**, pass on, kick the bucket (slang), croak (slang), expire (fml) Opposite: live **2 stop**, give out, go dead, break down, fail Opposite: start

die away v **fade**, fade away, dwindle, fizzle, ebb Opposite: revive

die down v **subside**, decrease, lessen, diminish, decline Opposite: revive

diehard adj **intransigent**, reactionary, conservative, traditionalist, dyed-in-the-wool Opposite: progressive ■ n **reactionary**, conservative, traditionalist, fogy, conformist Opposite: progressive

die of v **succumb**, fall victim, surrender, yield, submit Opposite: survive

die off v **die out**, become extinct, pass away, pass on, disappear Opposite: survive

die out v **become extinct**, disappear, vanish, die off, pass away Opposite: survive

diet n **1 food**, fare, nourishment, nutrition, sustenance **2 regime**, intake, supply, regimen **3 parliament**, legislature, assembly, council, congress ■ v **slim**, starve, fast, cut back, cut down Opposite: binge

dietary adj **nutritional**, dietetic, eating, alimentary, alimental

dieter n **slimmer**, weight watcher, faster, starver, abstainer

differ v **1 be different**, be unlike, be at variance, vary, fluctuate Opposite: match **2 disagree**, argue, quarrel, fall out, wrangle Opposite: agree. See COMPARE AND CONTRAST at **disagree**.

difference n **1 dissimilarity**, disparity, distinction, differentiation, divergence Opposite: similarity **2 change**, alteration, variance, modification, transformation Opposite: consistency **3 argument**, dispute, disagreement, quarrel, contretemps (fml)

different adj **1 dissimilar**, diverse, unlike,

clashing, poles apart *Opposite*: similar **2 distinct**, separate, discrete, another *Opposite*: same **3 unusual**, special, singular, distinctive, atypical *Opposite*: run-of-the-mill

differential *n* **difference**, discrepancy, disparity, gap, variance

differentiate *v* **distinguish**, discriminate, tell apart, set apart, discern *Opposite*: blend

differentiation *n* **1 distinction**, discrimination, delineation, demarcation, separation *Opposite*: assimilation **2 difference**, diversity, variation, distinction, discrepancy *Opposite*: similarity

differently *adv* **in a different way**, another way, in your own way, otherwise, inversely *Opposite*: similarly

differing *adj* **opposing**, contradictory, contrary, divergent, different *Opposite*: similar

difficult *adj* **1 hard**, tricky, complicated, thorny, complex *Opposite*: straightforward **2 challenging**, hard, tough, trying, grim *Opposite*: easy **3 incomprehensible**, unintelligible, impenetrable, involved, complicated *Opposite*: simple **4 obstinate**, stubborn, recalcitrant, intractable, fractious *Opposite*: amenable. *See* COMPARE AND CONTRAST *at* **hard**.

difficulty *n* **1 complexity**, complicatedness, intricacy, adversity, complication **2 problem**, snag, obstacle, impediment, stumbling block **3 trouble**, effort, struggle, exertion, strain *Opposite*: ease

diffidence *n* **shyness**, hesitancy, reserve, timidity, reticence *Opposite*: brashness

diffident *adj* **shy**, hesitant, insecure, timid, reticent *Opposite*: brash

diffract *v* **bend**, deflect, curve, divert, spread

diffraction *n* **deflection**, bending, curving, diversion, spreading

diffuse *v* **disperse**, spread, disseminate, distribute, circulate *Opposite*: concentrate ■ *adj* **1 dispersed**, spread, disseminated, distributed, circulated *Opposite*: concentrated **2 wordy**, verbose, prolix, long-winded, drawn-out *Opposite*: concise. *See* COMPARE AND CONTRAST *at* **wordy**.

diffusion *n* **dispersal**, dispersion, dissemination, distribution, circulation *Opposite*: concentration

dig *v* **1 break up**, plough, turn, hoe, till **2 excavate**, tunnel, hollow out, burrow, mine **3 prod**, nudge, push, shove, jab ■ *n* **1 poke**, prod, nudge, push, shove **2 gibe**, taunt, jeer, crack, insult *Opposite*: compliment

digest *v* **1 process**, assimilate, absorb, break down, consume **2 assimilate**, absorb, take in, take on board, grasp *Opposite*: ignore ■ *n* **1 abridgment**, résumé, summary, condensation, abstract **2 publication**, journal, magazine, periodical, book

digestible *adj* **edible**, palatable, eatable, consumable, comestible *(fml)* *Opposite*: indigestible

digestion *n* **assimilation**, ingestion, absorption, incorporation, breakdown

digestive *adj* **peptic**, gastric, intestinal, gastrointestinal, duodenal

digestive tract *see* **alimentary canal**

digger *n* **1 miner**, excavator, gravedigger, gold digger, prospector **2 excavator**, bulldozer, earthmover, crawler, backhoe

diggings *n* **excavation**, mine, quarry, pit, dig

dig into *v* **1 stick into**, push into, sink into, stab, prod **2 examine**, look at, delve into, investigate, go into *Opposite*: ignore

dig in your heels *v* **stand firm**, hold your ground, stand your ground, hold out, resist *Opposite*: give in

digit *n* **number**, numeral, figure, cipher, character

digital *adj* **numerical**, numerary, numeral, alphanumeric, cardinal

dignified *adj* **distinguished**, decorous, stately, noble, gracious *Opposite*: undignified

dignify *v* **distinguish**, honour, grace, glorify, venerate *Opposite*: degrade

dignitary *n* **notable**, VIP, worthy, celebrity, luminary *Opposite*: nobody

dignity *n* **1 self-respect**, self-esteem, pride, self-possession, self-worth *Opposite*: ignominy **2 formality**, gravity, solemnity, grandeur, decorum *Opposite*: informality **3 worthiness**, worth, nobility, nobleness, goodness *Opposite*: unworthiness

dig out *v* **1 uncover**, excavate, dig up, unearth, expose *Opposite*: bury **2** *(infml)* **retrieve**, find, discover, locate, reveal

digress *v* **deviate**, depart, wander, go off at a tangent, stray *Opposite*: focus

digression *n* **deviation**, departure, aside, parenthesis, detour *Opposite*: focus

digs *(dated infml)* *n* **lodgings** *(dated)*, lodging, accommodation, rooms, quarters

dig up *v* **1 unearth**, excavate, disinter, exhume, expose *Opposite*: bury **2** *(infml)* **bring to light**, dredge up, expose, reveal, find *Opposite*: hide

diktat *n* **command**, decree, edict, dictate, order

dilapidated *adj* **decrepit**, rundown, derelict, ramshackle, on its last legs *Opposite*: pristine

dilapidation *n* **disrepair**, dereliction, decrepitude, decay, ruin

dilate *v* **1 expand**, widen, open, enlarge, increase *Opposite*: contract **2 amplify**, expatiate, expand, dwell on, expound *Opposite*: abbreviate

dilation *n* **expansion**, opening, enlargement, increase, distension *Opposite*: contraction

dilatory *adj* **slow**, tardy, remiss, behindhand, slack *Opposite*: prompt

dilemma *n* **quandary**, tight spot, catch-22, predicament, impasse

dilettante *n* **amateur**, dabbler, abecedarian,

neophyte, novice *Opposite*: expert

diligence *n* **assiduousness**, meticulousness, conscientiousness, thoroughness, attentiveness *Opposite*: carelessness

diligent *adj* **industrious**, assiduous, painstaking, meticulous, conscientious *Opposite*: lazy

dilly-dally *v* **dawdle**, dally, delay, shilly-shally, drag your heels *Opposite*: hurry

dilute *v* **1 thin**, weaken, water down, adulterate *Opposite*: concentrate **2 reduce**, attenuate, temper, mitigate, water down *Opposite*: increase ∎ *adj* **weak**, watered down, thinned, watery, insipid *Opposite*: concentrated

dilution *n* **1 thinning**, weakening, watering down, watering **2 reduction**, attenuation, enfeeblement, erosion, weakening *Opposite*: strengthening **3 concentration**, strength, intensity, potency

dim *adj* **1 badly lit**, murky, gloomy, shadowy, dusky *Opposite*: bright **2 soft**, faint, muted, weak, diffuse *Opposite*: strong **3 indistinct**, vague, blurred, blurry, hazy *Opposite*: clear ∎ *v* **turn down**, lower, darken, reduce *Opposite*: turn up

dimension *n* **1 measurement**, length, height, width, breadth **2 aspect**, element, facet, feature, factor

dimensions *n* **size**, scope, extent, magnitude, proportions

diminish *v* **1 reduce**, lessen, make smaller, weaken, moderate *Opposite*: increase **2 shrink**, ebb, fade, fade away, fade out *Opposite*: grow

diminishing *adj* **lessening**, fading, waning, weakening, falling *Opposite*: increasing

diminution *n* **decrease**, reduction, lessening, attenuation, shrinking *Opposite*: growth

diminutive *adj* **small**, little, tiny, minuscule, miniature *Opposite*: huge

dimmer *n* **light switch**, dimmer switch, brightness control, regulator, rheostat

dimness *n* **1 softness**, faintness, weakness, diffuseness, dullness *Opposite*: brightness **2 murkiness**, gloom, gloominess, shadowiness, duskiness *Opposite*: brightness **3 indistinctness**, vagueness, blurriness, haziness, faintness *Opposite*: clearness

dimple *n* **hollow**, depression, pit, indentation, dent *Opposite*: bump

dimpled *adj* **1 dimply**, cleft, indented, dented, chubby *Opposite*: smooth **2 textured**, indented, dented, pocked, pockmarked *Opposite*: smooth

din *n* **noise**, hubbub, rumpus, racket *(infml)*, hullabaloo ∎ *v* **drum into**, hammer, inculcate, instil, impress

dine *v* **eat**, feast, banquet, consume, ingest

diner *n* **patron**, customer, guest

ding *n* **ringing**, ring, dong, ding-dong, ding-a-ling ∎ *v* **ring**, tinkle, dong, ding-dong

ding-dong *(infml)* *n* **argument**, spat, row, quarrel, tiff

dinge *n* **filth**, grime, mess, dirt, muck *(infml)* *Opposite*: cleanliness

dinginess *n* **1 dirtiness**, discoloration, griminess, dullness, dreariness *Opposite*: brightness **2 shabbiness**, drabness, squalidness, cheerlessness, seediness *Opposite*: neatness

dingy *adj* **1 dirty**, grimy, soiled, grubby, dull *Opposite*: clean **2 shabby**, drab, squalid, tatty, worn *Opposite*: bright

dinky *(infml)* *adj* **small**, compact, neat, natty, cute *Opposite*: hefty

dinnertime *n* **mealtime**, suppertime, lunchtime, tea-time

dinosaur *n* **relic**, museum piece, back number, fossil, has-been *(infml)*

WORD BANK
❏ **types of dinosaur** allosaurus, ankylosaur, apatosaurus, brachiosaurus, brontosaurus, cotylosaur, dicynodont, diplodocus, hadrosaur, ichthyosaur, iguanodon, megalosaur, mosasaur, oviraptor, pelycosaur, plesiosaur, pteranodon, pterodactyl, pterosaur, stegosaur, titanosaur, triceratops, tyrannosaur, velociraptor

dint *n* **indent**, dent, indentation, depression, hollow ∎ *v* **dent**, damage, mark, spoil, blemish

dip *v* **1 plunge**, immerse, dunk, douse, bathe **2 drop**, drop down, descend, decline, sink *Opposite*: rise **3 slope**, incline, slant, descend, fall away *Opposite*: level ∎ *n* **1 swim**, plunge, dunk, bathe **2 fall**, decline, drop, depression, falling off *Opposite*: rise **3 hollow**, depression, incline, slope, rise and fall

dip into *v* **skim**, flick through, flip through, glance, browse *Opposite*: study

diploma *n* **certificate**, qualification, credential

diplomacy *n* **1 international relations**, mediation, negotiation, peacekeeping **2 tact**, skill, subtlety, discretion, savoir-faire *Opposite*: tactlessness

diplomat *n* **1 civil servant**, envoy, representative, attaché, ambassador **2 tactician**, peacekeeper, negotiator, mediator, go-between

diplomatic *adj* **1 political**, ambassadorial, consular, embassy **2 tactful**, subtle, suave, discreet, sensitive *Opposite*: tactless

dipper *n* **ladle**, scoop, spoon

dire *adj* **terrible**, awful, dreadful, calamitous, horrible *Opposite*: wonderful

direct *v* **1 manage**, control, regulate, rule, oversee **2 aim**, point, turn, target, train **3 show the way**, guide, lead, put on the right track, point in the right direction **4** *(fml)* **order**, give orders, instruct, give instructions, command *Opposite*: request ∎ *adj* **1 straight**, shortest, through, unswerving, undeviating

Opposite: circuitous **2 precise**, exact, absolute, complete, unequivocal *Opposite*: vague **3 straightforward**, honest, open, candid, frank *Opposite*: devious ■ *adv* **directly**, straight, nonstop, right, in a straight line *Opposite*: indirectly. *See* COMPARE AND CONTRAST *at* guide.

direction *n* **1 management**, control, government, guidance, leadership **2 way**, course, track, route, path **3 trend**, course, route, focus, aim

directional *adj* **manoeuvring**, steering, turning, reversing, guiding

directions *n* **instructions**, information, orders, guidelines, commands

directive *n* **order**, command, instruction, direction, edict

directly *adv* **1 in a straight line**, straight, right, unswervingly, nonstop *Opposite*: indirectly **2 completely**, diametrically, absolutely, wholly, unequivocally **3 openly**, honestly, frankly, straightforwardly, truthfully *Opposite*: ambiguously **4** *(fml)* **immediately**, quickly, at once, promptly, without delay

direct mail *n* **promotional mailing**, mail shot, circular, junk mail, unsolicited mail

directness *n* **honesty**, openness, straightforwardness, truthfulness, sincerity *Opposite*: deviousness

director *n* **manager**, leader, executive, boss, administrator

directorate *n* **board of directors**, executive, executive board, executive committee, board

director-general *n* **president**, head, director, chairperson, chief executive

directorship *n* **director's post**, management post, executive post, managerial position, presidency

directory *n* **listing**, phone book, catalogue, inventory, register

dirge *n* **elegy**, requiem, funeral hymn, lament, chant

dirt *n* **1 grime**, filth, mud, dust, muck *(infml)* **2 soil**, earth, clay, loam, mud **3 gossip**, scandal, filth, smut, lowdown *(infml)*

dirt-cheap *(infml) adj* **cheap**, reduced, cut-price, bargain, inexpensive *Opposite*: dear ■ *adv* **cheaply**, at a knockdown price, at bargain-basement prices, for a song, for next to nothing

dirtiness *n* **griminess**, filthiness, messiness, muddiness, grubbiness *Opposite*: cleanliness

dirty *adj* **1 filthy**, grimy, soiled, grubby, squalid *Opposite*: clean **2 dishonest**, illegal, corrupt, unfair, immoral *Opposite*: honest **3 dull**, muted, muddy, cloudy, murky *Opposite*: clear ■ *v* **soil**, stain, pollute, foul, defile *(fml) Opposite*: clean

COMPARE AND CONTRAST CORE MEANING: not clean

dirty stained or marked with dirt; **filthy** extremely or disgustingly dirty; **grubby** slightly dirty; **grimy**

heavily ingrained with accumulated dirt; **soiled** stained or marked, especially during normal use; **squalid** insanitary and unpleasant; **unclean** dirty or impure, especially in moral or religious contexts.

dirty tricks *n* **unfair tactics**, foul play, deviousness, dishonesty, jiggery-pokery *(infml)*

dirty word *n* **swearword**, expletive, four-letter word, profanity, obscenity

disability *n* **incapacity**, infirmity, frailty, debility, ill health

disable *v* **incapacitate**, restrict, inactivate, deactivate, put out of action

disablement *n* **impairment**, incapacitation, deactivation, spiking *(infml)*

disabuse *v* **persuade out of**, disillusion, enlighten, set straight, shatter the illusions of

disadvantage *n* **difficulty**, drawback, shortcoming, weakness, hindrance *Opposite*: advantage

disadvantaged *adj* **deprived**, underprivileged, needy, destitute, poor *Opposite*: privileged

disadvantageous *adj* **detrimental**, damaging, hurtful, harmful, injurious *Opposite*: advantageous

disaffect *v* **estrange**, disillusion, disenchant, dissatisfy, alienate

disaffected *adj* **disillusioned**, dissatisfied, disgruntled, cynical, alienated *Opposite*: enthusiastic

disaffection *n* **disillusionment**, alienation, estrangement, dissatisfaction, cynicism *Opposite*: enthusiasm

disagree *v* **1 take issue with**, differ, demur, agree to differ, be at odds *Opposite*: agree **2 differ**, vary, diverge, deviate, contradict *Opposite*: agree **3 argue**, quarrel, wrangle, dispute, bicker *Opposite*: agree

COMPARE AND CONTRAST CORE MEANING: have or express a difference of opinion with somebody **disagree** have or put forward a different view or opinion; **differ** have different opinions about something; **argue** express disagreement, especially continuously or angrily; **dispute** have a heated argument; **take issue with** disagree strongly with; **contradict** argue against the truth or correctness of a statement or claim; **agree to differ** stop arguing and accept that the opposing viewpoints are irreconcilable; **be at odds** be in disagreement, especially over a period of time or about a particular issue.

disagreeable *adj* **1 displeasing**, distasteful, offensive, nasty, unpleasant *Opposite*: agreeable **2 bad-tempered**, unfriendly, unhelpful, difficult, contrary *Opposite*: pleasant

disagreement *n* **1 dispute**, difference of opinion, quarrel, argument, misunderstanding *Opposite*: agreement **2 difference**, divergence, incongruity, discrepancy, dissimilarity *Opposite*: agreement

disallow v 1 (fml) **reject**, refuse, deny, throw, disapprove Opposite: pass 2 **cancel**, prohibit, forbid, veto, bar Opposite: allow

disallowed adj **rejected**, forbidden, banned, excluded, vetoed Opposite: allowed

disappear v 1 **vanish**, fade, fade away, go, evaporate Opposite: appear 2 **cease to exist**, die out, die off, pass away, vanish Opposite: appear

disappearance n **vanishing**, evaporation, fading, loss, desertion Opposite: appearance

disappearing adj **vanishing**, waning, endangered, threatened, dying

disappoint v **let down**, disillusion, fail, dissatisfy, dishearten Opposite: please

disappointed adj **let down**, dissatisfied, disillusioned, upset, saddened Opposite: satisfied

disappointing adj **unsatisfactory**, unacceptable, second-rate, poor, below par Opposite: satisfactory

disappointment n 1 **dissatisfaction**, displeasure, distress, discontent, disenchantment Opposite: satisfaction 2 **setback**, failure, frustration, defeat, drawback

disapprobation (fml) n **disfavour**, condemnation, disapproval, dislike, displeasure Opposite: approval

disapproval n **condemnation**, displeasure, dissatisfaction, censure, discontentment Opposite: approval

disapprove v 1 **condemn**, censure, criticize, deplore, frown on Opposite: approve 2 (fml) **reject**, refuse, veto, turn down, deny Opposite: approve

COMPARE AND CONTRAST CORE MEANING: have an unfavourable opinion of something or somebody **disapprove** give a negative judgment based on personal standards; **frown on** express dislike or disapproval; **object** be opposed to something, or express opposition; **criticize** point out flaws or faults; **condemn** give an unfavourable judgment on somebody or something; **deplore** disapprove of something strongly; **denounce** criticize or condemn publicly and harshly; **censure** make a formal, often public or official, statement of disapproval.

disapproving adj **critical**, judgmental, negative, censorious, stern Opposite: approving

disarm v 1 **deactivate**, defuse, make safe, neutralize Opposite: arm 2 **win over**, charm, enchant, beguile, win the affection of Opposite: annoy

disarmament n **arms reduction**, nuclear disarmament, unilateral disarmament, decommissioning, demilitarization Opposite: rearmament

disarming adj **charming**, enchanting, attractive, appealing, captivating Opposite: unattractive

disarrange v **disorder**, disturb, jumble, dishevel, mix up Opposite: order

disarranged adj **disordered**, untidy, rumpled, messy, jumbled

disarray n 1 **confusion**, dismay, panic, alarm, hysteria Opposite: order 2 **mess**, disorder, chaos, confusion, untidiness Opposite: order

disassemble v **take apart**, take to bits, undo, take down, take to pieces Opposite: assemble

disassociate v 1 **dissociate**, separate, split, set apart, disentangle Opposite: associate 2 **distance**, detach, set apart, dissociate, draw back Opposite: implicate

disaster n 1 **tragedy**, ruin, adversity, catastrophe, calamity 2 (infml) **failure**, debacle, fiasco, shambles, farce Opposite: success

disastrous adj 1 **calamitous**, catastrophic, tragic, terrible, devastating 2 **unsuccessful**, unfortunate, luckless, doomed, unlucky Opposite: successful

disavow v **disown**, deny, renounce, reject, recant

disavowal (fml) n **repudiation**, denial, negation, renunciation, abjuration Opposite: avowal (fml)

disband v **break up**, split up, scatter, separate, part

disbar v **expel**, throw out, dismiss, banish, exclude

disbarment n **expulsion**, dismissal, banishment, exclusion, removal

disbelief n **incredulity**, doubt, distrust, mistrust, suspicion Opposite: faith

disbelieve v **distrust**, doubt, mistrust, suspect, be suspicious of Opposite: believe

disbeliever n **doubter**, agnostic, atheist, nonbeliever, sceptic Opposite: believer

disbelieving adj **unconvinced**, incredulous, suspicious, doubtful, distrustful Opposite: believing

disburse v **pay out**, pay, spend, expend, lay out

disbursement n **payment**, expenditure, expense, costs, distribution

discard v **throw away**, abandon, dispose of, remove, get rid of Opposite: keep

discarded adj **cast off**, thrown away, thrown out, rejected, dispensed with Opposite: kept

discern v 1 **make out**, notice, see, perceive, discover Opposite: miss 2 **understand**, perceive, distinguish, fathom, be aware of Opposite: miss 3 **distinguish**, tell the difference, separate, discriminate, differentiate

discernible adj **visible**, apparent, obvious, perceptible, noticeable

discerning adj **discriminating**, sharp, astute, judicious, sensitive Opposite: indiscriminate

discernment n **judgment**, acumen, discrimination, perspicacity, taste

discharge v 1 **emit**, send out, excrete, expel, ooze 2 **free**, release, set free, emancipate, liberate 3 **dismiss**, relieve of duty, let go, lay off, give somebody their cards Opposite:

retain 4 (fml) **pay off**, clear, settle, satisfy, liquidate ■ *n* 1 **emission**, flow, secretion, excretion, seepage 2 **release**, liberation, emancipation, expulsion, ejection

disciple *n* **follower**, believer, supporter, devotee, partisan

disciplinarian *n* **tyrant**, martinet, despot, authoritarian, stickler

disciplinary *adj* **punitive**, corrective, penal, penalizing

discipline *n* 1 **punishment**, correction, chastisement (fml), castigation (fml) 2 **regulation**, order, control, restraint, authority *Opposite*: chaos 3 **self-control**, self-restraint, restraint, control, regulation 4 **subject**, branch of learning, field ■ *v* 1 **punish**, chastise, correct, chasten, castigate (fml) 2 **instruct**, educate, exercise, drill, prepare

disciplined *adj* **controlled**, self-controlled, orderly, well-ordered, methodical *Opposite*: undisciplined

disclaim *v* **deny**, disown, renounce, reject, repudiate

disclaimer *n* 1 **rider**, proviso, qualification, provision, condition 2 **repudiation**, denial, renunciation, negation, disassociation

disclose *v* **reveal**, unveil, divulge, make known, relate *Opposite*: conceal

disclosure *n* **revelation**, exposé, discovery, leak, confession

discoloration *n* **staining**, stain, tint, mark, streak

discolour *v* **fade**, stain, colour, darken, tarnish

discoloured *adj* **stained**, dirty, tarnished, faded, streaked

discomfit (fml) *v* **embarrass**, unsettle, disconcert, distress, rattle *Opposite*: relax

discomfiting (fml) *adj* **disconcerting**, embarrassing, unsettling, disturbing, distressing *Opposite*: reassuring

discomfiture (fml) *n* **embarrassment**, awkwardness, confusion, unease, disconcertment

discomfort *n* 1 **ache**, pain, soreness, tenderness, irritation 2 **uneasiness**, worry, distress, anxiety, embarrassment *Opposite*: calmness

discomposure *n* **agitation**, upset, uneasiness, embarrassment, discomfort

disconcert *v* **unsettle**, perturb, rattle, fluster, unnerve *Opposite*: relax

disconcerted *adj* **unsettled**, thrown off balance, confused, flustered, taken aback *Opposite*: calm

disconcerting *adj* **disturbing**, alarming, confusing, perplexing, bewildering *Opposite*: soothing

disconnect *v* **cut off**, detach, separate, divide, disengage *Opposite*: connect

disconnected *adj* **detached**, severed, disengaged, separated, divided *Opposite*: attached

disconnection *n* 1 **stoppage**, interruption, cessation, cutting off, discontinuation *Opposite*: connection 2 **separation**, severance, decoupling, disengagement, break *Opposite*: connection

disconsolate *adj* **unhappy**, dejected, gloomy, melancholy, sad *Opposite*: content

discontent *n* **dissatisfaction**, unhappiness, displeasure, disgruntlement, sadness *Opposite*: contentment

discontented *adj* **dissatisfied**, unhappy, disgruntled, malcontent, displeased *Opposite*: contented

discontentment *n* **dissatisfaction**, discontent, displeasure, unhappiness, irritation *Opposite*: contentment

discontinuation *n* **cessation**, termination, suspension, withdrawal, stoppage *Opposite*: continuation

discontinue *v* **stop**, cease, halt, end, suspend *Opposite*: continue

discontinued *adj* **obsolete**, finished, superseded, out-of-date, withdrawn

discontinuity *n* **break**, gap, cutoff, cutout, disjointedness *Opposite*: continuity

discontinuous *adj* **intermittent**, sporadic, broken, irregular, disjointed *Opposite*: continuous

discord *n* 1 **disagreement**, conflict, dispute, argument, friction *Opposite*: accord 2 **dissonance**, cacophony, disharmony, inharmoniousness, discordance *Opposite*: harmony

discordant *adj* 1 **disagreeing**, conflicting, frictional, dissenting, acrimonious *Opposite*: amicable 2 **dissonant**, jarring, harsh, inharmonious, cacophonous *Opposite*: harmonious

discount *n* **reduction**, money off, markdown, price cut, cut rate ■ *v* 1 **disregard**, overlook, ignore, disbelieve, pass over *Opposite*: accept 2 **reduce**, mark down, lower, take off, deduct *Opposite*: put up

discounted *adj* **reduced**, on offer, cut-price, sale, on special offer

discourage *v* 1 **dissuade**, oppose, hinder, inhibit, prevent *Opposite*: encourage 2 **dispirit**, dishearten, cast down, depress, dismay *Opposite*: cheer

discouraged *adj* **disheartened**, dispirited, downcast, depressed, dejected *Opposite*: positive

discouragement *n* 1 **disappointment**, dismay, despair, depression, low spirits *Opposite*: hopefulness 2 **dissuasion**, caution, warning, opposition, deterrence *Opposite*: encouragement 3 **deterrent**, hindrance, obstacle, impediment, damper *Opposite*: incentive

discouraging *adj* **disheartening**, depressing, dispiriting, gloomy, unpromising *Opposite*: encouraging

discourse *n* 1 **dissertation**, treatise, homily,

sermon, address **2 dialogue**, conversation, discussion, communication, speech ■ *v (fml)* **converse**, debate, compare notes, have a word, have a discussion

discourteous *adj* **rude**, ill-mannered, impolite, insolent, uncivil *Opposite*: polite

discourteousness *see* **discourtesy**

discourtesy *n* **rudeness**, impoliteness, disrespect, incivility, insolence *Opposite*: politeness

discover *v* **1 find out**, learn, determine, notice, realize **2 come across**, find, turn up, uncover, unearth

discoverer *n* **inventor**, originator, pioneer, innovator, creator

discovery *n* **1 find**, innovation, breakthrough, invention, finding **2 detection**, finding, unearthing, sighting, encounter

discredit *v* **1 slur**, demean, smear, insult, humiliate **2 question**, doubt, disbelieve, query, suspect

discreditable *adj* **shameful**, disreputable, ignominious, disgraceful, reprehensible *Opposite*: honourable

discreet *adj* **1 tactful**, prudent, circumspect, cautious, careful *Opposite*: tactless **2 inconspicuous**, subtle, unnoticeable, unobtrusive, understated *Opposite*: obvious

discrepancy *n* **inconsistency**, difference, incongruity, divergence, disagreement *Opposite*: correspondence

discrete *adj* **separate**, distinct, disconnected, detached, isolated

discretion *n* **1 carefulness**, prudence, caution, canniness, maturity *Opposite*: tactlessness **2 freedom of choice**, will, pleasure, option, choice

discretionary *adj* **optional**, flexible, open, elective, unrestricted *Opposite*: mandatory

discriminate *v* **distinguish**, tell apart, differentiate, separate, categorize

discriminating *adj* **discerning**, sharp, astute, selective, judicious

discrimination *n* **1 bias**, prejudice, unfairness, inequity, bigotry **2 taste**, judgment, good taste, discernment, insight **3 distinction**, difference, differential, contrast

discriminatory *adj* **biased**, prejudiced, unfair, bigoted, inequitable *Opposite*: non-discriminatory

discursive *adj* **expansive**, lengthy, conversational, long-winded, circumlocutory *Opposite*: concise

discursiveness *n* **expansiveness**, long-windedness, roundaboutness, verbosity, circumlocution *Opposite*: concision

discuss *v* **talk over**, deliberate, debate, converse, confer

discussion *n* **conversation**, debate, argument, dialogue, chat

discussion group *n* **class**, seminar, tutorial, round table, committee

disdain *n* **scorn**, contempt, derision, condescension, disparagement *Opposite*: respect ■ *v* **despise**, scorn, spurn, hold in contempt, disparage *Opposite*: respect

disdainful *adj* **sneering**, scornful, derisive, condescending, aloof *Opposite*: respectful

disease *n* **illness**, sickness, ailment, infection, syndrome *Opposite*: health

diseased *adj* **unhealthy**, unwell, sickly, ill, sick *Opposite*: healthy

disembark *v* **come ashore**, go ashore, land, get off, arrive in port *Opposite*: embark

disembarkation *n* **arrival**, alighting, debarkation, landing, getting off

disembodied *adj* **ghostly**, spiritual, intangible, ethereal, immaterial *Opposite*: tangible

disembowel *v* **eviscerate**, gut, fillet, exenterate

disenchanted *adj* **disillusioned**, disappointed, dissatisfied, crestfallen, embittered *Opposite*: idealistic

disenchantment *n* **disillusionment**, disappointment, dissatisfaction, embitterment, bitterness *Opposite*: idealism

disenfranchise *v* **marginalize**, exclude, alienate, subjugate, disqualify *Opposite*: enfranchise

disenfranchisement *n* **marginalization**, exclusion, alienation, subjugation, disqualification *Opposite*: enfranchisement

disengage *v* **undo**, unfasten, unlock, untie, uncouple *Opposite*: fasten

disengagement *n* **1 withdrawal**, disentanglement, detachment, disconnection, extrication *Opposite*: engagement **2 release**, uncoupling, separation, extrication, withdrawal *Opposite*: attachment

disentangle *v* **unravel**, unscramble, untie, separate, straighten out *Opposite*: entangle

disequilibrium *n* **imbalance**, instability, uncertainty, flux, volatility *Opposite*: equilibrium

disestablish *v* **reform**, repudiate, renounce, re-evaluate, disclaim *Opposite*: establish

disfavour *n* **1 disrepute**, unpopularity, discredit, disgrace, obscurity *Opposite*: favour **2 distaste**, disdain, disapproval, displeasure, disapprobation *(fml) Opposite*: favour

disfigure *v* **mutilate**, scar, deface, mar, spoil *Opposite*: enhance

disfigurement *n* **scar**, mutilation, defacement, deformity, blemish *Opposite*: enhancement

disgorge *v* **expel**, eject, empty, pour out, spew *Opposite*: retain

disgrace *n* **shame**, discredit, scandal, ignominy, humiliation ■ *v* **bring shame on**, discredit, bring into disrepute, shame, degrade

disgraced *adj* **discredited**, shamed, condemned, humiliated, fallen *Opposite*: popular

disgraceful *adj* **shameful**, shocking, outrageous, scandalous, discreditable

disgruntle v **displease**, irritate, anger, annoy, dissatisfy Opposite: satisfy

disgruntled adj **discontented**, dissatisfied, resentful, displeased, unhappy Opposite: contented

disguise v **cover up**, hide, conceal, mask, masquerade Opposite: reveal ■ n **mask**, costume, camouflage, masquerade, cover

disguised adj **camouflaged**, masked, masquerading, cloaked, veiled Opposite: overt

disgust n **revulsion**, repugnance, abhorrence, repulsion, antipathy Opposite: attraction ■ v **sicken**, repulse, revolt, repel, shock Opposite: please. See COMPARE AND CONTRAST at **dislike**.

disgusted adj **sickened**, revolted, repulsed, repelled, offended Opposite: charmed

disgusting adj **revolting**, repulsive, sickening, ghastly, filthy Opposite: attractive

dish n **1 plate**, bowl, saucer **2 food item**, course, recipe

---

WORD BANK

❑ types of cooked dish bruschetta, burritos, casserole, cassoulet, ceviche, chop suey, chow mein, couscous, curry, fajitas, falafel, fish cake, fondue, fricassee, frijoles, frittata, fry-up, goulash, gruel, Irish stew, kedgeree, lasagne, meat loaf, mixed grill, moussaka, nachos, nasi goreng, paella, pilau, pirozhki, pizza, quiche, ragout, ratatouille, risotto, sambal, satay, sauerkraut, stew, stir-fry, tacos, tagine, tamale, tempura, teriyaki, tofu, yakitori

---

disharmonious adj **conflicting**, discordant, tense, uneasy, bitter Opposite: harmonious

disharmony n **conflict**, disagreement, discord, tension, unrest Opposite: harmony

dishcloth n **washing-up cloth**, kitchen cloth, towel, drying-up cloth, dishrag (US)

dishearten v **discourage**, depress, sadden, cast down, dismay Opposite: buoy up

disheartened adj **discouraged**, depressed, saddened, dismayed, dejected Opposite: encouraged

disheartening adj **intimidating**, off-putting, daunting, dispiriting, depressing Opposite: encouraging

dishevelled adj **unkempt**, wild and woolly, tousled, ruffled, untidy Opposite: well-groomed

dishevelment n **messiness**, scruffiness, untidiness, unruliness Opposite: tidiness

dishonest adj **lying**, deceitful, false, untruthful, fraudulent Opposite: honest

dishonesty n **deceit**, deceitfulness, fraudulence, lying, untruthfulness Opposite: honesty

dishonour n **disgrace**, shame, discredit, ignominy, disrepute Opposite: honour ■ v **shame**, disgrace, discredit, defame, bring into disrepute Opposite: honour

dishonourable adj **disgraceful**, disreputable,

discreditable, shameful, ignominious Opposite: honourable

dish out (infml) v **distribute**, parcel out, allot, hand out, deal out

dishy (infml) adj **good-looking**, nice-looking, cute, attractive, handsome Opposite: ugly

disillusion v **disenchant**, bring down to earth, disappoint, let down, dishearten Opposite: inspire

disillusioned adj **disenchanted**, disappointed, disheartened, cynical Opposite: starry-eyed

disillusionment n **disenchantment**, disappointment, cynicism, letdown, discouragement Opposite: gratification

disincentive n **deterrent**, discouragement, hindrance, impediment, encumbrance Opposite: incentive

disinclination n **reluctance**, unwillingness, opposition, hesitation, aversion Opposite: inclination

disincline v **put off**, deter, discourage, dissuade, prevent Opposite: encourage

disinclined adj **reluctant**, unwilling, opposed, unenthusiastic, loath Opposite: inclined. See COMPARE AND CONTRAST at **unwilling**.

disinfect v **sterilize**, sanitize, purify, fumigate, cleanse Opposite: contaminate

disinfectant n **antiseptic**, sterilizer, purifier, bleach, sanitizer

disinformation n **deception**, falsehood, propaganda, half-truth, misinformation Opposite: truth

disingenuous adj **dishonest**, insincere, untruthful, deceitful, hypocritical Opposite: honest

disingenuousness n **dishonesty**, insincerity, untruthfulness, deceit, hypocrisy Opposite: honesty

disinherit v **cut off**, disown, leave penniless, cut out, divest Opposite: bequeath

disintegrate v **crumble**, fragment, break, collapse, split Opposite: combine

disintegration n **breakdown**, breakup, collapse, fragmentation, crumbling

disinter v **1 exhume**, dig up, unearth Opposite: bury **2** (fml) **uncover**, unearth, bring to light, expose, reveal Opposite: cover up

disinterest n **indifference**, unconcern, apathy, disregard, heedlessness Opposite: interest

disinterested adj **fair-minded**, unbiased, impartial, without prejudice, neutral Opposite: biased

disinterestedness n **impartiality**, objectivity, fair-mindedness, neutrality, distance Opposite: bias

disinterment n **1 exhumation**, digging up, unearthing Opposite: interment **2** (fml) **exposure**, unearthing, discovery, revelation, uncovering Opposite: concealment

disjoint v **1 split**, separate, come apart, sever, divide Opposite: join **2 dislocate**, dislodge, move, relocate, separate *Opposite*: retain

disjointed *adj* **rambling**, fragmented, incoherent, disorganized, disorderly *Opposite*: coherent

disjointedness *n* **disjunction**, disjuncture, incoherence, dislocation, disconnection *Opposite*: coherence

dislikable *adj* **disagreeable**, unpleasant, offensive, repugnant, horrible *Opposite*: likable

dislike *v* **hate**, detest, loathe, frown on, disapprove *Opposite*: like ■ *n* **distaste**, antipathy, aversion, hatred, hate *Opposite*: liking

---

COMPARE AND CONTRAST CORE MEANING: a feeling of not liking somebody or something
dislike a feeling or attitude of disapproval; **distaste** mild dislike, mainly of behaviour and activities; **hatred** *or* **hate** intense dislike or hostility; **disgust** a feeling of horrified and sickened disapproval; **loathing** intense dislike; **repugnance** strong disgust, mainly of behaviour and activities; **abhorrence** a feeling of aversion or intense disapproval, mainly of behaviour and activities; **animosity** a feeling of hostility and resentment; **antipathy** a deep-seated dislike or hostility; **aversion** a strong feeling of dislike; **revulsion** a sudden violent feeling of disgust.

---

dislocate *v* **1 put out of place**, displace, put out of joint, disjoint, dislodge *Opposite*: replace **2 disrupt**, interrupt, disturb, upset, disorder *Opposite*: restore

dislocation *n* **1 displacement**, disarticulation, dislodgment **2 disruption**, interruption, disturbance, disorder, upset

dislodge *v* **remove**, get out, extricate, free, displace *Opposite*: wedge

disloyal *adj* **unfaithful**, treacherous, untrue, false, fickle *Opposite*: loyal

disloyalty *n* **unfaithfulness**, treachery, falseness, infidelity, betrayal *Opposite*: loyalty

dismal *adj* **miserable**, gloomy, depressing, dreary, dull *Opposite*: bright

dismay *v* **disappoint**, shock, sadden, depress, perturb *Opposite*: comfort ■ *n* **disappointment**, shock, consternation, apprehension, panic *Opposite*: comfort

dismayed *adj* **discouraged**, disheartened, demoralized, downcast, depressed *Opposite*: heartened

dismember *v* **tear limb from limb**, cut into pieces, cut up, dissect, tear apart

dismemberment *n* **taking apart**, mutilation, division, maiming, splitting off

dismiss *v* **1 discharge**, relieve of duty, give notice, give somebody the push, fire *(infml)* *Opposite*: retain **2 send away**, allow to go, release, send home *Opposite*: detain **3 reject**, set aside, think no more of, put out of your mind, shelve *Opposite*: dwell on

dismissal *n* **removal**, notice, discharge, release, sack *Opposite*: appointment

dismissive *adj* **flippant**, indifferent, unconcerned, trivializing, contemptuous *Opposite*: attentive

dismount *v* **get down**, get off, alight, climb down, descend *Opposite*: mount

disobedience *n* **defiance**, noncompliance, breaking the rules, insubordination, waywardness *Opposite*: obedience

disobedient *adj* **defiant**, noncompliant, rebellious, insubordinate, badly behaved *Opposite*: obedient

disobey *v* **defy**, refuse to comply, break the rules, contravene, violate *Opposite*: obey

disobliging *adj* **unhelpful**, uncooperative, unaccommodating, rude, unfriendly *Opposite*: obliging

disorder *n* **1 chaos**, disarray, confusion, mess, muddle *Opposite*: order **2 complaint**, illness, sickness, ailment, syndrome ■ *v* **disorganize**, disarrange, disturb, jumble, muddle *Opposite*: order

disordered *adj* **chaotic**, messy, muddled, topsy-turvy, higgledy-piggledy *Opposite*: well-ordered

disorderliness *n* **confusion**, messiness, muddle, chaos, disarray *Opposite*: orderliness

disorderly *adj* **1 unruly**, riotous, uncontrollable, rebellious, wild *Opposite*: orderly **2 muddled**, jumbled, confused, messy, unsystematic

disorganization *n* **inefficiency**, ineptitude, ineffectiveness, chaos, disorder *Opposite*: organization

disorganize *v* **muddle**, mix up, confuse, jumble, dislocate *Opposite*: organize

disorganized *adj* **muddled**, jumbled, confused, messy, unsystematic *Opposite*: organized

disorient *see* disorientate

disorientate *v* **confuse**, perplex, fox, befuddle, fuddle *Opposite*: orientate

disorientated *adj* **confused**, unsettled, bewildered, perplexed, thrown *(infml)* *Opposite*: clear-headed

disorientation *n* **puzzlement**, bafflement, stupefaction, bewilderment, confusion

disown *v* **renounce**, reject, wash your hands of, turn your back on, disclaim *Opposite*: acknowledge

disparage *v* **belittle**, laugh at, mock, ridicule, pour scorn on *Opposite*: praise

disparagement *n* **belittling**, mocking, ridicule, criticism, derision *Opposite*: praise

disparaging *adj* **critical**, unfavourable, disapproving, censorious, unsympathetic *Opposite*: approving

disparate *adj* **dissimilar**, unlike, different, incongruent, unrelated *Opposite*: similar

disparity *n* **difference**, inequality, discrepancy, disproportion, gap *Opposite*: parity

dispassion *n* **aloofness**, coolness, calmness, impassivity, serenity *Opposite*: enthusiasm

dispassionate *adj* **calm**, composed, unflustered, unemotional, detached *Opposite*: fiery

dispatch *v* **1 send off**, send out, post, mail, ship *Opposite*: keep **2 kill**, murder, assassinate, put to death, slaughter ■ *n* **message**, communication, notice, letter, report

dispatch rider *n* **courier**, messenger, deliverer

dispel *v* **dismiss**, chase away, drive out, disperse, scatter *Opposite*: attract

dispensable *adj* **expendable**, superfluous, unessential, unnecessary, replaceable *Opposite*: indispensable

dispensary *n* **chemist's**, pharmacy, drugstore (US)

dispensation *n* **indulgence**, allowance, special consideration, privilege, exemption

dispense *v* **give out**, hand out, distribute, allot, mete out *Opposite*: withhold

dispenser *n* **distributor**, slot machine, machine, vending machine

dispersal *n* **dispersion**, spreading, scattering, diffusion, distribution *Opposite*: concentration

disperse *v* **scatter**, go away, disband, break up, dissolve *Opposite*: concentrate

dispersion *n* **dispersal**, spreading, scattering, diffusion, distribution *Opposite*: concentration

dispirit *v* **dishearten**, discourage, dampen, depress, dismay *Opposite*: rouse

dispirited *adj* **disheartened**, discouraged, dejected, depressed, downhearted *Opposite*: cheerful

dispiriting *adj* **disheartening**, depressing, demoralizing, upsetting, saddening *Opposite*: uplifting

displace *v* **1 move**, relocate, shift, transfer, put out of place *Opposite*: restore **2 oust**, supplant, replace, supersede, succeed *Opposite*: restore

displacement *n* **movement**, dislocation, dislodgment, shift, supplanting

display *v* **1 show**, exhibit, put on show, present, put on view *Opposite*: conceal **2 flaunt**, parade, show off, strut, pose *Opposite*: conceal ■ *n* **show**, exhibition, presentation, demonstration, parade

displease *v* **anger**, annoy, irritate, upset, put out *Opposite*: please

displeased *adj* **annoyed**, dissatisfied, put out, irked, unhappy *Opposite*: pleased

displeasure *n* **anger**, annoyance, irritation, disapproval, discontentment *Opposite*: pleasure

disport (archaic) *v* **show off**, pose, swagger, strut, flaunt

disposable *adj* **throwaway**, one-use, non-refundable *Opposite*: reusable

disposal *n* **removal**, discarding, clearance, dumping, throwing away *Opposite*: retention

dispose *v* **1 incline**, influence, persuade, prompt, encourage **2 settle**, resolve, fix, decide, determine **3** (fml) **position**, place, set out, arrange, set

disposed *adj* **willing**, likely, liable, inclined, of a mind *Opposite*: unwilling

dispose of *v* **1 throw away**, throw out, dispense with, discard, get rid of *Opposite*: keep **2 transfer**, pass on, divest yourself of, relieve yourself of, sell *Opposite*: keep **3** (fml) **attend to**, determine, settle, sort out, sort **4 kill**, murder, execute, assassinate, dispatch **5** (fml) **consume**, demolish, get through, devour, use up

disposition *n* **nature**, character, temperament, temper, outlook

dispossess (archaic or fml) *v* **deprive**, divest, strip, rob, disinherit

dispossessed *adj* **evicted**, expelled, ejected, turned out, driven out

dispossession *n* **deprivation**, denial, withdrawal, removal

disproportion *n* **imbalance**, discrepancy, disparity, inequality, inconsistency *Opposite*: equality

disproportionate *adj* **uneven**, unequal, lopsided, inconsistent, top-heavy *Opposite*: corresponding

disproportionately *adv* **excessively**, unduly, unreasonably, extremely, too *Opposite*: slightly

disprove *v* **refute**, invalidate, contradict, challenge, negate (fml) *Opposite*: prove

disputable *adj* **arguable**, debatable, moot, questionable, uncertain *Opposite*: incontrovertible

disputation (fml) *n* **argument**, strife, conflict, debate, disagreement *Opposite*: agreement

disputatious (fml) *adj* **argumentative**, quarrelsome, awkward, difficult, contrary *Opposite*: conciliatory

disputative (fml) *adj* **argumentative**, quarrelsome, awkward, difficult, contrary *Opposite*: conciliatory

dispute *v* **1 argue**, debate, discuss, quarrel, wrangle *Opposite*: agree **2 challenge**, question, contest, query, doubt *Opposite*: accept ■ *n* **argument**, disagreement, quarrel, difference, clash *Opposite*: agreement. *See* COMPARE AND CONTRAST *at* disagree.

disqualification *n* **ineligibility**, banning, barring, disentitlement, debarment *Opposite*: entitlement

disqualified *adj* **ineligible**, banned, barred, debarred, prohibited *Opposite*: eligible

disqualify *v* **ban**, bar, debar, prohibit, exclude *Opposite*: allow

disquiet *n* **unrest**, uneasiness, concern, worry, anxiety *Opposite*: calmness

disquieting *adj* **worrying**, disturbing, alarming, unsettling, troubling *Opposite*: reassuring

disquisition (fml) n **essay**, tract, discussion, address, speech

disquisitional (fml) adj **verbose**, wordy, long-winded, rambling, digressive Opposite: concise

disregard v **ignore**, take no notice of, turn a blind eye to, discount, pay no attention to Opposite: heed ■ n **disrespect**, indifference, contempt, disdain, neglect Opposite: regard

disregarded adj **1 ignored**, omitted, overlooked, unheeded, unnoticed Opposite: acknowledged **2 snubbed**, slighted, marginalized, sidelined, dishonoured Opposite: respected

disrepair n **poor shape**, bad shape, bad condition, poor order, disorder

disreputable adj **notorious**, infamous, scandalous, disgraceful, seedy Opposite: reputable

disrepute n **disgrace**, ill repute, disrespect, disregard, discredit Opposite: esteem

disrespect n **disregard**, contempt, insolence, impertinence, impudence Opposite: respect ■ v **insult**, affront, belittle, disparage, denigrate Opposite: respect

disrespectable adj **dishonourable**, frowned on, disreputable, unpopular, infamous Opposite: respectable

disrespectful adj **rude**, impolite, bad-mannered, discourteous, insolent Opposite: respectful

disrobe (fml) v **strip**, undress, unclothe, uncover, divest (fml) Opposite: dress

disrupt v **disturb**, upset, interrupt, dislocate, disorder

disruption n **disturbance**, commotion, trouble, interruption, distraction

disruptive adj **troublesome**, unruly, disorderly, unsettling, disturbing

disruptiveness n **unruliness**, rowdiness, disorderliness, indiscipline, naughtiness

dissatisfaction n **displeasure**, discontent, disappointment, unhappiness, frustration Opposite: satisfaction

dissatisfied adj **disgruntled**, displeased, discontented, disappointed, unhappy Opposite: satisfied

dissatisfy v **disgruntle**, displease, disappoint, put out, frustrate Opposite: satisfy

dissect v **1 cut up**, cut apart, divide, dismember, slice up **2 scrutinize**, break down, examine, study, explore

dissection n **1 cutting up**, partition, division, separation, segmentation **2 examination**, analysis, investigation, scrutiny, observation

dissemble v **1 pretend**, mislead, act, put on an act, dissimulate **2 disguise**, conceal, hide, suppress, mask Opposite: disclose

disseminate v **distribute**, broadcast, circulate, spread, publicize. See COMPARE AND CONTRAST at **scatter.**

dissemination n **distribution**, broadcasting, diffusion, propagation, spreading

dissension n **opposition**, disagreement, dissent, discord, rebellion Opposite: consent

dissent v **disagree**, oppose, rebel, dispute, differ Opposite: agree ■ n **opposition**, disagreement, dissension, discord, rebellion Opposite: consent

dissenter n **rebel**, dissident, nonconformist, insurgent, mutineer

dissertation n **thesis**, paper, study, critique, essay

disservice n **damage**, harm, wrong, injury, difficulty Opposite: service

dissidence n **disagreement**, unorthodoxy, nonconformity, independence, rebellion Opposite: conformism

dissident n **dissenter**, rebel, nonconformist, protester, insurgent Opposite: conformist ■ adj **rebel**, rebellious, dissenting, unorthodox, nonconforming Opposite: conformist

dissimilar adj **unlike**, different, diverse, unrelated, disparate Opposite: similar

dissimilarity n **difference**, variation, distinction, contrast, divergence Opposite: similarity

dissimulate v **disguise**, conceal, hide, suppress, mask Opposite: disclose

dissimulation (fml) n **concealment**, suppression, disguise, camouflage, dishonesty Opposite: disclosure

dissipate v **1 dispel**, disperse, dissolve, scatter, drive away **2 squander**, waste, fritter away, throw away, blow (slang)

dissipated adj **dissolute**, degenerate, debauched, self-indulgent, immoral Opposite: upright

dissipation n **debauchery**, indulgence, rakishness, overindulgence, degeneracy Opposite: uprightness

dissociate v **distance**, detach, divorce, separate, disconnect Opposite: associate

dissociation n **detachment**, separation, disconnection, severance, alienation Opposite: association

dissolute adj **degenerate**, depraved, immoral, debauched, self-indulgent Opposite: upright

dissoluteness n **decadence**, overindulgence, extravagance, self-indulgence, degeneracy Opposite: temperance

dissolution n **closure**, disbanding, termination, ending, suspension Opposite: inauguration

dissolve v **1 melt**, soften, liquefy, thaw, run Opposite: solidify **2 disband**, close, break up, suspend, end Opposite: inaugurate **3 disappear**, dissipate, dispel, disperse, melt away Opposite: appear

dissonance n **discord**, disagreement, dissension, conflict, difference Opposite: harmony

dissonant *adj* **discordant**, unmusical, harsh, inharmonious, cacophonous *Opposite*: harmonious

dissuade *v* **deter**, put off, discourage, advise against, persuade against *Opposite*: persuade

dissuasion *n* **discouragement**, deterrence, persuasion, opposition, warning *Opposite*: encouragement

dissuasive *adj* **discouraging**, opposing, inhibitive, hindering *Opposite*: encouraging

distance *n* **1 coldness**, aloofness, detachment, reserve, remoteness *Opposite*: warmth **2 space**, expanse, void, vastness, gap *Opposite*: closeness ■ *v* **dissociate**, move away, detach, separate, avoid *Opposite*: associate

distant *adj* **1 faraway**, remote, far-off, far-flung, outlying *Opposite*: near **2 vague**, faint, indistinct, hazy, obscure *Opposite*: clear **3 aloof**, cold, unfriendly, detached, reserved *Opposite*: warm

distaste *n* **aversion**, dislike, antipathy, disgust, disfavour *Opposite*: love. *See* COMPARE AND CONTRAST *at* **dislike**.

distasteful *adj* **repugnant**, offensive, disgusting, repulsive, objectionable *Opposite*: pleasant

distastefulness *n* **unpleasantness**, offensiveness, nastiness, repulsiveness *Opposite*: pleasantness

distend *v* **swell**, bloat, balloon, inflate, swell up *Opposite*: deflate

distended *adj* **swollen**, bloated, inflated, enlarged, expanded

distension *n* **swelling**, expansion, enlargement, tumescence, dilation

distil *v* **1 purify**, refine, condense, extract, concentrate *Opposite*: dilute **2 extract**, garner, glean, cull, collect *Opposite*: expand

distillate *n* **essence**, tincture, concentrate, extract, distillation

distillation *n* **1 concentration**, condensation, refinement, purification, extraction *Opposite*: dilution **2 essence**, epitome, embodiment, summation, condensation **3 distillate**, tincture, extract, concentrate

distinct *adj* **1 separate**, different, dissimilar, discrete, diverse *Opposite*: same **2 clear**, definite, well-defined, noticeable, marked *Opposite*: unclear

distinction *n* **1 difference**, division, dissimilarity, discrepancy, otherness *Opposite*: similarity **2 feature**, characteristic, idiosyncrasy, peculiarity, trait **3 merit**, excellence, note, worth, accolade *Opposite*: disgrace

distinctive *adj* **characteristic**, idiosyncratic, distinguishing, individual, typical *Opposite*: common

distinctiveness *n* **uniqueness**, individuality, particularity, individualism, singularity *Opposite*: sameness

distinctly *adv* **definitely**, clearly, noticeably, markedly, particularly *Opposite*: vaguely

distinguish *v* **1 differentiate**, tell apart, between, discriminate, decide *Opposite*: homogenize **2 make out**, discern, see, recognize, perceive **3 set apart**, single out, characterize, mark, classify

distinguishable *adj* **1 different**, unique, distinct, special, divergent **2 discernible**, obvious, noticeable, clear, evident *Opposite*: indistinguishable

distinguished *adj* **illustrious**, eminent, famous, famed, well-known *Opposite*: undistinguished

distinguishing *adj* **unique**, individual, personal, distinctive, characteristic *Opposite*: typical

distort *v* **1 misrepresent**, interfere with, twist, alter, garble **2 deform**, disfigure, twist, warp, alter *Opposite*: straighten

distorted *adj* **1 one-sided**, slanted, partial, inaccurate, partisan *Opposite*: accurate **2 twisted**, malformed, warped, bent, contorted *Opposite*: straight **3 unrecognizable**, grotesque, unnatural, monstrous, bizarre

distortion *n* **1 bend**, buckle, twist, deformation, warp **2 misrepresentation**, alteration, lie, falsehood, falsification

distract *v* **1 sidetrack**, divert, confuse, addle, befuddle **2 entertain**, amuse, divert, absorb, engross

distracted *adj* **1 unfocused**, abstracted, preoccupied, sidetracked, diverted *Opposite*: attentive **2 troubled**, agitated, anxious, perplexed, confused *Opposite*: calm

distracting *adj* **off-putting**, disturbing, diverting, disrupting

distraction *n* **1 interruption**, disruption, commotion, disturbance, interference **2 diversion**, entertainment, hobby, pastime, leisure activity **3 agitation**, anxiety, bewilderment, confusion, desperation

distraught *adj* **distressed**, beside yourself, out of your mind, hysterical, upset *Opposite*: calm

distress *n* **1 suffering**, pain, sorrow, anguish, agony *Opposite*: peace **2 trouble**, danger, rigour, difficulty, misfortune ■ *v* **upset**, disturb, trouble, bother, afflict *Opposite*: soothe

distressed *adj* **1 upset**, distraught, troubled, concerned, worried *Opposite*: content **2 in pain**, suffering, anguished, tormented, miserable

distressing *adj* **upsetting**, worrying, difficult, stressful, painful

distress signal *n* **call for help**, cry for help, alarm bell, alarm, call

distribute *v* **1 deal out**, hand out, share out, allocate, give out *Opposite*: amass **2 deliver**, supply, circulate, spread out, spread *Opposite*: retain. *See* COMPARE AND CONTRAST *at* **scatter**.

distributer see distributor

distribution n 1 **sharing**, allocation, giving out, division, allotment 2 **delivery**, supply, circulation, transportation, dispersal 3 **spreading**, dispersal, dissemination, scattering

distributor n **supplier**, provider, wholesaler, broker, trader

district n **area**, locality, quarter, borough, ward

distrust n **suspicion**, disbelief, doubt, misgiving, cynicism Opposite: trust ▪ v **disbelieve**, doubt, be suspicious of, mistrust, suspect Opposite: trust

distrustful adj **suspicious**, doubting, wary, nervous, disbelieving Opposite: trusting

disturb v 1 **interrupt**, distract, bother, disrupt, annoy 2 **upset**, worry, bother, concern, perturb 3 **move**, transfer, shift, dislocate, remove 4 **spoil**, unsettle, upset, meddle, tamper. See COMPARE AND CONTRAST at **bother**.

disturbance n 1 **trouble**, commotion, riot, uproar, fracas 2 **annoyance**, interruption, intrusion, bother, disruption

disturbed adj 1 **troubled**, bothered, concerned, worried, distressed Opposite: unconcerned 2 **unstable**, troubled, traumatized, unbalanced, unhinged Opposite: stable

disturbing adj **worrying**, troubling, alarming, upsetting, distressing Opposite: reassuring

disunite v **split**, divide, separate, undo, dissolve Opposite: unite

disunity n **disagreement**, discord, divergence, dissent, conflict Opposite: unity

disuse n **neglect**, abandonment, unemployment, dereliction Opposite: use

disused adj **empty**, abandoned, neglected, derelict, deserted Opposite: occupied

ditch n **channel**, trench, dike, drain, waterway ▪ v (infml) **scrap**, get rid of, drop, split up with, discard

dither v **hesitate**, dally, dawdle, waste time, vacillate

ditherer n **vacillator**, dawdler, waverer, hesitater

dithering n **indecisiveness**, indecision, hesitation, irresolution, wavering Opposite: decisiveness

ditty n **song**, poem, rhyme, limerick, nursery rhyme

diurnal adj 1 **day**, daytime, daylight Opposite: nocturnal 2 **daily**, 24-hour, 24-hourly, circadian, quotidian (fml)

diva n prima donna, singer, chanteuse, soprano

divan n **settee**, couch, sofa

dive v 1 **jump**, leap, drop, lunge, submerge Opposite: surface 2 **plummet**, plunge, fall, nose-dive, crash Opposite: shoot up ▪ n 1 **lunge**, leap, drop, jump 2 **plunge**, fall, nosedive, crash, free-fall 3 (infml) **dump** (infml), hole (infml), fleapit (infml)

diver n **swimmer**, deep-sea diver, snorkeller, frogman, scuba diver

diverge v 1 **deviate**, move away, wander, depart, swerve Opposite: converge 2 **differ**, disagree, vary, conflict Opposite: concur 3 **digress**, ramble, stray, deviate

divergence n 1 **deviation**, departure, discrepancy, disagreement, separation Opposite: convergence 2 **difference**, difference of opinion, disagreement, variance, conflict Opposite: agreement

divergent adj **different**, differing, deviating, conflicting, contradictory Opposite: similar

diverse adj 1 **varied**, miscellaneous, assorted, sundry 2 **different**, dissimilar, unlike, distinct, separate Opposite: similar

diversely adv **varyingly**, variously, distinctly, separately, dissimilarly Opposite: similarly

diversification n **change**, divergence, variation, modification, broadening Opposite: specialization

diversify v **branch out**, expand, spread, broaden your horizons, vary Opposite: specialize

diversion n 1 **distraction**, entertainment, pastime, hobby, leisure activity 2 **change**, alteration, departure, digression, deviation

diversionary adj **distracting**, diverting, misleading, deflecting, deceptive

diversity n **variety**, assortment, multiplicity, range, mixture Opposite: uniformity

divert v 1 **redirect**, deflect, reroute, switch 2 **distract**, sidetrack, turn away, avert, deter Opposite: focus 3 **entertain**, amuse, please, delight, gladden

divest v **strip**, rid, dissociate, separate, part from Opposite: give

divide v 1 **split**, separate, partition, segregate, break up Opposite: join 2 **share**, share out, divide up, deal out, distribute 3 **cause a rift**, split up, break up, split, come between Opposite: unite ▪ n **gulf**, rift, division, split, gap

dividend n **bonus**, extra, payment, share, surplus

divider n **partition**, separator, screen

dividing line n **distinction**, margin, borderline, border, watershed

divination n **prophecy**, prediction, forecast, foretelling, insight

divine adj 1 **heavenly**, celestial, godly, godlike, deific (fml) Opposite: secular 2 (infml) **great**, exquisite, delightful, lovely, pleasing ▪ v **discover**, guess, presume, deduce, discern

divinity n **religion**, theology, religious studies, spirituality, mysticism

divisible adj **isolatable**, detachable, separable, dividable Opposite: inseparable

division n 1 **separation**, splitting up, partition, dissection, detachment Opposite: union 2 **sharing out**, distribution, allotment, allocation, apportionment 3 **split**, rift, disagreement, discord, break Opposite: unity

4 boundary, partition, border, dividing line, demarcation **5 category**, classification, type, class, grouping **6 department**, section, group, branch, sector

divisive *adj* **discordant**, troublesome, disruptive, conflict-ridden, contentious

divisiveness *n* **disruptiveness**, dissension, disagreement, discord, disunity

divorce *n* **separation**, split, breakup, split-up, annulment *Opposite*: marriage ■ *v* **dissociate**, disconnect, separate, distance, detach *Opposite*: associate

divorced *adj* **separated**, removed, unconnected, split, detached *Opposite*: together

divot *n* **turf**, sod, clump, clod, piece

divulge *v* **reveal**, tell, make known, disclose, let drop

divvy *(infml) v* **divide up**, divide, share out, deal out, distribute

dizzily *adv* **dazedly**, woozily, lightheadedly, shakily, unsteadily *Opposite*: steadily

dizziness *n* **faintness**, giddiness, wooziness, vertigo, shakiness

dizzy *adj* **1 faint**, giddy, woozy, shaky, lightheaded **2** *(infml)* **frivolous**, flippant, silly, lighthearted, flighty

DJ *n* **1 dinner jacket**, tuxedo, black tie, tux *(infml)* **2 disc jockey**, MC, radio presenter, broadcaster, deejay *(infml)*

do *v* **1 perform**, accomplish, act, carry out, complete **2 see to**, fix, prepare, sort out, look after **3 solve**, work out, resolve, figure out, puzzle out **4** *(infml)* **cheat**, trick, con, swindle, defraud ■ *n (infml)* **reception**, party, function, drinks party, cocktail party. *See* COMPARE AND CONTRAST *at* **perform**.

doable *adj* **achievable**, possible, workable, feasible, attainable *Opposite*: impossible

do a bunk *(infml) v* **disappear**, vanish, bolt, run away, scoot *Opposite*: hang about

do away with *v* **1 abolish**, dispense with, remove, dispose of, get rid of *Opposite*: retain **2** *(infml)* **kill**, murder, assassinate, finish off *(infml)*, do in *(infml)*

docile *adj* **quiet**, passive, unassuming, compliant, submissive *Opposite*: wild

docility *n* **quietness**, submissiveness, meekness, tameness, gentleness *Opposite*: fierceness

dock *n* **berth**, mooring, anchorage, wharf, quay ■ *v* **1 come in**, tie up, land, berth, moor **2 cut**, cut off, crop, stop, reduce *Opposite*: increase

docket *n* **1 tag**, sticker, label, marker, ticket **2 agenda**, programme, schedule, calendar, timetable ■ *v* **label**, tag, identify, disclose, declare

dockside *n* **wharf**, jetty, dock, quayside, quay

dockyard *n* **shipyard**, boatyard, dry dock

doctor *n* **1 medical practitioner**, physician, healer, doc *(infml)*, medic *(infml)* **2 academic**,

scholar, expert, specialist, Doctor of Philosophy ■ *v* **1 amend**, modify, adjust, meddle with, rework **2 treat**, care for, look after, cure, heal

doctorate *n* **higher degree**, research degree, university degree, PhD, Doctor of Philosophy

doctrinaire *adj* **rigid**, inflexible, stern, strict, unbending *Opposite*: liberal

doctrine *n* **policy**, principle, set of guidelines, canon, dogma

document *n* **text**, file, article, essay, paper ■ *v* **record**, keep a record, detail, write down, provide evidence

documentation *n* **certification**, papers, credentials, documents, citations

dodder *v* **1 tremble**, shake, waver, quake, quiver **2 totter**, reel, teeter, stagger, wobble *Opposite*: stride

doddering *adj* **tottering**, reeling, teetering, staggering, wobbling

doddery *adj* **shaky**, unsteady, tottery, feeble, frail *Opposite*: steady

doddle *(infml) n* **child's play**, piece of cake *(infml)*, cinch *(infml)*, pushover *(infml)*, breeze *(infml) Opposite*: challenge

dodge *v* **1 move**, cut, duck, move away, sidestep **2 avoid**, evade, shirk, elude, get out of

dodgy *(infml) adj* **1 dishonest**, suspect, unreliable, untrustworthy, doubtful *Opposite*: reliable **2 risky**, dangerous, hazardous, unsafe, chancy *Opposite*: safe

do down *(infml) v* **disparage**, smear, belittle, deride, pour scorn on

doer *n* **achiever**, dynamo, go-getter *(infml)*, live wire *(infml)*

doff *v* **take off**, lift, tip, tilt, remove *Opposite*: don

dog *n* **canine**, hound, doggy *(infml)*, mutt *(infml)*, pooch *(infml)* ■ *v* **1 follow**, pursue, chase, trail, track **2 bother**, beleaguer, harass, vex, plague

WORD BANK
❏ **types of large dog** Afghan hound, Alsatian, bloodhound, borzoi, boxer, bulldog, collie, dalmatian, Doberman pinscher, Great Dane, greyhound, guide dog, husky, Labrador, mastiff, Newfoundland, Old English sheepdog, Pyrenean mountain dog, retriever, Rottweiler, Saint Bernard, setter, sheepdog, wolfhound
❏ **types of small dog** affenpinscher, airedale, basenji, basset, beagle, Border terrier, bull terrier, cairn terrier, chihuahua, chow, corgi, dachshund, fox terrier, foxhound, Jack Russell, Pekingese, pomeranian, poodle, pug, Scottie, Sealyham, shar-pei, shih tzu, spaniel, terrier, whippet, Yorkshire terrier

dog-eared *adj* **damaged**, tattered, battered, well-read, worn *Opposite*: pristine

dogfight *n* **fight**, conflict, combat, encounter, raid

dogged *adj* **determined**, single-minded, unwavering, indefatigable, steadfast *Opposite*: half-hearted

doggedness *n* **perseverance**, persistence, single-mindedness, tenacity, resolve *Opposite*: apathy

doggerel *n* **1 verse**, poetry, rhyme, limerick, ditty **2 gibberish**, nonsense, prattle, rubbish, garbage

dogleg *n* **sharp bend**, angle, corner, curve, bend ▪ *v* bend, turn, curve, swerve

dogma *n* **creed**, doctrine, philosophy, canon, belief

dogmatic *adj* **rigid**, inflexible, unbending, strict, intransigent *Opposite*: flexible

dogmatism *n* **intransigence**, inflexibility, strictness, presumption, arrogance *Opposite*: openness

dog-tired *(infml)* *adj* **exhausted**, worn out, shattered, tired, all in *Opposite*: fresh

do in *(infml)* *v* **kill**, murder, assassinate, finish off *(infml)*, do away with *(infml)*

doings *(infml)* *n* **activities**, actions, events, happenings, deeds

doldrums *n* **1 stagnation**, sluggishness, boredom, lethargy, lassitude *Opposite*: energy **2 gloominess**, melancholy, dejection, despondency, pessimism *Opposite*: cheerfulness

doleful *adj* **unhappy**, miserable, sad, woeful, dejected *Opposite*: cheerful

dolefulness *n* **sadness**, unhappiness, misery, mournfulness, woefulness *Opposite*: cheerfulness

dole out *(infml)* *v* **share out**, dispense, distribute, allocate, allot *Opposite*: hoard

doll *n* **toy**, figurine, figure, model, puppet

dollar *n* **dollar bill**, buck *(infml)*, big one *(infml)*, greenback *(US slang)*

dollop *(infml)* *n* **blob**, spoonful, spoon, squirt, drop

doll up *(infml)* *v* **dress up**, smarten up, spruce up, titivate, smarten *Opposite*: tone down

dolly *(infml)* *see* doll

dolmen *n* **megalith**, obelisk, trilithon, monument, standing stone

domain *n* **area**, field, sphere, sphere of influence, province

dome *n* **vault**, cupola, roof, ceiling

domed *adj* **vaulted**, hemispherical, rounded, round

domestic *adj* **1 home**, family, house, household, familial *Opposite*: public **2 national**, local, internal, inland, native *Opposite*: international

domesticate *v* **tame**, break, bring under control, control, housetrain

domesticated *adj* **tame**, pet, trained, tamed, housetrained *Opposite*: wild

domestication *n* **taming**, training, housetraining, subjugation

domesticity *n* **home life**, family life, home comforts, married life, creature comforts

domestic partner *n* **cohabitee**, partner, significant other, spousal equivalent *(US)*

domicile *(fml)* *n* **home**, residence, house, flat, quarters

dominance *n* **supremacy**, ascendancy, domination, power, authority *Opposite*: weakness

dominant *adj* **1 domineering**, bossy, overbearing, officious, authoritarian *Opposite*: submissive **2 leading**, main, central, foremost, prevailing *Opposite*: minor

dominate *v* **1 control**, rule, lead, govern, direct **2 overlook**, overshadow, tower above, tower over, dwarf

domination *n* **power**, control, command, authority, dominion

domineering *adj* **bossy**, dominant, overbearing, officious, authoritarian *Opposite*: meek

dominion *n* **1 power**, authority, control, command, domination **2 territory**, colony, province, region, protectorate

don *v* **put on**, throw on, get into, pull on, dress in *Opposite*: take off ▪ *n* **university teacher**, lecturer, fellow, academic, tutor

donate *v* **give**, contribute, bequeath, provide, offer. *See* compare and contrast *at* give.

donation *n* **gift**, contribution, payment, bequest, endowment

done *adj* **complete**, completed, ended, finished, through

donkey's years *(infml)* *n* **years**, aeons, for ever, ages *(infml)*, yonks *(slang)*

donkeywork *(infml)* *n* **1 hard work**, heavy labour, hard graft **2 groundwork**, preparatory, work, preparation, research

donnish *adj* **academic**, bookish, dry, serious, intellectual

donor *n* **giver**, contributor, benefactor, patron, supporter

doodle *v* **draw**, sketch, scribble, squiggle ▪ *n* **drawing**, sketch, scribble, picture, squiggle

doom *n* **1 fate**, destiny, lot, kismet, portion *(literary)* **2 disaster**, trouble, end, death, tragedy

doomed *adj* **1 fated**, destined, damned, condemned, predestined **2 hopeless**, disaster-prone, ruined, lost, damned

doom-laden *adj* **gloomy**, pessimistic, dismal, depressing, despairing *Opposite*: upbeat *(infml)*

doomsday *n* **end of the world**, end of time, Last Judgment, Judgment Day, Day of Judgment

doomy *(infml)* *adj* **1 pessimistic**, despairing, gloomy, glum, melancholy *Opposite*: cheery **2 ominous**, threatening, portentous, worrying, troubling *Opposite*: hopeful

door *n* **entrance**, gate, entry, exit, access

doorplate *n* **name plate**, sign, plaque, house sign, plate

doorstep *n* **entrance**, threshold, access, doorway, front doorstep

doorway *n* **entrance**, door, front entrance, entry, front door

doppelgänger *n* **double**, mirror image, shadow, twin, clone

dormant *adj* **1 inactive**, asleep, sleeping, quiescent, quiet *Opposite*: active **2 latent**, undeveloped, hidden, unexpressed

dosage *n* **amount**, quantity, dose, measure, prescription

dose *n* **1 amount**, quantity, dosage, measure, prescription **2** (*infml*) **bout**, spell, period, attack, experience ■ *v* **treat**, give medicine to, dose up

doss *n* **sleep**, nap, catnap, siesta, snooze (*infml*)

dossier *n* **file**, record, report, folder, profile

dot *n* **spot**, point, mark, blotch, speck ■ *v* **speckle**, sprinkle, pepper, fleck, spot

doting *adj* **fond**, loving, devoted, affectionate, adoring

dotted *adj* **scattered**, sprinkled, spotted, speckled, spread

dotty *adj* **1 unconventional**, odd, eccentric, idiosyncratic, strange *Opposite*: normal **2 absurd**, impractical, illogical, foolish, nonsensical *Opposite*: practical **3** (*infml*) **crazy** (*infml*), fond, besotted, doting, infatuated

double *adj* **dual**, binary, twofold, duple, twin ■ *adv* **twice**, twofold, twice over, two times ■ *n* **1 duo**, pair, duet, couple **2 doppelgänger**, clone, alter ego, twin, stand-in ■ *v* **1 increase twofold**, double up, amplify, magnify, expand *Opposite*: lessen **2 bend**, fold, double up, bend over, fold up

double act *n* **pair**, twosome, duo, two-hander, couple

double agent *n* **spy**, mole, infiltrator, inside agent, secret agent

double-book *v* **overbook**, overfill, overextend, overstretch

double check *n* **second check**, reassessment, check, verification

double-check *v* **make sure**, ensure, reassure yourself, check, verify

double-cross *v* **betray**, con, let down, cheat, sell out ■ *n* **betrayal**, deception, swindle, trick, con

double-crosser *n* **swindler**, cheat, trickster, liar, fraudster

double-dealer *n* **swindler**, liar, cheat, fraudster, trickster

double-dealing *n* **duplicity**, betrayal, deceit, cheating, treachery *Opposite*: honesty ■ *adj* **duplicitous**, deceitful, double-faced, cheating, swindling *Opposite*: honest

double Dutch (*infml*) *n* **rubbish**, gibberish, gabble, nonsense, garbage

double-edged *adj* **ambiguous**, two-edged, disingenuous, ironic, sly *Opposite*: ingenuous

double-faced *adj* **insincere**, deceitful, dishonest, two-faced, false *Opposite*: honest

double-jointed *adj* **flexible**, supple, agile, lithe

double-quick (*infml*) *adj* **rapid**, swift, speedy, prompt, instant *Opposite*: slow ■ *adv* **rapidly**, swiftly, speedily, promptly, quickly *Opposite*: slowly

double talk *n* **1 gibberish**, nonsense, trash, rubbish, garbage **2 sophistry**, doublespeak, deceit, jargon, smoke and mirrors

double up *v* **bend**, fold, double, bend over, fold up

doubt *v* **disbelieve**, mistrust, suspect, have reservations, have doubts *Opposite*: believe ■ *n* **hesitation**, uncertainty, reservation, misgiving, distrust *Opposite*: certainty

doubter *n* **nonbeliever**, cynic, doubting Thomas, agnostic, pessimist *Opposite*: believer

doubtful *adj* **1 unsure**, uncertain, hesitant, in doubt, dubious *Opposite*: certain **2 unlikely**, unpromising, uncertain, insecure, shaky *Opposite*: probable **3 unreliable**, dubious, suspect, questionable, untrustworthy *Opposite*: reliable

---

COMPARE AND CONTRAST CORE MEANING: feeling doubt or uncertainty

doubtful undecided or feeling hesitant; **uncertain** or **unsure** lacking certainty or confidence; **in doubt** still undecided and liable to change; **dubious** doubtful and, often, suspicious; **sceptical** questioning the truth or likelihood of something.

---

doubtfully *adv* **uncertainly**, hesitantly, distrustfully, doubtingly, suspiciously *Opposite*: confidently

doubtfulness *n* **1 uncertainty**, hesitancy, indecision, doubt, distrust *Opposite*: certainty **2 unlikelihood**, improbability, chance in a million, slim chance *Opposite*: likelihood

doubting *adj* **hesitant**, doubtful, distrustful, suspicious, unbelieving *Opposite*: trusting

doubtless *adv* **no doubt**, without a doubt, probably, almost certainly, without question *Opposite*: possibly

doughty (*archaic*) *adj* **brave**, determined, tough, spirited, indomitable *Opposite*: feeble

dour *adj* **1 severe**, unfriendly, sour, stern, hard-faced *Opposite*: kindly **2 determined**, stubborn, set, purposeful, resolute *Opposite*: indecisive

dourness *n* **1 severity**, unfriendliness, sourness, sternness, grimness *Opposite*: kindness **2 determination**, stubbornness, purpose, drive, resoluteness *Opposite*: indecision

douse *v* **1 drench**, soak, wet, souse, cover **2 quench**, extinguish, put out, smother, snuff *Opposite*: kindle

dovetail *v* **fit together**, slot in, join together,

come together, unite *Opposite*: separate

dowdiness *n* **drabness**, plainness, dullness, dreariness, frumpiness

dowdy *adj* **plain**, frumpy, drab, unfashionable, dreary *Opposite*: fashionable

dowel *n* **rod**, pin, peg

do without *v* **abstain**, deny yourself, go without, keep off, forgo

down *prep* **along**, through, the length of ■ *adj* **1 listed**, nominated, scheduled, timetabled, tabled **2 depressed**, unhappy, miserable, dejected, downhearted *Opposite*: happy **3 out of action**, inoperative, not working, out of order *Opposite*: working **4 behind**, losing, short *Opposite*: winning ■ *v* **1 put down**, lay down, throw down, set down, lay aside *Opposite*: pick up **2 knock down**, floor, overpower, overcome, defeat **3 consume**, eat, drink, gulp down, swallow

down-and-out *adj* **destitute**, penniless, homeless, on the streets, broke *(infml)* *Opposite*: well-heeled *(infml)*

downbeat *adj* **1 pessimistic**, gloomy, dark, bleak, negative *Opposite*: upbeat *(infml)* **2** *(infml)* **casual**, informal, relaxed, unpretentious, laid-back *(infml)*

downcast *adj* **sad**, pessimistic, dejected, depressed, down *Opposite*: cheerful

downer *(infml)* *n* **disappointment**, shame, pity, letdown, discouragement

downfall *n* **failure**, ruin, fall, end, demise *(fml)* *Opposite*: success

downgrade *v* **demote**, reduce, lower, relegate *Opposite*: upgrade

downhearted *adj* **sad**, pessimistic, dejected, disappointed, depressed *Opposite*: cheerful

downhill *adj* **easy**, simple, effortless, plain sailing, straightforward *Opposite*: uphill

download *v* **transfer**, copy, move, take

downmarket *adj* **low quality**, inferior, cheap, low cost, second-rate *Opposite*: upmarket

down payment *n* **payment**, instalment, deposit, disbursement

downplay *v* **tone down**, moderate, restrain, soften, modulate *Opposite*: highlight

downpour *n* **heavy shower**, deluge, rainstorm, cloudburst, torrent

downright *adv* **positively**, undeniably, unquestionably, undoubtedly, totally *Opposite*: questionably

downside *n* **negative aspect**, shortcoming, weakness, snag, stumbling block *Opposite*: advantage

downsize *v* **slim down**, cut back, economize, rationalize, trim *Opposite*: expand

downstairs *adv* **below**, down the stairs, down, down below

downswing *n* **fall**, slump, decline, dip, downturn *Opposite*: upswing

downtime *n* **stoppage**, lost time, idle time, interruption

down-to-earth *adj* **practical**, realistic, sensible, matter-of-fact, pragmatic *Opposite*: fanciful

downtrodden *adj* **browbeaten**, subjugated, broken, oppressed, demoralized

downturn *n* **slump**, recession, dip, decline, depression *Opposite*: upturn

downward *adj* **descending**, down, downhill, sliding, descendent *Opposite*: upward

downy *adj* **silky**, soft, velvety, furry, feathery *Opposite*: rough

dowry *n* **wedding gift**, present, grant, settlement, portion

doyen *n* **leading figure**, senior member, leading light, notable, leader

doyenne *n* **leading figure**, senior member, leading light, notable, leader

do your homework *(infml)* *v* **prepare**, research, plan, find out

doze *v* **nap**, sleep, slumber, snooze *(infml)*, kip *(infml)* ■ *n* **nap**, slumber, sleep, snooze *(infml)*, kip *(infml)*

dozens *(infml)* *n* **lots**, loads *(infml)*, masses *(infml)*, tons *(infml)*, stacks *(infml)*

doze off *v* **fall asleep**, go to sleep, nod off, nod, drift off *Opposite*: wake up

dozily *adv* **sleepily**, tiredly, lethargically, sluggishly, drowsily *Opposite*: alertly

doziness *n* **sleepiness**, tiredness, lethargy, sluggishness, drowsiness *Opposite*: alertness

dozy *adj* **1 sleepy**, drowsy, tired, dozing, nodding *Opposite*: alert **2 silly**, foolish, dreamy, scatterbrained, daffy *(infml)*

drab *adj* **1 gloomy**, sombre, dull, grey, dingy *Opposite*: bright **2 uninteresting**, unexciting, monotonous, boring, dreary *Opposite*: interesting

drabness *n* **dullness**, plainness, dowdiness, dreariness, dinginess *Opposite*: brightness

draconian *adj* **harsh**, severe, strict, strong, austere *Opposite*: mild

draft *n* **outline**, sketch, summary, plan, rough copy ■ *v* **draw up**, prepare, sketch out, outline, write

drag *v* **1 pull**, haul, draw, heave, lug **2 dawdle**, lag, crawl, creep, loiter *Opposite*: fly. See COMPARE AND CONTRAST *at* pull.

dragging *adj* **slow**, tedious, tiresome, wearisome, uninteresting *Opposite*: interesting

draggy *(infml)* *adj* **1 sluggish**, slow, slow-moving, snail-paced, dawdling *Opposite*: brisk **2 tiresome**, tedious, dragging, wearisome, uninteresting *Opposite*: interesting

drag in *v* **bring in**, involve, allude to, mention, implicate *Opposite*: exclude

dragnet *n* **1 net**, mesh, trawl net, game net, trap **2 search**, hunt, pursuit, tracking operation, quest

dragoon *v* **coerce**, press, bully, intimidate, browbeat

drag out v extend, prolong, draw out, lengthen, stretch Opposite: cut short

drag up v return to, bring up, dredge up, revive, mention

drag your feet v hold back, hang back, drag your heels, take your time, stall

drain v use up, exhaust, consume, deplete, sap Opposite: replenish ■ n sewer, ditch, channel, culvert, conduit

drained adj exhausted, weak, weary, tired, worn out Opposite: energetic

draining adj exhausting, trying, wearing, tiring, gruelling

drama n 1 play, stage show, performance, production, spectacle 2 excitement, commotion, fuss, performance, crisis

dramatic adj 1 considerable, significant, radical, noticeable, spectacular Opposite: modest 2 affected, melodramatic, theatrical, histrionic, studied Opposite: natural

dramatics n histrionics, hysterics, excitement, commotion, fuss

dramatist n playwright, writer, author, scriptwriter

dramatization n staging, performance, production, adaptation

dramatize v exaggerate, sensationalize, play up, embellish, lay on Opposite: play down

drape v swathe, dress, wrap, cover, clothe

drapery n curtains, hangings, drapes, swags

drastic adj radical, severe, extreme, dire, sweeping Opposite: modest

draught n 1 current, flow, waft, breeze, breath 2 (dated) medicine, concoction, mixture, brew, tonic

draw v 1 sketch, illustrate, copy, depict, describe 2 pull, drag, haul, move, tow Opposite: shove 3 pull out, extract, withdraw, take out, unsheathe Opposite: put away 4 get, obtain, extract, derive, gain 5 attract, pull, lure, appeal, entice 6 finish equal, tie, equal, square, even ■ n 1 dead heat, tie, stalemate, deadlock, standoff 2 attraction, magnet, crowd puller, inducement, lure. See COMPARE AND CONTRAST at pull.

draw a veil over v conceal, keep quiet about, ignore, forget, hush up (infml) Opposite: expose

draw back v move away, draw away, withdraw, retreat, recoil Opposite: approach

drawback n disadvantage, problem, downside, negative, weakness Opposite: advantage

draw in v involve, implicate, engage, ensnare, hook

drawing n sketch, picture, illustration, diagram, portrayal

drawl n accent, twang, brogue, tones, pronunciation

drawn adj haggard, strained, pinched, tired, wan Opposite: relaxed

draw near v approach, get closer, come nearer, come up, creep up Opposite: move away

drawn-out adj protracted, lengthy, long, convoluted, interminable Opposite: swift

draw off v pour, siphon off, pull, drain off, suck up

draw on v use, employ, be inspired by, resort to, fall back on

draw out v prolong, extend, make last, lengthen, stretch Opposite: cut short

drawstring n tie, string, lace, belt

draw the short straw v get a raw deal, do badly, be unlucky, come off worst, lose out

draw up v draft, put together, assemble, prepare, write

dray n wagon, cart, low-loader, transporter, lorry

dread v fear, be afraid of, be terrified of, be frightened of, be worried about Opposite: look forward to ■ n terror, fear, trepidation, anxiety, dismay Opposite: confidence

dreadful adj terrible, awful, horrible, frightful, alarming Opposite: lovely

dreadfully adv extremely, very, terribly, awfully, really

dreadfulness n awfulness, horror, misery, ghastliness, gruesomeness

dream n 1 vision, daydream, reverie, nightmare, hallucination Opposite: reality 2 aspiration, wish, goal, hope, ambition 3 delight, joy, pleasure, marvel, ideal Opposite: nightmare ■ v fantasize, visualize, imagine, fancy, daydream

dreamer n visionary, idealist, romantic, fantasist Opposite: realist

dreaminess n 1 pensiveness, abstraction, vagueness, wistfulness, languor 2 perfection, beauty, exquisiteness, loveliness, gorgeousness

dreamland n paradise, heaven, nirvana, fairyland, fantasy world Opposite: real world

dreamlike adj unreal, fantastic, surreal, weird, bizarre Opposite: real

dream up v concoct, think up, invent, imagine, come up with

dream world n fantasy world, land of make-believe, fairyland, never-never land, cloud-cuckoo-land Opposite: real world

dreamy adj 1 pensive, vague, faraway, wistful, preoccupied Opposite: alert 2 wonderful, beautiful, superb, out of this world, fantastic Opposite: ordinary

dreariness n 1 dullness, monotony, tedium, boredom, routine Opposite: excitement 2 bleakness, misery, cheerlessness, grimness, gloominess Opposite: cheerfulness

dreary adj 1 dull, boring, monotonous, tedious, lifeless Opposite: interesting 2 bleak, dismal, miserable, grim Opposite: cheerful

dredge v search, scour, comb, ransack, rummage

dredge up v unearth, dig up, drag up, bring up, uncover Opposite: bury

dregs n residue, sediment, silt, lees, deposit

drench v soak, wet, saturate, douse, steep Opposite: dry out

drenched adj soaked, sodden, wet, inundated, saturated Opposite: dry

dress v 1 wear, put on, dress up, clothe, slip into Opposite: undress 2 adorn, decorate, deck out, ornament, trim ■ n 1 frock, gown, robe 2 clothing, clothes, costume, garb, wear

WORD BANK
❑ types of dress ballgown, cheongsam, cocktail dress, evening dress, gymslip, kaftan, kimono, muumuu, pinafore, robe, sari, shalwar-kameez, sheath, shift, shirtdress, sundress, wedding dress

dress down v scold, reprimand, lecture, rebuke, censure Opposite: praise

dressed adj turned out, robed, garbed, outfitted, kitted out (infml) Opposite: undressed

dressing n bandage, covering, gauze

dressing gown n housecoat, negligée, wrap, peignoir, robe

dressmaking n couture, tailoring, sewing

dress rehearsal n practice, run through, trial, dummy run, rehearsal

dress sense n flair, stylishness, fashion sense, panache, chic

dress up v disguise, revamp, embellish, decorate, titivate

dressy adj elegant, fashionable, stylish, chic, classy (infml) Opposite: sloppy

dribble v 1 drool, salivate, slobber, slaver, drivel 2 trickle, ooze, drip, seep, leak Opposite: gush

dried adj dehydrated, dried out, dried up, desiccated, dry

drift v float, flow, glide, coast, waft ■ n gist, meaning, point, sense, idea

drifter n wanderer, tramp, vagabond, rolling stone, vagrant

drifting adj wandering, nomadic, homeless, itinerant, travelling Opposite: settled

driftwood n flotsam, jetsam, wreckage, refuse, waste

drill n practice, exercise, discipline, training, instruction ■ v 1 bore, make a hole, pierce, puncture, penetrate 2 train, coach, school, discipline, instruct. See COMPARE AND CONTRAST at teach.

drily adv ironically, humorously, wittily, subtly, wryly

drink v swallow, down, sip, gulp, slurp ■ n 1 thirst-quencher, liquid refreshment, soft drink, cold drink, hot drink 2 alcoholic drink, alcohol, liqueur, nip, tipple (infml) 3 mouthful, taste, gulp, swallow, sip

drinkable adj fit to drink, safe to drink, filtered, potable

drinking fountain n water spout, jet, tap, faucet (US)

drip v dribble, trickle, drop, leak, seep Opposite: gush ■ n drop, trickle, dribble, leak Opposite: stream

drip-dry adj noniron, wash-and-wear, crease-resistant, permanent-press, easy-care

dripping adj wet, soaked, drenched, sodden, saturated Opposite: dry

drive v 1 steer, handle, guide, direct, operate 2 take, run, chauffeur, transport 3 power, run, cause to move, set in motion 4 force, make, coerce, constrain, impel 5 push, propel, urge, goad, send 6 hammer, push, force, plunge, sink ■ n 1 energy, determination, ambition, initiative, motivation Opposite: lethargy 2 urge, desire, need, instinct, passion 3 campaign, crusade, push, fundraiser, appeal

drivel n nonsense, balderdash, gibberish, bunkum (infml), hogwash (infml)

driven adj ambitious, determined, obsessed, motivated, compelled Opposite: apathetic

driver n chauffeur, motorist, operator

drive up the wall (infml) v exasperate, infuriate, make your blood boil, enrage, irritate

driving adj 1 heavy, pouring, lashing Opposite: light 2 powerful, dynamic, energetic, motivating, forceful

drizzle n light rain, trickle, shower, sprinkle (US) Opposite: downpour ■ v rain, spit, spot, shower, trickle Opposite: pour

drizzly adj damp, wet, rainy, misty

droll adj amusing, funny, comic, witty, humorous Opposite: dull

drone v hum, buzz, whine, whirr, murmur

drool v dribble, salivate, slobber, slaver, drivel

droop v 1 sag, wilt, bow, hang down, flop 2 tire, tire out, wear out, flag, wilt Opposite: perk up

droopiness n 1 tiredness, fatigue, weariness, exhaustion, apathy Opposite: freshness 2 floppiness, limpness, lifelessness, slackness, bagginess Opposite: stiffness

droopy adj 1 tired, tired out, worn out, fatigued, weary Opposite: fresh 2 hanging, floppy, limp, dangling, sagging Opposite: upright

drop v 1 fall, go down, plunge, plummet, crash Opposite: rise 2 let fall, let go, release, throw down 3 drip, trickle, ooze, seep, dribble Opposite: pour 4 abandon, stop, shelve, give up, discontinue Opposite: maintain ■ n 1 descent, fall, plunge, decline, dip Opposite: ascent 2 droplet, drip, bead, globule, dewdrop 3 reduction, decrease, decline, fall, cut Opposite: increase

drop a line v write, get in touch, correspond, contact, send a letter

drop back v fall behind, fall back, slow down, lag behind, straggle

drop behind *see* **drop back**

drop in *v* **call**, call by, call in, come round, drop by

droplet *n* **drop**, drip, bead, dewdrop, globule

drop off *(infml)* *v* **1 go to sleep**, nod off, fall asleep, doze off, drift off *Opposite*: wake up **2 deliver**, unload, deposit, leave *Opposite*: pick up

drop out *v* **leave**, give up, quit, withdraw, stop *Opposite*: carry on

dropper *n* **dispenser**, measurer, tube, glass dropper, eye dropper

droppings *n* **dung**, muck, stools, faeces, manure

dross *n* **rubbish**, trash, garbage, scum, waste

drought *n* **lack**, dearth, deficiency, scarcity, famine *Opposite*: abundance

drove *n* **throng**, horde, crowd, gaggle, multitude *Opposite*: trickle

droves *n* **multitudes**, hordes, crowds, scores, masses *(infml)*

drown *v* **1 go down**, go under, sink, die *Opposite*: float **2 drench**, overwater, soak, swamp, saturate *Opposite*: dry **3 cover**, mask, obscure, hide, overlie *Opposite*: amplify

drowse *v* **doze**, be sleepy, nap, have a nap, catnap *Opposite*: wake

drowsiness *n* **sleepiness**, lethargy, stupor, tiredness *Opposite*: wakefulness

drowsy *adj* **sleepy**, tired, dozy, lethargic, somnolent *Opposite*: awake

drub *v* **beat**, pound, thrash, defeat, hammer *(infml)*

drubbing *n* **beating**, thrashing, hammering *(infml)*, pasting *(infml)*, licking *(infml)*

drudge *n* **worker**, skivvy *(infml)*, menial *(fml)* *Opposite*: drone ■ *v* **work**, toil, labour, grind, plod

drudgery *n* **labour**, toil, work, chore, grind

drug *n* **medication**, medicine, painkiller

drum *n* **barrel**, cask, cylinder, container ■ *v* **pound**, beat, tap, thump, thud

drum into *v* **impress**, instil, drive into, teach, din in

drumming *n* **thudding**, pounding, beating, hammering, tapping

drum roll *n* **roll of drums**, tattoo, rattle, paradiddle, rumble

drum up *v* **gather**, stimulate, rally, foster, encourage *Opposite*: suppress

drunk *adj* **inebriated**, intoxicated, plastered *(infml)*, under the influence *(infml)*, smashed *(infml)* *Opposite*: sober

druthers *(infml)* *n* **preference**, free choice, first choice, fancy, cup of tea

dry *adj* **1 dehydrated**, dried out, dried up, arid, waterless *Opposite*: wet **2 thirsty**, dehydrated, parched, in need of a drink, gasping **3 deadpan**, wry, ironic, understated, droll *Opposite*: gushing **4 uninteresting**, dull,

tedious, boring, monotonous *Opposite*: interesting **5 teetotal**, abstinent, abstemious, temperate, prohibitionist ■ *v* **1 make dry**, rub, rub down, towel, wipe *Opposite*: wet **2 desiccate**, become dry, dry out, dry up, dehydrate *Opposite*: swell

---

COMPARE AND CONTRAST CORE MEANING: lacking moisture

dry having little or no moisture; **dehydrated** experiencing fluid loss, or preserved by drying; **desiccated** (used of products, especially food) free from moisture, or preserved by drying; **arid** (used of land) dry from lack of rain; **parched** dry from excessive heat or lack of rain; **shrivelled** dry, shrunken, and wrinkled; **sere** (*literary*) dry and withered.

---

dryad *n* **wood nymph**, fairy, naiad, pixie, nymph

dry-clean *v* **clean**, launder, wash, valet

dryer *n* **drying device**, hair dryer, tumble dryer, clothes dryer, clothes horse

dry-eyed *adj* **unemotional**, impassive, expressionless, unmoved, stoical *Opposite*: tearful

dry land *n* **solid ground**, shore, beach, terra firma *Opposite*: sea

dryness *n* **1 aridness**, aridity, dehydration, drought, desiccation *Opposite*: wetness **2 wryness**, irony, understatement, matter-of-factness, sarcasm

dry out *v* **1 air**, dry, dry off, tumble dry, tumble *Opposite*: damp **2 shrivel up**, curl up, dry up, wither, become dehydrated *Opposite*: soak

dry run *n* **rehearsal**, run-through, dummy run, trial run, trial

dry up *v* **1 desiccate**, become dry, dry out, dry, dehydrate *Opposite*: swell **2** *(infml)* **falter**, lose the thread, stop midstream, forget your lines, come to a halt *Opposite*: continue **3 fail**, run out, be used up, come to an end, disappear *Opposite*: continue

dual *adj* **double**, twin, twofold

dualism *n* **symmetry**, contrast, dichotomy, opposition, polarity

duality *n* **dichotomy**, division, dyad, contrast, opposition

dub *v* **call**, nickname, christen, hail as, label

dubbin *n* **polish**, wax, blacking, dressing, waterproofing

dubiety *(fml)* *n* **doubtfulness**, doubt, dubiousness, uncertainty, hesitancy *Opposite*: certitude

dubious *adj* **1 doubtful**, uncertain, unsure, undecided, unconvinced *Opposite*: certain **2 suspect**, untrustworthy, questionable, shady, unsavoury *Opposite*: trustworthy **3 ambiguous**, doubtful, debatable, uncertain, questionable *Opposite*: unambiguous. *See* COMPARE AND CONTRAST *at* **doubtful**.

dubiousness *n* **1 doubt**, doubtfulness, uncertainty, hesitancy, suspicion *Opposite*: certainty **2 fallibility**, unreliability, improbability, ambiguity, vagueness *Opposite*: reliability

duchy *n* **dukedom**, estate, territory, barony, principality

duck *n* **water bird**, waterfowl, diver ■ *v* **1 stoop**, bend, bow, bob, nod *Opposite*: straighten **2 avoid**, evade, dodge, sidestep, circumvent *Opposite*: confront

duckboard *n* **walkway**, boardwalk, path, planking, catwalk

duck out *v* **back out**, pull out, drop out, withdraw, get out

duct *n* **channel**, canal, pipe, tube, vessel

ductile *adj* **pliable**, malleable, elastic, pliant, plastic. *See* COMPARE AND CONTRAST *at* pliable.

dud *(infml)* *n* **failure**, fiasco, letdown, disappointment, flop *(infml)* *Opposite*: success ■ *adj* **useless**, worthless, ineffective, broken, no good *Opposite*: usable

due *adj* **1 expected**, scheduled, appointed, anticipated, looked-for **2 appropriate**, fitting, suitable, proper, right and proper *Opposite*: undue **3 owing**, unpaid, outstanding, payable, owed *Opposite*: paid ■ *adv* **directly**, exactly, direct, dead, straight *Opposite*: indirectly

duel *n* **contest**, fight, battle, gunfight, combat ■ *v* **fight**, clash, battle, contest, struggle

duellist *n* **fighter**, combatant, opponent, gunfighter, contender

dues *n* **fees**, subscription, payment, charge, levy

duet *n* **duo**, double act, twosome, couple, pair

due to *prep* **because of**, owing to, by reason of, as a result of, attributable to

duff *(infml)* *adj* **useless**, inferior, broken, faulty, rotten *Opposite*: excellent

dugout *n* **bunker**, trench, foxhole, ditch, hollow

dulcet *adj* **melodious**, melodic, honeyed, soothing, pleasant *Opposite*: harsh

dull *adj* **1 boring**, uninteresting, tedious, monotonous, dreary *Opposite*: interesting **2 cloudy**, overcast, gloomy, leaden, dismal *Opposite*: bright **3 dark**, dim, muted, faded, lacklustre *Opposite*: bright **4 stupid**, obtuse, plodding, sluggish, unintelligent *Opposite*: bright ■ *v* **deaden**, dampen, stultify, cloud, blunt *Opposite*: accentuate

dullness *n* **1 tediousness**, tedium, monotony, dreariness, dryness *Opposite*: liveliness **2 cloudiness**, gloom, half-light, gloominess, leadenness *Opposite*: brightness **3 darkness**, dimness, drabness, dowdiness, dinginess *Opposite*: brightness

duly *adv* **accordingly**, suitably, fittingly, appropriately, properly *Opposite*: unduly

dumbfound *v* **astonish**, amaze, astound, surprise, stagger

dumbfounded *adj* **astonished**, amazed, astounded, thunderstruck, staggered

dummy *n* **1 mannequin**, model, lay figure, figure, form **2 copy**, replica, imitation, fake, mock-up *Opposite*: original ■ *adj* **imitation**, fake, mock, pretend, replica *Opposite*: original

dummy run *n* **rehearsal**, run-through, dry run, trial run, trial

dump *v* **1 put**, leave, abandon, tip, throw **2 get rid of**, abandon, leave, dispose of, discard *Opposite*: keep **3** *(infml)* **abandon**, discard, leave, desert, walk out on *(infml)* *Opposite*: stand by ■ *n* **1 landfill**, junkyard, scrapyard, rubbish dump, tip **2** *(infml)* **eyesore**, mess, monstrosity, hovel, tip

dumper *n* **tipper**, fly-tipper, litterer, litter lout *(infml)*, litterbug *(infml)*

dune *n* **bank**, sandbank, hill, mound, ridge

dung *n* **manure**, droppings, slurry, muck, fertilizer

dungeon *n* **prison**, cell, jail, vault, oubliette

dunk *v* **dip**, submerge, immerse, soak, steep

duo *n* **pair**, twosome, couple, double act, two of a kind

dupe *v* **fool**, trick, deceive, con, take in ■ *n* **victim**, target, fool, sucker *(infml)*, mug *(slang)*

duplicate *v* **1 replicate**, copy, photocopy, reproduce, make two of **2 repeat**, replicate, reproduce, copy, do again ■ *n* **copy**, replacement, photocopy, spare, carbon copy *Opposite*: original ■ *adj* **identical**, matching, replica, replacement, spare *Opposite*: original. *See* COMPARE AND CONTRAST *at* copy.

duplication *n* **1 repetition**, replication, doubling, copying, photocopying **2 replica**, duplicate, copy, print, facsimile *Opposite*: original

duplicitous *adj* **double-dealing**, two-faced, tricky, deceitful, dishonest *Opposite*: honest

duplicity *n* **deceit**, deception, dishonesty, disloyalty, unfaithfulness *Opposite*: honesty

durability *n* **toughness**, sturdiness, strength, robustness, resilience *Opposite*: flimsiness

durable *adj* **tough**, hard-wearing, sturdy, strong, robust *Opposite*: flimsy

duration *n* **length**, extent, period, time, interval

duress *n* **pressure**, force, threat, coercion, compulsion *Opposite*: persuasion

during *prep* **throughout**, through, in, in the course of

dusk *n* **twilight**, sunset, nightfall, sundown, evening *Opposite*: dawn

dusky *adj* **shadowy**, dark, darkish, dim, hazy *Opposite*: bright

dust *n* **powder**, dirt, sand, earth, soil ■ *v* **1 clean**, clean up, wipe, wipe down, wipe up **2 sprinkle**, brush, cover, scatter, sift

dustbin *n* **bin**, litter bin, wheelie bin, waste-paper bin, rubbish bin

dust bowl *n* **desert**, waste, wasteland, wilderness

duster *n* **cloth**, rag, feather duster, dust cloth

dust jacket *n* **cover**, jacket, outer, dust cover, paper cover

dustpan *n* pan, scoop, shovel, receptacle, container

dustsheet *n* dust cover, cover, sheet, throw, cloth

dusty *adj* dirty, grimy, filthy, sandy, grubby *Opposite*: spotless

dutiful *adj* obedient, well-behaved, compliant, loyal, devoted *Opposite*: disobedient

duty *n* **1 responsibility**, obligation, onus, burden, calling **2 job**, task, function, responsibility, obligation **3 tax**, payment, levy, due, impost

duty-bound *adj* **constrained**, compelled, obliged, forced, obligated

duty-free *(infml)* *adj* **tax-free**, tax-exempt, untaxed, nontaxable

duvet *n* quilt, eiderdown, coverlet, comforter *(US)*

dwell *(literary)* *v* reside, live, have your home, stay, inhabit *Opposite*: leave

dweller *n* inhabitant, resident, occupant, occupier, tenant

dwelling *(fml)* *n* house, home, residence, place of abode, lodging

dwell on *v* think about, ponder, brood over, mull over, go on about *Opposite*: forget

dwindle *v* decrease, decline, diminish, fall off, drop *Opposite*: increase

dwindling *adj* declining, decreasing, diminishing, deteriorating, falling *Opposite*: burgeoning

dye *v* colour, stain, tint, change the colour of ■ *n* **1 colouring**, colour, stain, pigment **2 hair dye**, colour, tint, rinse, peroxide

dyed-in-the-wool *adj* long-established, confirmed, committed, dedicated, incorrigible

dying *adj* **1 last**, final, ultimate, closing, ending **2 disappearing**, failing, fading, vanishing, becoming extinct *Opposite*: thriving

dyke *n* **1 embankment**, dam, barrier, bank, wall **2 ditch**, watercourse, channel, drain, conduit

dynamic *adj* active, self-motivated, energetic, vibrant, forceful *Opposite*: lethargic

dynamics *n* **1 changing aspects**, subtleties, forces at work, dynamic forces, underlying forces **2 louds and softs**, dynamic range, changes in volume, dynamic contrast, crescendos

dynamism *n* vitality, vigour, energy, drive, enthusiasm *Opposite*: lethargy

dynamite *v* blow up, blast, explode, detonate, wreck

dynamo *n* **1 electric generator**, generator, motor, turbine **2** *(infml)* **extrovert**, live wire *(infml)*, go-getter *(infml)*, live one *(infml)*

dynastic *adj* hereditary, successional, imperial, sovereign, ruling

dynasty *n* **1 reign**, rule, empire, period, era **2 family**, house, line

dyspepsia *n* indigestion, heartburn, acid stomach, upset stomach, unsettled stomach

dysphemism *n* **1 offensiveness**, rudeness, vulgarity, obscenity, ribaldry *Opposite*: euphemism **2 obscenity**, swear word, expletive, oath, profanity *Opposite*: euphemism

dysphemistic *adj* vulgar, lewd, offensive, obscene, rude *Opposite*: euphemistic

E

each *pron* **every one**, each one, all, both ■ *adj* every, all, both, every single

eager *adj* keen, enthusiastic, excited, raring to go, ready *Opposite*: unenthusiastic

eagerness *n* keenness, enthusiasm, excitement, readiness, willingness *Opposite*: apathy

eagle-eyed *adj* observant, hawk-eyed, sharp-sighted, sharp-eyed, alert *Opposite*: unobservant

ear *n* **1 external ear**, outer ear, earhole, lug *(infml)*, shell-like *(infml)* **2 ability**, sensitivity, talent, knack, facility **3 attention**, hearing, heed, regard

WORD BANK
❏ **parts of an ear** anvil, auricle, cochlea, eardrum, hammer, incus, internal ear, malleus, middle ear, stapes, stirrup, tympanic membrane, tympanum, vestibule

earful *(infml)* *n* scolding, lecture, piece of your mind, reprimand, talking-to *(infml)*

earlier *adv* before, in advance, previously, formerly, beforehand *Opposite*: later ■ *adj* previous, former, past, prior *Opposite*: later

earliest *adj* first, initial, original *Opposite*: latest

early *adv* **1 early on**, at the beginning, before time, in advance, ahead of schedule *Opposite*: late **2 soon**, promptly, without delay, now, as soon as possible *Opposite*: later ■ *adj* **1 initial**, first, primary, premature *Opposite*: later **2 timely**, prompt, quick, speedy, immediate *Opposite*: tardy

early years *n* babyhood, infancy, childhood, youth, formative years *Opposite*: adulthood

earmark v **allocate**, assign, allot, set aside, put aside

earn v **1 make**, be paid, take home, receive, get **2 deserve**, work for, win, warrant, merit

earnest adj **1 serious**, solemn, grave, sober, intense Opposite: frivolous **2 sincere**, heartfelt, deep, intense, strong Opposite: superficial

earnestness n **sincerity**, seriousness, solemnity, intensity, feeling Opposite: facetiousness

earnings n **1 pay**, salary, wage, wages, income Opposite: expenditure **2 profit**, revenue, gain, return, dividend Opposite: loss

earphone see **earpiece**

earpiece n **receiver**, headset, headphones, earphone

earshot n **hearing range**, range, hearing distance, hearing

earsplitting adj **loud**, piercing, shrill, deafening, noisy Opposite: quiet

earth n **soil**, ground, dirt, mud, terrain

Earth n **world**, globe, planet

earthling n **human being**, human, earthly being, intelligent life-form, human life-form Opposite: extraterrestrial

earthly adj **1 worldly**, material, mortal, secular, everyday Opposite: heavenly **2 possible**, imaginable, conceivable

earthmover n **bulldozer**, digger, power shovel, excavator, steam shovel

earthquake n **tremor**, upheaval, trembling, shaking, seismic activity

earthshaking see **earthshattering**

earthshattering adj **momentous**, tremendous, remarkable, stunning, devastating Opposite: trivial

earthwards adv **towards the earth**, towards the ground, downwards, down, in a nose-dive Opposite: skyward

earthwork n **fortification**, rampart, bulwark, barrier

earthy adj **1 unpretentious**, down-to-earth, no-nonsense, simple, unsophisticated Opposite: refined **2 vulgar**, crude, gross, bawdy, rude

ease n **1 effortlessness**, simplicity, straightforwardness, facility, easiness Opposite: difficulty **2 comfort**, luxury, affluence, wealth, opulence Opposite: hardship ■ v **1 relieve**, alleviate, lessen, reduce, mitigate Opposite: worsen **2 slide**, slip, edge, push gently, draw out **3 make easier**, facilitate, help, aid, assist Opposite: hinder

easel n **stand**, frame, tripod, support, mount

ease up v **relax**, slow down, slacken off, calm down, ease off

easily adv **1 with no trouble**, without difficulty, without problems, effortlessly, simply **2 without doubt**, by far, by a long shot, by a long way, by a long chalk

easy adj **1 simple**, trouble-free, straightforward, effortless, uncomplicated Opposite: difficult **2 informal**, relaxed, calm, cool, tranquil Opposite: tense **3 comfortable**, affluent, luxurious, undemanding, leisurely Opposite: hard

easygoing adj **relaxed**, casual, tolerant, even-tempered, calm Opposite: anxious

easy-peasy (infml) adj **simple**, easy, straightforward, effortless Opposite: difficult

eat v **1 consume**, have, gobble, wolf, munch Opposite: starve **2 have a meal**, dine, lunch, breakfast, snack

eat away v **erode**, corrode, eat into, wear away, wear down

eater n **consumer**, feeder, diner, devourer, guzzler (infml)

eatery (infml) n **restaurant**, self-service restaurant, cafeteria, bistro, eating place

eat into v **1 use up**, eat up, gobble up, reduce, consume **2 corrode**, rust, pockmark, attack, destroy

eat up v **1 consume**, down, gobble, guzzle (infml), scoff (infml) **2 absorb**, obsess, take over, consume, dominate **3** (infml) **lap up**, love, applaud, enthuse about, rave about (infml) Opposite: hate

eat your heart out (infml) v **brood**, dwell on, grieve, pine

eat your words (infml) v **apologize**, retract, say sorry, eat humble pie, take it all back Opposite: stand firm

eau de cologne n **perfume**, cologne, fragrance, scent, toilet water

eavesdrop v **listen in**, overhear, tap, spy, pry

eavesdropper n **listener**, nosy parker (infml), spy, observer

ebb v **1 recede**, go out, flow away, retreat, fall away Opposite: come in **2 fade**, diminish, recede, fail, disappear Opposite: surge ■ n **receding tide**, ebb tide, outgoing tide, falling tide Opposite: flow

ebb and flow v **fluctuate**, vacillate, vary ■ n **shift**, fluctuation, vacillation, variation, flux

ebullience n **joviality**, enthusiasm, liveliness, happiness, cheerfulness Opposite: lugubriousness

ebullient adj **jovial**, enthusiastic, lively, happy, bouncy Opposite: lugubrious

e-cash n **electronic cash**, digital cash, smart card

eccentric adj **odd**, unconventional, unorthodox, unusual, peculiar Opposite: conventional ■ n **oddity**, character, original, case (infml)

eccentricity n **1 oddness**, unconventionality, peculiarity, strangeness, weirdness Opposite: conventionality **2 quirk**, peculiarity, foible, idiosyncrasy, oddity

ecclesiastic n **clergyman**, clergywoman, priest, cleric, minister

ecclesiastical *adj* **church**, clerical, religious, apostolic, papal *Opposite*: secular

echelon *n* **level**, rank, grade, tier, class

echo *n* **reverberation**, resonance, repeat, boom, ricochet ■ *v* **1 reverberate**, resonate, resound, boom, rebound **2 repeat**, reiterate, copy, parrot, confirm

echoing *adj* **resounding**, reverberating, reflecting, ringing, resonant

eclectic *adj* **heterogeneous**, varied, wide-ranging, extensive, diverse *Opposite*: narrow

eclecticism *n* **extensiveness**, range, diversity, scope, variety

eclipse *v* **1 hide**, conceal, obscure, cover, darken **2 outdo**, overshadow, outshine, surpass, overwhelm

ecofriendly *adj* **biodegradable**, green, environmentally friendly, sustainable

ecological *adj* **environmental**, environmentally friendly, natural, biological, organic

ecologist *n* **environmentalist**, biologist, natural scientist, naturalist, conservationist

e-commerce *n* **e-business**, e-tailing, cybermarketing, electronic transactions

economic *adj* **1 financial**, monetary, fiscal, pecuniary, commercial **2 profitable**, cost-effective, moneymaking, lucrative, efficient *Opposite*: uneconomic

economical *adj* **1 frugal**, parsimonious, thrifty, careful, sparing *Opposite*: wasteful **2 inexpensive**, cheap, cost-effective, low-cost, budget *Opposite*: expensive

economize *v* **cut back**, cut down, retrench, save, scrimp and save *Opposite*: spend

economy *n* **1 frugality**, thrift, cost-cutting, saving, parsimony *Opposite*: extravagance **2 saving**, cutback, retrenchment, reduction, scaling-down ■ *adj* **cheap**, budget, reduced, family, low-cost *Opposite*: expensive

WORD BANK
❏ **types of economic condition** austerity, boom, boom and bust, deflation, depression, downswing, downturn, hyperinflation, inflation, inflationary spiral, recession, recovery, reflation, slump, stagflation, upswing, upturn
❏ **types of economic system** collectivism, command economy, free enterprise economy, free market economy, market economy, mixed economy, new economy, planned economy, private economy, service economy

ecosystem *n* **natural environment**, biome, biota, ecology, environment

ecstasy *n* **1 joy**, delight, elation, bliss, rapture *Opposite*: misery **2 trance**, high, frenzy, state *(infml)* *Opposite*: stupor

ecstatic *adj* **1 overjoyed**, delighted, thrilled, elated, blissful *Opposite*: miserable **2 elated**, high, overexcited, frenzied, in a frenzy *Opposite*: calm

eddy *n* **whirlpool**, swirl, vortex, whirl, maelstrom

edge *n* **1 border**, rim, boundary, perimeter, periphery *Opposite*: centre **2 brink**, verge, threshold, point **3 sharpness**, bitterness, acidity, harshness, venom **4 advantage**, upper hand, superiority, control, authority ■ *v* **1 approach**, skirt, sidle, pick your way, creep **2 frame**, trim, fringe, enclose

edgeways *adv* **sideways**, side-on, crossways, across, laterally

edging *n* **border**, trim, fringe, hem, frill

edgy *adj* **nervous**, on edge, anxious, jumpy, jittery *Opposite*: relaxed

edible *adj* **eatable**, fit for human consumption, palatable, appetizing, comestible *(fml)* *Opposite*: poisonous

edict *n* **proclamation**, announcement, pronouncement, decree, statute

edification *n* **improvement**, education, enlightenment, instruction, elevation *Opposite*: obfuscation

edifice *n* **1 building**, construction, pile, structure, mansion **2 organization**, network, structure, association, group

edify *v* **enlighten**, inform, educate, instruct, improve *Opposite*: obfuscate

edifying *adj* **educational**, informative, illuminating, instructive, scholastic

edit *v* **1 rewrite**, revise, amend, rework, correct **2 oversee**, run, manage, be in charge of, direct

edited *adj* **1 amended**, corrected, revised, rewritten, redrafted *Opposite*: unedited **2 abridged**, concise, shortened, summarized, truncated *Opposite*: complete

edition *n* **version**, publication, copy, issue, impression

editor *n* **1 publishing supervisor**, publishing manager, editor in chief, managing editor, executive editor **2 subeditor**, copy editor, corrector, checker, cutter

editorial *n* **leader**, editorial column, viewpoint, perspective, essay

editorialize *v* **expound**, pontificate, spout, preach, sermonize

edit out *v* **delete**, remove, cut, omit, abridge

educate *v* **teach**, instruct, edify, tutor, train. *See* COMPARE AND CONTRAST *at* **teach**.

educated *adj* **1 well-informed**, well-read, learned, erudite, knowledgeable *Opposite*: uneducated **2 cultured**, cultivated, tasteful, sophisticated, refined *Opposite*: boorish

educated guess *n* **guess**, estimation, estimate, approximation, guesstimate

education *n* **teaching**, learning, schooling, tutoring, instruction

educational *adj* **instructive**, enlightening, didactic, edifying, informative

educator *n* **teacher**, instructor, lecturer, professor, educationalist

eerie *adj* **unnerving**, uncanny, weird, strange, peculiar

efface v **obliterate**, eradicate, destroy, wear away, rub out

effect n **1 result**, consequence, outcome, upshot, end product **2 influence**, weight, force, power, validity **3 impression**, meaning, sense, impact, purpose ■ v (fml) **achieve**, carry out, produce, bring about, realize

effective adj **1 successful**, efficient, productive, useful Opposite: ineffective **2 real**, actual, in effect, active, operative Opposite: nominal **3 operational**, operative, in force, in operation, in effect Opposite: inoperative

---

COMPARE AND CONTRAST CORE MEANING: producing a result

effective causing the desired or intended result; **efficient** capable of achieving the desired result with the minimum use of resources, time, and effort; **effectual** (fml) potentially successful in producing a desired or intended result; **efficacious** (fml) having the power to achieve the desired result, especially an improvement in somebody's physical condition.

---

effectively adv **1 efficiently**, successfully, productively, well, excellently Opposite: ineffectively **2 in reality**, to all intents and purposes, in point of fact, in all but name

effectiveness n **efficiency**, productiveness, efficacy, success, use Opposite: ineffectiveness

effects (fml) n **belongings**, property, personal property, possessions, things

effectual (fml) adj **effective**, worthwhile, successful, productive, helpful Opposite: ineffectual

effervesce v **hiss**, fizz, bubble, sparkle, froth

effervescence n **1 fizz**, bubbles, sparkle, froth, foam **2 vivacity**, vibrancy, vitality, animation, sparkle Opposite: languor

effervescent adj **1 fizzy**, sparkling, bubbly, aerated, bubbling Opposite: still **2 lively**, vibrant, bubbly, bouncy, sparkling Opposite: dull

efficacious (fml) adj **effective**, efficient, successful, productive, useful Opposite: ineffective

efficacy n **effectiveness**, efficiency, usefulness, productiveness, worth Opposite: ineffectiveness

efficiency n **competence**, efficacy, effectiveness, productivity, proficiency Opposite: inefficiency

efficient adj **1 well-organized**, effective, competent, capable, able Opposite: ineffective **2 inexpensive**, timesaving, labour-saving, economical, cost-effective Opposite: wasteful. See COMPARE AND CONTRAST at **effective**.

effigy n **image**, statue, icon, figure, figurine

effluent n **waste**, sewage, bilge water, seepage, runoff

effort n **1 exertion**, energy, determination, force, elbow grease (infml) Opposite: ease **2 attempt**, try, endeavour, go, shot

effortless adj **easy**, natural, unforced, graceful, unproblematic Opposite: strenuous

effortlessness n **ease**, naturalness, smoothness, simplicity, facility Opposite: difficulty

effrontery n **impudence**, nerve, gall, boldness, arrogance

effusion n **outpouring**, gush, rush, expression, declaration

effusive adj **gushing**, demonstrative, fulsome, vociferous, extravagant Opposite: reserved

e.g. adv **for example**, for instance, say, let's say, perhaps

egalitarian adj **equal**, classless, free, democratic, equal opportunities Opposite: classconscious

egg n **reproductive cell**, ovum, egg cell, ovule ■ v **urge**, incite, spur, encourage, push Opposite: dissuade

egghead (infml) n **brainbox**, intellectual, boffin (infml), brain (infml), bookworm (infml)

egg on v **encourage**, urge, push, incite, spur Opposite: dissuade

eggshell n **protective covering**, shell, case, casing, covering

ego n **personality**, character, self, self-image, self-worth

egocentric see egotistical

egoism, egoist, egoistic see egotism, egotist, egotistical

egomaniac see egotist

egoism n **self-centredness**, selfishness, conceit, vanity, arrogance Opposite: altruism

egotist n **narcissist**, self-seeker, individualist, self-publicist, self-aggrandizer

egotistical adj **selfish**, conceited, vain, selfcentred, self-important Opposite: altruistic

eiderdown n **quilt**, continental quilt, duvet, cover, bedspread

either adj **1 whichever**, either one, one or the other, any **2 each**, both Opposite: neither

eject v **1 expel**, emit, get rid of, spew, spout **2 expel**, banish, drive out, throw out, remove

eke out v **1 make something last**, spin out, make a little go a long way, draw out, use sparingly Opposite: squander **2 supplement**, complement, add to, pad out, make up Opposite: diminish **3 scrape**, scratch, scrape together, scratch out, make

elaborate adj **1 complex**, complicated, intricate, detailed, involved Opposite: straightforward **2 intricate**, sumptuous, extravagant, ornate, decorative Opposite: simple ■ v **1 expound**, expand, enlarge, go into detail, explain Opposite: condense **2 complicate**, work up, build on, develop, detail Opposite: simplify

elaboration n amplification, embellishment, explanation, expansion, development

elapse v pass, pass by, intervene, slip away, go by

elastic adj 1 stretchy, expandable, flexible, supple, resilient Opposite: rigid 2 flexible, adaptable, changeable, variable, mutable Opposite: inflexible. See COMPARE AND CONTRAST at pliable.

elasticated adj stretchy, elastic, expanding, expandable, stretchable Opposite: rigid

elate v exhilarate, thrill, excite, lift, uplift Opposite: dishearten

elated adj ecstatic, overjoyed, thrilled, delighted, euphoric Opposite: disheartened

elation n ecstasy, delight, euphoria, jubilation, excitement Opposite: despair

elbow n prod, jostle, nudge, shove, dig

elbowroom n 1 space, room, room to spare, room to manoeuvre 2 scope, freedom, leeway, room to manoeuvre, choice

elder n leader, head, chief

elderly adj aging, old, aged, mature, of advanced years Opposite: young

eldest adj oldest, first-born, first

elect v 1 vote for, return, vote into office, pick, select 2 choose, opt for, decide on, select, designate ■ adj designated, future, chosen, selected

elected adj chosen, designated, selected, voted, nominated

election n 1 vote, poll, ballot 2 selection, choice, appointment, designation, nomination

electioneer v campaign, whistle-stop, canvass, run

elective adj 1 voting, chosen by election, filled by election, passed by vote Opposite: appointed 2 optional, voluntary, free, selective, discretionary Opposite: compulsory

elector n voter, member of the electorate, voting member, constituent

electoral adj democratic, voting, election, polling, balloting

electorate n people, voters, registered voters, voting public, constituency

electric adj 1 electronic, electrically powered, mains powered, battery-operated, plug-in 2 absorbing, charged, exciting, thrilling, emotional Opposite: boring

electrical see electric

electricity n current, voltage, power, energy, electrical energy

electrified adj 1 electric, electrically powered, wired-up, connected 2 excited, captivated, thrilled, transfixed, awestruck Opposite: bored

electrify v captivate, transfix, thrill, excite, exhilarate Opposite: bore

electrifying adj exciting, stirring, thrilling, captivating, stimulating Opposite: boring

electrode n conductor, rod, anode, cathode, probe

electronic adj 1 electric, microelectronic, electrical, automated, computer-operated 2 computerized, high-tech, on-screen, online, computer

electronics n microchip technology, microelectronics, computer electronics, integrated circuit technology, semiconductor technology

elegance n grace, style, sophistication, chic, taste Opposite: inelegance

elegant adj sophisticated, stylish, graceful, chic, well-designed Opposite: inelegant

elegiac (fml) adj mournful, sad, melancholic, funereal, plaintive Opposite: cheerful

elegy n funeral song, dirge, requiem, poem, speech

element n 1 component, part, section, division, portion 2 hint, amount, quantity, touch, bit 3 factor, cause, feature, component, ingredient 4 habitat, environment, milieu, medium, domain

elemental adj rudimentary, basic, fundamental, essential, primary

elementary adj basic, simple, straightforward, uncomplicated, plain

elements n rudiments, basics, fundamentals, essentials, foundations

elephantine adj 1 ponderous, lumbering, clumsy, slow, heavy Opposite: dainty 2 huge, enormous, colossal, gigantic, massive Opposite: minute

elevate v 1 lift, lift up, raise, uplift, hoist Opposite: lower 2 promote, raise, advance, move up, further Opposite: demote

elevated adj 1 pre-eminent, eminent, important, prominent, high Opposite: lowly 2 raised, raised up, lifted, high, higher

elevation n 1 height, altitude, rise Opposite: depth 2 promotion, rise, advancement, boost Opposite: demotion

elevenses n snack, morning snack, mid-morning snack, nibble, bite

eleventh-hour adj ultimate, last-minute, last-ditch, final

elf n pixie, imp, sprite, fairy, gnome

elfin adj sylphlike, petite, dainty, tiny, waiflike

elicit v 1 provoke, cause, produce, bring about, occasion 2 draw out, draw, bring out, extract, obtain Opposite: repress

eligibility n suitability, aptness, entitlement, appropriateness, fitness Opposite: unsuitability

eligible adj 1 qualified, entitled, suitable, fit, appropriate Opposite: ineligible 2 single, unmarried, unattached, available

eliminate v 1 remove, eradicate, abolish, get rid of, do away with Opposite: retain 2 destroy, kill, exterminate, liquidate, wipe out *(infml) Opposite*: preserve **3 defecate,** urinate, excrete, expel, pass

elimination *n* **removal**, abolition, exclusion, rejection, eradication *Opposite*: preservation

elite *n* **best**, cream, cream of the crop, elect, crème de la crème *Opposite*: hoi polloi ■ *adj* **choice**, best, select, selective, leading *Opposite*: run-of-the-mill

elitism *n* **exclusiveness**, exclusivity, superiority, selectivity, selectiveness *Opposite*: equality

elitist *adj* **exclusive**, discriminatory, selective, superior, snobbish *Opposite*: egalitarian

elixir *n* **1 medicine**, tincture, solution, tonic, preparation **2 potion**, restorative, tonic, cure-all, snake oil

ellipsis *n* **abbreviation**, contraction, elision, truncation, abridgment

elliptical *adj* **1 oval**, ovoid, ovate, egg-shaped, elongated **2 concise**, succinct, cryptic, indirect, oblique *Opposite*: verbose

elocution *n* **diction**, articulation, pronunciation, enunciation, delivery

elongate *v* **lengthen**, draw out, extend, stretch, prolong *Opposite*: shorten

elongated *adj* **lengthened**, stretched out, extended, drawn-out, prolonged *Opposite*: shortened

elope *v* **run away**, run off, escape, decamp, abscond *Opposite*: return

elopement *n* **flight**, escape, desertion, decampment, truancy *Opposite*: return

eloquence *n* **expressiveness**, articulateness, articulacy, persuasiveness, expression *Opposite*: inarticulacy

eloquent *adj* **expressive**, fluent, articulate, well-spoken, persuasive *Opposite*: inarticulate

else *adj* **different**, new, other, experimental ■ *adv* **1 as well**, besides, in addition, other, more **2 other**, otherwise, differently, different, new

elucidate *v* **explain**, clarify, explicate, expound, illuminate *Opposite*: confuse

elucidation *n* **clarification**, illumination, exposition, explanation, explication *Opposite*: obfuscation

elude *v* **1 escape**, flee, evade, get away, dodge **2 baffle**, confound, foil, puzzle, stump

elusive *adj* **indefinable**, subtle, intangible, vague, indescribable *Opposite*: obvious

elusiveness *n* **indefinability**, subtlety, intangibility, vagueness, tenuousness *Opposite*: accessibility

emaciated *adj* **thin**, wasted, skeletal, withered, shrunken *Opposite*: plump. *See* COMPARE AND CONTRAST *at* thin.

emaciation *n* **thinness**, skinniness, gauntness, scrawniness, scragginess *Opposite*: plumpness

e-mail *n* **electronic post**, electronic message,

communication, correspondence ■ *v* send, flame, spam, ping, chat

emanate *v* **1 originate**, come, stem, spring, derive **2** *(fml)* **radiate**, emit, give off, give out, send out *Opposite*: absorb

emancipate *v* **liberate**, set free, free, release, unshackle *Opposite*: enslave

emancipation *n* **liberation**, freedom, release, deliverance *(fml)*, manumission *(fml)*

emasculate *(fml) v* **weaken**, enfeeble, undermine, enervate, unnerve *Opposite*: empower

emasculated *adj* **ineffectual**, powerless, helpless, impotent, weak *Opposite*: strong

embalm *v* **mummify**, conserve, preserve, fix, keep

embankment *n* **ridge**, bank, mound, defences, dam

embargo *n* **ban**, restriction, prohibition, restraint, block *Opposite*: permission ■ *v* **1 forbid**, prohibit, ban, stop, restrict *Opposite*: permit **2 confiscate**, sequestrate, seize, take away, expropriate

embark *v* **board**, get on, go aboard *Opposite*: disembark

embark on *v* **begin**, start, commence, engage in, set off on *Opposite*: abandon

embarrass *v* **humiliate**, mortify, shame, abash, show up *Opposite*: honour

embarrassed *adj* **uncomfortable**, self-conscious, ill at ease, nervous, ashamed *Opposite*: proud

embarrassing *adj* **awkward**, uncomfortable, uneasy, disconcerting, trying

embarrassment *n* **awkwardness**, blushes, humiliation, mortification, shame *Opposite*: pride

embassy *n* **consulate**, legation, mission, delegation, deputation

embed *v* **implant**, set in, insert, drive in, push in

embellish *v* **1 decorate**, adorn, embroider, beautify, ornament *Opposite*: simplify **2 exaggerate**, elaborate, overdo, aggrandize, enhance *Opposite*: understate

embellishment *n* **1 decoration**, adornment, ornamentation, embroidery, beautification **2 exaggeration**, elaboration, aggrandizement, enhancement, enlargement *Opposite*: understatement

ember *n* **cinder**, ash, coal

embezzle *v* **misappropriate**, misuse, appropriate, steal, cheat. *See* COMPARE AND CONTRAST *at* steal.

embezzlement *n* **misappropriation**, misuse, appropriation, theft, larceny *(dated)*

embezzler *n* **swindler**, fraud, thief, larcenist, fraudster

embitter *v* **disillusion**, poison, sour, estrange, alienate

embittered adj **disillusioned**, bitter, resentful, sour, disaffected Opposite: mellow

emblazon v **decorate**, adorn, embellish, ornament, illustrate

emblem n **symbol**, crest, logo, sign, badge

emblematic adj **symbolic**, representative, characteristic, illustrative, exemplary

emblematical see **emblematic**

embodiment n **personification**, example, quintessence, incarnation, epitome

embody v **exemplify**, symbolize, represent, personify, epitomize

embolden v **encourage**, hearten, buoy up, bolster, reassure Opposite: discourage

emboss v **stamp**, chase, tool, engrave, mark

embrace v **1 hug**, hold, enfold, cuddle, clasp Opposite: release **2 accept**, welcome, adopt, take up, support Opposite: reject **3 comprise**, contain, include, incorporate, involve Opposite: exclude ■ n **hold**, hug, cuddle, clinch, clasp Opposite: release

embroider v **1 sew**, stitch, cross-stitch, trim, decorate **2 elaborate**, embellish, exaggerate, overstate, inflate Opposite: understate

embroil v **involve**, entangle, enmesh, ensnare, entrap

embryo n **beginning**, rudiment, germ, kernel, seed

embryonic adj **developing**, emergent, nascent, primary, early Opposite: advanced

emcee (infml) n **MC**, master of ceremonies, compere, host, presenter ■ v **compere**, host, present, introduce

emend v **alter**, correct, amend, revise, rewrite

emerge v **1 come out**, appear, materialize, come into view, come into sight Opposite: disappear **2 come to light**, transpire, leak out **3 appear**, appear, occur, develop, begin

emergence n **appearance**, rise, advent, arrival, development Opposite: decline

emergency n **crisis**, disaster, tragedy, accident, danger ■ adj **spare**, extra, backup, alternative, reserve

emergent adj **developing**, up-and-coming, embryonic, growing, nascent Opposite: established

emigrant n **expatriate**, migrant, immigrant, settler, exile Opposite: native

emigrate v **trek**, migrate, travel, move away, leave Opposite: return

emigration n **migration**, expatriation, exile, relocation, exodus Opposite: return

eminence n **distinction**, renown, reputation, fame, importance Opposite: anonymity

eminent adj **well-known**, renowned, important, distinguished, famous Opposite: unknown

eminently adv **very**, highly, extremely, exceedingly, exceptionally

emir n **ruler**, commander, prince, leader, governor

emirate n **principality**, country, state, nation, land

emissary n **representative**, envoy, ambassador, messenger, agent

emission n **release**, production, discharge, emanation, secretion Opposite: absorption

emit v **produce**, release, give off, give out, send out Opposite: absorb

emollient adj **soothing**, palliative, placatory, calmative, calming Opposite: disruptive ■ n **balm**, lotion, moisturizer, ointment, salve Opposite: irritant

emolument (fml) n **payment**, remuneration, reward, fee, compensation. See COMPARE AND CONTRAST at **wage**.

emotion n **feeling**, sentiment, reaction, passion, excitement

emotional adj **1 moving**, touching, poignant, bittersweet, affecting **2 expressive**, open, demonstrative, emotive, sensitive Opposite: impassive

emotionless adj **impassive**, blank, unemotional, detached, cold Opposite: emotional

emotive adj **sensitive**, emotional, poignant, affecting, moving

empathize v **identify with**, understand, sympathize, commiserate, relate to Opposite: dismiss

empathy n **understanding**, sympathy, compassion, responsiveness, identification Opposite: indifference

emperor n **ruler**, tsar, sovereign, king, head of state Opposite: subject

emphasis n **stress**, importance, weight, accent, prominence

emphasize v **highlight**, stress, accentuate, call attention to, underline Opposite: understate

emphatic adj **1 forceful**, categorical, vigorous, definite, unequivocal Opposite: hesitant **2 resounding**, absolute, ringing, clear, evident Opposite: ambiguous

empire n **territory**, realm, kingdom, domain

empirical adj **experiential**, experimental, observed, pragmatic, practical Opposite: theoretical

empiricism n **pragmatism**, experimentation, observation, practicality

empiricist n **pragmatist**, observer, experimenter, realist, researcher Opposite: theorist

employ v **1 pay**, retain, use, hire, take on Opposite: dismiss **2 use**, utilize, make use of, occupy, spend Opposite: waste ■ n **employment**, service, pay, hire, engagement Opposite: unemployment. See COMPARE AND CONTRAST at **use**.

employed adj **working**, in a job, in employment, in work, engaged Opposite: unemployed

employee n **worker**, operative, servant, wage earner, member Opposite: employer

employer n **boss**, company, manager, owner, proprietor Opposite: employee

employment n 1 **service**, pay, hire, engagement, occupation *Opposite*: unemployment 2 **occupation**, job, profession, trade, work

emporium n **store**, retail store, department store, warehouse, bazaar

empower v 1 **authorize**, allow, sanction, permit, vest *Opposite*: forbid 2 **inspire**, embolden, encourage, galvanize, rouse *Opposite*: discourage

empowerment n 1 **authorization**, enabling, permission, consent, dispensation *Opposite*: embargo 2 **liberation**, enfranchisement, emancipation, inspiration, encouragement

empress n **ruler**, tsaritsa, tsarina, sovereign, queen *Opposite*: subject

emptiness n 1 **bareness**, barrenness, blankness, desolation, hollowness *Opposite*: fullness 2 **meaninglessness**, worthlessness, purposelessness, hollowness, futility *Opposite*: purpose

empty adj 1 **unfilled**, bare, blank, vacant, hollow *Opposite*: full 2 **idle**, futile, ineffectual, unproductive, insincere 3 **meaningless**, pointless, vain, hollow, futile *Opposite*: meaningful ■ v **drain**, clear, pour out, discharge, clear out *Opposite*: fill. *See* COMPARE AND CONTRAST *at* **vacant, vain**.

empty-handed adj **unsuccessful**, frustrated, thwarted, unrewarded, defeated *Opposite*: successful

empty-headed adj **stupid**, silly, vacuous, frivolous, inane *Opposite*: intelligent

emulate v 1 **imitate**, follow, copy, mimic, ape 2 **compete with**, vie with, contend with, rival, outdo. *See* COMPARE AND CONTRAST *at* **imitate**.

emulation n **imitation**, competition, rivalry, mimicry, simulation *Opposite*: originality

emulsify v **blend**, combine, beat together, stir together, mix *Opposite*: separate

emulsion n **suspension**, blend, mixture, cream, mix

enable v **allow**, permit, make possible, empower, qualify *Opposite*: prevent

enact v 1 **perform**, act out, play, portray, represent 2 **pass**, ratify, endorse, decree, sanction *Opposite*: reject

enactment n 1 **performance**, performing, acting out, portrayal, representation 2 **passing**, ratification, ratifying, endorsement, sanctioning

enamel n **coating**, varnish, veneer, glaze, lacquer ■ v **coat**, paint, varnish, lacquer, cover

enamoured adj **fond**, in love, charmed, taken with, captivated *Opposite*: repelled

en bloc adv **all together**, all at once, as one, collectively, en masse *Opposite*: separately

encamp v **set up camp**, set up, install, base, settle

encampment n **camp**, military camp, campsite, base camp, army camp

encapsulate v **sum up**, summarize, put in a nutshell, epitomize, condense *Opposite*: expand

encase v **cover**, enclose, sheathe, coat, wrap *Opposite*: uncover

encased adj **covered**, enclosed, sheathed, coated, wrapped *Opposite*: uncovered

enchant v **charm**, captivate, fascinate, enthral, entrance *Opposite*: disgust

enchanted adj **charmed**, enthralled, captivated, delighted, entranced *Opposite*: disgusted

enchanting adj **charming**, captivating, enthralling, alluring, delightful *Opposite*: disgusting

enchantment n **charm**, attraction, delight, fascination, allure

encircle v **surround**, enclose, ring, circle, enfold

enclave n 1 **region**, reserve, territory, commune, area 2 **group**, community, class, clique, clan *(infml)*

enclose v 1 **surround**, hem in, encircle, enfold, ring 2 **wall**, fence, hedge, pen, seal off 3 **include**, put in, attach, insert, add *Opposite*: leave out

enclosed adj **surrounded**, bounded, hemmed in, fenced, walled *Opposite*: open

enclosure n 1 **field**, arena, stockade, pen, paddock 2 **inclusion**, attachment, insertion, addition, insert

encode v **encrypt**, code, put into code, scramble, convert *Opposite*: decode

encompass v **include**, cover, take in, incorporate, involve *Opposite*: exclude

encore n **repeat**, extra, impromptu item, curtain call, reprise

encounter v 1 **meet**, come across, bump into, run into, come upon 2 **face**, confront, contend with, grapple with, combat *Opposite*: avoid ■ n 1 **meeting**, chance meeting, happenstance 2 **confrontation**, engagement, contest, argument, skirmish

encourage v 1 **inspire**, hearten, cheer, raise your spirits, buoy up *Opposite*: discourage 2 **support**, egg on, urge, animate, incite *Opposite*: discourage 3 **foster**, assist, help, aid, nurture *Opposite*: stifle

encouragement n **support**, backup, help, reassurance, inspiration *Opposite*: discouragement

encouraging adj **hopeful**, heartening, cheering, reassuring, promising *Opposite*: discouraging

encroach v **intrude**, infringe, invade, trespass, make inroads into *Opposite*: respect

encroachment n **infringement**, violation, advance, intrusion, invasion

encrusted adj **covered**, coated, thick, crusted, caked *Opposite*: bare

encrypt v **encode**, code, put into code, scramble, translate *Opposite*: decode

encumber v burden, hinder, hamper, impede, get in the way Opposite: facilitate

encumbrance n burden, hindrance, nuisance, impediment, handicap Opposite: help

encyclopaedia see encyclopedia

encyclopedia n reference work, compendium, compilation, fact file, information database

encyclopedic adj comprehensive, full, complete, in-depth, thorough Opposite: narrow

end n 1 finish, conclusion, ending, closing stages, last part Opposite: beginning 2 extremity, edge, side, tip, top Opposite: middle 3 purpose, aim, reason, objective, goal 4 death, downfall, decline, ruin, dissolution Opposite: birth 5 remnant, leftover, stub, scrap, remainder Opposite: whole 6 consequence, outcome, upshot, result, end result Opposite: cause ■ v 1 stop, finish, conclude, close, terminate Opposite: begin 2 result, finish, conclude, culminate, end up

endanger v put in danger, jeopardize, risk, compromise, threaten Opposite: protect

endangered adj rare, in danger of extinction, dying out, scarce, threatened Opposite: common

endear v commend, recommend, ingratiate, make appealing, insinuate Opposite: alienate

endearing adj appealing, attractive, charming, engaging, winning Opposite: unappealing

endearment n kind word, sweet nothing, compliment, blandishment, loving word Opposite: insult

endeavour v try, strive, attempt, make every effort, do your utmost Opposite: neglect ■ n 1 attempt, effort, try, exertion, best shot 2 enterprise, undertaking, bid, venture, foray

endemic adj widespread, prevalent, common, rife, rampant Opposite: rare

ending n end, finish, finale, conclusion, culmination Opposite: beginning

end it all v commit suicide, kill yourself, take your own life, do away with yourself, die by your own hand

endless adj 1 boundless, infinite, limitless, without end, interminable Opposite: finite 2 eternal, continual, continuous, nonstop, perpetual Opposite: temporary

endorse v 1 sanction, approve, ratify, recommend, countersign Opposite: reject 2 support, back, advocate, favour, subscribe to Opposite: denounce

endorsed adj permitted, recognized, sanctioned, recommended, authorized Opposite: disallowed

endorsement n 1 authorization, commendation, confirmation, countersignature, ratification 2 backing, support, advocacy, sanction, encouragement

endow v award, donate, give, bequeath, provide

endowment n 1 donation, gift, bequest, legacy, award 2 natural gift, talent, ability, capability, aptitude

end product n outcome, end result, result, upshot, product

end result n outcome, end product, result, upshot, product

end up v finish up, finish off, transpire, turn out, result in Opposite: start out

endurable adj tolerable, manageable, bearable, passable, sufferable Opposite: intolerable

endurance n 1 staying power, strength, stamina, fortitude, resolution Opposite: weakness 2 stamina, fortitude, tolerance, grit, guts (slang) 3 persistence, perseverance, tenacity, continuance, survival

endure v 1 bear, tolerate, undergo, put up with, go through Opposite: succumb 2 last, continue, go on, persist, survive Opposite: perish

enduring adj lasting, continuing, durable, stable, long-term Opposite: short-lived

end user n user, purchaser, shopper, consumer, client Opposite: producer

endways adv end on, endways on, jutting out, end foremost, end uppermost Opposite: lengthways

endwise see endways

enemy n opponent, adversary, rival, opposition, competitor Opposite: friend

energetic adj 1 lively, active, vigorous, brisk, animated Opposite: lethargic 2 strenuous, vigorous, brisk, dynamic, challenging Opposite: easy

energize v invigorate, strengthen, boost, galvanize, electrify Opposite: enervate

energizing adj invigorating, stimulating, enlivening, revitalizing, reviving Opposite: draining

energy n 1 vigour, liveliness, dynamism, vitality, drive Opposite: lethargy 2 power, force, strength, momentum, resources

enervate v weaken, debilitate, sap the strength of, drain, fatigue Opposite: invigorate

enervating adj exhausting, weakening, enfeebling, fatiguing, draining Opposite: invigorating

enfeeble v weaken, debilitate, enervate, deplete, exhaust Opposite: strengthen

enfold v enclose, surround, wrap, wrap up, envelop

enforce v 1 apply, carry out, impose, implement, make compulsory 2 coerce, oblige, compel, require, insist on

enforced adj compulsory, obligatory, forced, imposed, required Opposite: optional

enforcement n implementation, application, execution, putting into practice, administration

enfranchise v give somebody the vote,

empower, emancipate, liberate, naturalize *Opposite*: disenfranchise

enfranchisement *n* **empowerment**, naturalization, suffrage, manumission *(fml) Opposite*: disenfranchisement

engage *v* **1 involve**, occupy, engross, absorb, take part **2 appoint**, take on, employ, hire, contract *Opposite*: dismiss **3 battle**, fight, combat, contest, encounter **4 hold**, keep, absorb, charm, attract *Opposite*: repel **5 connect**, slot in, fit into place, interlock, join *Opposite*: disengage

engaged *adj* **1 busy**, occupied, unavailable, in use, being used *Opposite*: free **2 spoken for**, involved, promised, tied up, betrothed *(fml) Opposite*: unattached

engagement *n* **1 appointment**, meeting, rendezvous, assignation, visit **2 employment**, job, position, situation, post **3 battle**, fight, encounter, conflict, action. *See* COMPARE AND CONTRAST *at* fight.

engaging *adj* **attractive**, appealing, charming, winning, fetching *Opposite*: unattractive

engender *v* **1 produce**, cause, create, bring about, stimulate **2** *(fml)* **beget**, give birth to, generate, propagate, spawn

engine *n* **machine**, motor, turbine, mechanism, generator

WORD BANK
❏ **parts of an engine** alternator, ball bearing, cam, camshaft, cog, cogwheel, coil, crank, crankshaft, cylinder, distributor, gasket, gear, gearbox, gearing, lever, manifold, piston, pump, radiator, seal, shaft, solenoid, spark plug, starter, sump, tappet, valve

engineer *v* **bring about**, cause, contrive, concoct, plot

engorge *v* **swell up**, swell, puff up, expand, blow up *Opposite*: deflate

engrave *v* **etch**, score, scratch, carve, incise

engraving *n* **1 etching**, lithograph, print, reproduction, woodcut **2 engraved design**, carving, etching, linocut, inscription

engross *v* **absorb**, captivate, hold your attention, hold, engage *Opposite*: bore

engrossed *adj* **absorbed**, captivated, enthralled, gripped, held *Opposite*: bored

engrossing *adj* **absorbing**, captivating, enthralling, gripping, interesting *Opposite*: uninteresting

engulf *v* **swallow up**, overcome, overwhelm, immerse, submerge

enhance *v* **improve**, add to, increase, boost, develop *Opposite*: impair

enhanced *adj* **improved**, greater, strengthened, heightened, boosted *Opposite*: diminished

enhancement *n* **improvement**, augmentation, development, enrichment, heightening *Opposite*: detraction

enigma *n* **paradox**, conundrum, problem, mystery, puzzle

enigmatic *adj* **mysterious**, inscrutable, puzzling, perplexing, obscure *Opposite*: straightforward. *See* COMPARE AND CONTRAST *at* obscure.

enjoin *(fml)* *v* **order**, command, instruct, direct, tell *Opposite*: forbid

enjoy *v* **1 like**, delight in, appreciate, revel in, relish *Opposite*: dislike **2 benefit from**, have, experience, be blessed with, possess *Opposite*: lack

enjoyable *adj* **pleasant**, agreeable, pleasing, entertaining, amusing *Opposite*: boring

enjoyment *n* **pleasure**, delight, satisfaction, gratification, fun *Opposite*: boredom

enjoy yourself *v* **be amused**, be delighted, let yourself go, play, party *(infml)*

enlarge *v* **1 increase**, expand, broaden, widen, lengthen *Opposite*: decrease **2 detail**, elaborate, expand, amplify, flesh out *Opposite*: compress. *See* COMPARE AND CONTRAST *at* increase.

enlargement *n* **expansion**, extension, amplification, increase, widening *Opposite*: decrease

enlighten *v* **tell**, inform, explain to, instruct, edify

enlightened *adj* **1 rational**, unprejudiced, reasonable, logical, open-minded *Opposite*: irrational **2 educated**, aware, informed, knowledgeable, wise *Opposite*: unaware

enlightening *adj* **informative**, instructive, edifying, helpful, educational *Opposite*: uninformative

enlightenment *n* **explanation**, illumination, clarification, insight, information *Opposite*: ignorance

enlist *v* **1 join**, join up, sign on, sign up, volunteer **2 recruit**, conscript, procure, solicit, count on *Opposite*: reject

enliven *v* **liven up**, cheer up, invigorate, wake up, cheer *Opposite*: put a damper on

en masse *see* en bloc

enmesh *v* **entangle**, tangle, trap, catch, catch up *Opposite*: disentangle

enmity *n* **hostility**, hate, hatred, ill will, animosity *Opposite*: goodwill

ennui *n* **boredom**, languor, world-weariness, tedium, weariness *Opposite*: excitement

enormity *n* **1 atrociousness**, horror, monstrousness, wickedness, heinousness *Opposite*: goodness **2 atrocity**, abomination, outrage, evil, horror *Opposite*: kindness **3 size**, extent, vastness, scale, immensity

enormous *adj* **huge**, vast, massive, giant, mammoth *Opposite*: tiny

enormously *adv* **extremely**, very, a lot, a great deal, hugely *Opposite*: slightly

enough *adj* **sufficient**, adequate, ample, plenty, abundant *Opposite*: insufficient

enquire *v* **ask**, find out, query, investigate, probe *Opposite*: reply

enrage *v* **infuriate**, anger, make your blood

boil, madden, incense *Opposite*: calm

enraged *adj* **furious**, infuriated, angry, beside yourself, fuming *Opposite*: calm

enrapture *(fml)* *v* **entrance**, delight, captivate, enchant, mesmerize *Opposite*: bore

enrich *v* **improve**, supplement, enhance, deepen, develop *Opposite*: diminish

enrichment *n* **enhancement**, improvement, augmentation, amelioration, upgrading *Opposite*: diminution

enrol *v* **register**, sign up, put your name down, join, join up

enrolment *n* **registration**, matriculation, signing up, admission, acceptance *Opposite*: resignation

ensemble *n* **1 band**, company, troupe, group, corps **2 outfit**, suit, costume, coordinates, rig-out *(infml)* **3 collection**, assembly, aggregate, set, combination ■ *adj* **collaborative**, collective, joint, group, cooperative *Opposite*: solo

enshrine *v* **protect**, treasure, hallow, preserve, cherish

enshroud *v* **obscure**, hide, mask, shield, cover *Opposite*: expose

ensign *n* **flag**, pennant, banner, standard, colours

enslave *v* **subjugate**, dominate, subject, bind, yoke *Opposite*: liberate

ensnare *v* **enmesh**, embroil, catch, trap, entrap *Opposite*: set free

ensue *v* **1 follow**, succeed, follow on, result, arise *Opposite*: precede **2 result**, follow, proceed, arise, derive *Opposite*: precede

ensuing *adj* **resultant**, subsequent, succeeding, resulting, following *Opposite*: preceding

ensure *v* **make sure**, make certain, safeguard, guarantee, confirm

entail *v* **involve**, require, demand, need, necessitate

entangle *v* **1 tangle**, twist, intertwine, snarl up, catch up *Opposite*: disentangle **2 snare**, trap, catch, snag, enmesh *Opposite*: free

entanglement *n* **predicament**, tangle, muddle, morass, mess

enter *v* **1 go in**, go into, come in, come into, cross the threshold *Opposite*: leave **2 input**, insert, put in, record, register *Opposite*: delete **3 submit**, put in, propose, hand in, state **4 compete**, participate, take part, take up, try **5 join**, sign up, agree to, enlist, enrol **6 walk on**, come on, appear, make an entrance *Opposite*: exit

enter into *v* **become involved in**, take part in, join in, throw yourself into, participate in *Opposite*: withdraw

enter on *v* **start**, begin, enter upon, move into, start out on *Opposite*: finish

enterprise *n* **1 business**, company, firm, corporation, organization **2 venture**, project, activity, undertaking, endeavour **3 initiative**,

innovativeness, creativity, inventiveness, originality *Opposite*: apathy

enterprising *adj* **innovative**, inventive, imaginative, resourceful, adventurous *Opposite*: unadventurous

entertain *v* **1 amuse**, divert, distract, regale, interest *Opposite*: bore **2 accommodate**, wine and dine, feed, invite, regale *Opposite*: visit **3 consider**, think about, give thought to, contemplate, think over *Opposite*: reject

entertainer *n* **performer**, artiste, artist, talent, turn

WORD BANK

❏ **types of entertainer** actor, actress, busker, clown, co-star, comedian, comic, compere, conjurer, contortionist, dancer, DJ, double act, emcee *(infml)*, film star, impressionist, juggler, magician, mime, musician, popstar, rapper, singer, standup comedian, stooge, straight man, street entertainer, street musician, street performer, trapeze artist, ventriloquist

entertaining *adj* **amusing**, enjoyable, diverting, pleasurable, charming *Opposite*: dull

entertainment *n* **1 entertaining**, performing, acting, show business, theatre **2 amusement**, fun, diversion, distraction, enjoyment *Opposite*: boredom **3 show**, production, concert, attraction, performance

enter upon *v* **start**, begin, enter on, move into, start out on *Opposite*: finish

enthral *v* **captivate**, charm, mesmerize, beguile, fascinate *Opposite*: bore

enthralled *adj* **fascinated**, engrossed, gripped, captivated, absorbed *Opposite*: bored

enthralling *adj* **fascinating**, beguiling, engrossing, gripping, captivating *Opposite*: boring

enthrone *(fml)* *v* **crown**, instate, ordain, swear in, consecrate *Opposite*: dethrone

enthuse *v* **1 be enthusiastic**, be passionate, talk excitedly, show enthusiasm, be effusive **2 stimulate**, galvanize, excite, spur to action, impassion *Opposite*: bore

enthusiasm *n* **1 eagerness**, interest, passion, gusto, zeal *Opposite*: apathy **2 craze**, interest, hobby, passion, mania

enthusiast *n* **fan**, fanatic, buff, aficionado, aficionada

enthusiastic *adj* **eager**, keen, passionate, fervent, excited *Opposite*: apathetic

entice *v* **lure**, tempt, induce, seduce, bribe *Opposite*: put off

enticement *n* **lure**, temptation, incentive, inducement, bribery *Opposite*: deterrent

enticing *adj* **tempting**, alluring, inviting, attractive, appealing *Opposite*: off-putting

entire *adj* **1 whole**, complete, full, total, perfect *Opposite*: part **2 absolute**, complete, total, thorough, unqualified *Opposite*: partial

entirety *n* **sum**, whole, wholeness, totality, entireness *Opposite*: part

entitle v 1 **enable**, allow, permit, sanction, authorize Opposite: debar 2 **title**, call, name, dub, label

entitled adj 1 **permitted**, in your own right, eligible, allowed, enabled Opposite: barred 2 **titled**, called, named, dubbed, labelled

entitlement n **right**, power, prerogative, privilege, claim

entity n **object**, thing, article, being, unit Opposite: nonentity

entourage n **staff**, associates, following, followers, train

entrails n **guts**, intestines, bowels, viscera, innards (infml)

entrance n 1 **entry**, way in, doorway, door, opening Opposite: exit 2 **arrival**, entry, appearance, entering, ingress (fml) Opposite: departure 3 **admission**, entry, ticket, pass, admittance ■ v **captivate**, engross, fascinate, charm, delight Opposite: bore

entrance hall n **lobby**, foyer, reception area, hallway, vestibule

entrancing adj **captivating**, enchanting, enthralling, spellbinding, fascinating Opposite: boring

entrant n **applicant**, contestant, candidate, participant, competitor. See COMPARE AND CONTRAST at **candidate**.

entrap v **trick**, deceive, ensnare, trap, lure

entrapment n **trap**, frame, snare, trick, setup (infml)

entreat v **plead**, beg, pray, ask, request Opposite: demand

entreaty n **appeal**, plea, petition, supplication (fml) Opposite: demand

entrée n 1 **starter**, hors d'oeuvre, first course, appetizer, antipasto 2 **introduction**, induction, entrance, access, admittance Opposite: exclusion

entrench v **embed**, ensconce, ingrain, root, establish

entrepreneur n **businessperson**, trader, organizer, impresario, financier

entrepreneurial adj **business**, small-business, commercial, risk-taking, empire-building

entrust v **trust**, commend, delegate, assign, deliver Opposite: deprive

entry n 1 **admission**, entrance, access, pass, ticket 2 **entrance**, doorway, door, opening, access Opposite: exit 3 **record**, item, note, account, statement 4 **application**, submission, attempt, effort, go Opposite: withdrawal

entwine v **tangle**, entangle, twist, interweave, interlace Opposite: undo

enumerate v 1 **detail**, list, spell out, itemize, name 2 **count**, number, tally, compute, reckon Opposite: estimate

enunciate v 1 **pronounce**, articulate, voice, utter, speak Opposite: mumble 2 **express**, spell out, detail, state, put forward Opposite: suppress

enunciation n 1 **pronunciation**, articulation, diction, speech 2 **expression**, assertion, declaration, proclamation, clarification Opposite: suppression

envelop v **enclose**, encircle, encase, engulf, swathe Opposite: unwrap

envelope n **cover**, wrapper, covering, wrapping, casing

enviable adj **desirable**, fortunate, lucky, privileged, to die for Opposite: unenviable

envious adj **jealous**, green with envy, resentful, spiteful, covetous

environment n 1 **nature**, ecosystem, earth, world, natural world 2 **surroundings**, setting, situation, atmosphere, scene 3 **background**, upbringing, circumstances, conditions, situation

environmental adj **ecological**, conservation, conservational, environmentally friendly, ecofriendly

environmentalist n **ecologist**, conservationist, preservationist, green

environs n **vicinity**, surroundings, locality, environment, neighbourhood

envisage v **imagine**, visualize, foresee, predict, see

envision see **envisage**

envoy n **representative**, diplomat, attaché, emissary, herald

envy n **jealousy**, greed, bitterness, resentment, spite Opposite: goodwill ■ v **covet**, desire, resent, begrudge, grudge

epaulette n **decoration**, insignia, strap, chevron

ephemeral adj **short-lived**, passing, fleeting, brief, momentary Opposite: lasting. See COMPARE AND CONTRAST at **temporary**.

ephemeralness n **brevity**, transitoriness, transience, fleetingness, temporariness Opposite: timelessness

epic n **classic**, historical fiction, costume drama, period piece, extravaganza Opposite: short story ■ adj **marathon**, heroic, classic, larger-than-life, impressive Opposite: minuscule

epicure n **gourmet**, gastronome, connoisseur, bon vivant, epicurean

epicurean adj 1 **hedonistic**, decadent, pleasure-seeking, pleasure-loving, sensualist Opposite: ascetic 2 **gastronomic**, gourmet, culinary ■ n **gourmet**, gastronome, connoisseur, bon vivant, epicure

epidemic n 1 **plague**, outbreak, endemic, scourge, contagion 2 **spate**, wave, rash, craze, increase Opposite: decrease ■ adj **widespread**, wide-ranging, prevalent, rampant, sweeping Opposite: restricted. See COMPARE AND CONTRAST at **widespread**.

epidermis n **skin**, hide, flesh, cuticle, integument

epigram n **witticism**, saying, axiom, ditty, rhyme

epilogue *n* **conclusion**, coda, speech, monologue *Opposite*: prologue

episode *n* **1 incident**, affair, chapter, event, occurrence **2 chapter**, part, section, scene, instalment **3 occurrence**, incidence, attack, outbreak, bout

episodic *adj* **1 serialized**, discontinuous, divided **2 sporadic**, intermittent, periodic, discontinuous, irregular *Opposite*: regular

epistle *(fml) n* **letter**, missive, communication, message, communiqué

epitaph *n* **inscription**, legend, caption, epigraph

epithet *n* **nickname**, description, label, sobriquet, appellation *(fml)*

epitome *n* **essence**, personification, embodiment, model, quintessence *Opposite*: antithesis

epitomize *v* **typify**, characterize, exemplify, personify, embody

epoch *n* **era**, age, time, period, date

epoch-making *adj* **historic**, crucial, important, momentous, earthshattering *Opposite*: insignificant

equable *adj* **composed**, calm, easygoing, unflappable, placid *Opposite*: jumpy

equal *adj* **1 identical**, equivalent, like, alike, the same *Opposite*: unequal **2 on a par**, even, uniform, level, on level pegging *Opposite*: unequal ▪ *n* **match**, equivalent, counterpart, parallel, peer ▪ *v* **1 come to**, amount to, equate, make, correspond **2 match**, rival, keep pace with, copy, meet

equality *n* **parity**, fairness, equivalence, likeness, equal opportunity *Opposite*: inequality

equalize *v* **match**, level, even out, align, line up *Opposite*: differentiate

equally *adv* **1 similarly**, likewise, in the same way, by the same token, alike *Opposite*: conversely **2 evenly**, uniformly, regularly, equivalently, alike *Opposite*: unequally

equanimity *n* **composure**, calmness, levelheadedness, equability, self-control *Opposite*: volatility

equate *v* **associate**, liken, link, connect, parallel *Opposite*: contrast

equation *n* **reckoning**, calculation, comparison, equivalence, equality

equestrian *adj* **riding**, equine, show jumping, horseracing, horsey

equidistant *adj* **halfway between**, midway between, between, in between, intermediate

equilateral *adj* **symmetrical**, regular, square, rectangular, triangular

equilibrium *n* **balance**, symmetry, steadiness, stability, evenness *Opposite*: imbalance

equip *v* **1 provide**, endow, fit out, outfit, kit out **2 prepare**, train, school, qualify, ground

equipment *n* **tools**, apparatus, tackle, utensils, paraphernalia

equitable *(fml) adj* **fair**, evenhanded, reasonable, justifiable, rightful *Opposite*: unfair

equity *(fml) n* **fairness**, evenhandedness, impartiality, justice, fair play *Opposite*: injustice

equivalence *n* **correspondence**, sameness, likeness, similarity, equality *Opposite*: difference

equivalent *adj* **equal**, corresponding, correspondent, alike, same *Opposite*: different ▪ *n* **counterpart**, equal, opposite number, parallel, twin

equivocal *adj* **vague**, ambiguous, confusing, ambivalent, misleading *Opposite*: unambiguous

equivocate *v* **prevaricate**, vacillate, be evasive, quibble, beat about the bush *Opposite*: speak your mind

equivocation *n* **vagueness**, indirectness, ambiguity, prevarication, weasel words *(infml)* *Opposite*: directness

era *n* **age**, epoch, aeon, time, period

eradicate *v* **eliminate**, get rid of, destroy, exterminate, do away with *Opposite*: introduce

eradication *n* **abolition**, purge, annihilation, extermination, obliteration *Opposite*: introduction

erase *v* **rub out**, remove, delete, expunge, obliterate

erasure *n* **removal**, destruction, eradication, elimination, deletion

erect *v* **1 build**, construct, assemble, set up, raise *Opposite*: demolish **2 create**, set up, found, initiate, establish ▪ *adj* **straight**, upright, vertical, rigid, stiff *Opposite*: prone

erection *n* **1 construction**, building, assembly, creation, formation **2** *(fml)* **structure**, building, construction, edifice, pile

erode *v* **wear away**, wear down, corrode, eat away, eat into

eroded *adj* **weathered**, worn, weather-beaten, corroded, eaten away

erosion *n* **corrosion**, attrition, destruction, loss *Opposite*: accretion

erotic *adj* **sexy**, sensual, stimulating, suggestive, arousing

err *(fml) v* **go wrong**, blunder, stumble, go astray, get something wrong

errand *n* **task**, duty, run, chore, job

errant *adj* **wayward**, sinful, naughty, misbehaving, delinquent *Opposite*: well-behaved

erratic *adj* **unpredictable**, unreliable, inconsistent, irregular, changeable *Opposite*: consistent

erroneous *adj* **mistaken**, flawed, wrong, specious, inaccurate *Opposite*: correct

error *n* **mistake**, fault, blunder, inaccuracy, miscalculation. *See* COMPARE AND CONTRAST *at* **mistake**.

ersatz adj **faux**, artificial, substitute, reproduction, imitation *Opposite*: genuine

erstwhile adj **former**, previous, past, old, earlier *Opposite*: current

erudite adj **scholarly**, knowledgeable, well-educated, well-read, cultured *Opposite*: uneducated

erudition n **knowledge**, learnedness, education, learning, culture *Opposite*: ignorance

erupt v 1 **explode**, blow up, break out, flare up, go off *Opposite*: subside 2 **explode**, lose your temper, hit the roof *(infml)*, blow your top *(infml)*, blow a fuse *(infml)* *Opposite*: hold back

eruption n **outbreak**, outburst, explosion, upsurge, epidemic

escalate v **intensify**, worsen, heighten, go from bad to worse, deteriorate *Opposite*: de-escalate

escalating adj **mounting**, rising, intensifying, ever-increasing, swelling *Opposite*: diminishing

escalation n **rise**, growth, boom, increase, climb *Opposite*: reduction

escalator n **moving staircase**, staircase, stairway, stairs

escapade n **adventure**, jaunt, antic, caper, spree

escape v 1 **flee**, run away, get away, break out, run off *Opposite*: be captured 2 **leak out**, leak, drip, seep, flow 3 **avoid**, evade, dodge, elude, shake off *Opposite*: face ■ n 1 **seepage**, leakage, leak, outflow, discharge 2 **flight**, getaway, break, breakout, escaping *Opposite*: capture 3 **diversion**, distraction, pastime, leisure activity, escapism

escapee n **runaway**, fugitive, absconder, deserter, fleer

escapism n **diversion**, distraction, entertainment, relaxation, daydreaming

escapist adj **diverting**, distracting, entertaining, relaxing, fantasy *Opposite*: realistic

escarpment n **cliff**, bluff, scarp, ridge, incline

eschew v **avoid**, shun, have nothing to do with, steer clear of, give a wide berth to *Opposite*: embrace

escort n **guide**, attendant, minder, bodyguard, chaperon ■ v **accompany**, guide, usher, lead, attend

esoteric adj **obscure**, mysterious, abstruse, impenetrable, cryptic *Opposite*: straightforward

ESP n **extra-sensory perception**, psychic powers, clairvoyance, second sight, telepathy

especial adj **special**, unusual, exceptional, extraordinary, outstanding *Opposite*: ordinary

especially adv 1 **particularly**, in particular, specially, above all, more than ever 2 **exceptionally**, remarkably, notably, markedly, outstandingly

espousal n **adoption**, backing, support, championship, promotion *Opposite*: opposition

espouse v 1 **take up**, adopt, support, back, advocate *Opposite*: oppose 2 *(archaic)* **marry**, wed, take your vows, walk down the aisle, get hitched *(infml)*

essay n **paper**, thesis, dissertation, composition, article ■ v *(fml)* **try**, endeavour, strive, have a shot, attempt

essence n 1 **spirit**, core, heart, quintessence, crux 2 **concentrate**, extract, tincture, distillate, concentration

essential adj 1 **necessary**, vital, indispensable, important, crucial *Opposite*: unnecessary 2 **fundamental**, basic, elemental, key, central *Opposite*: secondary ■ n **necessity**, requisite, prerequisite, requirement, must *Opposite*: extravagance. *See* COMPARE AND CONTRAST *at* **necessary**.

essentially adv 1 **fundamentally**, basically, in essence, in effect, really 2 **effectively**, more or less, broadly, in the main, for the most part

essentials n **basics**, fundamentals, prerequisites, rudiments, necessities *Opposite*: frills

establish v 1 **set up**, found, institute, start, create *Opposite*: close down 2 **ascertain** *(fml)*, determine, find out, prove, confirm *Opposite*: disprove

established adj **recognized**, well-known, traditional, conventional, customary *Opposite*: new

establishment n 1 **founding**, formation, creation, setting up, institution *Opposite*: dissolution 2 **business**, firm, company, institution, concern 3 **authorities**, powers that be, the ruling classes, the established order, the system

estate n 1 **plantation**, land, park, lands, parkland 2 **area**, zone, industrial estate, business park, commercial centre 3 **assets**, property, holdings, worth, fortune

esteem v **appreciate**, cherish, hold dear, venerate, value *Opposite*: scorn ■ n **regard**, respect, admiration, high regard, reverence *Opposite*: contempt. *See* COMPARE AND CONTRAST *at* **regard**.

esteemed adj **respected**, valued, honoured, revered, admired *Opposite*: scorned

estimable adj **admirable**, worthy, deserving, laudable, venerable *Opposite*: unimpressive

estimate n 1 **quote**, price, estimation, valuation, costing *Opposite*: cost 2 **approximation**, estimation, guess, educated guess, evaluation ■ v **approximate**, guess, assess, reckon, value *Opposite*: calculate

estimated adj **projected**, assessed, valued, appraised, approximate

estimation n 1 **opinion**, assessment, inference, evaluation, view *Opposite*: fact 2 **educated guess**, approximation, estimate, guesstimate, evaluation

estranged *adj* **alienated**, separated, apart, at odds, on bad terms

estrangement *n* **separation**, hostility, rupture, distancing, disaffection *Opposite*: reconciliation

estuary *n* **river mouth**, bay, inlet, sound, creek *Opposite*: source

etc. *adv* **et cetera**, and so on, and so forth, and the like, and the rest

etch *v* **engrave**, scratch, scrape, cut, incise

etching *n* **engraving**, drawing, print, design, impression

eternal *adj* **everlasting**, undying, unending, never-ending, perpetual *Opposite*: transient

eternity *n* **1 time without end**, perpetuity, infinity, all time, ever and a day *(infml)* **a long time**, aeons, forever *(infml)*, ages *(infml)*, donkey's years *(infml)*

ethereal *adj* **1 ghostly**, otherworldly, unearthly, spectral, shadowy *Opposite*: earthly **2 waiflike**, frail, delicate, airy, insubstantial *Opposite*: substantial

ethic *n* **moral belief**, ethos, idea, principle, code

ethical *adj* **moral**, principled, right, fair, decent *Opposite*: unethical

ethics *n* **principles**, morals, beliefs, moral code, moral principles

ethnic *adj* **cultural**, traditional, folkloric, racial, indigenous

ethnicity *n* **culture**, way of life, origin, background, traditions

ethos *n* **philosophy**, beliefs, principles, code, character

etiquette *n* **manners**, good manners, protocol, custom, propriety *Opposite*: bad manners

eulogize *v* **praise**, extol, laud, sing the praises of, praise to the skies *Opposite*: criticize

eulogy *n* **tribute**, acclamation, acclaim, praise, homage *Opposite*: criticism

euphemism *n* **neutral term**, understatement, rewording, bowdlerization, code word *Opposite*: dysphemism

euphemistic *adj* **inoffensive**, polite, bowdlerized, cleaned up, neutral *Opposite*: dysphemistic

euphoria *n* **elation**, ecstasy, jubilation, rapture, excitement *Opposite*: despair

euphoric *adj* **overjoyed**, elated, ecstatic, joyful, joyous *Opposite*: despairing

evacuate *v* **1 empty**, abandon, withdraw from, leave, vacate *Opposite*: fill **2 send away**, remove from, move out of, clear from *Opposite*: bring in

evacuation *n* **removal**, clearing, emptying, withdrawal, flight *Opposite*: influx

evacuee *n* **refugee**, émigré, emigrant, migrant

evade *v* **1 avoid**, dodge, escape, elude, shirk *Opposite*: confront **2 equivocate**, prevaricate, hedge, stonewall *(infml)*, fudge *(infml)*

evaluate *v* **assess**, appraise, weigh up, gauge, estimate

evaluation *n* **assessment**, appraisal, estimation, calculation, valuation

evaluator *n* **assessor**, surveyor, inspector, judge

evanescent *adj* **short-lived**, fleeting, momentary, ephemeral, passing *Opposite*: permanent

evangelical *adj* **enthusiastic**, fervent, eager, zealous, keen *Opposite*: apathetic

evaporate *v* **vanish**, fade away, fade, disappear, melt away *Opposite*: solidify

evaporation *n* **vaporization**, drying up, loss, vanishing, disappearance

evasion *n* **1 avoidance**, dodging, elusion, circumvention, skirting **2 prevarication**, equivocation, hedging, stonewalling *(infml)*, fencing *(infml)*

evasive *adj* **elusive**, slippery, shifty, indirect, oblique *Opposite*: direct

evasiveness *n* **indirectness**, equivocation, shiftiness, elusiveness, ambiguousness *Opposite*: directness

eve *n* **day before**, evening before, night before

even *adj* **1 smooth**, flat, level, straight, unfluctuating *Opposite*: uneven **2 constant**, steady, uniform, unvarying, unchanging *Opposite*: fluctuating **3 equal**, similar, level, on a par, just as *Opposite*: unequal

evenhanded *adj* **fair**, impartial, unbiased, just, equal *Opposite*: biased

evenhandedness *n* **fairness**, impartiality, justice, neutrality, equity *(fml)* *Opposite*: partiality

even if *conj* **though**, albeit, although, even though, in spite of the fact that

evening *n* **twilight**, sunset, dusk, nightfall, late afternoon *Opposite*: morning

evenness *n* **consistency**, sameness, symmetry, uniformity, flatness *Opposite*: irregularity

even out *v* **1 flatten**, level, smooth, square, align **2 balance out**, balance, level out, balance up, equalize *Opposite*: unbalance

event *n* **occasion**, happening, occurrence, incident, affair

even-tempered *adj* **calm**, unflappable, equable, placid, imperturbable *Opposite*: temperamental

eventful *adj* **exciting**, action-packed, lively, busy, hectic *Opposite*: dull

eventual *adj* **ultimate**, final, last, ensuing, subsequent *Opposite*: immediate

eventuality *(fml)* *n* **possibility**, prospect, case, contingency, outcome

eventually *adv* **finally**, ultimately, sooner or later, in the end, in due course *Opposite*: immediately

even up *v* **equalize**, stabilize, even out, redress

the balance, balance up *Opposite*: unbalance

ever *adv* **always**, forever, eternally, all the time, constantly *Opposite*: never

evergreen *adj* **immortal**, perennial, ever popular, classic, old time favourite *Opposite*: stale

---

WORD BANK

❑ **types of evergreen tree** bay, bo tree, boxwood, bunya, carob, cedar, cola, cypress, eucalyptus, fir, fir tree, gum tree, holly, juniper, kahikatea, kauri, larch, laurel, mahogany, mangrove, monkey puzzle, pine, redwood, sandalwood, sequoia, spruce, yew

---

everlasting *adj* **eternal**, endless, ceaseless, never-ending, perpetual *Opposite*: transient

ever-present *adj* **ubiquitous**, chronic, pervasive, omnipresent

every *adj* **each**, all, every single, every one

everyday *adj* **ordinary**, average, normal, unremarkable, common *Opposite*: extraordinary

everyone *n* **everybody**, all, all and sundry, one and all, each person *Opposite*: no one

everything *n* **all**, the whole thing, the lot, the whole lot, the whole shebang *(infml)* *Opposite*: nothing

everywhere *adv* **all over**, ubiquitously, far and wide, the world over, universally

evict *v* **throw out**, expel, turn out, eject, remove *Opposite*: install

eviction *n* **removal**, expulsion, ejection, throwing out, exclusion

evidence *n* **1 indication**, sign, signal, mark, suggestion **2 proof**, confirmation, facts, data, substantiation ■ *v* **show**, demonstrate, evince, make clear, prove

evident *adj* **obvious**, plain, apparent, clear, manifest *Opposite*: obscure

evidently *adv* **1 obviously**, clearly, plainly, manifestly, palpably **2 apparently**, seemingly, as far as we know, it would seem, as far as one can tell

evil *adj* **1 wicked**, malevolent, sinful, malicious, criminal *Opposite*: good **2 foul**, vile, nasty, horrible, unpleasant *Opposite*: pleasant ■ *n* **wickedness**, malevolence, sin, iniquity, vice *Opposite*: good

evildoer *n* **wrongdoer**, sinner, criminal, offender, delinquent *Opposite*: benefactor

evilness *n* **wickedness**, badness, evil, immorality, sinfulness *Opposite*: goodness

evince *v* **show**, display, reveal, exhibit, manifest *Opposite*: conceal

evocation *n* **recreation**, elicitation, recall, air, hint

evocative *adj* **reminiscent**, suggestive, redolent, haunting

evoke *v* **call to mind**, bring to mind, suggest, call up, induce *Opposite*: suppress

evolution *n* **development**, fruition, growth, progress, progression *Opposite*: regression

evolve *v* **develop**, grow, progress, advance, go forward *Opposite*: regress

ewer *n* **jug**, pitcher, vessel, bottle, container

ex *adj* **former**, sometime, onetime, erstwhile, lapsed *Opposite*: future

exacerbate *v* **make worse**, worsen, aggravate, impair, intensify *Opposite*: soothe

exact *adj* **1 correct**, precise, accurate, strict, faithful *Opposite*: approximate **2 careful**, meticulous, precise, particular, thorough *Opposite*: careless ■ *v* **demand**, obtain, extort, extract, wrest

exacting *adj* **demanding**, testing, challenging, rigorous, tough *Opposite*: easy

exactitude *n* **precision**, correctness, accuracy, meticulousness, exactness *Opposite*: carelessness

exactly *adv* **precisely**, just, absolutely, quite, in every respect *Opposite*: approximately

exactness *n* **precision**, accuracy, exactitude, correctness, meticulousness *Opposite*: vagueness

exaggerate *v* **overstress**, embellish, embroider, make a mountain out of a molehill, inflate *Opposite*: understate

exaggerated *adj* **overstated**, inflated, embroidered, embellished, blown up *Opposite*: understated

exaggeration *n* **overstatement**, hyperbole, embellishment, embroidery, overemphasis *Opposite*: understatement

exalt *(fml)* *v* **1 promote**, raise, elevate, intensify, boost **2 praise**, laud, acclaim, applaud, pay tribute to *Opposite*: disparage

exaltation *(fml)* *n* **1 adulation**, adoration, acclaim, acclamation, praise *Opposite*: condemnation **2 excitement**, rapture, exhilaration, happiness, joy *Opposite*: despair

exalted *(fml)* *adj* **high**, lofty, glorious, dignified, illustrious *Opposite*: lowly

exam *n* **test**, assessment, examination, paper

examination *n* **1 inspection**, scrutiny, checkup, investigation, analysis **2 test**, assessment, exam, paper

examine *v* **1 look at**, inspect, scrutinize, observe, study **2 consider**, think about, look into, investigate, research **3 test**, assess, grade, judge, question

examiner *n* **inspector**, auditor, surveyor, superintendent, assessor

example *n* **1 sample**, instance, case, case in point, specimen **2 model**, pattern, paradigm, standard, paragon

exasperate *v* **infuriate**, madden, frustrate, annoy, irritate *Opposite*: placate. *See* COMPARE AND CONTRAST *at* annoy.

exasperating *adj* **infuriating**, maddening, frustrating, vexing, annoying *Opposite*: calming

exasperation *n* **frustration**, irritation, enragement, annoyance, vexation

excavate *v* **dig**, mine, quarry, dig out, exhume *Opposite*: bury

exceed v go beyond, surpass, go above, go over, top *Opposite*: fall short

exceedingly adv very, exceptionally, remarkably, extremely, extraordinarily *Opposite*: slightly

excel v shine, stand out, outshine, outclass, surpass *Opposite*: fall behind

excellence n fineness, brilliance, superiority, distinction, quality *Opposite*: mediocrity

excellent adj outstanding, brilliant, exceptional, admirable, superb *Opposite*: poor

except prep apart from, but, excluding, with the exception of, aside from *Opposite*: including

exception n exclusion, omission, exemption, concession, allowance

exceptionable (fml) adj offensive, obnoxious, rude, objectionable, repugnant *Opposite*: inoffensive

exceptional adj excellent, brilliant, special, extraordinary, incomparable *Opposite*: ordinary

exceptionality n rarity, infrequency, extraordinariness, uniqueness, remarkableness *Opposite*: normality

exceptionally adv very, remarkably, extremely, extraordinarily, outstandingly *Opposite*: slightly

excerpt n extract, passage, quote, quotation, selection

excess n 1 surplus, glut, overload, surfeit, overabundance *Opposite*: shortage 2 overindulgence, intemperance, dissipation, inordinateness, prodigality *Opposite*: moderation ■ adj extra, additional, surplus, spare, superfluous

excesses n extremes, dissipation, intemperance, overindulgence, prodigality

excessive adj extreme, too much, unnecessary, unwarranted, undue *Opposite*: moderate

excessively adv very, extremely, overly, exceptionally, markedly *Opposite*: moderately

excessiveness n extremeness, exorbitance, extravagance, immoderateness (fml), immoderation (fml) *Opposite*: moderation

exchange v switch, switch over, replace, trade, barter *Opposite*: keep ■ n 1 conversation, argument, talk, chat, discussion 2 trade, switch, barter, replacement, substitute

exchangeable adj redeemable, transferable, negotiable, commutable, interchangeable

exchange blows v fight, scuffle, go for each other, trade punches, brawl

excise v delete, remove, edit, cut out, expunge *Opposite*: insert

excision n editing, deletion, removal, cutting out, erasure *Opposite*: insertion

excitability n nervousness, edginess, volatility, fieriness, temper *Opposite*: coolness

excitable adj nervous, emotional, highly strung, edgy, impulsive *Opposite*: unflappable

excite v 1 stimulate, enthuse, animate, motivate, enliven *Opposite*: bore 2 incite, agitate, provoke, instigate, stir up *Opposite*: soothe

excited adj 1 happy, enthusiastic, eager, animated, motivated *Opposite*: indifferent 2 agitated, nervous, provoked, overwrought, hot and bothered *Opposite*: calm

excitement n 1 enthusiasm, eagerness, anticipation, pleasure, exhilaration *Opposite*: indifference 2 agitation, tension, unrest, ferment, restlessness *Opposite*: calm

exciting adj thrilling, exhilarating, stirring, stimulating, electrifying *Opposite*: boring

exclaim v cry out, cry, shout, call out, call *Opposite*: whisper

exclamation n shout, cry, yell, scream, howl *Opposite*: whisper

exclude v 1 keep out, bar, reject, leave out, prevent *Opposite*: welcome 2 reject, rule out, eliminate, discount, ignore *Opposite*: include

excluding prep exclusive of, not including, without, apart from *Opposite*: including

exclusion n 1 keeping out, barring, rejection, leaving out, prohibiting *Opposite*: welcome 2 ban, refusal, sanction, embargo, prohibition 3 rejection, elimination, marginalization, prohibition, veto *Opposite*: inclusion

exclusive adj 1 high-class, elite, select, restricted, limited *Opposite*: inclusive 2 sole, complete, undivided, full, whole *Opposite*: partial

exclusiveness n 1 luxury, sophistication, refinement, superiority, stylishness 2 selectiveness, selectivity, exclusivity, elitism, snobbery

excommunicate v exclude, bar, debar, expel, eject *Opposite*: admit

excommunication n exclusion, barring, debarring, expulsion, ejection *Opposite*: admission

excoriate v 1 skin, peel, pare, strip, flay 2 (fml) criticize, denounce, attack, berate, upbraid *Opposite*: commend

excrescence n monstrosity, eyesore, blot, growth, outgrowth

excruciating adj 1 agonizing, painful, unbearable, awful, terrible *Opposite*: pleasant 2 embarrassing, tedious, stultifying, irritating, infuriating *Opposite*: enthralling

exculpate (fml) v free, let off, excuse, clear, release *Opposite*: arraign

exculpation (fml) n acquittal, exoneration, discharge, pardon, clearing *Opposite*: arraignment

excursion n 1 trip, jaunt, outing, junket, tour 2 group, team, party, expedition 3 (fml)

digression, departure, detour, deviation, tangent

excusable *adj* **understandable**, forgivable, justifiable, explicable, pardonable *Opposite*: inexcusable

excuse *v* **1 forgive**, pardon, let off, acquit, absolve *Opposite*: blame **2 overlook**, make allowances for, pass over, tolerate, justify **3 exempt**, release, let off, free, relieve *Opposite*: oblige ■ *n* **justification**, reason, explanation, pretext, defence

excused *adj* **exempted**, released, exempt, let off, relieved *Opposite*: required

execrable *adj* **awful**, appalling, disgusting, repulsive, deplorable *Opposite*: excellent

execute *v* **1 carry out**, perform, implement, complete, accomplish **2 put to death**, kill, murder, hang, electrocute. *See* COMPARE AND CONTRAST *at* kill, perform.

execution *n* **1 putting to death**, capital punishment, the death sentence, killing, hanging **2 implementation**, performance, accomplishment, carrying out, completing

executive *n* **manager**, senior manager, director, administrator, official ■ *adj* **1 decision-making**, policymaking, managerial, management, administrative **2 expensive**, exclusive, high class, superior, select

executor *n* **doer**, prime mover, initiator, originator, architect

exemplary *adj* **1 admirable**, praiseworthy, excellent, perfect, ideal *Opposite*: shameful **2** *(fml)* **model**, archetypal, textbook, typical, classic

exemplify *v* **demonstrate**, typify, represent, illustrate, show

exempt *adj* **excused**, exempted, released, relieved, discharged *Opposite*: required ■ *v* **excuse**, free, let off, let go, release *Opposite*: oblige

exemption *n* **exception**, immunity, release, indemnity, exclusion *Opposite*: obligation

exercise *n* **1 physical activity**, working out, training, keep fit, drill *Opposite*: inactivity **2 move**, movement, drill, step, stretch **3** *(fml)* **implementation**, carrying out, use, application, employment *Opposite*: avoidance ■ *v* **1 work out**, train, keep fit, do exercises, drill **2 use**, put into effect, implement, apply, employ *Opposite*: avoid

exercises *n* **military exercises**, manoeuvres, drills, war games

exert *v* **bring to bear**, use, apply, exercise, make use of

exertion *n* **effort**, action, application, physical exertion, energy *Opposite*: ease

exert yourself *v* **make an effort**, try hard, push yourself, strive, labour

exhale *v* **breathe out**, blow out, puff out, let your breath out, respire *Opposite*: inhale

exhaust *v* **1 tire out**, wear out, drain, fatigue, weaken *Opposite*: refresh **2 use up**, use, wear out, consume, drain *Opposite*: renew

exhausted *adj* **tired**, worn out, shattered, fatigued, drained *Opposite*: refreshed

exhausting *adj* **tiring**, wearing, shattering, fatiguing, killing *Opposite*: refreshing

exhaustion *n* **tiredness**, fatigue, collapse, weariness, enervation *Opposite*: energy

exhaustive *adj* **thorough**, complete, comprehensive, in-depth, full *Opposite*: superficial

exhibit *v* **1 display**, show, unveil, put on a display, put on view *Opposite*: hide **2 show off**, parade, flaunt, expose, display ■ *n* **exhibition**, display, show, showcase, showing

exhibition *n* **1 display**, show, showing, demonstration, exposition **2 grant**, scholarship, bursary, award, fund

exhibitionist *n* **attention seeker**, braggart, extrovert, show-off *(infml)*

exhilarate *v* **excite**, elate, thrill, enliven, invigorate *Opposite*: bore

exhilarated *adj* **elated**, ecstatic, euphoric, overjoyed, delighted *Opposite*: indifferent

exhilaration *n* **excitement**, elation, high spirits, animation, happiness

exhort *v* **urge**, press, push, pressure, insist *Opposite*: forbid

exhortation *(fml)* *n* **appeal**, call, encouragement, urging, incitement

exhume *v* **dig up**, disinter, unearth, disentomb, disclose *Opposite*: bury

exigency *(fml)* *n* **need**, demand, requirement, emergency, necessity

exigent *(fml)* *adj* **1 urgent**, pressing, crucial, vital, important *Opposite*: unimportant **2 demanding**, tough, testing, challenging, taxing *Opposite*: easy

exile *n* **1 émigré**, tax exile, expatriate, deportee, refugee **2 banishment**, deportation, expulsion, separation, ostracism ■ *v* **banish**, send away, deport, expel, separate

exist *v* **1 be**, be real, be present, be existent, happen **2 live**, be, survive, continue living, stay alive

existence *n* **being**, life, reality, presence, survival

existent *(fml)* *adj* **existing**, current, present, extant, ongoing

existing *adj* **present**, current, in effect, prevailing, standing

exit *n* **1 way out**, door, outlet, egress *(fml)* *Opposite*: entrance **2 departure**, exodus, walking out, leaving, going away *Opposite*: arrival ■ *v* **go out**, leave, depart, go, walk out *Opposite*: enter

exodus *n* **mass departure**, departure, migration, emigration, flight *Opposite*: arrival

exonerate *v* **clear**, absolve, acquit, vindicate, forgive *Opposite*: blame

exoneration n 1 **pardon**, absolution, acquittal, vindication, exculpation (fml) Opposite: blame 2 **release**, freeing, liberation, exemption, discharge

exorbitant adj **excessive**, inflated, ridiculous, dear, overpriced Opposite: reasonable

exorcize v **get rid of**, get free of, banish, drive out, force out

exotic adj 1 **unusual**, out of the ordinary, novel, striking, interesting Opposite: ordinary 2 **foreign**, from abroad, tropical, alien, nonnative Opposite: familiar

expand v **make bigger**, get bigger, enlarge, increase, develop Opposite: contract. See COMPARE AND CONTRAST at **increase**.

expandable adj **stretchy**, elastic, foldup, foldout, pullout

expand upon v **enlarge on**, elaborate on, give details, embellish, amplify

expanse n **area**, breadth, stretch, span, region

expansion n **growth**, development, increase, extension, spreading out Opposite: contraction

expansive adj 1 **communicative**, generous, magnanimous, friendly, open Opposite: reserved 2 **extensive**, spread-out, spacious, roomy, sizable Opposite: cramped

expansively adv 1 **at length**, extensively, widely, comprehensively, broadly Opposite: briefly 2 **effusively**, lavishly, openly, generously, jovially

expansiveness n 1 **effusiveness**, lavishness, openness, generousness, enthusiasm Opposite: reserve 2 **size**, large size, mass, extent, reach

expat (infml) see **expatriate**

expatriate n **émigré**, tax exile, emigrant, refugee, colonial Opposite: native

expect v 1 **wait for**, anticipate, look forward to, await, look ahead 2 **imagine**, suppose, guess, think, believe 3 **demand**, require, insist on, count on, anticipate

expectancy n **anticipation**, expectation, hope, suspense, bated breath

expectant adj 1 **eager**, hopeful, in suspense, hoping, on tenterhooks 2 **pregnant**, expecting, in the family way (dated infml), in the club (slang)

expectation n **hope**, anticipation, expectancy, belief, prospect

expected adj **likely**, probable, foreseeable, predictable, awaited Opposite: surprising

expecting adj **pregnant**, expectant, in the club (slang), in the family way (dated infml)

expectorant n **cough medicine**, linctus, cough mixture, medicine, cough syrup

expediency n 1 **convenience**, practicality, pragmatism, usefulness, feasibility 2 **appropriateness**, suitability, fitness, advisability, convenience Opposite: unsuitability

expedient adj 1 **appropriate**, fitting, suitable, advisable, necessary Opposite: inappropriate 2 **advantageous**, convenient, practical, useful, beneficial Opposite: altruistic ■ n **measure**, means, method, manoeuvre, device

expedite (fml) v **speed up**, accelerate, hurry up, advance, further Opposite: impede

expedition n 1 **journey**, excursion, voyage, trip, outing 2 **team**, party, crew, group, company

expeditious adj **speedy**, prompt, quick, swift, hasty Opposite: slow

expel v 1 **dismiss**, fire, eject, oust, throw out 2 **drive out**, force out, push out, eject, flush out

expend v 1 **use up**, use, consume, spend, burn up Opposite: conserve 2 (fml) **spend**, disburse, pay out, lay out, pay Opposite: save

expendable adj 1 **consumable**, replaceable, throwaway, disposable, usable Opposite: durable 2 **dispensable**, disposable, superfluous, unessential, nonessential Opposite: indispensable

expenditure n **spending**, outgoings, expenses, payments, outflow Opposite: income

expense n 1 **cost**, expenditure, outlay, disbursement, outflow Opposite: income 2 **price**, rate, figure, amount, price tag 3 **sacrifice**, cost, detriment, disadvantage, loss

expenses n **expenditures**, outgoings, outlay, payments, costs Opposite: income

expensive adj 1 **costly**, dear, high-priced, steep (infml), pricey (infml) Opposite: cheap 2 **luxurious**, exclusive, affluent, lavish, classy (infml) Opposite: cheap

experience n 1 **involvement**, knowledge, skill, practice, understanding Opposite: inexperience 2 **occurrence**, incident, episode, encounter, event ■ v **feel**, go through, face, live through, undergo

experienced adj **knowledgeable**, skilled, practised, qualified, veteran Opposite: inexperienced

experiment n **trial**, test, investigation, research, experimentation ■ v **test**, try out, investigate, try, trial

experimental adj **new**, tentative, untried, trial, speculative Opposite: proven

experimentation n **testing**, research, investigation, trialling

expert n **specialist**, authority, professional, connoisseur, doyen Opposite: amateur ■ adj **skilled**, skilful, practised, proficient, professional Opposite: inexperienced

expertise n **skill**, knowledge, proficiency, capability, know-how (infml)

expertness n **skilfulness**, dexterity, knowledge, expertise, proficiency Opposite: inexperience

expiate v **make amends**, compensate, make up for, recompense, redress

expire v 1 **end**, run out, finish, terminate, conclude 2 *(fml)* **die**, pass away, pass on, perish, breathe your last *(literary)*

expiry n 1 **end**, ending, running out, finish, finishing *Opposite:* beginning 2 *(fml)* **death**, passing, end, dying, demise *(fml)*

explain v 1 **make clear**, describe, put in plain words, elucidate, clarify 2 **justify**, account for, defend, rationalize, vindicate

explanation n 1 **reason**, justification, rationalization, vindication, account 2 **description**, account, clarification, enlightenment, details

explanatory adj **descriptive**, instructive, illustrative, illuminating, clarifying

expletive n **swearword**, curse, oath, exclamation, obscenity

explicable adj **explainable**, understandable, reasonable, justifiable, rational *Opposite:* inexplicable

explicate v **explain**, elucidate, spell out, clarify, expound

explicit adj 1 **clear**, obvious, open, overt, plain *Opposite:* implicit 2 **definite**, precise, exact, specific, unequivocal *Opposite:* vague 3 **frank**, uninhibited, candid, open, graphic

explode v 1 **blow up**, go off, burst, erupt, burst out *Opposite:* implode 2 **get angry**, fly into a rage, hit the ceiling, hit the roof *(infml)*, blow up *(infml) Opposite:* calm down 3 **disprove**, prove wrong, discredit, invalidate, nullify *Opposite:* prove

exploit v 1 **take advantage of**, abuse, misuse, ill-use, manipulate 2 **use**, develop, make use of, take advantage of, utilize *Opposite:* waste ■ n **feat**, deed, adventure, activity, heroic act

exploitable adj 1 **gullible**, credulous, innocent, vulnerable *Opposite:* shrewd 2 **usable**, utilizable, consumable, available

exploitation n 1 **misuse**, mistreatment, taking advantage, manipulation 2 **use**, utilization, development, management, operation

exploitative adj **unfair**, unequal, abusive, manipulative *Opposite:* fair

exploration n 1 **examination**, investigation, survey, study, consideration 2 **travelling**, discovery, journeying, adventure, voyaging

exploratory adj **investigative**, examining, probing, tentative, experimental

explore v 1 **travel**, discover, reconnoitre, see the sights, sightsee 2 **investigate**, study, search, look at, survey

explorer n **traveller**, voyager, surveyor, pioneer, pathfinder

explosion n 1 **bang**, blast, detonation, eruption, burst 2 **outburst**, fit, eruption, paroxysm, burst 3 **upsurge**, leap, flood, outbreak, eruption *Opposite:* slump

explosive adj 1 **volatile**, unstable, unpredictable, dangerous *Opposite:* stable 2 **short-tempered**, quick-tempered, hotheaded, volatile, fiery *Opposite:* placid

WORD BANK
❏ **types of explosive material** dynamite, gelignite, gunpowder, napalm, nitroglycerine, plastic explosive, propellant, Semtex™, TNT
❏ **types of explosive weapon** A-bomb, antiballistic missile, atom bomb, ballistic missile, bomb, booby trap, bunker-buster, cruise missile, daisycutter, depth charge, firebomb, guided missile, hand grenade, hydrogen bomb, mine, missile, Molotov cocktail, nail bomb, neutron bomb, nuclear missile, nuclear warhead, nuclear weapon, petrol bomb, pipe bomb, smart bomb, torpedo, smoke bomb, warhead, time bomb, weapon of mass destruction

exponent n 1 **advocate**, proponent, promoter, fan, champion 2 **interpreter**, explainer, performer, practitioner

export v 1 **sell abroad**, sell overseas, send abroad, send overseas, ship *Opposite:* import 2 **spread**, transfer, carry across, pass on, disseminate

expose v 1 **open up**, reveal, uncover, bare, display *Opposite:* cover 2 **subject**, lay open to, put in danger, endanger, imperil *(fml)* 3 **blow the whistle on**, unmask, reveal, lay bare, bring to light *Opposite:* cover up

exposé n **disclosure**, revelation, leak, exposure, discovery

exposed adj **unprotected**, visible, uncovered, bare, out in the open *Opposite:* covered

exposition n 1 **description**, discussion, explanation, account, clarification 2 **exhibition**, fair, show, trade fair, display

expostulate v **disagree**, protest, object, reprove, remonstrate. *See* COMPARE AND CONTRAST *at* object.

exposure n 1 **contact**, experience, introduction, acquaintance, dealings 2 **revelation**, disclosure, revealing, unveiling, publicity *Opposite:* whitewash

expound v **explain**, expand on, talk about, develop, illustrate

express v 1 **state**, articulate, utter, voice, communicate 2 **squeeze out**, extract, press out, force out ■ adj 1 **fast**, rapid, direct, nonstop, prompt *Opposite:* slow 2 **precise**, explicit, definite, exact, specific *Opposite:* vague

expression n 1 **look**, face, air, appearance, countenance 2 **phrase**, idiom, turn of phrase, term, saying 3 **communication**, manifestation, illustration, example, demonstration 4 **extraction**, squeezing out, pressing out, forcing out

expressionless adj **straight-faced**, unresponsive, impassive, poker-faced, inexpressive *Opposite:* expressive

expressive adj 1 **communicative**, sensitive, open, easy-to-read, animated *Opposite:* impassive 2 **representative**, representing, demonstrating, signifying, indicative

expressively adv **meaningfully**, dramatically, emotionally, sensitively, vividly Opposite: blandly

expressivity n **articulacy**, eloquence, self-expression, fluency, clarity Opposite: inarticulacy

expressly adv **specifically**, particularly, explicitly, clearly, definitely

expropriate v **steal**, confiscate, seize, commandeer, appropriate

expulsion n **dismissal**, exclusion, throwing out, eviction, removal Opposite: admittance

expunge v **obliterate**, purge, erase, delete, rub out Opposite: insert

expurgated adj **cut down**, abridged, censored, edited, bowdlerized

exquisite adj **1 beautiful**, gorgeous, delicate, attractive, superb Opposite: ugly **2 excellent**, perfect, delightful, flawless, wonderful Opposite: flawed **3 discriminating**, discerning, sensitive, fastidious, refined **4 intense**, touching, moving, excruciating, poignant Opposite: dull

exquisiteness n **beauty**, delicacy, daintiness, perfection, attractiveness Opposite: ugliness

extant adj **existing**, in existence, present, living, surviving Opposite: lost. See COMPARE AND CONTRAST at **living**.

extemporaneous adj **extemporary**, extemporal, unrehearsed, impromptu, ad-lib Opposite: rehearsed

extempore adj **extemporaneous**, ad-lib, off-the-cuff, impromptu, unrehearsed Opposite: rehearsed ■ adv **extemporaneously**, ad lib, off the cuff, impromptu, spontaneously Opposite: rehearsed

extemporize v **ad-lib**, improvise, speak off the cuff, play it by ear, make it up as you go along Opposite: prepare

extend v **1 spread**, spread out, range, cover, encompass **2 continue**, reach, stretch, go on, run **3 make bigger**, expand, enlarge, make longer, lengthen Opposite: curtail **4 prolong**, stretch out, drag out, lengthen, postpone Opposite: cut short **5 increase**, expand, widen, broaden, add to Opposite: decrease **6 offer**, give, hold out, proffer, tender Opposite: withdraw. See COMPARE AND CONTRAST at **increase**.

extended adj **lengthy**, protracted, long, prolonged, stretched Opposite: cut short

extension n **1 additional room**, addition, lean-to, wing, conservatory **2 extra time**, delay, postponement, leeway, allowance **3 expansion**, enlargement, lengthening, broadening, increase Opposite: contraction

extensive adj **1 large**, huge, vast, massive Opposite: restricted **2 wide**, widespread, wide-ranging, general, all-embracing Opposite: narrow

extensively adv **1 significantly**, considerably, greatly, to a great extent, to a large extent Opposite: insignificantly **2 at length**, lengthily, widely, far, broadly Opposite: briefly

extensiveness n **breadth**, comprehensiveness, fullness, richness, vastness Opposite: narrowness

extent n **1 size**, area, coverage, limit, boundary **2 degree**, amount, level, range, scope

extenuating adj **mitigating**, explanatory, justifying, moderating, palliative

exterior adj **external**, outside, outdoor, peripheral, outward Opposite: interior ■ n **1 outside**, façade, elevation, surface, shell Opposite: interior **2 appearance**, look, aura, veneer, front

exterminate v **kill**, eliminate, annihilate, massacre, destroy

extermination n **extinction**, annihilation, execution, killing, slaughter Opposite: preservation

external adj **outside**, exterior, outdoor, peripheral, outward Opposite: internal

externalize v **express**, give voice to, utter, get off your chest, voice Opposite: internalize

externally adv **outwardly**, on the outside, on the exterior, on the surface, superficially Opposite: inwardly

extinct adj **nonexistent**, inexistent, died out, destroyed, vanished Opposite: living. See COMPARE AND CONTRAST at **dead**.

extinction n **death**, extermination, destruction, loss, annihilation Opposite: survival

extinguish v **1 douse**, quench, snuff, stub out, smother Opposite: light **2 end**, take away, destroy, snuff out, do away with **3 eclipse**, overshadow, outshine, obscure Opposite: show up

extol (fml or literary) v **praise**, commend, eulogize, admire, worship Opposite: deprecate

extort v **extract**, obtain under duress, obtain by threat, wrest, wring

extortion n **coercion**, threats, blackmail, squeezing, force

extortionate adj **expensive**, exorbitant, inflated, high, overpriced Opposite: reasonable

extra adj **additional**, further, added, spare, second ■ adv **1 more**, in addition, further, on top, spare **2 especially**, particularly, ultra, exceptionally, more ■ n **optional extra**, addition, add-on, supplement, bonus

extract v **1 take out**, remove, haul out, pull out, dig out Opposite: put in **2 obtain**, winkle out, unearth, extricate, root out **3 extort**, force, wrest, wheedle out, wring ■ n **excerpt**, cutting, quotation, citation, abstract

extraction n **1 removal**, taking out, withdrawal, pulling out, drawing out Opposite: insertion **2 origin**, birth, descent, ancestry, family

extracurricular adj **1 additional**, supplementary, optional, secondary, extra-mural Opposite: regular **2** (infml) **extramarital**, adulterous, clandestine, illicit, improper

extradite v **deport**, expel, banish, transfer, repatriate

extradition n **repatriation**, handing over, deportation, expulsion, return

extra-large adj **outsize**, outsized, giant, jumbo, oversized Opposite: undersized

extramarital adj **adulterous**, illicit, clandestine, improper, extracurricular (infml)

extramural adj **external**, extracurricular, additional, optional, vocational Opposite: intramural

extraneous adj **1 irrelevant**, unrelated, unconnected, inappropriate, beside the point Opposite: pertinent **2 inessential**, unimportant, unnecessary, superfluous, peripheral Opposite: essential

extraordinaire adj **excellent**, extraordinary, superb, exceptional, remarkable Opposite: ordinary

extraordinarily adv **1 strangely**, oddly, unusualy, bizarrely, abnormally Opposite: normally **2 extremely**, very, unusually, particularly, amazingly

extraordinary adj **1 strange**, odd, unusual, unexpected, astonishing Opposite: ordinary **2 special**, particular, exceptional, remarkable, great Opposite: normal

extrapolate v **infer**, generalize, induce, deduce, conclude

extrasensory adj **telepathic**, psychic, clairvoyant, mystic, mystical

extraterrestrial adj **celestial**, interplanetary, Martian, alien, interstellar Opposite: terrestrial ■ n **alien**, creature, creature from outer space, space invader, ET Opposite: earthling

extravagance n **1 profligacy**, overspending, wastefulness, excessiveness, lavishness Opposite: prudence **2 luxury**, indulgence, folly, nonessential, overindulgence Opposite: essential

extravagant adj **1 profligate**, wasteful, excessive, spendthrift, overgenerous Opposite: thrifty **2 exaggerated**, overstated, profuse, excessive, elaborate Opposite: restrained

extravaganza n **show**, musical, variety performance, gala, festival

extreme adj **1 great**, tremendous, severe, intense, acute Opposite: insignificant **2 radical**, fanatical, immoderate, zealous, excessive Opposite: moderate **3 farthest**, furthest, outermost, ultimate, maximum **4 dangerous**, life-threatening, thrilling, risky, exciting Opposite: safe ■ n **limit**, boundary, edge, end, pole

extremely adv **very**, tremendously, enormously, awfully, really Opposite: somewhat

extreme sport n **adrenaline sport**, alternative sport, Xtreme sport

extremism n **radicalism**, fanaticism, zealotry,

activism, intemperance Opposite: moderation

extremist n **radical**, fanatic, activist, revolutionary, rebel Opposite: moderate ■ adj **radical**, fanatical, revolutionary, rebel, terrorist Opposite: moderate

extremity n **1 edge**, limit, boundary, margin, extreme Opposite: centre **2 limb**, hand, foot, arm, leg

extricate v **get out**, extract, remove, disentangle, detach Opposite: engage

extrication n **disconnection**, detachment, disentanglement, disengagement, release Opposite: engagement

extroversion n **sociability**, friendliness, self-confidence, socialness, conviviality Opposite: introversion

extrovert n **outgoing person**, gregarious person, assertive person, socializer, befriender Opposite: introvert ■ adj **sociable**, outgoing, gregarious, friendly, social Opposite: introverted

exuberance n **enthusiasm**, excitement, liveliness, energy, high spirits Opposite: apathy

exuberant adj **enthusiastic**, excited, lively, energetic, high-spirited Opposite: lethargic

exude v **1 radiate**, give out, give off, display, show Opposite: absorb **2 secrete**, release, ooze, leak, discharge

exult v **revel**, take pride, gloat, glory, triumph Opposite: lament

exultant adj **jubilant**, overjoyed, triumphant, joyful, thrilled Opposite: miserable

exultation n **happiness**, triumph, joy, rejoicing, jubilation Opposite: misery

eye n **appreciation**, sense, taste, discrimination, discernment ■ v **look at**, stare at, gaze at, watch, observe

---

WORD BANK

❏ **parts of an eye** aqueous humour, cone, conjunctiva, cornea, eyeball, iris, lens, macula, optic nerve, pupil, retina, rod, vitreous humour

---

eyeball (infml) v **stare at**, glare at, have a good look at, look at, gaze at

eye-catching adj **striking**, noticeable, attention-grabbing, startling, arresting Opposite: unremarkable

eyeful (infml) n **look**, view, glance, squint (infml), gander (infml)

eyelet n **hole**, grommet, eyehole, perforation, loophole

eye opener n **revelation**, discovery, realization, surprise, shock

eyesight n **vision**, sight, sightedness, eye, view

eyesore n **blot on the landscape**, blot, monstrosity, blemish, fright

eyewitness n **witness**, observer, bystander, onlooker, looker-on

F

fable n tale, legend, parable, myth, story

fabled adj 1 **legendary**, wonderful, remarkable, extraordinary, famous Opposite: unknown 2 **fictitious**, mythical, imaginary, legendary, fairy-tale Opposite: factual

fabric n 1 **cloth**, material, textile, stuff, piece goods 2 **structure**, foundation, framework, basics, makeup 3 **brickwork**, stonework, masonry, structure, superstructure

WORD BANK
❏ **types of fabric from animals** alpaca, angora, astrakhan, baize, brocade, camel hair, cashmere, chenille, crepe de Chine, felt, flannel, fur, gabardine, horsehair, jersey, lambswool, leather, loden, mohair, pashmina, shahtoosh, silk, taffeta, tweed, vicuna, wool, worsted
❏ **types of fabric from plants** burlap, calico, canvas, chambray, cheesecloth, chintz, corduroy, cotton, cretonne, damask, denim, drill, flannelette, gauze, gingham, grosgrain, hessian, lawn, linen, madras, moleskin, muslin, organdy, poplin, sacking, sailcloth, seersucker, tarpaulin, terry, terry towelling, ticking, towelling, twill, velour, velvet, voile, winceyette
❏ **types of synthetic fabric** acrylic, chiffon, crêpe, fishnet, fleece, lamé, moquette, nylon, percale, polyester, PVC, rayon, sateen, satin, spandex, tulle, viscose

fabricate v 1 **invent**, make up, concoct, dream up, trump up 2 **construct**, make, manufacture, produce, engineer Opposite: destroy

fabricated adj **invented**, made-up, untrue, fictitious, fictional Opposite: genuine

fabrication n 1 **untruth**, lie, invention, falsehood, cock-and-bull story Opposite: truth 2 **construction**, manufacture, production, assembly, creation 3 **counterfeit**, forgery, fake, imitation. See COMPARE AND CONTRAST at **lie**.

fabulous adj 1 **excellent**, wonderful, tremendous, magnificent, marvellous Opposite: awful 2 **fictitious**, mythical, imaginary, legendary, fairy-tale Opposite: factual

façade n 1 **frontage**, portico, fascia, front 2 **pretence**, veneer, impression, front, face

face n 1 **countenance**, features, mug (slang), phiz (slang), phizog (slang) 2 (infml) **nerve**, gall, boldness, audacity, pluck 3 **expression**, look, appearance, air, aspect 4 **outside**, surface, aspect, façade, wall Opposite: back ■ v 1 **be opposite**, be in front of, stand in front of, stand facing, look toward 2 **confront**, tackle, meet, cope with, challenge Opposite: avoid 3 **accept**, admit, be realistic, realize, bite the bullet Opposite: deny

WORD BANK
❏ **parts of a face** brow, cheek, cheekbone, chin, chops (infml), eye, eyebrow, forehead, hairline, jaw, jawline, jowl, lips, mandible, mouth, nose, temple

faceless adj **impersonal**, featureless, unidentified, anonymous, nameless

facelift n 1 **plastic surgery**, cosmetic surgery, tuck 2 **renovation**, modernization, refurbishment, redecoration, restoration

face-off n **confrontation**, conflict, argument, showdown, challenge

face pack n **face mask**, facial, beauty treatment, mudpack

face-saving adj **dignified**, diplomatic, tactical, tactful, restorative Opposite: humiliating

facet n 1 **aspect**, feature, part, component, factor 2 **surface**, face, side, plane, façade

face the music v **accept responsibility**, face the storm, face up to your actions, take the flak, bite the bullet

facetious adj 1 **flippant**, silly, ill-timed, ill-judged, inappropriate Opposite: earnest 2 **lighthearted**, playful, humorous, witty, droll Opposite: serious

facetiousness n 1 **flippancy**, frivolousness, inappropriateness, silliness, inanity Opposite: earnestness 2 **lightheartedness**, wittiness, wit, drollness, humorousness Opposite: seriousness

face to face adv 1 **in person**, in the flesh, personally, head-on, person to person 2 **head on**, opposite, in confrontation, nose to nose, head to head

face up to v **accept**, admit, come to terms with, realize, confront Opposite: deny

facial n **beauty treatment**, face mask, face pack, makeover, massage

facile adj **superficial**, simplistic, flippant, trite, inane Opposite: profound

facilitate v **make easy**, ease, make possible, enable, smooth Opposite: impede

facilitation n **assistance**, help, furtherance, advancement, easing Opposite: obstruction

facilitator n **organizer**, architect, originator, prime mover, initiator

facilities n **amenities**, services, conveniences, restroom, toilet

facility n 1 **skill**, capability, capacity, talent, flair Opposite: inability 2 **service**, provision, resource, feature, advantage

facing *prep* **opposite**, in front of, fronting

facsimile *n* **copy**, duplicate, reproduction, replica, likeness

fact *n* **1 truth**, reality, actuality, verity *(fml)* *Opposite*: fiction **2 piece of information**, detail, point, circumstance, datum **3 happening**, deed, occurrence, event, act

faction *n* **1 section**, party, splinter group, bloc, division **2 conflict**, division, disunity, schism, disharmony *Opposite*: agreement

factional *adj* **1 sectarian**, dissenting, disaffected, separatist, schismatic *Opposite*: united **2 dramatized**, fictionalized, drama-documentary, semirealistic, documentary

factious *adj* **divisive**, sectarian, schismatic, discordant, contentious *Opposite*: unifying

factitious *adj* **contrived**, artificial, simulated, affected, unnatural *Opposite*: genuine

fact of life *n* **reality**, practicality, fact, truth, actuality

factor *n* **influence**, thing, feature, aspect, reason

factory *n* **plant**, works, installation, industrial unit, manufacturing plant

WORD BANK
❑ **types of factory** assembly plant, brewery, cannery, distillery, forge, foundry, machine shop, mill, mint, pottery, sawmill, smithy, steelworks, sweatshop, water mill, workshop

facts *n* **1 truth**, evidence, reality, actuality, proof **2 particulars**, details, specifics, essentials, data

fact sheet *n* **information sheet**, information leaflet, booklet, brochure, handout

factual *adj* **1 objective**, hard, verifiable, bona fide, authentic *Opposite*: subjective **2 truthful**, accurate, realistic, honest, true-life *Opposite*: fictional

faculty *n* **1 sense**, power, endowment, capability, function **2 ability**, facility, gift, talent, knack *Opposite*: inability **3 staff**, teaching body, teaching staff, teachers, professors

fad *n* **fashion**, craze, trend, whim, vogue

faddiness *n* **fussiness**, fastidiousness, pickiness, choosiness *(infml)*, pernicketiness *(infml)*

faddy *adj* **fussy**, finicky, picky, particular, choosy *(infml)*

fade *v* **1 become paler**, lighten, become lighter, lose colour, bleach *Opposite*: darken **2 disappear**, weaken, die away, diminish, fade away *Opposite*: grow **3 wane**, wither, die, waste away, wilt *Opposite*: flourish

fade away *v* **1 disappear**, vanish, fade, evaporate, dwindle *Opposite*: persist **2 waste away**, shrivel, wane, wither, atrophy *Opposite*: thrive

fading *adj* **disappearing**, declining, dying, vanishing, diminishing *Opposite*: growing

faff about *(infml) see* **faff around**

faff around *(infml) v* **waver**, hesitate, vacillate, shilly-shally, mess about *(infml)*

fail *v* **1 be unsuccessful**, nose-dive, miss the mark, go belly up, fall flat *Opposite*: succeed **2 fall short**, not make the grade, not be up to scratch, flunk *(infml)*, fluff *(infml) Opposite*: pass **3 stop working**, break down, crash, go down, stop **4 go out of business**, go bankrupt, crash, fold, go under *Opposite*: thrive **5 let down**, disappoint, neglect, forsake, desert *Opposite*: satisfy **6 weaken**, fade, diminish, dwindle, decline *Opposite*: rally

failed *adj* **unsuccessful**, botched, disastrous, futile, abortive *Opposite*: successful

failing *n* **shortcoming**, flaw, weakness, weak point, fault *Opposite*: forte ■ *prep* **without**, in the absence of, lacking ■ *adj* **deteriorating**, worsening, weakening, fading, waning *Opposite*: strengthening. *See* COMPARE AND CONTRAST *at* **flaw**.

fail-safe *adj* **foolproof**, guaranteed, dependable, reliable, unfailing *Opposite*: unreliable

failure *n* **1 disappointment**, letdown, catastrophe, fiasco, disaster *Opposite*: success **2 breakdown**, stoppage, malfunction, crash, collapse **3 bankruptcy**, closure, crash, collapse, insolvency

faint *adj* **1 dim**, weak, faded, indistinct, feeble *Opposite*: bright **2 dizzy**, giddy, woozy, unsteady, vertiginous **3 slight**, diminished, muffled, soft, low *Opposite*: loud ■ *v* **pass out**, collapse, black out, fall down, lose consciousness *Opposite*: come to

faint-hearted *adj* **fearful**, apprehensive, hesitant, cowardly, shy *Opposite*: bold. *See* COMPARE AND CONTRAST *at* **cowardly**.

faintly *adv* **1 dimly**, weakly, slightly, indistinctly, feebly *Opposite*: brightly **2 slightly**, softly, barely, indistinctly, imperceptibly *Opposite*: loudly

faintness *n* **1 dimness**, weakness, feebleness, indistinctness, haziness *Opposite*: brightness **2 slightness**, quietness, weakness, feebleness, softness *Opposite*: loudness **3 dizziness**, giddiness, wooziness, vertigo, lightheadedness

fair *adj* **1 reasonable**, just, fair-minded, open-minded, impartial *Opposite*: biased **2 light**, blond, fair-haired, flaxen, tow-headed *Opposite*: dark **3 adequate**, passable, average, reasonable, decent **4 pleasing**, attractive, good-looking, lovely, pretty *Opposite*: unattractive **5 good**, bright, sunny, clear, cloudless *Opposite*: inclement ■ *n* **1 travelling fair**, fairground, funfair, amusement park, theme park **2 festival**, sale, fête, exposition, bazaar

fairground *n* **fair**, funfair, theme park, amusement park, playground

fair-haired *adj* **fair**, blond, flaxen, tow-headed *Opposite*: dark

fairly *adv* **1 honestly**, justly, properly, legitimately, impartially *Opposite*: unfairly **2 moderately**, rather, quite, reasonably, somewhat **3 completely**, positively, literally, practically, absolutely

fair-minded adj fair, open-minded, even-handed, nondiscriminatory, impartial Opposite: prejudiced

fairness n justice, equality, evenhandedness, impartiality, fair-mindedness Opposite: unfairness

fairy n pixie, brownie, sprite, elf, leprechaun

fairyland n wonderland, dreamland, dream world, seventh heaven, heaven

fairy story n 1 myth, fairy tale, folktale, folk story, legend 2 invention, fabrication, lie, untruth, falsehood

fairy tale n 1 invention, fabrication, lie, untruth, falsehood 2 fairy story, folktale, folk story, myth, legend

fairy-tale adj 1 mythical, enchanted, magic, magical, imaginary Opposite: real 2 fortunate, happy, storybook, perfect, romantic Opposite: unhappy 3 fabricated, unbelievable, make-believe, made-up, highly coloured Opposite: truthful

faith n 1 trust, confidence, reliance, conviction, belief Opposite: disbelief 2 loyalty, devotion, faithfulness, commitment, dedication Opposite: disloyalty

faithful adj 1 loyal, devoted, trusty, trustworthy, staunch Opposite: faithless 2 correct, true, realistic, authentic, close Opposite: unrealistic

faithfulness n 1 loyalty, devotion, staunchness, dependability, reliability Opposite: faithlessness 2 correctness, closeness, realism, authenticity, accuracy Opposite: unreality

faithless adj dishonest, disloyal, untrustworthy, unfaithful, fickle Opposite: faithful

faithlessness n dishonesty, infidelity, inconstancy, fickleness, disloyalty Opposite: faithfulness

fake n imitation, copy, replica, simulation, mock-up Opposite: original ■ adj false, bogus, sham, phoney, counterfeit Opposite: genuine ■ v 1 falsify, copy, counterfeit, forge, replicate 2 simulate, feign, pretend, act, dissemble

faker n fraud, fake, liar, pretender, impostor

fall v 1 drop, go down, descend, plunge, plummet Opposite: ascend 2 tumble, fall over, fall down, drop, trip over 3 decrease, reduce, sink, come down Opposite: increase ■ n 1 reduction, decrease, drop, tumble, descent Opposite: increase 2 waterfall, rapids, cataract, cascade, white water

fall about (infml) v laugh, hoot, scream with laughter, guffaw, roar

fallacious adj mistaken, erroneous, misleading, deceptive, false Opposite: correct

fallacy n misconception, myth, error, mistake, delusion

fall apart v disintegrate, crumble, collapse, fall to pieces, fall to bits Opposite: come together

fall asleep v nod off, doze off, go to sleep,

drop off (infml) Opposite: wake up

fall back v 1 retreat, withdraw, draw back, run away, regroup Opposite: advance 2 drop behind, fall behind, drop back, lag, lag behind Opposite: catch up

fallback n replacement, contingency, alternative, stand-in, substitute

fall back on v resort to, rely on, turn to, depend on, have recourse to

fall behind v 1 drop back, drop behind, fall back, lag, lag behind Opposite: keep up 2 be delayed, be late, be in arrears, default, fail to pay

fall by the wayside v come to nothing, fold, collapse, fail, abandon

fall down v 1 collapse, fall over, tumble, trip over, trip 2 fail, be unsuccessful, disappoint, go wrong, flop (infml) Opposite: succeed

fall flat v fail, miss the target, be a disaster, flop (infml), bomb (infml) Opposite: succeed

fall for v 1 fall in love with, be attracted to, be taken with, be stuck on (infml), take a shine to (infml) Opposite: go off 2 be duped by, be deceived by, be tricked by, be taken in by, believe Opposite: see through

fall foul of v come into conflict with, tangle with, have a brush with, come up against

fall guy (infml) n 1 dupe, stooge, fool, gull, sucker (infml) 2 scapegoat, whipping boy, victim, butt, sucker (infml)

fallibility n imperfection, frailty, weakness, shortcoming, failure Opposite: infallibility

fallible adj imperfect, mortal, weak, frail, human Opposite: infallible

falling adj dwindling, dropping, deteriorating, tumbling, sinking Opposite: rising

falling-out n quarrel, fight, row, disagreement, misunderstanding Opposite: reconciliation

fall into place v work out, shape up, make sense, come together, sort itself out

fall in with v 1 meet, come across, bump into, run into, get to know Opposite: avoid 2 join, join forces with, team up with, collaborate with, band together with 3 agree with, accept, support, go along with, comply with Opposite: reject

fall off v decline, go down, decrease, plunge, reduce Opposite: increase

falloff n decrease, decline, falling off, reduction, drop Opposite: increase

fall out v quarrel, argue, disagree, come to blows, row Opposite: make up

fallout n consequence, result, outcome, effect, knock-on effect

fall over v tumble, fall down, collapse, trip, trip over

fallow adj 1 uncultivated, unploughed, unplanted, unseeded, unused Opposite: cultivated 2 inactive, unproductive, idle, sterile, infertile Opposite: creative

fall short v be deficient, be wanting, be lacking,

prove inadequate, not make the grade *Opposite*: succeed

fall through v fail, go wrong, come to nothing, miscarry, misfire *Opposite*: succeed

fall to bits *see* **fall to pieces**

fall to pieces v disintegrate, come apart, crumble, fall apart, break up

false adj 1 incorrect, untruthful, untrue, wrong, dishonest *Opposite*: true 2 mistaken, erroneous, fallacious, misleading, deceiving *Opposite*: correct 3 artificial, bogus, sham, phoney, counterfeit *Opposite*: real

falsehood n 1 lie, untruth, tale, fiction, invention 2 deception, dishonesty, mendacity, deceit, deceitfulness. *See* COMPARE AND CONTRAST *at* lie.

false impression n mistaken belief, misconception, misreading, wrong idea, misapprehension

falseness n 1 incorrectness, dishonesty, deceit, deceitfulness, speciousness *Opposite*: honesty 2 mistakenness, erroneousness, wrongness, fallaciousness, deceptiveness *Opposite*: rightness

falsification n fabrication, distortion, forgery, misrepresentation, deception *Opposite*: correction

falsified adj fabricated, forged, untrue, counterfeit, false *Opposite*: true

falsify v fabricate, fake, forge, rig, misrepresent

falsity n falseness, spuriousness, hollowness, inaccuracy, deceptiveness *Opposite*: correctness

falter v 1 hesitate, pause, waver, stammer, stutter *Opposite*: continue 2 fail, weaken, fade, wane, abate *(fml or literary)* *Opposite*: rally 3 stumble, trip up, stagger, totter, sway. *See* COMPARE AND CONTRAST *at* hesitate.

faltering adj hesitant, tentative, halting, timid, uncertain *Opposite*: confident

fame n renown, celebrity, reputation, distinction, recognition *Opposite*: obscurity

famed adj well-known, famous, celebrated, renowned, eminent *Opposite*: unknown

familial adj family, ancestral, household, domestic, matrimonial

familiar adj 1 well-known, recognizable, common, customary, habitual *Opposite*: unfamiliar 2 accustomed, habitual, usual, recurring, everyday *Opposite*: unusual 3 acquainted, conversant, accustomed, used to, at home with 4 friendly, intimate, easy, informal, personal *Opposite*: formal

familiarity n 1 knowledge, understanding, acquaintance, awareness, ease *Opposite*: unfamiliarity 2 intimacy, informality, friendship, ease, closeness *Opposite*: formality

familiarization n acquaintance, getting used to, adjustment, adaptation, becoming accustomed

familiarize v acquaint, tell, explain, make clear, train

familiarize yourself v get to know, adapt, get used to, acclimatize yourself, acquaint yourself

familiarly adv intimately, closely, informally, cosily, casually *Opposite*: distantly

family n 1 relations, relatives, folks, children, family unit 2 lineage, descendants, dynasty, ancestors, line 3 category, genus, species, type, kind ■ adj domestic, household, everyday, intimate, private

family circle n relatives, relations, family, folks, people *(infml)*

family name n surname, last name, maternal name, paternal name, name

family tree n ancestry, pedigree, genealogy, ancestors, descendants

family unit n family, household, house, ménage *(fml)*

famine n food shortage, shortage, scarcity, dearth, want *Opposite*: abundance

famished adj hungry, ravenous, underfed, unfed, starving *(infml)* *Opposite*: sated

famous adj well-known, famed, celebrated, renowned, eminent *Opposite*: unknown

famously adv notably, memorably, eminently, prominently, distinctively 2 well, excellently, superbly, like a house on fire, like nobody's business

fan n admirer, enthusiast, aficionado, aficionada, follower ■ v 1 waft, blow, cool, wave, percolate 2 stir up, stimulate, provoke, increase, fuel *Opposite*: defuse

fanatic n 1 extremist, zealot, radical, fundamentalist, crusader 2 fan, enthusiast, devotee, buff, follower ■ adj fanatical, obsessive, passionate, addicted, extreme *Opposite*: indifferent

fanatical adj enthusiastic, passionate, obsessive, dedicated, fervent *Opposite*: indifferent

fanaticism n extremism, radicalism, fervour, zeal, keenness *Opposite*: indifference

fanciful adj imaginary, fantastic, whimsical, unbelievable, out of this world *Opposite*: prosaic

fancy adj 1 elaborate, ornate, decorative, ornamental, intricate 2 expensive, upmarket, lavish, extravagant, posh *(infml)* *Opposite*: plain ■ v 1 *(infml)* like, want, be attracted to, wish for, desire 2 imagine, picture, think, conjure, believe ■ n notion, dream, hope, desire, fantasy

fancy-free adj free, at liberty, unfettered, unconstrained, at leisure *Opposite*: tied

fanfare n display, trumpet blast, salute, elaboration, flourish

fan out v spread out, separate, expand, broaden, disperse *Opposite*: assemble

fantasize v daydream, imagine, dream, picture, visualize

fantastic adj 1 **excellent**, superb, great, marvellous, fabulous Opposite: awful 2 **bizarre**, eccentric, imaginary, strange, fanciful Opposite: normal 3 **incredible**, unbelievable, implausible, improbable, unlikely Opposite: plausible 4 **large**, big, enormous, huge, great Opposite: tiny

fantasy n 1 **dream**, daydream, image, fancy, hope 2 **imagination**, unreality, fancy, caprice, power of invention Opposite: reality

fan the flames v **exacerbate**, aggravate, inflame, make worse, worsen Opposite: calm

far adv 1 **far off**, far away, far afield, far and wide, distantly Opposite: close 2 **much**, greatly, considerably, a lot, significantly Opposite: barely ■ adj **distant**, remote, far-off, faraway, far-flung Opposite: near

faraway adj 1 **remote**, far-off, far-flung, outlying, distant Opposite: nearby 2 **dreamy**, preoccupied, bemused, distant, in a world of your own Opposite: alert

farce n **shambles**, travesty, absurdity, circus, sham

farcical adj **absurd**, ridiculous, ludicrous, silly, nonsensical Opposite: solemn

fare n 1 **price**, tariff, ticket, cost, fee 2 **passenger**, customer, client, payer, rider 3 **food**, menu, meal, dishes, provisions ■ v **do**, get on, manage, cope, get by

farewell n **goodbye**, sendoff, departure, valediction (fml), leave-taking (literary) Opposite: greeting

far-fetched adj **unbelievable**, fantastic, implausible, incredible, fanciful Opposite: believable

far-flung adj 1 **widespread**, extensive, sweeping, diffuse, wide-ranging Opposite: restricted 2 **distant**, remote, far-off, faraway, outlying Opposite: nearby

far from prep **anything but**, unlike, different from, poles apart Opposite: near

farm n 1 **smallholding**, estate, plantation, ranch, spread 2 **farmhouse**, farmstead, homestead, grange, ranch ■ v **cultivate**, work, till, plough, grow

farmer n **agriculturalist**, grower, market gardener, crofter, smallholder

farm hand n **farmworker**, labourer, seasonal worker, harvester

farming n **agribusiness**, agriculture, husbandry, cultivation, market gardening

farm out v **delegate**, subcontract, contract out, send out, hand out

farmstead n **homestead**, farm, ranch, grange

farmyard n **yard**, barnyard, cattle yard, stable yard

far-off adj **distant**, remote, far, faraway, far-flung Opposite: nearby

farrago n **hotchpotch**, potpourri, mishmash, medley, mixture

far-reaching adj **extensive**, sweeping, broad, across-the-board, comprehensive Opposite: limited

farsighted adj **wise**, visionary, farseeing, provident, prophetic Opposite: short-sighted

farsightedness n **foresight**, providence, prescience, forethought, wisdom Opposite: short-sightedness

farthest adj **furthest**, utmost, uttermost, outermost, furthermost

fascinate v **captivate**, charm, attract, enthral, mesmerize Opposite: repel

fascinated adj **captivated**, rapt, spellbound, charmed, involved Opposite: uninterested

fascinating adj **captivating**, charming, attractive, enthralling, mesmerizing Opposite: repellent

fascination n **captivation**, charm, attraction, appeal, allure

fashion n 1 **style**, way, manner, mode, method 2 **trend**, craze, fad, vogue, mode ■ v **shape**, mould, form, make, fit

fashionable adj **chic**, stylish, designer, up-to-the-minute, in Opposite: dated

fashion-conscious adj **chic**, stylish, fashionable, elegant, modish Opposite: old-fashioned

fast adj 1 **quick**, speedy, rapid, swift, express Opposite: slow 2 **sudden**, sharp, fleeting, momentary, short-lived Opposite: long-lasting 3 **ahead**, gaining, in advance Opposite: slow 4 **firm**, steadfast, constant, unwavering, faithful Opposite: fickle 5 (infml) **debauched**, wild, reckless, dissolute, profligate ■ adv 1 **quickly**, speedily, rapidly, swiftly, promptly Opposite: slowly 2 **firmly**, firm, tightly, tight, stable Opposite: loosely ■ v **abstain**, starve yourself, go without Opposite: feast ■ n **diet**, abstention, starvation, cleansing, hunger strike

fasten v 1 **secure**, attach, fix, clip, clasp Opposite: detach 2 **shut**, close, tie, tie up, do up Opposite: undo

fastener n **clasp**, fastening, tie, closure, popper

fastening n **clasp**, tie, closure, fastener, clip

fastidious adj 1 **demanding**, fussy, finicky, faddy, picky Opposite: easygoing 2 **delicate**, refined, particular, dainty, squeamish Opposite: slovenly

fastidiousness n 1 **fussiness**, meticulousness, care, carefulness, neatness Opposite: carelessness 2 **delicacy**, delicateness, daintiness, squeamishness Opposite: crudeness

fastness n **speediness**, swiftness, alacrity, speed, haste

fast track n **push**, boost, way forward, advancement, furthering

fast-track v **advance**, accelerate, forge ahead, progress, develop

fat n **1 oil**, lard, grease, shortening *(US)* **2 flab**, adipose tissue, padding, insulation, blubber *(infml)* ■ adj **1 overweight**, plump, chubby, stout, portly *Opposite*: thin **2 fatty**, greasy, oily, oleaginous, blubbery *(infml) Opposite*: lean **3 thick**, hefty, sizable, big, large *Opposite*: slim **4 rich**, wealthy, affluent, well-off, prosperous *Opposite*: poor

fatal adj **1 deadly**, lethal, incurable, terminal, mortal **2 ruinous**, disastrous, destructive, serious, grave *Opposite*: beneficial **3 decisive**, critical, crucial, fateful, pivotal *Opposite*: unimportant. *See* COMPARE AND CONTRAST *at* **deadly**.

fatalism n **resignation**, passivity, acceptance, stoicism, pessimism

fatalistic adj **philosophical**, defeatist, resigned, stoic, stoical

fatality n **1 death**, accident, casualty, loss, decease *(fml)* **2 deadliness**, deathliness, lethalness, noxiousness, fatness

fate n **1 destiny**, fortune, providence, luck, doom **2 outcome**, consequence, result, upshot, end

fated adj **predetermined**, destined, predestined, preordained, meant

fateful adj **1 critical**, important, momentous, significant, crucial *Opposite*: insignificant **2 ominous**, unfortunate, inauspicious, unlucky, ill-fated *Opposite*: lucky

father n **1 dad** *(infml)*, daddy *(infml)*, pa *(infml)*, pater *(dated slang)*, pop *(US infml)* **2 ancestor**, forefather, forebear, predecessor, progenitor *Opposite*: descendant **3 founder**, originator, initiator, contriver, architect **4 priest**, vicar, minister, padre, pastor ■ v **1 beget**, sire, engender, procreate, spawn **2 protect**, comfort, advise, look after, nurture

fatherhood n **paternity**, parenthood, kinship *Opposite*: motherhood

fatherland n **homeland**, native land, home, motherland, mother country

fatherliness n **protectiveness**, benevolence, affection, supportiveness, kindness

fatherly adj **paternal**, protective, concerned, caring, loving

fathom v **1 sound**, measure, plumb, gauge, probe **2 comprehend**, understand, work out, figure out, grasp

fathomable adj **comprehensible**, understandable, penetrable, graspable, intelligible *Opposite*: unfathomable

fathomless adj **1 deep**, immeasurable, unfathomable, bottomless, inestimable *Opposite*: shallow **2 incomprehensible**, immeasurable, unfathomable, obscure, incalculable *Opposite*: fathomable

fatigue n **exhaustion**, tiredness, weariness, weakness, lethargy *Opposite*: energy

fatigued adj **exhausted**, weary, tired, drained, worn-out *Opposite*: fresh

fatness n **obesity**, plumpness, chubbiness, stoutness, portliness *Opposite*: thinness

fatten v **feed up**, stuff, plump, build up, feed *Opposite*: starve

fattening adj **calorific**, fatty, rich, greasy, oily *Opposite*: slimming

fatten up v **feed up**, stuff, build up, feed, fatten *Opposite*: starve

fatty adj **greasy**, fat, oily, blubbery *(infml) Opposite*: lean

fatuity *(fml)* n **unintelligence**, complacency, silliness, stupidity, childishness *Opposite*: sensibleness

fatuous adj **unintelligent**, complacent, unaware, silly, stupid *Opposite*: sensible

fatuousness n **unintelligence**, complacency, silliness, foolishness, stupidity *Opposite*: sensibleness

fault n **1 responsibility**, liability, burden, culpability, accountability **2 shortcoming**, failing, weakness, defect, flaw *Opposite*: strength **3 blemish**, defect, imperfection, flaw, mark *Opposite*: bonus **4 mistake**, error, blunder, slip, omission ■ v **blame**, criticize, condemn, find fault with, question *Opposite*: praise. *See* COMPARE AND CONTRAST *at* **flaw**.

faultfinder n **critic**, carper, complainer, grumbler, nitpicker

faultfinding n **criticism**, grumbling, nitpicking, whingeing *(infml)* ■ adj **critical**, reproachful, carping, damning, unfavourable *Opposite*: uncritical

faultless adj **flawless**, perfect, impeccable, immaculate, blameless *Opposite*: imperfect

faultlessness n **flawlessness**, perfection, purity, impeccability, immaculateness *Opposite*: imperfection

fault line n **crack**, rift, split, fissure, fault

faulty adj **1 out of order**, defective, broken-down, broken, on the blink *(infml) Opposite*: perfect **2 flawed**, imperfect, incorrect, incoherent, contradictory *Opposite*: sound

fauna n **animals**, creatures, wildlife, beasts

faux adj **fake**, artificial, unreal, reproduction, false *Opposite*: genuine

favour n **1 good turn**, errand, kindness, courtesy, service *Opposite*: disservice **2 approval**, regard, kindness, esteem, sympathy *Opposite*: disfavour **3 gift**, trinket, token, present, keepsake ■ v **1 prefer**, choose, support, back, approve *Opposite*: reject **2 help**, assist, aid, advance, promote *Opposite*: hinder. *See* COMPARE AND CONTRAST *at* **regard**.

favourable adj **1 advantageous**, helpful, beneficial, opportune, convenient *Opposite*: unfavourable **2 promising**, auspicious, encouraging, propitious, bright *Opposite*: inauspicious **3 approving**, positive, constructive, good, sympathetic *Opposite*: negative

favourite adj **chosen**, pet, beloved, favoured ■ n **1 pet**, darling, beloved **2 choice**, preference, pick

favouritism *n* **preferentialism**, preference, partiality, nepotism, bias *Opposite*: impartiality

fawn *v* **flatter**, grovel, toady, kowtow, crawl *(infml)*

fawning *adj* **flattering**, obsequious, smarmy, sycophantic, servile

fax *n* **facsimile**, message, document, transmission, copy ■ *v* **send**, transmit, convey, communicate, telex

faze *v* **fluster**, disconcert, disturb, put off, deter *Opposite*: encourage

fear *n* **1 fright**, alarm, trepidation, terror, dread *Opposite*: assurance **2 worry**, concern, anxiety, apprehension, misgiving ■ *v* **dread**, be afraid, be scared, be apprehensive, be frightened

fearful *adj* **1 frightening**, terrifying, terrible, frightful, horrific **2 worried**, afraid, scared, apprehensive, frightened *Opposite*: fearless **3** *(infml)* **terrible**, dreadful, appalling, awful, horrible *Opposite*: wonderful

fearfulness *n* **1 scariness**, terribleness, frightfulness, horror, terror **2 apprehension**, anxiety, awe, fear, dread *Opposite*: bravery **3** *(infml)* **terribleness**, atrociousness, dreadfulness, awfulness, horror

fearless *adj* **courageous**, brave, bold, unafraid, daring *Opposite*: cowardly

fearlessness *n* **courage**, bravery, boldness, heroism, valour *Opposite*: cowardice. *See* COMPARE AND CONTRAST *at* **courage**.

fearsome *adj* **1 frightening**, formidable, terrifying, alarming, awesome **2 impressive**, awesome, formidable, awe-inspiring, tremendous

feasibility *n* **viability**, possibility, probability, likelihood, practicability *Opposite*: impossibility

feasible *adj* **viable**, possible, practicable, achievable, reasonable *Opposite*: impossible

feast *n* **1 banquet**, dinner, meal, buffet, spread *(infml)* **2 delight**, treat, indulgence, pleasure, joy **3 celebration**, festival, holiday, feast day, holy day ■ *v* **eat**, dine, indulge, partake, gobble *Opposite*: fast

feat *n* **achievement**, accomplishment, deed, exploit, act

feathery *adj* **downy**, fluffy, soft, light, plumy

feature *n* **1 facial feature**, contour, lineament *(literary)* **2 characteristic**, trait, mark, attribute, quality **3 article**, piece, report, item, story ■ *v* **1 contain**, include, present, introduce, bring out **2 perform**, star, appear, act, turn up **3 highlight**, star, include, showcase, show **4 figure**, appear, participate, take part, play a part

featureless *adj* **dull**, drab, bland, uninspired, unremarkable *Opposite*: distinctive

febrile *adj* **feverish**, fevered, flushed, hot, delirious

feckless *adj* **good-for-nothing**, useless, hopeless, spineless, feeble *Opposite*: dynamic

fecklessness *n* **uselessness**, hopelessness, spinelessness, feebleness, irresponsibility *Opposite*: dynamism

fecund *adj* **1 productive**, creative, prolific, industrious, fruitful **2** *(fml)* **fertile**, prolific, productive, fruitful, rich *Opposite*: infertile

fecundity *n* **fertility**, productiveness, fruitfulness, richness, prolificacy *Opposite*: infertility

federal *adj* **central**, centralized, national, state, civic *Opposite*: regional

federate *v* **1 unite**, join, amalgamate, come together, merge *Opposite*: devolve **2 associate**, unite, combine, join, confederate *Opposite*: disassociate

federation *n* **1 combination**, union, association, confederation, amalgamation **2 alliance**, coalition, confederation, grouping, partnership

fee *n* **1 payment**, remuneration, salary, pay, stipend **2 charge**, subscription, toll, tariff, cost. *See* COMPARE AND CONTRAST *at* **wage**.

feeble *adj* **1 weak**, frail, delicate, shaky, thin *Opposite*: robust **2 unconvincing**, ineffectual, poor, half-hearted, ineffective *Opposite*: convincing. *See* COMPARE AND CONTRAST *at* **weak**.

feebleness *n* **1 weakness**, fragility, delicateness, frailty, shakiness *Opposite*: robustness **2 ineffectuality**, weakness, half-heartedness, ineffectiveness *Opposite*: effectiveness

feed *v* **1 nourish**, nurse, suckle, breast-feed, serve *Opposite*: starve **2 eat**, consume, partake, devour, swallow **3 support**, sustain, nourish, nurture, encourage ■ *n* **feedstuff**, food, fodder, forage, provender

feedback *n* **response**, reaction, comment, criticism, advice

feed into *v* **1 contribute**, add to, supplement, enhance, add weight *Opposite*: draw on **2 connect**, join up, flow into, lead into, merge

feel *v* **1 touch**, finger, handle, sense, fondle **2 sense**, experience, undergo, be aware of, bear **3 think**, believe, consider, comprehend, understand ■ *n* **1 sensation**, touch, texture, finish, sense **2 impression**, atmosphere, air, feeling, ambience

feeler *n* **sensor**, antenna, whisker

feel for *v* **sympathize**, feel sorry for, pity, commiserate, empathize

feel-good *adj* **optimistic**, positive, satisfying, cheering, upbeat *(infml)*

feeling *n* **1 sensation**, sense, sensitivity, touch *Opposite*: numbness **2 emotion**, sentiment, mood, reaction, sense **3 affection**, concern, regard, love, sympathy *Opposite*: antipathy **4 opinion**, view, point of view, belief, impression **5 air**, atmosphere, feel, ambience, mood **6 hunch**, instinct, suspicion, intuition, idea

feel like *v* **1 want**, desire, crave, wish, long for **2 seem**, appear, resemble, look like

feel sorry for *v* **pity**, empathize with, feel for,

commiserate with, sympathize with

feign v **pretend**, put on, fake, simulate, make believe

feigned adj **put on**, artificial, insincere, pretend, fake Opposite: genuine

feint n **trick**, stratagem, ploy, ruse, gambit

feisty (infml) adj **lively**, spirited, energetic, aggressive, hearty Opposite: feeble

felicitations (fml) n **congratulations**, compliments, best wishes, blessings, greetings

felicitous adj **1 appropriate**, apt, suitable, apposite, well-chosen Opposite: inapposite **2 fortunate**, lucky, fortuitous, timely, happy Opposite: unfortunate

felicity n **1 happiness**, contentment, joy, pleasure, luck Opposite: unhappiness **2 appropriateness**, aptness, suitability, appositeness, fittingness Opposite: inappropriateness

feline adj **graceful**, slinky, subtle, elegant, stealthy

fell v **1 cut down**, chop down, hew **2 knock down**, knock out, floor, demolish (infml), deck (infml) Opposite: set up

fellow n **1** (dated) **man**, boy, guy (infml), chap (infml), bloke (infml) **2** (dated) **companion**, colleague, associate, partner, comrade **3 member**, associate, researcher, academic

fellow feeling n **sympathy**, empathy, support, affinity, mutuality Opposite: hostility

fellowship n **1 communion**, companionship, camaraderie, comradeship, friendship Opposite: enmity **2 society**, association, college, affiliation, cooperative

felon n **criminal**, offender, lawbreaker, delinquent, villain (infml)

felony n **crime**, offence, misdemeanour, wrongdoing, lawbreaking

female adj **feminine**, womanly, ladylike, girlish Opposite: masculine ■ n **woman**, lady, girl Opposite: male

feminine adj **female**, womanly, ladylike, girlish Opposite: masculine

femininity n **femaleness**, feminineness, womanliness, girlishness Opposite: masculinity

feminism n **women's movement**, women's liberation, women's rights, women's suffrage, women's studies

feminist n **suffragist**, suffragette, activist, radical, campaigner

fen n **marsh**, wetland, fenland, bog, lowland

fence n **barrier**, boundary, hurdle, hedge, railing ■ v **1 enclose**, hedge, shut in, restrict, confine Opposite: open up **2 evade**, parry, feint, dodge, fight off

fencing n **1 fence**, railing, paling, barrier, palisade **2 repartee**, banter, wordplay, raillery, badinage

fender n **fireguard**, fire screen, guard, screen

fend for v **look after**, take care of, provide for, defend, support

fend for yourself v **take care of yourself**, look after yourself, support yourself, manage on your own, survive

fend off v **keep away**, repel, repulse, discourage, ward off Opposite: welcome

fenland n **marsh**, bog, fen, wetland, lowland Opposite: desert

feral adj **wild**, untamed, undomesticated, savage, uncontrollable Opposite: domesticated

ferment v **agitate**, inflame, stir up, incite, provoke ■ n **uproar**, tumult, confusion, excitement, commotion Opposite: peace

ferocious adj **1 fierce**, vicious, violent, cruel, brutal Opposite: gentle **2 intense**, strong, heated, raging, extreme Opposite: mild

ferociousness see **ferocity**

ferocity n **1 fierceness**, aggressiveness, viciousness, violence, brutality Opposite: gentleness **2 intensity**, strength, extremeness, severity Opposite: mildness

ferret v **hunt**, search, search out, rummage, dig out

ferret around v **look for**, search out, ferret about, delve, search around

ferret out v **1 discover**, uncover, find, reveal, unveil Opposite: conceal **2 track down**, flush out, uncover, hunt down, catch Opposite: hide

ferry v **transport**, carry, ship, convey, transmit

fertile adj **1 productive**, fruitful, prolific, generative, fecund (fml) Opposite: infertile **2 lush**, productive, abundant, rich, fruitful Opposite: barren

fertility n **fruitfulness**, richness, lushness, productiveness, fecundity Opposite: barrenness

fertilization n **1 insemination**, impregnation, pollination, artificial insemination, donor insemination **2 fertilizer application**, manuring, composting, top dressing, nourishment

fertilize v **1 inseminate**, impregnate, pollinate **2 manure**, feed, top-dress, compost, enrich Opposite: exhaust

fertilizer n **manure**, compost, top dressing, soil enricher, enricher

fervent adj **keen**, avid, ardent, eager, enthusiastic Opposite: indifferent

fervid adj **impassioned**, intense, heated, burning

fervour n **passion**, dedication, enthusiasm, eagerness, zeal Opposite: indifference

fester v **rankle**, irritate, gall, embitter, annoy

festival n **feast day**, holiday, celebration, anniversary, birthday

festive adj **celebratory**, cheerful, joyful, merry, happy Opposite: sad

festiveness n **merriness**, joyfulness, cheerfulness, happiness, jolliness Opposite: lugubriousness

festivities n **revels**, revelry, celebrations, merriment, partying

festivity n 1 **good cheer**, rejoicing, merriment, pleasure, enjoyment *Opposite*: sadness 2 **party**, event, do (*infml*), gala, carnival

festoon n **garland**, decoration, swag, ornament, chain ■ v **decorate**, adorn, swathe, hang, drape *Opposite*: strip

festooned adj **garlanded**, wreathed, hung, decorated, draped *Opposite*: unadorned

fetch v 1 **get**, obtain, bring, carry, bring back 2 **sell for**, make, raise, get, draw

fetching adj **attractive**, eye-catching, handsome, good-looking, stylish *Opposite*: unattractive

fete *see* **fête**

fête n 1 **bazaar**, celebration, event, fair, gala 2 **holiday**, anniversary, jubilee, centenary, feast day ■ v **honour**, commemorate, lionize, entertain, praise

fetid adj **rotten**, putrid, foul, rank, fusty *Opposite*: fresh

fetish n 1 **obsession**, fixation, mania, craze, engrossment *Opposite*: aversion 2 **talisman**, charm, idol, image, totem

fetishize v **make a fetish of**, worship, idolize, be obsessed by, get hung up on (*slang*)

fetter n **shackle**, bond, chain, yoke, handcuff ■ v **tie**, bind, chain, restrain, hamper *Opposite*: unfetter

feud n **dispute**, argument, row, quarrel, bad blood *Opposite*: friendship ■ v **fight**, argue, dispute, quarrel, disagree

feudal adj **out-of-date**, outdated, old-fashioned, medieval, primitive *Opposite*: modern

fever n 1 **temperature**, infection, disease, illness, malaise 2 **passion**, fervour, excitement, agitation, vehemence

fevered adj **feverish**, agitated, restless, frenzied, fanatical *Opposite*: calm

feverish adj **excited**, agitated, nervous, heated, intense *Opposite*: tranquil

few adj **insufficient**, a small number of, hardly any, not many, only some *Opposite*: many

fey adj **whimsical**, fanciful, otherworldly, unworldly, fantastical

fiasco n **debacle**, disaster, mess, shambles, failure *Opposite*: success

fiat n 1 **official sanction**, sanction, authorization, permission, agreement 2 **order**, command, decree, edict, instruction

fib (*infml*) n **untruth**, white lie, lie, tall tale, falsification *Opposite*: truth ■ v **lie**, not tell the truth, misrepresent, perjure yourself, tell stories *Opposite*: come clean (*infml*). See COMPARE AND CONTRAST *at* lie.

fibber (*infml*) n **liar**, deceiver, fabricator, prevaricator, perjurer

fibbing (*infml*) n **lying**, prevarication, falsification, evasion

fibre n 1 **thread**, strand, string, filament, twine 2 **makeup**, composition, structure, character,

stuff 3 **grit**, strength, fortitude, backbone, character *Opposite*: weakness

WORD BANK
❑ **types of fibre** cane, coconut matting, coir, fibreglass, jute, kapok, matting, raffia, ramie, rattan, seagrass, sisal, straw, wicker

fibrous adj **tough**, leathery, stringy, rubbery, chewy *Opposite*: tender

fickle adj **inconsistent**, changeable, capricious, inconstant, indecisive *Opposite*: constant

fickleness n **inconsistency**, changeability, capriciousness, inconstancy, indecisiveness *Opposite*: constancy

fiction n 1 **creative writing**, works of fiction, literature, narrative, novels *Opposite*: nonfiction 2 **work of fiction**, novel, fantasy, story, short story 3 **falsehood**, fabrication, lie, untruth, misrepresentation *Opposite*: fact 4 **invention**, fantasy, imagination, nonsense, illusion *Opposite*: reality

fictional adj **imaginary**, imagined, illusory, unreal, false *Opposite*: real

fictionalization n **fictional account**, fictional version, account, narrative, story

fictionalize v **dramatize**, novelize, recount, adapt

fictitious adj **untrue**, fabricated, invented, made-up, false *Opposite*: factual

fiddle n (*infml*) **swindle**, fraud, cheat, hoax, con ■ v 1 **fidget**, play, play around, toy, pick at 2 **meddle**, tamper, interfere, mess, mess about (*infml*) 3 **tinker**, manipulate, adjust, tweak, jiggle *Opposite*: leave alone 4 (*infml*) **defraud**, swindle, cheat, con, hoax 5 (*infml*) **falsify**, doctor, tamper with, manipulate, fix

fiddling adj **petty**, unimportant, trifling, trivial, insignificant *Opposite*: significant ■ n (*infml*) **fraud**, deception, cheating, fixing, swindling

fiddly (*infml*) adj **tricky**, awkward, difficult, complex, detailed *Opposite*: easy

fidelity n **loyalty**, faithfulness, reliability, trustworthiness, dependability *Opposite*: infidelity

fidget v 1 **twitch**, squirm, fret, shuffle, jiggle *Opposite*: freeze 2 **fiddle**, play, play around, toy, jiggle *Opposite*: leave alone

fidgetiness n **twitchiness**, fretfulness, restlessness, jitteriness, uneasiness *Opposite*: stillness

fidgety adj **twitchy**, fretful, restless, squirmy, uneasy *Opposite*: still

field n 1 **meadow**, pasture, grassland, grazing, lea (*literary*) 2 **sports ground**, playing field, pitch, turf, arena 3 **subject**, area, topic, discipline, theme ■ v 1 **catch**, retrieve, pick up, go after, fetch 2 **deal with**, handle, tackle, take care of, see to *Opposite*: ignore

fielder n **player**, cricketer, baseball player, sportsperson, outfielder *Opposite*: batter

field test n **field trial**, test, trial, clinical trial, pilot

field-test v **test**, try out, study, put through its paces, trial

fieldwork n **research**, information-gathering, investigation, fact-finding, exploration

fiend n **villain**, evil person, brute, beast, monster *Opposite*: angel

fiendish adj **1 cruel**, evil, brutal, monstrous, villainous *Opposite*: pleasant **2 cunning**, ingenious, clever, crafty, devilish **3 impossible**, tricky, difficult, hard, perplexing *Opposite*: straightforward

fiendishly adv **1 cruelly**, brutally, wickedly, inhumanly, maliciously *Opposite*: pleasantly **2 extremely**, excessively, extraordinarily, incredibly, impossibly

fierce adj **1 violent**, ferocious, aggressive, brutal, severe *Opposite*: gentle **2 intense**, violent, extreme, savage, ferocious *Opposite*: mild **3 strong**, powerful, profound, deep, turbulent *Opposite*: mild

fiercely adv **1 violently**, ferociously, aggressively, brutally, severely *Opposite*: gently **2 ferociously**, intensely, strongly, brightly, hotly *Opposite*: feebly **3 extremely**, exceedingly, very, passionately, resolutely *Opposite*: mildly

fierceness n **1 ferocity**, brutality, violence, aggressiveness, sternness *Opposite*: gentleness **2 intensity**, violence, strength, power, fury *Opposite*: mildness

fiery adj **1 burning**, blistering, sweltering, blazing, flaming *Opposite*: icy **2 fierce**, passionate, heated, angry, furious *Opposite*: mild

fiesta n **feast**, holiday, festival, carnival, celebration

fifth wheel n **supernumerary**, ghost at the feast, hanger-on *(infml)*, wallflower *(infml)*, gooseberry *(infml)*

fifty-fifty adv **half and half**, half each, two ways, equally, halfway

fight v **1 brawl**, box, stuff, scrap, wrestle **2 wage war**, clash, struggle, battle, skirmish **3 dispute**, oppose, struggle, contest, wrangle *Opposite*: accept ■ n **1 conflict**, battle, engagement, skirmish, clash **2 scrap**, tussle, brawl, fistfight, fisticuffs *(infml)* **3 argument**, dispute, wrangle, clash, row *Opposite*: reconciliation **4 contest**, match, bout, competition, round

COMPARE AND CONTRAST CORE MEANING: a struggle between opposing armed forces

fight a physical struggle between individuals or groups such as battalions or armies; **battle** a large-scale fight involving combat between opposing forces, warships, or aircraft as part of an ongoing war or campaign; **war** a state of hostilities between nations, states, or factions involving the use of arms and the occurrence of a series of battles; **conflict** warfare between opposing forces, especially a prolonged and bitter but sporadic struggle; **engagement** a hostile encounter involving military forces; **skirmish** a brief minor fight, usually one that is part of a larger conflict; **clash** a short fierce encounter, usually involving physical combat.

fight back v **1 retaliate**, defend yourself, put up a fight, riposte, resist *Opposite*: attack **2 repress**, control, hold back, suppress, push back *Opposite*: let out

fighter n **boxer**, wrestler, pugilist, prizefighter

fighting adj **aggressive**, belligerent, pugnacious, hostile, rebellious *Opposite*: pacifist ■ n **combat**, hostility, unrest, warfare, violence *Opposite*: peace

fight off v **fend off**, drive away, resist, repulse, repel *Opposite*: attack

fight shy of v **avoid**, evade, eschew, dodge *Opposite*: confront

figment n **fabrication**, creation, invention, illusion, fantasy

figurative adj **metaphorical**, symbolic, allegorical, nonliteral, emblematic *Opposite*: literal

figure n **1 number**, numeral, character, symbol, digit **2 amount**, cost, sum, quantity, total **3 shape**, form, outline, stature, build **4 person**, dignitary, celebrity, notable, individual **5 diagram**, chart, picture, table, illustration ■ v **1 play a part**, feature, appear, be included, be incorporated **2 reckon**, guess, believe, think, suppose *Opposite*: doubt

figure of speech n **expression**, symbol, idiom, image, rhetorical expression

WORD BANK
❑ **types of figure of speech** alliteration, antonomasia, assonance, chiasmus, hendiadys, hypallage, hyperbaton, hyperbole, litotes, meiosis, metaphor, metonymy, oxymoron, personification, prosopopoeia, simile, synecdoche, zeugma

figure out v **work out**, deduce, discover, fathom, decipher. *See* COMPARE AND CONTRAST *at* **deduce**.

figurine n **statuette**, figure, model, ornament, statue

filament n **thread**, strand, string, fibre, wire

filch *(infml)* v **steal**, rob, thieve, walk off with, snatch. *See* COMPARE AND CONTRAST *at* **steal**.

file n **1 folder**, sleeve, dossier, heading, box file **2 report**, dossier, profile, record, information **3 line**, queue, row, column, procession ■ v **1 record**, categorize, put on record, keep, file away **2 rub**, rasp, scrape, sand, smooth **3 march**, troop, parade, snake, walk in single file

filial adj **familial**, family, loving, devoted *Opposite*: parental

filigree n **tracery**, lacy pattern, lattice, latticework, lace

filing n **shaving**, particle, splinter, shard, shred

fill v **1 fill up**, pack, stuff, cram, jam *Opposite*: empty **2 pervade**, imbue, impart, permeate, saturate **3 plug**, block, block up, seal, stop *Opposite*: clear **4 satisfy**, fulfil, meet, satiate, provide for *Opposite*: fall short

filler n **1 padding**, stuffing, wadding, filling, packing **2 plaster**, grout, putty, caulking, pitch

fillet v **bone**, clean, prepare, gut, scale

fill in v 1 **complete**, fill out, write out, answer 2 **take somebody's place**, stand in, substitute, deputize, cover 3 **bring up to date**, put in the picture, give the latest, give the lowdown 4 **clog**, plug, choke, dam up, block

fill-in n **substitute**, stand-in, temp, replacement, temporary worker

filling n 1 **inside**, contents, guts, innards (infml) 2 **stuffing**, padding, bulk, wadding, packing ■ adj **satisfying**, substantial, big, heavy, rich Opposite: meagre

filling station n **petrol station**, garage, service station, services, service area

fillip n **boost**, tonic, spur, stimulus, impetus Opposite: knock

fill out v 1 **complete**, fill in, write out, answer 2 **put on weight**, fatten up, bulk up, grow, develop Opposite: waste away

fill up v 1 **refill**, fill, replenish, load, stock up Opposite: empty 2 **satisfy**, satiate, stuff, bloat, fill

film n 1 **picture**, big screen, silver screen, flick (infml), movie (US) 2 **layer**, coat, coating, covering, sheet ■ v **record**, video, tape, capture, shoot

film over v **mist over**, mist up, glaze over, steam up, cloud over Opposite: clear

filmy adj **light**, airy, translucent, transparent, diaphanous Opposite: solid

filter n **sieve**, strainer, colander, mesh, riddle ■ v 1 **sort**, sort out, separate out, stream, categorize Opposite: mingle 2 **sift**, sieve, strain, clean, clarify 3 **seep**, ooze, trickle, penetrate, permeate

filth n 1 **dirt**, grime, rubbish, refuse, soil 2 **smut**, rudeness, lewdness, immorality, obscenity

filthiness n 1 **dirtiness**, griminess, dirt, grubbiness, foulness Opposite: cleanliness 2 **lewdness**, rudeness, immorality, smut, obscenity Opposite: decency

filthy adj 1 **dirty**, grimy, muddy, soiled, grubby Opposite: clean 2 **rude**, indecent, lewd, obscene, offensive Opposite: decent. See COMPARE AND CONTRAST at **dirty**.

filtration n **percolation**, separation, purification, clarification, categorization

fin n 1 **appendage**, flipper, paddle, dorsal fin, organ 2 **projection**, stabilizer, blade, paddle, propeller

finagle (infml) v **trick**, cheat, manipulate, engineer, wheedle

final adj 1 **last**, concluding, closing, ending, finishing Opposite: first 2 **conclusive**, definitive, absolute, decisive, irrevocable Opposite: provisional ■ n **round**, match, game, decider, last leg

finale n **ending**, end, climax, culmination, finish Opposite: prelude

finalist n **qualifier**, contestant, challenger, runner-up, contender Opposite: also-ran

finality n **conclusiveness**, decisiveness, definiteness, inevitability, irrevocability Opposite: uncertainty

finalization n **completion**, conclusion, agreement, settlement, decision Opposite: commencement (fml)

finalize v **confirm**, settle, decide, firm up, complete Opposite: start

finally adv 1 **at last**, at length, at long last, ultimately, after all Opposite: initially 2 **conclusively**, completely, decisively, irrevocably, definitively Opposite: tentatively 3 **lastly**, in conclusion, to conclude, to finish, to end Opposite: firstly

finance n **money**, economics, business, investment, backing ■ v **back**, invest in, pay for, fund, support

finances n **money**, funds, assets, cash, capital

financial adj **monetary**, fiscal, economic, pecuniary, monetarist

financier n **banker**, investor, backer, sponsor, investment banker

find v 1 **discover**, locate, come across, hit upon, unearth 2 **recover**, regain, get back, retrieve, discover Opposite: lose 3 **realize**, understand, get, obtain, attain ■ n **discovery**, bargain, treasure trove, treasure, novelty

find fault with v **criticize**, nitpick, pick holes in, take to task, have a go at (infml) Opposite: praise. See COMPARE AND CONTRAST at **criticize**.

finding n 1 **discovery**, conclusion, result, verdict, outcome 2 **verdict**, ruling, result, sentence, decision

find out v 1 **discover**, learn, realize, observe, note 2 **catch**, expose, uncover, reveal, unmask

fine adj 1 **light**, slight, faint, thin, tenuous Opposite: heavy 2 (infml) **acceptable**, satisfactory, good, all right, okay (infml) Opposite: unsatisfactory 3 **tiny**, minute, light, delicate, small 4 **bright**, sunny, warm, beautiful, fair Opposite: dull 5 **delicate**, dainty, slender, refined, thin Opposite: coarse 6 **outstanding**, superb, excellent, superior, exceptional Opposite: poor 7 **subtle**, keen, sharp, skilled, refined Opposite: dull ■ n **penalty**, punishment, payment, forfeit, levy ■ v **penalize**, punish, levy, charge

fineness n 1 **excellence**, greatness, superiority, quality, distinction Opposite: poorness 2 **delicacy**, sheerness, thinness, narrowness, slenderness Opposite: thickness

finer points n **details**, minutiae, nuances, small print, nitty-gritty (infml)

finery n **regalia**, jewellery, evening dress, morning dress, dress uniform

finesse n 1 **skill**, flair, grace, poise, assurance Opposite: clumsiness 2 **subtlety**, delicacy, diplomacy, tact, discretion Opposite: tactlessness

finest adj **premium**, handpicked, optimum, best, supreme Opposite: worst

fine-tune v **adjust**, modify, tune, polish up, perfect

fine-tuning n **adjustment**, refinement, modification, perfection, tuning

finger n **1 digit**, limb, member, extremity **2 portion**, piece, slither, slice, bit *Opposite*: hunk ▪ v **handle**, touch, feel, manipulate, toy with

fingerprint n **1 impression**, print, mark, pattern, thumbprint **2 characteristic**, identification, evidence, pattern, diagnostic

fingertip adj **sensitive**, delicate, fine, sensitized, hair-trigger

finicky adj **fastidious**, fussy, picky, particular, choosy *(infml) Opposite*: sloppy. *See* COMPARE AND CONTRAST *at* careful.

finish v **1 end**, stop, terminate, close, cease *Opposite*: start **2 use up**, drain, exhaust, polish off, empty *Opposite*: stock up **3** *(infml)* **destroy**, ruin, annihilate, defeat, exhaust **4 polish**, buff, rub, varnish, lacquer ▪ n **1 end**, ending, close, conclusion, completion *Opposite*: start **2 surface**, texture, appearance, quality, varnish

finished adj **1 over**, ended, broken down, broken up, broken off **2 refined**, perfect, polished, elegant, professional *Opposite*: rough **3 polished**, buffed, varnished, glossed, gilded *Opposite*: unfinished **4 ruined**, wrecked, lost, destroyed, devastated

finish off v **1 complete**, conclude, finalize, bring to an end, wind up *Opposite*: start up **2 use up**, eat up, exhaust, polish off, demolish *(infml) Opposite*: stock up **3** *(infml)* **eliminate**, kill, exterminate, dispatch, dispose of

finite adj **limited**, restricted, determinate, fixed, set *Opposite*: infinite

fire n **1 blaze**, flames, bonfire, conflagration, inferno **2 combustion**, conflagration, ignition **3 passion**, ardour, fervour, excitement, enthusiasm *Opposite*: apathy ▪ v **1 shoot**, set off, detonate, trigger, launch **2 excite**, arouse, inspire, enthuse, enliven **3** *(infml)* **dismiss**, let go, lay off, throw out, sack *(infml) Opposite*: take on

fire alarm n **bell**, siren, klaxon, buzzer, warning

firearm n **gun**, weapon, handgun, pistol, rifle

fireball n **ball lightning**, ball of fire, flash, lightning

firebrand n **troublemaker**, agitator, hothead, revolutionary, demagogue

firebreak n **clearing**, opening, strip, break, barrier

fire drill n **fire practice**, drill, rehearsal, evacuation, exercise

fire escape n **stairway**, ladder, escape hatch, staircase, emergency exit

fireguard n **1 fire screen**, screen, guard, fender, frame **2 firebreak**, clearing, strip, glade, opening

firelight n **glow**, glimmer, flame, flare, blaze

fireplace n **hearth**, inglenook, fire, fireside, chimney corner

firepower n **weapons**, arms, guns, armaments, munitions

fire practice n **fire drill**, drill, practice, rehearsal, evacuation

fireproof adj **incombustible**, nonflammable, flame-retardant, fire-retardant, fire-resistant *Opposite*: combustible

fireside n **hearth**, inglenook, fireplace, chimney corner

firetrap n **fire hazard**, danger, deathtrap *(infml)*

fire up v **1 get going**, initiate, start off, set off, launch **2 ignite**, fire, light, kindle, set alight **3 enthuse**, motivate, incite, stimulate, excite

firewood n **logs**, kindling, wood, fuel

firing n **gunfire**, fire, shooting, shots

firing line n **1 front line**, front, battlefield, vanguard **2 forefront**, vanguard, lead, cutting edge, leading edge

firm adj **1 solid**, compact, hard, rigid, dense *Opposite*: soft **2 secure**, stable, fixed, strong, safe *Opposite*: unstable **3 determined**, certain, definite, fixed, resolved *Opposite*: uncertain ▪ v **harden**, stiffen, solidify, set, press down *Opposite*: soften ▪ n **company**, business, partnership, multinational, corporation

firmly adv **1 tightly**, securely, steadily, powerfully, strongly *Opposite*: loosely **2 resolutely**, inflexibly, determinedly, decisively, definitely *Opposite*: irresolutely

firmness n **1 hardness**, rigidity, compactness, density, stiffness *Opposite*: softness **2 stability**, steadiness, strength, safety *Opposite*: instability **3 determination**, steadfastness, resolve, resolution, decisiveness *Opposite*: uncertainty

firm up v **1 settle**, conclude, tie up, confirm, establish **2 stabilize**, balance, steady, settle *Opposite*: destabilize

first adj **1 initial**, primary, original, opening, earliest *Opposite*: last **2 chief**, head, principal, leading, major *Opposite*: minor **3 fundamental**, basic, key, elementary, primary *Opposite*: advanced ▪ adv **firstly**, initially, at the outset, in the beginning, to begin with *Opposite*: lastly

first aid n **emergency treatment**, medical treatment, medical care, resuscitation, mouth-to-mouth

first-class adj **best**, superb, first-rate, unrivalled, excellent *Opposite*: poor

firsthand adj **direct**, actual, immediate, personal *Opposite*: second-hand ▪ adv **directly**, personally, from the horse's mouth, straight *Opposite*: indirectly

first light n **dawn**, daybreak, sunrise, daylight, morning *Opposite*: dusk

firstly adv **to start with**, initially, first of all, at the outset, first *Opposite*: lastly

first name n name, Christian name, given name, moniker *(slang)* Opposite: surname

first-rate adj **best**, superb, first-class, unrivalled, excellent Opposite: poor

firth n estuary, inlet, fjord, sound, creek

fish v **1 catch fish**, angle, go fishing, trawl, cast a line **2 search**, seek, trawl, probe, dig around

WORD BANK
❏ **types of flatfish** angelfish, brill, flounder, halibut, lemon sole, manta ray, plaice, pompano, ray, skate, sole, stingray, turbot
❏ **types of freshwater fish** bass, bream, carp, catfish, crappie, goldfish, grayling, guppy, loach, minnow, mullet, Nile perch, perch, pike, piranha, roach, stickleback, tench, tilapia, trout
❏ **types of sea fish** anchovy, anglerfish, cod, coley, dogfish, eel, haddock, hake, herring, John Dory, ling, mackerel, monkfish, pilchard, salmon, sardine, sea bream, shark, sprat, sturgeon, whitebait, whiting
❏ **types of tropical sea fish** barracuda, flying fish, kingfish, mahi-mahi, marlin, pomfret, sailfish, sawfish, snapper, swordfish, tuna
❏ **parts of a fish** air bladder, anal fin, dorsal fin, fin, gill, pectoral fin, pelvic fin, roe, scale, tail

fish for v search for, angle for, be after, invite, hope for

fishing n angling, casting, trawling, harpooning, whaling

fishnet n mesh, netting, net, tulle, gauze

fish out *(infml)* v **pull out**, take out, haul out, drag out, dig out Opposite: put in

fishy *(infml)* adj dubious, suspicious, irregular, underhand, shady Opposite: aboveboard

fission n breaking up, separation, splitting, division, schism Opposite: fusion

fissure n crack, split, crevice, fracture, cleft

fist n **1** *(infml)* **hand**, knuckle, paw *(infml)*, duke *(slang)*, mitt *(slang)* **2 fistful**, handful, bunch, wad

fistfight n brawl, scrap, scuffle, fisticuffs, skirmish

fistful n handful, bunch, fist, wad

fit v **1 measure**, tailor, size, take in, take up **2 match**, suit, correspond, tally **3 install**, put in, mount, fix, provide with ■ adj **1 appropriate**, fitting, right, proper, acceptable Opposite: unfit **2 healthy**, well, fine, in fine fettle, hale and hearty Opposite: unfit ■ n convulsion, spasm, seizure, attack, turn

fitful adj disturbed, sporadic, broken, restless, irregular Opposite: undisturbed

fit in v **1 conform**, blend in, integrate, go well with, assimilate **2 find time for**, squeeze in, manage, cope with, take on

fitness n **1 health**, strength, robustness, vigour, wellbeing Opposite: weakness **2 suitability**, appropriateness, aptness, qualification, capability Opposite: inappropriateness

fit out v equip, supply, set up, kit out, outfit

fitted adj **1 tailored**, close-fitting, formfitting, trim, snug Opposite: baggy **2 built-in**, fixed, permanent, attached, incorporated Opposite: freestanding

fitting adj suitable, appropriate, right, correct, proper Opposite: inappropriate

fittingness n suitability, appropriateness, rightness, correctness, properness Opposite: inappropriateness

fittings n accessories, decorations, furniture, equipment

WORD BANK
❏ **types of general fittings** ceiling rose, chimneypiece, dado, fender, fireplace, looking glass, mantel, mantelpiece, mirror, picture rail, radiator, skirting board, socket, wainscot
❏ **types of plumbing fittings** ball cock, basin, bath, bathtub, bidet, drinking fountain, hand basin, hot tub, nozzle, plumbing, rose, sauna, shower, sink, sitz bath, spa, spout, sprinkler, tank, tap, toilet, towel rail, tub, vanity unit, wash-hand basin, washbasin, washbowl, whirlpool bath

fit up v equip, supply, set up, kit out, fit out

five o'clock shadow n beard, stubble, bristles

fix v **1 mend**, repair, correct, put to rights, make right **2** *(infml)* **prepare**, make ready, get ready, cook, rustle up *(infml)* **3 agree**, arrange, establish, organize, set up Opposite: cancel **4 fasten**, attach, glue, stick, secure Opposite: detach **5** *(infml)* **rig**, manipulate, massage, arrange, fiddle *(infml)* ■ n **1** *(infml)* **dilemma**, predicament, tight spot, quandary, corner **2** *(infml)* **solution**, answer, resolution, remedy **3** *(infml)* **con**, fraud, swindle, trick, setup *(infml)* **4** *(slang)* **dose**, injection, shot *(infml)*, hit *(slang)*

fixated adj obsessed, absorbed, fanatical, engrossed, paranoid Opposite: indifferent

fixation n obsession, fascination, mania, passion, addiction

fixative n **1 preservative**, preserver, spray, varnish, coating **2 glue**, adhesive, cement, paste, gum

fixed adj **1 secure**, immovable, immobile, static, motionless Opposite: fluid **2 set**, unchanging, flat, preset, predetermined Opposite: variable **3 rigid**, inflexible, hard-and-fast, cast-iron Opposite: flexible

fixedness n secureness, immovability, immobility, motionlessness, stability Opposite: fluidity

fixture n **1 match**, game, meeting, contest, clash **2 accessory**, decoration, fitting

fix up v **1 arrange**, schedule, plan, make plans for, organize **2 repair**, renew, refurbish, renovate, redecorate

fizz v effervesce, sparkle, bubble, froth, foam ■ n effervescence, sparkle, bubbles, froth, foam

fizzle v **1 fizz**, hiss, sizzle, spit, sputter **2 fail**, fade away, peter out, tail off, disappear Opposite: flourish

fizzy *adj* **effervescent**, sparkling, bubbly, carbonated, foamy *Opposite*: still

fjord *n* **inlet**, sound, creek, firth

flab *n* **fat**, podginess, chubbiness, plumpness, corpulence

flabbergast *(infml)* *v* **amaze**, astonish, astound, dumbfound, stun

flabbergasted *(infml) adj* **amazed**, astonished, astounded, dumbfounded, dumbstruck

flabbiness *(infml) n* **flaccidity**, looseness, softness, slackness, floppiness *Opposite*: firmness

flabby *(infml) adj* **flaccid**, loose, soft, slack, saggy *Opposite*: firm

flaccid *adj* **limp**, soft, loose, drooping, sagging *Opposite*: firm

flag *n* **standard**, ensign, pennant, pennon, colours ■ *v* 1 **weaken**, tire, weary, wane, fade *Opposite*: rally 2 **mark**, highlight, identify, label, signal

flagellate *v* **whip**, flog, scourge, lash, beat

flagellation *n* **whipping**, flogging, scourging, lashing, beating

flagging *adj* **weakening**, tiring, wearied, waning, fading *Opposite*: rallying

flagon *n* **bottle**, carafe, flask, canteen, carboy

flagpole *n* **flagstaff**, staff, pole, mast, post

flagrant *adj* **blatant**, scandalous, obvious, deliberate, brazen *Opposite*: covert

flagship *n* 1 **warship**, man-of-war, ship of the line, capital ship, battleship 2 **star**, leader, jewel, pearl, pièce de résistance ■ *adj* **prize**, star, lead, top, leading

flagstaff *see* **flagpole**

flagstone *n* **paving stone**, kerbstone, slab, block, paver

flag-waving *n* **patriotism**, chauvinism, jingoism, nationalism, loyalism

flail *v* 1 **thrash**, wave, whirl, flap, flounder 2 **flog**, beat, batter, hit, strike

flail about *v* **flounder**, writhe, struggle, squirm, stagger

flair *n* 1 **talent**, skill, aptitude, feel, gift *Opposite*: ineptitude 2 **elegance**, stylishness, style, chic, panache *Opposite*: inelegance. *See* COMPARE AND CONTRAST *at* **talent**.

flak *(infml) n* **criticism**, condemnation, censure, disapproval, hostility *Opposite*: support

flake *n* **shaving**, fleck, sliver, chip, scale ■ *v* **peel**, crumble, chip, come off, scale

flaky *adj* 1 **peeling**, crumbling, crumbly, chipped, scaly 2 *(infml)* **unreliable**, undependable, irresponsible, flighty, forgetful *Opposite*: reliable

flamboyance *n* **showiness**, ostentation, flashiness, gaudiness, luridness *Opposite*: modesty

flamboyant *adj* **showy**, ostentatious, flashy, gaudy, lurid *Opposite*: understated

flame *n* **fire**, blaze, flare, spark, flicker ■ *v* **burn**, blaze, light up, glow, flare

flameproof *adj* **nonflammable**, non-inflammable, incombustible, fireproof, fire-retardant *Opposite*: inflammable

flaming *adj* 1 **blazing**, burning, flaring, flickering, sparking *Opposite*: doused 2 **intense**, angry, passionate, blazing, heated *Opposite*: calm

flammable *adj* **inflammable**, combustible, incendiary, igneous *Opposite*: fireproof

flan *n* **quiche**, tart, tartlet, pie, pastry

flank *n* **side**, edge, verge, margin, border ■ *v* **border**, edge, line, skirt, fringe

flannel *(infml) v* **flatter**, beguile, sweet-talk *(infml)*, soft-soap *(infml)*, blarney *(infml)* ■ *n* **flattery**, sweet talk *(infml)*, soft soap *(infml)*, blarney *(infml)*, weasel words *(infml)*

flap *v* *(infml)* **panic**, fret, dither, fluster, worry *Opposite*: calm down ■ *n* 1 *(infml)* **panic**, fret, dither, fluster, state *(infml) Opposite*: calm 2 **tab**, fold, lappet, lap, tail 3 **flutter**, wave, flail, shake, wag

flare *v* 1 **burn**, blaze, flame, flicker, flash 2 **broaden**, splay, bell, widen, spread ■ *n* **flash**, blaze, flicker, flame, burst

flared *adj* **widening**, wide, spreading, broadening, flaring *Opposite*: tapered

flare up *v* **erupt**, break out, explode, heat up, blaze *Opposite*: die down

flare-up *(infml) n* **outbreak**, eruption, flash, outburst, explosion

flash *v* 1 **glint**, sparkle, twinkle, flare, flicker 2 **pass quickly**, rush, speed, race, zoom *Opposite*: crawl 3 *(infml)* **flaunt**, show, show off, display, exhibit ■ *n* 1 **blaze**, spark, flare, flicker, sparkle 2 **moment**, instant, second, twinkling, minute 3 **news flash**, update, bulletin, announcement, report ■ *adj* *(infml)* **showy**, ostentatious, flashy, gaudy, loud *Opposite*: understated

flashback *n* **memory**, recurrence, remembrance, recollection, hallucination

flash flood *n* **deluge**, downpour, cloudburst, spate, surge

flashpoint *n* 1 **crisis**, breaking point, climax, turning point, crossroads 2 **trouble spot**, hot spot, minefield, inferno, hornet's nest

flashy *adj* **showy**, ostentatious, glitzy, gaudy, loud *Opposite*: understated

flask *n* **bottle**, flagon, carafe, hip flask, decanter

flat *adj* 1 **level**, even, smooth, plane, horizontal *Opposite*: uneven 2 **unexciting**, dull, monotonous, tedious, boring *Opposite*: exciting 3 **fixed**, set, preset, invariable, nonnegotiable *Opposite*: variable 4 **categorical**, downright, absolute, out-and-out, emphatic *Opposite*: equivocal ■ *n* 1 **surface**, plane, level, face, blade 2 **suite**, rooms, maisonette, studio, penthouse

flatly *adv* 1 **categorically**, flat, absolutely,

unequivocally, emphatically *Opposite*: equivocally **2 dully**, monotonously, lifelessly, blandly, tediously *Opposite*: animatedly

flatmate *n* **cohabitant**, cohabitee, housemate, friend, roommate

flatness *n* **1 levelness**, evenness, smoothness, horizontalness, horizontality *Opposite*: unevenness **2 dullness**, monotony, monotonousness, tedium, boringness *Opposite*: excitement

flatten *v* **1 squash**, crush, level, even out, compress **2 knock over**, knock down, fell, poleaxe, crush

flatter *v* **compliment**, praise, cajole, sweet-talk *(infml)*, butter up *(infml)* *Opposite*: insult

flatterer *n* **toady**, sycophant, fawner, creep *(infml)*, crawler *(infml)* *Opposite*: critic

flattering *adj* **1 obsequious**, smooth, toadyish, sycophantic, unctuous *Opposite*: uncomplimentary **2 gratifying**, pleasing, satisfying, satisfactory, cheering *Opposite*: galling **3 becoming**, complimentary, kind, favourable, sympathetic *Opposite*: unbecoming

flattery *n* **sycophancy**, obsequiousness, toadyism, adulation, unctuousness *Opposite*: insult

flatulence *n* **pomposity**, pretentiousness, bombast, verbosity, grandiloquence *Opposite*: simplicity

flatulent *adj* **pompous**, pretentious, bombastic, verbose, grandiloquent *Opposite*: unpretentious

flaunt *v* **show off**, exhibit, display, parade, flourish *Opposite*: hide

flavour *n* **1 hint**, sense, feeling, feel, air **2 taste**, zest, tang, essence, aroma *Opposite*: tastelessness **3 additive**, seasoning, extract, spice, essence ■ *v* **1 season**, spice, lace, salt, ginger **2 characterize**, distinguish, mark, pervade, run through

flavourful *adj* **tasty**, tangy, appetizing, palatable, savoury *Opposite*: unappetizing

flavouring *n* **flavour**, additive, seasoning, extract, spice

flavourless *adj* **tasteless**, bland, insipid, flat, anodyne *(literary)* *Opposite*: tasty

flavoursome *adj* **tasty**, delicious, mouthwatering, appetizing, yummy *(infml)* *Opposite*: tasteless

flaw *n* **fault**, defect, blemish, imperfection, failing

COMPARE AND CONTRAST CORE MEANING: something that detracts from perfection

flaw an unintended mark or crack that prevents something from being totally perfect and detracts from its value, or a weakness in somebody's character or in a plan, theory, or system; **imperfection** a fault that makes a person or thing less than perfect; **fault** something that detracts from the integrity, functioning, or perfection of a thing, or a weakness in somebody's character, usually more serious than a flaw; **defect** a fault in a machine,

system, or plan, especially one that prevents it from functioning correctly, or a personal weakness; **failing** something that mars somebody or something in some way, especially an unfortunate feature of somebody's character; **blemish** a mark of some kind that detracts from the appearance of something, especially the appearance of something, or a feature that detracts from somebody's otherwise undamaged reputation or record.

---

flawed *adj* **faulty**, defective, damaged, blemished, imperfect *Opposite*: perfect

flawless *adj* **perfect**, faultless, immaculate, impeccable, unblemished *Opposite*: imperfect

flawlessness *n* **perfection**, faultlessness, immaculateness, impeccability, spotlessness *Opposite*: imperfection

flaxen *adj* **fair-haired**, fair, blond, blonde, golden-haired

flay *v* **1 whip**, lash, thrash, flog, beat **2 criticize**, censure, condemn, pillory, lambaste *Opposite*: endorse

fleapit *n* **cinema**, venue, theatre, picture house *(dated)*

fleck *n* **speck**, spot, speckle, dot, flyspeck

flecked *adj* **marked**, speckled, dotted, streaked, splashed

fledgling *n* **novice**, beginner, learner, tyro, neophyte *Opposite*: expert ■ *adj* **inexperienced**, new, untried, young, inexpert *Opposite*: experienced

flee *v* **run away**, escape, fly, take flight, run off *Opposite*: remain

fleece *(infml)* *v* **swindle**, con, cheat, take for a ride, defraud

fleeciness *n* **woolliness**, downiness, fluffiness, furriness, fuzziness

fleecy *adj* **woolly**, fluffy, flocculent, soft, shaggy

fleet *n* **navy**, flotilla, armada, convoy, task force

fleeting *adj* **brief**, transitory, short-lived, momentary, passing *Opposite*: permanent. *See* COMPARE AND CONTRAST *at* temporary.

flesh *n* **1 tissue**, soft tissue, muscle **2 skin**, surface, epithelium, epidermis, dermis **3 meat**, beef, lamb, pork, ham **4 pulp**, pulpiness, meat **5 relatives**, family, relations, blood relatives, kin **6 body**, flesh and blood, physicality, corporeality, corpus **7 substance**, details, information, reality, solidness

flesh and blood *n* **family**, relations, relatives, kith and kin, flesh

flesh-and-blood *adj* **real live**, human, real, sentient, animate

fleshiness *n* **beefiness**, stoutness, portliness, heftiness, corpulence

fleshly *adj* **1 bodily**, corporeal, physical, corporal, human *Opposite*: psychological **2 carnal**, bodily, erotic, animal, voluptuous *Opposite*: ascetic **3 worldly**, secular, material, human, mundane *Opposite*: spiritual

flesh out v amplify, elaborate, pad, pad out, expand Opposite: condense

fleshy adj plump, ample, overweight, fat, corpulent Opposite: slender

flex v 1 bend, loosen up, activate, move, warm up Opposite: straighten 2 contract, tense, tighten, control Opposite: relax

flexibility n suppleness, litheness, elasticity, give, plasticity Opposite: rigidity

flexible adj 1 supple, lithe, elastic, plastic, stretchy Opposite: rigid 2 adaptable, accommodating, variable, compliant, open Opposite: intractable

flick n (infml) film, picture, big screen, silver screen, movie (US) ■ v brush, tap, glance, flip, graze

flicker v sparkle, glimmer, flash, waver, sputter ■ n 1 glimmer, spark, sparkle, twinkle, glint Opposite: beam 2 trace, ghost, impression, flash, glimmer

flickering adj glimmering, shimmering, intermittent, irregular, flashing

flick through v look through, dip into, leaf through, flip through, riffle Opposite: scrutinize

flier n leaflet, handout, advertisement, notice, insert

flight n 1 trip, journey, airlift, voyage, tour 2 escape, departure, getaway, breakout, evasion

flightiness n capriciousness, changeability, frivolity, volatility, erraticism Opposite: reliability

flight of fancy n fantasy, pipe dream, fancy, dream, daydream

flighty adj unreliable, capricious, changeable, erratic, undependable Opposite: dependable

flimsiness n fragility, weakness, delicacy, frailty, feebleness Opposite: sturdiness

flimsy adj 1 fragile, weak, delicate, insubstantial, slight Opposite: sturdy 2 poor, feeble, unconvincing, inadequate, weak Opposite: sound. See COMPARE AND CONTRAST at fragile.

flinch v recoil, start, cringe, shy away, baulk Opposite: stand your ground. See COMPARE AND CONTRAST at recoil.

fling v throw, toss, hurl, pitch, lob ■ n (infml) romance, love affair, affair, involvement, relationship. See COMPARE AND CONTRAST at throw.

flinty adj hard, unemotional, stern, inflexible, pitiless Opposite: soft

flip v turn over, toss, flick, spin, overturn ■ adj (infml) flippant, casual, joking, jokey, dismissive Opposite: serious

flip over v tip, tip up, upset, upturn, flip

flippancy n levity, facetiousness, glibness, offhandedness, impertinence Opposite: seriousness

flippant adj facetious, offhand, glib, dismissive, frivolous Opposite: serious

flip through v leaf through, browse, flick through, skim through, scan

flirt v 1 trifle, toy, play, seduce, lead on 2 flick, jerk, toss, flip, propel

flirtation n romance, fling, love affair, entanglement, liaison

flirtatious adj playful, coy, seductive, suggestive, kittenish

flirt with v consider, toy with, entertain, think about, trifle with

flit v fly, flutter, dart, skim, flash

float v 1 sail, swim, drift, glide, tread water Opposite: sink 2 hover, soar, drift, glide, hang Opposite: drop 3 propose, suggest, put forward, promote, offer Opposite: reject

floating adj fluctuating, detached, variable, moving, free Opposite: fixed

flock n group, set, cluster ■ v gather, collect, congregate, assemble, cluster Opposite: disperse

WORD BANK
❑ **types of flock** bevy (of quail/larks), brood (of chickens), cast (of hawks), charm (of finches), clutch (of chickens), colony (of gulls), covey (of partridges), exaltation (of larks) (literary), flight (of doves/swallows), gaggle (of geese), herd (of swans), kettle (of hawks), mob (of emus), murmuration (of starlings) (literary), muster (of peacocks), rookery (of penguins), siege (of herons), skein (of geese), watch (of nightingales) (literary), wedge (of swans in flight), wisp (of snipe)

floe n ice floe, iceberg, ice field, icecap, ice sheet

flog v 1 whip, lash, beat, thrash, scourge 2 (infml) sell, vend, get rid of, trade, peddle Opposite: buy

flood n 1 deluge, overflow, downpour, torrent, tidal wave Opposite: drought 2 abundance, glut, excess, stream, rush Opposite: shortage ■ v inundate, submerge, overflow, swamp, saturate Opposite: ebb

flooded adj underwater, swamped, waterlogged, inundated, drowned

floodgate n head gate, sluicegate, water gate, lock, weir

floodlight n illumination, lighting, stream, flood, searchlight ■ v light up, illuminate, light, irradiate, spotlight

floodlit adj illuminated, lit up, lit, illumined (literary)

floodplain n plain, valley, delta, water meadow, fen

flood tide n 1 inflow, high tide, current 2 groundswell, swell, surge, wave, upsurge

floor n 1 storey, level, deck (US) 2 bottom, base, level, surface, flat ■ v astonish, stupefy, astound, stagger, confound

flooring n parquet, floorboards, terrazzo, tiles, floor tiles

floor manager n **supervisor**, overseer, manager, duty officer, line manager

floor plan n **layout**, plan, design, arrangement, allocation

flop v **1 collapse**, slump, fall down, slacken, sag *Opposite*: stand up **2** (*infml*) **fail**, fold, close, crash, nose-dive *Opposite*: succeed **3** (*infml*) **collapse**, slump, fall down, slacken, sag *Opposite*: stand up ■ n (*infml*) **failure**, fiasco, dead loss, loser, dud (*infml*) *Opposite*: hit

floppiness n **limpness**, droopiness, looseness, slackness, softness *Opposite*: firmness

floppy adj **limp**, droopy, lank, loose, flappy *Opposite*: firm

flora n **plants**, flowers, vegetation, plant life

floral adj **flowery**, flowered, flower-patterned, floral-patterned

floral-patterned *see* floral

floret n **floweret**, bud, blossom, bloom, flower

florid adj **1 ornate**, baroque, elaborate, fancy, flowery *Opposite*: plain **2 ruddy**, red, sanguine, rosy, heightened *Opposite*: pallid

flotation n **launch**, initiation, debut, inauguration, introduction

flotilla n **fleet**, armada, convoy, task force, navy

flotsam n **debris**, refuse, driftwood, jetsam, wreckage

flounce v **prance**, storm, stomp, strut, swagger

flounder v **1 splash**, struggle, thrash, wallow, stumble **2 dither**, hesitate, falter, get into difficulties, waver

flour v **dust**, cover, coat, sprinkle, dredge

WORD BANK
☐ **types of flour** cornflour, cornmeal, meal, plain flour, polenta, rice flour, self-raising flour, wheatmeal, wholemeal

flourish v **1 be successful**, succeed, thrive, grow, do well *Opposite*: decline **2 shake**, show, flaunt, display, wave ■ n **1 embellishment**, curl, curlicue, decoration, ornament **2 grand gesture**, display, fanfare, show, bravado

flourishing adj **doing well**, thriving, successful, booming, healthy *Opposite*: declining

floury adj **starchy**, crumbly, crumbling, farinaceous, floured

flout v **disobey**, break, ignore, defy, contravene *Opposite*: obey

flow v **1 run**, pour, flood, stream, gush **2 spring**, arise, emerge, emanate, issue ■ n **movement**, current, stream, course, drift

flower n **1 floret**, flower head, bud, blossom, bloom **2 best**, pick, height, choicest, elite *Opposite*: worst ■ v **1 bloom**, bud, blossom, open, come into bloom *Opposite*: fade **2 develop**, come to fruition, flourish, peak, blossom *Opposite*: wane

WORD BANK
☐ **types of annual flower** aster, forget-me-not, lobelia, love-in-a-mist, marigold, nasturtium, pansy, petunia, poppy, stock, sunflower, sweet pea
☐ **types of perennial flower** African violet, aquilegia, begonia, buttercup, carnation, chrysanthemum, cowslip, daisy, delphinium, foxglove, fuchsia, geranium, lily of the valley, lotus, love-lies-bleeding, lupin, orchid, pelargonium, peony, pink, primrose, rose, snapdragon, sweet william, violet, wallflower
☐ **parts of a flower** androecium, anther, bract, calyx, carpel, corolla, fall, filament, floret, glume, gynoecium, involucre, lemma, lip, nectary, ovary, ovule, palea, pedicel, peduncle, perianth, petal, pistil, receptacle, sepal, spur, stamen, stigma, style, tepal

flowerbed n **plot**, garden plot, patch, border, herbaceous border

flowered adj **floral**, flowery, flower-patterned, floral-patterned

flowering n **peak**, high point, acme, blossoming, pinnacle *Opposite*: nadir

flower-patterned adj **floral**, flowery, flowered, floral-patterned

flowerpot n **plant pot**, planter, tub, jardinière, urn

flowery adj **1 ornate**, ornamental, baroque, embellished, florid *Opposite*: plain **2 floral**, flowered, flower-patterned, floriated

flowing adj **graceful**, smooth, curving, sinuous, elegant *Opposite*: jerky

fluctuate v **vary**, alter, ebb and flow, rise and fall, come and go

fluctuating adj **changing**, changeable, shifting, mutable, unstable *Opposite*: constant

fluctuation n **variation**, vacillation, rise and fall, oscillation, flux *Opposite*: steadiness

flue n **vent**, chimney, outlet, shaft, duct

fluency n **effortlessness**, eloquence, articulacy, ease, facility *Opposite*: hesitancy

fluent adj **1 easy**, flowing, confident, assured, smooth *Opposite*: halting **2 articulate**, eloquent, voluble, smooth-spoken, smooth-tongued *Opposite*: tongue-tied

fluff v (*infml*) **do badly**, make a mess of, ruin, spoil, botch (*infml*) ■ n **fuzz**, lint, hair ■ v **fluff up**, plump up, ruffle, shake, pat

fluffiness n **1 furriness**, fuzziness, hairiness, woolliness, fleeciness **2 lightness**, airiness, softness, flimsiness, frothiness *Opposite*: heaviness

fluffy adj **1 fleecy**, cottony, feathery, downy, furry **2 frothy**, foamy, bubbly, soft, light

fluid n **1 liquid**, solution, water *Opposite*: solid ■ adj **1 runny**, liquid, watery, liquefied, molten *Opposite*: solid **2 effortless**, flowing, smooth, graceful, elegant *Opposite*: jerky **3 changeable**, fluctuating, unstable, adaptable, flexible *Opposite*: constant

fluidity n 1 **variability**, changeableness, changeability, flexibility, mutability Opposite: fixedness 2 **smoothness**, gracefulness, grace, agility, flexibility Opposite: jerkiness

fluke (infml) n **stroke of luck**, accident, coincidence, lucky break, chance occurrence Opposite: mischance

flummox (infml) v **confuse**, perplex, baffle, stump, bewilder

flummoxed (infml) adj **confused**, perplexed, confounded, baffled, stumped

flunk (infml) v **fail**, be unsuccessful, not pass, do badly, bomb (infml) Opposite: ace (infml)

flunkey (infml) see **flunky**

flunky (infml) n **minion**, sidekick, assistant, helper, subordinate

fluorescent adj **glowing**, bright, shining, luminous, flaming

flurry n 1 **burst**, spell, outbreak, bout, flood 2 **wind**, gust, puff, squall, shower ■ v **fluster**, agitate, disturb, disconcert, perturb Opposite: soothe

flush v 1 **redden**, blush, go red, colour, glow Opposite: pale 2 **clear**, wash out, cleanse, rinse, swill ■ n **blush**, high colour, redness, rosiness, ruddiness Opposite: pallor ■ adj 1 **even**, level, flat, true Opposite: uneven 2 (infml) **well off**, rich, in the money, in funds, rolling in it (infml)

flushed adj **red-faced**, rosy, red, blushing, glowing Opposite: pale

fluster v **disconcert**, agitate, confuse, upset, bother Opposite: soothe

flustered adj **harassed**, agitated, nervous, disconcerted, rattled Opposite: calm

flute n **groove**, channel, indentation, line, furrow Opposite: ridge

fluted adj **grooved**, channelled, corrugated, furrowed, lined Opposite: flat

flutter v **beat**, flap, wave, tremble, quiver ■ n 1 **fluster**, excitement, flurry, agitation, confusion Opposite: composure 2 (infml) **bet**, wager, stake

flux n **fluidity**, mutability, fluctuation, instability, unrest Opposite: stability

fly v 1 **hover**, soar, wing, take wing, take off 2 **zoom**, tear, dash, hurry, race Opposite: dawdle 3 **bolt**, run away, escape, flee, take flight Opposite: stand your ground

WORD BANK

❏ **types of flying insect** aphid, bee, blackfly, bluebottle, bumblebee, cicada, daddy longlegs, deer fly, dragonfly, firefly, fruit fly, gnat, grasshopper, greenfly, hornet, horsefly, locust, mayfly, midge, mosquito, tsetse fly, wasp, whitefly

flyaway adj **unmanageable**, unruly, uncontrollable, hard to handle, awkward Opposite: manageable

flyblown adj 1 **maggoty**, wormy, infested, worm-eaten, festering 2 **dirty**, filthy, contaminated, tainted, unclean Opposite: clean

fly-by-night adj **unscrupulous**, dubious, unreliable, shifty, questionable Opposite: reputable

flying adj 1 **hovering**, airborne, soaring, in the air, on the wing 2 **rapid**, brief, speedy, hurried, short

flying saucer n **UFO**, spaceship, spacecraft

fly in the face of v **challenge**, disagree with, go against, contradict, oppose Opposite: conform

fly in the ointment n **drawback**, complaint, impediment, snag, hitch

flyleaf n **front page**, first page, frontispiece, page, leaf

fly off the handle (infml) v **erupt**, explode, lose your temper, fly into a rage, hit the ceiling (infml) Opposite: calm down

flysheet n **flier**, handbill, handout, sheet, notice

fly the coop (infml) v **escape**, leave, run away, flee, bolt Opposite: remain

foal v **produce young**, produce offspring, breed, give birth, reproduce

foam n **bubbles**, froth, fizz, lather, suds ■ v **froth up**, effervesce, froth, bubble, fizz

foam at the mouth v **rage**, seethe, fume, boil, splutter

fob off v 1 **foist**, palm off, dump, pass on, offload 2 **mislead**, misinform, deceive, stall, pull the wool over somebody's eyes 3 **cheat**, con, palm off, rip off (infml), do (infml)

focal adj **principal**, pivotal, central, crucial, important Opposite: peripheral

focal point n **central point**, pivot, core, centre, focus Opposite: periphery

focus n 1 **emphasis**, attention, effort, concentration, motivation 2 **nub**, central point, core, spotlight, centre 3 **focal point**, heart, hub, nucleus, meeting point ■ v **concentrate**, direct, converge, meet, come together

focused adj **motivated**, concentrated, fixated, attentive, absorbed

fodder n **food**, silage, hay, feed, feedstuff

foe (fml) n **adversary**, enemy, antagonist, rival, opponent Opposite: friend

foetid see **fetid**

fog n 1 **mist**, vapour, smog, haze, miasma 2 **muddle**, confusion, daze, haze Opposite: clarity ■ v **obscure**, cloud, bewilder, confuse, stupefy Opposite: sharpen

fogginess n 1 **mistiness**, murkiness, haziness, cloudiness, gloom Opposite: brightness 2 **obscurity**, confusion, doubtfulness, bewilderment, perplexity Opposite: clarity

foggy adj 1 **hazy**, misty, cloudy, murky, smoggy Opposite: clear 2 **unclear**, vague, confused, muddled, bewildered Opposite: precise

foghorn n **horn**, siren, hooter, klaxon

foible *n* **weakness**, fault, shortcoming, quirk, idiosyncrasy *Opposite*: strength

foil *v* **stop**, throw a spanner in the works, frustrate, thwart, outwit

foist *v* **force upon**, inflict upon, thrust upon, impose, palm off

fold *v* **1 double over**, bend, fold up, fold over, double *Opposite*: straighten **2 go out of business**, close, shut down, go bankrupt, collapse ■ *n* **crinkle**, crease, wrinkle, pleat, doubling

foldaway *see* **folding**

folded *adj* **doubled**, doubled over, doubled up, bent over, turned under *Opposite*: outspread

folding *adj* **portable**, foldup, foldaway, collapsible, hinged

fold up *v* **bend flat**, bend, collapse, double, fold over *Opposite*: unfold

foldup *see* **folding**

foliage *n* **leaves**, greenery, vegetation, undergrowth, shrubbery

foliage plant *n* **houseplant**, pot plant, greenery

folk *adj* **traditional**, popular, common, widespread, vernacular ■ *n* **people**, folks, the people, the population, everyone

folklore *n* **myth**, legend, oral tradition, mythology, tradition

folks *n* **1** *(infml)* **people**, folk, everyone, the silent majority, society **2** *(infml)* **everyone**, everybody, ladies and gentlemen, you guys, friends **3 relations**, relatives, nearest and dearest, family, kinsfolk

folk singer *n* **singer**, folkie, balladeer, troubadour

folksy *adj* **simple**, unsophisticated, unpretentious, wholesome, traditional

folktale *n* **tale**, story, legend, myth, ballad

follicle *n* **sac**, cavity, gland, hair follicle

follow *v* **1 pursue**, chase, stalk, trail, shadow *Opposite*: precede **2 monitor**, check on, keep an eye on, track, chart **3 come out of**, ensue, result, develop, arise **4 keep on**, go along, stay on, keep to, stick to **5 enjoy**, admire, support, keep up with, be keen on **6 obey**, abide by, keep to, respect, adhere to *Opposite*: break **7 understand**, see, comprehend, grasp, get the gist

COMPARE AND CONTRAST CORE MEANING: go after **follow** take the same route behind another person, for example by walking down the street or driving along the same road, deliberately or by chance, and not necessarily with the intention of closing the gap; **chase** try to reach, catch, or overtake another person who is in front; **pursue** make an effort to catch up with the person being followed; **tail** *(infml)* to follow secretly for purposes of surveillance; **shadow** follow secretly, used especially to talk about the activities of spies and detectives; **stalk** follow or try to get close to a person or hunted animal unobtrusively, especially obsessively to follow and criminally harass a person;

trail follow tracks or traces left by a person or animal no longer in sight.

follower *n* **supporter**, fan, admirer, hanger-on, devotee

following *adj* **next**, subsequent, succeeding, ensuing, resulting *Opposite*: previous

follow-on *adj* **resulting**, consequent, resultant, ensuing, secondary ■ *n* **side effect**, continuation, consequence, result, repercussion

follow through *v* **complete**, see through, bring to completion, bring to the end, finish off *Opposite*: drop

follow-up *n* **continuation**, addition, supplement, complement, development

folly *n* **irrationality**, foolishness, madness, stupidity, idiocy *Opposite*: prudence

foment *v* **foster**, stir up, stimulate, incite, generate *Opposite*: dampen

fond *adj* **loving**, tender, affectionate, caring, warm *Opposite*: uncaring

fondle *v* **massage**, touch, stroke, caress, pet

fondness *n* **liking**, affection, weakness, soft spot, partiality *Opposite*: dislike. *See* COMPARE AND CONTRAST *at* **love**.

fond of *adj* **devoted to**, taken with, attached to, keen on, partial to *Opposite*: indifferent

font *n* **1** *(literary)* **source**, supply, wellspring, fount, basis **2** *(literary)* **fountain**, spring, water source, well, source **3 typeface**, lettering, type style, type

food *n* **1 nourishment**, nutrition, nutriment, diet, sustenance **2 staple**, foodstuff, fare, provisions, groceries

foodie *(infml) n* **gourmet**, connoisseur, epicurean, bon vivant, bon viveur

food lover *see* **foodie**

foodstuff *n* **food**, staple, essential, ingredient, provisions

fool *n* **dolt** *(infml)*, dope *(infml)*, boob *(infml)*, sucker *(infml)*, mug *(slang)* ■ *v* **mislead**, trick, deceive, take in, con

fool about *v* **1 clown**, act the fool, play around, fool around, horse around **2 tamper**, meddle, fiddle, mess around *(infml)*, fiddle around *(infml)*

fool around *v* **1 clown**, act the fool, play around, fool about, horse around **2 idle**, fiddle about, potter, muck about *(infml)*, mess about *(infml)*

foolhardiness *n* **recklessness**, imprudence, stupidity, idiocy, foolishness *Opposite*: prudence

foolhardy *adj* **reckless**, rash, imprudent, foolish, unwise *Opposite*: sensible

foolish *adj* **1 stupid**, silly, unwise, imprudent, thoughtless *Opposite*: wise **2 ridiculous**, laughable, silly, ludicrous, absurd

foolishness *n* **irrationality**, stupidity, idiocy, silliness, imprudence *Opposite*: wisdom

foolproof *adj* **secure**, safe, infallible, fail-safe, perfect *Opposite*: risky

foot n **base**, bottom, end Opposite: top

footage n **film**, shots, tape, videotape, material

football n **matter**, point, problem, issue, hot potato

footer n **addendum**, title, footnote, note, text Opposite: header

footfall n **footstep**, step, tread, sound

foothill n **hill**, slope, base, foot, bottom Opposite: summit

foothold n **position**, base, purchase, grip, toehold

footing n **1 stability**, equilibrium, purchase, foothold, grip **2 basis**, position, foundation, base, support

footle (infml) v **1 fool around**, idle, dawdle, potter, fiddle around (infml) **2 chatter**, prattle, blabber, blather (infml), blab (infml) ■ n **rubbish**, nonsense, prattle, balderdash, bunkum (infml)

footlights n **acting**, the stage, the theatre, the limelight

footling (infml) adj **trivial**, unimportant, insignificant, trifling, inconsequential Opposite: important

footloose adj **free**, unattached, uncommitted, unrestricted, single

footnote n **note**, annotation, cross-reference, appendix, addendum

footpath n **path**, trail, track, pathway, walkway

footprint n **footmark**, footstep, print, imprint, impression

footrest n **rail**, bar, stool, footstool, foot rail

footsore adj **tired**, weary, exhausted, aching, sore

footstep n **footfall**, sound, step, tread, pace

footstool n **footrest**, stool, support, ottoman

footway see footpath

footwork n **manoeuvring**, cunning, skill, negotiation, horse-trading

fop n **peacock**, narcissus, poseur, poser (infml), dandy (dated)

foppish adj **vain**, affected, preening, narcissistic, self-obsessed

for prep **1 aimed at**, intended for, designed for, meant for, used for **2 in favour of**, in support of, pro Opposite: against

forage n **1 food**, feed, fodder, silage **2 quest**, search for, hunt, exploration, foray ■ v **look for**, search, seek, scavenge, rummage

for all prep **despite**, in spite of, even with, notwithstanding (fml)

foray n **raid**, incursion, venture, sortie, expedition

forbear (fml) v **refrain**, restrain yourself, abstain, hold back, withhold

forbearance (fml) n **patience**, self-control, restraint, tolerance, moderation Opposite: impatience

forbearing (fml) adj **patient**, long-suffering, forgiving, tolerant, lenient Opposite: impatient

forbid v **prohibit**, ban, bar, prevent, outlaw Opposite: allow

forbidden adj **prohibited**, banned, outlawed, illegal, illicit Opposite: permissible

forbidding adj **1 hostile**, unfriendly, stern, harsh, unsympathetic Opposite: approachable **2 uninviting**, unpleasant, dismal, depressing, bleak Opposite: welcoming **3 threatening**, ominous, menacing, sinister, dangerous

force n **1 power**, strength, energy, might, vigour Opposite: weakness **2 influence**, weight, power, strength, intensity ■ v **1 compel**, oblige, make, impose, coerce **2 push**, shove, break down, break open, prise

forced adj **1 strained**, unnatural, affected, put on, artificial Opposite: natural **2 involuntary**, compulsory, required, obligatory, enforced Opposite: voluntary

force-feed v **1 feed up**, fatten, fatten up, feed, nourish **2 teach**, brainwash, programme, ram down somebody's throat, cram

forceful adj **1 powerful**, vigorous, strong, dynamic, potent Opposite: weak **2 persuasive**, convincing, compelling, valid, powerful Opposite: unconvincing

forcefulness n **1 strength**, power, vigour, dynamism, influence Opposite: weakness **2 persuasiveness**, validity, cogency, powerfulness, power

force out v **drive out**, expel, turn out, oust, evict

forces n **armed forces**, military, services, defence force

forcible adj **1 compulsory**, violent, aggressive, armed Opposite: peaceful **2 effective**, forceful, powerful, convincing, persuasive Opposite: weak

ford n **shallows**, crossing, passage, stepping stone ■ v **cross**, traverse, negotiate, cross over, wade

forearm v **prepare**, forewarn, prime, alert, tip off (infml)

forebear n **ancestor**, forerunner, antecedent, predecessor, grandparent Opposite: descendant

foreboding n **premonition**, presentiment, feeling, fear, intuition ■ adj **ominous**, menacing, threatening, sinister, forbidding Opposite: encouraging

forecast v **predict**, estimate, calculate, project, anticipate ■ n **prediction**, estimate, guess, calculation, conjecture

forecaster n **forward planner**, interpreter, analyst, prophet

foreclose (fml) v **exclude**, shut out, close out, ban, exile

forecourt n **space**, area, courtyard, concourse, square

forefront n **1 front**, head, vanguard, lead, van *Opposite*: back **2 foreground**, forepart, front, frontage, face *Opposite*: background

forego v **1** (fml) **precede**, come first, go before, herald, pave the way

foregoing adj **previous**, prior, preceding, earlier, former

foregone adj **inevitable**, predetermined, inescapable, unavoidable, fated *Opposite*: uncertain

foreground n **forefront**, front, centre, centre stage, focus *Opposite*: background

foreign adj **1 alien**, external, extraneous, imported, overseas *Opposite*: indigenous **2 strange**, unfamiliar, unknown, alien, exotic *Opposite*: familiar **3 unrelated**, extraneous, irrelevant, external, unconnected *Opposite*: relevant

foreigner n **stranger**, foreign person, alien, immigrant, newcomer *Opposite*: national

foreknowledge n **premonition**, prescience, feeling, foresight, intuition *Opposite*: hindsight

foreleg n **front leg**, forelimb, limb, leg, appendage

foremost adj **chief**, leading, primary, prime, notable

forename n **first name**, given name, Christian name, nickname, pet name *Opposite*: surname

forerunner n **1 portent**, indication, omen, sign, harbinger **2 forebear**, ancestor, antecedent, precursor, predecessor

foresee v **expect**, foretell, prophesy, divine, predict *Opposite*: look back

foreseeable adj **1 predictable**, probable, likely, imaginable, conceivable *Opposite*: unforeseeable **2 near**, immediate, imminent, prospective, impending *Opposite*: far-off

foreshadow v **presage**, indicate, suggest, warn of, augur

foreshore n **shore**, beach, mudflat, sand, shingle

foresight n **1 forethought**, prudence, far-sightedness, anticipation, sagacity *Opposite*: hindsight **2 premonition**, insight, prescience, intuition, foreknowledge *Opposite*: hindsight

forest n **woods**, woodland, forestry, plantation, jungle

forestall v **prevent**, avert, obviate, hinder, thwart

foretaste n **sample**, token, indication, example, taste *Opposite*: recollection

foretell (literary) v **predict**, prophesy, presage, portend, forecast *Opposite*: review

forethought n **anticipation**, consideration, foresight, prudence, planning *Opposite*: afterthought

forever adv **1 eternally**, for all time, in perpetuity, indefinitely, ad infinitum *Opposite*: momentarily **2** (infml) **incessantly**, persistently, repeatedly, continually, endlessly *Opposite*: never

forewarn v **warn**, caution, alert, prime, forearm

forewarning n **warning**, notice, notification, word of warning, signal

foreword n **preface**, introduction, prelude, preamble, prologue *Opposite*: conclusion

forfeit n **penalty**, forfeiture, loss, penalization, punishment ■ v **1 lose**, pay for, be deprived of, pay with, be stripped of **2 surrender**, sacrifice, give up, part with, go without

forfeiture n **penalty**, forfeit, loss, penalization, punishment

forge n **furnace**, hearth, oven ■ v **1 shape**, form, build, create, fashion **2 counterfeit**, fake, falsify, copy, imitate

forge ahead v **take the lead**, come to the fore, make progress, make headway, move forward *Opposite*: lag

forged adj **fake**, counterfeit, false, spurious, phoney *Opposite*: genuine

forger n **counterfeiter**, falsifier, faker, coiner, imitator

forgery n **fake**, counterfeit, sham, phoney, imitation *Opposite*: original

forget v **1 overlook**, disremember, fail to recall, be unable to remember, be unable to call to mind *Opposite*: remember **2 stop thinking about**, put out of your mind, disregard, put behind you, turn your back on *Opposite*: attend to. *See* COMPARE AND CONTRAST *at* **neglect**.

forgetful adj **1 absent-minded**, inclined to forget, vague, absent, oblivious *Opposite*: mindful **2 inattentive**, neglectful, negligent, wandering, careless *Opposite*: attentive

forgetfulness n **absent-mindedness**, amnesia, obliviousness, insensibleness, vagueness

forgettable adj **unmemorable**, unremarkable, undistinguished, mediocre, ordinary *Opposite*: unforgettable

forgivable adj **pardonable**, excusable, allowable, defensible, justifiable *Opposite*: unforgivable

forgive v **pardon**, excuse, forgive and forget, let off, absolve *Opposite*: blame

forgiveness n **1 pardon**, absolution, amnesty, exoneration, reconciliation *Opposite*: blame **2 clemency**, pity, mercy, compassion, understanding *Opposite*: ruthlessness

forgiving adj **merciful**, lenient, magnanimous, sympathetic, compassionate *Opposite*: unforgiving

forgo v **do without**, sacrifice, pass by, waive, relinquish *Opposite*: take up

forgotten adj **lost**, gone, neglected, disregarded, buried *Opposite*: immortal

fork n **divide**, split, divergence, junction, branch

forked adj **split**, cleft, divided, branched, pronged *Opposite*: undivided

forlorn adj **1 miserable**, sad, dejected, despondent, unhappy *Opposite*: cheerful **2 desolate**, neglected, abandoned, lonely, lost *Opposite*: cherished

form n **1 structure**, state, condition, nature, status **2 type**, variety, kind, mode, manner **3 document**, paper, questionnaire, pro forma, blank **4 procedure**, method, system, arrangement, formula **5 shape**, configuration, appearance, outline, look ■ v **1 develop**, take shape, materialize, come into being, arise **2 fashion**, shape, model, create, mould **3 start**, found, create, bring into being, establish

formal adj **1 official**, proper, prescribed, recognized, strict *Opposite*: informal **2 conventional**, reserved, stiff, prim, starched *Opposite*: relaxed

formality n **1 conventionalism**, reserve, stiffness, primness, correctness *Opposite*: informality **2 procedure**, requirement, regulation, custom, ritual

formalization n **validation**, ratification, solemnization, reinforcement, celebration

formalize v **validate**, ratify, solemnize, reinforce, honour

format n **structure**, presentation, organization, arrangement, setup ■ v **arrange**, lay out, organize, configure, set up

formation n **1 arrangement**, configuration, shape, structure, pattern **2 creation**, development, construction, establishment, foundation

formative adj **influential**, determinative, seminal, decisive, developmental

formative years n **childhood**, early life, early years, early childhood, infancy *Opposite*: maturity

former adj **previous**, past, ex-, earlier, prior *Opposite*: current

formerly adv **previously**, before, in the past, once, earlier

formidable adj **1 difficult**, tough, daunting, arduous, challenging *Opposite*: easy **2 alarming**, frightening, dreadful, fearsome, redoubtable *Opposite*: encouraging **3 awe-inspiring**, impressive, remarkable, astounding, awesome *Opposite*: uninspiring

formless adj **shapeless**, amorphous, unformed, unshaped, unstructured *Opposite*: distinct

formula n **1 method**, plan, modus operandi, recipe, prescription **2 cliché**, stock phrase, expression, phrase, formulation

formulaic adj **1 prescribed**, standard, rigid, fixed, set **2 unoriginal**, imitative, clichéd, overused, cookie-cutter *Opposite*: original

formulate v **1 devise**, invent, prepare, put together, make **2 express**, represent, present, frame, put into words

formulation n **1 preparation**, design, construction, creation, invention **2 representation**,

guise, form, presentation, manifestation

forsake v **1 abandon**, leave, disown, quit, desert *Opposite*: support **2 renounce**, relinquish, give up, turn your back on, sacrifice

forsaken adj **abandoned**, cast off, discarded, deserted, jilted *Opposite*: supported

fort n **fortification**, fortress, stronghold, citadel, castle

forte n **strong point**, speciality, strong suit, gift, strength *Opposite*: failing

forth (fml) adv **1 forwards**, ahead, onward *Opposite*: back **2 out**, into view, into the open, into the world *Opposite*: back

forthcoming adj **1 approaching**, impending, imminent, future, coming *Opposite*: distant **2 available**, ready, offered, supplied, in the offing *Opposite*: unavailable **3 helpful**, open, obliging, cooperative, informative *Opposite*: reticent

forthright adj **straightforward**, direct, frank, outspoken, plain-spoken *Opposite*: timid

forthrightness n **frankness**, candour, directness, candidness, outspokenness *Opposite*: timidity

forthwith adv **immediately**, without delay, at once, straightaway, right away *Opposite*: later

fortification n **1 defences**, ramparts, buttresses, walls, earthworks **2 strengthening**, defence, reinforcement, buttressing, building up *Opposite*: erosion

fortified adj **1 defended**, protected, walled, garrisoned, secured *Opposite*: exposed **2 reinforced**, strengthened, hardened, buttressed, toughened *Opposite*: unsupported **3 encouraged**, heartened, invigorated, reinvigorated, stimulated *Opposite*: drained

fortify v **1 defend**, protect, wall, garrison, secure *Opposite*: expose **2 make stronger**, strengthen, reinforce, brace, support *Opposite*: weaken **3 enrich**, boost, enhance, improve, mix *Opposite*: deplete **4 give a boost to**, revive, refresh, reinvigorate, invigorate *Opposite*: drain **5 build up**, boost, bolster, support, sustain *Opposite*: weaken

fortitude n **strength**, courage, resilience, staying power, grit *Opposite*: weakness

fortress n **stronghold**, fort, citadel, fortification, castle

fortuitous adj **accidental**, chance, casual, unexpected, unplanned *Opposite*: planned

fortunate adj **1 privileged**, lucky, blessed, well-off, prosperous *Opposite*: unfortunate **2 lucky**, providential, happy, opportune, auspicious *Opposite*: unfortunate. *See* COMPARE AND CONTRAST *at* **lucky.**

fortunately adv **1 as luck would have it**, by chance, luckily, providentially, opportunely *Opposite*: unfortunately **2 happily**, luckily, mercifully, thank goodness, thank heavens *Opposite*: unfortunately

fortune n **1 wealth**, riches, affluence, opulence,

prosperity *Opposite*: poverty **2 packet** *(infml)*, bomb *(infml)*, mint *(infml)*, pile *(infml)*, tidy sum *(infml)* *Opposite*: pittance **3 luck**, chance, providence, accident, fate *Opposite*: design **4 destiny**, fate, kismet, karma, future *Opposite*: past

fortune-teller *n* **clairvoyant**, seer, soothsayer, psychic, medium

forty winks *(infml)* *n* nap, doze, sleep, siesta, catnap

forum *n* **1 opportunity**, medium, environment, setting, scene **2 meeting**, debate, discussion, round table, conference

forward *adj* **1 onward**, advancing, frontwards, headlong, headfirst *Opposite*: backward **2 presumptuous**, self-assured, bold, familiar, brazen *Opposite*: reticent ■ *v* **1 send**, dispatch, post, send on, redirect **2 advance**, promote, further, progress, accelerate *Opposite*: hold back

forward-looking *adj* **progressive**, modern, forward-thinking, avant-garde, open-minded *Opposite*: backward-looking

forwardness *n* **boldness**, directness, brazenness, forthrightness, self-assurance *Opposite*: reticence

forwards *adv* **1 ahead**, frontwards, to the fore, up, onward *Opposite*: backwards **2 to the fore**, into view, into the open, up *Opposite*: backwards

forward-thinking *see* **forward-looking**

fossil *n* **relic**, remnant, vestige, remains

fossilization *n* **petrification**, preservation, calcification, hardening, solidification

fossilize *v* **turn into stone**, petrify, solidify, harden, calcify

foster *v* **1 look after**, take care of, care for, take in, bring up **2 promote**, further, advance, cultivate, forward *Opposite*: discourage ■ *adj* **stand-in**, substitute, adoptive, temporary, short-term *Opposite*: natural

foster child *n* **child**, dependant, adoptee, ward, looked after child

foster parent *n* **guardian**, substitute parent, foster father, foster mother, carer

foul *adj* **1 unpleasant**, disgusting, offensive, distasteful, filthy *Opposite*: pleasant **2 vulgar**, obscene, lewd, uncouth, unwholesome *Opposite*: decent **3 inclement**, stormy, wet, unpleasant, rotten *Opposite*: fair **4 unclean**, stinking, polluted, tainted, soiled *Opposite*: clean **5 dishonest**, shady, criminal, treacherous, dishonourable *Opposite*: legitimate **6** *(infml)* **horrible**, rotten, unpleasant, nasty, dreadful *Opposite*: charming ■ *v* **1 entangle**, tangle up, catch, ensnarl, snarl *Opposite*: free **2 pollute**, soil, make dirty, contaminate, taint

foul-mouthed *adj* **blasphemous**, crude, rude, dirty, vulgar *Opposite*: polite

foulness *n* **1 filth**, filthiness, squalor, pollution, dirt *Opposite*: cleanness **2 vulgarity**, obscenity, lewdness, profanity, uncouthness *Opposite*: decency

foul play *n* **1 deviousness**, unfairness, cheating, trickery, monkey business *(infml)* **2 criminal action**, treachery, dishonesty, villainy, violence *Opposite*: honesty

foul-smelling *adj* **smelly**, reeking, malodorous, fetid, rotten *Opposite*: sweet-smelling

foul-tasting *adj* **nasty**, disgusting, unpleasant, indigestible, revolting

foul-up *(infml)* *n* **blunder**, slip, mix-up, error, mistake *Opposite*: success

found *v* **originate**, set up, create, start, bring into being *Opposite*: close

foundation *n* **1 basis**, grounds, substance, groundwork, underpinning *Opposite*: superstructure **2 establishment**, institution, charity, institute, society

founder *n* **creator**, originator, initiator, organizer, forefather ■ *v* **1 sink**, go down, plunge, wallow, submerge *Opposite*: float **2 fail**, break down, come to nothing, fall through, miscarry *Opposite*: succeed

foundling *(dated)* *n* **orphan**, waif, stray, urchin, outcast

fount *(literary)* *n* **source**, fountain, well, spring, wellspring

fountain *n* **1 cascade**, water feature, spout, jet, spring **2 source**, origin, cause, beginning, fountainhead

fountainhead *see* **fountain**

four-letter word *n* **swearword**, vulgarity, vulgarism, obscenity, expletive *Opposite*: euphemism

foursome *n* **group of four**, quartet, group, ensemble

fourth *n* **quarter**, twenty-five percent, fourth part

fox *v* **1 confuse**, baffle, muddle, puzzle, perplex *Opposite*: enlighten **2 deceive**, trick, outwit, fool, con

foxy *adj* **sly**, cunning, crafty, sharp, wily *Opposite*: naive

foyer *n* **lobby**, vestibule, reception area, hall, entrance hall

fracas *n* **quarrel**, row, fight, brawl, melee *Opposite*: calm

fraction *n* **1 part**, portion, segment, section, division *Opposite*: whole **2 little bit**, little, small part, tiny proportion, small percentage

fractional *adj* **slight**, small, tiny, minuscule, insignificant *Opposite*: great

fractionally *adv* **slightly**, marginally, just, a little, a fraction *Opposite*: greatly

fractious *adj* **irritable**, peevish, restless, complaining, grumpy *Opposite*: even-tempered

fracture *n* **break**, breakage, crack, rupture, fissure *Opposite*: repair ■ *v* **crack**, break, rupture, splinter, split *Opposite*: mend

fragile adj 1 **delicate**, brittle, flimsy, breakable, frail Opposite: sturdy 2 **tenuous**, unstable, delicate, precarious, shaky Opposite: stable 3 **frail**, weak, delicate, infirm, feeble Opposite: strong

COMPARE AND CONTRAST CORE MEANING: easily broken or damaged
fragile not having a strong structure or not made of robust materials, and therefore easily broken or damaged; **delicate** similar to fragile, used especially of things that are beautiful or remarkable because of their fragility; **frail** easily broken or damaged, or physically weak and vulnerable to injury; **flimsy** too easily broken, torn, or damaged, especially used of badly or cheaply made goods, or of light and insubstantial clothing; **frangible** capable of being broken or easily damaged; **friable** easily reduced to tiny particles.

fragility n 1 **brittleness**, flimsiness, delicateness, delicacy, breakability Opposite: solidity 2 **tenuousness**, instability, delicacy, delicateness, precariousness Opposite: stability 3 **frailty**, weakness, feebleness, ill health, infirmity Opposite: strength

fragment n **piece**, portion, bit, splinter, sliver Opposite: whole ■ v **break**, divide, break up, disintegrate, crumble Opposite: fuse

fragmentary adj **incomplete**, disconnected, bitty, scrappy, patchy Opposite: entire

fragmentation n **disintegration**, destruction, shattering, breaking up, crumbling Opposite: fusion

fragmented adj **disjointed**, uneven, scrappy, bitty, patchy Opposite: continuous

fragrance n 1 **smell**, scent, perfume, bouquet, aroma 2 **cologne**, scent, perfume, toilet water, eau de toilette. See COMPARE AND CONTRAST at smell.

fragranced adj **perfumed**, scented, sweet-smelling, fragrant

fragrant adj **perfumed**, aromatic, scented, sweet-smelling, fragranced Opposite: smelly

frail adj 1 **weak**, infirm, delicate, feeble, puny Opposite: robust 2 **flimsy**, insubstantial, fragile, delicate, spindly Opposite: sturdy. See COMPARE AND CONTRAST at fragile, weak.

frailness see frailty

frailty n 1 **infirmity**, weakness, feebleness, fragility, ill health Opposite: robustness 2 **shortcoming**, weakness, imperfection, failing, defect Opposite: strength

frame n 1 **structure**, framework, scaffold, skeleton, support 2 **edge**, surround, border, mount, setting 3 **body**, form, build, physique, skeleton ■ v **enclose**, mount, border, edge, outline Opposite: inset

frame of mind n **mood**, mental state, mental condition, humour, temper

frame of reference n **context**, situation, standpoint, background, setting

framework n 1 **structure**, frame, scaffold, skeleton, support 2 **outline**, agenda, basis, context, background

franchise n **permit**, licence, contract, authorization, charter ■ v **license**, permit, contract, contract out, grant

frangible adj **breakable**, fragile, brittle, easily broken. See COMPARE AND CONTRAST at fragile.

frank adj **forthright**, free, honest, guileless, open Opposite: insincere

frankfurter n **hot dog**, sausage, wiener (US)

frankness n **honesty**, forthrightness, openness, bluntness, truthfulness Opposite: insincerity

frantic adj 1 **panicky**, hysterical, beside yourself, desperate, agitated Opposite: calm 2 **frenzied**, frenetic, hectic, feverish, wild Opposite: calm

fraternal adj 1 **sibling**, brotherly, brother's, familial, genealogical 2 **comradely**, brotherly, friendly, amicable, communal Opposite: hostile

fraternity n 1 **community**, network, group, world, clan (infml) 2 **brotherliness**, brotherhood, comradeship, mutual support, friendship Opposite: hostility

fraternization n **mixing**, socializing, intercourse, mingling, partying Opposite: avoidance

fraternize v **associate**, socialize, mix, hobnob, hang out (infml) Opposite: avoid

fraud n 1 **dishonesty**, deceit, deception, double-dealing, trickery Opposite: honesty 2 **impostor**, charlatan, hoaxer, swindler, cheat 3 **deception**, con, scheme, swindle, deceit

fraudster n **confidence trickster**, swindler, cheat, hoaxer, charlatan

fraudulence n **deceit**, duplicity, deceitfulness, illegitimacy, dishonesty Opposite: honesty

fraudulent adj **fake**, deceitful, untrue, duplicitous, dishonest Opposite: genuine

fraught adj 1 **full**, charged, filled, weighed down, laden Opposite: free 2 **tense**, anxious, nervous, troubled, apprehensive Opposite: calm

fray v **unravel**, ravel, wear, wear out, tatter Opposite: mend ■ n **fight**, argument, quarrel, fracas, dispute

frayed adj **threadbare**, worn, tattered, ragged, unravelled

frazzled (infml) adj **exhausted**, weary, tired out, drained, fatigued Opposite: lively

freak n 1 **curiosity**, rarity, oddity, one-off, aberration 2 (infml) **enthusiast**, fanatic, fiend, buff, lover 3 **chance**, surprise, happenstance, accident, fluke (infml)

freakish adj **variable**, volatile, changeable, unpredictable, inexplicable Opposite: stable

freaky adj **weird**, strange, amazing, grotesque, unexpected Opposite: commonplace

freckle n **spot**, mark, patch, speckle, speck

freckled adj **speckled**, freckly, dappled, spotted, stippled

free *adj* **1 allowed**, at liberty, permitted, able, welcome *Opposite*: restricted **2 liberated**, unbound, released, emancipated, freed *Opposite*: imprisoned **3 unrestricted**, unregimented, unconventional, loose, unstructured *Opposite*: conventional **4 gratis**, free of charge, without charge, at no cost, complimentary **5 relaxing**, off, available, unoccupied, on holiday *Opposite*: working **6 open**, uninhibited, uncontrolled, spontaneous, honest *Opposite*: inhibited ■ *v* **1 release**, let go, set free, liberate, emancipate *Opposite*: imprison **2 exempt**, rid, unburden, excuse, pardon

free-and-easy *adj* **indulgent**, overindulgent, lax, overfamiliar, relaxed *Opposite*: uptight *(infml)*

freebie *(infml)* *n* **free sample**, handout, perk, free gift, free offer

freedom *n* **1 liberty**, autonomy, lack of restrictions, self-determination, independence *Opposite*: restriction **2 looseness**, inventiveness, nonconformity *Opposite*: conformity **3 frankness**, openness, abandon, free expression, candour *Opposite*: inhibition

free fall *n* **1 skydive**, jump, descent, drop, fall **2 decline**, descent, collapse, confusion, turmoil *Opposite*: upturn

free-fall *v* **1 skydive**, drop, plummet, fall, descend *Opposite*: soar **2 drop**, plummet, collapse, decline, fall apart

free-for-all *(infml)* *n* **brawl**, fight, brouhaha, riot, scuffle

free gift *n* **free sample**, free offer, giveaway *(infml)*, freebie *(infml)*

freehand *adj* **without a pattern**, by eye, by hand, sketchy, free

freehanded *adj* **generous**, openhanded, unstinting, giving, liberal *Opposite*: stingy *(infml)*

freehold *n* **1 tenure**, ownership, right, occupancy **2 property**, estate, land, building, holding

freeholder *n* **property owner**, landowner, owner, holder, landlord

freeing *n* **release**, liberation, acquittal, emancipation, freedom *Opposite*: capture

freelance *adj* **self-employed**, temporary, irregular, casual, ad hoc *Opposite*: permanent

freeload *(infml)* *v* **live off others**, parasitize, take advantage, use others, sponge *(infml)*

freeloader *(infml)* *n* **slacker**, parasite, idler, hanger-on, user

freely *adv* **1 without restrictions**, at will, at liberty, easily, spontaneously **2 liberally**, generously, unreservedly, without restraint, without stinting *Opposite*: parsimoniously

free-range *adj* **unconfined**, free, loose, at large, uncaged *Opposite*: battery

free spirit *n* **individualist**, nonconformist, maverick, freethinker, rebel *Opposite*: conformist

freestanding *adj* **self-supporting**, unconnected, separate, detached, unattached *Opposite*: attached

freethinker *n* **individualist**, free spirit, nonconformist, nonbeliever, sceptic *Opposite*: conformist

freethinking *adj* **independent**, open-minded, enlightened, nonconformist, liberal *Opposite*: conformist

free time *n* **leisure**, leisure time, spare time, time off, recreation

free up *v* **1 make available**, empty, make space for, clear, liberate *Opposite*: occupy **2** *(infml)* **loosen**, unjam, unblock, unsnarl, unclog *Opposite*: snarl

freewheel *v* **1 coast**, sail, glide, cruise, roll along **2 take it easy**, drift, go with the flow, cruise *Opposite*: struggle

free will *n* **autonomy**, self-determination, choice, liberty, freedom *Opposite*: dependence

freeze *v* **1 turn to ice**, freeze up, ice up, ice over, solidify *Opposite*: thaw **2 refrigerate**, chill, cool, preserve *Opposite*: thaw **3 halt**, stop, stop in your tracks, stop dead, stiffen *Opposite*: relax **4 suspend**, stop, halt, hold, break off *Opposite*: resume **5 hold**, fix, restrict, stop, control ■ *n* **restriction**, halt, embargo, check, stoppage *Opposite*: resumption

freeze out *(infml)* *v* **exclude**, ostracize, ignore, shun, reject *Opposite*: welcome

freeze up *v* **ice over**, ice up, harden, solidify, freeze *Opposite*: thaw

freezing *adj* **cold**, subzero, icy, chilly, bitter *Opposite*: hot

freight *n* **1 cargo**, goods, merchandise, consignment, load **2 carriage**, shipping, conveyance, transport, transportation

frenetic *adj* **hectic**, bustling, busy, frantic, feverish *Opposite*: calm

frenzied *adj* **frantic**, hyperactive, hysterical, feverish, emotional *Opposite*: calm

frenzy *n* **1 fury**, turmoil, fever, rage, passion *Opposite*: calmness **2 whirl**, fit, tumult, rush, flurry

frequency *n* **incidence**, occurrence, regularity, rate of recurrence, rate

frequent *adj* **recurrent**, common, everyday, normal, numerous *Opposite*: infrequent ■ *v* **visit**, haunt, patronize, hang around, spend time at *Opposite*: avoid

fresco *n* **wall painting**, mural, frieze, wall, painting

fresh *adj* **1 at its best**, garden-fresh, crisp, moist, juicy *Opposite*: stale **2 new**, renewed, additional, replacement, other *Opposite*: old **3 clean**, bright, unmarked, unsullied, immaculate *Opposite*: soiled **4 wholesome**, crisp, pleasant, airy, refreshing *Opposite*:

musty **5 novel**, original, new, inventive, innovative *Opposite*: hackneyed **6 alert**, energetic, lively, vigorous, active *Opposite*: tired. *See* COMPARE AND CONTRAST *at* **new**.

freshen *v* **tidy**, neaten, dust, clean, air

freshen up *v* **wash**, shower, change, clean up, powder your nose *(infml)*

fresher *(infml)* *n* **first-year student**, first year, undergraduate, student, novice *Opposite*: finalist

fresh-faced *adj* **youthful**, young-looking, baby-faced, boyish, girlish

freshly *adv* **newly**, recently, just now, a moment ago, just this minute

freshness *n* **1 crispness**, juiciness, flavour, moistness *Opposite*: staleness **2 cleanness**, cleanliness, brightness, sparkle, brilliance *Opposite*: grubbiness **3 novelty**, originality, newness, inventiveness, innovation *Opposite*: tiredness

fret *v* **worry**, fuss, agonize, vex, trouble *Opposite*: calm down

fretful *adj* **worried**, restless, agitated, unsettled, distressed *Opposite*: calm

fretfulness *n* **anxiety**, restlessness, agitation, distress, unease *Opposite*: calmness

friable *adj* **crumbly**, powdery, workable, light *Opposite*: heavy. *See* COMPARE AND CONTRAST *at* **fragile**.

friary *n* **religious community**, monastery, religious foundation, fraternity, brotherhood

friction *n* **1 rubbing**, abrasion, contact, chafing, rasping **2 hostility**, conflict, tension, antagonism, disagreement *Opposite*: accord

friend *n* **1 comrade**, companion, mate, pal *(infml)*, chum *(infml)* *Opposite*: foe *(fml)* **2 acquaintance**, contact, colleague, associate, partner *Opposite*: stranger **3 ally**, helper, supporter, well-wisher, collaborator *Opposite*: rival

friendliness *n* **affability**, sociability, conviviality, amiability, approachability *Opposite*: reserve

friendly *adj* **1 affable**, sociable, approachable, outgoing, open *Opposite*: unfriendly **2 close**, familiar, intimate, congenial, amicable *Opposite*: frosty **3 beneficial**, helpful, favourable, welcoming, supportive *Opposite*: hostile

friendship *n* **1 bond**, relationship, alliance, attachment, acquaintance **2 companionship**, comradeship, camaraderie, closeness, familiarity *Opposite*: animosity

frieze *n* **decoration**, band, strip, panel, mural

fright *n* **1 fear**, terror, anxiety, foreboding, dread *Opposite*: composure **2 scare**, shock, start, turn, seizure

frighten *v* **scare**, terrify, alarm, startle, upset *Opposite*: soothe

frightened *adj* **scared**, afraid, terrified, alarmed, startled *Opposite*: calm

frightening *adj* **terrifying**, alarming, startling, fearsome, fearful *Opposite*: soothing

frightful *adj* **appalling**, horrible, unpleasant, dreadful, awful *Opposite*: pleasant

frightfully *adv* **terribly**, extremely, awfully, dreadfully, excessively

frightfulness *n* **awfulness**, atrociousness, severity, badness, hideousness *Opposite*: pleasantness

frigid *adj* **1 unfriendly**, standoffish, cold, distant, frosty *Opposite*: warm **2 cold**, frosty, chilly, icy, freezing *Opposite*: torrid

frigidity *n* **coldness**, frostiness, iciness, cold-heartedness, aloofness *Opposite*: warmth

frigidly *adv* **coldly**, icily, frostily, unemotionally, unfeelingly *Opposite*: warmly

frill *n* **1 decoration**, flounce, trimming, ruffle, ruche **2 extra**, add-on, luxury, decoration, accompaniment

frills *n* **accompaniments**, trappings, added extras, embellishments, add-ons *Opposite*: essentials

frilly *adj* **lacy**, ruched, gathered, pleated, fancy *Opposite*: plain

fringe *n* **1 tassel**, edging, edge, border, trimming **2 periphery**, edge, extreme, perimeter, border *Opposite*: centre ■ *adj* **1 peripheral**, outlying, marginal, far-flung, frontier *Opposite*: central **2 unconventional**, extreme, radical, marginal, extremist *Opposite*: mainstream

fringe benefit *n* **extra**, compensation, perk, privilege, reward

frisk *v* **1 play**, frolic, gambol, cavort, kick up your heels *Opposite*: plod **2 search**, pat down, body search, examine, inspect

friskiness *n* **playfulness**, excitability, excitement, liveliness, enthusiasm *Opposite*: lethargy

frisky *adj* **playful**, frolicsome, excitable, excited, lighthearted *Opposite*: lethargic

fritter away *v* **dissipate**, waste, squander, misspend, gamble away *Opposite*: conserve

frivolity *n* **1 playfulness**, perkiness, lightheartedness, merriment, gaiety *Opposite*: seriousness **2 triviality**, frivolousness, unimportance, inconsequentiality, superficiality *Opposite*: seriousness

frivolous *adj* **1 trivial**, silly, inconsequential, idle, shallow *Opposite*: serious **2 playful**, frolicsome, perky, lighthearted, silly *Opposite*: serious

frizz *v* **curl**, crimp, frizzle, perm, kink *Opposite*: straighten

frizzle *v* **1 burn**, shrivel, scorch, sear, dry up **2 frizz**, curl, perm, crimp, kink *Opposite*: straighten **3 sizzle**, fry, pan-fry, sauté, grill

frizzy *adj* **curled**, wiry, curly, kinky, frizzed *Opposite*: straight

frogmarch *v* **propel**, march, accompany, take, carry

frogspawn *n* eggs, spawn, tadpoles

frolic *v* play, skip, cavort, frisk, gambol *Opposite*: plod

frolicsome *adj* playful, frisky, frivolous, light-hearted, spirited *Opposite*: solemn

frond *n* leaf, branch, palm leaf, fern leaf

front *n* 1 façade, face, frontage, obverse, head *Opposite*: back 2 **impertinence**, cockiness, nerve, gall, temerity

frontage *n* front, façade, face, outlook, front part *Opposite*: rear

frontal *adj* forward, anterior, front, fore *(literary)* *Opposite*: posterior *(fml)*

front door *n* main entrance, main door, door, entrance, entry *Opposite*: back door

frontier *n* border, boundary, limit, edge, border line

frontispiece *n* illustration, print, picture, photograph, drawing

front line *n* 1 front, war zone, battle zone, combat zone, ground zero 2 **forefront**, cutting edge, leading edge, sharp end, vanguard

front-page *adj* headline, important, significant, momentous, attention-grabbing

frontrunner *(infml)* *n* leader, head, favourite, prime candidate, number one *(infml)* *Opposite*: also-ran

frontwards *adv* ahead, to the fore, forwards *Opposite*: backwards

frost *n* 1 ice, rime, hoar frost 2 **cold**, frostiness, iciness, coolness, frigidity *Opposite*: warmth

frosted *adj* ice-covered, frosty, iced, icy, snowy *Opposite*: thawed

frostily *adv* coldly, icily, coolly, frigidly, angrily *Opposite*: warmly

frostiness *n* 1 **iciness**, coldness, cold, chill, rawness *Opposite*: warmth 2 **coldness**, aloofness, frigidity, coolness, iciness *Opposite*: warmth

frosting *n* 1 **icing**, cake coating, decoration, royal icing, topping 2 **dullness**, opaqueness, opacity, matte finish, matte surface

frosty *adj* 1 **icy**, cold, chilly, freezing, frigid *Opposite*: warm 2 **cold**, unfriendly, cool, icy, frigid *Opposite*: friendly

froth *n* 1 **foam**, bubbles, lather, head, fizz 2 **triviality**, trivia, frivolity, superficiality, shallowness *Opposite*: substance ■ *v* **to become foamy**, foam, bubble, lather, lather up

frothiness *n* 1 **foaminess**, bubbliness, fizziness, fizz, soapiness 2 **triviality**, insubstantiality, lightness, frivolity, pettiness *Opposite*: seriousness

frothy *adj* 1 **foamy**, foam-covered, lathered, lathered up, bubbly 2 **light**, inconsequential, superficial, trivial, shallow *Opposite*: serious

frown *v* knit your brow, scowl, glare, glower, lower *Opposite*: smile ■ *n* scowl, glare, glower, grimace, puckered brow *Opposite*: smile

frown on *v* disapprove, take a dim view of, frown upon, condemn, dislike *Opposite*: favour. *See* COMPARE AND CONTRAST *at* **disapprove**.

frown upon *see* **frown on**

frowzy *adj* unkempt, dishevelled, frayed, messy, shabby *Opposite*: neat

frozen *adj* 1 ice-covered, cold, solid, freezing, iced up 2 **immobile**, stationary, unmoving, still, motionless *Opposite*: mobile

frugal *adj* thrifty, prudent, economical, sparing, penny-wise *Opposite*: profligate

frugality *n* thrift, stinginess, parsimony, prudence, economy *Opposite*: profligacy

fruit *n* 1 ovary, berry, pod, capsule, achene 2 **produce**, bounty, harvest, crop, yield 3 **product**, result, consequence, reward, fruition ■ *v* **produce fruit**, bear fruit, ripen, mature

WORD BANK

❏ **types of fruit** apple, apricot, avocado, banana, blackcurrant, cherry, citrus, damson, date, fig, grape, guava, kiwi fruit, kumquat, lychee, mango, melon, nectarine, olive, papaya, passion fruit, peach, pear, pineapple, plum, pomegranate, quince, raspberry, redcurrant, strawberry, watermelon

❏ **parts of a fruit** flesh, juice, kernel, peel, pip, pith, pulp, rind, seed, skin, stone

fruitful *adj* productive, fertile, rich, prolific, abundant *Opposite*: fruitless

fruitfulness *n* productivity, abundance, profitability, prosperity, fertility *Opposite*: fruitlessness

fruition *n* completion, maturity, readiness, realization, culmination

fruitless *adj* unsuccessful, futile, useless, unproductive, wasted *Opposite*: fruitful

fruitlessness *n* uselessness, futility, unproductiveness, failure, inadequacy *Opposite*: fruitfulness

fruity *adj* 1 **rich**, sweet, tangy, zesty, lemony 2 **mellow**, deep, rich, plummy, harmonious *Opposite*: shrill

frustrate *v* 1 **thwart**, prevent, foil, stop, block *Opposite*: promote 2 **discourage**, exasperate, irritate, upset, disturb *Opposite*: encourage

frustrated *adj* 1 **unfulfilled**, unsatisfied, irritated, upset, angry *Opposite*: satisfied 2 **foiled**, blocked, stymied, obstructed, hindered *Opposite*: successful

frustrating *adj* annoying, unsatisfying, exasperating, infuriating, maddening *Opposite*: satisfying

frustration *n* 1 **prevention**, hindrance, blocking, foiling, defeat *Opposite*: success 2 **dissatisfaction**, irritation, disturbance, annoyance, nuisance *Opposite*: satisfaction

fry *v* cook, sauté, stir-fry, fry up, deep-fry

frying pan *n* pan, skillet, omelette pan

fuddle v **confuse**, bewilder, stupefy, muddle, dull Opposite: clarify ■ n **muddle**, dither, mess, state (infml)

fuddy-duddy (infml) n **fogy**, reactionary, stick-in-the-mud (infml), stuffed shirt (infml)

fudge (infml) n **nonsense**, rubbish, garbage, verbiage, waffle (infml) ■ v **1 falsify**, alter, massage, doctor, fiddle (infml) **2 prevaricate**, evade the issue, stall, beat about the bush, waffle (infml)

fuel n **energy source**, fossil fuel, alternative fuel, renewable fuel ■ v **1 power**, fire, run, drive, operate **2 stimulate**, increase, promote, fire, energize Opposite: quell

fug n fog, smog, haze, smoke, miasma

fuggy adj **stuffy**, stale, airless, suffocating, foggy Opposite: bracing

fugitive n **escapee**, deserter, absconder, outlaw, runaway ■ adj **brief**, fleeting, elusive, short, quick

fugue n **fugue state**, blackout, amnesia, memory loss

fulcrum n **pivot**, hinge, swivel, support, point

fulfil v **1 achieve**, bear out, live up to, satisfy, justify **2 carry out**, execute, follow, obey, complete Opposite: neglect **3 satisfy**, meet, conform to, be in conformity with, accord with Opposite: fall short **4 complete**, finish, go through with, get through, make it through Opposite: abandon **5 supply**, fill, deliver, provide, furnish (fml) Opposite: renege **6 succeed**, do proud, gain fulfilment, make good, fulfil your potential Opposite: fail. See COMPARE AND CONTRAST at perform.

fulfilled adj **satisfied**, content, happy, pleased, rewarded Opposite: frustrated

fulfilling adj **satisfying**, rewarding, pleasing, gratifying, enjoyable Opposite: frustrating

fulfilment n **1 achievement**, realization, execution, completion, accomplishment Opposite: neglect **2 contentment**, serenity, inner peace, self-actualization, nirvana Opposite: dissatisfaction

full adj **1 occupied**, complete, bursting, packed, filled Opposite: empty **2 complete**, broad, extensive, comprehensive, detailed Opposite: sketchy **3 sonorous**, resonant, rich, deep, plummy Opposite: shrill **4 satiated**, satisfied, bursting, sated, replete Opposite: hungry **5 plump**, round, chubby, ample, broad Opposite: thin

full-blooded adj **vigorous**, hearty, thoroughgoing, forceful, robust Opposite: feeble

full-blown adj **complete**, full, full-scale, full-size, developed Opposite: incomplete

full-bodied adj **flavourful**, rich, intense, powerful, strong Opposite: insipid

full dress n **formal attire**, dress uniform, jacket and tie, evening dress, black tie

full-frontal (infml) adj **all-out**, unrestrained, wholehearted, uninhibited, concerted Opposite: half-hearted

full-length adj **1 ankle-length**, floor-length, long Opposite: short **2 head-to-toe**, whole-body, full, long, tall **3 unabridged**, complete, uncut, unedited, unexpurgated Opposite: abridged

fullness n **1 completeness**, richness, abundance Opposite: emptiness **2 roundness**, plumpness, chubbiness, ampleness, pudginess (infml) Opposite: thinness

full of adj **alive with**, awash with, thick with, resplendent with, crammed with Opposite: lacking in

full-scale adj **1 life-size**, full-size, complete, full **2 total**, full-blown, unrestrained, all-out, unlimited Opposite: partial

full-size adj **normal**, standard, regular, ordinary

full-time adj **around-the-clock**, permanent, twenty-four-hour, day and night, 24/7 Opposite: part-time

full-timer n **full-time employee**, full-time worker, full-time member of staff Opposite: part-timer

fully adv **completely**, entirely, wholly, totally, altogether Opposite: partially

fully-fledged adj **1 complete**, mature, well-developed, independent, self-sufficient **2 qualified**, out-and-out, full, genuine, actual

fully-grown adj **mature**, adult, full-sized, full, well-developed Opposite: immature

fulminate v **rail**, rant and rave, rage, rant, thunder Opposite: praise

fulsome adj **flattering**, excessive, immoderate, effusive, overgenerous

fumble v **1 grope**, scrabble, rummage, root, search **2 mishandle**, botch up, blunder, muddle, muddle up ■ n **mistake**, error, blunder, botched job, mess

fume v **seethe**, rage, bristle, be angry, be furious ■ n **1 emission**, vapour, miasma, smog, smoke **2 stench**, smell, stink, reek, odour

fumigate v **sterilize**, disinfect, decontaminate, delouse, smoke

fumigation n **disinfection**, decontamination, smoking, delousing, cleansing

fuming adj **furious**, irate, incensed, enraged, seething

fun n **amusement**, excitement, enjoyment, entertainment, merriment Opposite: boredom ■ adj (infml) **amusing**, entertaining, enjoyable, exciting, pleasurable Opposite: boring

function n **1 purpose**, meaning, role, job, occupation **2 event**, gathering, meeting, affair, party ■ v **work**, perform, operate, run, go Opposite: malfunction

functional adj **1 practical**, useful, handy, purposeful, efficient Opposite: useless **2 operational**, operative, running, going, working Opposite: inoperative

functionary n **official**, representative, bureaucrat, lackey, employee

fund n **1 supply**, stock, store, source, collection **2 reserve**, account, supply, endowment, stock ■ v **finance**, support, back, sponsor, subsidize

fundamental adj **1 basic**, primary, original, essential, elementary *Opposite*: secondary **2 central**, essential, vital, ultimate, major *Opposite*: superfluous

fundamentally adv **at heart**, at bottom, basically, essentially, primarily *Opposite*: superficially

fundamentals n **basics**, rudiments, essentials, ground rules, brass tacks

funding n **backing**, support, finance, subsidy, money

fundraiser n **1 campaigner**, crusader, supporter, representative, moneymaker **2 appeal**, campaign, crusade, push, drive

funeral n **service**, memorial, interment, burial, cremation

funereal adj **gloomy**, melancholy, sorrowful, mournful, sad *Opposite*: cheerful

funfair n **fair**, fairground, theme park, amusement park, carnival *(US)*

fungal adj **fungiform**, mycological, fungoid, fungous

funky *(infml)* adj **up-to-date**, fashionable, unconventional, trendy *(infml)*, cool *(infml)*

fun-loving adj **playful**, joyful, high-spirited, frivolous, exuberant *Opposite*: staid

funnel n **chimney**, pipe, flue, smokestack, conduit ■ v **channel**, direct, focus, guide, concentrate

funnily adv **1 strangely**, curiously, surprisingly, oddly, unusually **2 comically**, humorously, amusingly, hilariously, wittily

funniness n **humour**, comedy, comicalness, wit, wittiness *Opposite*: solemnity

funny adj **1 amusing**, humorous, comic, comical, hilarious *Opposite*: serious **2 strange**, odd, weird, curious, peculiar *Opposite*: normal **3 quaint**, unconventional, eccentric, quirky, odd **4 unwell**, sick, nauseous, off-colour, poorly *(infml)* *Opposite*: well ■ n *(infml)* **joke**, pun, witticism, bon mot, gag *(infml)*

COMPARE AND CONTRAST CORE MEANING: causing or intended to cause amusement
funny causing amusement or laughter, whether intentionally or not; **comic** used in the same way as *funny*, especially to describe books, poems, or plays; **comical** funny to the extent of being absurd, especially if this is unintentional; **droll** funny because it is whimsical or odd, or drily humorous; **facetious** supposed to be funny but ill-timed, inappropriate, or silly; **humorous** intended to make people laugh; **witty** using words in a clever, inventive, humorous way; **hilarious** extremely funny; **sidesplitting** very funny indeed, especially causing a great deal of uncontrollable laughter.

fur n **hair**, pelt, fleece, coat, fuzz

furious adj **1 angry**, livid, fuming, irate, infuriated *Opposite*: calm **2 energetic**, concerted, all-out, breakneck, violent

furiousness n **1 anger**, rage, fury, wrath, crossness **2 violence**, energy, vigour, ferocity, passion

furl v **roll up**, wrap up, curl, curl up, tie up *Opposite*: unfurl

furlough n **leave of absence**, leave, absence, holiday, R and R

furnace n **heater**, oven, kiln, boiler, blast furnace

furnish *(fml)* v **supply**, provide, equip, give, deliver *Opposite*: strip

furnished adj **equipped**, fitted out, well-appointed, well-found *Opposite*: unfurnished

furnishings n **furniture**, fittings, tables, chairs, cabinets

furniture n **fittings**, tables, chairs, cabinets, beds

furore n **1 uproar**, outcry, commotion, controversy, protest **2 excitement**, hysteria, hype, frenzy, ballyhoo

furred see furry

furriness n **hairiness**, fuzziness, woolliness, fleeciness, fluffiness *Opposite*: baldness

furrow n **channel**, groove, rut, undulation, gully ■ v **wrinkle**, crease, gather, draw, contract

furrowed adj **wrinkled**, crumply, creasy, wrinkly, crinkly *Opposite*: smooth

furry adj **hairy**, fuzzy, woolly, downy, furred

further adj **additional**, more, extra, added, supplementary ■ v **advance**, promote, foster, broaden, expand *Opposite*: prevent

furthermore adv **also**, in addition, besides, additionally, moreover

furthermost adj **farthest**, furthest, greatest, remotest, nethermost *(fml)*

furthest adj **farthest**, utmost, uttermost, outermost, furthermost

furtive adj **secretive**, stealthy, secret, sly, sneaky *Opposite*: open. See COMPARE AND CONTRAST at **secret**.

furtiveness n **1 secrecy**, stealth, covertness, surreptitiousness, discreetness *Opposite*: openness **2 sneakiness**, suspiciousness, guiltiness, slyness, craftiness *Opposite*: straightforwardness

fury n **anger**, rage, wrath, ferocity, ire *(fml)*. See COMPARE AND CONTRAST at **anger**.

fuse v **combine**, blend, mingle, meld, coalesce *Opposite*: fragment

fusion n **synthesis**, union, combination, mixture, blend *Opposite*: fission

fuss n **1 commotion**, excitement, bother, bustle, activity **2 worry**, concern, bother, trouble, hassle *(infml)* **3 protest**, controversy, argument, complaint, reaction ■ v **worry**, fret, stew, bother, niggle

fussiness n 1 **trivialness**, pedantry, obsessiveness, prissiness, hairsplitting 2 **meticulousness**, dogmatism, inflexibility, fastidiousness, exactness 3 **elaborateness**, frilliness, ornateness, overstatement

fusspot (infml) n **worrier**, neurotic, worryguts (infml)

fussy adj 1 **trivial**, pedantic, obsessive, prissy, assiduous 2 **picky**, particular, finicky, fastidious, selective Opposite: laid-back (infml) 3 **elaborate**, busy, frilly, ornate, overelaborate. See COMPARE AND CONTRAST at **careful**.

fusty adj 1 **stale**, mouldy, damp, fetid, musty Opposite: fresh 2 **stuffy**, antiquated, dull, boring, old-fashioned Opposite: trendy (infml)

futile adj **useless**, pointless, fruitless, unsuccessful, vain Opposite: useful

futility n **uselessness**, pointlessness, ineffectiveness, ineffectuality, vainness Opposite: usefulness

future n **prospect**, outlook, potential, time ahead, time to come Opposite: past ■ adj **forthcoming**, coming, imminent, yet to come, impending Opposite: past

futures n **stocks**, commodities, contracts, investments

futuristic adj **innovative**, revolutionary, ahead of its time, advanced, ultramodern Opposite: antiquated

fuzz n **down**, hair, fur, fluff

fuzziness n 1 **hairiness**, fluffiness, woolliness, down, wool 2 **blurriness**, nebulousness, haziness, vagueness, mistiness Opposite: clarity 3 **uncertainty**, vagueness, incoherence, ambiguity, indistinctness Opposite: certainty

fuzzy adj 1 **hairy**, furry, fluffy, downy, woolly 2 **blurry**, unclear, nebulous, hazy, vague Opposite: clear 3 **unsure**, ambiguous, unclear, indistinct, vague Opposite: clear

G

gab (infml) v **chatter**, chat, gossip, natter, prattle ■ n **chat**, chatter, talk, conversation, gossip

gabardine n **raincoat**, garment, mac (infml), mackintosh (dated)

gabble v **jabber**, rattle on, blabber, gibber, talk nineteen to the dozen ■ n **gibberish**, chatter, prattle, rubbish, nonsense

gabby (infml) adj **talkative**, chatty, garrulous, voluble, gushing Opposite: taciturn

gad v **socialize**, go partying, go clubbing, have a night on the town (infml), gallivant (infml)

gadabout n **pleasure-seeker**, fun lover, social butterfly, partygoer, raver (infml)

gadfly (dated) n **nuisance**, pest, irritator, tormentor, meddler

gadget n 1 **device**, tool, appliance, implement, contraption 2 **thingamajig** (infml), thingamabob (infml), gizmo (infml), doodah (infml), whatsit (infml)

gaffe n **blunder**, solecism, mistake, error, clanger (infml)

gaffer (infml) n **boss**, supervisor, owner, proprietor, manager Opposite: underling

gag n 1 **restraint**, curb, muzzle, tape, binding 2 **ban**, gagging order, injunction, restriction, interdiction 3 (infml) **joke**, one-liner, funny, shaggy dog story, quip ■ v 1 **muzzle**, stifle, muffle, restrain, curb 2 **suppress**, silence, interdict, prohibit, ban 3 **choke**, retch, suffocate, stifle, hyperventilate

gagging order n **restriction**, gag, injunction, prohibition, court order

gaggle n **crowd**, group, horde, throng, multitude

gaiety n **joyfulness**, lightheartedness, happiness, liveliness, merriment Opposite: misery

gaily adv **happily**, joyfully, cheerily, merrily, brightly Opposite: sadly

gain v 1 **get**, achieve, acquire, obtain, secure Opposite: lose 2 **increase**, add, put on, grow, expand Opposite: decrease ■ n 1 **achievement**, improvement, advantage, advance, increase Opposite: setback 2 **advantage**, profit, reward, benefit, return Opposite: loss. See COMPARE AND CONTRAST at **get**.

gain access v **get into**, enter, infiltrate, access, get permission

gainful adj **profitable**, advantageous, lucrative, rewarding, useful Opposite: unprofitable

gain ground v **progress**, advance, improve, expand, spread Opposite: fall back

gain on v **near**, close in on, approach, catch up on, close the gap

gainsay (fml) v **oppose**, contradict, argue, refute, deny Opposite: agree

gait n **walk**, step, pace, bearing, manner

gala n **festival**, celebration, party, ball, festivity

galactic adj 1 (infml) **huge**, enormous, immense, vast, extensive Opposite: infinitesimal 2 **celestial**, cosmic, planetary, astronomical, space *Opposite*: terrestrial

galaxy *n* **gathering**, assembly, meeting, cluster, collection

gale *n* **wind**, windstorm, storm, tempest, hurricane *Opposite*: breeze

gall *n* **1 audacity**, impudence, boldness, nerve, effrontery **2 sore**, irritation, lesion, wound, blister ■ *v* **irritate**, annoy, infuriate, anger, vex *Opposite*: please

gallant *adj* **1** *(literary)* **brave**, courageous, heroic, valiant, fearless *Opposite*: cowardly **2 courteous**, chivalrous, polite, gentlemanly, thoughtful *Opposite*: rude

gallantry *n* **1** *(literary)* **courage**, bravery, heroism, valour, daring *Opposite*: cowardice **2 courtesy**, thoughtfulness, chivalry, politeness, attentiveness *Opposite*: boorishness

gallery *n* **1 colonnade**, portico, arcade, galleria, corridor **2 balcony**, veranda, porch

galling *adj* **frustrating**, annoying, irritating, infuriating, exasperating *Opposite*: soothing

gallivant *(infml)* *v* **globetrot**, tour, travel around, gad, wander *Opposite*: stay put

gallons *n* **lots**, loads *(infml)*, tons *(infml)*, masses *(infml)*, heaps *(infml)* *Opposite*: handful

gallop *n* **sprint**, dash, charge, bolt, mad dash ■ *v* **dash**, career, hurtle, run, fly

gallows *n* **scaffold**, gibbet, gallows tree, crossbeam, arm

galore *adj* **abundant**, plentiful, copious, aplenty, plenteous *(literary)* *Opposite*: scant

galvanize *v* **stimulate**, spur, rouse, electrify, fire up *Opposite*: dampen

gambit *n* **stratagem**, manoeuvre, ploy, scheme, strategy

gamble *v* **1 bet**, wager, back, game, stake **2 risk**, stake, venture, hazard, chance *Opposite*: play safe ■ *n* **1 wager**, bet, stake, flutter *(infml)* **2 chance**, risk, hazard, venture, speculation

gamble away *v* **squander**, lose, fritter away, waste, throw away

gambler *n* **1 better**, high roller, wagerer, speculator, plunger *(infml)* **2 risk-taker**, adventurer, speculator, risker, chancer *(infml)*

gambling *n* **betting**, gaming, bookmaking

gambol *v* **frolic**, skip, hop, spring, leap

game *n* **1 pastime**, sport, diversion, amusement, entertainment **2 wild animals**, big game, game birds, game fish **3 match**, fixture, competition, contest, derby ■ *adj* **1 willing**, ready, up for, disposed, inclined *Opposite*: unwilling **2 brave**, spirited, plucky, gutsy *(infml)*, spunky *(infml)* *Opposite*: spiritless

WORD BANK

❏ **types of board game** backgammon, chess, Chinese chequers, dominoes, draughts, go, ludo, mahjongg, Monopoly™, pachisi, reversi, Scrabble™, snakes and ladders, solitaire

❏ **types of card game** baccarat, bridge, canasta, contract bridge, cribbage, euchre, gin rummy, hearts, patience, pinochle, poker, pontoon, rummy, whist

gamekeeper *n* **game warden**, breeder, keeper, handler, steward

gamely *adv* **bravely**, sportingly, spiritedly, stoically, determinedly *Opposite*: weakly

game plan *n* **plan**, strategy, scheme, stratagem, ploy

games *n* **sports**, competition, tournament, cup, sports event

gammy *(infml)* *adj* **sore**, stiff, painful, uncomfortable, aching

gamut *n* **range**, scale, length, scope, extent

gander *(infml)* *n* **look**, peek, glimpse, glance, dekko *(infml)*

gang *n* **1 mob**, band, ring, clique, posse *(slang)* **2 team**, squad, group, lineup, crew *(infml)*

gangland *n* **underworld**, criminal world, organized crime, vice, racketeering

gangling *adj* **lanky**, gangly, tall, rangy, awkward *Opposite*: elegant

ganglion *n* **swelling**, lump, knot, concentration, cyst

gangly *see* **gangling**

gangplank *n* **bridge**, walkway, footway, footbridge, gangway

gangrene *n* **infection**, decay, rot, decomposition, putrefaction ■ *v* **fester**, putrefy, decompose, decay, rot

gangrenous *adj* **infected**, festering, diseased, decaying, rotting *Opposite*: healthy

gangster *n* **criminal**, thug, hoodlum, racketeer, Mafioso

gang up on *v* **unite against**, join forces against, combine against, pick on, mob

gangway *n* **walkway**, footway, aisle, passage, passageway

gannet *(infml)* *n* **glutton**, gourmand, pig *(infml)*

gantry *n* **scaffold**, framework, support

gaol *see* **jail**

gap *n* **1 break**, opening, breach, slit, fissure **2 interval**, hiatus, pause, break, interruption *Opposite*: continuity **3 disparity**, difference, divergence, mismatch, inequality *Opposite*: parity **4 chasm**, gorge, ravine, canyon, rift

gape *v* **1 stare**, gaze, ogle, look hard, gawk *(infml)* **2 part**, separate, divide, yawn, break open. *See* COMPARE AND CONTRAST *at* gaze.

gaping *adj* **wide**, wide open, huge, yawning, cavernous *Opposite*: narrow

garage *n* **1 carport**, lockup, shed, outbuilding, parking garage **2 service station**, petrol station, gas station *(US)*

garb *n* **clothing**, dress, costume, apparel, outfit ■ *v* **clothe**, dress, do up, dress up, attire *(fml)*

garbage *n* **nonsense**, trivia, drivel, rubbish, hogwash *(infml)* *Opposite*: sense

garbed adj **arrayed**, clothed, dressed, robed, wearing

garble v **jumble**, confuse, muddle, mangle, distort

garbled adj **jumbled**, confused, muddled, distorted, mangled Opposite: clear

garden n 1 **plot**, allotment, patch, bower, yard (US) 2 **park**, gardens, public park, green, common ■ v **plant**, cultivate, tend, work, grow

---

WORD BANK

❑ **types of garden** bog garden, cottage garden, flower garden, herb garden, Japanese garden, kitchen garden, knot garden, orchard, potager, rock garden, rose garden, vegetable garden, vegetable plot, water garden

❑ **parts of a garden** arboretum, arbour, bed, border, container, flowerbed, lawn, patio, pergola, planter, rockery, shrubbery, water feature, window box

---

gardener n **horticulturist**, landscape gardener, grower, planter, weeder

gargantuan adj **huge**, large, gigantic, enormous, vast Opposite: tiny

gargle v 1 **rinse your mouth**, rinse, wash out, disinfect, freshen 2 **gurgle**, bubble, burble, glug (infml)

gargoyle n **ornament**, decoration, carving, figurehead, effigy

garish adj **gaudy**, showy, lurid, vulgar, brash Opposite: tasteful

garland n 1 **wreath**, chaplet, coronet, circlet, crown 2 **festoon**, swag, drape, chain, lei

garment n **clothing**, vestment, costume, dress, frock (dated)

WORD BANK

❑ **parts of a garment** brim, buckle, button, buttonhole, coat-tail, collar, cuff, décolletage, drawstring, gusset, hem, lace, lapel, leg, lining, neck, neckband, neckline, pocket, sash, sleeve, strap, turn-up, waistband, zip

---

garner v 1 **gather**, bring in, save, lay down, store Opposite: scatter 2 **acquire**, get, gain, collect, bring together Opposite: squander

garnish v **enhance**, improve, set off, embellish, decorate ■ n 1 **accompaniment**, sauce, relish, trimming, savoury 2 **embellishment**, decoration, adornment, ornament, trimming

garret n **attic**, loft, gable, penthouse, top storey

garrison n **barracks**, quarters, base, military base, casern. See COMPARE AND CONTRAST at **talkative**.

garrulous adj **talkative**, voluble, chatty, effusive, loquacious Opposite: taciturn. See COMPARE AND CONTRAST at **talkative**.

garrulousness n **verbosity**, volubility, chattiness, prattling, long-windedness Opposite: taciturnity

gas n 1 **air**, vapour, fume, smoke 2 (infml) **chatter**, prattle, chitchat (infml), gab (infml),

blather (infml) 3 (infml) **blast**, thrill, experience, trip (infml) Opposite: drag ■ v (infml) **chat**, gossip, chitchat (infml), natter (infml), yak (infml)

gaseous adj 1 **vaporous**, gassy, steamy, smoky, fumy 2 **carbonated**, fizzy, bubbly, sparkling, effervescent Opposite: still 3 (infml) **talkative**, verbose, long-winded, chatty, chattering Opposite: tight-lipped

gash n **wound**, slash, cut, tear, laceration ■ v **cut**, slash, wound, tear, lacerate

gasket n **seal**, washer, ring, liner, lining

gasp n **wheeze**, pant, huff, puff, breath

gasping adj 1 **out of breath**, puffed, winded, breathless, panting 2 **thirsty**, parched, dry, dehydrated, thirsting 3 **desperate**, dying, longing, craving, yearning

gassy adj 1 **carbonated**, fizzy, bubbly, sparkling, effervescent Opposite: still 2 **vaporous**, gaseous, steamy, smoky, fumy 3 (infml) **talkative**, verbose, long-winded, chatty, gossipy Opposite: tight-lipped

gastric adj **stomach**, abdominal, intestinal, digestive, gastrointestinal

gastrointestinal adj **stomach**, abdominal, intestinal, digestive, gastric

gastronome n **gourmet**, food lover, connoisseur, epicure, foodie (infml) Opposite: glutton

gastronomic adj **culinary**, cooking, food, gourmet, epicurean

gastronomy n **cookery**, cooking, cuisine, food, gourmet food

gasworks n **gas plant**, power station, installation, power plant

gate n 1 **entrance**, entry, door, gateway, opening 2 **attendance**, crowd, turnout, audience 3 **receipts**, takings, proceeds, revenue, take

gatecrash v **sneak in**, barge in, invade, intrude, crash (infml)

gatecrasher n **intruder**, interloper, trespasser, invader, partycrasher (US) Opposite: guest

gatepost n **support**, upright, post, frame, doorpost

gateway n 1 **entry**, doorway, entrance, opening, access 2 **opening**, first step, opportunity, access, way in

gather v 1 **meet**, get together, collect, congregate, assemble Opposite: disperse 2 **collect**, bring together, draw together, amass, pull together Opposite: distribute 3 **harvest**, pick, collect, garner, pluck Opposite: scatter 4 **understand**, conclude, assume, deduce, surmise Opposite: misunderstand 5 **pleat**, fold, pucker, ruche, shirr Opposite: smooth ■ n **fold**, pleat, pucker, wrinkle, ruck. See COMPARE AND CONTRAST at **collect**.

gathering n **meeting**, assembly, congregation, crowd, jamboree

gathering place n **meeting place**, centre, assembly point, forum

gather up v **pick up**, take up, draw up, scoop up, dredge up *Opposite*: put down

gauche adj **awkward**, uncouth, tactless, callow, graceless *Opposite*: poised

gaudiness n **showiness**, luridness, flamboyance, garishness, tawdriness *Opposite*: tastefulness

gaudy adj **garish**, flashy, kitschy, loud, showy *Opposite*: tasteful

gauge v **evaluate**, judge, assess, determine, measure ■ n **measurement**, estimate, assessment, measure, test

gaunt adj **thin**, skinny, lean, bony, emaciated *Opposite*: plump

gauntness n **thinness**, skinniness, leanness, boniness, scrawniness *Opposite*: plumpness

gauzy adj **thin**, delicate, filmy, see-through, gossamer *Opposite*: heavy

gawk (*infml*) v **stare**, gape, gaze, watch, goggle *Opposite*: ignore. *See* COMPARE AND CONTRAST *at* gaze.

gawkiness (*infml*) n **awkwardness**, clumsiness, inelegance, gracelessness, ungainliness *Opposite*: gracefulness

gawky (*infml*) adj **awkward**, clumsy, gangling, gangly, ungainly *Opposite*: graceful

gawp (*infml*) *see* gawk

gaze v **look**, stare, watch, contemplate, gape *Opposite*: ignore ■ n **stare**, look, contemplation, observation, scrutiny *Opposite*: glance

---

COMPARE AND CONTRAST CORE MEANING: look at somebody or something steadily or at length
gaze look for a long time with unwavering attention; **gape** look at somebody or something in surprise or wonder, usually with an open mouth; **gawk** or **gawp** (*infml*) stare stupidly or rudely; **ogle** look steadily at somebody for sexual enjoyment or to show sexual interest; **rubberneck** (*infml*) stare at somebody or something in an over-inquisitive or insensitive way; **stare** look at somebody or something directly and intently without moving the eyes away, as a result of curiosity or surprise or to express rudeness or defiance.

---

gazette n **newspaper**, paper, journal, periodical, newsletter

gear (*infml*) n 1 **kit**, stuff, things, paraphernalia, tackle 2 **clothes**, clothing, kit, outfit, togs (*infml*)

gear to v **adjust to**, align with, adapt to, tailor, modify

gear up v **get ready**, prepare, mobilize, ready yourself, psych yourself up (*infml*) *Opposite*: wind down

gel n **cream**, lotion, balm, ointment, salve ■ v 1 (*infml*) **come together**, take shape, crystallize, develop, form *Opposite*: fall apart 2 (*infml*) **see eye to eye**, relate, get on, get on like a house on fire, get along 3 **congeal**, thicken, coagulate, clot, harden *Opposite*: liquefy

gelatinous adj **viscous**, jellylike, gummy, gooey, sticky

geld v **castrate**, neuter, spay, sterilize, vasectomize

gem n 1 **jewel**, stone, precious stone, cut stone, gemstone 2 (*infml*) **treasure**, pearl, star, godsend, paragon

gemstone n **jewel**, stone, gem, precious stone, cut stone

WORD BANK

❏ **types of gemstone** agate, amethyst, aquamarine, beryl, bloodstone, carnelian, chalcedony, chrysoprase, diamond, emerald, garnet, jade, lapis lazuli, moonstone, mother-of-pearl, onyx, opal, pearl, ruby, sapphire, sard, topaz, tourmaline, turquoise

---

gender n **sex**, sexual category, sexual characteristics, masculinity, femininity

---

WORD BANK

❏ **types of female animal** bitch, cow, dam, doe, ewe, filly, heifer, hind, jenny, lioness, mare, nanny goat, sow, tigress, vixen

❏ **types of male animal** billy goat, boar, buck, bull, bullock, colt, hart, jackass, ram, stag, stallion, steer, tom, tomcat, wether

❏ **types of male or female bird** capon, cob, cock, cockerel, drake, duck, gander, goose, hen, pen, rooster

---

gene n **genetic factor**, inheritable factor, protein sequence, DNA segment

genealogical adj **hereditary**, ancestral, family, pedigree

genealogy n **family tree**, descent, lineage, pedigree, family

general adj 1 **overall**, universal, all-purpose, wide-ranging, broad *Opposite*: specific 2 **usual**, typical, conventional, customary, accustomed *Opposite*: unusual 3 **widespread**, common, blanket, across-the-board, sweeping *Opposite*: unique 4 **unspecific**, undefined, unclear, vague *Opposite*: specific

generality n 1 **generalization**, sweeping statement, simplification, oversimplification, overview *Opposite*: detail 2 **platitude**, cliché, banality, truism, axiom

generalization n **sweeping statement**, simplification, oversimplification, overview, generality *Opposite*: detail

generalize v **simplify**, oversimplify, take a broad view, make a sweeping statement *Opposite*: specify

generalized adj **widespread**, sweeping, comprehensive, general, global *Opposite*: isolated

generally adv **usually**, normally, in general, in the main, by and large *Opposite*: rarely

general public n **population**, populace, ordinary people, hoi polloi, rank and file *Opposite*: elite

generate v **make**, produce, create, cause, engender *Opposite*: prevent

generation n 1 **age group**, peer group, peers, cohort, compeers *(fml)* 2 **age**, era, epoch, period, aeon 3 **production**, making, creation, invention, initiation *Opposite*: destruction

generator n **producer**, maker, creator, originator, initiator

generic *adj* **general**, broad, common, basic, nonspecific *Opposite*: specific

generosity n **kindness**, big-heartedness, open-handedness, liberality, munificence *Opposite*: miserliness

generous *adj* 1 **kind**, big-hearted, liberal, openhanded, charitable *Opposite*: stingy *(infml)* 2 **substantial**, large, lavish, liberal, plentiful *Opposite*: meagre

COMPARE AND CONTRAST CORE MEANING: giving readily to others
generous willing to give money, help, or time freely; **liberal** free with money, time, or other assets; **magnanimous** very generous, kind, or forgiving; **munificent** very generous, especially on a grand scale; **bountiful** (*literary*) generous, particularly to less fortunate people.

genesis n **origin**, origins, beginning, start, birth

genetic *adj* **hereditary**, inherited, heritable, inherent, genomic *Opposite*: learned

genial *adj* **friendly**, amiable, warm, welcoming, hospitable *Opposite*: unfriendly

geniality n **friendliness**, warmth, cordiality, amiability, conviviality *Opposite*: hostility

genie n **sprite**, spirit, apparition, jinni, imp

genius n 1 **mastermind**, prodigy, intellect, virtuoso, whiz kid *(infml)* 2 **brilliance**, intellect, brains, virtuosity, intelligence *Opposite*: stupidity. *See* COMPARE AND CONTRAST *at* **talent**.

genocide n **killing**, slaughter, massacre, ethnic cleansing, liquidation

genre n **type**, sort, kind, category, field. *See* COMPARE AND CONTRAST *at* **type**.

gent *(dated infml)* n **gentleman**, man, bloke *(infml)*, guy *(infml)*, fellow *(dated)*

genteel *adj* 1 **refined**, proper, polite, courteous, discreet *Opposite*: vulgar 2 **pretentious**, snobbish, condescending, patronizing, affected *Opposite*: modest

gentility n **refinement**, propriety, manners, breeding, decorum *Opposite*: vulgarity

gentle *adj* 1 **mild**, calm, kind, tender, moderate *Opposite*: harsh 2 **soft**, light, soothing, mellow, restful *Opposite*: rough

gentleman n 1 **man**, male, chap *(infml)*, guy *(infml)*, bloke *(infml)* 2 **nobleman**, aristocrat, squire, grandee *Opposite*: cad

gentlemanly *adj* **chivalrous**, gallant, courteous, polite, civil *Opposite*: rude

gentleness n 1 **mildness**, calmness, kindness, tenderness, placidity *Opposite*: harshness 2 **quietness**, softness, lightness, smoothness, mellowness *Opposite*: harshness

gentrification n **redevelopment**, refurbishment, urban renewal, renovation, restoration *Opposite*: neglect

gentrify v **redevelop**, refurbish, renovate, restore, improve

gentry n **upper class**, nobility, aristocracy, elite, ruling class *Opposite*: working class

genuflect v 1 **kneel**, bow, curtsy, bend the knee, bob 2 **bow to**, defer to, kowtow, show respect for, grovel *Opposite*: disrespect

genuflection n **kneeling**, curtsy, bow, bob, dip

genuine *adj* 1 **real**, authentic, indisputable, true, unadulterated *Opposite*: fake 2 **sincere**, honest, frank, open, unaffected *Opposite*: false

genuineness n **authenticity**, realness, substance, legitimacy, validity

gen up *(infml)* v **research**, study, read up, revise, swot up *(infml)*

genus n **type**, kind, sort, species, class

geographic *see* geographical

geographical *adj* **physical**, topographical, terrestrial, earthly, environmental

geography n **topography**, natural features, characteristics, layout

geological division n **eon**, era, epoch, period

WORD BANK
❏ **types of eon (from oldest to most recent)** pre-Archaean, Archaean, Proterozoic, Phanerozoic
❏ **types of epoch (from oldest to most recent)** Palaeocene, Eocene, Oligocene, Miocene, Pliocene, Pleistocene, Holocene
❏ **types of era (from oldest to most recent)** Palaeozoic, Mesozoic, Cenozoic
❏ **types of period (from oldest to most recent)** Cambrian, Ordovician, Silurian, Devonian, Carboniferous, Permian, Triassic, Jurassic, Cretaceous, Tertiary, Quaternary

geometric *adj* **regular**, symmetrical, ordered, orderly, linear

geriatric *adj* **elderly**, aged, old, senior *Opposite*: young

germ n 1 **microbe**, microorganism, bacteria, virus, bug *(infml)* 2 **origin**, seed, embryo, rudiment, kernel

germane *adj* **relevant**, useful, connected, to the point, of interest *Opposite*: irrelevant

germ-free *adj* **sterile**, antiseptic, hygienic, sanitary, uninfected *Opposite*: contaminated

germinate v **sprout**, grow, develop, take root, evolve

germination n **sprouting**, propagation, incubation, growth, development

gestation n **development**, growth, incubation, maturation, pregnancy

gesticulate v **gesture**, wave, signal, motion, sign

gesticulation n **sign**, signal, gesture, wave, motion

gesture

gesture *n* **1 sign**, signal, gesticulation, motion, wave **2 act**, action, deed, token, intimation ■ *v* **gesticulate**, signal, shrug, nod, wave

get *v* **1 obtain**, acquire, secure, procure, gain **2 become**, grow, begin, have, attain **3 catch**, contract, acquire, develop, be infected with **4 cause**, make, induce, persuade, urge **5 move**, step, progress, walk, climb **6** *(infml)* **understand**, comprehend, grasp, follow, perceive

COMPARE AND CONTRAST CORE MEANING: come into possession of something

get become the owner of something or succeed in finding and possessing it; **acquire** get possession of something, sometimes suggesting that time or effort was involved; **obtain** get something, especially by making an effort or having the necessary qualifications; **gain** get something through effort, skill, or merit; **procure** get something, especially with effort or special care; **secure** get something, especially after using considerable effort to persuade somebody to grant or allow it.

get across *v* **put across**, put over, convey, impart, communicate

get a grip *(infml)* *v* **calm down**, get hold of yourself, compose yourself, control yourself, chill out *(infml)*

get ahead *v* **advance**, climb the ladder, progress, make progress, prosper *Opposite*: fail

get ahead of *v* **pass by**, be in front of, overtake *Opposite*: hold back

get along *v* **survive**, get by, manage, cope, live

get a move on *(infml)* *v* **speed up**, hurry up, get going, get moving, accelerate *Opposite*: slow down

get angry *v* **bristle**, bridle, explode, lose your cool, hit the roof *(infml)*

get a raw deal *v* **suffer**, draw the short straw, be hard done by, be put upon, come off badly

get at *v* **1 reach**, find, contact, speak to, write to **2 annoy**, tease, rub up the wrong way, irritate, get to

get away *v* **leave**, go away, escape, flee, depart

getaway *n* **escape**, exit, retreat, breakout, flight

get away from *v* **elude**, shake off, lose, escape from, outrun

get away with *v* **get off**, get off scot-free, escape, evade, elude *Opposite*: answer for

get a word in edgeways *v* **get a word in**, get a chance to speak, have your say, voice your opinion, say anything

get back *v* **retrieve**, recoup, repossess, regain, recuperate *Opposite*: lose

get back at *v* **get even**, turn the tables on, take revenge, get your own back, even the score

get behind *v* **support**, endorse, back, join forces, put in a good word for *Opposite*: oppose

get better *v* **recover**, recuperate, improve, turn the corner, bounce back *Opposite*: deteriorate

get bigger *v* **swell**, grow, inflate, mount, expand *Opposite*: shrink

get by *v* **survive**, manage, cope, scrape by, get on

get cracking *(infml)* *v* **get going**, make a start, get moving, get on, get a move on *(infml)*

get done *v* **accomplish**, achieve, complete, finish, do

get down *v* **descend**, get off, dismount, come down, climb down

get down to *v* **get to work**, begin, get on, start, concentrate *Opposite*: put off

get down to business *v* **get on with it**, get down to it, get down to brass tacks, get down to the nitty-gritty, stop beating about the bush

get even *v* **get your own back**, get back at, take revenge, turn the tables, even the score

get free of *v* **get rid of**, exorcize, escape, jettison, eliminate

get going *v* **1 start**, make a start, get on, hurry up, stir **2 start up**, turn on, activate, operate, power *Opposite*: turn off

get hitched *(infml)* *v* **get married**, marry, walk down the aisle, tie the knot *(infml)*, wed *(fml or literary)*

get hold of *v* **1 contact**, reach, find, get in touch with, talk to **2 obtain**, find, acquire, search out, lay hands on

get in *v* **1 arrive**, enter, appear, turn up *(infml)*, show up *(infml)* *Opposite*: depart **2 join**, be accepted, be included, make the grade, make the cut *(US)*

get in on the act *(infml)* *v* **take part**, join in, be included, be involved, jump on the bandwagon

get in the way *v* **obstruct**, hinder, impede, interfere, encumber

get into *v* **1 gain entry**, enter, open, access, hack into *Opposite*: get out of **2 put on**, slip into, don, change into, dress in *Opposite*: take off

get in touch with *v* **call**, get hold of, contact, reach, ring up

get into your stride *v* **get going**, get up to speed, get the hang of something, get off the ground

get involved *v* **interfere**, intervene, join in, be drawn in, put your oar in *Opposite*: hold back

get in with *v* **ingratiate yourself**, make friends with, curry favour, gain the favour of, associate with

get it *(infml)* *v* **understand**, see, get the drift, follow, comprehend *Opposite*: misunderstand

get it in the neck *(infml)* *v* **take the blame**, carry the can *(infml)*, take the rap *(slang)*

get it off your chest *v* **bare your soul**, tell somebody, let it out, unburden yourself, share *Opposite*: bottle up

get it wrong v **misunderstand**, blunder, get the wrong idea, get the wrong end of the stick, boob (infml)

get less v **subside**, die down, lessen, reduce, fall Opposite: grow

get longer v **lengthen**, elongate, grow, extend, spread out Opposite: shorten

get lost v **lose your way**, lose your bearings, go astray, go wrong, take a wrong turning

get married v **marry**, walk down the aisle, get hitched (infml), tie the knot (infml), wed (fml or literary)

get moving v **hurry up**, speed up, get going, make a move, get a move on (infml)

get off v **1 leave**, depart, exit, go, embark Opposite: arrive **2 dismount**, get down, descend, come down, climb off Opposite: get on

get on v **1 deal with**, handle, manage, accept, progress Opposite: mismanage **2 like**, be compatible, work well with, relate, gel (infml) Opposite: dislike **3 board**, climb on, mount, get on board, embark Opposite: get off **4 make a start**, get going, begin, start, get down to Opposite: defer

get on your high horse v **give yourself airs**, put on airs, lord it, get all high and mighty

get on your nerves v **annoy**, irritate, bother, put your back up, irk

get out v **leave**, depart, quit, evacuate, retreat Opposite: enter

get out of v **evade**, avoid, dodge, duck, get round Opposite: participate

get over v **1 recover**, live through, endure, survive, get beyond Opposite: succumb **2 come to terms with**, accept, surmount, overcome, conquer **3 convey**, communicate, impart, pass on, get across

get ready v **prepare**, steel, prime, brace, organize

get rid of v **dispose of**, discard, throw away, throw out, jettison Opposite: keep

get round v **1 become known**, break out, circulate, get out, be revealed **2 avoid**, go around, bypass, sidestep, evade

get smaller v **shrink**, shrivel up, narrow, deflate, recede Opposite: swell

get somewhere v **make headway**, make progress, make inroads, achieve something, make a breakthrough Opposite: fall behind

get the better of v **defeat**, beat, trounce, triumph over, get the upper hand

get the drift v **understand**, see, follow, get it (infml), get the message (infml)

get the hang of v **learn**, pick up, understand, master

get the message (infml) v **understand**, get the drift, take the hint, grasp, follow

get the most out of v **maximize**, make the most of, get the full benefit, exploit, milk (infml)

get the picture (infml) v **understand**, follow, see, grasp, get it (infml)

get the wrong end of the stick v **misconstrue**, misinterpret, make a mistake, misunderstand, misread

get the wrong idea v **misunderstand**, misread, misinterpret, misconstrue, misjudge

get thinner v **narrow**, taper, slim down, lose weight

get through v **1 survive**, come through, endure, weather, ride out **2 use**, consume, wear out, go through, expend **3 breach**, break through, penetrate, cross, pass

get to v **1 annoy**, irritate, bother, irk, affect **2 reach**, make, arrive at, attain

get-together (infml) n **meeting**, gathering, social, assembly, rendezvous

get to know v **become acquainted with**, be introduced to, meet, become familiar with

get to your feet v **stand up**, rise, stand, get up, arise (literary)

get under way v **begin**, start, proceed, launch, commence Opposite: come to a halt

getup (infml) n **outfit**, clothes, costume, suit, dress

get-up-and-go (infml) n **energy**, vitality, verve, life, drive

get used to v **become accustomed to**, get into the habit, adjust, adapt, acclimatize

get your bearings v **orient yourself**, find your way, find your feet, adjust, adapt

get your own back v **take revenge**, get even, retaliate, get back at, avenge yourself

geyser n **hot spring**, spring, natural spring, fountain, jet

ghastly adj **1 horrifying**, shocking, upsetting, distressing, grisly Opposite: pleasant **2 terrible**, horrible, appalling, dreadful, nasty Opposite: pleasant **3** (infml) **ill**, sick, unwell, dreadful, bad Opposite: well

gherkin n **pickled cucumber**, dill pickle, pickle

ghostlike adj **eerie**, spectral, ghostly, supernatural, ethereal

ghostly adj **ethereal**, spectral, indistinct, supernatural, eerie

ghostwrite v **cowrite**, write, compose, author, coauthor

ghostwriter n **cowriter**, writer, composer, author, coauthor

ghoulish adj **1 morbid**, macabre, dark, chilling, ghastly **2 cruel**, savage, brutal, fiendish, bloodthirsty Opposite: gentle

GI n **soldier**, private, enlisted person, volunteer, conscript

giant adj **huge**, enormous, vast, large, massive Opposite: tiny

gibber v **babble**, rant, prattle, jabber, gabble

gibberish n **nonsense**, prattle, babble, gabble, rubbish Opposite: sense

gibe n **jeer**, taunt, sneer, remark, joke ■ v **taunt**, mock, tease, jeer, ridicule

giblets n **guts**, offal, innards (infml)

giddiness n **1 dizziness**, unsteadiness, light-headedness, wooziness, shakiness *Opposite*: steadiness **2** *(dated)* **frivolity**, capriciousness, volatility, overexcitement, flightiness *Opposite*: seriousness

giddy adj **1 dizzy**, unsteady, off-balance, light-headed, woozy *Opposite*: steady **2** *(dated)* **frivolous**, scatterbrained, capricious, volatile, excited *Opposite*: serious

gift n **1 present**, donation, contribution, reward, bequest **2 talent**, skill, ability, flair, knack. *See* COMPARE AND CONTRAST *at* **talent**.

gifted adj **talented**, skilled, bright, able, intelligent. *See* COMPARE AND CONTRAST *at* **intelligent**.

giftwrap v **wrap**, wrap up, package

gigantic adj **huge**, enormous, massive, vast, gargantuan *Opposite*: tiny

giggle v **titter**, snigger, chuckle, laugh, chortle ■ n **snigger**, titter, chuckle, laugh, chortle

giggly adj **silly**, hysterical, immature, tittering, sniggering *Opposite*: serious

gilded adj **golden**, gold-plated, gilt, gold

gild the lily v **overdo it**, get carried away, go too far, lay it on thick, over-egg the pudding

gilt n **gold**, gold leaf, gold plate ■ adj **golden**, gold-plated, gilded, gold

gimmick n **trick**, ploy, stunt, device, promotion

gingerly adv **cautiously**, tentatively, warily, delicately, carefully *Opposite*: boldly

ginormous *(infml)* adj **huge**, enormous, vast, massive, immense *Opposite*: tiny

girder n **beam**, joist, bar, rafter, crossbeam

girdle n **belt**, sash, cummerbund, tie, drawstring

gird your loins v **brace yourself**, get ready, grit your teeth, prepare yourself, steel yourself

girlfriend n **partner**, lover, sweetheart, fiancée, ladyfriend *(infml)* *Opposite*: boyfriend

girlhood n **childhood**, youth, infancy, early years, adolescence

girlish adj **youthful**, adolescent, childlike, young

girth n **circumference**, breadth, width, span, thickness *Opposite*: height

gist n **idea**, essence, substance, general picture, point *Opposite*: minutiae

give v **1 provide**, offer, hand over, present, donate *Opposite*: take **2 grant**, award, accord, bestow *(fml)*, confer *(fml)* *Opposite*: withhold **3 impart**, convey, communicate, pass on, share *Opposite*: withhold **4 perform**, put on, stage, produce, organize **5 devote**, dedicate, give up, sacrifice, spend *Opposite*: withhold **6 yield**, collapse, break, go, split *Opposite*: hold up

COMPARE AND CONTRAST CORE MEANING: hand over something to somebody

give hand over a possession to somebody else to keep or use; **present** give something in a formal or ceremonial way; **confer** *(fml)* give somebody an honour, privilege, or award, often at a formal ceremony; **bestow** *(fml)* present somebody with something, especially something unexpected or undeserved; **donate** give a contribution to a charitable organization or another good cause, or, in a medical context, give blood for blood transfusions or organs for transplant; **grant** agree to allow a request, favour, or privilege, especially at the discretion of a person in authority, or formally or officially give money.

give a beating v **attack**, assault, batter, hit, smack

give a boost v **strengthen**, boost, lift, encourage, boost up *Opposite*: deflate

give a lift v **encourage**, boost, boost up, strengthen, fortify *Opposite*: deflate

give a miss *(infml)* v **stay away from**, abstain from, hold back from, give a wide berth, avoid

give-and-take *(infml)* n **cooperation**, compromise, reciprocity, collaboration, teamwork *Opposite*: selfishness

give away v **1 get rid of**, donate, offer, give, pass on *Opposite*: keep **2 disclose**, reveal, let slip, betray, divulge *Opposite*: keep secret

giveaway n **1 telltale sign**, clue, hint, indication, symptom **2** *(infml)* **gift**, special offer, free sample, trial offer, promotion ■ adj *(infml)* **bargain**, rock-bottom, low, introductory, special *Opposite*: exorbitant

give a wide berth v **steer clear**, keep well away, avoid, avoid like the plague, shun *Opposite*: seek out

give back v **return**, restore, hand back, repay, refund *Opposite*: keep

give chase *(fml)* v **pursue**, follow in hot pursuit, follow, go after, chase

give in v **1 lose**, admit defeat, surrender, concede, submit *Opposite*: stand your ground **2 hand over**, hand in, deliver, submit, present *Opposite*: withhold

give instructions v **direct**, inform, brief, instruct, tell

given adj **known**, assumed, agreed, specified, prearranged ■ prep **because of**, in view of, as a result of, taking into consideration, taking into account

given name n **first name**, Christian name, forename, name, moniker *(slang)*

given that conj **providing**, provided that, as long as, only if, assuming that

give off v **emit**, radiate, send out, discharge, exude

give out v **1 hand out**, distribute, provide, offer, allot *Opposite*: keep **2 declare**, announce, proclaim, pronounce, reveal *Opposite*: withhold **3 emit**, send out, transmit, give off, radiate **4 run out**, dry up, fail, come to an end, end *Opposite*: hold out **5 fail**, collapse, break, yield, go *Opposite*: hold

give over *(infml)* v **stop**, cease, desist, pack in

(infml), lay off *(infml) Opposite*: continue

give over to v dedicate, devote, allocate, reserve, allot

give permission v consent, agree, allow, let, authorize *Opposite*: forbid

give somebody the slip v lose, shake off, get away from, escape from, avoid

give the cold shoulder to v ignore, rebuff, exclude, look straight through, send to Coventry

give the lie to v contradict, belie, rebut, refute, conflict with

give the once-over *(infml)* v examine, inspect, check out, scrutinize, look at

give up v 1 admit defeat, give in, surrender, concede, submit *Opposite*: stand your ground 2 hand over, part with, surrender, relinquish, give away *Opposite*: keep 3 stop, quit, leave off, renounce, abstain from *Opposite*: stick with 4 despair, abandon, lose hope, give up on 5 devote, dedicate, give, surrender, sacrifice *Opposite*: withhold 6 reveal, disclose, divulge, tell, let slip *Opposite*: keep secret

give up on v 1 stop, give up, quit, abandon, leave off 2 despair, abandon, lose hope, give up

give your word v promise, vow, swear, pledge, assure

gizmo *(infml)* n gadget, device, contraption, appliance, thing

glacial adj 1 icy, ice-cold, freezing, biting, bitter *Opposite*: tropical 2 hostile, unfriendly, icy, cold, cool *Opposite*: warm

glacier n ice field, icecap, ice floe, iceberg, floe

glad adj 1 delighted, happy, pleased, content, grateful *Opposite*: sad 2 willing, ready, prepared, happy, eager *Opposite*: unwilling

gladden v delight, please, cheer, bring joy to, hearten *Opposite*: sadden

glade n clearing, opening, gap, open space, dell *(literary)*

gladiator n 1 fighter, fencer, sword fighter, warrior, battler 2 campaigner, lobbyist, supporter, advocate, champion

gladness n happiness, cheerfulness, delight, joy, pleasure *Opposite*: sadness

glad rags *(infml)* n best clothes, finery, black tie, Sunday best, best bib and tucker *(infml)*

glamorize v 1 romanticize, idealize, exaggerate, embellish, dress up *Opposite*: understate 2 beautify, decorate, adorn, do up, dress up

glamorous adj stylish, fashionable, glitzy, dazzling, splendid *Opposite*: drab

glamour n 1 allure, charm, appeal, fascination, attraction *Opposite*: dullness 2 good looks, beauty, glitz, glitziness, style *Opposite*: drabness

glance v 1 look, peep, peek, glimpse, squint *Opposite*: gaze 2 glint, shine, glimmer, gleam, glitter ■ n peep, look, glimpse, scan, squint *(infml) Opposite*: gaze

glance off v bounce off, ricochet, reflect, deflect, rebound

glancing adj sideways, sidelong, lateral, slanting, tangential

glare v 1 scowl, stare, glower, frown, look daggers 2 dazzle, flash, glimmer, glitter, shine 3 stand out, leap out, jump out, catch the eye, show ■ n 1 dirty look, stare, glower, scowl, frown 2 shine, brightness, dazzle, flash, shimmer *Opposite*: dullness

glaring adj 1 conspicuous, obvious, obtrusive, evident, blatant *Opposite*: inconspicuous 2 dazzling, brilliant, shimmering, bright, intense *Opposite*: dim 3 garish, brash, gaudy, loud, clashing *Opposite*: soft

glaringly adv blatantly, patently, flagrantly, clearly, extremely

glass n beaker, tumbler, wineglass, goblet, flute

glasses n spectacles, goggles, specs *(infml)*

WORD BANK
❏ **types of glasses** bifocals, dark glasses, monocle, pince-nez, shades *(infml)*, sunglasses, sunspecs *(infml)*

glassy adj 1 smooth, slippery, shiny, glossy, slick *Opposite*: dull 2 expressionless, glazed, dazed, blank, vacant *Opposite*: alert

glaze v varnish, finish, seal, coat, cover ■ n coating, varnish, finish, seal, cover

glazed adj 1 glassy, blank, fixed, expressionless, dull *Opposite*: alert 2 glossy, shiny, smooth, lustrous, varnished *Opposite*: dull

gleam v 1 shine, glow, beam, burn, blaze 2 flash, flicker, twinkle, shimmer, sparkle ■ n 1 glow, shine, beam, ray, blaze 2 flicker, flash, twinkle, shimmer, sparkle

gleaming adj shiny, polished, luminous, lustrous, glossy *Opposite*: dull

glee n 1 delight, happiness, pleasure, joy, elation *Opposite*: sadness 2 triumph, jubilation, smugness, exultance *Opposite*: despondency

gleeful adj 1 delighted, happy, pleased, joyful, elated *Opposite*: sad 2 triumphant, jubilant, smug, gloating, exultant *Opposite*: despondent

glen n valley, gorge, ravine, dale, vale *(literary)*

glib adj 1 persuasive, fluent, smooth, convincing, slick *Opposite*: hesitant 2 superficial, shallow, facile, casual, simplistic *Opposite*: profound

glibness n 1 persuasiveness, fluency, slickness, smoothness *Opposite*: hesitation 2 superficiality, shallowness, facileness, casualness *Opposite*: profoundness

glide v 1 slither, slide, slide along, slip, skate 2 fly, soar, wheel, drift, coast

glimmer v twinkle, shine, gleam, flicker, glow

■ n **shine**, twinkle, gleam, flicker, glow

glimpse n 1 **look**, glance, peep, sight, peek (infml) 2 **hint**, sight, foretaste, indication, pointer ■ ■ v **see**, catch sight of, glance at, peep at, look at

glint v **sparkle**, flash, wink, shine, twinkle ■ n **flash**, sparkle, shine, twinkle, spark

glisten v **gleam**, sparkle, glint, flash, reflect ■ n **sparkle**, gleam, glint, flash, shine

glistening adj **gleaming**, shining, sparkly, shiny, glittering

glitch n **hitch**, problem, malfunction, fault, anomaly

glitter v **gleam**, sparkle, shine, dazzle, shimmer ■ n 1 **sparkle**, gleam, shimmer, flash, twinkle 2 **tinsel**, sequins, spangles 3 **dazzle**, splendour, flashiness, glamour, showiness

glittering adj **impressive**, sparkling, dazzling, splendid, scintillating

glittery adj **shiny**, sparkly, shimmering, brilliant, dazzling

glitz n **glamour**, style, stylishness, glitziness, showiness

glitziness n 1 **glamour**, glitter, style, glitz, stylishness 2 **showiness**, tawdriness, flashiness, extravagance, tastelessness

glitzy adj **showy**, ostentatious, flashy, extravagant, swanky (infml)

gloat v **revel**, wallow, exult, smirk, delight

glob (infml) n **blob**, gobbet, drop, globule, lump

global adj 1 **worldwide**, international Opposite: local 2 **universal**, comprehensive, total, inclusive, overall

globally adv 1 **internationally**, worldwide, universally Opposite: locally 2 **altogether**, as a whole, generally, universally, totally

globe n 1 **sphere**, ball, orb 2 **earth**, world, planet

globetrot v **travel**, journey, tour, shuttle, backpack

globetrotter n **traveller**, tourist, backpacker, holidaymaker, journeyer

globular adj **spherical**, round, circular, bulbous, rotund

globule n **drop**, blob, bead, bubble, gobbet

gloom n 1 **darkness**, shade, murkiness, shadow, dimness Opposite: brightness 2 **pessimism**, despair, sadness, dejection, unhappiness Opposite: happiness

gloominess n 1 **dimness**, darkness, murkiness, shade, shadow Opposite: brightness 2 **despondency**, pessimism, gloom, depression, despair Opposite: happiness

gloomy adj 1 **dark**, depressing, dim, overcast, dull Opposite: bright 2 **depressed**, low, low-spirited, melancholy, miserable Opposite: cheerful

glorification n **adoration**, veneration, elevation, deification, praise Opposite: belittlement

glorify v **worship**, adore, lionize, deify, elevate Opposite: belittle

glorious adj **magnificent**, wonderful, splendid, celebrated, superb Opposite: shameful

glory n 1 **magnificence**, splendour, beauty, wonder, grandeur 2 **credit**, fame, praise, laurels, triumph Opposite: criticism

glory in v **enjoy**, lap up, wallow in, make the most of, revel in Opposite: despise

gloss n 1 **lustre**, polish, shine, brightness, sheen 2 **interpretation**, explanation, spin (slang) 3 **annotation**, commentary, footnote, explanation, comment

glossary n **lexicon**, dictionary, word list, vocabulary, thesaurus

glossiness n 1 **shininess**, smoothness, sheen, patina, lustre 2 (infml) **veneer**, surface, façade

gloss over v **skim over**, pass over, dismiss, evade, dodge Opposite: dwell on

glossy adj **sleek**, silky, silken, lustrous, shiny Opposite: dull

glow n **radiance**, ruddiness, light, luminosity, glimmering ■ v **burn**, blaze, flame, shine, smoulder

glower v **glare**, frown, scowl, look daggers, look hard

glowering adj **angry**, dark, scowling, sullen, surly

glowing adj 1 **bright**, shimmering, radiant, lustrous, shining Opposite: dull 2 **fulsome**, complimentary, flattering, appreciative, congratulatory Opposite: derogatory 3 **healthy-looking**, tanned, rosy, shining, radiant Opposite: pale

glue n **adhesive**, paste, superglue, cement, gum ■ v **paste**, stick, fasten, attach, join

gluey adj **sticky**, gummy, tacky, glutinous, thick

glum adj **gloomy**, down, morose, sad, low Opposite: cheerful

glumness n **pessimism**, unhappiness, misery, depression, dejection Opposite: cheerfulness

glut n **excess**, surplus, superfluity, flood, over-abundance Opposite: shortage

glutinous adj **sticky**, gluey, gooey, tacky, gummy

glutton n **overeater**, gourmand, greedy guts (infml), gannet (infml), pig (infml)

gluttonous adj **greedy**, voracious, insatiable, excessive, desirous (fml)

gluttony n **greed**, greediness, excess, pig-gishness, rapaciousness

gnarled adj **knotted**, twisted, bent, knotty, crooked Opposite: straight

gnash v **grind**, clench, grit, grate, rasp

gnash your teeth v **be fuming**, be upset, grind your teeth, be frustrated

gnat n **midge**, mosquito, fly, firefly, insect

gnaw v **worry**, trouble, bother, cause anxiety, concern *Opposite*: comfort

gnome n **elf**, sprite, goblin, troll, leprechaun

go v **1 leave**, go away, go off, depart, set off *Opposite*: come **2 move**, move on, proceed, progress, make for **3 work**, run, function, operate, move *Opposite*: stop **4 reach**, extend, stretch, spread **5 become**, get, grow, come to be **6 die**, pass away, pass on, depart *(fml)*, expire *(fml) Opposite*: live ■ n **1 energy**, liveliness, enthusiasm, spirit, verve *Opposite*: lethargy **2 try**, attempt, turn, chance, shot **3** *(infml)* **energy**, life, zest, zip *(infml)*, oomph *(infml)*

go about v **get on with**, perform, carry out, accomplish, transact

goad v **provoke**, prod, push, stir, stimulate *Opposite*: calm ■ n **1 stick**, prod, poker, rod, whip **2 stimulus**, impetus, driving force, spur, stimulation. *See* COMPARE AND CONTRAST *at* **motive**.

go adrift v **wander**, drift, stray, go astray, deviate

go after v **try for**, aim for, target, go all-out for, bend over backwards

go against v **violate**, disobey, fly in the face of, infringe, buck *(infml)*

go-ahead *(infml)* n **permission**, consent, approval, green light, support

goal n **1 objective**, aim, end, ambition, purpose **2 goalmouth**, penalty area, box, area, goal line

go along with v **acquiesce**, concur, agree, grant, accept *Opposite*: refuse

go around v **1 circulate**, spread, pass on, hand on, disseminate **2 travel**, go from place to place, ride, walk, move **3 revolve**, rotate, twirl, spin, twist

go around with *(infml)* v **accompany**, escort, tag along, spend time with, be together

go astray v **stray**, get lost, transgress, go off the rails, deviate

go away v **1 leave**, get away, move, depart, be off *Opposite*: stay **2 disappear**, vanish, fade, fade away, recede *Opposite*: stay

go back v **return**, turn back, revert, revisit, retrace your steps *Opposite*: advance

go back on v **change your mind**, backtrack, break your promise, have second thoughts, retract *Opposite*: keep your word

go back over v **reconsider**, re-examine, repeat, revise, return to

go backwards v **reverse**, retreat, regress, lose ground, fall back *Opposite*: advance

go bad v **decay**, go off, rot, decompose, putrefy

go bankrupt v **fail**, collapse, fold, go out of business, go to the wall

gobble v **1 devour**, bolt, wolf, guzzle *(infml)*, scoff *(infml) Opposite*: nibble **2** *(infml)* **use up**, go through, run through, consume, eat into *Opposite*: conserve

gobbledegook *(infml)* n **nonsense**, jargon, gibberish, drivel, rubbish

go berserk v **lose control**, lose your temper, lose your cool, go mad, be beside yourself

go-between n **mediator**, intermediary, broker, arbitrator, messenger

go beyond v **surpass**, outdo, rise above, overtake, pass

goblet n **glass**, cup, chalice, wineglass

goblin n **elf**, sprite, imp, gnome, troll

go bust *(infml)* v **go bankrupt**, go under, shut down, fail, go out of business

go by v **pass**, pass by, elapse, lapse

god n **deity**, divinity, idol, spirit, supernatural being

goddess n **deity**, divinity, idol, spirit, supernatural being

godlike adj **divine**, superhuman, transcendent, heavenly, holy

godliness n **1 religiousness**, holiness, devoutness, goodness, saintliness *Opposite*: wickedness **2 divinity**, holiness, heavenliness, transcendence, sacredness

godly *(fml)* adj **1 religious**, devout, holy, pious, saintly *Opposite*: wicked **2 divine**, holy, heavenly, transcendent, godlike

go down v **1 descend**, drop, sink, dive, plunge *Opposite*: go up **2 deteriorate**, decline, slip, go downhill, get worse *Opposite*: improve **3** *(infml)* **lose**, be defeated, be beaten, go under, fail *Opposite*: win

go downhill v **deteriorate**, worsen, fail, get worse, go down *Opposite*: improve

go down with *(infml)* v **catch**, become ill with, contract, pick up, come down with

godsend n **blessing**, boon, stroke of luck, bonus, windfall *Opposite*: disaster

go easy on *(infml)* v **1 treat gently**, indulge, sympathize, oblige, please *Opposite*: punish **2 take it easy**, slow down, take it steady, avoid, stint *Opposite*: overdo

gofer *(infml)* n **runner**, messenger, minion, assistant, lackey

go for v **1** *(infml)* **try for**, go after, target, aim for, set your sights on **2** *(infml)* **like**, enjoy, prefer, follow, love *Opposite*: dislike **3** *(infml)* **choose**, pick, select, prefer, opt for *Opposite*: refuse **4 attack**, lay into, set upon, assault, tear into

go forward v **advance**, progress, go on, move along, proceed *Opposite*: go back

go from bad to worse v **worsen**, take a turn for the worse, deteriorate, degenerate, go downhill *Opposite*: improve

go-getter *(infml)* n **achiever**, doer, self-starter, high-flier, live wire *(infml) Opposite*: layabout

go-getting *(infml)* adj **ambitious**, high-powered, determined, positive, single-minded

goggle v **stare**, gaze, gape, ogle, look

goggles *n* glasses, spectacles, specs (*infml*)

go hard *v* solidify, set, set hard, harden, stiffen *Opposite*: soften

go in *v* enter, set foot in, gain admittance, step in, access *Opposite*: leave

go in for *v* 1 enter, compete in, take part in, take up 2 like, prefer, follow, love, enjoy *Opposite*: dislike

going *n* 1 departure, exit, disappearance *Opposite*: arrival 2 conditions, circumstances, situation, case, setup ■ *adj* 1 successful, profitable, moneymaking, working *Opposite*: bankrupt 2 accepted, standard, valid, current, present 3 available, obtainable, ready, free, open *Opposite*: taken

going-over (*infml*) *n* 1 examination, inspection, check, investigation, analysis 2 overhaul, service, restoration, checkup, improvement 3 rebuke, reprimand, scolding, talking-to (*infml*), telling-off (*infml*)

going rate *n* market price, standard price, usual price, average price, price

goings-on (*infml*) *n* activity, comings and goings, affairs, business, toing and froing

go into *v* 1 discuss, go over, talk about, look into, examine *Opposite*: ignore 2 enter, go in, set foot in, gain admittance, step in *Opposite*: leave

go into detail *v* elaborate, enlarge on, amplify, expand, explain

go in with *v* partner, join, cooperate, merge, combine

gold *n* 1 treasure, bullion, ingots, gold plate, sovereigns 2 wealth, money, assets, resources, riches 3 (*infml*) first place, first prize, title, medal, trophy ■ *adj* gilded, gilt, gold-leaf, gold-plated, golden

gold brick *n* fake, fraud, fool's gold, counterfeit, swindle

golden *adj* 1 excellent, unique, first-rate, wonderful, superb 2 idyllic, best, peak, utopian, paradisaical 3 gold, gold-plated, gold-leaf, gilt, gilded 4 favoured, superior, special, elite, select

golden age *n* peak, pinnacle, apex, summit, zenith

golden mean *n* middle, midway, mean *Opposite*: extreme

golden opportunity *n* opportunity, advantage, chance, chance of a lifetime, good fortune

golden rule *n* standard, belief, tenet, code, guide

gold mine *n* moneymaker, treasure-trove, treasure house, money-spinner (*infml*)

gold-plated *adj* gilded, gilt, gold-leaf, golden, gold

gold standard *n* benchmark, system, yardstick, touchstone, criterion

go mad *v* lose your temper, blow up (*infml*), go off the deep end (*infml*), go haywire (*infml*), blow your top (*infml*)

go missing *v* disappear, vanish, abscond, escape, go AWOL

gone *adj* 1 (*infml*) dead, passed away, passed on, no more, deceased (*fml*) *Opposite*: alive 2 absent, away, left, disappeared, moved out *Opposite*: present 3 used up, spent, finished, consumed, depleted *Opposite*: remaining

gonfalon *n* pennant, banner, flag, standard, ensign

goo (*infml*) *n* 1 sludge, slush, slop, sticky stuff, gunge (*infml*) 2 slush, sentimentality, emotionalism, mush, corn (*infml*)

good *adj* 1 high-quality, first-class, superior, excellent, first-rate *Opposite*: poor 2 suitable, helpful, beneficial, sound, safe *Opposite*: useless 3 skilled, skilful, able, proficient, accomplished *Opposite*: bad 4 virtuous, decent, respectable, moral, upright *Opposite*: immoral 5 enjoyable, pleasant, nice, lovely, satisfactory *Opposite*: unpleasant 6 obedient, well-behaved, well-mannered, polite, well-brought-up *Opposite*: naughty 7 nice, lovely, clear, mild, pleasant *Opposite*: bad 8 effective, useful, valuable, right, appropriate *Opposite*: ineffective ■ *n* benefit, help, advantage, usefulness, profit

good cause *n* charitable organization, voluntary organization, deserving cause, charity, benefit

good deed *n* good turn, favour, kindness, service *Opposite*: sin

good faith *n* honesty, lawfulness, sincerity, probity, integrity

good fortune *n* luck, good luck, chance, a stroke of luck, lucky break *Opposite*: misfortune

good health *n* fitness, strength, healthiness, vigour, robustness *Opposite*: illness

goodhearted *adj* kind-hearted, kind, caring, generous, giving

good-humoured *adj* friendly, good-natured, good-tempered, easygoing, genial *Opposite*: ill-tempered

good judgment *n* judiciousness, acumen, astuteness, wisdom, perspicacity

good life *n* luxury, comfort, ease, life of ease, life of Riley

good-looking *adj* attractive, handsome, beautiful, lovely, pretty *Opposite*: unattractive

COMPARE AND CONTRAST CORE MEANING: having a pleasing facial appearance
good-looking having a pleasant personal, especially facial, appearance; **attractive** pleasing in appearance or manner, or sexually desirable; **beautiful** pleasing to the senses, especially pleasing to look at, and often used to describe women whose appearance is generally considered ideal or perfect; **handsome** with good facial features or a pleasing general appearance, generally used of men, but also of women who have strong but attractive features; **lovely** pleasing to look at, most often used of women; **pretty** with an attractive,

pleasant face that is appealing, rather than outstandingly beautiful, most often used of women.

good looks *n* **beauty**, attractiveness, prettiness, handsomeness, loveliness

goodly *adj* **large**, substantial, fair, considerable, reasonable

good manners *n* **propriety**, manners, courtesy, decorum, etiquette *Opposite*: bad manners

good name *n* **reputation**, credit, standing, status, prestige

good-natured *adj* **pleasant**, cheerful, friendly, kind, happy *Opposite*: disagreeable

goodness *n* **virtuousness**, decency, kindness, honesty, integrity *Opposite*: badness

good offices *n* **intervention**, intercession, support, mediation, help

goods *n* **1 wares**, stock, articles, produce, supplies **2 property**, personal property, belongings, goods and chattels, things **3 merchandise**, imports, exports, cargo, freight

good sense *n* **prudence**, reason, practicality, intelligence, nous (*infml*) *Opposite*: stupidity

good-sized *adj* **sizable**, generous, big, substantial, large *Opposite*: small

good taste *n* **discernment**, style, elegance, judgment, refinement *Opposite*: bad taste

good-tempered *adj* **placid**, good-natured, easygoing, good-humoured, amicable *Opposite*: bad-tempered

good thing *n* **advantage**, blessing, boon, benefit, plus (*infml*)

good turn *n* **favour**, kindness, good deed, service

goodwill *n* **kindness**, friendliness, helpfulness, benevolence, generosity *Opposite*: malice

good word *n* **recommendation**, testimonial, reference, character, defence

goody *n* **1 treat**, perk, bonus, reward, extravagance **2 hero**, winner, good guy (*US*) *Opposite*: baddie (*infml*) **3 titbit**, sweet, snack, candy (*US*)

goody-goody (*infml*) *n* **teacher's pet**, goody two-shoes (*infml*), bluenose (*US dated infml*) ■ *adj* **sanctimonious**, smug, self-satisfied, self-righteous, prudish

gooey *adj* **1 sticky**, viscous, thick, glutinous, gummy **2** (*infml*) **slushy**, corny, cloying, sentimental, mushy

goof (*infml*) *n* **error**, blunder, slip, gaffe, mistake ■ *v* **1 mistake**, get it wrong, make a blunder, blunder, go wrong **2 mix up**, muddle, botch (*infml*), mess up (*infml*), foul up (*infml*)

go off *v* **1 explode**, blow up, go up, detonate **2 leave**, go away, go, depart, set off *Opposite*: stay **3 go bad**, decay, rot, decompose, putrefy

go off the deep end *v* **lose your temper**, lose your cool, go berserk, lose control, hit the roof (*infml*) *Opposite*: calm down

go on *v* **1 continue**, last, keep on, keep up, persist *Opposite*: stop **2 occur**, happen, take place, come about **3 blabber**, chatter, prattle, blather (*infml*), blab (*infml*)

go on at (*infml*) *v* **whine**, complain, nag, criticize, grumble

go one better *v* **surpass**, outdo, top, crown, better

goose step *v* **strut**, stride, tramp, pace, walk

go out *v* **1 socialize**, meet friends, party (*infml*), go out on the town (*infml*), paint the town red (*infml*) **2 ebb**, recede, flow out

go out of business *v* **go bankrupt**, fold, close down, shut down, go belly up

go over *v* **discuss**, go into, examine, look at, study *Opposite*: ignore

go over the top *v* **overdo it**, get carried away, gild the lily, over-egg the pudding, go mad (*infml*)

gore *v* **wound**, pierce, stab, spear, stick ■ *n* **blood**, violence, bloodletting, slaughter, killing

gorge *n* **valley**, ravine, canyon, defile, gap ■ *v* **1 overeat**, stuff, binge, glut, sate **2 devour**, wolf, bolt, gobble, consume *Opposite*: nibble

gorgeous *adj* **beautiful**, magnificent, stunning, elegant, attractive *Opposite*: unattractive

gorgeousness *n* **elegance**, magnificence, beauty, splendour, exquisiteness

gorilla (*infml*) *n* **thug**, brute, bully, hoodlum, heavy (*slang*)

gormless (*infml*) *adj* **stupid**, unintelligent, dull, obtuse, brainless *Opposite*: bright

go round *v* **visit**, call on, look in, drop in, pop in

gory *adj* **1 bloody**, bloodstained, blood-soaked **2 violent**, gruesome, brutal, bloodthirsty, fierce *Opposite*: pleasant **3 disgusting**, grisly, unpleasant, ghastly *Opposite*: delightful

go-slow *n* **stoppage**, strike, slowdown (*US*)

gossamer *n* **filaments**, spider's web, cobwebs, threads (*US*) ■ *adj* **delicate**, flimsy, sheer, filmy, ethereal *Opposite*: robust

gossip *n* **1 rumour**, hearsay, tittle-tattle, scandal, chitchat **2 chatter**, chat, talk, conversation, chinwag (*infml*) **3 tattler**, telltale, gossipmonger, scandalmonger, rumourmonger ■ *v* **chatter**, talk, converse, chat, natter (*infml*)

gossipmonger *n* **tattler**, telltale, gossip, scandalmonger, rumourmonger

go the distance *v* **complete**, finish, achieve, accomplish, carry out *Opposite*: give up

Gothic *adj* **supernatural**, melodramatic, eerie, grotesque, gloomy

go through *v* **1 experience**, endure, undergo, bear, suffer **2 use**, get through, run through, consume, utilize *Opposite*: keep **3 examine**, look through, look over, go over, study

go through the roof v soar, rocket, rise, shoot up, spiral upwards *Opposite*: plummet

go to bed v retire, turn in *(infml)*, hit the hay *(infml)*, hit the sack *(infml)*

go to pieces v break down, crack, lose control, collapse, crumple

go to pot *(infml)* v deteriorate, disintegrate, fall apart, go downhill, go from bad to worse *Opposite*: improve

go to rack and ruin *(infml)* see **go to pot**

go to sleep v fall asleep, nod off, doze off, drift off, drop off *(infml)* *Opposite*: wake up

go to the dogs *(infml)* v go downhill, deteriorate, degenerate, decline, go from bad to worse *Opposite*: improve

go to the wall v go bankrupt, fold, go under, fail, close down

go to waste v be wasted, go down the drain, fall by the wayside, go to seed, go down the tube *(infml)*

gouge v scratch, score, scrape, mark, cut into ■ n score, scratch, gash, groove, hollow

gouge out v dig out, hollow out, press out, squeeze out, force out

go under v 1 collapse, go to the wall, fold, fail, go bust *(infml)* 2 lose consciousness, pass out, black out, faint

go up v explode, go off, detonate, blow up, ignite

go up in smoke v 1 burn, catch fire, burst into flames, burn to a crisp, burn to the ground 2 fail, fold, collapse, go wrong, go awry

gourmand n 1 glutton, overeater, greedy guts *(infml)*, gannet *(infml)*, pig *(infml)* 2 gastronome, food lover, connoisseur, gourmet, epicure

gourmet n gastronome, food lover, connoisseur, gourmand, epicure

govern v rule, preside over, oversee, administer, administrate

governess n tutor, teacher, instructor, schoolteacher, educator

government n administration, rule, management, direction, regime

governmental adj administrative, parliamentary, legislative, executive, constitutional

governor n director, ruler, manager, administrator, chief

governorship n administration, leadership, stewardship, directorship, captaincy

go wild *(infml)* v run riot, rampage, run amok, go on the rampage, run wild

go with v 1 *(infml)* date, go out with, see, socialize, go steady 2 adopt, accept, follow, run with, support

go without v not have, do without, be without, lack, want *Opposite*: have

gown n dress, robe, evening dress, wedding dress, ballgown

go wrong v 1 fail, break down, not work, not succeed, go awry *Opposite*: succeed 2 make a mistake, misjudge, blunder, slip up *(infml)*, goof *(infml)*

GP n family doctor, doctor, clinician, practitioner, medic *(infml)*

grab v 1 grasp, clutch, grip, take hold of, seize *Opposite*: let go 2 snatch, take, seize, remove, steal 3 *(infml)* affect, appeal, impress, attract, please

grab hold of v grab, grasp, grip, snatch, clutch

grace n 1 elegance, refinement, loveliness, beauty, polish *Opposite*: awkwardness 2 kindness, kindliness, decency, mercy, mercifulness *Opposite*: unkindness 3 blessing, prayer, thanks, thanksgiving ■ v 1 dignify, honour, favour, distinguish *Opposite*: demean 2 adorn, embellish, enhance, decorate, ornament *Opposite*: deface

graceful adj 1 elegant, beautiful, supple, agile, nimble *Opposite*: graceless 2 poised, dignified, polished, refined, stylish *Opposite*: awkward 3 flowing, fluid, smooth, easy on the eye, attractive *Opposite*: ugly

gracefulness n 1 elegance, grace, smoothness, fluidity, subtlety *Opposite*: inelegance 2 poise, dignity, refinement, grace, restraint *Opposite*: awkwardness

graceless adj 1 clumsy, ungainly, inelegant, awkward, maladroit *Opposite*: graceful 2 rude, impolite, ill-mannered, boorish, offensive *Opposite*: polite

gracelessness n 1 inelegance, awkwardness, clumsiness, ungainliness, unskilfulness *Opposite*: gracefulness 2 rudeness, impoliteness, mannerlessness, bad manners, boorishness *Opposite*: politeness

grace period n extra time, extension, overrun, overtime (US)

gracious adj 1 kind, polite, tactful, courteous, civil *Opposite*: rude 2 condescending, haughty, superior, patronizing, high and mighty *Opposite*: genuine 3 luxurious, elegant, comfortable, well-appointed, plush *(infml)* *Opposite*: modest 4 merciful, compassionate, lenient, humane, charitable *Opposite*: harsh

graciousness n kindness, courteousness, politeness, civility, affability *Opposite*: rudeness

gradation n nuance, degree, stage, progression, shift

grade n 1 score, mark, rating, ranking, evaluation 2 rank, position, status, standing, class ■ v classify, categorize, sort, arrange, order

gradient n slope, incline, ramp, hill, rise

gradual adj slow, measured, slow but sure, plodding, continuing *Opposite*: rapid

graduate v 1 progress, move up, advance, go forward, move on *Opposite*: fall back 2 mark off, measure off, divide up, regulate 3 arrange, order, categorize, classify, rank

graduation *n* **1 matriculation**, qualification, completion, validation, attainment **2 award ceremony**, graduation day, ceremony, passing out **3 mark**, division, line, unit, step **4 calibration**, division, measurement, marking up, marking out

graffiti *n* drawing, doodle, scrawl, scribble, writing

graft *n* **1 implant**, insert, transplant, scion, slip **2** (*infml*) **work**, labour, toil, slog, grind ■ *v* **1** (*infml*) **labour**, strive, work, slog, slave **2 splice**, attach, join, embed, implant

grain *n* **1 cereal**, wheat, corn, barley, maize **2 seed**, kernel, germ **3 particle**, speck, fragment, crumb, bit **4 pattern**, direction, configuration, arrangement, texture

grammar *n* syntax, sentence structure, language rules, parsing

grammatical *adj* **1 linguistic**, syntactic, structural **2 correct**, well-formed, right, proper, standard

gran (*infml*) *see* **grandmother**

granary *n* warehouse, barn, silo

grand *adj* **1 outstanding**, impressive, imposing, majestic, magnificent *Opposite*: humble **2 ambitious**, impressive, far-reaching, major, substantial *Opposite*: limited **3 distinguished**, illustrious, celebrated, well-known, famous *Opposite*: ordinary **4 wonderful**, fantastic, excellent, memorable, great *Opposite*: poor

granddad (*infml*) *see* **grandfather**

grandee *n* dignitary, notable, public figure, VIP, nob (*infml*) *Opposite*: upstart

grandeur *n* **splendour**, magnificence, sumptuousness, opulence, majesty *Opposite*: austerity

grandfather *n* granddad (*infml*), grandpa (*infml*), gramps (*infml*)

grandiloquence *n* pomposity, bombast, loftiness, fustian, rhetoric

grandiloquent *adj* pompous, lofty, haughty, bombastic, high-flown *Opposite*: plain

grandiose *adj* **1 pretentious**, pompous, flamboyant, ostentatious, extravagant *Opposite*: modest **2 magnificent**, lavish, splendid, impressive, stately *Opposite*: modest **3 elaborate**, ambitious, complex, impenetrable, unfathomable *Opposite*: simple

grandiosity *n* **1 pretentiousness**, pompousness, self-importance, affectedness, pomposity *Opposite*: unpretentiousness **2 magnificence**, lavishness, splendour, impressiveness, stateliness *Opposite*: modesty **3 elaborateness**, ambitiousness, complexity, impenetrability *Opposite*: simplicity

grandma (*infml*) *see* **grandmother**

grandmother *n* grandma (*infml*), nana (*infml*), gran (*infml*), granny (*infml*), nanny (*infml*)

grandness *n* magnificence, splendour, majesty, dignity, stateliness *Opposite*: simplicity

grandpa (*infml*) *see* **grandfather**

grange *n* **farmhouse**, country house, manor house, homestead, ranch

granny (*infml*) *see* **grandmother**

grant *v* **1 allow**, permit, agree to, consent to, approve of *Opposite*: prohibit **2 give**, accord, award, sign over, present ■ *n* **funding**, scholarship, endowment, contribution, donation. *See* COMPARE AND CONTRAST *at* **give**.

granular *adj* gritty, grainy, rough, coarse, granulated *Opposite*: smooth

granulated *adj* ground, coarse, grainy, gritty, rough

granule *n* grain, pellet, particle, morsel, crumb

grapevine *n* rumour mill, gossip, word of mouth, viral marketing, bush telegraph (*infml*)

graph *n* chart, diagram, grid, display

graphic *adj* **1 explicit**, realistic, vivid, striking, detailed *Opposite*: sketchy **2 illustrative**, pictorial, drawn, diagrammatic, decorative

grapple *v* **1 struggle**, wrestle, seize, grab, grasp **2 contend**, deal with, cope, face, handle

grasp *v* **1 take hold of**, clutch, grab, seize, grip *Opposite*: let go of **2 understand**, comprehend, see the point of, follow, get ■ *n* **1 grip**, hold, clutch, clasp, clench **2 understanding**, comprehension, knowledge, awareness, perception **3 reach**, scope, extent, range, capacity

grasping *adj* greedy, avaricious, covetous, selfish, acquisitive *Opposite*: generous

grass *n* grassland, meadow, pasture, prairie, sward

WORD BANK

❏ **types of grass** bamboo, beach grass, bluegrass, bulrush, couch grass, crab grass, esparto, fescue, Kentucky bluegrass, lyme grass, marram, meadow fescue, pampas grass, reed, rye-grass, spinifex, sugar cane, sword grass, timothy

---

grassland *n* plains, prairie, savanna, steppe, heath

grassroots *n* **1 masses**, hoi polloi, rank and file, ranks, also-rans **2 basis**, origin, foundation, base, root ■ *adj* **popular**, proletarian, public, common, ordinary

grassy *adj* green, verdant, lush

grate *n* grill, lattice, grille, trellis, grid ■ *v* **1 shred**, scrape, rasp, file, grind **2 irritate**, annoy, exasperate, vex, chafe *Opposite*: please

grateful *adj* thankful, appreciative, obliged, indebted, glad *Opposite*: ungrateful

gratefulness *n* thankfulness, appreciativeness, appreciation, gratitude, thanks *Opposite*: ingratitude

gratification *n* satisfaction, fulfilment, indulgence, enjoyment, delight *Opposite*: displeasure

gratify *v* **please**, satisfy, indulge, fulfil, oblige *Opposite*: displease

gratifying *adj* **rewarding**, satisfying, agreeable, heartwarming, acceptable *Opposite*: humiliating

grating *n* **grille**, grate, lattice, grid, screen ■ *adj* **1 rough**, harsh, raucous, strident, discordant *Opposite*: mellifluous **2 irritating**, annoying, infuriating, insensitive, vexing *Opposite*: pleasant

gratis *adj* **free**, free of charge, on the house, complimentary, for nothing

gratitude *n* **thanks**, thankfulness, appreciation, gratefulness, appreciativeness *Opposite*: ingratitude

gratuitous *adj* **1 unwarranted**, uncalled-for, wanton, unjustified, unnecessary *Opposite*: necessary **2 free**, gratis, complimentary, at no charge, on the house

gratuitously *adv* **unnecessarily**, pointlessly, unreasonably, needlessly, wantonly *Opposite*: necessarily

gratuity *n* **tip**, service charge, donation, token of appreciation, reward

grave *n* **tomb**, crypt, vault, burial chamber, mausoleum ■ *adj* **1 serious**, severe, weighty, momentous, crucial *Opposite*: minor **2 solemn**, serious, sombre, grim, earnest *Opposite*: cheerful **3 ominous**, foreboding, forbidding, fateful, dire *Opposite*: favourable

gravel *n* **stones**, pebbles, shingle, chippings

gravelly *adj* **1 croaky**, gruff, hoarse, rough, harsh *Opposite*: velvety **2 pebbly**, shingly, stony, rocky, gritty

gravely *adv* **1 grimly**, sternly, austerely, seriously, solemnly *Opposite*: cheerfully **2 fatally**, dangerously, critically, incurably, mortally

gravestone *n* **headstone**, marker, cenotaph, tombstone, memorial

graveyard *n* **cemetery**, churchyard, necropolis, burial ground, boneyard *(infml)*

gravitas *n* **seriousness**, gravity, sobriety, solemness, sombreness

gravitate *v* **1 incline**, lean, move, drift, be attracted *Opposite*: repel **2 sink**, settle, drop, fall, descend *Opposite*: rise

gravitation *n* **movement**, attraction, gravity

gravity *n* **1 gravitation**, gravitational force, pull, draw **2 seriousness**, importance, significance, severity, enormity *Opposite*: insignificance **3 solemnity**, grimness, sedateness, dignity, earnestness *Opposite*: cheerfulness

graze *v* **1 browse**, crop, nibble, forage, eat **2 scrape**, scratch, scuff, rub, skin **3 glance**, brush, skim, sweep, touch ■ *n* **scratch**, scrape, abrasion, lesion, scuff mark

grease *n* **fat**, lard, oil ■ *v* **lubricate**, oil, smear

greasiness *n* **fattiness**, griminess, sliminess, oiliness, oleaginousness

greasy *adj* **oily**, fatty, slippery, slimy, oleaginous

great *adj* **1 huge**, immense, enormous, vast, large *Opposite*: tiny **2 famous**, illustrious, eminent, distinguished, celebrated *Opposite*: ordinary **3 noble**, elevated, lofty, imposing, stately *Opposite*: lowly **4 wonderful**, fantastic, magnificent, excellent, incredible *Opposite*: awful **5 absolute**, utter, complete, downright, intense *Opposite*: slight **6 countless**, inordinate, prodigious, excessive, boundless *Opposite*: limited **7 important**, significant, momentous, critical, major *Opposite*: unimportant

greater *adj* **better**, superior, larger, bigger, more

greatest *adj* **most**, maximum, record, utmost, supreme

greatly *adv* **1 very much**, really, to a great extent, to the highest degree, deeply *Opposite*: hardly **2 importantly**, significantly, momentously, critically, seriously

greatness *n* **1 magnitude**, enormity, immensity, vastness, size **2 importance**, prominence, seriousness, significance, weightiness *Opposite*: insignificance **3 fame**, eminence, distinction, impressiveness, prominence *Opposite*: commonness

greed *n* **1 gluttony**, voracity, ravenousness, insatiability, hunger *Opposite*: moderation **2 avarice**, covetousness, materialism, acquisitiveness, greediness *Opposite*: generosity

greediness *see* **greed**

greedy *adj* **1 gluttonous**, voracious, ravenous, insatiable, hungry *Opposite*: moderate **2 avaricious**, covetous, grasping, materialistic, acquisitive *Opposite*: generous

greenery *n* **foliage**, vegetation, plants, leaves, greens (US)

greenfield *adj* **undeveloped**, green belt, out-of-town, rural, country *Opposite*: urban

greenhorn *n* **novice**, recruit, initiate, beginner, neophyte. *See* COMPARE AND CONTRAST *at* beginner.

greenhouse *n* **orangery**, glasshouse, hothouse, conservatory

green light *n* **permission**, clearance, consent, approval, stamp of approval *Opposite*: red light

greet *v* **1 welcome**, meet, make the acquaintance of, receive **2 address**, speak to, acknowledge, hail, salute *Opposite*: ignore **3 respond to**, react to, receive, meet, hail

greeting *n* **salutation**, welcome, welcoming, reception, acknowledgment

gregarious *adj* **outgoing**, sociable, social, extrovert, expressive *Opposite*: shy

gregariousness *n* **sociability**, friendliness, openness, unreservedness, conviviality *Opposite*: shyness

gremlin *(infml)* *n* **jinx**, malfunction, blip, glitch, bug *(infml)*

grid *n* **network**, lattice, net, web, gridiron

griddle *v* **grill**, sear, barbecue, cook

gridiron n grid, lattice, grating, framework, network

gridlock n 1 **traffic jam**, jam, holdup, tailback, snarl-up 2 **deadlock**, stalemate, standstill, logjam, impasse

grief n **sorrow**, heartache, anguish, misery, unhappiness Opposite: joy

grief-stricken adj **grieving**, distraught, traumatized, inconsolable, heartbroken Opposite: happy

grievance n 1 **complaint**, protest, criticism, objection, grumble 2 **injustice**, wrong, cause of distress, ill-treatment, unfairness

grieve v 1 **mourn**, feel sad, be sad, lament, be distressed Opposite: rejoice (literary) 2 **hurt**, afflict, pain, distress, upset Opposite: cheer

grievous adj 1 **serious**, significant, critical, dangerous, grave Opposite: slight 2 **dreadful**, awful, terrible, shameful, painful

grill v 1 (infml) **question**, interrogate, examine, press, probe 2 **cook**, barbecue, toast, brown, frizzle ■ n **griddle**, grate, barbecue, rotisserie. See COMPARE AND CONTRAST at question.

grille n grating, lattice, framework, grid, trellis

grim adj 1 **depressing**, bleak, dismal, gloomy, cheerless Opposite: hopeful 2 **forbidding**, ugly, unattractive, uninviting, grey Opposite: attractive 3 **stern**, serious, dour, severe, morose Opposite: kind 4 **shocking**, ghastly, horrible, horrific, gruesome Opposite: pleasant 5 (infml) **ill**, unwell, off-colour (infml), poorly (infml), indisposed (fml) Opposite: well 6 (infml) **shoddy**, bad, awful, dire, appalling Opposite: excellent

grimace n **scowl**, frown, smirk, sneer, pout Opposite: smile ■ v **frown**, scowl, smirk, sneer, pout Opposite: smile

grime n **filth**, dirt, stain, soot, dust

griminess n **dirtiness**, dinginess, filthiness, grubbiness, dustiness Opposite: cleanliness

grimness n 1 **bleakness**, cheerlessness, dismalness, ominousness, gloominess Opposite: brightness 2 **forbiddingness**, ugliness, unattractiveness, greyness, dinginess Opposite: attractiveness 3 **sternness**, seriousness, dourness, severity, moroseness Opposite: kindness 4 **gruesomeness**, horror, hideousness, grisliness, dreadfulness Opposite: pleasantness

grimy adj **dirty**, grubby, smudged, soiled, filthy Opposite: clean. See COMPARE AND CONTRAST at dirty.

grin v **smile**, beam, smirk, laugh, chortle Opposite: frown ■ n **beam**, smile, smirk, laugh, chortle Opposite: frown

grin and bear it (infml) v **put up with**, take the rough with the smooth, take the bad with the good, weather, lump it (infml)

grind v 1 **crush**, break up, mill, pound, mince 2 **grate**, rasp, gnash, scrape Opposite: glide 3 **sharpen**, file, whet, abrade, polish Opposite: blunt ■ n (infml) **toil**, chore, slog, tedium, routine

grind down v 1 **wear**, erode, eat away, abrade, rub 2 **oppress**, tyrannize, persecute, harass, weaken Opposite: nurture

grinder n **mill**, mincer, crusher, pounder, pulverizer

grinding adj 1 **crushing**, oppressive, relentless, unending, never-ending 2 **grating**, crunching, earsplitting, screeching, squealing Opposite: pleasant

grip n 1 **grasp**, hold, clasp, clutch Opposite: release 2 **control**, rule, command, authority, clutches 3 **understanding**, comprehension, grasp, command, appreciation Opposite: ignorance ■ v 1 **grasp**, clasp, clutch, catch, seize Opposite: release 2 **stick**, adhere, cling, hang on, cleave to (literary) 3 **overwhelm**, fill, pervade, suffuse, swamp 4 **fascinate**, enthral, spellbind, transfix, mesmerize Opposite: bore

gripe (infml) v **complain**, grumble, protest, object, moan (infml) ■ n **complaint**, grumble, grievance, protest, objection Opposite: compliment. See COMPARE AND CONTRAST at complain.

gripped adj **absorbed**, engrossed, rapt, obsessed, enthralled Opposite: bored

gripping adj **fascinating**, spellbinding, enthralling, mesmerizing, transfixing Opposite: boring

grisliness n **gruesomeness**, ghastliness, grimness, hideousness, dreadfulness Opposite: pleasantness

grisly adj **gruesome**, ghastly, horrible, horrific, horrid Opposite: pleasant

gristle n **cartilage**, tendon, sinew

gristly adj **tough**, chewy, sinewy, stringy, leathery Opposite: tender

grit n 1 **gravel**, stones, pebbles, sand, shingle 2 **determination**, perseverance, tenacity, bravery, fortitude Opposite: cowardice ■ v **clench**, grind, gnash, grate

gritty adj 1 **determined**, persistent, resolute, courageous, persevering Opposite: cowardly 2 **realistic**, graphic, harsh, stark, uncompromising Opposite: romantic 3 **grainy**, coarse, rough, granular, sandy Opposite: smooth

grit your teeth v **steel yourself**, nerve yourself, brace yourself, persevere, hold on tight Opposite: knuckle under

grizzle (infml) v 1 **cry**, whine, moan, whimper, snivel 2 **grumble**, complain, moan, mutter, go on

grizzly adj **fractious**, irritable, crying, whiny, whining

groan v 1 **moan**, cry out, whimper, grunt, growl Opposite: laugh 2 (infml) **grumble**, complain, carp, moan, gripe (infml) 3 **creak**, squeak, squeal, screech, grind

groceries n **food**, shopping, provisions, rations, victuals

grogginess n **tiredness**, fatigue, sleepiness, unsteadiness, bleariness Opposite: alertness

groggy *adj* tired, sleepy, slow, unsteady, bleary *Opposite*: alert

groom *v* 1 prime, train, coach, prepare, tutor *Opposite*: hinder 2 clean, clean up, brush, comb, tidy

groove *n* channel, furrow, rut, trench, indentation *Opposite*: ridge

grope *v* 1 fumble, feel, cast about, scrabble, flounder 2 *(infml)* fondle, touch, molest, caress, feel up *(infml)*

gross *adj* 1 aggregate, combined, whole, overall, total *Opposite*: net 2 flagrant, blatant, glaring, arrant, serious *Opposite*: minor 3 coarse, vulgar, crass, rude, crude *Opposite*: polite 4 uncultured, uncivilized, uncultivated, unsophisticated, unpolished *Opposite*: cultured 5 overweight, obese, fat, heavy, stout *Opposite*: slim 6 *(infml)* disgusting, unpleasant, sickening, foul, nasty *Opposite*: pleasant ■ *v* earn, make, take, receive, bring in

grossly *adv* 1 wholly, totally, completely, utterly, unacceptably *Opposite*: slightly 2 rudely, coarsely, uncouthly, crassly, crudely *Opposite*: politely 3 *(infml)* disgustingly, revoltingly, nauseatingly, vilely, hideously *Opposite*: pleasantly

grotesque *adj* 1 distorted, bizarre, misshapen, monstrous, gross *(infml) Opposite*: attractive 2 incongruous, ridiculous, ludicrous, laughable, outrageous *Opposite*: fitting

grotto *n* cavern, pothole, hollow, cave

grotty *(infml) adj* shabby, rundown, dingy, tatty, grubby *Opposite*: spotless

grouch *(infml) n* 1 complaint, grumble, whine, grouse *(infml)*, moan *(infml) Opposite*: praise 2 grumbler, complainer, malcontent, moaner *(infml)*, whinger *(infml)* ■ *v* complain, grumble, sulk, gripe *(infml)*, moan *(infml)*

grouchiness *(infml) n* peevishness, irritability, cantankerousness, crabbiness, bad temper *Opposite*: equanimity

grouchy *(infml) adj* bad-tempered, complaining, touchy, grumpy, crabby *Opposite*: eventempered

ground *n* 1 earth, soil, land, field, dry land 2 playing field, pitch, field, arena, stadium ■ *adj* crushed, pulverized, broken up, milled, minced ■ *v* 1 initiate, prepare, coach, instruct, tutor 2 base, substantiate, support, build, justify 3 punish, deal with, chastise

groundbreaking *adj* innovative, pioneering, revolutionary, radical, trailblazing *Opposite*: outdated

grounding *n* foundation, basis, preparation, training, instruction

groundless *adj* baseless, unsupported, unjustified, unwarranted, unfounded *Opposite*: sound

ground plan *n* 1 floor plan, plan, scale drawing, blueprint, diagram 2 outline, sketch, blueprint, draft, preliminary design

ground rule *n* fundamental, axiom, stipulation, point of departure, modus operandi

grounds *n* 1 basis, foundation, reason, justification, argument 2 estate, land, park, parkland, gardens 3 dregs, lees, sediment, residue, deposit

groundsheet *n* tarpaulin, sheeting, cover, throw, rug

groundswell *n* 1 swell, wave, storm, squall, heavy sea 2 upsurge, wave, outpouring, rise, swell

groundwork *n* foundation, basis, base, footing, underpinning

group *n* 1 collection, cluster, set, assemblage, assembly *Opposite*: individual 2 grouping, set, faction, crowd, company *Opposite*: individual 3 musical group, band, trio, duo, quartet *Opposite*: soloist 4 alliance, federation, consortium, amalgamation, confederation ■ *v* 1 classify, categorize, arrange, sort, bracket 2 gather, assemble, congregate, convene, cluster *Opposite*: disperse

groupie *(infml) n* follower, fan, enthusiast, supporter, aficionado

grouping *n* 1 alliance, federation, consortium, assemblage, alignment 2 category, class, set, type, group

grouse *(infml) v* complain, grumble, moan, gripe *(infml)*, bellyache *(infml)* ■ *n* complaint, grumble, objection, protest, moan *(infml)*. *See* compare and contrast *at* complain.

grout *n* mortar, filling, plaster, cement, putty ■ *v* fill, mortar, plaster, cement, render

grouts *n* dregs, lees, residue, sediment, deposit

grove *n* copse, coppice, orchard, wood, stand

grovel *v* 1 plead, beg, cringe, fawn, bow and scrape 2 crawl, crouch, stoop, kneel, creep *(infml) Opposite*: stand up

grow *v* 1 develop, grow up, mature, shoot up, sprout 2 expand, enlarge, swell, extend, spread *Opposite*: shrink 3 increase, multiply, intensify, escalate, strengthen *Opposite*: decrease 4 produce, cultivate, nurture, breed, raise

growing *adj* rising, mounting, upward, budding, emergent *Opposite*: decreasing

growl *v* roar, snarl, bark, howl, rumble

grow less *v* weaken, wear off, fade, subside, decrease *Opposite*: increase

grown *adj* grown-up, fully-fledged, adult, developed, mature *Opposite*: immature

grown-up *adj* adult, mature, developed, grown, responsible *Opposite*: immature

growth *n* 1 growing, development, evolution, progress, advance *Opposite*: decay 2 increase, enlargement, expansion, augmentation, development *Opposite*: reduction 3 tumour, cyst, lump, swelling, outgrowth

grow up *v* 1 grow, develop, mature, evolve,

flourish **2 take shape**, arise, be born, develop, come about

groyne *n* **breakwater**, mole, barrier, bulwark, jetty

grub *v* **1 dig**, burrow, root out, excavate, pull up **2 search**, hunt, rummage, ferret, forage ■ *n* **1 larva**, maggot, caterpillar, bug, creepy-crawly *(infml)* **2** *(infml)* **food**, victuals, sustenance, feed, nourishment

grubbiness *n* **1 dirtiness**, griminess, filthiness, muddiness, sloppiness *Opposite*: cleanness **2 sordidness**, squalidness, seediness, contemptibleness, despicableness *Opposite*: purity

grubby *adj* **1 dirty**, grimy, soiled, filthy, muddy *Opposite*: clean **2 sordid**, squalid, seedy, contemptible, despicable *Opposite*: honourable. *See* COMPARE AND CONTRAST *at* **dirty**.

grudge *n* **complaint**, bitterness, resentment, dislike, hatred ■ *v* **resent**, hold against, begrudge, loathe, mind

grudging *adj* **reluctant**, unwilling, complaining, resentful, rancorous *Opposite*: willing

gruelling *adj* **arduous**, exhausting, demanding, taxing, tough *Opposite*: easy

gruesome *adj* **grisly**, ghastly, horrible, horrific, horrid *Opposite*: pleasant

gruesomeness *n* **grisliness**, ghastliness, horror, dreadfulness, hideousness *Opposite*: pleasantness

gruff *adj* **1 bad-tempered**, grumpy, angry, impatient, brusque *Opposite*: friendly **2 hoarse**, husky, gravelly, rasping, harsh *Opposite*: soft

gruffness *n* **1 grumpiness**, crustiness, abruptness, curtness, sternness *Opposite*: pleasantness **2 hoarseness**, huskiness, thickness, throatiness, harshness *Opposite*: softness

grumble *v* **complain**, protest, mutter, object, moan *(infml)* ■ *n* **complaint**, protest, objection, moan *(infml)*, grouse *(infml)*. *See* COMPARE AND CONTRAST *at* **complain**.

grumbler *n* **complainer**, whiner, groaner, grouch *(infml)*, moaner *(infml)*

grumpiness *n* **bad-temperedness**, irritability, cantankerousness, petulance, crabbiness *Opposite*: cheerfulness

grumpy *adj* **bad-tempered**, irritable, sullen, cantankerous, ill-tempered *Opposite*: cheerful

grunge *(infml)* *n* **filth**, grime, dirt, mess, muck *(infml)* *Opposite*: cleanliness

grungy *(infml)* *adj* **shabby**, dirty, scruffy, unkempt, dilapidated *Opposite*: clean

grunt *v* **speak indistinctly**, mumble, groan, snort

guarantee *n* **1 assurance**, promise, pledge, agreement, security **2 warranty**, certification, undertaking, contract, agreement ■ *v* **assure**, ensure, promise, pledge, warrant

guaranteed *adj* **certain**, definite, sure, cast-iron, fail-safe *Opposite*: uncertain

guarantor *n* **backer**, sponsor, underwriter, supporter, patron. *See* COMPARE AND CONTRAST *at* **backer**.

guard *v* **protect**, defend, safeguard, shield, watch over ■ *n* **1 protector**, sentinel, sentry, picket, lookout **2 safeguard**, security, protection, shield, fortification. *See* COMPARE AND CONTRAST *at* **safeguard**.

guarded *adj* **1 wary**, cautious, careful, circumspect, hesitant *Opposite*: open **2 protected**, secured, watched over, defended, safeguarded *Opposite*: unprotected. *See* COMPARE AND CONTRAST *at* **cautious**.

guardhouse *n* **prison**, jail, lockup, cells, detention centre

guardian *n* **1 guard**, sentinel, keeper, custodian **2 carer**, protector, godparent

guardianship *n* **protection**, custody, care, responsibility, supervision

guardrail *n* **handrail**, rail, banister, railing, paling

guerrilla *n* **freedom fighter**, rebel, insurgent, irregular, paramilitary

guess *v* **1 predict**, solve, fathom, work out, conjecture **2 deduce**, presume, speculate, suppose, estimate ■ *n* **deduction**, conjecture, supposition, presumption, speculation

guesstimate *(infml)* *n* **guess**, estimate, conjecture, projection, reckoning ■ *v* **estimate**, guess, reckon, conjecture, project

guesswork *n* **conjecture**, deduction, presumption, speculation, estimation

guest *n* **visitor**, caller, invitee, boarder, lodger *Opposite*: host

guesthouse *n* **hotel**, hostel, bed and breakfast, inn, boarding house

guestroom *n* **room**, bedroom, spare room

guff *(infml)* *n* **nonsense**, rubbish, rigmarole, stuff, stuff and nonsense *Opposite*: sense

guffaw *v* **laugh**, chuckle, chortle, roar, fall about *(infml)* ■ *n* **chuckle**, laugh, chortle, roar, belly laugh

guidance *n* **1 leadership**, direction, supervision, management, control **2 help**, assistance, advice, support, counselling

guidance counsellor *n* **adviser**, counsellor, therapist, mediator

guide *v* **1 direct**, steer, lead, conduct, escort **2 steer**, drive, pilot, direct, handle ■ *n* **1 leader**, director, attendant, chaperon, controller **2 tour guide**, courier, leader, escort, conductor **3 influence**, standard, model, ideal, guiding light **4 guidebook**, handbook, manual, instructions, vade mecum

---

COMPARE AND CONTRAST CORE MEANING: show somebody the way to a place

guide take somebody in the right direction or give a tour of a particular place; **conduct** take somebody to or around a particular place, especially when the person showing the way has some kind of authority or specialized knowledge; **direct**

show or indicate the way; **lead** show the way to others, usually by going ahead of them; **steer** encourage somebody to take a particular course; **usher** escort somebody to or from a place, especially a seat.

guidebook *n* travel guide, vade mecum, gazeteer, guide, manual

guideline *n* advice, recommendation, standard, guide, parameter

guild *n* club, union, society, association, league

guile *n* cunning, treachery, astuteness, slyness, wiliness *Opposite*: frankness

guileful *adj* cunning, treacherous, sly, astute, wily *Opposite*: naive

guileless *adj* naive, frank, candid, ingenuous, straightforward *Opposite*: guileful

guillotine *v* behead, decapitate, execute, kill

guilt *n* **1** remorse, shame, self-reproach, conscience, contriteness **2** fault, responsibility, blame, culpability, guiltiness *Opposite*: innocence

guiltless *adj* innocent, blameless, faultless, unimpeachable, irreproachable *Opposite*: guilty

guilt-ridden *adj* guilty, fearful, anguished, tormented, haunted *Opposite*: unashamed

guilty *adj* **1** culpable, responsible, at fault, blameworthy, in the wrong *Opposite*: innocent **2** shamefaced, remorseful, embarrassed, mortified, guilt-ridden *Opposite*: unashamed

guilty conscience *n* guilt complex, conscience, twinge, pang, guilt trip *(slang)*

guise *n* **1** appearance, semblance, show, pretext, excuse **2** form, appearance, shape, light, phase **3** costume, disguise, dress, outfit, mask

gulf *n* **1** bight, bay, inlet, sound, cove **2** hole, abyss, chasm, gap, hollow

gullet *n* crop, maw, throat, craw, gorge

gullibility *n* trustfulness, innocence, credulity, unwariness, acceptance *Opposite*: shrewdness

gullible *adj* naive, susceptible, innocent, trusting, accepting *Opposite*: discerning

gully *n* **1** ravine, gorge, valley, gap, chasm **2** channel, ditch, furrow, rut, culvert

gulp *v* swallow, drink, toss down, guzzle *(infml)*, swig *(infml)* *Opposite*: sip ∎ *n* swallow, drink, mouthful, swig *(infml)*, slug *(infml)* *Opposite*: sip

gulp back *v* stifle, suppress, restrain, hold back, fight back

gulp down *v* wolf, swill, swallow, down, gobble *Opposite*: sip

gum *n* **1** secretion, exudate, resin, latex, juice **2** glue, adhesive, paste, cement, epoxy resin ∎ *v* stick, glue, paste, bond, cement *Opposite*: unstick

gummy *adj* sticky, gooey, gluey, tacky, adhesive

gumption *(infml)* *n* **1** common sense, sense, shrewdness, practicality, presence of mind *Opposite*: stupidity **2** courage, nerve, bravery, mettle, pluck

gun *n* firearm, handgun, shooter *(infml)*, piece *(slang)*

WORD BANK
❑ **types of gun** air pistol, air rifle, antiaircraft gun, automatic, bazooka, blunderbuss, cannon, carbine, flame-thrower, handgun, howitzer, machine gun, magnum, mortar, musket, pistol, revolver, rifle, sawn-off shotgun, semiautomatic, shotgun, submachine gun, Tommy gun *(infml)*

gun down *(infml)* *v* kill, assassinate, shoot, shoot down, mow down

gunfight *n* gun battle, shoot-out, firefight, fight, duel

gunfire *n* firing, shooting, gunshot, shots, bombardment

gunge *(infml)* *n* slime, dirt, mess, goo *(infml)*, gunk *(infml)*

gung ho *(infml)* *adj* **1** combative, belligerent, militaristic, bellicose, aggressive *Opposite*: peaceable **2** enthusiastic, eager, keen, zealous, ardent *Opposite*: reluctant

gungy *(infml)* *adj* slimy, dirty, filthy, messy, gunky *(infml)* *Opposite*: clean

gunk *(infml)* *n* grease, mess, filth, dirt, slime

gunky *(infml)* *see* gungy

gunman *n* **1** sniper, murderer, assassin, killer, gangster **2** marksman, markswoman, shot, crack shot, good shot

gunner *n* soldier, shooter, artilleryman, fusilier, rifleman

guns *n* weapons, ordnance, firepower, artillery, arms

gunshot *see* gunfire

gurgle *v* **1** bubble, slosh, splash, ripple, murmur **2** babble, burble, coo, warble, crow

guru *n* **1** spiritual leader, religious teacher, maharishi, spiritual guide, spiritual adviser **2** leader, authority, leading light, expert, pundit

gush *v* **1** pour, flood, stream, surge, spurt *Opposite*: trickle **2** be effusive, prattle, flatter, ooze, admire *Opposite*: criticize ∎ *n* flood, flow, spurt, jet, stream *Opposite*: trickle

gushing *adj* **1** pouring, flowing, overflowing, spouting, torrential *Opposite*: trickling **2** effusive, voluble, enthusiastic, emotional, sentimental *Opposite*: reserved

gusset *n* patch, insert, inset, reinforcement, support

gust *n* **1** squall, draught, flurry, breeze, blast *Opposite*: calm **2** burst, explosion, expulsion, eruption, outburst ∎ *v* blow, bluster, squall

gusto n **enjoyment**, delight, enthusiasm, passion, zest *Opposite*: apathy

gusty adj **windy**, breezy, squally, stormy, blustery *Opposite*: calm

gut v **1 disembowel**, eviscerate, clean, prepare, dress **2 ruin**, damage, destroy, burn, raze *Opposite*: build up **3 strip**, clear out, empty, empty out, plunder ■ adj **instinctive**, intuitive, emotional, automatic, unconscious *Opposite*: considered

gut feeling n **guess**, hunch, instinct, impression, intuition *Opposite*: fact

gutless adj **cowardly**, spineless, spiritless, weak, timid *Opposite*: plucky. *See* COMPARE AND CONTRAST *at* **cowardly**.

gut reaction *see* gut feeling

guts n **1 intestines**, bowels, stomach, viscera, entrails **2 interior**, recesses, bowels, inner workings, heart **3** (*infml*) **glutton**, gourmand, gannet (*infml*), pig (*infml*), greedy guts (*infml*)

gutsy (*infml*) adj **1 brave**, plucky, courageous, fearless, determined *Opposite*: cowardly **2 passionate**, impassioned, emotional, intense, fiery *Opposite*: insipid **3 greedy**, gluttonous, insatiable, voracious, piggish *Opposite*: ascetic

gutted adj **1 cleaned**, disembowelled, eviscerated, prepared, dressed **2** (*infml*) **devastated**, shattered, reeling, heartbroken, brokenhearted *Opposite*: pleased

gutter n **drain**, sewer, channel, trench, groove ■ v **flicker**, sputter, waver, drip, fade *Opposite*: flare

guttering n **gutters**, channels, trenches, grooves, sewers

guttural adj **harsh**, rough, rasping, throaty, deep *Opposite*: melodious

guv (*infml*) n **1 mate**, pal (*infml*), chum (*infml*), guvnor (*dated infml*), man (*slang*) **2 boss**, superior, manager, chief, gaffer (*infml*)

guvnor (*dated infml*) n **1 mate**, pal (*infml*), chum (*infml*), guv (*infml*), man (*slang*) **2 father**, pa (*infml*), dad (*infml*), pop (*infml*), papa (*dated*) **3 boss**, superior, manager, chief, gaffer (*infml*)

guy n **1** (*infml*) **man**, gentleman, boy, bloke (*infml*), chap (*infml*) **2 effigy**, figure, model, manikin, scarecrow ■ v (*infml*) **poke fun at**, imitate, tease, satirize, send up (*infml*) *Opposite*: respect

guyrope n **rope**, lashing, string, halyard, guy

guys (*infml*) n **people**, folks, gang, everybody

guzzle (*infml*) v **1 gulp**, gobble, wolf, stuff, swig (*infml*) *Opposite*: nibble **2 consume**, use, devour, burn up, use up *Opposite*: conserve

gym (*infml*) *see* gymnasium

gymkhana n **horse show**, riding show, equestrian show, showjumping competition, riding competition

gymnasium n **fitness centre**, exercise room, sports centre, leisure centre, sports club

gymnastic adj **1 athletic**, acrobatic, sporty, sporting **2 energetic**, athletic, lithe, supple *Opposite*: stiff

gymnastics n **physical exercises**, aerobics, callisthenics, keep fit, exercises

gymslip n **dress**, uniform, pinafore

gypsy n **nomad**, traveller, drifter, wanderer

gyrate v **rotate**, whirl, spin, revolve, twirl

gyration n **whirling**, twirling, spinning, turning, revolving

gyratory adj **spiral**, rotating, revolving, spinning, whirling *Opposite*: still

H

habit n **1 custom**, routine, tradition, convention, practice **2 tendency**, inclination, leaning, preference, fondness **3 addiction**, problem, dependency, weakness, fixation **4 uniform**, garb, apparel, outfit, garment

COMPARE AND CONTRAST CORE MEANING: established pattern of behaviour

habit an action or behaviour pattern that is regular, repetitive, often unconscious, and sometimes compulsive; **custom** the way somebody normally or routinely behaves in a situation, or a traditional practice in a particular community or group of people; **tradition** a long-established action or pattern of behaviour in a particular community or group of people, especially one that has been handed down from generation to generation; **prac-**tice an established way of doing something, especially one that has developed through experience and knowledge; **routine** a typical pattern of behaviour that is regularly followed on a day-to-day basis, sometimes with the suggestion that this is monotonous and tedious; **wont** (*fml*) something that somebody does regularly or habitually.

habitable adj **inhabitable**, livable, fit for human habitation, comfortable, fit to live in *Opposite*: uninhabitable

habitat n **home**, locale, environment, surroundings, territory

habitation n **1 occupancy**, occupation, tenancy, residence **2 house**, home, lodging, residence, place **3 building**, structure, housing, construction, architecture

habitual adj **1 regular**, usual, routine, customary, normal *Opposite*: unusual **2 persistent**, frequent, chronic, long-term, ongoing *Opposite*: occasional **3 characteristic**, usual, customary, typical, expected *Opposite*: uncharacteristic. *See* COMPARE AND CONTRAST *at* usual.

habituate v **familiarize**, adjust, accustom, inure, acclimatize *Opposite*: disorientate

habituation *(fml)* n **familiarization**, adjustment, acclimatization, orientation, adaptation *Opposite*: disorientation

hack v **1 cut**, chop, slash, lacerate, scythe *Opposite*: splice **2** *(infml)* **cope**, manage, handle, deal with, succeed ■ n **1** *(infml)* **drudge**, slave, factotum, flunky *(infml)*, dogsbody *(infml)* *Opposite*: specialist **2** *(infml)* **journalist**, reporter, scribbler, writer, stringer

hackneyed adj **trite**, clichéd, tired, stale, everyday *Opposite*: original

haemorrhage n **loss**, outflow, outpouring, seeping away, depletion ■ v **lose**, flow away, seep away, pour out, drain away

haggard adj **worn**, fatigued, tired, faded, exhausted *Opposite*: fresh

haggle v **bargain**, barter, quibble, negotiate, wrangle

hail n **storm**, volley, burst, flood, barrage ■ v **1 greet**, welcome, address, speak to, call to *Opposite*: ignore **2 acclaim**, acknowledge, salute, uphold, confirm *Opposite*: reject **3 summon**, call, call over, flag down, wave *Opposite*: dismiss

hair n **1 tresses**, curls, mop, shock, mane *(literary or infml)* **2 coat**, fur, wool, pelt, fleece

haircut n **1 trim**, cut, clip, restyle **2 hairstyle**, style, hairdo *(infml)*, coiffure *(fml)*

hairdo *(infml)* n **haircut**, hairstyle, style, coiffure *(fml)*

hairdresser n **stylist**, barber, hair stylist, cutter, coiffeur *(fml)*

hairdressing n **hair gel**, styling gel, mousse, hair cream, styling spray

hairiness n **furriness**, shagginess, fuzziness, hirsuteness, fluffiness *Opposite*: baldness

hairless adj **bald**, receding, thin on top, bald as a coot, shaved *Opposite*: hairy

hair-raising adj **terrifying**, horrifying, extraordinary, spine-tingling, frightening *Opposite*: calming

hairsplitting n **quibbling**, nitpicking, cavilling, pettifoggery, equivocation

hairstyle n **haircut**, style, cut, hairdo *(infml)*, coiffure *(fml)*

WORD BANK
❏ **types of hairstyle** Afro, beehive, big hair *(infml)*, bob, bouffant, braids, bun, bunches, chignon, cornrow, cowlick, crew cut, crop, dreadlocks, flat top, French pleat, fringe, mohican, mullet, pageboy, pigtail, plait, pompadour, ponytail, quiff, ringlet, topknot

hairy adj **1 hirsute**, bearded, bushy, furry, shaggy *Opposite*: hairless **2** *(infml)* **dangerous**, hazardous, treacherous, risky, perilous *Opposite*: safe

halcyon *(literary)* adj **untroubled**, calm, peaceful, still, tranquil *Opposite*: turbulent

hale adj **healthy**, well, fit, robust, in good shape *Opposite*: unhealthy

half-baked *(infml)* adj **1 unplanned**, ill-considered, impulsive, ill-conceived *Opposite*: considered **2 impractical**, silly, unrealistic, idealistic, starry-eyed *Opposite*: sensible

half-hearted adj **unenthusiastic**, perfunctory, lukewarm, indifferent, lackadaisical *Opposite*: wholehearted

half-light n **twilight**, semi-darkness, dusk, gloom, gloominess

halfway adv **1 midway**, centrally, in the middle, between, in-between **2 almost**, nearly, mostly, partially, partly *Opposite*: completely ■ adj **middle**, central, intermediate, mid, midway

hall n **1 corridor**, passageway, hallway, foyer, entrance **2 gallery**, great hall, room, public room, ballroom **3 mansion**, dormitory, manor, tower, castle

hallmark n **1 seal**, stamp, trademark, symbol, logo **2 characteristic**, feature, trait, property, quality

hall of residence n **residence**, dormitory, student house, hall, dorm *(infml)*

hallow v **consecrate**, sanctify, bless, deify, revere *Opposite*: desecrate

hallowed adj **sacred**, holy, sanctified, blessed, consecrated *Opposite*: profane

hallucinate v **see things**, have delusions, have visions, fantasize, be delirious

hallucination n **vision**, illusion, figment of the imagination, phantasm, mirage

hallway n **corridor**, passageway, hall, foyer, entrance

halo n **corona**, aureole, nimbus, aura, radiance

halt n **standstill**, stop, close, break, pause *Opposite*: start ■ v **stop**, pause, cease, freeze, come to an end *Opposite*: begin

halter n **bridle**, rein, strap, lead, noose

halting adj **hesitant**, uncertain, tentative, stumbling, faltering *Opposite*: firm

halve v **1 bisect**, divide, cut in two, cut in half *Opposite*: double **2 split**, split fifty-fifty, go halves on, share, share out **3 decrease**, reduce, cut, slash, cut down *Opposite*: double

ham v **overact**, lay it on thick, overplay, overdo it, mug

ham-fisted *(infml)* adj **clumsy**, inelegant, inept, blundering, awkward *Opposite*: dexterous

ham-fistedness *(infml)* n **clumsiness**, ineptness, awkwardness, heavy-handedness

ham-handed *(infml) see* ham-fisted

ham-handedness *(infml) see* **ham-fistedness**

hamlet *n* **village**, settlement, homestead, community, colony *Opposite*: city

hammer *v* 1 *(infml)* **batter**, beat, assault, attack, brutalize 2 *(infml)* **defeat**, beat, thrash, trounce, walk over *(infml)* 3 **strike**, pound, hit, knock, beat 4 *(infml)* **criticize**, disparage, condemn, censure, put down *(infml) Opposite*: praise

hammering *n* 1 **pounding**, buffeting, battering, beating, lashing 2 *(infml)* **defeat**, beating, thrashing, trouncing, hiding *(infml) Opposite*: victory

hammer out *v* 1 **beat**, pound, forge, shape, craft 2 **accomplish**, establish, arrive at, reach, produce

hamper *n* **basket**, picnic basket, pannier ■ *v* **hinder**, obstruct, get in the way of, impede, slow down *Opposite*: facilitate. *See* COMPARE AND CONTRAST *at* hinder.

hamstrung *adj* **constrained**, restricted, thwarted, confined, cramped *Opposite*: liberated

hand *n* 1 **pointer**, needle, indicator, arrow, finger 2 **influence**, part, share, role, involvement 3 **clap**, ovation, standing ovation, round of applause, burst of applause *Opposite*: boo 4 **handwriting**, writing, script, scrawl, scribble ■ *v* **give**, hand over, offer, pass, tender *Opposite*: take

handbag *n* **bag**, shoulder bag, clutch bag, backpack, purse *(US)*

handbill *n* **leaflet**, flier, pamphlet, advertisement, circular

handbook *n* **manual**, instruction manual, guide, guidebook, instruction book

handcuff *n* **manacles**, chains, shackles, fetters, irons ■ *v* **chain**, manacle, shackle, fasten, tie up *Opposite*: release

hand down *v* **leave**, bequeath, pass down, transmit, will

handful *n* 1 **some**, a few, one or two, not many, hardly any *Opposite*: many 2 *(infml)* **test**, trial, problem, nuisance, hard work

handicraft *n* **craft**, handcraft, handiwork, skill, art

WORD BANK

❏ **types of handicraft** appliqué, basketry, crochet, dressmaking, embroidery, knitting, lacemaking, macramé, needlepoint, needlework, quilting, sewing, smocking, stitching, tapestry, tatting, weaving

handily *adv* 1 **conveniently**, closely, accessibly, nearby, in easy reach *Opposite*: inconveniently 2 **skilfully**, dexterously, cleverly, neatly, ably *Opposite*: awkwardly

hand in *v* 1 **submit**, give, give in, tender, offer *Opposite*: withhold 2 **surrender**, return, give up, give back, hand over *Opposite*: withhold

handiness *n* 1 **convenience**, proximity, closeness, accessibility *Opposite*: inconvenience 2 **usefulness**, utility, efficacy, helpfulness,

practicality *Opposite*: uselessness 3 **skilfulness**, skill, dexterity, practicality, cleverness *Opposite*: awkwardness

handiwork *n* 1 **deed**, action, achievement, work, creation 2 **handicraft**, craft, skill, talent, art

handkerchief *n* **tissue**, paper handkerchief, facial tissue, hankie *(infml)*

handle *n* **grip**, holder, handgrip ■ *v* 1 **touch**, finger, feel, move, hold 2 **control**, deal with, run, cope with, conduct 3 **manage**, operate, conduct, supervise, take charge of 4 **trade in**, sell, buy, deal in, import

handler *n* **trainer**, coach, manager, supervisor

handling *n* **treatment**, management, conduct, supervision, control

hand-me-down *adj* **second-hand**, castoff, recycled, used, worn *Opposite*: brand-new

hand out *v* **dispense**, distribute, administer, give away, give out *Opposite*: take in

handout *n* 1 **windfall**, bonus, gift, donation, charity 2 **document**, fact sheet, leaflet, brochure, pamphlet

hand over *v* **give up**, tender, surrender, entrust, relinquish *Opposite*: withhold

handover *n* **delivery**, abdication, assignment, conferral, bestowal

handpicked *adj* **select**, elite, exclusive, finest, top-quality *Opposite*: run-of-the-mill

handrail *n* **banister**, rail, railing, guardrail, balustrade

handset *n* **receiver**, earpiece, mouthpiece, phone, telephone

hands-off *adj* **detached**, remote, distant, non-interventionist, laissez-faire *Opposite*: hands-on

handsome *adj* 1 **good-looking**, fine, attractive, striking, beautiful *Opposite*: ugly 2 **generous**, substantial, sizable, attractive, liberal *Opposite*: ungenerous. *See* COMPARE AND CONTRAST *at* good-looking.

handsomely *adv* **generously**, substantially, sizably, attractively, well

hands-on *adj* **practical**, active, applied, proactive, energetic *Opposite*: hands-off

handspring *n* **somersault**, cartwheel, flip, flip-flop, vault

hand-to-hand *adj* **unarmed**, close-range, face-to-face, direct, bareknuckle

handwork *n* **handiwork**, handicraft, skill, art, craft

handwriting *n* **script**, writing, calligraphy, penmanship, scrawl

handy *adj* 1 **convenient**, near, nearby, within reach, in easy reach *Opposite*: inconvenient 2 **useful**, helpful, practical, clever, usable *Opposite*: useless 3 **skilful**, dexterous, practical, clever, skilled *Opposite*: awkward

hang *v* 1 **suspend**, dangle, droop, drape, hang down *Opposite*: take down 2 **lynch**, suspend by the neck, execute, put to death, swing *(infml)* **3 droop**, flop, drape, sag, trail *Opposite*: stick up **4** *(infml)* **relax**, hang around, hang loose, chill out *(infml)*, hang out *(infml)*

hang about v **1 wait**, linger, loiter, dawdle, lie around *(infml)* **2 associate**, mix, socialize, spend time with, hang around

hang around see **hang about**

hang back v **hesitate**, drag your feet, drag your heels, linger, drop behind *Opposite*: forge ahead

hangdog adj **guilty**, dejected, furtive, intimidated, sheepish *Opposite*: chirpy *(infml)*

hang down v **sag**, dangle, droop, swing, hang *Opposite*: stick up

hanger n **coat hanger**, hook, peg, support, nail

hanger-on n **follower**, sycophant, disciple, proselyte, associate

hanging n **1 execution**, lynching, killing **2 wall hanging**, tapestry, drape, drapery, swag

hang on v **1 grip**, grasp, clutch, cling, hold on *Opposite*: let go **2 persevere**, keep it up, stick with it, stick it out, hold on *Opposite*: give up **3 depend on**, hinge on, follow from, turn on, rely on **4 wait**, linger, stay, hold on, remain *Opposite*: leave

hang out v **1 suspend**, dangle, drape, swing, hang up *Opposite*: take down **2** *(infml)* **spend time**, loiter, hang around, frequent, haunt **3** *(infml)* **associate**, mix, be friendly, hang around, interact **4** *(infml)* **relax**, hang around, loll around, hang about, laze about

hangout *(infml)* n **haunt**, den, retreat, meeting place, lair *(infml)*

hangover n **relic**, leftover, remnant, aftermath, aftereffect

hang together v **make sense**, add up, hold up, tell the complete story, give the full picture *Opposite*: fall apart

hang up v **1 suspend**, dangle, droop, drape, swing *Opposite*: take down **2 ring off**, put the phone down, disconnect, get off the phone, replace the receiver *Opposite*: pick up

hang-up *(infml)* n **anxiety**, worry, complex, inhibition, fixation

hank n **coil**, length, reel, skein, ball

hanker v **yearn**, crave, desire, long, ache

hankering n **yearning**, craving, longing, desire, ache *Opposite*: dislike

haphazard adj **random**, chaotic, slapdash, disorganized, messy *Opposite*: systematic

hapless adj **unfortunate**, unlucky, luckless, ill-fated, wretched *Opposite*: fortunate

haplessness n **misfortune**, bad luck, ill fortune, wretchedness, misery *Opposite*: luck

happen v **occur**, take place, go on, come about, ensue

happening n **occurrence**, event, incident, episode, phenomenon ■ adj *(infml)* **fashionable**, stylish, in, up-to-the-minute, edgy *Opposite*: old-fashioned

happenstance n **accident**, coincidence, chance, happenchance, fluke *(infml)*

happily adv **1 luckily**, fortunately, thankfully, as good luck would have it, opportunely *Opposite*: sadly **2 gladly**, willingly, cheerfully, freely, voluntarily *Opposite*: unwillingly **3 cheerfully**, contentedly, joyfully, gleefully, blissfully *Opposite*: sadly

happiness n **contentment**, pleasure, gladness, cheerfulness, joy *Opposite*: sadness

happy adj **1 content**, contented, pleased, glad, joyful *Opposite*: sad **2 lucky**, fortunate, favourable, opportune *Opposite*: unlucky

happy-go-lucky adj **carefree**, optimistic, easygoing, lighthearted, nonchalant *Opposite*: anxious

harangue v **berate**, lecture, criticize, rant, address ■ n **tirade**, diatribe, criticism, lecture, rant

harass v **annoy**, pester, bother, pursue, worry *Opposite*: leave alone

harassed adj **1 stressed**, under pressure, distraught, beleaguered, worried *Opposite*: relaxed **2 put upon**, pressured, persecuted, singled out, discriminated against

harassment n **pestering**, nuisance, annoyance, irritation, persecution

harbinger n **forerunner**, herald, portent, omen, indication

harbour n **port**, dock, anchorage, waterfront, wharf ■ v **1 believe**, entertain, hold, bear in mind, cherish **2 protect**, shelter, give refuge to, hide, conceal

hard adj **1 firm**, stiff, rigid, solid, tough *Opposite*: soft **2 difficult**, strenuous, laborious, tough, arduous *Opposite*: easy **3 problematical**, tricky, difficult, awkward, thorny *Opposite*: easy **4 intense**, fast, violent, brutal, fierce *Opposite*: gentle **5 cruel**, callous, harsh, severe, unkind *Opposite*: kind ■ adv **intensely**, fast, violently, fiercely, powerfully *Opposite*: gently

COMPARE AND CONTRAST CORE MEANING: requiring effort or exertion

hard requiring mental or physical effort or exertion to do or achieve; **difficult** requiring considerable planning or effort to accomplish; **strenuous** requiring physical effort, energy, stamina, or strength; **tough** needing a great deal of effort; **arduous** requiring hard work or continuous physical effort; **laborious** requiring unwelcome, often tedious, effort and exertion.

hard-bitten adj **tough**, hardened, cynical, stubborn, uncompromising

hard-boiled *(infml)* adj **unsentimental**, hardened, tough, cynical, case-hardened *Opposite*: sentimental

hard-core adj **uncompromising**, committed, dedicated, firm, staunch

harden v 1 **solidify**, set, freeze, consolidate, settle *Opposite*: soften 2 **toughen**, strengthen, reinforce, fortify, stabilize *Opposite*: weaken

hardened *adj* **hard-bitten**, toughened, tough, cynical, unsentimental

hardheaded *adj* **shrewd**, sharp, practical, no-nonsense, tough *Opposite*: impractical

hardhearted *adj* **callous**, cold, hard, insensitive, unfeeling *Opposite*: kind

hardheartedness n **callousness**, coldness, insensitivity, pitilessness, stoniness *Opposite*: kindness

hardiness n **toughness**, hardihood, stamina, durability, robustness *Opposite*: frailty

hardline *adj* **uncompromising**, inflexible, rigid, extreme, radical

hardly *adv* **barely**, only just, scarcely, by a hair's breadth, by the skin of your teeth

hardness n **rigidity**, stiffness, firmness, inflexibility, solidity *Opposite*: softness

hardship n **adversity**, privation, lack, poverty, destitution *Opposite*: comfort

hardware n **equipment**, apparatus, tackle, gear, kit

hard-wearing *adj* **durable**, long-lasting, strong, tough, resilient

hardy *adj* **robust**, resilient, enduring, tough, strong *Opposite*: frail

hark back v **go back to**, revisit, recall, relive, revive

harm n **damage**, hurt, injury, destruction, maltreatment *Opposite*: help ■ v **hurt**, damage, spoil, injure, impair *Opposite*: help

---

COMPARE AND CONTRAST CORE MEANING: weaken or impair something or somebody

harm cause physical or mental impairment or deterioration; **damage** cause physical deterioration that makes an object less useful, valuable, or able to function, or impair something abstract such as a chance or somebody's reputation; **hurt** cause physical or mental pain or harm to people and animals; **injure** cause physical harm to a person or animal, usually causing at least a temporary loss of function or use, or impair something abstract such as somebody's reputation or pride; **wound** inflict physical harm on somebody, especially as a result of the use of a weapon, a violent incident, or a serious accident, or upset or offend somebody.

---

harmed *adj* **injured**, damaged, hurt, wounded, impaired *Opposite*: untouched

harmful *adj* **damaging**, injurious, destructive, detrimental, dangerous *Opposite*: harmless

harmless *adj* 1 **inoffensive**, innocuous, innocent, meaningless, bland *Opposite*: offensive 2 **safe**, risk-free, nontoxic, nonhazardous, sound *Opposite*: harmful

harmlessness n 1 **inoffensiveness**, naivety, innocence, wholesomeness, blandness *Opposite*: offensiveness 2 **innocuousness**, safety, mildness, nontoxicity

harmonious *adj* 1 **musical**, melodious, tuneful, pleasant-sounding, sweet *Opposite*: discordant 2 **agreeable**, congruous, balanced, matching, corresponding *Opposite*: discordant 3 **friendly**, cordial, affable, congenial, agreeable *Opposite*: hostile

harmonize v 1 **go with**, match, blend, complement, tone *Opposite*: jar 2 **bring into line**, synchronize, standardize, make uniform, make conform

harmonized *adj* **in line**, consistent, coordinated, matched, in step *Opposite*: uncoordinated

harmonizing *adj* **consistent**, toning, matching, agreeing, coordinating *Opposite*: clashing

harmony n **agreement**, accord, concord, synchronization, congruence *Opposite*: discord

harness v 1 **tie together**, strap up, yoke, bind, attach *Opposite*: separate 2 **control**, exploit, employ, channel, utilize

harp on v **complain**, go on, keep on, whine, grumble

harried *adj* **harassed**, put upon, bothered, agitated, stressed *Opposite*: calm

harrowing *adj* **disturbing**, upsetting, traumatic, distressing, frightening *Opposite*: relaxing

harry v **harass**, bother, pester, badger, annoy

harsh *adj* 1 **severe**, bleak, austere, inhospitable, stark *Opposite*: mild 2 **cruel**, unkind, unsympathetic, insensitive, callous *Opposite*: kind 3 **punitive**, exacting, strict, stern, severe *Opposite*: lenient 4 **discordant**, loud, blaring, raucous, jangly *Opposite*: pleasant

harshness n 1 **severity**, austerity, ruggedness, bleakness, starkness *Opposite*: gentleness 2 **callousness**, cruelty, ruthlessness, strictness, severity *Opposite*: gentleness

harvest n **crop**, yield, produce, return, fruitage *Opposite*: sowing ■ v **reap**, gather, collect, bring in, pick *Opposite*: sow

hash v **chop**, cut up, mince, grind, shred

hassle (*infml*) n **bother**, annoyance, irritation, disturbance, stress ■ v **harass**, irritate, annoy, bother, get on your nerves *Opposite*: leave alone

haste n **speed**, swiftness, rapidity, alacrity, rush *Opposite*: slowness

hasten v **hurry**, make haste, rush, speed up, speed

hastiness n **impulsiveness**, impetuosity, rashness, thoughtlessness, carelessness *Opposite*: carefulness

hasty *adj* **quick**, speedy, hurried, swift, rapid *Opposite*: slow

hatch v 1 **devise**, come up with, originate, formulate, plan 2 **give forth**, emerge, produce, break open, come out 3 **shade**, mark, crisscross, crosshatch, highlight

hate v **detest**, loathe, despise, abhor, revile *Opposite*: love ■ n **hatred**, abhorrence, detestation, loathing, odium *Opposite*: love. *See* COMPARE AND CONTRAST *at* dislike.

hated adj **loathed**, detested, despicable, despised, unloved Opposite: loved

hateful adj **horrible**, detestable, vile, odious, unbearable Opposite: lovable

hatred n **hate**, abhorrence, detestation, loathing, odium Opposite: love. See COMPARE AND CONTRAST at dislike.

haughtiness n **arrogance**, conceit, pride, self-importance, overconfidence Opposite: modesty

haughty adj **supercilious**, proud, self-important, superior, high and mighty Opposite: humble

haul v **drag**, pull, tow, lug, tug Opposite: shove. See COMPARE AND CONTRAST at pull.

haul over the coals v **rebuke**, scold, reprimand, take to task, tell off (infml)

haunch n **1 upper leg**, hip, buttock, thigh, loin **2 side**, flank, hindquarter, thigh, rump

haunt v **1 walk**, roam, frequent, prowl, inhabit Opposite: leave **2 trouble**, disturb, worry, bother, preoccupy Opposite: soothe ■ n **meeting place**, rendezvous, stamping ground (infml), hangout (infml)

haunted adj **1 eerie**, ghostly, weird, sinister, spooky (infml) **2 troubled**, preoccupied, worried, disturbed, anxious Opposite: relaxed

haunting adj **lingering**, melancholy, poignant, evocative, moving Opposite: forgettable

hauteur n **haughtiness**, arrogance, superiority, loftiness, snobbishness Opposite: humility

haut monde n **elite**, crème de la crème, high society, rich and famous, aristocracy Opposite: masses

have v **1 possess**, own, boast, exhibit, enjoy Opposite: lack **2 must**, need, ought to, should, require **3 receive**, obtain, grasp, get, gain Opposite: lose **4 consume**, take, partake, eat, drink Opposite: abstain **5 think of**, come up with, devise, develop, entertain **6 experience**, undergo, partake, engage in, take part in **7 be affected by**, suffer from, suffer with, be afflicted with, be ill with **8 organize**, carry out, arrange, hold, give **9 tolerate**, put up with, allow, permit, endure **10 produce**, bear, give birth to, bring forth

have a go at (infml) v **find fault with**, flay, criticize, get angry with, reprimand Opposite: praise

have a hand in v **partake in**, play a part in, play a role in, participate, be part of

have a horror of v **fear**, dread, be frightened of, be afraid of, be scared of

have in mind v **propose**, suggest, be thinking of, come up with, intend

have it in for v **persecute**, harass, bully, victimize, target Opposite: favour

haven n **1 refuge**, safe place, place of safety, sanctuary, shelter **2** (literary) **harbour**, port, anchorage, dock, port of call

have-nots n **disadvantaged**, poor, deprived, underprivileged, underclass Opposite: privileged

have on v **1 wear**, be dressed in, be clothed in, show off, flaunt **2** (infml) **tease**, kid, fool, joke, pull somebody's leg (infml)

haversack n **rucksack**, backpack, pack, knapsack, shoulder bag

have second thoughts v **change your mind**, go back on, reconsider, think better of, get cold feet

have to do with v **relate to**, concern, involve, be regarding, be in connection with

have up (infml) v **prosecute**, try, take to court, arrest, charge

have your eye on v **want**, desire, aim for, be after, hanker

havoc n **chaos**, destruction, disorder, turmoil, disaster Opposite: order

hawk v **sell**, peddle, vend, deal, market Opposite: buy

hawker n **dealer**, vendor, seller, marketer, salesperson Opposite: client

hawk-eyed adj **eagle-eyed**, sharp-eyed, sharp-sighted, observant, perceptive Opposite: unobservant

hawkish adj **aggressive**, belligerent, warmongering, warlike, militant Opposite: peaceable

hawser n **cable**, rope, chain, towline, tow

hay n **straw**, feed, fodder, dry feed, winter feed

hayrack n **rack**, trough, manger, feeder

haywire (infml) adj **wild**, out of order, erratic, nonfunctional, confused Opposite: functional

hazard n **danger**, threat, risk, peril, menace Opposite: safeguard ■ v **1 suggest**, proffer, put forward, propose **2 risk**, take a chance, chance, gamble, venture Opposite: protect

hazardous adj **dangerous**, unsafe, harmful, risky, lethal Opposite: safe

haze n **mist**, fog, miasma, cloud, vapour ■ v **become cloudy**, mist over, cloud over, darken Opposite: clear

haziness n **1 mistiness**, fogginess, cloudiness, obscurity, smokiness Opposite: clarity **2 confusion**, muddle, uncertainty, indistinctness, vagueness Opposite: clarity

hazy adj **1 misty**, foggy, cloudy, obscure, blurred Opposite: clear **2 unclear**, indistinct, muddled, confused, obscure Opposite: distinct

head n **1 skull**, cranium, dome, crown, nut (infml) **2 mind**, intelligence, intellect, sense, brain **3 boss**, leader, chief, president, controller **4 top**, peak, crown, promontory, apex Opposite: base **5 introduction**, beginning, start, opening, heading Opposite: end ■ v **1 come first**, lead, be first, precede, be foremost Opposite: follow **2 control**, rule, regulate, have control over, lead **3 go**, move, journey, advance, proceed

headache (infml) n **annoyance**, pain, bother, bore, nuisance Opposite: relief

headband n **hairband**, Alice band, sweatband, bandeau, circlet

header n **1 shot**, pass, goal **2 heading**, title, caption, slogan, legend Opposite: footer

headfirst adv **headlong**, head over heels, diving, pitching, plunging

headily adv **1 exhilaratingly**, thrillingly, invigoratingly, excitingly, stimulatingly Opposite: dully **2 pungently**, aromatically, strongly, richly, spicily Opposite: mildly **3 impetuously**, impulsively, recklessly, rashly, hastily Opposite: cautiously

heading n **1 title**, caption, headline, banner, header **2 direction**, bearing, course, route, trajectory

headland n **promontory**, cape, peninsula, point, bluff

headline n **caption**, banner, title, heading, header

headlong adv **1 headfirst**, head over heels, diving, pitching, plunging **2 impetuously**, rashly, recklessly, hastily, hurriedly Opposite: carefully ■ adj **impetuous**, rash, reckless, hasty, hurried Opposite: considered

head off v **1 divert**, reroute, redirect, turn back, intercept **2 forestall**, block, prevent, stop, avert Opposite: encourage **3 leave**, go away, depart, take off, commence Opposite: remain

head office see **headquarters**

head of state n **premier**, president, leader, ruler, sovereign

head-on adv **1 straight on**, straight ahead, frontally, directly, full steam ahead **2 unflinchingly**, uncompromisingly, with guns blazing, confrontationally, bluntly Opposite: indirectly ■ adj **face-to-face**, frontal, uncompromising, direct, confrontational Opposite: indirect

headpiece n **header**, heading, design, ornament, decoration

headquarters n **HQ**, control centre, nerve centre, head office, command centre

headset n **headphones**, receiver, earpiece, earphones

headship n **leadership**, direction, management, control, regime

head start n **advantage**, edge, lead, helping hand, help Opposite: disadvantage

headstone n **tombstone**, gravestone, stone, slab, memorial

headstrong adj **obstinate**, wilful, stubborn, inflexible, mulish Opposite: docile

head teacher n **principal**, head, headmaster, headmistress, rector

head-to-head adv **adjacent**, next to, end-to-end, in line, together ■ adj **one-to-one**, face-to-face, direct, intimate, personal ■ n **encounter**, meeting, discussion, dialogue, confrontation

headway n **progress**, movement, advance, progression, improvement

headwind n **breeze**, wind, gale, gust

heady adj **1 exhilarating**, thrilling, invigorating, exciting, stimulating Opposite: dull **2 pungent**, aromatic, strong, rich, spicy Opposite: mild **3 impetuous**, imprudent, impulsive, reckless, rash Opposite: cautious

heal v **1 cure**, restore to health, make well, nurse, mend Opposite: worsen **2 make good**, settle, patch up, reconcile, set right Opposite: damage

healer n **doctor**, faith healer, naturopath, homeopath, therapist

healing n **recovery**, restoration, recuperation, therapy, treatment ■ adj **curative**, remedial, therapeutic, medicinal, restorative

health n **wellbeing**, fitness, condition, healthiness, strength

healthful adj **healthy**, good for your health, good for you, beneficial, wholesome Opposite: unhealthy

healthiness n **health**, good condition, robustness, wellbeing, fitness

healthy adj **1 fit**, well, strong, vigorous, in good physical shape Opposite: sick **2 healthful**, good for your health, good for you, beneficial, nourishing Opposite: unhealthy

heap n **mound**, pile, stack, mountain, bundle ■ v **pile up**, pile, layer, mound, mass

heaps (infml) n **lots**, loads (infml), masses (infml), tons (infml), piles (infml) ■ adv **a lot**, very much, a great deal, loads, lots

heap up v **1 pile up**, pile, mound, mass, stack **2 collect**, amass, gather, accumulate, stockpile

hear v **1 make out**, catch, get, overhear, pick up **2 gather**, learn, find out, understand, pick up **3 listen to**, catch, get, pick up, receive **4 understand**, pay attention to, attend to, heed, take notice of Opposite: miss **5 sit in judgment**, try, judge, preside over, examine

hear from v **have news of**, have contact with, be in touch with, be contacted by, have a call from

hearing n **1 earshot**, range, hearing distance, reach **2 trial**, inquiry, investigation, examination, consideration

hear of v **consider**, conceive, tolerate, permit, admit

hearsay n **rumour**, gossip, tittle-tattle, idle talk, word of mouth Opposite: fact

heart n **1 core**, heart of hearts, mind, sentiment, soul **2 compassion**, sympathy, empathy, feeling, sensitivity Opposite: cruelty **3 spirit**, courage, bravery, fortitude, pluck

heartache n **sorrow**, sadness, distress, anguish, despair Opposite: joy

heart attack n **1 cardiac arrest**, coronary, seizure **2** *(infml)* **shock**, fright, scare, turn, fit

heartbreak n grief, despair, anguish, sorrow, pain *Opposite*: joy

heartbreaking adj tragic, distressing, upsetting, sad, heartrending *Opposite*: uplifting

heartbroken adj **inconsolable**, forlorn, despairing, dejected, disconsolate *Opposite*: thrilled

heartburn n **stomach pain**, acid stomach, indigestion, colic, dyspepsia

hearten v encourage, inspire, raise your spirits, uplift, buoy *Opposite*: dishearten

heartening adj **encouraging**, promising, cheering, optimistic, reassuring *Opposite*: disheartening

heartfelt adj sincere, genuine, earnest, warm, cordial *Opposite*: superficial

hearth n **1 fireside**, fireplace, inglenook, grate **2 family life**, home sweet home, home, household

heartiness n **vigour**, enthusiasm, gusto, energy, cheerfulness

heartland n centre, core, hub, nucleus, focus *Opposite*: hinterland

heartless adj callous, cruel, unfeeling, cold-blooded, merciless *Opposite*: caring

heartlessness n cruelty, callousness, cold-bloodedness, mercilessness, unkindness *Opposite*: kindness

heartrending adj heartbreaking, tragic, distressing, pitiful, pathetic *Opposite*: uplifting. *See* COMPARE AND CONTRAST *at* **moving**.

heart-searching n soul-searching, self-examination, self-analysis, introspection, deep thought

heart-to-heart adj frank, honest, open, candid, forthright ■ n talk, tête-à-tête, one-to-one, chat, discussion

heartwarming adj cheering, positive, encouraging, heartening, pleasing *Opposite*: depressing

hearty adj **1 enthusiastic**, sincere, whole-hearted, emphatic, vigorous *Opposite*: half-hearted **2 jovial**, cheerful, warm, genial, welcoming **3 strong**, sincere, abiding, deep, profound **4 substantial**, nourishing, filling, plentiful, abundant *Opposite*: meagre

heat n **1 warmth**, high temperature, temperature, hotness, warmness *Opposite*: coldness **2 passion**, emotion, fervour, ardour, intensity *Opposite*: indifference ■ v warm, heat up, warm through, warm up, reheat *Opposite*: cool

heated adj animated, frenzied, impassioned, fiery, intense *Opposite*: calm

heater n fire, stove, radiator, electric fire, electric heater *Opposite*: air conditioner

heating n **1 warming**, warming up, heating up, reheating, microwaving **2 central heating**, heating system, solar heating, space heating *Opposite*: air conditioning

WORD BANK
❑ **types of heating appliance** boiler, electric fire, furnace, heater, heat pump, immersion heater, quartz heater, radiator, space heater, storage heater

heat wave n **hot spell**, Indian summer, drought, scorcher *(infml)*, sizzler *(infml)*

heave v **1 haul**, drag, pull, yank, lug *Opposite*: push **2** *(infml)* **throw**, toss, pitch, fling, chuck *(infml)* **3 rise and fall**, throb, palpitate, swell, surge. *See* COMPARE AND CONTRAST *at* **throw**.

heaven n **1 bliss**, paradise, ecstasy, rapture, cloud nine *Opposite*: hell **2 air**, sky, cosmos, ether *(literary)*, firmament *(literary)*

heavenly adj **1 divine**, holy, angelic, cherubic, saintly **2 wonderful**, blissful, delightful, lovely, fantastic *Opposite*: dreadful

heavenwards adv upward, skyward, up, into the air, into the sky *Opposite*: earthwards

heaviness n weight, bulk, mass, substance, solidity *Opposite*: lightness

heaving adj crowded, bursting at the seams, full to overflowing, busy, packed

heavy adj **1 weighty**, hefty, substantial, heavyweight *Opposite*: light **2 thick**, dense, full, viscous, compact *Opposite*: thin **3 demanding**, onerous, burdensome, tiring, tedious *Opposite*: easy **4 busy**, packed, tight, hectic, frenetic *Opposite*: light **5 powerful**, forceful, violent, hard, jarring *Opposite*: weak

heavy-duty adj **1 hard-wearing**, forceful, tough, durable, long-lasting *Opposite*: lightweight **2** *(infml)* **serious**, important, intensive, intense, high-level

heavy-handed adj **1 clumsy**, rough, careless, awkward, uncoordinated *Opposite*: dexterous **2 oppressive**, harsh, forceful, hard, severe

heavy-handedness n **1 clumsiness**, roughness, carelessness, awkwardness, gaucheness **2 oppressiveness**, harshness, forcefulness, severity, brutality

heavyset adj stocky, well-built, sturdy, solid, thickset *Opposite*: slight

heavyweight n **1 muscleman**, bodyguard, bouncer, heavy *(slang)* **2 big name**, leader, leading light, key player, colossus

heckle v jeer, interrupt, butt in, boo, shout down *Opposite*: cheer

heckler n critic, jeerer, interrupter, protester, troublemaker *Opposite*: supporter

heckling n **criticism**, jeering, interruption, protest, repartee

hectic adj frantic, frenzied, excited, confused, chaotic *Opposite*: calm

hector v bully, intimidate, harass, badger, hassle *(infml)*

hedge n hedgerow, privet, border, verge, windbreak ■ v 1 **ring**, fence, protect, encircle, surround 2 **evade**, prevaricate, stall, beat about the bush, fudge (infml)

hedgerow n **hedge**, border, verge, windbreak, shrubbery

hedonism n **pleasure-seeking**, high-living, intemperance, self-indulgence, profligacy Opposite: asceticism

hedonist n **pleasure-seeker**, rake, degenerate, sybarite, epicure Opposite: ascetic

hedonistic adj **self-indulgent**, pleasure-seeking, profligate, debauched, sybaritic Opposite: ascetic

heed v **pay attention to**, listen to, take note of, observe, notice Opposite: ignore ■ n **attention**, notice, note, regard, mindfulness Opposite: disregard

heedful adj **mindful**, vigilant, watchful, thoughtful, careful Opposite: heedless

heedless adj **neglectful**, oblivious, without regard, rash, reckless Opposite: careful

heedlessness n **thoughtlessness**, recklessness, carelessness, neglectfulness, rashness Opposite: carefulness

heel v **repair**, resole, mend, fix, reinforce

heel in v **dig in**, put in, bury, cover

heftiness n **robustness**, burliness, stoutness, heaviness, stockiness

hefty adj 1 **bulky**, large, robust, sturdy, stocky Opposite: slight 2 **heavy**, weighty, substantial, cumbersome, awkward

hegemony n **domination**, control, supremacy, dominion, power

height n 1 **tallness**, stature, altitude, loftiness, elevation Opposite: depth 2 **pinnacle**, summit, peak, top, apex Opposite: nadir

heighten v **intensify**, amplify, increase, enhance, add to

heinous adj **monstrous**, atrocious, odious, dreadful, shocking

heir n **successor**, inheritor, beneficiary, legatee, recipient

heirloom n **family treasure**, inheritance, valuable, gift, bequest

helideck see helipad

helipad n **landing pad**, landing strip, helideck, heliport, helistop

heliport, helistop see helipad

helix n **spiral**, coil, corkscrew, spring, ringlet

hell n 1 **Hades**, underworld, perdition, inferno, abyss Opposite: heaven 2 **torture**, misery, torment, agony, anguish

help v 1 **aid**, assist, help out, lend a hand, be of assistance Opposite: hinder 2 **relieve**, improve, ease, alleviate, amend Opposite: worsen 3 **avoid**, evade, dodge, stop, refrain from ■ n **assistance**, aid, benefit, support, service Opposite: hindrance

helper n **assistant**, aid, aide, collaborator, coworker. See COMPARE AND CONTRAST at assistant.

helpful adj 1 **useful**, beneficial, advantageous, of use, effective Opposite: useless 2 **obliging**, accommodating, supportive, caring, cooperative Opposite: unhelpful

helpfulness n 1 **usefulness**, effectiveness, utility, benefit, advantageousness Opposite: uselessness 2 **kindness**, neighbourliness, goodwill, concern, care Opposite: unhelpfulness

helping n **serving**, plateful, portion, ration, selection

helping hand n **help**, assistance, support, aid, boost

helpless adj **powerless**, weak, feeble, dependent, vulnerable Opposite: self-reliant

helplessness n **powerlessness**, weakness, feebleness, vulnerability, dependence Opposite: confidence

helpmate n **assistant**, associate, spouse, partner, coworker

help out v **help**, lend a hand, abet, aid, assist

help yourself v **use**, make use of, appropriate, take, have

helter-skelter adv **hurriedly**, in confusion, carelessly, haphazardly, pell-mell Opposite: calmly ■ adj **chaotic**, disorganized, confused, haphazard Opposite: ordered

hem v **edge**, turn up, shorten, lengthen, sew up Opposite: let down

hem in v **enclose**, close in, encircle, confine, restrict Opposite: release

hence (fml) adv 1 **therefore**, for this reason, consequently, that's why, and so 2 **from now on**, from this time, henceforth, later, in future

henceforth adv **from now on**, from this time, in future, hereafter (fml), henceforward (fml)

henhouse n **coop**, pen, barn, shelter, shed

herald n 1 **messenger**, crier, announcer, proclaimer, courier 2 (literary) **sign**, harbinger, indication, omen, portent ■ v 1 **proclaim**, announce, give out, publish, tout 2 **signal**, prefigure, foreshadow, presage, indicate

herculean adj **superhuman**, colossal, enormous, phenomenal, extraordinary Opposite: small

herd n 1 **people**, masses, mob, crowd, sheep 2 **group**, set, cluster ■ v 1 **round up**, steer, gather together, collect, drove 2 **shepherd**, usher, direct, guide, funnel

WORD BANK

❏ **types of herd** bale (of turtles), band (of gorillas), bevy (of roe deer), colony (of ants/sea lions), drove (of sheep), flock (of sheep), gam (of whales), gang (of elk), kennel (of dogs), leash (of foxes), litter (of cubs/kittens), mob (of kangaroos), pack (of wolves), pod (of porpoises/seals/walrus/whales), pride (of lions), rookery (of seals), school (of porpoises/whales), skulk (of foxes), troop (of kangaroos/monkeys)

here adv **at this time**, at this point, now, at this juncture

hereabouts adv **nearby**, near, around here, close

hereafter (fml) adv **after this**, in future, henceforth, from now on, from this time

hereditary adj **1 genetic**, transmissible, inborn, inbred, innate **2 inherited**, heritable, traditional, family

heresy n **dissent**, deviation, unorthodoxy, sacrilege, profanation (fml)

heretical adj **unorthodox**, profane, sacrilegious, dissenting, unconventional

herewith adv **with this**, together with this, enclosed, with, attached

heritable adj **inheritable**, transferable, transmissible, hereditary

heritage n **inheritance**, legacy, tradition, birthright, custom

hermaphrodite adj **androgynous**, epicene, intersexual

hermetic adj **airtight**, enclosed, closed

hermit n **recluse**, loner, solitary

hero n **1 superman**, champion, conqueror, idol Opposite: loser **2 male lead**, leading actor, leading man, star, protagonist

heroic adj **daring**, stout, valiant, brave, epic

heroics n **recklessness**, rashness, irresponsibility, going over the top, overdoing it Opposite: timidity

heroine n **1 superwoman**, champion, conqueror, idol **2 female lead**, leading actress, leading lady, star, protagonist

heroism n **valour**, bravery, courageousness, fearlessness, boldness

hero worship n **adulation**, idolization, idealization, admiration, glorification

hesitancy n **indecision**, caution, uncertainty, tentativeness, timidity Opposite: decisiveness

hesitant adj **cautious**, tentative, timid, shy, undecided Opposite: decisive. See COMPARE AND CONTRAST at **unwilling**.

hesitate v **1 be uncertain**, be indecisive, vacillate, waver, falter **2 be unwilling**, think twice, scruple, have qualms, be reluctant

COMPARE AND CONTRAST CORE MEANING: show uncertainty or indecision

hesitate be slow in doing something, or take a short break in an activity, as a result of uncertainty or reluctance; **pause** stop doing something briefly before carrying on, or wait intentionally for a short period before doing something; **falter** show a loss of confidence, especially speak or say something with a series of short stoppages, for example because of nervousness, fear, awkwardness, or incompetence; **stumble** speak or act hesitatingly, confusedly, or incompetently; **waver** become unsure or begin to change from a previous opinion; **vacillate** be indecisive or irresolute, changing between one opinion and another.

hesitation n **1 uncertainty**, indecision, vacillation, wavering, faltering Opposite: decisiveness **2 unwillingness**, qualms, reluctance, disinclination, hesitancy Opposite: willingness

heterogeneous adj **varied**, mixed, assorted, diverse, various Opposite: homogeneous

heuristic adj **experiential**, empirical, experimental, investigative, exploratory

hew v **1 cut**, chop, fell, cleave, axe **2 carve**, fashion, sculpt, shape, model

hex n **curse**, spell, jinx, voodoo

heyday n **prime**, zenith, glory days, peak, halcyon days (literary)

hiatus n **pause**, break, interruption, space, lull

hibernate v **lie dormant**, take cover, overwinter, hide, hide away

hiccup (infml) n **hitch**, glitch, interruption, delay, setback

hidden adj **1 concealed**, out of sight, unseen, secreted, veiled **2 unknown**, secret, mysterious, clandestine, covert

hidden agenda n **ulterior motive**, secret plan, motivation, driving force, impetus

hide v **1 conceal**, put out of sight, hide from view, secrete, veil Opposite: flaunt **2 go underground**, take cover, disappear, keep cover, hole up (slang) **3 keep secret**, withhold, hold back, keep back, suppress Opposite: disclose

hideaway n **hiding place**, refuge, sanctuary, asylum, retreat

hidebound adj **narrow-minded**, prejudiced, conservative, conventional, parochial Opposite: broad-minded

hideous adj **1 ugly**, unattractive, grotesque, repellent, unsightly Opposite: attractive **2 revolting**, repugnant, repulsive, gruesome, shocking Opposite: pleasant. See COMPARE AND CONTRAST at **unattractive**.

hideousness n **ugliness**, repulsiveness, unsightliness, gruesomeness, dreadfulness

hideout n **safe house**, refuge, sanctuary, retreat, den

hidey-hole (infml) n **hiding place**, hideaway, safe house, safe place, shelter

hiding (infml) n **beating**, whacking, thumping, smacking, spanking

hiding place n **hideaway**, hole, place of escape, den, safe house

hierarchical adj **ranked**, graded, tiered, ordered, classified

hierarchy n **chain of command**, ladder, pecking order, grading, order

hieroglyph n **symbol**, pictograph, picture, ideogram, cipher

hifalutin (infml) see **highfalutin**

hi-fi n **sound system**, stereo system, stereo, CD player, cassette recorder

higgledy-piggledy adj **untidy**, topsy-turvy, in a mess, jumbled, confused Opposite: ordered

high adj **1 tall**, lofty, elevated, towering, soaring *Opposite*: low **2 in height**, from top to bottom, from head to foot, from top to toe, tall **3 above average**, great, extraordinary, elevated, extreme *Opposite*: normal **4 high-pitched**, shrill, piercing, penetrating, sharp *Opposite*: low-pitched **5 important**, eminent, prominent, high-ranking, superior *Opposite*: low ■ n **1 high point**, peak, climax, summit, high spot *Opposite*: low point **2** (*infml*) **thrill**, boost, tonic, lift, excitement

high achiever n **high flier**, success, star, winner, success story

highbrow adj **intellectual**, cultured, academic, scholarly, exclusive *Opposite*: lowbrow ■ n **intellectual**, academic, scholar, philosopher, sage (*literary*)

high-class adj **high-quality**, fancy, formal, elegant, superior *Opposite*: cheap

high court n **court**, principal court, supreme court (*US*)

highest adj **top**, topmost, utmost, ultimate, premier

highfalutin (*infml*) adj **pretentious**, pompous, affected, grandiose, snobbish *Opposite*: down-to-earth

high-flier n **high achiever**, success, winner, success story, star *Opposite*: plodder

high-flown adj **affected**, pretentious, grandiose, high-sounding, grandiloquent *Opposite*: down-to-earth

high-grade adj **high-quality**, quality, finest, superior, prime *Opposite*: low-grade

high ground n **1 upland**, highland, plateau, hillside, hilltop *Opposite*: lowland **2 principled stance**, moral stand, high road (*US*)

high-handed adj **bossy**, autocratic, dominant, undemocratic, domineering

high-handedness n **bossiness**, arrogance, imperiousness, inconsiderateness, overbearingness

high jinks (*infml*) n **mischief**, mischievousness, trouble, no good, nonsense

highland n **upland**, plateau, high ground, hilltop, moorland *Opposite*: lowland

high-level adj **sophisticated**, elevated, advanced, complex, top *Opposite*: unsophisticated

high life n **good life**, life of Riley, life of ease, lap of luxury, easy street

highlight n **high point**, climax, high spot, best part, best bit ■ v **emphasize**, draw attention to, underline, stress, focus on *Opposite*: downplay

highly adv **1 extremely**, very, exceedingly, very much, greatly *Opposite*: modestly **2 favourably**, approvingly, kindly, warmly, graciously *Opposite*: unfavourably

highly-strung adj **excitable**, edgy, tense, jittery, easily upset *Opposite*: laid-back (*infml*)

high-minded adj **principled**, worthy, moral, noble, upright *Opposite*: base

high-pitched adj **shrill**, high, piercing, penetrating, sharp

high point n **best moment**, high spot, best bit, climax, icing on the cake *Opposite*: low point

high-powered adj **successful**, dynamic, driven, ambitious, energetic

high-pressure adj **stressful**, difficult, relentless, pressured, intense *Opposite*: easy

high profile n **prominence**, conspicuousness, eminence, celebrity, notoriety *Opposite*: anonymity

high-profile adj **prominent**, prestigious, conspicuous, famous, eminent *Opposite*: discreet

high-rise adj **multistorey**, high, tall, big, lofty *Opposite*: low-rise ■ n **skyscraper**, block of flats, apartment block, tower block, office block

high society n **upper classes**, elite, polite society, beautiful people, upper crust (*infml*)

high-sounding adj **imposing**, high-flown, grandiloquent, grandiose, lofty

high-spirited adj **lively**, exuberant, merry, cheerful, vivacious *Opposite*: lethargic

high spirits n **liveliness**, exuberance, merriness, cheerfulness, vivacity *Opposite*: depression

high spot n **best moment**, high point, best bit, best part, climax

high-tech adj **advanced**, technological, computerized, digital, modern

high-up (*infml*) n **boss**, manager, director, big boss, bigwig (*infml*)

hijack v **1 take over**, seize, commandeer, capture, skyjack **2** (*infml*) **steal**, appropriate, take over, commandeer, borrow ■ n **takeover**, skyjacking, capture, seizure

hijinks (*infml*) *see* high jinks

hike v **ramble**, trek, walk, climb

hiker n **walker**, rambler, backpacker, trekker

hilarious adj **funny**, sidesplitting, comic, comical, humorous

hilariousness n **humour**, humorousness, uproariousness, comicalness, mirthfulness

hilarity n **amusement**, laughter, merriment, mirth, glee *Opposite*: sadness

hill n **1 mountain**, peak, mount, knoll, mound *Opposite*: valley **2 gradient**, slope, incline, rise *Opposite*: drop

hillock n **mound**, hump, hill, knoll

hilltop n **top**, summit, peak, pinnacle, brow *Opposite*: base

hilly adj **mountainous**, undulating, bumpy, alpine, craggy *Opposite*: flat

hind adj **back**, rear, rearmost, posterior (*fml*), hindmost (*literary*) *Opposite*: fore (*literary*)

hinder v **hold back**, obstruct, impede, block, hamper *Opposite*: facilitate

COMPARE AND CONTRAST CORE MEANING: put difficulties in the way of progress
hinder delay or restrict the development or progress of something, either accidentally or by deliberate interference; **block** prevent movement through, into, or out of something, or prevent something from taking place; **hamper** restrict the free movement or action of somebody or something; **hold back** keep something from happening or restrain somebody from doing something; **impede** interfere with the movement, progress, or development of somebody or something; **obstruct** cause a serious delay in action or progress, or cause a major physical blockage in a road or passageway.

hindquarters n **back**, rear, rear legs, hind legs *Opposite*: front

hindrance n **1 obstruction**, impediment, barrier, obstacle, encumbrance **2 interference**, interruption, limitation, prevention, sabotage *Opposite*: assistance

hindsight n **reflection**, retrospection, perception, observation, remembrance *Opposite*: foresight

hinge n **pivot**, axis, fulcrum, joint, centre

hinge on v **depend on**, hang on, turn on, be dependent on, rest on

hint v **suggest**, intimate, insinuate, imply, mention ■ n **1 suggestion**, clue, intimation, mention, indication **2 tip**, advice, pointer, suggestion, clue **3 trace**, tinge, suggestion, dash, taste

hinterland n **vicinity**, environs, surroundings, neighbourhood *Opposite*: heartland

hire v **1 employ**, appoint, take on, contract, sign up *Opposite*: fire **2 rent**, lease, let, charter, engage *Opposite*: purchase

hire out v **rent out**, rent, lend, lend out, lease

hirsute adj **hairy**, bearded, bushy, furry, long-haired *Opposite*: bald

hiss v **1 jeer**, boo, hoot, mock, ridicule *Opposite*: cheer **2 whisper**, murmur, rustle, whistle, susurrate

historic adj **1 significant**, momentous, notable, famous, remarkable *Opposite*: insignificant **2 past**, old, ancient, antique, historical *Opposite*: modern

historical adj **past**, old, ancient, antique, historic *Opposite*: modern

historically adv **1 in history**, over all, factually, archaeologically **2 traditionally**, generally, usually, as a rule, in the main

history n **1 past**, times gone by, times past, olden times, antiquity *Opposite*: present **2 account**, record, chronicle, narration, memoir

histrionic adj **theatrical**, dramatic, exaggerated, melodramatic, unrestrained *Opposite*: restrained

histrionics n **dramatics**, tantrums, hysterics, melodrama, drama

hit v **1 strike**, punch, thump, slap, beat **2 crash into**, strike, bang into, bump into, collide with **3 affect**, afflict, damage, hurt, disadvantage ■ n **1 blow**, knock, smack, slap, bump **2 success**, winner, triumph, sensation, market leader *Opposite*: flop (*infml*)

hit-and-miss adj **haphazard**, random, unpredictable, unplanned, careless *Opposite*: planned

hit back v **retaliate**, get even, strike back, react, even the score

hitch n **snag**, catch, drawback, glitch, delay ■ v **1 fasten**, hook, harness, join, tether *Opposite*: undo **2 hitchhike**, get a lift, be given a lift, thumb a lift, put your thumb out

hitchhike v **hitch**, get a lift, be given a lift, thumb a lift, put your thumb out

hitherto adv **up till now**, up till then, until now, until then, till now

hit it off (*infml*) v **get on well**, connect, get on, make friends, take to each other *Opposite*: clash

hit on v **think of**, chance upon, discover, realize, arrive at

hit out v **1 criticize**, attack, assail, condemn, lambaste **2 strike out**, lash out, lunge, go for, attack

hit the hay (*infml*) v **go to bed**, say goodnight, get to sleep, get some rest, retire

hit the roof v **lose your temper**, be angry, fly into a rage, go berserk, see red (*infml*) *Opposite*: calm down

hit the sack (*infml*) *see* **hit the hay**

hit upon v **stumble on**, chance upon, discover, realize, arrive at

hive v **store**, put away, save, put aside, hoard *Opposite*: discard

hive off v **cream off**, skim off, transfer, separate, split off *Opposite*: merge

hoard v **save**, store, amass, stockpile, accumulate *Opposite*: throw away ■ n **store**, pile, mass, reserve, supply. *See* COMPARE AND CONTRAST *at* **collect**.

hoarder n **collector**, saver, accumulator, miser, squirrel (*infml*)

hoarding n **billboard**, notice board, advertisement, placard, poster

hoar frost n **frost**, ice, rime

hoarse adj **croaky**, gruff, gravelly, husky, rough *Opposite*: smooth

hoarseness n **croakiness**, gruffness, huskiness, roughness, harshness *Opposite*: smoothness

hoary adj **1 overused**, old, ancient, age-old, stale *Opposite*: fresh **2 white**, snow-white, whitened, snowy, grey

hoax n **trick**, deception, practical joke, joke, swindle ■ v **deceive**, trick, con, swindle, mislead

hoaxer *n* **trickster**, practical joker, fraudster, joker, swindler

hobble *v* **limp**, hop, shuffle, shamble, totter ■ *n* **limp**, shuffle, stagger, shamble, stumble

hobby *n* **pastime**, leisure pursuit, diversion, relaxation, sideline *Opposite*: job

hobbyhorse *n* **favourite subject**, pet topic, bee in your bonnet, obsession, idée fixe

hobgoblin *n* **goblin**, imp, elf, pixie, sprite

hobnob *v* **socialize**, mix, fraternize, associate, go around *Opposite*: shun

hobo *n* **traveller**, itinerant, vagrant, tramp, drifter

hoe *v* **turn over**, weed, dig, dig out, loosen

hog *(infml)* *v* **monopolize**, take over, help yourself, take the lion's share of, hang onto

hogwash *(infml)* *n* **nonsense**, gibberish, humbug, garbage, rubbish

hoi polloi *n* **common herd**, general public, masses, ordinary people, proletariat *Opposite*: aristocracy

hoist *v* **lift**, raise, pull, heave, erect ■ *n* **winch**, crane, lift, elevator, pulley

hoity-toity *(infml)* *adj* **haughty**, arrogant, snobbish, proud, disdainful *Opposite*: down-to-earth

hold *v* **1 grasp**, clutch, grip, clasp, seize *Opposite*: release **2 fix**, secure, fasten, bind, attach **3 embrace**, hug, cuddle, enfold, squeeze **4 contain**, accommodate, stow, carry, take in **5 detain**, restrain, confine, shut in, imprison *Opposite*: let go **6 arrange**, convene, call, conduct, have **7 possess**, have, keep, retain, own **8 believe**, think, maintain, presume, consider **9 sustain**, maintain, continue, keep up, carry on **10 wait**, hold on, hang on, stay on the line *Opposite*: hang up ■ *n* **1 grip**, grasp, clasp, clutch, embrace **2 control**, power, influence, claim, sway **3 storage space**, storeroom, cargo bay, compartment, storage

holdall *n* **bag**, case, suitcase, portmanteau, carryall *(US)*

hold back *v* **1 restrain**, inhibit, suppress, repress, hamper *Opposite*: let go **2 keep back**, retain, keep, reserve, keep hold of *Opposite*: release. *See* COMPARE AND CONTRAST *at* hinder.

hold close *v* **hug**, embrace, hold tight, cuddle, enfold *Opposite*: release

hold down *(infml)* *v* **keep**, retain, maintain, manage, hang onto *Opposite*: lose

holder *n* **1 container**, pouch, receptacle, vessel, box **2 owner**, possessor, proprietor, controller, bearer

hold forth *v* **speak out**, harangue, preach, lecture, discourse *Opposite*: bottle up

hold in *v* **1 keep in check**, restrain, keep back, hold back, control *Opposite*: release **2 restrain**, keep the lid on, control, bridle, suppress *Opposite*: let out

holding *n* **1 land**, field, property, farm, croft

2 stock, investment, share, property, interest

hold in high regard *v* **revere**, respect, venerate, idolize, esteem *Opposite*: despise

hold off *v* **1 refrain**, desist, leave off, abstain, avoid *Opposite*: speed up **2 resist**, fend off, keep away, keep off, repel *Opposite*: yield

hold on *v* **1 wait**, hang on, be patient, wait a minute, hold your horses *(infml)* **2 grasp**, grip, keep hold of, hold fast, stick to *Opposite*: let go **3 persist**, persevere, keep on, stand your ground, stand firm *Opposite*: give up

hold onto *v* **1 retain**, keep, hang onto, save, hoard *Opposite*: give up **2 grasp**, clasp, clutch, grip, stick *Opposite*: release

hold out *v* **1 extend**, give, present, offer, proffer *Opposite*: withdraw **2 endure**, stand your ground, persist, stand firm, withstand *Opposite*: give in

hold out on *v* **not tell**, keep something from, hide something from, withhold something from *Opposite*: tell

hold over *v* **defer**, delay, postpone, put off, suspend *Opposite*: bring forward

hold sway *v* **have authority**, have influence, have power, be in power, be in control

hold the fort *v* **look after things**, take care of things, take over, take charge, mind things

hold up *v* **1 delay**, slow down, slow up, impede, hinder *Opposite*: speed up **2 rob**, raid, mug, do *(slang)*, stick up *(US infml)* **3 survive**, bear up, keep up, endure, keep going *Opposite*: give up **4 support**, shore up, keep up, prop, sustain *Opposite*: bring down

holdup *n* **1 theft**, raid, robbery, assault, mugging **2 delay**, hitch, glitch, snag, stoppage

hold with *v* **approve of**, endorse, support, subscribe to, agree with *Opposite*: disapprove

hold your own *v* **1 match up**, stand your ground, stand firm, look after yourself, take care of yourself **2 bear up**, persevere, be stable, be comfortable, persist *Opposite*: succumb

hole *n* **1 cavity**, hollow, void, chasm, gulf **2 aperture**, gap, opening, crack, break **3 burrow**, lair, retreat, run, sett **4 flaw**, weakness, fault, error, defect *Opposite*: strength **5** *(infml)* **hovel**, slum, shack, pigsty *(infml)*, fleapit *(infml)*

hole-and-corner *adj* **secret**, secretive, hidden, clandestine, private *Opposite*: public

hole-in-the-wall *(infml)* *n* **restaurant**, bar, bistro, café, dive *(infml)*

holey *adj* **leaky**, porous, perforated, worn, torn

holiday *n* **1 day off**, day's leave, personal day *(US)* **2 leave**, time off, break, sabbatical, hols *(infml)* *Opposite*: work **3 festival**, anniversary, feast, saint's day, carnival ■ *v* **be on holiday**, stay, relax, sojourn *(literary)*, vacation *(US)* *Opposite*: work

holidaymaker *n* **traveller**, sightseer, visitor,

tourist, day tripper *Opposite*: resident

holier-than-thou *(infml)* adj **self-righteous**, pious, smug, superior, sanctimonious *Opposite*: self-effacing

holiness *n* **sanctity**, sacredness, piety, godliness, religiousness

holistic *adj* **all-inclusive**, rounded, full, complete, general

holler *(infml)* v **shout**, yell, scream, shriek, howl *Opposite*: whisper

hollow *adj* **1 empty**, void, unfilled, vacant, unoccupied *Opposite*: solid **2 concave**, depressed, sunken, indented, cavernous *Opposite*: convex **3 resonating**, echoing, deep, low, dull *Opposite*: high-pitched **4 insincere**, empty, worthless, futile, vain *Opposite*: sincere ■ *n* **1 cavity**, recess, indentation, cup, nook *Opposite*: bulge **2 valley**, crater, dip, depression, basin *Opposite*: hill ■ *v* **excavate**, scoop, dig out, gouge, tunnel *Opposite*: fill. *See* COMPARE AND CONTRAST *at* **vain**.

hollowness *n* **1 void**, empty space, cavity, emptiness, concavity *Opposite*: solidity **2 insincerity**, emptiness, worthlessness, futility, vainness *Opposite*: sincerity

holy *adj* **1 sacred**, consecrated, hallowed, sanctified, blessed **2 saintly**, righteous, devout, religious, godly *Opposite*: irreligious

homage *n* **deference**, reverence, respect, service, duty *Opposite*: disrespect

home *n* **1 residence**, house, habitat, quarters, address **2 family**, household, family circle, family unit, background **3 birthplace**, place of birth, homeland, home town, native land **4 institution**, residence, residential home, children's home, rest home ■ *adj* **1 internal**, domestic, inland, interior, local *Opposite*: foreign **2 home-based**, household, homegrown, family, domestic *Opposite*: industrial ■ *adv* **homewards**, back home, in, home sweet home

homecoming *n* **return**, arrival, repatriation, visit, revisiting *Opposite*: emigration

home help *n* **domestic**, cleaner, maid, au pair, carer

home in *v* **focus**, zoom in, move in, aim, take aim *Opposite*: draw back

homeland *n* **native country**, mother country, native land, fatherland, motherland

homeless *adj* **on the streets**, living rough, dispossessed, destitute, vagrant *Opposite*: housed

homely *adj* **1 cosy**, simple, plain, ordinary, unpretentious *Opposite*: fancy **2 unattractive**, plain, unappealing, ugly, mousy *Opposite*: attractive. *See* COMPARE AND CONTRAST *at* **unattractive**.

home rule *n* **self-government**, autonomy, self-rule, independence, separatism

homesick *adj* **nostalgic**, sad, melancholy, pining, unsettled *Opposite*: content

homespun *adj* **plain**, simple, ordinary,

unsophisticated, down-to-earth *Opposite*: sophisticated

homestead *n* **farm**, farmstead, ranch, smallholding, croft

home town *n* **birthplace**, home, home base, back yard, home ground

home truth *n* **fact**, truth, bitter pill, criticism *Opposite*: lie

homework *n* **1 schoolwork**, exercise, lesson, study, assignment **2** *(infml)* **preparation**, reading, research, groundwork, reading up

homicidal *adj* **murderous**, destructive, killer, killing, bloodthirsty *Opposite*: harmless

homicide *n* **killing**, murder, slaughter, manslaughter, assassination

homily *n* **lecture**, sermon, talk, speech, discourse

hominid *n* **primate**, hominoid, anthropoid

hominoid *see* **hominid**

homogeneity *n* **1 sameness**, similarity, equality, consistency, regularity *Opposite*: dissimilarity **2 uniformity**, constancy, consistency, stability, regularity *Opposite*: variability

homogeneous *adj* **1 same**, similar, standardized, consistent, equal *Opposite*: heterogeneous **2 uniform**, consistent, constant, stable, regular *Opposite*: variable

homogeneousness *see* **homogeneity**

homogenize *v* **1 smooth**, emulsify, mix, beat, whip *Opposite*: separate out **2 standardize**, normalize, even out, regulate, make the same *Opposite*: distinguish

hone *v* **1 improve**, refine, enhance, polish, perfect *Opposite*: impair **2 sharpen**, whet, file, grind, polish *Opposite*: blunt

honest *adj* **1 upright**, trustworthy, moral, good, decent *Opposite*: immoral **2 truthful**, authentic, true, sincere, frank *Opposite*: untruthful

honestly *adv* **1 fairly**, justly, in all conscience, decently, reliably *Opposite*: immorally **2 really**, truly, truthfully, candidly, openly *Opposite*: untruthfully

honesty *n* **1 uprightness**, morality, trustworthiness, goodness, scrupulousness *Opposite*: immorality **2 sincerity**, truthfulness, integrity, frankness, candour *Opposite*: dishonesty

honeyed *adj* **1 ingratiating**, sugarcoated, cloying, flattering, fawning *Opposite*: sharp **2 melodious**, soft, dulcet, sweet, pleasing *Opposite*: harsh

honk *v* **beep**, hoot, toot, blare, blast

honorarium *n* **payment**, fee, grant, scholarship, exhibition. *See* COMPARE AND CONTRAST *at* **wage**.

honorary *adj* **1 nominal**, token, symbolic, titular **2 unpaid**, voluntary, unwaged, unsalaried, amateur *Opposite*: salaried

honour *n* **1 integrity**, decency, morality, righteousness, rectitude *Opposite*: baseness **2 respect**, admiration, esteem, regard, reverence *Opposite*: scorn **3 dignity**, distinction, nobility, pride, decorum **4 reputation**, image, good name, name, renown *Opposite*: disgrace **5 distinction**, award, tribute, credit, accolade *Opposite*: blot ■ *v* **1 keep**, stick to, fulfil, carry out *Opposite*: break **2 esteem**, respect, admire, take your hat off to, revere *Opposite*: disparage

honourable *adj* **1 moral**, upright, noble, worthy, right *Opposite*: immoral **2 respectable**, decent, admirable, praiseworthy, worthy *Opposite*: shameful

honoured *adj* **privileged**, pleased, flattered, grateful, thrilled *Opposite*: insulted

hoodlum *n* **gangster**, criminal, lawbreaker, thug, vandal

hoodwink *v* **trick**, deceive, dupe, delude, take in

hooey *(infml)* *n* **nonsense**, rubbish, humbug, gibberish, garbage *Opposite*: fact

hook *n* **peg**, hanger, nail, knob, catch ■ *v* **fasten**, attach, secure, join, tie *Opposite*: unhook

hook and eye *n* **fastener**, fastening, clasp, catch, clip

hooked *adj* **bent**, curved, bowed, curving, angular *Opposite*: straight

hook up *v* **1 connect**, link up, plug in, wire up, electrify *Opposite*: disconnect **2** *(infml)* **get together**, take up with, meet up, meet, pair off *Opposite*: part

hooligan *(infml)* *n* **criminal**, gangster, lawbreaker, thug, hoodlum

hoop *n* **ring**, loop, band, circle, round

hoot *v* **1 toot**, beep, honk, blare, blow **2 shout**, howl, whoop, roar, cry out

hop *v* **1 jump**, skip, leap, spring, bound ■ *n* **1 leap**, jump, skip, bound **2** *(infml)* **flight**, journey, trip, stage, leg **3** *(dated infml)* **dance**, party, disco, barn dance, social

hope *v* **want**, expect, trust, anticipate, wish *Opposite*: despair ■ *n* **1 confidence**, expectation, optimism, anticipation, faith *Opposite*: despair **2 likelihood**, prospect, possibility, promise, potential *Opposite*: impossibility **3 desire**, aspiration, dream, expectation, plan

hopeful *adj* **1 confident**, expectant, optimistic, positive, encouraged *Opposite*: pessimistic **2 promising**, encouraging, positive, rosy, propitious *Opposite*: discouraging **3 aspiring**, prospective, would-be, potential, budding ■ *n* **aspirant**, candidate, applicant, contender, seeker

hopefully *adv* **1 confidently**, expectantly, optimistically, positively, buoyantly *Opposite*: despairingly **2 with any luck**, with a bit of luck, all being well

hopefulness *n* **1 confidence**, hope, optimism, expectation, anticipation *Opposite*: despair **2 promise**, encouragement, positiveness, positivity, rosiness

hopeless *adj* **1 impossible**, desperate, unprom-

ising, fruitless, bleak *Opposite*: promising **2 despairing**, desperate, in despair, despondent, disheartened *Opposite*: positive **3 useless**, bad, pathetic, inept, incompetent *Opposite*: excellent

hopelessly *adv* **1 despairingly**, in despair, desperately, despondently, downheartedly *Opposite*: positively **2 terribly**, desperately, badly, completely, totally *Opposite*: slightly

hopelessness *n* **1 impossibility**, desperateness, fruitlessness, bleakness, futility *Opposite*: promise **2 despair**, desperation, despondency, bleakness, depression *Opposite*: hope **3 uselessness**, ineptness, ineptitude, incompetence, inability *Opposite*: excellence

horde *n* **throng**, crowd, mass, gang, group

horizon *n* **skyline**, distance, vanishing point, vista, prospect

horizontal *adj* **level**, flat, straight, plane *Opposite*: vertical

horn *n* **1 siren**, klaxon, hooter, alarm, buzzer **2 antler**, spine, barb, projection, tusk

horn of plenty *n* **cornucopia**, abundance, treasure chest, ready supply, never-ending supply *Opposite*: famine

horrendous *adj* **1 dreadful**, awful, terrible, dire, unbearable *Opposite*: wonderful **2** *(infml)* **outrageous**, exorbitant, sky-high, shocking, dreadful

horrible *adj* **unpleasant**, bad, awful, vile, nasty *Opposite*: pleasant

horribly *adv* **1 unpleasantly**, dreadfully, badly, terribly, unbearably *Opposite*: pleasantly **2 extremely**, greatly, very, totally, utterly

horrid *adj* **1 disgusting**, awful, dreadful, nasty, vile *Opposite*: pleasant **2 dreadful**, shocking, appalling, horrific, frightful

horridness *n* **1 nastiness**, beastliness, unpleasantness, hatefulness, meanness *Opposite*: pleasantness **2 disgustingness**, loathsomeness, vileness, dreadfulness, unpleasantness *Opposite*: attractiveness **3 dreadfulness**, frightfulness, terribleness, awfulness, horror

horrific *adj* **appalling**, dreadful, awful, horrendous, horrifying *Opposite*: wonderful

horrified *adj* **1 appalled**, shocked, aghast, sickened, disgusted *Opposite*: delighted **2 dismayed**, depressed, shocked, perplexed, disturbed

horrify *v* **1 appal**, disgust, revolt, shock, sicken *Opposite*: delight **2 dismay**, depress, shock, perplex, disturb

horrifying *adj* **1 horrific**, horrible, horrendous, terrible, sickening *Opposite*: delightful **2 shocking**, upsetting, disturbing, perplexing, perturbing

horror *n* **fear**, shock, revulsion, dismay, disgust *Opposite*: delight

horror-stricken *see* **horror-struck**

horror-struck *adj* **petrified**, scared stiff, terrified, horrified, stunned

hors d'oeuvre n **appetizer**, starter, entrée, crudités, first course

horse n **mount**, pony, charger, steed *(literary)*

WORD BANK

❏ **types of horse** Arabian horse, bronco, brood mare, carthorse, charger, cob, hack, hunter, mustang, pacer, packhorse, pony, racehorse, saddle horse, Shetland pony, shire horse, thoroughbred, trotter, warhorse, workhorse

❏ **parts of a horse** croup, fetlock, flank, foreleg, forelock, hindquarters, hock, hoof, mane, pastern, shank, withers

---

horse around v **fool around**, play around, clown, act the fool, cavort

horseman n **rider**, jockey, equestrian, huntsman, knight

horseplay n **rough-and-tumble**, boisterousness, play, fun, horsing around

horse sense *(infml)* n **common sense**, good sense, sense, wit, judgment

horseshoe n 1 **lucky charm**, talisman, mascot, amulet, token 2 **crescent**, curve, arc, loop, bend

horsewoman n **rider**, jockey, equestrian, huntswoman

horticultural adj **gardening**, garden, market garden, agricultural, nursery

horticulture n **gardening**, cultivation, propagation, agriculture, market gardening

hose n **tube**, pipe, line, hosepipe, garden hose ■ v **rinse**, water, spray, sluice, wash

hose down v **wash**, clean, sluice, rinse, hose *Opposite*: dry

hosepipe n **tube**, pipe, line, hose, garden hose

hospice n **nursing home**, hospital, rest home, sanatorium, clinic

hospitable adj **welcoming**, friendly, warm, open, generous *Opposite*: unfriendly

hospital n **infirmary**, sanatorium, rest home, hospice, sickbay

hospitality n **welcome**, friendliness, warmth, kindness, generosity *Opposite*: unfriendliness

host n 1 **entertainer**, master of ceremonies, MC, presenter, compere 2 **crowd**, swarm, cloud, congregation, mass ■ v **accommodate**, lay on, hold, present, introduce

hostage n **captive**, prisoner, detainee, victim

hostel n 1 **inn**, hotel, bed and breakfast, guesthouse, motel 2 **shelter**, refuge, boarding house, single room occupancy, dosshouse *(slang)*

hostess n **entertainer**, MC, presenter, compere, emcee *(infml)*

hostile adj 1 **unfriendly**, aggressive, intimidating, antagonistic, unreceptive *Opposite*: friendly 2 **adverse**, harsh, unwelcoming, unfavourable, unpleasant *Opposite*: pleasant

hostilities n **fighting**, warfare, conflict, battle, aggression

hostility n **aggression**, anger, unfriendliness, resentment, antagonism *Opposite*: friendliness

hot adj 1 **warm**, burning, boiling, searing, fiery *Opposite*: cold 2 **sweltering**, stifling, muggy, sultry, boiling *Opposite*: chilly 3 **spicy**, peppery, piquant, pungent, fiery *Opposite*: bland 4 **passionate**, fierce, angry, emotional, strong *Opposite*: dispassionate

hot air *(infml)* n **nonsense**, rubbish, drivel, stuff and nonsense, lies

hotbed n **breeding ground**, source, focus, hothouse, centre

hot-blooded adj **passionate**, volatile, hot-tempered, ardent, fierce *Opposite*: cold-blooded

hotchpotch n **jumble**, mixture, mishmash, mixed bag, miscellany

hotelier n **innkeeper**, landlord, landlady, proprietor, manager

hotfoot adv **immediately**, at once, without delay, instantly, urgently *Opposite*: slowly

hothead n **firebrand**, tearaway, madcap, loose cannon *(slang)*

hotheaded adj **impetuous**, volatile, rash, irascible, on a short fuse *Opposite*: prudent

hothouse n **greenhouse**, glasshouse, orangery, conservatory, winter garden

hotly adv **passionately**, fiercely, ardently, fervently, vehemently *Opposite*: dispassionately

hotness n 1 **heat**, high temperature, temperature, warmness, warmth *Opposite*: coldness 2 **overheating**, sweatiness, stickiness, warmness, warmth 3 **spiciness**, heat, fieriness, piquancy, pepperiness *Opposite*: mildness

hot potato n **difficulty**, controversy, tricky problem, thorny problem, knotty problem

hotshot *(infml)* n **high-flier**, achiever, star, expert, go-getter *(infml)*

hot-tempered adj **excitable**, fiery, hot-blooded, volatile, quick-tempered *Opposite*: relaxed

hot up *(infml)* v **intensify**, liven up, quicken, increase, speed up *Opposite*: cool down

hot water *(infml)* n **trouble**, bother, difficulty, controversy, conflict

hound n **dog**, wolfhound, deerhound, basset hound, foxhound ■ v **pursue**, chase, harass, pester, persecute

hour n 1 **60 minutes**, time, period, o'clock 2 **time**, period, era, age, day

house n 1 **residence**, home, address, building, pad *(dated slang)* 2 **household**, family, dynasty, community, line 3 **company**, firm, organization, business, establishment ■ v 1 **accommodate**, lodge, shelter, give shelter to, take in 2 **contain**, keep, store, hold, retain

---

WORD BANK

❏ **types of apartment** bedsit, flat, garden flat, loft, maisonette, penthouse, studio flat

---

❏ **types of house** bothy, bungalow, cabin, chalet, chateau, cottage, country house, detached house, farmhouse, grange, hacienda, homestead, igloo, lodge, manor, manor house, mansion, mobile home, palace, pied-à-terre, ranch, semidetached, shack, starter home, stately home, terraced house, timeshare, town house, villa

housecoat *n* **robe**, wrap, dressing gown, kimono, gown

house guest *n* **visitor**, guest, lodger, boarder

household *n* **family**, home, family circle, family unit, house ▪ *adj* **domestic**, home, family, everyday, domiciliary *Opposite*: industrial

household name *n* **celebrity**, star, superstar, megastar, luminary *Opposite*: unknown

housekeeping *n* **housework**, chores, cleaning, tidying, tidying up

house of worship *n* **house of God**, church, cathedral, synagogue, mosque

houseplant *n* **pot plant**, plant, indoor plant, foliage plant

WORD BANK
❏ **types of houseplant** aspidistra, coleus, fern, moss, poinsettia, rubber plant, sansevieria, spider plant, yucca

housing *n* **1 accommodation**, lodging, shelter, board, home **2 cover**, covering, case, casing, frame

housing estate *n* **estate**, development, urban development, residential area, council estate

hovel *n* **slum**, shack, squat, fleapit *(infml)*, dump *(infml)*

hover *v* **1 float**, hang, drift, soar, fly *Opposite*: descend **2 linger**, stay close, hang around, wait, remain *Opposite*: leave

how *adv* **in what way**, by what means, by what method, in what manner, just how

however *adv* **though**, but, on the other hand, yet, still *Opposite*: also

howl *v* **yowl**, bay, cry, wail, scream *Opposite*: murmur

howl down *v* **drown out**, shout down, boo, jeer, mock *Opposite*: cheer

howler *(infml)* *n* **blunder**, gaffe, error, malapropism, mistake

howling *adj* **violent**, whistling, gale-force, hurricane-force, breathtaking *Opposite*: gentle

hub *n* **1 centre**, middle, boss, pivot *Opposite*: spoke **2 centre**, heart, focus, focal point, nucleus *Opposite*: periphery

hubbub *n* **noise**, hullabaloo, din, uproar, clamour *Opposite*: silence

huddle *n* **group**, cluster, knot, crowd, clump *Opposite*: scattering ▪ *v* **1 gather together**, crowd together, throng together, cluster, come together *Opposite*: scatter **2 crouch**, bend, cower, nestle, hunch

hue *n* **1 colour**, tint, tinge, tone, shade **2 type**, kind, sort, description, manner

hue and cry *n* **uproar**, furore, commotion, protest, public outcry *Opposite*: acceptance

huff *n* **sulk**, mood, bad mood, temper, fit of pique ▪ *v* **1 bluster**, grumble, complain, rant, gripe *(infml)* *Opposite*: calm down **2 puff**, pant, wheeze, gasp, blow

huffy *adj* **touchy**, sensitive, moody, grumpy, sulky *Opposite*: good-natured

hug *v* **embrace**, hold close, enfold, cuddle, clasp ▪ *n* **cuddle**, clinch, clasp, bear hug, embrace

huge *adj* **1 enormous**, vast, gigantic, massive, giant *Opposite*: tiny **2** *(infml)* **incredible**, awesome, phenomenal, amazing, mind-blowing *(infml)*

hugely *adv* **enormously**, immensely, overwhelmingly, vastly, tremendously *Opposite*: slightly

hulk *n* **1 giant**, goliath, colossus, titan, ogre **2 shell**, skeleton, frame, carcass, wreck

hulking *adj* **bulky**, vast, massive, colossal, enormous *Opposite*: dainty

hull *n* **body**, exterior, underside, keel, casing *Opposite*: interior

hullaballoo *see* hullabaloo

hullabaloo *n* **noise**, hubbub, din, uproar, clamour *Opposite*: silence

hum *v* **1 drone**, whine, purr, buzz, whirr **2** *(infml)* **smell**, stink, reek, whiff *(infml)*, pong *(infml)* ▪ *n* **1 whine**, drone, purr, buzz, whirr **2** *(infml)* **smell**, stink, odour, whiff *(infml)*, pong *(infml)*

human *n* **person**, being, human being, individual, creature ▪ *adj* **humanoid**, hominid, hominoid, anthropological, anthropoid *Opposite*: animal

human being *n* **person**, human, being, individual, creature

humane *adj* **compassionate**, caring, kind, gentle, humanitarian *Opposite*: cruel

humanitarian *adj* **caring**, charitable, benevolent, philanthropic, public-spirited *Opposite*: uncaring

humanity *n* **1 mankind**, people, human race, mortality, homo sapiens **2 kindness**, charity, compassion, sympathy, mercy *Opposite*: cruelty

humanize *v* **1 anthropomorphize**, personify, personalize **2 civilize**, cultivate, improve, soften, refine *Opposite*: brutalize

humanizing *adj* **civilizing**, improving, progressive, refining, softening *Opposite*: brutalizing

humankind *n* **human race**, humanity, people, mortality, homo sapiens

humanly *adv* **at all**, feasibly, physically, realistically, in any way

human race *n* **humankind**, humanity, people, mortality, homo sapiens

human rights *n* **basic rights**, civil liberties, civil rights, citizens' rights, inalienable rights

humble *adj* **1 modest**, unassuming, retiring,

meek, self-effacing *Opposite*: arrogant **2 respectful**, subservient, servile, deferential, obliging *Opposite*: aloof **3 lowly**, poor, modest, simple, underprivileged *Opposite*: privileged ■ *v* **1 humiliate**, chasten, shame, bring down a peg, force to eat humble pie *Opposite*: glorify **2 degrade**, debase, demean, lower, reduce *Opposite*: exalt *(fml)*

humbled *adj* **shamed**, chastened, crestfallen, mortified, sheepish *Opposite*: proud

humbleness *n* **humility**, modesty, meekness, self-effacement, shyness *Opposite*: arrogance

humbling *adj* **1 chastening**, awe-inspiring, awesome, overwhelming *Opposite*: uplifting *(fml)* **2 mortifying**, embarrassing, shaming, sobering, crushing *Opposite*: heartening

humbug *n* **1 nonsense**, rubbish, gibberish, garbage, claptrap *(infml)* *Opposite*: fact **2 deception**, hypocrisy, lies, deceit, propaganda *Opposite*: sincerity

humdrum *adj* **dull**, boring, routine, unexciting, everyday *Opposite*: exciting

humid *adj* **moist**, damp, steamy, tropical, sticky *Opposite*: arid

humidify *v* **moisten**, dampen, saturate, impregnate *Opposite*: dry out

humidity *n* **moisture**, moistness, dampness, clamminess, stickiness *Opposite*: aridity

humiliate *v* **chasten**, embarrass, demean, degrade, disgrace *Opposite*: dignify

humiliated *adj* **chastened**, humbled, shamed, mortified, disgraced *Opposite*: proud

humiliating *adj* **chastening**, humbling, embarrassing, mortifying, shameful *Opposite*: gratifying

humiliation *n* **disgrace**, shame, mortification, embarrassment, dishonour *Opposite*: dignity

humility *n* **self-effacement**, unpretentiousness, humbleness, modesty, meekness *Opposite*: arrogance

humming *adj* **1 droning**, whining, purring, buzzing, whirring *Opposite*: silent **2** *(infml)* **smelly**, reeking, stinking, malodorous, stinky *(infml)*

hummock *n* **hillock**, mound, knoll, hill, rise *Opposite*: dip

humongous *(infml)* *adj* **enormous**, gigantic, colossal, massive, ginormous *(infml)* *Opposite*: tiny

humorist *n* **1 comedian**, comic, standup comedian, impressionist, entertainer **2 joker**, wit, satirist, punster, clown

humorous *adj* **funny**, amusing, entertaining, hilarious, comical *Opposite*: serious

humour *n* **1 funniness**, wit, comedy, comicality, comicalness *Opposite*: seriousness **2 wit**, wittiness, sparkle, drollness, sense of humour *Opposite*: dourness **3 comedy**, satire, black humour, spoof, slapstick ■ *v* **go along with**,

pacify, indulge, accommodate, please *Opposite*: oppose

humourless *adj* **1 sullen**, serious, po-faced, sour, dour *Opposite*: merry **2 unfunny**, unamusing, dull, straight, serious *Opposite*: funny

hump *n* **bulge**, bump, lump, swelling, protuberance *Opposite*: dip

humungous *see* **humongous**

hunch *n* **feeling**, gut feeling, sixth sense, premonition, intuition ■ *v* **bend**, huddle, stoop, crouch, lean forwards *Opposite*: straighten

hunger *n* **1 appetite**, emptiness, craving, hungriness, ravenousness **2 starvation**, food shortage, lack of food, malnutrition, famine *Opposite*: surfeit **3 craving**, desire, need, wish, yearning ■ *v* **crave**, yearn, long, desire, hanker *Opposite*: spurn

hungrily *adv* **1 ravenously**, greedily, voraciously, raveningly **2 eagerly**, impatiently, keenly, enthusiastically, excitedly *Opposite*: nonchalantly

hungry *adj* **1 famished**, ravenous, empty, ravening, voracious *Opposite*: full **2** *(infml)* **ambitious**, driven, thrusting, power-hungry, aggressive *Opposite*: content **3 avid**, eager, keen, greedy, thirsty *Opposite*: nonchalant

hunk *n* **chunk**, piece, lump, slab, wedge

hunker *v* **squat**, squat down, hunker down, crouch, crouch down *Opposite*: stand

hunky *(infml)* *adj* **muscular**, well-built, masculine, stocky, solid *Opposite*: puny

hunt *v* **1 chase**, pursue, stalk, follow, track *Opposite*: flee **2 seek out**, hunt down, track down, chase, pursue *Opposite*: evade **3 search**, seek, rummage, look, ferret about *Opposite*: find ■ *n* **search**, quest, chase, pursuit, expedition

hunt down *v* **find**, catch, track down, capture, get hold of *Opposite*: flee

hunted *adj* **panic-stricken**, alarmed, startled, frightened, unsettled *Opposite*: relaxed

hunter *n* **1 stalker**, predator, tracker, pursuer, chaser *Opposite*: prey **2 seeker**, searcher, quester, forager, scout *Opposite*: prey

hunting *n* **blood sport**, fox hunting, deer stalking, hare coursing, shooting

hurdle *n* **obstacle**, difficulty, problem, stumbling block, snag *Opposite*: aid ■ *v* **jump**, leap, jump over, leap over, clear

hurl *v* **throw**, fling, launch, toss, heave. *See* COMPARE AND CONTRAST *at* **throw**.

hurly-burly *n* **commotion**, chaos, turmoil, confusion, bustle *Opposite*: peace

hurricane *n* **storm**, gale, tempest, tropical storm, tornado

hurried *adj* **1 quick**, rushed, speedy, swift, sudden *Opposite*: leisurely **2 rushed**, pressurized, under pressure, harried, hassled *(infml)* *Opposite*: relaxed

hurry *v* **1 rush**, speed, hasten, run, dash *Oppo-*

site: delay **2 speed up**, accelerate, quicken, hasten, hustle ■ *n* **1 haste**, rush, dash, flurry, frenzy **2 urgency**, time pressure, panic, rush, haste

hurry up *v* **speed up**, accelerate, quicken, hasten, hustle *Opposite*: slow down

hurt *v* **1 injure**, harm, wound, damage, mar *Opposite*: benefit **2 ache**, be sore, be painful, throb, trouble *Opposite*: soothe **3 offend**, upset, insult, injure, cause offence *Opposite*: comfort **4 impair**, damage, mar, spoil, ruin *Opposite*: improve ■ *n* **1 upset**, pain, distress, sadness, offence *Opposite*: gratification **2 injury**, damage, harm, pain, soreness *Opposite*: benefit ■ *adj* upset, offended, wounded, unhappy, indignant *Opposite*: gratified. *See* COMPARE AND CONTRAST *at* **harm**.

hurtful *adj* **upsetting**, unkind, cruel, spiteful, cutting *Opposite*: kind

hurting *adj* **sad**, aching, heartbroken, broken-hearted, down *Opposite*: happy

hurtle *v* **dash**, career, tear, race, plunge *Opposite*: plod

husband *n* **spouse**, partner, other half, significant other, mate *Opposite*: wife

hushed *adj* **quiet**, silent, muted, soft, whispered *Opposite*: loud

hush-hush *(infml) adj* **secret**, confidential, top-secret, cloak-and-dagger, clandestine *Opposite*: public

hush money *(infml) n* **bribe**, pacifier, incentive, sweetener *(infml)*, backhander *(infml)*

hush up *(infml) v* **cover up**, suppress, conceal, keep quiet, keep secret *Opposite*: reveal

husk *n* **shell**, casing, pod, covering, skin *Opposite*: kernel

huskiness *n* **throatiness**, hoarseness, dryness, roughness, gruffness *Opposite*: clearness

husky *adj* **throaty**, hoarse, dry, rough, gruff *Opposite*: clear

hustle *v* **1 propel**, jostle, manhandle, push, shove **2** *(infml)* **hurry**, hurry up, get going, get cracking, get a move on *(infml) Opposite*: slow down

hustle and bustle *n* **commotion**, chaos, turmoil, confusion, hurly-burly *Opposite*: calm

hut *n* **shed**, lean-to, cabin, shelter, shack

hutzpah *see* **chutzpah**

hybrid *n* **cross**, crossbreed, mix, amalgam, mixture

hydroplane *v* **skid**, slide, swerve, aquaplane, slew

hygiene *n* **cleanliness**, sanitation, sanitariness, cleanness, sterility

hygienic *adj* **clean**, sterile, disinfected, sanitary, germ-free *Opposite*: unhygienic

hymn *n* **song**, chant, carol, chorus, anthem ■ *v* **praise**, celebrate, eulogize, extol, laud *Opposite*: criticize

hype *n* **publicity**, propaganda, buildup, excitement, puff ■ *v* **publicize**, advertise, build up, tout, push

hyper *(infml) adj* **1 hyperactive**, restless, frenzied, agitated, overactive *Opposite*: placid **2 excitable**, hotheaded, on the edge, highly strung, volatile *Opposite*: calm

hyperactive *adj* **restless**, agitated, frenzied, overactive, manic *(infml) Opposite*: placid

hyperbole *n* **exaggeration**, overstatement, overemphasis, magnification, inflation *Opposite*: understatement

hypercritical *adj* **overcritical**, censorious, nitpicking, finicky, pedantic *Opposite*: lenient

hypersensitive *adj* **touchy**, oversensitive, thin-skinned, easily offended, easily hurt *Opposite*: thick-skinned

hypnotic *(infml) adj* **fascinating**, mesmerizing, entrancing, spellbinding, compelling *Opposite*: uninteresting

hypnotize *v* **fascinate**, mesmerize, spellbind, entrance, enthral *Opposite*: bore

hypocrisy *n* **insincerity**, double standard, pretence, duplicity, two-facedness *Opposite*: sincerity

hypocrite *n* **charlatan**, fraud, phoney, double-dealer, pretender

hypocritical *adj* **insincere**, two-faced, duplicitous, deceitful, phoney *Opposite*: genuine

hypothesis *n* **theory**, premise, suggestion, supposition, proposition

hypothesize *v* **imagine**, conjecture, put forward, assume, theorize

hypothetical *adj* **theoretical**, imaginary, supposed, conjectural, proposed *Opposite*: real

hysteria *n* **panic**, hysterics, frenzy, madness, emotion *Opposite*: calm

hysterical *adj* **1 panic-stricken**, out of control, agitated, overexcited, feverish *Opposite*: composed **2 uncontrollable**, frenzied, intense, violent, unrestrained *Opposite*: controlled **3** *(infml)* **hilarious**, uproarious, highly amusing, sidesplitting, comical *Opposite*: sad

hysterically *adv* **1 frantically**, feverishly, frenziedly, frenetically, agitatedly *Opposite*: calmly **2 uncontrollably**, violently, wildly, frenziedly, unrestrainedly *Opposite*: quietly **3** *(infml)* **uproariously**, hilariously, sidesplittingly, riotously, screamingly *Opposite*: mildly

hysterics *n* **1** *(infml)* **fits**, fits of laughter, stitches, laughter **2 hysteria**, panic, frenzy, agitation, distraction *Opposite*: calmness

I

ice *n* frost, snow, hoar frost, rime, black ice ■ *v* **1 freeze up**, freeze, freeze solid, freeze over, ice over *Opposite*: thaw **2 decorate**, finish off, frost, embellish, adorn **3 chill**, cool, cool down *Opposite*: heat

icebreaker *n* opener, starter, opening, introduction

ice-cold *adj* freezing, frozen, icy, subzero, chilled *Opposite*: boiling

ice cream *n* ice, cone, ice-cream cone, sherbet, sorbet

iced *adj* chilled, cool, refrigerated, frozen, cold *Opposite*: hot

ice over *v* freeze, freeze over, freeze up, harden, solidify *Opposite*: thaw

ice pack *n* compress, cold compress, wrapping, poultice

ice up *v* freeze, freeze over, freeze up, ice over, frost up *Opposite*: thaw

iciness *n* **coldness**, coolness, frostiness, unfriendliness, hostility *Opposite*: warmth

icing *n* **1 frosting**, decoration, glaze, glazing, ganache **2 freezing**, freezing over, freezing up

icky *(infml) adj* **1 nasty**, unpleasant, horrid, uncomfortable, horrible **2 sticky**, gooey, tacky, messy, disgusting **3 sentimental**, too much, saccharine, over-the-top *(infml)*, sloppy *(infml)*

icon *n* **1 idol**, star, model, symbol, embodiment **2 image**, likeness, representation, sign, picture

iconoclast *n* **revolutionary**, radical, free thinker, subversive, individualist *Opposite*: conservative

iconoclastic *adj* **radical**, revolutionary, subversive, individualistic, freethinking *Opposite*: conservative

icy *adj* **1 freezing**, frozen, frosty, ice-cold, subzero **2 unfriendly**, frosty, hostile, distant, aloof *Opposite*: warm

ID *n* **identification**, identity card, passport, papers, documents

idea *n* **1 opinion**, belief, view, viewpoint, outlook **2 suggestion**, design, plan, scheme, proposal **3 concept**, impression, notion, understanding, perception **4 plan**, inspiration, solution, brainchild, notion **5 aim**, objective, plan, object, goal **6 gist**, précis, outline, sketch, overview

ideal *n* **1 epitome**, model, archetype, essence, stereotype **2 principle**, standard, belief, value ■ *adj* **best**, model, ultimate, idyllic, supreme

idealism *n* **1 naivety**, romanticism, impracticality, optimism *Opposite*: realism **2 perfectionism**, fundamentalism, commitment, principle, morality

idealist *n* **1 perfectionist**, fundamentalist, crusader, zealot, fanatic **2 romantic**, optimist, dreamer *Opposite*: realist

idealistic *adj* **1 naive**, unrealistic, romantic, impractical, optimistic *Opposite*: realistic **2 uncompromising**, principled, committed, unswerving, unwavering

idealize *v* **romanticize**, put on a pedestal, view through rose-tinted spectacles, venerate, overemphasize

idealized *adj* **perfect**, flawless, faultless, ideal, unrealistic

ideally *adv* **1 in an ideal world**, preferably, if possible, if at all possible **2 perfectly**, supremely, superlatively, well

idée fixe *n* **obsession**, pet topic, hobbyhorse, fixation, bee in your bonnet

idem *adv* **the same**, the same thing, the same as before

identical *adj* **same**, indistinguishable, equal, matching, alike *Opposite*: different

identifiable *adj* **recognizable**, distinguishable, perceptible, discernible, detectable

identification *n* **1 recognition**, classification, naming, detection, discovery **2 ID**, documentation, proof of identity, papers, credentials **3 empathy**, sympathy, affinity, rapport, bonding

identify *v* **1 recognize**, classify, name, find, categorize **2 equate**, connect, relate, link, associate

identify with *v* **empathize with**, sympathize with, relate to, feel for, have sympathy for

identity *n* **individuality**, uniqueness, distinctiveness, self, character

identity card *n* **pass**, card, passport, ID card *(infml)*

ideological *adj* **conceptual**, philosophical, moral, political, ethical

ideology *n* **philosophy**, belief, creed, dogma, line

idiolect *n* **speech pattern**, turn of phrase, style, dialect, idiom

idiom *n* **1 expression**, phrase, set phrase, turn of phrase, saying **2 language**, dialect, speech, style, vernacular

idiomatic *adj* **natural**, fluent, colloquial, vernacular, native *Opposite*: stilted

idiosyncrasy n **quirk**, peculiarity, eccentricity, foible, habit

idiosyncratic adj **characteristic**, personal, individual, distinctive, eccentric

idle adj **1 inactive**, inoperative, unoccupied, at rest, still Opposite: working **2 lazy**, indolent, shiftless, workshy, slothful Opposite: diligent **3 frivolous**, futile, pointless, worthless, vain **4 unfounded**, baseless, groundless, frivolous, meaningless **5 empty**, hollow, ineffectual, impotent, meaningless ■ v **1 laze**, laze around, hang around, sit around, sit about **2 turn over**, run, tick over (infml). See COMPARE AND CONTRAST at **vain**.

idle away v **while away**, fritter away, waste, pass, spend

idleness n **laziness**, sloth, inertia, indolence, apathy Opposite: activity

idler n **slacker**, loafer, malingerer, timewaster, shirker Opposite: workaholic

idly adv **1 lazily**, indolently, shiftlessly, slothfully (fml) Opposite: diligently **2 frivolously**, futilely, pointlessly, worthlessly, uselessly Opposite: seriously

idol n **1 hero**, star, pin-up, obsession, ideal **2 icon**, graven image, statue, carving, sculpture

idolater n **fan**, admirer, fanatic, devotee, hero-worshipper

idolatry n **worship**, hero worship, adoration, admiration, veneration Opposite: denigration

idolization see **idolatry**

idolize v **worship**, hero-worship, adore, look up to, admire Opposite: denigrate

idyll n **nirvana**, honeymoon, honeymoon period, heaven, paradise Opposite: nightmare

idyllic adj **1 peaceful**, calm, tranquil, restful, relaxing Opposite: nightmarish **2 picturesque**, scenic, unspoiled, beautiful, charming

i.e. adv **that is to say**, that is, namely, viz, to be precise

if n **1 doubt**, uncertainty, question mark, unknown, unknown quantity **2 stipulation**, condition, rider, proviso, qualification

iffy (infml) adj **1 risky**, chancy, shaky, suspicious, dubious Opposite: reliable **2 unsure**, undecided, doubtful, hesitant, up in the air Opposite: certain

ignite v **1 catch fire**, catch light, go up in flames, burst into flames, flare up Opposite: go out **2 set fire to**, light, put a match to, set light to, set alight Opposite: put out **3 stir up**, stir, inflame, fan the flames of, kindle Opposite: dampen

ignition n **explosion**, detonation, eruption, burst, blastoff

ignoble adj **dishonourable**, shameful, despicable, immoral, dastardly Opposite: honourable

ignominious adj **humiliating**, embarrassing, shameful, disgraceful, reprehensible Opposite: honourable

ignominy n **humiliation**, embarrassment, shame, disgrace, infamy Opposite: honour

ignorance n **unawareness**, unfamiliarity, obliviousness, inexperience, witlessness Opposite: knowledge

ignorant adj **unaware**, uninformed, ill-informed, unfamiliar, oblivious Opposite: aware

ignore v **pay no attention to**, take no notice of, close your eyes to, pay no heed to, disregard Opposite: notice

ignored adj **overlooked**, unnoticed, disregarded, discounted, unheeded Opposite: noted

ilk n **type**, like, sort, kind, class

ill adj **1 unwell**, sick, under the weather, laid up, in poor health Opposite: well **2 unkind**, unfriendly, hostile, harsh, mean Opposite: good **3 harmful**, adverse, detrimental, unfavourable, unpropitious Opposite: good **4 wicked**, evil, immoral, bad, iniquitous Opposite: good ■ adv **1 unkindly**, hostilely, harshly, cruelly, unpleasantly Opposite: well **2 unfavourably**, adversely, unpropitiously, inauspiciously, ominously Opposite: well **3 hardly**, barely, scarcely Opposite: well ■ n **harm**, evil, misfortune, trouble, mischief Opposite: good

ill-advised adj **foolish**, foolhardy, misguided, rash, reckless Opposite: well-advised

ill-assorted adj **incompatible**, mismatched, unsuited, incongruous, antagonistic Opposite: compatible

ill-bred adj **rude**, impolite, boorish, bad-mannered, ill-mannered Opposite: well-bred

ill-conceived adj **doomed**, impractical, vague, ill-judged, half-baked (infml)

ill-considered adj **careless**, reckless, irresponsible, rash, hasty Opposite: prudent

ill-defined adj **imprecise**, vague, hazy, unclear, nebulous Opposite: clear

ill-disguised adj **obvious**, blatant, clear, apparent, plain Opposite: concealed

ill-disposed adj **hostile**, unfriendly, cold, cool, antagonistic Opposite: well-disposed

illegal adj **against the law**, unlawful, illicit, illegitimate, prohibited Opposite: legal. See COMPARE AND CONTRAST at **unlawful**.

illegality n **1 unlawfulness**, illicitness, illegitimacy, impropriety, wrongfulness Opposite: legality **2 crime**, misdemeanour, offence, felony, infraction

illegible adj **unreadable**, indecipherable, scrawled, scribbled, spidery Opposite: legible

illegitimate adj **unlawful**, illegal, illicit, prohibited, banned Opposite: legitimate

ill-fated adj **doomed**, ill-starred, unlucky,

unfortunate, hapless *Opposite*: lucky

ill-favoured *adj* **unattractive**, ugly, repulsive, repellent, hideous *Opposite*: good-looking

ill feeling *n* **animosity**, hostility, ill will, antagonism, enmity *Opposite*: friendliness

ill-founded *adj* **illogical**, false, inaccurate, trumped-up, unreliable *Opposite*: reliable

ill-gotten *adj* **illegal**, illicit, fraudulent, contraband, unlawful

ill health *n* **infirmity**, illness, sickness, disease, frailty *Opposite*: good health

ill humour *n* **bad mood**, mood, bad temper, foul mood, sulk

illiberal *adj* **1 intolerant**, bigoted, narrow-minded, reactionary, parochial *Opposite*: liberal **2** *(fml)* **mean**, parsimonious, miserly, niggardly, tight *Opposite*: generous

illicit *adj* **illegal**, unlawful, illegitimate, dishonest, criminal *Opposite*: legal. *See* COMPARE AND CONTRAST *at* **unlawful**.

illiterate *adj* **uneducated**, untaught, unschooled, untrained, uninformed *Opposite*: literate

ill-judged *adj* **misguided**, injudicious, inappropriate, unwise, imprudent *Opposite*: prudent

ill-mannered *adj* **rude**, bad-mannered, impolite, discourteous, disrespectful *Opposite*: well-mannered

ill-natured *adj* **unpleasant**, disagreeable, ill-tempered, bad-tempered, irascible *Opposite*: good-natured

illness *n* **1 disease**, sickness, complaint, ailment, infection **2 ill health**, sickness, disease, infirmity, disability *Opposite*: good health

illogical *adj* **1 irrational**, unreasoned, unscientific, specious, unsound *Opposite*: logical **2 unreasonable**, senseless, absurd, ludicrous, nonsensical *Opposite*: logical

illogicality *n* **1 irrationality**, speciousness, unsoundness, inconsistency, contradiction **2 unreasonableness**, senselessness, absurdity, ludicrousness, nonsensicality

ill-omened *adj* **inauspicious**, unlucky, unfortunate, ominous, fateful *Opposite*: blessed

ill-starred *adj* **unlucky**, doomed, ill-fated, unfortunate, hapless *Opposite*: lucky

ill-tempered *adj* **bad-tempered**, short-tempered, irascible, irritable, grumpy *Opposite*: good-tempered

ill-timed *adj* **inopportune**, mistimed, untimely, inconvenient, intrusive *Opposite*: opportune

ill-treat *v* **abuse**, harm, mistreat, misuse, ill-use *Opposite*: look after. *See* COMPARE AND CONTRAST *at* **misuse**.

ill-treated *adj* **abused**, harmed, mistreated, maltreated, ill-used *Opposite*: cherished

ill-treatment *n* **abuse**, harm, maltreatment, mistreatment, cruelty *Opposite*: care

illuminate *v* **1 light up**, light, brighten, lighten, irradiate *Opposite*: darken **2 clarify**, elucidate, explain, clear up, illustrate *Opposite*: confuse

illuminating *adj* **enlightening**, revealing, informative, instructive, educational *Opposite*: confusing

illumination *n* **1 light**, lighting, lights, brightness, brilliance **2 enlightenment**, clarification, explanation, insight, knowledge *Opposite*: confusion

illuminations *n* **lights**, Christmas lights, coloured lights, decorations, fairy lights

ill-use *v* **abuse**, harm, mistreat, maltreat, treat badly *Opposite*: look after

ill-used *adj* **mistreated**, maltreated, badly treated, abused, hurt *Opposite*: cherished

illusion *n* **1 fantasy**, daydream, figment of your imagination, chimera, mirage *Opposite*: reality **2 impression**, semblance, appearance, feeling, sensation **3 delusion**, misapprehension, deception, misconception, magic

illusive *see* **illusory**

illusory *adj* **deceptive**, false, imagined, misleading, unreal *Opposite*: real

illustrate *v* **exemplify**, demonstrate, show, point up, prove

illustration *n* **1 picture**, drawing, figure, diagram, photograph **2 example**, demonstration, instance, case in point, exemplification

illustrative *adj* **descriptive**, explanatory, graphic, expressive, demonstrative

illustrious *adj* **distinguished**, celebrated, renowned, famous, eminent *Opposite*: obscure

ill will *n* **animosity**, hostility, ill feeling, antagonism, enmity *Opposite*: goodwill

image *n* **1 picture**, representation, drawing, icon, figure **2 impression**, picture, idea, concept, notion **3 copy**, twin, double, duplicate, carbon copy **4 appearance**, look, persona, aura, air

imagery *n* **images**, pictures, descriptions, metaphors, similes

imaginable *adj* **conceivable**, possible, thinkable, supposable, presumable *Opposite*: unimaginable

imaginary *adj* **fantasy**, make-believe, made-up, unreal, invented *Opposite*: real

imagination *n* **1 mind's eye**, mind, head, thoughts, dreams **2 resourcefulness**, ingenuity, creativity, inventiveness, vision

imaginative *adj* **creative**, inventive, original, ingenious, artistic *Opposite*: unimaginative

imaginativeness *n* **creativeness**, inventiveness, originality, ingeniousness, resourcefulness

imagine *v* **1 picture**, envisage, visualize, see, conjure up **2 make up**, dream, dream up, invent, make believe **3 suppose**, think, expect, assume, presume

imagined adj **fictional**, imaginary, abstract, unreal, illusory Opposite: real

imbalance n **inequity**, disparity, unevenness, disproportion, inequality Opposite: balance

imbibe (fml) v **drink**, down, swallow, take in, absorb

imbroglio n **mess**, embarrassment, entanglement, complication, enmeshment

imbue v **instil**, fill, permeate, infuse, saturate

imitate v 1 **reproduce**, copy, duplicate, replicate, rip off (infml) 2 **mimic**, copy, ape, emulate, take off (infml)

COMPARE AND CONTRAST CORE MEANING: adopt the behaviour of another person
imitate copy another's behaviour, voice, or manner, sometimes in order to make fun of him or her; **copy** do exactly what somebody else does; **emulate** try to equal or surpass somebody else who is successful or admired; **mimic** imitate somebody in a deliberate and exaggerated way, especially to amuse people; **take off** (infml) imitate somebody to amuse people; **ape** imitate somebody in an absurd or grotesque way.

imitation n 1 **simulation**, reproduction, replication, copy, facsimile 2 **impersonation**, impression, skit, parody, sendup (infml) ■ adj **mock**, fake, simulated, artificial, pretend Opposite: real

imitative adj **unoriginal**, derivative, plagiarized, copied, second-hand Opposite: original

imitator n 1 **follower**, sheep, copier, clone, imitation Opposite: original 2 **impersonator**, impressionist, mimic, double, actor

immaculate adj 1 **spotless**, perfect, neat and tidy, clean, tidy Opposite: messy 2 **perfect**, flawless, faultless, pristine, pure Opposite: flawed

immanent (fml) adj **inherent**, intrinsic, innate, ingrained, internal

immaterial adj **irrelevant**, unimportant, of no importance, of no consequence, inconsequential Opposite: relevant

immature adj 1 **young**, undeveloped, small, unformed, juvenile Opposite: mature 2 **childish**, babyish, infantile, juvenile, adolescent Opposite: mature

immaturity n 1 **adolescence**, infancy, reproductive immaturity, youth, babyhood Opposite: maturity 2 **childishness**, irresponsibility, naivety, ingenuousness, silliness Opposite: maturity 3 **naivety**, inexperience, greenness, rawness, awkwardness Opposite: maturity

immeasurable adj **vast**, beyond measure, endless, infinite, incalculable Opposite: slight

immeasurably adv **extremely**, infinitely, vastly, incalculably, inestimably Opposite: slightly

immediate adj 1 **instant**, direct, instantaneous, abrupt, fast 2 **direct**, close, near, proximate

Opposite: distant 3 **urgent**, current, pressing, high priority, burning

immediately adv 1 **right away**, straightaway, at once, without delay, instantly Opposite: later 2 **directly**, closely, nearly, proximately Opposite: distantly ■ conj **as soon as**, the moment, the instant, the minute, the second

immemorial adj **ancient**, age-old, old, centuries old, timeworn

immense adj **huge**, vast, enormous, massive, gigantic Opposite: tiny

immensely adv **hugely**, vastly, enormously, immeasurably, greatly

immensity n **hugeness**, vastness, enormity, sheer size, extent

immerse v 1 **submerge**, dip, plunge, duck, dunk 2 **engross**, throw yourself into, absorb yourself in, engage, occupy

immersed adj **engrossed**, wrapped up, absorbed, deep, occupied Opposite: distracted

immersion n 1 **involvement**, engagement, absorption, entanglement, preoccupation 2 **dipping**, soaking, wetting, dunking, steeping

immigrant n **settler**, émigré, migrant, refugee, colonist Opposite: emigrant

immigrate v **settle**, arrive, colonize, discover, found Opposite: emigrate

immigration n **migration**, settlement, arrival, entry, colonization

imminent adj **impending**, forthcoming, pending, looming, about to happen Opposite: distant

immobile adj 1 **motionless**, stationary, still, stock-still, inert Opposite: mobile 2 **fixed**, immovable, secure, steady, permanent Opposite: mobile

immobility n **stillness**, motionlessness, immovability, fixity, stasis Opposite: mobility

immobilize v **stop**, halt, restrain, arrest, bring to a halt Opposite: mobilize

immoderate adj **excessive**, extreme, intemperate, extravagant, unrestrained Opposite: moderate

immoderateness (fml) see immoderation

immoderation (fml) n **excess**, intemperance, extravagance, prodigality, abandon Opposite: moderation

immodest adj **boastful**, arrogant, conceited, ostentatious, bombastic Opposite: modest

immodesty n **arrogance**, conceit, boastfulness, pretentiousness, ostentatiousness Opposite: modesty

immolate (literary) v 1 **sacrifice**, offer up, slaughter, make an offering of, kill 2 **give up**, sacrifice, renounce, do without, forgo

immoral adj **wicked**, depraved, corrupt, dissolute, dishonest Opposite: moral

immorality n **wickedness**, sin, depravity, corruption, dissoluteness *Opposite*: morality

immortal *adj* 1 **eternal**, everlasting, undying, perpetual, enduring *Opposite*: mortal 2 **memorable**, well-known, famous, illustrious, unforgettable *Opposite*: forgotten

immortalize *v* **commemorate**, celebrate, preserve, make immortal, memorialize

immovable *adj* 1 **fixed**, immobile, secure, steady, permanent *Opposite*: movable 2 **resolute**, unbending, rigid, stubborn, obstinate *Opposite*: irresolute

immune *adj* 1 **resistant**, protected, invulnerable, safe, insusceptible *(fml)* *Opposite*: susceptible 2 **exempt**, excepted, absolved, excused, not liable *Opposite*: liable 3 **impervious**, invulnerable, untouchable, untouched, unaffected *Opposite*: vulnerable

immune system *n* **body's defences**, natural defences, immune response, white blood cells, natural resistance

immunity *n* 1 **resistance**, protection, invulnerability, imperviousness, insusceptibility *(fml)* *Opposite*: susceptibility 2 **exemption**, exception, liberty, freedom, protection *Opposite*: liability

immunization *n* **vaccination**, inoculation, injection, shot *(infml)*, jab *(infml)*

immunize *v* **vaccinate**, inoculate, inject, protect, jab *(infml)*

immure *(literary)* *v* **imprison**, confine, shut away, shut up, hold captive *Opposite*: free

immutable *adj* **unchanging**, irreversible, fixed, absolute, unchangeable *Opposite*: mercurial

imp *n* 1 **elf**, goblin, pixie, sprite, fairy 2 **mischief**, urchin, rascal, scamp *(infml)*, scallywag *(dated infml)*

impact *n* 1 **crash**, collision, shock, bang, blow 2 **influence**, impression, effect, bearing, power

impacted *adj* **wedged**, stuck, jammed, squeezed, obstructed

impair *v* **damage**, harm, spoil, weaken, worsen *Opposite*: enhance

impaired *adj* **reduced**, lessened, decreased, weakened, diminished *Opposite*: unimpaired

impairment *n* **damage**, injury, hurt, loss, weakening *Opposite*: enhancement

impale *v* **spear**, pierce, stab, bayonet, spike

impalpable *(fml)* *adj* **intangible**, shadowy, vague, unclear, indefinable *Opposite*: palpable

impart *v* **communicate**, inform, tell, convey, divulge

impartial *adj* **neutral**, fair, unbiased, independent, objective *Opposite*: biased

impartiality *n* **neutrality**, fairness, independence, objectivity, detachment *Opposite*: bias

impassable *adj* **blocked**, impenetrable, closed, obstructed, inaccessible *Opposite*: open

impasse *n* **stalemate**, standoff, deadlock, gridlock, bottleneck

impassioned *adj* **emotional**, ardent, fervent, passionate, heated *Opposite*: impassive

impassive *adj* 1 **expressionless**, blank, inexpressive, poker-faced, deadpan *Opposite*: expressive 2 **unemotional**, unmoved, stolid, stoic, phlegmatic *Opposite*: impassioned

COMPARE AND CONTRAST CORE MEANING: showing no emotional response or interest
impassive showing no outward sign of emotion, especially on the face; **apathetic** not taking any interest in anything, or not bothering to do anything; **phlegmatic** generally unemotional and difficult to arouse; **stolid** solemn, unemotional, and not easily excited or upset; **stoic** showing admirable patience and endurance in the face of adversity without complaining or getting upset; **unmoved** showing no emotion, surprise, or excitement when this would normally have been expected.

impatience *n* 1 **annoyance**, irritation, edginess, intolerance, displeasure *Opposite*: patience 2 **eagerness**, keenness, anxiety, hurry, haste *Opposite*: patience

impatient *adj* 1 **annoyed**, irritated, edgy, intolerant, exasperated *Opposite*: patient 2 **eager**, keen, raring, anxious, in a hurry *Opposite*: patient

impeach *v* **indict**, accuse, arraign, charge, inculpate *(fml)*

impeccable *adj* **perfect**, flawless, faultless, unimpeachable, above reproach *Opposite*: flawed

impecunious *adj* **poor**, impoverished, penniless, poverty-stricken, destitute *Opposite*: wealthy

impede *v* **obstruct**, hinder, hamper, slow down, delay *Opposite*: facilitate. *See* COMPARE AND CONTRAST *at* hinder.

impediment *n* 1 **obstacle**, obstruction, barrier, hurdle, hindrance 2 **impairment**, disablement, weakness, disorder, inhibition

impel *v* 1 **compel**, urge, force, drive, coerce *Opposite*: hold back 2 *(fml)* **propel**, force, drive, throw, push

impend *(fml)* *v* **loom**, approach, be on the horizon, be imminent, be in the offing *Opposite*: recede

impending *adj* **imminent**, looming, in the near future, approaching, coming *Opposite*: far-off

impenetrability *n* 1 **impassability**, impermeability, density, denseness, thickness 2 **incomprehensibility**, complexity, opacity, intricacy, obscurity *Opposite*: lucidity

impenetrable *adj* 1 **impassable**, dense, tightly packed, thick, solid 2 **incomprehensible**, unfathomable, indecipherable, inscrutable, unsolvable *Opposite*: understandable

impenitent *adj* **unrepentant**, unremorseful,

unapologetic, defiant, shameless *Opposite*: remorseful

imperative *adj* **1 necessary**, vital, crucial, essential, urgent *Opposite*: unimportant **2** *(fml)* **commanding**, domineering, bossy, imperious, overbearing *Opposite*: subservient ■ *n* **priority**, essential, requirement, necessity, obligation *Opposite*: option

imperceptible *adj* **slight**, gradual, subtle, invisible, undetectable *Opposite*: obvious

imperceptibly *adv* **slightly**, gradually, invisibly, subtly, little by little *Opposite*: obviously

imperfect *adj* **faulty**, defective, deficient, damaged, flawed *Opposite*: perfect

imperfection *n* **1 fault**, defect, deficiency, blemish, flaw **2 faultiness**, inadequacy, limitation, deficiency, failure *Opposite*: perfection. *See* compare and contrast *at* **flaw**.

imperial *adj* **grand**, majestic, imposing, regal, stately

imperialism *n* **expansionism**, colonialism, empire-building, colonization, interventionism

imperil *(fml)* *v* **endanger**, put in danger, risk, put at risk, jeopardize *Opposite*: protect

imperious *adj* **domineering**, authoritative, commanding, arrogant, superior *Opposite*: humble

imperiousness *n* **haughtiness**, overbearingness, arrogance, superiority, bossiness *Opposite*: humility

imperishability *n* **durability**, resilience, stability, endurance, hardiness

imperishable *adj* **1 permanent**, durable, indestructible, resilient, stable **2** *(literary)* **enduring**, eternal, everlasting, permanent, immortal *Opposite*: transient

impermanence *n* **transience**, transitoriness, evanescence, ephemerality, temporariness *Opposite*: permanence

impermanent *adj* **temporary**, transitory, passing, transient, evanescent *Opposite*: permanent

impermeability *n* **watertightness**, airtightness, waterproofness, protection, impenetrability *Opposite*: permeability

impermeable *adj* **resistant**, impervious, waterproof, water-resistant, rainproof *Opposite*: permeable

impersonal *adj* **1 objective**, cool, detached, measured, careful *Opposite*: personal **2 anonymous**, faceless, soulless, featureless, grey **3 unfriendly**, cool, cold, aloof, frosty *Opposite*: friendly

impersonate *v* **1 mimic**, imitate, ape, copy, satirize **2 pretend to be**, pose as, masquerade as, personate, pass off

impersonation *n* **1 impression**, parody, caricature, takeoff *(infml)*, sendup *(infml)* **2 imitation**, masquerade, personation, pretence, imposture *(fml)*

impertinence *n* **impudence**, insolence, disrespect, impoliteness, brazenness *Opposite*: respect

impertinent *adj* **impudent**, insolent, disrespectful, impolite, brazen *Opposite*: respectful

imperturbable *adj* **calm**, cool, unflappable, collected, composed *Opposite*: excitable

impervious *adj* **1 unreceptive**, unbending, unyielding, unwavering, rigid *Opposite*: responsive **2 impermeable**, solid, resistant, waterproof, water-resistant *Opposite*: permeable

imperviousness *n* **1 obduracy**, unyieldingness, rigidity, inflexibility *Opposite*: responsiveness **2 impermeability**, resistance, invulnerability, watertightness, solidity *Opposite*: permeability

impetuosity *n* **impulsiveness**, rashness, hastiness, hotheadedness, recklessness *Opposite*: consideration

impetuous *adj* **impulsive**, rash, hasty, hotheaded, unthinking *Opposite*: considered

impetuousness *see* impetuosity

impetus *n* **1 push**, motivation, incentive, energy, stimulus **2 force**, momentum, impulsion, thrust, forward motion *Opposite*: inertia

impiety *n* **irreverence**, sin, wickedness, transgression, immorality *Opposite*: piety

impinge *(fml)* *v* **impose**, intrude, interrupt, encroach, impact

impious *adj* **sinful**, irreverent, wicked, immoral, irreligious *Opposite*: pious

impish *adj* **mischievous**, naughty, wicked, playful, puckish

impishness *n* **mischievousness**, naughtiness, wickedness, playfulness, puckishness

implacability *n* **pitilessness**, mercilessness, relentlessness, ruthlessness, cruelty *Opposite*: kindness

implacable *adj* **pitiless**, merciless, relentless, ruthless, cruel *Opposite*: kind

implant *v* **establish**, embed, plant, insert, instil

implantation *n* **embedding**, establishment, grafting, attaching, joining

implausibility *n* **improbability**, unlikelihood, inconceivability, doubtfulness, questionability *Opposite*: plausibility

implausible *adj* **unlikely**, improbable, unbelievable, incredible, fantastic *Opposite*: plausible

implement *n* **tool**, device, gadget, instrument, contrivance ■ *v* **carry out**, put into practice, apply, realize, execute

implementation *n* **carrying out**, application, putting into practice, operation, execution *Opposite*: proposal

implicate *v* **1 connect**, involve, associate, link, incriminate *Opposite*: clear **2** *(fml)* **imply**, suggest, assume, hint at, point to

implication n **1 insinuation**, inference, suggestion, innuendo, hint **2 involvement**, association, connection, link, part **3 consequence**, repercussion, outcome, result

implicit adj **1 understood**, implied, unspoken, tacit, hidden Opposite: explicit **2 unreserved**, absolute, total, complete, utter Opposite: qualified

implicitly adv **1 indirectly**, covertly, tacitly, obliquely, subtly **2 unreservedly**, absolutely, totally, completely, wholly

implied adj **indirect**, understood, implicit, unspoken, tacit

implode v **collapse**, fail, cave in, fall in, subside Opposite: explode

implore (fml) v **beg**, plead, pray, appeal, entreat

imploring (fml) adj **pleading**, desperate, longing, heartfelt, suppliant (fml)

implosion n **collapse**, falling-in, subsidence, cave-in, disintegration Opposite: explosion

imply v **1 suggest**, hint at, point to, indicate, insinuate **2 involve**, entail, mean, denote

impolite adj **rude**, ill-mannered, bad-mannered, boorish, disrespectful Opposite: polite

impoliteness n **rudeness**, bad manners, loutishness, boorishness, disrespect Opposite: politeness

impolitic adj **unwise**, inappropriate, misguided, ill-advised, ill-judged Opposite: wise

imponderable adj **unknown**, unquantifiable, incalculable, indeterminable, inestimable ■ n **unknown**, mystery, enigma, paradox, uncertainty

import v **bring in**, introduce, trade in, smuggle Opposite: export ■ n **1 introduction**, importation, ingress (fml) Opposite: export **2 significance**, importance, meaning, consequence (fml)

importance n **1 significance**, meaning, weight, magnitude, import Opposite: triviality **2 rank**, position, standing, status, reputation

important adj **1 significant**, vital, imperative, central, chief Opposite: trivial **2 high-ranking**, eminent, worthy, notable, prominent Opposite: insignificant

importantly adv **significantly**, notably, crucially, critically, vitally

importation n **import**, introduction, ingress (fml) Opposite: export

importer n **trader**, shipper, carrier, haulier, distributor

importunate (fml) adj **persistent**, demanding, unrelenting, annoying, overeager

importune (fml) v **bother**, pester, badger, harass, plague

importunity (fml) n **1 persistence**, insistence, obstinacy, doggedness, stubbornness **2 demand**, request, entreaty, appeal, petition

impose v **1 enforce**, levy, exact, execute, carry out **2 inflict**, force, foist, dump, insist **3 intrude**, be in the way, be a nuisance, disturb, trespass

imposing adj **impressive**, striking, grand, magnificent, stately Opposite: unimpressive

imposition n **burden**, nuisance, annoyance, bother, obligation

impossibility n **unfeasibility**, impracticality, hopelessness, ridiculousness, unlikelihood Opposite: possibility

impossible adj **1 irresolvable**, irresoluble, unfeasible, impracticable, unattainable Opposite: possible **2 unbearable**, terrible, dreadful, intolerable, insufferable Opposite: manageable

impossibly adv **dreadfully**, terribly, hopelessly, unbearably, ridiculously Opposite: reasonably

impostor n **deceiver**, imitator, impersonator, pretender, fake Opposite: the real McCoy (infml)

imposture (fml) n **deception**, impersonation, pretence, masquerade, imitation

impotence n **ineffectiveness**, incapability, ineffectualness, feebleness, powerlessness Opposite: strength

impotent adj **powerless**, weak, helpless, unable, incapable Opposite: powerful

impound v **confiscate**, seize, lock up, take away, hold Opposite: release

impoverish v **deprive**, ruin, bankrupt, diminish, weaken Opposite: enrich

impoverished adj **needy**, poor, penniless, disadvantaged, underprivileged Opposite: rich

impoverishment n **1 destitution**, failure, disadvantage, poverty, insolvency Opposite: prosperity **2 diminishment**, ruination, decline, depletion, degeneration Opposite: enrichment

impracticability n **unworkability**, impossibility, impracticality, impracticableness, unworkableness Opposite: feasibility

impracticable adj **unviable**, useless, unrealistic, unfeasible, unpractical Opposite: viable

impractical adj **1 unpractical**, unreasonable, unviable, unfeasible, unworkable Opposite: practical **2 unrealistic**, idealistic, starry-eyed, not down to earth, clueless (infml) Opposite: realistic

impracticality n **unviability**, unfeasibility, impracticability, inconvenience, hopelessness Opposite: practicality

imprecate (fml) v **curse**, revile, call down, execrate (literary or fml), maledict (literary)

imprecation (fml) n **1 oath**, insult, swearword, expletive, curse **2 swearing**, cursing, blasphemy, profanity, cussing (infml)

imprecise adj **sketchy**, vague, inexact, rough, inaccurate Opposite: precise

imprecision n **fuzziness**, roughness, sketchiness, inaccuracy, inexactitude *Opposite*: accuracy

impregnable adj **unassailable**, invincible, secure, unconquerable, impenetrable *Opposite*: vulnerable

impregnate v **saturate**, soak, steep, infuse, permeate *Opposite*: dry out

impresario n **manager**, producer, promoter, agent, entrepreneur

impress v 1 **excite**, move, amaze, influence, affect *Opposite*: disappoint 2 **emphasize**, stress, drive home, drum into, din into *Opposite*: gloss over

impression n 1 **feeling**, idea, notion, thought, sense *Opposite*: certainty 2 **imprint**, dent, mark, print, hollow 3 **mark**, impact, effect, influence, reaction 4 **impersonation**, imitation, parody, takeoff *(infml)*, sendup *(infml)*

impressionable adj **susceptible**, suggestible, vulnerable, receptive, sensitive *Opposite*: unreceptive

impressionist n **impersonator**, mimic, imitator, comic, entertainer

impressionistic adj **ill-defined**, rough, loose, unfocused, imprecise *Opposite*: detailed

impressive adj **imposing**, inspiring, striking, remarkable, notable *Opposite*: unimpressive

impressiveness n **grandeur**, splendour, magnificence, brilliance, eminence

imprint n 1 **impression**, print, mark, indentation, hollow 2 **stamp**, inscription, name, print, printer's mark 3 **hallmark**, emblem, stamp, seal, sign 4 **indication**, mark, impression, effect, sign ■ v **impress**, fix, establish, drive home, drum into

imprison v **confine**, detain, intern, lock up, lock away

imprisoned adj **confined**, jailed, captive, restrained, trapped *Opposite*: free

imprisonment n **custody**, captivity, detention, term, internment

improbability n **unlikelihood**, implausibility, dubiousness, doubtfulness, questionability *Opposite*: probability

improbable adj **unlikely**, doubtful, implausible, questionable, dubious *Opposite*: likely

impromptu adj **unprepared**, unrehearsed, unplanned, spontaneous, spur-of-the-moment *Opposite*: prepared

improper adj 1 *(fml)* **indecorous**, inappropriate, unsuitable, out of place, unfitting *Opposite*: fitting 2 **rude**, shocking, indecent, inappropriate, unacceptable *Opposite*: proper 3 **dishonest**, irregular, shady, illegal, criminal *Opposite*: honest

impropriety n **rudeness**, indecency, unseemliness, immodesty, indecorum *Opposite*: propriety

improve v 1 **look up**, perk up, get better, rally, mend *Opposite*: worsen 2 **better**, enhance,

ameliorate, enrich, upgrade *Opposite*: deteriorate 3 **correct**, adjust, touch up, titivate, amend

improved adj **better**, enhanced, amended, upgraded, developed *Opposite*: deteriorated

improvement n 1 **amendment**, correction, development, upgrade, enhancement *Opposite*: deterioration 2 **recovery**, recuperation, rally, progress, advance *Opposite*: decline

improve on v **better**, go one better, top, beat, exceed

improvident adj **imprudent**, careless, reckless, negligent, irresponsible *Opposite*: prudent

improvisation n 1 **inventiveness**, invention, creativeness, lateral thinking 2 **extemporization**, ad-libbing, standup

improvise v 1 **ad-lib**, extemporize, create, make up, invent *Opposite*: orchestrate 2 **contrive**, concoct, invent, create, devise

improvised adj **unpremeditated**, ad hoc, unplanned, makeshift, spontaneous *Opposite*: prepared

imprudence n **profligacy**, carelessness, indiscretion, rashness, injudiciousness *Opposite*: prudence

imprudent adj **foolish**, impulsive, indiscreet, irresponsible, rash *Opposite*: prudent

impudence n **impertinence**, boldness, insolence, nerve, effrontery *Opposite*: respect

impudent adj **bold**, brazen, insolent, rude, disrespectful *Opposite*: respectful

impugn *(fml)* v **question**, dispute, call into question, doubt, query

impulse n 1 **instinct**, desire, urge, whim, compulsion *Opposite*: aversion 2 **propulsion**, motive power, drive, stimulus, pressure 3 **tick**, pulse, nerve, pulsation, beat

impulsion n 1 **push**, propulsion, thrust, momentum, impetus 2 **desire**, yen, compulsion, instinct, whim *Opposite*: aversion

impulsive adj **unwary**, thoughtless, impetuous, imprudent, precipitate *Opposite*: cautious

impulsively adv **unwarily**, thoughtlessly, on impulse, impetuously, spontaneously *Opposite*: deliberately

impulsiveness n **precipitateness**, suddenness, thoughtlessness, impetuosity, spontaneity *Opposite*: deliberation *(fml)*

impunity n **exemption**, freedom, licence, liberty, latitude

impure adj **contaminated**, adulterated, mixed, tainted, polluted *Opposite*: pure

impurity n **contamination**, pollution, adulteration, uncleanness, infection *Opposite*: purity

imputation n **accusation**, assertion, attribution, reproach, complaint

impute v 1 **credit**, chalk up, attribute, accredit, assign 2 **complain**, accuse, implicate, allege, assert

in *prep* **inside**, within, around *Opposite*: outside ■ *adv* **around**, inside, accessible, available, at home *Opposite*: out ■ *adj* **cutting-edge**, fashionable, popular, now, in vogue *Opposite*: out

inability *n* **incapability**, incapacity, powerlessness, helplessness, failure *Opposite*: ability

inaccessibility *n* **1 unreachability**, remoteness, distance, isolation, unapproachability *Opposite*: approachability **2 unattainability**, unavailability, unaffordability, impossibility, confidentiality *Opposite*: accessibility **3 difficulty**, obscurity, obscureness, obliqueness, impenetrability *Opposite*: lucidity

inaccessible *adj* **1 unreachable**, out-of-the-way, unapproachable, hard to find, remote *Opposite*: approachable **2 difficult**, obscure, esoteric, abstruse, oblique *Opposite*: simple

inaccuracy *n* **1 imprecision**, inexactness, mistakenness, wrongness, erroneousness *Opposite*: precision **2 error**, mistake, slip, flaw, blunder. *See* COMPARE AND CONTRAST *at* mistake.

inaccurate *adj* **imprecise**, inexact, mistaken, erroneous, wrong *Opposite*: precise

inaction *n* **1 failure to act**, indecision, procrastination, fumbling, delay *Opposite*: decisiveness **2 inactivity**, laziness, idleness, inertia, apathy *Opposite*: energy

inactivate *v* **deactivate**, put out of action, incapacitate, disable, turn off *Opposite*: set in motion

inactive *adj* **1 motionless**, stationary, unmoving, immobile, stopped *Opposite*: moving **2 idle**, dormant, out of action, unused, inoperative *Opposite*: working **3 sedentary**, lazy, slothful, indolent, sluggish *Opposite*: energetic

inactivity *n* **1 motionlessness**, immobility, stillness *Opposite*: motion **2 idleness**, dormancy, inoperativeness *Opposite*: activity **3 sedentariness**, laziness, sloth, indolence, sluggishness *Opposite*: energy

in addition to *prep* **as well as**, along with, on top of, besides, over and above

inadequacy *n* **1 insufficiency**, meagreness, scantiness, lack, shortage *Opposite*: sufficiency **2 fault**, failure, failing, incompetence, defectiveness *Opposite*: asset

inadequate *adj* **1 insufficient**, scarce, derisory, laughable, poor *Opposite*: sufficient **2 incompetent**, lacking, deficient, ineffective, inefficient *Opposite*: capable

inadmissible *adj* **unacceptable**, prohibited, excluded, barred, disallowed *Opposite*: acceptable

inadvertence *n* **1 carelessness**, inattention, negligence, thoughtlessness, laxity **2 oversight**, omission, error, mistake, blunder

inadvertency *see* inadvertence

inadvertent *adj* **unintentional**, careless, unintended, involuntary, unplanned *Opposite*: intentional

inadvisable *adj* **ill-advised**, imprudent, unwise, foolish, injudicious *Opposite*: wise

inalienable *(fml) adj* **unchallengeable**, absolute, immutable, unassailable, incontrovertible *Opposite*: disputable

in all *adv* **ultimately**, altogether, all in all, as a whole, all told

inane *adj* **silly**, unintelligent, absurd, ridiculous, stupid *Opposite*: sensible

inanimate *adj* **1 lifeless**, dead, nonliving, inorganic, inert *Opposite*: alive **2 inactive**, dull, unresponsive, apathetic, listless *Opposite*: spirited

inanity *n* **1 meaninglessness**, senselessness, stupidity, ridiculousness, absurdity *Opposite*: logic **2 silliness**, foolishness, frivolousness, stupidity, ridiculousness *Opposite*: sensibleness

inapplicability *n* **unsuitability**, inappropriateness, irrelevance, inaptness, wrongness *Opposite*: suitability

inapplicable *adj* **unsuitable**, irrelevant, inappropriate, inapposite, inapt *Opposite*: suitable

inapposite *adj* **unsuitable**, out of place, inappropriate, inapt, unfitting *Opposite*: suitable

inappositeness *n* **unsuitability**, inappropriateness, inaptness, wrongness, irrelevance *Opposite*: suitability

inappreciable *adj* **insignificant**, imperceptible, negligible, unimportant, immaterial *Opposite*: significant

inappreciably *adv* **insignificantly**, imperceptibly, negligibly, immaterially, microscopically *Opposite*: significantly

inappropriate *adj* **unsuitable**, unfitting, untimely, inapt, wrong *Opposite*: fitting

inappropriateness *n* **unsuitability**, impropriety, wrongness, incorrectness, unseemliness *Opposite*: appropriateness

inarticulacy *n* **1 incoherence**, hesitation, lack of fluency, stumbling, stuttering *Opposite*: eloquence **2 unintelligibility**, incomprehensibility, inaudibility, indistinctness, unclearness *Opposite*: clarity

inarticulate *adj* **1 tongue-tied**, incoherent, mumbling, hesitant, faltering *Opposite*: eloquent **2 garbled**, muttered, incoherent, unintelligible, incomprehensible *Opposite*: clear

inasmuch as *conj* **because**, insofar as, considering that, since, as

inattention *n* **inattentiveness**, daydreaming, woolgathering, distraction, abstraction *Opposite*: concentration

inattentive *adj* **careless**, distracted, abstracted, daydreaming, woolgathering *Opposite*: careful

inattentiveness *n* **carelessness**, inattention,

daydreaming, distraction, abstraction *Opposite*: attention

inaudibility *n* **quietness**, faintness, imperceptibility, noiselessness, silence *Opposite*: audibility

inaudible *adj* **quiet**, low, faint, soft, silent *Opposite*: perceptible

inaugural *adj* **opening**, initial, first, introductory, foundational

inaugurate *v* **1 swear in**, install, induct, instate, initiate *Opposite*: dismiss **2 open**, launch, dedicate, initiate, unveil *Opposite*: close **3 initiate**, establish, put in place, set up, start up *Opposite*: terminate *(fml)*

inauguration *n* **1 induction**, investiture, installation, swearing in, inaugural ceremony *Opposite*: dismissal **2 opening**, launch, opening ceremony, initiation ceremony, start *Opposite*: closure **3 initiation**, creation, introduction, setting up, conception *Opposite*: closedown

inauspicious *adj* **unpromising**, discouraging, ill-starred, ill-fated, ominous *Opposite*: promising

inauthentic *adj* **false**, imitation, fake, forged, counterfeit *Opposite*: genuine

in between *prep* **between**, next to, sandwiched by, in the middle of, amid

in-between *adj* **intermediate**, separating, isolating, halfway, indeterminate ■ *adv* **meanwhile**, in the interval, in the intervening time, between times, at the same time

inborn *adj* **innate**, natural, instinctive, intuitive, inherited *Opposite*: acquired

inbound *adj* **incoming**, arriving, inward bound, coming in, heading towards

inbred *adj* **congenital**, inherited, hereditary, ingrained, deep-seated *Opposite*: acquired

in brief *adv* **briefly**, in a few words, in short, to sum up, in a word

in-built *adj* **1 innate**, natural, inborn, inherent, instinctive *Opposite*: learned **2 incorporated**, integral, intrinsic, included, integrated *Opposite*: add-on

incalculable *adj* **1 countless**, without number, innumerable, infinite, multitudinous *Opposite*: finite **2 unpredictable**, unforeseeable, indeterminable, uncertain, haphazard *Opposite*: predictable

incalculably *adv* **greatly**, infinitely, immeasurably, inestimably, immensely

incandesce *v* **glow**, radiate, shine, luminesce, fluoresce

incandescence *n* **glow**, luminosity, light, luminescence, fluorescence

incandescent *adj* **glowing**, radiant, luminous, shining, bright

incantation *n* **chant**, invocation, prayer, spell, charm

incapable *adj* **1 unable**, powerless, inept, inexpert, unqualified *Opposite*: able **2 helpless**, weak, vulnerable, feeble, frail *Opposite*: strong

incapacitate *v* **debilitate**, injure, harm, disable, lay up *Opposite*: enable

incapacitated *adj* **debilitated**, injured, harmed, disabled, laid up *Opposite*: fit

incapacity *n* **1 inability**, ineffectiveness, incapability, powerlessness, weakness *Opposite*: ability **2 disability**, infirmity, frailty, ill health

incarcerate *(fml)* *v* **imprison**, jail, lock up, hold prisoner, intern *Opposite*: free

incarceration *(fml)* *n* **imprisonment**, confinement, custody, captivity, internment *Opposite*: freedom

incarnate *adj* **personified**, in person, in the flesh, alive, embodied

incarnation *n* **personification**, embodiment, manifestation, avatar, living form

in case *conj* **just in case**, in the event, lest, if, whether or no

incautious *adj* **careless**, rash, reckless, impetuous, impulsive *Opposite*: careful

incendiary *adj* **1 inflammable**, combustible, flammable **2 inflammatory**, provocative, rabble-rousing, aggressive, stirring *Opposite*: conciliatory ■ *n* **1** *(fml)* **troublemaker**, agitator, demagogue, activist, firebrand **2 arsonist**, pyromaniac, burner, firebomber, fire raiser

incense *v* **enrage**, anger, exasperate, infuriate, annoy *Opposite*: calm

incensed *adj* **enraged**, angry, exasperated, infuriated, irate *Opposite*: calm

incentive *n* **inducement**, enticement, motive, motivation, encouragement *Opposite*: disincentive. *See* COMPARE AND CONTRAST *at* **motive**.

inception *(fml)* *n* **beginning**, start, inauguration, initiation, foundation *Opposite*: culmination

incessant *adj* **nonstop**, never-ending, ceaseless, continuous, continual *Opposite*: sporadic

inch *v* **creep**, crawl, shuffle, edge

in charge *adj* **in command**, in control, at the helm, responsible, giving the orders

inchoate *(fml)* *adj* **undeveloped**, incipient, immature, beginning, budding *Opposite*: mature

incidence *n* **occurrence**, frequency, rate, commonness, prevalence

incident *n* **1 event**, occurrence, occasion, happening, episode **2 confrontation**, clash, skirmish, fight, episode

incidental *adj* **related**, accompanying, secondary, subsidiary, supplementary *Opposite*: essential

incidentally *adv* **by the way**, by the by, while we're on the subject, before I forget, parenthetically

incinerate *v* **burn**, burn up, set fire to, cremate, reduce to ashes

incinerator n **furnace**, brazier, kiln, oven, burner

incipient adj **emerging**, initial, embryonic, budding, early *Opposite*: final

incise v **cut**, slit, notch, score, carve

incision n **cut**, slit, opening, notch, scratch

incisive adj **keen**, perceptive, insightful, sharp, penetrating *Opposite*: dull

incite v **provoke**, inflame, rouse, goad, spur *Opposite*: quell

incitement n **provocation**, stimulation, agitation, encouragement, goad *Opposite*: deterrent

incivility n **rudeness**, impoliteness, discourteousness, discourtesy, lack of respect *Opposite*: politeness

inclement adj **intemperate**, extreme, severe, bad, foul *Opposite*: pleasant

inclination n **1 feeling**, predisposition, disposition, leaning, proclivity *Opposite*: antipathy **2 slope**, slant, incline, gradient, pitch

incline v **1 dispose**, persuade, prejudice, bias, lean *Opposite*: deter **2 slant**, slope, tilt, rise, fall ■ n **slope**, slant, gradient, rise, ascent

inclined adj **1 motivated**, persuaded, tending, disposed, apt *Opposite*: averse *(fml)* **2 leaning**, sloping, slanting, tilting, orientated

include v **1 contain**, comprise, take in, consist of, take account of *Opposite*: omit **2 bring in**, incorporate, add in, enter, involve *Opposite*: reject

included adj **contained within**, counted in, comprised, encompassed, involved *Opposite*: omitted

including prep **counting**, as well as, with, together with, plus *Opposite*: excluding

inclusion n **presence**, addition, enclosure, insertion, annexation *Opposite*: absence

inclusive adj **comprehensive**, wide-ranging, all-encompassing, complete, broad *Opposite*: restricted

incognito adv **in disguise**, disguised, undercover, anonymously, secretly *Opposite*: openly

incoherence n **unintelligibility**, inarticulateness, disjointedness, illogicality, confusedness *Opposite*: coherence

incoherent adj **1 disjointed**, confused, jumbled, illogical, all over the place *(infml)* *Opposite*: clear **2 inarticulate**, unintelligible, incomprehensible, garbled, mumbled *Opposite*: articulate

incombustible adj **fireproof**, flameproof, fire-resistant, flame-resistant, fire-retardant *Opposite*: flammable

income n **profits**, proceeds, returns, revenue, earnings *Opposite*: expenditure

incomer n **settler**, immigrant, colonist, migrant, newcomer

income tax n **tax**, toll, duty, excise, tariff

incoming adj **1 inbound**, inward bound, homeward bound, arriving, entering *Opposite*: outgoing **2 new**, next, succeeding, newly appointed, newly elected *Opposite*: outgoing

incommensurate adj **disproportionate**, unequal, inadequate, insufficient, lacking parity *Opposite*: proportionate

incommode *(fml)* v **inconvenience**, trouble, disturb, bother, put out

incommodious *(fml)* adj **1 cramped**, restricted, confined, tiny, small *Opposite*: roomy **2 inconvenient**, troublesome, awkward, annoying, bothersome

incommunicado adj **not in contact**, out of touch, not in communication, not able to communicate, unwilling to communicate

incomparable adj **unequalled**, unrivalled, unparalleled, unsurpassed, unmatched *Opposite*: ordinary

incompatibility n **1 mismatch**, unsuitability, discordancy, inharmoniousness, irreconcilability **2 inconsistency**, illogicality, irreconcilability, incongruity, mismatch *Opposite*: consistency

incompatible adj **mismatched**, unsuited, discordant, dissenting, irreconcilable *Opposite*: like-minded

incompetence n **ineptitude**, unskilfulness, inability, ineffectiveness, stupidity *Opposite*: ability

incompetent adj **inept**, useless, unskilled, ineffectual, hopeless *Opposite*: able

incomplete adj **1 imperfect**, partial, unfinished, inadequate, half-finished *Opposite*: entire **2 unfinished**, undeveloped, curtailed, shortened, deficient *Opposite*: finished

incomprehensible adj **unintelligible**, unfathomable, impenetrable, inexplicable, inconceivable *Opposite*: understandable

incomprehension n **disbelief**, incredulity, incredulousness, perplexity, blankness *Opposite*: understanding

inconceivable adj **unimaginable**, unthinkable, beyond belief, unbelievable, incredible *Opposite*: imaginable

inconclusive adj **indecisive**, questionable, unconvincing, unsatisfying, unsettled *Opposite*: decisive

in confidence adv **in secret**, confidentially, between ourselves, in private, privately *Opposite*: openly

incongruity n **oddness**, strangeness, absurdity, inappropriateness, inaptness *Opposite*: consistency

incongruous adj **odd**, strange, out of place, incompatible, inappropriate *Opposite*: consistent

in conjunction with prep **together with**, combined with, along with, with, in addition to *Opposite*: apart from

in consequence *(fml)* adv **accordingly**, as a

result, consequently, therefore, so

inconsequence *n* **unimportance**, irrelevance, insignificance, triviality, inconsequentiality *Opposite*: importance

inconsequential *adj* **unimportant**, trivial, petty, negligible, minor *Opposite*: important

inconsequentiality *n* **unimportance**, insignificance, triviality, frivolity, inconsequence *Opposite*: importance

inconsiderable *adj* **small**, minor, tiny, paltry, negligible *Opposite*: sizable

inconsiderate *adj* **selfish**, thoughtless, insensitive, uncharitable, unkind *Opposite*: caring

inconsistency *n* **1 discrepancy**, contradiction, variation, variance, irregularity **2 changeability**, unpredictability, unreliability, fickleness, capriciousness *Opposite*: consistency

inconsistent *adj* **1 conflicting**, contradictory, incompatible, incongruous, paradoxical *Opposite*: consistent **2 unpredictable**, variable, unreliable, erratic, changeable *Opposite*: constant

inconsolable *adj* **grief-stricken**, broken-hearted, devastated, desolate, despairing *Opposite*: ecstatic

inconspicuous *adj* **unobtrusive**, discreet, unremarkable, ordinary, modest *Opposite*: obvious

inconstant *adj* **changeable**, variable, irregular, unpredictable, fluctuating *Opposite*: unchanging

incontestable *adj* **indisputable**, incontrovertible, irrefutable, unquestionable, indubitable *Opposite*: arguable

incontrovertible *adj* **undeniable**, unquestionable, irrefutable, incontestable, indisputable *Opposite*: questionable

inconvenience *n* **1 troublesomeness**, tiresomeness, inopportuneness, untimeliness, awkwardness *Opposite*: benefit **2 problem**, trouble, bother, difficulty, nuisance ■ *v* **disrupt**, put out, trouble, bother, disturb *Opposite*: help

inconvenient *adj* **troublesome**, tiresome, inopportune, problematic, untimely *Opposite*: beneficial

in cooperation with *prep* **together with**, in association with, in collaboration with, alongside, in conjunction with

incorporate *v* **1 include**, integrate, assimilate, fit in, add in *Opposite*: exclude **2 merge**, combine, feature, contain, include *Opposite*: divide

incorporated *adj* **combined**, united, unified, merged, fused *Opposite*: separate

incorporation *n* **combination**, amalgamation, integration, assimilation, merger *Opposite*: separation

incorporeal *(fml) adj* **intangible**, ethereal, spiritual, unreal, disembodied *Opposite*: tangible

incorrect *adj* **1 erroneous**, wrong, mistaken, untrue, inaccurate *Opposite*: right **2 improper**, unfitting, inappropriate, unseemly, unbecoming *Opposite*: proper

incorrectness *n* **1 erroneousness**, error, fallacy, wrongness, mistakenness *Opposite*: correctness **2 impropriety**, inappropriateness, unsuitability, unseemliness, indecorousness *Opposite*: propriety

incorrigible *adj* **irredeemable**, habitual, inveterate, dyed-in-the-wool, persistent *Opposite*: tractable

incorruptible *adj* **1 moral**, principled, just, straight, honourable *Opposite*: venal **2 imperishable**, everlasting, immortal, indestructible, unchanging *Opposite*: perishable

increase *v* **enlarge**, extend, expand, amplify, swell *Opposite*: decrease ■ *n* **upsurge**, surge, rise, growth, intensification *Opposite*: decrease

COMPARE AND CONTRAST CORE MEANING: make larger or greater

increase become or cause to become larger in number, quantity, degree, or scope; **expand** become or cause to become larger or more extensive; **enlarge** become or cause to become larger generally, or broaden in scope and detail; **extend** make larger in terms of length, area, period of time, or other existing limits; **augment** *(fml)* add to something in order to make it larger or more substantial; **intensify** become or cause to become greater in strength or degree; **amplify** become or cause to become louder, or greater in intensity or scope.

incredible *adj* **1 unbelievable**, implausible, improbable, far-fetched, absurd *Opposite*: believable **2 amazing**, astonishing, extraordinary, staggering, unbelievable *Opposite*: unremarkable **3** *(infml)* **excellent**, superb, tremendous, prodigious, phenomenal *Opposite*: mediocre

incredibly *adv* **1 unbelievably**, implausibly, inconceivably, absurdly, improbably *Opposite*: believably **2** *(infml)* **very**, extremely, unbelievably, amazingly, really

incredulity *n* **disbelief**, amazement, astonishment, doubt, scepticism *Opposite*: belief

incredulous *adj* **disbelieving**, sceptical, unbelieving, doubtful, doubting *Opposite*: believing

increment *n* **increase**, addition, rise, growth, boost *Opposite*: cut

incriminate *v* **implicate**, impeach, give away, lay the blame on, convict *Opposite*: exonerate

in-crowd *(infml) n* **inner circle**, beau monde, high society, clique, elite

incrustation *n* **coating**, crust, layer, covering, accumulation

incubate *v* **hatch**, gestate, raise, rear, nurture

incubation *n* **development**, gestation, cultivation, nurture, growth *Opposite*: destruction

inculcate *v* **impress upon**, teach, drum into, instruct, drill into

incumbency *n (fml)* **1 tenure**, period of office, term of office, term, time **2 post**, position, office, appointment **3 duty**, obligation, responsibility, office, task

incumbent *adj (fml)* **obligatory**, mandatory, compulsory, binding, unavoidable *Opposite*: optional ■ *n* **official**, office holder, occupant, appointee, officer

incur *v* **1 experience**, suffer, sustain, bring upon yourself, lay yourself open to *Opposite*: avoid **2 sustain**, meet with, encounter, experience, suffer

incurable *adj* **1 terminal**, fatal, deadly, inoperable, untreatable *Opposite*: curable **2 irredeemable**, inveterate, incorrigible, hopeless, undying *Opposite*: redeemable

incurious *adj* **uninterested**, indifferent, unmoved, unconcerned, detached *Opposite*: inquisitive

incursion *n* **1 raid**, night raid, attack, sortie, invasion *Opposite*: retreat **2** *(fml)* **intrusion**, invasion, spread, infiltration, arrival

in custody *adj* **under arrest**, in prison, in detention, detained, remanded

indebted *adj* **obligated**, obliged, grateful, thankful, in somebody's debt *Opposite*: ungrateful

indebtedness *n* **obligation**, gratitude, appreciation, thankfulness, gratefulness *Opposite*: ingratitude

indecency *n* **1 offensiveness**, coarseness, crudeness, lewdness, obscenity *Opposite*: decency **2 impropriety**, unsuitability, unseemliness, indecorousness, indelicacy *Opposite*: propriety

indecent *adj* **1 offensive**, coarse, rude, crude, obscene *Opposite*: decorous **2 improper**, unsuitable, unseemly, indecorous, unbecoming *Opposite*: proper

indecipherable *adj* **1 illegible**, incomprehensible, unintelligible, unreadable, indistinct *Opposite*: legible **2 impenetrable**, inscrutable, obscure, unfathomable, enigmatic *Opposite*: clear

indecision *n* **irresolution**, hesitancy, indecisiveness, uncertainty, vacillation *Opposite*: decisiveness

indecisive *adj* **1 irresolute**, in two minds, vacillating, wavering, hesitant *Opposite*: decisive **2 inconclusive**, indefinite, indeterminate, tentative, unclear *Opposite*: conclusive

indecisiveness *n* **1 irresolution**, hesitancy, hesitation, vacillation, uncertainty *Opposite*: decisiveness **2 indefiniteness**, inconclusiveness, woolliness, vagueness, indeterminacy *Opposite*: certainty

indecorous *adj* **impolite**, rude, shocking, inappropriate, unseemly *Opposite*: polite

indecorum *n* **impoliteness**, bad behaviour, rudeness, offensiveness, impropriety *Opposite*: politeness

indeed *adv* **1 in reality**, in fact, actually, in truth, as a matter of fact **2 certainly**, really, to be sure, undeniably, definitely

indefatigable *adj* **untiring**, unflagging, unrelenting, remorseless, unfaltering *Opposite*: half-hearted

indefensible *adj* **1 inexcusable**, unpardonable, unforgivable, unjustifiable, unwarrantable *Opposite*: excusable **2 invalid**, untenable, unsustainable, shaky, weak *Opposite*: valid **3 unprotected**, exposed, vulnerable, undefended, unfortified *Opposite*: impregnable

indefinable *adj* **indescribable**, inexpressible, vague, indefinite, obscure

indefinite *adj* **1 unlimited**, unfixed, unspecified, unknown, indeterminate *Opposite*: specified **2 unclear**, imprecise, vague, hazy, woolly *Opposite*: precise **3 vague**, uncertain, undecided, unclear, noncommittal *Opposite*: certain

indefinitely *adv* **until further notice**, for the foreseeable future, for life, forever, ad infinitum

indelible *adj* **1 permanent**, fixed, ineradicable, fast, stubborn *Opposite*: temporary **2 unforgettable**, deep-seated, deep-rooted, lasting, enduring *Opposite*: temporary

indelibly *adv* **permanently**, ineradicably, lastingly, forever, for good *Opposite*: temporarily

indelicacy *n* **tactlessness**, offensiveness, tastelessness, crudeness, unseemliness *Opposite*: politeness

indelicate *adj* **tactless**, offensive, improper, unseemly, impolite *Opposite*: polite

indemnify *v* **1 insure**, underwrite, cover, assure, protect **2 reimburse**, compensate, repay, pay, refund

indemnity *n* **1 insurance**, protection, cover, life assurance, security **2 compensation**, reimbursement, remuneration, reparation, payment

indent *v* **1 hollow out**, dent, depress, stave in, scoop **2 notch**, serrate, nick, pink, incise

indentation *n* **1 hollow**, dent, depression, scoop, gouge **2 notch**, groove, serration, nick, incision

indenture *n* **contract**, arrangement, pact, deal, agreement

independence *n* **1 self-government**, sovereignty, autonomy, self-rule, self-determination *Opposite*: subjection **2 self-sufficiency**, self-reliance, self-determination, freedom, autonomy *Opposite*: helplessness **3 individuality**, freedom, liberation, unconventionality *Opposite*: conventionality **4 impartiality**, objectivity, disinterest, neutrality, disinterestedness *Opposite*: partiality

independent *adj* **1 self-governing**, sovereign,

autonomous, self-determining, self-regulating *Opposite*: dependent **2 self-sufficient**, self-reliant, autonomous, self-supporting, self-contained *Opposite*: dependent **3 free**, liberated, individual, individualistic, unconventional *Opposite*: conventional **4 impartial**, detached, objective, dispassionate, neutral *Opposite*: partial

in-depth *adj* **painstaking**, detailed, exhaustive, thorough, comprehensive *Opposite*: superficial

indescribable *adj* **1 indefinable**, inexpressible, unutterable, incommunicable, unspeakable **2 extreme**, great, tremendous, intense, dramatic

indestructible *adj* **1 abiding**, durable, everlasting, imperishable, eternal *Opposite*: perishable **2 unbreakable**, nonbreaking, resistant, shatterproof, rock-solid *Opposite*: fragile

indeterminable *adj* **1 unknowable**, indefinable, indescribable, impalpable *(fml) Opposite*: knowable **2 unresolvable**, unanswerable, uncountable *Opposite*: answerable

indeterminate *adj* **1 unknown**, unpredictable, undefined, unspecified, unstipulated *Opposite*: known **2 vague**, imprecise, uncertain, unclear, inexact *Opposite*: definite

index *n* **1 catalogue**, directory, guide, file, key **2 indication**, indicator, symbol, pointer, sign

indicate *v* **1 point to**, point at, point out, show, point towards **2 denote**, signify, be a sign of, imply, suggest **3 make known**, demonstrate, show, display, express **4 signal**, wink, flash

indication *n* **sign**, suggestion, signal, hint, warning

indicative *adj* **revealing**, symptomatic, telling, telltale, suggestive

indicator *n* **pointer**, needle, gauge, dial, display

indict *v* **accuse**, impeach, summons, prosecute, arraign *Opposite*: exonerate

indictable *adj* **criminal**, unlawful, illegal, chargeable, felonious

indictment *n* **1 accusation**, impeachment, summons, prosecution, arraignment *Opposite*: exoneration **2 condemnation**, denunciation, criticism, comment, censure *Opposite*: praise

indifference *n* **1 apathy**, coldness, coolness, unconcern, disinterest *Opposite*: concern **2 unimportance**, insignificance, inconsequence, meaninglessness, irrelevance *Opposite*: importance

indifferent *adj* **1 uncaring**, uninterested, unresponsive, apathetic, unsympathetic *Opposite*: concerned **2 average**, mediocre, moderate, undistinguished, middling *Opposite*: exceptional

indigence *(fml) n* **poverty**, need, penury, deprivation, destitution *Opposite*: wealth

indigenous *adj* **native**, original, aboriginal,

homegrown, local *Opposite*: immigrant. *See* COMPARE AND CONTRAST *at* **native**.

indigent *(fml) adj* **poor**, needy, impoverished, poverty-stricken, penniless *Opposite*: wealthy

indigestible *adj* **1 heavy**, rich, tough, inedible, stodgy *(infml) Opposite*: edible **2 incomprehensible**, impenetrable, unreadable, complex, obscure *Opposite*: readable

indigestion *n* **heartburn**, stomachache, upset stomach, colic, gastritis

indignant *adj* **angry**, furious, vexed, irate, outraged *Opposite*: mollified

indignation *n* **anger**, resentment, outrage, annoyance, exasperation *Opposite*: delight. *See* COMPARE AND CONTRAST *at* **anger**.

indignity *n* **humiliation**, shame, disgrace, mortification, embarrassment *Opposite*: glory

indirect *adj* **1 circuitous**, roundabout, rambling, circumlocutory, tortuous *Opposite*: straight **2 unintended**, unplanned, secondary, ancillary, subsidiary *Opposite*: intended **3 devious**, oblique, implicit, tacit, implied *Opposite*: overt

indiscernible *adj* **imperceptible**, invisible, inaudible, unnoticeable, undetectable *Opposite*: perceptible

indiscipline *n* **disorderliness**, rowdiness, unruliness, insubordination, disruptiveness *Opposite*: control

indiscreet *adj* **1 careless**, injudicious, imprudent, incautious, unthinking *Opposite*: careful **2 tactless**, undiplomatic, unsubtle, garrulous, indelicate *Opposite*: tactful

indiscretion *n* **1 carelessness**, injudiciousness, imprudence, lack of caution, recklessness *Opposite*: carefulness **2 tactlessness**, garrulousness, indelicateness, nosiness *(infml)* **3 transgression**, impropriety, peccadillo, misdeed, lapse

indiscriminate *adj* **1 unselective**, undiscriminating, undiscerning, uncritical, broad *Opposite*: selective **2 haphazard**, random, arbitrary, wholesale, blanket *Opposite*: planned

indispensable *adj* **necessary**, essential, crucial, vital, required *Opposite*: unnecessary. *See* COMPARE AND CONTRAST *at* **necessary**.

indisposed *(fml) adj* **1 sick**, unwell, ill, laid up, under the weather *Opposite*: well **2 unwilling**, disinclined, reluctant, loath, loth *Opposite*: willing

indisposition *n* **1 illness**, complaint, condition, problem, debility *Opposite*: health **2 reluctance**, unwillingness, disinclination, refusal, resistance *Opposite*: willingness

indisputable *(fml) adj* **indubitable**, unquestionable, undeniable, incontrovertible, irrefutable *Opposite*: debatable

indissoluble *adj* **binding**, unbreakable, enduring, everlasting, eternal *Opposite*: temporary

indistinct adj 1 **unclear**, hazy, dim, misty, blurred Opposite: clear 2 **inaudible**, imperceptible, faint, soft, low Opposite: audible 3 **vague**, imprecise, inexact, indefinite, indeterminate Opposite: definite

indistinctive adj **ordinary**, dull, everyday, unexceptional, unmemorable Opposite: unique

indistinctness n 1 **blurriness**, haziness, fuzziness, mistiness, dimness Opposite: clarity 2 **unclearness**, inarticulacy, faintness, softness Opposite: audibility

indistinguishable adj 1 **undifferentiated**, homogeneous, identical, the same, interchangeable Opposite: separable 2 **vague**, blurry, hazy, fuzzy, misty Opposite: clear 3 **inaudible**, inarticulate, unintelligible, faint, soft Opposite: clear

individual n **person**, human being, entity, character, personality ■ adj 1 **separable**, singular, separate, discrete, distinct 2 **particularized**, special, private, exclusive, particular Opposite: collective 3 **unusual**, distinctive, original, idiosyncratic, individualistic Opposite: ordinary

individualism n **uniqueness**, egoism, individuality, independence, selfishness Opposite: conformity

individualist n **free spirit**, nonconformist, eccentric, rebel, maverick Opposite: conformist

individuality n **independence**, uniqueness, eccentricity, personality, distinctiveness Opposite: conformity

individualize v **adapt**, modify, customize, personalize, convert

individually adv **separately**, independently, alone, on your own, by yourself Opposite: together

indivisible adj **inseparable**, united, amalgamated, blended, conjoined (fml) Opposite: separable

indoctrinate v **instruct**, programme, train, teach, coach

indoctrination n **instruction**, programming, propaganda, brainwashing, training

indolence n **laziness**, idleness, lethargy, sloth, inactivity Opposite: energy

indolent adj **lazy**, lethargic, idle, sluggish, slothful Opposite: energetic

indomitable adj **unconquerable**, strong, resolute, determined, stubborn Opposite: submissive

indoor adj **inside**, interior, covered, enclosed, internal Opposite: outdoor

indoors adv **inside**, in, within, at home, in the house Opposite: outside

indubitable adj **unquestionable**, definite, certain, positive, undoubted Opposite: questionable

induce v 1 **persuade**, encourage, tempt, make, bring Opposite: dissuade 2 **bring on**, bring about, provoke, stimulate, produce Opposite: deter

inducement n **stimulus**, incentive, encouragement, carrot, enticement Opposite: disincentive. See COMPARE AND CONTRAST at motive.

induct v 1 **inaugurate**, swear in, initiate, welcome, receive 2 **introduce**, initiate, train, instruct, educate

induction n 1 **bringing on**, stimulation, generation, production, provocation 2 **inauguration**, instalment, investiture, reception, swearing in 3 **introduction**, initiation, training, instruction, orientation

indulge v **treat**, spoil, pamper, pander, cosset Opposite: deny

indulgence n 1 **treat**, luxury, extravagance, pleasure Opposite: necessity 2 **tolerance**, lenience, understanding, clemency, sympathy Opposite: strictness

indulgent adj **permissive**, kind, lenient, tolerant, generous Opposite: strict

industrial adj 1 **manufacturing**, engineering, trade, business, work 2 **developed**, built-up, industrialized, mechanized, manufacturing

industrial action n **strike**, stoppage, work-to-rule, go-slow, general strike

industrial espionage n **espionage**, spying, intelligence gathering, surveillance, bugging

industrial estate n **trading estate**, science park, enterprise zone, industrial zone, industrial development

industrialist n **manufacturer**, entrepreneur, magnate, mogul, captain of industry

industrialization n **industrial development**, economic development, development, economic growth, progress

industrialize v **change**, mechanize, develop, mass-produce, automate

industrialized adj **industrial**, developed, technologically advanced, manufacturing, commercial Opposite: agrarian

industrial tribunal n **hearing**, court, tribunal

industrious adj **diligent**, hard-working, busy, productive, conscientious Opposite: indolent

industriousness n **diligence**, hard work, application, conscientiousness, productiveness Opposite: indolence

industry n 1 **manufacturing**, business, commerce, trade, engineering 2 (fml or literary) **hard work**, diligence, productiveness, conscientiousness, activity Opposite: indolence

inebriated adj **drunk**, intoxicated, plastered (infml), smashed (infml), under the influence (infml) Opposite: sober

inedible adj **uneatable**, indigestible, unpalatable, revolting, bad Opposite: edible

ineffable (fml) adj **indescribable**, inexpressible, unutterable, beyond words, overwhelming

ineffective adj **unsuccessful**, unproductive, useless, vain, futile Opposite: successful

ineffectiveness n **unsuccessfulness**, unproductiveness, uselessness, futility, hopelessness Opposite: success

ineffectual adj **incompetent**, indecisive, weak, feeble, useless Opposite: competent

ineffectuality n **incompetence**, indecisiveness, inadequacy, uselessness, feebleness Opposite: competence

inefficiency n **1 unproductiveness**, wastefulness, laxness Opposite: efficiency **2 disorganization**, incompetence, inadequacy, ineptitude, ineffectiveness Opposite: competence

inefficient adj **1 unproductive**, wasteful, uneconomical, lax, timewasting Opposite: efficient **2 incompetent**, inept, disorganized, ineffectual, inadequate Opposite: competent

inelastic adj **inflexible**, rigid, unbendable, stiff, unyielding Opposite: stretchy

inelegance n **1 unsophistication**, lack of style, tastelessness, bad taste, vulgarity Opposite: stylishness **2 clumsiness**, awkwardness, gracelessness, coarseness, roughness Opposite: grace

inelegant adj **1 unstylish**, unsophisticated, tasteless, vulgar, unpolished Opposite: stylish **2 clumsy**, awkward, ungainly, maladroit, graceless Opposite: graceful

ineligible adj **unqualified**, disqualified, barred, disallowed, banned Opposite: entitled

inept adj **incompetent**, inexpert, clumsy, useless, hopeless Opposite: competent

ineptitude n **incompetence**, clumsiness, uselessness, ineffectiveness, lack of ability Opposite: competence

ineptness see ineptitude

inequality n **disparity**, dissimilarity, variation, difference, discrimination Opposite: parity

inequitable adj **unfair**, unjust, unbalanced, undemocratic, unequal Opposite: fair

inequity (fml) n **unfairness**, injustice, discrimination, inequality, bias Opposite: fairness

ineradicable adj **indelible**, enduring, lasting, ingrained, stubborn Opposite: fleeting

inert adj **1 motionless**, still, lifeless, immobile, unmoving Opposite: moving **2 sluggish**, slow, inactive, passive, torpid Opposite: active

inertia n **apathy**, inactivity, torpor, lethargy, inaction Opposite: activity

inescapable adj **inevitable**, unavoidable, bound to happen, certain, patent Opposite: avoidable

inessential adj **unnecessary**, unneeded, superfluous, redundant, dispensable Opposite: necessary

inestimable adj **incalculable**, immeasurable, great, fathomless, enormous Opposite: measurable

inevitability n **unavoidability**, predictability, certainty, inescapability, irrevocability

inevitable adj **unavoidable**, predictable, expected, foreseeable, to be expected Opposite: avoidable

inevitably adv **unavoidably**, inescapably, without doubt, certainly, predictably

inexact adj **imprecise**, inaccurate, vague, rough, approximate Opposite: precise

inexactness n **imprecision**, vagueness, uncertainty, roughness, approximation Opposite: precision

in excess of prep **more than**, beyond, above, over and above, exceeding Opposite: below

inexcusable adj **unpardonable**, unforgivable, uncalled-for, intolerable, indefensible Opposite: excusable

inexhaustible adj **everlasting**, infinite, unlimited, never-ending, bottomless Opposite: limited

inexorability (fml) n **inevitability**, unavoidability, inescapability, relentlessness, certainty

inexorable adj **1** (fml) **unstoppable**, inevitable, unavoidable, inescapable, unchangeable **2 adamant**, obstinate, obdurate, unyielding, unbending

inexorableness (fml) see inexorability

inexpedient adj **1 inconvenient**, impractical, inopportune, untimely, ill-timed Opposite: convenient **2** (fml) **inadvisable**, inappropriate, unwise, unsuitable, injudicious Opposite: advisable

inexpensive adj **cheap**, low-cost, low-priced, economical, budget Opposite: costly

inexperience n **greenness**, rawness, innocence, immaturity, naivety Opposite: experience

inexperienced adj **green**, inexpert, raw, new, innocent Opposite: seasoned

inexpert adj **unskilled**, clumsy, inept, inexperienced, untrained Opposite: skilled

inexplicable adj **unaccountable**, mysterious, incomprehensible, unfathomable, bizarre Opposite: explicable

inexplicit adj **imprecise**, vague, ambiguous, hazy, sketchy Opposite: precise

inexpressible adj **indescribable**, beyond words, overwhelming, deep, indefinable

inexpressive adj **emotionless**, impassive, soulless, deadpan, unemotional Opposite: animated

inextricable adj **complicated**, complex, tricky, involved, knotty Opposite: simple

inextricably adv **indissolubly**, inseparably, indistinguishably, intimately, indivisibly

infallibility n **1 perfection**, rightness, flawlessness, correctness, exactitude Opposite: inaccuracy **2 dependability**, soundness, reliability, trustworthiness, steadiness Opposite: fallibility

infallible adj **1 perfect**, right, correct, exact, accurate Opposite: imperfect **2 dependable**, unfailing, foolproof, reliable, sound Opposite: unreliable

infallibly adv **dependably**, unfailingly, without fail, reliably, always Opposite: unreliably

infamous adj **1 notorious**, disreputable, ill-famed, ill-reputed, dishonourable Opposite: reputable **2 abominable**, villainous, wicked, iniquitous, loathsome Opposite: illustrious

infamy n **1 notoriety**, ill repute, ill fame, shame, disrepute Opposite: esteem **2 disgrace**, scandal, outrage, abomination, atrocity Opposite: good deed

infancy n **1 babyhood**, childhood, early years, youth, immaturity Opposite: adulthood **2 beginning**, early stages, embryonic stage, initial stages, first phase Opposite: conclusion

infant n **baby**, child, newborn, babe in arms, toddler Opposite: adult

infantile adj **1 childish**, babyish, immature, puerile, juvenile Opposite: mature **2 childhood**, juvenile, infant, baby, youthful Opposite: adult

infatuated adj **in love**, lovesick, obsessed, besotted, captivated Opposite: disenchanted

infatuation n **passion**, obsession, craze, love, fascination Opposite: disenchantment. See COMPARE AND CONTRAST at **love**.

in favour of prep **for**, all for, supporting, on the side of, supportive of Opposite: against

infect v **1 contaminate**, pollute, taint, poison, blight Opposite: cleanse **2 pervert**, corrupt, deprave, debase, defile (fml) Opposite: redeem **3 influence**, affect, afflict, touch, inspire

infected adj **1 contaminated**, polluted, tainted, poisoned, impure Opposite: pure **2 ill**, diseased, sick, infested, disease-ridden Opposite: healthy **3 septic**, festering, weeping, pussy, pus-filled Opposite: healthy **4 affected**, influenced, touched, inspired, moved Opposite: untouched

infection n **1 contagion**, contamination, pollution, taint, poison **2 disease**, illness, virus, blight, bug (infml) **3 corruption**, perversion, depravity, debasement, debauchery (fml)

infectious adj **1 communicable**, catching, transferable, transmittable, transmissible **2 irresistible**, compelling, captivating, alluring, contagious

infective adj **infectious**, communicable, catching, transferable, transmittable

infer v **1 conclude**, deduce, suppose, gather, understand **2 imply**, suggest, insinuate, hint

inference n **1 conclusion**, deduction, supposition, conjecture, presumption **2 implication**, extrapolation, corollary, interpretation, reading

inferior adj **1 lower**, junior, secondary, subordinate, subsidiary Opposite: superior **2 mediocre**, lesser, lower, substandard, poorer Opposite: superior ■ n **junior**, subordinate, underling, vassal, menial (fml) Opposite: superior

inferiority n **1 lowliness**, humbleness, subordination, subservience, subsidiarity Opposite: superiority **2 mediocrity**, weakness, inadequacy, shoddiness, meanness Opposite: superiority

inferiority complex n **inadequacy**, anxiety, phobia, depression, obsession

inferno n **1 conflagration**, blaze, fire, firestorm, flames **2 hellhole**, hell, underworld, perdition, fire and brimstone Opposite: heaven

infertile adj **sterile**, unproductive, barren, unfruitful, childless Opposite: fertile

infertility n **sterility**, barrenness, childlessness, aridity, unproductiveness Opposite: fertility

infest v **overrun**, fill, invade, infiltrate, pervade

infestation n **plague**, invasion, swarm, influx, infiltration

infidelity n **unfaithfulness**, faithlessness, disloyalty, betrayal, adultery Opposite: faithfulness

infighting n **rivalry**, internal strife, competitiveness, backbiting, squabbling

infiltrate v **penetrate**, permeate, gain access to, break into, creep into

infiltration n **penetration**, permeation, access, intrusion, insinuation

infiltrator n **mole**, spy, secret agent, double agent, subversive

infinite adj **1 immeasurable**, never-ending, endless, countless, unbounded Opposite: limited **2 extreme**, stupendous, great, immense, large Opposite: slight

infinitely adv **markedly**, a great deal, substantially, enormously, by a long way Opposite: slightly

infinitesimal adj **tiny**, minute, minuscule, microscopic, insignificant Opposite: huge

infinity n **eternity**, immensity, endlessness, infinitude, boundlessness

infirm adj **unwell**, sick, ill, frail, in poor health Opposite: healthy. See COMPARE AND CONTRAST at **weak**.

infirmary n **hospital**, sanatorium, sickbay, hospice, medical centre

infirmity n **ill health**, illness, frailty, disability, weakness Opposite: health

inflame v **1 arouse**, anger, fan, provoke, stir up Opposite: calm **2 exacerbate**, aggravate, fuel, intensify, increase Opposite: diminish

inflamed adj **reddened**, swollen, irritated, tender, sore

inflammable adj **flammable**, combustible, ignitable, incendiary Opposite: non-flammable

inflammation n **irritation**, swelling, soreness, tenderness, redness

inflammatory adj **provocative**, seditious, rabble-rousing, fiery, stirring Opposite: placatory

inflatable adj **blow-up**, pump-up, expandable

inflate v 1 **blow up**, pump up, fill with air, expand, fill Opposite: deflate 2 **exaggerate**, amplify, embellish, magnify, overestimate Opposite: understate 3 **increase**, go up, drive up, escalate, boost Opposite: deflate

inflated adj **exaggerated**, overstated, overblown, puffed up, magnified Opposite: understated

inflation n **price rises**, rise, increase, price increases Opposite: deflation

inflationary adj **price-raising**, price-increasing, spiralling

inflect v **change**, modulate, vary, adjust, modify

inflection n **modulation**, nuance, variation, variety, accent

inflexibility n 1 **stubbornness**, obstinacy, intransigence, rigour, dogmatism Opposite: tractability 2 **rigidity**, stiffness, hardness, firmness, tautness Opposite: flexibility

inflexible adj 1 **unbending**, stubborn, obstinate, uncompromising, strict Opposite: tractable 2 **rigid**, stiff, hard, unbendable, firm Opposite: bendable

inflict v **impose**, exact, mete out, wreak, perpetrate Opposite: remove

in-flight adj **onboard**, mid-flight, airborne, midair

inflow n **influx**, arrival, invasion, incursion, introduction Opposite: outflow

influence n 1 **effect**, inspiration, impact, stimulus, encouragement 2 **power**, sway, authority, weight, control ■ v 1 **sway**, manipulate, persuade, induce, win over 2 **affect**, motivate, inspire, shape, have an effect on

influential adj **powerful**, important, significant, persuasive, dominant Opposite: ineffectual

influenza n **flu**, cold, virus, infection, respiratory tract infection

influx n **arrival**, invasion, incursion, flood, entry Opposite: outflow

info (infml) n 1 **information**, data, statistics, facts, figures 2 **news**, report, tidings, word, communication

infomercial n **commercial**, advertisement, promotional film, ad (infml), promo (infml)

inform v 1 **tell**, notify, let know, update, bring up-to-date Opposite: keep in the dark 2 **blow the whistle on**, betray, sneak on, denounce, tell on Opposite: keep mum (infml)

informal adj 1 **relaxed**, casual, familiar, easy, comfortable Opposite: ceremonious 2 **unofficial**, off-the-record, unauthorized, unsanctioned, confidential Opposite: official 3 **colloquial**, idiomatic, vernacular, everyday, familiar Opposite: formal

informality n **casualness**, familiarity, ease, unpretentiousness, lack of formality Opposite: formality

informally adv 1 **casually**, nonchalantly, easily, unceremoniously, offhandedly Opposite: ceremoniously 2 **unofficially**, off the record, confidentially Opposite: officially

informant n 1 **source**, guide, interpreter, adviser, tipster 2 **informer**, sneak, spy, mole, grass (slang)

information n 1 **data**, statistics, facts, figures, material 2 **news**, report, tidings, word, communication

information processing n **data processing**, data handling, data manipulation, data analysis, data transmission

information retrieval n **data storage and retrieval**, data storage, data retrieval, data processing, computer processing

information sheet n **newsletter**, brochure, leaflet, bulletin, communiqué

information superhighway n **Internet**, World Wide Web, infobahn, the Net (infml), the Web (infml)

information technology n **IT**, computing, telecommunications, computer technology, electronic technology

informative adj **educational**, revealing, edifying, enlightening, useful Opposite: uncommunicative

informed adj **knowledgeable**, well-versed, conversant, up-to-date, educated Opposite: ignorant

informer n **informant**, sneak, spy, mole, grass (slang)

infraction n **breach**, violation, infringement, contravention, transgression

infrastructure n 1 **substructure**, organization, structure, setup, arrangement 2 **public services**, communications, public transport, power supplies, water supplies

infrequency n **rarity**, irregularity, uncommonness, paucity, scarcity Opposite: frequency

infrequent adj **rare**, uncommon, occasional, intermittent, sporadic Opposite: frequent

infringe v 1 **disobey**, disregard, breach, break, violate Opposite: obey 2 **encroach on**, intrude on, interfere with, trespass, invade Opposite: respect

infringement n 1 **breach**, violation, contravention, transgression, flouting Opposite: compliance 2 **encroachment**, intrusion, invasion, interference, trespass

in front of prep 1 **before**, ahead of, facing, opposite Opposite: behind 2 **in the presence of**, with, in the company of, before, watched by

infuriate v **enrage**, madden, incense, make your blood boil, annoy Opposite: calm

infuriated adj **enraged**, exasperated, furious, angry, incensed Opposite: calm

infuriating adj **maddening**, annoying, irritating, exasperating, galling Opposite: calming

infuse v 1 **pervade**, fill, permeate, suffuse, imbue 2 **instil**, impart, introduce, inculcate, imbue 3 **steep**, soak, brew, immerse, saturate Opposite: drain

infusion n **brew**, tea, distillation, fermentation, drink

ingenious adj 1 **inventive**, clever, imaginative, resourceful, original Opposite: unimaginative 2 **effective**, cunning, inspired, clever, nifty (infml)

ingenuity n **inventiveness**, cleverness, resourcefulness, imagination, originality

ingenuous adj 1 **innocent**, unworldly, artless, unsophisticated, naive Opposite: artful 2 **honest**, direct, frank, open, straightforward Opposite: dishonest

ingenuousness n 1 **innocence**, unpretentiousness, unworldliness, gullibility, simplicity Opposite: artfulness 2 **openness**, straightforwardness, directness, honesty, frankness Opposite: dishonesty

ingest v **absorb**, swallow, take in, consume, eat Opposite: vomit

inglenook n **hearthside**, fireside, nook, corner, recess

inglorious adj **shameful**, dishonourable, disgraceful, humiliating, unsuccessful Opposite: glorious

ingoing adj **incoming**, new, inward Opposite: outgoing

ingot n **slab**, nugget, lump, brick, block

ingrain v **impress**, etch, drill in, fix, root

ingrained adj **deep-seated**, in-built, entrenched, fixed, deep-rooted Opposite: superficial

ingratiate v **insinuate yourself**, toady, get in with, grovel, curry favour Opposite: alienate

ingratiating adj **sycophantic**, insinuative, obsequious, smarmy, deferential Opposite: proud

ingratitude n **rudeness**, unmannerliness, lack of appreciation, ungratefulness, thanklessness Opposite: gratitude

ingredient n **element**, component, part, constituent, factor

ingress (fml) n **entry**, entrance, opening, door, admission

in-group n **clique**, gang, faction, circle, elite

ingrowing adj **ingrown**, impacted, malformed, deformed

inhabit v **live**, reside, populate, occupy, squat

inhabitable adj **habitable**, civilized, usable, hospitable, livable Opposite: uninhabitable

inhabitant n **occupant**, resident, citizen, native, denizen

inhabited adj **populated**, populous, tenanted Opposite: uninhabited

inhalation n **breath**, gulp, gasp, pant, mouthful

inhale v **breathe in**, gasp, gulp, huff, pant Opposite: exhale

inhaler n **bronchodilator**, nebulizer, spray

in hand adj 1 **under control**, receiving attention, under consideration, under deliberation, being dealt with Opposite: pending 2 **unused**, remaining, spare, superfluous, available

inharmonious adj 1 **discordant**, clashing, harsh, jarring, unmusical Opposite: harmonious 2 **argumentative**, clashing, incompatible, disagreeable, antagonistic Opposite: cordial

inherent adj **characteristic**, essential, innate, natural, intrinsic Opposite: acquired

inherit v **receive**, accede to, come into, succeed to, take over Opposite: bequeath

inheritance n **heirloom**, tradition, legacy, bequest, birthright

inhibit v 1 **slow**, stop, hold back, restrain, hinder 2 **constrain**, hinder, prevent, impede, obstruct

inhibited adj **self-conscious**, reserved, introverted, repressed, subdued Opposite: uninhibited

inhibition n **reserve**, shyness, embarrassment, self-consciousness, reticence Opposite: spontaneity

inhospitable adj 1 **unwelcoming**, unfriendly, unreceptive, uncongenial, uninviting Opposite: hospitable 2 **harsh**, forbidding, bleak, desolate, barren Opposite: inviting

inhuman adj 1 **cruel**, vicious, cold-blooded, inhumane, brutal Opposite: kind 2 **cold-hearted**, unfeeling, insensitive, merciless, callous Opposite: sensitive 3 **otherworldly**, weird, strange, unearthly, eerie Opposite: earthly

inhumane adj **cold-hearted**, cold-blooded, cruel, callous, brutal Opposite: humane

inhumanity n **cruelty**, cold-heartedness, mercilessness, viciousness, ruthlessness Opposite: humanity

inimical adj 1 **unfavourable**, contrary, opposed, adverse, detrimental Opposite: favourable 2 **hostile**, unfriendly, unwelcoming, cold, ill-disposed Opposite: friendly

inimitable adj **unique**, matchless, unmatched, incomparable, peerless Opposite: common

iniquitous adj **wicked**, heinous, sinful, bad, evil Opposite: good

iniquity n **wickedness**, evil, sin, vice, immorality Opposite: goodness

initial adj **first**, early, original, preliminary, opening Opposite: final

initialize v **reset**, prime, prepare, set, make ready Opposite: disable

initiate v 1 **start**, introduce, originate, begin, open Opposite: finish 2 **instruct**, induct, admit, introduce, teach Opposite: expel

initiation n 1 **beginning**, start, opening, instigation, launch Opposite: end 2 **introduction**, admission, induction, admittance, instruction Opposite: expulsion

initiative n 1 **inventiveness**, creativity, wits, enterprise, resourcefulness 2 **plan**, proposal, scheme, idea, programme 3 **pole position**, upper hand, advantage, edge, lead

initiator n **motivator**, inventor, originator, author, creator

inject v 1 **vaccinate**, inoculate, give a jab (infml), give a shot (infml) 2 **bring**, add, introduce, insert, instil Opposite: remove

injection n 1 **inoculation**, dose, vaccination, booster, jab (infml) 2 **addition**, instillation, instilment, insertion, introduction Opposite: removal

in-joke n **private joke**, running joke, witticism

injudicious adj **ill-advised**, unwise, foolish, imprudent, careless Opposite: judicious

injudiciousness n **indiscretion**, imprudence, foolishness, rashness, impulsiveness Opposite: prudence

injunction n **ban**, sanction, embargo, restriction, order

injure v **damage**, harm, hurt, wound, cut Opposite: heal. See COMPARE AND CONTRAST at harm.

injured adj **hurt**, incapacitated, wounded, battered, bruised Opposite: unscathed

injurious adj **harmful**, distressing, damaging, adverse, detrimental Opposite: beneficial

injury n **wound**, damage, grievance, wrong, hurt

injury time n **extra time**, extension, overtime (US)

injustice n **discrimination**, unfairness, inequality, bias, prejudice Opposite: justice

in keeping with prep **consistent with**, suitable for, in accordance with, in line with, according to

inkling n **suspicion**, hint, clue, hunch, feeling Opposite: certainty

inkwell n **jar**, inkstand, pot, container, well

inlaid adj **decorated**, veneered, enamelled, ornamented, mosaic

inland adj **interior**, internal, upcountry, inward, central Opposite: coastal ■ adv **within**, inwards, inshore, upcountry, inside

inlay n 1 **enamel**, tile, piece, ornament, inset 2 **pattern**, decoration, ornament, mosaic, enamelling

inlet n **bay**, cove, creek, fjord, tidal creek

in line with prep **in agreement with**, according to, in keeping with, corresponding to, consistent with

inmate n **prisoner**, internee, patient, convict, jailbird (slang)

in memoriam prep **in memory of**, in remembrance of, as a memorial to, in commemoration of, for

inmost see **innermost**

innards (infml) n **entrails**, guts, intestines, bowels, viscera

innate adj **essential**, inborn, native, distinctive, natural

inner adj 1 **innermost**, inward, internal, inside, central Opposite: outer 2 **private**, secret, intimate, deep, hidden Opposite: public

inner city n **city centre**, centre, town centre, downtown (US)

inner-city adj **city**, metropolitan, town, central, inner Opposite: suburban

innermost adj **deepest**, private, secret, intimate, inmost Opposite: outermost

innings n **runs**, turn, batting, score, round

innocence n 1 **blamelessness**, goodness, guiltlessness, incorruptibility, virtue Opposite: guilt 2 **naivety**, inexperience, unworldliness, unsophistication, gullibility Opposite: experience

innocent adj 1 **blameless**, acquitted, guiltless, cleared, not guilty Opposite: guilty 2 **harmless**, unknowing, unintended, unintentional, inoffensive Opposite: malicious 3 **virtuous**, untouched, unsullied, chaste, immaculate Opposite: tainted 4 **unsophisticated**, unworldly, artless, harmless, naive Opposite: worldly

innocuous adj **inoffensive**, harmless, innocent, safe, mild Opposite: offensive

innovate v **invent**, modernize, originate, revolutionize, transform Opposite: stagnate

innovation n **novelty**, invention, revolution, modernization, origination Opposite: stagnation

innovative adj **groundbreaking**, advanced, state-of-the-art, pioneering, inventive Opposite: outdated

innuendo n **insinuation**, ambiguity, double entendre, inference, intimation

innumerable adj **countless**, uncountable, numerous, incalculable, immeasurable

inoculate v **immunize**, vaccinate, inject, protect, give a shot (infml) Opposite: infect

inoculation n **vaccination**, injection, booster, immunization, jab (infml)

inoffensive adj **innocuous**, harmless, bland, dull, safe Opposite: offensive

inoperable adj 1 **incurable**, untreatable, terminal, grave, fatal Opposite: operable 2 **impracticable**, unworkable, unfeasible, impossible, unachievable Opposite: doable

inoperative adj **out of action**, out of order, out of use, broken, broken down Opposite: operative

inopportune adj **ill-timed**, unfortunate, inconvenient, mistimed, untimely Opposite: opportune

in order to conj **so as to**, to, with the intention of, with the purpose of, with the aim of

inordinate adj **excessive**, undue, unwarranted, immoderate, unreasonable *Opposite*: moderate

inorganic *adj* **mineral**, inanimate, inert, lifeless *Opposite*: organic

in particular *adv* **specifically**, especially, specially, particularly, above all *Opposite*: generally

input *n* **contribution**, effort, say, participation, involvement ■ *v* **enter**, key, key in, record, store

inquest *n* **investigation**, inquiry, examination, postmortem, autopsy

inquire *v* **ask**, query, request, question, find out

inquire into *v* **investigate**, go into, delve into, look into, probe into

inquiring *adj* **1 inquisitive**, interested, curious, questioning, analytical *Opposite*: incurious **2 searching**, questioning, penetrating, probing, prying

inquiry *n* **1 review**, postmortem, autopsy, investigation, examination **2 request**, question, query, interrogation, quiz

inquisition *n* **inquiry**, inquest, investigation, examination, interrogation

inquisitive *adj* **1 curious**, inquiring, interested, questioning, probing *Opposite*: indifferent **2 prying**, intrusive, prurient, meddlesome, officious *Opposite*: incurious

inquisitiveness *n* **1 curiosity**, interest, keenness, desire for knowledge, thirst for knowledge *Opposite*: indifference **2 prurience**, meddlesomeness, prying, questioning, officiousness *Opposite*: indifference

inquisitor *n* **cross-examiner**, examiner, investigator, interrogator, questioner

inquisitorial *adj* **interrogational**, cross-examining, investigative, interviewing, questioning

inquorate *adj* **insufficient**, inadequate, not enough, too few, under strength

insalubrious *(fml) adj* **unhealthy**, unsavoury, unwholesome, harmful, unhygienic *Opposite*: healthy

ins and outs *n* **details**, fine points, particulars, facts, minutiae

insane *adj* **1 of unsound mind**, mentally disordered, mentally ill, deranged *Opposite*: sane **2 foolish**, silly, stupid, irrational, impractical *Opposite*: sensible

insanitary *adj* **unhygienic**, dirty, unclean, contaminated, unhealthy *Opposite*: hygienic

insanity *n* **foolishness**, stupidity, irrationality, folly, senselessness *Opposite*: common sense

insatiability *n* **voraciousness**, greed, greediness, gluttony, ravenousness

insatiable *adj* **voracious**, greedy, avid, ravenous, unquenchable

inscribe *v* **1 engrave**, carve, etch, cut, scratch *Opposite*: erase **2 list**, enter, record, register, enrol *Opposite*: delete **3 dedicate**, autograph, address, sign, assign

inscription *n* **1 writing**, caption, label, engraving, legend **2 dedication**, autograph, signature, personal note, initials

inscrutability *n* **mystique**, mystery, mysteriousness, enigma, incomprehensibility *Opposite*: clarity

inscrutable *adj* **enigmatic**, sphinx-like, unfathomable, mysterious, impenetrable *Opposite*: transparent

insect *n* **bug**, fly, pest, creature, creepy-crawly *(infml)*

WORD BANK
❑ **parts of an insect** abdomen, antenna, feeler, proboscis, thorax, wing
❑ **types of stage of insect development** caterpillar, chrysalis, glowworm, grub, imago, larva, maggot, nit, pupa, silkworm, woodworm

insecure *adj* **1 unconfident**, anxious, self-doubting, uncertain, timid *Opposite*: confident **2 vulnerable**, unprotected, unguarded, undefended, at risk *Opposite*: secure **3 shaky**, rickety, unstable, unsteady, loose *Opposite*: steady

insecurity *n* **lack of confidence**, anxiety, uncertainty, timidity, self-doubt *Opposite*: confidence

insensate *adj* **unconscious**, comatose, inert, anaesthetized, numb *Opposite*: animate

insensible *adj* **1 unconscious**, comatose, inert, insentient, numb *Opposite*: conscious **2 unaware**, unresponsive, insensitive, oblivious, numb *Opposite*: sensitive **3 imperceptible**, indiscernible, unnoticeable, indistinguishable, inappreciable *Opposite*: obvious

insensitive *adj* **1 tactless**, thoughtless, inconsiderate, uncaring, unsympathetic *Opposite*: sensitive **2 numb**, unfeeling, insensate, insensible, dead *Opposite*: sensitive **3 unresponsive**, oblivious, unmoved, inured to, indifferent *Opposite*: responsive

insensitivity *n* **selfishness**, thoughtlessness, inconsiderateness, tactlessness, inattentiveness *Opposite*: sensitivity

insentient *adj* **lifeless**, inert, inanimate, insensate, unconscious *Opposite*: sentient

inseparable *adj* **1 close**, devoted, intimate, joined at the hip, in each other's pocket *Opposite*: distant **2 indivisible**, indissoluble, inextricable, united, conjoined *(fml) Opposite*: independent

insert *v* **1 introduce**, implant, inject, put in, place in *Opposite*: take out **2 add**, include, enclose, append, incorporate *Opposite*: extract ■ *n* **supplement**, pullout, addition, enclosure, inset

insertion *n* **1 addition**, inclusion, incorporation, enclosure, attachment *Opposite*: extraction **2 supplement**, pullout, addition, inset, inset

in-service *adj* **work-related**, occupational, professional, vocational, job-related

inset v **insert**, put in, add, include, incorporate Opposite: extract ■ n **supplement**, insert, pullout, insertion, inclusion

inshore adv **landwards**, coastwards, ashore, shorewards

inside adv **indoors**, in, within, in the interior, at home Opposite: outside ■ adj **1 confidential**, privileged, secret, private, exclusive **2 inner**, innermost, inmost, inward Opposite: outer **3 indoor**, interior, internal Opposite: outside **4** (infml) **locked up**, imprisoned, put away (infml), banged up (infml), doing time (slang) ■ n **interior**, inner recesses, inner parts, contents Opposite: outside ■ prep **in**, within, surrounded by, contained by Opposite: outside

insides (infml) n **internal organs**, guts, entrails, bowels, viscera

insidious adj **sinister**, treacherous, crafty, sneaky, deceptive Opposite: harmless

insight n **vision**, understanding, awareness, intuition, perception

insightful adj **perceptive**, astute, shrewd, understanding, discerning Opposite: unperceptive

insightfulness n **perspicacity**, perceptiveness, astuteness, discernment, sensitivity

insignia n **emblem**, crest, badge, sign, symbol

insignificance n **unimportance**, irrelevance, inconsequentiality, triviality, paltriness Opposite: significance

insignificant adj **unimportant**, irrelevant, immaterial, inconsequential, trivial Opposite: significant

insincere adj **dishonest**, two-faced, hypocritical, disingenuous, deceitful Opposite: sincere

insincerity n **dishonesty**, disingenuousness, hypocrisy, deceit, mendacity Opposite: sincerity

insinuate v **1 imply**, suggest, hint, intimate, indicate Opposite: declare **2 ingratiate yourself**, worm your way in, wheedle, cosy up, curry favour Opposite: insult

insinuation n **suggestion**, implication, hint, intimation, allusion Opposite: statement

insipid adj **1 dull**, bland, characterless, trite, tame Opposite: exciting **2 bland**, tasteless, unappetizing, flavourless, watery Opposite: tasty

insipidness n **1 dullness**, blandness, feebleness, characterlessness, colourlessness **2 tastelessness**, lack of flavour, blandness, wateriness, weakness Opposite: tastiness

insist v **1 maintain**, claim, assert, contend, swear Opposite: deny **2 require**, demand, press for, stipulate, enforce

insistence n **persistence**, resolve, firmness, perseverance, doggedness

insistent adj **1 adamant**, firm, persistent, unrelenting, resolute Opposite: half-hearted

2 incessant, repeated, persistent, relentless, unrelenting Opposite: occasional

insofar as conj **inasmuch as**, insomuch as, to the extent that, to the degree that, because

insolence n **impudence**, impertinence, rudeness, audacity, disrespect Opposite: respect

insolent adj **impudent**, rude, disrespectful, brazen, impertinent (fml) Opposite: respectful

insolubility n **mysteriousness**, indecipherability, intricacy, difficulty, impenetrability Opposite: solubility

insoluble adj **inexplicable**, mysterious, insolvable, unfathomable, indecipherable Opposite: solvable

insolvency n **bankruptcy**, liquidation, indebtedness, ruin, collapse Opposite: solvency

insolvent adj **bankrupt**, ruined, in debt, in receivership, broke (infml) Opposite: solvent

insomnia n **sleeplessness**, wakefulness, restlessness

insomuch as conj **insofar as**, inasmuch as, to the extent that, to the degree that, because

insouciance n **carefreeness**, nonchalance, indifference, happiness, unconcern Opposite: worry

inspect v **look at**, review, examine, scrutinize, look over Opposite: ignore

inspection n **review**, examination, scrutiny, assessment, check

inspector n **examiner**, superintendent, overseer, assessor, supervisor

inspiration n **1 stimulus**, spur, motivation, stimulation, encouragement Opposite: disincentive **2 creativeness**, inventiveness, brilliance, vision, creativity **3 insight**, flash, idea, revelation, brain wave (infml)

inspirational adj **stimulating**, inspiring, stirring, rousing, moving Opposite: boring

inspire v **stimulate**, motivate, stir, move, encourage Opposite: bore

inspired adj **1 brilliant**, outstanding, superb, exceptional, dazzling Opposite: uninspired **2 stimulated**, stirred, moved, encouraged, motivated Opposite: uninspired

inspiring adj **inspirational**, stirring, rousing, moving, exciting Opposite: uninspiring

in spite of prep **despite**, regardless of, in the face of, notwithstanding (fml)

instability n **unpredictability**, variability, uncertainty, unsteadiness, volatility Opposite: stability

install v **1 connect**, fit, put in, set up, fix Opposite: remove **2 ordain**, establish, inaugurate, instate, induct Opposite: oust **3 settle in**, settle, settle down, ensconce, position

installation n **1 connection**, fitting, setting up, fixing, putting in Opposite: removal **2 system**, mechanism, machinery, equipment, apparatus **3 appointment**, ordination, inauguration, investiture, instatement Opposite: removal

instalment n 1 **payment**, segment, portion, part, section 2 **part**, episode, chapter

instance n **example**, case, case in point, occurrence, illustration

instant adj 1 **prompt**, immediate, sudden, swift, instantaneous Opposite: gradual 2 **prepared**, precooked, premixed, powdered, microwavable 3 **urgent**, pressing, immediate ■ n **moment**, second, split second, the twinkling of an eye, minute

instantaneous adj **prompt**, rapid, sudden, immediate, instant Opposite: gradual

instantly adv **promptly**, right away, instantaneously, immediately, directly Opposite: gradually

instate v **appoint**, ordain, inaugurate, establish, install Opposite: oust

instead adv **in its place**, as an alternative, as a substitute, as a replacement

instead of prep **in place of**, rather than, as opposed to, in preference to

instigate v **bring about**, prompt, initiate, start, activate Opposite: stifle

instigation n 1 **start**, beginning, initiation, establishment, commencement (fml) Opposite: end 2 **initiation**, prompting, urging, encouragement, provocation Opposite: discouragement

instigator n **initiator**, prime mover, mastermind, troublemaker, ringleader

instil v 1 **impart**, inculcate, drum into, drive into, impress upon 2 **drip**, pour, infuse, inject, introduce

instinct n 1 **nature**, character, makeup, predisposition, disposition 2 **drive**, reflex, feeling, impulse, urge Opposite: reason 3 **feeling**, intuition, gut feeling, sixth sense, sense 4 **talent**, knack, gift, flair, ability

instinctive adj 1 **involuntary**, automatic, reflex, natural, unconscious Opposite: conscious 2 **natural**, intuitive, innate, inherent, inborn Opposite: learned

instinctively adv **impulsively**, mechanically, on impulse, automatically, unconsciously

institute v **introduce**, establish, set up, bring about, found ■ n **organization**, institution, establishment, foundation, association

institution n 1 **establishment**, organization, body, association, society 2 **tradition**, custom, convention, ritual 3 **introduction**, establishment, setting up, foundation, creation

institutional adj 1 **official**, recognized, formal, established, organized Opposite: unofficial 2 **utilitarian**, uniform, dull, functional, ordinary Opposite: unique

institutionalized adj **established**, existing, long-standing, traditional, entrenched Opposite: innovative

instruct v 1 **teach**, train, coach, tutor, educate 2 **command**, order, tell, give orders to, charge. See COMPARE AND CONTRAST at **teach**.

instruction n 1 **teaching**, training, lessons, tuition, education 2 **order**, command, direction, directive

instructive adj **informative**, educational, useful, helpful, enlightening

instructor n **teacher**, coach, tutor, trainer, mentor

instrument n 1 **tool**, gadget, device, utensil, apparatus 2 **means**, channel, vehicle, method, medium

instrumental adj **contributory**, active, involved, helpful, influential Opposite: tangential

instrumentalist n **musician**, player, performer

instrumentation n 1 **arrangement**, composition, musical arrangement, music, score 2 **instrument panel**, equipment, instruments, controls, console

insubordinate adj **disobedient**, defiant, rebellious, mutinous, unruly Opposite: obedient

insubordination n **disobedience**, defiance, rebelliousness, mutiny, unruliness Opposite: obedience

insubstantial adj **flimsy**, light, slight, weak, frail Opposite: weighty

insubstantiality n **weakness**, fragility, thinness, flimsiness, lightness Opposite: robustness

insufferable adj **excruciating**, unbearable, intolerable, insupportable, unendurable

insufficiency n 1 **lack**, deficiency, dearth, absence, shortage 2 **inadequacy**, deficiency, unfitness, failure, inefficiency Opposite: adequacy

insufficient adj **inadequate**, deficient, lacking, in short supply, scarce Opposite: surplus

insular adj **inward-looking**, blinkered, narrow-minded, narrow, limited Opposite: open-minded

insularity n **narrow-mindedness**, narrowness, parochialism, intolerance, small-mindedness Opposite: openness

insulate v 1 **lag**, wad, line, fill, pad 2 **cloister**, protect, shield, cut off, isolate Opposite: expose

insulation n 1 **lining**, lagging, wadding, padding, filling 2 **protection**, isolation, separation, segregation, sequestration Opposite: exposure

insulator n **insulation**, padding, sound-proofing, lagging

insult v **offend**, affront, abuse, slur, slight Opposite: praise ■ n **affront**, offence, slight, slur, rudeness Opposite: compliment

insulting adj **abusive**, offensive, rude, insolent, wounding Opposite: polite

insuperable adj **insurmountable**, impossible, unbeatable, challenging, overwhelming Opposite: easy

insupportable adj **unbearable**, intolerable, unendurable, insufferable, unspeakable Opposite: bearable

insurance n **cover**, indemnity, assurance, protection, coverage

insurance policy n 1 **document**, contract, cover, agreement, guarantee 2 **safety net**, safeguard, precaution, protection, provision

insure v **protect**, cover, assure, indemnify, underwrite

insurer n **underwriter**, broker, guarantor

insurgence see **insurgency**

insurgency n **uprising**, rebellion, revolt, insurrection, revolution

insurgent n **rebel**, insurrectionary, revolutionary, guerrilla, mutineer ■ adj **mutinous**, rebellious, rebel, insurrectionary

insurmountable adj **unbeatable**, insuperable, unassailable, invincible, impossible Opposite: easy

insurrection n **uprising**, rebellion, revolt, insurgency, revolution

intact adj **complete**, whole, unbroken, in one piece, integral Opposite: broken

intake n 1 **consumption**, eating, drinking, ingestion 2 **entry**, entrants, students 3 **opening**, pipe, tube, aperture, inlet Opposite: outlet

intangibility n 1 **imperceptibility**, immateriality, immaterialness, untouchability, insubstantiality Opposite: tangibility 2 **indescribability**, elusiveness, vagueness, subtlety, abstractness

intangible adj 1 **imperceptible**, immaterial, insubstantial, incorporeal (fml), impalpable (fml) Opposite: concrete 2 **unquantifiable**, elusive, vague, ethereal, subtle

integer n **whole number**, number, numeral, digit, figure Opposite: fraction

integral adj 1 **essential**, vital, important, basic, fundamental 2 **connected**, internal, central, at the heart of Opposite: unimportant 3 **complete**, whole, intact, undivided, unbroken

integrate v 1 **mix**, fit in, join in, assimilate, take part 2 **put together**, mix, incorporate, add, join together Opposite: separate 3 **open up**, desegregate, combine, mix, assimilate

integrated adj 1 **combined**, united, joined, unified, cohesive Opposite: separated 2 **open**, desegregated, multiethnic, multicultural, multilingual Opposite: segregated

integration n **addition**, mixing, incorporation, combination, amalgamation

integrity n **honesty**, truth, truthfulness, honour, veracity Opposite: dishonesty

intellect n **intelligence**, brainpower, brain, brains, mind Opposite: emotion

intellectual adj **knowledgeable**, intelligent, highbrow, academic, cerebral ■ n **philosopher**, thinker, academic, scholar, highbrow

intelligence n 1 **brain**, cleverness, aptitude, intellect, brains Opposite: stupidity 2 **information**, news, reports, communication, word

intelligence quotient n **IQ**, mental ability, aptitude

intelligent adj 1 **clever**, bright, smart, quick, able Opposite: stupid 2 **sensible**, rational, wise, logical, perceptive Opposite: irrational

COMPARE AND CONTRAST CORE MEANING: having the ability to learn and understand easily **intelligent** quick to learn and understand; **bright** showing an ability to think, learn, or respond quickly, especially used of younger people; **quick** alert, perceptive, and able to respond quickly; **smart** showing intelligence and mental alertness but sometimes suggesting insolent intelligence; **clever** having sharp mental abilities, sometimes suggesting showy or superficial cleverness; **able** capable or talented, also used in educational circles of children who are intelligent; **gifted** talented, especially artistically or creatively, also used in educational circles of children who are exceptionally intelligent.

intelligentsia n **intellectuals**, academics, highbrows, cognoscenti, literati (fml)

intelligible adj **comprehensible**, understandable, clear, plain, lucid Opposite: unintelligible

intemperance n **self-indulgence**, overindulgence, excess, hedonism, gluttony Opposite: moderation

intemperate adj **self-indulgent**, uncontrolled, unrestrained, inordinate, immoderate Opposite: moderate

intend v **mean**, aim, propose, plan, have in mind

intended adj 1 **envisioned**, future, planned, proposed, projected 2 **planned**, intentional, deliberate, on purpose, premeditated Opposite: accidental ■ n (dated) **fiancé**, fiancée, husband-to-be, wife-to-be, girlfriend

intense adj **penetrating**, strong, powerful, forceful, concentrated Opposite: moderate

intensely adv **forcefully**, powerfully, strongly, deeply, extremely Opposite: mildly

intensification n **strengthening**, increase, rise, escalation, spiralling Opposite: reduction

intensify v **strengthen**, deepen, step up, exaggerate, increase Opposite: weaken. See COMPARE AND CONTRAST at **increase**.

intensity n **strength**, concentration, power, force, passion Opposite: moderation

intensive adj **concentrated**, rigorous, exhaustive, severe, thorough Opposite: easy

intensive care n **monitoring**, nursing, specialist care, 24-hour care, one-to-one care

intent n (fml) **intention**, aim, goal, target, objective ■ adj 1 **concentrated**, absorbed, focused, directed, fixed 2 **intending to**, bent on, determined, resolved, set on

intention n **aim**, purpose, goal, target, objective

intentional adj **deliberate**, planned, intended, premeditated, calculated Opposite: accidental

intently adv **closely**, fixedly, carefully, keenly, attentively Opposite: abstractedly

intentness n **attentiveness**, concentration, focus, attention, close attention Opposite: abstraction

inter v **bury**, entomb, lay to rest

interact v **interrelate**, act together, cooperate, relate, intermingle

interaction n **communication**, contact, interface, dealings, relations

interactive adj **communicating**, collaborating, cooperating, collaborative, cooperative

interbreed v **breed**, reproduce, multiply, mate, produce

intercalate v **insert**, introduce, interpolate, add, interpose Opposite: extrapolate

intercede v **intervene**, mediate, plead, negotiate, arbitrate

intercept v **cut off**, catch, interrupt, stop, seize

interception n **capture**, seizure, interruption, interference, intervention

intercession n **intervention**, mediation, arbitration, negotiation

interchange v **switch**, trade, exchange, substitute, trade off ■ n **1 trading**, exchange, transaction, substitution, trade-off **2 crossroads**, junction, intersection

interchangeable adj **substitutable**, identical, the same, compatible, transposable Opposite: incompatible

intercommunicate v **talk**, communicate, converse, discuss, contact

interconnect v **join**, intersect, connect, interrelate, interlock

intercontinental adj **international**, transnational, global, worldwide, large-scale Opposite: national

intercourse n **dealings**, contact, communication, interaction, association

intercut v **interpose**, insert, alternate, interweave, interject

interdependent adj **symbiotic**, dependent, reliant, codependent

interdict n **order**, court order, ban, prohibition, veto ■ v **ban**, prohibit, forbid, veto, embargo Opposite: permit

interest n **1 attention**, notice, curiosity, concentration, awareness Opposite: indifference **2 hobby**, activity, pursuit, pastime, leisure activity **3 concern**, importance, significance, relevance, note **4 good**, advantage, benefit, gain, profit ■ v **attract**, draw, appeal, fascinate, be of interest Opposite: bore

interested adj **absorbed**, attentive, involved, concerned, attracted Opposite: indifferent

interest group n **1 alliance**, association, cartel, trade union, pressure group **2 club**, association, group, society

interesting adj **stimulating**, thought-provoking, motivating, exciting, fascinating Opposite: boring

interface n **border**, boundary, line, crossing point, edge

interfere v **1 pry**, intrude, meddle, disturb, intervene **2 delay**, inhibit, restrict, affect, get in the way

interference n **1 meddling**, intrusion, prying, interfering, intervention **2 restriction**, obstruction, hindrance, obstacle, delay

interfering adj **intrusive**, meddlesome, prying, inquisitive, meddling

intergalactic adj **interstellar**, interplanetary, space

intergovernmental adj **interstate**, international, diplomatic, foreign, high-level

interim adj **temporary**, provisional, short-term, intervening, acting Opposite: permanent ■ n **interlude**, pause, break, interval, pause in the action

interior n **inside**, centre, core, heart Opposite: outside ■ adj **internal**, inner, central, inland, inside Opposite: peripheral

interior decoration n **decoration**, furnishings, decorating scheme, colour scheme, interior design

interject v **butt in**, exclaim, interrupt, interpose, cut in

interjection n **1 exclamation**, outburst, cry, utterance, shout **2 interruption**, interpolation, introduction, addition, insertion

interlace v **interweave**, intertwine, interlock, entwine, knit

interlard v **interpose**, insert, introduce, intersperse, interweave

interleave v **slot in**, put in, enclose, interweave, add

interlink v **interweave**, intertwine, interlace, interconnect, knit

interlock v **mesh**, dovetail, link, join, interconnect

interlocutor n **speaker**, talker, discusser, panelist, converser

interloper n **1 intruder**, trespasser, gatecrasher, persona non grata, impostor **2 meddler**, busybody (infml), snoop (infml), nosy parker (infml)

interlude n **interval**, break, rest, pause, interim

intermediary n **intercessor**, arbitrator, negotiator, go-between, mediator ■ adj **intermediate**, middle, midway, in-between, transitional

intermediate adj **middle**, midway, in-between, transitional, halfway Opposite: extreme

interment n **burial**, entombment, committal, funeral, funeral rites Opposite: disinterment

intermesh v **join**, interlink, knit, mesh, interconnect

interminable adj **endless**, ceaseless, everlasting, perpetual, never-ending Opposite: finite

intermingle v **intermix**, mingle, interact, combine, fuse

intermission *n* **intermezzo**, interval, break, interlude, pause

intermittent *adj* **spasmodic**, periodic, sporadic, occasional, irregular *Opposite*: constant. *See* COMPARE AND CONTRAST *at* **periodic**.

intermix *v* **meld**, intermingle, mix, mingle, blend *Opposite*: separate

intern *v* **imprison**, detain, confine, hold, jail *Opposite*: release ■ *n* **medical student**, doctor, student doctor, med student, medic *(infml)*

internal *adj* **1 interior**, inner, inside *Opposite*: external **2 domestic**, in-house, home, intramural *Opposite*: external

internalize *v* **1 adopt**, affect, take on, assume, co-opt **2 stew**, mull over, bottle up, suppress *Opposite*: externalize

international *adj* **global**, worldwide, intercontinental, universal, transnational *Opposite*: domestic

internecine *adj* **1 internal**, inner, civil, domestic **2 destructive**, devastating, decimating, deadly, injurious

internee *n* **prisoner**, captive, detainee, hostage, inmate

Internet *n* **World Wide Web**, information superhighway, cyberspace, the Net *(infml)*, the Web *(infml)*

WORD BANK

❏ **types of Internet facilities and activities** bot, browser, bulletin board, chat room, cookie, home page, instant messaging, ISP, newsgroup, portal, robot, router, search engine, service provider, URL, web page, web site, webcast, webconferencing, webzine

---

internment *n* **imprisonment**, captivity, confinement, custody, detention *Opposite*: release

interpersonal *adj* **relational**, social, personal, interactive *Opposite*: solitary

interplanetary *adj* **space**, planetary, interstellar, intergalactic, astronomical

interplay *n* **chemistry**, interaction, relationship, interchange, back-and-forth

interpolate *v* **1 insert**, interpose, intercalate, incorporate, include **2 interrupt**, interject, interpose, throw in, cut in

interpose *v* **1 interrupt**, cut in, throw in, interpolate, interject **2 intervene**, interfere, intercede, meddle, butt in

interpret *v* **1 explain**, clarify, account for, elucidate, make clear **2 take to mean**, understand, read, construe, infer *Opposite*: misread **3 translate**, decode, decipher, unravel, figure out

interpretation *n* **clarification**, understanding, reading, explanation, analysis

interpretative *adj* **explanatory**, revelatory, informational, informative, revealing

interpreter *n* **1 translator**, linguist, transcriber, polyglot, explainer **2 performer**, portrayer, exponent, promoter, medium

interpretive *see* **interpretative**

interracial *adj* **mixed**, of mixed race, multicultural, multiethnic, integrated *Opposite*: segregated

interregnum *n* **interval**, pause, lag, lapse, wait

interrelate *v* **interconnect**, relate, connect, link up, correlate

interrogate *v* **question**, cross-examine, quiz, interview, debrief. *See* COMPARE AND CONTRAST *at* **question**.

interrogation *n* **questioning**, examination, cross-examination, grilling, interview

interrogative *adj* **questioning**, curious, inquisitive, inquiring, probing

interrogator *n* **questioner**, interviewer, investigator, examiner

interrupt *v* **1 butt in**, barge in, interject, disturb, intrude **2 break off**, cut short, disrupt, break up, stop

interruption *n* **break**, pause, disruption, stoppage, disturbance *Opposite*: continuity

intersect *v* **cross**, interconnect, meet, traverse, overlap

intersection *n* **1 connection**, meeting, node, joint, joining **2 junction**, crossroads, fork, interchange, roundabout

intersperse *v* **mix together**, combine, intermingle, sprinkle, scatter

interstate *adj* **regional**, national, federal, political, administrative

interstellar *adj* **interplanetary**, space, star, intergalactic, stellar

interstice *n* **space**, gap, crack, opening, aperture

intertwine *v* **interweave**, entwine, interlace, link, interleave *Opposite*: divide

interval *n* **1 intermission**, break, pause, interlude, recess **2 gap**, space, distance, hiatus, separation

intervene *v* **1 intercede**, arbitrate, mediate, interfere, get involved *Opposite*: hold back **2 happen**, occur, take place, ensue, succeed

intervention *n* **interference**, involvement, intrusion, intercession, interposition

interview *n* **meeting**, talk, consultation, conference, discussion ■ *v* **question**, interrogate, talk to, converse with, put questions to

interviewee *n* **applicant**, candidate, hopeful, aspirant, contender *Opposite*: interviewer

interviewer *n* **1 examiner**, assessor, questioner, interrogator, evaluator *Opposite*: interviewee **2 presenter**, questioner, correspondent, personality, journalist

interweave *v* **intertwine**, interlace, mingle, intermingle, entwine

intestate *adj* **without a will**, unrepresented, unaccounted for, voiceless, unheard

intestinal *adj* **duodenal**, colonic, abdominal, stomach, bowel

in that *conj* **because**, as, since, given that

in the face of prep **despite**, in spite of, regardless of, notwithstanding (fml)

in the light of prep **taking into consideration**, in view of, considering, taking into account, with regard to

in the name of prep **on behalf of**, for, for the benefit of, for the sake of, on the authority of

intimacy n 1 **familiarity**, closeness, understanding, confidence, caring Opposite: distance 2 **quietness**, seclusion, privacy, informality, friendliness Opposite: formality

intimate adj 1 **close**, dear, near, warm, friendly Opposite: distant 2 **cosy**, quiet, informal, friendly, warm Opposite: formal 3 **personal**, confidential, private, secret, innermost Opposite: public 4 **thorough**, detailed, in-depth, profound, firsthand Opposite: superficial ■ v **suggest**, hint, insinuate, imply, indicate

intimately adv 1 **closely**, warmly, familiarly, confidentially, personally Opposite: distantly 2 **quietly**, informally, cosily, warmly, comfortably Opposite: formally 3 **thoroughly**, very well, fully, in detail, closely Opposite: superficially

intimation n **hint**, allusion, insinuation, suggestion, warning

intimidate v **threaten**, frighten, bully, coerce, terrorize

intimidated adj **daunted**, scared, frightened, overwhelmed, unsettled Opposite: relaxed

intimidating adj **threatening**, unapproachable, frightening, daunting, menacing Opposite: approachable

intimidation n **coercion**, pressure, bullying, threats, terrorization

into (infml) adj **addicted to**, interested in, obsessed by, mad about, keen on

intolerable adj **unbearable**, insufferable, impossible, unendurable, insupportable Opposite: bearable

intolerance n **bigotry**, prejudice, narrow-mindedness, fanaticism, narrowness Opposite: tolerance

intolerant adj **bigoted**, prejudiced, narrow-minded, fanatical, blinkered Opposite: tolerant

intonation n 1 **pitch**, inflection, lilt, cadence, timbre 2 **chanting**, chant, incantation, invocation, intoning

intone v 1 **say**, utter, speak, articulate, pronounce 2 (fml) **chant**, sing, croon, drone, hum

intoxicating adj 1 (fml) **alcoholic**, strong, powerful, heady, mind-altering Opposite: soft 2 **exciting**, invigorating, stimulating, exhilarating, fascinating Opposite: dull

intoxication n **alcoholism**, drunkenness, inebriation, intemperance, heavy drinking

intractability n 1 (fml) **unmanageability**, uncontrollability, obstinacy, stubbornness, pigheadedness Opposite: tractability 2 **difficulty**, knottiness, complexity, awkwardness, unwieldiness Opposite: simplicity

intractable adj 1 (fml) **stubborn**, obstinate, obdurate, wilful, headstrong Opposite: easygoing 2 **difficult**, problematic, troublesome, awkward, knotty Opposite: easy. See COMPARE AND CONTRAST at **unruly**.

intramural adj **internal**, inner, in-house, college, school Opposite: extramural

intransigence n **inflexibility**, stubbornness, narrow-mindedness, obstinacy, unyieldingness Opposite: flexibility

intransigent adj **inflexible**, stubborn, obdurate, obstinate, uncompromising Opposite: flexible ■ n (fml) **conservative**, dinosaur, diehard, reactionary, extremist Opposite: progressive

intravenous adj **venous**, vein, arterial, blood, circulatory

in-tray n **tray**, pigeonhole, in-box (US)

intrepid adj **fearless**, brave, bold, courageous, heroic Opposite: cowardly

intricacies n **details**, ins and outs, workings, particulars, minutiae

intricacy n **complexity**, difficulty, obscurity, sophistication, convolutedness

intricate adj **complicated**, complex, involved, difficult, elaborate Opposite: simple

intrigue n 1 **plotting**, conspiracy, manoeuvring, trickery, scheming 2 **conspiracy**, plot, deception, scheme, stratagem ■ v **interest**, fascinate, charm, attract, captivate

intriguing adj **interesting**, fascinating, exciting, stimulating, absorbing Opposite: uninteresting

intrinsic adj **basic**, essential, inherent, fundamental, central Opposite: acquired

introduce v 1 **present**, make known to, acquaint with, familiarize, announce 2 **host**, present, preside over, lead, head 3 **bring in**, set up, initiate, usher in, pioneer Opposite: conclude 4 **make somebody aware of**, bring to somebody's attention, acquaint somebody with, turn somebody on to, get somebody into

introduction n 1 **foreword**, opening, preface, prologue, preamble Opposite: conclusion 2 **outline**, overview, primer, summary, starter 3 **institution**, presentation, insertion, ushering in

introductory adj 1 **preliminary**, initial, opening, starting, early Opposite: final 2 **basic**, entry-level, preliminary, first, simple

introspection n **self-examination**, contemplation, brooding, meditation, self-analysis

introspective adj **self-examining**, self-absorbed, inward-looking, contemplative, brooding

introversion n **introspection**, self-absorption, contemplation, navel-gazing, shyness Opposite: extroversion

introvert n recluse, hermit, loner, homebody (infml), shrinking violet (infml) Opposite: extrovert ▪ adj **introverted**, shy, withdrawn, reclusive, reserved Opposite: extrovert

introverted adj **shy**, withdrawn, reclusive, reserved, reticent Opposite: extrovert

intrude v **encroach**, break in, interrupt, interfere, impose

intruder n **interloper**, burglar, trespasser, prowler, stalker

intrusion n **disturbance**, interruption, imposition, interference, invasion

intrusive adj **invasive**, indiscreet, interfering, insensitive, upsetting Opposite: discreet

intuit v **sense**, perceive, discern, feel, understand

intuition n 1 **instinct**, perception, insight, sixth sense, awareness 2 **hunch**, feeling, inkling, suspicion, sense

intuitive adj 1 **instinctive**, spontaneous, innate, in-built, instinctual Opposite: cerebral 2 **perceptive**, sensitive, shrewd, discerning, insightful

intuitively adv **instinctively**, automatically, by instinct, spontaneously, naturally

intuitiveness n **instinct**, perceptiveness, perception, insightfulness, insight

inundate v 1 **flood**, deluge, drown, immerse, submerge Opposite: drain 2 **overwhelm**, snow under, swamp, overburden, beseige

inundation n 1 **deluge**, flood, sea, stream, shower Opposite: trickle 2 **flood**, blizzard, sea, wave, barrage

inure v **harden**, toughen, accustom, season, acclimatize

inurement n **hardening**, toughening, acclimatization, seasoning, desensitization

invade v 1 **attack**, occupy, enter, conquer, annex 2 **overrun**, infect, infest, plague, colonize

invader n **attacker**, aggressor, raider, intruder, assailant

invalid adj 1 **null and void**, unacceptable, unenforceable, illegal, worthless Opposite: valid 2 **unsound**, untrue, unfounded, illogical, untenable Opposite: valid 3 **infirm**, enfeebled, debilitated, disabled, sick Opposite: well ▪ n **convalescent**, patient, sick person

invalidate v **overturn**, cancel, annul, nullify, undo Opposite: validate. See COMPARE AND CONTRAST at **nullify**.

invalidation n **annulment**, undoing, overthrow, nullification, cancellation Opposite: validation

invalidity n 1 **unsoundness**, inaccuracy, baselessness, irrationality, falsehood Opposite: validity 2 **illegality**, inoperativeness, ineffectiveness, unsoundness, voidness Opposite: legality

invaluable adj **priceless**, irreplaceable, vital, instrumental, precious Opposite: worthless

invaluableness n **pricelessness**, irreplaceability, helpfulness, importance, value Opposite: worthlessness

invariable adj **constant**, set, unchanging, inflexible, consistent Opposite: erratic

invasion n **attack**, assault, incursion, raid, foray Opposite: withdrawal

invasive adj 1 **aggressive**, offensive, hostile, warlike, bellicose 2 **intrusive**, disturbing, interfering, insensitive, imposing Opposite: discreet

invective (fml) n **diatribe**, tirade, attack, broadside, counterblast Opposite: eulogy

inveigh v **protest**, complain, fulminate, criticize, rail

inveigle v **persuade**, entice, charm, cajole, trick

invent v 1 **create**, devise, formulate, originate, conceive 2 **make up**, think up, concoct, fabricate, contrive

invented adj **false**, made-up, fictitious, imaginary, pretend Opposite: real

invention n 1 **device**, innovation, contraption, gadget, design 2 **creation**, discovery, development, brainchild, origination 3 **fabrication**, forgery, falsehood, deceit, lies Opposite: truth 4 **creativity**, imagination, ingenuity, inventiveness, resourcefulness

inventive adj **creative**, imaginative, ingenious, resourceful, original Opposite: unimaginative

inventiveness n **ingenuity**, resourcefulness, originality, creativity, imagination

inventor n **discoverer**, originator, creator, architect, author

inventory n 1 **list**, record, account, register, catalogue 2 **supply**, range, array, stock, accounting

inverse adj **opposite**, converse, reverse, contrary, counter Opposite: same ▪ n **reverse**, opposite, other, contrary, converse

inversion n 1 **reversal**, overturn, downturn, upturn 2 **reverse**, transposition, antithesis, contrary, converse

invert v **turn over**, upset, capsize, overturn, reverse Opposite: right

invest v 1 **capitalize**, put in, devote, advance, finance 2 **endow**, provide, supply, empower, authorize 3 (fml) **appoint**, ordain, instate, inaugurate, establish

investigate v **examine**, look into, explore, inspect, study

investigation n **study**, examination, analysis, research, survey

investigative adj **analytical**, exploratory, undercover, fact-finding, research

investigator n **detective**, private detective, private investigator, agent, private eye (infml)

investiture n **installation**, inauguration, swearing-in, instatement, admission

investment n 1 **savings**, speculation, venture,

asset, share **2** *(fml)* **investiture**, swearing-in, instatement, installation, enthronement

investor *n* **1** saver, shareholder, depositor, stakeholder, financier **2** **backer**, sponsor, patron, guarantor, security

inveterate *adj* **chronic**, confirmed, hardened, ingrained, incurable *Opposite*: occasional

invidious *adj* **unpleasant**, discriminatory, unenviable, unfair, undesirable *Opposite*: pleasant

in view of *prep* **considering**, bearing in mind, taking into consideration, taking into account, in consideration of *(fml)* *Opposite*: notwithstanding *(fml)*

invigilate *v* **supervise**, monitor, inspect, observe, check

invigilator *n* **supervisor**, inspector, monitor, overseer, scrutineer

invigorate *v* **energize**, revitalize, refresh, stimulate, enliven *Opposite*: exhaust

invigorated *adj* **strengthened**, fortified, energized, refreshed, restored *Opposite*: weakened

invigorating *adj* **bracing**, brisk, stimulating, refreshing, revitalizing *Opposite*: enervating

invincibility *n* **strength**, insuperability, invulnerability, impregnability, indomitability *Opposite*: vulnerability

invincible *adj* **unbeatable**, invulnerable, unconquerable, indomitable, impregnable *Opposite*: vulnerable

inviolable *adj* **unbreakable**, sacred, sacrosanct, firm, unchallengeable

inviolate *adj* **1 unaltered**, unchanged, unbroken, intact, entire *Opposite*: altered **2 pure**, unsullied, untouched, whole, intact *Opposite*: contaminated

invisibility *n* **hiddenness**, inconspicuousness, indiscernibility, faintness, indistinctness *Opposite*: visibility

invisible *adj* **1 imperceptible**, unseen, indistinguishable, indiscernible, undetectable *Opposite*: visible **2 hidden**, concealed, disguised, unnoticed, obscured *Opposite*: obvious **3 imaginary**, nonexistent, intangible, shadowy, insubstantial *Opposite*: palpable

invitation *n* **1 offer**, request, call, summons, bidding **2 encouragement**, inducement, provocation, incitement, enticement *Opposite*: discouragement

invite *n* *(infml)* **invitation**, request, call, summons, offer ■ *v* **1 ask**, request, call, summon, bid *(archaic)* *Opposite*: blackball **2 provoke**, incite, induce, attract, encourage *Opposite*: forbid

inviting *adj* **attractive**, appealing, alluring, tempting, welcoming *Opposite*: unappealing

invocation *n* **prayer**, call, request, entreaty, petition

invoice *n* **bill**, account, statement, demand,

proof of purchase *Opposite*: receipt ■ *v* **bill**, debit, charge

invoke *v* **1 cite**, quote, use, refer, mention **2 appeal**, call upon, call up, beg, summon **3 evoke**, call to mind, conjure up, incite, arouse

involuntarily *adv* **unwillingly**, reluctantly, unhappily, against your will, compulsorily *Opposite*: willingly

involuntary *adj* **1 compulsory**, obligatory, forced, unwilling, reluctant *Opposite*: willing **2 instinctive**, spontaneous, reflex, unintentional, automatic *Opposite*: intentional

involve *v* **1 contain**, include, take in, comprise, consist of **2 concern**, have to do with, affect, interest, encompass **3 implicate**, draw in, mix up, get into, embroil **4 engage**, engross, absorb, grip, occupy *Opposite*: bore **5 imply**, mean, entail, necessitate, require

involved *adj* **1 complicated**, complex, intricate, elaborate, knotty *Opposite*: simple **2 concerned**, caught up, mixed up, occupied, implicated *Opposite*: uninvolved

involvement *n* **1 attachment**, interest, concern, enthusiasm, commitment *Opposite*: detachment **2 participation**, association, connection, contribution, engrossment

invulnerable *adj* **untouchable**, invincible, unassailable, safe, impenetrable *Opposite*: vulnerable

inward *adj* **1 inner**, innermost, inmost, private, deep *Opposite*: external **2 internal**, interior, inner, inner-directed, innermost *Opposite*: outer **3 incoming**, ingoing, entering, inward bound, inflowing *Opposite*: outward

inwardly *adv* **secretly**, privately, to yourself, silently, deeply *Opposite*: openly

inwards *adv* **within**, inwardly, inside, in *Opposite*: outwards

iota *n* **jot**, bit, scrap, speck, grain *Opposite*: lot

IQ *n* **intelligence quotient**, level of intelligence, intelligence, intellect, brains

irascible *adj* **quick-tempered**, irritable, petulant, hot-tempered, short-tempered *Opposite*: easygoing

irate *adj* **angry**, incensed, furious, mad, irritated *Opposite*: calm

ire *(literary)* *n* **fury**, rage, anger, wrath, annoyance *Opposite*: calmness. See COMPARE AND CONTRAST at **anger**.

iridescent *adj* **lustrous**, rainbow-like, shimmering, shimmery, colourful *Opposite*: monochrome

irk *v* **annoy**, vex, displease, trouble, bother *Opposite*: please. See COMPARE AND CONTRAST at **bother**.

irksome *adj* **annoying**, irritating, exasperating, tiresome, tedious *Opposite*: pleasant

iron *v* **press**, smooth out, iron out, smooth, flatten *Opposite*: crumple ■ *adj* **firm**, hard, strong, determined, tough *Opposite*: soft

iron curtain n **obstacle**, impediment, hurdle, line, border

ironic adj **1 caustic**, dry, biting, sarcastic, satirical **2 incongruous**, paradoxical, poignant, peculiar, odd. See COMPARE AND CONTRAST at **sarcastic**.

ironical see **ironic**

iron out v **sort out**, resolve, smooth over, clear up, settle

ironwork n **wrought iron**, metalwork, ironmongery, ironware, iron object

irony n **1 satire**, dryness, causticness, sardonicism, sarcasm Opposite: sincerity **2 paradox**, incongruity, fatefulness, dramatic irony, contrariety

irradiate v **1 light up**, light, illuminate, brighten, cast light on Opposite: darken **2 enlighten**, clarify, inform, instruct, inspire Opposite: obfuscate

irradiation n **1 radioactivity**, radiation, contamination, X-ray, treatment **2 preservation**, treatment, sterilization, purification

irrational adj **illogical**, unreasonable, foolish, ridiculous, absurd Opposite: rational

irrationality n **illogicality**, unreasonableness, foolishness, ludicrousness, absurdity Opposite: sense

irreconcilable adj **incompatible**, irresoluble, conflicting, opposing, opposed Opposite: compatible

irrecoverable adj **1 irretrievable**, gone, lost, given up, written off (infml) **2 irreparable**, beyond repair, irreversible, irredeemable, irremediable

irredeemable adj **hopeless**, unalterable, absolute, complete, incorrigible Opposite: redeemable

irreducible adj **complex**, complicated, involved, intricate, difficult

irrefutable adj **indisputable**, certain, unquestionable, overwhelming, unassailable Opposite: disputable

irregular adj **1 uneven**, unequal, asymmetrical, unbalanced, rough Opposite: even **2 erratic**, variable, random, haphazard, intermittent Opposite: regular **3 improper**, unacceptable, abnormal, wrong, unsuitable Opposite: proper

irregularity n **1 unevenness**, inequality, variability, randomness, haphazardness Opposite: regularity **2 indiscretion**, abnormality, wrongdoing, misdeed, anomaly

irrelevance n **1 insignificance**, unimportance, inappropriateness, worthlessness, triviality Opposite: relevance **2 inconsequence**, side issue, detail, technicality, red herring

irrelevant adj **immaterial**, neither here nor there, unrelated, inappropriate, extraneous Opposite: relevant

irreligious adj **ungodly**, unspiritual, non-religious, blasphemous, sacrilegious Opposite: devout

irremediable adj **irreparable**, irreversible, irredeemable, beyond repair, irrevocable

irreparable adj **beyond repair**, irreversible, irretrievable, severe, lasting

irreplaceable adj **unique**, inimitable, matchless, exceptional, rare Opposite: common

irrepressible adj **uncontrollable**, out of control, wild, unruly, disorderly Opposite: contained

irreproachable adj **blameless**, faultless, flawless, perfect, impeccable Opposite: blameworthy

irresistible adj **1 overwhelming**, overpowering, uncontrollable, compelling, strong Opposite: weak **2 desirable**, tempting, appealing, enticing, alluring Opposite: unappealing

irresolute adj **indecisive**, vacillating, unsure, weak, undetermined Opposite: determined

irresolution n **indecision**, indecisiveness, vacillation, weakness, hesitancy Opposite: determination

irrespective adv **regardless**, nevertheless, nonetheless, heedlessly, notwithstanding (fml)

irrespective of prep **regardless of**, despite, no matter, in spite of, heedless of Opposite: considering

irresponsibility n **recklessness**, carelessness, inattention, negligence, rashness Opposite: responsibility

irresponsible adj **reckless**, careless, negligent, rash, foolish Opposite: responsible

irretrievable adj **irreparable**, irreversible, irrevocable, severe, irrecoverable

irreverence n **disrespect**, mockery, derision, impertinence, impudence Opposite: respect

irreverent adj **disrespectful**, mocking, derisive, rude, impudent Opposite: respectful

irreversible adj **irreparable**, irretrievable, irrevocable, unalterable, irremediable Opposite: temporary

irrevocable adj **binding**, irreversible, final, unalterable, unchangeable Opposite: flexible

irrevocably adv **irreversibly**, forever, permanently, once and for all, for all time

irrigate v **water**, flood, wet, moisten, hose down Opposite: dry out

irritability n **touchiness**, bad temper, petulance, cantankerousness, tetchiness (infml) Opposite: equanimity

irritable adj **bad-tempered**, short-tempered, ill-tempered, cross, petulant Opposite: easy-going

irritant n **nuisance**, annoyance, aggravation, irritation, bane Opposite: balm

irritate v **1 annoy**, infuriate, bother, exasperate, aggravate (infml) Opposite: soothe **2 inflame**, rub, chafe, sting, hurt Opposite: soothe. See COMPARE AND CONTRAST at **annoy**.

irritated adj **annoyed**, cross, angry, exasperated, wound up (infml) Opposite: unperturbed

irritating *adj* **annoying**, exasperating, irksome, infuriating *Opposite*: soothing

irritation *n* **1 annoyance**, frustration, impatience, exasperation, aggravation *(infml)* *Opposite*: calmness **2 nuisance**, bother, irritant, bane, pain *(infml)* **3 inflammation**, soreness, tenderness, itchiness, rash. *See* COMPARE AND CONTRAST *at* anger.

island *n* **isle**, islet, atoll, desert island, key *Opposite*: mainland

islander *n* **inhabitant**, local, resident, occupant, native

island-hop *v* **travel around**, tour, sail around, sail, cruise

isle *n* **island**, islet, atoll, desert island, key

islet *see* **isle**

ism *(infml)* *n* **doctrine**, ideology, belief, belief system, creed

isolate *v* **cut off**, separate, segregate, detach, set apart *Opposite*: include

isolated *adj* **1 remote**, cut off, inaccessible, lonely, secluded *Opposite*: nearby **2 lonely**, alone, solitary, insular, friendless **3 one-off**, exceptional, unique, solitary, unrepeated *Opposite*: common

isolation *n* **separation**, segregation, remoteness, loneliness, seclusion *Opposite*: inclusion

isolationism *n* **separateness**, remoteness, seclusion, independence, standoffishness

isometrics *n* **exercise**, body building, workout, keep fit

isotope *n* **element**, form, variant, version

issue *n* **1 subject**, matter, question, topic, problem **2 copy**, number, edition, back number, back copy **3 production**, release, distribution, circulation, publication **4 progeny**, offspring, children, young, descendants ■ *v* **1 supply**, give out, hand out, deliver, distribute **2 announce**, broadcast, send out, make, declare **3 publish**, release, broadcast, disseminate, distribute *Opposite*: withdraw **4 emanate**, emerge, issue forth, gush, flow **5 originate**, stem, spring, arise, rise

isthmus *n* **strip**, neck, bridge, peninsula, spit

IT *n* **information technology**, computer science, data processing, information processing, data retrieval

italic *adj* **sloping**, slanted, oblique *Opposite*: roman

itch *v* **1 irritate**, prickle, scratch, tickle, crawl *Opposite*: soothe **2 long**, desire, wish, hanker, yearn ■ *n* **1 itchiness**, tickle, irritation, prickling, tingling **2 desire**, longing, wish, eagerness, hankering

itchiness *n* **irritation**, tickle, inflammation, tingling, prickliness

itching *adj* **eager**, longing, dying, keen, burning *Opposite*: reluctant

itchy *adj* **prickly**, tickly, scratchy, uncomfortable, irritated

item *n* **1 thing**, article, piece, entry, point **2 couple**, pair, twosome, match, duo

itemize *v* **list**, detail, enumerate, record, document

iterate *v* **repeat**, restate, reiterate, go over, retell

iteration *n* **repetition**, restatement, reiteration, rehearsal, duplication

itinerant *adj* **peripatetic**, roving, wandering, nomadic, roaming *Opposite*: settled

itinerary *n* **route**, schedule, journey, circuit, tour

itsy-bitsy *(infml)* *adj* **tiny**, little, small, minute, minuscule *Opposite*: huge

ivory tower *n* **seclusion**, isolation, retreat, remoteness, academic world *Opposite*: real world

J

jab *v* **stab**, prod, thrust, dig, poke ■ *n* **1 prod**, stab, thrust, dig, poke **2** *(infml)* **injection**, immunization, inoculation, vaccination, booster

jabber *v* **chatter**, babble, prattle, gabble, ramble

jacket *n* **cover**, covering, casing, sheathing, sheath

jack in *(infml)* *v* **stop**, give up, resign, abandon, leave *Opposite*: take up

jackknife *v* **turn**, skid, swerve, veer, swivel

jackpot *n* **prize**, bonanza, winnings, windfall, rollover

jack up *v* **1 lift**, lift up, raise, raise up, put up *Opposite*: lower **2 increase**, raise, put up, hike up, boost *Opposite*: slash

jaded *adj* **1 bored**, world-weary, jaundiced, cynical, fed up *(infml)* *Opposite*: enthusiastic **2 tired**, weary, exhausted, worn-out, lacklustre *Opposite*: fresh

jagged *adj* **1 uneven**, rough, ragged, crude, irregular *Opposite*: even **2 sharp**, pointed, pointy, rough, serrated *Opposite*: smooth

jaggedness *n* **1 unevenness**, raggedness, roughness, irregularity, bumpiness *Opposite*: evenness **2 sharpness**, pointedness, pointiness, roughness, serration *Opposite*: smoothness

jail *n* **prison**, lockup, open prison, dungeon, borstal ■ *v* **imprison**, lock up, lock away, put behind bars, confine *Opposite*: free

jailbreak *n* **breakout**, escape, getaway, exodus, flight

jailer *n* **prison officer**, guard, governor, keeper, prison guard *Opposite*: liberator

jalopy *(dated infml)* *n* **wreck**, banger *(infml)*, tin lizzie *(infml)*, rattletrap *(infml)*, heap *(slang)*

jam *v* **1 push**, squash, cram, stuff, pack **2 fill**, fill up, throng, pack, block **3 stop**, seize, seize up, grind to a halt, stick ■ *n* **1 traffic jam**, gridlock, bottleneck, logjam, roadblock **2** *(infml)* **predicament**, mess, quandary, pickle *(infml)*, fix *(infml)*

jamb *n* **upright**, post, support, column, door-post

jamboree *n* **celebration**, party, carnival, fête, garden party

jammed *adj* **1 stuck**, wedged, stuck fast, lodged, caught *Opposite*: free **2 blocked**, congested, thronged, packed, crammed *Opposite*: deserted

jammy *(infml)* *adj* **lucky**, fortunate, comfortable, easy *Opposite*: unlucky

jam-packed *(infml)* *adj* **crowded**, full, full up, packed, filled to capacity *Opposite*: empty

jangle *v* **rattle**, jingle, clank, clink, clatter

jar *n* **pot**, container, vessel, crock, urn ■ *v* **1 shake**, jolt, jerk, bump, hit **2 irritate**, grate, annoy, irk, get on somebody's nerves *Opposite*: harmonize

jargon *n* **1 terminology**, slang, argot, parlance, language **2 nonsense**, verbiage, cant, mumbo jumbo *(infml)*, waffle *(infml)*

jarring *adj* **1 irritating**, grating, annoying, unpleasant, unbearable *Opposite*: calming **2 disturbing**, unsettling, shocking, destabilizing, uncomfortable *Opposite*: reassuring **3 clashing**, incongruous, uncharacteristic, discordant, inharmonious *Opposite*: harmonious

jaundiced *adj* **cynical**, pessimistic, sceptical, unenthusiastic, jaded

jaunt *n* **outing**, trip, excursion, break, day out

jauntiness *n* **cheerfulness**, jolliness, gaiety, dash, spryness

jaunty *adj* **carefree**, cheerful, cheery, jolly, spry

javelin *n* **spear**, projectile, missile, lance, harpoon

jaw *n* **chin**, jawbone, jawline, jowl, mouth

jawbone *n* **jaw**, chin, maxilla, mandible

jaywalk *v* **cross**, cross over, walk across, stroll across, go across

jaywalker *n* **pedestrian**, walker, crosser, traverser, stroller

jazz up *(infml)* *v* **enhance**, spice, spice up, liven up, enliven

jealous *adj* **1 envious**, covetous, resentful, green with envy, green **2 protective**, suspicious, wary, watchful, mistrustful *Opposite*: trusting

jealousy *n* **1 envy**, covetousness, resentment, resentfulness, desirousness *(fml)* **2 protectiveness**, suspicion, suspiciousness, wariness, watchfulness

jeer *v* **boo**, hiss, heckle, catcall, taunt *Opposite*: applaud ■ *n* **hiss**, boo, taunt, catcall, hoot

jeer at *v* **insult**, taunt, sneer, mock, deride *Opposite*: cheer

jeering *n* **derision**, mockery, name-calling, mocking, taunting *Opposite*: applause ■ *adj* **derisive**, scornful, mocking, sardonic, contemptuous

jejune *adj* **1 boring**, undemanding, uninteresting, lightweight, insubstantial *Opposite*: interesting **2 childish**, immature, adolescent, unsophisticated, crude *Opposite*: mature

jell *v* **1 solidify**, set, congeal, firm, harden *Opposite*: liquefy **2 take shape**, shape up, crystallize, come together, firm up *Opposite*: disintegrate **3 bond**, get on, be compatible, be on the same wavelength, click *(infml)* *Opposite*: clash

jellied *adj* **gelatinous**, set, solid, congealed

jellify *v* **set**, gelatinize, congeal, jell, gel *Opposite*: liquefy

jelly *n* **1 gelatin**, aspic, gel **2 petroleum jelly**, lubricant, ointment ■ *v* **set**, thicken, jellify, gelatinize, congeal *Opposite*: liquefy

jemmy *v* **lever**, open, force, prise, crowbar

jeopardize *v* **put at risk**, risk, put in danger, endanger, expose

jeopardy *n* **danger**, risk, threat, peril, hazard

jerk *v* **1 yank**, tug, pull, wrench, haul **2 lurch**, jolt, shudder, judder, bump **3 twitch**, shudder, tremble, shake ■ *n* **1 pull**, tug, yank, wrench, haul **2 jolt**, bump, shudder, judder, lurch **3 spasm**, twitch, shudder, tremble, shake

jerkin *n* **jacket**, body warmer, tunic, waistcoat, gilet

jerkiness *n* **bumpiness**, jumpiness, bounciness, lurching, shuddering *Opposite*: smoothness

jerky *adj* **irregular**, spasmodic, erratic, fitful, bumpy *Opposite*: smooth

jerry-build *v* **throw up**, fling up, throw together *(infml)*, knock together *(infml)*

jerry-built *adj* **poor**, shoddy, jerry-rigged, cheap and nasty, flimsy

jerry can *n* **can**, container, canister

jest *(literary)* *n* **joke**, prank, hoax, quip, spoof ■ *v* **banter**, joke, kid, tease, quip

jester *n* **fool**, clown, comedian, entertainer, comic

jet *n* **spurt**, spout, fountain, squirt, stream

jetsam *n* **odds and ends**, flotsam, debris, detritus, rubbish

jet set (infml) n glitterati, high society, rich and famous, beautiful people, idle rich Opposite: hoi polloi

jettison v throw away, throw out, get rid of, abandon, discard Opposite: keep

jetty n dock, breakwater, quay, landing stage, pier

jewel n 1 gemstone, gem, precious stone, semi-precious stone, crystal 2 ornament, trinket, accessory

jib v baulk, stop short, pull up, recoil, retreat

jibe see gibe

jiffy (infml) n moment, second, minute, flash, instant

jig v jerk, skip, hop, caper, leap

jiggle v wiggle, waggle, shake, joggle, rattle

jigsaw n puzzle, jigsaw puzzle, picture puzzle, Chinese puzzle, tangram

jigsaw puzzle see jigsaw

jilt v reject, turn down, break up, split up, walk out Opposite: stick by

jingle n tune, song, refrain, chorus, ditty ■ v tinkle, rattle, ring, clink, clank

jingoism n chauvinism, patriotism, nationalism, xenophobia, hostility

jingoistic adj chauvinistic, patriotic, nationalistic, xenophobic, hostile

jinx n curse, plague, evil eye, spell, bad luck

jinxed adj unlucky, luckless, hapless, unfortunate, star-crossed Opposite: lucky

jitters (infml) n nervousness, agitation, uneasiness, anxiety, apprehension Opposite: calmness

jittery adj nervous, jumpy, on edge, edgy, fidgety Opposite: calm

job n 1 occupation, work, line, line of work, trade 2 task, duty, responsibility, chore, assignment 3 position, post, appointment, vacancy, role

jobbing adj casual, occasional, freelance, part-time, temporary Opposite: regular

jobless adj unemployed, out of work, laid off, unwaged, on benefit Opposite: employed

job-sharing n part-time work, work-sharing, sharing

jockey n rider, equestrian, steeplechaser, showjumper, competitor ■ v 1 ride, race, steeplechase, showjump, compete 2 manoeuvre, compete, contend, fight, struggle 3 manipulate, cajole, trick, deceive, talk into

jocular adj funny, joking, jokey, jovial, playful Opposite: solemn

jocularity n wittiness, comicality, humour, playfulness, jokiness Opposite: solemnity

jog v 1 trot, run, train, exercise, keep fit 2 nudge, prod, bump, push, bang

jogger n runner, sprinter, cross-country runner, harrier, athlete

joggle v shake, wiggle, waggle, jiggle, jerk

joie de vivre n vitality, enthusiasm, liveliness, exuberance, high-spiritedness Opposite: lethargy

join v 1 fasten, connect, link, unite, stick Opposite: separate 2 connect, link up, merge, bring together, unite Opposite: disengage 3 sign up, enrol, enlist, join up, go in with Opposite: leave ■ n joint, seam, connection, intersection, link

joined adj 1 bonded, fixed together, hinged, hitched, linked Opposite: detached 2 associated, allied, affiliated, twinned, connected Opposite: independent

joinery n woodwork, cabinetmaking, furniture making, carving, carpentry

join forces v team up, collaborate, get together, come together, rally Opposite: split

join in v participate, become involved, take part, enter into, take a turn Opposite: leave

joint adj combined, dual, shared, multiparty, united Opposite: individual ■ n join, linkage, link, junction, intersection

join together v merge, amalgamate, integrate, dovetail, associate Opposite: split

join up v 1 enlist, enrol, sign up, join, subscribe Opposite: quit 2 meet up, link, team up, come together, get together

joist n beam, spar, truss, support

joke n 1 witticism, shaggy dog story, tall story, pun, anecdote 2 laughing stock, butt, object of ridicule, fool, buffoon 3 prank, trick, practical joke, stunt, hoax ■ v kid, pretend, clown, play the fool, pull somebody's leg (infml)

joker n clown, fool, buffoon, comedian, comic

jokey adj amusing, good-humoured, light-hearted, flippant, funny Opposite: serious

joking adj jokey, playful, flippant, light-hearted, facetious Opposite: serious ■ n clowning, teasing, raillery, fooling around, fooling about

jollification n festivity, revelry, celebration, merrymaking, party

jolliness see jollity

jollity n cheerfulness, fun, hilarity, joviality, jolliness Opposite: seriousness

jolly adj cheerful, happy, fun, jovial, bright Opposite: sad ■ adv (dated infml) very, really, tremendously, hugely, terrifically

jolt v shake, jerk, bump, joggle, nudge ■ n 1 bump, shake, jerk, joggle, bounce 2 shock, surprise, bolt from the blue, blow, reminder

josh (infml) v tease, make fun of, chaff, ridicule, mock

jostle v push, knock, bump, elbow, shove

jot n iota, atom, bit, speck, tittle

jot down v write down, make a note of, scribble down, put on paper, put down

jotter n notepad, notebook, pad, personal organizer, writing pad

journal n 1 periodical, magazine, paper,

weekly, monthly **2 diary**, log, chronicle, record, register

journalism *n* **reporting**, reportage, broadcasting, commentary, fourth estate

journalist *n* **correspondent**, reporter, broadcaster, newsreader, columnist

journalistic *adj* **reporting**, editorial, newspaper, current affairs

journey *n* **trip**, voyage, expedition, ride, flight ■ *v* **travel**, tour, go, trek, voyage

joust *v* **fight**, tilt, compete, battle, engage *Opposite*: agree

jovial *adj* **cheerful**, jolly, good-humoured, fun-loving, breezy *Opposite*: glum

joviality *n* **cheerfulness**, jollity, jolliness, cheeriness, bonhomie *Opposite*: glumness

jovialness *see* joviality

jowl *n* **jaw**, chin, jawbone, jawline, muzzle

joy *n* **1 happiness**, delight, enjoyment, bliss, ecstasy *Opposite*: sadness **2 delight**, jewel, treasure, pearl, angel

joyful *adj* **1 happy**, elated, ecstatic, thrilled, pleased *Opposite*: sad **2 wonderful**, blissful, pleasurable, fantastic, enjoyable *Opposite*: unpleasant

joyfulness *n* **happiness**, enjoyment, bliss, ecstasy, merriment *Opposite*: sadness

joyless *adj* **miserable**, cheerless, depressing, bleak, desolate *Opposite*: happy

joylessness *n* **cheerlessness**, misery, gloom, unhappiness, bleakness *Opposite*: happiness

joyous *adj* **happy**, merry, blissful, festive, cheerful *Opposite*: glum

joyousness *n* **happiness**, pleasure, bliss, joyfulness, jubilation *Opposite*: glumness

joyrider *n* **carjacker**, car thief, speeder, twoccer *(slang)*, hot-rodder *(slang)*

joyriding *n* **carjacking**, car theft, speeding, hot-rodding *(slang)*

JP *n* **Justice of the Peace**, magistrate, justice, judge, arbitrator

jubilant *adj* **triumphant**, proud, thrilled, ecstatic, delighted *Opposite*: disappointed

jubilation *n* **elation**, triumph, joyousness, euphoria, delight *Opposite*: disappointment

jubilee *n* **anniversary**, celebration, commemoration, festival, festivity

judder *v* **shake**, vibrate, shudder, quiver, tremble ■ *n* **shudder**, vibration, quiver, tremor, jerk

judge *n* **1 magistrate**, justice, justice of the peace, judge advocate **2 arbitrator**, adjudicator, moderator, umpire, referee **3 evaluator**, critic, reviewer, arbiter, expert ■ *v* **1 arbitrate**, adjudicate, mediate, referee, umpire **2 assess**, evaluate, weigh, weigh up, look at **3 consider**, reckon, think, believe, maintain **4 estimate**, guess, consider, say, assess **5 condemn**, criticize, sneer at, belittle, pass judgment on

judgment *n* **1 verdict**, ruling, decision, finding, sentence **2 discernment**, good sense, shrewdness, wisdom, common sense **3 opinion**, view, considered opinion, feeling, thoughts

judgmental *adj* **critical**, hypercritical, condemnatory, negative, disapproving *Opposite*: complimentary

judicial *adj* **legal**, court, justice, official

judiciary *n* **judges**, bench, courts, magistrates

judicious *adj* **sensible**, wise, careful, shrewd, astute *Opposite*: foolish

judiciousness *n* **wisdom**, prudence, shrewdness, sense, care *Opposite*: foolishness

jug *n* **pitcher**, ewer, carafe, crock

juggernaut *n* **giant**, titan, leviathan, behemoth, goliath

juggle *v* **1 fit in**, manage, cope with, run, deal with **2 manipulate**, falsify, alter, misrepresent, tamper with

juice *n* **extract**, sap, liquid, fluid, liquor

juiciness *n* **succulence**, ripeness, lusciousness, moistness *Opposite*: dryness

juicy *adj* **1 succulent**, luscious, thirst-quenching, moist, ripe *Opposite*: dry **2** *(infml)* **titillating**, scandalous, salacious, exciting, sensational *Opposite*: dull

jumble *v* **mix up**, muddle, clutter, disarrange, shuffle *Opposite*: tidy ■ *n* **1 muddle**, heap, clutter, hotchpotch, mishmash **2 unwanted items**, odds and ends, second-hand goods, castoffs, junk *(infml)*

jumbled *adj* **untidy**, topsy-turvy, muddled, chaotic, disorderly *Opposite*: orderly

jumbo *adj* **oversize**, outsize, huge, enormous, giant-sized *Opposite*: tiny

jump *v* **1 bound**, leap, hop, skip, soar **2 be startled**, be surprised, start, get a fright, be frightened **3** *(infml)* **obey**, do as you are told, conform, toe the line, play the game ■ *n* **1 leap**, bound, hop, skip, spring **2 obstacle**, hurdle, fence, wall, hedge **3 start**, jolt, jerk, lurch, jar

jump back *v* **rebound**, recoil, bounce back, ricochet

jumper *n* **athlete**, high jumper, long jumper, hurdler, steeplechaser

jump in *v* **make a start**, take the plunge, get going, leap in, take the bull by the horns

jumpiness *n* **1 jitteriness**, anxiety, nervousness, agitation, edginess *Opposite*: calmness **2 jerkiness**, erraticism, unsteadiness, suddenness, abruptness *Opposite*: smoothness

jump-start *v* **1 kick-start**, start up, get going, set in motion, bump-start **2 stimulate**, trigger, set off, start up, kick-start ■ *n* **1 kick-start**, bump-start, push-start, startup, start **2 stimulus**, momentum, spur, drive, impetus

jumpy *adj* **1 jittery**, anxious, nervous, worried, tense *Opposite*: calm **2 jerky**, erratic, unsteady, sudden, abrupt *Opposite*: smooth

junction *n* **connection**, intersection, seam, link, joint

juncture *n* **1 point in time**, stage, moment, occasion, interval **2** *(fml)* **join**, connection, joint, link, seam

jungle *n* **1 tropical forest**, rain forest, forest, wilderness, bush **2 tangle**, muddle, maze, jumble, mess

junior *adj* **low-ranking**, subordinate, inferior, lower, low-grade *Opposite*: senior ■ *n* **subordinate**, underling, beginner, trainee, novice *Opposite*: old hand

junk *(infml)* *n* **1 rubbish**, scrap, debris, litter, refuse **2 second-hand goods**, jumble, unwanted items, castoffs, odds and ends ■ *v* **discard**, throw away, throw out, get rid of, scrap *Opposite*: keep

junket *n* **trip**, excursion, visit, outing, spree

junk food *n* **snack food**, convenience food, fast food, TV dinner

junk mail *n* **fliers**, leaflets, brochures, direct mail, mailshot

junta *n* **1 military government**, military rule, regime, martial law, government **2 cabal**, faction, clique, gang, band **3 council**, committee, legislative body, assembly, forum

jurisdiction *n* **1 authority**, dominion, influence, power, control **2 area**, state, extent of power, territory, province

juror *n* **jury member**, assessor, estimator, judge, adjudicator

jury *n* **adjudicators**, judges, bench, panel, board

just *adv* **1 a minute ago**, a moment ago, a second ago, only this minute, in the past few minutes **2 at this moment**, now, immediately, presently, in a minute **3 only**, merely, simply, solely, purely **4 barely**, hardly, scarcely, slightly **5 simply**, really, truly, definitely, emphatically **6 exactly**, precisely, absolutely, emphatically, completely ■ *adj* **1 fair**, impartial, objective, unbiased, unprejudiced *Opposite*: unfair **2 correct**, moral, ethical, good, appropriate *Opposite*: unjust **3 reasonable**, valid, sensible, sound, balanced

just deserts *n* **what you deserve**, what was coming to you, just reward, comeuppance *(infml)*

justice *n* **1 fairness**, reasonableness, impartiality, evenhandedness, righteousness *Opposite*: unfairness **2 validity**, legitimacy, rightfulness, acceptability, reasonableness **3 judge**, magistrate, justice of the peace, judge advocate

justifiable *adj* **defensible**, admissible, justified, reasonable, correct *Opposite*: indefensible

justification *n* **defence**, reason, reasoning, explanation, validation

justified *adj* **warranted**, defensible, vindicated, correct, right *Opposite*: unwarranted

justify *v* **1 defend**, validate, explain, rationalize, excuse **2 align**, adjust, straighten up, line up

justly *adv* **1 fairly**, impartially, rightly, reasonably, honestly *Opposite*: unfairly **2 correctly**, morally, deservedly, reasonably, justifiably *Opposite*: unjustly

just reward *see* just deserts

jut *v* **stick out**, protrude, overhang, poke out, project

juvenile *adj* **1 youthful**, young, immature, adolescent, fresh-faced *Opposite*: mature **2 childish**, infantile, babyish, puerile, immature *Opposite*: grown-up ■ *n* **youngster**, adolescent, young person, teenager, youth *Opposite*: adult

juxtapose *v* **put side by side**, put together, put next to, put beside, put adjacent to

juxtaposition *n* **collocation**, association, apposition, comparison, contrast

K

kaleidoscope *n* **1 complex pattern**, phantasmagoria, display, mixture, medley **2 series**, web, set, chain reaction, domino effect

kaleidoscopic *adj* **colourful**, variegated, multicoloured, many-coloured, motley *Opposite*: monochromatic

kangaroo *(infml)* *v* **jerk**, jump, leap, bump, jolt *Opposite*: glide

kaolin *n* **clay**, kaolinite, argil, potter's clay, potter's earth

kaput *(infml)* *adj* **broken**, ruined, wrecked, finished, ended *Opposite*: working

karaoke *n* **singing**, singsong, karaoke night, music, entertainment

karma *n* **1 destiny**, fate, kismet, fortune, providence **2** *(infml)* **atmosphere**, aura, feeling, ambience, vibrations *(infml)*

kebab *n* **skewer**, brochette, grill stick

keel *v* **capsize**, turn upside down, upset, overturn, turn over *Opposite*: right

keel over *(infml)* *v* **1 collapse**, fall over, faint, pass out, lose consciousness *Opposite*: come to **2 capsize**, keel, turn upside down, upset, overturn *Opposite*: right

keen *adj* **1** eager, enthusiastic, willing, fanatical, dedicated *Opposite*: indifferent **2 acute**, quick, clever, perceptive, alert *Opposite*: dull **3 sensitive**, responsive, finely honed, finely tuned, well-developed *Opposite*: insensitive **4 intense**, strong, acute, deep, powerful *Opposite*: mild **5** (*literary*) **sharp**, sharpened, whetted, bright, steely *Opposite*: blunt **6 icy**, bitter, cold, chilly, wintry *Opposite*: mild **7 competitive**, low, cheap, attractive, affordable *Opposite*: prohibitive ■ *v* **cry out**, wail, howl, weep, sob

keenness *n* **1 enthusiasm**, eagerness, zeal, passion, willingness *Opposite*: reluctance **2 fondness**, attraction, devotion, partiality, liking *Opposite*: aversion **3 acuteness**, perception, quickness, cleverness, perceptiveness *Opposite*: dullness **4 intensity**, intenseness, strength, acuteness, depth *Opposite*: mildness **5** (*literary*) **sharpness**, razor-sharpness, brightness, steeliness *Opposite*: bluntness **6 iciness**, bitterness, coldness, chill, wintriness *Opposite*: mildness **7 competitiveness**, lowness, cheapness, attractiveness, affordability

keen on *adj* partial to, taken with, fond of, wild about, gone on (*infml*)

keen-sighted *adj* **sharp-sighted**, sharp-eyed, eagle-eyed, hawk-eyed

keep *v* **1** hold onto, hang onto, save, retain, have *Opposite*: let go **2 hide**, conceal, repress, withhold, hold back *Opposite*: let out **3 maintain**, hold, sustain, preserve, conserve *Opposite*: abandon **4 store**, hold, stash, stack, shelve *Opposite*: get rid of **5 continue**, go on, carry on, keep on, persist in *Opposite*: stop **6 honour**, fulfil, carry out, comply with, obey *Opposite*: break **7 detain**, delay, hold up, hold back, keep back *Opposite*: release **8 take care of**, care for, tend, look after, watch over **9 stay**, remain, be, keep yourself *Opposite*: become **10 own**, look after, care for, farm, rear

keep abreast *v* **stay current**, keep up, keep up to date, be well-informed, stay in touch

keep an eye on *v* **1 watch closely**, keep a close watch on, observe, spy on, watch **2 look after**, watch over, keep in check, mind, take care of

keep a secret *v* **not tell a soul**, be discreet, keep quiet, be the soul of discretion, keep mum (*infml*) *Opposite*: spill the beans (*infml*)

keep a straight face *v* **show no emotion**, have a poker face, look blank, dissemble, keep a stiff upper lip (*infml*)

keep at *v* **persevere**, persist, soldier on, keep your nose to the grindstone, stick to *Opposite*: give up

keep at bay *v* **hold off**, keep away, ward off, stave off, fend off *Opposite*: encourage

keep away *v* **hold off**, ward off, keep at bay, stave off, fend off *Opposite*: encourage

keep back *v* **1 withhold**, keep secret, suppress, omit, hide *Opposite*: reveal **2 reserve**, conserve, hold on to, save, withhold *Opposite*: use up **3 restrain**, curb, control, restrict, limit

keep count *v* **record**, note, keep a record of, note down, keep a note of *Opposite*: lose track of

keep down *v* **1 oppress**, suppress, repress, subjugate, subdue *Opposite*: liberate **2 limit**, curb, restrain, control, check

keeper *n* **custodian**, warder, guard, guardian, caretaker

keep fit *n* **physical exercise**, exercise, working out, aerobics, gymnastics ■ *v* **keep in shape**, exercise, work out, train, keep in trim

keep from *v* **1 withhold**, omit, hide, conceal, keep back *Opposite*: reveal **2 prevent**, restrain, stop, deter, prohibit *Opposite*: allow **3 protect**, shield, shelter, save, cushion *Opposite*: expose

keep going *v* **persevere**, carry on, persist, hold up, last *Opposite*: stop

keep in *v* **hold in**, repress, withhold, hold back, retain *Opposite*: let out

keep in check *v* **control**, restrict, restrain, curb, limit

keeping *n* **charge**, custody, possession, care, trust

keep in mind *v* **bear in mind**, remember, recall, retain *Opposite*: forget

keep in the dark *v* **keep in ignorance**, withhold information from, keep something back from, hold something back from, conceal something from *Opposite*: inform

keep mum (*infml*) *v* **keep quiet**, not tell a soul, be discreet, keep secret, keep under wraps *Opposite*: spill the beans (*infml*)

keep off *v* **1 hold back**, separate, shut out, ward off *Opposite*: encourage **2 abstain**, do without, go without, avoid, not touch *Opposite*: indulge

keep on *v* **continue**, persist, persevere, carry on, go on *Opposite*: give up

keep on at (*infml*) *v* **nag**, badger, pester, harp on, harass *Opposite*: give up on

keep out *v* **exclude**, shut out, bar, ban, deny entry *Opposite*: admit

keepsake *n* **memento**, reminder, souvenir, gift, token

keep secret *v* **withhold**, suppress, sit on, keep from, keep under wraps *Opposite*: let slip

keep the ball rolling *v* **continue**, keep things moving, keep things going, keep up the momentum, maintain momentum *Opposite*: stop

keep the lid on *v* **keep under control**, contain, control, suppress, restrain

keep to *v* **obey**, comply with, abide by, stick to, adhere to

keep track of v **follow**, keep an eye on, keep up with, monitor, keep up to date with *Opposite*: lose track of

keep under control v **keep in check**, restrain, contain, keep the lid on, suppress

keep under wraps v **keep secret**, keep to yourself, keep back, keep quiet, hide *Opposite*: reveal

keep up v **1 continue**, sustain, maintain, carry on, persevere *Opposite*: stop **2 stay beside**, keep abreast, keep pace, stay even, match *Opposite*: fall behind **3 stay in touch**, keep in touch, keep in contact, keep abreast, keep up to date *Opposite*: lose touch

keep your chin up v **make the best of things**, take the bad with the good, look on the bright side, make the best of a bad job, not let things get the better of you *Opposite*: go under

keep your cool (infml) v **stay calm**, keep your head, calm down, simmer down, cool off

keep your word v **be as good as your word**, keep your promise, deliver on a promise, be true to your word, keep your side of the bargain *Opposite*: go back on

keg n **barrel**, cask, tub, firkin, drum

ken n **knowledge**, acquaintance, understanding, awareness, comprehension

kennel n **house**, hut, shelter

kerfuffle (infml) n **commotion**, disturbance, disorder, agitation, hubbub

kernel n **1 pip**, pit, stone *Opposite*: husk **2 core**, nub, root, heart, essence

kettle n **pot**, pan, cauldron, steamer, fish kettle

kettle of fish n **mess**, predicament, difficulty, problem, quagmire

key n **1 skeleton key**, master key, passe-partout, passkey, latchkey **2 pitch**, register, tone, scale, note **3 button**, knob, control **4 solution**, answer, explanation, means, secret ■ adj **important**, main, crucial, significant, vital *Opposite*: unimportant ■ v **input**, keyboard, enter, key in, type

keyboard n **control panel**, console, controls ■ v **type**, key, key in, input, enter

keyboarder n **keyboard operator**, typist, typesetter, data entry clerk (US)

keyhole n **hole**, aperture, spyhole, peephole, opening

key in v **key**, type, input, enter, typeset

keynote n **theme**, essence, idea, gist, core ■ adj **important**, crucial, major, essential, defining

key player n **leading light**, principal, kingpin (infml), big cheese (infml)

keystone n **foundation**, basis, bedrock, underpinning, grounding

kibbutz n **collective**, commune, cooperative, community, settlement

kick v **1 boot**, strike, hack, put the boot in **2 dribble**, punt, place-kick, kick off **3 jolt**, jerk, recoil, flex, reflex **4** (infml) **give up**, quit, end, cease, stop *Opposite*: take up ■ n **1 recoil**, rebound, return, reaction, reflex **2** (infml) **thrill**, boost, pleasure, excitement, frisson

kick back (infml) v **relax**, take it easy, lounge, loaf, veg out (infml)

kickback n **bribe**, softener, payment, reward, inducement

kick in v **1 break down**, smash, demolish, flatten, destroy **2** (infml) **take effect**, come on-stream, get going, get underway, start *Opposite*: run out

kick in the teeth n **setback**, blow, shock, betrayal, letdown *Opposite*: boost

kick off (infml) v **start**, begin, start the ball rolling, get underway, commence *Opposite*: end

kickoff (infml) n **start**, beginning, opening, initiation, commencement (fml) *Opposite*: end

kick out (infml) v **throw out**, sling out, eject, force out, make redundant *Opposite*: appoint

kick-start v **1 start up**, start, get going, turn over, crank up *Opposite*: stop **2 restart**, start, revive, resuscitate, jump-start ■ n (infml) **fillip**, shot in the arm, spur, stimulus, boost

kick up a fuss v **protest**, rampage, make a scene, make a fuss, complain *Opposite*: smooth over

kid n (infml) **child**, teenager, adolescent, youngster, toddler *Opposite*: adult ■ v **1 tease**, joke, poke fun at, make fun of, mock **2** (infml) **fool**, trick, delude, hoodwink, con. *See* COMPARE AND CONTRAST *at* youth.

kidder n **joker**, tease, trickster, clown, prankster

kiddy (infml) n **youngster**, child, baby, tot (infml), kid (infml)

kidnap v **abduct**, take hostage, capture, take prisoner, hijack *Opposite*: release

kid's stuff n **child's play**, piece of cake, pushover, doddle (infml)

kill v **1 murder**, assassinate, execute, put to death, slaughter *Opposite*: revive **2** (infml) **switch off**, shut down, deactivate, disconnect, cut *Opposite*: start up

COMPARE AND CONTRAST CORE MEANING: deprive of life

kill cause the death of a person or animal; **murder** take the life of another person deliberately and not in self-defence in a serious criminal act; **assassinate** murder a public figure by a sudden violent attack; **execute** take somebody's life as part of a judicial or extrajudicial process; **put to death** deliberately take somebody's life, especially in accordance with a legal death sentence; **slaughter** kill farm animals for food, or kill a person or large numbers of people brutally; **slay** (fml or literary) kill a person or animal; **put down** or **put to sleep** kill a sick or injured animal, especially when done by a vet.

killer n 1 murderer, assassin, slaughterer, executioner, exterminator 2 disease, destroyer, natural disaster, predator

killing n murder, assassination, butchery, slaughter, carnage

killjoy n spoilsport, party pooper (infml), sourpuss (infml), wet blanket (infml), misery (infml) Opposite: merrymaker

kill off v put an end to, stop, halt, destroy, end Opposite: set up

kill time v pass the time, waste time, wait, loiter, twiddle your thumbs

kill yourself v commit suicide, end it all, take your own life, top yourself (slang)

kill yourself laughing v laugh your head off, double over, have hysterics (infml), split your sides (infml), crease up (infml)

kiln n oven, furnace, forge

kilt v pleat, gather, fold, crease, smock

kimono n dressing gown, negligée, peignoir, bathrobe, robe

kin n family, relatives, relations, nearest and dearest

kind adj caring, nice, generous, gentle, compassionate Opposite: inhumane ■ n type, sort, class, variety, category. See COMPARE AND CONTRAST at type, generous.

kind-hearted adj kind, caring, sympathetic, nice, gentle

kind-heartedness n kindness, sympathy, compassion, benevolence, thoughtfulness Opposite: cruelty

kindle v 1 encourage, stimulate, stir up, fire up, promote Opposite: quench 2 spark, light, set alight, burn, ignite Opposite: douse

kindliness n kindness, compassion, sympathy, amiability, gentleness Opposite: cruelty

kindly adj friendly, sympathetic, generous, caring, kind ■ adv gently, compassionately, sympathetically, benevolently, kind-heartedly Opposite: cruelly

kindness n compassion, gentleness, sympathy, kind-heartedness, benevolence Opposite: cruelty

kind of (infml) adv rather, somewhat, fairly, in a way, quite

kindred adj associated, close, like, alike, allied Opposite: dissimilar ■ n 1 kinship, family, kin, blood, ties 2 family, relations, relatives, kinsfolk, nearest and dearest

king n 1 monarch, sovereign, ruler, rajah, tsar Opposite: subject 2 ruler, chief, head, leader, dictator 3 leader, star, superstar, luminary, leading light

kingdom n realm, empire, monarchy, territory, domain

kingly adj magnificent, stately, grand, majestic, regal

kingpin (infml) n key player, leading light, principal, superstar, linchpin

kingship n monarchy, sovereignty, crown, power, authority

king-size adj extra-large, outsize, enormous, huge, giant Opposite: miniature

kink n bend, twist, crook, hook, bow

kinky adj 1 (infml) unusual, strange, idiosyncratic, quirky, unnatural Opposite: conventional 2 crinkled, crinkly, twisty, knotted, twisted Opposite: straight

kinsfolk n family, relatives, relations, kindred, kith and kin

kinship n 1 relationship, connection, tie, link, bond 2 relatedness, understanding, empathy, affiliation, affinity

kinsman (fml) n relative, relation, family member

kinswoman (fml) n relative, relation, family member

kiosk n booth, stall, stand, hut

kip (infml) n nap, sleep, doze, forty winks (infml), snooze (infml)

kismet n fate, fortune, luck, destiny, doom

kiss v 1 peck, smooch (infml), canoodle (infml), osculate (fml), neck (dated) 2 touch, brush, glance, graze, caress ■ n 1 caress, light touch, contact, graze, pat 2 peck, embrace, smacker (infml), smooch (infml), canoodle (infml)

kiss-and-tell (infml) adj revealing, exposing, divulging, sensational, scandalous

kit n 1 tackle, tools, equipment, implements, supplies 2 set of clothes, dress, strip, apparel, costume 3 belongings, things, stuff, baggage, luggage

kitbag n canvas bag, knapsack, backpack, rucksack, duffel bag

kitchen n kitchenette, galley, scullery

kith and kin n relations, family, relations, kinsfolk, flesh and blood

kit out v equip, prepare, provide, fit out, supply

kitsch n 1 vulgarity, tastelessness, sentimentality, ostentation, showiness Opposite: tastefulness 2 trash, frippery, junk (infml), tack (infml) ■ adj tasteless, in poor taste, vulgar, common, loud Opposite: tasteful

kittenish adj 1 playful, frisky, lively, coltish, frolicsome Opposite: staid 2 flirtatious, coy, frisky, cute, coquettish (literary)

kitty n 1 (infml) cat, kitten, puss (infml), pussy (infml), pussycat (infml) 2 fund, pool, stake, ante, pot (US infml)

klaxon n horn, siren, alarm, signal

knack n ability, skill, talent, flair, aptitude. See COMPARE AND CONTRAST at talent.

knapsack n bag, shoulder bag, rucksack, backpack, daypack

knead v massage, rub, work, mould, manipulate

knee-deep *adj* **involved**, occupied, engrossed, absorbed, immersed *Opposite*: uninvolved

knee-jerk *(infml) adj* **1 unthinking**, automatic, reflex, habitual, immediate *Opposite*: considered **2 predictable**, prejudging, prejudiced, biased, dyed-in-the-wool *Opposite*: unpredictable

kneel *v* **go down on your knees**, genuflect, kneel down, kowtow *Opposite*: rise

knees-up *(infml) n* **party**, celebration, festivity, fiesta, bash *(infml)*

knell *n* **toll**, ring, peal, sound, ringing

knick-knack *n* **trinket**, ornament, curio, souvenir, object

knife *v* **stab**, spear, stick, wound, lacerate

WORD BANK
❏ **types of knife** bread knife, butcher's knife, carving knife, clasp knife, cleaver, flick knife, jackknife, paperknife, paring knife, penknife, steak knife, table knife

knife-edge *n* **critical point**, decisive point, turning point, watershed, crisis

knight *n* **cavalier**, caballero, knight-errant, adventurer

knit *v* **1 heal**, mend, set, join, meld **2 unite**, join, interweave, weave, interlace

knob *n* **1 handle**, doorknob, dial, button, handhold **2 lump**, bump, bulge, protuberance, protrusion

knobbly *adj* **lumpy**, bumpy, ridged, bony, protuberant *Opposite*: smooth

knock *v* **1 hit**, bump, collide, bang, thump **2** *(infml)* **criticize**, disparage, condemn, censure, belittle *Opposite*: praise ■ *n* **1 blow**, collision, hit, bump, bang **2** *(infml)* **setback**, blow, upset, misfortune, kick in the teeth

knock about *(infml) v* **1 beat**, hit, mistreat, abuse, batter **2 spend time**, kick about *(infml)*, hang about *(infml)*, hang out *(infml)*, hang around *(infml)*

knockabout *adj* **1 physical**, slapstick, boisterous, rowdy, rough *Opposite*: decorous **2 sturdy**, stout, strong, solid, substantial *Opposite*: flimsy ■ *n* **1 slapstick**, physical comedy, visual comedy, clowning, buffoonery **2** *(infml)* **game**, informal game, friendly, friendly game, knock-up

knock back *(infml) v* **down**, gulp, swallow, drink, put back

knock down *v* **1 floor**, fell, knock over, hit, strike **2 destroy**, demolish, dismantle, bulldoze, pull down *Opposite*: build **3 reduce the price of**, discount, mark down, lower, reduce *Opposite*: put up

knockdown *adj* **cheap**, reduced, low, rockbottom, bargain *Opposite*: inflated

knocker *n* **1 door fixture**, knob, handle, bell, doorbell **2** *(infml)* **critic**, faultfinder, detractor, carper, caviller *Opposite*: admirer

knock off *(infml) v* **1 stop work**, finish, call it a day, down tools, leave *Opposite*: start **2 deduct**, take off, discount, subtract, reduce *Opposite*: add **3 mass-produce**, churn out, knock out, turn out, rattle off

knockoff *(infml) n* **copy**, fake, forgery, reproduction, counterfeit *Opposite*: original

knock-on effect *n* **consequence**, outcome, result, upshot, conclusion

knock out *v* **1 make unconscious**, hit, floor, fell, knock down **2 eliminate**, put out, defeat, overcome, beat **3 surprise**, amaze, astound, impress, overwhelm

knockout *(infml) n* **big success**, hit, sensation, triumph, winner *Opposite*: flop *(infml)*

knock over *v* **1 upset**, topple, overturn, tip over, spill **2** *(infml)* **surprise**, amaze, astound, impress, overwhelm

knock together *(infml) v* **assemble**, improvise, make up, concoct, cobble together

knock up *(infml) v* **improvise**, assemble, make up, concoct, knock together *(infml)*

knoll *n* **hill**, hillock, hummock, mound, mount

knot *n* **1 tie**, loop, reef knot, granny knot **2 lump**, bump, bulge, protuberance, nub **3 cluster**, huddle, clutch, band, collection ■ *v* **join**, tie, bind, tether, secure *Opposite*: untie

knotted *adj* **tied**, tense, secured, taut, tangled *Opposite*: relaxed

knotty *adj* **tricky**, awkward, complicated, complex, thorny *Opposite*: simple

know *v* **1 understand**, be aware of, be knowledgeable about, comprehend, appreciate **2 experience**, go through, undergo **3 be acquainted with**, be familiar with, distinguish, see, have knowledge of

knowable *adj* **intelligible**, comprehensible, understandable, coherent, identifiable *Opposite*: unknowable

know-all *(infml) n* **smart aleck** *(infml)*, clever Dick *(infml)*, clever clogs *(infml)*, smartypants *(infml)*, wiseacre *(infml)*

know backwards *v* **know well**, know back to front, know inside out, know like the back of your hand

know-how *(infml) n* **knowledge**, experience, expertise, savoir-faire, proficiency

knowing *adj* **1 meaningful**, significant, expressive, eloquent, perceptive *Opposite*: innocent **2 deliberate**, intentional, intended, conscious, calculating *Opposite*: unconscious

knowledge *n* **1 acquaintance**, familiarity, awareness, understanding, comprehension *Opposite*: ignorance **2 information**, facts, data, gen *(infml)* **3 wisdom**, learning, education, scholarship, erudition

knowledgeable *adj* **well-informed**, au fait, conversant, familiar, informed *Opposite*: ignorant

known *adj* **recognized**, identified, acknowledged, accepted, branded *Opposite*: unknown

knuckle *n* **protuberance**, projection, lump, prominence, bulge

knuckle down *(infml)* *v* **work hard**, apply yourself, get down to it, get your head down, buckle down *(infml)*

knuckle under *v* **give in**, give up, admit defeat, concede defeat, concede *Opposite*: continue

kohl *n* **eyeliner**, eye pencil, mascara

kosher *(infml) adj* **1 genuine**, authentic, true, real, bona fide *Opposite*: fake **2 lawful**, acceptable, legitimate, aboveboard, proper *Opposite*: unlawful

kowtow *v* **1 kneel**, bow, genuflect, prostrate oneself, salaam *Opposite*: stand up **2 grovel**, be servile, be obsequious, show deference, bow and scrape *Opposite*: lord it over ■ *n* **bow**, genuflection, prostration, salaam, homage

kudos *n* **glory**, praise, credit, fame, admiration *Opposite*: discredit

L

laager *n* **camp**, encampment, settlement, defensive position, shelter

lab *(infml) n* **workroom**, workshop, test bed, test centre, laboratory

label *n* **1 tag**, ticket, sticker, marker, sticky label **2 make**, brand name, trade name, trademark, mark **3 description**, categorization, classification, characterization ■ *v* **1 put a label on**, mark, identify, stamp **2 consider**, regard, describe, categorize, class

laboratory *n* **workroom**, workshop, test bed, test centre, research laboratory

laborious *adj* **arduous**, backbreaking, strenuous, hard, tough *Opposite*: easy. *See* COMPARE AND CONTRAST *at* **hard**.

laboriousness *n* **difficulty**, arduousness, hardness, toughness, tedium *Opposite*: ease

labour *n* **1 work**, toil, hard work, manual labour, efforts **2 workers**, workforce, employees, labour force, hands *Opposite*: management **3 task**, job, chore, effort, exertion **4 childbirth**, delivery, giving birth, contractions, confinement *(dated)* ■ *v* **1 strive**, strain, grind away, endeavour, keep at it *Opposite*: idle **2 struggle**, exert, grapple, wrestle, agonize **3 malfunction**, strain, complain, play up, seize up **4 drag yourself**, stagger, plod, trudge, trail *Opposite*: skip **5 overemphasize**, go on, dwell on, exaggerate, drive home *Opposite*: skim

laboured *adj* **tortured**, tortuous, forced, strenuous, arduous *Opposite*: effortless

labourer *n* **manual worker**, blue-collar worker, hand, workhand, worker

labour force *n* **workforce**, workers, labour, hands, staff

labour under *v* **suffer from**, struggle with, be disadvantaged by, be burdened with, be swayed by

labyrinth *n* **maze**, warren, web, tangle, jumble

labyrinthine *adj* **complex**, convoluted, intricate, complicated, tortuous *Opposite*: straightforward

lace *n* **tie**, shoelace, bootlace, cord ■ *v* **1 do up**, tie up, lace up, fasten *Opposite*: undo **2 spike**, mix, fortify

lacerate *v* **slash**, tear, cut, score, scratch

laceration *n* **cut**, slash, graze, scratch, tear

lack *n* **shortage**, absence, want, dearth, deficiency *Opposite*: surplus ■ *v* **be short of**, not have, be deficient in, want for, need *Opposite*: have

---

COMPARE AND CONTRAST CORE MEANING: an insufficiency or absence of something

lack a complete absence of a particular thing; **shortage** a lack of something that is needed or required; **deficiency** a shortfall in the amount of something necessary, e.g. a particular nutrient in the human body, or an inadequacy in the supply or performance of something; **deficit** the amount by which something falls short of a target amount or level; **want** *or* **dearth** a scarcity or absence of something.

---

lackadaisical *adj* **apathetic**, careless, indifferent, relaxed, half-hearted *Opposite*: enthusiastic

lackey *n* **minion**, lapdog, sycophant, toady, creature

lacking *adj* **missing**, not there, wanting, absent *Opposite*: present

lacking in *adj* **short of**, without, not having, bereft of, devoid of *Opposite*: full of

lacklustre *adj* **dull**, lifeless, dreary, unexciting, uninspiring *Opposite*: dazzling

laconic *adj* **terse**, brief, short, concise, economical *Opposite*: long-winded

lacquer *n* **polish**, varnish, gloss

lacy *adj* **delicate**, lacelike, net, filigree, fine

lad *n* **1 boy**, young man, youngster, youth, teenager *Opposite*: lass **2** *(infml)* **man**, guy, *(infml)*, fella *(infml)*, bloke *(infml)*, chap *(infml)* Opposite: lass

ladder n **1 stepladder**, folding ladder, loft ladder, roof ladder, steps **2 ranking**, tree, table, pecking order, hierarchy ■ v **run**, rip, tear, snag

laddie *(infml) see* **lad**

laddish *(infml) adj* **male**, masculine, macho, sexist, chauvinist

laden *adj* **weighed down**, burdened, overloaded, loaded Opposite: empty

la-di-da *(infml) adj* **affected**, pretentious, snobbish, put-on, full of airs and graces Opposite: common

lady n **woman**, female, matron

lag v **1 drop back**, drop behind, fall back, fall behind, trail Opposite: lead **2 insulate**, wrap, wad, protect, pad ■ n **interval**, wait, delay, intermission, pause

laggard n **straggler**, dawdler, shirker, slacker, idler Opposite: leader

lagging n **insulation**, wadding, padding, sleeve, skin

lagoon n **1 inlet**, creek, cove, bay **2 lake**, pond, pool, loch, lough

lah-di-dah *(infml) see* **la-di-da**

laid-back *(infml) adj* **relaxed**, easygoing, easy, phlegmatic, cool Opposite: tense

lair *(infml)* n **hideout**, den, haunt, retreat, hideaway

laird n **landowner**, lord, landlord, property owner, owner

laissez-faire n **noninterventionism**, nonintervention, noninvolvement, laxity Opposite: intervention ■ *adj* **noninterventionist**, unrestrictive, permissive, freewheeling, lax Opposite: proactive

laity n **1 laypeople**, flock, congregation, worshippers Opposite: clergy **2 nonprofessionals**, outsiders, amateurs, uninitiated

lake n **pond**, lagoon, loch, tarn, water

lakeside n **shore**, waterside, water's edge, bank, land

lama n **monk**, priest, brother, father, clergyman

lambaste v **attack**, upbraid, reprimand, criticize, reprove Opposite: praise

lambent *adj* **brilliant**, scintillating, witty, sharp, rapier-like Opposite: leaden

lament v **mourn**, grieve, weep, cry for, bemoan Opposite: celebrate ■ n **lamentation**, cry, dirge, crying, weeping Opposite: celebration

lamentable *adj* **regrettable**, deplorable, inexcusable, execrable, appalling Opposite: laudable

lamentation n **lament**, dirge, cry, weeping, crying Opposite: celebration

laminate v **cover**, seal, coat, protect, enclose

laminated *adj* **plastic-coated**, coated, covered, bonded, composite

lampoon v **ridicule**, satirize, make fun of, parody, caricature ■ n **satire**, parody, skit, sketch, caricature

lamppost n **streetlight**, streetlamp, light

lance n **spear**, weapon, bayonet, javelin ■ v **cut**, pierce, prick, slice into, slice open

land n **1 earth**, ground, terrain, countryside **2 property**, plot, parcel, lot, acreage **3 homeland**, nation, country, territory ■ v **1 arrive**, set down, alight, come down, touch down Opposite: take off **2 acquire**, get, annex, gain, obtain Opposite: lose

landed *adj* **property-owning**, landowning, wealthy, propertied, rich Opposite: landless

landfall n **1 arrival**, landing, touchdown, docking, mooring **2 land**, dry land, mainland, terra firma, shore

land forces n **army**, ground forces, troops, infantry, soldiers

landholder n **landowner**, landlord, property-owner, proprietor, owner

landing n **1 arrival**, alighting, touchdown, docking, mooring **2 mooring**, pier, jetty, quay, landing stage **3 mezzanine**, half floor, top of the stairs

landing field *see* **landing strip**

landing stage n **jetty**, quay, mooring, landing

landing strip n **runway**, airstrip, airfield, aerodrome, landing field

landlady n **1 property owner**, landowner, landholder, proprietor, owner Opposite: tenant **2 licensee**, proprietor, manager, hotelier, innkeeper

landless *adj* **dispossessed**, evicted, ousted, powerless Opposite: landed

landline n **cable**, line, phone line, wire, link

landlocked *adj* **closed in**, blocked-in, non-coastal, interior Opposite: coastal

landlord n **1 property owner**, landowner, landholder, proprietor, owner Opposite: tenant **2 licensee**, proprietor, manager, hotelier, innkeeper

landmark n **1 marker**, sight, attraction, sign, signpost **2 breakthrough**, milestone, revolution, innovation, benchmark ■ *adj* **milestone**, breakthrough, momentous, revolutionary, innovative Opposite: run-of-the-mill

landmass n **continent**, land, landform, island, mainland

land on your feet v **come out on top**, succeed, get lucky, come through unscathed, find yourself Opposite: fail

landowner n **property owner**, landlord, owner, proprietor, landlady Opposite: tenant

landscape n **1 scenery**, countryside, land, site, scene **2 painting**, picture, watercolour, oil painting, drawing **3 background**, backdrop, circumstances, situation, setting ■ v **design**, model, form, shape, plan out

landslide n **1 avalanche**, landslip, rock fall,

---

mudslide **2 victory**, rout, win, success, triumph

landslip *n* **landslide**, avalanche, rock fall, mudslide

landward *adj* **inland**, inward, inward-looking, inner, innermost

landwards *adv* **inland**, ashore, inwards, in

land with (*infml*) *v* **saddle with**, burden, dump with, encumber, load

lane *n* **traffic lane**, right-hand lane, right lane, fast lane, slow lane

language *n* **1 tongue**, idiom, dialect, parlance, lingo (*infml*) **2 communication**, speech, talking **3 words**, vocabulary, writing, prose, poetry

COMPARE AND CONTRAST CORE MEANING: communication by words

language the human use of spoken or written words as a communication system, or the particular system of communication prevailing in a specific country, nation, or community; **vocabulary** the body of words that make up a particular language; **tongue** a particular language used by a specific country, nation, or community; **dialect** a form of a language spoken in a particular region or by members of a particular social class or profession; **slang** words and expressions used instead of standard terms in casual speech or writing, or by a particular group of people; **jargon** terms associated with a particular specialized activity, profession, or culture, especially terms that are not generally understood by outsiders; **parlance** the style of speech or writing used by people in a particular context or profession; **lingo** (*infml*) the way of speaking associated with a particular, usually specialized, group of people; **-speak** a suffix added to nouns to describe the language used by a particular group of people or in a particular context, suggesting that this way of speaking or writing is obscure or difficult to follow; **-ese** a suffix added to nouns to describe the language associated with a group of people, especially when it resembles jargon.

languid *adj* **unhurried**, relaxed, languorous, lazy, indolent *Opposite*: vigorous

languish *v* **1 suffer**, weaken, fail, flag, deteriorate *Opposite*: thrive **2 decline**, fail, sink, teeter, fade away *Opposite*: thrive **3 pine**, pine away, long for, grieve

languor *n* **tiredness**, listlessness, lethargy, sluggishness, dreaminess *Opposite*: vigour

languorous *adj* **tired**, listless, lethargic, languid, sluggish *Opposite*: vigorous

laniard *see* **lanyard**

lank *adj* **limp**, lifeless, dull, thin, floppy

lanky *adj* **gangling**, gangly, long-legged, leggy, angular *Opposite*: rotund

lanyard *n* **rope**, cord, line, cable, halyard

lap *n* **1 circuit**, tour, round, circle **2 stage**, leg, part, segment, section ■ *v* **lick up**, slurp, lap up, drink

lapdog *n* **minion**, toady, sycophant, lackey, creature

lap of luxury *n* **bed of roses**, life of Riley, life of ease, Easy Street

lapse *n* **1 error**, slip, failure, mistake, blunder **2 interval**, space, break, delay, pause ■ *v* **1 decline**, tumble, descend, drop, fall *Opposite*: rise **2 slip**, tail off, trail off, drift, falter *Opposite*: start up **3 come to an end**, end, fail, give up, stop *Opposite*: renew

lapsed *adj* **failed**, onetime, former, erstwhile, recent *Opposite*: current

lapse into *v* **1 slide into**, slip into, fall into, drift into, resort to *Opposite*: choose **2 revert**, regress, backslide, relapse, fall back *Opposite*: progress

lap up *v* **1 lick up**, slurp up, lap **2 enjoy**, soak up, bask in, love, glory in *Opposite*: hate **3 swallow**, fall for, believe, be fooled by, take in *Opposite*: disbelieve

larceny (*dated*) *n* **theft**, stealing, robbery, thieving, embezzlement

larder *n* **pantry**, cold-room, storeroom, room, cupboard

large *adj* **1 big**, huge, great, sizable, immense *Opposite*: tiny **2 well-built**, outsized, hefty, bulky, ample *Opposite*: small **3 sizable**, considerable, not inconsiderable, significant, substantial *Opposite*: insignificant

large-hearted *adj* **generous**, giving, kind, kindly, kind-hearted *Opposite*: mean-spirited

largely *adv* **mainly**, in the main, mostly, for the most part, principally *Opposite*: particularly

largeness *n* **size**, bulk, expansiveness, mass, extent *Opposite*: smallness

larger-than-life *adj* **flamboyant**, confident, impressive, exaggerated, overstated *Opposite*: understated

large-scale *adj* **major**, important, significant, extensive, sweeping *Opposite*: small-scale

largesse *n* **1 generosity**, charity, liberality, munificence, benevolence *Opposite*: miserliness **2 gifts**, handouts, aid, assistance, donations

lark *n* **game**, joke, prank, caper, high jinks (*infml*)

lark about *v* **fool about**, play the fool, fool around, mess about (*infml*), mess around (*infml*) *Opposite*: behave

lark around *see* **lark about**

lash *n* **1 hit**, whip, blow, stroke, whiplash **2 cat-o'-nine-tails**, cat, whip, belt, switch ■ *v* **1 smash**, pound, beat, impact, bump **2 criticize**, lambaste, upbraid, condemn, slate (*infml*) **3 whip**, flog, flay, thrash, strike **4 shake**, jerk, thrash, twitch, thump **5 tie**, bind, fasten, knot, secure *Opposite*: loosen

lashings *n* **lots**, plenty, loads (*infml*), heaps (*infml*), piles (*infml*) *Opposite*: little

lash out *v* **1** (*infml*) **spend**, fritter, squander, run through, shell out *Opposite*: save **2 attack**, strike out, hit out, let fly, flail around **3 criti-**

cize, lambaste, berate, hit out, tear into *Opposite*: praise

lass *n* girl, miss, young woman, daughter, lassie *(infml) Opposite*: lad

lassie *see* lass

lassitude *n* weariness, listlessness, apathy, lethargy, fatigue *Opposite*: liveliness

lasso *n* noose, rope, loop, tether, riata

last *adj* 1 previous, latter, past, preceding, latest *Opposite*: next 2 final, end, ultimate, closing, concluding *Opposite*: first 3 remaining, surviving, extant, final, sole remaining *Opposite*: original ■ *v* keep, stay fresh, keep going, carry on, go on *Opposite*: die out

last-ditch *adj* eleventh-hour, desperate, emergency, frantic, frenzied

lasting *adj* permanent, long-lasting, long-term, lifelong, eternal *Opposite*: temporary

lastly *adv* finally, last of all, to finish, to conclude, to end *Opposite*: firstly

last minute *n* eleventh hour, final moment, last ditch, last gasp

last-minute *adj* late, tardy, delayed, overdue, belated *Opposite*: prompt

last name *n* surname, family name, name, patronymic, matronymic *Opposite*: given name

last out *v* survive, live, go on, continue, persist *Opposite*: fail

last resort *n* last chance, only hope, last-ditch effort, fallback

last straw *n* final straw, limit, end, breaking point, deciding factor

latch *n* fastener, handle, bolt, key, bar

latch on *(infml) v* understand, grasp, comprehend, get *(infml)*, catch on *(infml)*

latch onto *v* 1 stay with, stick to, fasten onto, befriend, take up with *Opposite*: abandon 2 take to, discover, get into, go in for, pursue

late *adj* 1 delayed, tardy, overdue, belated, unpunctual *Opposite*: early 2 later, delayed, deferred, postponed *Opposite*: early 3 late-night, nighttime, evening, twilight *Opposite*: early 4 dead, much lamented, late lamented, deceased *(fml)*, dear departed *(fml or literary) Opposite*: living 5 last-minute, eleventh-hour, last-ditch, final *Opposite*: early ■ *adv* belatedly, unpunctually, tardily, behind schedule, behind time *Opposite*: early 2 at the last minute, too late, late on, finally, at the end *Opposite*: early 3 at night, in the small hours, in the dead of night, in the evening, after dark *Opposite*: early 4 recently, until recently, lately, of late, latterly. *See* COMPARE AND CONTRAST *at* dead.

latecomer *n* straggler, dawdler, laggard

lately *adv* recently, of late, these days, latterly, currently

latency *n* dormancy, inactivity, potential, expectancy, underdevelopment *Opposite*: expression

lateness *n* tardiness, unpunctuality, delay, belatedness, deferment *Opposite*: promptness

latent *adj* 1 hidden, covert, buried, concealed, invisible *Opposite*: manifest 2 dormant, inactive, lurking, embryonic, underlying

later *adv* later on, in a while, shortly, soon, afterwards *Opposite*: earlier

lateral *adj* side, on the side, adjacent, crossways, horizontal

latest *adj* newest, up-to-the-minute, hottest, state-of-the-art, modern *Opposite*: outdated

latex *n* sap, fluid, liquid

lather *n* 1 foam, suds, froth, bubbles, soapsuds 2 *(infml)* agitation, anxiety, panic, dither, pother *Opposite*: calmness ■ *v* soap, lather up, soap up

latitude *n* 1 parallel, position, location, coordinate *Opposite*: longitude 2 leeway, freedom, autonomy, liberty, room *Opposite*: restriction

latter *adj* last, final, concluding, second, end *Opposite*: former

latter-day *adj* modern, modern-day, contemporary, current *Opposite*: former

latterly *adv* 1 recently, lately, up till now, currently, of late *Opposite*: formerly 2 at the end, towards the end, in the last part, finally *Opposite*: initially

lattice *n* frame, mesh, framework, web, matrix

laud *v* praise, applaud, extol, acclaim, glorify *Opposite*: criticize

laudable *adj* admirable, praiseworthy, creditable, worthy, commendable *Opposite*: despicable

laudatory *adj* admiring, congratulatory, praising, complimentary, approving *Opposite*: damning

laugh *v* chuckle, chortle, guffaw, giggle, snigger *Opposite*: cry ■ *n* 1 chuckle, chortle, guffaw, giggle, hoot 2 *(infml)* fun, joke, teasing, giggle, lark

laughable *adj* pathetic, pitiful, derisory, inadequate, ridiculous *Opposite*: impressive

laugh at *v* sneer, jeer, mock, make fun of, ridicule *Opposite*: respect

laughing stock *n* figure of fun, joke, fool, buffoon, butt

laugh off *v* downplay, trivialize, shrug off, joke about, dismiss *Opposite*: face up to

laugh out of court *v* ridicule, mock, make fun of, scoff at, pour scorn on

laughter *n* happiness, amusement, hilarity, mirth, merriment *Opposite*: sadness

launch *v* 1 dispatch, send off, send, shoot, fire 2 open, start, begin, commence, initiate 3 introduce, present, inaugurate, unveil, reveal 4 hurl, throw, toss, fling, propel ■ *n* presentation, introduction, promotion, unveiling, inauguration

launching pad n **takeoff point**, springboard, start, base, foundation

launch into v **embark on**, get going on, break into, begin, commence

launch out v **1 start**, start afresh, start anew, start out, begin Opposite: finish **2** (infml) **treat yourself**, indulge yourself, spend money like water, go mad, splash out Opposite: stint

launder v **1 wash**, clean, dry-clean, valet **2 legalize**, filter, clean, decontaminate

laundry n **washing**, wash, clean washing, dirty washing

laurels n **success**, glory, honour, achievements

lavish adj **1 abundant**, plentiful, sumptuous, copious, prolific Opposite: scanty **2 extravagant**, profligate, wasteful, unrestrained, excessive Opposite: frugal ■ v **heap**, pour, smother, cover, load Opposite: deprive

law n **1 rule**, regulation, decree, act, edict **2 principle**, theory, formula, rule

law-abiding adj **honest**, straight, upright, upstanding, peaceable Opposite: crooked (infml)

law and order n **1 law enforcement**, keeping the peace, order, orderliness, policing Opposite: crime **2 stability**, harmony, peace, peace and quiet, peacefulness Opposite: unrest

lawbreaker n **criminal**, felon, wrongdoer, convict, offender

lawful adj **legal**, legalized, legitimate, official, endorsed Opposite: unlawful. See COMPARE AND CONTRAST at **legal**.

lawgiver see **lawmaker**

lawless adj **unruly**, anarchic, uncontrolled, unregulated, ungovernable Opposite: law-abiding

lawlessness n **anarchy**, chaos, disorder, unruliness, mayhem (infml) Opposite: order

lawmaker n **legislator**, policymaker, lawgiver

lawsuit n **court case**, proceedings, litigation, process

lawyer n **legal representative**, notary, solicitor, barrister, trial lawyer

lax adj **1 lenient**, soft, tolerant, permissive, accepting **2 negligent**, slack, careless, slipshod, sloppy Opposite: strict **3 limp**, loose, flaccid, relaxed, floppy Opposite: tense

laxity n **1 leniency**, tolerance, permissiveness, softness, forbearance (fml) Opposite: severity **2 carelessness**, negligence, sloppiness, slackness, indifference Opposite: vigilance

laxness see **laxity**

lay v **put down**, place, rest, put, arrange Opposite: pick up ■ adj **untrained**, amateur, nonprofessional, uninitiated, unqualified Opposite: professional

lay about v **strike out**, hit out, thrash about, flail around, hit

layabout n **slacker**, shirker, timewaster, idler, lounger Opposite: go-getter (infml)

lay bare v **reveal**, explain, show, expose, display Opposite: cover up

lay before v **set before**, present, put before, submit, set out Opposite: withdraw

lay bets v **bet**, gamble, wager, stake money on

lay claim to v **appropriate**, claim, stake a claim to, demand, insist on Opposite: renounce

lay down v **1 put down**, lay aside, put aside, give up, surrender Opposite: take up **2 decree**, set down, put down, formulate, rule

lay down the law v **order**, boss, order around, boss around, dictate to

layer n **1 level**, tier, seam, gradation, stratum (fml) **2 coating**, coat, sheet, film, deposit

layette n **baby clothes**, babywear, baby linen, nursery equipment

lay in v **store**, acquire, hoard, save, stock up Opposite: use up

lay into v **1** (infml) **criticize**, attack, lambaste, get at, round on Opposite: praise **2 hit**, attack, beat, thump, thrash Opposite: protect

lay it on v **exaggerate**, embroider, embellish, overdo, pile on Opposite: understate

lay it on the line (infml) v **be honest**, be direct, be blunt, be straight, be clear Opposite: lie

lay off v **1 dismiss**, suspend, make redundant, sack, let go Opposite: take on **2** (infml) **stop**, cease, desist, discontinue, cut out Opposite: continue

layoff n **1 dismissal**, redundancy, downsizing, rationalization, streamlining **2 unemployment**, career break, inactivity, rest, joblessness Opposite: employment

lay on v **provide**, supply, make available, organize, cater

lay out v **1 explain**, present, describe, outline, set out **2 design**, plan, arrange, organize, prepare

layout n **plan**, design, arrangement, outline, draft

lay to rest v **bury**, entomb, inter (fml)

laze v **idle**, lounge, loaf, bask, relax Opposite: toil

laze about see **laze**

laze around see **laze**

laziness n **idleness**, lethargy, indolence, languor, sluggishness Opposite: energy

lazy adj **indolent**, idle, lethargic, languid, sluggish Opposite: energetic

lazybones (infml) n **layabout**, slacker, shirker, loafer, idler Opposite: worker

leach v **leak**, filter, percolate, trickle, seep

lead v **1 guide**, indicate, direct, escort, pilot Opposite: follow **2 be in charge of**, run, control, command, direct **3 be in the lead**, take the lead, be the forerunner, be in front, have an advantage Opposite: trail

■ *n* **1 leader**, spearhead, leading light, trailblazer, groundbreaker **2 advantage**, advance start, head start, flying start **3 precedent**, example, style, pattern, model **4 clue**, tip, indication, information, hint **5 leash**, chain, tether, restraint, rope ■ *adj* **principal**, chief, main, central, prime. *See* COMPARE AND CONTRAST *at* **guide**.

lead astray *v* **mislead**, misinform, lead on, hoodwink, delude

leaden *adj* **1 steely**, ashen, dull, grim, dark *Opposite*: bright **2 heavy**, ponderous, weighty, sluggish, stodgy *(infml) Opposite*: light **3 laboured**, slow, sluggish, dragging, crawling *Opposite*: quick **4 lifeless**, dull, dreary, flat, monotonous *Opposite*: lively

leader *n* **1 guide**, director, organizer, mentor, guru *Opposite*: disciple **2 spearhead**, leading light, trailblazer, groundbreaker, lead **3 head**, chief, manager, superior, principal *Opposite*: underling

leadership *n* **management**, control, guidance, headship, direction

lead-in *n* **introduction**, preamble, preface, prelude, preliminary *Opposite*: conclusion

leading *adj* **prominent**, foremost, important, principal, chief *Opposite*: secondary

leading article *n* **editorial**, leader, opinion, view, comment

leading edge *n* **forefront**, cutting edge, sharp end, vanguard, avant-garde

leading light *n* **big name**, top name, star, superstar, celebrity *Opposite*: unknown

lead off *v* **begin**, start, start off, commence, open *Opposite*: end

lead on *v* **entice**, lure, tempt, seduce, attract

lead the way *v* **blaze a trail**, set a trend, originate, break new ground, break through

lead time *n* **notice**, run-up, advance notice, warning, notification

lead to *v* **cause**, bring about, make possible, initiate, set in motion

lead up to *v* **1 prepare for**, prepare the way, prepare the ground, sow the seeds, gear up **2 approach**, come to, get to, get round to

leaf *n* **1 foliage**, greenery, sprig, spray, frond **2 page**, sheet, folio, side **3 sheet**, foil, plate, lamina, film **4 flap**, foldout, projection, section, piece

leaflet *n* **booklet**, brochure, pamphlet, flier, handbill

leaf through *v* **look through**, flick through, skim, browse, flip

leafy *adj* **green**, verdant, lush, luxuriant, rank *Opposite*: bare

league *n* **association**, group, union, confederation, club

leak *n* **1 escape**, seepage, leakage, outflow, drip **2 disclosure**, betrayal, giveaway, revelation, release ■ *v* **1 seep**, escape, pour out, trickle, drip **2 disclose**, reveal, give away,

betray, uncover *Opposite*: keep under wraps *(infml)*

leakage *n* **leak**, escape, seepage, outflow, drip

leak out *v* **emerge**, get out, slip out, come out, come to light

leakproof *adj* **watertight**, waterproof, sealed, hermetic, rainproof *Opposite*: leaky

leaky *adj* **1 leaking**, holey, sieve-like, dripping, drippy *Opposite*: watertight **2** *(infml)* **unsecured**, unsafe, indiscreet, loose, lax *Opposite*: secure

lean *v* **1 bend**, bend over, bend forwards, incline, tilt **2 rest**, prop, support, place, put **3 tend**, incline, be disposed, favour, prefer ■ *adj* **thin**, slender, slim, wiry, sinewy *Opposite*: stout. *See* COMPARE AND CONTRAST *at* **thin**.

leaning *n* **inclination**, tendency, bent, affinity, preference *Opposite*: aversion

lean on *v* **1 depend on**, rely on, trust, count on **2** *(infml)* **intimidate**, pressurize, put pressure on, oblige, coerce

leap *v* **1 jump**, bound, dive, soar, fly **2 increase**, rise, shoot up, go up, jump *Opposite*: drop ■ *n* **1 bound**, jump, dive, spring, hop **2 rise**, increase, jump, hike, climb *Opposite*: drop

leap at *v* **jump at**, seize, grab, clutch, accept *Opposite*: baulk

leapfrog *v* **1 jump**, vault, leap, bound, spring **2 advance**, shoot ahead, get ahead, pull ahead, catapult **3 overtake**, pass, leave behind, outstrip, leave standing **4 circumvent**, evade, avoid, sidestep, bypass

leap out *v* **stand out**, stick out, jump out, hit somebody in the face, impact

learn *v* **1 study**, absorb, pick up, acquire, cram *(infml) Opposite*: teach **2 find out**, hear, discover, realize, gather

learned *adj* **erudite**, educated, scholarly, academic, cultured *Opposite*: uneducated

learner *n* **beginner**, apprentice, student, pupil, novice *Opposite*: expert

learning *n* **knowledge**, education, erudition, scholarship, culture *Opposite*: ignorance

lease *v* **rent**, rent out, hire, hire out, let

lease out *see* **lease**

leash *n* **lead**, chain, tether, string, rope

least *adj* **smallest**, slightest, tiniest, minimum *Opposite*: most

leastways *(infml) adv* **in any case**, anyway, at least, at any rate, in spite of

leastwise *see* **leastways**

leave *v* **1 go away**, depart, go, run off, abscond *Opposite*: stay **2 put down**, set down, put, put away, place *Opposite*: remove **3 bequeath**, pass on, hand down, donate, entrust *Opposite*: withhold **4 result in**, cause, bring about, effect *(fml)* **5 delay**, defer, put off, avoid, hold off *Opposite*: bring forward **6 abandon**, desert, renounce, forsake, ditch *(infml) Opposite*: stand by **7 set aside**, allow, give, permit, assign ■ *n* **1 holiday**, sabbatical time off, leave of absence, vacation **2** *(fml)* **permission**, consent, authority, authorization, dispensation

leave alone *v* **let alone**, let be, leave well enough alone, pay no attention, ignore *Opposite*: harass

leave be *see* **leave alone**

leave behind *v* **1 overtake**, outstrip, outpace, surpass, leave standing *Opposite*: fall behind **2 put behind you**, escape, evade, get away from, put to one side *Opposite*: suffer **3 abandon**, get rid of, cast off, leave, forget *Opposite*: retain

leave cold *v* **bore**, do nothing for, bore rigid, bore stiff, bore to tears *Opposite*: inspire

leave in peace *see* **leave alone**

leave much to be desired *v* **be unsatisfactory**, disappoint, let down, not make the grade, fall short *Opposite*: pass muster

leave no stone unturned *v* **do all you can**, do your utmost, pull out all the stops, spare no effort, try everything

leave of absence *n* **sabbatical**, time off, time out, leave

leave off *v* **stop**, desist, cease, refrain, discontinue *Opposite*: carry on

leave out *v* **omit**, exclude, count out, ignore, overlook *Opposite*: include

leavings *n* **leftovers**, scraps, remnants, remains, castoffs

lecherous *adj* **lewd**, lustful, lascivious, libidinous, lusty

lectern *n* **bookstand**, reading stand, reading desk, stand, bookrest

lecture *n* **1 talk**, address, sermon, speech, homily **2 reprimand**, dressing-down, scolding, tongue-lashing, ticking-off *(infml)* ▪ *v* **1 teach**, address, instruct, talk, hold forth **2 harangue**, criticize, scold, reprove, censure

lecturer *n* **1 speaker**, public speaker, speechmaker, orator, presenter **2 teacher**, professor, instructor, academic, don

ledge *n* **1 shelf**, sill, niche, ridge, rack **2 outcrop**, ridge, sill, shelf, foothold

ledger *n* **book**, account book, record book, record, register

lee *n* **shelter**, cover, protection, shadow, shade

leer *v* **smirk**, ogle, eye, sneer, stare ▪ *n* **sneer**, grimace, smirk, evil eye, stare

leery *(infml) adj* **suspicious**, wary, doubting, doubtful, circumspect *Opposite*: confident

lees *n* **dregs**, remains, leftovers, remnants

leeward *adj* **protected**, sheltered, shielded *Opposite*: upwind

leeway *n* **scope**, flexibility, margin, freedom, latitude

left-hand *adj* **left**, leftward, port *Opposite*: right-hand

left-handed *adj* **anticlockwise**, right to left, circular, round, helical *Opposite*: right-handed

leftover *n* **relic**, hangover, vestige, remnant, remainder

leftovers *n* **scraps**, remains, what's left, table scraps, leavings

left-wing *adj* **progressive**, reformist, leftist, socialist, communist *Opposite*: right-wing

left-winger *n* **progressive**, reformist, leftist, socialist, communist *Opposite*: right-winger

leg *n* **1 limb**, foreleg, member, extremity, hind leg **2 pole**, foot, support, stand, base **3 stage**, phase, lap, step, part

WORD BANK

❏ **parts of a leg or foot** ankle, big toe, calf, haunch, heel, instep, knee, lap, little toe, shin, sole, thigh, toe, toenail

legacy *n* **1 bequest**, inheritance, heirloom, heritage, birthright **2 relic**, hangover, vestige, remnant, remainder ▪ *adj* **superseded**, obsolete, discontinued, outdated, antiquated *Opposite*: up-to-date

legal *adj* **lawful**, permissible, permitted, allowed, authorized *Opposite*: illegal

COMPARE AND CONTRAST CORE MEANING: describes something that is permitted, recognized, or required by law
legal permitted, recognized, or required by law; **lawful** a less common word meaning legal; **decriminalized** no longer categorized as a criminal offence; **legalized** previously categorized as illegal and now declared legal; **legitimate** complying with the law, or under the law; **licit** *(fml)* a rarely used word meaning legal.

legalese *n* **jargon**, cant, mumbo jumbo *(infml)*, gobbledegook *(infml)*

legality *n* **validity**, lawfulness, rightfulness, legitimacy *Opposite*: illegality

legalization *n* **ratification**, authorization, certification, validation, endorsement *Opposite*: criminalization

legalize *v* **decriminalize**, authorize, sanction, allow, permit *Opposite*: prohibit

legate *n* **representative**, envoy, ambassador, emissary, diplomat

legend *n* **1 fable**, myth, tale, lore, folklore **2 star**, celebrity, big name, icon, personality *Opposite*: unknown

legendary *adj* **1 fabled**, mythical, mythological, imaginary, fabulous *Opposite*: real-life **2 famous**, renowned, well-known, celebrated, great *Opposite*: unknown

legible *adj* **clear**, readable, intelligible, decipherable, understandable *Opposite*: illegible

legion *n* **multitude**, host, team, crowd, throng

legislate *v* **enact**, pass, establish, lay down the law, decree

legislation *n* **1 lawmaking**, lawgiving, legislature, regulation **2 laws**, legal code, body of law, bill, rule

legislative *adj* lawmaking, parliamentary, governmental, judicial, jurisdictive

legislature *n* government, parliament, administration, senate, assembly

legit *(slang) see* legitimate

legitimacy *n* 1 legality, lawfulness, validity, rightfulness, justice 2 acceptability, rightfulness, correctness 3 sincerity, genuineness, realness, authenticity, validity

legitimate *adj* 1 lawful, rightful, valid, legal, legit *(slang) Opposite:* unlawful 2 reasonable, acceptable, justifiable, logical, valid *Opposite:* unreasonable 3 genuine, sincere, real, valid, authentic *Opposite:* spurious

leg-pull *(infml) n* joke, practical joke, deception, trick, tease

legroom *n* room, space, freedom, elbowroom *(infml)*

legume *n* leguminous plant, pulse, pea, bean

legwarmer *n* sock, stocking, legging, gaiter, puttee

legwork *(infml) n* research, preparation, homework, groundwork, spadework

lei *n* garland, wreath, chaplet, coronet, circlet

leisure *n* free time, spare time, time off, leisure time, R and R *Opposite:* work

leisure centre *n* sports centre, gymnasium, sports club, swimming pool, gym *(infml)*

leisured *adj* rich, wealthy, affluent, moneyed, propertied *Opposite:* poor

leisurely *adj* unhurried, easy, relaxed, restful, relaxing *Opposite:* frantic

leisurewear *n* sportswear, casualwear, casual clothes, casuals, mufti

leitmotif *n* motif, theme, strand, element, topic

lemming *n* conformist, sheep, imitator, follower, copycat *(infml) Opposite:* nonconformist

lemon *n* 1 lemonade, bitter lemon, fruit juice, squash, cordial 2 *(infml)* failure, dud *(infml)*, nonstarter *(infml)*, washout *(infml)*, flop *(infml) Opposite:* winner

lemony *adj* lemon-flavoured, lemon, citrus *Opposite:* sweet

lend *v* 1 loan, advance, give, offer *Opposite:* borrow 2 provide, offer, give, impart, add *Opposite:* take away

lend a hand *v* help, help out, give somebody a hand, do your bit, assist *Opposite:* hinder

lend an ear *v* listen, pay attention, hang on the words of, listen up *(slang)*

lender *n* giver, moneylender, financier, creditor, investor

length *n* 1 distance, span, measurement, extent, dimension 2 duration, time, time span, extent 3 piece, strip, segment, section, bit

lengthen *v* grow, increase, extend, elongate, stretch *Opposite:* shorten

lengthways *adv* lengthwise, along, end to end, sideways, laterally *Opposite:* endways

lengthwise *see* lengthways

lengthy *adj* long, long-lasting, extensive, prolonged, protracted *Opposite:* brief

lenience *see* leniency

leniency *n* clemency, mercy, compassion, humanity, tolerance *Opposite:* severity

lenient *adj* compassionate, merciful, humane, tolerant, indulgent *Opposite:* severe

leonine *adj* impressive, imposing, majestic, proud, dignified

leotard *n* one-piece, body, body stocking, all-in-one, bodysuit *(US)*

leper *n* outcast, untouchable, pariah, outsider, exile

leprechaun *n* sprite, elf, imp, pixie, dwarf

lèse majesté *see* lese majesty

lese majesty *n* 1 disrespect, disregard, dishonour, contempt, disdain *Opposite:* respect 2 treason, high treason, sedition, betrayal, treachery *Opposite:* loyalty

lesion *n* wound, injury, cut, graze, scratch

less *adj* a smaller amount of, not as much of, a lesser amount of, a reduced amount of *Opposite:* more ■ *prep* minus, take away, with a reduction of, excluding *Opposite:* plus

lessen *v* diminish, decrease, decline, tail off, ease off *Opposite:* increase

lesser *adj* smaller, slighter, minor, reduced *Opposite:* greater

lesson *n* 1 class, lecture, session, tutorial, seminar 2 example, message, moral, warning, object lesson

lest *(fml) conj* in case, for fear that, so as not to

let *v* 1 allow, give permission, permit, agree to, consent to *Opposite:* forbid 2 rent, rent out, lease, lease out, hire ■ *n* 1 *(fml)* problem, difficulty, hindrance, impediment, complication 2 lease, tenancy, occupancy, rent, agreement

let alone *see* let be

let be *v* leave alone, leave in peace, leave be, leave off, leave well enough alone *Opposite:* pester

let down *v* 1 lower, drop, sink, let fall, move down *Opposite:* raise 2 deflate, empty, drain *Opposite:* inflate 3 disappoint, fail, abandon, betray, disillusion 4 lengthen, extend, let out, expand, enlarge *Opposite:* take up

letdown *n* disappointment, anticlimax, failure, disillusionment, discouragement *Opposite:* success

let drop *v* disclose, reveal, divulge, let slip, let out

let fly *v* 1 lose your temper, explode, rage, hit the roof *(infml)*, see red *(infml) Opposite:* keep your cool *(infml)* 2 throw, fling, toss, hurl, pitch

let go *v* release, liberate, set free, free, set loose *Opposite:* retain

lethal adj **deadly**, fatal, mortal, poisonous, toxic. See COMPARE AND CONTRAST at **deadly**.

lethargic adj **sluggish**, tired, weary, exhausted, lacklustre Opposite: energetic

lethargy n **sluggishness**, tiredness, weariness, exhaustion, fatigue Opposite: energy

let in v **admit**, allow in, open the door to, show in, receive Opposite: keep out

let in for (infml) v **involve in**, entangle in, ensnare in, mix up in, entrap in Opposite: get out of

let in on v **make aware of**, tell, acquaint with, reveal to, disclose to Opposite: keep from

let into v 1 **let in on**, fill in on, share, tell, inform of Opposite: keep from 2 **admit to**, welcome into, usher into, take into, show into 3 **accept into**, receive into, allow into, enlist into, enrol into

let know v **tell**, inform, advise, alert, warn Opposite: keep in the dark

let loose v **let out**, let go, set free, set loose, release Opposite: confine

let off v 1 **excuse**, pardon, release, free, acquit Opposite: punish 2 **fire**, explode, detonate, set off, shoot

let on v 1 **admit**, disclose, divulge, reveal, declare Opposite: conceal 2 **pretend**, make out, claim, profess, act Opposite: come clean (infml)

let out v 1 **emit**, give, utter, release, produce Opposite: suppress 2 **free**, let go, release, set free, let loose Opposite: keep in 3 **enlarge**, expand, extend, widen, broaden Opposite: take in 4 **let slip**, reveal, divulge, disclose, blurt out Opposite: conceal

let-out n **loophole**, escape clause, way out, technicality, window

let pass v 1 **ignore**, let go, overlook, let ride, pay no attention to Opposite: pick up on (infml) 2 **let through**, let by, let past, stand aside for, make way for Opposite: bar

let ride v **ignore**, close your eyes to, turn a blind eye to, let go, let pass Opposite: stop

let slip v 1 **reveal**, disclose, divulge, give away, let out Opposite: hold back 2 **let go**, lose, lose track of, lose sight of, take your eyes off Opposite: keep an eye on

letter n 1 **communication**, note, message, memo, dispatch 2 **character**, symbol, sign, capital, capital letter

letterbox n **post office box**, postbox, mailbox (US)

letter card n **note card**, notelet, note, card

lettered adj **educated**, knowledgeable, cultured, cultivated, literary Opposite: uneducated

lettering n **writing**, print, calligraphy, letters, inscription

letters n **literature**, culture, cultivation, knowledge, education

let the cat out of the bag v **talk**, let on, tell a

secret, tell, spill the beans (infml) Opposite: keep mum (infml)

let through v **make way for**, stand aside for, clear the way for, let pass, let past Opposite: block

let up v **ease off**, ease, ease up, lessen, slacken Opposite: intensify

let-up (infml) n **respite**, break, rest, relief, interval Opposite: intensification

let up on v **ease up on**, ease off on, slack off on, soften up on, spare

let your hair down (infml) v **relax**, have a good time, enjoy yourself, let yourself go, have fun

let yourself go v 1 **unwind**, relax, mellow, let your hair down, throw caution to the winds 2 **give up**, lose heart, go downhill, lose your self-respect, go to the dogs (infml)

levee n 1 **embankment**, earthwork, bank, wall, rampart 2 **reception**, royal reception, royal function, court reception, court function

level adj 1 **flat**, smooth, flat as a pancake, even, dead flat Opposite: bumpy 2 **horizontal**, parallel with the ground, even, flat Opposite: slanted 3 **equal**, neck and neck, side by side, close, near ■ n 1 **height**, altitude, stage, point, plane 2 **intensity**, quantity, concentration, amount, degree ■ v 1 **flatten**, smooth, steamroll, press flat, even out 2 **aim**, direct, point, turn 3 **demolish**, knock down, raze, blow up, raze to the ground Opposite: rebuild

level crossing n **railway crossing**, crossing, grade crossing (US)

level-headed adj **sensible**, calm, sound, even-tempered, reliable Opposite: rash

level-headedness n **composure**, equanimity, calmness, good sense, reliability Opposite: rashness

levelly adv 1 **calmly**, steadily, sensibly, evenly, equably Opposite: excitedly 2 **smoothly**, flatly, evenly Opposite: unevenly

level off v **stabilize**, even out, settle, settle down, smooth out

level out v **settle down**, stabilize, settle, even out, even up

level pegging n **equality**, parity, same score, tie, draw Opposite: inequality

lever n **handle**, control, regulator, knob

leverage n **influence**, power, force, control, weight

leviathan n **giant**, colossus, behemoth, monster

levitate v **float**, rise up, ascend, drift up, soar Opposite: sink

levitation n **defiance of gravity**, rising, raising, hovering, floating

levity n **lightheartedness**, cheerfulness, humour, lightness, flippancy Opposite: gravity

levy v **impose**, tax, collect, put, charge ■ n **tax**, rates, toll, duty, tariff

lewd adj **salacious**, obscene, crude, vulgar, indecent

lexical *adj* **verbal**, word, vocabulary, philological, etymological

lexicon *n* **1 vocabulary**, vocabulary list, word list, glossary, dictionary **2 language**, lexis, idiolect

ley *n* **1 grassland**, pasture, pastureland, pasturage, grazing **2 path**, pathway, footpath, bridle path, track

liability *n* **1 legal responsibility**, obligation, accountability, responsibility, charge **2 disadvantage**, problem, burden, millstone, jinx

liable *adj* **1 legally responsible**, accountable, answerable, responsible *Opposite*: unaccountable **2 likely**, apt, predisposed, prone *Opposite*: unlikely

liaise *v* **act as a go-between**, communicate, link, bridge, mediate

liaison *n* **link**, connection, contact, cooperation, relationship

liar *n* **deceiver**, fast talker, perjurer, fibber *(infml)*, storyteller *(infml)*

libation *n* **1 drink**, alcoholic drink, potion, brew *(infml)*, bevvy *(slang)* **2 offering**, oblation, offertory, sacrifice, tribute

libel *n* **defamation**, vilification, slander, smear, denigration *Opposite*: praise ■ *v* **defame**, vilify, sully, tarnish, malign *Opposite*: praise. *See* COMPARE AND CONTRAST *at* **malign**.

libellous *adj* **defamatory**, vilifying, slanderous, unfounded *Opposite*: admiring

liberal *adj* **1 open-minded**, broad-minded, moderate, noninterventionist, freethinking *Opposite*: narrow-minded **2 generous**, copious, abundant, profuse, substantial *Opposite*: meagre. *See* COMPARE AND CONTRAST *at* **generous**.

liberalism *n* **tolerance**, broad-mindedness, open-mindedness, moderation, freethinking *Opposite*: narrow-mindedness

liberalize *v* **relax**, slacken, loosen, ease up, open *Opposite*: tighten

liberate *v* **release**, free, set free, unshackle, unfetter *Opposite*: imprison

liberated *adj* **unconventional**, open-minded, freethinking, modern, enlightened *Opposite*: unenlightened

liberation *n* **freedom**, liberty, release, discharge, emancipation *Opposite*: captivity

liberator *n* **deliverer**, saviour, emancipator, releaser *Opposite*: captor

liberty *n* **1 freedom**, independence, autonomy, emancipation, liberation *Opposite*: captivity **2 right**, freedom, authorization, authority, permission *Opposite*: suppression

libidinous *adj* **lustful**, lecherous, lusty, lascivious, salacious

library *n* **collection**, archive, books, papers, records

librettist *n* **libretto writer**, lyricist, songwriter, writer, author

licence *n* **1 certificate**, authorization, warrant, pass, card **2 excess**, abandon, lawlessness, unrestraint, immoderation *(fml)* **3 freedom**, liberty, carte blanche, authority, permission

license *v* **certify**, permit, allow, authorize, accredit

licensed *adj* **approved**, qualified, certified, accredited, registered

licentiate *n* **licence holder**, licensee, certified professional, qualified practitioner

licentious *adj* **immoral**, degenerate, decadent, dissipated, depraved

licit *adj* **lawful**, legitimate, legal, valid, right *Opposite*: illegal. *See* COMPARE AND CONTRAST *at* **legal**.

lick *(infml)* *v* **defeat**, conquer, get the better of, overcome, thrash

lickety-split *(infml)* *adv* **quickly**, fast, at high speed, at a rate of knots, at a lick *(infml)* *Opposite*: sluggishly

licking *(infml)* *n* **trouncing**, thrashing, drubbing, hammering *(infml)*, pasting *(infml)*

lick your lips *v* **relish**, salivate, drool, anticipate, await

lid *n* **top**, cover, cap, closure

lido *n* **1 outdoor pool**, outdoor swimming pool, open-air pool, public swimming pool **2 public beach**, bathing beach, beach

lie *v* **1 recline**, stretch out, lounge, lie down, slouch **2 be positioned**, be arranged, be placed, be situated, sit **3 remain**, rest, stay, be, stop **4 tell lies**, tell untruths, perjure yourself, tell stories, be economical with the truth *Opposite*: tell the truth ■ *n* **untruth**, falsehood, fabrication, white lie, fib *(infml)* *Opposite*: truth

COMPARE AND CONTRAST CORE MEANING: something that is not true

lie a false statement made deliberately; **untruth** something that is presented as being true but is actually false; **falsehood** a lie or an untruth; **fabrication** an invented statement, story, or account devised with intent to deceive; **fib** *(infml)* an insignificant harmless lie; **white lie** a minor harmless lie, usually told to avoid hurting somebody's feelings.

lie about *see* **lie around**

lie around *(infml)* *v* **1 laze**, laze about, lounge around, flop about, sit around **2 be scattered about**, be all over the place, clutter up the place, be distributed, litter

lie back *v* **recline**, stretch out, lounge, sprawl, relax

lie down *v* **recline**, rest, stretch out, relax, lounge *Opposite*: stand up

lie-down *(infml)* *n* **sleep**, nap, rest, doze, snooze *(infml)*

lie in *(infml)* *v* **sleep late**, stay in bed, get up late, rise late

lie-in *(infml)* *n* **late sleep**, late rise, rest, doze, long sleep

lie in wait v **lurk**, hide, conceal yourself, ambush, prowl

lie off v **remain near**, remain close, stay near, stay close, lie near

lie of the land (infml) n **general state**, general situation, prospect, state of affairs, picture

life n **1 existence**, being, living Opposite: death **2 lifetime**, life span, life cycle, life expectancy, natural life **3 verve**, vivacity, animation, energy, excitement

life-and-death adj **critical**, crucial, vital, pivotal, paramount Opposite: unimportant

lifeblood n **essential**, essence, quintessence, sine qua non, necessity

life cycle n **life span**, development, maturation, growth

life expectancy n **life span**, lifetime, allotted span, natural life

lifeguard n **rescuer**, beach attendant, swimming pool attendant, pool attendant, lifesaver (infml)

lifeless adj **1 dead**, unconscious, unresponsive, unmoving, inert Opposite: alive **2 unexciting**, dull, uninteresting, tedious, listless Opposite: animated. See COMPARE AND CONTRAST at dead.

lifelike adj **realistic**, natural, believable, convincing, credible Opposite: unrealistic

lifeline n **salvation**, link, help, support, helping hand

lifelong adj **enduring**, all-time, permanent, ultimate, lasting Opposite: temporary

life-or-death see **life-and-death**

life-size adj **full-scale**, full-size, actual size Opposite: miniature

life span n **natural life**, lifetime, life cycle, life expectancy, life

lifestyle n **way of life**, standard of living, existence, routine, life

life's work n **achievement**, accomplishment, success, attainment

life-threatening adj **dangerous**, serious, severe, grave, incurable

lifetime n **1 life**, time, life span, natural life, life cycle **2 era**, generation, time, period, epoch **3** (infml) **days**, eternity (infml), forever (infml), ages (infml), donkey's years (infml)

lift v **1 winch up**, haul up, elevate, boost, raise **2 revoke**, cancel, take back, relax, rescind Opposite: impose **3 lighten**, buoy up, brighten, elate, uplift **4** (infml) **steal**, walk off with, help yourself, pocket, take ■ n **boost**, revitalization, tonic, encouragement, kick (infml)

ligature n **1 cord**, string, rope, tie, line **2** (fml) **bond**, connection, link, linkage, union

light n **glow**, beam, brightness, luminosity, daylight Opposite: darkness ■ adj **1 bright**, sunny, sunlit, well-lit Opposite: dark **2 pastel**, subtle, neutral, fair, pale Opposite: deep **3 weightless**, buoyant, fluffy, insub-

stantial, frothy Opposite: heavy **4 gentle**, delicate, soft, noiseless, featherlike Opposite: heavy **5 nimble**, graceful, dainty, elegant, agile Opposite: awkward **6 carefree**, happy, cheerful, untroubled, joyful Opposite: oppressive **7 easy**, manageable, undemanding, simple, effortless Opposite: demanding **8 entertaining**, lightweight, fun, frivolous, amusing Opposite: sombre ■ v **set alight**, set on fire, ignite, strike, set fire to Opposite: extinguish

WORD BANK

❏ **types of light** arc lamp, chandelier, floodlight, fluorescent lamp, footlights, headlight, hurricane lamp, lamp, lamppost, lantern, LED, light bulb, neon light, nightlight, penlight, searchlight, spotlight, streetlamp, streetlight, sunlamp, torch, torchlight, traffic light, uplighter

light-coloured adj **pale**, light, pastel, subtle, fair

lighten v **1 ease**, lessen, alleviate, reduce, lift Opposite: overload **2 cheer up**, improve, lift, refresh, buoy up Opposite: depress

lighten up (infml) v **relax**, take it easy, loosen up, unwind, cool it (infml)

lightface adj **faint**, light Opposite: boldface

light-fingered adj **thieving**, kleptomaniacal, larcenous, dishonest, sticky-fingered (infml)

light-footed adj **nimble**, graceful, dainty, elegant, agile Opposite: clumsy

lightheaded adj **dizzy**, faint, giddy, woozy, unsteady

lighthearted adj **1 carefree**, happy-go-lucky, happy, cheerful, cheery Opposite: troubled **2 cheerful**, jokey, cheery, funny, bright Opposite: gloomy **3 enjoyable**, entertaining, amusing, diverting, fun Opposite: serious

lighting n **illumination**, light, lights

light into (infml) v **attack**, tear into, set upon, lay into, let have it Opposite: defend

lightly adv **1 gently**, softly, delicately, imperceptibly, quietly Opposite: heavily **2 flippantly**, frivolously, jokily, informally, casually Opposite: seriously **3 nimbly**, gracefully, trippingly, adeptly, dexterously Opposite: awkwardly

light-minded adj **frivolous**, silly, foolish, vacuous, inane Opposite: serious-minded

lightness n **1 weightlessness**, buoyancy, fluffiness, frothiness, flimsiness Opposite: heaviness **2 nimbleness**, precision, grace, agility, dexterity Opposite: clumsiness

lightning n **flash of lightning**, forked lightning, sheet lightning, lightning bolt, lightning strike ■ adj **fast**, quick, speedy, whirlwind, sudden Opposite: slow

light out (infml) v **run away**, run off, leave in a hurry, cut and run, run for it

lights out n **1 bedtime**, time for bed, sleep time, bye-byes (infml) **2 signal**, taps, bugle call, curfew, last post Opposite: reveille

light up v 1 **illuminate**, light, cast light on, shed light on, shine a light on *Opposite*: darken 2 **shine**, glow, gleam, beam, burn *Opposite*: darken 3 **cheer up**, brighten up, perk up, liven up, brighten

lightweight *adj* **frivolous**, trivial, insubstantial, inconsequential, unimportant *Opposite*: serious ■ *n* **person of little consequence**, small fry, little man, little guy, pawn

likable *adj* **pleasant**, nice, affable, agreeable, amiable *Opposite*: unpleasant

like *prep* **similar to**, akin to, approximating to, in the vein of, reminiscent of *Opposite*: unlike ■ *adj* **similar**, comparable, alike, corresponding, identical *Opposite*: dissimilar ■ *v* **be fond of**, love, be keen on, enjoy, be partial to *Opposite*: dislike

likelihood *n* **probability**, possibility, prospect, chance, chances

likely *adj* 1 **probable**, possible, expected, prospective, to be expected *Opposite*: unlikely 2 **liable**, apt, prone, tending, having a tendency to

like-minded *adj* **in agreement**, concurring, compatible, in accord, of one mind *Opposite*: incompatible

liken *v* **compare**, equate, relate, associate *Opposite*: contrast

likeness *n* 1 **similarity**, resemblance, correspondence 2 **portrait**, image, reproduction, picture, rendering

likewise *adv* **similarly**, the same, equally, also, as well

liking *n* **taste**, fondness, partiality, love, penchant *Opposite*: dislike. *See* COMPARE AND CONTRAST *at* **love**.

lilt *n* **intonation**, inflection, rise and fall, cadence, stress

lily-livered *(dated) adj* **cowardly**, faint-hearted, spineless, weak, chicken *(infml) Opposite*: courageous

limb *n* 1 **extremity**, appendage, member 2 **branch**, bough, spur

limber *adj* **lithe**, supple, agile, nimble, lissom *Opposite*: stiff

limber up *v* **warm up**, loosen up, exercise, practise, prepare

limelight *n* **attention**, public interest, public eye, fame, renown

limit *n* 1 **boundary**, bounds, border, edge, perimeter 2 **threshold**, cutoff point, check, cap, constraint ■ *v* **control**, regulate, restrain, curb, constrain *Opposite*: deregulate

limitation *n* **drawback**, inadequacy, imperfection, weakness, weak point

limited *adj* **incomplete**, imperfect, partial, inadequate, restricted *Opposite*: boundless

limited company *n* **limited liability company**, public limited company, joint-stock company, company, corporation

limited edition *n* **special edition**, limited printing, limited issue, limited print run, deluxe edition

limiter *n* **regulator**, controller, control, restraint, check

limitless *adj* **boundless**, unbounded, immeasurable, infinite, vast *Opposite*: limited

limits *n* **bounds**, restrictions, confines, parameters, boundaries

limp *v* **hobble**, shuffle, shamble, stagger, wobble ■ *adj* **floppy**, wilted, flaccid, lifeless, drooping *Opposite*: stiff

limpid *adj* 1 **transparent**, clear, translucent, diaphanous, see-through *Opposite*: opaque 2 **lucid**, clear, crystal clear, clear as day, understandable *Opposite*: obscure

limpness *n* **floppiness**, flaccidity, droopiness, lifelessness, sagginess *Opposite*: stiffness

limy *adj* **lime-flavoured**, lime, citrus

linchpin *n* **keystone**, cornerstone, hub, essential, kingpin *(infml) Opposite*: accessory

line *n* 1 **row**, column, procession, lineup, queue 2 **streak**, stripe, contour, mark, stroke 3 **boundary**, limit, border, edge, frontier 4 **link**, route, track, connection, course 5 **string**, cable, rope, thread, twine 6 **ancestry**, family, lineage, descent, race 7 **edge**, profile, contour, outline, silhouette 8 **policy**, attitude, method, approach, ideology 9 **area**, occupation, field, interest, speciality ■ *v* **coat**, cover, face, reinforce, pad

lineage *n* **ancestry**, family, line, heredity, extraction

linear *adj* 1 **in lines**, lined, line 2 **straight**, rectilinear, direct, undeviating, right

lined *adj* 1 **wrinkled**, creased, wizened, furrowed, crinkled *Opposite*: smooth 2 **ruled**, feint *Opposite*: plain

line manager *n* **manager**, production manager, sales manager, boss, superior

line of attack *n* **stratagem**, tactic, technique, method, modus operandi

line officer *n* **combat officer**, frontline officer, fighting officer, field officer, officer

line of sight *n* **sightline**, line of vision, view

line of work *n* **profession**, career, job, occupation

liner *n* **lining**, pool liner, facing, bin liner, insert

line up *v* 1 **assemble**, queue, gather together, collect, align 2 **form ranks**, fall into line, marshal, order, align 3 **plan**, organize, arrange, prepare, set up 4 **arrange**, collect, order, organize, place *Opposite*: disarrange

lineup *n* 1 **team list**, roster, team, listing, side 2 **schedule**, listing, programme 3 **group**, team, alliance, association, league

linger *v* **remain**, stay behind, hang on, loiter, stay *Opposite*: leave

lingerie *n* **underwear**, underclothes, underclothing, undergarments, undies *(infml)*

lingering *adj* 1 **drawn-out**, spun-out, slow, protracted, long-drawn-out *Opposite*: quick

2 lasting, remaining, persistent, enduring, haunting

lingo (infml) n **language**, speech, idiom, vernacular, jargon

linguistic adj **language**, verbal, philological, dialectal, etymological

liniment n **ointment**, cream, unguent, rub, salve

lining n **coating**, liner, insert, facing

link n **connection**, relation, association, relationship, linkage ▪ v **connect**, relate, associate, bring together, link up Opposite: separate

linkage n **connection**, relation, association, relationship, link

linked adj **related**, connected, accompanying, allied, associated Opposite: unrelated

linkup n **connection**, association, link, linkage, bond Opposite: separation

lionhearted adj **brave**, courageous, stouthearted, bold, audacious Opposite: cowardly

lionize v **glorify**, idolize, praise, fete, celebrate Opposite: censure

lion's share n **largest part**, bulk, most, majority, mass

lip n **edge**, rim, brim, brink

lip-smacking adj **delicious**, delectable, tasty, flavourful, flavoursome

liquefy v **dissolve**, soften, melt, run, thaw Opposite: solidify

liquescent adj **melting**, runny, gooey, liquefying Opposite: solid

liquid n **fluid**, water, juice, solution, liquor ▪ adj **runny**, fluid, gooey, watery, melted Opposite: solid

liquidate v **1 settle**, clear up, pay, honour, pay off **2 shut down**, sell out, sell off, bankrupt, wind up **3 kill**, murder, execute, eliminate, assassinate

liquidation n **insolvency**, bankruptcy, closing, winding up, selling out

liquidator n **receiver**, official receiver, sequestrator, administrative receiver, overseer

liquidity n **1 liquidness**, fluidity, fluidness, wateriness Opposite: solidity **2 assets**, liquid assets, convertible assets, resources, financial resources

liquidize v **purée**, blend, pulverize, mash, pulp

liquor n **1 alcohol**, spirits, strong drink **2 liquid**, fluid, solution, juice

lissom adj **1 lithe**, supple, flexible, willowy, svelte Opposite: stiff **2 agile**, nimble, lively, quick, light Opposite: awkward

lissome see lissom

list n **1 catalogue**, register, record, roll, listing **2 tilt**, slant, slope, gradient, lean ▪ v **1 record**, catalogue, register, itemize, enumerate **2 slant**, tilt, incline, lean, bank

listed adj **registered**, recorded, itemized, enumerated Opposite: unlisted

listen v **lend an ear**, pay attention, take note, attend, pin your ears back (infml) Opposite: ignore

listener n **hearer**, radio listener, audience member, audiophile, eavesdropper

listen in v **eavesdrop**, monitor, wiretap, bug, snoop (infml)

listening post n **observation post**, lookout post, surveillance post, sentry post

listen up (infml) v **listen**, pay attention, attend, heed, pay heed Opposite: ignore

listing n **1 citation**, item, entry **2 list**, catalogue, register, record, roll

listings n **schedule**, programme, guide

listless adj **languid**, lethargic, indolent, enervated, limp Opposite: energetic

litany n **1 prayers**, liturgical prayers, petitions, invocations, responses **2 list**, listing, catalogue, series, recital

lite adj **low-fat**, slimming, light, diet, low-calorie Opposite: fattening

literacy n **1 reading ability**, the three Rs, literateness **2 knowledge**, learning, mastery, nous, savvy (infml)

literal adj **1 factual**, truthful, honest, exact, accurate Opposite: figurative **2 word for word**, verbatim, accurate, exact, correct Opposite: inaccurate

literary adj **1 fictional**, mythical, legendary, storybook, fictitious Opposite: historical **2 bookish**, erudite, scholarly, well-read, literate

literate adj **well-educated**, well-read, knowledgeable, cultured, erudite Opposite: illiterate

literati (fml) n **1 intellectuals**, intellects, highbrows, intelligentsia, academics **2 authors**, writers, poets, playwrights, editors

literature n **1 writings**, works, collected works, texts, books **2 information**, sources, reading matter, brochures, pamphlets

lithe adj **supple**, flexible, lissom, agile, nimble Opposite: stiff

litigable adj **responsible**, liable, accountable, answerable, actionable

litigate v **take proceedings**, sue, contest, file, petition

litigation n **court case**, proceedings, lawsuit, legal action, legal process

litmus test n **acid test**, proof, confirmation, test, measure

litter n **1 waste**, rubbish, debris, refuse, trash (US) **2 disorder**, confusion, jumble, clutter, untidiness **3 offspring**, young, progeny, brood, family ▪ v **drop litter**, scatter, spoil, strew, clutter Opposite: clean up

litterbug (infml) see litter lout

litter lout (infml) n **litterer**, fly-tipper, dumper, litterbug (infml)

little *adj* **1 small**, slight, petite, diminutive, tiny *Opposite*: large **2 unimportant**, trivial, slight, petty, trifling *Opposite*: major ■ *pron* **bit**, touch, spot, some, pittance *Opposite*: lot ■ *adv* **not very**, not much, not sufficiently, insufficiently, inadequately *Opposite*: well

little folk *see* little people

little green man *n* **supernatural beings**, Martian, extra-terrestrial

little people *n* **supernatural beings**, imaginary beings, fairies, elves, pixies

littoral *adj* **coastal**, shoreline, seaside *Opposite*: inland ■ *n* **shore**, coast, seaside, shoreline, beach

liturgy *n* **church service**, mass, ritual, religious ceremony, rite

livable *adj* **1 habitable**, functional, civilized, comfortable, agreeable *Opposite*: uninhabitable **2 bearable**, endurable, acceptable, tolerable, worthwhile *Opposite*: intolerable

live *v* **1 exist**, be alive, be in this world, survive, subsist *Opposite*: die **2 reside**, stay, have your home, inhabit, settle ■ *adj* **living**, animate, conscious, breathing, aware *Opposite*: dead

liveable *see* livable

lived-in *adj* **1 homely**, comfortable, relaxed, dishevelled, laid-back (*infml*) **2 careworn**, haggard, worn, lined, tired

live down *v* **get over**, recover from, shake off, forget

livelihood *n* **1 living**, income, source of revenue, means of support, maintenance **2 employment**, occupation, trade, business, work

liveliness *n* **energy**, sparkle, vigour, joie de vivre, vivacity *Opposite*: lethargy

lively *adj* **energetic**, vigorous, sparkling, active, vivacious *Opposite*: lethargic

liven *v* **perk up**, cheer up, boost, quicken, energize *Opposite*: depress

liven up *v* **enliven**, stimulate, revive, cheer up, perk up

live off *v* **rely on**, depend on, impose on, sponge (*infml*), mooch (*infml*)

live on *v* **1 remain**, continue, survive, persist, prevail *Opposite*: die away **2 survive on**, get by on, exist on, subsist on, eke out a living

liveried *adj* **uniformed**, costumed, dressed up, caparisoned

liverish *adj* **irritable**, bad-tempered, moody, irascible, ill-humoured

livery *n* **1** (*literary*) **insignia**, colours, corporate colours, racing colours **2 uniform**, dress, costume, vestments, regalia

livestock *n* **animals**, cattle, stock

live through *v* **survive**, come through, get through, experience, undergo *Opposite*: succumb

live up to *v* **match**, achieve, reach, come up to, meet

live wire (*infml*) *n* **doer**, activist, high-flier, extrovert, go-getter (*infml*)

live with *v* **tolerate**, put up with, bear, endure, manage

livid *adj* **1 discoloured**, bruised, purple, black-and-blue, contused **2 furious**, enraged, up in arms, beside yourself, incensed *Opposite*: delighted

living *adj* **alive**, breathing, existing, live, active *Opposite*: dead ■ *n* **livelihood**, income, living wage, source of revenue, subsistence

---

COMPARE AND CONTRAST CORE MEANING: having life or existence

living not dead, or, of inanimate things, still in existence; **alive** not dead; **animate** used especially to distinguish living animals and plants from inanimate objects such as rocks, water, or buildings; **extant** still in existence.

---

living thing *n* **creature**, being, living being, life form, organism

load *n* **weight**, cargo, freight, consignment, shipment ■ *v* **1 fill**, pack, stack, load up, pile *Opposite*: unload **2 put in**, insert, slot in, pop in (*infml*) *Opposite*: eject **3 burden**, encumber, weigh down, overload, oppress *Opposite*: alleviate

loaded *adj* **1 laden**, weighed down, encumbered, burdened, overloaded *Opposite*: empty **2 biased**, leading, deceptive, trick, manipulative *Opposite*: innocent

loads (*infml*) *n* **many**, much, lots, tons (*infml*), heaps (*infml*) *Opposite*: handful

load up *v* **fill up**, stack, pack, pile, fill *Opposite*: unload

loaf *v* **be idle**, be unoccupied, hang about, laze, loiter

loafer *n* **idler**, slacker, shirker, sloth, loiterer

loan *n* **advance**, credit, finance, mortgage ■ *v* **lend**, advance, give a loan, give an advance, allow *Opposite*: borrow

loath *adj* **wary**, unwilling, reluctant, chary, against *Opposite*: eager. *See* COMPARE AND CONTRAST *at* unwilling.

loathe *v* **hate**, dislike, detest, despise, scorn *Opposite*: adore

loathing *n* **hate**, hatred, antipathy, repugnance, dislike *Opposite*: love. *See* COMPARE AND CONTRAST *at* dislike.

loathsome *adj* **hateful**, despicable, disgusting, repugnant, detestable *Opposite*: delightful

lob *v* **1 throw**, toss, fling, pitch, hurl **2 hit**, knock, strike, bat, whack ■ *n* **toss**, throw, pitch, hit, ball

lobby *n* **1 entrance hall**, foyer, reception area, vestibule, atrium **2 pressure group**, interest group, ginger group, campaign group, special interest group ■ *v* **petition**, press your case, try to influence, apply pressure, sway opinion

lobby group *n* **pressure group**, campaign group, interest group, lobby, alliance

lobe *n* **part**, section, portion, hemisphere

local *adj* **1 restricted**, limited, confined, narrow, insular *Opposite*: universal **2 home**, neighbouring, neighbourhood, community, district *Opposite*: national **3 native**, indigenous, resident, homegrown *Opposite*: foreign ■ *n* **resident**, inhabitant, citizen, native *Opposite*: stranger

locale *n* **location**, place, setting, site, spot

locality *n* **1 area**, district, region, neighbourhood, zone **2 position**, place, site, spot, setting

localize *v* **1 restrict**, confine, limit, focus, contain **2 pinpoint**, locate, identify, find exactly, narrow down

localized *adj* **contained**, limited, restricted, confined, local *Opposite*: generalized

locally *adv* **nearby**, close by, in the vicinity, in the neighbourhood

locate *v* **1 find**, trace, discover, track down, detect *Opposite*: lose **2 place**, put, position, situate, set

location *n* **site**, place, position, spot, setting

loch *n* **1 lake**, tarn, lough, broad **2 inlet**, fjord, firth, creek, sea loch

lock *n* **1 security device**, padlock, mortise lock, safety catch, combination lock **2 curl**, strand, tuft, wisp, ringlet ■ *v* **1 fasten**, bolt, secure, lock up, padlock *Opposite*: unlock **2 fix in place**, lodge, wedge, secure, confine *Opposite*: free **3 brace**, clench, stiffen, tighten *Opposite*: flex **4 link**, clasp, intertwine, join, unite

lock away *v* **1 imprison**, lock up, jail, send to prison, sentence to prison *Opposite*: release **2 shut away**, keep safe, secure, seal up, hide away *Opposite*: bring out

lock horns *v* **argue**, row, disagree, fight, contest

lock on *v* **home in on**, track, follow, shadow

lock up *v* **imprison**, put in jail, put in prison, put behind bars, confine *Opposite*: release

lockup *n* **jail**, prison, detention centre, reformatory, slammer *(slang)*

locomotion *n* **movement**, motion, propulsion, kinetic energy, kinesis *Opposite*: immobility

locomotive *n* **train**, engine, steam engine, tank engine

lodge *n* **1 small house**, cabin, cottage, chalet, hunting lodge **2 hotel**, inn, resort, motel ■ *v* **1 stay**, live, board, be a lodger, take lodgings **2 accommodate**, board, billet, put up, quarter **3 fix in place**, embed, implant, stick, catch

lodger *n* **tenant**, boarder, paying guest, co-tenant, lessee

lodging *n* **accommodation**, room, space, place to stay, housing

lodgings *(dated)* *n* **rooms**, quarters, accommodation, digs *(dated infml)*

loftiness *n* **1 haughtiness**, superior manner, disdain, arrogance, condescension *Opposite*: humility **2 grandeur**, nobility, dignity *Opposite*: baseness **3 height**, elevation, altitude

lofty *adj* **1 supercilious**, superior, disdainful, lordly, arrogant *Opposite*: humble **2 grand**, elevated, noble, admirable, distinguished *Opposite*: base **3 tall**, high, towering, soaring, high-ceilinged *Opposite*: low

log *n* **record**, journal, notes, minutes, logbook ■ *v* **make a note of**, chart, record, note down, note

logbook *n* **record**, record book, log, journal, report

loge *n* **box**, enclosure, box seat *(US)*

logic *n* **reason**, judgment, sense, common sense, lucidity

logical *adj* **1 plausible**, reasonable, obvious, sensible, understandable *Opposite*: implausible **2 rational**, reasonable, sound, commonsense, commonsensical *Opposite*: illogical

log in *v* **gain access**, open up, start, switch on, sign in

logjam *n* **1 deadlock**, standstill, standoff, stalemate, impasse **2 traffic jam**, holdup, tailback, buildup, snarl-up

logo *n* **symbol**, sign, emblem, badge, insignia

log off *v* **leave**, quit, exit, log out, close down *Opposite*: log on

log on *v* **gain access**, open up, start, switch on, sign in *Opposite*: log off

log out *see* **log off**

loiter *v* **1 amble**, stroll, wander, drift, dally **2 wait**, linger, lurk, skulk, hang around

loll *v* **1 lie**, lounge, lie back, sprawl, slouch **2 droop**, hang down, dangle, sag, flop

lollop *v* **1 bound**, bounce, bumble, stride, lope **2 relax**, take it easy, lounge, veg out *(infml)*, lie about *(infml)*

lolly *(infml)* *n* **1 money**, cash, ready money, readies *(infml)*, dosh *(infml)* **2 ice lolly**, ice, lollipop

lone *adj* **1 solitary**, single, single-handed, solo *Opposite*: accompanied **2 only**, sole, unique, singular **3 isolated**, lonely, separate, distinct, discrete

loneliness *n* **aloneness**, solitude, isolation, seclusion *Opposite*: companionship

lonely *adj* **1 forlorn**, lost, alone, friendless, without a friend in the world **2 isolated**, solitary, secluded, cut off, deserted

loner *n* **recluse**, hermit, lone wolf, outsider

long *adj* **1 extended**, extensive, elongated, lengthy, stretched *Opposite*: short **2 time-consuming**, protracted, lengthy, slow, prolonged *Opposite*: brief ■ *v* **long for**, want, yearn, crave, desire. *See* COMPARE AND CONTRAST *at* **want**.

long-ago *adj* **past**, old, historic, early, pre-historic *Opposite*: modern

long-drawn-out *adj* **protracted**, prolonged, lengthy, drawn-out, dragged-out *Opposite*: brief

long-established *adj* **age-old**, time-honoured, timeworn, ancient, old *Opposite*: new

longevity *n* **long life**, permanence, durability, endurance

long haul *(infml)* *n* **1** ordeal, marathon, trial, struggle, endurance test **2** trek, hike, distance, way, schlep *(US infml)*

longing *n* **desire**, wish, yearning, hunger, craving

longitude *n* **position**, meridian, coordinate, location *Opposite*: latitude

long-lasting *adj* **long-term**, continuing, enduring, long-standing, long-running *Opposite*: short-lived

long-life *adj* **UHT**, tinned, canned *Opposite*: fresh

long-lived *adj* **long-lasting**, long-standing, prolonged, abiding, long-term *Opposite*: short-lived

long-lost *adj* **lost**, gone, forgotten, missing

long-range *adj* **long-term**, future, distant, far-off

long shot *n* **slim chance**, long odds, poor prospect, remote possibility, outside chance

long-standing *adj* **established**, age-old, ancient, enduring, ongoing

long-suffering *adj* **forgiving**, resigned, tolerant, accommodating, patient *Opposite*: intolerant

long-term *adj* **lasting**, long-standing, enduring, continuing, durable *Opposite*: short-term

long-winded *adj* **long-drawn-out**, rambling, interminable, wordy, prolix *Opposite*: concise. *See* COMPARE AND CONTRAST *at* **wordy**.

loofah *n* **sponge**, scrubber, exfoliator

look *v* **1** observe, watch, see, view, regard **2** examine, inspect, scrutinize, pore over, study **3** seem, appear, come across, seem to be **4** explore, investigate, examine, consider, discuss **5** focus on, gaze, stare, glare, glance ■ *n* appearance, expression, air, aspect, guise

look after *v* **care for**, take care of, see to, watch over, guard *Opposite*: neglect

look ahead *v* **look forward**, project, plan, anticipate, think about *Opposite*: look back

lookalike *(infml)* *n* **double**, twin, doppelgänger, mirror image, duplicate

look back *v* **1** remember, reminisce, recall, recollect, relive *Opposite*: look ahead **2** review, check, return, revisit

look daggers *v* **glare**, glower, scowl, give somebody a dirty look

look down on *v* **scorn**, disdain, despise, frown on, abhor *Opposite*: look up to

looked-for *adj* **anticipated**, expected, awaited, foreseen, hoped-for *Opposite*: unexpected

looker *n* **observer**, watcher, spectator, viewer, onlooker

look for *v* **search for**, seek, hunt for, rummage

look forward to *v* **anticipate**, hope for, expect, await, wait for *Opposite*: dread

looking glass *n* **mirror**, glass, hand mirror, shaving mirror

look into *v* **investigate**, go into, check out, research, study

look like *v* **resemble**, be like, be similar to, mimic, seem like

look on the bright side *v* **be positive**, be optimistic, make the best of something, make the best of a bad job, make the best of things *Opposite*: despair

look out *v* **1** watch out, beware, take care, pay attention, be alert **2** look over, look on to, look out on, give on to, front

lookout *n* **1** guard, sentry, sentinel, watch **2** viewpoint, vantage point, lookout tower, crow's nest, belvedere

look over *v* **inspect**, examine, check, peruse, scan

lookover *(infml)* *n* **inspection**, examination, scan, check, scrutiny

look-see *(infml)* *n* **look**, glance, glimpse, peep, peek

look through *v* **ignore**, take no notice of, give the cold shoulder, snub, cut *Opposite*: acknowledge

look up *v* **1** search, hunt, research, find, consult **2** get better, improve, take a turn for the better, mend, recuperate *Opposite*: worsen **3** visit, call on, contact, get in touch, locate

look up to *v* **admire**, respect, esteem, worship, adore *Opposite*: look down on

loom *v* **1** appear, emerge, come out, materialize, show *Opposite*: recede **2** hang over, approach, come up, threaten, menace *Opposite*: recede

looming *adj* **impending**, pending, forthcoming, coming up, approaching

loop *n* **ring**, coil, twist, circlet, hoop ■ *v* **wind**, twist, coil, entwine, encircle

loophole *n* **dodge**, get-out, gap, ambiguity, excuse

loose *adj* **1** movable, slack, wobbly, unfastened, free *Opposite*: fixed **2** floppy, relaxed, supple, slack, droopy *Opposite*: tight **3** loose-fitting, baggy, unrestricting, flowing, roomy *Opposite*: tight **4** free, freed, at liberty, unchained, untied *Opposite*: secure **5** assorted, diverse, free, miscellaneous, eclectic **6** *(dated)* irresponsible, lax, slack, relaxed, free *Opposite*: strict

loose-fitting *adj* **loose**, baggy, voluminous, roomy, ample *Opposite*: tight

loose-limbed *adj* **supple**, lissom, agile, lithe, elastic *Opposite*: stiff

loosen v come loose, work loose, untie, undo, release Opposite: tighten

looseness n 1 bagginess, shapelessness, roominess, ampleness Opposite: tightness 2 (dated) irresponsibility, laxity, slackness, freeness, carelessness Opposite: strictness

loosen up v 1 warm up, limber up, stretch, exercise, prepare 2 relax, take it easy, kick back (infml), let your hair down (infml), chill out (infml)

loot n 1 booty, spoils, plunder, swag (slang) 2 (infml) money, cash, wealth, assets, dosh (infml) ■ v burgle, plunder, ransack, pillage, rob

looter n robber, raider, plunderer, burglar, thief

lop v 1 cut, chop, hack, sever, crop Opposite: graft 2 cut off, chop off, slice off, remove, amputate Opposite: attach 3 deduct, take off, subtract, discount, reduce Opposite: add

lope v pace, stride, step, gait, tread ■ v stride, move, walk, lollop, yomp (infml)

lopsided adj uneven, askew, crooked, cock-eyed, wonky (infml) Opposite: even

lopsidedness n unevenness, crookedness, skewedness, imbalance, disproportionateness Opposite: evenness

loquacious adj talkative, garrulous, chatty, voluble, verbose Opposite: silent. See COMPARE AND CONTRAST at talkative.

lore n wisdom, tradition, teachings, knowledge, experience

lose v 1 misplace, be unable to find, mislay, drop, miss Opposite: find 2 be defeated, be beaten, go under, fail, suffer defeat Opposite: win 3 shake off, evade, give somebody the slip, leave behind, get away from 4 waste, squander, exhaust, use up, consume Opposite: save

lose consciousness v faint, black out, pass out, swoon, collapse Opposite: come to

lose control v lose your temper, get carried away, go berserk, hit the roof (infml), lose it (infml) Opposite: keep your cool (infml)

lose heart v become despondent, become demoralized, give up, give in, lose motivation Opposite: take heart

lose it (infml) see lose control

lose out (infml) v miss out, get the worst of it, come off second best, fail to benefit, miss the boat Opposite: gain

loser n failure, also-ran, underdog, dud (infml), has-been (infml) Opposite: achiever

lose the thread v get off the point, lose the point, digress, go off at a tangent, deviate Opposite: follow

lose touch v lose contact, drift apart, lose track of, be out of the loop (infml) Opposite: keep up

lose track of v misplace, lose sight of, lose, be unable to follow, mislay Opposite: keep track of

lose weight v diet, go on a diet, slim, watch your weight, count the calories

lose your bearings v get lost, lose your way, stray, become disorientated, go wrong

lose your cool (infml) v lose control, go off the deep end, go berserk, lose your head, lose your rag (infml) Opposite: keep your cool (infml)

lose your footing v stumble, trip, trip up, fall over, slip

lose your nerve v go to pieces, break down, get flustered, give up, fall apart Opposite: keep your cool (infml)

lose your patience v flare up, snap, hit the roof (infml), lose your cool (infml), lose it (infml) Opposite: keep your cool (infml)

lose your rag (infml) see lose your temper

lose your temper v fly into a rage, explode, hit the roof (infml), go mad (infml), fly off the handle (infml) Opposite: keep your cool (infml)

lose your way v lose your bearings, get lost, become disorientated, stray, go wrong

losing adj behind, trailing, bringing up the rear, down Opposite: winning

loss n 1 deprivation, removal, withdrawal, forfeiture, depletion 2 bereavement, passing, passing away, death, demise (fml) 3 deficit, debit, deficiency, shortfall Opposite: profit 4 damage, harm, injury, cost, hurt 5 defeat, beating, thrashing, trouncing, hammering (infml) Opposite: victory

lossmaking adj uneconomic, running at a loss, unprofitable, not viable, inefficient Opposite: profitable

loss of consciousness n blackout, faint, fainting fit, swoon, collapse

lost adj 1 misplaced, mislaid, missing, gone, nowhere to be found Opposite: found 2 off-course, disorientated, adrift, astray 3 confused, bewildered, bemused, at sea, stumped 4 forlorn, vulnerable, abandoned, alone, aimless 5 deep in thought, spellbound, entranced, rapt, engrossed

lot n 1 batch, set, assortment, grouping, bundle 2 ration, share, slice, proportion, percentage 3 fate, destiny, luck, kismet, fortune

loth see loath

lotion n oil, ointment, liniment, unguent, rub

lots n plenty, many, heaps (infml), bags (infml), loads (infml) Opposite: a few

lottery n 1 draw, sweepstake, raffle, lotto, bingo 2 risk, gamble, chance, fortune, luck Opposite: certainty

lotus-eater n lazy person, hedonist, dreamer, daydreamer, idler

louche adj disreputable, shady, dubious, immoral, suspect Opposite: respectable

loud adj 1 noisy, deafening, piercing, strident, thunderous Opposite: quiet 2 vociferous, rowdy, boisterous, raucous, noisy *Opposite*: gentle **3 lurid**, flamboyant, brash, flashy, gaudy *Opposite*: muted

loudmouthed *(infml) adj* **blustering**, loud, noisy, vociferous, voluble *Opposite*: quiet

loudness *n* **volume**, noise, decibels, level, intensity *Opposite*: quietness

lough *n* **1 lake**, tarn, broad, water, loch **2 inlet**, fjord, firth, creek, sea loch

lounge *n* **living room**, drawing room, sitting room, family room, salon ■ *v* **sprawl**, recline, laze, loaf, loll

lounger *n* **reclining seat**, recliner, sunbed, folding chair, deck chair

lousy *(infml) adj* **1 awful**, rotten, miserable, dreadful, abysmal *Opposite*: great **2 useless**, worthless, stupid, second-rate, mean *Opposite*: great

lout *n* **bully**, thug, rogue, boor, hoodlum

loutish *adj* **coarse**, impolite, rough, uncouth, rude *Opposite*: genteel

loutishness *n* **uncouthness**, rudeness, incivility, vulgarity, boorishness *Opposite*: politeness

lovable *adj* **endearing**, adorable, enchanting, attractive, delightful

love *v* **1 feel affection for**, adore, worship, be in love with, be devoted to *Opposite*: hate **2 like**, enjoy, appreciate, be keen on, be partial to *Opposite*: dislike ■ *n* **1 affection**, fondness, passion, liking, tenderness *Opposite*: hatred **2 darling**, dear, dearest, sweetheart, honey *(US infml)*

COMPARE AND CONTRAST CORE MEANING: a strong positive feeling towards somebody or something

love an intense feeling of tender affection and compassion, especially strong romantic or sexual feelings between people; **liking** a feeling of enjoying something or of finding it pleasant, or personal taste or choice; **affection** fond or tender feelings towards somebody or something; **fondness** a feeling of affection or preference; **passion** intense or overpowering emotion, either love for somebody, usually of a strong sexual nature, or strong liking or enthusiasm for something; **infatuation** an intense but short-lived, often unrealistic love for somebody, usually of a romantic or sexual nature; **crush** *(infml)* a temporary romantic infatuation, especially in teenagers and young people.

---

loved *adj* **precious**, treasured, respected, important, adored *Opposite*: detested

loved ones *n* **family**, nearest and dearest, relations, relatives, kin

loveless *adj* **harsh**, hard, unhappy, unkind, cruel *Opposite*: loving

loveliness *n* **beauty**, attractiveness, good looks, exquisiteness, charm *Opposite*: ugliness

lovely *adj* **1 beautiful**, attractive, pretty, good-looking, gorgeous *Opposite*: ugly **2 pleasant**,

agreeable, delightful, perfect, wonderful *Opposite*: unpleasant. *See* COMPARE AND CONTRAST *at* **good-looking**.

lovesick *adj* **infatuated**, sentimental, overly affectionate, obsessed, pining

loving *adj* **affectionate**, tender, fond, devoted, caring *Opposite*: cold

low *adj* **1 near to the ground**, close to the ground, low down, short, small *Opposite*: high **2 depleted**, at a low level, down, short, in short supply *Opposite*: high **3 soft**, muted, soothing, muffled, subdued *Opposite*: loud **4 sad**, miserable, unhappy, down, depressed *Opposite*: cheerful ■ *n* **low point**, slump, depression, depths, nadir *Opposite*: peak

lowbrow *adj* **popular**, mass-market, philistine, undemanding, middle-of-the-road *Opposite*: highbrow

lowdown *(infml) n* **facts**, fundamentals, basics, ins and outs, particulars

lower *adj* **inferior**, subordinate, lesser, junior, poorer *Opposite*: superior ■ *v* **1 let down**, drop, let fall, hand down, sink *Opposite*: raise **2 lessen**, drop, cut, bring down, decrease *Opposite*: raise

lower class *n* **working class**, masses, hoi polloi, lower classes, proletariat *Opposite*: upper class

lower-class *adj* **working-class**, blue-collar, plebeian, popular *Opposite*: aristocratic

lowermost *adj* **lowest**, bottommost, deepest, bottom, last

lower yourself *v* **deign**, condescend, cheapen yourself, stoop, humiliate yourself

low-grade *adj* **low-quality**, inferior, cheap, substandard, second-rate *Opposite*: premium

low-key *adj* **simple**, unglamorous, unspectacular, understated, subdued *Opposite*: elaborate

lowland *n* **plain**, fen, flat, valley, swamp *Opposite*: high ground

lowliness *n* **humbleness**, meekness, submissiveness, inferiority, commonness *Opposite*: eminence

lowly *adj* **humble**, poor, deprived, ordinary, modest *Opposite*: exalted *(fml)*

low-lying *adj* **low**, lowland, sea-level, below sea level, coastal *Opposite*: high

low-minded *adj* **coarse**, common, vulgar, base, uncouth *Opposite*: refined

low-pitched *adj* **low**, deep, throaty, gruff *Opposite*: high-pitched

low point *n* **low**, all-time low, nadir, rock bottom *Opposite*: high point

low-rise *adj* **double-storey**, single-storey, small, low *Opposite*: high-rise

loyal *adj* **faithful**, trustworthy, devoted, reliable, dependable *Opposite*: disloyal

loyalist *n* **stalwart**, partisan, supporter, devotee, advocate *Opposite*: rebel

loyalty *n* **faithfulness**, allegiance, constancy,

fidelity, devotion *Opposite*: disloyalty

lozenge *n* pastille, tablet, pill

lubricate *v* oil, grease, loosen

lucid *adj* **1 articulate**, clear, well-spoken, silver-tongued, smooth-tongued *Opposite*: incoherent **2 rational**, sane, sober, clear-headed, compos mentis *Opposite*: delirious **3 luminous**, shining, luminescent, limpid, translucent *Opposite*: dull

lucidity *n* **1 intelligibility**, perspicuity, fluency, eloquence, lucidness *Opposite*: ambiguousness **2 rationality**, lucidness, clarity, reason, sanity *Opposite*: confusion **3 luminousness**, luminescence, limpidness, lucidness, translucence *Opposite*: dullness

lucidness *see* lucidity

luck *n* **1 good fortune**, good luck, stroke of luck, windfall, blessing *Opposite*: misfortune **2 chance**, fate, fortune, destiny, providence

luckless *adj* hapless, unlucky, unfortunate, jinxed, ill-fated *Opposite*: lucky

lucky *adj* **fortunate**, blessed, auspicious, propitious, providential *Opposite*: unlucky

COMPARE AND CONTRAST CORE MEANING: relating to advantage or good fortune

lucky bringing or experiencing success or advantage, especially when this seems to happen by chance; **fortunate** bringing or experiencing unexpectedly great success or advantage; **happy** resulting in something pleasant or welcome; **providential** happening at a favourable time; **serendipitous** favourable and happening entirely by chance.

lucky break *n* opportunity, opening, chance, blessing, boon

lucky charm *n* amulet, mascot, good luck charm, juju, talisman

lucky dip *n* raffle, draw, lottery, tombola, lotto

lucrative *adj* profitable, rewarding, worthwhile, beneficial, well-paid *Opposite*: unprofitable

ludicrous *adj* absurd, ridiculous, preposterous, nonsensical, comical *Opposite*: sensible

ludicrousness *n* absurdity, ridiculousness, unreasonableness, foolishness, nonsensicalness *Opposite*: sensibleness

lug *v* drag, heave, cart, carry, haul

luggage *n* baggage, bags, cases, suitcases, stuff

luggage compartment *n* hold, boot, locker, trunk (*US*)

lugubrious *adj* sad, mournful, gloomy, depressing, doleful *Opposite*: cheerful

lugubriousness *n* moroseness, gloominess, melancholy, depression, sadness *Opposite*: cheerfulness

lukewarm *adj* **1 tepid**, warm, cool, hand-hot **2 unenthusiastic**, half-hearted, cool, unexcited, indifferent *Opposite*: enthusiastic

lull *v* soothe, calm, reassure, quieten, settle down *Opposite*: rouse ■ *n* quiet, calm, stillness, silence, pause *Opposite*: storm

lullaby *n* cradlesong, song, ditty, child's bedtime song, serenade

lumbago *n* backache, back pain, bad back

lumber *v* **1** (*infml*) **burden**, encumber, weigh down, land, impose *Opposite*: relieve **2 trudge**, shamble, hobble, plod, clump

lumbering *adj* awkward, clumsy, unwieldy, hulking, graceless *Opposite*: dainty

luminary *n* celebrity, star, achiever, personality, personage *Opposite*: nobody

luminosity *n* glow, light, brilliance, radiance, shine

luminous *adj* **glowing**, shining, brilliant, bright, radiant *Opposite*: dull

lump *n* **1 bump**, swelling, protuberance, knob, inflammation *Opposite*: dent **2 piece**, chunk, morsel, block, section ■ *v* **1 group**, collect, combine, join, amalgamate *Opposite*: split **2** (*infml*) **put up with**, deal with, take, endure, bear

lumpy *adj* **1 clumpy**, uneven, bumpy, knobbly **2 cumbersome**, awkward, lumbering, unwieldy, graceless *Opposite*: graceful

lunge *n* swipe, grab, swing, thrust, stab ■ *v* **1 attack**, dive, spring, leap, charge **2 grab**, swipe, swing, thrust, stab

lurch *v* **1 pitch**, stagger, rock, tilt, list **2 totter**, stagger, stumble, sway, reel

lure *v* entice, tempt, attract, decoy, draw in ■ *n* bait, trap, decoy, enticement, temptation

lurid *adj* **1 shocking**, explicit, sensational, vivid, juicy (*infml*) *Opposite*: bland **2 loud**, garish, gaudy, bright, colourful *Opposite*: dull

luridness *n* **1 explicitness**, sensationalism, vividness, juiciness (*infml*) **2 garishness**, brightness, vividness, gaudiness, colourfulness

lurk *v* lie in wait for, loiter, prowl, hang about, skulk

luscious *adj* juicy, moist, delicious, succulent, sweet *Opposite*: dry

lusciousness *n* juiciness, succulence, moistness, palatability, sweetness *Opposite*: dryness

lush *adj* **1 verdant**, abundant, green, flourishing, thriving *Opposite*: arid **2 luxurious**, lavish, opulent, sumptuous, deluxe *Opposite*: downmarket

lushness *n* **1 greenness**, abundance, fertility, leafiness, luxuriance *Opposite*: aridity **2 luxury**, lavishness, sumptuousness, opulence, richness

lust *n* desire, envy, covetousness, longing, yearning ■ *v* yearn, desire, long, hanker, hunger

lustful *adj* lecherous, libidinous, lascivious, passionate, amorous

lustre *n* sheen, shine, patina, gleam, glint *Opposite*: dullness

lustreless *adj* dull, mat, drab, faded, unpolished *Opposite*: shiny

lustrous adj shiny, glossy, radiant, gleaming, shimmering Opposite: dull

lusty adj hearty, healthy, vigorous, forceful, robust Opposite: feeble

luxuriance n lavishness, luxury, extravagance, abundance, richness

luxuriant adj 1 lush, flourishing, thriving, exuberant, rank Opposite: sparse 2 abundant, lavish, plentiful, copious, ample Opposite: meagre

luxuriate v enjoy, wallow, indulge, bask, relish

luxurious adj 1 deluxe, sumptuous, opulent, expensive, lavish Opposite: simple 2 extravagant, indulgent, decadent, prodigal, epicurean Opposite: simple

luxuriousness n expensiveness, luxury, sumptuousness, magnificence, fulsomeness

luxury n 1 treat, extra, extravagance, indulgence, bonus Opposite: necessity 2 lavishness, comfort, sumptuousness, opulence, magnificence

lying adj deceitful, dishonest, two-faced, insincere, untruthful Opposite: truthful ■ n dishonesty, deceit, duplicity, falseness, untruthfulness Opposite: truthfulness

lynch v hang, string up, murder, mob, assassinate

lynchpin see linchpin

lyric adj 1 poetic, romantic, emotional, expressive, inspired 2 musical, melodic, harmonious, tuneful, lilting

lyrical adj poetic, romantic, emotional, expressive, inspired

lyricism n poeticality, expressiveness, eloquence, floweriness

lyrics n words, lines, libretto

M

ma (infml) n mother, mum (infml), mummy (infml), mam (infml), mama (infml)

macabre adj ghoulish, ghastly, grisly, chilling, gruesome

macadam n asphalt, tar, bitumen, Tarmac, blacktop (US)

macerate v 1 soften, soak, steep, marinate, marinade 2 break up, separate, soak, mash, pulp 3 waste away, starve, fast, slim down, lose weight

Machiavellian adj cunning, unscrupulous, tricky, amoral, devious Opposite: honest

machinate v plot, scheme, conspire, intrigue, hatch

machination n intrigue, plotting, manoeuvring, scheming, planning

machine n 1 mechanism, engine, appliance, apparatus, contraption 2 system, machinery, structure, procedure, mechanism 3 automaton, robot, cyborg, android

machine-gun v shoot, kill, fire at, blaze, strafe ■ adj staccato, rapid, abrupt, fast, quick Opposite: slow

machinery n 1 mechanism, moving parts, workings, works, cogs 2 machines, apparatus, tackle, gear, technology 3 organization, system, procedure, machine, structure

machinist n machine operator, operator, factory worker, operative, technician

machismo n manliness, masculinity, masculineness, maleness, virility

macho adj manly, masculine, virile, laddish

macro n instruction, command, key code, function, short cut

macrobiotic adj wholefood, vegan, vegetarian, organic, wholegrain

macrocosm n system, structure, formation, composition, whole Opposite: microcosm

mad adj 1 angry, furious, livid, irate, infuriated Opposite: calm 2 uncontrolled, frenzied, frenetic, panic-stricken, frantic Opposite: calm 3 passionate, wild about, mad on, keen on, infatuated with Opposite: indifferent

madcap adj silly, zany, chaotic, wild, crazy (infml) Opposite: sensible

madden v infuriate, enrage, annoy, anger, irritate Opposite: pacify

maddened adj infuriated, incensed, annoyed, angered, enraged Opposite: calm

maddening adj infuriating, annoying, irritating, exasperating, frustrating Opposite: pleasing

made-to-measure adj tailor-made, custom-made, customized, custom-built, bespoke Opposite: off-the-peg

made-to-order see made-to-measure

made-up adj pretend, invented, concocted, fictional, fictitious Opposite: real

madly adv 1 intensely, extremely, strongly, deeply, very 2 wildly, frantically, frenetically, rashly, riotously Opposite: calmly

madness n folly, foolishness, stupidity, foolhardiness

maelstrom n tumult, turbulence, flurry, whirl, turmoil

maestro n genius, talent, virtuoso, marvel, expert Opposite: amateur

mafia n **clique**, gang, coterie, faction, set

magazine n **1 periodical**, publication, glossy magazine, journal, weekly **2 arsenal**, depot, repository, ordnance, stockpile

magic n **1 enchantment**, sorcery, witchcraft, voodoo, augury **2 conjuring**, tricks, trickery, illusion, sleight of hand **3 mystery**, charm, appeal, allure, attraction ■ adj **1 enchanted**, magical, fairylike, charmed, dreamlike **2 supernatural**, magical, paranormal, mysterious, miraculous Opposite: normal **3 thrilling**, magical, enchanting, delightful, wonderful Opposite: mundane **4 powerful**, special, key, all-important, famous

magical adj **1 enchanted**, magic, fairylike, charmed, dreamlike **2 supernatural**, magic, paranormal, mysterious, miraculous Opposite: normal **3 thrilling**, magic, enchanting, delightful, wonderful Opposite: mundane

magician n **1 conjurer**, illusionist, entertainer, escape artist, performer **2 sorcerer**, wizard, warlock, enchanter, necromancer (literary) **3 genius**, virtuoso, expert, wizard, marvel

magisterial adj **1 commanding**, authoritative, majestic, stately, dignified Opposite: lightweight **2 overbearing**, arrogant, superior, domineering, imperious Opposite: diffident **3 authoritative**, expert, able, knowledgeable, scholarly

magistrate n **law officer**, justice of the peace, judge, JP, justice

magma n **molten rock**, lava, tuff, igneous rock, pumice

magnanimity n **nobility**, high-mindedness, fairness, generousness, generosity Opposite: pettiness

magnanimous adj **generous**, benevolent, bighearted, openhanded, altruistic Opposite: petty. See COMPARE AND CONTRAST at **generous**.

magnate n **tycoon**, mogul, entrepreneur, industrialist, baron

magnet n **1 magnetic body**, lodestone, horseshoe magnet, electromagnet, bar magnet **2 lure**, draw, attraction, crowd puller, inducement

magnetic adj **attractive** ■, charming, compelling, alluring, captivating Opposite: repellent

magnetism n **1 magnetic field**, attraction, pull **2 charisma**, appeal, allure, charm, magic

magnetize v **attract**, charm, influence, draw, fascinate Opposite: repel

magnification n **exaggeration**, intensification, enlargement, increase, amplification Opposite: reduction

magnificence n **splendour**, glory, brilliance, radiance, majesty

magnificent adj **superb**, wonderful, splendid, glorious, brilliant Opposite: unimpressive

magnify v **1 enlarge**, blow up, expand, amplify, increase Opposite: shrink **2** (fml) **worship**, praise, extol, laud, glorify

magnitude n **1 greatness**, size, extent, degree, amount **2 importance**, significance, enormity, weight, consequence (fml) Opposite: triviality

magnum n **bottle**, jeroboam, demijohn

magpie (infml) n **1 chatterer**, babbler, prattler, talker, gossip **2 collector**, hoarder, saver, accumulator, squirrel (infml)

maharishi n **religious teacher**, guru, mahatma, prophet, evangelist Opposite: follower

maiden n **girl**, lass, young woman, young lady, damsel (literary) ■ adj **first**, earliest, initial, original

mail n **letters**, correspondence, packages, parcels, post

mailbag n **1 postbag**, sack, bag, satchel, shoulder bag **2 correspondence**, feedback, mail, letters, postbag

mailer n **envelope**, padded envelope, carton, mailing tube, container

mailing list n **distribution list**, register, circulation list, newsgroup, address book

mail order n **home shopping**, electronic shopping, cybershopping, online shopping, teleordering

mailshot n **advertisement**, circular, leaflet, letter, brochure

maim v **wound**, injure, hurt, mutilate, damage

main adj **major**, chief, key, foremost, core Opposite: minor

mainland n **landmass**, continent, land Opposite: island

main line n **rail route**, principal route, major route

mainline adj **main**, chief, central, inter-city, principal Opposite: local

mainly adv **mostly**, largely, chiefly, for the most part, primarily

mainspring n **driving force**, motive force, motivating force, chief reason, chief motive

mainstay n **cornerstone**, linchpin, keystone, foundation, basis

mainstream adj **normal**, typical, conventional, ordinary, middle-of-the-road Opposite: unconventional

maintain v **1 uphold**, keep, keep up, continue, sustain Opposite: destroy **2 argue**, claim, insist, assert, hold Opposite: deny **3 look after**, care for, take care of, keep up, keep in good condition Opposite: neglect

maintenance n **1 preservation**, upholding, protection, continuation, continuance Opposite: destruction **2 repairs**, upkeep, looking after, care, keep Opposite: neglect **3 alimony**, allowance, child support, child maintenance, grant

majestic adj **1 impressive**, superb, grand, wonderful, splendid Opposite: modest **2 regal**, royal, grand, stately, imposing Opposite: humble

majesty n **magnificence**, splendour, dignity, grandeur, illustriousness

major adj **1** main, chief, key, foremost, leading Opposite: minor **2** significant, important, weighty, substantial, crucial Opposite: trivial **3** serious, grave, life-threatening Opposite: minor

majority n **1** bulk, preponderance, mass, greater part, lion's share **2** margin, difference, gap, advantage, lead **3** adulthood, maturity, manhood, womanhood, adult years Opposite: childhood ■ adj mainstream, popular, common, widely held, middle-of-the-road Opposite: minority

make v **1** create, fashion, compose, craft, build Opposite: destroy **2** put together, assemble, make up, put up, cobble together **3** manufacture, produce, fabricate, churn out, yield Opposite: consume **4** cause, bring about, create, give rise to, occasion **5** cook, prepare, concoct, produce, create **6** earn, bring in, get, take home, get paid Opposite: spend **7** force, compel, pressurize, pressure, command Opposite: ask **8** become, turn into, change into, be **9** appoint, elect, designate, nominate, name **10** achieve, get into, get on to, succeed, progress to Opposite: miss **11** form, make up, constitute, comprise, be **12** manage, accomplish, find time for, fit in, finish **13** reach, get to, make it to, get as far as, arrive at ■ n sort, type, kind, style, variety

make a beeline for v make straight for, go directly to, head for, target

make a big thing of v make a mountain out of a molehill, make a point of, make a show of, make a big deal out of (infml) Opposite: play down

make a clean breast of things v admit, confess, own up, tell all, tell the truth

make a difference v have an effect, matter, be important, change things

make a dog's breakfast/dinner of v make a mess of, make a pig's ear of, botch (infml), bungle (infml), foul up (infml)

make a fool of v con, deceive, dupe, fool, mislead

make a fool of yourself v appear foolish, embarrass yourself, expose yourself to ridicule, humiliate yourself, make an exhibition of yourself

make a fuss v complain, fuss, make a scene, kick up a fuss, make a mountain out of a molehill

make a fuss of v make much of, indulge, spoil, cosset, coddle Opposite: ignore

make a hash of (infml) v muddle, confuse, jumble, spoil, mix up

make allowances v take into account, bear in mind, consider, take into consideration, allow for

make amends v compensate, make reparations, make up for, pay back, recompense

make a mess of v do badly, make a dog's dinner of, manage badly, mishandle, mismanage

make a mountain out of a molehill v exaggerate, make a big thing of, make a fuss, make too much of, overstate

make a name for yourself v succeed, rise to fame, make it to the top, become known, gain respect

make an effort v attempt, endeavour, put yourself out, try, work hard

make an exhibition of yourself v make a fool of yourself, expose yourself to ridicule, embarrass yourself, behave foolishly, show off

make a note of v **1** mark, memorize, notice, observe, remark upon **2** write down, jot down, take down, keep a record of

make a point of v **1** let people know about, make a big thing of, make a fuss, make a show of, make a song and dance about (infml) **2** make sure to, not forget to, take care to, remember to, make an effort to

make a scene v be angry, carry on, make an exhibition of yourself, make a fuss, throw a tantrum

make a splash v make an impression, impress, get noticed, make an impact, turn heads

make a stab at (infml) v attempt, try, strive, endeavour, have a go at (infml)

make a start v begin, get going, jump in, start, get cracking (infml) Opposite: procrastinate

make a statement v say something, send a message, catch the eye, turn heads, make an impact

make available v free up, find, set aside, release, provide Opposite: refuse

make believe v pretend, imagine, fantasize, daydream, muse

make-believe n fantasy, pretence, role-playing, play-acting, story Opposite: reality ■ adj pretend, imaginary, fantasy, made-up, invented Opposite: real

make better v cure, heal, treat, alleviate, relieve

make certain v check, double-check, ensure, make sure, be in no doubt

make clear v clarify, elucidate, spell out, explain, give details Opposite: obscure

make contact v speak to, approach, communicate, touch base, get in touch Opposite: drop

make contacts v meet people, exchange cards, introduce yourself, make friends, network

make do v manage, put up with, cope, accept, tolerate

make ends meet v cope, manage, pay your bills, break even, get by

make enquiries see make inquiries

make for v **1** head for, head towards, go towards, proceed towards, aim for **2** produce, create, bring about, give rise to, generate

make friends v befriend, take up with, get

in with, get to know, become acquainted *Opposite*: repel

make fun of v mock, poke fun at, laugh at, tease, ridicule *Opposite*: respect

make good v succeed, arrive, be somebody, do well, become successful *Opposite*: fail

make happen v cause, bring about, realize, make real, produce

make headway v make progress, progress, get somewhere, get on, make ground

make inquiries v research, investigate, explore, look into, inspect

make inroads v 1 produce a result, have an effect on, get somewhere, make something happen, make headway 2 encroach, creep up on, dent, overstep, infringe

make it *(infml)* v succeed, achieve, accomplish, attain, manage *Opposite*: give up

make known v publicize, announce, communicate, proclaim, broadcast

make light of v play down, make little of, minimize, underestimate, understate *Opposite*: overstate

make mincemeat of v defeat heavily, thrash, rout, overwhelm, overpower

make much of v make a fuss of, mollycoddle, baby, pet, pat

make off v run away, run off, decamp, make a break for it, make a run for it *Opposite*: come back

make off with v appropriate, run away with, steal, remove, pilfer *Opposite*: return

make out v 1 distinguish, see, hear, perceive, pick out 2 understand, work out, decipher, decode, figure out 3 fill in, write out, make, compose, draw up 4 imply, suggest, give the impression, make somebody believe, insinuate 5 get by, get on, manage, fare, do

makeover n 1 transformation, change, restyling, cosmetic treatment, beautification 2 renovation, restoration, transformation, alteration, conversion

make progress v 1 make headway, progress, advance, get somewhere, forge ahead *Opposite*: stall 2 recover, get well, get better, improve, be on the mend *Opposite*: deteriorate

make public v publicize, publish, release, put out, reveal

maker n creator, manufacturer, fabricator, producer, architect *Opposite*: destroyer

make sense v add up, fit, seem sensible, seem right

make sense of v understand, decode, decipher, follow, grasp *Opposite*: misunderstand

makeshift adj rough-and-ready, crude, temporary, improvised, provisional *Opposite*: permanent

make short work of v make short shrift of, do quickly, dash through, rush through, dash off *(infml)*

make somebody's acquaintance v meet for the first time, meet, get to know, become acquainted, bump into

make somebody's blood boil v anger, annoy, exasperate, irritate, enrage *Opposite*: delight

make somebody's hackles rise v anger, antagonize, get up somebody's nose, annoy, get somebody's back up *Opposite*: placate

make sure v validate, confirm, certify, take care, ensure *Opposite*: assume

make the best of a bad job *see* make the best of things

make the best of things v take the bad with the good, look on the bright side, keep your chin up, keep smiling, take the rough with the smooth *Opposite*: complain

make the grade v meet the standards, be good enough, measure up, hit the mark, satisfy *Opposite*: fail

make the most of v capitalize on, take advantage of, maximize, profit from, make hay while the sun shines *(infml)* *Opposite*: squander

make tracks *(infml)* v leave, depart, go away, make a move, hit the road *Opposite*: stay

make up v 1 prepare, make ready, get ready, set up, put together 2 contribute, add, supply, come up with, provide *Opposite*: deduct 3 form, comprise, constitute, add up to, make 4 invent, concoct, forge, fabricate, think up 5 top up, subsidize, complete, supplement, round up 6 be reconciled, make peace, forgive and forget, kiss and make up, bury the hatchet *Opposite*: fall out 7 compensate, make amends, make good, recompense, redeem

makeup n 1 cosmetics, face paint, greasepaint, powder and paint, maquillage 2 composition, constitution, structure, formation, construction 3 temperament, character, personality, nature, disposition

make up your mind v decide, come to a decision, resolve, determine

make use of v utilize, use, draw on, take advantage of, avail yourself of. *See* COMPARE AND CONTRAST *at* use.

make waves v kick up a fuss, create a stir, rock the boat, dissent, revolt

makeweight n 1 counterpoise, weight, counterbalance, ballast, counterweight 2 extra, complement, supplement, compensation, reinforcement

make your mark v succeed, arrive, make an impact, make an impression, make your presence felt

make yourself known v introduce yourself, say who you are, identify yourself, give your name, come forward

make yourself useful v help out, be of service, lend a hand, assist, rally round *Opposite*: hinder

make your way v go, move, head, wend your way, pick your way

making n **creation**, manufacture, production, construction, assembly

makings n 1 **ingredients**, requirements, components, elements, materials 2 **qualities**, potential, wherewithal, what it takes, assets

maladjusted adj **disturbed**, neurotic, unstable, confused, alienated Opposite: well-adjusted

maladjustment n **instability**, disturbance, confusion, alienation, estrangement Opposite: stability

maladroit adj **awkward**, clumsy, inept, gauche, ungainly Opposite: dexterous

maladroitness n **clumsiness**, insensitivity, awkwardness, ineptitude, gaucheness Opposite: gracefulness

malady n **sickness**, illness, disease, disorder, condition

malaise n 1 **sickness**, illness, disease, disorder, condition 2 **dissatisfaction**, discontent, unease, disquiet, anxiety

malcontent n **complainer**, mischief-maker, protester, rebel, whiner ■ adj **discontented**, disgruntled, dissatisfied, unhappy, complaining Opposite: content

male adj **masculine**, mannish, manlike, manly, virile Opposite: feminine ■ n **man**, boy, guy (infml), bloke (infml), fella (infml) Opposite: female

malediction (fml) n **curse**, spell, blight, charm, hex Opposite: blessing

malefactor (fml) n **lawbreaker**, wrongdoer, criminal, outlaw, offender

malevolence n **wickedness**, malice, ill will, evil, spite Opposite: benevolence

malevolent adj **malicious**, spiteful, wicked, nasty, mean Opposite: benevolent

malformation n **deformity**, defect, fault, abnormality, distortion

malformed adj **misshapen**, deformed, abnormal, crooked, distorted Opposite: perfect

malfunction v **act up**, break down, crash, fail, play up Opposite: function ■ n **fault**, breakdown, failure, error, blip

malice n **hatred**, spite, malevolence, meanness, nastiness Opposite: kindness

malicious adj **hateful**, spiteful, malevolent, mean, nasty Opposite: kind

malign v **criticize**, defame, vilify, denigrate, disparage Opposite: praise ■ adj **harmful**, hurtful, damaging, destructive, negative Opposite: benign

COMPARE AND CONTRAST CORE MEANING: say or write something damaging about somebody **malign** criticize somebody in a spiteful and false or misleading way; **defame** make an attack on somebody's good name or reputation with a view to damaging or destroying it; **slander** in legal terms, make spoken false accusations about somebody that are damaging to the person's reputation; **libel** in legal terms, make false damaging accusations about somebody in writing, signs, or pictures; **vilify** make viciously defamatory statements about somebody.

malignancy n 1 **spite**, malevolence, menace, evil, malice Opposite: kindness 2 **melanoma**, tumour, disease, growth, cancer

malignant adj 1 **evil**, malevolent, hateful, spiteful, malicious Opposite: kind 2 **cancerous**, spreading, harmful, fatal, life-threatening Opposite: benign

malinger v **shirk**, duck, sidestep, go AWOL, play hooky (infml)

malleability n 1 **bendiness**, ductility, flexibility, plasticity, pliability Opposite: rigidity 2 **impressionability**, pliability, manipulability, compliance, acquiescence Opposite: inflexibility

malleable adj 1 **soft**, supple, flexible, bendy, pliable Opposite: rigid 2 **impressionable**, compliant, acquiescent, manipulable, biddable. See COMPARE AND CONTRAST at **pliable**.

malnourished adj **underfed**, undernourished, underweight, starving, famished Opposite: well-fed

malnutrition n **undernourishment**, malnourishment, underfeeding, starvation, famine

malodorous adj **foul-smelling**, fetid, reeking, smelly, stinking Opposite: fragrant

malpractice n **misconduct**, negligence, abuse, dereliction, mismanagement

maltreat v **hurt**, injure, harm, damage, misuse. See COMPARE AND CONTRAST at **misuse**.

maltreatment n **mistreatment**, abuse, ill-treatment, harm, damage

mama (infml) n **mother**, mummy (infml), mum (infml), mam (infml), mammy (infml)

mamma (infml) see **mama**

mammal n **animal**, marsupial, placental mammal, marine mammal

---

WORD BANK
❏ **types of large mammal** alpaca, bactrian camel, bear, bison, boar, buffalo, camel, dromedary, elephant, giraffe, hippopotamus, llama, panda, polar bear, rhinoceros, wart hog
❏ **types of marine mammal** dolphin, dugong, grampus, manatee, narwhal, porpoise, sea lion, seal, walrus, whale
❏ **types of small mammal** anteater, armadillo, badger, ferret, hare, hedgehog, hyrax, marten, mink, mongoose, otter, pine marten, polecat, porcupine, rabbit, raccoon, skunk, sloth, stoat, weasel, wolverine

---

mammon n **ambition**, greed, loot, money, riches

mammoth adj **enormous**, huge, massive, immense, epic Opposite: tiny

man n **gentleman**, male, fella (infml), guy (infml), bloke (infml) Opposite: woman ■ v **operate**, staff, crew, work, command

manacle n **handcuff**, chain, shackle, bond, fetter ■ v **bind**, chain, chain up, fetter, handcuff Opposite: release

manage v 1 **achieve**, accomplish, succeed, be

able to, bring about *Opposite*: fail **2 cope**, fare, get on, do, get by *Opposite*: give up **3 run**, direct, administer, supervise, be in charge **4 handle**, deal with, control, cope with **5 control**, discipline, master, dominate, boss

manageable *adj* **1 feasible**, doable, practicable, viable, possible *Opposite*: unmanageable **2 controllable**, handy, user-friendly, adaptable, easy to use *Opposite*: unwieldy

management *n* **1 organization**, running, administration, supervision, managing **2 directors**, managers, executives, employers, board

manager *n* **boss**, director, executive, administrator, supervisor

managerial *adj* **executive**, management, supervisory, directorial, decision-making

mandarin *n* **bureaucrat**, official, public servant, civil servant, manager

mandate *n* **1 order**, command, directive, decree, dictate **2 authority**, authorization, consent, permission, support **3 term of office**, reign, tenure, stay ■ *v* **assign**, authorize, command, delegate, instruct

mandatory *adj* **obligatory**, compulsory, required, fixed, binding *Opposite*: optional

mandible *n* **jaw**, jawbone, maxilla, mouth, mouthpart

mane (*literary or infml*) *n* **tresses**, curls, shock, head of hair, locks (*literary*)

man-eating *adj* **carnivorous**, ferocious, fierce, wild, aggressive

man friend (*infml*) *n* **male companion**, boyfriend, partner

manful *adj* **brave**, strong, resolute, bold, determined *Opposite*: cowardly

manger *n* **trough**, feeding-box, container, crib

mangle *v* **crush**, mash, smash, contort, twist

mangy (*infml*) *adj* **dirty**, shabby, disgusting, filthy, foul *Opposite*: pristine

manhandle *v* **push**, shove, jostle, hustle, move

manhood *n* **1 maturity**, independence, adulthood **2 strength**, courage, determination, virility, boldness *Opposite*: unmanliness **3 men**, menfolk, males

mania *n* **obsession**, desire, love, craze, passion

maniac *n* **enthusiast**, fanatic, zealot, fiend, freak (*infml*)

manic (*infml*) *adj* **overexcited**, agitated, hectic, frenzied, busy *Opposite*: calm

manicure *v* **trim**, file, shape, cut, clip

manifest *adj* **apparent**, unmistakable, clear, plain, obvious *Opposite*: unclear ■ *v* **make plain**, establish, demonstrate, display, reveal

manifestation *n* **sign**, indication, index, indicator, appearance

manifesto *n* **declaration**, statement, policy, guidelines, proposal

manifold *adj* **various**, diverse, many, multiple, assorted *Opposite*: uniform

manipulate *v* **1 operate**, work, use, deploy, employ **2 influence**, control, bias, direct, sway **3 manoeuvre**, direct, control, stage-manage, engineer

manipulation *n* **1 operation**, handling, management, use, guidance **2 running**, control, exploitation, persuasion, scheming **3 falsification**, forgery, alteration, misuse, tampering **4 osteopathy**, massage, movement, flexing, rubbing

manipulative *adj* **scheming**, calculating, controlling, devious, unscrupulous

manipulator *n* **Machiavelli**, exploiter, schemer, Svengali, wheeler-dealer (*infml*)

mankind *n* **1** (*dated*) **men**, menfolk, manhood, males **2 human race**, humankind, humanity, human beings, people

manliness *n* **masculinity**, machismo, manhood *Opposite*: unmanliness

manly *adj* **virile**, mannish, male, masculine, macho

man-made *adj* **artificial**, synthetic, manufactured, substitute, imitation *Opposite*: natural

manna *n* **1 food**, sustenance, victuals, fodder, provisions **2 godsend**, blessing, boon, gift, help

mannequin *n* **dummy**, model, figure, tailor's dummy, dressmaker's dummy

manner *n* **1 way**, means, method, style, custom **2 type**, kind, sort, class, category **3 behaviour**, conduct, demeanour, bearing, comportment (*fml*)

mannered *adj* **affected**, artificial, put-on, false, simpering *Opposite*: natural

mannerism *n* **1 gesture**, trait, characteristic, gesticulation, habit **2 affectation**, show, act, display, pretence

mannerly *adj* **well-behaved**, polite, refined, well-mannered, respectful *Opposite*: rude

manners *n* **1 etiquette**, protocol, good manners **2 conduct**, deportment, manner, behaviour, demeanour

manoeuvre *n* **1 move**, movement, operation, exercise **2 ploy**, trick, plot, tactic, plan ■ *v* **manipulate**, plot, contrive, plan, scheme

manqué *adj* **failed**, near, would-be, unfulfilled, unsuccessful *Opposite*: successful

mansard *n* **attic**, loft, roof, eaves, rafters

manse *n* **vicarage**, rectory, parsonage, residence, church house

manslaughter *n* **murder**, homicide, killing, assassination, slaying

mantle (*fml*) *n* **responsibility**, function, role, position, duty

mantra *n* **chant**, intonation, repetition, refrain, hymn

manual *adj* **physical**, labour-intensive, blue-collar *Opposite*: mental ■ *n* **instruction booklet**, guide, handbook, guidebook, instruction manual

manufacture v **build**, assemble, construct, produce, create ■ n **production**, making, creation, building, assembly

manufactured adj **factory-made**, mass-produced, industrial, man-made, synthetic

manufacturer n **builder**, producer, constructor, creator, industrialist

manufacturing n **production**, manufacture, making, assembly, construction

manure n **dung**, compost, guano, muck, fertilizer

manuscript n **document**, copy, text, script

many adj **a lot of**, lots of, numerous, countless, several Opposite: a few

many-sided adj **multifaceted**, complex, complicated, deep, multidimensional Opposite: one-dimensional

map n **plan**, chart, atlas, record, drawing ■ v **chart**, plot, plan, record, draw

map out v **work out**, plan, devise, outline, arrange

map reading n **route-planning**, routing, direction-finding, orienteering, navigation

mar v **deface**, ruin, mutilate, damage, disfigure Opposite: repair

marathon adj **lengthy**, epic, long-drawn-out, gruelling, difficult

maraud v **raid**, plunder, ransack, loot, pillage

marauder n **raider**, robber, bandit, pillager, plunderer

marble n **glass ball**, agate, cat's eye

marbled adj **veined**, streaked, mottled, lined, shot through

march v 1 **parade**, file, step, troop, process 2 **stride**, stomp, storm, sweep, flounce ■ n 1 **hike**, trek, walk, tramp, trudge 2 **protest**, picket, mass lobby, rally, demonstration

marcher n **demonstrator**, protester, walker, campaigner, supporter

marchpast n **parade**, review, muster, procession

margin n 1 **boundary**, border, brim, sideline, edge 2 **surplus**, room, leeway, allowance, scope

marginal adj 1 **negligible**, minimal, low, minor, slight Opposite: major 2 **irrelevant**, insignificant, unimportant, borderline, fringe Opposite: central

marginalization n **relegation**, sidelining, demotion, downgrading, disregarding

marginalize v **relegate**, sideline, demote, downgrade, disregard Opposite: include

marginally adv **slightly**, a little, a touch, a bit (infml), a tad (infml)

marina n **harbour**, port, dock, quay, yacht haven

marinade n 1 **dressing**, sauce, flavouring, juices, infusion 2 see **marinate**

marinate v **steep**, soak, infuse, immerse, douse

marine adj 1 **saltwater**, seawater, sea, aquatic 2 **nautical**, oceangoing, naval, seafaring, seagoing

mariner n **sailor**, seafarer, seadog, old salt, tar (archaic infml)

marital adj **conjugal**, nuptial, wedded, spousal, matrimonial

maritime adj 1 **nautical**, naval, oceanic, seafaring, seagoing 2 **seaside**, coastal, shoreline, littoral

mark n 1 **spot**, scratch, dent, stain, smear 2 **sign**, indication, feature, characteristic, symbol 3 **score**, point, assessment, evaluation, grade ■ v 1 **stain**, scratch, smudge, smear, blot 2 **indicate**, denote, show, demonstrate, evidence 3 **celebrate**, commemorate, keep, observe, solemnize 4 **correct**, assess, evaluate, score, grade (US)

markdown n **discount**, price cutting, reduction, concession Opposite: mark-up

marked adj **clear**, apparent, evident, noticeable, conspicuous

marker n **indicator**, sign, indication, symbol, pointer

market n **marketplace**, souk, bazaar, arcade, fair ■ v **sell**, promote, advertise, peddle, trade

marketable adj **in demand**, sought-after, wanted, vendible, merchantable

marketing n **advertising**, selling, presentation, publicizing, promotion

marketplace n 1 **bazaar**, market, souk, flea market, open market 2 **trading floor**, sphere, arena, market

marking n **pattern**, coloration, design

mark out v 1 **outline**, demarcate, sketch, delimit, delineate 2 **distinguish**, differentiate, single out, identify, characterize

mark-up n **price increase**, rise, hike, profit, profit margin Opposite: markdown

maroon v **abandon**, leave high and dry, leave, cast aside, cast adrift

marooned adj **stranded**, deserted, abandoned, isolated, stuck

marque n **make**, label, trademark, brand

marquee n **tent**, pavilion, canvas, shelter, erection (fml)

marquetry n **inlay**, pattern, design, veneer

marred adj **blemished**, flawed, stained, disfigured, tarnished Opposite: unblemished

marriage n 1 **wedding**, matrimony, wedding ceremony, marriage ceremony, nuptials (fml) Opposite: divorce 2 **union**, fusion, combination, coming together, alliance Opposite: separation

marriageability n **eligibility**, suitability, availability, fitness

marriageable adj **eligible**, suitable, available, adult, grown-up

married adj **wedded**, matrimonial, nuptial, conjugal, marital

marry v **get married**, join in matrimony, walk down the aisle, tie the knot (infml), get hitched (infml)

marsh n **bog**, swamp, quagmire, swampland, marshland

marshal n **officer**, deputy, law officer, sheriff (US) ■ v **1 assemble**, position, gather together, collect, shepherd Opposite: disperse **2 arrange**, order, sort out, put in order, organize Opposite: muddle

marshland n **bog**, swamp, swampland, marsh, wetland

marshy adj **boggy**, swampy, soggy, muddy, peaty Opposite: dry

mart n **auction**, sale, market, store, trading place

martial adj **1 military**, soldierly, warlike, battle-hardened, fighting Opposite: civilian **2 warlike**, fierce, aggressive, belligerent, hostile Opposite: peaceful

martial law n **state of emergency**, militarism, junta, dictatorship, emergency powers

Martian n **alien**, extraterrestrial, ET, spaceman, invader Opposite: terrestrial

martinet n **disciplinarian**, stickler, despot, hardliner, perfectionist Opposite: softy (infml)

martyr n **1 sacrifice**, sacrificial victim, victim, scapegoat, ransom (literary) **2 idealist**, witness, believer, supporter **3 sufferer**, invalid, patient

martyrdom n **1 death**, killing, slaughter, torture, ritual murder **2 suffering**, misery, pain, sacrifice, torment

marvel n **1 wonder**, miracle, spectacle, sight, curiosity **2 genius**, prodigy, phenomenon, wunderkind, whiz (infml) ■ v **be amazed**, be surprised, be impressed, admire, wonder Opposite: deride

marvellous adj **1 amazing**, impressive, remarkable, magnificent, superb Opposite: ordinary **2 great**, brilliant, wonderful, fantastic, fabulous

mascot n **symbol**, charm, talisman, amulet, periapt Opposite: hex

masculine adj **male**, manly, mannish, macho, virile Opposite: feminine

masculinity n **maleness**, manliness, mannishness, manhood, boyhood Opposite: femininity

mash n **purée**, pulp, mush ■ v **pulp**, squash, pound, crush, smash

mask n **cover**, disguise, guise, façade, front ■ v **hide**, conceal, disguise, cover, camouflage Opposite: expose

masked adj **1 disguised**, incognito, camouflaged, concealed, screened Opposite: exposed **2 undetectable**, imperceptible, latent, hidden, invisible Opposite: detectable

masonry n **stonework**, brickwork, building materials, granite, sandstone

masque n **1 performance**, allegory, theatricals, play, opera **2 masquerade**, dance, ball, masked ball

masquerade n **1 pretence**, deception, cover-up, subterfuge, ruse **2 masked ball**, masque, ball, dance ■ v **pretend to be**, impersonate, pose, disguise yourself, make believe

mass n **1 form**, figure, frame, physique, build **2 quantity**, corpus, amount, area, reservoir **3 bulk**, main part, essence, majority, better part ■ v **gather**, assemble, group, congregate, collect Opposite: disperse ■ adj **general**, widespread, common, universal, wholesale

massacre n **extermination**, annihilation, carnage, butchery, mass slaughter ■ v **slaughter**, murder, exterminate, butcher, mow down

massage n **manipulation**, pressure, kneading, rubbing, reflexology ■ v **1 knead**, manipulate, rub, rub down **2 falsify**, manipulate, alter, amend, misrepresent

masses n **1 common people**, crowd, multitude, commonality, hoi polloi Opposite: elite **2** (infml) **lots**, loads (infml), tons (infml), heaps (infml), oodles (infml)

massif n **mountain range**, chain, sierra, ridge, line

massive adj **1 bulky**, heavy, solid, weighty, hulking Opposite: slight **2 huge**, enormous, gigantic, immense, colossal Opposite: tiny

massively (infml) adv **enormously**, immensely, hugely, tremendously, vastly Opposite: slightly

mass-produce v **churn out**, turn out, manufacture, process, knock out

mass-produced adj **high-street**, off-the-peg, ready-to-wear, off-the-shelf, ready-made Opposite: personalized

master n **1 controller**, ruler, leader, chief, boss Opposite: underling **2 expert**, virtuoso, maestro, genius, prodigy Opposite: novice **3 teacher**, guru, tutor, instructor, guide Opposite: pupil ■ adj **chief**, principal, main, major, leading Opposite: secondary ■ v **1 conquer**, gain control of, overcome, subdue, get the better of **2 become skilled at**, become proficient at, grasp, learn, understand Opposite: fail

masterful adj **1 expert**, skilled, proficient, skilful, accomplished Opposite: incompetent **2 authoritative**, commanding, imposing, assured, forceful Opposite: weak

masterly adj **skilled**, skilful, proficient, talented, gifted Opposite: incompetent

mastermind n **brains**, architect, organizer, instigator, brain (infml) ■ v **plan**, engineer, oversee, organize, devise Opposite: carry out

masterpiece n **work of art**, magnum opus, tour de force, stroke of genius, masterwork

masterwork see **masterpiece**

mastery n **1 expertise**, skill, knowledge, proficiency, command **2 control**, power, supremacy, authority, command

masthead *n* title, banner, strip, logo, header

masticate *v* chew, munch, crunch, champ, grind

mastication *n* **chewing**, munching, eating, grinding, champing

mat *n* **1 rug**, carpet, doormat, bathmat, floor-covering **2 table mat**, place mat, doily, coaster, pad ▪ *v* tangle, entwine, entangle, intertwine, knot *Opposite*: disentangle

match *n* **1 competition**, bout, contest, game, tie **2 equal**, counterpart, equivalent, pair, partner ▪ *v* **1 be alike**, correspond, be identical, tally, fit *Opposite*: differ **2 go with**, complement, harmonize, accord, coordinate *Opposite*: clash

matching *adj* **1 corresponding**, identical, similar, alike, same *Opposite*: different **2 toning**, harmonizing, complementary, coordinative, coordinating *Opposite*: clashing

matchless *adj* **peerless**, outstanding, unrivalled, unparalleled, incomparable *Opposite*: ordinary

matchmaker *n* **marriage broker**, go-between, fixer, intermediary, cupid

mate *n* **1 friend**, companion, comrade, pal *(infml)*, chum *(infml)* *Opposite*: rival **2 helper**, assistant, colleague, partner, coworker ▪ *v* breed, reproduce, couple *(fml)*, copulate *(fml)*

material *n* **1 substance**, matter, raw material, stuff **2 data**, information, ideas, facts, notes **3 fabric**, textile, stuff, cloth, yard goods ▪ *adj* **1 physical**, substantial, solid, factual, quantifiable *Opposite*: insubstantial **2 significant**, relevant, pertinent, important, central *Opposite*: immaterial

materialism *n* acquisitiveness, avariciousness, avarice, covetousness, avidity *Opposite*: detachment

materialistic *adj* **money-orientated**, grasping, acquisitive, avaricious, covetous *Opposite*: spiritual

materialization *n* **appearance**, arrival, advent, embodiment, manifestation *Opposite*: disappearance

materialize *v* **1 come into existence**, happen, occur, exist, take shape *Opposite*: evaporate **2 appear**, turn up, show up, arrive, reveal yourself *Opposite*: disappear

materially *adv* **significantly**, considerably, substantially, importantly, essentially *Opposite*: slightly

materials *n* **resources**, supplies, ingredients, constituents, equipment

maternal *adj* **1 motherly**, parental, nurturing, protective, guiding **2 caring**, devoted, kind, tender, gentle *Opposite*: uncaring

maternity *n* **motherhood**, childbearing, parenthood

matey *adj* **friendly**, comradely, companionable, warm, amiable *Opposite*: unfriendly

mathematical *adj* **1 arithmetical**, numerical, arithmetic, geometric, algebraic **2 exact**, precise, scientific, accurate, measured *Opposite*: random

mathematics *n* **calculation**, reckoning, maths, algebra, arithmetic

matinée *n* **afternoon showing**, show, performance, presentation

matriarch *n* **mother**, matron, grandmother, older woman, materfamilias *(fml)* *Opposite*: patriarch

matriculate *v* **1 admit**, register, enrol, enlist, inscribe *Opposite*: strike off **2 be admitted**, sign up, join, be enrolled, register *Opposite*: drop out

matriculation *n* **admission**, registration, admittance, enrolment, enlistment *Opposite*: expulsion

matrimonial *adj* **marital**, wedded, married, nuptial, conjugal

matrimony *n* **marriage**, wedlock, wedding, ceremony, service *Opposite*: divorce

matrix *n* **1 substance**, medium, carrier, solution, base **2 situation**, environment, milieu, conditions, background **3 template**, mould, format, pattern, mint

matron *n* **older woman**, mature woman, middle-aged woman, matriarch, doyenne

matronly *adj* **full-figured**, plump, portly, stout, well-rounded

matte *adj* **dull**, lustreless, nonglossy, muted *Opposite*: glossy

matted *adj* **tangled**, entwined, entangled, dishevelled, intertwined

matter *n* **1 subject**, topic, theme, issue, affair **2 trouble**, problem, difficulty, worry, concern **3 substance**, stuff, stock, staple, material ▪ *v* **be of importance**, be important, count, signify, be significant. *See* COMPARE AND CONTRAST *at* subject.

matter-of-fact *adj* **1 down-to-earth**, straightforward, rational, unemotional, realistic **2 factual**, unvarnished, down-to-earth, literal, unembroidered *Opposite*: fictional

matting *n* **floorcovering**, tatami, mats, coconut matting, rush matting

mattress *n* **futon**, air mattress, air bed, pallet, pad

maturation *n* **maturing**, ripening, mellowing, development, growth

mature *adj* **1 grown-up**, adult, fully-grown, middle-aged, older *Opposite*: immature **2 experienced**, responsible, prudent, wise, sensible *Opposite*: naive **3 established**, developed, advanced, settled, matured *Opposite*: undeveloped **4 ripe**, ripened, ready, strong, sweet *Opposite*: young ▪ *v* **grow up**, develop, ripen, mellow, age

matured *adj* **mature**, ripe, ripened, mellowed, aged *Opposite*: young

maturely *adv* **wisely**, sensibly, responsibly, prudently *Opposite*: immaturely

maturity *n* **1 adulthood**, prime of life, middle age, old age *Opposite*: youth **2 ripeness**, mellowness, development, age *Opposite*: youth **3 wisdom**, experience, responsibility, reliability, sensibleness *Opposite*: inexperience

maudlin *adj* **oversentimental**, mawkish, slushy, mushy, syrupy *Opposite*: unemotional

maul *v* **1 claw**, attack, ill-treat, paw, mangle **2 criticize**, attack, savage, slate *(infml)*, slam *(infml)*

mauling *n* **criticism**, disparagement, censure, barrage, blast

mausoleum *n* **tomb**, vault, sepulchre, crypt, resting place

maverick *n* **nonconformist**, eccentric, individualist, rebel, odd one out *Opposite*: conformist

mawkish *adj* **oversentimental**, slushy, mushy, syrupy, overemotional *Opposite*: unemotional

mawkishness *n* **sentimentality**, tearfulness, mushiness, slushiness, weepiness *(infml)* *Opposite*: detachment

maxi *adj* **large**, mega, big, jumbo, king-size *Opposite*: mini

maxim *n* **1 saying**, adage, proverb, saw, aphorism **2 rule**, tenet, guideline, truth, principle

maximal *adj* **best**, greatest, most, utmost, highest *Opposite*: minimal

maximization *n* **expansion**, growth, enlargement, extension, intensification

maximize *v* **1 make the most of**, make best use of, exploit, take full advantage of, capitalize on *Opposite*: minimize **2 increase**, expand, amplify, make bigger, boost *Opposite*: minimize

maximum *n* **1 most**, greatest, highest, utmost *Opposite*: minimum **2 limit**, ceiling, greatest extent, top figure, upper limit *Opposite*: minimum

maybe *adv* **perhaps**, possibly, it could be, perchance *(literary)*, mayhap *(archaic)* *Opposite*: definitely

mayday *n* **SOS**, distress signal, emergency call, distress call, 999 call

mayhem *(infml)* *n* **chaos**, disorder, confusion, turmoil, havoc *Opposite*: order

maypole *n* **column**, post, pole, support

maze *n* **1 labyrinth**, warren, web, network **2 confusion**, muddle, jumble, mess, intricacy *Opposite*: order

MC *n* **master of ceremonies**, host, toastmaster, moderator, presenter *(infml)*

meadow *n* **field**, pasture, paddock, grazing land, lea *(literary)*

meagre *adj* **small**, slight, insufficient, inadequate, sparse *Opposite*: plentiful

meagreness *n* **insufficiency**, inadequacy, scantness, sparseness, stinginess *(infml)* *Opposite*: abundance

meal *n* **food**, bite, snack, something to eat

WORD BANK

❏ **types of meal** banquet, barbecue, breakfast, brunch, buffet, clambake, continental breakfast, dinner, elevenses, English breakfast, high tea, lunch, luncheon, picnic, ready-made meal, snack, supper, takeaway, tea, titbit, TV dinner

❏ **parts of a meal** afters *(infml)*, antipasto, aperitif, appetizer, canapé, delicacy, dessert, entrée, hors d'oeuvre, main course, meze, nibbles, pudding, side dish, starter, sweet, sweet course, tapas, pud *(infml)*

mealtime *n* **breakfast time**, lunchtime, dinnertime, suppertime, tea-time

mealy-mouthed *adj* **hypocritical**, insincere, euphemistic, indirect, devious *Opposite*: frank

mean *v* **1 denote**, signify, indicate, stand for, represent **2 intend**, propose, aim, plan, want **3 entail**, involve, require, lead to, necessitate ■ *adj* **1 miserly**, tightfisted, parsimonious, ungenerous, stingy *Opposite*: generous **2** *(archaic)* **humble**, lowly, poor, simple, underprivileged **3 nasty**, unkind, cruel, callous, vile *Opposite*: kind **4 paltry**, derisory, meagre, miserable, scanty *Opposite*: plentiful **5 poor**, shabby, squalid, humble, lowly *Opposite*: comfortable **6 middle**, mid, average, normal, standard *Opposite*: extreme ■ *n* **average**, norm, median, middle, midpoint *Opposite*: extremity

COMPARE AND CONTRAST CORE MEANING: referring to somebody or something below normal standards of decency

mean unkind or malicious; **nasty** showing spitefulness, malice, or ill-nature; **vile** despicable or shameful; **low** without principles or morals; **base** lacking proper social values or moral principles; **ignoble** dishonourable and contrary to the high standards of conduct expected.

mean business *v* **be serious**, mean what you say, mean it, be determined, be deadly serious

meander *v* **1 wind**, zigzag, twist and turn, twist, snake **2 wander**, roam, amble, ramble, stroll *Opposite*: rush

meandering *adj* **twisting**, winding, twisty, tortuous, snaking *Opposite*: straight

meanie *(infml)* *n* **miser**, skinflint, penny pincher *(infml)*, scrooge *(infml)*, cheapskate *(infml)*

meaning *n* **1 sense**, connotation, denotation, import, gist **2 significance**, importance, implication, worth, value *Opposite*: insignificance

meaningful *adj* **1 expressive**, evocative, telling, eloquent, speaking **2 significant**, important, consequential, momentous, deep *Opposite*: meaningless

meaningfulness n meaning, importance, significance, seriousness, relevance *Opposite*: meaninglessness

meaningless *adj* **1** empty, worthless, throwaway, hollow, pointless *Opposite*: meaningful **2** unimportant, trivial, inconsequential, irrelevant, insignificant *Opposite*: significant

meaninglessness n emptiness, insignificance, futility, purposelessness, worthlessness *Opposite*: importance

mean it v be in earnest, not be joking, be deadly serious, mean business, mean what you say

meanness n **1** nastiness, unkindness, cruelty, callousness, spitefulness *Opposite*: kindness **2** miserliness, niggardliness, parsimoniousness, tightfistedness, close-fistedness *(infml)* *Opposite*: generosity

means n **1** way, method, process, measures, channel **2** income, earnings, resources, revenue, funds

mean-spirited *adj* ungenerous, uncharitable, harsh, mean, unkind *Opposite*: generous

meant *adj* **1** inevitable, preordained, fated, predestined, destined *Opposite*: accidental **2** intended, designed, planned, aimed, targeted *Opposite*: unexpected

meantime n interim, intervening time, period in-between, the time being

mean well v have good intentions, have your heart in the right place, try to do the right thing, try hard, have the best intentions

meanwhile *adv* in the meantime, for the meantime, in the interim, in the intervening time, for now

measly *(infml)* *adj* meagre, ungenerous, mean, derisory, paltry *Opposite*: ample

measurable *adj* **1** quantifiable, assessable, gaugeable, computable, calculable *Opposite*: indeterminate **2** considerable, appreciable, noticeable, detectable, perceptible *Opposite*: imperceptible

measurably *adv* noticeably, evidently, significantly, demonstrably, obviously *Opposite*: insignificantly

measure n **1** amount, degree, quantity, portion, ration **2** measuring device, gauge, meter, counter ■ v gauge, calculate, compute, determine, assess

measured *adj* **1** deliberate, calculated, precise, exact, careful *Opposite*: unthinking **2** slow, unhurried, unrushed, restrained, stately *Opposite*: hurried

measurement n dimension, size, extent, quantity, amount

WORD BANK
❏ **types of metric unit** centigram, centilitre, centimetre, decagram, decalitre, decametre, decigram, decilitre, decimetre, gram, hectare, hectogram, hectolitre, hectometre, kilogram, kilolitre, kilometre, litre, metre, microgram, micrometre, milligram, millilitre, millimetre, tonne
❏ **types of nonmetric unit** acre, barrel, bushel,

degree Fahrenheit, dram, fluid dram, fluid ounce, foot, furlong, gallon, gill, inch, mile, ounce, peck, pint, pound, quart, rod, ton, yard
❏ **types of SI unit** becquerel (radioactivity), coulomb (electric charge), degree Celsius (temperature), farad (capacitance), gray (radiation dose), henry (inductance), hertz (frequency), joule (energy), lumen (luminous flux), lux (illuminance), newton (force), ohm (electric resistance), pascal (pressure), siemens (electric conductance), sievert (radiation effects), tesla (magnetic flux density), volt (electric potential), watt (power), weber (magnetic flux)

measure up v hit the mark, satisfy, deliver, fulfil requirements, do *Opposite*: fall short

measuring device n gauge, measure, meter, counter

WORD BANK
❏ **types of measuring device** altimeter, anemometer, aneroid barometer, balance, barograph, barometer, callipers, clock, compass, dipstick, dividers, dropper, Geiger counter, measuring tape, micrometer, mileometer, pipette, protractor, quadrant, rule, scale, speedo, speedometer, spirit level, statoscope, tachometer, tape, tape measure, theodolite, thermometer, weather vane, weighbridge, weighing machine, weighing scales, wind gauge, windsock

meat n **1** flesh, food, carrion **2** substance, heart, gist, pith, kernel

WORD BANK
❏ **types of cut** best end, breast, brisket, chop, chuck, chump, cutlet, drumstick, flank, foreshank, hock, joint, leg, loin, neck, rasher, rib, round, scrag end, shoulder, side, silverside, sparerib, steak, topside, wing
❏ **types of meat** beef, chicken, duck, gammon, goat, goose, grouse, hare, lamb, mutton, partridge, pheasant, pork, rabbit, turkey, veal, venison, wild boar
❏ **types of processed meat** bacon, beefburger, bratwurst, bresaola, burger, chorizo, foie gras, frankfurter, ground beef, ground meat, ham, hamburger, jerky, liver sausage, meat loaf, meatball, merguez, mince, minced beef, minced meat, mincemeat, mortadella, pancetta, parma ham, pastrami, pâté, patty, pepperoni, rissole, salami, sausage, saveloy
❏ **types of steak** Chateaubriand, fillet, porterhouse steak, rump, sirloin, T-bone steak, tenderloin

meaty *adj* **1** brawny, burly, muscular, fleshy, hunky *(infml)* *Opposite*: weedy **2** substantial, profound, deep, weighty, solid *Opposite*: lightweight

mecca n focus, focal point, magnet, hub, centre

mechanical *adj* **1** motorized, powered, power-driven, machine-driven, automated *Opposite*: manual **2** automatic, perfunctory, unconscious, unthinking, reflex

mechanics n workings, technicalities, procedure, mechanism, process

mechanism n 1 **device**, instrument, apparatus, machine, machinery 2 **means**, method, system, procedure, process

mechanistic adj **automatic**, mechanical, machine-like, automatous, robotic

mechanization n **automation**, computerization, streamlining, modernization, systematization

mechanize v **automate**, power, systematize, industrialize, program

mechanized adj **automated**, mechanical, industrialized, automatic, computerized

medal n **award**, decoration, honour, distinction, laurel

medallion n **medal**, decoration, pendant, ornament

medallist n **champion**, winner, victor, runner-up

meddle v **interfere**, butt in, stick your nose in, intrude, put your oar in

meddler n **troublemaker**, nuisance, gossip, interferer, busybody (infml)

meddlesome adj **interfering**, intrusive, meddling, officious, prying Opposite: detached

meddling n **interference**, inquisitiveness, intrusion, prying, intrusiveness ■ adj **interfering**, meddlesome, inquisitive, intrusive, prying Opposite: uninterested

media n **mass media**, television, radio, newspapers, magazines

median n **mean**, midpoint, middle, norm, standard

mediate v **arbitrate**, intercede, facilitate, intermediate, referee Opposite: provoke

mediation n **arbitration**, intercession, conciliation, intervention, negotiation Opposite: provocation

mediator n **go-between**, intermediary, third party, arbitrator, negotiator

medic (infml) n **doctor**, medical student, houseman, physician, registrar

medical adj **medicinal**, remedial, health, homeopathic, curative ■ n **checkup**, physical, health check, examination

WORD BANK
❏ **types of complementary therapy** acupressure, acupuncture, Alexander technique, Ayurvedic medicine, Bach flower remedy, chiropractic, colour therapy, cranial osteopathy, flotation, herbal medicine, homeopathy, hydrotherapy, hypnotherapy, iridology, kinesiology, massage, music therapy, naturopathy, neurolinguistic programming, osteopathy, Pilates, reflexology, reiki, shiatsu, T'ai Chi, yoga
❏ **types of medical procedure** amniocentesis, amputation, anesthesia, angioplasty, appendectomy, biopsy, booster, bypass, Caesarean section, CAT scan, checkup, chemotherapy, diagnosis, dialysis, endoscopy, facelift, graft, hysterectomy, immunization, keyhole surgery,

laparoscopy, manipulation, mastectomy, operation, physiotherapy, plastic surgery, radiotherapy, resuscitation, sedation, tracheotomy, transfusion, ultrasound scan, vaccination, vasectomy, X-ray
❏ **types of medical specialty** anaesthetics, cardiology, dermatology, endocrinology, gastroenterology, general medicine, geriatrics, gynaecology, haematology, infectious diseases, internal medicine, neurology, obstetrics, oncology, ophthalmology, paediatrics, psychiatry, radiology, rheumatology, surgery

medicament n **medicine**, remedy, treatment, pharmaceutical, curative

medicated adj **medicinal**, antiseptic, antibacterial, antiviral, analgesic

medication n **drug**, pharmaceutical, pill, tablet, capsule

medicinal adj **medicated**, remedial, healing, therapeutic, curative

medicine n **drug**, remedy, medication, treatment, prescription

medieval adj **old-fashioned**, out-of-date, primitive, feudal, unenlightened Opposite: modern

mediocre adj **middling**, average, unexceptional, ordinary, middle-of-the-road Opposite: excellent

mediocrity n **patchiness**, unevenness, poorness, weakness, averageness Opposite: excellence

meditate v **contemplate**, ponder, think, consider, deliberate

meditation n **thought**, consideration, contemplation, reflection, rumination

meditative adj **thoughtful**, reflective, contemplative, pensive, introspective Opposite: active

medium adj **average**, intermediate, middle, middling, standard Opposite: extraordinary ■ n **means**, vehicle, channel, mode, method

medley n **mixture**, combination, assortment, mix, jumble

meek adj 1 **mild**, quiet, humble, gentle, docile Opposite: overbearing 2 **timid**, compliant, weak, cowed, fearful Opposite: assertive

meekness n 1 **humbleness**, quietness, docility, humility, gentleness 2 **timidity**, submissiveness, fearfulness, compliance, weakness Opposite: assertiveness

meet v 1 **come across**, encounter, bump into, run into, chance on Opposite: avoid 2 **be introduced to**, make somebody's acquaintance, get to know, greet, become acquainted with 3 **gather**, get together, come together, convene, assemble Opposite: disperse 4 **experience**, encounter, come across, endure, go through 5 **touch**, contact, connect, join, converge Opposite: separate

meeting n 1 **business meeting**, conference, assembly, summit, seminar 2 **encounter**, introduction, reunion, appointment, engagement

megalith n prehistoric monument, standing stone, menhir, dolmen, sarsen

megalomania n power lust, overbearingness, tyranny, totalitarianism, autocracy

megalomaniac n tyrant, dictator, autocrat, despot ■ adj power-hungry, power-crazy, self-important, tyrannical, dictatorial

megaphone n loudhailer, voice amplifier, bullhorn (US)

melancholic adj dejected, sad, unhappy, miserable, forlorn Opposite: cheerful

melancholy adj sad, downhearted, miserable, down, low Opposite: cheerful ■ n sadness, unhappiness, dejection, sorrow, the blues Opposite: cheerfulness

meld v mix, merge, blend, fuse, combine Opposite: separate ■ n combination, mix, mixture, blend, amalgamation

melee n 1 fight, commotion, brawl, fracas, uproar 2 muddle, jumble, mix, confusion, mixture

mellifluous adj pleasant, soothing, sweet, melodious, honeyed Opposite: jarring

mellow adj 1 smooth, rich, full, warm, soft Opposite: harsh 2 mature, full-flavoured, ripe, aged, strong Opposite: young 3 easygoing, good-humoured, tolerant, approachable, genial Opposite: uptight (infml) ■ v 1 calm down, ease up, settle down, relax, soften 2 mature, soften, develop, ripen, improve Opposite: deteriorate

mellowness n 1 smoothness, richness, warmth, fullness, mellifluousness Opposite: harshness 2 ripeness, sweetness, fullness, matureness, maturity Opposite: rawness 3 geniality, equanimity, amiability, warmth, affability

melodic see melodious

melodious adj tuneful, harmonious, musical, easy on the ear, mellow Opposite: discordant

melodiousness n tunefulness, musicalness, pleasantness, euphoniousness, euphony Opposite: cacophony

melodrama n 1 fuss, drama, scene, storm in a teacup, exaggeration 2 play, drama, tragedy, stage show, act

melodramatic adj histrionic, overdramatic, overemotional, exaggerated, sensational Opposite: low-key

melody n tune, song, air, phrase, strain

melt v 1 thaw, thaw out, dissolve, soften, liquefy Opposite: freeze 2 disappear, dissolve, fade, vanish, evaporate Opposite: materialize

meltdown (infml) n collapse, breakdown, failure, disaster, disintegration Opposite: success

melting adj tender, sweet, loving, sentimental, soft Opposite: harsh

melting pot n mixture, mix, mishmash, blend, hotchpotch

member n 1 associate, affiliate, fellow, adherent, participant 2 limb, appendage, organ, extremity, leg 3 part, constituent, component, element, portion

membership n 1 association, affiliation, involvement, connection, relationship Opposite: exclusion 2 members, associates, affiliates, fellows, adherents

membrane n skin, film, sheath, casing, tissue

memento n souvenir, reminder, vestige, keepsake, token

memo n memorandum, note, minute, letter, message

memoir n 1 account, biography, history, chronicle, description 2 essay, article, report, paper, thesis

memoirs n autobiography, journal, life story, life history, diary

memorabilia n collectables, collector's items, souvenirs, mementos, ephemera

memorability n importance, note, momentousness, uncommonness, impressiveness Opposite: inconsequence

memorable adj unforgettable, notable, remarkable, outstanding, impressive Opposite: forgettable

memorandum n memo, note, minute, letter, message

memorial n monument, cenotaph, statue, bust, plaque

memorize v learn by heart, learn by rote, learn, commit to memory, remember Opposite: forget

memory n 1 reminiscence, recollection, recall, remembrance, retention 2 commemoration, remembrance, celebration, memorial

menace n 1 threat, danger, hazard, peril, jeopardy Opposite: reassurance 2 (infml) thorn in the flesh, nuisance, troublemaker, annoyance, bother ■ v 1 endanger, threaten, jeopardize, hang over, loom over 2 threaten, intimidate, terrorize, frighten, alarm Opposite: reassure

menacing adj threatening, ominous, frightening, alarming, intimidating Opposite: reassuring

menagerie n zoo, zoological gardens, city farm, farm park

mend v 1 repair, fix, put right, put back together, restore Opposite: break 2 stitch, sew, sew up, patch, patch up Opposite: rip 3 improve, amend, rectify, reform, transform 4 recover, get better, get well, recuperate, heal Opposite: deteriorate ■ n patch, darn, repair

mendacious adj 1 untruthful, dishonest, deceitful, unreliable, lying Opposite: truthful 2 untrue, misleading, false, spurious, untruthful Opposite: true

mendaciously *adv* **untruthfully**, dishonestly, deceitfully, falsely, unreliably *Opposite*: truthfully

mendacity *n* **lies**, deception, deceit, falsehood, fabrication *Opposite*: truthfulness

mendicant *adj* **homeless**, vagrant, vagabond, begging, penniless ■ *n (fml)* **beggar**, vagrant, tramp, down-and-out, homeless person

mending *n* **sewing**, darning, stitching, fixing, patching

menfolk *n* **kinsmen**, men, boys, husbands, sons

menial *adj* **unskilled**, boring, tedious, basic, lowly *Opposite*: skilled

menswear *n* **men's clothing**, sportswear, outerwear

mental *adj* **psychological**, cerebral, rational, intellectual, spiritual *Opposite*: physical

mentality *n* **attitude**, approach, outlook, mindset, state of mind

mention *v* **talk about**, state, say, cite, bring up *Opposite*: conceal ■ *n* **reference**, indication, discussion, remark, comment

mentor *n* **adviser**, counsellor, guide, tutor, teacher *Opposite*: pupil

menu *n* **bill of fare**, carte du jour, tariff, blackboard, set menu

mercantile *adj* **merchant**, commercial, trade, trading, business

mercenary *n* **soldier of fortune**, soldier, legionnaire, freedom fighter, dog of war ■ *adj* **acquisitive**, grasping, greedy, avaricious, covetous *Opposite*: altruistic

merchandise *n* **goods**, products, produce, commodities, stock ■ *v* **sell**, retail, trade in, deal in, handle

merchant *n* **1 retailer**, seller, vendor, shopkeeper, tradesperson **2 wholesaler**, dealer, trader, supplier, broker

merciful *adj* **1 compassionate**, kind, lenient, humane, generous *Opposite*: hardhearted **2 thankful**, fortunate, welcome, lucky, happy *Opposite*: unfortunate

merciless *adj* **cruel**, hardhearted, pitiless, harsh, heartless *Opposite*: kind

mercilessness *n* **cruelty**, hardheartedness, pitilessness, harshness, heartlessness *Opposite*: kindness

mercurial *adj* **changeable**, unpredictable, lively, active, impulsive *Opposite*: consistent

mercy *n* **1 compassion**, pity, clemency, kindness, leniency *Opposite*: cruelty **2 blessing**, relief, kindness, stroke of luck, piece of luck *Opposite*: blow

mere *adj* **1 ordinary**, simple, sheer, plain, unadorned **2 scant**, meagre, paltry, mean, miserable

merely *adv* **just**, only, simply, purely

meretricious *adj* **1** *(fml)* **superficial**, flashy, vulgar, tawdry, showy **2 specious**, plausible, deceptive, insincere, glib *Opposite*: genuine

merge *v* **1 combine**, unite, come together, join, amalgamate *Opposite*: separate **2 blend**, meld, blur, fuse, unify *Opposite*: separate

merger *n* **1 amalgamation**, union, combination, joining, fusion *Opposite*: separation **2 blend**, meld, blur, fusion, union *Opposite*: separation

merit *n* **1 value**, worth, quality, excellence, distinction **2 advantage**, good point, pro, plus point, asset *Opposite*: disadvantage **3 ability**, accomplishment, capability, aptitude, skill *Opposite*: ■ *v* **deserve**, warrant, earn, call for, be worthy of

meritorious *adj* **commendable**, praiseworthy, estimable, admirable, laudable *Opposite*: despicable

merriment *n* **cheerfulness**, happiness, fun, high spirits, jollity *Opposite*: misery

merry *adj* **cheerful**, happy, cheery, jolly, joyful *Opposite*: miserable

merry-go-round *n* **whirl**, round, series, succession, string

merrymaker *n* **partygoer**, party guest, life and soul of the party, social butterfly, reveller *Opposite*: killjoy

merrymaking *n* **celebration**, revels, partying, jollification, jollity *Opposite*: misery

mesa *n* **butte**, hill, mound, tor, peak

mesh *n* **net**, web, network, netting, webbing ■ *v* **interlock**, interconnect, engage, fit together, enmesh *Opposite*: separate

mesmeric *adj* **fascinating**, absorbing, compelling, compulsive, mesmerizing *Opposite*: boring

mesmerize *v* **hypnotize**, fascinate, absorb, entrance, enthral *Opposite*: bore

mesmerizing *see* **mesmeric**

mess *n* **1 untidiness**, muddle, chaos, confusion, clutter *Opposite*: order **2 tight spot**, tight corner, predicament, quandary, dilemma **3 canteen**, refectory, dining room, dining hall, restaurant

mess about *(infml) see* **mess around**

message *n* **1 communication**, memo, memorandum, note, letter **2 meaning**, significance, point, lesson, moral

mess around *(infml)* *v* **1 waste time**, fool around, play, mess about *(infml)*, muck about *(infml) Opposite*: behave **2 relax**, laze around, lounge around, loll around, rest up **3 tamper**, fiddle, meddle, interfere, mess **4 hang around**, associate, go around, go out, spend time **5 joke**, have a laugh, fool around, play the fool, act the fool **6 mistreat**, treat badly, treat unfairly, fool with, muck about *(infml)* **7 potter**, tinker, dabble, fiddle, mess about *(infml)*

messenger *n* **courier**, envoy, go-between, emissary, herald

messiah *n* **champion**, liberator, leader, defender, saviour

messiness n **1 untidiness**, disorderliness, scruffiness, dirtiness, scrappiness Opposite: neatness **2 unpleasantness**, acrimony, bitterness, awkwardness, nastiness

mess up (infml) v **1 spoil**, ruin, wreck, scupper, blunder **2 make untidy**, muddle up, mix up, make a mess, clutter Opposite: tidy up **3 upset**, confuse, put out, put somebody off their stride, throw (infml) Opposite: sort out

mess-up (infml) n **muddle**, mix-up, mess, confusion, muddle-up

messy adj **1 untidy**, muddled, chaotic, cluttered, in disarray Opposite: neat **2 unpleasant**, acrimonious, bitter, awkward, complicated Opposite: amicable

metabolism n **breakdown**, absorption, digestion, uptake, use

metabolize v **break down**, absorb, digest, take up, make use of

metallic adj **1 metal**, iron, steel, copper, brass **2 shiny**, reflective, glossy, glittering, polished Opposite: dull **3 tinny**, brassy, ringing, clanging, sharp Opposite: soft

metamorphose v **change**, transform, transmute, mutate, alter

metamorphosis n **transformation**, change, mutation, conversion, alteration

metaphor n **symbol**, image, figure of speech, allegory, comparison

metaphorical adj **figurative**, symbolic, allegorical, emblematic, representational Opposite: literal

metaphysical adj **abstract**, theoretical, philosophical, hypothetical, conjectural

meteoric adj **dramatic**, sudden, swift, spectacular, impressive Opposite: gradual

meteorological adj **climatological**, climatic, atmospheric, weather, weather-related

meteorology n **weather forecasting**, climatology, weather prediction, weathercasting

mete out v **give out**, deal out, allocate, impose, exact

meter n **measuring device**, gauge, counter

method n **1 means**, way, process, system, procedure **2 orderliness**, organization, order, form, structure

methodical adj **systematic**, logical, disciplined, precise, orderly Opposite: haphazard

methodological adj **procedural**, organizational, working, running, operational

methodology n **organizing system**, practice, procedure, organization, policy

meticulous adj **careful**, scrupulous, thorough, particular, painstaking Opposite: careless. See COMPARE AND CONTRAST at **careful**.

meticulously adv **exactly**, accurately, precisely, squarely, methodically Opposite: carelessly

meticulousness n **care**, thoroughness, strictness, diligence, perfectionism Opposite: carelessness

métier n **vocation**, occupation, profession, calling, sphere

metre n **rhythm**, beat, tempo, pulse, pattern

metropolis n **city**, conurbation, capital, metropolitan area, megalopolis. See COMPARE AND CONTRAST at **city**.

metropolitan adj **city**, urban, municipal, civic

mettle n **courage**, bravery, determination, spirit, grit. See COMPARE AND CONTRAST at **courage**.

mettlesome adj **lively**, spirited, high-spirited, courageous, plucky Opposite: lethargic

mew v **cry**, miaow, sob, whimper, yowl

mezzanine n **mezzanine floor**, entresol, storey, level

miaow v **cry**, purr, mew, caterwaul, whimper

miasma n **mist**, fog, haze, cloud, murk

microbe n **microorganism**, germ, bug (infml)

microbiological adj **biological**, bacteriological, fungal, viral, microparasitic

microcosm n **small-scale version**, version in miniature, miniature copy, miniature Opposite: macrocosm

micromanage v **interfere**, intervene, nitpick, breathe down somebody's neck, control

microorganism n **microbe**, germ, bug (infml)

microscopic adj **tiny**, minute, infinitesimal, minuscule, atomic Opposite: gigantic

microscopically adv **meticulously**, minutely, closely, carefully, painstakingly

microwave v **heat**, heat up, warm, warm up, warm through

mid adj **middle**, median, medium, midway, central Opposite: extreme

midair adj **1 air**, airborne, in-flight, mid-flight, midcourse **2 in the air**, up in the air, in the sky, overhead, above the ground

midday n **noon**, noontime, twelve noon, lunchtime, the middle of the day

middle n **1 centre**, heart, focus, core, hub Opposite: circumference **2 midpoint**, halfway point, median, mean, norm ■ adj **1 central**, mid, internal, intermediate, inside **2 median**, average, intermediate, medium, middling

middlebrow (infml) adj **unintellectual**, conventional, unchallenging, middle-of-the-road, mediocre

middleman n **1 trader**, distributor, wholesaler, retailer, broker **2 intermediary**, agent, go-between, mediator, negotiator

middle-of-the-road adj **normal**, mainstream, majority, standard, typical

middling adj **1 usual**, typical, ordinary, average, run-of-the-mill Opposite: unusual **2 adequate**, all right, tolerable, fair, passable Opposite: exceptional

midnight n **twelve o'clock**, twelve midnight, middle of the night, night, nighttime Opposite: noon

midpoint n **centre**, middle, nucleus, median, mean

midriff *n* **waist**, stomach, belly, middle, abdomen

midst *n* **middle**, centre, heart, focus, core

midstream *adv* **halfway through**, midway, in the middle, in full flow

midsummer *n* **middle of the summer**, summertime, summer solstice, dog days, the height of summer *Opposite*: midwinter

midway *adj* **central**, middle, mid, halfway ■ *adv* **halfway**, in the middle, midstream, in full flow, halfway through

midwinter *n* **middle of winter**, wintertime, winter solstice, the winter months, the depths of winter *Opposite*: midsummer

mien *(fml)* *n* **appearance**, bearing, expression, manner, look

miff *(infml)* *v* **irritate**, upset, annoy, vex, peeve *(infml)*

miffed *(infml)* *adj* **annoyed**, displeased, put out, chagrined, bothered

might *n* **strength**, power, force, capacity, valour

mightily *adv* **tremendously**, greatly, extremely, awfully, decidedly *Opposite*: slightly

mighty *adj* **1 powerful**, strong, forceful, potent, great *Opposite*: weak **2 huge**, enormous, vast, expansive, massive *Opposite*: insignificant

migrant *n* **1 wanderer**, traveller, nomad, itinerant, wayfarer *(literary)* *Opposite*: resident **2 refugee**, immigrant, emigrant, asylum seeker ■ *adj* **migratory**, travelling, wandering, drifting, itinerant *Opposite*: resident

migrate *v* **travel**, journey, wander, drift, roam

migration *n* **relocation**, immigration, emigration, exodus, movement

migratory *adj* **travelling**, wandering, drifting, migrant, itinerant

mild *adj* **1 gentle**, kind, soft, easygoing, meek *Opposite*: harsh **2 weak**, bland, tasteless, insipid, flat *Opposite*: strong **3 slight**, unimportant, insignificant, trifling, trivial *Opposite*: serious **4 warm**, balmy, pleasant, clement, temperate *Opposite*: harsh

mildly *adv* **1 gently**, kindly, meekly, placidly, calmly *Opposite*: harshly **2 slightly**, a little, somewhat, a touch, insignificantly *Opposite*: considerably

mild-mannered *adj* **gentle**, kind, polite, good-natured, placid *Opposite*: fierce

mildness *n* **gentleness**, kindness, leniency, tenderness, warmth *Opposite*: harshness

mileage *n* **1 distance**, travelling distance, range, extent, way **2** *(infml)* **benefit**, profit, advantage, usefulness, assistance

milepost *n* **marker**, sign, mark, indicator, signpost

miles *(infml)* *n* **a long way**, a great distance, miles and miles, miles away, a long way away ■ *adv* **much**, very much, lots, a lot, far

milestone *n* **1 sign**, signpost, indicator, mark, marker **2 landmark**, highlight, high point, achievement, record

milieu *n* **setting**, environment, scene, background, surroundings

militancy *n* **aggressiveness**, combativeness, belligerence, forcefulness, violence

militant *adj* **confrontational**, aggressive, radical, revolutionary, combative *Opposite*: peaceable ■ *n* **activist**, revolutionary, radical, fighter, supporter

militarism *n* **belligerence**, aggression, aggressiveness, pugnaciousness, bellicosity

militarist *adj* **bellicose**, aggressive, warmongering, martial, military *Opposite*: pacific

militaristic *see* **militarist**

militarized *adj* **mobilized**, armed, battle-ready, prepared, organized

military *adj* **armed**, martial, soldierly, fighting *Opposite*: civilian ■ *n* **services**, forces, armed forces, military establishment, army

militate *v* **influence**, inspire, affect, work, act on

militia *n* **territorial army**, reservists, local militia, paramilitaries, mercenaries

milk *(infml)* *v* **exploit**, drain, tap, take advantage of, cash in on

milky *adj* **cloudy**, chalky, creamy, pale, translucent *Opposite*: clear

millennial *adj* **utopian**, idealistic, visionary, romantic, optimistic

millennium *n* **epoch**, era, age, period, time

millionaire *n* **tycoon**, mogul, magnate, billionaire, baron *Opposite*: pauper

millions *n* **many**, lots, masses, loads *(infml)*, heaps *(infml)*

millstone *n* **burden**, weight, dead weight, albatross, shackle

mime *v* **1 act out**, represent, simulate, express, symbolize **2 mimic**, satirize, caricature, parody, ape

mimetic *adj* **imitative**, derivative, copied, representational, simulated *Opposite*: original

mimic *v* **1 caricature**, ape, satirize, parody, mock **2 imitate**, impersonate, represent, mirror, simulate ■ *n* **impersonator**, impressionist, imitator, caricaturist, parodist. *See* COMPARE AND CONTRAST *at* imitate.

mimicry *n* **imitation**, impersonation, impression, parody, caricature

minaret *n* **turret**, tower, spire

mince *v* **shred**, cut up, chop up, crumble, hash ■ *n* **mincemeat**, minced meat, minced beef, ground beef, ground meat

mincemeat *n* **mince**, minced meat, minced beef, ground beef, ground meat

mincing *adj* **affected**, foppish, dainty, prim, fussy

mind *n* **1 brain**, intellect, wits, brains, brainpower **2 attention**, concentration, thoughts, awareness, observance **3 point of view**, mentality, opinion, thinking, view **4 thinker**, intellect, intellectual, brain *(infml)*, egghead *(infml)* ■ v **1 pay attention**, take care, beware, heed, be careful **2 object**, care, take offence, demur, resent *Opposite*: approve **3 look after**, tend, care for, attend to, take care of

mind-bending *see* **mind-boggling**

mind-blowing *(infml) adj* **astonishing**, amazing, incredible, inconceivable, astounding *Opposite*: unexceptional

mind-boggling *(infml) adj* **overwhelming**, complex, difficult, complicated, puzzling *Opposite*: simple

minded *(fml) adj* **inclined**, of a mind to, intent, set, prepared *Opposite*: disinclined

minder *n* **1** *(infml)* **guard**, guardian, escort, lookout, attendant **2 child minder**, carer, sitter, babysitter

mindful *adj* **watchful**, aware, wary, heedful, alert *Opposite*: unwary. *See* COMPARE AND CONTRAST *at* **aware**.

mindless *adj* **1 tedious**, dull, boring, monotonous, mechanical *Opposite*: enthralling **2 senseless**, gratuitous, unnecessary, pointless, needless

mindlessly *adv* **1 automatically**, mechanically, unconsciously, unthinkingly, robotically *Opposite*: deliberately **2 senselessly**, stupidly, thoughtlessly, carelessly, foolishly *Opposite*: thoughtfully

mind-numbing *adj* **boring**, dull, tedious, tiresome, wearisome *Opposite*: interesting

mindset *n* **attitude**, outlook, mind, mentality, way of thinking

mind your own business *v* **keep your nose out of it**, keep off, keep out of it, keep yourself to yourself, mind your own beeswax *(US)* *Opposite*: snoop

mine *n* **1 pit**, excavation, colliery, coalfield, coalmine **2 source**, repository, fund, gold mine, store *Opposite*: dearth ■ v **extract**, excavate, quarry, dig, dig out

minefield *n* **problem**, trial, test, ordeal, hazard

miner *n* **tunneller**, sapper, coalminer, collier, driller

mingle *v* **1 mix**, blend, fuse, join, unite *Opposite*: separate **2 circulate**, associate, intermingle, socialize, mix

mingy *(infml) adj* **mean**, ungenerous, inadequate, sparse, stingy *(infml) Opposite*: generous

mini *(infml) adj* **small**, miniature, baby, diminutive, tiny *Opposite*: maxi

miniature *adj* **small-scale**, small, tiny, minute, little *Opposite*: enormous

miniaturization *n* **reduction**, shrinking, contraction, diminishment *Opposite*: enlargement

miniaturize *v* **reduce**, scale down, shrink, contract, diminish *Opposite*: enlarge

minibar *n* **bar**, fridge, cupboard, cooler, cocktail cabinet

minibreak *(infml) n* **long weekend**, weekend, holiday, break, vacation

minimal *adj* **1 negligible**, trifling, slight, nominal, token *Opposite*: significant **2 least**, smallest, minimum, tiniest, minutest *Opposite*: maximum

minimalism *n* **simplicity**, plainness, cleanness, austereness, starkness *Opposite*: elaboration

minimalist *adj* **simple**, uncluttered, understated, discreet, plain *Opposite*: baroque

minimize *v* **1 minimalize**, diminish, curtail, lessen, reduce *Opposite*: maximize **2 play down**, make light of, reduce, dismiss, shrug off *Opposite*: exaggerate

minimum *n* **least**, bare minimum, smallest amount, iota, jot *Opposite*: maximum ■ *adj* **smallest**, least, lowest, tiniest, minutest *Opposite*: maximum

minion *n* **follower**, assistant, hanger-on, underling, crony *Opposite*: superior

miniseries *n* **series**, serial, soap, drama, serialization

minister *n* **priest**, vicar, rector, parson, reverend ■ v *(fml)* **attend**, look after, care for, tend, nurse *Opposite*: neglect

ministerial *adj* **governmental**, parliamentary, cabinet, official, legislative

ministration *(fml) n* **care**, support, attention, nurture, aid *Opposite*: neglect

ministry *n* **office**, bureau, department, agency, organization

minnow *n* **small fry**, little man, little guy, nobody, sprat

minor *adj* **1 slight**, small, negligible, inconsequential, trivial *Opposite*: major **2 lesser**, inferior, junior, secondary, lower *Opposite*: major ■ *n* **juvenile**, youth, adolescent, child, teenager *Opposite*: adult

minority *n* **section**, faction, interest group, pressure group, subgroup ■ *adj* **alternative**, underground, marginal, sectional, smaller *Opposite*: majority

minstrel *n* **musician**, troubadour, wandering minstrel, player, entertainer

mint *n* *(infml)* **fortune**, millions, billions, pile *(infml)*, packet *(infml) Opposite*: pittance ■ v **cast**, issue, imprint, make, strike

minus *prep* **1 less**, take away, excluding, reduced by, with the subtraction of *Opposite*: plus **2 without**, lacking, excluding, exclusive of, with the exception of *Opposite*: including ■ *n* **1 deficiency**, loss, drop, fall, decrease *Opposite*: addition **2 disadvantage**, detriment, handicap, hindrance, drawback *Opposite*: plus

minuscule *adj* **tiny**, minute, microscopic, infinitesimal, little *Opposite*: gigantic

minute *n* **moment**, instant, second, flash, sec *(infml) Opposite*: ages *(infml)* ■ v **record**, summarize, write down, précis, transcribe ■ *adj* **1 miniature**, tiny, minuscule, microscopic, infinitesimal *Opposite*: enormous

2 close, detailed, thorough, exhaustive, painstaking *Opposite*: cursory

minuteness *n* **smallness**, tininess, shortness, compactness

minutes *n* **notes**, record, proceedings, transcript, transcription

minutiae *n* **details**, niceties, intricacies, particulars, ins and outs *Opposite*: gist

miracle *n* **wonder**, phenomenon, marvel, sensation, vision

miraculous *adj* **amazing**, astounding, astonishing, incredible, unbelievable *Opposite*: mundane

mirage *n* **hallucination**, optical illusion, illusion, vision, delusion *Opposite*: reality

mire *n* **swamp**, marsh, mud, sludge, slush

mirror *n* **glass**, hand mirror, shaving mirror, looking glass *(dated)* ■ *v* **1 reflect**, echo, copy, parallel, emulate **2 represent**, symbolize, illustrate, typify, signify

mirror image *n* **double**, twin, copy, replica, likeness

mirth *n* **laughter**, hilarity, humour, jollity, fun *Opposite*: sadness

mirthful *adj* **joyful**, merry, gleeful, jovial, cheery *Opposite*: mirthless

mirthless *adj* **cheerless**, dour, gloomy, grim, dismal *Opposite*: cheerful

misadventure *n* **accident**, mishap, misfortune, disaster, calamity

misaligned *adj* **askew**, skewed, awry, cock-eyed, crooked *Opposite*: straight

misalliance *n* **mismatch**, inequality, bad match, disparity, mésalliance

misanthropic *adj* **cynical**, pessimistic, distrustful, disdainful, sardonic *Opposite*: philanthropic

misanthropy *n* **cynicism**, pessimism, distrust, disdain, sardonicism *Opposite*: philanthropy

misapplication *n* **misuse**, abuse, misemployment, mishandling, exploitation

misapply *v* **misuse**, abuse, misemploy, mishandle, mismanage

misapprehend *v* **mistake**, misunderstand, misinterpret, misconstrue, misjudge

misapprehension *n* **misunderstanding**, misinterpretation, wrong idea, false impression, misconception *Opposite*: comprehension

misappropriate *v* **steal**, embezzle, pocket, take, help yourself *Opposite*: reimburse. *See* COMPARE AND CONTRAST *at* **steal**.

misappropriation *n* **embezzlement**, misuse, stealing, dishonesty, fraud

misbegotten *adj* **ill-conceived**, bad, inappropriate, foolish, deplorable

misbehave *v* **be naughty**, be bad, play up, act up, behave badly *Opposite*: behave

misbehaviour *n* **naughtiness**, misconduct, mischief, disobedience, waywardness

miscalculate *v* **misjudge**, underestimate, overestimate, get it wrong, overvalue

miscalculation *n* **error**, mistake, inaccuracy, blunder, slip

miscarriage *(fml)* *n* **failure**, lapse, breakdown, insufficiency, mistake

miscarriage of justice *n* **wrongful conviction**, unfair ruling, injustice, judicial error, mistake

miscarry *(fml)* *v* **fail**, founder, backfire, go wrong, go amiss

miscellaneous *adj* **various**, varied, assorted, mixed, diverse *Opposite*: homogeneous

miscellany *n* **assortment**, collection, selection, grouping, medley

mischance *n* **misfortune**, ill fortune, bad luck, ill luck, misadventure

mischief *n* **1 misbehaviour**, naughtiness, trouble, disobedience, waywardness **2 harm**, damage, trouble, disruption, injury **3 troublemaker**, nuisance, rascal, scamp *(infml)*, monkey *(infml)*

mischief-maker *n* **meddler**, troublemaker, gossip, ringleader, instigator

mischievous *adj* **1 naughty**, playful, impish, roguish, badly behaved *Opposite*: well-behaved **2** *(fml)* **harmful**, damaging, malicious, wicked, negative *Opposite*: harmless. *See* COMPARE AND CONTRAST *at* **bad**.

mischievousness *n* **1 naughtiness**, bad behaviour, impishness, playfulness, disobedience **2** *(fml)* **malice**, hatred, harm, animosity, spite

misconceive *v* **misunderstand**, misapprehend, misinterpret, get the wrong impression, get the wrong idea *Opposite*: understand

misconceived *adj* **ill-conceived**, ill-thought-out, flawed, misguided, inappropriate

misconception *n* **fallacy**, delusion, misapprehension, misconstruction, mistaken belief *Opposite*: fact

misconduct *n* **bad behaviour**, misbehaviour, delinquency, transgression, wrongdoing

misconstruction *n* **misinterpretation**, misunderstanding, misreading, false impression, misjudgment *Opposite*: understanding

misconstrue *v* **misinterpret**, misunderstand, misread, get the wrong idea about, get the wrong impression about *Opposite*: understand

miscount *v* **lose count**, miscalculate, make a mistake, underestimate, overestimate

misdeed *n* **misdemeanour**, crime, offence, wrong, transgression

misdemeanour *n* **1 petty larceny**, crime, offence, malfeasance **2 misdeed**, wrongdoing, lapse, transgression, foul

misdirect *v* **1 point in the wrong direction**, lead astray, send off course, send on a wild goose chase *Opposite*: direct **2 misallocate**, misuse, misapply, waste, misemploy

miser *n* **1** hoarder, accumulator, saver, collector, squirrel *(infml)* **2** skinflint, pinchpenny, penny pincher *(infml)*, cheapskate *(infml)*, scrooge *(infml)* *Opposite*: spendthrift

miserable *adj* **1** unhappy, sad, depressed, down, despondent *Opposite*: happy **2** depressing, cheerless, wretched, desolate, gloomy *Opposite*: cheery **3** inadequate, paltry, derisory, miserly, mean *Opposite*: generous **4** gloomy, dull, grey, overcast, dreary *Opposite*: bright

miserliness *n* parsimoniousness, greed, greediness, tightfistedness, avariciousness *Opposite*: generosity

miserly *adj* **1** mean, tightfisted, parsimonious, tight, niggardly *Opposite*: generous **2** paltry, derisory, mean, miserable, meagre *Opposite*: generous

misery *n* **1** unhappiness, sadness, depression, desolation, gloom *Opposite*: happiness **2** deprivation, destitution, distress, poverty, privation **3** *(infml)* grumbler, whiner, wet blanket *(infml)*, grouch *(infml)*, moaner *(infml)*

misfire *v* go wrong, backfire, fail, fall through, not come off *Opposite*: succeed

misfit *n* oddity, eccentric, loner, odd one out, nonconformist *Opposite*: conformist

misfortune *n* disaster, calamity, trial, tribulation, misadventure *Opposite*: opportunity

misgiving *n* scruple, qualm, doubt, niggle, suspicion

misguided *adj* mistaken, foolish, ill-advised, unwise, erroneous *Opposite*: wise

mishandle *v* **1** mismanage, make a mess of, misapply, misuse, botch *(infml)* **2** abuse, mistreat, exploit, ill-treat, rough up *(infml)*

mishap *n* accident, calamity, misfortune, disaster, catastrophe

mishear *v* hear wrong, get wrong, pick up wrong, not get, be mistaken

mishit *v* miss, nick, clip, hit a foul, slice ■ *n* error, slice, hook, miss, nick

mishmash *n* hotchpotch, jumble, muddle, miscellany, mixture

misinform *v* mislead, deceive, lie to, lead on, lead astray

misinformation *n* propaganda, dishonesty, distortion, fabrication, bending of the truth *Opposite*: fact

misinterpret *v* misconstrue, misunderstand, misread, get the wrong idea about, get the wrong impression about *Opposite*: understand

misinterpretation *n* misunderstanding, misconception, misapprehension, misreading, confusion *Opposite*: understanding

misjudge *v* miscalculate, underestimate, overestimate, be wrong about, get the wrong idea

misjudgment *n* **1** poor judgment, error of judgment, error, miscalculation, slip **2** wrong impression, misinterpretation, miscon-

struction, false reading, prejudice *Opposite*: understanding

mislaid *adj* lost, missing, nowhere to be found, gone astray, misplaced

mislay *v* lose, misplace, be unable to find, miss, put in the wrong place *Opposite*: find

mislead *v* give the wrong impression, misinform, deceive, lie, delude

misleading *adj* deceptive, ambiguous, confusing, false, disingenuous *Opposite*: truthful

mismanage *v* mishandle, make a mess of, misuse, manage badly, botch *(infml)*

mismanagement *n* mishandling, misconduct, negligence, malpractice, maladministration *Opposite*: efficiency

mismatch *n* incongruity, discrepancy, gap, disparity, misalliance *Opposite*: harmony

mismatched *adj* incompatible, unequal, uneven, unjust, one-sided

misnomer *n* misleading term, inaccurate term, poor description, loose term, contradiction

misplace *v* lose, mislay, be unable to put your hands on, drop, leave behind *Opposite*: find

misplaced *adj* **1** inappropriate, erroneous, misdirected, out-of-place, inapt *Opposite*: appropriate **2** mislaid, nowhere to be found, missing, lost, gone astray

misprint *n* typographical error, error, mistake, blunder, oversight

mispronounce *v* say wrong, distort, mangle, make a mess of, stumble through *Opposite*: articulate

mispronunciation *n* distortion, error, misstatement, slip, blunder

misquote *v* put words in somebody's mouth, misreport, misrepresent, misattribute, quote out of context

misread *v* misjudge, misinterpret, misunderstand, misconstrue, get the wrong idea *Opposite*: interpret

misrepresent *v* parody, pervert, twist, distort, pass off

misrepresentation *n* parody, caricature, distortion, falsification, twisting

misrule *n* **1** misgovernment, mishandling, corruption, maladministration, mismanagement **2** lawlessness, anarchy, unruliness, chaos, turmoil *Opposite*: order

miss *v* **1** overlook, fail to spot, let pass, fail to notice, fail to see *Opposite*: see **2** skip, fail to attend, escape, avoid, forget *Opposite*: attend **3** forego, lose, pass up, let pass, let go *Opposite*: take up **4** pine for, long for, yearn for, wish for, grieve for ■ *n* **1** omission, oversight, delinquency, neglect, mistake **2** failure, false step, error, slip, miscue

missal *n* service book, prayer book, liturgical book, breviary, Psalter

misshapen *adj* distorted, twisted, deformed, malformed, warped *Opposite*: shapely

missing adj **lost**, absent, gone astray, misplaced, mislaid *Opposite*: present

mission n 1 **assignment**, task, job, work, undertaking 2 **calling**, vocation, purpose, goal, aim 3 **delegation**, deputation, task force, legation, embassy

missionary n 1 **evangelist**, proselytizer, preacher, minister, priest 2 **campaigner**, champion, crusader, proselytizer, propagandist

missive n **letter**, communiqué, note, communication, memo

miss out v 1 **omit**, leave out, disregard, miss, exclude *Opposite*: include 2 **fail to benefit**, forgo, miss the boat, miss an opportunity, miss a chance *Opposite*: benefit

misspelling n **spelling mistake**, wrong spelling, misspelt word, slip, error

misspend v **squander**, fritter away, waste, throw away, misuse *Opposite*: save

misspent adj **wasted**, squandered, frittered away, misused, thrown away *Opposite*: profitable

misstep n **mistake**, slip, gaffe, blunder, error

miss the boat v **miss an opportunity**, miss a chance, miss out, fail to benefit, forego

miss the point v **misunderstand**, misinterpret, misconstrue, fail to understand, misread *Opposite*: understand

mist n **haze**, fog, vapour, smog, spray

mistake n 1 **blunder**, gaffe, slip, lapse, miscalculation 2 **error**, fault, inaccuracy, oversight, misspelling ■ v 1 **misunderstand**, misjudge, misinterpret, misconstrue, confuse *Opposite*: understand 2 **confuse with**, take for, mix up with, confound, mix *Opposite*: recognize

---

COMPARE AND CONTRAST CORE MEANING: something incorrect or improper

mistake an unwise decision or an error resulting from a lack of care; **error** something that unintentionally deviates from a recognized standard or guide; **inaccuracy** something that is incorrect because it has been measured, calculated, copied, or conveyed incorrectly; **slip** a minor mistake or oversight, especially one caused by carelessness; **blunder** a serious or embarrassing mistake, usually the result of carelessness or ignorance; **faux pas** (*literary*) an embarrassing mistake that breaks a social convention.

---

mistaken adj **wrong**, incorrect, false, erroneous, faulty *Opposite*: correct

mistime v **misjudge**, miss the boat, anticipate, jump the gun, pre-empt *Opposite*: coordinate

mistiness n 1 **haziness**, murkiness, duskiness, cloudiness, fogginess *Opposite*: clearness 2 **vagueness**, indistinctness, obscurity, opacity, lack of clarity *Opposite*: clarity

mist over v **mist**, mist up, fog over, become hazy, become clouded *Opposite*: clear

mistreat v **abuse**, misuse, ill-treat, harm, mishandle *Opposite*: pamper. *See* COMPARE AND CONTRAST *at* **misuse**.

mistreated adj **abused**, neglected, wronged, injured, victimized *Opposite*: pampered

mistreatment n **maltreatment**, exploitation, abuse, ill-treatment, neglect *Opposite*: pampering

mistress n 1 **lover**, concubine, courtesan, kept woman, ladyfriend (*infml*) *Opposite*: wife 2 **owner**, trainer, keeper, rider 3 **expert**, specialist, queen, doyenne, leading exponent *Opposite*: novice 4 **teacher**, schoolmistress, governess, instructress, schoolteacher *Opposite*: pupil 5 **manager**, employer, controller, proprietor, owner *Opposite*: servant

mistrial n **invalid trial**, unfair trial, miscarriage of justice, travesty, injustice

mistrust n **suspicion**, distrust, doubt, wariness, uncertainty *Opposite*: trust ■ v **distrust**, doubt, suspect, be wary of, be suspicious of *Opposite*: trust

mistrustful adj **distrustful**, wary, suspicious, doubtful, sceptical *Opposite*: trusting

misty adj 1 **hazy**, foggy, murky, cloudy, steamy *Opposite*: clear 2 **indistinct**, vague, obscure, dim, opaque *Opposite*: clear

misty-eyed adj 1 **tearful**, emotional, teary, teary-eyed, close to tears *Opposite*: dry-eyed 2 **sentimental**, nostalgic, romantic, weepy (*infml*), soppy (*infml*) *Opposite*: unsentimental

misunderstand v **get the wrong idea**, misinterpret, misread, misconstrue, get the wrong impression *Opposite*: understand

misunderstanding n 1 **mistake**, mix-up, confusion, misinterpretation, misconstruction 2 **quarrel**, row, argument, difference of opinion, disagreement *Opposite*: agreement

misunderstood adj **unacknowledged**, unrecognized, unappreciated, undervalued, misjudged *Opposite*: valued

misuse n **misappropriation**, misapplication, waste, ill use, mismanagement ■ v 1 **waste**, misappropriate, squander, misapply, mishandle 2 **abuse**, exploit, mistreat, maltreat, ill-treat *Opposite*: cherish

---

COMPARE AND CONTRAST CORE MEANING: treat somebody or something wrongly or badly

misuse put something to an inappropriate use or purpose, or treat a person or animal badly or harshly; **abuse** use in a wrong or inappropriate way something that should be used responsibly, for example a power, privilege, or a substance such as alcohol or a drug. It is also used to refer to cruel or violent treatment of a person or animal, especially on a regular or habitual basis; **ill-treat** or **maltreat** behave cruelly towards a person or animal, or treat something roughly and carelessly; **mistreat** treat a person badly, inconsiderately, or unfairly, not necessarily in a way involving physical cruelty, or treat something roughly and carelessly.

mite *(dated)* n **jot**, bit, scrap, speck, grain

mitigate v **alleviate**, lessen, ease, allay, moderate *Opposite*: aggravate

mitigating adj **justifying**, extenuating, modifying, qualifying, vindicating *Opposite*: aggravating

mitigation n **1 extenuation**, vindication, justification, qualification, moderation **2 alleviation**, easing, improvement, lessening, relief *Opposite*: intensification

mix v **1 mix up**, mingle, intermingle, blend, intersperse *Opposite*: separate **2 combine**, blend, unite, merge, join *Opposite*: separate out **3 fraternize**, mingle, associate, get together, socialize **3 go together**, accord, agree, fit, harmonize *Opposite*: clash ▪ n **combination**, mixture, blend, assortment, fusion

mixed adj **1 varied**, diverse, assorted, sundry, miscellaneous *Opposite*: uniform **2 cosmopolitan**, integrated, international, interracial, multiracial *Opposite*: segregated

mixed bag n **ragbag**, assortment, combination, jumble, variety

mixed-up *(infml)* adj **1 confused**, muddled, bewildered, puzzled, perplexed *Opposite*: clear **2 disturbed**, maladjusted, confused, troubled, rebellious *Opposite*: well-adjusted

mixture n **combination**, mix, blend, amalgam, concoction

COMPARE AND CONTRAST CORE MEANING: something formed by mixing materials

mixture a number of elements or ingredients brought together; **blend** something formed by putting together two or more different kinds of things, especially in a skilled way, to form a new whole in which the original elements lose their distinctness; **combination** something formed by the association of two or more things that retain their distinctness; **compound** a technical word for a chemical formed from two or more elements, also used generally to describe anything composed of two or more separate parts; **alloy** a technical word for a metal such as steel that is formed by combining two or more different metallic elements; **amalgam** a technical word for an alloy formed by combining mercury with another metal, also used generally to describe something that is a mixture of two or more elements or characteristics.

---

mix up v **1 confuse**, misunderstand, muddle, confound, mistake *Opposite*: straighten out **2 mix**, combine, merge, blend, fuse *Opposite*: separate

mix-up n **mistake**, muddle, misunderstanding, confusion, error

mnemonic n **memory aid**, reminder, prompt, cue, aide-mémoire *(fml)*

mo *(infml)* n **tick** *(infml)*, sec *(infml)*, half a tick *(infml)*, half a sec *(infml)*, moment

moan v **1 groan**, sigh, whine, whimper, wail **2** *(infml)* **complain**, grumble, whinge *(infml)*, whine, gripe *(infml)* ▪ n *(infml)* **complaint**, grumble, gripe *(infml)*, whinge *(infml)*, grouse *(infml) Opposite*: compliment

moaner *(infml)* n **grumbler**, complainer, whiner, wailer, objector

moat n **ditch**, trench, fosse, channel, dyke *Opposite*: bank

mob n **1 crowd**, horde, mass, multitude, throng **2** *(infml)* **masses**, populace, plebs, hoi polloi, rabble *Opposite*: elite ▪ v **1 besiege**, descend on, crowd round, surround, swarm around *Opposite*: attack, jostle, pester, set upon, set about *Opposite*: defend

mobile adj **1 active**, flexible, limber, supple, agile *Opposite*: immobile **2 expressive**, changing, changeable, lively, communicative *Opposite*: inexpressive **3 movable**, portable, transportable, itinerant, peripatetic *Opposite*: fixed **4 upwardly mobile**, successful, ambitious, aspiring, rising *Opposite*: unambitious

mobility n **1 flexibility**, freedom of movement, agility, suppleness, movement *Opposite*: stasis **2 progress**, social mobility, upward mobility, success, promotion

mobilization n **enlistment**, deployment, armament, organization, utilization *Opposite*: demobilization

mobilize v **rally**, assemble, muster, drum up, gather together *Opposite*: demobilize

mock v **1 ridicule**, tease, make fun of, laugh at, poke fun at *Opposite*: praise **2 mimic**, imitate, parody, ape, simulate ▪ adj **fake**, pretend, simulated, imitation, artificial *Opposite*: genuine. See COMPARE AND CONTRAST at **ridicule**.

mocker n **ridiculer**, derider, scorner, scoffer, caricaturist

mockery n **1 ridicule**, scorn, derision, contempt, disdain *Opposite*: respect **2 travesty**, charade, farce, sham, caricature *Opposite*: exemplar *(literary)*

mocking adj **scornful**, derisive, contemptuous, disdainful, sardonic *Opposite*: respectful

mock-up n **replica**, copy, model, sample, dummy

mode n **form**, style, manner, method, means

model n **1 replica**, mock-up, representation, copy, reproduction **2 type**, sort, style, kind, version **3 example**, paradigm, pattern, standard, prototype ▪ v **1 demonstrate**, show, exhibit, display, show off **2 sculpt**, mould, form, shape, fashion ▪ adj **perfect**, classical, prototypical, typical, archetypal *Opposite*: atypical

moderate adj **1 reasonable**, modest, sensible, restrained, judicious *Opposite*: excessive **2 average**, medium, normal, balanced, middling *Opposite*: extraordinary ▪ v **1 curb**, control, tone down, play down, diminish *Opposite*: intensify **2 arbitrate**, mediate, referee, facilitate, umpire

moderately adv **reasonably**, rather, somewhat, fairly, comparatively Opposite: excessively

moderation n **restraint**, control, self-control, temperance, fairness Opposite: excess

moderator n **mediator**, go-between, arbiter, arbitrator, referee

modern adj **1 contemporary**, current, up-to-date, up-to-the-minute, recent Opposite: old-fashioned **2 state-of-the-art**, latest, cutting-edge, leading-edge, novel Opposite: outdated **3 progressive**, enlightened, forward-looking, avant-garde, advanced Opposite: traditional. See COMPARE AND CONTRAST at **new**.

modern-day adj **contemporary**, modern, current, recent, present-day Opposite: past

modernism n **innovation**, innovativeness, novelty, originality, modernization Opposite: traditionalism

modernistic adj **ultramodern**, modern, radical, futuristic, avant-garde Opposite: traditional

modernity n **modernism**, innovation, innovativeness, freshness, newness Opposite: traditionalism

modernization n **transformation**, upgrading, innovation, reconstruction, renewal

modernize v **update**, renovate, streamline, revolutionize, reform

modernizer n **innovator**, pacesetter, trendsetter, new broom, visionary

modest adj **1 self-effacing**, humble, reserved, discreet, unpretentious Opposite: arrogant **2 shy**, meek, diffident, quiet, reserved Opposite: overbearing **3 unexceptional**, ordinary, humble, unpretentious, plain Opposite: showy **4 moderate**, reasonable, acceptable, small, low Opposite: excessive

modesty n **humility**, reserve, reticence, diffidence, shyness Opposite: arrogance

modicum n **little**, bit, degree, scrap, ounce

modification n **change**, alteration, adjustment, amendment, reform

modified adj **adapted**, altered, changed, improved, revised Opposite: unmodified

modify v **1 alter**, change, adapt, adjust, amend Opposite: maintain **2 lessen**, reduce, restrain, moderate, curb Opposite: intensify. See COMPARE AND CONTRAST at **change**.

modish adj **fashionable**, stylish, in, chic, up-to-the-minute Opposite: unfashionable

modular adj **linked**, flexible, integrated, prefabricated, segmental

modulate v **1 adjust**, alter, amend, vary, modify **2 moderate**, curb, control, tone down, play down Opposite: intensify

modulation n **1 adjustment**, change, alteration, swing, variation **2 inflection**, intonation, accent, lilt, cadence Opposite: flatness

module n **unit**, component, part, element, section

modus operandi n **method**, formula, technique, way, protocol

modus vivendi n **1 compromise**, arrangement, settlement, deal, bargain **2 practice**, way of life, lifestyle, standard of living, habit

moggy (infml) n **cat**, puss (infml), pussy (infml)

mogul n **tycoon**, entrepreneur, magnate, industrialist, dynast

moist adj **damp**, wet, humid, soggy, clammy Opposite: dry

moisten v **dampen**, wet, moisturize, humidify, sprinkle Opposite: dry

moistness n **dampness**, humidity, wetness, clamminess, sogginess Opposite: aridity

moisture n **damp**, dampness, wetness, humidity, moistness Opposite: dryness

moisturize v **1 nourish**, soothe, oil, condition, treat Opposite: dry **2 moisten**, dampen, wet, humidify, spray

moisturizer n **cold cream**, cream, lotion, conditioner, night cream

molasses n **syrup**, treacle, golden syrup, black treacle, blackstrap molasses

mole n **spy**, infiltrator, secret agent, undercover agent, plant

molecule n **particle**, bit, iota, speck, shred

molest v **1 assault**, mistreat, abuse, attack, feel up (infml) **2 bother**, pester, annoy, torment, harass

mollify v **pacify**, calm, placate, appease, calm down Opposite: enrage

mollycoddle v **pamper**, fuss over, spoil, overprotect, cosset

molten adj **melted**, liquefied, liquid, fluid, heated Opposite: solid

moment n **1 instant**, second, minute, split second, flash Opposite: age **2** (fml) **importance**, significance, weight, import, substance

momentarily adv **for a moment**, briefly, temporarily, fleetingly, transitorily

momentary adj **brief**, fleeting, passing, temporary, transitory Opposite: interminable

momentous adj **important**, significant, historic, earthshattering, crucial Opposite: insignificant

momentum n **impetus**, thrust, energy, force, drive Opposite: brake

monarch n **ruler**, sovereign, crowned head, emperor, king Opposite: subject

monarchism n **royalism**, imperialism, elitism, tsarism, traditionalism Opposite: republicanism

monarchist n **royalist**, loyalist, counter-revolutionary, traditionalist, imperialist Opposite: revolutionary

monarchy n **realm**, kingdom, dominion, domain, empire Opposite: republic

monastery n **religious foundation**, religious community, cloister, friary, abbey

monastic adj **austere**, reclusive, simple, spartan, frugal

monetary adj financial, fiscal, economic, monetarist, pecuniary

money n 1 cash, currency, ready money, ready cash, coinage 2 capital, funds, riches, means, wherewithal

moneybags (infml) n millionaire, multimillionaire, billionaire, tycoon, mogul

money box n piggy bank, cash box, collecting box, safe

moneyed adj wealthy, rich, affluent, prosperous, comfortable

moneylender n lender, financier, banker, pawnbroker, loan shark

moneymaker n 1 tycoon, speculator, magnate, investor, mogul 2 hit, success, gold mine, profit centre, money-spinner (infml)

moneymaking adj profitable, commercial, economic, fruitful, lucrative

money-spinner (infml) n hit, moneymaker, cash cow (slang), going concern, success

money-spinning (infml) adj economic, profitable, lucrative, fruitful, worthwhile

mongrel n dog, cur, hound, crossbreed, pyedog Opposite: pedigree

monitor n 1 screen, display, VDU, television set 2 observer, supervisor, overseer, inspector, invigilator ■ v observe, keep an eye on, supervise, scrutinize, examine

monk n holy man, religious, monastic, friar, abbot

monkey (infml) n 1 fool, laughing stock, dupe, ass, butt 2 mischief, rogue, rascal, scamp (infml), scallywag (dated infml)

monkey around v fool around, joke, play the fool, clown around, lark

monkey business (infml) n tricks, mischief, trouble, pranks, high jinks (infml)

monkey with v tamper, meddle, interfere, fiddle, tinker

monkish adj reclusive, austere, withdrawn, cloistered, simple Opposite: worldly

monochromatic adj 1 unicolour, homochromous, self-coloured, homochromatic, shaded 2 dull, indistinct, neutral, uniform, toneless Opposite: colourful

monochrome adj 1 unicolour, homochromous, homochromatic, self-coloured, monochromatic 2 neutral, colourless, dull, indeterminate, toneless Opposite: colourful

monocle n eyeglass, glass, lens

monogamous adj faithful, exclusive, committed, married, steady Opposite: bigamous

monogamy n exclusivity, fidelity, commitment, marriage, coupledom Opposite: bigamy

monogram n initials, signet, logo, seal, stamp ■ v mark, initial, sign, seal, identify

monograph n book, article, paper, essay, thesis

monolith n standing stone, menhir, megalith, sarsen, stone

monolithic adj colossal, monumental, massive, uniform, immovable

monologue n 1 soliloquy, speech, prologue, epilogue, aside Opposite: dialogue 2 harangue, rant, speech, running commentary, lecture Opposite: conversation

monopolistic adj anticompetitive, unchallenged, controlling, autocratic, exploitative Opposite: competitive

monopolization n control, domination, appropriation, takeover, expropriation Opposite: cooperation

monopolize v control, dominate, take over, corner, exploit Opposite: share

monopoly n control, domination, cartel, corner, trust (US)

monosyllabic adj uncommunicative, curt, gruff, brief, short Opposite: verbose

monosyllable n word, syllable, grunt, squeak Opposite: polysyllable

monotheism n theism, deism Opposite: polytheism

monotone n drone, whine, chant, intonation, mutter

monotonous adj dull, repetitious, uninteresting, repetitive, boring Opposite: varied

monotony n 1 tedium, dullness, boredom, flatness, dreariness Opposite: excitement 2 uniformity, repetitiousness, sameness, repetitiveness, predictability Opposite: variety

monsoon n rainy season, wet season, rains

monster n 1 fiend, ogre, beast, brute 2 giant, behemoth, leviathan, whopper (infml), biggie (infml) ■ adj huge, enormous, giant, monstrous, gigantic Opposite: small

monstrosity n eyesore, blot on the landscape, atrocity, sight, horror

monstrous adj 1 atrocious, outrageous, horrific, immoral, evil 2 huge, enormous, giant, monster, gigantic Opposite: small 3 hideous, grotesque, gruesome, ugly, horrible Opposite: lovely

monstrously adv preposterously, shockingly, offensively, unbelievably, prodigiously Opposite: unexceptionally

montage n mosaic, tableau, medley, mixture, pastiche

monthly adj 1 regular, periodic, frequent, once-a-month, scheduled Opposite: occasional 2 month-long, 30-day, period, season, medium-term ■ adv regularly, once a month, periodically, frequently, at monthly intervals Opposite: irregularly ■ n magazine, publication, periodical, journal, bulletin

monument n 1 headstone, marker, tombstone, gravestone 2 memorial, testimonial, testament, tribute

monumental adj 1 colossal, epic, immense, massive, enormous Opposite: small 2 historic, classic, significant, important, epic Opposite: minor

mooch *(infml)* *v* **wheedle**, beg, sponge *(infml)*, cadge *(infml)*, scrounge *(infml)*

moocher *(infml)* *n* **scrounger**, taker, sponger *(infml)*, cadger *(infml)*, freeloader *(infml)*

mood *n* **1 frame of mind**, disposition, temper, attitude, temperament **2 temper**, bad temper, sulk, the doldrums, anger **3 atmosphere**, feel, air, feeling, ambience

moodiness *n* **sulkiness**, changeableness, sullenness, grumpiness, glumness *Opposite*: cheeriness

moody *adj* **temperamental**, morose, sulky, sullen, glum *Opposite*: predictable

moon *v* **1 wander**, drift, meander, amble, dawdle **2** *(literary)* **fantasize**, dream, daydream, languish, pine

moonbeam *n* **ray**, moonlight, shaft of light, moonshine, glint *Opposite*: sunbeam

moonlight *(infml)* *v* **do work on the side**, do two jobs, supplement your income, have a second job, have a night job

moonscape *n* **wasteland**, desert, wilderness, barren land, waste

moonshine *n* **1** *(infml)* **poteen**, bootleg alcohol, home-brew, firewater *(dated slang)*, white lightning *(US)* **2 nonsense**, fantasy, silliness, fiction, gibberish

moonshot *n* **rocket launch**, launch, lunar expedition, lunar exploration, mission

moonstruck *(infml)* *adj* **dazed**, confused, irrational, distracted, in a daze *Opposite*: alert

moor *n* **heath**, moorland, common, upland, fell ■ *v* **tie**, fix, secure, chain, attach *Opposite*: untie

mooring *n* **anchorage**, berth, tie-up, bay, reserved space

moot *adj* **debatable**, arguable, doubtful, controversial, unresolved *Opposite*: established ■ *v* **propose**, put forward, suggest, bring up, introduce

mop *v* **wipe**, clean, swab, dust, mop up

mope *v* **brood**, languish, pine, sulk, pout

moppet *(infml)* *n* **child**, toddler, little one, tot *(infml)*, kid *(infml)*

mop up *v* **1 wipe up**, clear up, mop, wipe, swab **2** *(infml)* **finish off**, dispose of, see to, deal with, polish off

moraine *n* **glacial deposit**, debris, rubble, residue

moral *adj* **ethical**, good, right, honest, decent *Opposite*: immoral ■ *n* **message**, meaning, significance, rule, maxim

morale *n* **confidence**, self-esteem, spirits, self-confidence, assurance *Opposite*: aimlessness

moralist *n* **1 moralizer**, censor, preacher, critic, philosopher **2 virtuous person**, upright person, puritan, saint, prude

moralistic *adj* **moralizing**, didactic, strait-laced, serious, upright

morality *n* **1 ethics**, morals, principles, standards, scruples **2 goodness**, decency, probity, honesty, integrity *Opposite*: wickedness

moralize *v* **preach**, lecture, sermonize, criticize, nag

moralizing *n* **lecturing**, sermonizing, instruction, remonstration, admonishment ■ *adj* **lecturing**, critical, preaching, exhorting, hectoring *Opposite*: unprincipled

morals *n* **ethics**, morality, standards, scruples, principles

morass *n* **1 bog**, marsh, mire, swamp, wetland **2 mess**, chaos, muddle, quagmire, mire

moratorium *n* **suspension**, freeze, halt, pause, cessation

morbid *adj* **1 morose**, gloomy, dark, moody, melancholic *Opposite*: cheerful **2 gruesome**, dark, sinister, macabre, perverse

morbidity *n* **illness**, injury, disease, ill health, indisposition *Opposite*: health

mordant *adj* **caustic**, astringent, acerbic, penetrating, sarcastic *Opposite*: gentle

more *adj* **additional**, extra, supplementary, added, further *Opposite*: less

moreish *(infml)* *adj* **tasty**, delectable, tempting, delicious, yummy *(infml)* *Opposite*: bland

moreover *adv* **furthermore**, what is more, in addition, besides, also

mores *n* **customs**, values, habits, traditions, patterns

morgue *n* **mortuary**, undertaker's, chapel of rest, funeral home *(US)*

moribund *adj* **1 dying**, failing, expiring, on your last legs, at death's door *Opposite*: well **2 declining**, on the way out, waning, past its best, on its last legs *Opposite*: thriving

morning *n* **dawn**, daybreak, sunrise, break of day, first light *Opposite*: evening

morose *adj* **miserable**, glum, depressed, down, low *Opposite*: cheery

morph *v* **transform**, alter, switch, convert, adapt

morphology *n* **shape**, form, contours, formation

morsel *n* **scrap**, crumb, bit, piece, fragment *Opposite*: chunk

mortal *adj* **1 earthly**, worldly, human, corporeal, finite *Opposite*: immortal **2 deadly**, fatal, lethal, life-threatening, terminal **3 extreme**, great, grave, severe, serious *Opposite*: mild ■ *n* **human being**, human, person, individual, soul. *See* COMPARE AND CONTRAST *at* **deadly**.

mortality *n* **humanity**, death, transience, impermanence

mortally *adv* **1 fatally**, lethally, incurably, terminally **2 extremely**, severely, seriously, greatly, very *Opposite*: mildly

mortgage *n* **loan**, bank loan, advance, secured loan, debt ■ *v* **pledge**, forfeit, offer as security, use as a guarantee, pawn

mortification n shame, degradation, indignity, embarrassment, chagrin

mortified adj ashamed, embarrassed, humiliated, horrified, offended Opposite: proud

mortify v degrade, humiliate, take down, embarrass, crush

mortifying adj humiliating, shameful, embarrassing, degrading, chastening Opposite: uplifting

mortuary n morgue, undertaker's, chapel of rest, funeral home (US)

mosaic n medley, assortment, mixture, variety, montage

mosey (infml) v saunter, wander, amble, stroll, dawdle Opposite: rush

mossy adj moss-covered, moss-grown, moss-topped, overgrown, green

most pron the majority, nearly everyone, nearly all, a good number, a large amount Opposite: few ■ adv very, highly, extremely, really, truly Opposite: fairly

mostly adv 1 for the most part, above all, mainly, generally, on the whole 2 usually, more often than not, normally, typically, commonly Opposite: rarely

mote n speck, particle, jot, iota, bit Opposite: mass

mothball v 1 postpone, delay, put on the back burner, put aside, put on ice 2 shut up, pack away, decommission, put into storage, put out of commission Opposite: open up

moth-eaten adj tattered, threadbare, tatty, dog-eared, worn Opposite: brand-new

mother v look after, care for, protect, nurse, tend Opposite: neglect

motherhood n maternity, parenthood, kinship Opposite: fatherhood

motherland n mother country, native country, birthplace, homeland, fatherland

motherly adj maternal, protective, caring, loving, kind Opposite: uncaring

motif n 1 design, pattern, image, decoration, shape 2 theme, idea, subject, topic, keynote

motion n 1 movement, action, activity, change, mobility Opposite: stillness 2 gesture, wave, signal, sign, gesticulation 3 proposal, suggestion, proposition, submission, recommendation ■ v signal, indicate, wave, gesture, beckon

motionless adj stationary, immobile, still, stock-still, static Opposite: moving

motionlessness n stillness, calm, immobility, paralysis, rigidity Opposite: mobility

motion picture n film, picture, feature film, video, flick (infml)

motivate v 1 cause, prompt, provoke, induce, spur Opposite: deter 2 inspire, stimulate, encourage, egg on, persuade Opposite: discourage

motivated adj interested, driven, inspired, moved, stirred Opposite: unmotivated

motivating adj stimulating, interesting, inspiring, galvanizing, encouraging Opposite: uninspiring

motivation n 1 incentive, inspiration, enthusiasm, impetus, stimulus Opposite: disincentive 2 reason, cause, motive, purpose, rationale

motivator n instigator, persuader, promoter, cheerleader, stimulus

motive n reason, motivation, spur, incentive, inducement Opposite: deterrent

---

COMPARE AND CONTRAST CORE MEANING: something that prompts action

motive the reason for doing something or behaving in a particular way; **incentive** something external, often some kind of reward, that inspires extra enthusiasm or effort; **inducement** something external that persuades or attracts somebody to a particular course of action, especially something that is offered as a reward; **spur** something such as the hope of a reward or the fear of punishment that encourages action or effort or energy; **goad** a stimulus that motivates somebody or stirs somebody into action, often against his or her will.

---

motiveless adj unprovoked, gratuitous, wanton, senseless, unwarranted Opposite: justified

motley adj assorted, miscellaneous, diverse, varied, mixed Opposite: uniform

motocross n scramble, cross-country race, motorcycle race, trail biking, motorcycle racing

motor n engine, petrol engine, diesel engine, internal combustion engine, electric motor ■ adj motorized, motor-powered, petrol-powered, diesel-powered, electrically powered ■ v 1 (fml) drive, travel, proceed, journey, ride 2 (infml) zoom, speed, tear along, race, zip (infml) Opposite: dawdle

motorcade n convoy, procession, parade, file, escort

motorist n driver, car driver, car user, car owner, chauffeur Opposite: passenger

motorized adj motor, motor-powered, petrol-powered, diesel-powered, electrically powered

mottled adj dappled, spotted, spotty, blotchy, speckled Opposite: plain

motto n slogan, saying, maxim, aphorism, adage

mould n 1 cast, container, form, die, tin 2 frame, pattern, template, stencil, outline 3 conformation, character, type, variety, vein 4 mildew, fungus, fungal growth, decay, rust ■ v 1 shape, fashion, style, sculpt, form 2 influence, change, guide, form, shape 3 cling, hug, follow, fit around, wrap around

moulder v rot, gather dust, disintegrate, crumble, decay

mouldiness n decay, disintegration, mustiness, mildew, rottenness

moulding n **decoration**, detail, cornice, beading, dado

mouldy adj **1 mildewed**, festering, fungal, decaying, decayed Opposite: fresh **2 stale**, neglected, dirty, musty, fusty Opposite: fresh **3 boring**, dull, dreary, drab, insipid Opposite: exciting

moult v **shed**, cast, peel, slough, scale

mound n **1 knoll**, hillock, embankment, bank, hill Opposite: valley **2 pile**, stack, mass, bundle, mountain

mount v **1 prepare**, set up, produce, launch, arrange **2 rise**, mount up, increase, accumulate, grow Opposite: decrease **3 get on**, climb on, jump on, board, go on Opposite: dismount **4 climb**, ascend, go up, climb up, clamber up Opposite: descend **5 frame**, box, encase, inset, affix ■ n **1 base**, stand, support, pedestal, plinth **2 horse**, mule, ass, donkey, pony

mountain n **1 peak**, mount, crag, fell, massif Opposite: valley **2 pile**, mass, stack, bundle, mound

mountaineer n **climber**, alpinist, rock climber

mountainous adj **1 hilly**, high, steep, precipitous, rocky Opposite: flat **2 huge**, enormous, immense, monumental, gigantic Opposite: tiny

mountainside n **slope**, shoulder, gradient, incline, hillside

mountaintop n **peak**, summit, pike, crest, hilltop Opposite: bottom

mounted adj **1 on horseback**, equestrian, astride, straddling, riding Opposite: on foot **2 attached**, fixed, affixed, screwed on, displayed Opposite: loose

mounting adj **rising**, increasing, growing, swelling, escalating Opposite: decreasing

mourn v **grieve**, lament, grieve for, grieve over, weep for Opposite: rejoice (literary)

mourner n **bereaved person**, funeral-goer, griever, widow, widower

mournful adj **sad**, sorrowful, sombre, woeful, doleful Opposite: cheerful

mournfulness n **sadness**, sombreness, melancholy, gloominess, despondency Opposite: cheerfulness

mourning n **grief**, bereavement, sorrow, sadness, lamentation Opposite: rejoicing

mouth n **1 maw**, trap (infml), gob (slang), cakehole (slang) **2 entrance**, opening, door, doorway, aperture **3 estuary**, outlet, bay, inlet **4** (infml) **insolence**, impertinence, rudeness, cheek (infml), backchat (infml) ■ v **say**, mime, state, utter, reply

WORD BANK
❏ **parts of a mouth** adenoids, denture, gum, lip, palate, roof, soft palate, taste bud, tongue, tonsils, tooth, uvula

mouthful n **1 bite**, taste, piece, spoonful, forkful **2 harangue**, sermon, lecture, tirade, earful (infml)

mouthpiece n **spokesperson**, representative, agent, ambassador, delegate

mouth-to-mouth n **artificial respiration**, kiss of life, resuscitation, cardiopulmonary resuscitation, CPR

mouthwash n **gargle**, rinse, breath freshener, mouth spray

mouthwatering adj **delicious**, delectable, lipsmacking, luscious, tasty Opposite: revolting

movable adj **1 portable**, transportable, transferable, mobile, detachable Opposite: fixed **2 changeable**, variable, mutable, impermanent, adjustable Opposite: fixed

move v **1 reposition**, shift, budge, shove, stir **2 go**, progress, transport, walk, step **3 relocate**, transfer, redeploy, change, shift Opposite: stay put **4 cause**, provoke, persuade, encourage, prod **5 affect**, touch, stir the emotions, impress, upset ■ n **1 movement**, action, motion, gesture, transfer **2 attempt**, effort, step, action, activity **3 shift**, realignment, rearrangement, repositioning, relocation

move ahead v **progress**, move on, press forward, go on, move forward Opposite: retreat

move along v **1 proceed**, hasten, go on, advance, press on **2 move aside**, move over, make way, make room, shift Opposite: stay put

move away v **retreat**, back off, diverge, distance, deviate

move back v **recoil**, recede, shrink back, retreat, regress Opposite: advance

move fast v **streak**, zoom, speed, tear, whiz

move forward v **advance**, progress, push on, go ahead, proceed Opposite: fall back

move heaven and earth v **do your utmost**, pull out all the stops, make every effort, move mountains, leave no stone unturned

move in on v **approach**, surround, converge, come closer, draw near Opposite: retreat

move into v **enter**, start, enter on, begin, set the ball rolling Opposite: back out

movement n **1 motion**, mobility, locomotion, circulation Opposite: stillness **2 move**, action, motion, gesture, lift **3 drive**, programme, crusade, undertaking, measure **4 pressure group**, association, society, lobby, faction **5 progress**, advance, development, improvement, headway Opposite: stagnation

movements n **actions**, activities, travels, schedule, arrangements

move on v **1 leave**, depart, go, make off, set off Opposite: stay put **2 progress**, get going, go on, take the next step, uproot Opposite: backtrack

move out v **leave**, depart, go, relocate, move on Opposite: stay put

move over v **move aside**, make way, make room, shift, step aside Opposite: stay put

mover n **1 motivator**, driving force, agent, doer, goer **2 initiator**, proposer, presenter, introducer, advocate *Opposite*: seconder

move towards v **come closer**, draw near, move in on, approach, converge *Opposite*: move away

move up v **go up**, rise, increase, progress, advance *Opposite*: drop

moving adj **touching**, poignant, affecting, pathetic, heartrending

COMPARE AND CONTRAST CORE MEANING: arousing emotion

moving causing deep feelings, especially of sadness or compassion; **pathetic** arousing feelings of compassion and pity, often centred on somebody who is vulnerable, helpless, or unfortunate; **pitiful** arousing compassion and pity, or arousing contempt or derision; **poignant** causing strong, often bittersweet feelings of sadness, pity, or regret; **touching** causing feelings of warmth, sympathy, and tenderness; **heartwarming** inspiring warm or kindly feelings, usually by showing life and human nature in a positive and reassuring light; **heartrending** causing intense sadness or distress, especially in sympathy with somebody else's unhappiness or hardship because it involves suffering or tragic events.

moving parts n **mechanism**, machinery, workings, components, gears

mow v **cut**, scythe, cut down, shear, trim

mow down v **1 shoot**, kill, slaughter, massacre, butcher **2 knock down**, run over, knock over, floor, topple

much adv **1 significantly**, noticeably, considerably, greatly, substantially **2 often**, frequently, over and over again, time and again, repeatedly ■ adj **a good deal of**, a great deal of, lots of, abundant, ample

much-loved adj **adored**, favourite, preferred, chosen, desired

muck n **1 manure**, sewage, waste, sludge, dung **2** (infml) **dirt**, mess, grime, mud, filth

muck about (infml) v **fool about**, lark about, mess about (infml), mess around (infml), waste time

muckiness (infml) n **filthiness**, muddiness, dirtiness, grubbiness, griminess

muckraker n **scandalmonger**, gossipmonger, troublemaker, mudslinger, slanderer

muckraking n **scandalmongering**, dishing the dirt, mudslinging, slander, libel

muck up (infml) v **spoil**, ruin, damage, make a mess of, botch (infml)

mucky (infml) adj **dirty**, muddy, messy, grubby, grotty (infml) *Opposite*: clean

mucous adj **self-lubricating**, slimy, slippery, lubricated

mucus n **slime**, secretion, saliva, lubricant, phlegm

mud n **mire**, sludge, dirt, muck (infml)

muddiness n **1 dirtiness**, grubbiness, filthiness, griminess, muckiness (infml) *Opposite*: cleanness **2 cloudiness**, murkiness, dullness, opacity, thickness *Opposite*: clarity

muddle v **1 mix up**, jumble, disorder, disorganize, disarrange *Opposite*: disentangle **2 confuse**, bewilder, baffle, puzzle, perplex *Opposite*: clarify ■ n **disorder**, jumble, confusion, mix-up, chaos *Opposite*: order

muddled adj **1 jumbled**, scrambled, mixed up, topsy-turvy, upside down *Opposite*: ordered **2 confused**, befuddled, bewildered, bemused, perplexed *Opposite*: clear

muddleheaded adj **1 baffled**, mixed up, confused, befuddled, bewildered *Opposite*: clear-headed **2 inept**, illogical, impractical, random, ineffective *Opposite*: logical

muddle up v **mix up**, jumble, disorder, disorganize, disarrange

muddy adj **1 mud-spattered**, dirty, grubby, grimy, filthy *Opposite*: clean **2 cloudy**, murky, unclear, opaque, thick *Opposite*: clear

mud flap n **mudguard**, flap, shield, guard, cover

mudpack n **face mask**, facial, face pack, treatment, beauty treatment

mudslinger n **slanderer**, defamer, denigrator, character assassin, attacker

mudslinging n **defamation**, backbiting, slander, denigration, character assassination *Opposite*: praise

muff v **1 miss**, drop, fumble, mishit, mishandle **2 get wrong**, mishandle, botch (infml), bungle (infml), mess up (infml)

muffle v **deaden**, dampen, quieten, silence, mute *Opposite*: amplify

muffled adj **stifled**, muted, inaudible, soft, lowered *Opposite*: loud

mufti n **casuals**, civilian clothes, ordinary clothes, street clothes, casual wear *Opposite*: uniform

mug v **attack**, assault, rob, ambush, hold up

mugger n **robber**, assailant, thug, attacker, assaulter

mugginess n **humidity**, closeness, clamminess, oppressiveness, warmth *Opposite*: freshness

mugging n **attack**, assault, bag-snatch, robbery, ambush

muggy adj **humid**, close, sultry, clammy, oppressive *Opposite*: fresh

mug shot n **photo**, photograph, close-up, police photo, passport photo

mug up (infml) v **learn**, study, absorb, cram (infml), swot (infml)

mulch n **covering**, protection, insulation, organic matter, leaves ■ v **cover**, protect, insulate, dress, top dress

mulish adj **stubborn**, obstinate, defiant, headstrong, obdurate *Opposite*: amenable

mulishness n **stubbornness**, obstinacy, defiance, obduracy, determination *Opposite*: amenability

mulled adj **spiced**, flavoured, warmed, sweetened, warm

mull over v **ponder**, consider, contemplate, think over, think about

multicolour adj **colourful**, rainbow, variegated, many-hued, polychrome

multicultural adj **diverse**, multiethnic, multiracial, inclusive, all-inclusive

multifaceted adj **multilayered**, complex, complicated, many-sided, polygonal Opposite: simple

multifarious adj **diverse**, varied, assorted, mixed, miscellaneous Opposite: homogeneous

multilateral adj 1 **many-sided**, polygonal, multifaceted, multidimensional 2 **mutual**, all-party, multiparty, joint, bilateral Opposite: unilateral

multilingual adj **polyglot**, trilingual, bilingual

multimedia n 1 **hypermedia**, software, interactive program, program 2 **collage**, combination, montage, assemblage, construction

multimillionaire n **millionaire**, magnate, billionaire, tycoon, mogul

multinational adj **international**, cosmopolitan, transnational, global, worldwide Opposite: national ■ n **conglomerate**, corporation, transnational, international business, international company

multipartite adj **multiple**, multifarious, multifaceted, composite, compound

multiple adj **manifold**, numerous, many, several, various Opposite: few

multiplex n **multiscreen cinema**, cinema complex, picture house (dated)

multiplication n **increase**, growth, development, reproduction, duplication Opposite: decrease

multiplicity n **array**, diversity, variety, large quantity, range Opposite: dearth

multiply v **increase**, grow, reproduce, swell, proliferate Opposite: decrease

multipurpose adj **versatile**, flexible, adaptable, multiuse Opposite: dedicated

multiracial adj **interracial**, multicultural, multiethnic, inclusive, all-inclusive Opposite: exclusive

multistorey adj **high-rise**, multilevel, tall, high, towering Opposite: low-rise

multitude n 1 **crowd**, horde, host, mass, throng Opposite: handful 2 **variety**, assortment, array, collection, wealth Opposite: few

mum (infml) n **mother**, mummy (infml), mama (infml), ma (infml), mammy (infml) ■ adj **silent**, tight-lipped, mute, quiet, dumb Opposite: communicative

mumble v **mutter**, murmur, drone, intone, gabble Opposite: enunciate

mumbled adj **muttered**, murmured, muffled, inaudible, slurred Opposite: enunciated

mumbo jumbo (infml) n **jargon**, gibberish, doublespeak, cant, technobabble Opposite: sense

mummify v 1 **embalm**, preserve, wrap up, prepare, dress 2 **shrivel**, dry out, dry up, wrinkle, wither Opposite: flourish

mummy n 1 **mummified body**, body, cadaver, corpse

munch v **chew**, masticate, crunch, grind, eat

mundane adj **ordinary**, dull, routine, everyday, commonplace Opposite: exotic

mundaneness n **ordinariness**, routine, tedium, flatness, unimaginativeness Opposite: excitement

municipal adj **civic**, public, community, urban, metropolitan Opposite: private

municipality n **city**, metropolis, town, borough, burg (US). See COMPARE AND CONTRAST at **city**.

munificence n **generosity**, largesse, benevolence, kindness, philanthropy Opposite: miserliness

munificent adj **generous**, liberal, magnanimous, unstinting, unsparing Opposite: miserly. See COMPARE AND CONTRAST at **generous**.

munitions n **weaponry**, ammunition, arms, guns, armaments

mural n **wall painting**, fresco, frieze, painting

murder n **homicide**, manslaughter, assassination, killing, slaying ■ v **kill**, assassinate, execute, put to death, slaughter. See COMPARE AND CONTRAST at **kill**.

murderer n **killer**, assassin, butcher, slaughterer, executioner

murderous adj 1 **fatal**, lethal, mortal, deadly, homicidal 2 (infml) **difficult**, testing, arduous, rigorous, exhausting Opposite: easy

murk n **gloom**, darkness, shadows, dark, dimness Opposite: light

murkiness n **darkness**, fogginess, mistiness, cloudiness, gloom Opposite: brightness

murky adj **dark**, gloomy, foggy, misty, cloudy Opposite: clear

murmur v 1 **whisper**, mutter, mumble, purr, croon Opposite: bray 2 **complain**, grumble, grouch, mutter, grouse (infml) Opposite: praise

muscle n 1 **sinew**, brawn, musculature, thew (archaic) 2 **influence**, power, authority, force, control 3 (infml) **strength**, vigour, power, force, elbow grease (infml)

WORD BANK

❏ types of muscle or tendon abdominals, Achilles tendon, biceps, diaphragm, hamstring, pectoral, quadriceps, sinew, smooth muscle, sphincter, striated muscle, tendon, triceps

---

muscle in (infml) v **intrude**, intervene, barge in, butt in, interfere

muscular adj **brawny**, beefy, well-built, burly, well-developed Opposite: puny

muse v **think**, ponder, consider, mull over, deliberate

museum n **gallery**, exhibition hall, arts centre, academy, institution

mush n **1 pap**, purée, mash, paste, slop **2 sentimentality**, sentimentalism, slush, sugariness, slop (infml)

mushroom v **grow**, increase, expand, flourish, swell Opposite: decline

mushy adj **1 soggy**, soft, squashy, squishy, squidgy Opposite: firm **2 oversentimental**, mawkish, maudlin, syrupy, romantic

music n **melody**, tune, harmony, composition, song

WORD BANK
❏ **types of musical form** anthem, aria, bagatelle, ballad, cantata, canticle, capriccio, chorale, coloratura, concerto, étude, fantasia, fugue, hymn, intermezzo, madrigal, mass, nocturne, oratorio, overture, prelude, requiem, rondo, scherzo, sinfonia, sonata, song, suite, symphony, tone poem, waltz
❏ **types of musical register** alto, baritone, bass, countertenor, falsetto, mezzo-soprano, soprano, tenor
❏ **types of musical term** a cappella, adagio, allegro, andante, appassionato, arpeggio, capriccioso, con brio, con moto, crescendo, diminuendo, forte, fortissimo, grave, larghetto, largo, legato, lentissimo, lento, moderato, pianissimo, piano, pizzicato, rubato, sotto voce, staccato
❏ **types of classical music** Baroque, chamber music, comic opera, early music, opera, operetta, Romantic, twelve-tone
❏ **types of dance music** acid house, acid jazz, big beat, boogie, broken beat, disco, drum 'n' bass, funk, garage, hard core, hip hop, house, jungle, ragga, ragamuffin, rap, rave, reggae, rock steady, ska, speed garage, techno, trance, two step
❏ **types of electronic music** ambient, breakbeat, breaks and beats, chillout, downtempo, dub, electro, electronica, new age, trip hop
❏ **types of jazz music** bebop, boogie-woogie, cool jazz, dixieland, honky-tonk, jazz, jazz funk, jazz fusion, jazz rock, jive, modal jazz, New Orleans jazz, ragtime, swing, trad jazz
❏ **types of pop and vocal music** bluegrass, blues, britpop, country and western, doowop, easy listening, folk, gangsta rap, gospel, lounge, Motown, new wave, northern soul, pop, R&B, rap metal, rockabilly, soul, spiritual
❏ **types of rock music** grunge, heavy metal, indie, metal, punk, rock, rock 'n' roll, thrash metal
❏ **types of world music** afrobeat, bhangra, calypso, flamenco, Latin, mento, raga, rai, roots, salsa, yodel

musical adj **melodic**, harmonious, melodious, tuneful, easy on the ear Opposite: discordant

musician n **performer**, instrumentalist, player, artiste, composer

musing n **thinking**, reflection, reverie, daydream, consideration ■ adj **thoughtful**, reflective, pensive, contemplative, absorbed

musk n **perfume**, scent, smell, fragrance, aroma

musky adj **pungent**, perfumed, scented, odorous, aromatic

must v **have to**, have got to, be obliged to, ought to, should ■ n **necessity**, obligation, duty, essential, requirement Opposite: option

muster v **gather**, gather together, congregate, collect, get together Opposite: disperse ■ n **gathering**, assembly, meeting, congregation, congress

mustiness n **dankness**, staleness, mouldiness, stuffiness, fustiness Opposite: freshness

musty adj **mildewed**, stale, mouldy, fusty, stuffy Opposite: fresh

mutable adj **changeable**, alterable, changing, variable, fluctuating Opposite: fixed

mutant adj **distorted**, misshapen, malformed, transformed, altered

mutate v **change**, alter, transform, transmute, metamorphose

mutation n **change**, alteration, transformation, transmutation, metamorphosis

mute adj **silent**, speechless, voiceless, unspeaking, quiet Opposite: vocal

muted adj **subdued**, hushed, soft, quiet, gentle Opposite: loud

mutilate v **maim**, injure, hurt, disfigure, harm

mutilation n **disfigurement**, defacement, damage, injury, maiming

mutineer n **rebel**, insurgent, rioter, radical, insurrectionist

mutinous adj **rebellious**, revolutionary, seditious, subversive, disobedient Opposite: obedient

mutiny n **rebellion**, revolt, sedition, uprising, insubordination

mutter v **1 mumble**, murmur, drone, burble, slur Opposite: speak up **2 complain**, grouch, grumble, murmur, grouse (infml) Opposite: praise

mutual adj **joint**, shared, common, communal, reciprocated

muzzle v **silence**, gag, hush, stifle, suppress

muzzy adj **1 vague**, fuzzy, out of focus, blurred, bleary Opposite: clear **2 fuzzy**, woozy, groggy, bleary, shaky Opposite: clear-headed

myopia n **1 short-sightedness**, poor sight, near-sightedness (US) **2 bigotry**, prejudice, bias, intolerance, narrow-mindedness

myopic adj **1 short-sighted**, owlish, nearsighted (US) **2 narrow-minded**, bigoted, parochial, prejudiced, intolerant Opposite: broad-minded

myriad adj **countless**, innumerable, numberless, numerous, many Opposite: few ■ n **multitude**, mass, host, army, crowd Opposite: few

mysterious adj **1 strange**, unexplained, inexplicable, unsolved, odd **2 secretive**, enigmatic, shadowy, furtive, cryptic *Opposite*: open

mysteriousness *n* **strangeness**, oddness, weirdness, curiousness, inexplicableness *Opposite*: normality

mystery *n* **1 problem**, puzzle, conundrum, enigma, riddle **2 secrecy**, obscurity, ambiguity, inscrutability, vagueness ■ *adj* **unknown**, anonymous, unidentified, secret, clandestine ■ *n* **whodunit**, detective novel, thriller, crime novel

mystic *n* **spiritualist**, medium, shaman, sorcerer, wizard ■ *adj* **mystical**, spiritual, supernatural, magical, cabalistic

mystical *adj* **spiritual**, mystic, magical, supernatural, magic

mystification *n* **bewilderment**, confusion, perplexity, bafflement, puzzlement

mystified *adj* **puzzled**, confused, bewildered, baffled, perplexed *Opposite*: enlightened

mystify *v* **puzzle**, confuse, bewilder, confound, baffle

mystifying *adj* **mysterious**, baffling, inexplicable, puzzling, confusing

mystique *n* **air of mystery**, air of secrecy, aura, charisma, magic

myth *n* **1 legend**, fable, saga, fairy story, fairy tale **2 falsehood**, fiction, illusion, invention, fabrication *Opposite*: fact

WORD BANK
❏ **types of mythical being** Abominable Snowman, Bigfoot, bogey, bogeyman, bugaboo, daemon, demon, dryad, giant, gnome, goblin, gremlin (*infml*), hobgoblin, leprechaun, naiad, nymph, ogre, sasquatch, sylph, troll, wood nymph, yeti

mythic *see* **mythical**

mythical *adj* **1 legendary**, mythological, fabled, fabulous, storybook *Opposite*: factual **2 imaginary**, untrue, fictitious, fictional, made-up *Opposite*: real

mythological *adj* **mythical**, mythic, fabulous, fairy-tale, fabled *Opposite*: factual

mythology *n* **myths**, legends, folklore, tradition, mythos

N

nab *v* **1** (*infml*) **arrest**, seize, capture, detain, catch **2 steal**, walk off with, rip off (*infml*), swipe (*infml*), lift (*infml*)

nadir *n* **lowest point**, all-time low, depths of despair, depths, base *Opposite*: zenith

naff (*infml*) *adj* **tasteless**, unfashionable, unstylish, ridiculous, crass *Opposite*: fashionable

nag *v* **1 badger**, pester, plague, harass, harry **2 criticize**, find fault, carp, grumble, complain **3 irritate**, annoy, worry, trouble, torment. *See* compare and contrast *at* **complain**.

nagging *adj* **irritating**, niggling, troublesome, distressing, irksome

nail *n* **pin**, spike, tack, peg ■ *v* **tack**, pin, fix, fasten, attach

nail-biting *adj* **nerve-racking**, tense, exciting, stressful, anxious *Opposite*: relaxing

nail down *v* **pin down**, get an agreement on, get a decision on, settle, confirm

naive *adj* **1 simple**, trusting, innocent, childlike, inexperienced *Opposite*: suspicious **2 unsophisticated**, gullible, wet behind the ears, green, foolish *Opposite*: shrewd

naivety *n* **innocence**, ingenuousness, candour, artlessness, naturalness *Opposite*: sophistication

naked *adj* **1 bare**, nude, undressed, unclothed, with nothing on *Opposite*: clothed **2 uncovered**, unprotected, exposed, unsheathed, unwrapped *Opposite*: covered **3 open**, undisguised, unadorned, unadulterated, unvarnished *Opposite*: hidden

COMPARE AND CONTRAST CORE MEANING: devoid of clothes or covering
naked not covered or concealed, especially not covered by clothing on any part of the body; **bare** without the usual furnishings or decorations, or not covered by clothing; **nude** not wearing any clothes at all, especially in artistic contexts; **undressed** not wearing any or many clothes, used especially when clothes have just been removed or are about to be put on.

nakedly *adv* **openly**, blatantly, starkly, obviously, overtly *Opposite*: covertly

nakedness *n* **1 nudity**, bareness, state of undress **2 defencelessness**, helplessness, exposure, vulnerability **3 blatancy**, obviousness, openness, overtness, starkness *Opposite*: covertness

namby-pamby (*infml insult*) *adj* **feeble**, soft, spineless, ineffectual, pathetic (*infml*) *Opposite*: tough

name *n* **1 first name**, Christian name, forename, surname, family name **2 designation**, term, tag, title, label **3 reputation**, renown, character, respectability, fame *Opposite*: notoriety **4 celebrity**, star, big name, public figure, VIP *Opposite*: nobody ■ *v* **1 call**, christen, baptize, nickname, label **2 identify**, specify, refer to, mention, cite *Opposite*: conceal

3 nominate, appoint, assign, choose, suggest *Opposite*: reject

name-calling *n* **abuse,** insults, foul language, swearing, invective *(fml)*

named *adj* **called,** baptized, christened, entitled, titled *Opposite*: nameless

name-drop *v* **boast,** brag, show off, vaunt, swank *(infml)*

name-dropper *n* **boaster,** bragger, braggart, show-off *(infml)*, bigmouth *(infml)*

nameless *adj* **1 anonymous,** unknown, unidentified, unnamed, unspecified *Opposite*: named **2 indescribable,** awful, dreadful, horrible, ghastly

namely *adv* **that is,** that is to say, viz, specifically, explicitly

nameplate *n* **plate,** sign, plaque, notice, panel

naming *n* **identification,** designation, nomenclature, christening, baptism

nanny *n* **1 child minder,** au pair, carer, minder, caretaker *(US)* **2** *(infml)* **grandmother,** nana *(infml)*, nan *(infml)*, granny *(infml)*, gran *(infml)*

nanosecond *n* **moment,** split second, second, instant, trice

nap *n* **1 doze,** catnap, siesta, sleep, rest **2 pile,** surface, finish, weave, texture ■ *v* **sleep,** catnap, have a siesta, doze, drowse

napkin *n* **serviette,** bib, paper towel, table linen, napery *(archaic)*

narcissism *n* **self-love,** self-absorption, egotism, conceit, self-importance *Opposite*: selflessness

narcissistic *adj* **vain,** self-absorbed, egotistic, egotistical, selfish *Opposite*: selfless

nark *(infml)* *v* **1 provoke,** incense, drive mad *(infml)*, aggravate *(infml)*, madden *Opposite*: please **2 complain,** grumble, whine, whinge *(infml)*, carp

narrate *v* **relate,** recount, tell, describe, recite

narration *n* **1 telling,** recitation, relating, unfolding, recounting **2 tale,** account, description, chronicle, history

narrative *n* **1 tale,** account, description, chronicle, history **2 plot,** story line, sequence of events

narrator *n* **storyteller,** speaker, raconteur, teller of tales, relator *Opposite*: listener

narrow *adj* **thin,** fine, slim, slender, slight *Opposite*: wide ■ *v* **1 get thinner,** get smaller, taper, contract, tighten *Opposite*: widen **2 restrict,** limit, narrow down, confine, focus *Opposite*: broaden

narrow down *v* **focus,** restrict, limit, confine, concentrate *Opposite*: broaden

narrow escape *n* **close call,** near miss, close shave, lucky escape, near thing *(infml)*

narrowing *n* **tapering,** contraction, thinning, reduction, tightening

narrowly *adv* **1 only just,** barely, hardly, scarcely, by a hair's breadth **2 closely,** intently, carefully, attentively, assiduously

narrow-minded *adj* **bigoted,** blinkered, insular, intolerant, prejudiced *Opposite*: broad-minded

narrow-mindedness *n* **bigotry,** insularity, prejudice, bias, intolerance *Opposite*: broad-mindedness

narrowness *n* **thinness,** fineness, slimness, slightness, constriction *Opposite*: width

narrow squeak *see* narrow escape

nascent *adj* **budding,** promising, embryonic, emerging, blossoming *Opposite*: moribund

nastiness *n* **spite,** meanness, malice, viciousness, cruelty *Opposite*: kindness

nasty *adj* **1 spiteful,** mean, malicious, vicious, cruel *Opposite*: kind **2 foul,** horrid, horrible, revolting, offensive *Opposite*: pleasant **3 severe,** painful, horrible, serious, grave *Opposite*: slight **4** *(infml)* **obscene,** offensive, indecent, vulgar, crude **5** *(infml)* **difficult,** tricky, hard, complicated, knotty. *See* COMPARE AND CONTRAST *at* **mean.**

nation *n* **1 state,** country, land, realm, homeland **2 people,** population, inhabitants, residents, populace

national *adj* **1 nationwide,** countrywide, state, general, coast-to-coast *Opposite*: local **2 state,** public, nationalized, state-run, state-owned *Opposite*: private ■ *n* **resident,** citizen, inhabitant, subject, native *Opposite*: visitor

nationalism *n* **1 independence,** autonomy, home rule, self-rule, self-government **2 patriotism,** chauvinism, jingoism, xenophobia

nationalist *n* **separatist,** autonomist, separationist

nationalistic *adj* **patriotic,** jingoistic, chauvinistic, xenophobic

nationality *n* **people,** population, race, ethnic group

nationalize *v* **make public,** take over, municipalize *Opposite*: privatize

nationalized *n* **state-owned,** publicly owned, public sector, state, national *Opposite*: private

nationally *adv* **countrywide,** all over the country, on a national scale, nationwide, generally *Opposite*: locally

nation-state *n* **state,** country, land, nation, sovereign state

nationwide *adj* **countrywide,** general, national, state, coast-to-coast *Opposite*: local ■ *adv* **nationally,** countrywide, all over the country, on a national scale, generally *Opposite*: locally

native *adj* **1 innate,** natural, inborn, instinctive, inherent *Opposite*: acquired **2 indigenous,** local, aboriginal, resident, autochthonous *Opposite*: foreign ■ *n* **inhabitant,** resident, local, citizen, subject *Opposite*: foreigner

COMPARE AND CONTRAST CORE MEANING: originating in a particular place
native born or originating in a particular place; **aboriginal** existing in a region from the earliest known times; **indigenous** originating in and typical of a region or country; **autochthonous** originating where currently found, especially used of rocks and minerals that were formed in their present position, or flora, fauna, or inhabitants descended from those present in a region from earliest times.

native land *n* **land of origin**, land of birth, birthplace, native country, motherland

nativity *n* **origin**, birth, genesis, conception, dawn *Opposite*: demise *(fml)*

natter *(infml) v* **have a chat**, chat, chatter, gossip, talk ■ *n* **chat**, conversation, gossip, talk, chinwag *(infml)*

natty *adj* **smart**, fashionable, trim, dapper, chic *Opposite*: unfashionable

natural *adj* **1 usual**, normal, ordinary, accepted, expected *Opposite*: unusual **2 physical**, biological, environmental, ecological, geographical *Opposite*: technological **3 innate**, native, inborn, instinctive, effortless *Opposite*: learned **4 unaffected**, unpretentious, spontaneous, genuine, artless *Opposite*: affected **5 untreated**, unprocessed, pure, raw, crude *Opposite*: artificial **6 biological**, physical, birth, true, actual *Opposite*: adoptive

naturalistic *adj* **realistic**, real, true-to-life, natural, lifelike

naturalize *v* **1 accept**, adopt, enfranchise **2 adapt**, become established, grow wild, grow naturally, acclimatize

naturally *adv* **1 of course**, obviously, logically, as expected, unsurprisingly *Opposite*: surprisingly **2 innately**, inherently, instinctively, intuitively, effortlessly **3 unaffectedly**, unpretentiously, spontaneously, genuinely, artlessly *Opposite*: pretentiously **4 in nature**, physically, biologically, geographically, geologically *Opposite*: artificially

naturalness *n* **unaffectedness**, spontaneity, genuineness, artlessness, sincerity *Opposite*: affectedness

natural resource *n* **raw material**, mineral, mineral deposit, reserve, resource

natural world *n* **environment**, nature, biosphere, ecosphere

nature *n* **1 Mother Nature**, countryside, natural surroundings, wildlife, flora **2 class**, kind, sort, type, description **3 character**, personality, temperament, disposition, spirit

naughtiness *n* **disobedience**, bad behaviour, wickedness, ill-discipline, waywardness *Opposite*: obedience

naughty *adj* **disobedient**, bad, badly behaved, wicked, ill-disciplined *Opposite*: good. See COMPARE AND CONTRAST *at* **bad**.

nausea *n* **1 biliousness**, queasiness, sickness, vomiting, unsettled stomach **2** *(literary)* **revul**-sion, repugnance, repulsion, abhorrence, disgust

nauseate *v* **1 sicken**, turn your stomach, make you feel sick *Opposite*: please **2** *(literary)* **disgust**, repel, revolt, upset, put off *Opposite*: attract

nauseating *(literary) adj* **disgusting**, sickening, repellent, revolting, repulsive *Opposite*: pleasant

nauseous *adj* **1 sick**, bilious, queasy, unwell, nauseated *Opposite*: well **2 disgusting**, sickening, repellent, revolting, repulsive *Opposite*: pleasant

nautical *adj* **maritime**, seafaring, sailing, marine, naval

naval *see* **nautical**

navel *n* **umbilicus**, tummy button *(infml)*, bellybutton *(infml)*

navel-gazing *n* **self-analysis**, reflection, rumination, brooding, self-absorption

navigable *adj* **1 passable**, negotiable, crossable, traversable *Opposite*: impassable **2 manoeuvrable**, controllable, seaworthy, sturdy, steerable

navigate *v* **1 find the way**, plot a course, plot a route, map read, follow the map **2 sail across**, circumnavigate, steer, pilot, take the helm

navigation *n* **direction finding**, steering, course plotting, map reading, celestial navigation

navigational *adj* **directional**, direction-finding, course-plotting, route-finding

navigator *n* **guide**, autopilot, skipper, pilot, direction finder

navvy *(dated) n* **manual worker**, labourer, manual labourer, worker, hand

navy *n* **fleet**, armada, flotilla, merchant navy, merchant marine *(US)*

near *prep* **1 close to**, by, next to, in close proximity to, in the vicinity of *Opposite*: far from **2 like**, close to, similar to, resembling, approaching **3 on the verge of**, approaching, nearing, close to, bordering on ■ *adv* **1 nearby**, close, close by, close at hand, in close proximity **2 almost**, nearly, virtually, practically, just about ■ *adj* **close**, nearby, neighbouring, adjacent, adjoining *Opposite*: far ■ *v* **approach**, reach, draw up to, draw near to, go up to *Opposite*: leave

nearby *adj* **close**, near, neighbouring, adjacent, adjoining *Opposite*: distant ■ *adv* **near**, close, close by, close at hand, in close proximity

nearly *adv* **closely**, approximately, almost, near, virtually

near miss *n* **lucky escape**, close thing, close call, close shave, narrow escape

nearness *n* **immediacy**, imminence, proximity, closeness, juxtaposition *Opposite*: distance

nearside *adj* **passenger**, kerbside, inside

near thing *(infml) see* **near miss**

neat adj **1 well-ordered**, in order, straight, arranged, tidy Opposite: untidy **2 well-organized**, organized, methodical, systematic, careful Opposite: disorganized **3 straight**, undiluted, unmixed, full-strength, pure Opposite: diluted **4 simple**, ingenious, elegant, clever, convenient **5 graceful**, effortless, practised, precise, deft Opposite: clumsy **6 natty**, trim, compact, well-designed, elegant Opposite: cumbersome

neaten v **order**, tidy, tidy up, arrange, sort out Opposite: mess up (infml)

neatness n **1 tidiness**, orderliness, carefulness, efficiency, precision Opposite: messiness **2 ingeniousness**, elegance, cleverness, effectiveness, handiness Opposite: ineffectiveness **3 gracefulness**, effortlessness, preciseness, deftness, skilfulness Opposite: clumsiness **4 simplicity**, elegance, nattiness, trimness, compactness

nebulous adj **unclear**, vague, imprecise, hazy, unformulated Opposite: precise

necessary adj **essential**, indispensable, needed, vital, requisite (fml) Opposite: optional

COMPARE AND CONTRAST CORE MEANING: describes something that is required

necessary important in order to achieve a desired result, or required by authority or convention; **essential** of the highest importance for achieving something; **vital** extremely important to the survival or continuing effectiveness of something; **indispensable** absolutely essential, or extremely desirable or useful; **requisite** (fml) necessary for a particular purpose; **needed** required or desired.

necessitate v **require**, demand, need, call for, dictate

necessitude n **need**, necessity, demand, requirement, want

necessity n **1 essential**, requirement, prerequisite, basic, necessary Opposite: luxury **2 need**, requirement, inevitability, obligation, stipulation

neck n **narrow part**, stem, shank, shaft ■ v (dated infml) **kiss**, cuddle, hug, smooch (infml), embrace

neckerchief (dated) n **bandanna**, cravat, scarf, tie, band

necklace n **chain**, string, choker, band, necklet

necklet see **necklace**

necropolis n **cemetery**, burial ground, graveyard, resting place, churchyard

nectar n **liquid**, juice, sap, fluid, syrup

née adj **formerly**, previously, originally

need v **1 demand**, require, call for, want, necessitate **2 have to**, must, should, ought ■ n **1 essential**, necessity, requirement, want, prerequisite Opposite: option **2 privation**, poverty, want, hardship, neediness Opposite: luxury. See COMPARE AND CONTRAST at **necessary**.

needed adj **necessary**, desired, required, wanted. See COMPARE AND CONTRAST at **necessary**.

needful adj **1** (fml or archaic) **necessary**, obligatory, compulsory, mandatory, essential **2** (fml) **requiring**, necessitating, demanding, calling for, needing

neediness n **need**, poverty, want, penury, destitution

needle n **1 pointer**, indicator, hand **2 spine**, spike, prickle, barb, pine needle ■ v (infml) **irritate**, provoke, annoy, pester, niggle

needless adj **unnecessary**, pointless, uncalled-for, useless, unneeded Opposite: necessary

needlessness n **uselessness**, unhelpfulness, fruitlessness, impracticality, pointlessness Opposite: usefulness

needy adj **poor**, in need, deprived, disadvantaged, destitute

ne'er-do-well (dated) n **layabout**, waster, idler, slacker, shirker

nefarious adj **wicked**, evil, despicable, immoral, reprehensible Opposite: reputable

negate (fml) v **1 refute**, contradict, disprove, disavow, deny Opposite: affirm **2 invalidate**, cancel, reverse, render null and void, nullify Opposite: validate. See COMPARE AND CONTRAST at **nullify**.

negation n **1 denial**, annulment, nullification, repudiation, cancellation Opposite: affirmation **2 opposite**, contrary, absence, lack, antithesis Opposite: confirmation

negative adj **1 unenthusiastic**, unconstructive, unhelpful, pessimistic, downbeat (infml) Opposite: encouraging **2 bad**, undesirable, adverse, harmful, damaging Opposite: positive ■ n **rejection**, rebuff, veto, no, refusal Opposite: approval

negatively adv **1 in the negative**, with a no, with a refusal, with a denial Opposite: affirmatively **2 damagingly**, harmfully, destructively, undesirably, adversely Opposite: positively **3 offputtingly**, discouragingly, unenthusiastically, unconstructively, unhelpfully Opposite: encouragingly

negativity n **unconstructiveness**, unhelpfulness, pessimism, disapproval Opposite: enthusiasm

neglect v **1 abandon**, desert, forget, forsake, ignore Opposite: look after **2 omit**, forget, overlook, ignore, disregard ■ n **negligence**, abandonment, desertion, disregard, inattention Opposite: care

COMPARE AND CONTRAST CORE MEANING: fail to do something

neglect fail to give the proper or required care and attention to somebody or something, or fail to do something, especially because of carelessness, forgetfulness, or indifference; **forget** fail, or fail to remember, to give due attention to somebody or something; **omit** fail to do something, either deliberately or accidentally; **overlook** fail to notice or check something as a result of inattention, preoccupation, or haste.

neglected adj **deserted**, abandoned, unkempt, uncared for, mistreated Opposite: looked after

neglectful adj **negligent**, careless, slipshod, remiss, lax Opposite: attentive

negligée n **nightdress**, nightgown, dressing gown, peignoir, nightie (infml)

negligence n **neglect**, inattention, disregard, laxity, slackness Opposite: attention

negligent adj **1 neglectful**, careless, inattentive, slipshod, remiss Opposite: careful **2** (literary) **nonchalant**, relaxed, casual, informal, easy Opposite: formal

negligible adj **insignificant**, tiny, small, slight, unimportant Opposite: significant

negligibly adv **not noticeably**, just, insignificantly, trivially, marginally Opposite: significantly

negotiable adj **1 open to discussion**, unfixed, flexible, open-ended, up for grabs (infml) Opposite: non-negotiable **2 transferable**, exchangeable, convertible, assignable, movable **3 passable**, navigable, crossable, traversable, accessible Opposite: impassable

negotiate v **1 talk**, discuss, confer, consult, bargain **2 sell**, transfer, exchange, convert, convey **3 get past**, pass, navigate, go around, cross

negotiation n **arbitration**, mediation, discussion, cooperation, diplomacy

negotiations n **talks**, discussions, conference, consultation, dialogue

negotiator n **speaker**, representative, envoy, delegate, mediator

neighbourhood n **area**, district, region, locality, quarter

neighbouring adj **nearby**, local, adjoining, surrounding, bordering Opposite: distant

neighbourliness n **friendliness**, kindness, helpfulness, consideration, sociability Opposite: unfriendliness

neighbourly adj **helpful**, kind, pleasant, sociable, friendly Opposite: antisocial

nemesis (literary) n **1 avenger**, retaliator, revenger, vindicator **2 punishment**, vengeance, retribution, fate, doom

neologism n **new word**, coinage, buzzword (infml)

neonatal adj **newborn**, new, brand-new

neophyte n **novice**, beginner, recruit, learner, trainee

nepotism n **favouritism**, preferential treatment, partiality, bias, preference

nerve n **1 courage**, bravery, spirit, audacity, bravado Opposite: cowardice **2 boldness**, impudence, insolence, effrontery, bravado. See COMPARE AND CONTRAST at **courage**.

nerve centre n **hub**, centre of operations, control room, headquarters, HQ

nerve-racking adj **worrying**, anxious, tense, stressful, scary (infml)

nerves (infml) n **anxiety**, worry, tension, stress, mental strain

nerve-wracking see **nerve-racking**

nerviness n **edginess**, anxiety, jumpiness, tenseness, uneasiness Opposite: calmness

nervous adj **anxious**, worried, edgy, jumpy, panicky Opposite: calm

nervousness n **anxiety**, edginess, jumpiness, tenseness, uneasiness Opposite: calmness

nervy (infml) adj **nervous**, anxious, worried, edgy, jumpy Opposite: calm

nest egg n **savings**, reserve, capital, fund, store

nestle v **1 cosy up**, cuddle up, huddle, nuzzle, settle **2 cushion**, place, lie, soften, shelter

net n **mesh**, web, netting, lattice, grid ■ v **1** (infml) **get**, catch, achieve, obtain, procure **2 earn**, make, gain, make a profit of, profit ■ adj **remaining**, disposable, clear, after deductions, left Opposite: gross

nether (fml) adj **rear**, hind, hinder, back, after

nether world (fml) n **hell**, inferno, purgatory, underworld, perdition

netting n **mesh**, net, web, fabric, meshwork

nettle (infml) v **irritate**, annoy, infuriate, bother, exasperate

network n **net**, system, grid, web, link

neurological adj **nervous**, nerve, neural

neurosis n **quirk**, complex, obsession, inhibition, idiosyncrasy

neurotic adj **anxious**, fearful, phobic, fixated, disturbed Opposite: rational

neuter v **spay**, sterilize, castrate, fix

neutral adj **1 unbiased**, impartial, disinterested, dispassionate, middle-of-the-road Opposite: biased **2 drab**, indistinct, indeterminate, pale, light-coloured Opposite: colourful

neutrality n **impartiality**, detachment, objectivity, noninvolvement, disinterest Opposite: bias

neutralization n **cancelling out**, nullification, off-setting, frustration, counteraction Opposite: activation

neutralize v **counteract**, counterbalance, defuse, deactivate, nullify

never adv **1 not ever**, not once, on no occasion, at no time Opposite: always **2 certainly not**, under no circumstances, by no means, in no way, not at all

never-ending adj **endless**, everlasting, continual, continuous, nonstop

nevertheless adv **yet**, but, however, nonetheless, on the other hand

new adj **1 novel**, newfangled, original, innovative, fresh Opposite: old **2 recent**, latest, up-to-the-minute, contemporary, up-to-date Opposite: outmoded **3 brand-new**, pristine, newborn, in mint condition, newfound Opposite: used **4 another**, additional, extra, further, different **5 inexperienced**, new to the job, just starting out, wet behind the ears, green *Opposite*: experienced

COMPARE AND CONTRAST CORE MEANING: never experienced before or having recently come into being
new recently invented, discovered, made, bought, experienced, or not previously known or encountered; **fresh** excitingly or refreshingly different from what has been done or experienced previously; **modern** of the latest kind, or characterized by up-to-date ideas, techniques, design, or equipment; **newfangled** puzzlingly or worryingly new or different, especially because it seems gimmicky or overcomplicated; **novel** new and different, often in an interesting, unusual, or inventive way; **original** unique and not copied or derived from anything else.

newborn *adj* **1 new**, brand-new, neonatal **2 newfound**, new, brand-new, fresh, recent *Opposite*: established ■ *n* **baby**, infant, child, neonate, babe *(literary)*

newcomer *n* **1 new arrival**, stranger, Johnny-come-lately *(infml)* **2 novice**, recruit, beginner, neophyte, trainee *Opposite*: old hand

newfangled *adj* **new**, innovative, up-to-date, up-to-the-minute *Opposite*: old-fashioned. *See* COMPARE AND CONTRAST *at* **new**.

newly *adv* **1 recently**, lately, freshly, just now, just this minute **2 afresh**, anew, again, once more

newlyweds *n* **just marrieds**, wedding couple, happy couple, bride and groom

newness *n* **novelty**, innovation, originality, freshness, inventiveness

news *n* **1 information**, reports, intelligence, gossip, rumour **2 news bulletin**, news broadcast, newscast, news summary, news flash

newscast *n* **news**, news bulletin, news broadcast, news summary, news flash

newsletter *n* **information sheet**, newssheet, bulletin, circular

newspaper *n* **1 paper**, broadsheet, daily, weekly, tabloid **2 newsprint**, printing paper, coarse paper

newsprint *n* **newspaper**, printing paper, coarse paper

newsreader *n* **presenter**, broadcaster, anchor, anchorperson

newsreel *n* **news film**, documentary, news report, news bulletin, news footage

newsroom *n* **news studio**, broadcasting studio, TV studio

newssheet *n* **newsletter**, bulletin, press release, information sheet, data sheet

newsstand *n* **kiosk**, stand, stall, booth

newsworthy *adj* **interesting**, exciting, remarkable, out of the ordinary, extraordinary *Opposite*: unremarkable

newsy *adj* **chatty**, gossipy, friendly, interesting, informative

next *adv* **after that**, then, afterwards, after, thereafter *Opposite*: first

next-door *adj* **adjacent**, adjoining, neighbouring, flanking, next

next of kin *n* **close relative**, blood relation, blood relative, spouse, partner

nexus *n* **connection**, link, tie, relationship, node

nib *n* **tip**, point, end

nibble *v* **chew**, nip, peck, gnaw, bite *Opposite*: chomp *(infml)* ■ *n* **bite**, morsel, titbit, crumb, speck

nibbles *n* **snacks**, finger food, canapés, appetizers, hors d'oeuvres

nice *adj* **1 enjoyable**, agreeable, pleasant, good, lovely *Opposite*: unpleasant **2 polite**, considerate, friendly, courteous, charming *Opposite*: nasty **3 respectable**, proper, refined, virtuous, genteel *Opposite*: improper **4 attractive**, lovely, pleasant, delightful, appealing *Opposite*: unattractive **5 precise**, exact, fine-drawn, meticulous, narrow *Opposite*: broad **6 discriminating**, painstaking, particular, scrupulous, precise

nice-looking *adj* **good-looking**, pretty, lovely, attractive, handsome *Opposite*: unattractive

nicely *adv* **1 suitably**, effectively, satisfactorily, accurately, carefully *Opposite*: unsatisfactorily **2 agreeably**, kindly, well, politely, courteously *Opposite*: unpleasantly **3 carefully**, meticulously, finely, subtly, narrowly *Opposite*: broadly

nicety *n* **1 distinction**, precision, detail, small point, refinement **2 delicacy**, tactfulness, particularity, finesse, polish

niche *n* **1 alcove**, bay, nook, cubbyhole, recess **2 place**, position, slot, function, role

nick *n* **1 incision**, groove, mark, notch, cut **2** *(slang)* **prison**, jail, custody ■ *v* **1 score**, incise, mark, cut, scratch **2** *(slang)* **misappropriate**, steal, walk off with, make off with, make away with. *See* COMPARE AND CONTRAST *at* **steal**.

nick-nack *see* knick-knack

nickname *n* **name**, pet name, epithet, sobriquet, diminutive ■ *v* **label**, call, name, designate, dub

nifty *adj* **1 good**, quick, clever, skilful, neat *Opposite*: clumsy **2 smart**, attractive, well-designed, neat, natty *Opposite*: unattractive **3 useful**, handy, convenient, effective, ingenious *Opposite*: useless

niggardly *adj* **1 ungenerous**, mean, miserly, tight, parsimonious *Opposite*: generous **2 miserable**, meagre, wretched, insufficient, paltry

niggle *v* **1 criticize**, cavil, carp, nag, nitpick **2 trouble**, bother, nag, annoy, irritate ■ *n* **1 complaint**, grumble, objection, grievance, criticism **2 doubt**, anxiety, twinge, misgiving, concern

niggling adj 1 trivial, petty, unimportant, inconsequential, insignificant Opposite: important 2 irritating, awkward, finicky, troublesome, difficult

nigh adj imminent, close, near, at hand, approaching Opposite: remote

night n 1 nighttime, hours of darkness, dark, darkness, nightfall Opposite: day 2 early hours, small hours, middle of the night

nightcap n 1 drink, bedtime drink, hot drink, hot toddy 2 sleeping cap, hat, cap

nightclothes n pyjamas, nightwear, sleepwear (US)

nightdress n nightgown, nightshirt, negligée, nightie (infml)

nightfall n dusk, twilight, evening, sunset, end of the day Opposite: daybreak

nightlife n nightspots, social life, entertainment, club scene, discos

nightly adj night, evening, nocturnal ■ adv every night, night by night, once a night, through the night

nightmare n dream, bad dream, hallucination, vision, incubus ■ adj traumatic, frightening, dreadful, terrible, horrendous Opposite: wonderful

nightmarish adj nightmare, frightening, terrifying, horrendous, terrible Opposite: lovely

nightspot n bar, nightclub, disco, club

nighttime n night, evening, dark, hours of darkness, middle of the night Opposite: daytime

nightwear n sleepwear, nightclothes, pyjamas

nihilism n negativism, pessimism, nothingness, emptiness, anarchism

nihilist n pessimist, existentialist, anarchist, revolutionary, radical

nihilistic adj negativistic, pessimistic, existentialist, destructive, anarchic

nil n nothing, zero, none, null, nullity

nimble adj sprightly, lithe, deft, agile, quick Opposite: awkward

nimbleness n sprightliness, litheness, agility, quickness, dexterity Opposite: awkwardness

nimbus n circle of light, halo, corona, aura, radiance

nip v 1 squeeze, compress, grasp, grab, grip 2 (infml) race, hurry, dash, rush, run Opposite: dawdle 3 peck, nibble, snap, gnaw, bite ■ n 1 pinch, tweak, grasp, grab, squeeze 2 sip, drink, swallow, tot, swig (infml) 3 peck, bite, nibble, snippet, clipping

nip in the bud (infml) v stop, prevent, hinder, block, thwart Opposite: encourage

nipper n 1 pincer, claw, gripper, appendage 2 (infml) baby, child, little one, toddler, rug rat (US infml)

nippy adj 1 cold, chilly, freezing, biting, icy

Opposite: warm 2 quick, fast, speedy, rapid, swift Opposite: slow

nirvana n 1 enlightenment, spiritual enlightenment, state of grace 2 bliss, heaven, joy, paradise, pleasure Opposite: hell

nitpick v cavil, complain, quibble, find fault, criticize. See COMPARE AND CONTRAST at criticize.

nitpicker n faultfinder, critic, carper, nagger, pedant

nitpicking n criticism, faultfinding, carping, hairsplitting, quibbling ■ adj critical, faultfinding, carping, finicky, fussy

nitty-gritty (infml) n essentials, brass tacks, fundamentals, basics, crux of the matter

no adv on no account, not at all, certainly not, definitely not, by no means ■ n rejection, negative, denial, rebuff, refusal ■ adj not any, not one, not at all

nob (infml) n VIP, grandee, toff (infml), big shot (infml), bigwig (infml)

no ball n foul throw, misthrow, foul ball (US)

nobble (infml) v 1 persuade, win over, sway, convince, influence 2 coerce, affect, force, intimidate, bribe 3 dope, incapacitate, fix, tamper with, drug 4 accost, waylay, confront, approach, detain

nobility n 1 aristocracy, upper class, landed gentry, upper crust (infml) Opposite: hoi polloi 2 dignity, graciousness, decency, goodness, nobleness Opposite: baseness

noble adj 1 honourable, principled, moral, decent, upright Opposite: unprincipled 2 magnificent, impressive, imposing, fine, splendid Opposite: unimpressive 3 aristocratic, patrician, blue-blooded, titled, upper-class ■ n aristocrat, peer, nobleman, noblewoman, patrician Opposite: commoner

nobleness n honourableness, honour, morality, magnanimity, dignity

nobody pron not one person, not a single person, no one, not a soul Opposite: everybody ■ n nonentity, mediocrity, unknown, upstart, nothing Opposite: somebody

nocturnal adj nighttime, night, nightly Opposite: diurnal

nod v move, bow, bob, jiggle, dip ■ n permission, affirmation, signal, sign, gesture

noddle (dated infml) n head, nut (infml), bonce (infml), skull (infml), noggin (dated infml)

node n 1 bulge, protuberance, lump, swelling, bump 2 meeting point, join, connection, intersection, point

nod off v doze off, fall asleep, drift off, doze, catnap Opposite: wake up

nod to v acknowledge, greet, signal to, salute

nodule n node, knot, knob, lump, bump

no end (infml) pron a lot, a great deal, very much, enormously, greatly

no-frills *(infml) adj* **basic**, utilitarian, unadorned, economy, generic *Opposite*: luxury

noggin *(dated infml) n* **head**, noddle *(dated infml)*, bonce *(infml)*, skull *(infml)*, nut *(infml)*

noise *n* **sound**, din, clamour, clatter, blast *Opposite*: silence

noiseless *adj* **soundless**, silent, muted, hushed, quiet *Opposite*: noisy

noisome *adj* **foul**, offensive, disgusting, repulsive, repellent *Opposite*: pleasant

noisy *adj* **loud**, deafening, earsplitting, piercing, raucous *Opposite*: quiet

nomad *n* **wanderer**, traveller, itinerant, migrant, drifter

nomadic *adj* **itinerant**, travelling, roaming, wandering, roving

nom de plume *n* **pen name**, pseudonym, alias, assumed name, nom de guerre

nomenclature *n* **1 classification**, taxonomy, codification, categorization, organization **2 terminology**, vocabulary, language, terms, jargon

nominal *adj* **1 supposed**, ostensible, so-called, in name only, titular *Opposite*: actual **2 small**, trifling, token, minimal, insignificant *Opposite*: great

nominate *v* **1 propose**, put forward, suggest, name, submit *Opposite*: reject **2 appoint**, elect, designate, choose, select *Opposite*: reject

nomination *n* **1 proposal**, suggestion, recommendation, submission **2 choice**, selection, appointment, nominee, candidate

nominee *n* **candidate**, entrant, applicant, nomination, contender

nonaggression *n* **pacifism**, peaceful coexistence, nonviolence, inaction *Opposite*: aggression

nonalcoholic *adj* **soft**, lite, low-alcohol *Opposite*: alcoholic

nonaligned *adj* **neutral**, independent, unallied, unconnected, unrelated *Opposite*: aligned

nonalignment *n* **neutrality**, independence, autonomy, self-determination, impartiality *Opposite*: alignment

nonattendance *n* **1 truancy**, playing truant, skiving *(infml)*, bunking off *(infml)*, wagging *(slang)* *Opposite*: attendance **2 absence**, default, absenteeism, nonappearance *Opposite*: presence

nonbeliever *n* **disbeliever**, unbeliever, doubter, sceptic, agnostic *Opposite*: believer

nonchalance *n* **indifference**, detachment, disinterest, calmness, dispassion *Opposite*: interest

nonchalant *adj* **casual**, imperturbable, offhand, cool, calm *Opposite*: concerned

noncombatant *n* **civilian**, citizen, conscientious objector *Opposite*: soldier

noncommittal *adj* **guarded**, evasive, vague, wary, tactful *Opposite*: definite

noncompliance *n* **nonconformity**, refusal, failure, denial, defiance *Opposite*: compliance

noncompliant *adj* **disobedient**, recalcitrant, rebellious, uncooperative, dissenting *Opposite*: cooperative

nonconformist *adj* **unconventional**, eccentric, alternative, rebellious, radical *Opposite*: conformist ■ *n* **rebel**, dissenter, maverick, radical, eccentric *Opposite*: conformist

nonconformity *n* **1 unconventionality**, originality, eccentricity, idiosyncrasy, individuality *Opposite*: conformity **2 noncooperation**, noncompliance, divergence, variation, difference *Opposite*: conformity

noncooperation *n* **defiance**, disobedience, insubordination, rebellion, rebelliousness *Opposite*: cooperation

nondescript *adj* **unremarkable**, ordinary, unexceptional, dull, uninteresting *Opposite*: special

nondiscriminatory *adj* **fair**, equal, unbiased, evenhanded, just *Opposite*: discriminatory

none *pron* **1 no one**, nobody, not a soul, not a single person *Opposite*: everyone **2 not any**, nothing, not a bit, not an iota, not a hint *Opposite*: some

nonentity *n* **nobody**, unknown, mediocrity, nothing *Opposite*: somebody

nonessential *adj* **luxury**, extra, supplementary, additional, dispensable *Opposite*: essential ■ *n* **extra**, luxury, perk *Opposite*: essential

nonetheless *adv* **however**, nevertheless, even so, on the other hand

nonevent *n* **failure**, anticlimax, disappointment, letdown, flop *Opposite*: success

nonexistence *n* **1 absence**, lack, want, dearth, deficiency **2 nothingness**, unreality, fictionality *Opposite*: existence

nonexistent *adj* **missing**, unreal, fictional, imaginary, absent *Opposite*: existent *(fml)*

nonfiction *adj* **factual**, true-life, reference, fact-based *Opposite*: fiction

nonflammable *adj* **noninflammable**, fireproof, flameproof, fire-retardant, fire-resistant *Opposite*: inflammable

nonintervention *n* **inaction**, noninvolvement, noninterventionism, laissez-faire, abstention *Opposite*: intervention

noninterventionist *adj* **laissez-faire**, noninterfering, nonaligned, nonpartisan, neutral

noniron *adj* **crease-resistant**, easy-care, drip-dry, wash-and-wear, permanent-press

nonjudgmental *adj* **indulgent**, lax, easygoing, relaxed, lenient *Opposite*: judgmental

nonmember *n* **outsider**, visitor, guest *Opposite*: member

nonnegotiable *adj* **1 firm**, immutable, unchanging, inflexible, fixed *Opposite*: negotiable **2 nontransferable**, unmarketable, nonsalable, nonexchangeable, nonconvertible

no-no *(infml)* *n* **taboo**, forbidden thing, breaking of convention, social restriction

no-nonsense *adj* **straightforward**, plain, practical, down-to-earth, plain-speaking *Opposite*: airy-fairy *(infml)*

nonpareil *adj* **unparalleled**, peerless, best, unequalled, unique *Opposite*: common

nonpartisan *adj* **unbiased**, impartial, unprejudiced, independent, neutral *Opposite*: partisan

nonpayment *n* **defaulting**, evasion, default, avoidance *Opposite*: payment

nonplus *v* **unnerve**, befuddle, stump, bewilder, mystify

nonplussed *adj* **confused**, baffled, bewildered, puzzled, stumped

nonprofessional *adj* **amateur**, blue-collar, manual, lay *Opposite*: professional

nonprofitmaking *adj* **charitable**, public, state, not-for-profit *Opposite*: profitmaking

nonproliferation *n* **limitation**, reduction, control, prevention *Opposite*: proliferation

nonresident *adj* **transient**, visiting, commuting, holidaying, vacationing *(US)* *Opposite*: resident ■ *n* **visitor**, transient, guest, holidaymaker, tourist *Opposite*: resident

nonsense *n* **rubbish**, drivel, gibberish, noise, babble *Opposite*: sense

nonsensical *adj* **ridiculous**, stupid, senseless, absurd, illogical *Opposite*: sensible

nonspecific *adj* **generic**, general, broad, broad-based, broad-spectrum *Opposite*: specific

nonstandard *adj* **unusual**, out of the ordinary, atypical, special, modified *Opposite*: standard

nonstarter *(infml)* *n* **hopeless case**, loser, failure, nonrunner, dud *(infml)* *Opposite*: winner

nonstick *adj* **coated**, protected, surfaced, covered

nonstop *adj* **continuous**, never-ending, uninterrupted, around-the-clock, constant *Opposite*: intermittent

nontoxic *adj* **harmless**, safe, nonhazardous, innocuous, risk-free *Opposite*: toxic

nonviolence *n* **pacifism**, passivity, non-aggression, civil disobedience *Opposite*: aggression

nonviolent *adj* **peaceful**, nonaggressive, pacific, peaceable, passive *Opposite*: violent

nook *n* **corner**, alcove, cranny, niche, recess

noon *n* **midday**, twelve noon, noontime, noonday *(literary)*

noonday *(literary) see* **noon**

no one *pron* **not one person**, not a single person, nobody, not a soul *Opposite*: everyone

noose *n* **1 loop**, lasso, halter, rope, riata **2 snare**, trap, booby trap, trick, con

norm *n* **standard**, average, custom, rule, model *Opposite*: exception

normal *adj* **usual**, standard, ordinary, typical, customary *Opposite*: abnormal

normality *n* **routine**, regularity, status quo, normalcy *(US)*

normalization *n* **regularization**, standardization, stabilization, regulation, control *Opposite*: deviation

normalize *v* **regularize**, standardize, regulate, put on a normal footing, control *Opposite*: destabilize

normally *adv* **1 usually**, in general, as a rule, on the whole, by and large *Opposite*: rarely **2 as normal**, as usual, naturally, unexceptionally, conventionally *Opposite*: abnormally

nose *n* **snout**, muzzle, beak, proboscis, conk *(slang)* ■ *v* *(infml)* **poke around**, watch, sneak, pry, snoop *(infml)*

nosebleed *n* **bloody nose**, blood, blood loss, haemorrhage

nosedive *n* **1 dive**, fall, drop, plunge, tumble *Opposite*: ascent **2 decrease**, fall, deterioration, drop, crash *Opposite*: increase

nose-dive *v* **1 plummet**, drop, plunge, dive, tumble *Opposite*: ascend **2 decrease**, deteriorate, plummet, drop, slump *Opposite*: rocket

nosegay *n* **posy**, spray, bouquet, bunch, sprig

nosh *(infml)* *n* **snack**, food, rations, tuck, goodies ■ *v* *(infml)* **eat**, munch, champ, eat up, consume

no-show *n* **absentee**, nonattender, dropout

nosh-up *(infml)* *n* **big meal**, feast, binge, blowout *(slang)*

nostalgia *n* **homesickness**, reminiscence, wistfulness, longing, melancholy

nostalgic *adj* **sentimental**, wistful, misty, longing, yearning *Opposite*: expectant

nostrum *n* **remedy**, plan, scheme, big idea, solution

nosy *(infml)* *adj* **inquisitive**, curious, interfering, prying, meddlesome

notability *n* **1 famous person**, celebrity, dignitary, VIP, notable *Opposite*: nobody **2 significance**, importance, relevance, import, weight

notable *adj* **noteworthy**, distinguished, outstanding, prominent, extraordinary *Opposite*: insignificant ■ *n* **celebrity**, dignity, VIP, personality, somebody *Opposite*: nobody

notarize *v* **authenticate**, certify, endorse, validate, rubber stamp

notary *n* **lawyer**, solicitor, legal official, legal clerk, attorney *(US)*

notation *n* **1 representation**, symbolization,

system, code, cipher **2 note**, footnote, jotting, memo, annotation

notch n **1** nick, indentation, cut, mark, slash **2 level**, degree, step, stage, rung

not counting prep apart from, excluding, aside from, besides, except

note n **1** letter, memo, memorandum, message, communication **2 footnote**, annotation, gloss, comment, addendum **3 tone**, edge, tinge, shade, hint ■ v **1 notice**, take note of, take notice of, take in, observe Opposite: disregard **2 mention**, observe, state, say, remark **3 make a note of**, note down, write down, record, jot down

noted adj renowned, well-known, famous, distinguished, celebrated

notelet n card, note card, letter card

notepad n writing pad, pad of paper, memo pad, pad, jotter

notepaper n writing paper, writing pad, stationery, headed paper, letterhead

noteworthy adj **of note**, notable, striking, remarkable, important Opposite: insignificant

nothing pron **nought**, nil, zero, zilch (infml) ■ n nonentity, nobody, unknown

nothingness n oblivion, nothing, emptiness, void, vacuum

notice n **1** sign, poster, announcement, advertisement, bill **2 warning**, notification, announcement, communication ■ v **become aware of**, see, take in, observe Opposite: close your eyes to

noticeable adj **obvious**, clear, visible, perceptible, conspicuous Opposite: inconspicuous

noticeboard n **display board**, information board, bulletin board (US)

notification n announcement, notice, warning, statement, report

notify v inform, alert, advise, warn, report

notion n **1** idea, view, concept, belief, conception **2 impulse**, urge, whim, fancy, instinct

notional adj **1 theoretical**, estimated, speculative, academic, hypothetical **2 imaginary**, unreal, fancied, fanciful, whimsical Opposite: real

not mince words v **be direct**, speak plainly, call a spade a spade, be blunt, speak your mind Opposite: prevaricate

notoriety n disrepute, infamy, dishonour, bad reputation, bad name

notorious adj **1 infamous**, disreputable, dishonourable, tarnished Opposite: reputable **2** (archaic) **famous**, renowned, eminent, familiar, recognized Opposite: unknown

notoriously adv **particularly**, especially, extremely, very

notwithstanding (fml) prep despite, in spite of, aside from, excluding, setting aside ■

adv **nevertheless**, all the same, nonetheless, anyhow

nought n zero, nothing, nil, zilch (infml)

nourish v **1 nurture**, give food to, sustain, suckle, feed **2 encourage**, promote, cultivate, support, foster

nourishing adj **nutritious**, wholesome, beneficial, healthful Opposite: unhealthy

nourishment n food, sustenance, diet, nutrition

nous n **1** (infml) **common sense**, good sense, sense, wisdom, horse sense **2 intellect**, ability, intelligence, rationality, reason

novel n book, narrative, work of fiction, tale, story ■ adj **original**, new, fresh, different, innovative Opposite: well-worn. See COMPARE AND CONTRAST at **new**.

novelist n writer, author, story writer

novella n **short story**, short novel, novelette, tale, fable

novelty n **innovation**, originality, newness, freshness, uniqueness

novice n beginner, learner, trainee, apprentice, greenhorn Opposite: old hand. See COMPARE AND CONTRAST at **beginner**.

now adv **1 at the present**, at the moment, at this time, currently, presently Opposite: then **2 immediately**, right away, straightaway, at once, instantly Opposite: later

nowadays adv **these days**, today, now, at the present time, at the moment Opposite: formerly

noxious adj **1 harmful**, toxic, poisonous, deadly, lethal Opposite: harmless **2 nasty**, unpleasant, offensive, foul, horrible Opposite: pleasant

nozzle n spout, jet, control valve, spigot, outlet

nuance n tone, gradation, distinction, tinge, hint

nub n crux, crucial point, essence, core, heart

nuclear adj atomic, nuclear-powered, fissile, fissionable

nucleus n centre, basis, core, heart, nub

nude adj unclothed, in the nude, undressed, in a state of undress, stripped Opposite: clothed. See COMPARE AND CONTRAST at **naked**.

nudge v push, bump, elbow, shove, jolt ■ n prod, push, shove, bump, jolt

nudity n bareness, nakedness, undress, deshabille

nugatory adj trifling, petty, insignificant, trivial, unimportant Opposite: significant

nugget n piece, bit, chunk, lump, hunk

nuisance n irritation, annoyance, bother, trouble, irritant Opposite: boon

null adj **1 invalid**, null and void, void, unacceptable, unsound Opposite: valid **2 worthless**, valueless, unimportant, insignificant, useless Opposite: useful

null and void adj invalid, void, null, unacceptable, flawed Opposite: valid

nullify v **invalidate**, annul, cancel out, abolish, negate (fml) Opposite: validate

COMPARE AND CONTRAST CORE MEANING: put an end to the effective existence of something **nullify** make something legally invalid or ineffective, or cancel something out; **abrogate** (fml) end an agreement or contract formally and publicly; **annul** declare something officially or legally invalid or ineffective; **repeal** end a law officially; **invalidate** deprive something of its legal force or value, e.g., by failing to comply with certain terms and conditions; **negate** (fml) render something ineffective, e.g., by doing something that counterbalances its force or effectiveness.

numb adj 1 **frozen**, anaesthetized, dead, deadened, unfeeling 2 **emotionless**, shocked, dazed, disoriented, distressed Opposite: animated ■ v **deaden**, freeze, anaesthetize, stun, dull

number n 1 **figure**, numeral, digit, integer 2 **amount**, quantity, sum ■ v **come to**, add up to, total, amount to, run to

numberless adj **countless**, innumerable, numerous, endless, myriad Opposite: few

number one adj 1 **first**, top, leading, best, most important 2 (infml) **excellent**, high quality, first-rate, top, top quality ■ n 1 (infml) **important person**, key player, linchpin, leader, prime candidate 2 (infml) **chief executive officer**, managing director, chief executive, boss, chief

numbing adj 1 **deadening**, freezing, anaesthetizing 2 **shocking**, distressing, dazing, upsetting, traumatic

numbness n 1 **deadness**, unresponsiveness, lack of sensation Opposite: sensation 2 **emotionlessness**, impassiveness, coldness, detachment, shock

numeracy n **mathematical ability**, numerical competence, skill, proficiency, expertise

numeral n **number**, figure, digit, cipher

numerate adj **mathematically competent**, good with numbers, proficient, accomplished, competent

numerical adj **mathematical**, arithmetic, arithmetical, statistical

numerous adj **many**, frequent, plentiful, abundant, several Opposite: few

numinous (fml) adj **mystic**, magical, magic, supernatural, transcendent

nunnery n **convent**, monastery, abbey, religious foundation, religious community

nuptial adj **marriage**, wedding, bridal, matrimonial, marital

nuptials (fml) n **wedding**, marriage, happy day

nurse v 1 **care for**, look after, take care of, tend, foster Opposite: neglect 2 **harbour**, cherish, nurture, have, foster

nursery n 1 **nursery school**, day nursery, playgroup, kindergarten 2 **plant sales outlet**, garden centre, plant market

nurture v 1 **care for**, look after, take care of, raise, rear 2 **cultivate**, cherish, develop, support, encourage

nut (infml) n 1 **skull**, cranium, dome, crown, bonce (infml) 2 **enthusiast**, fan, aficionado, aficionada, buff

WORD BANK
❑ **types of nut** acorn, almond, brazil nut, cashew, chestnut, cob, cobnut, coconut, cola nut, groundnut, hazelnut, hickory nut, horse chestnut, macadamia nut, monkey nut, peanut, pecan, pine nut, pistachio, walnut

nutrition n **nourishment**, diet, food, sustenance

nutritional adj **nutritious**, nourishing, nutritive, dietary, alimentary

nutritious adj **nourishing**, healthy, wholesome, healthful, beneficial Opposite: unhealthy

nutritive adj 1 **nutritional**, dietary, dietetic, alimentary, food 2 **nutritious**, nourishing, healthy, wholesome, healthful Opposite: unhealthy

nuts and bolts (infml) n **basics**, brass tacks, nitty-gritty (infml), practicalities, fundamentals

nutshell n **husk**, casing, shell

nuzzle v **nestle**, cuddle, burrow, snuggle, push

nymph n **fairy**, sprite, spirit, dryad, elf

oaf n **bumbler**, buffoon, lummox (infml), klutz (US slang)

oar n **paddle**, scull, sweep, blade

oasis n **retreat**, refuge, haven, sanctuary, escape

oath n 1 **promise**, pledge, vow, word, assur-ance 2 **curse**, swearword, expletive, four-letter word, imprecation (fml)

obduracy n **obstinacy**, stubbornness, inflexibility, mulishness, pigheadedness Opposite: compliance

obdurate adj 1 **obstinate**, stubborn, inflexible,

unyielding, unbending *Opposite*: compliant
2 hardhearted, callous, unfeeling, heartless,
pitiless *Opposite*: warm-hearted

obedience *n* **compliance**, agreement, submission, respect, duty *Opposite*: disobedience

obedient *adj* **compliant**, dutiful, submissive,
respectful, biddable *Opposite*: disobedient

obeisance *n* 1 *(fml)* **bow**, curtsy, bob, nod,
genuflection **2 homage**, respect, deference,
duty, loyalty

obelisk *n* **pillar**, column, pylon, needle, tower

obese *adj* **fat**, overweight, heavy, stout,
plump *Opposite*: underweight

obesity *n* **plumpness**, fatness, stoutness, portliness, corpulence *Opposite*: thinness

obey *v* **do as you are told**, submit, follow,
comply with, act upon *Opposite*: disobey

obfuscate *v* **obscure**, complicate, confuse,
muddy, cloud *Opposite*: clarify

obfuscation *n* **complication**, mystification,
confusion, muddying, clouding *Opposite*:
clarification

obituary *n* **tribute**, article, announcement,
eulogy, epitaph ■ *adj* **funerary**, funereal,
memorial, epitaphic, death

object *n* 1 **thing**, article, item, entity, body
2 purpose, objective, aim, point, idea ■
v **oppose**, protest, challenge, expostulate,
demur *Opposite*: approve

COMPARE AND CONTRAST CORE MEANING: indicate opposition to something

object be opposed or averse to something, or
express opposition to it; **protest** express strong
disapproval of or disagreement with something,
or refuse to obey or accept something, often by
making a formal statement or taking action in
public; **demur** raise objections in a hesitant or
tentative way; **remonstrate** reason or argue forcefully with somebody about something; **expostulate**
express disagreement or disapproval vehemently,
or attempt to dissuade somebody from doing
something.

---

objectify *v* 1 **actualize**, realize, represent,
portray, reify **2 diminish**, reduce, simplify,
trivialize

objection *n* 1 **opposition**, protest, protestation,
hostility, demurral *Opposite*: approval
2 doubt, concern, problem, worry, niggle
Opposite: confidence

objectionable *adj* **offensive**, obnoxious, horrible, unpleasant, intolerable *Opposite*:
inoffensive

objective *adj* 1 **impartial**, detached, neutral,
unbiased, unprejudiced *Opposite*: subjective
2 factual, actual, tangible, fact-based, demonstrable *Opposite*: subjective ■ *n* **object**,
purpose, aim, point, idea

objectivity *n* **impartiality**, detachment, independence, neutrality, fairness *Opposite*: subjectivity

objet d'art *n* **work of art**, masterpiece, creation,
piece, ornament

obligate *v* **compel**, oblige, force, make, require
Opposite: request

obligation *n* 1 **debt**, contract, commitment,
promise, agreement **2 duty**, responsibility,
requirement, compulsion, commitment
Opposite: option

obligatory *adj* 1 **required**, statutory, mandatory, binding, the law *Opposite*: discretionary **2 compulsory**, required, necessary,
essential, de rigueur *(fml) Opposite*: optional

oblige *v* 1 **compel**, obligate, force, make,
require *Opposite*: request **2 gratify**, please,
indulge, accommodate, help *Opposite*: disappoint

obliged *adj* **grateful**, thankful, appreciative,
gratified, indebted

obliging *adj* **helpful**, kind, considerate, willing,
agreeable *Opposite*: unhelpful

oblique *adj* 1 **slanting**, slanted, tilted, sloping,
leaning *Opposite*: upright **2 indirect**, implicit, implied, roundabout, circuitous *Opposite*: direct

obliqueness *n* 1 **tilt**, inclination, slant, steepness, lean **2 indirectness**, circuitousness, circumlocution, obscureness, opaqueness
Opposite: directness

obliterate *v* **destroy**, demolish, eliminate,
eradicate, annihilate *Opposite*: create

obliteration *n* **destruction**, annihilation, eradication, elimination, abolition *Opposite*: creation

oblivion *n* 1 **forgetfulness**, unconsciousness,
stupor, insensibility, obliviousness *Opposite*: awareness **2 obscurity**, extinction, the
past, the annals of history, nothingness
Opposite: existence

oblivious *adj* **unaware**, unconscious, unmindful, ignorant, insensible *Opposite*: conscious

obnoxious *adj* **loathsome**, hateful, horrible,
insufferable, intolerable *Opposite*: delightful

obscene *adj* 1 **indecent**, lewd, explicit, offensive, crude *Opposite*: decent **2 disgusting**,
nauseating, sickening, offensive, rude *Opposite*: decent **3 tasteless**, foul-mouthed,
crude, loutish, boorish

obscenity *n* 1 **indecency**, lewdness, offensiveness, explicitness, crudeness *Opposite*:
decency **2 offensiveness**, atrocity, tastelessness, vulgarity, rudeness *Opposite*: tastefulness **3 curse**, swearword, four-letter
word, expletive, cuss word *(US infml)*

obscurantism *n* **conservatism**, traditionalism,
dogmatism, reaction, illiberalism *Opposite*:
liberalism

obscurantist *adj* **reactionary**, conservative,
backward-looking, traditionalist, old-fashioned *Opposite*: liberal ■ *n* **conservative**, reactionary, traditionalist, diehard, dogmatist
Opposite: liberal

obscure *adj* 1 **incomprehensible**, unclear,

vague, ambiguous, abstruse *Opposite*: clear **2 indistinct**, faint, shadowy, murky, blurry *Opposite*: clear **3 unknown**, little-known, minor, unseen, unheard of *Opposite*: famous ■ *v* **1 confuse**, disguise, conceal, complicate, obfuscate *Opposite*: clarify **2 darken**, cloak, mask, hide, shroud *Opposite*: disclose

COMPARE AND CONTRAST CORE MEANING: difficult to understand

obscure difficult to understand because it is expressed in a complicated way or because it involves areas of knowledge or study that are not known to most people; **abstruse** not easy to understand, often because it involves specialist knowledge or is expressed in specialist language; **recondite** requiring a high degree of scholarship or specialist knowledge to be understood; **arcane** requiring information that is secret or known only to a few people in order to be understood; **cryptic** deliberately mysterious or ambiguous and seeming to have a hidden meaning; **enigmatic** having a quality of mystery and ambiguity that makes it difficult to understand and interpret.

obscurity *n* **1 anonymity**, insignificance, unimportance, inconspicuousness, oblivion *Opposite*: fame **2 incomprehensibility**, vagueness, ambiguousness, doubt, opacity *Opposite*: clarity

obsequious *adj* **servile**, sycophantic, flattering, toadying, submissive *Opposite*: assertive

obsequiousness *n* **sycophancy**, servility, flattery, submissiveness, compliance *Opposite*: assertiveness

observable *adj* **noticeable**, visible, apparent, evident, obvious *Opposite*: imperceptible

observance *n* **1 adherence**, compliance, execution, performance, observation *Opposite*: violation **2 ritual**, ceremony, ceremonial, rite, celebration

observant *adj* **sharp-eyed**, alert, attentive, watchful, vigilant *Opposite*: unobservant

observation *n* **1 surveillance**, scrutiny, watching, inspection, examination *Opposite*: neglect **2 remark**, comment, opinion, thought, reflection

observatory *n* **building**, station, laboratory, telescope, viewpoint

observe *v* **1 detect**, perceive, witness, see, spot *Opposite*: miss **2 watch**, view, scrutinize, monitor, study *Opposite*: ignore **3 remark**, comment, say, declare, state **4 abide by**, respect, follow, comply with, heed *Opposite*: violate **5 celebrate**, keep, remember, take part in, perform *Opposite*: break

observer *n* **spectator**, witness, viewer, onlooker, bystander *Opposite*: participant

obsess *v* **preoccupy**, grip, consume, fixate, possess *Opposite*: bore

obsessed *adj* **fanatical**, gripped, preoccupied, infatuated, fixated *Opposite*: indifferent

obsession *n* **mania**, fascination, fixation, passion, preoccupation *Opposite*: indifference

obsessive *adj* **compulsive**, fanatical, fixated, infatuated, neurotic *Opposite*: easygoing

obsolescence *n* **outmodedness**, unfashionableness, oldness, undesirability, uselessness *Opposite*: modernity

obsolescent *see* **obsolete**

obsolete *adj* **archaic**, outmoded, antiquated, passé, unfashionable *Opposite*: up-to-date

obstacle *n* **1 problem**, difficulty, hindrance, impediment, complication *Opposite*: help **2 obstruction**, barrier, blockage, blockade, impediment *Opposite*: passage

obstinacy *n* **stubbornness**, determination, pigheadedness, inflexibility, unreasonableness *Opposite*: compliance

obstinate *adj* **stubborn**, determined, pigheaded, fixed, inflexible *Opposite*: compliant

obstreperous *adj* **disruptive**, rowdy, disorderly, loud, noisy *Opposite*: demure. See COMPARE AND CONTRAST *at* **unruly**.

obstruct *v* **1 block**, barricade, impede, hold up, stop *Opposite*: clear **2 hinder**, thwart, frustrate, hamper, complicate *Opposite*: assist. See COMPARE AND CONTRAST *at* **hinder**.

obstruction *n* **obstacle**, barrier, block, blockade, barricade *Opposite*: help

obstructionism *n* **timewasting**, stalling, filibustering, sabotage, hindrance *Opposite*: helpfulness

obstructionist *adj* **stalling**, timewasting, filibustering, delaying, delay ■ *n* **staller**, timewaster, filibusterer, wrecker, saboteur

obstructive *adj* **disruptive**, uncooperative, unhelpful, obstreperous, awkward *Opposite*: helpful

obtain *v* **get**, get hold of, acquire, procure, attain *Opposite*: lose. See COMPARE AND CONTRAST *at* **get**.

obtainable *adj* **available**, accessible, reachable, attainable, at hand *Opposite*: unavailable

obtrude *v* **1 interfere**, impose, meddle, pry, interrupt **2 extend**, thrust, stick out, push out

obtrusive *adj* **1 conspicuous**, unmistakable, blatant, prominent, garish *Opposite*: inconspicuous **2 interfering**, intruding, meddlesome, forward, presumptuous

obtuse *adj* **insensitive**, dull-witted, simpleminded, imperceptive, stupid *Opposite*: astute

obverse *n* **1 front**, head, heads, side, face **2 counterpart**, complement, opposite, equivalent, opposite number ■ *adj* **1 front**, forward-facing, opposite, visible, anterior *Opposite*: reverse **2 equivalent**, complementary, opposite, other, opposing

obviate *v* **do away with**, avoid, remove, forestall, prevent

obvious *adj* **clear**, understandable, palpable,

noticeable, apparent *Opposite*: obscure

obviousness *n* **clearness**, certainty, overtness, unmistakability, conspicuousness *Opposite*: obscurity

occasion *n* **1 time**, juncture, case, instance, event **2 possibility**, opportunity, opening, season, contingency **3 reason**, cause, motive, justification, rationale ∎ *v* **cause**, motivate, give rise to, bring about, induce

occasional *adj* **infrequent**, irregular, chance, sporadic, rare *Opposite*: regular. *See* COMPARE AND CONTRAST *at* **periodic**.

occlude *v* **1 block**, stop up, close off, seal, shut off *Opposite*: free **2 cut off**, cut out, close, block off, shut *Opposite*: open

occlusion *n* **1 blocking**, obstruction, stopping up, closing off, sealing **2 cutting off**, cutting out, closure, blocking, sealing

occupancy *n* **tenancy**, tenure, habitation, possession, residence *Opposite*: vacancy

occupant *n* **inhabitant**, tenant, lodger, resident, occupier

occupation *n* **1 job**, profession, work, career, livelihood **2 activity**, pursuit, enterprise, task

occupational *adj* **work-related**, job-related, professional, industrial, working

occupied *adj* **1 busy**, engaged, employed, unavailable, working *Opposite*: free **2 in use**, full, engaged, tied down, taken *Opposite*: empty **3 conquered**, subjugated, subject, dominated, ruled *Opposite*: liberated

occupier *n* **inhabitant**, resident, tenant, occupant, lodger

occupy *v* **1 live in**, inhabit, reside in, dwell in *(literary)*, lodge *(dated)* *Opposite*: vacate **2 interest**, engage, divert, take up, entertain **3 conquer**, subjugate, dominate, rule, seize *Opposite*: liberate

occur *v* **1 happen**, take place, arise, come about, transpire **2 hit**, strike, cross your mind, appear, come to mind

occurrence *n* **1 incidence**, rate, amount, existence, manifestation **2 happening**, event, incident, episode, occasion

ocean *n* **sea**, deep, water, briny ∎ *adj* **marine**, sea, deep-sea, oceanic

oceangoing *adj* **seagoing**, sea, seaworthy, maritime, seafaring

oceanic *adj* **sea**, deep-sea, ocean, saltwater, marine

ocular *adj* **visual**, optical, ophthalmic

odd *adj* **strange**, peculiar, unusual, abnormal, anomalous *Opposite*: ordinary

oddity *n* **1 peculiarity**, quirk, foible, idiosyncrasy, twist **2 strangeness**, peculiarity, quirkiness, oddness, bizarreness *Opposite*: normality **3 eccentric**, character, original, exception, misfit **4 curiosity**, rarity, phenomenon, freak

oddments *n* **1 odds and ends**, leftovers, offcuts, bits, fragments **2 knick-knacks**, notions, sundries, curios, gewgaws

oddness *n* **strangeness**, peculiarity, mysteriousness, incongruity, weirdness *Opposite*: normality

odds *n* **chances**, probability, likelihood, balance

odds and ends *n* **remnants**, leftovers, loose ends, offcuts, fragments

odds-on *(infml)* *adv* **probably**, most likely, like enough, likely, dependably *Opposite*: unlikely

ode *n* **poem**, elegy, verse, sonnet, song *(literary)*

odious *adj* **hateful**, horrible, loathsome, revolting, detestable *Opposite*: delightful

odium *n* **abhorrence**, hatred, disgust, revulsion, hate *Opposite*: approval

odour *n* **1 scent**, perfume, stink, smell, stench **2 air**, aura, atmosphere, flavour, spirit. *See* COMPARE AND CONTRAST *at* **smell**.

odourless *adj* **unscented**, fragrance-free, neutral *Opposite*: scented

odyssey *n* **journey**, trek, crusade, pilgrimage, wanderings

oeuvre *(fml)* *n* **work**, piece, composition, opus, works

off *adj* **rotten**, rancid, bad, tainted, mouldy *Opposite*: fresh

offbeat *adj* **unusual**, unconventional, eccentric, quirky, bizarre *Opposite*: typical

off-centre *adj* **1 asymmetrical**, skewed, uneven, unbalanced, eccentric **2 off-the-wall** *(infml)*, quirky, eccentric, unconventional, odd

off chance *n* **likelihood**, probability, possibility, chance, prospect

off-colour *adj* **1 unwell**, sick, ill, unfit, under the weather *Opposite*: well **2** *(infml)* **risqué**, indecorous, suggestive, improper, indiscreet

offence *n* **1 crime**, wrongdoing, felony, fault, violation **2 insult**, affront, outrage, slight, slur **3 umbrage**, resentment, pique, indignation **4 attack**, offensive, assault, onslaught, bombardment *Opposite*: defence

offend *v* **1 hurt somebody's feelings**, upset, insult, affront, be rude to **2 commit an offence**, commit a crime, commit a felony, transgress, break the law

offended *adj* **affronted**, insulted, hurt, upset, slighted

offender *n* **criminal**, wrongdoer, reprobate, delinquent, lawbreaker

offensive *adj* **1 unpleasant**, distasteful, disgusting, odious, hateful *Opposite*: agreeable **2 insulting**, rude, impolite, provoking, provocative *Opposite*: courteous **3 aggressive**, attacking, violent, invasive, belligerent *Opposite*: peaceful

offensiveness *n* **rudeness**, impoliteness, indecency, vulgarity, abusiveness *Opposite*: politeness

offer *v* **1 proffer**, tender, present, bid **2 propose**, suggest, pose, recommend, put forward *Opposite*: withdraw ■ *n* **proposal**, suggestion, bid, proposition, bargain

offering *n* **contribution**, gift, donation, present, submission

off-guard *adj* **unready**, unawares, napping, unprepared *Opposite*: ready

offhand *adj* **1 impromptu**, extemporaneous, improvised, unrehearsed, spontaneous *Opposite*: premeditated **2 informal**, casual, nonchalant, easygoing, indifferent *Opposite*: serious

office *n* **bureau**, workplace, administrative centre, headquarters, agency

office holder *n* **official**, officer, politician, public servant, elected official

officer *n* **1 police officer**, constable, bobby (*infml*), cop (*slang*) **2 official**, bureaucrat, representative, administrator, office holder

official *n* **bureaucrat**, administrator, representative, spokesperson, officer ■ *adj* **authorized**, certified, endorsed, sanctioned, allowed *Opposite*: informal

officialdom (*infml*) *n* **the powers that be**, bureaucracy, administrative system, red tape (*infml*)

officiate *v* **preside**, manage, perform official duties, carry out official duties, solemnize

officious *adj* **meddlesome**, bossy, bureaucratic, self-important, overbearing

off-key *adj* **out of key**, tuneless, out of tune, discordant, screeching *Opposite*: melodious ■ *adv* **tunelessly**, out of tune, discordantly, unmusically *Opposite*: melodiously

off-limits *adj* **forbidden**, prohibited, proscribed, outlawed, verboten *Opposite*: permitted

off-line *adj* **off**, disconnected, down *Opposite*: online

offload *v* **1 discharge**, unload, deposit, dump, leave *Opposite*: load **2 pass on**, get rid of, dump, deposit, devolve *Opposite*: keep **3** (*infml*) **relieve of**, divest, rid, free from, unburden

off-putting *adj* **1 repellent**, repulsive, disgusting, distasteful, offensive *Opposite*: attractive **2 forbidding**, disconcerting, upsetting, disturbing, daunting *Opposite*: comforting

offset *n* **counterbalance**, balance, counterpoise, equalizer, counterweight ■ *v* **counterweigh**, counterbalance, make up for, counteract, compensate

offshoot *n* **1 sideshoot**, sprout, sucker, branch, twig **2 derivative**, subsidiary, consequence, result, outcome

offspring *n* **descendants**, progeny, children, issue, young

WORD BANK
❏ **types of offspring** only child, quadruplet, quintuplet, singleton, triplet, twin

off-the-cuff *adj* **impromptu**, spontaneous, improvised, unprepared, unrehearsed

off-the-peg *adj* **ready-made**, ready-to-wear, standard-size, mass-produced, prêt-à-porter *Opposite*: made-to-measure

off-the-shelf *adj* **standard**, regular, mass-produced, ordinary, run-of-the-mill *Opposite*: bespoke

off-the-wall (*infml*) *adj* **bizarre**, strange, eccentric, unusual, unconventional

often *adv* **frequently**, over and over again, time and again, repeatedly, habitually *Opposite*: seldom

ogle *v* **look at**, eye, leer, stare, gaze *Opposite*: ignore. *See* COMPARE AND CONTRAST *at* gaze.

ogre *n* **giant**, troll, tyrant, monster, fiend

oil *n* **1 lubricant**, emollient, grease **2 grease**, fat, lard ■ *v* **apply oil**, lubricate, smear with oil, grease, loosen

WORD BANK
❏ **types of cooking fat and oil** butter, canola oil, corn oil, dripping, ghee, lard, margarine, olive oil, peanut oil, rape oil, sesame oil, suet, sunflower oil, vegetable oil

oily *adj* **greasy**, fatty, slick, slippery, oleaginous

ointment *n* **gel**, liniment, lotion, balm, salve

old *adj* **1 aged**, elderly, mature, getting on, not getting any younger *Opposite*: young **2 from the past**, ancient, from way back, long-standing, long forgotten *Opposite*: recent **3 previous**, last, other, former, erstwhile *Opposite*: current

old-fashioned *adj* **1 antiquated**, outdated, unfashionable, behind the times, archaic *Opposite*: up-to-date **2 fogyish**, traditional, conservative, conventional, old-school *Opposite*: modern

COMPARE AND CONTRAST CORE MEANING: no longer in current use or no longer considered fashionable

old-fashioned no longer considered fashionable or suitable because of changes in taste or technology, or nostalgically favouring or maintaining the style of a former time; **outdated** no longer relevant to modern life because it has been superseded by something better, more fashionable, or more technologically advanced; **antiquated** regarded as in need of updating or replacing, though still functioning or in use; **archaic** belonging to a much earlier period of time, often suggesting a lack of relevance to modern life; **obsolete** superseded by something new, and in some cases therefore no longer in use; **passé** dismissed as no longer current or fashionable; **antediluvian** (*infml*) extremely old-fashioned and outdated.

old hand *n* **veteran**, expert, professional, connoisseur, authority *Opposite*: novice

old-style *adj* **traditional**, outdated, outmoded, out-of-date, old *Opposite*: modern

old-time *adj* **old-fashioned**, outdated, outmoded, traditional, old-style *Opposite*: modern

old-world *adj* **outdated**, outmoded, quaint, traditional, old-style *Opposite*: modern

olive branch *n* **peace offering**, compromise, concession, gesture, apology

omen *n* **sign**, portent, warning, forecast, premonition

ominous *adj* **threatening**, warning, worrying, gloomy, portentous *Opposite*: promising

omission *n* **1 oversight**, lapse, slip, error, blunder **2 exclusion**, exception, absence, leaving out, hiatus *Opposite*: inclusion

omit *v* **1 leave out**, miss out, pass over, skip, skip over *Opposite*: include **2 neglect**, forget, not take the trouble, not bother, overlook *Opposite*: remember. *See* COMPARE AND CONTRAST at neglect.

omnibus *n* **compilation**, collection, anthology, edition, album

omnipotence *n* **authority**, power, all-powerfulness, supremacy, influence *Opposite*: powerlessness

omnipotent *adj* **almighty**, all-powerful, invincible, unstoppable, supreme *Opposite*: powerless

omnipresent *adj* **ubiquitous**, all-pervading, universal, ever-present, pervasive *Opposite*: absent

omniscience *n* **knowledge**, awareness, insight, wisdom, sapience *Opposite*: ignorance

omniscient *adj* **all-knowing**, all-seeing, wise, well-informed, sagacious

on *prep* **1 sitting on**, on top of, resting on, lying on, upon *Opposite*: under **2 at**, next to, by the side of, by ■ *adv* **1 happening**, taking place, scheduled, arranged, proceeding *Opposite*: off **2 without stopping**, continuously, without a break, constantly, unceasingly

on account of *prep* **owing to**, because of, due to, through, as a result of

once *adv* **1 some time ago**, formerly, previously, a long time ago, once upon a time *Opposite*: now **2 as soon as**, when, after, the minute

once-over *(infml)* *n* **examination**, inspection, check, review, survey

oncoming *adj* **approaching**, looming, nearing, advancing, onrushing

one *adj* **unique**, single, solitary, lone, individual

one and all *pron* **everyone**, everybody, all, all and sundry, ladies and gentlemen *Opposite*: nobody

one-dimensional *adj* **superficial**, lacking in depth, simplistic, simple-minded, basic

one-liner *n* **joke**, witticism, quip, bon mot, epigram

oneness *n* **1 singleness**, cohesion, coherence *Opposite*: diversity **2 agreement**, unanimity,

unity, togetherness, solidarity *Opposite*: divergence

one-off *adj* **unique**, once-in-a-lifetime, never-to-be-repeated, limited-edition, special ■ *n* **rarity**, limited edition, one in a million

onerous *adj* **difficult**, burdensome, arduous, heavy, tiring *Opposite*: easy

one-sided *adj* **biased**, unfair, prejudiced, weighted, unrepresentative *Opposite*: balanced

one-sidedness *n* **bias**, partiality, unfairness, prejudice, unrepresentativeness

onetime *adj* **former**, previous, ex, past, old *Opposite*: current

one-to-one *adj* **1 individual**, private, personal, intimate, personalized **2 corresponding**, identical, matching ■ *adv* **individually**, privately, personally, alone ■ *n* **conversation**, heart-to-heart, tête-à-tête, gossip, discussion

one-way *adj* **single**, outward *Opposite*: return

ongoing *adj* **continuing**, rolling, in progress, current, open-ended

online *adj* **connected**, on, operational, working, available *Opposite*: off-line

onlooker *n* **bystander**, spectator, viewer, observer, witness

only *adv* **merely**, simply, just, barely, no more than ■ *adj* **single**, lone, solitary, individual, one

onrush *n* **surge**, rush, wave, tide, deluge

onrushing *adj* **oncoming**, surging, rushing, approaching, nearing

on-screen *adj* **televised**, television, live, on-air, televisual

onset *n* **start**, beginning, arrival, inception *(fml)*, commencement *(fml)* *Opposite*: conclusion

onside *adj* **legal**, safe, clear, in the clear ■ *adv* **legally**, safely, legitimately

onslaught *n* **attack**, assault, offensive, ambush, blitz

on the other hand *adv* **instead**, conversely, alternatively, then again, in contrast

on the strength of *prep* **because of**, on the basis of, on account of, by reason of, by virtue of *Opposite*: notwithstanding *(fml)*

on the subject of *prep* **concerning**, with reference to, regarding, as regards, re

on the threshold of *prep* **on the brink of**, on the point of, at the start of, verging on, bordering on

onus *n* **responsibility**, burden, obligation, duty

onward *adj* **forward**, headlong *Opposite*: backward ■ *adv* **on**, forwards, ahead, headlong, straight on *Opposite*: backwards

onwards *see* onward

oodles *(infml)* *n* **plenty**, lots, loads *(infml)*, heaps *(infml)*, piles *(infml)*

oomph *n* **energy**, enthusiasm, life, dynamism, vivacity

ooze v 1 seep, leach, leak, trickle, dribble 2 exude, be full of, reek of, radiate, overflow with

opacity n 1 opaqueness, imperviousness, impenetrability, denseness, cloudiness Opposite: transparency 2 obscurity, obtuseness, impenetrability, complexity, vagueness Opposite: transparency

opaque adj 1 impervious, cloudy, muddy, milky, misty Opposite: transparent 2 obscure, unclear, incomprehensible, impenetrable, difficult Opposite: clear

open adj 1 unlocked, ajar, wide open, gaping Opposite: closed 2 exposed, uncluttered, sweeping, undeveloped, unspoilt Opposite: built-up 3 accessible, public, unrestricted, free Opposite: restricted 4 approachable, friendly, amenable, receptive, amicable Opposite: standoffish 5 honest, unguarded, direct, straight, frank Opposite: guarded 6 vulnerable, exposed, undefended, unprotected, unguarded Opposite: safe ■ v 1 begin, start, commence, initiate, launch Opposite: conclude 2 unlock, unbolt, undo, unfasten, release Opposite: close

open-air adj outside, outdoor, alfresco, uncovered Opposite: indoor

open-and-shut adj simple, clear, straightforward, clear-cut, obvious Opposite: ambiguous

open-ended adj open, flexible, undecided, unrestricted, fluid Opposite: fixed

opener n 1 bottle opener, tin opener, can opener, corkscrew 2 (infml) starter, introduction, icebreaker, preamble

openhanded adj generous, unstinting, lavish, unselfish, philanthropic Opposite: miserly

openhandedness n generosity, lavishness, unselfishness, philanthropy, bounty (literary) Opposite: miserliness

openhearted adj sincere, genuine, honest, open, kind

openheartedness n sincerity, genuineness, honesty, kindness, love

opening n 1 gap, breach, aperture, hole, fissure 2 start, beginning, introduction, lead-in, prologue Opposite: end 3 opportunity, chance, lucky break, break (infml)

openly adv candidly, explicitly, frankly, honestly, plainly Opposite: secretly

open-minded adj unbiased, unprejudiced, tolerant, liberal, progressive Opposite: narrowminded

open-mindedness n broad-mindedness, impartiality, tolerance, liberalism, progressiveness Opposite: narrow-mindedness

open-mouthed adj astonished, amazed, astounded, horrified, aghast

openness n honesty, directness, frankness, sincerity, candidness Opposite: reticence

open out v 1 unfold, spread out, open, open up, stretch out Opposite: fold up 2 spread out,

radiate, separate, divide 3 expand, flower, spread, spread wide, get bigger

open up v 1 unfold, expand, spread out, open out, stretch 2 excavate, cut through, open, dig out, expose 3 unwrap, open, uncover, expose 4 speak freely, bare your soul, unwind, speak your mind, speak openly Opposite: clam up (infml) 5 open fire, start firing, start shooting 6 begin trading, open, unlock Opposite: close 7 (infml) accelerate, open the throttle, speed up, step on it, put your foot down Opposite: slow down

operable adj 1 treatable, curable, nonfatal Opposite: inoperable 2 practicable, doable, possible, feasible, workable Opposite: impracticable

operate v 1 function, work, run, go, activate 2 trade, work, manage, run, carry on

operation n 1 control, management, use, controlling, manoeuvring 2 business, company, venture, undertaking, outfit (infml) 3 process, action, act, procedure, manoeuvre 4 campaign, manoeuvre, procedure, raid, attack

operational adj in use, in operation, in order, working, active

operative adj in effect, functioning, working, effective, operational Opposite: inoperative ■ n worker, operator, machinist, hand, technician

operator n worker, operative, machinist, hand

operose (fml) adj arduous, taxing, difficult, strenuous, hard Opposite: easy

opine (fml) v pronounce, hold forth, discourse, lecture, preach

opinion n view, estimation, belief, judgment, attitude

opinionated adj voluble, bigoted, narrowminded, partisan, prejudiced Opposite: open-minded

opinion poll n survey, poll, questionnaire, investigation

opponent n adversary, enemy, rival, challenger, antagonist Opposite: ally

opportune adj favourable, fitting, appropriate, apt, right Opposite: inopportune

opportunism n resourcefulness, unscrupulousness, cunning, deviousness, speculation

opportunist n speculator, freebooter, fortune hunter, buccaneer, swashbuckler

opportunistic adj unscrupulous, resourceful, unprincipled, devious, cunning Opposite: principled

opportunity n occasion, opening, prospect, chance, break (infml) Opposite: misfortune

oppose v 1 be against, resist, fight, contest, combat Opposite: support 2 compete with, face, compete against, do battle with, clash with

opposed adj opposite, different, contrasting,

divergent, conflicting *Opposite*: similar

opposing *adj* 1 **opposite**, contrasting, differing, disparate, conflicting *Opposite*: similar 2 **rival**, opposite, hostile, competing, antagonistic *Opposite*: allied

opposite *adj* 1 **far**, other, furthest, facing, opposing *Opposite*: adjacent 2 **conflicting**, contradictory, differing, reverse, contrary *Opposite*: matching ■ *n* **contrary**, reverse, converse, inverse, opposite number *Opposite*: same ■ *prep* **facing**, across from, in front of, overlooking *Opposite*: beside

opposite number *n* **counterpart**, equivalent, parallel, equal, match

opposition *n* 1 **resistance**, antagonism, hostility, disapproval, disagreement *Opposite*: friendliness 2 **opponent**, challenger, competitor, enemy, rival

oppress *v* 1 **keep down**, coerce, tyrannize, dominate, repress *Opposite*: liberate 2 **afflict**, worry, torment, depress, distress *Opposite*: relieve

oppression *n* **domination**, coercion, cruelty, tyranny, repression

oppressive *adj* 1 **cruel**, harsh, domineering, tyrannical, repressive *Opposite*: fair 2 **overwhelming**, crushing, depressing, distressing, stressful *Opposite*: relaxing 3 **humid**, hot, close, muggy, stifling *Opposite*: fresh

oppressor *n* **autocrat**, despot, persecutor, bully, tyrant *Opposite*: liberator

opprobrious *adj* 1 **scornful**, contemptuous, damning, dismissive, reproachful *Opposite*: approving 2 **shameful**, humiliating, ignominious, embarrassing, belittling *Opposite*: glorious

opprobriousness *n* 1 **scorn**, contempt, censoriousness, dismissiveness, reproachfulness *Opposite*: approval 2 **shamefulness**, shame, humiliation, ignominy, embarrassment *Opposite*: glory

opprobrium *n* 1 **scorn**, contempt, condemnation, criticism, reproach *Opposite*: approval 2 **shame**, disgrace, ignominy, humiliation, embarrassment *Opposite*: glory

opt *v* **choose**, elect, decide, determine, plump for

optical *adj* **visual**, ocular, ophthalmic, photo-sensitive

optical illusion *n* 1 **illusion**, impression, effect, visual effect, mirage 2 **trick**, illusion, trick of the light, special effect, visual effect

optimal *adj* **best**, ideal, optimum, top, finest *Opposite*: worst

optimism *n* 1 **hopefulness**, sanguinity, confidence, positiveness, assurance *Opposite*: pessimism 2 **cheerfulness**, enthusiasm, buoyancy, sunniness, brightness *Opposite*: pessimism

optimist *n* **idealist**, romantic, utopian, visionary, hoper *Opposite*: pessimist

optimistic *adj* **hopeful**, positive, bright, cheerful, expectant *Opposite*: pessimistic

optimize *v* **enhance**, improve, adjust, heighten, elevate

optimum *n* **ideal situation**, best-case scenario, goal, ideal, best ■ *adj* **best**, ideal, optimal, top, finest *Opposite*: worst

option *n* **choice**, alternative, possibility, route, opportunity *Opposite*: imperative

optional *adj* **elective**, voluntary, discretionary, possible, free *Opposite*: compulsory

opt out *(infml)* *v* **bow out**, bail out, withdraw, get out, leave

opulence *n* 1 **wealth**, affluence, riches, prosperity, fortune *Opposite*: poverty 2 **lavishness**, luxury, richness, magnificence, sumptuousness *Opposite*: simplicity

opulent *adj* 1 **wealthy**, lavish, luxurious, rich, magnificent *Opposite*: poor 2 **abundant**, ample, lavish, profuse, rich *Opposite*: sparse

opus *n* **composition**, work, piece, production, brainchild

oracle *n* 1 **prophet**, augur, soothsayer, seer, visionary 2 **prophesy**, vision, revelation, foreshadowing, prediction

oral *adj* **spoken**, verbal, uttered, said, verbalized *Opposite*: written. *See* COMPARE AND CONTRAST *at* **verbal**.

orangery *n* **greenhouse**, glasshouse, hothouse, conservatory, winter garden

orate *v* 1 **speak**, lecture, make a speech, take the floor, discourse 2 *(fml)* **hold forth**, preach, lecture, speak, declaim

oration *n* **speech**, discourse, address, lecture, sermon

orator *n* **speaker**, debater, lecturer, raconteur, storyteller

oratorical *adj* **rhetorical**, debating, declamatory, speechmaking, eloquent *Opposite*: halting

oratory *n* 1 **debating**, discussion, rhetoric, declamation, speechifying *(infml)* 2 **eloquence**, persuasiveness, cogency, skill, style 3 **pomposity**, prolixity, grandiloquence, verbosity, speechifying *(infml)*

orb *n* **globe**, sphere, planet, ball, round

orbit *n* 1 **path**, track, trajectory, flight path, course 2 **scope**, range, compass, influence, ambit ■ *v* **circle**, circumnavigate, loop, encircle, revolve

orchard *n* **plantation**, wood, copse, grove, coppice

orchestral *adj* **instrumental**, classical, symphonic, musical

orchestrate *v* 1 **score**, arrange, compose, write, rewrite 2 **plan out**, work out, arrange, coordinate, organize *Opposite*: improvise

orchestration *n* 1 **instrumentation**, transposition, arrangement, scoring, composition 2 **planning**, organization, stage-management, arrangement, preplanning *Opposite*: improvisation

ordain *(fml)* v order, decree, proclaim, enact, command *Opposite*: suggest

ordeal n trial, torment, suffering, tribulation, test

order n **1 instruction**, command, directive, direction, demand *Opposite*: suggestion **2 sequence**, succession, rank, classification, arrangement *Opposite*: chaos **3 orderliness**, neatness, tidiness, method, regulation *Opposite*: disorder **4 stability**, calm, harmony, peace, peacefulness *Opposite*: upheaval **5 contract**, purchase, sale, request, requisition **6 sect**, organization, group, class, lodge ■ v **1 command**, instruct, tell, require, charge *Opposite*: request **2 requisition**, request, ask for, send for, send off for *Opposite*: supply **3 arrange**, organize, regulate, classify, categorize *Opposite*: confuse

ordered adj **1 well-ordered**, neat, tidy, methodical, well-organized *Opposite*: disorganized **2 controlled**, regimented, consistent, steady, efficient *Opposite*: irregular

orderliness n **neatness**, order, tidiness, method, organization *Opposite*: disorderliness

orderly adj **1 obedient**, disciplined, well-behaved, decorous, compliant *Opposite*: disorderly **2 arranged**, tidy, methodical, neat, logical *Opposite*: disorderly

ordinance n **decree**, order, rule, regulation, law

ordinarily adv **normally**, usually, generally, customarily, in general *Opposite*: unusually

ordinariness n **1 normality**, commonplaceness, usualness, commonness, familiarity **2 dullness**, triteness, drabness, dreariness, predictability

ordinary adj **1 normal**, commonplace, usual, regular, common *Opposite*: unusual **2 dull**, trite, drab, dreary, predictable *Opposite*: extraordinary

ordination n **investiture**, consecration, ceremony, conferment, installation

ordnance n **weapons**, artillery, arms, guns, weaponry

ordure *(fml)* n **excrement**, filth, dung, manure, faeces

ore n **mineral**, rock, metal, element, aggregate

organ n **1 body part**, tissue, structure **2** *(fml)* **agency**, organization, body, representative, voice **3** *(fml)* **publication**, mouthpiece, newspaper, magazine, periodical

organic adj **1 carbon-based**, biological, living, animate, animal *Opposite*: inorganic **2 gradual**, natural, spontaneous, slow, unforced *Opposite*: artificial **3 natural**, unprocessed, unrefined, untreated, raw *Opposite*: synthetic

organism n **living thing**, creature, animal, plant, virus

organization n **1 group**, body, society, association, party **2 arrangement**, configuration, design, format, composition **3 orderliness**, order, method, regulation, neatness *Opposite*: chaos

organizational adj **structural**, administrative, legislative, executive, logistic

organize v **1 establish**, form, shape, unify, unite **2 coordinate**, manage, control, run, set up **3 systematize**, arrange, sort out, classify, categorize *Opposite*: disarrange

organized adj **1 prearranged**, structured, ordered, systematized, well thought-out *Opposite*: spontaneous **2 methodical**, logical, orderly, reasonable, sensible *Opposite*: disorganized

organizer n **1 manager**, director, coordinator, planner, controller **2 diary**, appointment book, PDA, personal digital assistant, daybook

orient *see* orientate

orientate v **1 position**, turn, angle, face, place **2 familiarize**, adjust, learn about, orient, adapt

orientation n **1 location**, alignment, direction, positioning, angle **2 emphasis**, focus, character, slant, thrust **3 leaning**, tendency, proclivity, preference, inclination **4 adjustment**, acclimatization, assimilation, acclimation, settling in **5 initiation**, briefing, induction, training, introduction

oriented adj **concerned with**, in favour of, focused on, preoccupied with, slanted towards

orifice *(literary)* n **opening**, hole, vent, cavity, outlet

origin n **source**, derivation, provenance, cause, root

COMPARE AND CONTRAST CORE MEANING: the beginning of something
origin the beginning of something in terms of the time, place, situation, or idea from which it arose, or somebody's ancestry, social background, or country; **source** the place, person, or thing through which something has come into being or from which it has been obtained; **derivation** the origin or source of something, especially a word, phrase, or name; **provenance** the place of origin of something, or the source and ownership history of a work of art or archaeological artefact; **root** the fundamental cause, basis, or origin of something, especially a feeling or a problem.

original adj **1 first**, initial, previous, fundamental, primary *Opposite*: last **2 unique**, innovative, novel, inventive, creative *Opposite*: unoriginal ■ n **prototype**, genuine article, pattern, archetype, template *Opposite*: copy. See COMPARE AND CONTRAST at **new**.

originality n **innovation**, novelty, uniqueness, inventiveness, creativity *Opposite*: unoriginality

originally adv **first**, initially, in the beginning, formerly, at first *Opposite*: eventually

originate v 1 **begin**, derive, stem from, start, commence Opposite: finish 2 **create**, invent, initiate, instigate, inaugurate

originator n **inventor**, creator, instigator, designer, maker

ornament n 1 **knick-knack**, figurine, objet d'art, bauble, decoration 2 **embellishment**, adornment, enhancement, enrichment, trimming ■ v **adorn**, decorate, beautify, embellish, paint

ornamental adj **decorative**, attractive, for show, ornate, patterned Opposite: functional

ornamentation n **decoration**, adornment, embellishment, enhancement, garnishing

ornate adj 1 **decorative**, overelaborate, baroque, elaborate, ornamental Opposite: unadorned 2 **high-flown**, flowery, wordy, verbose, elaborate Opposite: plain

orotund (fml) adj 1 **loud**, clear, strong, ringing, stentorian Opposite: soft 2 **wordy**, verbose, grandiloquent, pompous, bombastic Opposite: humble

orphan n **child**, baby, boy, girl, waif ■ v **bereave**, leave alone, leave all alone, make an orphan

orphanage n **home**, residential home, hostel, poorhouse, workhouse

orthodox adj **conventional**, accepted, traditional, mainstream, conformist Opposite: unorthodox

orthodoxy n **accepted view**, convention, accepted belief, prevailing attitude, tenet

oscillate v 1 **swing**, move back and forth, move to and fro, move backwards and forwards, fluctuate 2 **waver**, hesitate, vacillate, blow hot and cold, dither

oscillation n **swaying**, fluctuation, vacillation, alternation, swinging

osculate (fml) v **kiss**, give a kiss, give a smacker (infml), canoodle with (infml), smooch (infml)

ossify v **petrify**, fossilize, harden, become inflexible, become fixed

ossuary (fml) n **vault**, grave, tomb, crypt, charnel house

ostensible adj **ostensive**, apparent, professed, supposed, perceived Opposite: real

ostentation n **flashiness**, showiness, display, flamboyance, pretension Opposite: modesty

ostentatious adj **flashy**, showy, flamboyant, affected, pretentious Opposite: modest

ostracism n **shunning**, snubbing, exclusion, barring, keeping out Opposite: inclusion

ostracize v **coldshoulder**, exclude, banish, shun, ignore Opposite: include

other adj **additional**, new, more, fresh, extra

otherness n **strangeness**, difference, uniqueness, distinctiveness, oddness Opposite: normality

otherwise adv **or else**, if not, else, alternatively

otiose adj **futile**, ineffectual, useless, impractical, ineffective Opposite: effective

ottoman n **divan**, couch, day bed, chaise lounge, settee

oubliette n **prison cell**, dungeon, prison, cell

ounce n **grain**, jot, scrap, small amount, modicum

oust v **expel**, throw out, get rid of, drive out, exile Opposite: appoint

ouster n **removal**, ejection, dismissal, expulsion, coup

out adv **outdoors**, out-of-doors, in the open, in the open air, alfresco Opposite: indoors ■ adj 1 **elsewhere**, not in, not at home, away, away from home Opposite: in 2 **exposed**, revealed, given away, made known, shown Opposite: hidden 3 **available**, on view, obtainable, ready, on show Opposite: unavailable 4 **unacceptable**, impossible, improbable, not worth it, not on Opposite: acceptable 5 **old-fashioned**, unfashionable, outdated, dated, passé Opposite: fashionable 6 **banned**, prohibited, disallowed, barred, prevented Opposite: legitimate 7 **unconscious**, out cold, asleep, comatose, dazed Opposite: conscious

out-and-out adj **complete**, blatant, obvious, outright, utter

outback n **wilderness**, scrubland, wilds, desert, badlands

outbid v **offer more than**, outspend, outdo, leave standing, overpay

outboard adj **external**, on the outside, outside, outward, exterior

outbrave (archaic) v **defy**, confront, brave, stand up to, face up to

outbreak n **eruption**, outburst, epidemic, occurrence, rash

outbuilding n **shed**, outhouse, lean-to, barn, shack

WORD BANK

❏ **types of outbuilding** barn, booth, byre, carport, conservatory, cowshed, garage, garden shed, gatehouse, gazebo, glasshouse, greenhouse, guardhouse, hothouse, hut, kiosk, lean-to, lodge, orangery, outhouse, pavilion, potting shed, privy (infml), sentry box, shed, stall, stand, summerhouse

outburst n **outpouring**, upsurge, surge, eruption, explosion

outcast n **untouchable**, exile, pariah, recluse, outsider

outclass v **surpass**, outshine, excel, do better than, better

outcome n **consequence**, result, ending, product, conclusion

outcrop n **rocky outcrop**, crag, ridge, bluff, boulder

outcry n 1 **protest**, disagreement, objection, chorus of disapproval, quarrel Opposite:

acceptance **2 uproar**, hullabaloo, hue and cry, turmoil, clamour

outdated *adj* **antiquated**, passé, outmoded, obsolete, dated *Opposite*: up-to-date. *See* COMPARE AND CONTRAST *at* **old-fashioned**.

outdistance *v* **outdo**, beat, do better than, outrun, outstrip

outdo *v* **exceed**, surpass, top, outdistance, outshine

outdoor *adj* **outside**, open-air, out-of-doors, alfresco *Opposite*: indoor

outdoors *adv* **out-of-doors**, outside, in the open, in the open air, alfresco *Opposite*: indoors

outer *adj* **outside**, external, on the outside, surface, superficial *Opposite*: inner

outermost *adj* **furthest**, farthest, remotest, outmost *Opposite*: innermost

outer space *n* **space**, the heavens, the universe, the solar system, the cosmos

outface *v* **1 stare out**, outstare, psych out (*infml*), stare down (*US*) *Opposite*: give in **2 brave**, stand up to, face up to, defy, confront *Opposite*: capitulate

outfall *n* **vent**, mouth, duct, channel, culvert

outfit *n* **1 suit**, clothes, clothing, ensemble, dress **2** (*infml*) **company**, team, business, group, unit ■ *v* **supply**, equip, fit out, arm, kit out

outflank *v* **1 go around**, attack from behind, attack from the rear, outmanoeuvre **2 outwit**, outmanoeuvre, outdo, bypass, outclass

outflow *n* **1 discharge**, drainage, seepage, leakage, depletion *Opposite*: influx **2 expenditure**, debit, expenses, spending, outlay *Opposite*: income

outfox *v* **defeat**, outwit, get the better of, outflank, take in

outgoing *adj* **1 outward-bound**, outbound, outward, departing, leaving *Opposite*: incoming **2 retiring**, leaving, departing, withdrawing, resigning *Opposite*: incoming **3 sociable**, friendly, gregarious, extrovert, genial *Opposite*: introvert

outgoings *n* **expenses**, expenditure, costs, overhead, outlay *Opposite*: income

outgrow *v* **1 get too large for**, grow too big for, get too big for, enlarge, grow up **2 move beyond**, be too grown-up for, be too old for, mature, develop **3 grow bigger than**, grow larger than, grow faster than, grow quicker than, outnumber

outgrowth *n* **extension**, result, development, product, consequence

outing *n* **visit**, excursion, trip, day trip, jaunt

outjockey *v* **outfox**, outdo, outwit, outmanoeuvre, outflank

outlandish *adj* **unusual**, bizarre, peculiar, strange, eccentric *Opposite*: usual

outlast *v* **outlive**, survive, live longer than, last longer than, endure

outlaw *n* **runaway**, criminal, fugitive, bandit, desperado ■ *v* **forbid**, ban, prohibit, proscribe, veto *Opposite*: allow

outlay *n* **expenditure**, expense, cost, spending, sum *Opposite*: return ■ *v* **expend**, spend, lay out, pay out, disburse

outlet *n* **1 opening**, passage, vent, exit, channel **2 means**, channel, conduit, vent, instrument **3 department store**, shop, retailer, market, store

outline *n* **1 shape**, form, figure, contour, silhouette **2 plan**, rough draft, summary, sketch, rough idea ■ *v* **1 draw round**, sketch, draw, delineate, chart *Opposite*: fill in **2 summarize**, sketch out, delineate, run through, give a rough idea *Opposite*: expand

outlive *v* **live longer than**, outlast, survive, last longer than, endure

outlook *n* **1 viewpoint**, view, attitude, position, point of view **2 future**, prospect, time to come, time ahead **3 view**, panorama, vista

outlying *adj* **remote**, out-of-the-way, distant, faraway, far-off *Opposite*: neighbouring

outmanoeuvre *v* **get the better of**, outsmart, outfox, outwit, outflank

outmoded *adj* **1 unfashionable**, dated, passé, old-fashioned, out-of-date *Opposite*: fashionable **2 obsolete**, out of use, out of commission, archaic, antiquated

outmost *adj* **outermost**, remotest, furthest, most remote, extreme

outnumber *v* **be more than**, be more numerous than, outstrip

out-of-date *adj* **outdated**, obsolete, outmoded, old-fashioned, dated *Opposite*: up-to-date

out-of-doors *adv* **outdoors**, outside, in the open, in the open air, alfresco *Opposite*: indoors

out of the blue *adv* **unexpectedly**, without warning, all of a sudden, suddenly, surprisingly

out-of-the-way *adj* **1 distant**, off the beaten track, remote, isolated, desolate *Opposite*: accessible **2 uncommon**, unconventional, different, out of the ordinary, special *Opposite*: common

outpace *v* **outstrip**, outperform, overtake, outdo, beat

outperform *v* **outdo**, outstrip, outpace, outclass, beat *Opposite*: underperform

outpost *n* **garrison**, base, station, settlement, colony

outpouring *n* **expression**, outburst, torrent, spate, flood

output *n* **production**, productivity, amount produced, yield, harvest

outrage *n* **1 crime**, barbarity, disgrace, scandal, horror **2 indignation**, anger, rage, fury, annoyance ■ *v* **infuriate**, offend, insult, anger, enrage *Opposite*: placate

outraged *adj* **angry**, incensed, livid, infuriated, furious *Opposite*: calm

outrageous adj **disgraceful**, shameful, shocking, offensive, contemptible Opposite: commendable

outré adj **shocking**, eccentric, unconventional, excessive, too much

outride v **1 outpace**, outstrip, outclass, beat, overtake **2 survive**, last out, endure, ride out, make it through

outrider n **patrol**, guard, bodyguard, attendant, escort

outright adv **1 completely**, entirely, totally, fully, absolutely Opposite: partially **2 immediately**, straightaway, right away, without hesitation, at once Opposite: hesitantly **3 openly**, unreservedly, frankly, forthrightly, unequivocally Opposite: equivocally ■ adj **1 absolute**, complete, total, utter, out-and-out Opposite: partial **2 out-and-out**, clear, transparent, obvious, direct

outrun v **1 outpace**, outstrip, outclass, beat, overtake **2 leave behind**, flee, run faster than, elude, get away from **3 go beyond**, overrun, exceed, excel, surpass

outsell v **beat**, overtake, outpace, outstrip, sell more than Opposite: underperform

outset n **beginning**, start, onset, kickoff (infml), inception (fml)

outshine v **surpass**, outdo, outstrip, outperform, do better than

outside adv **1 outdoors**, in the open air, alfresco, out of doors, in the fresh air **2 beyond**, out there, elsewhere, yonder ■ adj **1 outdoor**, external, separate, open-air, exterior **2 external**, unknown, unfamiliar, independent, freelance **3 slight**, faint, remote, scarce, slim Opposite: strong ■ prep **beyond**, out of, further than, farther than, past Opposite: within ■ n **exterior**, outer surface, surface, external surface Opposite: inside

outsider n **stranger**, foreigner, unknown, interloper, outcast

outsize adj **enormous**, massive, huge, immense, gigantic

outsized see outsize

outskirts n **border**, fringes, periphery, bounds, outer reaches Opposite: centre

outsmart v **outwit**, outfox, outmanoeuvre, get the better of, overcome

outspoken adj **frank**, opinionated, honest, candid, open Opposite: tactful

outspokenness n **frankness**, honesty, candour, openness, bluntness Opposite: tact

outspread adj **extended**, spread-out, stretched, widely spread, open Opposite: folded ■ v **extend**, expand, stretch, spread, spread out Opposite: close in

outstanding adj **1 exceptional**, wonderful, stupendous, dazzling, marvellous Opposite: abysmal **2 unresolved**, unsettled, unpaid, remaining, owing Opposite: settled

outstandingly adv **exceptionally**, terrifically,

wonderfully, stupendously, marvellously Opposite: abysmally

outstay v **outlast**, outlive, survive, stay longer than

outstretched adj **outspread**, extended, stretched out, spread-out, stretched Opposite: folded

outstrip v **outdo**, outshine, surpass, exceed, do better than Opposite: fall behind

outward adj **visible**, external, apparent, obvious, noticeable Opposite: inward

outwards adv **out**, outward, away, centrifugally Opposite: inwards

outweigh v **overshadow**, be more important than, prevail over, be greater than, dwarf

outwit v **outsmart**, outfox, outmanoeuvre, get the better of, take in

outworn adj **obsolete**, outmoded, out-of-date, antiquated, archaic Opposite: current

ovate adj **oval**, egg-shaped, ellipsoid

ovation n **standing ovation**, cheer, vote of confidence, endorsement, thumbs-up (infml)

over prep **1 throughout**, around, the length and breadth of, round, across **2 in excess of**, more than, greater than, larger than, above Opposite: under **3 on top of**, above, on, upon Opposite: beneath (fml) ■ adj **ended**, finished, done, completed, concluded

overabundance n **excess**, surplus, glut, superfluity, flood Opposite: shortage

overact v **ham it up**, ham, overdo it, exaggerate, overplay

overactive adj **feverish**, overexcited, overcharged, intense, fervid

overall adj **general**, complete, total, global, inclusive ■ adv **on the whole**, in general, generally, taken as a whole, largely Opposite: in particular

over and above prep **in addition to**, besides, as well as, added to, on top of

overarching adj **all-embracing**, main, all-encompassing, predominant, principal

overawe v **intimidate**, scare, impress, subdue

overbearing adj **arrogant**, domineering, bossy, imperious, pompous Opposite: meek

overblown adj **1 overdone**, excessive, exaggerated, unrestrained, immoderate Opposite: understated **2 pretentious**, pompous, puffed-up, extravagant Opposite: unassuming

overburden v **overload**, overtax, overstrain, burden, load

overcast adj **cloudy**, grey, gloomy, dark, dull Opposite: bright

overcharge v **charge too much**, take advantage of, cheat, swindle, rip off (infml)

overcome v **1 overwhelm**, overpower, incapacitate, disable, knock out **2 carry away**, affect, move to tears, reduce to tears, grip **3 surmount**, prevail over, rise above, triumph over, conquer *Opposite*: yield. *See* COMPARE AND CONTRAST *at* defeat.

overcompensate v overreact, overcorrect, overplay, give too much weight to, try too hard

overconfidence n arrogance, overoptimism, boldness, pride, nerve *Opposite*: caution

overconfident adj arrogant, full of yourself, brash, overoptimistic, bullish *(infml)* *Opposite*: modest

overcook v overdo, stew, burn, char, spoil

overcooked adj overdone, burnt, well done, chewy, hard *Opposite*: underdone

overcritical adj harsh, hypercritical, censorious, severe, critical

overcrowded adj filled to capacity, congested, overloaded, teeming, swarming *Opposite*: deserted

overcrowding n congestion, overloading, overpopulation, excess, excess numbers

overdo v 1 overcook, burn, stew, char, spoil 2 exaggerate, overstate, overplay, overemphasize, take to extremes *Opposite*: play down

overdone adj 1 overcooked, burnt, stewed, charred, spoilt *Opposite*: underdone 2 exaggerated, overstated, overplayed, overemphasized, extreme *Opposite*: restrained

overdo things v strain yourself, burn the candle at both ends, overtax yourself, overexert yourself, overdo it *Opposite*: relax

overdrawn adj in debt, in the red, overspent, insolvent, over your limit *Opposite*: in credit

overdue adj late, tardy, unpaid, unsettled, belated *Opposite*: early

overeat v overindulge, eat too much, gorge, stuff yourself, binge

overemotional adj emotional, sentimental, melodramatic, maudlin, histrionic *Opposite*: unemotional

overemphasize v exaggerate, overstate, overstress, stress, go over the top about

overenthusiasm n fanaticism, mania, obsessiveness, obsession, ardour

overenthusiastic adj overzealous, carried away, fanatical, obsessive, obsessional

overestimate v 1 misjudge, overrate, miscalculate, overvalue, allow too much for *Opposite*: underestimate 2 overrate, expect too much of, misjudge, miscalculate, overemphasize *Opposite*: underestimate

overexcite v work up, excite, get in a state, get carried away, wind up *(infml)* *Opposite*: calm down

overexcited adj carried away, high, frenzied, in a frenzy, feverish *Opposite*: calm

overexcitement n frenzy, mania, feverishness, anxiety, emotion

overextend v overstretch, overreach, go too far, bite off more than you can chew, exceed your limit

overflow v run over, flood, spill over, brim over, pour out ■ n excess, runoff, extra, surfeit, surplus *Opposite*: lack

overflowing adj spilling over, teeming, swarming, brimming, abundant *Opposite*: empty

overflow with v be full of, brim with, abound with, bubble with, be bursting at the seams with *Opposite*: lack

overgrown adj dense, thick, overrun, lush, untidy *Opposite*: tidy

overhang v project, extend, jut out, hang over, extend beyond ■ n projection, extension, outcrop, ledge, outcropping

overhaul v 1 repair, renovate, fix, refit, refurbish 2 overtake, surpass, leave behind, outdo, pass *Opposite*: fall behind ■ n service, refit, refurbishment

overhead adv above, in the air, upstairs, directly above, above your head *Opposite*: below

overheads n costs, outgoings, expenses, payments, business costs

overhear v eavesdrop, listen in, hear, eavesdrop on, listen to

overheated adj excited, impassioned, agitated, inflamed, hot and bothered *Opposite*: calm

overindulge v overeat, eat too much, stuff yourself, gorge, gorge yourself

overindulgence n excess, greed, intemperance, hedonism, gluttony

overindulgent adj excessive, greedy, immoderate, intemperate, hedonistic

overjoyed adj delighted, joyful, elated, ecstatic, jubilant *Opposite*: disappointed

overkill n excess, too much, overstatement, overegging the pudding, too much of a good thing *Opposite*: restraint

overladen adj overloaded, overfilled, crammed, overburdened, weighed down

overlap v 1 partly cover, overlie, meet, touch, cover 2 coincide, correspond, intersect, meet, come together ■ n 1 overlay, intersection, edge, join, connection 2 correspondence, connection, similarity, common ground, commonality

overlay n cover, coat, put over, overlap, drape

overload v overburden, overwork, tax, strain, weigh down ■ n excess, surplus, overwork, burden, overkill *Opposite*: lack

overloaded adj weighed down, weighted down, loaded, laden, full

overlook v 1 ignore, miss, forget, skip, neglect *Opposite*: notice 2 excuse, condone, spare, let pass, pardon *Opposite*: punish 3 give onto, be opposite, face, back onto 4 supervise, oversee, superintend, boss, watch 5 inspect, survey, examine, peruse, scan. *See* COMPARE AND CONTRAST *at* neglect.

overly adv excessively, too, desperately, exaggeratedly, exceedingly *Opposite*: slightly

overmuch *adv* **excessively**, too much, very much, unnecessarily, overly ■ *adj* **excessive**, extreme, too much, immoderate, extravagant ■ *n* **excess**, superfluity, surplus, overage

overnight *adv* **suddenly**, at once, quickly, instantly, abruptly *Opposite*: gradually ■ *adj* **instant**, immediate, abrupt, instantaneous, sudden *Opposite*: gradual

overpitch *v* **exaggerate**, overdo, overcompensate, overplay, overemphasize

overplay *v* **overemphasize**, exaggerate, overdo, overstress, overstate *Opposite*: underplay

overpower *v* **1 subdue**, override, suppress, subjugate, conquer *Opposite*: yield **2 overwhelm**, overshadow, floor, overcome, dumbfound

overpowering *adj* **overwhelming**, intense, overriding, uncontrollable, consuming *Opposite*: weak

overpoweringly *adv* **irresistibly**, overwhelmingly, devastatingly, strongly, intensely

overprice *v* **overrate**, overvalue, hike up, write up, mark up *Opposite*: underprice

overpriced *adj* **high-priced**, costly, extortionate, expensive, exorbitant *Opposite*: cheap

overprotect *v* **cosset**, fuss over, cocoon, indulge, protect *Opposite*: neglect

overrate *v* **overprize**, overestimate, exaggerate, overvalue *Opposite*: underrate

overrated *adj* **overvalued**, overestimated, hyped, puffed up, glorified *Opposite*: underrated

overreach *v* **1 overdo**, bite off more than you can chew, overstretch, overextend, go too far **2 overstrain**, overextend, overdo, overstress **3 outwit**, outsmart, outfox, outplay, deceive

overreact *v* **exaggerate**, make a big deal, make something out of nothing, make a mountain out of a molehill, make a drama out of a crisis

override *v* **1 disregard**, overrule, defy, flout, countermand *Opposite*: follow **2 supersede**, dominate, prevail, predominate, overrule

overriding *adj* **overruling**, superseding, intervening, dominant, prevailing *Opposite*: insignificant

overrule *v* **1 override**, cancel, rule against, refuse, make null and void **2 master**, exercise authority, domineer, pull rank

overrun *v* **invade**, attack, assail, assault, besiege ■ *adj* **swarming**, infested, teeming, flooded, swamped

overseas *adj* **foreign**, external, ultramarine *(literary)* ■ *adv* **abroad**, out of the country, in foreign parts

oversee *v* **supervise**, manage, superintend, run, direct

overseer *n* **supervisor**, manager, administrator, chief, boss

oversell *v* **exaggerate**, overvalue, overrate, hype, overstate *Opposite*: undersell

oversensitive *adj* **emotional**, thin-skinned, hypersensitive, vulnerable, touchy *Opposite*: thick-skinned

oversentimental *adj* **slushy**, mawkish, syrupy, maudlin, sad *Opposite*: callous

overshadow *v* **outshine**, outdo, dominate, surpass, eclipse

overshoot *v* **pass**, exceed, overreach, overpass, overrun *Opposite*: hit

oversight *n* **1 mistake**, failure to notice, slip, omission, misunderstanding **2 supervision**, control, overseeing, management, administration

oversimplify *v* **generalize**, overgeneralize, simplify, distort *Opposite*: complicate

oversize *adj* **extra large**, large, huge, king-size, oversized

oversized *see* **oversize**

oversleep *v* **sleep in**, sleep late, lie in *(infml)*

overspill *n* **flood**, overflow, runoff, excess, surplus ■ *v* **spill over**, overflow, brim over, pour out, flood

overstate *v* **exaggerate**, make too much of, overdo, overstress, overemphasize *Opposite*: understate

overstated *adj* **exaggerated**, extravagant, excessive, inflated, overelaborate *Opposite*: understated

overstatement *n* **exaggeration**, hyperbole, overemphasis *Opposite*: understatement

overstay *v* **prolong**, protract, spin out, extend

overstep *v* **1 exceed**, go beyond, pass, surpass, step over **2 transgress**, violate, disregard, disobey, contravene *Opposite*: obey

overstrain *v* **overstretch**, overstress, overreach, overtax, overload

overstress *v* **1 overemphasize**, exaggerate, overplay, overpitch, overstate **2 overstretch**, overstrain, overreach, overtax, overload ■ *n* **overstating**, overplaying, overdoing, dwelling on, going on about

overstretch *v* **1 overstrain**, overstress, overreach, overdo **2 overburden**, overtax, overload, overdo, overreach

overstrung *adj* **nervous**, tense, oversensitive, highly-strung, temperamental *Opposite*: placid

overstuffed *adj* **brimming**, overfilled, brimful, overflowing, bursting at the seams *Opposite*: empty

oversupply *n* **overflow**, excess, surplus, glut, superfluity ■ *v* **glut**, overwhelm, flood, inundate, swamp

overt *adj* **obvious**, unconcealed, explicit, evident, open *Opposite*: covert

overtake *v* **1 pass**, go beyond, go past, overhaul, leave behind *Opposite*: fall behind **2 hit**, sweep over, engulf, assail, strike

overtax v **strain**, overload, overdo it, overstretch, overstrain

over-the-hill adj **old**, past your prime, past your sell-by date, ancient, decrepit *Opposite*: up-and-coming

over-the-top (*infml*) adj **exaggerated**, excessive, overdone, extravagant, overblown *Opposite*: understated

overthrow v **conquer**, defeat, dethrone, bring down, depose *Opposite*: uphold

overtime n **extra pay**, extra hours, time and a half, additional hours, double time ■ adv **energetically**, tirelessly, actively, strenuously, intensely

overtone n **implication**, association, hint, undertone, connotation

overturn v **1 turn over**, knock over, tip over, upend, capsize *Opposite*: right **2 nullify**, abolish, invalidate, annul, reverse

overuse n **misuse**, abuse, overconsumption ■ v **overdo**, go to extremes, overplay, do to death, misuse

overused adj **overworked**, clichéd, hackneyed, commonplace, trite

overvalue v **overrate**, overprize, overestimate *Opposite*: undervalue

overview n **indication**, summary, outline, gestalt, synopsis

overweening adj **arrogant**, conceited, pompous, presumptuous, haughty *Opposite*: unassuming

overweight adj **too heavy**, heavy, big, large, weighty *Opposite*: underweight

overwhelm v **overpower**, overcome, engulf, devastate, crush

overwhelmed adj **1 overcome**, overawed, speechless, dazed, stunned *Opposite*: unimpressed **2 overpowered physically**, overcome, beaten, conquered, crushed **3 inundated**, snowed under, swamped, flooded, exhausted

overwhelming adj **irresistible**, overpowering, devastating, crushing, awe-inspiring *Opposite*: insignificant

overwinter v **hibernate**, lie dormant, stagnate, vegetate, lie fallow

overwork v **burn the midnight oil**, overdo it, work your fingers to the bone, overburden, overtax

overwrought adj **tense**, stressed, distraught, emotional, strained *Opposite*: calm

owe v **be beholden**, be obligated *Opposite*: repay

owed adj **owing**, unpaid, outstanding, due, payable *Opposite*: paid

owing adj **in arrears**, owed, due, in the red *Opposite*: paid

owing to prep **because of**, due to, on account of, thanks to, as a result of

owlish adj **owl-like**, serious, wise, solemn, bespectacled

own adj **individual**, private, particular, peculiar, specific ■ v **1 possess**, have, have possession of, keep, retain **2** (*fml*) **confess**, admit, own up, acknowledge, profess *Opposite*: deny

owner n **proprietor**, landlord, possessor, holder, titleholder

ownership n **possession**, rights, tenure, title, proprietorship

own goal n **self-defeating action**, blunder, mistake, misjudgment, miscalculation

own up v **confess**, admit, profess, express, utter

ox n **bull**, bullock, steer

oxidization n **reaction**, rust, tarnishing, corrosion, verdigris

oxidize v **react**, rust, tarnish, corrode, dissolve

P

PA n **public-address system**, loudspeaker, speaker, amplifier, amp

pace n **1 speed**, rapidity, swiftness, velocity, rate of knots **2 rate**, speed, tempo, time, regularity **3 step**, stride, leap, bound, hop ■ v **1 walk**, stride, march, walk back and forth, walk up and down **2 govern**, regulate, restrict, manage, limit

pacemaker n **leader**, pacesetter, pacer, innovator, trendsetter

pacific adj **1 soothing**, appeasing, conciliatory, comforting *Opposite*: antagonistic **2 tranquil**, peaceful, calm, untroubled, gentle *Opposite*: violent

pacifist n **peace lover**, conscientious objector, dove, peacemaker, peacekeeper ■ adj **pacific**, appeasing, conciliatory, placatory, comforting *Opposite*: antagonistic

pacify v **calm**, soothe, mollify, placate, calm down *Opposite*: antagonize

pack v **1 store**, arrange, put, place, sort **2 package**, wrap, wrap up, box, bundle *Opposite*: unpack **3 fill**, cram, stuff, jam, load **4 compact**, press, compress, squash, flatten ■ n **1 carton**, packet, box, parcel, container **2 folder**, packet, wallet, dossier, file **3 set**, bunch, group, quantity, collection **4 bag**, rucksack, backpack, haversack, daypack **5 crowd**, horde, mob, gang, bunch

package n **1 parcel**, packet, box, envelope, padded bag **2 set**, bundle, suite, raft, compendium ■ v **1 pack**, wrap, wrap up, parcel, box *Opposite*: unwrap **2 promote**, present, market, advertise, put across

packaging n **wrapping**, packing, wrapper, packet, box

packed adj **crowded**, crammed, full, full to capacity, heaving *Opposite*: empty

packet n **pack**, package, sachet, container, carton

pack in v **1 attract**, interest, excite, fill the seats, be a box office success *Opposite*: flop *(infml)* **2** *(infml)* **stop**, give up, quit, abandon, drop *Opposite*: take up

packing n **stuffing**, filling, filler, wadding, padding

pack up v **1 stop**, give up, quit, abandon, drop *Opposite*: start **2** *(infml)* **stop working**, break down, fail, seize up, jam

pact n **deal**, agreement, treaty, contract, accord

pad n **1 cushion**, cloth, wad, swab, pack **2 notepad**, sketchpad, notebook, jotter, sketchbook ■ v **1 creep**, tiptoe, steal, walk, sneak **2 line**, cover, fill, stuff, wad **3 fill out**, flesh out, amplify, lengthen, expand

padding n **1 stuffing**, filling, wadding, lining, packing **2 verbiage**, circumlocution, periphrasis, garbage, rubbish

paddle n **oar**, scull, sweep, blade ■ v **row**, scull, propel

page n **1 sheet**, piece of paper, sheet of paper, side, leaf **2 call**, beep, summons, message ■ v **call**, contact, bleep, summon, beep *(US)*

pageant n **procession**, parade, cavalcade, display, carnival

pageantry n **spectacle**, display, pomp, ceremony, ritual

paid adj **waged**, salaried, professional, funded *Opposite*: unpaid

pain n **1 discomfort**, agony, aching, hurt, ache *Opposite*: pleasure **2 grief**, sorrow, anguish, ache, torture *Opposite*: joy **3** *(infml)* **nuisance**, bother, bind, menace, drag *(infml)* *Opposite*: pleasure ■ v **sadden**, distress, upset, disturb, grieve *Opposite*: hearten

pained adj **hurt**, aggrieved, indignant, wounded, injured

painful adj **1 tender**, aching, raw, throbbing, excruciating *Opposite*: painless **2 sorrowful**, distressing, anguished, heartbreaking, upsetting *Opposite*: pleasant **3 laborious**, troublesome, awkward, laboured, tedious *Opposite*: easy **4 awful**, excruciating, dire, dreadful, agonizing *Opposite*: wonderful

painkiller n **analgesic**, sedative, anaesthetic, drug

painkilling adj **analgesic**, calming, sedative, deadening, numbing

painless adj **effortless**, easy, trouble-free, simple, unproblematic *Opposite*: problematic

pains n **care**, effort, trouble, lengths

painstaking adj **thorough**, careful, meticulous,

conscientious, scrupulous *Opposite*: careless. *See* COMPARE AND CONTRAST *at* **careful**.

paint v **1 coat**, decorate, smear, daub, splatter **2 portray**, capture, catch, show, render *(fml)*

painter n **artist**, watercolourist, portraitist, miniaturist

painting n **1 picture**, work of art, image, canvas, oil painting **2 art**, fine art, portraiture, landscape, oils

paint the town red *(infml)* v **celebrate**, have a good time, have fun, revel, go out

pair n **couple**, duo, twosome, brace, set ■ v **pair off**, team up, join up, match up, put together *Opposite*: separate

pal *(infml)* n **friend**, comrade, mate, crony, chum *(infml)*

palatable adj **1 edible**, pleasant, tasty, appetizing, toothsome *Opposite*: inedible **2 acceptable**, agreeable, satisfactory, pleasant, passable *Opposite*: disagreeable

palatial adj **luxurious**, lavish, grand, impressive, splendid *Opposite*: miserable

palaver n **1 fuss**, bother, trouble, nuisance, commotion **2 chatter**, chat, gossip, talk, chit-chat *(infml)*

pale adj **1 light**, pastel, soft, whitish, insipid *Opposite*: dark **2 pallid**, fair, colourless, ashen, white *Opposite*: deep **3 faint**, dim, feeble, weak, watery *Opposite*: bright ■ v **1 go white**, whiten, go pale, blanch, bleach *Opposite*: colour **2 diminish**, reduce, recede, lessen *Opposite*: intensify **3 lose colour**, fade, become washed out, soften, lighten *Opposite*: deepen

pall v **lose its attraction**, fade, diminish, wither, go sour ■ n **1 cloud**, blanket, shroud, sheet, wall **2 gloom**, despair, sadness, depression, melancholy

palliative adj **1 analgesic**, painkilling, anaesthetic, sedative **2 soothing**, calming, relaxing, comforting, mollifying

pallid adj **pale**, white, ashen, pasty, colourless *Opposite*: dark

pallor n **paleness**, whiteness, pastiness, wanness, sallowness *Opposite*: bloom

palpable adj **1 intense**, tangible, physical, real, deep *Opposite*: intangible **2 obvious**, clear, demonstrable, unmistakable, evident *Opposite*: hidden

palpitate v **flutter**, pound, race, tremble, quiver

paltry adj **1 worthless**, trivial, trifling, miserable, insignificant *Opposite*: substantial **2 despicable**, wretched, mean, miserable, contemptible

pamper v **spoil**, indulge, coddle, mollycoddle, cosset *Opposite*: mistreat

pamphlet n **leaflet**, brochure, booklet, guide, tract

pan n **pot**, saucepan, casserole, wok, frying pan ■ v *(infml)* **criticize**, berate, disparage, deride, slate *(infml)* *Opposite*: praise

panacea n **cure-all**, cure, solution, answer, remedy

panache n **flair**, flamboyance, style, spirit, confidence Opposite: awkwardness

pandemic n **epidemic**, plague, contagion, sickness, disease

pandemonium n **chaos**, bedlam, uproar, hubbub, mayhem (infml)

pander to v **indulge**, satisfy, gratify, bow to, go along with Opposite: resist

pane n **windowpane**, glass, window, sheet, panel

panel n **1 piece**, board, pane, sheet, plate **2 board**, team, jury, group, council

pang n **twinge**, spasm, paroxysm, shooting pain, cramp

panic n **fear**, anxiety, fright, terror, dread Opposite: calm ■ v **1 be frightened**, be terrified, lose your nerve, go to pieces, get flustered Opposite: calm down **2 terrify**, unnerve, scare, frighten, fluster

panicky adj **frightened**, scared, alarmed, fearful, anxious Opposite: calm

panic-stricken adj **terrified**, unnerved, frightened, fearful, scared out of your wits Opposite: calm

panoply n **display**, array, show, parade, exhibition

panorama n **view**, scene, vista, outlook, landscape

pan out (infml) v **turn out**, work out, develop, end up, resolve itself

pant v **gasp**, puff, wheeze, blow, gasp for air

pantomime (infml) n **farce**, joke, rigmarole, drama

pap n **drivel**, nonsense, rubbish, trash, garbage

paper n **1 newspaper**, daily, weekly, broadsheet, tabloid **2 document**, manuscript, thesis, dissertation, essay

paperback n **book**, softback, softcover, novel

paper over v **1 wallpaper**, cover, cover up, obscure, disguise Opposite: strip **2 conceal**, sweep under the carpet, hide, cover up, make light of Opposite: highlight

paperwork n **form-filling**, accounts, bookkeeping, correspondence, administration

papery adj **flimsy**, frail, thin, paper-thin, delicate

par n **average**, standard, norm, the usual

parable n **allegory**, fable, moral tale, folktale, tale

parade n **procession**, pageant, cavalcade, display, carnival ■ v **1 process**, march, file, strut, turn out **2 show off**, exhibit, display, trumpet, flaunt Opposite: hide **3 walk**, stalk, march, strut, stroll Opposite: skulk

paradigm n **1 model**, template, prototype, standard, pattern **2 epitome**, archetype, model, example, exemplar (literary) Opposite: antithesis

paradise n **1 heaven**, seventh heaven, nirvana, happy hunting ground Opposite: hell **2** (infml) **dream world**, wonderland, cloud nine, utopia, bliss

paradox n **inconsistency**, absurdity, irony, contradiction, contradiction in terms

paradoxical adj **inconsistent**, absurd, ironic, contradictory, illogical Opposite: logical

paradoxically adv **1 illogically**, absurdly, inconsistently, puzzlingly, unexpectedly Opposite: logically **2 strangely enough**, oddly enough, funnily enough, surprisingly, ironically

paragon n **model**, shining example, epitome, archetype, quintessence Opposite: rake

paragraph n **1 section**, subsection, passage, part, clause **2 article**, piece, item, story, editorial

parallel adj **similar**, equivalent, corresponding, analogous, matching Opposite: dissimilar ■ n **1 counterpart**, match, equal, equivalent, peer Opposite: opposite **2 similarity**, correspondence, equivalence, resemblance, analogy Opposite: dissimilarity

paramedic n **first aider**, first responder, emergency worker, rescue worker

parameter n **limit**, boundary, limitation, restriction, constraint

paramilitary adj **guerrilla**, rebel, revolutionary, terrorist ■ n **rebel**, revolutionary, terrorist, guerrilla, fighter

paramount adj **supreme**, utmost, dominant, chief, principal Opposite: minimal

paranoia n **fear**, suspicion, mistrust, distrust, obsession Opposite: confidence

paranoid adj **suspicious**, fearful, mistrustful, distrustful, obsessed Opposite: trusting

paraphernalia n **things**, stuff, equipment, kit, trappings

paraphrase v **rephrase**, summarize, reword, interpret, translate ■ n **summary**, rewording, précis, translation, interpretation

parasite n **1 pest**, bug, bloodsucker, insect, flea Opposite: host **2 leech**, scrounger (infml), sponger (infml), freeloader (infml)

WORD BANK
❏ **types of parasitic insect** bedbug, botfly, chigoe, crab louse, deer tick, flea, gadfly, harvest mite, head louse, louse, mite, sandfly, tapeworm, tick

parasitic adj **1 biting**, bloodsucking, dependent, opportunistic Opposite: host **2 dependent**, lazy, scrounging (infml), sponging (infml), freeloading (infml)

parasol n **sunshade**, umbrella, shade, brolly (infml)

parcel n **1 package**, packet, bundle, carton, box **2 tract**, plot, section, portion ■ v **pack**, package, wrap, wrap up, box Opposite: unwrap

parcel out v **distribute**, divide, share out, give out, hand out

parcel up v wrap up, wrap, parcel, bundle, pack *Opposite*: unwrap

parch v dry, dry out, scorch, dehydrate, desiccate

parched adj 1 dry, arid, dried up, dried out, scorched *Opposite*: waterlogged 2 *(infml)* thirsty, gasping, dehydrated, dry, panting *Opposite*: refreshed. *See* COMPARE AND CONTRAST at dry.

pardon v 1 forgive, absolve, exonerate, let off, acquit *Opposite*: condemn 2 excuse, forgive, overlook, let pass, take no notice of *Opposite*: resent ■ n forgiveness, absolution, exoneration, amnesty, mercy

pare v 1 cut, trim, clip, cut back, tidy up *Opposite*: grow 2 peel, skin, strip, trim, shave

pare down v cut back, cut down, reduce, scale down, pare *Opposite*: increase

parentage n 1 ancestry, background, pedigree, origin, derivation 2 parents, paternity, maternity

parental adj parent, maternal, paternal *Opposite*: filial

parenthesis n digression, afterthought, addition, aside, comment

parenthood n parentage, fatherhood, motherhood, parenting, paternity

parenting n childcare, child-rearing, babycare, nurturing, child raising

parish n community, neighbourhood, district, village, locality

parity n equivalence, equality, uniformity, similarity, correspondence *Opposite*: disparity

park n gardens, botanical gardens, common, green, grounds ■ v *(infml)* sit, settle, plonk, plunk, put

parking n car park, parking bay, parking space, parking place, parking spot

parkland n grassland, land, fields, meadows, estate

parlance n idiom, turn of phrase, phraseology, phrasing, jargon

parley v confer, negotiate, talk, discuss, deliberate ■ n conference, meeting, discussion, negotiations, consultation

parliament n government, legislative body, legislature, assembly, MPs

parliamentarian n member of parliament, MP, politician, backbencher, legislator

parliamentary adj governmental, legislative, lawmaking, congressional, senatorial

parlour n business premises, salon, business establishment, shop, studio

parlous *(archaic)* adj dangerous, perilous, risky, unsafe, uncertain *Opposite*: comfortable

parochial adj narrow, narrow-minded, closed-minded, provincial, insular *Opposite*: broad-minded

parochialism n narrow-mindedness, provincialism, insularity, closed-mindedness, narrowness *Opposite*: broad-mindedness

parodist n satirist, humorist, imitator, lampooner, burlesquer

parody n 1 caricature, imitation, lampoon, satire, burlesque 2 distortion, travesty, misrepresentation, perversion, pale imitation *Opposite*: model ■ v 1 distort, pervert, misrepresent, twist 2 lampoon, imitate, caricature, satirize, burlesque

parole n conditional release, early release, bail, liberation ■ v release on parole, release conditionally, liberate, bail, give terms

paroxysm n 1 outburst, fit, frenzy, outpouring, explosion 2 convulsion, spasm, fit, seizure, attack

paroxysmal adj convulsive, violent, spasmodic, uncontrollable, involuntary

parquet n flooring, parquetry, floor, floorboards, inlay

parrot n imitator, mimic, impersonator, impressionist, copier ■ v mimic, imitate, copy, impersonate, echo

parrot-fashion *(infml)* adv mindlessly, by rote, mechanically, automatically, unthinkingly

parry v 1 deflect, block, fend off, shield yourself from, dodge *Opposite*: take 2 evade, avoid, dodge, elude, sidestep *Opposite*: answer

parse v analyse, describe, break down, explain, construe

parsimonious adj thrifty, mean, frugal, ungenerous, miserly *Opposite*: extravagant

parsimoniousness *see* parsimony

parsimony n stinginess, thrift, thriftiness, meanness, frugality *Opposite*: extravagance

parson n cleric, priest, minister, pastor, parish priest

parsonage n church house, rectory, vicarage, manse, residence

part n 1 portion, division, section, fraction, piece *Opposite*: whole 2 feature, ingredient, element, component, bit 3 share, portion, fragment, slice, chunk *Opposite*: whole 4 function, role, duty, job, position ■ v divide, separate, open, split, segregate *Opposite*: join

partake v 1 *(fml)* consume, dine, eat, drink, taste *Opposite*: abstain 2 participate, share, contribute, take part, play a part *Opposite*: refrain

partial adj 1 incomplete, fractional, limited, restricted, unfinished *Opposite*: complete 2 biased, prejudiced, subjective, one-sided, inequitable *Opposite*: impartial

partiality n 1 fondness, liking, penchant, inclination, affection *Opposite*: dislike 2 bias, prejudice, preference, leaning, favouritism *Opposite*: impartiality

partially adv partly, in part, incompletely, to

some extent, somewhat *Opposite*: completely

partial to *adj* **keen on**, fond of, into *(infml)*

participant *n* **member**, contributor, contestant, applicant, partaker *Opposite*: observer

participate *v* **contribute**, partake, take part, join, join in *Opposite*: observe

participation *n* **contribution**, input, sharing, partaking, involvement *Opposite*: observation

participatory *adj* **taking part**, participating, sharing, partaking, hands-on

particle *n* **1 bit**, speck, spot, crumb, grain **2 iota**, bit, jot, scrap, shred

parti-coloured *adj* **variegated**, multicoloured, pied, piebald, rainbow *Opposite*: monochrome

particular *adj* **1 specific**, precise, certain, exact, actual *Opposite*: vague **2 individual**, distinct, noteworthy, special, unique *Opposite*: general **3 exacting**, meticulous, scrupulous, fastidious, fussy *Opposite*: relaxed

particularity *n* **1 fastidiousness**, meticulousness, fussiness, carefulness, discrimination *Opposite*: carelessness **2 peculiarity**, characteristic, trait, idiosyncrasy, quirk **3 individuality**, distinctiveness, idiosyncrasy, singularity, originality *Opposite*: similarity

particularize *v* **detail**, itemize, specify, enumerate, stipulate

particularly *adv* **1 chiefly**, mainly, above all, predominantly, mostly **2 exceptionally**, intensely, acutely, especially, specifically *Opposite*: unexceptionally

particulars *n* **details**, facts, information, essentials, basics

parting *n* **leaving**, departure, separation, going, goodbye *Opposite*: reunion

parting shot *n* **final remark**, Parthian shot, last word, retort, hostile remark

partisan *n* **supporter**, follower, adherent, fan, member *Opposite*: opponent ■ *adj* **biased**, prejudiced, opinionated, one-sided, bigoted *Opposite*: impartial

partisanship *n* **1 support**, devotion, membership, sponsorship, adherence **2 bias**, prejudice, bigotry, narrow-mindedness, one-sidedness *Opposite*: impartiality

partition *n* **1 divider**, panel, dividing wall, screen, sliding doors **2 separation**, division, rift, split, dividing up ■ *v* **divide**, separate, wall off, fence off, split

partly *adv* **partially**, in part, somewhat, partway, moderately *Opposite*: wholly

partner *n* **1 spouse**, wife, husband, mate, other half **2 associate**, colleague, collaborator, equal, mate *Opposite*: superior ■ *v* **team up**, unite, join, link up, accompany

partner in crime *n* **accessory**, accomplice, crony, associate, sidekick *(infml)*

partnership *n* **1 affiliation**, association, collaboration, companionship, alliance *Opposite*: opposition **2 company**, business, firm, corporation, enterprise

part-time *adj* **job-sharing**, evening, weekend, freelance, casual *Opposite*: full-time

part-timer *n* **part-time worker**, job-sharer, freelance, freelancer, casual *Opposite*: full-timer

partway *adv* **partly**, partially, halfway, in part, somewhat *Opposite*: completely

party *n* **1 social gathering**, gathering, festivity, revelry, event **2 faction**, political party, interest group, society, splinter group **3 participant**, accomplice, accessory, partaker, contributor **4 company**, band, gang, crew, contingent **5** *(fml)* **individual**, person, one, person concerned, someone ■ *v* *(infml)* **celebrate**, have fun, revel, whoop it up *(infml)*, paint the town red *(infml)*

partygoer *n* **celebrator**, socializer, guest, sociable person, attendee

party line *n* **official policy**, official position, party policy, official line, dogma

party pooper *(infml)* *n* **spoilsport**, killjoy, bore, wet blanket *(infml)*, misery guts *(infml)*

parvenu *n* **upstart**, nouveau riche, social climber, arriviste, pretender

pass *v* **1 go by**, overtake, exceed, outdo, surpass *Opposite*: stop **2 throw**, kick, hit, toss, lob **3 hand over**, give, deliver, hand, forward *Opposite*: withhold **4 elapse**, go by, pass by, lapse, go **5 succeed**, qualify, make the grade, excel, exceed *Opposite*: fail **6 approve**, ratify, adopt, permit, accept **7 happen**, occur, arise, take place, come about ■ *n* **1 permit**, licence, authorization, card, documentation *Opposite*: ban **2 toss**, kick, hit, throw, lob **3 passage**, gorge, route, corridor, valley **4 state of affairs**, state, plight, predicament, circumstances

passable *adj* **1 acceptable**, adequate, good enough, all right, respectable *Opposite*: unacceptable **2 traversable**, crossable, drivable, safe, penetrable *Opposite*: impassable

passage *n* **1 corridor**, pathway, walkway, hall, hallway **2 way through**, way, road, channel, course **3 section**, part, chapter, paragraph, segment **4 migration**, movement, exodus, flood, transit **5 journey**, voyage, transfer, run, crossing **6 approval**, enactment, passing, ratification, acceptance

passageway *n* **passage**, corridor, pathway, hallway, hall

pass away *v* **1 die**, succumb, pass on, kick the bucket *(slang)*, depart *(fml)* **2 come to an end**, finish, end, cease, terminate

pass by *v* **1 disregard**, overlook, pass over, ignore, look the other way **2 overtake**, go by, pass, surpass, leave behind **3 reject**, turn down, decline, refuse, ignore

passé *adj* **out-of-date**, old, faded, aged, worn-out *Opposite*: fashionable

passenger n traveller, customer, fare, commuter, rail user

passer-by n onlooker, bystander, spectator, witness, pedestrian

pass for v impersonate, pass as, look like, go as, do as

passim *(fml)* adv here and there, throughout, frequently, in various places, in several places

passing adj 1 transitory, short-lived, ephemeral, fleeting, fly-by-night Opposite: permanent 2 cursory, quick, casual, superficial, surface Opposite: thorough ■ n 1 departure, departing, leaving, disappearance, desertion 2 death, dying, passing away, end, departure. See COMPARE AND CONTRAST at **temporary**.

passion n 1 fervour, ardour, obsession, infatuation, love 2 desire, hunger, thirst, appetite, craving 3 rage, fury, outburst, fever, furore. See COMPARE AND CONTRAST at **love**.

passionate adj 1 fervent, ardent, zealous, avid, obsessive Opposite: indifferent 2 fiery, quick-tempered, incensed, inflamed, enraged Opposite: easygoing

passionately adv fervently, ardently, avidly, single-mindedly, overpoweringly Opposite: indifferently

passionless adj loveless, detached, unromantic, emotionless, frigid Opposite: passionate

passive adj inert, inactive, unreceptive, reflexive, flaccid Opposite: active

passiveness see **passivity**

passivity n inactivity, inaction, non-participation, indifference, apathy Opposite: activeness

pass judgment v give an opinion, judge, criticize, condemn, deliver judgment

pass muster v measure up, be all right, check out, qualify, do

pass off v masquerade, pretend, misrepresent, palm off, falsify

pass on v convey, send, forward, impart, communicate

pass out v 1 faint, black out, lose consciousness, have a fainting fit, swoon Opposite: come to 2 distribute, hand out, give out, assign, deal out

pass over v ignore, neglect, discount, disregard, let go Opposite: consider

passport n 1 official document, travel document, ID, papers, permit 2 access, gateway, entry, opening, door

pass the buck *(infml)* v shift the blame, evade responsibility, lay something at somebody's door

pass through v cross, go through, lead through, traverse, move across

password n code word, open sesame, secret word, PIN, key

past adj 1 elapsed, completed, accomplished, over and done, done Opposite: ongoing 2 previous, historical, earlier, former, bygone Opposite: future ■ n history, earlier period, ancient times, times of yore, antiquity Opposite: future

paste n 1 adhesive, glue, gum, fixative, wallpaper paste 2 slime, goo *(infml)*, gunk *(infml)*, gloop *(infml)*, gunge *(infml)* 3 pie crust, dough, pastry ■ v glue, stick, gum, fix, bond

pastel adj pale, light, soft, muted, neutral Opposite: vivid ■ n crayon, chalk, coloured chalk, oil pastel

pasteurization n sterilization, heat treatment, purification, decontamination, disinfection

pasteurize v sterilize, heat, purify, decontaminate, disinfect

pasteurized adj sterilized, treated, purified, decontaminated, disinfected

pastiche n imitation, spoof, satire, lampoon, parody

pastime n hobby, interest, activity, pursuit, amusement

pasting *(infml)* n beating, defeat, thrashing, drubbing, pounding

past love n first love, ex *(infml)*, old flame *(infml)*, blast from the past *(infml)*

pastor n minister, priest, vicar, clergyman, cleric

pastoral adj rural, rustic, countryside, countrified, idyllic Opposite: urban

pastry n 1 paste, dough, pie crust 2 pie, tart, tartlet, flan, Danish pastry

pasture n meadow, meadowland, fallow, grassland, prairie

pasty n pie, Cornish pasty, meat pie, sausage roll, steak pie ■ adj pale, unhealthy-looking, ashen, pallid, wan

pasty-faced adj pasty, pale, unhealthy-looking, ashen, pallid

pat v 1 tap, touch, stroke, caress, massage 2 shape, smooth, mould, work, knead ■ n touch, tap, stroke ■ adv perfectly, faultlessly, fluently, impeccably, by heart

patch n 1 cover, reinforcement, covering, square 2 area, spot, blotch, bit, smear 3 badge, award, stripe, tag, square ■ v repair, cover, mend, strengthen, reinforce

patchiness n 1 unevenness, intermittence, bittiness, sparseness Opposite: evenness 2 variability, inconsistency, unreliability, irregularity, unevenness Opposite: consistency

patchouli n aromatic oil, oil, perfume, scent, essential oil

patch up v mend, repair, fix, strengthen, reinforce

patchwork n mixture, mix, collage, assortment, potpourri

patchy adj 1 occasional, irregular, sporadic, intermittent, sparse 2 variable, inconsistent, unreliable, erratic, unpredictable

pate (archaic) n **head**, crown, cranium, skull, bonce (infml)

patent n **copyright**, charter, right ■ adj **clear**, obvious, blatant, flagrant, barefaced Opposite: unclear

paterfamilias n **father**, head of household, head, headman, paternalist

paternal adj **fatherly**, parental, nurturing, protective, guiding

paternalism n **authoritarianism**, interventionism, protectiveness, overprotectiveness, control

paternalistic adj **authoritarian**, patriarchal, protective, overprotective

paternity n **fatherhood**, parenthood, role, status, responsibility

path n **1 track**, trail, pathway, footpath, route **2 course**, route, way, orbit, direction

pathetic adj **1 pitiful**, sad, moving, tragic, doleful **2** (infml) **contemptible**, useless, risible, derisory, laughable. See COMPARE AND CONTRAST at moving.

pathfinder n **leader**, trailblazer, scout, pioneer, guide

pathological adj **1 medical**, clinical, scientific, diagnostic, immunological **2 morbid**, systemic, allergic, viral, bacteriological **3 extreme**, compulsive, uncontrolled, unreasonable, unreasoning

pathos n **sadness**, tragedy, bleakness, despair, anguish

pathway n **trail**, path, way, lane, alleyway

patience n **1 endurance**, staying power, stamina, persistence, perseverance Opposite: impatience **2 tolerance**, fortitude, serenity, imperturbability, unflappability Opposite: impatience

patient adj **1 enduring**, persistent, persevering, easygoing **2 tolerant**, long-suffering, serene, fortitudinous, imperturbable

patina n **1 discoloration**, tarnishing, staining, coating, verdigris **2 sheen**, shine, lustre, gloss **3 layer**, veneer, covering, coating, coat

patois n **1 dialect**, vernacular, idiom, language, speech **2 jargon**, slang, cant, patter, argot

pat on the back (infml) n **handshake**, round of applause, endorsement, seal of approval

patriarch n **1 head of family**, paterfamilias, father, head, headman Opposite: matriarch **2 bishop**, archbishop, prelate, leader

patriarchal adj **male-controlled**, male, masculine, macho

patrician n **aristocrat**, noble, peer, squire ■ adj **aristocratic**, refined, upper-class, noble, blue-blooded

patricide n **1 murder**, killing, parricide, slaughter, manslaughter **2 murderer**, killer, parricide, slaughterer, homicide

patriot n **nationalist**, loyalist, flag-waver

patriotic adj **nationalistic**, loyal, jingoistic, xenophobic, chauvinistic

patriotism n **loyalty**, partisanship, nationalism, jingoism, xenophobia

patrol n **1 tour**, round, beat, circuit, perambulation **2 unit**, detachment, squad, troop, group ■ v **guard**, watch, tour, make the rounds, walk the beat

patron n **1 sponsor**, benefactor, supporter, investor, backer **2 customer**, client, user, shopper, diner. See COMPARE AND CONTRAST at backer.

patronage n **investment**, backing, aid, sponsorship, benefaction

patronize v **1 be condescending to**, demean, denigrate, belittle, talk down to **2** (fml) **frequent**, shop at, use, utilize, visit

patronizing adj **condescending**, superior, denigrating, belittling, full of yourself

patter n **1 tapping**, drumming, beating, pitter-patter, rhythm **2 speech**, script, talk, spiel (infml) **3 jargon**, slang, cant, patois, argot ■ v **1 tap**, drum, beat, pitter-patter, knock **2 jabber**, prattle, rattle on, rant, go on and on

pattern n **1 design**, decoration, shape, outline, form **2 prototype**, outline, model, example, blueprint

patterned adj **decorated**, spotted, lined, squared, dotted

patty n **1 cake**, burger, rissole **2 pie**, pasty, pastry, meat pie

paucity n **dearth**, scarcity, rareness, scantiness, lack

paunch n **stomach**, belly, gut, potbelly, pot (infml)

paunchy adj **potbellied**, portly, corpulent, fleshy, plump

pauper n **poor person**, down-and-out, bankrupt, indigent (fml) Opposite: millionaire

pause v **1 stop**, wait, break off, rest, stop what you're doing Opposite: continue **2 linger**, stop, rest, tarry, halt Opposite: move on **3 hesitate**, falter, waver, wait, hold back ■ n **1 break**, recess, suspension, intermission, hiatus Opposite: continuation **2 silence**, awkward moment, hiatus, gap. See COMPARE AND CONTRAST at hesitate.

pave v **cover**, surface, floor, tile, flag

paved adj **cemented**, flagged, surfaced, covered, tiled

pavement n **path**, footpath, pathway, roadside, sidewalk (US)

paving n **flagging**, tiling, flooring, concrete, stonework

paw n (infml) **hand**, fist, mitt (slang) ■ v **maul**, molest, fondle, stroke, pet

pawn v **trade in**, wager, put up, place as collateral, pledge Opposite: redeem

pay v **disburse**, reimburse, compensate, forfeit, recompense Opposite: receive ■ n **wage**, salary, recompense, reimbursement, earnings. See COMPARE AND CONTRAST at wage.

payable adj **owed**, billed, due, to be paid, mature

pay back v 1 **repay**, reimburse, pay off, settle up, restore Opposite: keep 2 **retaliate**, get even, take revenge, give tit for tat, settle scores

payback n 1 **return**, reimbursement, profit, remuneration, repayment 2 (infml) **revenge**, retaliation, retribution, vengeance, reprisal

pay cheque n **wages**, salary, pay, payment, earnings

PAYE n **pay-as-you-earn**, income tax, revenue, tax, tax at source

payee n **recipient**, beneficiary, receiver, collector, acceptor Opposite: payer

payer n **spender**, financier, customer, client, paymaster Opposite: payee

pay in v **deposit**, bank, put away, put in, save Opposite: withdraw

payload n **cargo**, load, freight, shipment, consignment

payment n **sum**, expense, compensation, recompense, disbursement

pay off v 1 **settle**, square, repay, pay back, reimburse 2 **succeed**, bear fruit, work, be effective, prosper

payoff (infml) n 1 **payment**, settlement, reckoning, payout, remuneration 2 **bribe**, graft, take, inducement, bribery

payout n 1 **disbursement**, expenditure, expenses, outgoing, charge Opposite: income 2 **payment**, pay, wages, money, cash

pay packet n **wages**, salary, paycheque, payment, earnings

payroll n **employees**, personnel, staff, workforce, workers

payslip n **statement**, slip, record, note, pay

pdq (infml) adv **immediately**, at once, quickly, fast, right away Opposite: later

peace n 1 **concord**, peacetime, harmony, armistice, reconciliation Opposite: war 2 **harmony**, calm, quiet, stillness, tranquillity Opposite: uproar

peaceable adj 1 **peace-loving**, amiable, agreeable, easygoing, willing to please Opposite: aggressive 2 **tranquil**, peaceful, serene, harmonious, calm Opposite: chaotic

peace agreement n **treaty**, truce, ceasefire, armistice, agreement

peaceful adj 1 **quiet**, serene, calm, still, peaceable Opposite: disordered 2 **nonviolent**, passive, diplomatic, peaceable, pacific Opposite: violent

peacekeeper n **intermediary**, mediator, go-between, diplomat, pacifist

peacekeeping n **mediation**, intermediation, diplomacy, pacification, negotiation

peacemaker n **negotiator**, arbitrator, diplomat, mediator, intermediary Opposite: fighter

peacemaking n **reconciliation**, conciliation, mediation, arbitration, appeasement

peace offering n **olive branch**, apology, overture, approach, gesture

peacetime n **peace**, harmony, armistice, truce, ceasefire

peach (infml) n **beauty**, pearl, wow (infml), cracker (infml), humdinger (slang) Opposite: dud (infml)

peachy adj 1 **peachlike**, downy, fuzzy, velvety, soft 2 (infml) **excellent**, wonderful, nice, splendid, great Opposite: terrible

peacock n **egoist**, exhibitionist, fop, show-off (infml), dandy (dated)

peak n 1 **mountain**, mountaintop, summit, crest, point Opposite: valley 2 **tip**, pinnacle, zenith, top, summit Opposite: base ■ v **climax**, crest, top, max out (US) Opposite: dip ■ adj **top**, highest, crowning, topmost, ultimate Opposite: bottom

peaked adj **pointed**, sharp, pointy, spiky, tipped Opposite: rounded

peaky adj **sickly-looking**, pale, thin, wan, emaciated

peal n **clangour**, ringing, tolling, din, clang

peanuts (infml) n **a small sum**, a trifling amount, a trifle, a trifling sum, a paltry sum Opposite: fortune

pearl n **treasure**, precious thing, nugget, prize, gem (infml) Opposite: dud (infml)

pearly adj **iridescent**, lustrous, gleaming, shining, translucent Opposite: dull

pear-shaped adj **bottom-heavy**, broadening, widening, bulging, rotund Opposite: top-heavy

peasant n 1 **farmer**, labourer, farm hand, farmworker, crofter 2 **country-dweller**, rustic, provincial, bumpkin (infml), hillbilly (US infml)

peat n **mulch**, moss, compost, fertilizer, turf

pebble n **stone**, nugget, grit, shingle

pebbledash n **facing**, finish, plaster, roughcast, encrustation

peccadillo n **sin**, offence, failing, indulgence, crime Opposite: virtue

peck v 1 **strike**, bite, jab, poke, dig 2 **nibble**, pick at, eat, play with, toy with Opposite: gobble 3 (infml) **kiss**, brush, caress, osculate (fml), buss (dated) ■ n 1 **bite**, blow, stroke, jab, dig 2 (infml) **kiss**, brush, caress, smack, osculation (fml)

pecking order n **hierarchy**, class structure, social order, social structure, ladder

peckish (infml) adj **hungry**, famished, ravenous, starving (infml), starved (infml) Opposite: full

peculiar adj 1 **unusual**, odd, strange, weird, irregular Opposite: normal 2 **unique**, idiosyncratic, local, individual, special Opposite: universal

peculiarity n 1 **individuality**, idiosyncrasy, distinctiveness, particularity, uniqueness 2 **oddness**, strangeness, weirdness, eccentricity, abnormality Opposite: normality

peculiarly adv **1 uniquely**, abnormally, unusually, curiously, strangely Opposite: typically **2 particularly**, especially, extremely, very, extraordinarily Opposite: slightly

pecuniary adj **monetary**, financial, fiscal, economic, commercial

pedagogic see **pedagogical**

pedagogical adj **educational**, academic, instructive, tutorial, didactic

pedagogue n **teacher**, educator, schoolteacher, instructor, tutor

pedagogy n **teaching**, education, instruction, training, tutoring

pedal n **lever**, device, control, treadle ■ v **1 cycle**, ride, drive, steer, travel **2 ride**, operate, propel, control, guide

pedant n **doctrinaire**, obfuscator, nitpicker, sophist, hairsplitter Opposite: dilettante

pedantic adj **finicky**, plodding, obscure, arcane, dull Opposite: dilettante

pedantry n **literalism**, laboriousness, sophistry, meticulousness, thoroughness Opposite: creativity

peddle v **1 sell**, tout, hawk, vend, retail **2 promote**, market, hype, espouse, advocate

pedestal n **base**, plinth, stand, dais, platform

pedestrian n **walker**, rambler, ambler, hiker, strider ■ adj **dull**, ordinary, unimaginative, uninspired, prosaic Opposite: exciting

pedestrian crossing n **crossing**, pelican crossing, crosswalk (US), zebra crossing

pedestrianized adj **traffic-free**, pedestrian, closed off

pedicure n **beauty treatment**, foot massage, cosmetic treatment, cosmetic session, chiropody treatment

pedigree n **lineage**, family background, ancestry, derivation, history ■ adj **purebred**, full-blooded, thoroughbred, noble, aristocratic

pedlar n **seller**, dealer, street trader, trader, vendor

peek v **peep**, glance, peer, steal a look, sneak a quick look Opposite: stare ■ n **look**, glance, peep, glimpse, once-over (infml) Opposite: gaze

peel v **1 skin**, strip, pare, hull, bark **2 flake**, come off in layers, shed, desquamate **3 unwrap**, remove, strip off, take off ■ n **skin**, rind, peelings, covering, shell

peeler n **potato peeler**, carrot peeler, paring knife, scraper

peeling adj **flaking**, shedding, cracking, coming off, coming loose Opposite: smooth

peelings n **parings**, skin, peel, rind, shavings

peep v **1 peek**, peer, steal a look, glance, sneak a look Opposite: gaze **2 chirp**, twitter, tweet, chirrup, squeak ■ n **1 peek**, glance, glimpse, look, gander (infml) **2 sound**, utterance, noise, word

peephole n **1 opening**, crack, hole, aperture, knothole **2 spyhole**, eyehole, keyhole

peer n **1 equal**, colleague, contemporary, friend, match **2 noble**, aristocrat, lord, patrician, peer of the realm ■ v **look**, scrutinize, gaze, stare, examine Opposite: glance

peerage n **1 peers**, aristocracy, nobility, nobles, aristocrats **2 hereditary peerage**, life peerage, title, honour

peer group n **cohort**, coequals, generation, age group, classmates

peerless adj **incomparable**, matchless, unequalled, unrivalled, without equal Opposite: commonplace

peeve (infml) v **vex**, annoy, irritate, irk, upset Opposite: please ■ n **gripe** (infml), bugbear, irritation, vexation, nuisance Opposite: pleasure

peeved (infml) adj **annoyed**, irritated, irked, piqued, upset Opposite: pleased

peevish (infml) adj **irritable**, crabby, bad-tempered, cross, grumpy Opposite: good-tempered

peevishness n **irritability**, crabbiness, spitefulness, crossness, grumpiness

peewee (infml) adj **toy**, miniature, undersized, tiny, small Opposite: jumbo

peg n **pin**, fastener, dowel, hook, bolt ■ v **1 fasten**, secure, attach, fix, hang Opposite: detach **2 mark**, keep score, track, gauge, measure **3 freeze**, fix, set, control, limit Opposite: free

pejorative (fml) adj **disapproving**, judgmental, harsh, scornful, derogatory Opposite: positive

pelican crossing n **crossing**, zebra crossing, pedestrian crossing, crosswalk (US)

pell-mell adv **1 helter-skelter**, hurriedly, headlong, recklessly, tumultuously Opposite: carefully **2 untidily**, higgledy-piggledy, haphazardly, chaotically, topsy-turvily Opposite: neatly

pelmet n **valance**, decoration, drapery, board, frill

pelt n **hide**, fur, skin, hair, coat ■ v **1 bombard**, assail, assault, strafe, attack **2 pour**, cascade, come down in sheets (infml), bucket down (infml), rain cats and dogs (infml) Opposite: drizzle

pen n **enclosure**, run, cage, coop ■ v **1 scribble**, jot, compose, scrawl, write **2 confine**, shut in, hold in, trap, capture Opposite: release

WORD BANK
❏ **types of pen** ballpoint, felt-tipped pen, fountain pen, highlighter, marker, quill, rollerball

penal adj **punitive**, punishing, disciplinary, corrective

penalization n **punishment**, disciplining, fining, discipline, correction Opposite: rewarding

penalize v **punish**, discipline, fine, reprimand, correct Opposite: let off

penalty n **1 punishment**, fine, sentence, penalization 2 **consequence**, disadvantage, drawback, forfeit, price *Opposite*: advantage

penance n self-punishment, reparation, forfeit, atonement, amends

penchant n liking, fondness, partiality, taste, proclivity *Opposite*: antipathy

pencil v write, draw, mark, colour, sketch

pendent adj hanging, suspended, dangling, sagging, pendulous

pending adj 1 undecided, incomplete, awaiting, unresolved, pendent *(fml or literary) Opposite*: in hand 2 **imminent**, impending, expected, approaching, forthcoming ■ prep 1 awaiting, until, till 2 during, throughout, in the course of

pendulous adj 1 hanging, swinging, overhanging, drooping, loose 2 **undecided**, wavering, vacillating, uncommitted, uncertain *Opposite*: decided

pendulum n weight, bob, plumb, swing

penetrate v 1 enter, pass through, go through, go in, break in 2 diffuse, seep in, soak in, infiltrate, imbue 3 work out, solve, decipher, figure out, understand 4 grasp, see into, perceive, figure out, comprehend

penetrating adj 1 all-pervading, powerful, pungent, sharp, piercing 2 **probing**, piercing, searching, questioning, inquiring 3 **sharp**, intelligent, astute, perceptive, insightful *Opposite*: obtuse 4 **piercing**, shrill, high-pitched, earsplitting, sharp

penetration n 1 diffusion, infiltration, saturation, dispersion, dissemination 2 **perception**, astuteness, understanding, discernment, comprehension 3 **incursion**, access, breach, entrance, infringement

penetrative adj 1 penetrating, piercing, penetrant, permeating, pervasive 2 **keen**, perceptive, insightful, acute, sharp *Opposite*: unperceptive

pen friend n correspondent, letter writer, friend, acquaintance, pal *(infml)*

peninsula n neck of land, finger of land, cape, point, headland

penitence n shame, repentance, contrition, atonement, remorse *Opposite*: shamelessness

penitent adj repentant, repenting, contrite, remorseful, regretful *Opposite*: unrepentant

penitential see penitent

pen name n pseudonym, nom de plume, alias, nom de guerre

pennant n banner, flag, ensign, emblem, streamer

penniless adj poor, impoverished, impecunious, destitute, bankrupt *Opposite*: rich

pennon n flag, pennant, banner, standard, emblem

penny pincher *(infml)* n skinflint, miser, pinchpenny, cheapskate *(infml)*, scrooge *(infml) Opposite*: spendthrift

penny-pinching *(infml)* adj frugal, thrifty, tightfisted, parsimonious, tight *Opposite*: generous

pen pal *(infml)* n pen friend, correspondent, letter writer

penpusher *(infml)* n bureaucrat, clerk, writer, scribe, office worker

pension n retirement pension, retirement fund, annuity, income, retirement income

pensioner n retiree, retired person, senior citizen, senior, OAP

pensive adj thoughtful, meditative, contemplative, thinking, brooding

pensiveness n thoughtfulness, dreaminess, wistfulness, meditativeness, reflectiveness

pent-up adj repressed, stifled, unexpressed, contained, constrained *Opposite*: voiced

penultimate adj last but one, one before the last, next to last, second to last *(US)*

penumbra n 1 shadow, shade, darkness 2 **obscurity**, uncertainty, cloudiness, indistinctness

pen up v cage, round up, shut within, enclose, hold *Opposite*: free

penury n poverty, pennilessness, destitution, neediness, impoverishment *Opposite*: luxury

people n 1 nation, community, nationality, populace, population 2 **persons**, folks, individuals, public, general public 3 *(infml)* relatives, relations, family, folks, ancestors ■ v populate, fill, inhabit, immigrate, colonize

pep *(infml)* n energy, liveliness, vigour, perkiness, zest

pepper v 1 sprinkle, shower, spray, scatter, speckle 2 **intersperse**, sprinkle, interleave, infuse, scatter

pepper-and-salt adj flecked, streaked, greying, grizzled, patchy

peppery adj spicy, piquant, hot, fiery, pungent *Opposite*: mild

peppy *(infml)* adj lively, vigorous, sprightly, perky, frisky *Opposite*: lethargic

pep talk *(infml)* n team talk, speech, support, encouragement, inspiration

pep up *(infml)* v spice up, add zest, liven up, make something swing, give a bit of zing *(infml)*

per prep for each, apiece, for every, each, per capita

perambulator *(fml)* n pram, buggy, pushchair, stroller *(US)*, baby buggy *(US)*

perceive v 1 notice, observe, see, take in, remark *Opposite*: ignore 2 **understand**, comprehend, sense, feel, become aware of

percent adv out of a hundred, out of each hundred, in each hundred, in a hundred, per hundred ■ n percentage, part, proportion, ratio, percentile

percentage n 1 fraction, proportion, ratio,

part, section **2** *(infml)* **commission**, proportion, fraction, take, profit

perceptible *adj* **noticeable**, traceable, observable, appreciable, visible *Opposite*: imperceptible

perception *n* **1 reading**, view, opinion, picture, take **2 insight**, acuity, awareness, discernment, observation

perceptive *adj* **discerning**, sensitive, insightful, keen, observant *Opposite*: insensitive

perceptiveness *n* **insight**, insightfulness, understanding, intuition, discernment

perch *v* **rest**, sit, settle, balance, alight

percipience *n* **insight**, insightfulness, perceptiveness, discernment, understanding *Opposite*: insensitivity

percipient *adj* **insightful**, perceptive, observant, discerning, understanding *Opposite*: insensitive

percolate *v* **1 drip**, filter, trickle, ooze, leach **2 seep into**, infiltrate, permeate, penetrate, get into

percolator *n* **coffeepot**, coffee maker, coffee machine

percussion *(fml)* *n* **drumming**, beating, striking, hitting, bass beat

perdition *n* **hell**, purgatory, punishment, damnation, abyss

peremptory *adj* **1 dictatorial**, authoritative, unconditional, absolute, dogmatic *Opposite*: polite **2 decisive**, no-nonsense, quick, hasty, direct *Opposite*: roundabout

perennial *adj* **recurrent**, returning, perpetual, constant, persistent *Opposite*: occasional

perestroika *n* **restructuring**, reform, reconstruction, reorganization, modernization

perfect *adj* **1 faultless**, flawless, textbook, picture-perfect, seamless *Opposite*: flawed **2 complete**, absolute, unqualified, whole, finished *Opposite*: incomplete **3 ideal**, just right, just the thing, wonderful, just what the doctor ordered *Opposite*: wrong **4 precise**, exact, accurate, on target, just right ■ *v* **1 improve**, refine, hone, tighten up, work on *Opposite*: spoil **2 achieve**, finish, complete, finalize, reach the summit of

perfection *n* **1 excellence**, rightness, faultlessness, exactness, precision **2 accomplishment**, fulfilment, completion, realization, achievement *Opposite*: abandonment

perfectionism *n* **fastidiousness**, fussiness, nitpicking, hairsplitting, pedantry *Opposite*: carelessness

perfectionist *n* **stickler**, purist, pedant, obsessive, quibbler

perfectly *adv* **1 flawlessly**, faultlessly, impeccably, effortlessly, seamlessly *Opposite*: badly **2 completely**, entirely, wholly, absolutely, utterly *Opposite*: partially

perfidious *(fml)* *adj* **disloyal**, treacherous, deceitful, dishonest, lying *Opposite*: honest

perfidy *(fml)* *n* **treachery**, disloyalty, deceit, duplicity, betrayal *Opposite*: honesty

perforate *v* **puncture**, prick, pierce, hole, go through

perforation *n* **hole**, puncture, tear, rip, slash

perform *v* **1 do**, carry out, fulfil, accomplish, execute **2 present**, act, play, put on, stage **3 function**, work, behave, act, go

---

COMPARE AND CONTRAST CORE MEANING: complete a task

perform complete an action or accomplish a task, especially when this requires skill or care or when it forms part of a set procedure; **do** complete an action or accomplish a task of any kind; **carry out** complete any action or task; **fulfil** do what is necessary to achieve the successful accomplishment or realization of something planned, promised, or anticipated; **discharge** *(fml)* complete duties or responsibilities successfully; **execute** put an instruction or plan into effect, or complete an action or procedure that requires skill and expertise.

---

performance *n* **1 presentation**, recital, act, routine, concert **2 functioning**, implementation, execution, performing, carrying out **3 feat**, deed, act, accomplishment, occurrence

performer *n* **1 player**, actor, musician, recitalist, actress *Opposite*: spectator **2 doer**, perpetrator, executor, architect, operator

perfume *n* **1 fragrance**, scent, cologne, body spray, toilet water **2 smell**, aroma, scent, odour, fragrance *Opposite*: stench ■ *v* **scent**, fragrance, imbue, freshen, lace. *See* COMPARE AND CONTRAST *at* smell.

perfumed *adj* **scented**, sweet-smelling, sweet-scented, aromatic, fragrant

perfunctory *adj* **1 unthinking**, automatic, mechanical, dutiful, obligatory *Opposite*: thoughtful **2 hasty**, superficial, quick, fleeting, hurried *Opposite*: thorough

pergola *n* **arch**, trellis, framework, arbour, structure

perhaps *adv* **maybe**, possibly, conceivably, feasibly, imaginably *Opposite*: definitely

peril *n* **danger**, threat, risk, hazard, jeopardy *Opposite*: safety

perilous *adj* **dangerous**, unsafe, hazardous, risky, death-defying *Opposite*: safe

perimeter *n* **boundary**, border, edge, limit, outskirts

period *n* **1 interval**, episode, interlude, phase, cycle **2 era**, age, epoch, stage, phase

periodic *adj* **1 episodic**, intermittent, interrupted, sporadic, occasional *Opposite*: constant **2 cyclic**, recurring, recurrent, serial, regular *Opposite*: irregular

COMPARE AND CONTRAST CORE MEANING: recurring over a period of time
periodic recurring or reappearing from time to time with a degree of regularity; **intermittent** occurring at irregular intervals; **occasional** occurring infrequently at irregular intervals; **sporadic** occurring irregularly and unpredictably.

periodical n **journal**, bulletin, magazine, review, publication

peripatetic adj **itinerant**, travelling, nomadic, wandering, roving Opposite: settled

peripheral adj **1 outlying**, marginal, fringe, bordering, exterior Opposite: major **2 minor**, incidental, tangential, marginal, unimportant Opposite: central

periphery n **boundary**, margin, edge, sideline, border Opposite: centre

perish (literary) v **die**, pass away, take your last breath, succumb, depart this life (fml) Opposite: live

perishable adj **unpreserved**, fresh, untreated Opposite: preserved

perished (infml) adj **cold**, freezing, frozen, shivering, perishing Opposite: boiling

perishing adj **cold**, freezing, bitter, raw, chilly Opposite: boiling

periwig n **wig**, hairpiece, toupee, rug (infml), peruke (archaic)

perjure v **lie**, bear false witness, commit perjury, fabricate, stretch the truth Opposite: tell the truth

perjury n **lying**, untruthfulness, lie, falsehood, untruth Opposite: honesty

perk n **bonus**, benefit, incentive, perquisite, extra Opposite: disadvantage

perk up v **1 liven up**, cheer up, brighten up, wake up, awaken **2 stick up**, stand up, prick up, cock up, pop up Opposite: droop

perky adj **1 lively**, cheerful, energetic, jaunty, pert Opposite: despondent **2 overconfident**, confident, self-confident, self-important, self-assured Opposite: timid

perm v **curl**, wave, kink, crimp, frizz Opposite: straighten

permanence n **perpetuity**, durability, durableness, longevity, solidity Opposite: transience

permanency see **permanence**

permanent adj **perpetual**, enduring, lasting, eternal, everlasting Opposite: temporary

permeability n **porousness**, penetrability, perviousness, absorbency, sponginess Opposite: impermeability

permeable adj **porous**, penetrable, pervious, absorbent, absorptive Opposite: impermeable

permeate v **1 infuse**, flood, fill, infiltrate, invade **2 filter**, seep, leak, pervade, penetrate

permeation n **1 infusion**, pervasion, flood, infiltration, invasion **2 filtration**, seepage, leakage, penetration, percolation

permissible adj **allowable**, allowed, permitted, acceptable, accepted Opposite: unacceptable

permission n **consent**, authorization, approval, agreement, acquiescence Opposite: embargo

permissive adj **tolerant**, lenient, liberal, accommodating, lax Opposite: strict

permit v **authorize**, allow, let, approve, consent to Opposite: forbid ■ n **licence**, document, certification, certificate, authorization

permitted adj **allowed**, allowable, permissible, acceptable, accepted Opposite: forbidden

permutation n **variation**, transformation, version, arrangement, rearrangement

pernicious adj **1 malicious**, wicked, evil, malevolent, malign Opposite: benign **2 destructive**, harmful, deadly, fatal, insidious Opposite: harmless

perniciousness n **1 maliciousness**, malice, wickedness, evil, malevolence Opposite: benignity **2 destructiveness**, harmfulness, deadliness, insidiousness, ruinousness Opposite: harmlessness

pernickety (infml) adj **1 meticulous**, exacting, demanding, finicky, fussy Opposite: slapdash **2 detailed**, exacting, painstaking, precise, finicky Opposite: straightforward

peroration (fml) n **speech**, oration, discourse, address, talk

peroxide n **hydrogen peroxide**, bleaching agent, bleach, tint ■ v **bleach**, tint, lighten, dye, colour

perpendicular adj **vertical**, at right angles, upright, bolt upright, erect Opposite: parallel

perpetrate v **commit**, carry out, do, be responsible for, be behind

perpetration n **commission**, enactment, transaction, action, responsibility

perpetrator n **culprit**, criminal, wrongdoer, guilty party, offender

perpetual adj **continuous**, everlasting, uninterrupted, lasting, unending Opposite: temporary

perpetuate v **continue**, preserve, prolong, carry on, spread Opposite: stop

perpetuation n **continuation**, continuance, preservation, prolongation, spread Opposite: ending

perpetuity n **eternity**, time without end, all time, infinity, permanence

perplex v **puzzle**, baffle, confuse, stun, mystify Opposite: enlighten

perplexed adj **puzzled**, baffled, confused, at a loss, stunned Opposite: comprehending

perplexing adj **puzzling**, baffling, confusing, mystifying, confounding Opposite: simple

perplexity n **puzzlement**, bafflement, confusion, bewilderment, mystification Opposite: comprehension

perquisite *(fml)* n **privilege**, gratuity, perk, bonus, benefit *Opposite*: disadvantage

persecute v **1 oppress**, hound, harass, maltreat, pursue *Opposite*: protect **2 pester**, harass, torment, bother, bait *Opposite*: leave alone

persecution n **1 oppression**, harassment, maltreatment, pursuit, discrimination *Opposite*: protection **2 harassment**, torment, annoyance, irritation, suffering

persecutor n **1 oppressor**, harasser, pursuer, bully, torturer *Opposite*: protector **2 pesterer**, harasser, tormentor, nuisance, baiter

perseverance n **persistence**, determination, resolve, resolution, doggedness

persevere v **persist**, continue, keep at, keep it up, keep on *Opposite*: give up

persevering adj **persistent**, determined, resolute, resolved, dogged *Opposite*: irresolute

persist v **1 persevere**, continue, keep at, keep it up, keep on *Opposite*: give up **2 continue**, endure, live on, stay, go on *Opposite*: fade away

persistence n **1 perseverance**, determination, tenacity, resolve, resolution **2 continuance**, continuation, endurance, permanence, preservation *Opposite*: transience

persistent adj **1 tenacious**, determined, obstinate, insistent, dogged *Opposite*: irresolute **2 continuing**, continual, continued, unrelenting, incessant *Opposite*: fleeting

person n **1 being**, human being, individual, creature, soul **2 body**, form, frame, figure **3** *(fml)* **appearance**, persona, personality, character, ego

persona n **1 character**, figure, person, role, part **2 identity**, role, guise, personality, character

personable adj **amiable**, friendly, pleasant, affable, agreeable *Opposite*: disagreeable

personage *(fml)* n **VIP**, celebrity, star, public figure, dignitary *Opposite*: nobody

personal adj **1 individual**, private, own, special, particular *Opposite*: public **2 offensive**, rude, derogatory, familiar, intrusive *Opposite*: complimentary

personal ad n **advertisement**, announcement, public notice, ad *(infml)*, advert *(infml)*

personal assistant n **PA**, secretary, assistant, administrative assistant, administrator

personal computer n **PC**, computer, terminal, laptop, notebook

personal effects n **belongings**, possessions, personal property, things, stuff

personality n **1 character**, nature, disposition, temperament, makeup **2 celebrity**, star, public figure, somebody, VIP *Opposite*: nobody

personalize v **1 initial**, monogram, mark, engrave, identify **2 customize**, individualize, differentiate, distinguish, specify *Opposite*: generalize

personally adv **1 for myself**, in my opinion, in my view, for my part, myself *Opposite*: generally **2 in person**, face to face, individually, myself, directly *Opposite*: indirectly

personal organizer n **1 diary**, planner, appointment book, address book, engagement book **2 hand-held computer**, electronic planner, palmtop, electronic organizer

personification n **epitome**, image, embodiment, incarnation, representation

personify v **1 epitomize**, embody, incarnate, exemplify, characterize **2 anthropomorphize**, humanize, personalize, give a human face, bring alive

personnel n **workers**, staff, employees, workforce, human resources

perspective n **1 viewpoint**, standpoint, outlook, view, perception **2 proportion**, scale, ratio, size, depth **3 vista**, view, prospect, scene, lookout

perspicacious adj **discerning**, perceptive, astute, insightful, wise *Opposite*: obtuse

perspicacity n **discernment**, perceptiveness, astuteness, shrewdness, clear-sightedness

perspiration n **sweat**, fluid, exudate, secretion, moisture

perspire v **sweat**, exude, ooze, swelter, drip

persuade v **1 encourage**, coax, influence, induce, motivate *Opposite*: dissuade **2 convince**, win over, sway, convert, bring round

persuasion n **1 persuading**, encouragement, coaxing, influence, urging **2 affiliation**, belief, order, denomination, faith

persuasive adj **convincing**, influential, winning, swaying, believable *Opposite*: unconvincing

persuasiveness n **persuasion**, influence, cogency, smoothness, eloquence

pert adj **lively**, flippant, impudent, perky, breezy

pertain to v **relate**, refer to, apply to, belong to, affect

pertinacious adj **resolute**, stubborn, obstinate, persistent, headstrong *Opposite*: malleable

pertinence n **relevance**, relatedness, appositeness, appropriateness, suitability *Opposite*: irrelevance

pertinent adj **relevant**, related, apposite, appropriate, germane *Opposite*: irrelevant

pertness n **cheekiness**, liveliness, flippancy, perkiness, breeziness

perturb v **trouble**, bother, disturb, worry, agitate

perturbation n **alarm**, worry, agitation, disquiet, trepidation *Opposite*: composure

perturbed adj **troubled**, disturbed, worried, anxious, disconcerted *Opposite*: composed

perusal n **examination**, scrutiny, inspection, checking, readthrough

peruse *v* read, examine, scan, pore over, scrutinize *Opposite*: skim

pervade *v* permeate, pass through, saturate, spread through, infuse

pervasive *adj* extensive, universal, general, inescapable, prevalent *Opposite*: localized

pervasiveness *n* extensiveness, universality, generality, ubiquity, ubiquitousness

perverse *adj* 1 aberrant, irrational, deviant, abnormal, unreasonable *Opposite*: obliging 2 obstinate, wilful, stubborn, headstrong, pertinacious *Opposite*: malleable

perverseness *n* 1 aberrance, irrationality, deviance, disobedience, unreasonableness 2 wilfulness, stubbornness, contrariness, recalcitrance *Opposite*: malleability

perversion *n* distortion, misinterpretation, twisting, corruption, misapplication

perversity *n* obstinacy, wilfulness, stubbornness, unreasonableness, contrariness *Opposite*: malleability

pervert *v* 1 deprave, corrupt, lead astray, spoil, warp 2 distort, misinterpret, twist, misrepresent, alter

perverted *adj* 1 depraved, corrupt, debauched, warped, degenerate 2 distorted, misinterpreted, twisted, garbled, changed *Opposite*: undistorted

pervious *adj* 1 porous, penetrable, absorbent, permeable *Opposite*: impervious 2 receptive, amenable, responsive, flexible, open *Opposite*: impervious

pessimism *n* negativity, cynicism, doubt, distrust, gloom *Opposite*: optimism

pessimist *n* cynic, doubter, worrier, nihilist, defeatist *Opposite*: optimist

pessimistic *adj* negative, cynical, doubtful, distrustful, gloomy *Opposite*: optimistic

pest *n* 1 vermin, bug, insect, fly, mosquito 2 *(infml)* bother, nuisance, annoyance, vexation, irritant

pester *v* annoy, harass, worry, beleaguer, disturb *Opposite*: delight

pestilence *(archaic)* *n* plague, epidemic, virus, disease, bubonic plague

pestilent *adj* 1 infected, plague-ridden, contaminated, polluted, bug-ridden *Opposite*: healthy 2 deadly, lethal, fatal, virulent, killer *Opposite*: mild

pet *n* 1 animal, domestic animal, domesticated animal, tame animal, companion 2 favourite, darling, treasure, jewel, idol 3 dear, love, precious, darling, dearest 4 sulk, huff, pique, temper, tantrum ■ *adj* favourite, special, cherished, indulged, preferred ■ *v* 1 stroke, pat, fondle, caress, nuzzle 2 indulge, pamper, cosset, mollycoddle, spoil

peter out *v* disappear, dwindle, fade, recede, decrease *Opposite*: grow

petite *adj* small, diminutive, short, little, tiny *Opposite*: big

petition *n* request, appeal, entreaty, requisition, application ■ *v* appeal, lobby, request, beg, plead

petitioner *n* lobbyist, activist, campaigner, requester, asker

pet name *n* name, nickname, sobriquet, diminutive, epithet

petrified *adj* 1 frightened, terrified, scared, alarmed, scared stiff *Opposite*: reassured 2 fossilized, hardened, solidified, fixed, calcified

petrify *v* 1 frighten, terrify, scare, alarm, fill with fear *Opposite*: reassure 2 fossilize, harden, solidify, ossify, fix

petrifying *adj* frightening, terrifying, horrifying, shocking, spine-chilling *Opposite*: reassuring

petrol station *n* filling station, garage, service station, gas station *(US)*

pettifogging *adj* trivial, petty, unimportant, minor, insignificant *Opposite*: important

pettiness *n* 1 triviality, unimportance, inconsequence, paltriness, irrelevance *Opposite*: importance 2 petty-mindedness, mean-mindedness, triviality, pettifoggery, narrow-mindedness 3 spitefulness, grudgingness, resentfulness, maliciousness, vindictiveness

pettish *adj* peevish, irritable, sulky, bad-tempered, petulant *Opposite*: even-tempered

petty *adj* 1 trivial, unimportant, inconsequential, insignificant, paltry *Opposite*: important 2 petty-minded, mean-minded, niggling, narrow-minded, trivial 3 spiteful, grudging, resentful, malicious, vindictive *Opposite*: generous

petty cash *n* cash fund, office fund, float, coffee fund *(US)*

petulance *n* sulkiness, crabbiness, peevishness, sullenness, moodiness *Opposite*: affability

petulant *adj* sulky, crabby, peevish, grumpy, sullen *Opposite*: affable

pew *n* bench, form, seat, bleacher *(US)*

phalanx *n* group, body, mass, unit, formation

phantasm *n* ghost, spirit, apparition, spectre, phantom

phantasmagoria *n* image, dream, hallucination, optical illusion, mirage

phantasmagoric *adj* dreamlike, bizarre, surreal, psychedelic, fantastical

phantasmagory *see* phantasmagoria

phantom *n* ghost, apparition, spirit, spectre, phantasm

Pharaoh *n* ruler, king, sovereign, monarch, emperor

pharmaceutical *adj* medicinal, medical, pharmacological, therapeutic, curative ■ *n* drug, medicine, medication, treatment, narcotic

pharmacist *n* pharmacologist, chemist, posologist, dispensing chemist, apothecary *(archaic)*

pharmacy n chemist's, dispensary, dispensing chemist's, apothecary (archaic)

phase n stage, point, chapter, time, segment

phenomenal adj 1 remarkable, extraordinary, impressive, prodigious, outstanding Opposite: unremarkable 2 (infml) fantastic, wonderful, amazing, brilliant, sensational Opposite: moderate

phenomenon n 1 occurrence, fact, experience, happening, incident 2 marvel, wonder, singularity, miracle, spectacle 3 prodigy, genius, bright star, enfant terrible, whiz kid (infml)

phial n vial, bottle, vessel, flask, flagon

philanderer n flirt, Casanova, adulterer, lady-killer, ladies' man

philanthropic adj charitable, benevolent, humanitarian, generous, big-hearted Opposite: misanthropic

philanthropist n patron, humanitarian, donor, sponsor, promoter Opposite: misanthropist

philanthropy n charity, compassion, humanity, patronage, generosity Opposite: misanthropy

philippic n diatribe, tirade, discourse, denunciation, insult

philistine n barbarian, boor, vulgarian Opposite: aesthete ■ adj uncultured, unsophisticated, uninformed, untutored, boorish Opposite: cultured

philistinism n barbarism, unsophistication, boorishness, ignorance

philosopher n theorist, thinker, logician, truth-seeker, academic Opposite: realist

philosophic see philosophical

philosophical adj 1 logical, ethical, metaphysical, moral, theoretical 2 deep-thinking, learned, thoughtful, studious, enlightened Opposite: shallow 3 calm, resigned, restrained, stoical, patient Opposite: emotional

philosophize v moralize, speculate, theorize, pronounce, meditate

philosophy n beliefs, viewpoint, thinking, values, attitude

phlegm n 1 mucus, catarrh, rheum 2 calmness, composure, unflappability, self-possession, imperturbability Opposite: nervousness

phlegmatic adj calm, unemotional, composed, impassive, placid Opposite: nervous. See COMPARE AND CONTRAST at **impassive**.

phobia n fear, terror, dread, horror, fright

WORD BANK
❏ **types of phobia** acrophobia (fear of high places), agoraphobia (fear of public or open spaces), ailurophobia (fear of cats), arachnophobia (fear of spiders), claustrophobia (fear of confined or enclosed spaces), hydrophobia (fear of water), necrophobia (fear of death or dead bodies), nyctophobia (fear of night or darkness), photophobia (fear of light or lighted spaces), pyrophobia (fear of fire), technophobia (fear of new technology or computerization), zoophobia (fear of animals)

phobic adj 1 fearful, scared, terrified, nervous, anxious Opposite: unconcerned 2 irrational, neurotic, obsessed, disturbed, fixated Opposite: rational

phone n telephone, mobile phone, mobile, cellphone, cellular phone ■ v call, ring, ring up, telephone, make a call

phoney adj 1 false, fake, counterfeit, bogus, artificial Opposite: genuine 2 affected, pretentious, insincere, deceptive, sham Opposite: sincere ■ n fake, impostor, hypocrite, fraud, sham

phony see phoney

photo see photograph

photocopy n copy, duplicate, reproduction, print ■ v copy, reproduce, make a copy of, run off, duplicate

photo finish n close contest, close thing, tie, neck-and-neck finish (infml)

photogenic adj camera-friendly, attractive, picturesque, appealing, good-looking

photograph n picture, snap, shot, snapshot, print ■ v photo, snap, shoot, get on film

photographer n professional photographer, press photographer, paparazzo, amateur photographer, photojournalist

photographic adj 1 pictorial, graphic, picturesque, photogenic, camera-friendly 2 vivid, clear, accurate, exact, detailed

photography n cinematography, filmmaking, picture making, shooting, camerawork

WORD BANK
❏ **parts of a camera** autofocus, diaphragm, exposure meter, film, filter, fisheye lens, flash, lens, lens cap, rangefinder, shutter, telephoto lens, viewfinder, zoom lens
❏ **types of photographic equipment** box camera, camera, cine camera, developer, disc camera, enlarger, headcam, microfiche, microfilm, pinhole camera, printer, projector, reflex camera, single-lens reflex, speed camera, tripod, twin-lens reflex

photojournalism n photography, news photography, reportage, camerawork, filmmaking

photo opportunity n media event, photo shoot, photo op, public-relations exercise, publicity event

photosensitive adj light sensitive, sensitive, reactive, light reactive, hypersensitive

phrasal adj linguistic, verbal, expressive, semantic, phraseological

phrase n expression, saying, idiom, axiom, slogan ■ v express, couch, put, say, put into words

phrase book n glossary, bilingual dictionary, foreign-language dictionary, dictionary, lexicon

phraseology n phrasing, wording, choice of words, word choice, terminology

phrasing n wording, turn of phrase, style, word choice, diction

physical adj 1 **bodily**, corporeal, animal, corporal, fleshly Opposite: mental 2 **substantial**, material, objective, natural, real Opposite: ethereal 3 **brute**, instinctive, visceral, instinctual, basic Opposite: refined

physical education n **sports**, gymnastics, games, exercise, aerobics

physically adv **bodily**, actually, in the flesh, really, materially Opposite: mentally

physician n **doctor**, medical doctor, doctor of medicine, general practitioner, GP

physics n **dynamics**, forces, physical processes, interactions, properties

physiognomy n **appearance**, face, features, characteristics, physical appearance

physiological adj **physical**, bodily, biological, functional

physiotherapy n **remedial exercise**, exercise, rehabilitation, physio (infml), physical therapy (US)

physique n **build**, body type, physical type, figure, form

piazza n **square**, forum, gathering place, village square, town square

picaresque adj **roguish**, mischievous, rascally, impish, villainous

pick v 1 **harvest**, gather, cut, collect, pluck 2 **select**, single out, choose, pick and choose, make a choice ■ n **best choice**, top choice, choice, cream of the crop, pick of the litter

picked adj **chosen**, selected, select, elect, hand-picked

picket n 1 **stake**, post, fence post, peg, rod 2 **striker**, protester, boycotter, blockader 3 **lookout**, sentinel, watch, sentry, guard ■ v 1 **protest**, strike, demonstrate, strike against, demonstrate at 2 **enclose**, fence, restrain, hedge in, pen in

pick holes in v **find fault with**, fault, criticize, attack, tear to shreds Opposite: praise

pickings n **earnings**, profits, takings, proceeds, spoils

pickle n 1 **chutney**, relish, pickled vegetables 2 (infml) **difficulty**, bind, predicament, plight, quandary ■ v **preserve**, marinate, cure, keep, conserve

WORD BANK
❏ **types of pickle** chutney, cornichon, gherkin, piccalilli, pickled cucumber, sweet pickle

pickled adj **preserved**, marinated, soused

pick-me-up (infml) n **refreshment**, stimulant, tonic, boost, lift

pick on v **tease**, make fun of, bully, harass, criticize

pick out v 1 **choose**, make a choice, select, pick, pull out 2 **identify**, distinguish, isolate, recognize, single out 3 **highlight**, outline, emphasize

pickpocket n **thief**, sneak thief, robber, bag-snatcher, crook (infml)

pick up v 1 **lift**, raise, hoist, raise up, elevate Opposite: put down 2 (infml) **improve**, recover, bounce back, buck up, change for the better Opposite: deteriorate 3 **give a ride to**, give a lift to, collect, come and get, call for Opposite: drop off (infml) 4 **learn**, understand, grasp, get the hang of, remember 5 **speed up**, accelerate, go faster, get better, improve Opposite: slow down 6 **restart**, take up again, continue, carry on, jump back in Opposite: drop

pick up on (infml) v **notice**, point out, focus on, single out, call attention to Opposite: miss

picky adj **fastidious**, fussy, hard to please, finicky, particular Opposite: easygoing

picnic n (infml) **nothing**, doddle (infml), walk-over (infml), cinch, piece of cake (infml) ■ v **have a picnic**, eat al fresco, eat outside

pictograph n **symbol**, hieroglyph, primitive writing, character, drawing

pictographic adj **graphic**, symbolic, pictorial, illustrative, visual

pictorial adj **graphic**, symbolic, illustrative, pictographic, clear

picture n 1 **image**, depiction, portrait, representation, photograph 2 **film**, feature, flick (infml), movie (US), motion picture (US) 3 **embodiment**, epitome, perfect example, essence, personification ■ v 1 **imagine**, create in your mind, visualize, see, conceive of 2 **describe**, depict, illustrate, draw, show

picture book n **illustrated book**, children's book, story book, annual, coffee-table book

picture-postcard adj **picturesque**, attractive, pretty, chocolate-box, scenic Opposite: unattractive

picturesque adj 1 **attractive**, pretty, scenic, charming, chocolate-box Opposite: unattractive 2 **pictorial**, graphic, symbolic, pictographic, vivid

piddling (infml) adj **small**, petty, puny, paltry, trifling Opposite: enormous

pidgin n **lingua franca**, creole, patois, dialect, lingo (infml)

piebald adj **parti-coloured**, pied, skewbald, spotted, mottled Opposite: plain

piece n 1 **part**, fragment, bit, member, part of a set Opposite: whole 2 **bit**, portion, hunk, wedge, slice Opposite: whole 3 **example**, case, sample, instance, occurrence ■ v **patch**, mend, repair, restore, fix

piecemeal adv 1 **gradually**, by degrees, little by little, a little at a time, a bit at a time Opposite: together 2 **piece by piece**, bit by bit, one by one, separately, one at a time ■ adj **fragmentary**, disjointed, disconnected, disorganized, haphazard Opposite: cohesive

piece of cake (infml) n **doddle** (infml), child's play, nothing, breeze (infml), cinch (infml)

piece of music n **composition**, creation, tune, melody, work

piece of writing *n* article, essay, composition, report, discourse

piece out *v* apportion, mete out, share out, dispense, hand out

piece together *v* 1 **work out**, reconstruct, restore, make sense of, rationalize 2 assemble, join, fix, repair, mend *Opposite*: take apart

piecework *n* freelance work, part-time work, casual work, commission

piechart *n* graph, chart, diagram, illustration, figure

pied *adj* multicoloured, variegated, mottled, piebald, flecked *Opposite*: plain

pied-à-terre *n* second home, city apartment, holiday home, studio, town flat

pier *n* dock, wharf, berth, jetty, landing-stage

pierce *v* 1 bore into, stab, impale, cut, penetrate 2 hurt, sting, pain, wound, affront *Opposite*: heal

piercing *adj* 1 penetrating, intense, sharp, loud, earsplitting *Opposite*: soothing 2 perceptive, searching, shrewd, acute, keen *Opposite*: gentle 3 cold, bitter, freezing, wintry, raw *Opposite*: mild

piety *n* 1 piousness, devoutness, devotion, religiousness, virtue *Opposite*: impiety 2 sanctimoniousness, moralizing, hypocrisy, smugness, self-righteousness

piffle *(infml)* *n* nonsense, garbage, rubbish, twaddle *(infml)*, bunkum *(infml)* *Opposite*: sense

piffling *(infml)* *adj* trifling, unimportant, trivial, insignificant, petty *Opposite*: important

pig *(infml)* *n* 1 **glutton**, gourmand, greedy pig *(infml)*, guzzler *(infml)*, greedy guts *(infml)* 2 brute, beast, monster, rat *(slang)*

pigeon *(infml)* *n* easy target, dupe, sitting duck *(infml)*, sucker *(infml)*, chump *(dated infml)*

pigeon-breasted *adj* barrel-chested, top-heavy, stout

pigeonhole *n* 1 cubbyhole, compartment, box, shelf, slot 2 category, class, slot, classification, compartment ■ *v* categorize, class, classify, label, compartmentalize

piggish *adj* 1 greedy, gluttonous, hoggish, self-indulgent *Opposite*: abstemious 2 stubborn, uncooperative, obstructive, selfish, self-centred *Opposite*: considerate

piggy *adj* greedy, gluttonous, hoggish, self-indulgent, piggish *Opposite*: abstemious

piggyback *adj* allied, attached, associated, linked, added

piggy bank *n* money box, cash box, collecting box, savings box

piggy in the middle *n* go-between, pig in the middle, mediator, intermediary, negotiator

pigheaded *adj* stubborn, obstinate, mulish, dogged, single-minded *Opposite*: flexible

pigheadedness *n* stubbornness, obstinacy, mulishness, single-mindedness, intransigence *Opposite*: flexibility

pigment *n* colour, dye, stain, tint, colouring

pigmentation *n* colouring, coloration, skin-colour, pigment, colour

pig out *(infml)* *v* gobble, gorge, devour, eat, guzzle *(infml)*

pigsty *n* untidy place, mess, pit *(infml)*, tip *(infml)*, hole *(infml)*

pigswill *n* slops, pig food, scraps, mash, leftovers

pile *n* 1 **mound**, mountain, quantity, mass, heap 2 *(infml)* big money, fortune, mint *(infml)*, packet *(infml)*, bomb *(infml)* 3 stake, post, support, pillar, column 4 soft surface, down, nap, fibre, fur ■ *v* heap, load, stack, pile up, amass *Opposite*: scatter

pile up *v* stack, heap up, amass, mound, collect *Opposite*: scatter

pile-up *(infml)* *n* crash, car crash, collision, road accident, smash-up

pilfer *v* steal, rob, thieve, poach, take. *See* COMPARE AND CONTRAST *at* **steal**.

pilferer *n* thief, petty thief, sneak thief, robber, shoplifter

pilgrim *n* hajji, traveller, tourist, visitor, wayfarer *(literary)*

pilgrimage *n* journey, trip, visit, hajj, tour

pill *n* tablet, capsule, medication

pillage *v* plunder, sack, rob, loot, steal ■ *n* loot, spoils, plunder, booty, prize

pillager *n* plunderer, robber, looter, raider, thief

pillar *n* 1 support, column, post, prop, mast 2 rock, mainstay, tower of strength, stalwart

pillar box *n* postbox, letterbox, mailbox *(US)*, maildrop *(US)*

pillbox *n* 1 box, tin, container, étui 2 lookout post, shelter, gun emplacement, gun shelter

pillory *v* ridicule, denounce, scorn, deride, humiliate *Opposite*: praise

pillow *n* cushion, support, pad, bolster, head rest ■ *v* protect, support, prop up, hold up

pillowcase *n* pillowslip, slipcover, slipcase, bedding, slip

pilot *v* guide, conduct, control, navigate, lead ■ *adj* experimental, trial, model, test, preliminary

pimple *n* spot, blemish, blackhead, boil, pustule

pimply *adj* spotty, blemished, acned *Opposite*: clear

pin *n* 1 brooch, badge, stick pin 2 *(dated infml)* iota, tittle, pinch, bit, dash ■ *v* 1 fasten, attach, fix, secure 2 hold, pin down, hold down, restrain, stick

pinafore *n* apron, overall, pinny *(infml)*

pinch *v* 1 squeeze, nip, tweak, grasp, press 2 *(infml)* steal, take, make off with, pilfer, thieve ■ *n* touch, dash, soupçon, bit, taste. *See* COMPARE AND CONTRAST *at* **steal**.

pinched *adj* haggard, gaunt, drawn, pale, thin

pinchpenny *adj* **ungenerous**, miserly, tight-fisted, mean, stingy *(infml)* Opposite: generous ■ *n* **miser**, skinflint, penny pincher *(infml)*, scrooge *(infml)*, meanie *(infml)*

pin down *v* 1 **identify**, determine, locate, pinpoint, isolate 2 **hold down**, restrain, trap, pinion, pin

pine *v* 1 **long**, yearn, ache, want, wish 2 **waste away**, fade, fade away, suffer, go downhill Opposite: thrive

pine cone *n* **cone**, fir cone, seed case

ping *v* **sound**, ring, ding, beep, tinkle

pinion *v* **hold down**, trap, restrain, pin down, immobilize

pink *adj* 1 **flushed**, red, rosy, glowing, blushing 2 **undercooked**, rare, underdone, raw

---

WORD BANK
❏ **types of pink** cerise, coral, fuchsia, raspberry, rose, salmon pink, shell pink, shocking pink

---

pin money *n* **pocket money**, spending money, allowance, change, small change

pinnacle *n* 1 **summit**, peak, height, top, apex Opposite: base 2 **high point**, peak, acme, zenith, apex Opposite: nadir

pinpoint *v* **locate**, identify, pin down, isolate, find

pinprick *n* **hole**, puncture, pinhole, perforation, prick

pins and needles *n* **tingling**, prickling, numbness

pint-size *(infml) adj* **miniature**, pocket-sized, pocket-size, little, minuscule

pioneer *n* **innovator**, inventor, forerunner, developer, creator ■ *v* **lead the way**, open up, forge, found, initiate

pioneering *adj* **groundbreaking**, revolutionary, cutting-edge, inventive, innovative

pious *adj* 1 **devout**, religious, virtuous, moral, spiritual Opposite: impious 2 **self-righteous**, sanctimonious, moralizing, hypocritical, smug

piousness *n* 1 **piety**, devoutness, devotion, religiousness, virtue Opposite: impiety 2 **self-righteousness**, sanctimoniousness, moralizing, hypocrisy, smugness

pip *n* 1 **seed**, fruit seed, stone, nut, kernel 2 **spot**, speck, blemish, dot, mark 3 **peep**, beep, bleep, ping, ding ■ *v (infml)* **beat**, defeat, pip to the post *(infml)*

pipe *n* **tube**, cylinder, channel, conduit, pipeline ■ *v* 1 **supply**, channel, convey, transmit, bring in 2 **whistle**, twitter, tweet, cheep, peep

pipe down *(infml) v* **quiet down**, keep it down, be quiet, hush, shut up *(infml)*

pipe dream *n* **fantasy**, aspiration, ambition, castle in the air, castle in Spain

pipeline *n* **conduit**, pipe, duct, channel, tube

pipe up *v* **speak up**, speak, make yourself heard, have your say, chip in *(infml)*

piping *n* 1 **pipes**, tubing, plumbing 2 **edging**, trimming, fringing ■ *adj* **high-pitched**, shrill, piercing, penetrating, high

piquancy *n* **spiciness**, tastiness, sharpness, tang, kick Opposite: blandness

piquant *adj* 1 **spicy**, tasty, sharp, hot, tangy Opposite: bland 2 **stimulating**, provocative, interesting, exciting 3 **critical**, biting, severe, sharp, harsh

pique *n* **temper**, resentment, annoyance, anger, ill will ■ *v* 1 **irritate**, annoy, upset, offend, bother 2 **interest**, intrigue, attract, stimulate, arouse Opposite: bore

piqued *adj* **resentful**, irritated, annoyed, upset, in high dudgeon

piratic *adj* **freebooting**, marauding, attacking, robbing, lawless

pirouette *n* **spin**, twirl, whirl, turn, revolution ■ *v* **twirl**, rotate, spin, turn, whirl

pit *n* 1 **hole**, ditch, well, crater, trench 2 **coal mine**, mine, quarry, colliery 3 **dent**, pock, indentation, hollow, depression 4 **nadir**, bottom, depths 5 *(infml)* **untidy place**, mess, dump *(infml)*, hole *(infml)*, pigsty *(infml)* ■ *v* **set as rivals**, set against, fight, oppose

pitch *v* 1 **throw**, hurl, lob, toss, fling Opposite: catch 2 **erect**, set up, fix, plant, put up 3 **sway**, move, teeter, fall, stumble 4 **slope**, slant, fall away, descend, dip 5 **roll**, lurch, plunge, rock, buck 6 **propose**, sell, throw, offer, deliver ■ *n* 1 **playing field**, area, terrain, field, arena 2 **tone**, highness, lowness, note

pitch-black *adj* **black**, inky, jet-black, black as night, dark Opposite: pale

pitch-dark *adj* **unlit**, pitch-black, dark, black, jet-black Opposite: light

pitched battle *n* **argument**, disagreement, fight, head-to-head, battle

pitcher *n* **jug**, decanter, carafe

pitchfork *v* 1 **turn**, lift, fork, toss 2 **thrust**, push, force, propel, drive

pitching *adj* **rolling**, lurching, plunging, rocking, bucking

piteous *adj* **pathetic**, pitiful, wretched, sad, pitiable Opposite: enviable

pitfall *n* **drawback**, snare, snag, danger, downside Opposite: advantage

pith *n* **essence**, crux, heart, nub, core

pithead *n* **colliery**, pit, coalmine, mineshaft, mine

pithiness *n* **concision**, terseness, brevity, succinctness, briefness Opposite: verbosity

pithy *adj* **concise**, terse, to the point, brief, succinct Opposite: long-winded

pitiable *adj* 1 **contemptible**, wretched, deplorable, disgraceful, miserable Opposite: admirable 2 **pitiful**, pathetic, unfortunate, sad, piteous Opposite: heartening

pitiful *adj* 1 **disgraceful**, deplorable, contemptible, abject, despicable Opposite: admirable 2 **piteous**, pathetic, pitiable, unfortunate, sad *Opposite*: heartening **3 meagre**, inadequate, derisory, small, paltry *Opposite*: magnanimous

pitiless *adj* **merciless**, heartless, callous, hard, unfeeling *Opposite*: compassionate

pitilessness *n* **mercilessness**, heartlessness, callousness, ruthlessness, harshness *Opposite*: compassion

pit stop *n* **refuelling stop**, stop, break, servicing stop, rest

pittance *n* **subsistence wage**, small change, trifle, nothing, mite *Opposite*: fortune

pitted *adj* **potholed**, rutted, eroded, rough, bumpy *Opposite*: smooth

pity *n* **1 sympathy**, compassion, mercy, mercifulness, kindliness *Opposite*: pitilessness **2 shame**, disappointment, bad luck, tough luck, letdown *Opposite*: luck ■ *v* **sympathize**, commiserate, empathize, be there for somebody, show concern *Opposite*: blame

pitying *adj* **sympathetic**, understanding, compassionate, concerned, solicitous *Opposite*: unsympathetic

pivot *n* **hinge**, axle, axis, swivel, spindle ■ *v* **spin**, revolve, twist, rotate, whirl

pivotal *adj* **essential**, key, crucial, fundamental, critical *Opposite*: unimportant

pixie *n* **fairy**, elf, sprite, hobgoblin, Puck

pizzazz *(infml)* *n* **vitality**, spark, zest, style, glamour *Opposite*: dullness

placard *n* **poster**, sign, board, advertisement, notice

placate *v* **appease**, pacify, mollify, propitiate, conciliate *Opposite*: enrage

placation *n* **appeasement**, pacification, mollification, conciliation, satisfaction

placatory *adj* **appeasing**, mollifying, conciliatory, calming, soothing *Opposite*: inflammatory

place *n* **1 space**, spot, position, point, area **2 location**, spot, area, position, locality **3 home**, house, residence, room, habitation **4 status**, rank, position, station, circumstance ■ *v* **1 assign**, hire, employ, engage, retain *Opposite*: fire **2 position**, put, set, lay, leave *Opposite*: jettison **3 consign**, identify, file, locate, arrange

placebo *n* **dummy**, palliative, control, sample, try-on *(infml)* *Opposite*: treatment

place mat *n* **table mat**, mat, cover, cloth, coaster

placement *n* **1 siting**, positioning, location, arrangement, situation **2 location**, settlement, assignment, situation, employment

place setting *n* **setting**, cover, place, tableware, cutlery

placid *adj* **calm**, equable, even-tempered, imperturbable, easygoing *Opposite*: excitable

placidity *n* **calmness**, equability, serenity, imperturbability, even-temperedness *Opposite*: excitability

plagiarism *n* **copy**, piracy, theft, bootlegging, fraud

plagiarist *n* **copyist**, pirate, bootlegger, imitator, cheat *Opposite*: originator

plagiarize *v* **copy**, pirate, bootleg, steal, pass off as your own *Opposite*: originate

plague *n* **1 epidemic**, disease, infection, pandemic, wave **2 curse**, affliction, scourge, blight, visitation *Opposite*: blessing ■ *v* **1 afflict**, trouble, pursue, hound, harass *Opposite*: bless **2 pester**, badger, bother, harass, trouble *Opposite*: leave alone

plaid *adj* **checked**, chequered, tartan *Opposite*: plain

plain *adj* **1 simple**, basic, unadorned, natural, pure *Opposite*: elaborate **2 clear**, evident, obvious, apparent, manifest *Opposite*: obscure **3 blunt**, straightforward, direct, frank, open *Opposite*: evasive **4 plain-featured**, ordinary, unattractive, unappealing, homely *Opposite*: pretty ■ *n* **prairie**, savanna, steppe, pampas. *See* COMPARE AND CONTRAST *at* **unattractive**.

plain-clothes *adj* **undercover**, secret, disguised, out of uniform

plainly *adv* **1 simply**, normally, basically, naturally, purely *Opposite*: elaborately **2 clearly**, evidently, obviously, apparently, palpably *Opposite*: obscurely **3 bluntly**, straightforwardly, directly, frankly, openly *Opposite*: evasively

plainness *n* **1 simplicity**, ordinariness, naturalness, purity, bareness **2 clarity**, clearness, palpability, tangibility, transparency *Opposite*: obscurity **3 bluntness**, straightforwardness, directness, frankness, openness *Opposite*: evasiveness

plain-spoken *adj* **direct**, frank, blunt, forthright, bald *Opposite*: mealy-mouthed

plaint *n* **plea**, charge, accusation, complaint, action *Opposite*: defence

plaintiff *n* **accuser**, applicant, complainant, petitioner, litigant *Opposite*: defendant

plaintive *adj* **mournful**, lamenting, nostalgic, sorrowful, wistful *Opposite*: cheerful

plait *v* **braid**, interweave, weave, intertwine, crisscross *Opposite*: unravel

plan *n* **1 strategy**, scheme, project, plan of action, tactic **2 idea**, proposal, plot, scheme, aspiration **3 design**, diagram, layout, blueprint, outline ■ *v* **1 work out**, arrange, scheme, plot, organize *Opposite*: improvise **2 intend**, propose, mean, line up, schedule

plane *n* **aircraft**, aeroplane, crate *(dated infml)*, airplane *(US)*

planet *n* **Earth**, world, globe

WORD BANK
❏ **types of planet** Earth, Jupiter, Mars, Mercury, Neptune, Pluto, Saturn, Uranus, Venus

---

planned *adj* **deliberate**, intentional, prearranged, strategic, premeditated *Opposite*: unplanned

planner n 1 **town planner**, organizer, developer, city planner, designer 2 **diary**, calendar, appointment book, wall chart, planning aid

planning n **preparation**, setting up, development, arrangement, scheduling

plant n 1 **shrub**, bush, flower, herb, pot plant 2 **factory**, works, installation, industrial unit, manufacturing plant 3 *(infml)* **spy**, informant, infiltrator, secret agent, mole ■ v 1 **sow**, seed, scatter, root, transplant 2 **place**, fix, stand, transplant, deposit 3 **introduce**, lodge, establish, implant, fix Opposite: erase 4 *(infml)* **conceal**, hide, bury

plantation n **estate**, farm, homestead, farmstead, manor

planter n **pot**, flower pot, container, window box, urn

plaque n **sign**, panel, commemoration, inscription, plate

plaster n **sticking plaster**, covering, dressing, bandage, adhesive bandage *(US)* ■ v **surface**, coat, cover, face, plaster over

plasterwork n **plaster**, stuccowork, stucco, pargeting, moulding

plastic adj 1 **malleable**, soft, pliable, elastic, flexible Opposite: hard 2 **artificial**, fake, synthetic, false, forced Opposite: genuine

WORD BANK
❏ **types of plastic** acetate, celluloid, epoxide, latex, melamine, neoprene, polystyrene, polythene, polyurethane, PVC, vinyl

plasticity n **malleability**, softness, pliability, elasticity, flexibility Opposite: hardness

plate n 1 **dish**, platter, salver, serving dish, bowl 2 **number plate**, registration, license plate *(US)* ■ v **cover**, coat, overlay, protect, shield

plateau n 1 **upland**, highland, hill, mesa, tableland 2 **level**, stage, period, phase

plated adj **coated**, overlaid, gold-plated, covered, finished Opposite: solid

platform n 1 **stage**, display place, raised area, podium, stand 2 **policy**, proposal, manifesto, programme

plating n 1 **electroplating**, silver-plating, gilding, coating, lustre 2 **armour**, armour plate, cladding, metal casing, outer casing Opposite: core

platitude n 1 **cliché**, inanity, tired expression, commonplace, banality 2 **dullness**, boredom, insipidity, triteness, plainness

platitudinous adj **clichéd**, trite, banal, corny, hackneyed Opposite: original

platonic adj **spiritual**, companionable, friendly, nonsexual, nonphysical

platoon n **squad**, legion, team, detachment, subdivision

platter n **plate**, serving dish, salver, dish, tray

plaudit n **applause**, approval, praise, positive feedback, appreciation Opposite: criticism

plausibility n **believability**, credibility, reasonableness, probability, conceivability Opposite: implausibility

plausible adj **believable**, credible, reasonable, probable, conceivable Opposite: implausible

play v 1 **enjoy yourself**, occupy yourself, amuse yourself, have fun, frolic 2 **joke**, tease, fool around, fool about, mess about *(infml)* 3 **participate**, take part, join in, compete, engage in 4 **perform**, act, play-act, portray, star as ■ n 1 **recreation**, amusement, fun, diversion, games Opposite: work 2 **production**, drama, show, piece, performance

play-act *(infml)* v **pretend**, ham it up, put it on, put on an act, play to the gallery

playback n **replay**, rerun, reshowing, repetition, reproduction Opposite: recording

play down v **minimize**, make light of, underplay, underestimate, make little of Opposite: accentuate

player n 1 **participant**, team member, competitor, contestant 2 **actor**, thespian, performer, entertainer, play-actor

playfellow *(archaic)* n **friend**, playmate, mate, chum *(infml)*, pal *(infml)* Opposite: enemy

playful adj 1 **lively**, bouncy, full of fun, full of life, frisky Opposite: subdued 2 **good-humoured**, lighthearted, good-natured, teasing, jokey Opposite: serious

playfulness n 1 **liveliness**, bounce, bounciness, friskiness, spirit 2 **good humour**, lightheartedness, teasing, mischief, impishness Opposite: seriousness

play games with v **deceive**, trick, confuse, mistreat, abuse

playgoer n **theatre buff**, theatregoer, spectator, punter *(slang)*

playground n 1 **park**, play area, community playground, adventure playground, outdoor play area *(US)* 2 **school yard**, school grounds, play area, recreation area, concourse Opposite: classroom

play hooky *(infml)* v **play truant**, truant, skip classes, miss school, absent yourself Opposite: attend

playhouse n 1 **theatre**, auditorium, studio, venue 2 **Wendy house**, tree house, den

playing field n **sports ground**, sports field, pitch, park, ground

playmate n **friend**, mate, pal *(infml)*, chum *(infml)*, playfellow *(archaic)* Opposite: enemy

play off v **oppose**, set against, pit against, go against, challenge

play-off n **final**, final round, semifinal, quarterfinal, tiebreaker

play safe v **take no risks**, hedge your bets, take care, be cautious, be careful Opposite: gamble

playschool n **playgroup**, nursery, preschool, kindergarten *(US)*

play the game v **toe the line**, follow the rules,

conform, comply, obey *Opposite*: act up

plaything *n* **toy**, doll, bauble, curio, knick-knack

playtime *n* **break**, interval, free time, leisure time, lunchtime

play to the gallery *v* **show off**, play up, posture, perform, play to the crowd

play up *v* **1 exaggerate**, emphasize, embellish, highlight, draw attention to *Opposite*: play down **2 misbehave**, act up, malfunction, go wrong *Opposite*: behave

play up to *v* **flatter**, toady, ingratiate yourself with, win the favour of, butter up *(infml)*

playwright *n* **dramatist**, writer, author, tragedian, dramaturge

play your cards close to your chest *v* **be secretive**, be a dark horse, keep quiet, keep secret, keep under wraps

plaza *n* **square**, piazza, marketplace, court, mall *(US)*

plea *n* **1 appeal**, entreaty, prayer, request, petition *Opposite*: demand **2 statement**, claim, defence, declaration, assertion *Opposite*: denial **3 excuse**, pretext, reason, explanation, alibi

plea-bargain *v* **plead guilty**, do a deal, negotiate, come to an agreement, contract

plead *v* **1 beg**, appeal, pray, entreat, request *Opposite*: demand **2 declare**, assert, claim, state, put forward **3 support**, defend, argue, contend, vindicate

pleading *adj* **begging**, piteous, persuasive, suppliant *(fml)*, imploring *(fml)*

pleasant *adj* **1 enjoyable**, agreeable, pleasing, lovely, nice *Opposite*: unpleasant **2 amiable**, friendly, congenial, likable, genial *Opposite*: nasty

pleasantness *n* **1 appeal**, loveliness, niceness, pleasurableness, satisfaction *Opposite*: unpleasantness **2 amiability**, friendliness, congeniality, likability, likableness *Opposite*: nastiness

pleasantries *n* **small talk**, chat, gossip, banter, conversation

pleasantry *n* **remark**, civility, banality, politeness, observation *Opposite*: insult

please *v* **1 satisfy**, gratify, make happy, delight, thrill *Opposite*: displease **2 like**, prefer, choose, desire, wish *Opposite*: dislike

pleased *adj* **satisfied**, happy, content, delighted, contented *Opposite*: displeased

pleasing *adj* **agreeable**, pleasant, enjoyable, lovely, nice *Opposite*: disagreeable

pleasurable *adj* **agreeable**, enjoyable, pleasing, pleasant, gratifying *Opposite*: disagreeable

pleasure *n* **1 enjoyment**, happiness, delight, bliss, contentment *Opposite*: displeasure **2 gratification**, indulgence, hedonism, decadence, sensuality **3 amusement**, recreation, fun, leisure, diversion *Opposite*: work

pleat *n* **crease**, fold, tuck, gather, crimp ■ *v* **fold**, crease, tuck, gather, crimp

plebiscite *n* **referendum**, poll, vote, ballot, opinion poll

pledge *n* **1 vow**, oath, promise, assurance, guarantee **2 security**, deposit, guarantee, warranty, collateral ■ *v* **promise**, vow, swear, guarantee, give your word

plenary *adj (fml)* **full**, complete, entire, whole, unlimited ■ *n* **meeting**, session, general assembly, plenary meeting, plenary session

plenipotentiary *adj* **presiding**, all-powerful, in charge, officiating, supreme *Opposite*: powerless ■ *n* **minister**, minister plenipotentiary, ambassador, special envoy, envoy *Opposite*: pawn

plenteous *(literary) see* **plentiful**

plentiful *adj* **abundant**, copious, overflowing, ample, lavish *Opposite*: scarce

plenty *n* **prosperity**, abundance, copiousness, profusion, plethora *Opposite*: insufficiency ■ *adj (infml)* **ample**, a lot, lots, a load, sufficient *Opposite*: inadequate

plenum *n* **general assembly**, meeting, session, plenary meeting, plenary session

plethora *n* **overabundance**, excess, surfeit, glut, surplus *Opposite*: shortage

pliability *n* **1 flexibility**, bendability, pliancy, softness *Opposite*: rigidity **2 compliance**, pliancy, adaptability, flexibility, obedience *Opposite*: inflexibility

pliable *adj* **1 flexible**, bendable, workable, pliant, plastic *Opposite*: rigid **2 compliant**, pliant, docile, flexible, yielding *Opposite*: inflexible

COMPARE AND CONTRAST CORE MEANING: able to be bent or moulded

pliable flexible and easily bent or moulded; **ductile** describes metals that can be easily drawn out into a long continuous wire or hammered into thin sheets; **malleable** describes metals that can be hammered or pressed into various shapes without breaking or cracking; **elastic** describes substances or materials that can be stretched without breaking and then return to their original shape; **pliant** supple and springy and therefore easily bent.

pliancy *n* **1 pliability**, flexibility, suppleness, elasticity, plasticity *Opposite*: stiffness **2 compliance**, pliability, adaptability, flexibility, obedience *Opposite*: obstinacy

pliant *adj* **1 supple**, springy, bendy, pliable, flexible *Opposite*: stiff **2 compliant**, pliable, adaptable, flexible, accommodating *Opposite*: inflexible. *See* COMPARE AND CONTRAST *at* **pliable**.

plight *n* **dilemma**, trouble, predicament, difficulty, quandary

plinth *n* **pedestal**, platform, base, stand, support

plod *v* **trudge**, slog, tread, lumber, tramp *Opposite*: race

plodder n snail, toiler, slogger, idler, slow-coach (infml) Opposite: high-flier

plodding adj slow, dull, slow but sure, ponderous, tedious Opposite: rapid

plonk v place, put, put down, set down, dump ■ n (infml) wine, house wine, vin de table, vino (infml)

plop v place, put, put down, set down, plonk

plop down v flop down, sit down heavily, collapse, subside, plonk down

plot n 1 conspiracy, plan, scheme, subversion, strategy 2 story line, action, scenario, outline, narrative 3 area, section, parcel, piece, lot ■ v 1 plan, scheme, strategize, conspire, design 2 chart, map, draw, mark, map out

plotter n schemer, conspirator, conniver, contriver, strategist

plough v cultivate, till, turn over, work

plough into v crash into, bang into, drive into, run into, career into

plough on v keep at it, struggle on, persevere, plug away (infml), keep your nose to the grindstone

plough through v keep at, struggle through, plough on with, persevere, persist

plough under v bury, cover, cover over, turn over Opposite: dig up

ploy n trick, manoeuvre, strategy, plan, ruse

pluck v 1 pull, tug, pick at, grasp, take 2 pull out, remove, yank, tweak, uproot 3 pick, collect, gather, harvest 4 strum, play, twang, plunk, pick ■ n courage, determination, bravery, fortitude, nerve Opposite: cowardice. See COMPARE AND CONTRAST at courage.

pluckiness n bravery, courage, pluck, fearlessness, boldness Opposite: cowardice

pluck up courage v dare, take the plunge, brace yourself, take a deep breath, steel yourself Opposite: lose your nerve

plucky adj brave, courageous, fearless, bold, audacious Opposite: cowardly

plug n 1 stopper, cork, cap, bung, top 2 (infml) socket, outlet, power point, wall outlet, point 3 (infml) advertisement, recommendation, mention, puff, advert (infml) 4 sample, core, piece, wedge, extract 5 wad, mass, lump, wadding, padding ■ v 1 (infml) work, carry on, keep at it, keep going, persevere 2 (infml) puff, hype, sell, push, spin Opposite: run down 3 stop, cap, bung, cork, seal Opposite: unplug

plugged-in (infml) adj informed, involved, connected, in tune, in touch

plughole n outlet, bunghole, drain, hole

plug in v connect, link up, hook up (infml) Opposite: unplug

plum (infml) n reward, award, bonus, windfall, trophy ■ adj desirable, choice, covetable, prestigious, profitable

plumage n feathers, down, fluff, fuzz

plumb adv (infml) exactly, precisely, right, bang, slap (infml) ■ adj perpendicular, upright, vertical, true, aligned Opposite: horizontal ■ v 1 comprehend, understand, fathom, grasp, know 2 experience, undergo, face, suffer, go through

plumbing n drains, sanitation, drainage system, water system, heating system

plume n trail, cloud, spiral, column, curl

plummet v plunge, drop, dive, tumble, crash Opposite: climb

plummy adj 1 resonant, mellow, rich, sonorous Opposite: reedy 2 upper-class, public-school, patrician, affected, posh (infml) Opposite: common

plump adj fat, overweight, chubby, stout, fleshy Opposite: slender ■ v flop down, drop, plop down, flop, fall Opposite: stand up

plump for v choose, decide on, opt for, take, settle on

plumpness n fatness, chubbiness, fleshiness, curviness, obesity Opposite: slenderness

plump up v fatten, shake up, plump, fluff up

plunder v steal, rob, loot, pillage, raid ■ n stolen goods, loot, booty, spoils, ill-gotten gains

plunge v 1 thrust, force, throw, push, pitch 2 rush, jump, leap, lurch, throw yourself Opposite: hesitate 3 drop, dive, plummet, sink, nose-dive Opposite: soar ■ n dive, drop, plummet, nosedive, fall Opposite: climb

plunging adj 1 plummeting, dipping, dropping, tumbling, reducing Opposite: rising 2 low, low-cut, revealing, décolleté Opposite: high

plunk v twang, strum, plonk, play, pick

pluralism n variety, diversity, multiplicity, heterogeneity Opposite: homogeneity

pluralistic adj varied, mixed, diverse, multicultural, multiethnic Opposite: homogeneous

plurality n number, range, variety, multiplicity, multitude Opposite: single

plus prep in addition to, added to, as well as, along with, together with Opposite: minus ■ adj 1 desirable, positive, advantageous, favourable, good Opposite: minus 2 and above, and over, and more ■ n (infml) advantage, bonus, benefit, boon, plus point (infml) Opposite: minus

plush (infml) adj lush, luxurious, expensive, rich, lavish

plutocrat n tycoon, magnate, mogul, big shot (infml)

ply v 1 work, practise, pursue, carry out, wage 2 use, work with, apply, utilize, employ 3 supply, pile, load, provide, furnish (fml) 4 badger, hound, harass, overwhelm, bombard ■ n layer, thickness, strand, tier

p.m. adj afternoon, after lunch, evening, night Opposite: a.m.

pneumatic adj air-filled, inflated, inflatable, air Opposite: solid

poach v 1 **steal**, thieve, rustle, pilfer, plunder 2 **simmer**, boil, steam, braise

poacher n thief, rustler, robber, pilferer

pocked adj **pitted**, pockmarked, dented, cratered, scarred Opposite: unblemished

pocket n **pouch**, compartment, receptacle, sack, bag ■ v **help yourself to**, steal, appropriate, take, snaffle (infml) ■ adj **concise**, abridged, reduced, short, small

pocket money n **spending money**, pin money, expenses, extra cash, personal money

pocket-size see pocket-sized

pocket-sized adj **little**, small, handy, compact, portable Opposite: bulky

pockmark n **blemish**, scar, indentation, hollow, blotch

pockmarked adj **pitted**, pocked, dented, cratered, scarred Opposite: unblemished

pod n **shell**, husk, peapod, case, hull

podgy adj **fat**, overweight, chubby, stout, fleshy Opposite: slim

podium n **dais**, platform, stage, plinth

poem n **verse**, rhyme, ode, sonnet, elegy Opposite: prose

poet n **writer**, lyricist, rhymester, versifier, composer

poetic adj 1 **lyrical**, elegiac, graceful, rhythmical, flowing Opposite: prosaic 2 **sensitive**, full of feeling, profound, deep, moving Opposite: insensitive

poeticality n **lyricism**, expressivity, eloquence

poetry n **verse**, rhyme, poems, rhymes, lyrics Opposite: prose

po-faced adj **disapproving**, solemn, serious, strait-laced, humourless Opposite: jovial

pogrom n **persecution**, extermination, massacre, devastation, slaughter

poignance see poignancy

poignancy n **pathos**, sadness, tragedy, nostalgia, tenderness

poignant adj **moving**, emotional, touching, distressing, sad Opposite: unemotional. See COMPARE AND CONTRAST at moving.

point n 1 **opinion**, fact, idea, argument, theme 2 **instant**, time, stage, moment, juncture (fml) 3 **aim**, meaning, central theme, intention, heart 4 **purpose**, advantage, use, sense, object 5 **argument**, statement, line of reasoning, thrust, viewpoint 6 **detail**, item, feature, aspect, thing 7 **position**, spot, place, situation, site 8 **tip**, end, top, summit, peak 9 **headland**, cape, promontory, spit, peninsula 10 **socket**, power point, plug, contact, outlet ■ v **direct**, aim, face, indicate, draw attention to

point-blank adv 1 **at close range**, straight on, dead on, close up, close to 2 **frankly**, bluntly, outright, straightforwardly, directly Opposite: indirectly

pointed adj 1 **sharp**, piercing, keen, pointy, jagged Opposite: blunt 2 **barbed**, critical,

meaningful, incisive, sharp Opposite: mild

pointedly adv **deliberately**, purposely, intentionally, meaningfully, openly Opposite: subtly

pointer n 1 **cane**, baton, stick, pole 2 **needle**, indicator, hand, cursor 3 **tip**, advice, hint, suggestion, warning

pointing n **mortar**, cement, grout, filling

pointless adj **useless**, futile, senseless, meaningless, worthless Opposite: useful

pointlessness n **uselessness**, futility, senselessness, meaninglessness, worthlessness Opposite: usefulness

point of view n **opinion**, attitude, standpoint, viewpoint, position

point out v 1 **indicate**, show, reveal, point at, identify 2 **call attention to**, draw attention to, highlight, indicate, mention Opposite: hide

point-to-point n **steeplechase**, horse race, equestrian event, cross-country racing (US)

point up v **emphasize**, draw attention to, underline, make clear, show

poise n 1 **composure**, dignity, self-assurance, self-confidence, self-control Opposite: insecurity 2 **grace**, bearing, deportment, good posture, composure Opposite: clumsiness ■ v **hover**, balance, float, perch, hang

poised adj 1 **ready**, prepared, primed, in position, in place Opposite: unprepared 2 **balanced**, suspended, hovering, on the edge, on the brink 3 **composed**, dignified, self-assured, self-confident, controlled Opposite: insecure

poison n **venom**, toxin, contagion, toxic substance Opposite: antidote ■ v 1 **kill**, murder, exterminate, destroy, harm 2 **pollute**, taint, corrupt, contaminate, adulterate

poisoner n **murderer**, killer, exterminator, assassin, slaughterer

poisonous adj 1 **toxic**, venomous, noxious, fatal, lethal Opposite: harmless 2 **malicious**, evil, wicked, nasty, spiteful Opposite: kindly

poke v 1 **jab**, stab, push, prod, thrust 2 **protrude**, stick out, project, jut, extend 3 **search through**, look through, root, browse, rummage ■ n **stab**, jab, push, prod, thrust

poke fun at v **make fun of**, ridicule, tease, mock, laugh at

poker-faced adj **expressionless**, blank, impassive, emotionless, deadpan Opposite: expressive

poky (infml) adj **small**, tiny, cramped, restricted, tight Opposite: spacious

polar adj **glacial**, Arctic, Antarctic Opposite: tropical

polarity n **division**, split, schism, divergence, polarization Opposite: convergence

polarization n **divergence**, separation, division, opposition, schism Opposite: union

polarize v **diverge**, split, drive apart, separate, create a rift in Opposite: unite

pole

378

pole n 1 opposite, extreme, extremity, limit, end 2 rod, shaft, stick, post, dowel ▪ v push, propel, raft, punt, shove

poleaxe v astonish, amaze, stupefy, stun, shock

polemic n argument, plea, diatribe, speech, discourse ▪ adj controversial, outspoken, impassioned, uncompromising, bold Opposite: dispassionate

polemicist n debater, orator, speaker, essayist, lecturer

pole position n prime position, lead, front, advantage, catbird seat (US infml) Opposite: rear

pole-vault v jump, vault, leap, bound

police n police force, force, constabulary, law, crime squad ▪ v regulate, control, keep watch over, monitor, patrol

policeman see police officer

police officer n officer, police constable, PC, copper (dated infml), bobby (dated infml)

policewoman see police officer

policy n 1 course of action, rule, strategy, plan, guiding principle 2 contract, document, certificate, statement, papers

polish v 1 shine, buff, buff up, rub, clean Opposite: tarnish 2 improve, enhance, refine, perfect, hone ▪ n 1 shine, lustre, gleam, sheen, brilliance Opposite: dullness 2 refinement, skill, control, sophistication, grace

polished adj 1 refined, elegant, cultured, sophisticated, graceful Opposite: coarse 2 practised, skilful, accomplished, professional, impeccable Opposite: amateur 3 smooth, shiny, gleaming, glossy, slippery Opposite: dull

polish off v finish, finish off, dispose of, complete, eliminate Opposite: leave

polish up v 1 shine, buff, rub, clean, dust Opposite: tarnish 2 refine, improve, practise, brush up, work on Opposite: let go

polite adj 1 well-mannered, good-mannered, civil, well-bred, gracious Opposite: rude 2 refined, cultured, sophisticated, polished, elegant Opposite: coarse

politeness n good manners, graciousness, manners, civility, breeding Opposite: rudeness

politic adj tactful, diplomatic, prudent, wise, expedient Opposite: foolish

political adj 1 governmental, administrative, electoral, civil, diplomatic 2 party-political, politically aware, radical, partisan, dogmatic

political correctness n appropriateness, sensitivity, awareness, tactfulness, inclusiveness Opposite: insensitivity

politically correct adj inclusive, sensitive, tactful, inoffensive, appropriate Opposite: politically incorrect

politically incorrect adj exclusive, insensitive, inappropriate, unaware, tactless Opposite: politically correct

politician n political figure, representative, candidate, official, legislator

politicization n awareness raising, consciousness raising, lobbying

politicize v raise awareness of, put on the agenda, debate, discuss, air Opposite: depoliticize

politicking n campaigning, speechmaking, lobbying, politics, scheming

politics n 1 government, political affairs, affairs of state, policy, policymaking 2 beliefs, principles, opinions, views, theory

polity n political entity, organization, institution, state, society

poll n election, census, survey, opinion poll, sample ▪ v sample, survey, question, ask, interview

pollinate v fertilize, cross-fertilize, self-fertilize, cross-pollinate, self-pollinate

pollination n fertilization, cross-fertilization, self-fertilization, cross-pollination, self-pollination

polling n voting, casting your vote, balloting, going to the polls

polling booth n cubicle, voting booth, booth, stall, box

pollutant n contaminant, impurity, toxin, poison, waste product

pollute v 1 contaminate, poison, adulterate, infest, infect Opposite: clean 2 corrupt, pervert, demoralize, violate, damage Opposite: purify

polluted adj contaminated, dirty, poisoned, adulterated, unclean Opposite: clean

polluter n contaminator, dumper, poisoner, emitter, fly-tipper Opposite: environmentalist

pollution n 1 contamination, infection, adulteration, corruption 2 contaminant, toxic waste, effluence, greenhouse gasses, smog

poltergeist n ghost, spirit, manifestation, apparition, spectre

polyglot n linguist, multilingual person, bilingual person

polygonal adj many-sided, multilateral, triangular, quadrilateral, pentagonal

polygraph n detector, lie detector, recorder, tester

polymath n fount of knowledge, Renaissance man, Renaissance woman, walking encyclopedia, mine of information Opposite: specialist

polyp n growth, tumour, cyst, nodule, swelling

polysyllabic adj long, compound, complex, multisyllabic Opposite: monosyllabic

polysyllable n long word, compound, complex word Opposite: monosyllable

polytechnic *n* **college**, technical college, university, tech *(infml)*, poly *(infml)*

polytheism *n* **dualism**, animism, pantheism *Opposite*: monotheism

pomp *n* **splendour**, spectacle, display, ceremony, show *Opposite*: understatement

pompom *n* **bobble**, tassel, powder puff, decoration, detail

pomposity *n* **self-importance**, arrogance, pretentiousness, pretension, snobbishness *Opposite*: modesty

pompous *adj* **1 self-important**, arrogant, pretentious, snobbish, affected *Opposite*: modest **2 showy**, flaunting, spectacular, magnificent, grand *Opposite*: modest

pompousness *see* pomposity

poncho *n* **cloak**, cape, wrap

pond *n* **pool**, tarn, fishpond, millpond, mere *(literary)*

ponder *v* **consider**, think about, contemplate, deliberate, wonder about

ponderable *adj* **appreciable**, significant, considerable, substantial, weighty *Opposite*: insignificant

ponderous *adj* **1 heavy**, laborious, lumbering, weighty, unwieldy *Opposite*: light **2 tedious**, boring, laborious, tiresome, dull *Opposite*: lively

pong *(infml)* *n* **stink**, smell, whiff *(infml)*, niff *(slang)*, reek ■ *v* **smell**, stink, whiff *(infml)*, niff *(slang)*, reek

pongy *(infml)* *adj* **smelly**, stinky *(infml)*, whiffy *(infml)*, niffy *(slang)*, cheesy *Opposite*: fragrant

pontiff *n* **pope**, bishop of Rome, Holy Father

pontifical *adj* **1 episcopal**, papal, prelatic **2 pompous**, self-important, pontificating, grandiose, portentous *Opposite*: humble

pontificate *v* **hold forth**, preach, go on, sound off

pontoon *n* **platform**, float, buoy, support, base

pony-trekking *n* **hacking**, horse-riding, riding, riding out, equitation *(fml)*

pooch *(infml)* *n* **dog**, lapdog, canine companion, canine, hound

pooh-pooh *v* **reject**, dismiss, spurn, scorn, scoff at *Opposite*: praise

pool *n* **1 pond**, puddle, lake, swimming pool, tarn **2 team**, band, collection, consortium, collective **3 kitty**, fund, pot *(US infml)* ■ *v* **share**, combine, bring together, put together, assemble *Opposite*: ration out

pooped *(infml)* *adj* **exhausted**, tired out, worn out, drained, ready to drop *Opposite*: invigorated

poor *adj* **1 destitute**, needy, poverty-stricken, impoverished, penniless *Opposite*: rich **2 deprived**, unfortunate, underprivileged, meagre, reduced *Opposite*: privileged **3 weak**, inadequate, feeble, meagre, bad *Opposite*: superior **4 humble**, lowly, modest, insignificant *Opposite*: noble

poorly *adv* **badly**, inadequately, weakly, feebly, scantily *Opposite*: well ■ *adj* *(infml)* **ill**, unwell, under the weather, sick, out of sorts *Opposite*: healthy

poorness *n* **1 poverty**, impoverishment, destitution, pennilessness, neediness *Opposite*: wealth **2 weakness**, inadequacy, feebleness, inferiority, poor quality *Opposite*: superiority

poor quality *n* **cheapness**, tawdriness, mediocrity, inferiority, weakness *Opposite*: quality

poor-quality *adj* **cheap**, shoddy, trashy, second-class, second-rate *Opposite*: first-rate

pop *n* **explosion**, bang, crack, report, snap ■ *v* **1 explode**, burst, go off, crack **2** *(infml)* **dash**, dart, go, call, nip *(infml)* **3** *(infml)* **put**, place, insert, drop, shove ■ *adj* *(infml)* **popular**, modern, current, accessible, easy

pope *n* **pontiff**, bishop of Rome, Holy Father

popeyed *adj* **goggle-eyed**, swollen-eyed, wide-eyed, bug-eyed *(infml)*

pop in *(infml)* *v* **visit**, go, stop at, look in, call in

poppet *(infml)* *n* **dear**, love, lovey *(infml)*, darling, sweetie *(infml)*

poppycock *(dated infml)* *n* **nonsense**, absurdity, untruth, rubbish, twaddle *(infml)*

populace *n* **public**, population, general public, common people, lay people

popular *adj* **1 well-liked**, accepted, admired, in style, all the rage *Opposite*: unpopular **2 common**, general, prevalent, widely held, current *Opposite*: rare

popularity *n* **admiration**, approval, acceptance, fame, status *Opposite*: infamy

popularization *n* **1 promotion**, spread, commercialization, propagation, universalization **2 simplification**, vulgarization, interpretation, explanation, universalization

popularize *v* **1 make popular**, promote, spread, propagate, commercialize **2 simplify**, interpret, vulgarize, put in layperson's terms, explain

popularly *adv* **generally**, commonly, prevalently, readily, widely

populate *v* **inhabit**, people, settle, colonize, fill *Opposite*: desert

population *n* **inhabitants**, populace, people, residents

populist *adj* **mainstream**, majority, democratic, general, accessible *Opposite*: elitist

populous *adj* **crowded**, overcrowded, populated, full of people, packed *Opposite*: desolate

pop-up *adj* **spring-operated**, automatic, self-opening, folding, foldaway

porcine *adj* **piggy**, piggish, swinish, hoglike

pore *n* **hole**, opening, aperture, stoma

pore over *v* **examine**, scour, read, study, go over

porous *adj* **absorbent**, permeable, leaky, spongy *Opposite*: impermeable

porridge *n* **breakfast cereal**, gruel, oatmeal, oats

port *n* **seaport**, anchorage, dock, harbour, haven *(literary)*

portability *n* **movability**, transportability, transferability, lightness, compactness *Opposite*: bulkiness

portable *adj* **movable**, transportable, transferable, handy, convenient *Opposite*: fixed

portcullis *n* **gate**, door, grating, drawbridge, entry

portend *v* **foreshadow**, foretell, signify, mean, warn of

portent *n* **1 omen**, sign, presage, warning, indication **2** *(fml)* **marvel**, phenomenon, prodigy, wonder, miracle

portentous *adj* **1 significant**, important, crucial, ominous, fateful *Opposite*: trivial **2 pompous**, pretentious, self-important, haughty, arrogant *Opposite*: modest

porter *n* **gatekeeper**, doorkeeper, concierge, janitor, receptionist

portfolio *n* **1 range**, collection, selection, group, set **2 case**, folder, file, wallet

portico *n* **porch**, entrance, doorway, entry, entranceway

portion *n* **1 helping**, share, slice, serving, percentage **2 fraction**, piece, bit, part, segment *Opposite*: whole ■ *v* **divide**, distribute, allocate, assign, share out

portliness *n* **stoutness**, stockiness, roundness, heaviness, heftiness *Opposite*: slimness

portly *adj* **overweight**, stout, stocky, round, heavy *Opposite*: slim

portmanteau *n* **suitcase**, case, bag, valise, holdall ■ *adj* **multiple**, combination, hybrid, blended, general-purpose

portrait *n* **picture**, representation, portrayal, likeness, photograph

portraiture *n* **portrait making**, portrait painting, photography, painting, drawing

portray *v* **depict**, represent, describe, show, interpret

portrayal *n* **representation**, interpretation, depiction, picture, description

pose *v* **1 model**, stand, sit, sit for, posture **2 impersonate**, pretend, play the part of, masquerade, profess **3 ask**, put, put forward, present, propound **4 present**, cause, create, set, establish ■ *n* **1 posture**, stance, position, attitude, carriage *(fml)* **2 pretence**, sham, fake, front, façade

poser *n* **1** *(infml)* **poseur**, show-off, exhibitionist, posturer, narcissist **2 problem**, question, puzzle, conundrum, challenge

poseur *n* **exhibitionist**, posturer, narcissist, swaggerer, peacock

posh *(infml) adj* **1 upmarket**, elegant, fashionable, expensive, luxurious *Opposite*: downmarket **2 upper-class**, well-to-do, genteel, aristocratic *Opposite*: common

posit *(fml) v* **put forward**, postulate, suggest, theorize, speculate

position *n* **1 location**, place, site, spot, point **2 posture**, stance, pose, arrangement, attitude **3 rank**, status, standing, station **4 view**, opinion, policy, stance, perception ■ *v* **put**, place, locate, stand, sit

positive *adj* **1 sure**, certain, clear, convinced, assured *Opposite*: uncertain **2 irrefutable**, definite, explicit, clear-cut, conclusive *Opposite*: dubious **3 optimistic**, confident, constructive, helpful, encouraging *Opposite*: negative

positively *adv* **1 definitely**, absolutely, completely, really, certainly **2 encouragingly**, confidently, optimistically, supportively, constructively *Opposite*: negatively

posse *(infml) n* **gang**, band, party, group, company

possess *v* **1 own**, have, hold, enjoy, keep *Opposite*: lack **2 take control**, influence, take, occupy, seize

possessed *adj* **controlled**, influenced, obsessed, crazed, overcome

possession *n* **ownership**, control, tenure, custody, proprietorship

possessions *n* **property**, belongings, wealth, goods, assets

possessive *adj* **1 domineering**, jealous, controlling, overprotective, covetous *Opposite*: trusting **2 selfish**, greedy, grasping, tightfisted, mean *Opposite*: generous

possessiveness *n* **1 selfishness**, greed, tightfistedness, meanness, greediness *Opposite*: generosity **2 jealousy**, jealousness, suspiciousness, overprotectiveness, insecurity

possessor *n* **owner**, holder, bearer, keeper, proprietor

possibility *n* **likelihood**, prospect, risk, chance, probability

possible *adj* **1 likely**, conceivable, imaginable, thinkable, probable *Opposite*: unlikely **2 achievable**, doable, feasible, viable, workable *Opposite*: impossible

possibly *adv* **perhaps**, maybe, probably, conceivably, feasibly *Opposite*: certainly

post *n* **1 pole**, column, stake, upright, marker **2 position**, placement, job, station, place ■ *v* **1 display**, announce, advertise, put up, publish **2 send**, dispatch, forward, airmail, mail *Opposite*: receive

postage *n* **stamp price**, postage fee, postage charge, postage cost, first-class postage

postbag *n* **1 sack**, mailbag, bag, satchel, delivery bag **2 correspondence**, mail, letters, mailbag, postal communications

postbox *n* **letterbox**, posting box, pillar box, collection box, collection point

postcard *n* **card**, picture postcard, message, note, letter

poster n 1 **picture**, print, reproduction, artwork, photograph 2 **advertisement**, placard, notice, bill, announcement

posterior adj 1 **rear**, hind, back, hindmost Opposite: front 2 (fml) **latter**, subsequent, following, next, later Opposite: former

posterity n **future generations**, later generations, generations to come, successors, future

postgraduate n **student**, postgraduate student, graduate student, PhD student, graduate

post-haste adv **fast**, immediately, right away, quickly, straight away Opposite: slowly

posthumous adj **subsequent**, retrospective, delayed, following, postmortem

posting n **placement**, relocation, position, post, military posting

postmark n **date stamp**, frank, stamp, mark, rubber stamp ■ v **frank**, stamp, date, mark, rubber-stamp

postmortem n 1 **autopsy**, postmortem examination, medical examination, examination, inquest 2 **investigation**, analysis, examination, inquest, review

postnatal adj **postpartum**, post-delivery, perinatal Opposite: antenatal

post office n 1 **PO**, GPO, sorting office, mailroom, mail depot (US) 2 **mail system**, mail service, postal service, postal communications, mail

postpone v **delay**, put off, put back, shelve, put on the back burner Opposite: bring forward

postponement n **delay**, rescheduling, rearrangement, deferment, adjournment

postscript n **afterthought**, addition, supplement, afterword, epilogue Opposite: preface

postulate v 1 **assume**, guess, hypothesize, suggest, claim 2 (fml) **nominate**, propose, select, choose, put forward

posture n **bearing**, stance, attitude, position, pose

posturing n **self-importance**, pomposity, swagger, bravado, bluster

posy n **bouquet**, bunch of flowers, spray, nosegay, arrangement

pot n **container**, pan, vessel, jar, tub ■ v 1 **shoot**, bag, catch, get, hit 2 **preserve**, seal, pickle, can, tin

potable adj **drinkable**, clean, filtered, fit to drink, drinking

potato n **tuber**, new potato, seed potato, spud (infml), tater (infml)

WORD BANK
❏ **types of processed potato** chip, crisp, croquette, French fries, fries, jacket potato, knish, latke, mash, potato cake, potato chips, potato pancake, rösti

poteen n **bootleg alcohol**, spirit, bootleg

whisky, whisky, moonshine (infml)

potency n **strength**, force, power, might, vigour Opposite: weakness

potent adj 1 **strong**, effective, powerful, forceful, mighty Opposite: weak 2 **persuasive**, convincing, influential, forceful

potentate n **monarch**, ruler, leader, emperor, sovereign

potential n **ability**, capacity, possibility, makings, what it takes ■ adj **possible**, hypothetical, conceivable, likely, probable Opposite: unlikely

pothole n 1 **rut**, hole, dip, depression, fault 2 **cave**, cavern, catacomb, pit, hole

potholed adj **rutted**, pitted, holed, eroded, uneven Opposite: smooth

potholer n **speleologist**, caver, spelunker

potion n **liquid**, medicine, concoction, mixture, brew

potluck n **luck of the draw**, whatever is going, whatever is on offer, chance, whatever is available

potpourri n **miscellany**, mixture, assortment, collection, jumble

pots (infml) n **bags**, heaps (infml), piles (infml), tons (infml), loads (infml)

potshot n **shot**, pot, go, aim, try

potted adj 1 **preserved**, sealed, conserved, pickled, canned Opposite: fresh 2 (infml) **abridged**, summarized, brief, concise, shortened Opposite: full

potter v 1 **dabble**, mess, fiddle, tinker, toy 2 **go slowly**, dawdle, shuffle, amble, toddle (infml) Opposite: hurry

pottery n **ceramic objects**, earthenware, stoneware, ceramics

WORD BANK
❏ **types of pottery** bone china, ceramic, china, delft, Dresden china, earthenware, enamel, faience, Limoges, porcelain, Sèvres, stoneware, terracotta

potty (infml) adj **foolish**, irrational, eccentric, silly, ridiculous Opposite: sensible

pouch n **bag**, pocket, money bag, purse, sack

pouf n **stool**, beanbag, seat, cushion, floor cushion

poultice n **dressing**, compress, bandage, plaster

pounce v 1 **spring**, swoop, leap, jump, dive Opposite: recoil 2 **attack**, seize upon, seize, tackle, ambush ■ n **leap**, jump, spring, bound, swoop

pound n **pound sterling**, quid (infml), smacker (infml), nicker (slang) ■ v 1 **hit**, strike, batter, beat, hammer 2 **throb**, thump, beat, pulsate, pulse 3 **grind**, crush, pulverize, bruise, mash

pounding n 1 **throbbing**, thumping, pulsation, pulse, hammering 2 **beating**, thrashing, drubbing, defeat, pasting (infml)

pour v 1 decant, drizzle, dispense, discharge, transfer 2 spill out, gush, stream, flow, rush *Opposite*: trickle 3 rain, drench, lash, sheet down, rain cats and dogs *(infml)* *Opposite*: drizzle 4 swarm, crowd, teem, stream, rush *Opposite*: trickle

pouring adj torrential, heavy, sheeting down, hammering, driving *Opposite*: light

pour out v reveal, blurt out, disclose, give away, tell

pour scorn on v disparage, ridicule, deride, sneer at, mock

pour with rain v pour down, teem, come down in torrents, rain cats and dogs *(infml)*, bucket *(infml)*

pout v 1 purse your lips, pucker, frown, scowl, glower *Opposite*: smile 2 sulk, mope, glower, scowl, grouch *(infml)* *Opposite*: smile

poverty n 1 neediness, destitution, hardship, deprivation, privation *Opposite*: affluence 2 lack, deficiency, scarcity, shortage, dearth *Opposite*: surplus

poverty-stricken adj destitute, in need, poor, penniless, impoverished *Opposite*: rich

powder n fine particles, dust, residue, precipitate, ash ■ v crush, grind, pound, pulverize, mill

powdered adj ground, crushed, pulverized, milled, processed *Opposite*: whole

powder keg n tinderbox, minefield, time bomb, recipe for disaster, explosive combination

powdery adj fine, crumbly, chalky, dusty, dry

power n 1 ability, capacity, faculty, potential, capability *Opposite*: inability 2 strength, force, might, energy, brawn *Opposite*: weakness 3 control, influence, authority, supremacy, rule *Opposite*: powerlessness 4 authority, right, prerogative, licence, privilege *Opposite*: powerlessness 5 nation, country, state, player, superpower

power base n stronghold, seat of power, headquarters, home base, base

powerful adj 1 influential, commanding, authoritative, controlling, prevailing *Opposite*: powerless 2 strong, mighty, brawny, muscular, sturdy *Opposite*: weak 3 effective, potent, strong, pungent, overwhelming *Opposite*: impotent 4 persuasive, compelling, forceful, effective, convincing *Opposite*: unimpressive

powerhouse *(infml)* n driving force, heart, centre, dynamo, live wire *(infml)*

powerless adj helpless, incapable, unable, weak, feeble *Opposite*: powerful

powerlessness n helplessness, hopelessness, weakness, feebleness, ineffectiveness

power line n electricity cable, overhead cable, cable, wire, overhead wire

power point n socket, point, electric socket, plug, hookup

practicability n feasibility, viability, workability, attainability, operability *Opposite*: impossibility

practicable adj feasible, realistic, possible, workable, attainable *Opposite*: impossible

practical adj 1 applied, real-world, hands-on, everyday, real *Opposite*: theoretical 2 useful, sensible, feasible, sound, workable 3 realistic, down-to-earth, level-headed, sensible, pragmatic *Opposite*: unrealistic 4 everyday, workaday, serviceable, functional, plain *Opposite*: decorative 5 handy, step-by-step, helpful, user-friendly, useful

practicality n 1 usefulness, sensibleness, feasibility, soundness, workability *Opposite*: uselessness 2 realism, common sense, level-headedness, pragmatism, sensibleness *Opposite*: impracticality

practical joke n trick, prank, joke, lark, hoax

practically adv 1 almost, nearly, virtually, just about, nigh on 2 realistically, sensibly, rationally, reasonably, level-headedly *Opposite*: unrealistically

practice n 1 repetition, rehearsal, exercise, preparation, training 2 habit, custom, tradition, way, system. *See* COMPARE AND CONTRAST *at* habit.

practise v 1 rehearse, prepare, exercise, go through, run through *Opposite*: perform 2 do, put into practice, live out, carry out, perform *Opposite*: reject

practised adj skilful, experienced, trained, expert, adept *Opposite*: untrained

practitioner n doctor, medical practitioner, general practitioner, GP, physician

pragmatic adj practical, realistic, logical, rational, reasonable *Opposite*: idealistic

pragmatism n practicality, realism, logicality, rationality, reasonableness *Opposite*: idealism

pragmatist n practical person, down-to-earth person, realist, doer, rationalist *Opposite*: idealist

prairie n plain, savanna, steppe, pampas

praise n 1 admiration, commendation, approval, acclaim, tribute *Opposite*: criticism 2 worship, honour, adoration, devotion, thanks *Opposite*: vilification ■ v 1 admire, commend, extol, compliment, honour *Opposite*: criticize 2 glorify, honour, laud, worship, adore *Opposite*: vilify

praiseworthy adj admirable, commendable, laudable, worthy, exemplary *Opposite*: blameworthy

pram n buggy, pushchair, perambulator *(fml)*, stroller *(US)*, baby carriage *(US)*

prance v 1 cavort, dance, frolic, gambol, caper 2 swagger, strut, parade, flounce, sashay

prang *(infml)* v crash, smash, write off, bump, bash *(infml)*

prank n trick, practical joke, hoax, joke, lark

prankster n trickster, joker, practical joker, mischief-maker, imp

prate v chatter, gibber, prattle, babble, jabber

prattle v prate, gibber, chatter, jabber, babble ■ n chatter, gibber, drivel, nonsense, jabber

pray v 1 meditate, contemplate, say your prayers, call upon, invoke 2 hope, wish, cross your fingers, hope against hope, yearn 3 request, plead, beg, crave, ask

prayer n 1 invocation, meditation, contemplation, devotions, chant 2 entreaty, appeal, plea, request, desire

preach v 1 give a sermon, speak, discourse, talk, deliver an address 2 advise, lecture, sermonize, moralize, advocate

preacher n minister, pastor, missionary, lay preacher, vicar

preamble n introduction, preface, foreword, prelude, overture Opposite: postscript

prearrange v organize, set up, arrange, plan, settle upon

prearranged adj planned, arranged, agreed, preset, specified Opposite: chance

precarious adj shaky, unstable, insecure, wobbly, unsteady Opposite: stable

precaution n protection, safety measure, preventive measure, insurance, safeguard

precautionary adj protective, defensive, safety, cautionary, preventive Opposite: remedial

precede v lead, come first, go before, pave the way, herald Opposite: follow

precedence n superiority, priority, preference, primacy, antecedence

precedent n example, model, guide, pattern, standard

preceding adj previous, earlier, prior, former, past Opposite: following

precept (fml) n principle, teaching, rule, guideline, instruction

precinct n district, zone, area, sector, quarter

precincts n grounds, confines, area, limits, boundaries

precious adj 1 valuable, costly, expensive, dear, treasurable Opposite: worthless 2 valued, loved, beloved, important, dear Opposite: despised 3 fastidious, affected, overrefined, fussy, self-conscious Opposite: natural

preciousness n 1 valuableness, value, costliness, expensiveness, dearness Opposite: worthlessness 2 fastidiousness, affectation, fussiness, self-consciousness, daintiness Opposite: naturalness

precious stone n gemstone, jewel, stone, gem, sparkler (infml)

precipice n rock face, cliff, crag, sheer drop, abyss

precipitate adj 1 rash, impulsive, impetuous, careless, reckless Opposite: considered 2 hurried, hasty, swift, quick, rapid Opposite: slow 3 abrupt, sudden, unexpected, surprising, unforeseen Opposite: expected ■ v hasten, bring on, cause, lead to, occasion Opposite: retard

precipitation n rain, rainfall, snow, sleet, hail

precipitous adj 1 rash, quick, hurried, swift, impulsive Opposite: careful 2 steep, sheer, abrupt, high, vertical Opposite: gentle

précis n summary, synopsis, résumé, abstract, sketch ■ v summarize, sum up, condense, outline, abridge Opposite: expand

precise adj 1 exact, detailed, accurate, specific, particular Opposite: vague 2 meticulous, scrupulous, particular, careful, fastidious Opposite: careless

precision n exactness, accuracy, exactitude, care, meticulousness Opposite: vagueness

preclude (fml) v prevent, impede, stop, rule out, exclude Opposite: permit

preclusion (fml) n prevention, exclusion, disqualification, prohibition, deterrence Opposite: permission

precocious adj advanced, developed, intelligent, bright, gifted Opposite: immature

precociousness see precocity

precocity n talent, cleverness, brightness, intelligence, precociousness Opposite: immaturity

precognition n clairvoyance, foreknowledge, premonition, foresight, second sight

preconceived adj fixed, set, defined, rigid, inflexible Opposite: unprejudiced

preconception n prejudice, bias, fixed idea, presumption, notion

precondition n condition, requirement, prerequisite, qualification, must

precook v parboil, soften, blanch

precursor n forerunner, ancestor, predecessor, antecedent, pioneer Opposite: successor

predate v precede, go before, antedate, exist before, pre-exist

predator n marauder, killer, hunter, pillager, raider

predatory adj greedy, destructive, rapacious, grasping, voracious

predecessor n precursor, forerunner, ancestor, antecedent, prototype Opposite: successor

predestination n destiny, fate, doom, kismet, lot Opposite: free will

predestine v destine, fate, preordain, doom, predetermine

predestined adj fated, destined, bound, preordained, appointed

predetermination n 1 prearrangement, arrangement, intention, decision, resolution 2 predestination, preordination, preordainment, lot, destiny Opposite: free will

predetermine v 1 set, programme, encode, determine, decide 2 predestine, destine, fate, preordain, doom

predetermined adj **1 prearranged**, programmed, encoded, fixed, determined **2 predestined**, destined, fated, bound,
preordained

predicament n **difficulty**, quandary, dilemma,
tight spot, tight corner

predicate (fml) v **base**, establish, found,
ground, build

predict v **forecast**, foresee, envisage, expect,
guess

predictability n **1 likelihood**, probability, sureness, certainty, liability Opposite: unpredictability **2 unoriginality**, banality, triteness,
obviousness, staleness Opposite: originality

predictable adj **1 foreseeable**, expectable,
expected, likely, probable Opposite: unlikely
2 unsurprising, unoriginal, banal, trite,
obvious Opposite: original

predictableness see **predictability**

predicted adj **foretold**, forecast, foreseen,
prophesied, projected Opposite: unforeseen

prediction n **forecast**, guess, calculation, estimate, prophecy

predictive adj **prognostic**, extrapolative,
prophetic, projecting, foretelling

predilection (fml) n **liking**, preference, fondness, partiality, penchant Opposite: dislike

predispose (fml) v **incline**, dispose, prompt,
influence, prejudice

predisposed (fml) adj **inclined**, disposed,
subject, liable, susceptible Opposite: unwilling

predisposition n **tendency**, disposition, inclination, penchant, bias

predominance n **1 superiority**, power, dominance, control, supremacy **2 majority**, prevalence, preponderance, numerousness Opposite: minority

predominant adj **main**, major, chief, principal,
prime Opposite: minor

predominantly adv **mainly**, mostly, largely,
chiefly, principally Opposite: partially

predominate v **prevail**, dominate, outweigh,
preponderate, be in the majority

pre-eminence n **superiority**, authority, excellence, eminence, renown Opposite: obscurity

pre-eminent adj **distinguished**, outstanding,
excellent, eminent, renowned Opposite:
obscure

pre-eminently adv **to a great extent**, in large
part, first and foremost, predominantly,
principally Opposite: partly

pre-empt v **forestall**, anticipate, obstruct,
block, prevent Opposite: react

pre-emption n **preemptive action**, preventive
action, preventive measures, prevention,
anticipation Opposite: reaction

pre-emptive adj **preventive**, preventative, proactive, anticipatory, blocking Opposite:
reactive

preen v **groom**, smarten, clean, tidy, smooth

pre-exist v **predate**, precede, antecede, go
before, prelude

pre-existing adj **previous**, prior, earlier,
former, established Opposite: new

prefabricate v **manufacture**, make up, assemble, produce, mass-produce

preface n **foreword**, preamble, introduction,
prologue, prelude Opposite: postscript ■
v **prefix**, precede, introduce, start, begin

prefect n **senior pupil**, monitor, captain, head
boy, head girl

prefer v **favour**, have a preference, like better,
wish, desire

preferable adj **better**, desirable, nicer, superior, choice Opposite: inferior

preference n **favourite**, first choice, partiality,
penchant, fondness Opposite: dislike

preferential adj **special**, favoured, privileged,
superior, better Opposite: disadvantageous

preferment (fml) n **promotion**, upgrading,
appointment, advancement, elevation Opposite: demotion

preferred adj **favoured**, favourite, chosen,
number one, in

prefigure v **anticipate**, herald, foreshadow,
portend, presage

prefix v **preface**, precede, begin, start, start off

pregnancy n **1 gestation**, antenatal period, prenatal period, perinatal period, gravidity
2 significance, importance, import, meaning

pregnant adj **1 expectant**, prenatal, gravid,
expecting (infml), in the club (infml) **2 charged**,
significant, weighty, meaningful, pointed

preheat v **heat**, heat up, warm, warm up, turn
on Opposite: cool

prehistoric adj **1 primeval**, primitive, antediluvian, early, ancient **2 old-fashioned**, out-
of-date, ancient, outmoded, antiquated
Opposite: modern

prehistory n **early history**, olden days, times
gone by, dawn of time, Stone Age

prejudge v **jump to conclusions**, presume, presuppose, anticipate, assume

prejudice n **1 bias**, preconception, pre-
judgment, predisposition, partiality Opposite: impartiality **2 bigotry**, chauvinism,
narrow-mindedness, discrimination, intolerance Opposite: tolerance ■ v **influence**, bias,
sway, slant, distort

prejudiced adj **biased**, intolerant, bigoted,
narrow-minded, discriminatory Opposite:
tolerant

prejudicial adj **harmful**, detrimental, hurtful,
damaging, injurious Opposite: helpful

prelate n **archbishop**, cardinal, bishop, abbot

preliminary n **initial**, first, opening, pilot,
introductory Opposite: closing ■ n **beginning**,
first round, introduction, opening, groundwork Opposite: finale

prelude *n* **introduction**, overture, prologue, preface, foreword *Opposite*: finale

premature *adj* **early**, untimely, hasty, rash, precipitate *Opposite*: overdue

premeditated *adj* **planned**, deliberate, intentional, calculated, thought-out *Opposite*: spontaneous

premeditation *n* **1 planning**, calculation, coldbloodedness, coldness, contemplation *Opposite*: impulsiveness **2 reflection**, contemplation, thought, consideration, cogitation *(fml)* *Opposite*: spontaneity

premier *adj* **best**, first, leading, foremost, highest *Opposite*: worst ■ *n* **prime minister**, PM, first minister, president, head of state

premiere *n* **opening**, first night, first performance, first showing, debut

premiership *n* **1 prime ministership**, presidency, leadership, term of office, tenure **2 premier league championship**, competition, sports tournament

premise *n* **1 evidence**, principle, idea, foundation, ground **2 proposition**, supposition, hypothesis, assertion, thesis

premises *n* **building**, grounds, location, site, property

premium *n* **payment**, percentage, bonus, reward, perk ■ *adj* **best**, top, finest, quality, first-class *Opposite*: low-grade

premonition *n* **1 intuition**, presentiment, feeling, hunch, fear **2 warning**, omen, sign, portent, indication

premonitory *adj* **1 intuitive**, predictive, clairvoyant, prophetic, precognitive **2 warning**, prognostic, precautionary, cautionary, sobering

preoccupation *n* **worry**, obsession, anxiety, concern, fixation

preoccupied *adj* **worried**, anxious, lost in thought, elsewhere, inattentive *Opposite*: carefree

preoccupy *v* **worry**, concern, disturb, trouble, consume

preordained *adj* **inevitable**, fated, predetermined, destined, doomed

preparation *n* **1 groundwork**, training, grounding, homework, research **2 planning**, provision, arrangement, formulation, organization

preparatory *adj* **introductory**, foundation, preliminary, elementary, opening *Opposite*: final

prepare *v* **1 get ready**, arrange, organize, plan, set up **2 train**, groom, coach, prime, make ready **3 make**, cook, get ready, concoct, formulate

prepared *adj* **ready**, set, equipped, geared up, organized

preparedness *n* **readiness**, preparation, alertness, attentiveness, awareness

prepare yourself *v* **steel yourself**, brace yourself, nerve yourself, compose yourself, get ready

prepayment *n* **advance payment**, down payment, payment, advance, deposit *Opposite*: debt

preponderance *(fml)* *n* **1 majority**, mass, great number, multitude, many *Opposite*: minority **2 dominance**, superiority, prevalence, predominance, weight

preponderant *adj* **greater**, more numerous, more powerful, more important, more significant *Opposite*: lesser

preponderantly *adv* **generally**, largely, in the main, by and large, for the most part

prepossessing *(fml)* *adj* **attractive**, pleasant, alluring, good-looking, nice-looking *Opposite*: unattractive

preposterous *adj* **outrageous**, absurd, ridiculous, ludicrous, unbelievable *Opposite*: sensible

preposterousness *n* **outrageousness**, absurdity, ridiculousness, ludicrousness, silliness *Opposite*: sensibleness

preproduction *n* **planning**, groundwork, organization, scheduling, planning stage

prepubescent *adj* **preadolescent**, preteen, preteenager, young, childish *Opposite*: adult ■ *n* **youngster**, preadolescent, preteenager, preteen, subteen *Opposite*: adult

prequel *n* **prelude**, prologue, spin-off *Opposite*: sequel

prerecord *v* **record**, tape, film, copy, video

prerequisite *n* **precondition**, requirement, condition, qualification, criterion

prerogative *n* **right**, privilege, due, entitlement, birthright

presage *n* **portent**, omen, sign, warning, signal ■ *v* **foretell**, foreshadow, portend, bode, augur

preschool *adj* **young**, toddler, infant, kindergarten, nursery

prescience *n* **foresight**, precognition, clairvoyance, prophecy, prediction *Opposite*: hindsight

prescient *adj* **prophetic**, psychic, clairvoyant, discerning, perceptive

prescribe *v* **1 recommend**, suggest, advise, propose, advocate **2 lay down**, stipulate, impose, order, set down

prescribed *adj* **set**, agreed, arranged, prearranged, given

prescript *(fml)* *n* **rule**, regulation, law, convention, canon

prescription *n* **medicine**, treatment, drug, preparation, remedy

prescriptive *adj* **narrow**, rigid, strict, unbending, inflexible *Opposite*: lax

prescriptiveness *n* **narrowness**, rigidity, strictness, inflexibility, dogmatism *Opposite*: laxity

presence *n* **1 attendance**, company, occurrence, incidence, existence *Opposite*: absence **2 dignity**, charisma, aura, authority, poise **3 ghost**, apparition, spirit, ghoul, manifestation

presence of mind *n* **nerve**, composure, level-headedness, common sense, sense

present *v* **1 give**, hand over, award, donate, offer *Opposite*: deny **2 show**, display, exhibit, put on view, reveal **3 cause**, represent, pose, raise, produce **4 portray**, represent, depict, cast, show **5 appear**, report, arrive, turn up, visit **6 put forward**, bring forward, introduce, announce, offer for consideration **7 exhibit**, mount, stage, put on view, organize ■ *n* **1 gift**, offering, grant, dowry, largesse **2 now**, here and now, present day, today, nowadays *Opposite*: past ■ *adj* **1 current**, contemporary, present-day, existing, extant *Opposite*: past **2 there**, here, in attendance, at hand, near *Opposite*: absent. *See* COMPARE AND CONTRAST *at* **give**.

presentable *adj* **1 respectable**, personable, fit to be seen, smart, well-dressed *Opposite*: scruffy **2 reasonable**, acceptable, satisfactory, good enough, passable *Opposite*: unsatisfactory

presentation *n* **1 performance**, exhibition, demonstration, appearance, arrangement **2 award**, donation, giving, offer, bestowal **3 talk**, lecture, seminar, speech, address

present day *n* **now**, here and now, present, today, nowadays *Opposite*: past

present-day *adj* **contemporary**, current, existing, present, modern *Opposite*: past

presenter *n* **announcer**, broadcaster, anchor, TV presenter, radio presenter

presentiment *n* **feeling**, intuition, foreboding, fear, sense

presently *adv* **1 soon**, shortly, in a short time, in a while, before long **2 currently**, at the moment, at present, right now, now

preservation *n* **1 protection**, conservation, safeguarding, defence, conservancy *Opposite*: destruction **2 maintenance**, continuation, perpetuation, keeping, upholding *Opposite*: abolition

preservative *adj* **preserving**, conserving, protective, antibacterial, antifungal *Opposite*: destructive ■ *n* **additive**, preserver, E number, stabilizer

preserved *adj* **1 conserved**, well-looked-after, well-maintained, well-preserved, well-kept-up *Opposite*: dilapidated **2 treated**, pickled, frozen, dried, salted *Opposite*: fresh

preserver *n* **protector**, guard, guardian, saviour, conserver *Opposite*: destroyer

preset *adj* **set**, predetermined, fixed, stipulated, specific

preside *v* **take the chair**, chair, control, supervise, head

presidency *n* **premiership**, leadership, term of office, tenure

president *n* **leader**, premier, head, head of state, chair

presidential *adj* **1 political**, constitutional, high-level, governmental, top-level **2 dignified**, authoritative, monarchic, judicious, regal

presidium *n* **executive committee**, committee, council, group, body

press *v* **1 push**, depress, force down, bear down on, compress *Opposite*: pull **2 iron**, smooth, steam, flatten, hot-press **3 pursue**, lobby, beg, entreat, enjoin **4 force**, urge, push, compel, oblige ■ *n* **1 journalists**, reporters, correspondents, newspapers, media **2 crowd**, horde, throng, mob, multitude

press conference *n* **news conference**, question and answer session, interview, conference, photo opportunity

pressed *adj* **busy**, pushed, hard-pressed, constrained, compelled

press for *v* **demand**, seek, urge, push for, campaign for

press-gang *v* **force**, coerce, bully, pressure, make

pressing *adj* **1 urgent**, important, serious, crucial, vital *Opposite*: unimportant **2 persistent**, insistent, unrelenting, unyielding, demanding *Opposite*: half-hearted

press officer *n* **spokesperson**, media spokesperson, press liaison officer, press agent

press on *v* **continue**, push on, forge ahead, keep going, carry on *Opposite*: give up

press release *n* **statement**, document, announcement, bulletin

press stud *n* **popper**, press fastener, fastening, fastener, stud

press together *v* **squeeze together**, force together, clamp, join together, close *Opposite*: pull apart

pressure *n* **1 force**, weight, heaviness, burden, compression **2 stress**, anxiety, weight, strain, tension ■ *v* **coerce**, force, bully, insist, compel

pressured *adj* **worried**, stressed, under pressure, overstretched, edgy *Opposite*: relaxed

pressurize *v* **force**, coerce, compel, make, bully

prestige *n* **status**, standing, stature, kudos, esteem *Opposite*: notoriety

prestigious *adj* **admired**, respected, significant, important, impressive *Opposite*: insignificant

presumably *adv* **most probably**, I assume, I imagine, in all probability, most likely

presume *v* **1 believe**, assume, guess, deduce, imagine *Opposite*: know **2 venture**, dare, be so bold, take the liberty, make free

presumption *n* **1 belief**, assumption, conjecture, supposition, presupposition **2 impertinence**, audacity, nerve, gall, impudence

presumptive *(fml) adj* **probable**, likely, plausible, convincing, reasonable *Opposite*: implausible

presumptuous *adj* **presuming**, audacious, rude, insolent, bold *Opposite*: modest

presumptuousness *n* **rudeness**, arrogance, impropriety, disrespect, inappropriateness *Opposite*: modesty

presuppose *v* **assume**, take for granted, take as read, take as fact, presume

presupposition *n* **assumption**, supposition, conjecture, belief, guess

prêt-à-porter *adj* **off-the-peg**, ready-made, ready-to-wear, mass-produced *Opposite*: made-to-measure

pretence *n* **1 trick**, con, sham, hoax, fabrication **2 claim**, suggestion, allegation, hint, supposition **3 make-believe**, fantasy, fancy, imagination, castles in the air *Opposite*: reality

pretend *v* **1 make believe**, imagine, fantasize, make up, play **2 feign**, put on, affect, profess, simulate ■ *adj* **imaginary**, make-believe, made-up, invented, false *Opposite*: real

pretender *n* **aspirant**, aspiring leader, candidate, opponent, claimant

pretend to be *v* **impersonate**, masquerade as, pose as, imitate, pass for

pretension *n* **affectation**, airs, posing, posturing, pretence *Opposite*: humility

pretentious *adj* **affected**, ostentatious, showy, exaggerated, pompous *Opposite*: down-to-earth

pretentiousness *see* **pretension**

pretext *n* **excuse**, cause, con, ploy, ruse

prettify *v* **smarten up**, do up, beautify, improve, adorn *Opposite*: mess up *(infml)*

prettiness *n* **good looks**, handsomeness, attractiveness, beauty, loveliness *Opposite*: ugliness

pretty *adj* **attractive**, beautiful, handsome, good-looking, appealing *Opposite*: unattractive ■ *adv* **rather**, fairly, reasonably, quite, moderately. *See* COMPARE AND CONTRAST *at* **good-looking**.

prevail *v* **1 triumph**, win through, succeed, be victorious, overcome *Opposite*: fail **2** *(fml)* **exist**, reign, be happening, occur, predominate

prevailing *adj* **1 current**, existing, customary, established, popular **2 usual**, main, dominant, predominant, principal *Opposite*: underlying

prevail on *v* **persuade**, convince, cajole, sway, coax into

prevalence *n* **occurrence**, commonness, pervasiveness, incidence, frequency

prevalent *adj* **common**, dominant, predominant, widespread, rampant *Opposite*: rare. *See* COMPARE AND CONTRAST *at* **widespread**.

prevaricate *v* **hedge**, evade, lie, quibble, stall *Opposite*: call a spade a spade

prevarication *n* **evasiveness**, evasion, equivocation, avoidance, hedging *Opposite*: forthrightness

prevent *v* **stop**, avert, avoid, foil, thwart *Opposite*: encourage

preventable *adj* **avoidable**, needless, unnecessary, avertible, escapable *Opposite*: inevitable

prevention *n* **1 avoidance**, deterrence, stoppage, inhibition, hindrance *Opposite*: promotion **2 obstacle**, hindrance, impediment, inhibition, restraint

preventive *adj* **anticipatory**, pre-emptive, defensive, prophylactic, deterrent ■ *n* **protection**, defence, anticipatory measure, pre-emptive measure, deterrent

preview *n* **1 showing**, performance, broadcast, screening, opening **2 trailer**, clip, foretaste, extract, coming attraction ■ *v* **1 show**, perform, broadcast, screen, promote **2 review**, describe, introduce, advertise, trail

previous *adj* **preceding**, earlier, prior, former, past *Opposite*: subsequent

prey *n* **quarry**, victim, target, kill, game *Opposite*: hunter

prey on *v* **1 live on**, live off, feed on, hunt, kill **2 worry**, preoccupy, bother, haunt, oppress **3 take advantage of**, exploit, victimize, intimidate, bully

price *n* **1 cost**, worth, fee, face value, amount **2 penalty**, cost, punishment, consequences, fine ■ *v* **set a price**, assess, estimate, rate, evaluate

priceless *adj* **1 invaluable**, inestimable, beyond price, incalculable, costly *Opposite*: worthless **2** *(infml)* **hilarious**, funny, comic, amusing, entertaining

pricey *(infml) adj* **costly**, expensive, dear, high-priced, exorbitant *Opposite*: cheap

prick *v* **pierce**, stab, puncture, perforate, jab ■ *n* **hole**, puncture, perforation, pinhole

prickle *n* **1 spike**, spine, barb, thorn, quill **2 itch**, tickle, sting, irritation, tingling ■ *v* **sting**, itch, tickle, prick, irritate

prickling *n* **scratchiness**, pricking, itchiness, itching, prickle

prickly *adj* **1 spiny**, thorny, barbed, bristly, spiky *Opposite*: smooth **2 itchy**, tickly, scratchy, stinging, tingling **3** *(infml)* **sensitive**, snappy, irritable, grumpy, snappish *Opposite*: impervious

pride *n* **1 arrogance**, conceit, smugness, superiority, self-importance *Opposite*: humility **2 satisfaction**, delight, gratification, enjoyment, joy **3 self-respect**, dignity, self-esteem, honour

pride and joy *n* **most prized possession**, the apple of your eye, treasure, pride, showpiece

pride yourself on *v* **be proud of**, take satisfaction in, revel in, take pride in, glory in

priest *n* **minister**, pastor, vicar, rector, presbyter

priesthood *n* **clergy**, ministry, cloth *Opposite*: laity

prim *adj* **1 prudish**, prissy, strait-laced, puritanical, moralistic *Opposite*: broad-minded **2 formal**, proper, dignified, starchy, stiff *Opposite*: informal **3 tidy**, orderly, precise, meticulous, fussy *Opposite*: messy

primacy *n* **pre-eminence**, importance, predominance, dominance, prevalence

primal *adj* **primitive**, primeval, aboriginal, primordial, prehistoric *Opposite*: new

primarily *adv* **first and foremost**, above all, chiefly, mainly, principally

primary *adj* **1 first**, initial, top, leading, foremost *Opposite*: last **2 main**, chief, most important, key, prime *Opposite*: secondary **3 basic**, core, central, fundamental, essential *Opposite*: minor

primate *n* **1 ape**, monkey, hominid, human **2 archbishop**, bishop, prelate, cardinal

WORD BANK
❑ types of primate aye-aye, baboon, Barbary ape, bonnet monkey, capuchin, chimp, chimpanzee, colobus, gibbon, gorilla, lemur, macaque, mandrill, marmoset, orang-utan, proboscis monkey, rhesus monkey, spider monkey

prime *adj* **1 top**, superior, superlative, best, premier *Opposite*: inferior **2 major**, main, key, chief, leading ■ *n* **peak**, zenith, heyday, summit, high point *Opposite*: nadir ■ *v* **1 prepare**, ready, get ready, make ready **2 brief**, fill in, instruct, give somebody the lowdown *(infml)*

primed *adj* **1 prepared**, ready, set, in position, poised **2 aware**, well-informed, geared up, informed, in the picture *Opposite*: unprepared

prime minister *n* **premier**, chief minister, head of cabinet, PM, head of government

primer *n* **textbook**, reader, grammar, introduction, how-to *(infml)*

primeval *adj* **1 prehistoric**, original, ancient, archaic *Opposite*: modern **2 primitive**, primordial, primal, basic, instinctive *Opposite*: considered

primitive *adj* **1 embryonic**, primeval, original, aboriginal, nascent *Opposite*: developed **2 simple**, basic, uncomplicated, unsophisticated, crude *Opposite*: sophisticated **3 prehistoric**, ancient, primordial, primal, archaic *Opposite*: modern

primitiveness *n* **1 antiquity**, ancientness, primitive stage, early stage, primeval stage **2 crudeness**, simplicity, roughness, coarseness, unsophisticatedness *Opposite*: sophistication

primness *n* **1 prudishness**, narrowness, shockability, oversensitivity, strait-lacedness *Opposite*: broad-mindedness **2 formality**, properness, starchiness, propriety, stiffness *Opposite*: informality **3 neatness**, tidiness, orderliness, fastidiousness, meticulousness *Opposite*: messiness

primordial *adj* **1 primeval**, prehistoric, primal, ancient, primitive **2 embryonic**, developing, early, nascent

primp *v* **fuss**, fuss over, groom, preen, adorn

prince *n* **leader**, leading figure, leading light, doyen, big shot *(infml)*

princely *adj* **generous**, handsome, large, significant, huge *Opposite*: measly *(infml)*

principal *adj* **main**, major, chief, most important, primary ■ *n* **1 head of school**, headmaster, headmistress, dean, provost **2 leader**, chief, doyenne, doyen, head *Opposite*: follower

principality *n* **princedom**, territory, country, domain

principally *adv* **mainly**, chiefly, above all, first and foremost, primarily

principle *n* **1 rule**, theory, notion, concept, tenet **2 code**, standard, belief, attitude, value **3 source**, wellspring, origin, cause, basis

principled *adj* **honourable**, righteous, upright, ethical, just *Opposite*: unethical

print *n* **1 pattern**, design, motif **2 reproduction**, copy, lithograph, photograph, photocopy ■ *v* **1 turn out**, produce, make, issue, run off **2 publish**, carry, make known, advertise, broadcast **3 stamp**, imprint, engrave, emboss

printed *adj* **in print**, in black and white, on paper, published, reproduced

printing *n* **1 production**, reproduction, lithography, offset lithography, letterpress **2 text**, lettering, words, writing, wording **3 lettering**, capitals, upper case, lower case, block lettering *Opposite*: script **4 edition**, print run, impression

prior *adj* **previous**, preceding, past, erstwhile, former *Opposite*: subsequent

prioritization *n* **ordering**, ranking, arranging, arrangement, listing

prioritize *v* **1 order**, rank, arrange, list, line up **2 concentrate on**, give precedence to, select, highlight, rank first

priority *n* **importance**, precedence, urgency, import, significance

prior to *prep* **before**, previous to, earlier than, preceding, in advance of *Opposite*: after

priory *n* **monastery**, convent, religious community, abbey, ashram

prise *v* **1 lever**, open, force, work loose, work free **2 extract**, drag out, wheedle, coax, cajole

prison *n* **1 jail**, detention centre, young offenders' institution, secure unit, house of correction **2 imprisonment**, confinement, solitary confinement, detention, custody

prisoner *n* **1 detainee**, inmate, convict, political prisoner, prisoner of war **2 captive**, hostage, kidnap victim

prissiness *n* **primness**, prudishness, properness, starchiness, stiffness *Opposite*: informality

prissy *adj* **prim**, prudish, proper, starchy, stiff *Opposite*: informal

pristine *adj* **1 immaculate**, perfect, faultless, spotless, pure *Opposite*: soiled **2 unspoiled**, untouched, primeval, original, virgin *Opposite*: developed

privacy *n* **1 solitude**, time alone, space, seclusion, isolation *Opposite*: company **2 confidentiality**, discretion, secrecy, concealment *Opposite*: disclosure

private *adj* **1 confidential**, secret, concealed, undisclosed, classified *Opposite*: public **2 secluded**, set apart, isolated, remote, cloistered **3 privileged**, restricted, reserved, exclusive, not in the public domain *Opposite*: public **4 secretive**, reserved, reticent, tight-lipped, self-contained *Opposite*: forthcoming

private detective *n* private investigator, private eye *(infml)*, sleuth *(infml)*, PI *(US)*

private eye *(infml) see* private detective

private investigator *see* private detective

privately *adv* **confidentially**, in confidence, in private, secretly, in secret *Opposite*: publicly

privation *n* **hardship**, deprivation, adversity, poverty, need

privatization *n* **sale**, transfer, denationalization

privatize *v* **sell**, transfer, denationalize, go public *Opposite*: nationalize

privilege *n* **1 freedom**, licence, opportunity, dispensation, advantage **2 honour**, source of pride, treat, pleasure, joy ■ *v* **favour**, show partiality towards, benefit *Opposite*: persecute

privileged *adj* **1 advantaged**, lucky, fortunate, honoured *Opposite*: disadvantaged **2 confidential**, private, restricted, controlled, limited *Opposite*: public

privy *adj* **in the know**, sharing in, aware of, party to, partaking of ■ *n (infml)* **outside toilet**, outside lavatory, outside loo, latrine, garderobe

prize *n* **award**, reward, trophy, medal, accolade ■ *v* **treasure**, cherish, value, respect, esteem

prized *adj* **award-winning**, high-quality, valued, respected, esteemed

prizewinning *adj* **award-winning**, victorious, successful, triumphant, winning *Opposite*: unsuccessful

pro *prep* **for**, in favour of, all for, in support of *Opposite*: against ■ *n* **professional**, authority, expert, specialist, ace *(infml) Opposite*: amateur

proactive *adj* **practical**, taking the initiative, hands-on, active, down to business *Opposite*: passive

probability *n* **likelihood**, prospect, odds, possibility, chance *Opposite*: improbability

probable *adj* **likely**, credible, possible, feasible, plausible *Opposite*: unlikely

probate *n* **certification**, validation, confirmation, validity

probation *n* **trial**, test, audition, experimentation, tryout

probationary *adj* **provisional**, trial, test, experimental, sample *Opposite*: permanent

probe *n* **investigation**, inquiry, review, examination, analysis ■ *v* **investigate**, research, delve, inquire, look into

probing *adj* **searching**, penetrating, analytical, inquisitive, curious *Opposite*: cursory

probity *n* **correctness**, scrupulousness, rectitude, righteousness, integrity *Opposite*: immorality

problem *n* **1 difficulty**, setback, hitch, drawback, glitch *Opposite*: boost **2 puzzle**, poser, riddle, conundrum, challenge *Opposite*: solution ■ *adj* **problematic**, tricky, unruly, badly-behaved, delinquent *Opposite*: easy

COMPARE AND CONTRAST CORE MEANING: something difficult to solve or understand

problem a difficult situation, matter, or person; **mystery** an event or situation that has never been fully explained or understood, or a person who is puzzling or mysterious; **puzzle** a problem whose solution requires ingenuity, or a situation that it is difficult to resolve, or somebody whose behaviour or motives are difficult to understand; **riddle** a perplexing or confusing issue; **conundrum** something puzzling, confusing, or mysterious; **enigma** somebody or something that is mysterious and hard to understand.

problematic *adj* **tricky**, challenging, sticky, awkward, knotty *Opposite*: easy

problematical *see* problematic

proboscis *n* **nose**, snout, feeler, trunk, antenna

procedural *adj* **technical**, practical, bureaucratic, routine, ritual

procedure *n* **process**, modus operandi, way, technique, method

proceed *v* **go on**, carry on, continue, ensue, advance *Opposite*: recede

proceedings *n* **1 events**, actions, measures, trial, procedures **2 minutes**, record, account, report, chronicle

proceeds *n* **profits**, income, earnings, takings, gate

process *n* **procedure**, course, activity, development, progression ■ *v* **deal with**, handle, treat, sort out, administer

procession *n* **1 march**, parade, pageant, march-past, motorcade **2 sequence**, succession, string, series, line

processional *adj* **ceremonial**, ritual, commemorative, celebratory, sacred

proclaim *v* **state publicly**, announce, declare, state, make known

proclamation *n* **public statement**, announcement, declaration, decree, assertion

proclivity n **liking**, appetite, taste, penchant, inclination

procrastinate v **put off**, delay, postpone, adjourn, dally *Opposite*: make a start

procrastination n **deferment**, putting off, postponement, stalling, delay *Opposite*: action

procure v **obtain**, acquire, secure, get hold of, get. *See* COMPARE AND CONTRAST *at* **get**.

procurement n 1 **gaining**, obtaining, finding, locating, tracking down *Opposite*: giving up 2 **buying**, purchasing, ordering, obtaining *Opposite*: selling

procurer n **buyer**, purchaser, customer, client, consumer

prod v 1 **elbow**, nudge, dig, jab, push 2 **urge**, stimulate, stir, prompt, provoke ■ n **nudge**, elbow, dig, jab, push

prodigal adj **wasteful**, reckless, dissolute, profligate, uncontrolled *Opposite*: cautious

prodigious adj 1 **huge**, vast, copious, giant, gigantic *Opposite*: small 2 **abnormal**, extraordinary, phenomenal, unusual, exceptional *Opposite*: average

prodigy n **genius**, sensation, phenomenon, wonder, star

produce v 1 **create**, make, manufacture, construct, fabricate 2 **give**, give off, yield, churn out, be the source of ■ n **crop**, foodstuffs, harvest, products, goods

producer n **creator**, manufacturer, maker, fabricator

product n 1 **manufactured article**, commodity, artefact 2 **output**, merchandise, goods, wares 3 **result**, outcome, upshot, consequence, effect *Opposite*: cause 4 **creation**, invention, achievement, work

production n **manufacture**, making, construction, creation, invention

productive adj 1 **creative**, prolific, fecund, industrious, fruitful *Opposite*: destructive 2 **useful**, helpful, constructive, beneficial, valuable *Opposite*: negative

productiveness n **usefulness**, constructiveness, use, utility, fruitfulness

productivity n **output**, efficiency, yield, production, throughput

profane adj **blasphemous**, irreverent, irreligious, disrespectful, wicked *Opposite*: sacred

profanity n **blasphemy**, oath, vulgarity, curse, swearword

profess v 1 **declare**, announce, state, affirm, proclaim 2 **claim**, maintain, make out, feign 3 **admit**, own up, confess, acknowledge, agree

professed adj 1 **declared**, acknowledged, open, stated, blatant *Opposite*: unspoken 2 **supposed**, alleged, so-called, ostensible, seeming *Opposite*: proven

profession n **job**, work, occupation, line of work, career

professional adj **specialized**, qualified, proficient, skilled, trained *Opposite*: amateur ■ n **specialist**, expert, authority, pro, maven (US) *Opposite*: amateur

professionalism n **skill**, competence, expertise, proficiency, efficiency *Opposite*: incompetence

professor n **university teacher**, lecturer, fellow, don, tutor

professorial adj **academic**, pedagogical, intellectual, educational, senior

proffer v **offer**, hold out, extend, tender, volunteer *Opposite*: withdraw

proficiency n **skill**, ability, talent, expertise, aptitude *Opposite*: incompetence

proficient adj **capable**, talented, expert, gifted, adroit *Opposite*: incompetent

profile n 1 **outline**, side view, shape, silhouette, contour 2 **summary**, sketch, outline, report, précis ■ v **summarize**, sum up, sketch, outline, report

profit n 1 **income**, earnings, revenue, proceeds, turnover *Opposite*: loss 2 **advantage**, gain, benefit, use, reward *Opposite*: loss ■ v 1 **earn**, bring in, make, make money on, turn a profit *Opposite*: lose 2 **benefit**, gain, be of advantage to, help, aid

profitability n 1 **success**, effectiveness, productivity, viability, cost-effectiveness 2 **usefulness**, worth, fruitfulness, use, value *Opposite*: uselessness

profitable adj 1 **lucrative**, moneymaking, gainful, commercial, cost-effective *Opposite*: unprofitable 2 **advantageous**, beneficial, rewarding, useful, valuable *Opposite*: unhelpful

profiteer v **exploit**, take advantage of, make use of, racketeer, abuse ■ n **swindler**, racketeer, embezzler, crook (infml), con man (slang)

profitmaking adj **profitable**, viable, moneymaking, economic, cost-effective *Opposite*: draining

profligacy n **wastefulness**, recklessness, dissolution, decadence, extravagance *Opposite*: parsimony

profligate adj 1 **wasteful**, reckless, spendthrift, squandering, decadent *Opposite*: parsimonious 2 **dissolute**, licentious, immoral, wicked, shameless

profound adj 1 **deep**, thoughtful, reflective, philosophical, weighty *Opposite*: superficial 2 **intense**, great, overpowering, overwhelming, extreme *Opposite*: shallow

profoundly adv **intensely**, greatly, extremely, strongly, very much

profoundness see profundity

profundity n 1 **understanding**, perceptiveness, wisdom, acuity, perspicacity *Opposite*: superficiality 2 **complexity**, abstruseness, difficulty, depth, intricacy *Opposite*: simplicity 3 **intensity**, greatness, strength, seriousness, enormity *Opposite*: mildness 4 **depth**, immensity, fathomlessness, extent, reach

profuse adj **plentiful**, copious, abundant, teeming, generous Opposite: scanty

profusion n **abundance**, large amount, excess, cornucopia, plethora Opposite: dearth

progenitor n 1 **ancestor**, forebear Opposite: descendant 2 **antecedent**, originator, forerunner, prototype, predecessor Opposite: copy

progeny n **offspring**, children, young, descendants, issue

prognosis n **forecast**, prediction, projection, scenario, diagnosis

prognosticate v 1 **predict**, divine, foresee, foretell, forecast Opposite: recall 2 **indicate**, suggest, point to, augur, signify Opposite: prove

prognostication n 1 **prediction**, prognosis, projection, divination, foreseeing Opposite: recollection 2 **indication**, suggestion, pointer, token, portent Opposite: proof

prognosticator n **predictor**, diviner, prophet, seer, clairvoyant

program n **setting**, option, cycle, mode, instruction ■ v **write instructions**, load instructions, write software, load software, set

programme n 1 **plan**, agenda, schedule, timetable, list 2 **broadcast**, production, show, transmission, game show 3 **brochure**, booklet, synopsis, listing, timetable 4 **system**, procedure, course, series, setup ■ v 1 **schedule**, arrange, lay on, book, plan 2 **train**, condition, compel, brainwash, hypnotize

programmed adj **automatic**, involuntary, planned, automated, set Opposite: spontaneous

programmer n **computer operator**, computer programmer, computer scientist, program writer, systems analyst

programming n **software design**, program design, user interface design, program writing, software development

progress n **development**, improvement, advancement, evolution, growth Opposite: regression ■ v 1 **improve**, develop, advance, evolve, increase Opposite: regress 2 **move forward**, advance, proceed, continue, make progress Opposite: retreat

progression n 1 **development**, evolution, movement, advance, advancement Opposite: regression 2 **series**, sequence, succession, string, chain

progressive adj 1 **gradual**, ongoing, increasing, continuing, developing Opposite: sudden 2 **liberal**, reformist, open-minded, broad-minded, radical Opposite: reactionary

progressively adv **increasingly**, more and more, with time, gradually, little by little Opposite: suddenly

progressiveness n **liberalism**, reformism, progressivism, modernism, tolerance

progressivism n **liberalism**, reformism, modernism, radicalism, leftism

prohibit v **forbid**, ban, proscribe, disallow, veto Opposite: permit

prohibited adj **forbidden**, banned, verboten, illegal, proscribed Opposite: permitted

prohibition n **ban**, exclusion, embargo, prevention, veto Opposite: permission

prohibitive adj **high-priced**, excessive, exorbitant, extortionate, unaffordable Opposite: affordable

project n **assignment**, task, undertaking, job, plan ■ v 1 **forecast**, predict, estimate, foresee, foretell 2 **stick out**, jut out, protrude, bulge, distend 3 **throw**, launch, shoot, propel, cast 4 **plan**, envisage, propose, intend, anticipate

projected adj **estimated**, planned, proposed, outlined, expected Opposite: actual

projection n 1 **forecast**, prediction, plan, prognosis, estimate Opposite: outcome 2 **outcrop**, protuberance, bulge, protrusion, ledge

proletarian adj **popular**, grassroots, people's, working-class, blue-collar Opposite: aristocratic

proletariat n **hoi polloi**, rank and file, grassroots, working class, workers Opposite: gentry

proliferate v 1 **multiply**, thrive, flourish, boom, increase Opposite: dwindle 2 **reproduce**, propagate, multiply, breed, procreate Opposite: die out

proliferation n **propagation**, explosion, spread, multiplying, production

prolific adj 1 **productive**, creative, fertile, inexhaustible, high-volume Opposite: unproductive 2 (fml) **abundant**, abounding, plentiful, copious, profuse Opposite: scarce

prolix adj **wordy**, verbose, long-winded, flowery, protracted Opposite: concise. See COMPARE AND CONTRAST at wordy.

prologue n **introduction**, preface, foreword, preamble, opening Opposite: epilogue

prolong v **extend**, lengthen, protract, draw out, spin out Opposite: curtail

prolongation n **continuation**, perpetuation, drawing out, protraction, extension Opposite: curtailment

prolonged adj **lengthy**, protracted, long, continued, extended Opposite: curtailed

prom (infml) n **promenade**, seafront, walkway, path, esplanade

promenade n 1 **walkway**, seafront, path, boardwalk, esplanade 2 (fml) **stroll**, walk, saunter, amble, constitutional ■ v (fml) **walk**, stroll, amble, saunter, wander

prominence n 1 **fame**, importance, distinction, celebrity, eminence Opposite: obscurity 2 **bump**, lump, bulge, swelling, protrusion Opposite: crater

prominent adj 1 **protuberant**, protruding, pro-

jecting, bulbous, bulging *Opposite*: flat
2 noticeable, conspicuous, obvious, blatant,
flagrant *Opposite*: subtle **3 famous**, well-
known, important, high-flying, top *Opposite*: obscure

promiscuous *adj* **immoral**, loose, licentious,
wanton, uninhibited

promise *v* **1 assure**, swear, vow, undertake,
guarantee **2 suggest**, augur, bode, look like,
show all the signs ■ *n* **1 assurance**, undertaking, guarantee, contract, word *Opposite*:
threat **2 potential**, possibilities, aptitude,
ability, capacity

promising *adj* **1 talented**, gifted, capable, able
2 auspicious, hopeful, likely, encouraging,
favourable *Opposite*: disappointing

promisingly *adv* **favourably**, auspiciously,
hopefully, well, nicely *Opposite*: dis-
appointingly

promo *(infml) n* **promotion**, advertisement, publicity stunt, publicity, profile-raiser

promontory *n* **cape**, headland, peninsula,
outcrop, point

promote *v* **1 advance**, upgrade, further,
elevate, put forward *Opposite*: demote
2 endorse, encourage, help, support, stimulate *Opposite*: suppress **3 advertise**, publicize, make known, market, tout *Opposite*:
defame **4 further**, progress, move forward,
develop, encourage *Opposite*: hinder
5 stage, put on, organize, arrange

promoter *n* **organizer**, agent, sponsor, advocate, supporter

promotion *n* **1 upgrade**, advancement, elevation, rise, preferment *(fml) Opposite*:
demotion **2 advertising**, marketing, publicity,
publicity campaign, public relations
3 endorsement, encouragement, help,
support, stimulation **4 offer**, special promotion, deal, loss leader

promotional *adj* **publicity**, advertising, public
relations, PR, positive

prompt *adj* **1 quick**, rapid, swift, without delay,
speedy *Opposite*: slow **2 punctual**, on time,
at the appointed time, without delay, timely
Opposite: late ■ *v* **1 stimulate**, encourage,
provoke, incite, urge *Opposite*: prevent
2 bring about, induce, occasion, set off,
trigger *Opposite*: prevent ■ *n* **stimulus**, prod,
goad, reminder, aide-mémoire *(fml)*

prompting *n* **encouragement**, warning, pressure, motivation, instigation

promptness *n* **1 speed**, rapidity, swiftness,
alacrity, velocity *Opposite*: slowness **2 punctuality**, timeliness, timekeeping *Opposite*:
tardiness

promulgate *(fml) v* **1 declare**, proclaim, decree,
announce, pronounce *Opposite*: withdraw
2 publicize, spread, disseminate, circulate,
transmit *Opposite*: suppress

promulgation *(fml) n* **1 declaration**, proclamation, decree, announcement, pronouncement *Opposite*: withdrawal

2 publicizing, spreading, dissemination, circulation, broadcasting *Opposite*: suppression

prone *adj* **1 disposed**, predisposed, liable,
inclined, likely **2 flat**, horizontal, flat out,
face down, motionless *Opposite*: upright

prong *n* **point**, spike, spine, tine

pronounce *v* **1 say**, speak, utter, articulate,
voice **2 state**, assert, declare, announce,
decree

pronounced *adj* **marked**, noticeable, distinct,
definite, obvious *Opposite*: subtle

pronouncement *n* **statement**, assertion, declaration, announcement, decree

pronto *(infml) adv* **straightaway**, right away,
quick, quickly, at once *Opposite*: sluggishly

pronunciation *n* **articulation**, accent, elocution,
intonation, enunciation

proof *n* **evidence**, testimony, verification, confirmation, attestation ■ *adj* **resistant**, resilient, impervious, immune *Opposite*:
vulnerable

proofread *v* **check**, correct, check through,
check over, look through

proofreader *n* **checker**, reader, editor, copy
editor, corrector

prop *n* **support**, leg, crutch, buttress, pile ■
v **hold up**, support, prop up, sustain, buttress
Opposite: destabilize

propaganda *n* **1 publicity**, advertising, marketing, literature, information **2 misinformation**, disinformation, party line, half-
truths, cant

propagandist *n* **1 publicist**, polemicist, essayist, writer, speaker **2 partisan**, apologist,
mouthpiece, sophist, spin doctor *(slang)* ■
adj **slanted**, distorted, one-sided, polemical,
partisan

propagate *v* **1 breed**, grow, raise, reproduce,
proliferate **2 spread**, broadcast, proliferate,
circulate, disseminate

propagation *n* **1 breeding**, reproduction, proliferation, procreation **2 spread**, circulation,
dissemination, transmission, proliferation

propagator *n* **1 spreader**, broadcaster, trans-
mitter, communicator, diffuser **2 tray**, box,
seed tray, cloche, cold frame

propel *v* **push**, drive, force, boost, thrust

propensity *n* **tendency**, inclination, partiality,
bent, proclivity

proper *adj* **1 good**, correct, appropriate, suitable, right *Opposite*: wrong **2 polite**, modest,
decorous, prim, genteel *Opposite*: improper
3 own, personal, characteristic, identifiable,
individual

properly *adv* **correctly**, right, appropriately, as
it should be, by the book *Opposite*: incorrectly

propertied *adj* **property-owning**, land-owning,
landed, affluent, moneyed *Opposite*: dispossessed

property n **1 possessions**, belongings, goods, assets, material goods **2 land**, home, house, estate, acreage

property owner n **proprietor**, owner, landowner, homeowner, property holder *Opposite*: tenant

prophecy n **prediction**, forecast, divination, foretelling, insight

prophesy v **predict**, forecast, divine, foretell, see the future

prophet n **clairvoyant**, forecaster, fortune teller, seer, prescient

prophetic adj **visionary**, farsighted, predictive, foretelling, forewarning

propinquity (fml) n **nearness**, closeness, proximity, convenience, relationship *Opposite*: remoteness

propitiate v **appease**, placate, mollify, pacify, soothe *Opposite*: provoke (infml)

propitiation (fml) n **placation**, appeasement, mollification, pacification, soothing *Opposite*: provocation

propitiatory adj **placatory**, conciliatory, soothing, mollifying, calming *Opposite*: provocative

proponent n **advocate**, supporter, exponent, protagonist, follower *Opposite*: opponent

proportion n **1 amount**, quantity, part, share, percentage **2 ratio**, comparison, relative amount, relationship

proportional adj **relative**, comparative, relational, related, proportionate

proportionate adj **balanced**, proportional, comparable, equal, equivalent

proposal n **suggestion**, offer, application, tender, bid

propose v **1 suggest**, offer, recommend, proposition, advise **2 intend**, plan, have in mind, aim, mean

proposer n **nominator**, supporter, sponsor, advocate, advocator

proposition n **proposal**, plan, scheme, intention, suggestion

propound v **put forward**, advocate, submit, set out, offer

proprietary adj **1 branded**, exclusive, patented, registered, trademarked *Opposite*: generic **2 private**, privately owned, privately run, privately operated, commercial **3 protective**, jealous, territorial, possessive, suspicious

proprietor n **owner**, manager, administrator, landowner, property owner

proprietorial adj **possessive**, protective, jealous, suspicious, territorial

propriety n **1 politeness**, decorum, modesty, good manners, respectability *Opposite*: impropriety **2 correctness**, aptness, appropriateness, decency, suitability *Opposite*: impropriety

propulsion n **force**, forward motion, thrust, impulsion, momentum

prop up v **hold up**, support, prop, sustain, buttress *Opposite*: destabilize

prosaic adj **1 straightforward**, matter-of-fact, simple, plain, ordinary **2 banal**, mundane, everyday, dull, humdrum *Opposite*: extraordinary

proscribe v **ban**, bar, forbid, exclude, veto *Opposite*: permit

proscribed adj **prohibited**, banned, forbidden, verboten, inadmissible *Opposite*: permissible

proscription (fml) n **prohibition**, banning, exclusion, forbidding, interdiction

prose n **writing style**, style, text *Opposite*: poetry

prosecute v **put on trial**, impeach, arraign, indict, take legal action

prosecution n **trial**, action, suit, case, examination

proselytization n **preaching**, evangelization, agitation, propagandizing, campaigning

proselytize v **1 preach**, evangelize, spread the word, make somebody see the light, convert **2 persuade**, cajole, lecture, bend somebody's ear, talk into

proselytizer n **preacher**, evangelist, missionary, zealot, agitator

prospect n **1 view**, scene, vision, outlook, panorama **2 hope**, possibility, expectation, outlook, likelihood ■ v **search**, mine, dig, seek, pan

prospective adj **potential**, future, forthcoming, likely, probable

prospectus n **brochure**, list, document, booklet, leaflet

prosper v **1 flourish**, thrive, do well, get on, grow *Opposite*: decline **2 succeed**, make money, show a profit, be in the black

prosperity n **wealth**, affluence, opulence, riches, success *Opposite*: poverty

prosperous adj **1 wealthy**, affluent, rich, well-off, well-to-do *Opposite*: poor **2 flourishing**, thriving, successful, booming *Opposite*: failing

prostrate adj **1 flat**, face down, horizontal, level, prone *Opposite*: upright **2 drained**, exhausted, desperate, powerless, at a low ebb

prostrate yourself v **bow**, genuflect, bend low, humble yourself, grovel

prostration n **1 bowing**, kneeling, falling down, worship, adoration **2 incapacitation**, breakdown, exhaustion, helplessness, weakness *Opposite*: robustness

protagonist n **character**, hero, central character, leading role, good guy (US infml)

protean adj **variable**, changeable, mutable, adjustable, fluctuating *Opposite*: constant

protect v **defend**, guard, keep, safeguard, look after *Opposite*: neglect. *See* COMPARE AND CONTRAST *at* **safeguard**.

protected *adj* **1 endangered**, threatened, nearing extinction, dwindling *Opposite*: thriving **2 sheltered**, safe, secure, safeguarded, shielded *Opposite*: exposed **3 locked**, tamper-proof, inaccessible, sealed, impenetrable *Opposite*: open

protection *n* **1 safeguard**, defence, guard, fortification, shield **2 security**, safety, defence, asylum, sanctuary *Opposite*: exposure

protectionism *n* **isolationism**, protection, tariff barriers, trade barriers

protectionist *n* **isolationist**, nationalist, patriot, xenophobe ■ *adj* **protective**, isolationist, nationalist, preferential, xenophobic

protective *adj* **defensive**, caring, shielding, protecting, defending

protective covering *n* **shell**, armour, cladding, shield

protectiveness *n* **1 safety**, security, secureness, strength, robustness **2 solicitousness**, jealousy, possessiveness, suspicion **3 protectionism**, isolationism, protection, tariff barriers, trade barriers

protector *n* **1 shield**, armour, mask, apron **2 guard**, guardian, minder, defender, handler

protectorate *n* **dominion**, colony, dependency, region, territory

protégé *n* **ward**, pupil, dependant, apprentice, student *Opposite*: protector

protest *v* **1 complain**, object, remonstrate, dissent, dispute **2 declare**, affirm, assert, insist, claim ■ *n* **1 complaint**, objection, remonstration, dissent, dispute **2 demonstration**, march, rally, campaign, dispute. *See* COMPARE AND CONTRAST *at* complain, object.

protestation *n* **assertion**, declaration, affirmation, pronouncement, disclosure

protester *n* **activist**, campaigner, demonstrator, marcher, picketer *Opposite*: supporter

protest march *n* **demonstration**, march, rally, protest, demo *(infml)*

protest rally *see* protest march

protocol *n* **procedure**, etiquette, conventions, code of behaviour, rules

prototype *n* **example**, sample, model, original, archetype *Opposite*: copy

protract *v* **draw out**, prolong, extend, spin out, drag out *Opposite*: shorten

protracted *adj* **long-drawn-out**, prolonged, extended, lingering, expanded *Opposite*: brief

protraction *n* **1 extension**, lengthening, drawing out, continuation *Opposite*: shortening **2 scale drawing**, plan, elevation, blueprint, diagram

protrude *v* **stick out**, jut, project, overhang, obtrude

protrusion *n* **lump**, lip, flange, overhang, outcrop

protrusive *adj* **1 prominent**, bulging, swelling, jutting, extending *Opposite*: sunken **2 brash**, forward, presumptuous, rude, fresh *(infml)* *Opposite*: retiring

protuberance *n* **swelling**, bulge, bump, lump, knob

protuberant *adj* **sticking out**, prominent, bulging, swelling, popping *Opposite*: concave

proud *adj* **1 pleased**, satisfied, gratified, honoured, delighted *Opposite*: ashamed **2 impressive**, stately, majestic, noble, magnificent **3 arrogant**, conceited, smug, superior, self-important *Opposite*: humble **4 independent**, self-sufficient, dignified, scrupulous, honourable **5 rewarding**, satisfying, pleasurable, pleasing, uplifting **6 projecting**, prominent, jutting, bulging, protrusive *Opposite*: sunken

---

COMPARE AND CONTRAST CORE MEANING: describing somebody who is pleased with himself or herself

proud justifiably pleased and satisfied about a situation, or self-satisfied and having an exaggerated opinion of self-worth; **arrogant** feeling or showing self-importance and contempt for others; **conceited** showing excessive satisfaction with one's personal qualities or abilities; **egotistic** having an inflated sense of self-importance, especially when this is shown through constantly talking or thinking about oneself; **vain** excessively self-satisfied, especially suggesting that somebody is overly concerned with and admires his or her own personal appearance.

---

proudly *adv* **1 delightedly**, happily, triumphantly, joyfully *Opposite*: ashamedly **2 arrogantly**, conceitedly, smugly, self-importantly, pompously *Opposite*: humbly

provable *adj* **demonstrable**, verifiable, watertight, incontestable, unarguable

prove *v* **1 show**, establish, confirm, demonstrate, verify *Opposite*: disprove **2 turn out**, develop, grow, grow up, be

proven *adj* **established**, confirmed, demonstrated, verified, recognized *Opposite*: unproven

provenance *n* **origin**, derivation, attribution, source, birthplace. *See* COMPARE AND CONTRAST *at* origin.

provender *n* **1** *(archaic)* **fodder**, feed, hay, forage, silage **2** *(literary)* **food**, fare, provisions, victuals, grub *(infml)*

proverb *n* **maxim**, axiom, adage, saying, aphorism

proverbial *adj* **1 well-known**, axiomatic, familiar, legendary, famous **2 archetypal**, clichéd, typical, regular, common *Opposite*: novel

provide *v* **1 give**, supply, present, endow, grant *Opposite*: withhold **2 make available**, deliver, offer, arrange for, run *Opposite*: withdraw **3 stipulate**, postulate, specify, require **4 take care of**, support, look after, care for, keep *Opposite*: neglect

provided *see* **provided that**

provided that *conj* **on condition that**, if, only if, as long as, so long as

providence *n* **1 wisdom**, foresight, prudence, sense, frugality **2 fate**, luck, destiny, fortune, divine intervention

provident *adj* **1 prudent**, foresighted, well-prepared, wise, careful *Opposite*: improvident **2 frugal**, thrifty, cautious, careful, sparing *Opposite*: spendthrift

providential *adj* **1 preordained**, destined, fated, God-given, divine *Opposite*: arbitrary **2 fortunate**, lucky, beneficial, advantageous, convenient *Opposite*: unfortunate. *See* COMPARE AND CONTRAST *at* **lucky**.

provider *n* **1 supplier**, source, contributor, donor, bringer *Opposite*: beneficiary **2 breadwinner**, wage-earner, earner, worker, benefactor *Opposite*: dependant

providing *conj* **on condition that**, if, only if, as long as, so long as

province *n* **1 area**, sphere, field, jurisdiction, domain **2 region**, area, state, county, prefecture

provinces *n* **outlying areas**, countryside, backwaters, hinterland, shires *Opposite*: capital

provincial *adj* **1 local**, regional, county, district, small-town *Opposite*: central **2 unsophisticated**, unfashionable, simple, outmoded, parochial *Opposite*: worldly

provincialism *n* **lack of sophistication**, lack of refinement, parochialism, narrow-mindedness, insularity *Opposite*: worldliness

provision *n* **1 delivery**, facility, running, setting up, establishment **2 anticipation**, prearrangement, forethought, wherewithal, readiness **3 stipulation**, rider, condition, proviso, if

provisional *adj* **temporary**, interim, conditional, makeshift, short-term *Opposite*: permanent

provisions *n* **supplies**, necessities, requirements, food, rations

proviso *n* **stipulation**, rider, condition, provision, if

provisory *adj* **conditional**, subject to, dependent upon, provisional, contingent *Opposite*: unconditional

provocation *n* **1 incitement**, needling, goading, baiting, niggling *Opposite*: appeasement **2 vexation**, frustration, irritation, annoyance, affront

provocative *adj* **1 challenging**, provoking, stimulating, inflammatory, incendiary *Opposite*: conciliatory **2 suggestive**, enticing, seductive, alluring, encouraging *Opposite*: forbidding

provoke *v* **1 incite**, needle, goad, bait, irritate *Opposite*: soothe **2 cause**, elicit, produce, trigger, bring about *Opposite*: prevent

provoked *adj* **irritated**, annoyed, angered, goaded, frustrated *Opposite*: unaffected

provoking *adj* **infuriating**, irritating, annoying, frustrating, maddening *Opposite*: soothing

provost *n* **principal**, director, head, chancellor, leader

prowess *n* **1 ability**, skill, expertise, competence, dexterity *Opposite*: incompetence **2 bravery**, heroism, gallantry, courage, daring *Opposite*: cowardice

prowl *v* **stalk**, lurk, skulk, lie in wait, hang about

prowler *n* **stalker**, pursuer, intruder, tormentor, Peeping Tom

proximity *n* **nearness**, closeness, juxtaposition, vicinity, immediacy *Opposite*: remoteness

proxy *n* **1 indirect means**, substitution, deputation, commission, delegation **2 substitute**, stand-in, deputy, delegate, understudy

prudence *n* **1 practicality**, carefulness, caution, discretion, forethought *Opposite*: imprudence

prudent *adj* **practical**, careful, cautious, sensible, discreet *Opposite*: imprudent. *See* COMPARE AND CONTRAST *at* **cautious**.

prudential *adj* **sensible**, wise, sagacious, provident, practical *Opposite*: foolish

prudery *n* **primness**, stuffiness, reserve, puritanism, prudishness *Opposite*: broadmindedness

prudish *adj* **prim**, stuffy, strait-laced, starchy, formal *Opposite*: relaxed

prudishness *see* **prudery**

prune *v* **1 clip**, trim, snip, cut back, cut **2 shorten**, cut, abridge, condense, tighten up *Opposite*: expand

prurient *adj* **unwholesome**, unhealthy, immodest, indecent, salacious *Opposite*: healthy

pry *v* **interfere**, poke your nose in, meddle, inquire, peer *Opposite*: leave alone

prying *adj* **interfering**, inquisitive, curious, meddling, peeping *Opposite*: incurious

PS *adv* **postscript**, addendum, afterthought, addition, stop press

psalm *n* **sacred song**, hymn, poem, canticle, prayer

Psalter *n* **book of psalms**, prayer book, breviary, hymnal, missal

pseud *n* **fraud**, fake, know-all *(infml)*, poser *(infml)*

pseudonym *n* **alias**, false name, assumed name, fictitious name, stage name

psyche *n* **1 soul**, spirit, inner self, essence, being **2 mind**, consciousness, awareness, ego, intellect

psychedelic *adj* **1 hallucinogenic**, mind-altering, mind-expanding, mood-altering, mind-blowing *(infml)* **2 coloured**, patterned, vibrant, vivid, loud *Opposite*: dull

psychic *adj* **1 mental**, cerebral, intellectual, cognitive, psychosomatic **2 supernatural**, extrasensory, mysterious, unexplained, paranormal *Opposite*: physical **3 telepathic**, clairvoyant, intuitive, second-sighted, star-gazing ■ *n* **clairvoyant**, spiritualist, soothsayer, sensitive, diviner

psychical *adj* **supernatural**, paranormal, spiritual, extrasensory, subliminal *Opposite*: physical

psychological *adj* **mental**, emotional, inner, spiritual, psychosomatic *Opposite*: physical

psychology *n* **mind**, thinking, mindset, makeup, sensibility

psychosomatic *adj* **self-induced**, mental, psychological, inner, all in the mind

psych up *(infml)* *v* **nerve**, steel, gear up, wind up, prepare

PT *n* **physical training**, games, physical education, PE, gymnastics

puberty *n* **sexual maturity**, adolescence, youth, teens

pubescent *adj* **pubertal**, teenage, adolescent, teen *(infml)*

public *adj* **1 community**, civic, communal, municipal, free *Opposite*: private **2 freely available**, shared, known, open, in the public domain *Opposite*: secret ■ *n* **everyone**, people, populace, community, society

publication *n* **book**, magazine, newspaper, journal, periodical

public disgrace *n* **dishonour**, disgrace, ignominy, humiliation, exposure

public figure *n* **celebrity**, name, personality, personage, household name

public image *n* **façade**, front, public face, persona, identity

publicity *n* **advertising**, promotion, exposure, hype, media hype

publicize *v* **make public**, make known, broadcast, advertise, announce *Opposite*: suppress

publicly *adv* **openly**, in public, overtly, widely, freely *Opposite*: secretly

public relations *n* **image management**, publicity, media, relations, PR

public-spirited *adj* **philanthropic**, charitable, altruistic, humanitarian, benevolent *Opposite*: selfish

publish *v* **1 issue**, put out, bring out, print, distribute **2 make public**, make known, announce, broadcast, advertise *Opposite*: keep secret

publisher *n* **producer**, originator, commissioner, editor, issuer

publishing *n* **publication**, printing, issuing, reproducing, dissemination

pucker *v* **wrinkle**, crease, gather, pull together, ruck up *Opposite*: smooth ■ *n* **gather**, wrinkle, crease, ruck, pull

puckish *adj* **mischievous**, playful, naughty, impish, elfin

pudding *n* **dessert**, sweet, afters *(infml)*

puddle *n* **pool**, slick, wet patch ■ *v* **1 potter**, mosey around, dawdle, idle, lounge about **2 splash**, dabble, paddle, splosh, wade

pudgy *(infml)* *adj* **fat**, chubby, stubby, podgy, heavy

puerile *adj* **childish**, immature, infantile, foolish, silly *Opposite*: mature

puerility *n* **immaturity**, childishness, silliness, foolishness, inanity

puff *n* **1 gust**, breath, draught, current, flurry **2 cloud**, wisp, waft, billow **3 praise**, recommendation, advertisement, publicity, blurb *(slang)* ■ *v* **1 blow**, exhale, breathe out, breathe *Opposite*: inhale **2 pant**, breathe heavily, wheeze, gasp, gasp for breath

puffed *adj* **out of breath**, breathless, breathing heavily, panting, gasping

puffed-up *adj* **pompous**, self-important, arrogant, conceited, boastful *Opposite*: humble

puffiness *n* **1 swelling**, enlargement, inflammation, oedema, distension **2 pomposity**, pompousness, arrogance, haughtiness, pride *Opposite*: humility

puffing *n* **wheezing**, wheeziness, breathlessness, heavy breathing, breathing ■ *adj* **breathless**, out of breath, panting, gasping, winded

puff out *see* puff up

puff up *v* **enlarge**, swell, inflate, expand, bulge *Opposite*: deflate

puffy *adj* **swollen**, distended, inflated, bloated, bulbous

pugilism *n* **boxing**, fighting, prizefighting

pugilist *n* **boxer**, fighter, prizefighter, pug *(infml)*

pugnacious *adj* **aggressive**, confrontational, belligerent, truculent, argumentative *Opposite*: peaceable

pugnaciousness *see* pugnacity

pugnacity *n* **aggression**, fierceness, forcefulness, hostility, confrontational attitude

pukka *adj* **1 fine**, well-made, excellent, high-quality, first-class **2** *(infml)* **genuine**, authentic, real, correct, proper **3** *(infml)* **respectable**, high-class, upper-class, well-placed, superior

pull *v* **1 drag**, draw, heave, haul, tow *Opposite*: push **2 tug**, jerk, yank, wrench, pluck **3 attract**, draw, bring in, pull in, lure *Opposite*: put off **4 strain**, sprain, damage, injure, tear **5 remove**, extract, withdraw, draw out, pluck out *Opposite*: put in ■ *n* **1** *(infml)* **attraction**, appeal, power, influence, draw **2 jerk**, tug, yank, twitch, tweak

COMPARE AND CONTRAST CORE MEANING: move something towards you or in the same direction as you

pull move something towards you or in the same direction as you; **drag** move something large or heavy with effort across a surface; **draw** pull something with a smooth movement; **haul** pull something with a steady strong movement, often involving strenuous effort; **tow** pull something along behind by means of a rope or chain; **tug** pull at something with a sharp forceful movement, without necessarily moving the object; **yank** pull something suddenly and sharply with a single strong movement.

pull apart v disintegrate, tear apart, dismantle, pull to pieces, demolish *Opposite*: assemble

pull back v recoil, shrink, shrink away, back off, retract

pull down v demolish, tear down, destroy, fell, flatten *Opposite*: build up

pulley n winch, hoist, block and tackle

pull in v attract, draw, bring in, pull, entice *Opposite*: put off

pull-in (dated) n roadside café, transport café, service area, service station

pull off (infml) v achieve, succeed, be successful, accomplish, carry out *Opposite*: fail. See COMPARE AND CONTRAST at **accomplish**.

pull out v 1 remove, extract, withdraw, draw out, pluck out *Opposite*: insert 2 leave, depart, abandon, drop out, go away *Opposite*: remain

pullout n 1 insert, flier, supplement, enclosure, addendum 2 retreat, withdrawal, departure

pull out all the stops v do your utmost, go all-out, move heaven and earth, make a supreme effort, do all you can

pull somebody's leg (infml) v tease somebody, joke, have a joke on somebody, have a laugh, tell stories

pull the plug v end, discontinue, close down, cut off, wind up

pull the wool over somebody's eyes v deceive, delude, hoodwink, swindle, con

pull through v recover, get better, pick up, survive, get through

pull together v 1 unite, join forces, rally, cooperate, team up 2 organize, arrange, assemble, draw together, bring together

pull to pieces v 1 dismantle, pull to bits, pull apart, take to pieces, rip to pieces 2 criticize, vilify, make short work of, make mincemeat of, rip to shreds

pull up v 1 stop, halt, draw to a halt, brake, pull in 2 criticize, reprimand, rebuke, take to task, have words with

pull yourself together (infml) v compose yourself, regain your composure, think straight, calm down, regain your self-control

pulmonary adj pulmonic, lung, respiratory

pulp n 1 soft tissue, fleshy tissue, tissue, flesh 2 paste, mush, mash, blend, soft mass ■ v mash, crush, squash, pound, grind

pulpit n 1 podium, dais, stand, lectern, reading desk 2 clergy, church, church authorities

pulsate v throb, beat, pulse, thump, thud

pulsation n throb, beat, pulse, rhythm, pounding

pulse n 1 throb, pulsation, rhythm, pounding,

thump 2 legume, leguminous plant, bean, pea ■ v throb, beat, pulsate, pound, palpitate

WORD BANK
❑ **types of pulse** bean, black bean, black-eyed bean, broad bean, butter bean, chickpea, French bean, garbanzo, haricot, kidney bean, lentil, lima bean, mangetout, mung bean, pea, petits pois, pinto bean, runner bean, soya bean, string bean

pulverization n 1 maceration, liquidization, crushing, reduction, grinding 2 (infml) defeat, humiliation, thrashing, beating, whipping

pulverize v 1 grind, crush, macerate, pulp, mash 2 (infml) thrash, crush, annihilate, destroy, defeat

pummel v beat, thump, thrash, pound, punch

pump v 1 force, drive, impel, propel, thrust 2 question, interrogate, quiz, probe, debrief

pump out v produce, give off, generate, churn out, emit

pump up v inflate, blow up, puff up, puff out, expand *Opposite*: deflate

pun n witticism, joke, double entendre, quip, bon mot ■ v play with words, joke, quip, make a joke, banter

punch v 1 stamp, press, perforate, cut, pierce 2 hit, beat, strike, pummel, thump ■ n 1 blow, hit, thump, clout, knock 2 vigour, drive, energy, power, verve

punch-drunk (infml) adj dazed, confused, bewildered, stupefied, stunned *Opposite*: alert

punchiness n vigour, energy, verve, liveliness, drive *Opposite*: lethargy

punch-up (infml) n fight, scrap (infml), brawl, set-to (infml), fistfight

punchy (infml) adj 1 pithy, hard-hitting, forceful, terse, effective *Opposite*: bland 2 dazed, confused, bewildered, stupefied, stunned *Opposite*: alert

punctilious adj 1 correct, seemly, courteous, polite, civil *Opposite*: boorish 2 fastidious, scrupulous, painstaking, assiduous, meticulous *Opposite*: sloppy (infml). See COMPARE AND CONTRAST at **careful**.

punctiliousness n 1 propriety, courteousness, correctness, politeness, decorum *Opposite*: boorishness 2 fastidiousness, precision, correctness, exactitude, efficiency *Opposite*: carelessness

punctual adj on time, in good time, prompt, on the dot *Opposite*: late

punctuality n promptness, timekeeping, reliability, regularity *Opposite*: lateness

punctuate v 1 mark, edit, correct, mark up, proofread 2 interrupt, intersperse, scatter, interpose, pepper

puncture n hole, perforation, wound, lesion, pinhole ■ v 1 pierce, stab, perforate, prick, stick in 2 undermine, deflate, erode, ruin, destroy *Opposite*: inflate

pundit *n* **expert**, specialist, authority, commentator, guru

pungency *n* **1 spiciness**, strong flavour, bitterness, sharpness, tanginess *Opposite*: blandness **2 pithiness**, pointedness, wit, force, bite *Opposite*: mildness

pungent *adj* **1 strong**, powerful, spicy, hot, overpowering *Opposite*: bland **2 caustic**, pithy, pointed, witty, forceful *Opposite*: mild

punish *v* **chastise**, discipline, penalize, reprove, rebuke *Opposite*: commend

punishable *adj* **disciplinary**, indictable, bookable, hanging, capital

punishing *adj* **gruelling**, exhausting, demanding, tiring, arduous *Opposite*: undemanding

punishment *n* **1 sentence**, penalty, reprimand, retribution, penance *Opposite*: reward **2 rough treatment**, abuse, mistreatment, heavy use, stick *(infml)*

punitive *adj* **disciplinary**, penal, corrective, retaliatory, retributive

punk *(infml) adj* **inferior**, second rate, cheap, nasty, poor

punnet *n* **basket**, tray, carton, box, container

punt *n* **bet**, gamble, stake, wager, flutter ■ *v* **kick**, hit, strike, boot, shoot

puny *adj* **1 small**, weak, tiny, feeble, frail *Opposite*: robust **2 inadequate**, trifling, paltry, minor, feeble *Opposite*: considerable

pup *n* **upstart**, brat, puppy, know-all *(infml)*, smart aleck *(infml)* ■ *v* **whelp**, litter, bear, deliver, give birth

pupil *n* **acolyte**, understudy, follower, apprentice, student *Opposite*: teacher

puppet *n* **1 marionette**, dummy, doll, glove puppet, hand puppet **2 pawn**, lackey, instrument, tool, lapdog

puppy *n* **upstart**, brat, pup, smart aleck *(infml)*, know-all *(infml)*

purchase *v* **1 buy**, pay for, acquire, obtain, procure *Opposite*: sell **2 obtain**, win, gain, secure, acquire ■ *n* **1 acquisition**, buying, obtaining, procurement, securing *Opposite*: sale **2 buy**, acquisition, goods, merchandise, item **3 grip**, grasp, hold, leverage, foothold

purchaser *n* **buyer**, procurer, customer, client, consumer *Opposite*: seller

purdah *n* **1 seclusion**, withdrawal, separation, retirement, isolation **2 screen**, curtain, barrier, divider, shield

pure *adj* **1 unmixed**, one hundred per cent, genuine, real, authentic **2 uncontaminated**, unadulterated, unpolluted, clean, untainted *Opposite*: tainted **3 sheer**, complete, utter, absolute, downright **4** *(literary)* **chaste**, unsullied, uncorrupted, innocent, sinless *Opposite*: corrupt **5 clear**, vivid, strong, vibrant, rich *Opposite*: weak **6 theoretical**, abstract, fundamental, basic, higher *Opposite*: applied

purebred *adj* **thoroughbred**, pedigree, pure

purée *n* **pulp**, paste, mush, pap, sauce ■ *v* **mash**, blend, process, liquidize, pound

purely *adv* **1 entirely**, wholly, totally, thoroughly, completely *Opposite*: partly **2 merely**, only, simply, just, solely **3 chastely**, virtuously, decently, morally, innocently *Opposite*: indecently

pureness *n* **1 cleanliness**, wholesomeness, spotlessness, clarity, transparency *Opposite*: dirtiness **2 clarity**, vividness, strength, vibrancy, richness

purgative *(fml) n* **enema**, emetic, suppository, laxative, purge ■ *adj* **cleansing**, emetic, laxative, emptying, purging

purgatory *n* **agony**, limbo, hell, anguish, despair

purge *v* **1 get rid of**, eliminate, remove, eradicate, do away with **2** *(fml)* **pardon**, exonerate, absolve, forgive, excuse *Opposite*: castigate *(fml)* **3 wash out**, cleanse, clean, flush out, sluice ■ *n* **1 laxative**, cathartic, emetic, purgative *(fml)* **2 elimination**, removal, eradication, expulsion, ridding

purification *n* **cleansing**, sanitization, decontamination, distillation, sterilization

purifier *n* **cleanser**, filter, sterilizer, disinfectant, antiseptic

purify *v* **cleanse**, disinfect, sanitize, decontaminate, clean *Opposite*: contaminate

purist *n* **traditionalist**, perfectionist, stickler, pedant, conformist

purity *n* **1 cleanliness**, spotlessness, clarity, transparency, limpidness *Opposite*: dirtiness **2 innocence**, wholesomeness, virtue, virtuousness, chasteness

purl *n* **1 thread**, gold thread, silver thread, wire, filigree **2 border**, edge, frill, trim, fringe

purlieu *n* **1 suburb**, commuter belt, outskirts, suburbia, vicinity **2** *(fml)* **ghetto**, shanty town, slum

purloin *(fml) v* **steal**, walk off with, pocket, help yourself to, thieve. *See* COMPARE AND CONTRAST *at* steal.

purple *adj* **elaborate**, exaggerated, florid, overwritten, ornate

WORD BANK

❏ **types of purple** amethyst, aubergine, heliotrope, lavender, lilac, mauve, plum, violet

purport *v* **1 claim**, assert, allege, profess, contend **2** *(fml)* **intend**, aim, mean, plan ■ *n* **1** *(fml)* **sense**, significance, importance, meaning, implication **2** *(fml)* **purpose**, intention, aim, design, plan

purported *adj* **supposed**, claimed, alleged, ostensible, unsupported

purpose *n* **1 intention**, aim, object, objective, goal **2 determination**, resolution, resolve, persistence, perseverance *Opposite*: indifference

purpose-built adj **tailor-made**, custom-made, custom-built, individual, exclusive Opposite: standard

purposeful adj **focused**, determined, decisive, resolute, firm Opposite: indecisive

purposefulness n **determination**, resolution, single-mindedness, commitment, tenacity Opposite: aimlessness

purposeless adj **1 pointless**, irrational, useless, illogical, unreasonable **2 empty**, aimless, pointless, meaningless, senseless Opposite: meaningful

purposely adv **deliberately**, intentionally, on purpose, knowingly, wittingly Opposite: accidentally

purr v **vibrate**, hum, whirr, rumble, buzz

purse n **1 wallet**, pouch, money bag, change purse (US) **2 reward**, winnings, takings, prize ■ v **pucker**, tighten, squeeze, press, compress Opposite: relax

pursuance (fml) n **enactment**, undertaking, achievement, acquirement, fulfilment

pursue v **1 follow**, chase, hunt, trail, track **2 practise**, engage in, work at, go in for, take up. See COMPARE AND CONTRAST at **follow**.

pursuer n **follower**, chaser, hunter, trailer, tracker

pursuit n **1 chase**, hunt, search, quest, detection **2 hobby**, recreation, activity, pastime, interest

purulent adj **infected**, pus-filled, pussy, weeping, oozing

purvey v **1 sell**, provide, supply, deal in, furnish (fml) Opposite: buy **2 gossip**, tattle, whisper, spread, tell

purveyor (fml) n **1 supplier**, stockist, seller, vendor, outlet **2 spreader**, gossipmonger, teller, tattler, source

pus n **discharge**, secretion, excretion, fluid, infection

push v **1 shove**, thrust, ram, press, set in motion Opposite: pull **2 impel**, urge, goad, force, make Opposite: restrain **3 advocate**, promote, advance, endorse, boost Opposite: oppose ■ n **ambition**, energy, force, impetus, motivation Opposite: apathy

push-button adj **automatic**, high-tech, remote-control, electronic Opposite: manual

pushcart n **barrow**, cart, handcart, trolley, wagon

pushchair n **buggy**, stroller, carriage, baby carriage (US)

pushed (infml) adj **1 lacking**, short, short of cash, strapped (infml), hard up (infml) **2 hard-pressed**, pressed, busy, struggling, hard at it

push in v **cut in**, barge in, shove in, squeeze in, jump the queue

pushiness n **forcefulness**, nerve, aggressiveness, assertiveness, brashness Opposite: reluctance

pushing adj **1 approaching**, nearly, almost, just about, roughly Opposite: exactly **2 assertive**, forceful, aggressive, strident, brash Opposite: retiring

push off v **1** (infml) **go away**, leave, depart, get going, set out Opposite: remain **2 cast off**, shove off, embark, depart, set sail

pushover (infml) n **dupe**, soft touch, gull, target, softy (infml)

push through v **put into force**, enforce, enact, introduce, force through

pushy (infml) adj **assertive**, forceful, aggressive, strident, brash Opposite: retiring

pusillanimity n **timidity**, fear, cowardice, nervousness, hesitation Opposite: confidence

pusillanimous adj **timid**, cowardly, faint-hearted, weak, spineless Opposite: brave. See COMPARE AND CONTRAST at **cowardly**.

pussy n (infml) **cat**, kitten, puss (infml), pussy-cat (infml), kitty (infml) ■ adj **infected**, purulent, pus-filled, weeping, oozing

pussycat n **1 cat**, kitten, pussy (infml), puss (infml), kitty (infml) **2 dear**, soft touch, pushover, softy (infml), sweetie (infml)

pussyfoot (infml) v **1 hesitate**, waver, wander, prevaricate, procrastinate **2 tiptoe**, creep, steal, pick your way, ghost

pustule n **boil**, abscess, eruption, pimple, carbuncle

put v **place**, set, lay, position, situate Opposite: remove

put about v **spread**, circulate, tell, inform, give out Opposite: keep secret

put across v **get across**, express, transmit, articulate, explain

put a damper on v **deflate**, spoil, mar, subdue, depress Opposite: enliven

put a match to v **set alight**, set fire to, set on fire, light, ignite Opposite: put out

put an end to v **stop**, discontinue, halt, suspend, call a halt to Opposite: continue

put a premium on v **value**, appreciate, prize, favour, rate highly

put aside v **1 save**, earmark, allocate, put by, set aside **2 disregard**, ignore, close your eyes to, forget, waive **3 set down**, set aside, deposit, lay down, put down

put a spanner in the works v **foil**, thwart, cause, havoc, put a spoke in somebody's wheel Opposite: help

put a spoke in somebody's wheel v **foil**, thwart, frustrate, put a spanner in the works, sabotage Opposite: help

put a stop to v **put an end to**, stop, bring to an end, pull the plug on, call a halt Opposite: continue

putative adj **1 supposed**, reputed, alleged, assumed, presumed **2 accepted**, acknowledged, recognized, known, believed

put at risk v endanger, jeopardize, gamble with, risk, imperil *(fml)*

put away v 1 tidy up, pack away, clear up, tidy away, pack up *Opposite*: scatter 2 *(infml)* consume, eat, drink, swallow, devour 3 save, put aside, keep, stash away, put by 4 *(infml)* imprison, jail, commit, confine

put back v 1 postpone, defer, suspend, put on hold, put off 2 drink, throw back, put away, gulp down, swallow down 3 put away, replace, pack away, return, clear away 4 pay back, repay, reimburse, compensate, recompense

put back together v mend, repair, reassemble, rebuild, reconstruct *Opposite*: take apart

put behind you v forget, get over, recover from, put down to experience, get out of your system *Opposite*: brood

put by v save, put aside, stash away, earmark, put away

put down v 1 set down, lay down, down, deposit, leave *Opposite*: pick up 2 enter, write down, put in writing, record, log 3 quell, crush, suppress, quash, repress 4 *(infml)* ridicule, mock, criticize, deride, disparage *Opposite*: praise 5 attribute, ascribe, lay at the door of, impute, blame on 6 kill, put to death, dispatch, destroy

putdown *(infml)* n insult, attack, gibe, criticism, dig *Opposite*: compliment

put forth *(fml)* v 1 state, make known, publish, present, give 2 leave, set out, depart, head off, start out

put forward v 1 state, make known, publish, present, give 2 suggest, propose, present, submit, offer

put in v 1 donate, contribute, dedicate, allocate, give *Opposite*: take out 2 present, submit, offer, make, claim *Opposite*: withdraw 3 interrupt, break in, interpose, interject, butt in

put in an appearance v attend, drop in, appear, turn up, be present

put in danger v endanger, jeopardize, hazard, risk, compromise

put in the shade v outshine, be head and shoulders above, eclipse, be streets ahead of, surpass

put into v invest in, plough into, sink in, tie up in, devote to

put into action v implement, put into practice, apply, realize, carry out

put into effect v enforce, put into practice, exercise, apply, carry out

put into operation v implement, put into action, put into practice, apply, set up

put into practice v carry out, do, practise, realize, implement

put into words v phrase, articulate, formulate, express, convey

put in writing v put down on paper, put down in black and white, put down, confirm in writing, write down

put off v 1 postpone, delay, defer, shelve, suspend *Opposite*: bring forward 2 disgust, repel, offend, sicken, revolt *Opposite*: attract 3 confuse, distract, divert, disconcert, fluster 4 hinder, discourage, delay, obstruct, prevent

put on v 1 dress in, wear, change into, get into, don *Opposite*: take off 2 pretend, feign, simulate, fake, play-act 3 stage, present, produce, mount, direct 4 gain, add, increase, accumulate, acquire *Opposite*: lose

put-on adj pretend, false, fake, sham, feigned *Opposite*: genuine ■ n *(infml)* deception, simulation, trick, hoax, con

put on a brave front v put a brave face on it, keep up appearances, be brave, keep your chin up, keep a stiff upper lip *(infml)*

put on an act v pretend, put it on, put on a pretence, sham, feign

put on a pedestal v elevate, idolize, worship, admire, regard highly

put on hold v put off, delay, postpone, adjourn, defer

put on ice *see* put on hold

put on the back burner *see* put on hold

put on the market v offer for sale, put up for sale, market, advertise

put out v 1 extinguish, douse, snuff out, stifle, snuff *Opposite*: light 2 make public, make known, publicize, circulate, spread *Opposite*: keep secret 3 annoy, irritate, slight, offend, exasperate *Opposite*: please

putrefaction n decay, decomposition, rot, breakdown, corruption

putrefy v rot, decay, decompose, go bad, become rancid

putrid adj rotten, rotting, decayed, decaying, decomposed *Opposite*: fresh

putsch n coup, insurrection, uprising, revolution, revolt

put somebody's back up *(infml)* v annoy, irritate, get on somebody's nerves, get on the wrong side of somebody, alienate

putt v hit, tap, stroke, knock, push ■ n tap, stroke, hit, knock, push

put to death v kill, execute, murder, assassinate, liquidate. *See* COMPARE AND CONTRAST *at* kill.

put together v 1 assemble, piece together, construct, build, fabricate 2 draw up, formulate, devise, develop, prepare

put to good use v use, apply, exploit, exercise, make use of *Opposite*: discard

put to sleep v knock out, sedate, put under, numb, dope

put under v sedate, put to sleep, anaesthetize, put out, knock out *Opposite*: bring round

put up v 1 erect, raise, build, construct, create *Opposite*: tear down 2 accommodate, house, lodge, take in *Opposite*: evict **3 offer**, provide, proffer, extend, advance

put-upon *adj* **overburdened**, exploited, used, overworked, abused

put up to *v* **induce**, persuade, encourage, make, cause *Opposite*: dissuade

put up with *v* **tolerate**, endure, bear, stand, submit

put your back into *v* **try hard**, give your all, work hard, give it your best shot, give it all you've got

put your faith in *v* **trust**, rely on, count on, have confidence in, bank on

put your feet up *v* **relax**, rest, nap, lounge around, lie down

put your foot down *v* **demand**, stand firm, stand fast, be resolute, be determined

put your foot in it *(infml)* *v* **blunder**, goof, speak out of turn, be indiscreet, be tactless

put your foot in your mouth *(infml)* *see* **put your foot in it**

put your oar in *v* **interfere**, meddle, stick your nose in, intrude, butt in

puzzle *v* **1 mystify**, bewilder, perplex, baffle, confuse **2 wonder**, mull, brood, ponder ■ *n* **mystery**, enigma, conundrum, problem, dilemma *Opposite*: explanation. *See* COMPARE AND CONTRAST *at* **question**.

puzzled *adj* **mystified**, bewildered, perplexed, baffled, confused *Opposite*: enlightened

puzzlement *n* **bafflement**, perplexity, uncertainty, disorientation, bemusement *Opposite*: understanding

puzzle out *v* **work out**, solve, figure out, resolve, decipher

puzzler *n* **conundrum**, puzzle, mystery, riddle, brainteaser

puzzling *adj* **mystifying**, bewildering, perplexing, baffling, confusing *Opposite*: enlightening

pygmy *adj* **miniature**, small, tiny, dwarf, little

pylon *n* **tower**, mast, post, pillar

pyre *n* **fire**, bonfire, furnace

pyromaniac *n* **fire raiser**, fire setter, arsonist, torcher

Q

QC *n* **Queen's Counsel**, counsel, barrister, brief *(infml)*

quack *n* **imposter**, charlatan, fraud, fake, pretender

quackery *n* **deception**, trickery, dishonesty, fraud, deceit *Opposite*: honesty

quad *(infml)* *n* **quadrangle**, courtyard, yard, square, patio

quadrangle *n* **1 courtyard**, yard, square, patio, piazza **2 four-sided figure**, rectangle, oblong, quadrilateral, parallelogram

quadrilateral *n* **rectangle**, oblong, square, parallelogram, rhombus ■ *adj* **four-sided**, rectangular, square, quadrangular, quadrate

quadruped *n* **animal**, four-footed animal, tetrapod

quadruple *v* **increase fourfold**, multiply, times, magnify, augment *Opposite*: decrease

quagmire *n* **1 swamp**, marsh, bog, mire, quicksand **2 predicament**, dilemma, quandary, sticky situation, muddle

quail *v* **flinch**, recoil, cringe, baulk. *See* COMPARE AND CONTRAST *at* **recoil**.

quaint *adj* **1 old-world**, old-fashioned, picturesque, antiquated, charming *Opposite*: modern **2 strange**, peculiar, odd, curious, bizarre *Opposite*: ordinary

quake *v* **1 quail**, tremble, shudder, quaver, cower **2 shake**, tremble, quiver, shudder, shiver ■ *n* *(infml)* **earthquake**, tremor, seismic wave, seismic activity, temblor *(US)*

qualification *n* **1 credential**, diploma, certificate, licence **2 skill**, quality, attribute, ability, aptitude *Opposite*: failing **3 requirement**, condition, prerequisite, criterion, sine qua non **4 restriction**, reservation, modification, limitation, tempering

qualified *adj* **1 trained**, licensed, registered, certified, recognized *Opposite*: unqualified **2 suitable**, eligible, capable, competent, skilled *Opposite*: unsuitable **3 limited**, contingent, modified *Opposite*: unconditional

qualify *v* **1 be suitable**, be in the running, meet the requirements, be eligible, make the grade *Opposite*: fail **2 train**, certify, license, empower, entitle **3 restrict**, limit, modify, temper, moderate

quality *n* **1 characteristic**, feature, attribute, property, trait **2 standard**, grade, level, calibre, class **3 excellence**, superiority, distinction, merit, eminence *Opposite*: inferiority

qualm *n* **1 scruple**, pang of conscience, remorse, contrition, compunction **2 misgiving**, doubt, pang, fear, apprehensiveness

quandary *n* **dilemma**, predicament, difficulty, cleft stick, catch-22

quantifiable *adj* **calculable**, computable, measurable, assessable, determinable *Opposite*: unquantifiable

quantify *v* **calculate**, count, enumerate, measure, compute

quantitative *adj* **1 numerical**, enumerative, arithmetical, mathematical, variable **2 measurable**, quantifiable, calculable, numerical, computable *Opposite*: unquantifiable

quantity *n* **amount**, number, measure, extent, size

quantum *adj* **major**, dramatic, significant, important, considerable *Opposite*: minor

quarantine *n* **isolation**, seclusion, confinement, solitary confinement, cordon sanitaire *Opposite*: integration ■ *v* **1 isolate**, seclude, set apart, confine, separate *Opposite*: integrate **2 detain**, imprison, hold, lock up, intern *Opposite*: release

quarrel *n* **1 argument**, dispute, disagreement, row, squabble *Opposite*: reconciliation **2 complaint**, grievance, grumble, problem *(infml)*, bone to pick *(infml)* ■ *v* **argue**, row, fall out, clash, fight *Opposite*: make up

quarrelsome *adj* **argumentative**, cantankerous, irritable, petulant, confrontational *Opposite*: agreeable

quarry *n* **1 excavation**, mine, pit, diggings **2 prey**, victim, target, kill, game *Opposite*: hunter ■ *v* **mine**, dig out, extract, excavate, dig up

quarter *n* **1 fourth**, division, part, section, quadrant **2 district**, neighbourhood, sector, zone, locality ■ *v* **1 divide**, subdivide, cut up, section, split up **2 lodge**, house, billet, accommodate, put up *Opposite*: evict

quarterfinal *n* **round**, heat, leg, match, game

quarterly *adj* **three-monthly**, trimestral, four times a year ■ *n* **magazine**, periodical, journal, publication, glossy magazine

quarters *n* **rooms**, accommodation, billet, housing, lodgings *(dated)*

quash *v* **1 put down**, suppress, quell, subdue, crush *Opposite*: allow **2 nullify**, cancel, repeal, overturn, annul *Opposite*: validate

quasi *adj* **virtual**, to all intents and purposes, pseudo, would-be, self-styled *Opposite*: through and through

quatrain *n* **verse**, stanza, rhyme

quaver *v* **1 tremble**, shudder, shake, quiver, quake **2 trill**, warble, wobble, vibrate, quiver

quay *n* **dockside**, wharf, dock, pier, seafront

quayside *see* quay

queasily *adv* **nauseously**, biliously, dizzily, groggily, woozily

queasiness *n* **nausea**, sickness, biliousness, vomiting, upset stomach

queasy *adj* **1 nauseous**, sick, ill, indisposed, seasick *Opposite*: well **2 uneasy**, uncomfortable, doubtful, dubious, troubling *Opposite*: reassuring

queen *n* **1 monarch**, sovereign, ruler, crowned head, empress **2 icon**, star, prima donna, doyenne **3 epitome**, model, essence, ideal, crème de la crème

queenly *adj* **majestic**, royal, regal, dignified, stately

queen-size *adj* **large**, largish, medium-large

queer *adj* **1** *(dated)* **unusual**, unexpected, strange, surprising, funny *Opposite*: commonplace **2** *(dated)* **unwell**, sick, nauseous, queasy, faint *Opposite*: well **3** *(dated)* **eccentric**, unconventional, idiosyncratic, curious, bizarre *Opposite*: normal **4** *(dated infml)* **eccentric**, unconventional, idiosyncratic, curious, bizarre *Opposite*: normal

quell *v* **1 suppress**, put down, subdue, crush, quash *Opposite*: incite **2 allay**, assuage, alleviate, mollify, mitigate *Opposite*: aggravate

quench *v* **1 slake**, satisfy, satiate, reduce, sate *Opposite*: stimulate **2 extinguish**, put out, douse, smother, stifle *Opposite*: ignite

querulous *adj* **1 complaining**, carping, critical, difficult, hard to please *Opposite*: equable **2 whining**, cantankerous, grumbling, complaining, whingeing *(infml)* *Opposite*: good-natured

querulousness *n* **peevishness**, negativity, cantankerousness, criticalness, argumentativeness

query *n* **1 inquiry**, question, request, interrogation, demand *Opposite*: answer **2 doubt**, uncertainty, reservation, question, question mark *Opposite*: certainty ■ *v* **1 question**, cast doubt on, doubt, suspect, challenge *Opposite*: trust **2 inquire**, ask, interrogate, quiz, demand *Opposite*: answer

quest *n* **mission**, expedition, pursuit, search, hunt ■ *v* **search**, hunt, seek, chase, pursue *Opposite*: find

question *n* **1 inquiry**, query, request, interrogation, demand *Opposite*: answer **2 uncertainty**, doubt, reservation, query, question, question mark *Opposite*: certainty **3 issue**, subject, matter, point at issue, problem *Opposite*: resolution ■ *v* **1 interrogate**, quiz, probe, grill *(infml)*, give somebody the third degree *(infml)* *Opposite*: reply **2 query**, cast doubt on, doubt, suspect, challenge *Opposite*: trust

COMPARE AND CONTRAST CORE MEANING: ask for information

question ask for information on a particular topic, especially formally or officially; **quiz** question somebody to persistent questions; **interrogate** question somebody systematically and intensively in a formal or official context, such as in a police investigation or court case; **grill** *(infml)* question somebody intensively; **give the third degree** *(infml)* question somebody intensively, especially in an aggressive way.

questionable *adj* **dubious**, doubtful, open to discussion, open to doubt, moot *Opposite*: indisputable

questioner n interviewer, interrogator, cross-examiner, asker, inquirer Opposite: interviewee

questioning adj **interrogative**, inquisitorial, searching, quizzical, inquiring Opposite: responsive

question mark n **doubt**, uncertainty, reservation, query, question Opposite: certainty

question master n **host**, questioner, chair, interviewer, examiner Opposite: contestant

questionnaire n **survey**, opinion poll, inquiry form, form, feedback form

queue n 1 **line**, file, row, crocodile, column 2 **tailback**, backlog, logjam ■ v **line up**, queue up, form a queue, get in line, wait your turn

queue-jump v **push in**, move ahead, leapfrog, overtake, butt in

quibble v **equivocate**, hedge, split hairs, nitpick, cavil Opposite: agree ■ n **objection**, cavil, equivocation, quiddity (fml)

quiche n **tart**, egg pie, flan, tartlet, pastry

quick adj 1 **rapid**, fast, speedy, swift, nippy Opposite: slow 2 **intelligent**, clever, bright, quick-thinking, quick-witted 3 **nimble**, lively, sprightly, spry, agile Opposite: sluggish 4 **sudden**, immediate, instant, prompt, abrupt Opposite: delayed 5 **brief**, short, cursory, fleeting, momentary Opposite: lasting. See COMPARE AND CONTRAST at **intelligent**.

quicken v **speed up**, accelerate, hasten, pick up speed, go faster Opposite: slow down

quick-fire adj **rapid**, swift, successive, automatic, fast Opposite: measured

quickly adv 1 **rapidly**, fast, speedily, swiftly, hurriedly Opposite: slowly 2 **suddenly**, immediately, promptly, without delay, at once Opposite: slowly 3 **briefly**, cursorily, fleetingly, momentarily, passingly Opposite: lastingly

quickness n 1 **rapidity**, speed, speediness, swiftness, promptness Opposite: sluggishness 2 **alertness**, cleverness, quick-wittedness, adroitness, sharpness

quicksand n **swamp**, marsh, quagmire, bog, mire

quicksilver adj **volatile**, mercurial, changeable, inconstant, unpredictable Opposite: constant

quick-tempered adj **fiery**, temperamental, excitable, volatile, passionate Opposite: calm

quick-witted adj **smart**, intelligent, clever, bright, sharp

quick-wittedness n **adroitness**, inventiveness, sharpness, intelligence, cleverness

quid pro quo n **deal**, trade, agreement, exchange, trade-off

quiescence (fml) n **inactivity**, rest, stillness, inertness, calm Opposite: action

quiescent (fml) adj **calm**, inactive, dormant, gentle, sluggish Opposite: active

quiet adj 1 **silent**, noiseless, inaudible, low, soft Opposite: noisy 2 **peaceful**, still, tranquil, uninterrupted, undisturbed Opposite: noisy 3 **private**, discreet, unofficial, off-the-record, confidential Opposite: public 4 **trouble-free**, straightforward, uncomplicated, simple, easy 5 **relaxing**, restful, leisurely, peaceful, pleasant Opposite: busy 6 **discreet**, modest, subtle, subdued, muted Opposite: showy ■ n **silence**, hush, peace, stillness, tranquillity Opposite: noise. See COMPARE AND CONTRAST at **silent**.

quieten v 1 **fall silent**, calm down, settle down, calm, hush Opposite: animate 2 **alleviate**, allay, soothe, assuage, quell Opposite: aggravate

quieten down v **stop talking**, fall silent, keep it down, quieten, shut up (infml)

quietly adv 1 **silently**, gently, inaudibly, softly, in silence Opposite: loudly 2 **calmly**, peacefully, tranquilly, serenely, uninterrupted Opposite: noisily 3 **peacefully**, tranquilly, pleasantly, agreeably, restfully

quietness n 1 **silence**, softness, quiet, noiselessness, inaudibility Opposite: noise 2 **peace**, stillness, tranquillity, serenity, calm

quill n **feather**, plume, barb, spine, spike

quilt n **duvet**, bedspread, eiderdown, coverlet, bedcover

quintessence n **essence**, embodiment, epitome, personification, soul

quintessential adj **typical**, essential, archetypal, prototypical, model Opposite: atypical

quip n **witticism**, joke, gibe, one-liner, clever remark ■ v **joke**, gibe, remark, banter, retort

quirk n 1 **twist of fate**, coincidence, accident, chance, oddity 2 **idiosyncrasy**, peculiarity, foible, oddity, habit

quirky adj **idiosyncratic**, individual, unusual, peculiar, odd Opposite: normal

quit v 1 **resign**, leave, walk out, abandon, vacate Opposite: stay 2 **give up**, stop, relinquish, refrain from, renounce Opposite: take up

quite adv 1 **fairly**, rather, moderately, relatively, reasonably Opposite: extremely 2 **very**, entirely, completely, totally, utterly Opposite: slightly

quits (infml) adj **even**, square, settled, level, even-steven (infml)

quitter (infml) n **defeatist**, deserter, loser, pessimist, coward Opposite: go-getter (infml)

quiver v **tremble**, shake, shudder, shiver, quake ■ n **shudder**, shiver, tremble, palpitation, tremor

quivering adj **trembling**, quaking, quavering, unsteady, shaky Opposite: steady ■ n **pulsation**, vibration, spasm, palpitation, tremor

quixotic adj **romantic**, unrealistic, idealistic, impractical, dreamy Opposite: down-to-earth

quiz n test, puzzle, game, contest, competition ■ v question, interrogate, cross-examine, interview, examine. See COMPARE AND CONTRAST at question.

quizzical adj questioning, curious, puzzled, surprised, perplexed

quorum n minimum, minimum number, least, required number, lower limit

quota n share, allocation, allowance, part, ration

quotation n 1 quote, citation, line, passage, extract 2 estimate, price, figure, costing, quote

quote v 1 cite, recite, repeat, refer to, mention 2 give an estimate, estimate, bid, give a price, give a figure ■ n 1 quotation, citation, line, passage, extract 2 estimate, price, figure, costing, quotation

quotient n proportion, measure, amount, share, percentage

R

rabbi n religious leader, scholar, teacher, official, leader

rabbit n bunny, coney, cottontail ■ v (infml) chat, chatter, gossip, go on, run on

rabble n mob, crowd, swarm, throng, horde

rabble-rouser n troublemaker, agitator, demagogue, activist, firebrand

rabble-rousing n troublemaking, sedition, provocation, agitation, activism ■ adj provocative, inflammatory, seditious, incendiary, troublemaking

rabid adj 1 foaming at the mouth, diseased, sick, ill, infected Opposite: well 2 fanatical, extreme, radical, uncompromising, militant Opposite: lukewarm 3 intense, fervent, ardent, violent, zealous Opposite: moderate

rabidly adv fervently, ardently, intensely, single-mindedly, zealously Opposite: moderately

race n 1 contest, competition, heat, sprint, marathon 2 ethnic group, nation, tribe, line, people (infml) 3 struggle, fight, rivalry, battle, competition ■ v 1 compete, take part, run, sprint, contest Opposite: withdraw 2 speed, go fast, run, sprint, hurry Opposite: crawl

racecourse n track, turf, course, hippodrome

racer n competitor, contender, entrant, sprinter, runner

racetrack n track, stadium, running track, circuit, speedway

raceway n 1 channel, race, conduit, canal, course 2 track, circuit, course, stadium, racetrack

racial adj ethnic, cultural, tribal, national

racism n racial discrimination, discrimination, prejudice, bigotry, intolerance

racist adj chauvinistic, bigoted, xenophobic, prejudiced, discriminatory Opposite: tolerant

rack n stand, frame, framework, holder, shelf ■ v 1 afflict, torment, plague, torture, beset Opposite: comfort 2 shake, rock, devastate, play havoc with, wreck Opposite: restore

3 store, shelve, stack, stow, put away Opposite: unpack

racket (infml) n 1 row, noise, ruckus, din, rumpus 2 swindle, con, fraud, sting (infml), fiddle (infml)

racketeer n criminal, swindler, hoodlum, fraudster, shark (infml)

rack up (infml) v accumulate, chalk up, score, make, achieve

rack your brains v try to remember, think hard, concentrate, make an effort, focus

raconteur n narrator, storyteller, conversationalist, after-dinner speaker, wit

racy adj indecent, risqué, indelicate, improper, sexy Opposite: clean

radar n detector, locater, sensor, locating system, position finder

raddled adj haggard, debauched, worn-out, dishevelled, unkempt Opposite: fresh

radial adj circular, outward, centrifugal, radiated, outspread

radiance n 1 happiness, sparkle, joy, vivacity, joie de vivre Opposite: dullness 2 light, brightness, glow, luminosity, brilliance

radiant adj 1 happy, healthy, glowing, beaming, sunny Opposite: unhappy 2 shining, luminous, brilliant, bright, dazzling Opposite: dull

radiate v 1 give out, give off, emit, discharge, issue 2 exude, emanate, glow with, bristle with, brim with 3 spread out, branch out, diverge, spread, circulate

radiation n particle emission, energy, radioactivity, fallout, contamination

radiator n heater, room heater, storage heater, space heater

radical adj 1 basic, fundamental, essential, profound, deep-seated 2 sweeping, pervasive, thorough, far-reaching, wide-ranging Opposite: minor 3 revolutionary, extreme, extremist, uncompromising, militant Opposite: conservative ■ n extremist, activist, militant, revolutionary, fanatic *Opposite*: conservative

radicalism *n* extremism, militancy, fanaticism, ardour, zealotry

radio *n* radio set, transistor, receiver, boom box (*infml*), wireless (*dated*)

radioactive *adj* emitting radiation, dangerous, harmful, hot, active

radioactivity *n* radiation, particle emission, energy, fallout

radio-controlled *adj* remote-controlled, automatic, remote

radius *n* 1 line, distance, length 2 area, range, circle, ambit, extent 3 scope, area of influence, umbrella, reach, remit

raffia *n* straw, fibre, grass, natural fibre

raffish *adj* 1 unconventional, dashing, rakish, disreputable, louche *Opposite*: conventional 2 showy, ostentatious, gaudy, loud, garish *Opposite*: discreet

raffle *n* lottery, draw, tombola, sweepstake, drawing ■ *v* offer, give away, award, present, donate

raft (*infml*) *n* bundle, number, tranche, portfolio, range

rafter *n* beam, roof beam, support, joist, strut

rag *n* 1 scrap, shred, wisp, tatter, thread 2 (*infml*) newspaper, paper, daily, tabloid, red-top (*infml*) ■ *v* (*dated*) tease, taunt, make fun of, call names, poke fun at

ragamuffin (*dated*) *n* urchin, waif, child

ragbag (*infml*) *n* mixture, mixed bag, miscellany, jumble, hotchpotch

rage *n* fury, anger, wrath, temper, frenzy *Opposite*: calmness ■ *v* fume, rant and rave, storm, seethe, thunder. *See* COMPARE AND CONTRAST *at* anger.

ragged *adj* 1 tattered, torn, worn-out, raggedy, in tatters *Opposite*: pristine 2 unkempt, untidy, shabby, raggedy, in rags *Opposite*: neat 3 jagged, serrated, uneven, irregular, rough *Opposite*: even

raggedness *n* 1 untidiness, shabbiness, scruffiness, sloppiness, messiness *Opposite*: neatness 2 unevenness, jaggedness, roughness, irregularity, sharpness *Opposite*: smoothness

raggedy *see* ragged

raging *adj* powerful, intense, furious, strong, rampant *Opposite*: mild

ragtag *adj* 1 motley, disparate, assorted, miscellaneous, multifarious 2 untidy, shabby, unkempt, scruffy, ragged *Opposite*: neat

raid *n* attack, search, forced entry, break-in, incursion ■ *v* 1 storm, attack, invade, search, break into 2 rob, loot, plunder, hold up, burgle

raider *n* attacker, thief, robber, marauder, invader

rail *n* railing, handrail, banister, bar, support ■ *v* protest, complain, object, criticize, condemn *Opposite*: accept

railhead *n* terminus, starting point, end of the line

railing *n* fence, paling, barrier, balustrade, boundary line

raillery *n* teasing, joking, banter, repartee, kidding *Opposite*: bullying

railroad (*infml*) *v* push, force, steamroller, bulldoze, shove

railway *n* 1 track, line, train track, route, railroad (*US*) 2 rail network, rail transport system, train system, train network, railroad (*US*)

WORD BANK

❏ **types of railway** cable railway, funicular railway, light railway, metro, monorail, tramway, underground

❏ **types of rail vehicle** cable car, funicular, locomotive, metro, steam engine, TGV, train, tram, tube

❏ **parts of a train** cabin, car, carriage, coach, compartment, freight car, locomotive, luggage compartment, Pullman, restaurant car, sleeper, sleeping car, smoker, smoking car, smoking carriage, smoking compartment, steam engine, tank engine, wagon

---

rain *n* 1 rainfall, drizzle, shower, torrent, precipitation 2 volley, hail, stream, torrent, flood ■ *v* 1 pour, drizzle, spit, pelt down, shower 2 lavish, shower, pour, deluge, overwhelm

rainbow *n* arc, arch, bow ■ *adj* multicoloured, colourful, variegated, spectral, polychromatic *Opposite*: monochrome

rain cats and dogs (*infml*) *v* pour with rain, teem, pour down, come down in torrents, come down in buckets

rainfall *n* rain, shower, drizzle, Scotch mist, torrent *Opposite*: sunshine

rain off *v* postpone, cancel, put back, call off, move on *Opposite*: bring forward

rainproof *adj* impermeable, water-resistant, waterproof, showerproof, impervious *Opposite*: permeable

rainstorm *n* cloudburst, downpour, deluge, thunderstorm, shower

rainwater *n* rain, precipitation, rainfall, raindrops

rainy *adj* wet, raining, drizzling, showery, drizzly *Opposite*: dry

raise *v* 1 hoist, lift up, uplift, elevate, move up *Opposite*: let down 2 look after, bring up, foster, grow, breed *Opposite*: neglect 3 increase, put up, inflate, boost, jack up *Opposite*: lower 4 build, erect, set up, construct, put up 5 improve, better, enhance, uplift, advance *Opposite*: deteriorate 6 mention, bring up, present, put forward, moot *Opposite*: withdraw 7 solicit, canvass, obtain, bring in, procure 8 lift, end, terminate, conclude *Opposite*: impose 9 cause, elicit, stimulate, induce, excite *Opposite*: quell

raise objections *v* **object**, protest about, demur, remonstrate, contest *Opposite*: agree

raise your spirits *v* **cheer up**, lift your spirits, gladden, hearten, buoy up *Opposite*: depress

raison d'être *n* **meaning**, purpose, rationale, motivation, inspiration

rajah *n* **king**, prince, maharajah, chief, ruler *Opposite*: subject

rake *v* **1 gather**, clear up, scrape, collect, scrape up *Opposite*: scatter **2 enfilade**, pepper, spray, shoot **3 search through**, go through, sift, rummage, comb *Opposite*: find ▪ *n* **reprobate**, degenerate, prodigal, profligate, squanderer *Opposite*: paragon

rake-off (*infml*) *n* **bribe**, kickback, favour, backhander (*infml*), sweetener (*infml*) *Opposite*: cost

rake up (*infml*) *v* **mention**, drag up, dredge up, bring up, dig up *Opposite*: keep mum (*infml*)

rakish *adj* **1 dashing**, stylish, natty, sporty, jaunty *Opposite*: bland **2 dissolute**, profligate, degenerate, louche, dubious *Opposite*: upright

rally *n* **1 gathering**, meeting, assembly, convention, demonstration **2 resurgence**, revival, comeback, recovery, revitalization ▪ *v* **1 come together**, gather, call together, bring together, unite *Opposite*: disperse **2 revive**, improve, recover, pull through, get better *Opposite*: decline

ram *v* **1 strike**, hit, bump, slam, collide with **2 force**, stuff, jam, cram, compress

ramble *v* **1 go on**, digress, go off at a tangent, ramble on, rattle on *Opposite*: focus **2 walk**, hike, wander, roam, go for a walk ▪ *n* **hike**, walk, roam, stroll, wander

ramble on *v* **go on**, ramble, digress, go off at a tangent, rattle on *Opposite*: focus

rambler *n* **walker**, hiker, backpacker, roamer, wanderer

rambling *adj* **1 long-winded**, wordy, discursive, digressive, incoherent *Opposite*: concise **2 spread out**, sprawling, trailing, straggling, irregular *Opposite*: compact. *See* COMPARE AND CONTRAST *at* wordy.

rambunctious *adj* **rowdy**, high-spirited, lively, disorderly, riotous *Opposite*: mellow

ramekin *n* **dish**, pot, container, vessel, baking dish

ramequin *see* ramekin

ram home *v* **emphasize**, stress, accentuate, drive home, underline *Opposite*: pass over

ramification *n* **complication**, difficulty, consequence, result, implication

ramify *v* **1 branch**, divide, subdivide, fork, split *Opposite*: unite **2 complicate**, confuse, confound, compound, intensify *Opposite*: simplify

ramp *n* **1 slope**, incline, rise, upgrade, gradient **2 hump**, ridge, bump, speed bump, rumble strip

rampage *n* **riot**, uproar, tumult, furor, turmoil ▪ *v* **run riot**, riot, rage, run amok, tear

rampant *adj* **1 unchecked**, unrestrained, threatening, out of control, uncontrolled *Opposite*: contained **2 wild**, widespread, extensive, lush, rambling *Opposite*: tamed

rampart *n* **fortification**, embankment, bastion, wall, earthwork

ram-raid *v* **loot**, break in, force an entry, plunder, rob

ram-raider *n* **burglar**, robber, looter, thief, plunderer

ramshackle *adj* **rickety**, tumbledown, dilapidated, broken down, falling to pieces *Opposite*: sturdy

ranch *n* **farm**, smallholding, farmstead, estate, stud

rancher *n* **farmer**, livestock farmer, smallholder, landowner, squire

rancid *adj* **reeking**, fetid, sour, off, bad *Opposite*: fresh

rancidness *n* **sourness**, rankness, fetidness, rottenness, smelliness *Opposite*: freshness

rancorous *adj* **acrimonious**, bitter, malicious, resentful, vindictive *Opposite*: amicable

rancorousness *see* rancour

rancour *n* **acrimony**, bitterness, malice, resentment, vindictiveness

random *adj* **haphazard**, arbitrary, accidental, casual, hit and miss *Opposite*: deliberate

randomness *n* **haphazardness**, arbitrariness, casualness, chanciness, unpredictability *Opposite*: predictability

range *n* **1 variety**, choice, series, assortment, array **2 scope**, span, breadth, reach, extent ▪ *v* **vary between**, fluctuate, vacillate, oscillate, alternate

ranger *n* **1 wanderer**, roamer, rambler, walker, hiker **2 park ranger**, steward, overseer, guardian, guard

rangy *adj* **long-legged**, tall, lanky, gangling, gangly *Opposite*: thickset

rani *n* **queen**, princess, maharani, consort

rank *n* **status**, title, category, position, level ▪ *v* **rate**, position, place, categorize, class ▪ *adj* **1 sheer**, utter, complete, blatant, absolute *Opposite*: minimal **2 vigorous**, rampant, exuberant, abundant, flourishing *Opposite*: sparse **3** (*literary*) **pungent**, fetid, stinking, smelly, bad *Opposite*: fresh

ranking *n* **position**, status, place, standing, rank

rankle *v* **irritate**, fester, gnaw, eat up, irk *Opposite*: soothe

ransack *v* **1 search**, go through, rummage, turn upside down, turn out *Opposite*: find **2 rob**, despoil, vandalize, strip, loot

ransom *n* **payment**, money, sum, deal, exchange ▪ *v* **redeem**, buy back, set free, strike a deal, pay up

rant v rage, go on, bluster, fume, seethe Opposite: sweet-talk (infml) ▪ n **outburst**, tirade, histrionics, bombast, bluster

rant and rave v rage, go on, keep on, bluster, shout Opposite: calm down

rap v **hit**, thwack, strike, tap, crack ▪ n 1 **blow**, tap, knock, smack, crack Opposite: caress 2 **rebuke**, criticism, reprimand, reproach, tongue-lashing

rapacious adj 1 **grasping**, greedy, avid, voracious, avaricious Opposite: temperate 2 **destructive**, vicious, harmful, aggressive, dangerous Opposite: harmless

rapaciousness n 1 **voraciousness**, greediness, unscrupulousness, greed, avarice 2 **destructiveness**, violence, viciousness, harmfulness, aggressiveness Opposite: gentleness

rapid adj **swift**, quick, fast, speedy, hasty Opposite: slow

rapidity n **swiftness**, quickness, speed, speediness, haste Opposite: slowness

rapids n **fast-moving water**, white water, torrents, waterfall, fall

rap on/over the knuckles (infml) v **reprimand**, scold, rebuke, censure, upbraid Opposite: praise

rap out v **bark**, shout, snap, bawl, yell Opposite: whisper

rapper n **singer**, vocalist, rhymer, performer

rapport n **relationship**, bond, understanding, link, affinity Opposite: friction

rapprochement n **reconciliation**, reunion, understanding, settlement, compromise Opposite: hostility

rapt adj 1 **engrossed**, fascinated, absorbed, captivated, gripped Opposite: bored 2 **happy**, blissful, delighted, content, joyful Opposite: sullen

rapture n **bliss**, ecstasy, euphoria, delight, joy Opposite: depression

rapturous adj **delighted**, enthusiastic, thrilled, overjoyed, elated Opposite: unenthusiastic

rare adj 1 **infrequent**, occasional, sporadic, intermittent, erratic Opposite: frequent 2 **valuable**, unique, singular, scarce, exceptional Opposite: common 3 **underdone**, bloody, juicy, red, pink Opposite: overcooked

rarefied adj **esoteric**, abstruse, exclusive, obscure, complex Opposite: simple

rarely adv **seldom**, infrequently, on the odd occasion, hardly ever, not often Opposite: often

rareness n 1 **scarcity**, paucity, dearth, lack, scarceness Opposite: abundance 2 **uniqueness**, matchlessness, exclusivity, exceptionality, individuality Opposite: commonness

rarified see rarefied

raring adj **enthusiastic**, eager, keen, ready, impatient Opposite: reluctant

rarity n 1 **infrequency**, shortage, scarcity, uncommonness, fewness 2 **one-off**, find, unusual object, curiosity, oddity

rascal n 1 **tease**, joker, prankster, trickster, jester 2 **rogue**, mischief, mischief-maker, scoundrel, scamp (infml)

rascally adj 1 **mischievous**, impish, naughty, puckish, playful Opposite: well-behaved 2 **dishonest**, wicked, bad, mean, untrustworthy Opposite: good

rash adj **impetuous**, thoughtless, hasty, impulsive, reckless Opposite: sensible ▪ n 1 **eruption**, spots, reaction, itchiness, inflammation 2 **outbreak**, flush, spate, string, eruption Opposite: incident

rashness n **impetuousness**, thoughtlessness, haste, recklessness, foolishness Opposite: prudence

rasp n **file**, scraper, tool ▪ v 1 **scrape**, rub, grate, chafe, grind Opposite: smooth 2 **grate**, bark, snarl, growl Opposite: murmur

rasping adj **harsh**, rough, grating, hoarse, jarring Opposite: smooth

ratchet n **notch**, cog, wheel, pawl ▪ v **intensify**, inflame, step up, stir up, increase Opposite: lessen

rate n 1 **speed**, tempo, pace, velocity 2 **amount**, frequency, level, degree, proportion 3 **charge**, fee, price, tariff, toll ▪ v **value**, regard, rank, esteem, appraise

rather adv 1 **quite**, somewhat, to a certain extent, slightly, pretty 2 **very**, considerably, significantly, noticeably, extremely Opposite: hardly 3 **sooner**, preferably, instead, by preference

ratification n **approval**, sanction, endorsement, confirmation, authorization Opposite: rejection

ratify v **approve**, sanction, endorse, confirm, authorize Opposite: reject

rating n 1 **assessment**, score, evaluation, grade, ranking 2 **sailor**, seaman, hand

ratio n **proportion**, relative amount, relation, percentage, share

ration n **share**, portion, allowance, quota, allotment ▪ v **restrict**, control, limit, put a ceiling on, regulate Opposite: lavish

rational adj 1 **reasonable**, sensible, logical, realistic, sound Opposite: illogical 2 **lucid**, balanced, sane, normal, cogent Opposite: irrational

rationale n **reasoning**, basis, foundation, justification, motivation

rationality n **logic**, reason, shrewdness, judgment, lucidity Opposite: irrationality

rationalization n 1 **streamlining**, restructuring, reorganization, rearrangement, reshuffling 2 **justification**, explanation, reasoning, validation, excuse

rationalize v 1 **adjust**, tune, level, straighten out, unravel 2 **justify**, give good reason for, vindicate, excuse, explain 3 **make more effi-**

cient, reduce, downsize, streamline, slim down *Opposite*: increase

ration out v distribute, share out, apportion, divide up, allot *Opposite*: pool

rations n provisions, supplies, food, consignment, distribution

rat on (infml) v 1 betray, tell on, inform on, set up, spill the beans on (infml) 2 abandon, give up on, go back on, renege on, let down *Opposite*: stick to

rattily (infml) adv 1 irritably, crabbily, tetchily, grumpily (infml), testily (infml) 2 messily, shabbily, tattily, raggedly, scruffily *Opposite*: tidily

rattle v 1 shake, clatter, bang, crash, jangle 2 unnerve, fluster, faze, shock, disconcert *Opposite*: calm

rattle off v say quickly, reel off, run through, list, recite *Opposite*: stammer

rattle on v chatter, go on and on, drone on, talk nineteen to the dozen, jabber *Opposite*: clam up (infml)

rattle through v rush through, dash through, make short work of, dash off (infml) *Opposite*: labour

rattletrap (infml) n wreck, banger (infml), boneshaker (infml), rust bucket (infml), heap (slang)

rattling adj quick-fire, pacey, fast, brisk, lively *Opposite*: plodding

ratty (infml) adj 1 irritable, short-tempered, bad-tempered, crabby, irascible *Opposite*: easygoing 2 messy, unkempt, shabby, seedy, tatty *Opposite*: tidy

raucous adj loud, harsh, rough, hoarse, disorderly *Opposite*: subdued

raucousness n boisterousness, wildness, disorderliness, unruliness, riotousness *Opposite*: quietness

ravage v 1 wreck, devastate, destroy, ruin, damage *Opposite*: create 2 despoil, pillage, plunder, sack, lay waste *Opposite*: restore

ravages n effects, consequences, results, aftereffects

rave v 1 rant, rage, fume, fulminate, hold forth *Opposite*: reason 2 (infml) enthuse, praise, go on about, laud, extol *Opposite*: criticize ■ n party, bash, event, revelry, festivity

ravel v tangle, knot, twist, snag, catch *Opposite*: untangle

ravening adj voracious, greedy, hungry, predatory, vicious *Opposite*: sated

ravenous adj 1 hungry, famished, starving (infml), starved (infml) *Opposite*: sated 2 greedy, voracious, rapacious, ravening, predatory *Opposite*: generous

ravenousness n greediness, insatiability, hunger, greed, gluttony

raver (infml) n partygoer, hedonist, clubber, party animal (infml), sybarite (literary)

ravine n valley, gorge, gap, gully, canyon

raving adj frenzied, gibbering, crazed, raging, delirious *Opposite*: controlled

ravish v overwhelm, overcome, transport, overpower, delight

ravishing adj beautiful, stunning, gorgeous, striking, eye-catching *Opposite*: plain

raw adj 1 uncooked, fresh, rare, red, underdone *Opposite*: cooked 2 unprocessed, unrefined, untreated, crude, basic *Opposite*: processed 3 painful, sore, sensitive, tender, bleeding *Opposite*: healed 4 inexperienced, green, untrained, wet behind the ears, untried *Opposite*: experienced 5 bitter, chilly, perishing, bleak, freezing *Opposite*: mild 6 visceral, brutal, crude, rude, primal *Opposite*: bland

rawness n 1 inflammation, painfulness, soreness, pain, redness 2 inexperience, naivety, ingenuousness, innocence, immaturity *Opposite*: poise 3 cold, chill, bitterness, iciness, chilliness *Opposite*: mildness 4 brutality, crudeness, rudeness, primitiveness, atavism *Opposite*: polish

ray n beam, shaft, gleam, glimmer, flicker

raze v destroy, demolish, annihilate, level, flatten *Opposite*: build

razor v shave, cut, trim, style, clip

razzmatazz n showiness, flashiness, hype, razzle-dazzle, glitziness *Opposite*: dullness

re prep on the subject of, with regard to, with reference to, concerning, regarding

reach v 1 stretch, touch, get hold of, grasp, extend 2 go, move, feel, fumble, lunge 3 arrive at, get to, attain, make, achieve 4 influence, touch, affect, impact on, get to 5 contact, get in touch with, access, get through to, get hold of ■ n scope, spread, range, orbit, grasp

reachable adj within reach, on hand, nearby, easy to get to, accessible *Opposite*: remote

react v 1 respond, counter, retort, answer, reply *Opposite*: ignore 2 change, alter, oxidize, reduce, bond

reaction n response, repercussion, comeback, feedback, blowback (infml)

reactionary adj backward-looking, conservative, right-wing, illiberal, unreceptive *Opposite*: progressive ■ n conservative, right-winger, dinosaur, diehard, extremist *Opposite*: progressive

reactivate v restart, reboot, galvanize, resuscitate, revitalize *Opposite*: deactivate

reactive adj responsive, sensitive, oversensitive, volatile, mercurial *Opposite*: phlegmatic

read v 1 understand, comprehend, make sense of, follow 2 peruse, scan, glance at, look at, study 3 read out, recite, deliver, speak, declaim 4 interpret, decipher, figure out, translate, convert 5 study, take, do, do a degree in, research

readable adj clear, legible, decipherable,

understandable, comprehensible *Opposite*: illegible

reader *n* booklover, bibliophile, bookworm (*infml*)

readership *n* circulation, audience, distribution, market share, niche

readily *adv* 1 willingly, gamely, eagerly, voluntarily, gladly *Opposite*: grudgingly 2 promptly, unhesitatingly, quickly, straightaway, at once *Opposite*: belatedly 3 without difficulty, easily, effortlessly, with no trouble, smoothly *Opposite*: painfully

readiness *n* 1 willingness, gameness, eagerness, keenness, enthusiasm *Opposite*: unwillingness 2 promptness, speediness, quickness, alacrity, skill *Opposite*: delay

reading *n* 1 understanding, comprehension, construing, interpretation, analysis 2 recitation, recital, rendition, performance, presentation

readjust *v* 1 get used to, settle, settle in, accommodate, come to terms with 2 rearrange, realign, modify, calibrate, rectify *Opposite*: leave alone

readjustment *n* rearrangement, change, modification, alteration, reformation

read out *v* announce, recite, deliver, declaim, reel off

read-out *n* 1 data, information, figures, statistics, details 2 display, retrieval, record, screen, monitor

read up *v* study, find out about, look into, investigate, research

ready *adj* 1 prepared, set, all set, complete, standing by *Opposite*: unprepared 2 likely to, about to, on the verge of, on the point of, liable to *Opposite*: unlikely 3 willing, eager, prepared, disposed, keen *Opposite*: unwilling 4 quick, prompt, apt, timely, swift *Opposite*: slow 5 perceptive, discerning, attentive, wide-awake, astute *Opposite*: dull ∎ *v* prepare, set, arrange, prime, make plans for

ready-made *adj* off-the-peg, prêt-à-porter, retail, high-street, convenient *Opposite*: personalized

ready-to-wear *see* ready-made

reaffirm *v* repeat, reassert, confirm, reiterate, endorse *Opposite*: contradict

reaffirmation *n* restatement, repetition, reiteration, endorsement, confirmation *Opposite*: contradiction

reagent *n* substance, component, element, chemical, mixture

real *adj* 1 actual, factual, material, tangible, physical *Opposite*: nonexistent 2 genuine, original, authentic, bona fide, valid *Opposite*: false 3 sincere, unfeigned, genuine, frank, heartfelt *Opposite*: artificial

realign *v* readjust, straighten, manipulate, rearrange, restore *Opposite*: disarrange

realignment *n* readjustment, rearrangement, shift, repositioning, relocation

realism *n* practicality, pragmatism, level-headedness, common sense, sanity *Opposite*: impracticality

realist *n* pragmatist, doer, experimenter, radical, stoic *Opposite*: idealist

realistic *adj* 1 practical, sensible, pragmatic, down-to-earth, level-headed *Opposite*: impractical 2 convincing, lifelike, representative, truthful, accurate *Opposite*: unnatural

reality *n* 1 realism, authenticity, truth, certainty, veracity *Opposite*: idealism 2 actuality, the everyday, experience, existence, life *Opposite*: make-believe

realizable *adj* achievable, attainable, realistic, viable, possible *Opposite*: unattainable

realization *n* 1 understanding, comprehension, consciousness, awareness, recognition *Opposite*: ignorance 2 achievement, fulfilment, accomplishment, carrying out, attainment *Opposite*: failure

realize *v* 1 understand, comprehend, become conscious, appreciate, grasp *Opposite*: misunderstand 2 achieve, fulfil, accomplish, carry out, bring to fruition *Opposite*: fail. *See* COMPARE AND CONTRAST *at* **accomplish**.

real-life *adj* actual, true, factual, real, realistic *Opposite*: imaginary

reallocate *v* redistribute, reshuffle, reorganize, transfer, rationalize

really *adv* 1 actually, in fact, in truth, in reality, truly 2 very, thoroughly, truly, genuinely, sincerely *Opposite*: hardly

realm *n* 1 scope, area, range, domain, sphere 2 kingdom, monarchy, dominion, empire, land

realness *n* reality, actuality, authenticity, genuineness, sincerity

realty *n* real property, land, property, estate, real estate (*US*)

real world *n* reality, life, everyday, the world, actuality *Opposite*: ivory tower

real-world *adj* practical, actual, everyday, real, real-life *Opposite*: imaginary

ream *n* quantity, amount, pack, pile

reanimate *v* revive, restore, reawaken, awaken, resuscitate *Opposite*: deaden

reap *v* 1 gather, harvest, garner, collect, pick *Opposite*: sow 2 obtain, acquire, gain, earn, secure *Opposite*: lose

reaper *n* gatherer, harvester, cutter, gleaner, mower

reappear *v* come back, recur, resurface, return, come again *Opposite*: disappear

reappearance *n* recurrence, repetition, reemergence, return, comeback *Opposite*: disappearance

reappraisal *n* reassessment, re-evaluation, re-examination, review, reconsideration

reappraise v **reassess**, re-evaluate, check, reconsider, re-examine

rear v **raise**, bring up, care for, nurture, take care of *Opposite*: neglect ■ n **back**, stern, tail, tail end, back end *Opposite*: front

rearguard n **tail end**, rear, back end, tail, back *Opposite*: vanguard

rear its head v **appear**, loom, turn up, materialize, rise up *Opposite*: disappear

rearm v 1 **arm**, equip, provide, supply, sell 2 **re-equip**, build up, upgrade, reinforce, fortify *Opposite*: disarm

rearmament n 1 **equipment**, armament, provision, supply, sale 2 **buildup**, re-equipment, upgrade, fortification, reinforcement *Opposite*: disarmament

rearmost adj **backmost**, last, final, ultimate, hinder *Opposite*: foremost

rearrange v 1 **reorder**, reorganize, reposition, move, move around *Opposite*: leave 2 **reschedule**, change the date, postpone, delay, adjourn

rearrangement n 1 **reorganization**, reordering, movement, change, relocation 2 **rescheduling**, postponement, change of date, delay, adjournment

rearwards adv **backwards**, towards the back, behind, back, to the rear *Opposite*: forwards ■ adj **backward**, behind, back, to the rear, over your shoulder *Opposite*: forward

reason n 1 **justification**, explanation, basis, grounds, cause 2 **motive**, cause, aim, end, goal 3 **thought**, judgment, logic, sense, mind 4 **sanity**, right mind, mind, wits, senses *Opposite*: insanity ■ v 1 **think**, rationalize, deduce, work out, figure out 2 **argue**, debate, discuss, influence, persuade. *See* COMPARE AND CONTRAST *at* deduce.

reasonable adj 1 **sensible**, rational, acceptable, practical, realistic *Opposite*: unreasonable 2 **inexpensive**, affordable, cheap, moderate, economical *Opposite*: expensive 3 **not bad**, quite good, passable, tolerable, all right *Opposite*: appalling. *See* COMPARE AND CONTRAST *at* valid.

reasonableness n **sensibleness**, rationality, equanimity, fairness, common sense *Opposite*: irrationality

reasonably adv 1 **sensibly**, rationally, judiciously, level-headedly, soundly *Opposite*: irrationally 2 **quite**, fairly, moderately, rather, relatively *Opposite*: extremely

reasoned adj **rational**, coherent, logical, lucid, analytic *Opposite*: illogical

reasoning n **analysis**, logic, calculation, reckoning, interpretation

reassemble v 1 **put back together**, reconstruct, rebuild, repair, mend *Opposite*: take apart 2 **meet again**, reconvene, reunite, get back together, congregate *Opposite*: disperse

reassert v **restate**, reaffirm, repeat, reiterate, confirm *Opposite*: abandon

reassertion n **reaffirmation**, restatement, repetition, reiteration, confirmation *Opposite*: abandonment

reassess v **reconsider**, review, re-evaluate, re-examine, have another look at

reassessment n **reconsideration**, review, re-evaluation, check, revision

reassurance n **comfort**, assurance, support, encouragement, hope *Opposite*: discouragement

reassure v **assure**, comfort, support, encourage, set your mind at rest *Opposite*: discourage

reassuring adj **encouraging**, comforting, supportive, cheering, heartening *Opposite*: discouraging

reawaken v **stir up**, revive, bring back, rekindle, resuscitate *Opposite*: obliterate

rebadge v **give another name**, change the name of, rename, retitle, rebrand

rebarbative (fml) adj **unpleasant**, unattractive, objectionable, annoying, forbidding *Opposite*: pleasant

rebate n **refund**, repayment, return, discount, reimbursement *Opposite*: supplement

rebel n **protester**, objector, campaigner, agitator, radical *Opposite*: loyalist ■ v 1 **revolt**, rise up, mutiny, resist, mount the barricades *Opposite*: comply with 2 **protest**, campaign, agitate, defy, dissent *Opposite*: obey

rebellion n **revolt**, uprising, insurgence, upheaval, mutiny *Opposite*: compliance

rebellious adj 1 **revolutionary**, militant, armed, treacherous, mutinous *Opposite*: law-abiding 2 **disobedient**, unruly, insubordinate, recalcitrant, defiant *Opposite*: obedient

rebelliousness n 1 **revolution**, insurrection, sedition, mutiny, treachery *Opposite*: compliance 2 **disobedience**, unruliness, recalcitrance, insubordination, defiance *Opposite*: obedience

rebirth n 1 **regeneration**, renewal, restoration, revitalization, rejuvenation *Opposite*: degeneration 2 **revival**, renaissance, reawakening, renascence, return *Opposite*: disappearance

reboot v **restart**, start up again, open again, boot up

reborn adj **born again**, recreated, regenerated, renewed, revitalized

rebound v 1 **spring back**, recoil, ricochet, jump back, return 2 **recover**, bounce back, rally, pick up, return to normal

rebuff v **reject**, snub, refuse, repulse, slight *Opposite*: accept ■ n **rejection**, refusal, snub, slight, denial *Opposite*: acceptance

rebuild v 1 **reconstruct**, build, restructure, re-erect, remake *Opposite*: destroy 2 **restore**, renovate, recreate, reconstitute, do up *Opposite*: neglect

rebuke v **reprimand**, reprove, censure,

reproach, take to task *Opposite*: praise ■ *n* **reproach**, reproof, censure, reprimand, scolding *Opposite*: compliment

rebut *v* **refute**, disprove, deny, invalidate, contradict *Opposite*: accept

rebuttal *n* **refutation**, disproof, denial, negation, contradiction *Opposite*: endorsement

recalcitrance *n* **resistance**, noncooperation, stubbornness, obstinacy, obduracy *Opposite*: cooperation

recalcitrant *adj* **unruly**, refractory, disobedient, wayward, headstrong *Opposite*: cooperative. *See* COMPARE AND CONTRAST *at* unruly.

recall *v* **1 remember**, bring to mind, evoke, call to mind, recollect *Opposite*: forget **2 call back**, call in, take back, withdraw, take out ■ *n* **memory**, recollection, remembrance, reminiscence *Opposite*: amnesia

recant *v* **take back**, renounce, repudiate, disavow, retract *Opposite*: avow *(fml)*

recantation *n* **denial**, withdrawal, repudiation, retraction, revocation *Opposite*: affirmation

recap *v* **sum up**, summarize, go over, run through, review ■ *n* **summary**, outline, summing up, review, restatement

recapitulate *(fml) v* **sum up**, recap, summarize, run through, review

recapitulation *(fml) n* **recap**, summary, restatement, review, outline

recapture *v* **1 regain**, retake, take back, reclaim, repossess **2 summon up**, recall, evoke, bring back, recollect

recast *v* **1 reorganize**, re-present, re-form, modify, alter **2 reassign**, reallocate, reselect, redistribute

recede *v* **1 move away**, retreat, go back, withdraw, draw back *Opposite*: advance **2 diminish**, lessen, decline, wane, fade *Opposite*: increase

receding *adj* **retreating**, withdrawing, disappearing, ebbing, declining *Opposite*: growing

receipt *n* **1 acknowledgment**, proof of purchase, slip, voucher, chit *(dated) Opposite*: invoice **2 receiving**, reception, delivery, unloading, acceptance *Opposite*: dispatch

receive *v* **1 get**, obtain, accept, take, have *Opposite*: dispatch **2 hear**, catch, sense, gather, grasp **3 entertain**, have round, greet, welcome, meet

receivership *n* **bankruptcy**, insolvency, liquidation, failure, ruin

recent *adj* **new**, of late, fresh, current, topical *Opposite*: old

recently *adv* **lately**, only just, in recent times, a moment ago, a short time ago

receptacle *n* **container**, vessel, holder, repository, magazine

reception *n* **1 welcome**, greeting, reaction, response, treatment **2 party**, function, drinks

party, cocktail party, gathering **3 signal**, clarity, picture, sound **4 receipt**, receiving, delivery, unloading, acceptance *Opposite*: dispatch

receptionist *n* **receiver**, welcomer, greeter, telephonist, switchboard operator

receptive *adj* **1 open**, amenable, accessible, interested, approachable *Opposite*: hostile **2 alert**, sensitive, responsive, sharp, bright *Opposite*: slow

receptiveness *n* **1 approachability**, friendliness, openness, accessibility, interest *Opposite*: hostility **2 alertness**, sensitivity, responsiveness, acuteness, brightness *Opposite*: slowness

receptivity *see* **receptiveness**

recess *n* **1 alcove**, nook, indentation, niche, bay **2 break**, vacation, time off, rest, retreat

recession *n* **depression**, slump, downturn, collapse, decline *Opposite*: boom

recessionary *adj* **falling**, declining, failing, in slump, in depression *Opposite*: booming

recessive *adj* **1 receding**, falling, retreating, ebbing, declining *Opposite*: growing **2 latent**, suppressed, dormant, hidden, masked *Opposite*: dominant

recharge *v* **renew**, refresh, boost, revive, revitalize *Opposite*: drain

recherché *adj* **rare**, exotic, obscure, exquisite, unusual *Opposite*: ordinary

recidivism *n* **reoffending**, backsliding, lapse, regression, degeneracy

recidivist *n* **reoffender**, hardened criminal, repeat offender, backslider, lawbreaker

recipe *n* **formula**, guidelines, instructions, method, steps

recipient *n* **receiver**, beneficiary, heir, addressee, inheritor *Opposite*: donor

reciprocal *adj* **mutual**, joint, shared, equal, common *Opposite*: one-sided

reciprocate *v* **give in return**, respond, return, give back, counter

reciprocation *n* **giving in return**, correspondence, exchange, trade, interchange

reciprocity *n* **mutual benefit**, mutuality, exchange, trade, trade-off *Opposite*: isolation

recital *n* **performance**, concert, presentation, reading, recitation

recitation *n* **recital**, reading, performance, narration, presentation

recitative *n* **declamation**, narrative, oratorio, opera, singing

recite *v* **1 declaim**, narrate, perform, rehearse, speak publicly **2 list**, enumerate, reel off, regurgitate, itemize

reckless *adj* **irresponsible**, wild, thoughtless, uncontrolled, out of control *Opposite*: cautious

reckon *v* **1 calculate**, add up, total, tot up, count **2 regard**, consider, judge, rate, deem *(fml)* **3 think**, believe, suppose, imagine, feel *Opposite*: know

reckonable *adj* **calculable**, countable, quantifiable, finite, measurable *Opposite*: incalculable

reckoning *n* **1 calculation**, estimate, weighing up, computation, arithmetic **2 opinion**, judgment, view, estimation

reckon on *(infml)* *v* **depend**, rely, count on, bank on, be prepared for

reckon with *v* **allow for**, bargain for, be prepared for, expect, anticipate

reclaim *v* **get back**, regain, retrieve, recover, repossess

reclamation *n* **recovery**, retrieval, repossession, recuperation, renovation

recline *v* **lie down**, lie back, stretch out, loll, lounge *Opposite*: stand

recluse *n* **hermit**, loner, outsider, lone wolf, solitary

reclusive *adj* **isolated**, cloistered, solitary, withdrawn, secluded *Opposite*: sociable

recognition *n* **1 identification**, detection, distinguishing, perception, differentiation **2 credit**, gratitude, acknowledgment, thanks, appreciation *Opposite*: blame **3 acceptance**, admission, concession, acknowledgement *Opposite*: denial

recognizable *adj* **familiar**, identifiable, decipherable, detectable, distinguishable *Opposite*: unfamiliar

recognize *v* **1 know**, identify, distinguish, make out, be familiar with **2 acknowledge**, credit, cherish, value, have appreciation for **3 accept**, acknowledge, appreciate, understand, admit *Opposite*: deny

recognized *adj* **1 documented**, familiar, known, standard, predictable *Opposite*: unknown **2 established**, acclaimed, professional, accepted, important

recoil *v* **shrink**, withdraw, quail, wince, flinch *Opposite*: confront ■ *n* **shrinking**, wince, withdrawal, start, retreat

COMPARE AND CONTRAST CORE MEANING: draw back in fear or distaste
recoil draw back suddenly or react mentally in fear, horror, disgust, or distaste; **flinch** draw back physically because of fear or pain, or avoid confronting something unpleasant; **quail** tremble or cower with fear or apprehension; **shrink** move away physically from something because of fear or disgust, or feel reluctance to do something because of fear or apprehension; **wince** make an involuntary movement away from something in response to a stimulus such as pain or embarrassment.

recollect *v* **remember**, recall, call to mind, summon up, think of *Opposite*: forget

recollection *n* **memory**, recall, remembrance, reminiscence, calling to mind

recommence *v* **begin again**, restart, resume, take up again, continue

recommend *v* **1 suggest**, advocate, propose, advise, urge *Opposite*: oppose **2 endorse**, commend, vouch for, mention, put in a good word for *Opposite*: criticize

COMPARE AND CONTRAST CORE MEANING: put forward ideas to somebody deciding on a course of action
recommend put forward a course of action as being worthy of acceptance in the circumstances; **advise** give advice in a relatively open and objective way; **advocate** support or speak in favour of something; **counsel** *(fml or literary)* advise somebody on a particular course of action; **suggest** propose something in a tentative way as a possible course of action for somebody else to consider.

recommendation *n* **1 reference**, endorsement, commendation, blessing, approval *Opposite*: disparagement **2 advice**, proposal, suggestion, counsel *(fml or literary)*

recompense *v* **reward**, compensate, repay, pay, remunerate *Opposite*: charge ■ *n* **payment**, reward, remuneration, repayment, return *Opposite*: cost

reconcile *v* **settle**, bring together, square, reunite, resolve *Opposite*: fall out

reconciliation *n* **settlement**, understanding, squaring off, resolution, compromise *Opposite*: conflict

recondite *adj* **obscure**, abstruse, complex, out-of-the-way, little known *Opposite*: mainstream. *See* COMPARE AND CONTRAST *at* **obscure**.

recondition *v* **overhaul**, service, tune, clean, repair. *See* COMPARE AND CONTRAST *at* **renew**.

reconnaissance *n* **investigation**, scouting, inspection, exploration, survey

reconnect *v* **connect up**, rewire, rejoin, join up, put together again *Opposite*: sever

reconnection *n* **connecting again**, connecting up, rejoining, rewiring, recombination *Opposite*: severance

reconnoitre *v* **explore**, scout, investigate, survey, search ■ *n* **investigation**, reconnaissance, exploration, survey, scouting

reconsider *v* **reassess**, re-evaluate, review, think again, go back over

reconsideration *n* **reassessment**, re-evaluation, review, re-examination

reconstitute *v* **1 reconstruct**, rebuild, re-form, put back together, build again *Opposite*: take apart **2 alter**, change, reorganize, modify, revise *Opposite*: maintain

reconstitution *n* **1 reconstruction**, rebuilding, re-formation, putting back together, building again *Opposite*: breakup **2 alteration**, modification, reorganization, revision, change

reconstruct *v* **rebuild**, renovate, recreate, redo, restructure *Opposite*: take apart

reconstructed *adj* **rebuilt**, recreated, reassembled, restored, renovated *Opposite*: original

reconstruction *n* **rebuilding**, renovation, reform, modernization, renewal

reconvene v resume, come together again, call together again, gather again, call again

record n 1 **account**, report, archive, chronicle, document 2 **past performance**, track record, reputation, background, history 3 **personal best**, top score, high, world record, best ■ v 1 **note down**, make a note, keep a note, take notes, keep details 2 **make a recording**, tape, video, film, pick up

recording n **footage**, video recording, copy, soundtrack, tape

recount v **tell**, narrate, relate, report, describe

re-count n **verification**, second opinion, check ■ v **count again**, verify, tally up, check

recoup v **get back**, earn, make back, recover, regain Opposite: lose

recourse n **option**, alternative, remedy, way out, choice

recover v 1 **get well**, get better, pull through, recuperate, make progress Opposite: deteriorate 2 **get back**, claim, regain, recuperate, recoup Opposite: lose

recovery n 1 **revival**, upturn, recuperation, mending, healing Opposite: deterioration 2 **retrieval**, salvage, recapture, repossession, regaining Opposite: loss

re-create v **reproduce**, copy, redesign, reinvent, reconstruct. See COMPARE AND CONTRAST at **copy**.

recreation n 1 **leisure**, hobby, pastime, exercise, play Opposite: work 2 **regeneration**, rebirth, reformation, restoration, restitution Opposite: exhaustion

recreational adj **leisure**, spare time, fun, frivolous, entertaining

recreation room n **playroom**, games room, den (US)

recrimination n **accusation**, blame, reproach, allegation, retort Opposite: appeasement

recriminatory adj **counter-accusatory**, accusing, retaliatory, counterattacking Opposite: placatory

recrudescence n **reactivation**, recurrence, breaking out again, repetition, happening again

recruit v **employ**, take on, enlist, engage, conscript Opposite: fire (infml) ■ n **employee**, trainee, beginner, novice, newcomer Opposite: old hand

recruitment n **staffing**, employment, enrolment, conscription, enlistment Opposite: dismissal

rectangular adj **four-sided**, quadrilateral, quadrangular, oblong

rectification n **correction**, improvement, adjustment, minor adjustment, modification

rectify v **put right**, set right, correct, remedy, cure Opposite: damage

rectilinear adj **straight-lined**, with straight lines, direct, unbending, uncurving Opposite: serpentine

rectitude n 1 **righteousness**, morality, goodness, correctness, decency Opposite: immorality 2 (fml) **correctness**, rightness, precision, accuracy, exactness

rector n 1 **minister**, cleric, parson, priest, vicar 2 **principal**, head, director, chancellor, dean

rectory n **vicarage**, manse, church house, residence

recumbent (literary) adj **lying down**, leaning, lying back, reclining, resting Opposite: upright

recuperate v 1 **convalesce**, build up your strength, recover, get better, get well Opposite: deteriorate 2 **get back**, retrieve, reclaim, recover, recapture Opposite: lose

recuperation n 1 **convalescence**, healing, recovery, getting better, restoration Opposite: deterioration 2 **retrieval**, recovery, repossession, salvage, reclamation Opposite: loss

recuperative adj **curative**, restorative, invigorating, convalescent, healing

recur v **happen again**, persist, return, come back, reappear Opposite: cease

recurrence n **reappearance**, return, repetition, relapse Opposite: cessation

recurrent adj **repeated**, persistent, frequent, periodic, intermittent Opposite: finished

recurring see **recurrent**

recurvate adj **curved**, bowed, arched, rounded, bent Opposite: straight

recycle v **reprocess**, salvage, reuse, recover, reutilize Opposite: throw away

red-blooded adj **vigorous**, strong, robust, hearty, lusty Opposite: weak

red-carpet adj **preferential**, VIP, no-expense-spared, special, favoured

redden v **flush**, blush, colour, glow Opposite: redden

redecorate v **revamp**, spruce up, refurbish, restore, repaint

redeem v 1 **cash in**, cash, trade in, exchange, convert Opposite: keep 2 **compensate for**, make up for, make amends for, restore, redress 3 **release**, liberate, free, emancipate, deliver Opposite: arrest

redeemable adj **exchangeable**, valid, good, convertible, equivalent Opposite: irredeemable

redeeming adj **saving**, good, positive, abiding, compensatory

redemption n 1 **salvation**, rescue, release, liberation, emancipation Opposite: downfall 2 **improvement**, recovery, renovation, reclamation, refurbishment Opposite: deterioration 3 **exchange**, use, conversion, trade-in, buying back

redemptive adj **liberating**, redeeming, saving, rescuing, delivering

redeploy v **redistribute**, divert, post, send, dispatch

redeployment n redistribution, posting, reorganization, relocation, rearrangement

redevelop v improve, revitalize, renovate, revamp, restore Opposite: neglect

redevelopment n improvement, renovation, revitalization, revamping, restoration Opposite: neglect

red-faced adj 1 blushing, flushed, embarrassed, hot and bothered, sweating 2 ruddy, weather-beaten, rosy, florid, rubicund (literary)

redheaded adj auburn, chestnut-haired, auburn-haired, ginger, strawberry blonde

red herring n decoy, trick, ploy, lure, diversion

red-hot adj burning, boiling, scalding, fiery, scorching (infml) Opposite: cold

redirect v forward, send, readdress, send on, transmit

redirection n sending on, resending, rerouting, transferral, forwarding

rediscover v find again, revive, experience again, remember, relive

rediscovery n finding again, discovering again, reawakening, seeing afresh, rekindling

redistribute v reallocate, reorder, sort out, restructure, rearrange

redistribution n redeployment, rearrangement, relocation, reorganization, restructuring

red-letter day n special day, day to remember, occasion, event, turning point

red light n 1 traffic light, warning signal, warning light, stop light, stop sign Opposite: green light 2 (infml) rejection, disapproval, refusal, no, prohibition Opposite: approval

redness n 1 blush, flush, rosiness, glow, pinkness Opposite: pallor 2 soreness, rawness, tenderness, inflammation, painfulness

redo v rebuild, do from scratch, do again, recreate, start again

redolence n suggestion, hint, trace, evocation, reminiscence

redolent adj 1 suggestive, reminiscent, evocative, indicative, recalling 2 scented, aromatic, fragrant, sweet-smelling, perfumed

redouble v intensify, renew, increase, multiply, amplify Opposite: reduce

redoubtable adj formidable, impressive, terrible, mighty, fearsome Opposite: unimpressive

redraft n rewrite, reworking, alteration, modification, change ■ v rewrite, reword, rework, revise, rephrase

redress n compensation, reparation, damages, recompense, reimbursement ■ v 1 restore, level out, equalize, right, rectify 2 reimburse, repay, pay damages, pay reparations, remunerate

red tape (infml) n formalities, bureaucracy, paperwork, official procedure, rules and regulations

reduce v 1 decrease, lessen, diminish, cut, trim down Opposite: increase 2 downgrade, cut down, demote, degrade, slash Opposite: upgrade 3 lose weight, slim, slim down, go on a diet, diet

reduced adj cheap, bargain, cut-price, low-price, on sale

reduction n discount, decrease, lessening, drop, saving Opposite: increase

redundancy n unemployment, job loss, dismissal, severance, termination Opposite: employment

redundant adj 1 laid off, let go, out of work, out of a job, jobless Opposite: employed 2 superfluous, outmoded, disused, surplus, unneeded Opposite: needed

reduplicate v repeat, double, copy, redo, recast

reduplication n repetition, copying, imitation, doubling, duplication

reed n cane, stalk, stem

reediness n squeakiness, shrillness, stridency, screechiness, squawkiness Opposite: sonority

re-educate v retrain, reskill, re-equip, requalify, reinstruct

re-education n retraining, reskilling, re-equipping, requalification, reinstruction

reedy adj 1 high-pitched, thin, shrill, high, feeble Opposite: full-bodied 2 thin, narrow, slim, skinny, long Opposite: squat

reef n ridge, bar, bank, mound, range

reek v 1 stink, smell, pong (infml) 2 show signs, smack, smell, suggest, be redolent of ■ n stench, stink, smell, odour, whiff. See COMPARE AND CONTRAST at smell.

reel n roll, spool, cylinder, bobbin, roller ■ v 1 lurch, stagger, totter, stumble, wobble 2 wind, whirl, spin, go round and round, revolve

re-elect v vote in again, reappoint, reconfirm, endorse, reinstall

re-election n reappointment, endorsement, confirmation

reel off v recite, rattle off, list, repeat, go through

re-enter v return, retrace one's steps, go back into, withdraw into, retire into Opposite: leave

re-entry n return, going back into, going into again, going in again

re-establish v establish again, create again, regenerate, reinvent, rebuild

re-examination n reappraisal, reconsideration, reassessment, re-evaluation, rechecking

re-examine v reconsider, go back over, review, reassess, check

ref (infml) n referee, umpire, arbitrator, adjudicator, mediator

refectory n cafeteria, dining hall, mess hall, lunchroom (US)

refer v **1 consult**, check, turn to, look up, examine **2 mention**, denote, talk about, bring up, speak of **3 signify**, mean, indicate, suggest, insinuate **4 send to**, direct to, pass on to, consign to, turn over to **5 apply to**, relate to, concern, belong, be relevant to

referee n **umpire**, arbitrator, judge, arbiter, adjudicator *Opposite*: partisan ■ v **arbitrate**, adjudicate, umpire, mediate, judge

reference n **1 orientation**, position, situation, location, locus **2 allusion**, mention, suggestion, indication, citation **3 recommendation**, testimonial, character reference, endorsement, commendation

referendum n **vote**, poll, plebiscite, survey, ballot

referral n **transfer**, recommendation, appointment, medical appointment

refill v **replenish**, top up, fill up, restock, stock up *Opposite*: empty

refine v **1 purify**, process, treat, filter, distil *Opposite*: contaminate **2 improve**, polish, perfect, hone, enhance *Opposite*: coarsen

refined adj **1 sophisticated**, advanced, superior, polished, distinguished *Opposite*: coarse **2 purified**, processed, treated, filtered, distilled

refinement n **1 modification**, alteration, minor change, improvement, enhancement **2 sophistication**, finesse, class, maturity, delicacy *Opposite*: vulgarity

refining n **1 purifying**, sanitizing, decontaminating, cleansing, filtering *Opposite*: adulterating **2 improving**, cultivating, educating, taming, enlightening *Opposite*: coarsening ■ adj **improving**, educating, cultivating, civilizing, enlightening *Opposite*: coarsening

refit v **overhaul**, renovate, re-equip, service, repair ■ n **overhaul**, re-equipping, repair, refurbishment, service

reflate v **expand**, increase, stimulate, spur on, build up *Opposite*: deflate

reflation n **expansion**, increase, stimulation, boost, advance *Opposite*: deflation

reflect v **1 reproduce**, mirror, imitate, replicate, redirect **2 be a sign of**, reveal, expose, suggest, signal **3 think**, consider, ponder, mull over, contemplate

reflection n **1 indication**, sign, manifestation, suggestion, expression **2 consideration**, thinking, thought, contemplation, meditation *Opposite*: impulse **3 mirror image**, likeness, echo, image, replication

reflective adj **thoughtful**, pensive, wistful, meditative, contemplative *Opposite*: impulsive

reflex n **reaction**, impulse, instinct, spontaneous effect, response

reflexive adj **automatic**, impulsive, spontaneous, involuntary, instinctive *Opposite*: premeditated

reform v **improve**, restructure, revolutionize, remodel, modernize ■ n **improvement**, reorganization, restructuring, modification, transformation

re-form v **recreate**, reconstruct, re-fashion, rebuild, remake

reformation n **improvement**, renovation, reorganization, restructuring, overhaul

reformatory n **institution**, detention centre, secure unit, jail, prison

reformed adj **rehabilitated**, transformed, changed, converted, renewed

reformer n **improver**, campaigner, activist, crusader, agitator *Opposite*: conservative

refract v **bend**, divert, change course, detour, deflect

refraction n **bending**, change of direction, change of course, diversion, detour

refractory adj **headstrong**, stubborn, rebellious, obstinate, wayward *Opposite*: placid

refrain v **desist**, abstain, hold back, leave off, cease *Opposite*: persist ■ n **chorus**, strain, theme

refresh v **revive**, cool down, enliven, invigorate, rejuvenate *Opposite*: wear out

refresher n **reminder**, revision, update, review

refreshing adj **stimulating**, uplifting, inspirational, invigorating, energizing *Opposite*: draining

refreshment n **drink**, food, nourishment, sustenance, nutriment

refreshments n **food and drink**, snacks, drinks, nibbles, hors d'oeuvres

refrigerate v **keep cold**, store at a low temperature, cool, ice, chill *Opposite*: heat

refrigeration n **cooling**, chilling, preservation, freezing, conserving

refuel v **refill**, replenish, top up, restock, resupply *Opposite*: run down

refuge n **haven**, sanctuary, shelter, harbour, protection

refugee n **person in exile**, immigrant, migrant, expatriate, exile

refund v **repay**, reimburse, give back, pay back, compensate *Opposite*: keep ■ n **repayment**, reimbursement, money back, compensation, recompense *Opposite*: payment

refurbish v **renovate**, restore, refit, fix up, spruce up

refurbishment n **restoration**, renovation, overhaul, renewal, repair

refusal n **negative response**, snub, denial, rejection, negation *Opposite*: acceptance

refuse v **say no**, decline, reject, snub, rebuff *Opposite*: accept ■ n **waste**, garbage, rubbish, litter, debris

refutation n **repudiation**, disproof, negation, rejection, contradiction *Opposite*: confirmation

refute v disprove, contest, rebut, counter, repudiate *Opposite*: prove

regain v recover, get back, recuperate, recoup, reclaim *Opposite*: lose

regal adj royal, majestic, noble, imperial, stately

regale v entertain, amuse, delight, divert

regalia n symbols of office, ceremonial objects, ceremonial dress, insignia

regard v 1 look upon, stare, observe, gaze at, view 2 consider, hold, think, see, view 3 relate to, concern, touch on, connect with, have to do with ■ n 1 respect, esteem, favour, admiration, honour *Opposite*: disregard 2 *(fml)* look, stare, gaze, glance

COMPARE AND CONTRAST CORE MEANING: appreciation of the worth of somebody or something **regard** a mixture of liking and appreciation of somebody or something; **admiration** warm approval and appreciation of somebody or something, often suggesting a desire to copy or resemble somebody; **esteem** a high opinion and appreciation of somebody or something; **favour** a liking and preference for somebody or something; **respect** a strong acknowledgment and appreciation of somebody's abilities and achievements; **reverence** a feeling of deep respect and devotion combined with a slight sense of awe; **veneration** a profound feeling of respect and awe.

regarding prep concerning, about, on the subject of, on the topic of, as regards

regardless adv anyway, anyhow, no matter what, whatever happens, nevertheless

regardless of prep in spite of, despite, apart from, not considering, notwithstanding

regatta n boat race, race, gala, competition, contest

regenerate v renew, restore, revive, redevelop, reinforce *Opposite*: degenerate

regeneration n renewal, rebirth, revival, renaissance, rejuvenation

regenerative adj growing back, reformative, recreating, re-forming, recovering *Opposite*: degenerative

regent n substitute, proxy, replacement, protector

regime n 1 government, command, rule, administration, management 2 routine, system, regimen, treatment, course of therapy

regimen n routine, schedule, treatment, regime, course of therapy

regiment n military unit, troop, squadron, battalion, brigade ■ v 1 control strictly, regulate, oppress, suppress, order *Opposite*: liberate 2 organize systematically, arrange, order, file, organize

regimental adj strict, rigid, disciplined, harsh, ordered *Opposite*: lax

regimentation n control, regulation, oppression, suppression, organization

regimented adj 1 controlled, disciplined, restricted, strict, rigid *Opposite*: undisciplined 2 well-ordered, neatly arranged, organized, systematic, structured *Opposite*: disordered

region n area, district, county, section, province

regional adj local, area, district, provincial, county *Opposite*: national

regionalism n 1 regional loyalty, regional prejudice, decentralization, home loyalty, area loyalty 2 linguistic feature, local expression, dialect word

register n list, record, catalogue, roll, index ■ v 1 enter, list, record, catalogue, keep details 2 enrol, join, sign up, matriculate, enlist 3 reach, touch, record, measure, indicate 4 reveal, disclose, show, convey, score *Opposite*: hide

registrar n 1 public official, recorder, public administrator, record-keeper, clerk 2 administrative officer, school administrator, university official, administrator, bursar 3 senior hospital doctor, specialist, consultant

registration n 1 registering, recording, record-keeping, cataloguing, listing 2 enrolment, enlisting, signing up, signing on, course enrolment

registry n records office, register office, archive, administrative office, office

regress v 1 relapse, revert, lapse, backslide, retrogress *Opposite*: progress 2 go back, lose headway, lose ground, retreat, move back *Opposite*: advance

regression n 1 recession, retreat, retrogression, return *Opposite*: advance 2 reversion, deterioration, relapse, worsening, getting worse *Opposite*: progression

regressive adj reverting, returning, going back, degenerating, deteriorating *Opposite*: progressive

regret v 1 be sorry, be apologetic, apologize for, be repentant, feel sorry 2 *(fml)* be disappointed, be unhappy, lament, be remorseful, express grief ■ n 1 remorse, guilt, repentance, compunction, pang of conscience *Opposite*: shamelessness 2 disappointment, sorrow, unhappiness, grief, distress *Opposite*: contentment

regretful adj 1 apologetic, remorseful, repentant, sorry, penitent *Opposite*: unapologetic 2 disappointed, unhappy, sorrowful, sad *Opposite*: content

regrettable adj unfortunate, deplorable, lamentable, undesirable, unwelcome *Opposite*: fortunate

regroup v re-form, recover, rearrange, recuperate, reorder *Opposite*: scatter

regular adj 1 even, steady, unvarying, consistent, systematic *Opposite*: irregular

2 recurring, recurrent, frequent, repeated, fixed *Opposite*: intermittent **3 ordered**, methodical, even, consistent, reliable *Opposite*: inconsistent **4 usual**, normal, standard, ordinary, customary *Opposite*: unusual ■ n **soldier**, combatant, legionnaire, squaddie *(slang)*, GI *(US)*

regularity n orderliness, symmetry, uniformity, consistency, constancy *Opposite*: inconsistency

regularize v standardize, normalize, make conform, legalize, regulate

regulate v **1 control**, order, adjust, set, synchronize *Opposite*: deregulate **2** *(fml)* **direct**, control, guide, manage, handle

regulation n **1 rule**, directive, guideline, parameter, instruction **2 control**, adjustment, adaptation, alteration, management

regulator n **1 device**, valve, mechanism, controller, rheostat **2 watchdog**, controller, supervisory body, manager, supervisor

regulatory adj controlling, supervisory, governing, monitoring, directing

regurgitate v **1 bring up**, vomit, spew up, spit up, throw up *(infml) Opposite*: ingest **2 repeat**, rehearse, go over, do again, reiterate

regurgitation n **1 bringing up**, vomiting, sicking up, spitting out, spewing **2 repetition**, rehearsal, restating, churning out, recitation

rehabilitate v **1 restore**, recover, mend, repair, re-establish **2 assimilate**, acclimatize, re-educate, naturalize, reorient

rehabilitation n **reintegration**, restoration, therapy, recuperation, convalescence

rehash v rework, reuse, do again, go over, repeat

rehearsal n practice, preparation, trial, run-through, dummy run *Opposite*: performance

rehearse v practise, go over, run through, prepare, train

rehearsed adj practised, prepared, learned, studied, planned out *Opposite*: ad-lib

reheat v heat up, warm up, warm through, warm, heat

rehouse v move, transfer, relocate, resettle

reign n rule, sovereignty, control, supremacy, sway ■ v rule, hold sway, govern, control, lead

reimburse v repay, pay back, give money back, compensate, refund

reimbursement n repayment, compensation, recompense, settlement, damages

rein n bridle, restraint, harness, leash, lead

reincarnate v revive, bring back, revitalize, rejuvenate, reawaken

reincarnation n re-embodiment, rebirth, re-creation, reawakening, restoration

reinforce v **1 strengthen**, support, underpin, buttress, bolster *Opposite*: underplay

2 emphasize, underline, highlight, add force to, boost *Opposite*: weaken

reinforcement n **1 strengthening**, support, underpinning, fortification, buttressing *Opposite*: weakening **2 emphasis**, underlining, underscoring, corroboration, backup *Opposite*: underplaying

rein in v hold back, cut back, restrain, reduce, decrease *Opposite*: unleash

reinstate v restore, return, give back, re-establish, put back

reinstatement n restoration, return, recall, replacement, re-establishment

reinsurance n provision, extra cover, protection

reinsure v take out extra cover, transfer, make extra provision

reintroduce v introduce again, bring into effect again, reinstate, restore, re-establish

reintroduction n reinstatement, restoration, re-establishment

reinvigorated adj revitalized, refreshed, restored, recharged, fresh *Opposite*: exhausted

reissue v rerelease, redistribute, recirculate, republish, send out again ■ n new issue, reprint, rerelease, new edition, new copy

reiterate v repeat, go over, restate, stress, reinforce

reiteration n repetition, replication, restatement, echo, recap

reject v refuse, rebuff, decline, snub, throw out *Opposite*: accept

rejection n refusal, denial, rebuff, denunciation, refutation *Opposite*: acceptance

rejig *(infml)* v rearrange, alter, readjust, reorganize, change

rejoice *(literary)* v celebrate, be pleased about, cheer, exult, be glad *Opposite*: lament

rejoin *(fml)* v reply, answer, respond, retort, return

rejoinder *(fml)* n response, answer, reply, comeback, retort. *See* COMPARE AND CONTRAST *at* **answer**.

rejuvenate v revitalize, invigorate, revive, make younger, revivify

rejuvenation n revitalization, reinvigoration, regeneration, renewal, renovation

rekindle v renew, reawaken, revive, regenerate, relight *Opposite*: kill

relapse v go back to, revert, deteriorate, degenerate, fall back *Opposite*: improve ■ n deterioration, decline, degeneration, reversion, waning *Opposite*: improvement

relate v **1 connect**, link, associate, correlate, link up **2 interact**, get on, form a relationship, connect, cooperate **3 tell**, narrate, speak about, recount, relay

related adj connected, linked, associated, correlated, interrelated *Opposite*: unconnected

relating to *prep* about, regarding, re, apropos of, in relation to

relation *n* family member, relative, next of kin

relations *n* **1** kith and kin, kin, family members, relatives, family **2** relationships, dealings, associations, affairs, contact

relationship *n* association, connection, affiliation, rapport, liaison

relative *adj* comparative, qualified, virtual *Opposite*: absolute ■ *n* family member, relation, next of kin

relative to *prep* in relation to, compared with, proportionate to, corresponding to

relativism *n* contingency, belief, doctrine *Opposite*: absolutism

relativist *n* equivocator, fence sitter, agnostic, waverer, vacillator ■ *adj* contingent, dependent, relative

relativity *n* relativeness, dependence, contingency

relax *v* **1** loosen, slacken, ease, let up on, let out *Opposite*: tense **2** rest, put your feet up, take it easy, have a break, lie down **3** unwind, calm down, slow down, let go, loosen up **4** lessen, decrease, diminish, lower, ease *Opposite*: increase

relaxation *n* **1** recreation, leisure, entertainment, rest, repose **2** reduction, lessening, easing, slackening, moderation *Opposite*: increase

relaxed *adj* **1** tranquil, calm, comfortable, stress-free, unperturbed *Opposite*: tense **2** lenient, easygoing, untroubled, casual, laid-back *(infml) Opposite*: strict

relaxing *adj* calming, soothing, comforting, peaceful, tranquil *Opposite*: harrowing

relay *v* communicate, pass on, transmit, spread, convey

release *v* **1** let go, free, discharge, liberate, let loose *Opposite*: hold **2** make public, make available, announce, publish, circulate *Opposite*: withhold ■ *n* **1** relief, discharge, freedom, liberation, emancipation *Opposite*: arrest **2** announcement, issue, statement, publication, proclamation

relegate *v* demote, downgrade, transfer, consign, refer *Opposite*: promote

relegation *n* demotion, sending down, transfer down, lowering of rank, downgrade *Opposite*: promotion

relent *v* give in, cave in, change your mind, concede, yield *Opposite*: stand firm

relentless *adj* **1** ceaseless, unremitting, persistent, endless, steady **2** remorseless, merciless, pitiless, ruthless, heartless

relentlessness *n* **1** ceaselessness, unremittingness, persistence, intensity, steadiness **2** remorselessness, mercilessness, pitilessness, ruthlessness, harshness

relevance *n* significance, bearing, application, importance, weight *Opposite*: irrelevance

relevant *adj* pertinent, applicable, germane, related, appropriate *Opposite*: unrelated

reliability *n* dependability, consistency, steadfastness, trustworthiness *Opposite*: untrustworthiness

reliable *adj* dependable, consistent, steadfast, unswerving, unfailing *Opposite*: unreliable

reliance *n* dependence, confidence, trust, belief, faith *Opposite*: independence

reliant *adj* dependent, needful, conditional, subject to, contingent *Opposite*: independent

relic *n* historical object, artefact, remnant, remains, vestige

relief *n* **1** assistance, aid, help, reinforcement, support **2** respite, release, reprieve, break, liberation

relieve *v* **1** ease, release, alleviate, reduce, mitigate *Opposite*: exacerbate **2** take the place of, take over for, substitute for, stand in for, replace **3** dismiss, release, let go, discharge, get rid of *Opposite*: appoint

relieved *adj* reassured, thankful, calmed, pleased, comforted *Opposite*: worried

religion *n* faith, belief, creed, conviction, denomination

religious *adj* **1** theological, sacred, holy, consecrated, church *Opposite*: secular **2** spiritual, devout, pious, holy, observant *Opposite*: irreligious **3** thorough, conscientious, dutiful, faithful, reliable *Opposite*: unreliable

religiousness *n* devoutness, piousness, spirituality, sense of God, faithfulness

relinquish *v* give up, surrender, hand over, abandon, renounce *Opposite*: retain

reliquary *n* repository, casket, container, shrine

relish *v* enjoy, delight in, savour, take pleasure in, like *Opposite*: dislike ■ *n* enjoyment, delight, pleasure, elation, appreciation *Opposite*: displeasure

relive *v* experience again, go through again, live through again, remember, recall *Opposite*: forget

reload *v* refill, fill, load again, replenish, recharge *Opposite*: unload

relocate *v* move, change place, reposition, transfer, displace *Opposite*: remain

relocation *n* transfer, moving, rearrangement, repositioning, replacement

reluctance *n* unwillingness, lack of enthusiasm, disinclination, hesitancy, foot-dragging *(infml) Opposite*: enthusiasm

reluctant *adj* unwilling, unenthusiastic, disinclined, loath, hesitant *Opposite*: enthusiastic. *See* COMPARE AND CONTRAST *at* unwilling.

rely *v* depend on, bank on, count on, trust, be sure of *Opposite*: distrust

remain *v* **1** stay, stay put, stay behind, stay on, linger *Opposite*: leave **2** continue, keep on, endure, persist, go on *Opposite*: stop

remainder *n* rest, residue, remnants, remains, leftovers

remaining *adj* residual, outstanding, left over, excess, lingering

remains *n* 1 leftovers, remnants, relics, remainder, ruins 2 dead body, corpse, cadaver, ashes, carcass

remake *n* new version, cover version, cover, new edition, re-creation ■ *v* produce again, recreate, re-form, change the format, reshape

remand *v* return to custody, return to prison, commit to custody, imprison, jail ■ *n* return to custody, return to prison, committal to custody, custody, prison

remark *n* comment, statement, observation, aside, mention ■ *v* say, comment, state, observe, pronounce

remarkable *adj* extraordinary, amazing, notable, outstanding, noteworthy *Opposite*: ordinary

remarry *v* get married again, marry again, get wed again, re-wed, wed again (*fml or literary*)

rematch *n* replay, a second go, another game

remedial *adj* corrective, counteractive, helpful, educative, curative *Opposite*: precautionary

remedy *n* 1 solution, cure, answer, antidote, resolution 2 medicine, medication, preparation, mixture, therapy ■ *v* 1 cure, relieve, improve, alleviate, ease 2 resolve, deal with, correct, improve, make better *Opposite*: exacerbate

remember *v* 1 keep in mind, bear in mind, retain, memorize, learn *Opposite*: forget 2 recall, think of, recollect, dredge up, hark back to *Opposite*: forget

remembrance *n* commemoration, memory, tribute, recollection, reminiscence

remind *v* 1 be reminiscent, strike a chord, take you back, jog your memory, ring a bell (*infml*) 2 repeat, retell, prompt, recap, run by again

reminder *n* 1 cue, notice, prompt, recap, aide-mémoire (*fml*) 2 souvenir, token, memento, knick-knack, keepsake

reminisce *v* recall, talk about, hark back to, muse over, evoke

reminiscence *n* 1 nostalgia, recollection, looking back, musing, rumination 2 memory, recollection, reminder

reminiscent *adj* suggestive, evocative, resonant, redolent, similar

remiss *adj* careless, negligent, lax, slipshod, slapdash *Opposite*: diligent

remission *n* reduction, decrease, lessening, diminution, cutback

remissive *adj* pardoning, forgiving, absolving, exonerating

remit *v* 1 send, forward, dispatch, pay, settle 2 submit, refer, pass on *Opposite*: handle 3 slacken, decrease, lessen, diminish, cancel *Opposite*: increase ■ *n* responsibility, concern, sphere of activity, job, brief

remittance *n* 1 payment, transfer of funds,

transmittal, fee, transfer 2 release, dispatch, discharge (*fml*)

remix *v* produce a new version of, rehash, reproduce, alter, change ■ *n* new recording, different version, new version, latest version, revised version

remnant *n* remainder, remains, relic, residue, trace

remodel *v* alter, modify, modernize, adapt, adjust

remonstrance *n* 1 argument, evidence, backup, proof, case 2 protest, complaint, objection, petition, dispute

remonstrate *v* argue, protest, object, oppose, complain *Opposite*: agree. *See* COMPARE AND CONTRAST *at* object.

remorse *n* regret, sorrow, repentance, penitence, guilt

remorseful *adj* regretful, repentant, penitent, contrite, apologetic *Opposite*: unrepentant

remorseless *adj* 1 pitiless, ruthless, merciless, callous, cruel *Opposite*: merciful 2 inexorable, implacable, indefatigable, unbending, unyielding

remote *adj* 1 distant, isolated, inaccessible, far-flung, far-off *Opposite*: nearby 2 aloof, detached, withdrawn, reserved, cool *Opposite*: approachable 3 slight, outside, slim, unlikely, improbable *Opposite*: likely

remotely *adv* 1 slightly, tenuously, marginally, minimally, a little *Opposite*: closely 2 at all, in the least, the least bit, the slightest bit *Opposite*: greatly

remoteness *n* 1 isolation, seclusion, distance, solitude, inaccessibility *Opposite*: closeness 2 aloofness, detachment, reserve, inaccessibility, coolness *Opposite*: approachability 3 slightness, improbability, faintness, slimness *Opposite*: likelihood

remount *v* get on again, get back on, mount again, ride again, get back in the saddle

removable *adj* detachable, not fixed, can be removed, changeable, transferable *Opposite*: attached

removal *n* taking away, elimination, exclusion, subtraction, deletion *Opposite*: addition

remove *v* 1 take away, get rid of, eliminate, do away with, eradicate *Opposite*: add 2 take off, detach, cut off, amputate, disconnect

remunerate *v* pay, reward, compensate, recompense, repay

remuneration *n* payment, fee, salary, wage, compensation. *See* COMPARE AND CONTRAST *at* wage.

renaissance *n* rebirth, new start, new beginning, resurgence, revitalization *Opposite*: decline

rename *v* give a new name, retitle, rechristen, nickname, change the name of

renascent *adj* becoming active, budding, burgeoning, appearing, becoming popular

rend v **tear**, tear apart, rip, come apart, split *Opposite*: mend. *See* COMPARE AND CONTRAST *at* tear.

render v 1 (fml) **provide**, give, deliver, submit, make available 2 (fml) **portray**, depict, represent, execute, translate 3 (fml) **decide**, decree, judge, adjudicate, declare 4 **make**, cause, cause to become 5 **melt down**, reduce, condense, concentrate, boil down *Opposite*: solidify

rendering n 1 **portrayal**, depiction, picture, image, portrait 2 **version**, translation, interpretation, interpreting, execution 3 **plaster coating**, plaster, pebbledash, coating, cladding

rendezvous n 1 **engagement**, meeting, appointment, tryst, assignation 2 **meeting place**, meeting point, assembly point, location, site ■ v **meet**, come together, make contact, get together, assemble

rendition n **version**, interpretation, performance, rendering, execution

renegade n **apostate**, traitor, rebel, turncoat, betrayer *Opposite*: loyalist

renege v **go back on**, break your word, break a promise, back out, default

renew v 1 **return to**, reintroduce, repeat, restart, begin again 2 **rekindle**, revitalize, rejuvenate, refresh, revive 3 **recondition**, renovate, refurbish, revamp, restore

COMPARE AND CONTRAST CORE MEANING: improve the condition of something
renew replace something worn or broken; **recondition** bring something such as a machine or appliance back to a good condition or working state by means of repairs or replacement of parts; **renovate** bring something such as a building back to a former better state by means of repairs, redecoration, or refurbishment; **restore** bring something back to an original state after it has been damaged or fallen into a bad condition; **revamp** improve the appearance or condition of something.

renewal n **regeneration**, restitution, rekindling, revitalization, rejuvenation

renounce v 1 **relinquish**, surrender, hand over, give up, abdicate *Opposite*: accept 2 **disavow**, repudiate, reject, abandon, forsake *Opposite*: embrace

renovate v **renew**, recondition, modernize, refurbish, repair *Opposite*: wear out. *See* COMPARE AND CONTRAST *at* **renew**.

renovation n **facelift**, revamp, makeover, restoration, redecoration

renown n **fame**, celebrity, notoriety, prominence, popularity *Opposite*: obscurity

renowned adj **famous**, well-known, celebrated, prominent, popular *Opposite*: unknown

rent n 1 **rental**, rent payment, hire charge, fee, payment 2 **hole**, tear, rip, split, slash ■ v **let**, hire out, lend out, rent out, charter

rental n **rent payment**, fee, payment, hire charge, charge

renunciation n 1 **repudiation**, abandonment, denial, renouncement, rejection *Opposite*: acceptance 2 **surrender**, disowning, relinquishment, abdication

reorder v **rearrange**, reorganize, regroup, restructure, move around

reorganization n **reform**, restructuring, reshuffle, redeployment, reformation

reorganize v **regroup**, move around, reorder, rearrange, restructure

rep (infml) n **representative**, agent, courier, delegate, deputy

repaint v **redecorate**, renovate, touch up, patch up, freshen up

repair v **mend**, fix, patch up, restore, darn *Opposite*: damage ■ n **overhaul**, reparation, restoration, patch-up, mending

reparation n **amends**, compensation, damages, recompense, reimbursement

repartee n **banter**, wit, wordplay, badinage, raillery

repast (literary) n **meal**, banquet, feast, buffet, collation

repatriate v **send home**, deport, send back, banish, exile

repatriation n **sending home**, going home, deportation, return, exile

repay v **pay**, pay back, reimburse, refund, pay off

repayment n **payment**, refund, reimbursement, settlement, compensation

repeal v **cancel**, revoke, rescind, annul, nullify *Opposite*: enact

repeat v 1 **reiterate**, recap, go over, echo, retell 2 **do again**, replicate, duplicate, show again, copy ■ n **recurrence**, replication, reiteration, duplication, reappearance

repeated adj **recurrent**, frequent, recurring, repetitive, constant *Opposite*: rare

repel v 1 **disgust**, revolt, nauseate, repulse, make you feel sick 2 **keep away**, fend off, drive back, keep at bay, deter *Opposite*: attract

repellent adj 1 **disgusting**, revolting, nauseating, repulsive, repugnant *Opposite*: attractive 2 **impervious**, impermeable, resistant, proof, tight

repent v **regret**, be sorry, apologize, ask forgiveness, feel sorrow

repentance n **regret**, sorrow, remorse, penitence, atonement *Opposite*: shamelessness

repentant adj **regretful**, remorseful, apologetic, penitent, rueful *Opposite*: unrepentant

repercussion n **consequence**, effect, upshot, impact, aftermath

repertoire n **repertory**, collection, selection, series, stock

repertory n 1 **staging**, production, performance **2 theatre company**, theatre group, company, repertory theatre, theatre **3 repertoire**, selection, series, stock, range

repetition *n* **recurrence**, replication, duplication, reiteration, reappearance

repetitious *adj* **boring**, monotonous, tedious, dull, repetitive *Opposite*: innovative

repetitive *see* repetitious

repetitively *adv* **repeatedly**, continually, over and over again, cyclically, frequently *Opposite*: infrequently

rephrase *v* **restate**, retell, say differently, express in other words, put another way

replace *v* **1 substitute**, trade, use instead, exchange, switch **2 replenish**, put back, restore, return, reinstate

replacement *n* **substitute**, stand-in, substitution, proxy, surrogate *Opposite*: original

replay *v* **play again**, rerun, repeat, retell, reiterate ■ *n* **rerun**, repetition, reiteration, echo, repeat

replenish *v* **replace**, refill, fill, stock up, top up *Opposite*: deplete

replenishment *n* **replacement**, refill, top up, renewal

replete *adj* **1 full**, complete, supplied, abounding, brimming *Opposite*: lacking **2 sated**, satisfied, satiated, full, full up *Opposite*: hungry

repletion *n* **fullness**, surfeit, glut, satiety

replica *n* **copy**, reproduction, imitation, model, facsimile *Opposite*: original

replicate *v* **duplicate**, repeat, copy, imitate, reproduce. *See* COMPARE AND CONTRAST *at* copy.

replication *n* **repetition**, duplication, imitation, copying, reproduction

reply *v* **respond**, answer, retort, answer back, react *Opposite*: ask ■ *n* **response**, account, answer, retort, riposte *Opposite*: question. *See* COMPARE AND CONTRAST *at* answer.

report *v* **1 give an account**, tell, state, describe, give details **2 register**, check in, present yourself, turn up, show up ■ *n* **1 tale**, statement, description, testimony, story **2 loud noise**, bang, boom, crash, explosion

reportage *n* **news coverage**, reporting, coverage, mention, analysis

reportedly *adv* **allegedly**, supposedly, apparently, seemingly, so they say *Opposite*: actually

reporter *n* **foreign correspondent**, special correspondent, journalist, correspondent, writer

repose *n* **1 inactivity**, sleep, rest, relaxation, restfulness *Opposite*: activity **2 calmness**, peace, stillness, tranquillity, calm *Opposite*: agitation ■ *v* *(fml)* **relax**, rest, take it easy, recline, put your feet up

reposition *v* **shift**, transpose, move, relocate

repositioning *n* **transposition**, relocation, moving, move

repository *n* **1 store**, container, storage area, storage place, receptacle **2 source**, fountain, mine, storehouse, origin

repossess *v* **recoup**, take back, reclaim, recover, recuperate

repossession *n* **recovery**, reclamation, retrieval, taking back, seizure

repot *v* **transplant**, transfer, replant, pot, pot on

reprehensible *adj* **wrong**, bad, disgraceful, shameful, inexcusable *Opposite*: praiseworthy

reprehension *n* **criticism**, censure, condemnation, telling off, admonition *Opposite*: praise

reprehensive *adj* **condemnatory**, reproachful, accusing, reproving, critical *Opposite*: praiseworthy

represent *v* **1 act for**, speak for, stand for, stand in for **2 stand for**, symbolize, correspond to, signify, exemplify *Opposite*: misrepresent

representation *n* **1 picture**, image, symbol, depiction, illustration **2 statement**, complaint, submission, argument **3 account**, version, portrayal, description, interpretation

representational *adj* **realistic**, representative, figurative, depictive, mimetic *Opposite*: abstract

representative *n* **1 envoy**, delegate, agent, spokesperson, diplomat **2 agent**, courier, delegate, deputy, rep *(infml)* ■ *adj* **1 symbolic**, descriptive, illustrative, evocative, expressive **2 illustrative**, typical, characteristic, demonstrative, archetypal

repress *v* **1 curb**, block, suppress, contain, keep inside *Opposite*: express **2 dominate**, subdue, overpower, subjugate, quell

repressed *adj* **1 stifled**, bottled-up, suppressed, blocked, curbed *Opposite*: expressed **2 intimidated**, crushed, suppressed, subjugated, overpowered *Opposite*: liberated

repression *n* **suppression**, subjugation, domination, authoritarianism, tyranny

repressive *adj* **oppressive**, suppressive, tyrannical, authoritarian, brutal *Opposite*: liberal

reprieve *v* **let off**, pardon, grant a stay of execution, acquit, stay *Opposite*: punish ■ *n* **official pardon**, stay of execution, amnesty, pardon, acquittal

reprimand *v* **chastise**, reproach, lecture, scold, admonish *Opposite*: praise ■ *n* **rebuke**, admonishment, warning, dressing-down, reproof

reprint *v* **reissue**, print again, publish again, produce again, republish ■ *n* **reissue**, copy, edition

reprisal *n* **retaliation**, revenge, act of vengeance, punishment, payback *(infml)*

reprise *n* **reappearance**, echo, recap, repeat,

repetition ■ v **repeat**, reinterpret, re-enact, re-present

reproach v **admonish**, accuse, reprove, criticize, scold Opposite: praise ■ n **criticism**, censure, reprimand, blame, accusation Opposite: praise

reproachful adj **censorious**, accusing, disapproving, reproving, critical Opposite: approving

reprobate n **degenerate**, rascal, troublemaker, sinner, wrongdoer

reprocess v **process again**, reuse, recycle, recover, reclaim

reproduce v 1 **copy**, replicate, duplicate, repeat, imitate 2 **have children**, produce offspring, produce young, breed, give birth. See COMPARE AND CONTRAST at copy.

reproduction n 1 **copy**, imitation, replica, duplicate, facsimile Opposite: original 2 **breeding**, procreation, propagation, generation, multiplication ■ adj **imitation**, replica, fake, faux Opposite: genuine

reproductive adj **generative**, multiplicative, procreative, procreant, propagative

reproof n **criticism**, blame, accusation, rebuke, scolding Opposite: compliment

reprove v **criticize**, take to task, accuse, rebuke, scold Opposite: praise

reproving adj **disapproving**, condemnatory, reproachful, admonitory, censorious Opposite: approving

reptilian adj **cold-blooded**, unfriendly, emotionless, inhuman, stony Opposite: warm

republic n **state**, nation, democracy Opposite: monarchy

republican n **antiroyalist**, antimonarchist Opposite: monarchist ■ adj **pro-republic**, antiroyalist, antimonarchist Opposite: monarchist

republicanism n **antimonarchism**, antiroyalism, political belief Opposite: monarchism

repudiate v 1 **reject**, renounce, retract, disavow, turn your back on Opposite: acknowledge 2 **deny**, refute, contradict, gainsay, disclaim Opposite: accept

repudiation n 1 **retraction**, renunciation, rejection, abandonment, disavowal (fml) Opposite: acknowledgment 2 **denial**, refutation, negation, disclaimer, contradiction Opposite: acceptance

repugnance n **disgust**, revulsion, hatred, hate, abhorrence Opposite: attraction. See COMPARE AND CONTRAST at dislike.

repugnant adj 1 **offensive**, objectionable, distasteful, unacceptable, obnoxious Opposite: agreeable 2 **disgusting**, revolting, nauseating, repulsive, hideous Opposite: attractive

repulse v 1 **repel**, drive away, force away, hold back, hold off Opposite: yield 2 **disgust**, sicken, nauseate, repel, appal 3 **reject**, rebuff, resist, spurn, snub Opposite: welcome

repulsed adj **disgusted**, nauseated, revolted, repelled, sickened Opposite: attracted

repulsion n **disgust**, revulsion, nausea, loathing, repugnance Opposite: attraction

repulsive adj **disgusting**, revolting, nauseating, hideous, vile Opposite: attractive

repulsiveness n **hideousness**, repugnance, foulness, abhorrence, vileness Opposite: attractiveness

reputable adj **highly regarded**, trustworthy, well-thought-of, sound, upright Opposite: disreputable

reputation n **standing**, status, name, character, repute (fml)

repute (fml) see **reputation**

reputed adj **supposed**, alleged, presumed, apparent, believed Opposite: actual

request v **ask for**, apply for, call for, entreat, invite Opposite: demand ■ n **appeal**, call, application, entreaty, invitation Opposite: demand

requiem n 1 **service**, Mass, funeral, funeral Mass, service for the dead 2 **funeral music**, lament, dirge, funeral hymn, funeral song

require v 1 **need**, necessitate, want, have need of, entail 2 **oblige**, compel, demand, expect, force

required adj **necessary**, obligatory, compulsory, mandatory, essential Opposite: optional

requirement n **obligation**, condition, prerequisite, must, necessity Opposite: option

requisite (fml) adj **necessary**, mandatory, vital, essential, indispensable Opposite: optional. See COMPARE AND CONTRAST at necessary.

requisition n **demand**, request, application, summons ■ v 1 **take over**, commandeer, seize, take possession of, appropriate Opposite: relinquish 2 **demand**, apply for, call for, request, put in for

reread v **revise**, look back over, check through, go through, read again

rerun v **replay**, repeat, play again, air again, show again ■ n **repeat**, repeat showing, replay

reschedule v **postpone**, rearrange, defer, reorganize, suspend Opposite: bring forward

rescheduling n **postponement**, deferment, putting off, rearrangement, rearranging

rescind v **withdraw**, annul, cancel, repeal, overturn Opposite: authorize

rescue v **save**, free, set free, liberate, release Opposite: abandon ■ n **release**, liberation, saving, salvage Opposite: capture

rescuer n **saviour**, champion, liberator, salvation, redeemer Opposite: captor

research n **investigation**, study, exploration, examination, enquiries ■ v **investigate**, study, explore, do research, delve into

researcher n **investigator**, academic, scholar, scientist, student

resemblance n **similarity**, likeness, semblance, sameness, alikeness Opposite: difference

resemble v **look like**, bear a resemblance to, be similar to, be like, look a lot like Opposite: differ

resembling adj **like**, similar to, not unlike, close to, reminiscent of

resent v **1 begrudge**, bear a grudge, feel bitter about, have hard feelings about, feel aggrieved Opposite: accept **2 dislike**, not like, hate, be offended by, show antipathy towards Opposite: like

resentful adj **angry**, bitter, indignant, offended, aggrieved

resentment n **anger**, bitterness, dislike, hatred, antipathy. See COMPARE AND CONTRAST at anger.

reservation n **1 advance booking**, booking, registration, reserved seat, arrangement **2 protected area**, sanctuary, refuge, game reserve, game park **3 unwillingness**, reluctance, hesitation, distance, aloofness Opposite: enthusiasm **4 condition**, proviso, rider, corollary, stipulation

reservations n **misgivings**, doubts, hesitation, questions, uncertainties

reserve v **1 set aside**, keep, keep back, hold back, put to one side Opposite: use **2 book**, retain, put your name down for, make a reservation Opposite: cancel ■ n **1 store**, cache, hoard, stock, emergency supply **2 reservation**, park, game park, protected area, game reserve **3 substitute**, stand-in, fallback, replacement, locum

reserved adj **1 booked**, retained, taken, engaged Opposite: free **2 earmarked**, kept, set aside, held in reserve, kept back Opposite: used **3 aloof**, reticent, standoffish, snobbish, distant Opposite: outgoing

reserves n **1 assets**, funds, contingency fund, financial resources, capital **2 stocks**, supplies, hoard, resources, stores

reservist n **soldier**, reserve, reserve member, part-time soldier, Territorial

reservoir n **tank**, pool, basin, lake, artificial lake

reset v **rearrange**, reorganize, retune, change, right

resettle v **relocate**, transfer, transplant, emigrate, immigrate

resettlement n **relocation**, immigration, emigration, migration, transfer

reshape v **redesign**, reform, rewrite, restructure, reformat

reshuffle n **reorganization**, rearrangement, rationalization, reallocation, reordering ■ v **reorganize**, rearrange, rationalize, reallocate, reorder

reside v **1 live**, live in, inhabit, have your home, be a resident of **2 exist in**, be inherent in, be located in, be a feature of, be present in

residence n **house**, home, seat, habitation, dwelling (fml)

residency n **placement**, position, job, post, internship

resident n **occupant**, inhabitant, denizen, tenant, occupier

residential adj **domestic**, suburban, housing, domiciliary Opposite: business

residual adj **left over**, remaining, lingering, left behind, outstanding

residue n **remains**, remainder, rest, deposit, scum

resign v **leave**, leave your job, quit, walk out, give notice Opposite: sign on

resignation n **1 notice**, notification, letter of resignation **2 acceptance**, acquiescence, acknowledgment, submission, forbearance (fml) Opposite: defiance

resigned adj **reconciled**, accepting, acquiescent, submissive, stoic Opposite: resistant

resign yourself v **accept**, acknowledge, give in to, yield to, reconcile yourself Opposite: resist

resilience n **1 buoyancy**, spirit, hardiness, toughness, resistance Opposite: defeatism **2 pliability**, flexibility, elasticity, suppleness, bounciness Opposite: rigidity

resilient adj **1 hardy**, strong, tough, robust, buoyant Opposite: defeatist **2 elastic**, pliable, flexible, supple, resistant Opposite: rigid

resin n **mastic**, gum, balm, kauri gum, gamboge

resinous adj **sticky**, viscous, tacky, gummy

resist v **1 fight**, battle, struggle, fight back, attack Opposite: surrender **2 oppose**, defy, stand firm, contest, challenge Opposite: accept **3 withstand**, survive, endure, weather, be proof against Opposite: succumb **4 keep from**, avoid, refuse, refrain, withstand Opposite: give in

resistance n **1 confrontation**, fight, battle, fighting, struggle Opposite: surrender **2 opposition**, defiance, challenge, endurance Opposite: acceptance

resistant adj **1 opposed**, dead set against, unwilling, defiant, challenging Opposite: accepting **2 resilient**, hardy, unaffected, impervious, tough Opposite: weak

resistor n **regulator**, rheostat, controller

resit n **retake**, re-examination, re-test, repeat ■ v **take again**, retake, repeat, sit again

resolute adj **firm**, staunch, unyielding, stubborn, unbendable Opposite: irresolute

resoluteness n **firmness**, determination, steadfastness, staunchness, single-mindedness Opposite: indecisiveness

resolution n **1 decree**, declaration, decision, motion, ruling **2 promise**, pledge, oath, vow

3 resolve, determination, steadfastness, tenacity, firmness *Opposite*: indecision **4 solution**, answer, end, upshot, outcome

resolve *v* **1 make up your mind**, decide, determine, make a decision, undertake **2 solve**, get to the bottom of, sort out, put an end to, settle ■ *n* **resolution**, determination, steadfastness, tenacity, doggedness *Opposite*: indecision

resolved *adj* **determined**, set, resolute, fixed, committed *Opposite*: undecided

resonance *n* **1 timbre**, character, quality, tone, reverberation **2 significance**, meaning, importance, suggestion, echo

resonant *adj* **1 booming**, ringing, echoing, reverberating, resounding *Opposite*: tinny **2 significant**, meaningful, important, evocative, indicative *Opposite*: insignificant

resonate *v* **reverberate**, vibrate, resound, ring, echo

resort *n* **option**, recourse, alternative, course of action, possibility

resort to *v* **turn to**, give in to, have recourse to, fall back on, avail yourself of

resound *v* **echo**, resonate, boom, ring, reverberate

resounding *adj* **1 loud**, booming, echoing, ringing, resonant *Opposite*: weak **2 unqualified**, categorical, unambiguous, definite, unquestionable *Opposite*: qualified

resource *n* **reserve**, supply, source, means, store

resourceful *adj* **ingenious**, imaginative, inventive, practical, quick-witted *Opposite*: unimaginative

resourcefulness *n* **ingenuity**, imagination, inventiveness, wits, originality

resources *n* **capital**, income, possessions, wealth, property

respect *n* **1 admiration**, high opinion, regard, esteem, reverence *Opposite*: disrespect **2 detail**, regard, matter, particular, point ■ *v* **1 value**, revere, think a lot of, esteem, defer to *Opposite*: disrespect **2 show consideration for**, appreciate, regard, have a high regard for, recognize *Opposite*: disregard **3 follow**, abide by, comply with, obey, acknowledge *Opposite*: deny. *See* COMPARE AND CONTRAST *at* regard.

respectability *n* **decency**, propriety, uprightness, decorum, morality *Opposite*: indecency

respectable *adj* **1 reputable**, highly regarded, well-thought-of, decent, good *Opposite*: disreputable **2 adequate**, decent, reasonable, acceptable, satisfactory *Opposite*: inadequate

respected *adj* **reliable**, authoritative, distinguished, venerable, esteemed

respectful *adj* **deferential**, reverential, reverent, humble, dutiful *Opposite*: disrespectful

respectfulness *n* **deference**, respect, regard, consideration, honour *Opposite*: contemptuousness

respecting *prep* **with regard to**, regarding, with respect to, in respect of, relating to

respective *adj* **own**, individual, particular, separate, corresponding

respects *n* **compliments**, good wishes, greetings, salutations *(fml)*

respiration *n* **breathing**, inhalation, exhalation

respirator *n* **breathing apparatus**, ventilator, gas mask, oxygen mask

respiratory *adj* **breathing**, lung, respirational

WORD BANK
❑ **parts of a respiratory system** air sac, airway, alveolus, bronchial tube, bronchiole, bronchus, larynx, lung, pharynx, throat, trachea, vocal cords, voice box, windpipe

respire *v* **breathe**, take breaths, inhale, exhale

respite *n* **1 interval**, break, breathing space, lull, relief **2 reprieve**, delay, adjournment, hiatus, break

resplendent *adj* **splendid**, dazzling, magnificent, glorious, brilliant *Opposite*: unimpressive

respond *v* **1 reply**, answer, retort, answer back, rejoin *(fml)* **2 react**, act in response, take action, counter, act *Opposite*: ignore

respondent *n* **defendant**, accused, plaintiff

response *n* **reply**, answer, retort, comeback, reaction. *See* COMPARE AND CONTRAST *at* answer.

responsibility *n* **1 accountability**, duty, charge, concern, obligation *Opposite*: irresponsibility **2 blame**, liability, guilt, answerability, fault **3 task**, remit, brief, assignment, concern

responsible *adj* **1 accountable**, in charge, in control, in authority, answerable **2 to blame**, liable, guilty, at fault, blamable **3 dependable**, conscientious, trustworthy, reliable, sensible *Opposite*: irresponsible

responsive *adj* **receptive**, open, approachable, reactive, quick to respond *Opposite*: sluggish

responsively *adv* **sensitively**, quick-wittedly, instinctively, positively, favourably

responsiveness *n* **receptiveness**, openness, reaction, sensitivity, awareness *Opposite*: sluggishness

rest *n* **1 break**, respite, time out, relaxation, recreation **2 remainder**, residue, leftovers, remnants, surplus **3 stand**, support, holder, rack, frame ■ *v* **1 relax**, take it easy, have a rest, take a break, have a break **2 lie**, lean, lay, place, put

restart *v* **1 resume**, take up, start again, pick up, start over *(US)* **2 revive**, resurrect, save, renew, reopen *Opposite*: wind down

restate *v* **repeat**, reaffirm, reiterate, say again, regurgitate

rested *adj* **refreshed**, relaxed, restored, reinvigorated, revitalized *Opposite*: exhausted

restful *adj* **soothing**, relaxing, soporific, calming, peaceful *Opposite*: stimulating

restitution *n* **1 compensation**, recompense, reimbursement, amends, repayment **2 restoration**, return, reinstatement

restive *see* **restless**

restiveness *n* **restlessness**, impatience, agitation, edginess, nervousness *Opposite*: calmness

restless *adj* **fidgety**, agitated, edgy, impatient, on edge *Opposite*: relaxed

restlessness *n* **agitation**, impatience, restiveness, edginess *Opposite*: calmness

restock *v* **refill**, replenish, top up, fill up, replace

rest on *v* **hinge on**, turn on, depend on, rely, hang on

restoration *n* **1 reinstatement**, re-establishment, return, restitution, reinstallation *Opposite*: abolition **2 refurbishment**, renovation, repair, renewal, rebuilding

restorative *adj* **healing**, uplifting, invigorating, soothing, recuperative *Opposite*: draining

restore *v* **1 reinstate**, re-establish, bring back, return, give back **2 refurbish**, renovate, repair, renew, recondition. *See* COMPARE AND CONTRAST *at* **renew**.

restrain *v* **1 hold back**, prevent, stop, keep, deter **2 control**, bring under control, keep under control, keep in check, check **3 confine**, detain, jail, lock up, imprison *Opposite*: free

restrained *adj* **reserved**, controlled, in control of yourself, self-possessed, calm *Opposite*: demonstrative

restraining order *n* **injunction**, court order, gagging order, stay

restraint *n* **1 self-control**, control, command, self-possession, self-discipline *Opposite*: self-indulgence **2 limit**, limitation, curb, ceiling, restriction **3 captivity**, arrest, imprisonment, confinement, detention *Opposite*: freedom **4 belt**, chain, shackle, fetter, bond

restrict *v* **limit**, confine, put a ceiling on, curb, control *Opposite*: loosen

restricted *adj* **1 limited**, controlled, constrained, regulated, delimited *Opposite*: open **2 classified**, top-secret, secret, confidential, privileged *Opposite*: public

restriction *n* **limit**, constraint, restraint, control, ceiling

restrictive *adj* **preventive**, obstructive, limiting, deterring, restraining *Opposite*: free

restructure *v* **rearrange**, reorganize, reform, reshuffle, redistribute

restructuring *n* **rearrangement**, reorganization, shake-up, reform, reshuffle

result *n* **1 consequence**, outcome, upshot, effect, product **2 mark**, grade, score, outcome **3 calculation**, solution, answer, findings, conclusion ■ *v* **1 cause**, bring about, give rise to, occasion, lead to **2 ensue**, be caused by, stem, rise, be brought about by

resultant *adj* **subsequent**, ensuing, resulting, consequential, follow-on

resulting *adj* **subsequent**, resultant, ensuing, consequential, follow-on

resume *v* **1 recommence**, start again, continue, begin again, pick up where you left off *Opposite*: stop **2 return**, go back, reoccupy, take up again

résumé *n* **précis**, review, outline, rundown, summary

resumption *n* **recommencement**, continuation, carrying on, renewal, reopening

resurface *v* **1 float up**, come up, break the surface, rise *Opposite*: sink **2 reappear**, come back, rematerialize, re-emerge, return **3 coat**, cover, skim, overlay, surface

resurgence *n* **revival**, renaissance, rebirth, resurrection, recovery *Opposite*: disappearance

resurgent *adj* **burgeoning**, growing, rising, increasing, reviving

resurrect *v* **1 resuscitate**, bring back to life, raise from the dead, restore to life, revive *Opposite*: kill **2 save**, breathe new life into, revive, revivify, restart

resurrection *n* **revival**, renaissance, rebirth, revivification, reappearance

resuscitate *v* **1 give the kiss of life to**, give artificial respiration to, bring round, save *Opposite*: asphyxiate **2 breathe new life into**, revive, revivify, resurrect, boost

resuscitation *n* **1 artificial respiration**, cardiac massage, revival, recovery **2 restoration**, resurgence, renewal, revival, revitalization

retail *n* **trade**, selling, marketing, merchandising, wholesale ■ *v* **sell**, trade, put on the market, put up for sale, vend

retailer *n* **1 shop**, store, retail outlet **2 seller**, vendor, merchant, trader, dealer

retain *v* **1 keep**, keep hold of, hold on to, hold, hang on to *Opposite*: let go **2 recall**, recollect, keep in mind, remember, hold *Opposite*: forget

retainer *n* **deposit**, down payment, fee, payment

retake *v* **1 take back**, recapture, regain, reconquer, win back **2 repeat**, redo, resit ■ *n* **resit**, exam, examination, repeat

retaliate *v* **hit back**, strike back, get even, even the score, react *Opposite*: forgive

retaliation *n* **reprisal**, revenge, vengeance, retribution *Opposite*: forgiveness

retaliatory *adj* **tit-for-tat**, reciprocal, reactive, punitive, revengeful *Opposite*: forgiving

retard *v* **delay**, slow down, hold up, hold back, hinder *Opposite*: speed up

retardation n delay, check, obstruction, hindrance, obstacle Opposite: acceleration

retarded adj **underdeveloped**, slow, stunted, arrested, lagging Opposite: accelerated

retch v vomit, gag, be sick, heave (infml), throw up (infml)

retell v repeat, restate, go over, reiterate, recite

retention n **1 holding**, retaining, preservation, withholding, maintenance Opposite: release **2 remembering**, memorizing, recalling, memory, recollection Opposite: forgetting

retentive adj retaining, absorbent, spongy

rethink v reconsider, change your mind, change direction, change tack, change course ■ n reconsideration, change of mind, change of heart, second thoughts, volte-face

reticence n **1 reserve**, silence, uncommunicativeness, discretion, restraint Opposite: openness **2 shyness**, bashfulness, reserve, quietness, modesty Opposite: boldness

reticent adj reserved, discreet, restrained, unforthcoming, uncommunicative Opposite: talkative. See COMPARE AND CONTRAST at silent.

retinue n entourage, followers, attendants, servants, aides

retire v **1 give up work**, stop working, step down, be pensioned off, be superannuated **2 go to bed**, call it a day, turn in (infml), hit the sack (infml), hit the hay (infml) **3 leave**, take your leave, withdraw, go away, go off

retired adj **superannuated**, pensioned off, discharged, emeritus, emerita Opposite: working

retirement n **1 superannuation**, departure, leaving, giving up work, stepping down **2 withdrawal**, retreat, sequestration, seclusion

retiring adj reticent, self-effacing, unassuming, shy, reserved

retort v reply, answer, respond, counter, rejoin (fml) ■ n reply, response, riposte, answer, squelch (slang). See COMPARE AND CONTRAST at answer.

retouch v touch up, correct, restore, renovate, improve

retrace v review, redo, go back over, repeat

retract v **1 draw in**, draw back, pull in, pull back, withdraw Opposite: extend **2 deny**, take back, withdraw, apologize, recant Opposite: stand by

retractable adj telescopic, folding, collapsible

retraction n withdrawal, refutation, disclaimer, denial, negation Opposite: confirmation

retreat n **1 departure**, withdrawal, flight, evacuation Opposite: advance **2 haven**, hideaway, sanctuary, refuge, shelter ■ v move away, move back, draw back, back away, run away Opposite: advance

retrench v cut back, economize, save, save money, tighten your belt

retrenchment n cutback, economizing, cuts, cost-cutting, belt-tightening

retribution n vengeance, revenge, reprisal, reckoning, justice

retributive adj punitive, retaliatory, vengeful, punishing, revengeful

retrieval n recovery, repossession, rescue, reclamation, salvage Opposite: loss

retrieve v save, get back, recover, regain, repossess Opposite: lose

retro adj period, old-fashioned, dated, historical, passé

retrograde adj **1 backward**, reversing, rearward Opposite: forward **2 regressive**, declining, worsening, getting worse, deteriorating Opposite: improving

retrogress v **1 regress**, decline, revert, degenerate, worsen Opposite: progress **2 move backwards**, reverse, go back, retreat, draw back Opposite: move forward

retrogression n decline, regression, return, relapse, deterioration Opposite: progression

retrogressive adj **1 regressive**, reverting, degenerating, worsening, getting worse Opposite: progressive **2 reversing**, retreating, withdrawing, moving back, drawing back

retrospect n recollection, remembrance, review, reconsideration, survey Opposite: prospect

retrospective adj **1 reviewing**, reflective, surveying, reconsidering **2 retroactive**, backdated, ex post facto **3 backward-looking**, nostalgic, retrograde, traditional, conservative Opposite: forward-thinking ■ n exhibition, show, presentation, showcase, display

retrospectively adv on reflection, in retrospect, with hindsight, with the benefit of hindsight, on second thoughts

return v **1 revisit**, come back, go again, come again, go back Opposite: depart **2 send back**, take back, replace, restore Opposite: retain **3 resume**, go back, revert, revisit, begin again Opposite: stop **4 repay**, pay back, refund, reimburse, give back Opposite: keep ■ n **1 coming back**, reappearance, reoccurrence, arrival, homecoming Opposite: departure **2 profit**, earnings, yield, revenue, proceeds

returns n revenue, earnings, yield, proceeds, takings Opposite: outlay

reunification n reunion, reconsolidation, amalgamation, recombination, reintegration

reunify v reunite, come together, rejoin, bring together, reintegrate

reunion n **1 gathering**, meeting, event, get-together (infml) **2 reunification**, reintegration, recombination, reconsolidation

reunite v reunify, unite, bring together, unify, come together Opposite: split

reusable adj refillable, returnable, recyclable, green, ecofriendly Opposite: disposable

reuse v recycle, reclaim, reprocess, salvage Opposite: discard

rev n revolution, cycle, rotation, turn, revolution per minute ■ v **race**, roar, scream, increase power, accelerate

revaluation n revision, reappraisal, reassessment, readjustment, redefinition

revalue v 1 raise, increase, up, enhance, augment (fml) Opposite: devalue 2 **reappraise**, re-evaluate, adjust, reset, change

revamp v restore, make over, renew, refurbish, give a facelift ■ n **facelift**, refurbishment, restoration, renovation, overhaul. See COMPARE AND CONTRAST at renew.

reveal v 1 **make known**, disclose, divulge, expose, make public Opposite: conceal 2 **expose**, uncover, show, bare, bring to light Opposite: cover up

revealing adj 1 skimpy, see-through, figure-hugging, close-fitting, tight-fitting 2 **enlightening**, illuminating, telling, telltale, informative Opposite: obscure

revealingly adv tellingly, significantly, interestingly, importantly, conspicuously

reveille n 1 **wake-up call**, early-morning call, bugle call Opposite: lights out 2 **early morning**, daybreak, dawn, sunrise, the crack of dawn Opposite: dusk

revel v 1 delight, enjoy, take pleasure in, luxuriate, bask 2 **make merry**, celebrate, have fun, socialize, let your hair down (infml) ■ n **celebration**, party, festivities, carnival, merrymaking

revelation n 1 exposé, exposure, disclosure, leak, admission 2 **surprise**, shock, eye opener

reveller n partygoer, roisterer, merrymaker, pleasure-seeker, celebrator

revelry n festivities, revels, celebrations, partying, merriment

revenge n retaliation, vengeance, retribution, settling of scores, reprisal ■ v **requite**, avenge, even the score, get your own back, retaliate

revenue n income, proceeds, profits, returns, takings Opposite: expenses

reverberate v echo, resound, ring, vibrate, resonate

reverberating adj resounding, echoing, resonant, rich, rumbling

reverberation n echo, sound, noise, boom

reverberations n aftershock, aftereffects, impact, shock

revere v admire, respect, look up to, hold in the highest regard, be in awe of Opposite: despise

revered adj 1 respected, valued, illustrious, distinguished, esteemed Opposite: vilified 2 **holy**, sacred, blessed, venerated, hallowed Opposite: vilified

reverence n respect, admiration, worship, veneration, regard Opposite: contempt. See COMPARE AND CONTRAST at regard.

reverend adj 1 (fml) respected, revered, venerated, worthy, noble 2 **ecclesiastical**, clerical, priestly (literary), ministerial ■ n vicar, priest, cleric, minister, parson

reverent see reverential

reverential adj respectful, deferential, worshipful, humble, awed Opposite: disrespectful

reverie n daydream, dream, trance, musing, contemplation

reversal n 1 turnaround, U-turn, volte-face, about-turn, about-face (US) 2 **setback**, hitch, problem, reverse, blow

reverse v 1 overturn, turn round, undo, annul, invalidate Opposite: carry out 2 **move backwards**, back up, drive backwards, go backwards, retreat Opposite: advance 3 **transpose**, switch, invert, reorder, rearrange ■ n 1 **contrary**, opposite, antithesis, converse 2 **back**, rear, underneath, other side, opposite side Opposite: front 3 **setback**, reversal, hitch, problem, misfortune ■ adj **opposite**, contrary, converse, inverse Opposite: same

reversible adj 1 rescindable, revocable, alterable, adjustable, changeable Opposite: irreversible 2 **two-sided**, dual-purpose, multipurpose, double-sided, two-in-one

reversion n 1 return, decline, deterioration, degeneration, retreat 2 **reversal**, turnaround, about-turn, U-turn, volte-face

revert v 1 return, go back, take a step back, relapse, regress 2 **go back**, revisit, go over again, take another look at, return 3 **regress**, change back, return, mutate, degenerate 4 **lapse**, backslide, go back to your old ways, slip back, reoffend 5 **be returned**, pass, pass back, return, go back

review v 1 reconsider, re-examine, reassess, go over, check 2 **appraise**, evaluate, assess, look at, examine ■ n 1 **publication**, magazine, journal, periodical 2 **appraisal**, evaluation, assessment, examination, analysis 3 **reconsideration**, re-examination, reassessment, check, re-evaluation

reviewer n critic, commentator, assessor, referee

revile v insult, abuse, scorn, condemn, censure Opposite: praise

revise v 1 amend, modify, adjust, alter, change 2 **study**, brush up, go over, look over, go through

revision n 1 amendment, reconsideration, modification, adjustment, alteration 2 **study**, revising, homework

revisionism n reassessment, reconsideration, reinterpretation, pragmatism, alteration

revisionist adj pragmatic, heretical, progressive, modernizing, controversial ■ n **pragmatist**, modernizer, heretic, liberal

revisit v 1 return to, go back to, come back to, retreat to, re-enter Opposite: abandon

2 reconsider, re-examine, reassess, re-evaluate, rethink

revitalization n **renewal**, renaissance, revival, new life, recovery Opposite: decline

revitalize v **refresh**, invigorate, revive, rejuvenate, regenerate Opposite: wear out

revitalizing adj **energizing**, vitalizing, stimulating, uplifting, invigorating

revival n **1 revitalization**, renewal, restoration, stimulation, reinforcement Opposite: disappearance **2 resuscitation**, recovery, waking, bringing round, coming to Opposite: relapse

revive v **1 resuscitate**, come round, recover, come to, bring round Opposite: lose consciousness **2 recover**, pick up, perk up, resume, develop Opposite: die down **3 revitalize**, renew, breathe life into, restore, refresh Opposite: kill **4 put on**, stage, restage, perform, redo

revivify v **rejuvenate**, breathe new life into, refresh, resurrect, resuscitate Opposite: exhaust

revocation n **cancellation**, withdrawal, reversal, overturning, annulment Opposite: enactment

revoke v **cancel**, annul, rescind, withdraw, retract

revolt v **1 rebel**, rise up, mutiny, riot **2 repel**, repulse, sicken, nauseate, turn your stomach Opposite: attract ■ n **rebellion**, revolution, uprising, upheaval, insurgency

revolted adj **nauseated**, appalled, horror-struck, horror-stricken, dismayed Opposite: charmed

revolting adj **disgusting**, repellent, repulsive, sickening, nauseating Opposite: appealing

revolution n **1 rebellion**, revolt, uprising, upheaval, insurgency **2 transformation**, conversion, alteration, upheaval, development **3 rotation**, turn, spin, cycle, circle

revolutionary adj **1 rebellious**, radical, insurgent, mutinous, anarchist **2 radical**, groundbreaking, world-shattering, innovative, avant-garde Opposite: conventional ■ n **rebel**, radical, insurgent, rioter, mutineer

revolutionize v **transform**, transfigure, reform, alter, change Opposite: maintain

revolve v **rotate**, turn, spin, circle, orbit

revolving adj **rotating**, turning, spinning, circling, gyrating

revue n **variety show**, show, skit, sketch show, satire

revulsion n **disgust**, repulsion, repugnance, distaste, dislike Opposite: attraction

reward n **recompense**, payment, repayment, return, remuneration Opposite: penalty ■ v **recompense**, pay, repay, remunerate, compensate Opposite: penalize

rewarding adj **satisfying**, worthwhile, gratifying, pleasing, fulfilling Opposite: disappointing

rewind v **wind back**, spool back, reverse

rewire v **redo**, renovate, renew, refurbish, revamp

reword v **rephrase**, redraft, rewrite, rework, revise

rework v **amend**, revise, alter, modify, change

rewrite v **redraft**, rephrase, reword, rework, revise ■ n **revision**, amendment, alteration, modification

rhapsodic adj **ecstatic**, enthusiastic, lyrical, rapturous, fervent Opposite: unenthusiastic

rhapsodize v **enthuse**, be ecstatic, eulogize, go on about, go over the top (infml)

rhapsody n **ecstasy**, rapture, bliss, enthusiasm, eagerness Opposite: gloom

rheostat n **control**, regulator, resistor, controller

rhetoric n **1 oratory**, public speaking, speech-making, speechifying (infml) **2 bombast**, pomposity, grandiloquence, fustian, loftiness **3 language**, expression, style, idiom, words

rhetorical adj **1 bombastic**, pompous, pretentious, periphrastic, voluble **2 oratorical**, verbal, linguistic, stylistic

rhetorician n **orator**, speaker, public speaker, debater, advocate

rheumatic adj **stiff**, aching, sore, inflexible, rigid Opposite: flexible

rhinestone n **paste**, strass, diamanté

rhizome n **stem**, shoot, root, tuber, corm

rhomboid see **rhombus**

rhombus n **diamond**, lozenge, parallelogram, rhomboid

rhyme n **1 assonance**, consonance, rhyming **2 poem**, verse, nursery rhyme, jingle, limerick

rhyme or reason n **sense**, logic, meaning, pattern

rhythm n **1 beat**, pace, tempo, time, measure **2 regularity**, pattern, progression, sequence

rhythmic adj **1 recurring**, regular, periodic, recurrent **2 musical**, cadenced, metrical

rib n **beam**, strut, spoke, spine, spar ■ v (infml) **tease**, make fun of, laugh at, mock, kid

ribald adj **coarse**, vulgar, bawdy, rude, lewd Opposite: refined

ribaldry n **coarseness**, vulgarity, bawdiness, rudeness, lewdness Opposite: refinement

ribbed adj **grooved**, corrugated, ridged, bumpy, uneven

ribbon n **1 band**, tie, trimming, decoration, tape **2 strip**, stretch, band, length **3 decoration**, award, honour, badge of honour, medal

rich adj **1 wealthy**, well-off, affluent, prosperous, moneyed Opposite: poor **2 full**, abounding, plentiful, stuffed, heavy Opposite: lacking **3 opulent**, gorgeous, lush, luxuriant, splendid Opposite: shabby **4 heavy**, indigestible, calorific, cloying, unhealthy *Opposite*: light **5 productive**, fertile, abundant, plentiful, fruitful *Opposite*: infertile **6 intense**, deep, strong, full, powerful *Opposite*: weak **7** (*infml*) **ironic**, amusing, irritating, annoying, ridiculous

riches *n* **resources**, treasures, reserves, materials, raw materials

richly *adv* **1 opulently**, luxuriantly, luxuriously, splendidly, ornately *Opposite*: shabbily **2 thoroughly**, fully, completely, totally, deeply *Opposite*: barely

richness *n* **1 prosperity**, fortune, affluence, wealth *Opposite*: poverty **2 opulence**, luxury, sumptuousness, splendour, luxuriousness *Opposite*: shabbiness **3 fertility**, fruitfulness, productivity, lushness, fullness *Opposite*: infertility **4 intensity**, depth, strength, fullness, power *Opposite*: weakness

rick *v* twist, pull, sprain, crick, put out

rickety *adj* **shaky**, unsteady, unstable, rocky, unbalanced *Opposite*: firm

ricochet *v* **recoil**, rebound, glance off, bounce off, reflect ■ *n* **rebound**, recoil, reverberation, reflection, echo

rictus *n* **grimace**, grin, fixed expression, contortion

rid *v* **1** (*archaic*) **free**, clear, purge, liberate, cleanse **2 get rid of**, dispense with, do away with, divest, drop

riddle *n* **puzzle**, conundrum, question, brainteaser, problem ■ *v* **1 pierce**, perforate, puncture, pepper, damage **2 sift**, screen, sieve, separate. *See* COMPARE AND CONTRAST *at* **problem**.

ride *v* **1 gallop**, canter, trot, jockey **2 travel**, journey, go, be carried, be conveyed *Opposite*: walk **3 depend on**, rest on, centre on, rely on, be contingent on ■ *n* **trip**, outing, jaunt, journey, cycle

ride out *v* **endure**, brave, stick out, survive, live through *Opposite*: succumb

rider *n* **proviso**, qualification, provision, condition, stipulation

ride up *v* **roll up**, slide up, wriggle up, move up, wrinkle *Opposite*: fall down

ridge *n* **crest**, point, edge, rim, elevation ■ *v* **fold**, crumple, crinkle, crease, wrinkle

ridicule *v* **belittle**, mock, deride, scorn, scoff at ■ *n* **mockery**, scorn, derision, laughter, mimicry

COMPARE AND CONTRAST CORE MEANING: belittle by making fun of somebody or something **ridicule** make fun of somebody or something in a cruel contemptuous way; **deride** trivialize somebody or something; **laugh at** make scornful fun of somebody or their behaviour; **mock** treat somebody or something with scorn, often by cruel mimicking; **send up** (*infml*) parody or mimic somebody or something.

ridiculous *adj* **ludicrous**, preposterous, absurd, silly, outlandish *Opposite*: sensible

ridiculousness *n* **ludicrousness**, preposterousness, absurdity, irrationality, outlandishness *Opposite*: sense

riding *n* **show jumping**, racing, hunting, dressage, cross-country

rife *adj* **1 widespread**, common, endemic, extensive, prevalent *Opposite*: rare **2 full**, abounding, bursting, laden, loaded *Opposite*: lacking. *See* COMPARE AND CONTRAST *at* **widespread**.

riff *n* **phrase**, refrain, melody, tune, groove ■ *v* **play**, jam, improvise, strum, perform

riffle *v* **1 flick through**, turn the pages of, peruse, glance at, scan **2 shuffle**, mix, mix up, randomize, jumble up **3 ripple**, roughen, undulate, get choppy, ruffle ■ *n* **flick**, quick look, glance, perusal, skim

rifle *v* **ransack**, search, search through, rummage, go through

rift *n* **1 crack**, hole, fissure, split, crevice **2 disagreement**, difference, conflict, falling-out, quarrel

rig *v* **1 fix**, engineer, arrange, prepare, fit **2 improvise**, fix up, invent, set up, assemble *Opposite*: plan **3 manipulate**, falsify, mock up, fix, set up ■ *n* **1 oil rig**, platform, derrick **2** (*infml*) **dress**, clothes, clothing, outfit, rig-out (*infml*)

rigging *n* **ropes**, chains, wires, supports, pulleys

right *adj* **1 correct**, accurate, true, exact, precise *Opposite*: wrong **2 appropriate**, respectable, fitting, proper, desirable *Opposite*: inappropriate **3 just**, proper, fair, moral, honourable *Opposite*: immoral **4 well**, healthy, in shape, fit, very well *Opposite*: ill ■ *adv* **1 correctly**, exactly, accurately, precisely, directly *Opposite*: inexactly **2 appropriately**, as it should be, acceptably, suitably, properly *Opposite*: unsuitably **3** (*infml*) **utterly**, entirely, completely, absolutely, totally ■ *n* **1 truth**, honesty, goodness, morality, fairness *Opposite*: wrong **2 entitlement**, privilege, due, birthright, justification ■ *v* **redress**, rectify, amend, remedy, correct

right-angled *adj* **angled**, square, perpendicular, ninety-degree, right-angle

righteous *adj* **virtuous**, moral, good, just, blameless *Opposite*: sinful

righteousness *n* **virtue**, morality, justice, decency, uprightness *Opposite*: wickedness

rightful *adj* **fair**, correct, legal, due, just *Opposite*: unlawful

rightfulness *n* **truth**, fairness, correctness, legality, lawfulness

right hand *n* **assistant**, aide, deputy, lieutenant, helper

right-hand *adj* **1 right**, rightward, starboard *Opposite*: left-hand **2 trusted**, important, reliable, principal, main

right-handed *adj* **clockwise**, left to right, circular, round, helical *Opposite*: left-handed

rightio *(dated infml)* *see* **righto**

rightist *adj* **right-wing**, conservative, traditionalist

rightly *adv* **1 correctly**, truly, exactly, accurately, precisely *Opposite*: wrongly **2 justly**, fittingly, justifiably, suitably, rightfully *Opposite*: unreasonably **3** *(infml)* **for certain**, without a shadow of a doubt, for sure, certainly, positively

right-minded *adj* **reasonable**, sensible, fairminded, decent, rational

rightness *n* **1 rectitude**, correctness, faultlessness, truth, precision **2 aptness**, suitability, appropriateness, timeliness, properness *Opposite*: inappropriateness

righto *(dated infml)* *adv* **right**, all right, okay *(infml)*, OK *(infml)*, okeydokey *(infml)*

right-wing *adj* **conservative**, rightist, traditionalist *Opposite*: left-wing

right-winger *n* **conservative**, rightist, traditionalist *Opposite*: liberal

rigid *adj* **1 unbending**, inflexible, stiff, firm, set *Opposite*: floppy **2 severe**, strict, harsh, stern, inflexible *Opposite*: lax

rigidity *n* **1 stiffness**, inflexibility, hardness, firmness, rigour *Opposite*: floppiness **2 inflexibility**, firmness, severity, strictness, stringency *Opposite*: laxity

rigmarole *n* **1 explanation**, account, excuse, palaver, verbiage **2 fuss**, bother, ritual, business, hassle *(infml)*

rigorous *adj* **1 hard**, severe, harsh, demanding, laborious *Opposite*: mild **2 exact**, thorough, precise, meticulous, painstaking *Opposite*: slapdash

rigorousness *n* **1 strictness**, discipline, severity, harshness, difficulty *Opposite*: leniency **2 exactness**, thoroughness, discipline, meticulousness, scrupulousness *Opposite*: negligence

rigour *n* **1 severity**, strictness, harshness, intransigence, dogmatism *Opposite*: flexibility **2 thoroughness**, consistency, exactitude, precision, meticulousness *Opposite*: negligence **3 hardship**, difficulty, adversity, hard time, difficult time *Opposite*: mildness **4 stiffness**, rigidity, unresponsiveness, stiffening, rigor mortis *Opposite*: flexibility

rig out *(infml)* *v* **1 equip**, provide, prepare, arrange, fit out **2 dress up**, kit out, clothe, get up *(infml)*, attire *(fml)*

rig up *v* **improvise**, cobble together, set up, assemble, fix up *Opposite*: plan

rile *(infml)* *v* **anger**, enrage, annoy, irritate, irk *Opposite*: placate

rim *n* **edge**, border, lip, perimeter, circumference *Opposite*: centre

rime *n* **frost**, hoar frost, ice

rind *n* **peel**, skin, husk, crust, coat *Opposite*: flesh

ring *n* **1 circle**, loop, hoop, band, halo **2 group**, band, gang, organization, team **3 impression**, semblance, appearance, feel, air **4 call**, phone call, telephone call, buzz *(infml)*, bell *(infml)* ■ *v* **1 encircle**, enclose, circle, surround **2 peal**, tinkle, chime, toll, ding-dong **3 call**, phone, telephone, give a ring, ring up **4 resonate**, resound, ring out, reverberate, echo

ring a bell *(infml)* *v* **strike a chord**, jog somebody's memory, sound familiar, be reminiscent, remind

ring-fence *v* **set aside**, isolate, restrict, stipulate, protect ■ *n* **1 restriction**, limitation, specification, separation, reservation **2 fence**, barrier, boundary, perimeter, border

ringleader *n* **gang leader**, leader of the pack, agitator, instigator, inciter

ringlet *n* **curl**, lock, twist, coil, spiral

ringmaster *n* **master of ceremonies**, MC, host, chair, chairperson

ring off *v* **hang up**, put the receiver down, finish, go *Opposite*: hang on

ring out *v* **be heard**, sound, rise, pierce the silence, blast out

ringside *adj* **front row**, grandstand, touchline, unimpeded, unobstructed

ring up *v* **call**, phone, telephone, ring, give a tinkle

rink *n* **arena**, floor, space, area

rinse *n* **1 wash**, clean, bathe, sluice, dip **2 solution**, colourant, dye, tint, bleach

riot *n* **1 uprising**, insurrection, disturbance, unrest, demonstration **2** *(infml)* **laugh** *(infml)*, scream *(infml)*, gas *(infml)*, hoot *(slang)* ■ *v* **mutiny**, demonstrate, run riot, rebel, protest

rioter *n* **demonstrator**, rebel, revolutionary, insurgent, protester

riotous *adj* **1 violent**, disorderly, unruly, uncontrolled, uproarious *Opposite*: peaceful **2 wild**, debauched, uncontrolled, out of control, hedonistic *Opposite*: subdued

riotously *adv* **1 hilariously**, madly, side-splittingly, screamingly, wildly **2 raucously**, rowdily, wildly, rambunctiously, noisily *Opposite*: quietly

rip *v* **1 tear**, split, cleave, shred, scratch *Opposite*: mend **2 snatch**, tear, seize, grab, pluck *Opposite*: give **3 speed**, tear, dash, rush, fly *Opposite*: amble ■ *n* **tear**, split, scratch, cleft, slash. *See* COMPARE AND CONTRAST *at* tear.

ripcord *n* **cord**, line, string, cable, rope

ripe *adj* **1** *(infml)* **pungent**, strong, sour, strong-smelling, off *Opposite*: sweet **2 mature**, ready, grown, fully grown, matured *Opposite*: unripe **3 ready**, suitable, prepared, crying out, disposed

ripen *v* **mature**, season, grow, develop, evolve

ripeness *n* **maturity**, readiness, mellowness, age

rip off *(infml)* *v* **overcharge**, cheat, swindle, dupe, deceive

rip-off *(infml)* n **swindle**, con, cheat, diddle *(infml)*, swizz *(infml)*

riposte n **reply**, retort, comeback, response, answer ■ v **retort**, reply, come back, return, counter. *See* COMPARE AND CONTRAST *at* **answer**.

ripple v **undulate**, swell, flow, move, rise and fall ■ n **wave**, undulation, swell, current, wrinkle *Opposite*: stillness

rip-roaring *(infml)* adj **exciting**, uproarious, boisterous, rollicking, energetic *Opposite*: boring

rip up v **tear up**, shred, pull apart, chew up, pull to pieces *Opposite*: piece together

rise v 1 **stand up**, get up, get to your feet, arise *(literary) Opposite*: sit down 2 **go up**, increase, climb, mount, get higher *Opposite*: drop 3 **rebel**, revolt, mutiny, rise up, riot *Opposite*: conform 4 **originate**, begin, start, come out of, be set in motion *Opposite*: end 5 **emerge**, come up, appear, arise, be apparent *Opposite*: disappear 6 **wake up**, get up, get out of bed, arise, awaken *Opposite*: retire ■ n 1 **increase**, growth, upsurge, intensification, escalation *Opposite*: decrease 2 **growth**, spread, development, expansion, advance *Opposite*: decline 3 **hill**, slope, incline, acclivity, elevation *Opposite*: hollow 4 **climb**, ascent, elevation *Opposite*: fall 5 **increase**, promotion, advance, elevation

rise above v **surmount**, overcome, conquer, triumph over, surpass

rise and fall n **swell**, undulation, ripple, movement, rolling *Opposite*: stability

rise to *(infml)* v **respond**, meet, shine, succeed, perform

rise to the bait v **respond**, react, get angry, be provoked, answer *Opposite*: ignore

rise up v 1 **rebel**, revolt, riot, rise, mutiny 2 **emerge**, stand up, float up, soar, arise *(literary) Opposite*: sink

risibility n 1 *(fml)* **humorousness**, sense of humour, happiness, wit, humour *Opposite*: soberness 2 **ridiculousness**, ludicrousness, absurdity, laughableness, stupidity *Opposite*: seriousness

risible adj 1 **laughable**, ludicrous, absurd, ridiculous, stupid *Opposite*: serious 2 *(fml)* **humorous**, good-humoured, happy, cheerful, cheery *Opposite*: sombre

rising adj **increasing**, growing, going up, mounting, getting higher *Opposite*: falling ■ n **uprising**, rebellion, revolt, mutiny, riot

risk n 1 **danger**, jeopardy, peril, hazard, menace *Opposite*: safety 2 **possibility**, chance, danger, hazard, gamble ■ v 1 **endanger**, jeopardize, lay bare, expose, imperil *(fml) Opposite*: protect 2 **chance**, hazard, attempt, gamble, venture *Opposite*: play safe

riskiness n **hazardousness**, perilousness, precariousness, dangerousness, audaciousness *Opposite*: safety

risky adj **dangerous**, hazardous, chancy, precarious, perilous *Opposite*: safe

risqué adj **racy**, rude, lewd, salacious, naughty *Opposite*: decorous

rite n 1 **ritual**, ceremony, formal procedure, service, sacrament 2 **custom**, habit, practice, routine, procedure

ritual n 1 **rite**, ceremony, service, formal procedure, sacrament 2 **custom**, habit, practice, routine, procedure ■ adj 1 **ceremonial**, procedural, ceremonious, sacramental, formal 2 **customary**, habitual, usual, normal, expected

ritualistic adj **ceremonial**, formalized, formulaic, ritualized, sacred

rival n 1 **competitor**, opponent, adversary, contender, challenger *Opposite*: ally 2 **equal**, match, counterpart, peer, equivalent ■ v 1 **match**, equal, be the equal of, be similar to, compare with 2 **oppose**, compete with, challenge, go up against, be against 3 **outdo**, surpass, exceed, beat, top ■ adj **competing**, opposing, challenging, contending, enemy

rivalry n **competition**, opposition, contention, competitiveness, enmity *Opposite*: cooperation

river n **stream**, waterway, tributary, canal, watercourse

riverside n **waterside**, water's edge, bank, shore

rivet n **pin**, nail, fastener, press stud, bolt ■ v 1 *(infml)* **fascinate**, enthral, entrance, interest, mesmerize *Opposite*: bore 2 **fasten**, hold, pin, bolt, nail

riveting *(infml)* adj **fascinating**, enthralling, exciting, spellbinding, entrancing *Opposite*: boring

rivulet n **stream**, burn, gully, brook *(literary)*, creek *(US)*

RNA n **nucleic acid**, ribonucleic acid, genetic material

road n **street**, thoroughfare, lane, way

WORD BANK
❏ **types of major road** A-road, artery, avenue, boulevard, bypass, clearway, dual carriageway, flyover, main road, motorway, parkway, ring road, toll road, trunk road, turnpike
❏ **types of minor road** access road, access strip, alley, alleyway, B-road, backstreet, blind alley, byroad, byway, cart track, corniche, cul-de-sac, dead end, dirt track, driveway, esplanade, frontage road, lane, mews, parade, path, promenade, service road, side street, slip road, street, track

roadblock n **barricade**, barrier, sentry post, obstruction, blockade

roadhouse *(dated)* n **hotel**, pub, bar, transport café, tavern

road show n 1 **radio show**, live broadcast, open-air broadcast, broadcast, tour 2 **campaign**, publicity campaign, advertising campaign, media circus *(infml)*, dog-and-pony show *(US)*

road sign n **sign**, signpost, notice, stop sign, one-way sign

road-test v **try out**, test, test drive, trial, run

roadway n **road**, street, thoroughfare, highway

roadworks n **road repairs**, carriageway repairs, maintenance work, construction work, repair work

roadworthiness n **safety**, soundness, reliability, working order

roadworthy adj **safe**, fit, legal, driveable, suitable

roam v **wander**, rove, travel, journey, stray Opposite: settle

roamer n **wanderer**, traveller, rover, itinerant, nomad

roaming adj **wandering**, roving, itinerant, nomadic, peripatetic Opposite: stationary

roaring adj **1 busy**, thriving, prosperous, active Opposite: slack **2 noisy**, loud, deafening, boisterous, thunderous Opposite: quiet

roast v **bake**, cook, heat

roasting (infml) adj **boiling**, hot, red-hot, sweltering, burning up Opposite: cool

rob v **1 steal from**, take from, hold up, raid, mug **2 deprive**, cheat, strip, drain, fleece (infml)

robber n **thief**, burglar, pickpocket, shoplifter, mugger

robbery n **theft**, burglary, break-in, mugging, stealing

robe n **dressing gown**, negligée, housecoat, bathrobe, gown

robot n **automaton**, android, machine, computer, mechanical device

robotic adj **1 mechanical**, mechanized, automated, automatic, cybernetic **2 machine-like**, mechanical, unresponsive, unfeeling, humourless Opposite: warm

robotics n **cybernetics**, automation, engineering, manufacturing, science

robust adj **healthy**, vigorous, hearty, strong, tough Opposite: weak

robustness n **heftiness**, sturdiness, strength, toughness, forcefulness Opposite: weakness

rock n **1 stone**, boulder, pebble **2 pillar**, mainstay, tower of strength, stalwart ■ v **1 sway**, swing, shake, move up and down, pitch **2** (infml) **astound**, shock, shake, stun, disturb

rock bottom n **the lowest**, the bottom, the depths, all-time low, nadir

rocker n **1 biker**, greaser, Hell's Angel, motorcyclist, youth **2** (infml) **rock star**, rock musician, rock singer, rock and roller, pop star **3** (infml) **rock fan**, groupie (infml), headbanger (slang)

rockery n **garden**, rock garden, alpine garden, terrace

rocket v **1 speed**, whiz, hurtle, fly, zoom **2** (infml) **shoot up**, soar, increase rapidly, go through the roof (infml), go sky-high (infml) Opposite: plummet

rock face n **cliff face**, face, precipice, crag, cliff

rock garden n **garden**, rockery, alpine garden, terrace

rock-hard adj **solid**, firm, cast-iron, hard as nails, like granite Opposite: soft

rockiness n **shakiness**, unsteadiness, uncertainty, insecurity, instability Opposite: steadiness

rock-solid adj **1 firm**, unshakable, solid, rigid, unyielding Opposite: shaky **2 durable**, unbreakable, strong, firm, enduring Opposite: breakable

rock-strewn adj **stony**, rocky, gravelly, pebbly, rough Opposite: smooth

rock the boat (infml) v **cause an argument**, cause an upset, cause trouble

rocky adj **1 stony**, rock-strewn, pebbly, gravelly **2 difficult**, troubled, uncertain, not easy, hard Opposite: easy **3 shaky**, unsteady, wobbly, unsound, insecure Opposite: stable

rod n **bar**, pole, stick, shaft, dowel

rodeo n **competition**, display, festival, meet, fair

rogue n **scoundrel**, rascal, reprobate, ne'er-do-well (dated), cad (dated)

roguery n **1 dishonesty**, deceit, unscrupulousness, double-dealing, sharp practice Opposite: honesty **2 mischief**, mischievousness, playfulness, naughtiness, tricks

roguish adj **1 dishonest**, deceitful, unscrupulous, double-dealing, criminal Opposite: honest **2 mischievous**, naughty, impish, wicked, malicious

roguishness n **1 unscrupulousness**, dishonesty, deceit, double-dealing, sharp practice Opposite: honesty **2 mischievousness**, mischief, playfulness, naughtiness, tricks

roister v **1 revel**, make merry, celebrate, drink, party (infml) **2 brag**, boast, show off, swagger, gloat

roisterer n **1 reveller**, partygoer, merrymaker, pleasure-seeker, celebrator **2 braggart**, boaster, show-off (infml), loudmouth (infml), bigmouth (infml)

role n **1 part**, character, person, title role, starring role **2 position**, function, responsibility, job, task

role model n **example**, model, paradigm, exemplar (literary)

role-play v **act**, act out, enact, play, imagine

role-playing n **acting**, acting out, game-playing, imagination, play-acting

roll v **1 bowl**, trundle, troll, set rolling, roll along **2 revolve**, turn, turn over, turn round, spin ■ n **reel**, cylinder, spool, tube, bolt

roll call n **attendance check**, register check, checkup, check, monitoring

roller n **breaker**, wave, whitecap

roller-skate v **skate**, blade, Rollerblade

rollicking adj **boisterous**, rowdy, loud, carefree, swashbuckling ■ n (infml) **reprimand**, scolding, dressing-down, telling-off (infml), talking-to (infml)

roll in v arrive, enter, land, roll up, appear Opposite: leave

rolling adj 1 **undulating**, rising and falling, gently sloping Opposite: steep 2 **progressing**, continuing, ongoing, continuous, constant

roll out v **introduce**, launch, inaugurate, issue, bring out

roll out the red carpet v treat like royalty, give a hero's welcome, lionize, make a fuss of, welcome

roll up v 1 **appear**, turn up, ride up, show up, roll in Opposite: leave 2 **turn up**, push back, furl Opposite: unroll

roman adj 1 **upright**, straight, plain Opposite: italic 2 **in classical style**, classical, ancient

romance n 1 **relationship**, love affair, affair, involvement, fling (infml) 2 **love**, passion, amorousness, ardour, sex 3 **allure**, excitement, adventure, nostalgia, feeling 4 **fascination**, enthusiasm, passion, love, love affair 5 **love story**, romantic story, romantic tale, weepie (infml), tearjerker (infml) Opposite: tragedy 6 **adventure story**, adventure, tale, story, narrative 7 **fantasy**, story, tall tale, fiction, daydream ■ v 1 **tell stories**, fantasize, romanticize 2 **be romantic**, act romantically, swoon, daydream, be in love 3 **court** (dated), woo (literary), pay court to (dated) 4 **have an affair with**, have a love affair with, have a relationship with, date, have a fling with

romantic adj 1 **loving**, passionate, tender, amorous, adoring Opposite: platonic 2 **idealistic**, dreamy, quixotic, impractical, starry-eyed Opposite: prosaic

romanticism n idealization, fantasy, nostalgia, soft focus, rose-tinted glasses

romanticize v 1 **idealize**, glamorize, sentimentalize, put on a pedestal, view through rose-tinted spectacles 2 **daydream**, swoon, gush, dream, rhapsodize

Romeo n Don Juan, Casanova, seducer, wolf, womanizer

romp v 1 **cavort**, frolic, horse around, caper, prance 2 **sail**, steam, coast, cruise, whiz Opposite: struggle 3 (infml) **win**, coast, excel yourself, surpass yourself, walk it (infml) Opposite: lose ■ n 1 **frolic**, frisk, gambol, run, scramble 2 (infml) **page-turner**, thriller, chiller, potboiler Opposite: bore 3 (infml) **foregone conclusion**, one-horse race, piece of cake (infml), cinch (infml), walkover (infml)

roofed adj **covered**, enclosed, vaulted, topped Opposite: open

roofing n tiling, slating, tiles, slates, thatch

rooftop n roof, top, tiles, slates, gable

room n 1 **space**, extent, span, capacity, volume 2 **compartment**, apartment (fml), chamber (literary) 3 **scope**, opportunity, possibility, occasion, chance

WORD BANK
❑ **types of room in public buildings** antechamber, anteroom, ballroom, banqueting hall, boardroom, cell, changing room, classroom, cloakroom, dining hall, dormitory, dressing room, entrance hall, foyer, gallery, games room, hall, lavatory, library, lobby, lounge, meeting room, office, powder room, reception room, refectory, rest room, schoolroom, stateroom, surgery, vault, waiting room, ward
❑ **types of room in the home** atelier, attic, bathroom, bedchamber (literary), bedroom, boudoir, boxroom, day room, den, dining room, drawing room, family room, garret, guestroom, kitchen, kitchenette, laundry room, living room, loft, parlour, playroom, recreation room, salon, scullery, sitting room, sleeping quarters, spare room, study, sun lounge, toilet, utility room

roominess n **spaciousness**, largeness, capaciousness, generousness, sizableness Opposite: smallness

roommate n **flatmate**, housemate, lodger, cotenant, roomie (US infml)

rooms n **housing**, quarters, place, accommodation, lodgings (dated)

roomy adj **spacious**, large, generous, sizable, capacious Opposite: cramped

roost v settle, rest, stay, perch, sleep

root n 1 **stem**, rhizome, tuber, radicle, radix 2 **origin**, cause, source, basis, starting place ■ v 1 **dig**, grub, rootle, forage, delve 2 **search**, delve, rifle, burrow, rummage 3 **cheer**, shout, applaud, yell, clap Opposite: jeer. See COMPARE AND CONTRAST at origin.

rooted adj **entrenched**, ingrained, fixed, deep-rooted, deep-seated

rootless adj **drifting**, freewheeling, roving, nomadic, itinerant Opposite: rooted

root out v 1 **eradicate**, remove, get rid of, do away with, eliminate 2 **find**, discover, locate, turn up, unearth Opposite: hide

roots n **origins**, ancestry, background, heritage, pedigree

rope n **cord**, line, cable, lead, twine ■ v **tie**, fasten, lash, secure, attach Opposite: untie

ropy (infml) adj 1 **poor**, shoddy, trashy, cheap and nasty, rubbishy Opposite: excellent 2 **ill**, unwell, sick, bad, off-colour Opposite: healthy

rose n 1 **design**, rosette, ornament, representation, emblem 2 **sprinkler**, jet, nozzle, spray, attachment 3 **ceiling rose**, fitting, boss, connector, socket

roseate adj **reddish**, rose, fuchsia, magenta, rose-coloured

rosebud n **bud**, bloom, rose, flower, blossom

rose-coloured adj **optimistic**, idealistic, assured, sanguine, trusting Opposite: pessimistic

rose-tinted see **rose-coloured**

rosette n 1 **badge**, decoration, prize 2 **ornament**, design, rose, shape, representation

rosiness n **blush**, flush, pinkness, redness, glow

roster n **rota**, list, schedule, roll, register

rostrum n **platform**, podium, stage, dais, stand

rosy adj 1 **pink**, reddish, pinkish, rose, roseate 2 **blushing**, flushed, glowing, healthy, ruddy Opposite: pale 3 **promising**, auspicious, successful, happy, favourable Opposite: unpromising 4 **optimistic**, idealistic, unrealistic, hopeful, encouraging Opposite: pessimistic

rot v **decompose**, decay, putrefy, disintegrate, go off ■ n 1 **decay**, deterioration, putrefaction, decomposition, corrosion 2 (infml) **nonsense**, balderdash, rubbish, garbage, twaddle (infml) Opposite: sense

rota n **roster**, list, schedule, register, roll

rotary adj **rotating**, turning, revolving, rotational, gyratory

rotate v 1 **turn**, revolve, go, spin, swivel 2 **replace**, switch, alternate, exchange, swap (infml) 3 **take turns**, alternate, interchange, switch, swap (infml)

rotation n 1 **revolution**, turning, spin, gyration 2 **replacement**, switching, cycle, sequence 3 **alternation**, variation, interchange

rote n **repetition**, memorization, routine, habit, rotation

rotisserie n **spit**, skewer, brochette, grill, barbecue

rotor n **blade**, propeller, aerofoil

rotten adj 1 **decayed**, putrid, bad, decomposed, rotted Opposite: fresh 2 (infml) **awful**, bad, nasty, terrible, unpleasant Opposite: pleasant 3 (infml) **inferior**, poor, bad, dreadful, incompetent Opposite: good 4 (infml) **unwell**, ill, sick, off-colour, poorly (infml) Opposite: healthy (infml) 5 (infml) **unhappy**, uncomfortable, guilty, embarrassed, bad Opposite: happy 6 **unfair**, unethical, immoral, unprincipled, dishonest Opposite: just ■ adv (infml) **terribly**, unduly, excessively, overly, outrageously Opposite: slightly

rottenness n 1 **decay**, mouldiness, dry rot, wet rot, badness Opposite: freshness 2 (infml) **unpleasantness**, awfulness, dreadfulness, hideousness, ghastliness Opposite: pleasantness 3 (infml) **beastliness**, nastiness, cruelness, cruelty, horridness Opposite: goodness

rotter (dated infml) n **scoundrel**, liar, swindler, cheat, cad (dated) Opposite: angel

rotting adj **decomposing**, decaying, putrid, bad, contaminated Opposite: fresh

rotund adj **overweight**, stout, fat, plump, corpulent Opposite: slender

rotunda n **pavilion**, tower, dome, cupola

rotundity n **roundness**, sphericalness, rotundness, overweight, stoutness Opposite: slenderness

rouge (dated) n **blusher**, lipstick, makeup, face paint, colouring ■ v **make up**, redden, highlight, paint, beautify

rough adj 1 **uneven**, bumpy, irregular, jagged, lumpy Opposite: even 2 **coarse**, shaggy, hairy, bristly, bushy Opposite: smooth 3 **turbulent**, stormy, tempestuous, squally, wild Opposite: calm 4 **rugged**, wild, uncultivated, rocky, hilly Opposite: cultivated 5 **violent**, forceful, tough, physical, forcible Opposite: gentle 6 **boorish**, unrefined, rough-and-ready, coarse, crude Opposite: refined 7 **harsh**, grating, jarring, discordant, rasping Opposite: melodious 8 **approximate**, sketchy, vague, estimated, imprecise Opposite: exact 9 (infml) **unwell**, sickly, ill, out of sorts, seedy (infml) Opposite: well 10 **difficult**, trying, challenging, unpleasant, uncomfortable Opposite: easy 11 **rowdy**, boisterous, noisy, violent, tough Opposite: quiet ■ n **outline**, sketch, summary, draft, mock-up

roughage n **bulk**, cellulose, bran, fibre

rough-and-ready adj 1 **crude**, simple, basic, primitive, serviceable Opposite: sophisticated 2 **down-to-earth**, unpretentious, honest, rough-hewn, kind-hearted Opposite: refined

rough-and-tumble n **hurly-burly**, cut and thrust, infighting, sparring, fracas

roughcast n **coating**, cladding, facing, plasterwork, rendering

rough copy n **outline**, sketch, summary, draft, rough

roughen v **coarsen**, toughen, scratch, abrade, rough Opposite: soften

rough-hewn adj 1 **rough**, unfinished, undressed, incomplete 2 **crude**, basic, primitive, simple, rough Opposite: polished 3 **rugged**, rough, unrefined, coarse, crude

roughhouse (infml) n **rowdiness**, boisterousness, rough-and-tumble, horseplay, roughness

roughneck (infml) n **thug**, hoodlum, rowdy, yobbo (infml), hooligan (infml)

roughness n 1 **unevenness**, coarseness, bumpiness, irregularity, jaggedness Opposite: smoothness 2 **coarseness**, shagginess, hairiness, bristliness, bushiness Opposite: smoothness 3 **turbulence**, storminess, tempestuousness, wildness Opposite: calmness 4 **ruggedness**, wildness, rockiness, hilliness, cragginess Opposite: gentleness 5 **violence**, force, toughness, power, brutality Opposite: gentleness 6 **brusqueness**, rudeness, gruffness, harshness, coarseness Opposite: refinement 7 **harshness**, discordance, astringency, gruffness, raucousness Opposite: smoothness 8 **vagueness**, sketchiness, ambiguity, inexactness, haziness Opposite: exactness 9 **rowdiness**, boisterousness, noisiness, violence, toughness Opposite: quietness

rough out v **draft**, outline, prepare, sketch, block out Opposite: finalize

rough up *(infml)* v **maltreat**, mistreat, abuse, batter, manhandle *Opposite*: take care of

round n **circle**, disc, slice, ring, band ■ v **turn**, circumnavigate, negotiate, skirt round, skirt ■ *prep* **surrounding**, around, about, encircling, encompassing ■ *adv* **around**, about, near, on all sides

round about *prep* **around**, about, circa, say, in the region of

roundabout n **1 merry-go-round**, carousel, ride, attraction **2 traffic island**, traffic junction, junction, intersection, crossroads ■ *adj* **indirect**, oblique, circuitous, winding, meandering *Opposite*: direct

rounded *adj* **curved**, smoothed, smooth-edged, round, curvy *Opposite*: pointed

round-eyed *adj* **open-mouthed**, amazed, gaping, staring, fascinated

roundly *adv* **severely**, forcefully, completely, utterly, bluntly

roundness n **roundedness**, plumpness, chubbiness *Opposite*: slenderness

round-shouldered *adj* **stooping**, hunched, slouching, bent, bent over *Opposite*: erect

round table n **discussion**, negotiation, debate, forum, meeting

round-the-clock *adj* **24-hour**, day-and-night, 24/7, continuous, constant

round trip n **both ways**, return journey, return trip, return, circuit

round up v **capture**, gather together, collect, arrest, amass *Opposite*: disperse

round-up n **1 assembly**, capture, hunt, herding, rodeo *Opposite*: release **2 summary**, rundown, review, summing up, recap

rouse v **1 stir**, wake up, revive, awaken, disturb *Opposite*: lull **2 stir up**, provoke, incite, move, galvanize *Opposite*: lull

rousing *adj* **stirring**, inspiring, moving, exciting, stimulating *Opposite*: soothing

rout n **1 retreat**, flight, stampede, surrender, collapse *Opposite*: advance **2 defeat**, massacre, landslide, thrashing, beating *Opposite*: victory **3 tumult**, disorder, riot, disturbance, hubbub ■ v **beat back**, overpower, overwhelm, beat, defeat *Opposite*: retreat

route n **1 road**, path, way, track, itinerary **2 course**, means, method, way, direction ■ v **direct**, send, transmit, move, channel

routine n **1 procedure**, practice, habit, custom, sequence **2 tedium**, monotony, mundaneness, dullness, dreariness *Opposite*: variety ■ *adj* **1 usual**, standard, everyday, normal, customary *Opposite*: unusual **2 monotonous**, dull, tedious, repetitive, humdrum *Opposite*: exciting. *See* COMPARE AND CONTRAST *at* **habit**.

rove v **wander**, roam, range, meander, travel

rover n **wanderer**, traveller, rolling stone, nomad, drifter

roving *adj* **1 roaming**, travelling, wandering, rambling, nomadic *Opposite*: stationary **2 erratic**, wandering, fickle, capricious, inconsistent *Opposite*: steady

row n **1 line**, chain, string, file, queue **2 disagreement**, dispute, quarrel, controversy, argument *Opposite*: agreement **3 noise**, rumpus, din, commotion, racket *(infml)* *Opposite*: lull ■ v **1 paddle**, scull, punt, take the oars, propel **2 fight**, quarrel, have a row, disagree, argue *Opposite*: agree

rowdiness n **disorderliness**, unruliness, noisiness, loudness, raucousness *Opposite*: restraint

rowdy *adj* **disorderly**, unruly, noisy, loud, raucous *Opposite*: restrained

rower n **oarsperson**, sculler, coxswain, cox

royal *adj* **1 regal**, imperial, majestic, stately, noble **2 magnificent**, splendid, noble, excellent, grand *Opposite*: ordinary

royalist n **monarchist**, traditionalist, constitutionalist, conservative, loyal subject *Opposite*: republican

royals n **royalty**, crowned heads, monarchs, sovereigns, royal family

royalty n **1 royals**, crowned heads, monarchs, sovereigns, royal family **2 fee**, payment, percentage, credit, token

RP n **Received Pronunciation**, BBC English, the Queen's English, Standard English, British English

RSI n **repetitive strain injury**, tenosynovitis, carpal tunnel syndrome, industrial injury, work-related injury

rub v **1 massage**, stroke, caress, knead, pat **2 polish**, wipe, buff, shine, clean **3 chafe**, hurt, gall, irritate, scrape *Opposite*: soothe

rubber n **India rubber**, foam rubber, neoprene, gum, elastic

rubberneck *(infml)* v **stare**, gaze, gape, goggle, ogle. *See* COMPARE AND CONTRAST *at* **gaze**.

rubbernecking *(infml)* n **staring**, gazing, gaping, ogling, gawking *(infml)*

rubber stamp n **stamping device**, stamp, seal, stamper, signet

rubber-stamp v **approve**, sanction, pass, let through, nod through *(infml)* *Opposite*: veto

rubbery *adj* **tough**, elastic, chewy, hard, overcooked *Opposite*: tender

rubbing n **1 impression**, brass rubbing, copy, reproduction, relief **2 friction**, scraping, abrasion, resistance, chafing **3 soreness**, chafing, irritation, blistering, saddle sores

rubbish n **1 refuse**, debris, litter, waste, junk *(infml)* **2 nonsense**, drivel, garbage, claptrap *(infml)*, hogwash *(infml)* ■ v *(infml)* **pooh-pooh**, criticize, dismiss, ridicule, disparage *Opposite*: praise

rubbish bin n **dustbin**, bin, wheelie bin, waste bin, waste paper bin

rubbishy *adj* **inferior**, poor quality, poor, bad, dodgy *(infml)* *Opposite*: quality

rubble n debris, ruins, wreckage, remains, bricks

rub down v 1 finish, wipe down, sand, scour, prepare 2 massage, rub, go over, oil, stroke 3 dry, rub, dry off, towel dry, towel

rub out v erase, delete, wipe, expunge, efface

rubric n 1 title, heading, header, head, introduction 2 rules, instructions, guidelines, directions, rulebook 3 custom, tradition, practice, system, convention 4 class, category, classification, division, type

rub up the wrong way v irritate, annoy, make somebody's hackles rise, infuriate, offend

ruched adj pleated, gathered, frilled, frilly, edged Opposite: plain

ruck n 1 mass, pile, heap, accumulation, conglomeration 2 crease, wrinkle, crumple, fold, rumple ■ v wrinkle, crease, fold, crumple, gather Opposite: smooth

rucksack n backpack, haversack, knapsack, frame rucksack, daypack

ruckus n commotion, disturbance, rumpus, riot, uproar

ruction n quarrel, fight, dispute, disturbance, row

ructions n rumpus, fuss, uproar, dispute, controversy

ruddiness n redness, rosiness, glow, blush, flush Opposite: pallor

ruddy adj reddish, rosy, flushed, glowing, healthy-looking Opposite: pale

rude adj 1 impolite, discourteous, insolent, bad-mannered, ill-mannered Opposite: polite 2 foul, crude, offensive, vulgar, foulmouthed Opposite: polite

rudeness n impoliteness, insolence, discourtesy, offensiveness, vulgarity Opposite: politeness

rudimentary adj basic, elementary, simple, fundamental, primary Opposite: advanced

rudiments n basics, essentials, fundamentals, principles, beginnings

rue v regret, lament, repent, deplore, feel sorry about

rueful adj regretful, remorseful, apologetic, repentant, contrite Opposite: cheerful

ruffian (dated) n thug, tough guy, gangster, hooligan (infml), hood (US slang)

ruffle v 1 disturb, tousle, rumple, upset, dishevel Opposite: smooth 2 perturb, upset, annoy, disrupt, distress Opposite: calm

rug n 1 carpet, mat, hearth rug, sheepskin, runner 2 (infml) wig, toupee, hairpiece, periwig 3 blanket, car rug, throw, cover, bedspread

rugged adj 1 rocky, rough, craggy, uneven, jagged Opposite: rolling 2 strong-featured, craggy, chiselled, weathered, furrowed 3 strong, hardy, tough, robust, resilient Opposite: weak 4 testing, demanding, difficult, harsh, tough Opposite: easy 5 well-built, sturdy, tough, robust, strong Opposite: flimsy

ruggedness n 1 roughness, rockiness, harshness, jaggedness, cragginess Opposite: smoothness 2 strong features, cragginess, handsomeness, manliness, masculinity Opposite: roundness 3 toughness, resilience, stamina, endurance, strength Opposite: weakness 4 unforgiving nature, difficulty, harshness, toughness, severity Opposite: gentleness 5 resilience, sturdiness, toughness, robustness, strength Opposite: flimsiness

rug rat (US infml) n child, infant, toddler, sprog (slang)

ruin n 1 remains, wreck, debris, wreckage, shell 2 devastation, shambles, decay, destruction, collapse Opposite: regeneration 3 decline, downfall, defeat, fall, disaster Opposite: improvement ■ v damage, wreck, spoil, destroy, devastate Opposite: mend

ruination n 1 destruction, loss, ruin, calamity, devastation Opposite: salvation 2 undoing, downfall, ruin, curse, destruction Opposite: making

ruined adj 1 tumbledown, crumbling, derelict, abandoned, uninhabited Opposite: renovated 2 bankrupt, insolvent, out of business, broke (infml), cleaned out (infml) Opposite: solvent

ruinous adj disastrous, damaging, harmful, devastating, catastrophic Opposite: advantageous

rule n 1 instruction, law, regulation, decree, statute 2 regime, power, control, leadership, reign ■ v govern, reign, run, administrate, have power over Opposite: follow

rulebook n manual, rules, instructions, directory, rubric

rule out v 1 exclude, dismiss, reject, discount, discard Opposite: consider 2 prevent, exclude, ban, prohibit, forbid Opposite: facilitate

ruler n monarch, sovereign, leader, head of state, potentate Opposite: subject

WORD BANK
❏ **types of ruler** chief, chieftain, emir, emperor, empress, governor, head of state, king, maharajah, maharani, Pharoah, president, queen, rajah, rani, regent, sultan, tsar, tsarina, tsaritsa

rule the roost v be in control, be in charge, reign supreme, lord it, hold sway

ruling adj presiding, reigning, governing, dominant, sovereign Opposite: subordinate ■ n decision, verdict, edict, judgment, declaration

ruling body n council, administration, government, assembly, legislative body

rum (dated infml) adj odd, strange, extraordinary, weird, bizarre Opposite: usual

rumble v **grumble**, thunder, crash, growl, roll

rumbling (infml) n **indication**, early sign, beginning, warning sign, rumour

rumbustious adj **boisterous**, exuberant, swashbuckling, swaggering, rambunctious Opposite: reticent

ruminate v **1 chew**, graze, browse, crop, pasture **2 ponder**, think over, reflect, chew over, meditate

rumination n **1 chewing**, grazing, browsing, chewing the cud **2 reflection**, pondering, contemplation, musing, thought

ruminative adj **thoughtful**, pensive, reflective, contemplative, speculative Opposite: blithe

rummage v **search**, look through, grope, fumble, poke around

rumour n **1 unconfirmed report**, claim, report, tale, allegation Opposite: fact **2 speculation**, opinion, gossip, talk, tittle-tattle ■ v **say**, believe, allege, claim, speculate Opposite: confirm

rumoured adj **supposed**, thought, whispered, alleged, believed Opposite: true

rumour mill n **grapevine**, network, newsmongers, gossips, tattlers

rumourmonger n **gossip**, telltale, scandalmonger, gossipmonger, tattletale (US)

rump n **hindquarters**, back end, rear, buttocks, rear end

rumple v **wrinkle**, crumple, crease, crinkle, pucker Opposite: tidy

rumpled adj **crumpled**, creased, untidy, messy, bedraggled Opposite: tidy

rumpus n **disturbance**, commotion, furore, brouhaha, fuss

run v **1 sprint**, jog, lope, scuttle, scamper **2 compete**, enter, participate, take part, contend **3 operate**, function, process **4 manage**, administer, govern, administrate, lead **5 flow**, stream, trickle, course, pour out **6 proceed**, happen, go, progress, move along **7 move**, pass, cast, throw **8 continue**, extend, reach, stretch, go ■ n **1 outing**, trip, ride, excursion, visit **2 sequence**, series, chain, string, list **3 course**, track, route, lane, path **4 enclosure**, pen, cage, coop, paddock **5 sprint**, race, lope, dart, dash

runabout n **wanderer**, rover, rolling stone, nomad, traveller

run after v **pursue**, chase, go after, follow, hound

run along v **go away**, go, leave, depart, take leave Opposite: stay

run amok v **go berserk**, be in a frenzy, run riot, go on the rampage, rampage

run a risk v **take a risk**, play a dangerous game, sail close to the wind, court disaster, play Russian roulette

run around v **associate**, spend time, keep company, hang out (infml), hang (slang)

run away v **escape**, flee, run off, abscond, elope

runaway n **escapee**, absentee, absconder, fugitive ■ adj (infml) **bestselling**, blockbusting, hit, roaring, huge

runaway success n **big hit**, smash, smash hit, blockbuster (infml), barnburner (US infml)

run by v **explain**, describe, tell, impart, acquaint

run down v **1 bring to an end**, close down, wind up, shut down, peter out Opposite: start **2 belittle**, criticize, knock, disparage, put down Opposite: praise

rundown n **background**, details, information, lowdown (infml), info (infml)

run-down adj **1 exhausted**, tired, weak, wearied, worn-out Opposite: energetic **2 under the weather**, worn out, tired, weary, washed out Opposite: well **3 dilapidated**, ramshackle, shabby, neglected, derelict Opposite: well-kept

rune n **character**, letter, symbol, sign, hieroglyph

rung n **step**, stair, tread, stage

run-in (infml) n **argument**, confrontation, quarrel, clash, disagreement

run into v **1 come across**, bump into, meet by chance, encounter **2 hit**, bump into, crash into, collide with, run over Opposite: miss

runner n **1 sprinter**, jogger, racer, contender, competitor **2 candidate**, contender, entrant, participant, competitor **3 messenger**, courier, gofer (infml)

runner-up n **second place**, person in second place, silver medallist, second to finish, next best person

running n **management**, administration, organization, operation, controlling ■ adv **in a row**, consecutively, on the trot, successively, in succession

runny adj **liquid**, fluid, gooey, soft, thin Opposite: set

run off v **flee**, escape, run away, decamp, scarper (slang)

run-of-the-mill adj **mediocre**, ordinary, middling, average, undistinguished Opposite: extraordinary

run on v **go on**, carry on, continue, keep going Opposite: stop

run out v **end**, expire, come to an end, finish

run over v **1 crush**, hit, squash, flatten, collide with **2 explain**, summarize, go over, run through, cover

run rings around v **outshine**, beat, outdo, outstrip, outperform

run rings round see **run rings around**

run riot v **run amok**, go on the rampage, riot, go berserk, rampage

runt n **smallest**, weakest, littlest

run the gauntlet v **undergo**, experience, face, suffer, endure

run through v **1 use up**, exhaust, eat through, go through, deplete Opposite: conserve

2 review, go over, examine, consider, look over **3 pervade**, spread through, underlie, permeate **4 rehearse**, practise, try out, go through **5 infect**, contaminate, pollute

run-through n **1 rehearsal**, practice, dry run, test run, test **2 review**, survey, summary, overview, résumé

run up v **1 accumulate**, amass, collect, incur, build up *Opposite*: discharge **2 sew**, create, make, put together

run-up n **1 approach**, advance, run **2 buildup**, introduction, lead-in

runway n **landing strip**, airstrip, landing field, taxiway, flight strip

rupture n **1 break**, crack, tear, split, fissure **2 disagreement**, falling-out, split, breakup, separation ■ v **break**, crack, burst, come apart, rip apart

rural adj **country**, rustic, pastoral, bucolic, countryside *Opposite*: urban

ruse n **trick**, dodge, subterfuge, wile, con

rush v **1 hurry**, precipitate, hasten, dash, bolt **2 run**, hurry, dash, sprint, flash *Opposite*: dawdle ■ n **1 blast**, current, gale, gust, blow **2 haste**, hurry, urgency, flash

rushed adj **hurried**, quick, swift, hasty *Opposite*: leisurely

rushes n **unedited prints**, dailies, first prints, raw footage, footage

rust n **corrosion**, oxidation, erosion, corruption, decomposition ■ v **corrode**, oxidize, tarnish, erode, decompose

rustic adj **rural**, country, pastoral, bucolic, countryside *Opposite*: urban

rustle v **crunch**, crackle, whisper, swish

rustler n **thief**, poacher, robber, horse thief, cattle thief

rustle up *(infml)* v **prepare**, concoct, put together, make, produce

rustproof adj **nonrusting**, rust-free, rust-proofed, stainless-steel, corrosion-proof ■ v **seal**, make rustproof, waterproof, coat, paint

rusty adj **1 corroded**, oxidized, tarnished, eroded **2 out of practice**, out of form, unpractised, unaccustomed, off form

rut n **furrow**, groove, channel, runnel, pothole

ruthless adj **cruel**, callous, brutal, pitiless, merciless *Opposite*: merciful

ruthlessness n **callousness**, cruelty, mercilessness, brutality, heartlessness *Opposite*: mercy

rutted adj **uneven**, furrowed, potholed, bumpy *Opposite*: smooth

RV n **recreational vehicle**, camper, motor caravan, mobile home, trailer

S

sabbatical n **study leave**, leave, time off, retreat, leave of absence

sabotage n **disruption**, damage, vandalism, interference, interruption ■ v **disrupt**, damage, vandalize, interfere with, interrupt

saboteur n **vandal**, terrorist, ecowarrior, computer hacker, hunt saboteur

sabre rattling n **display of force**, bravado, empty, threats, bluffing

sac n **bag**, sack, pouch, case, pod

saccharine adj **1 sugary**, sickly, sweet, syrupy, treacly *Opposite*: sour **2 sentimental**, slushy, gushy, miserable, mawkish, cloying *Opposite*: unsentimental

sacerdotal adj **clerical**, ecclesiastic, religious, spiritual, priestly *(literary)*

sachet n **envelope**, packet, pouch

sack n **1 bag**, brown bag, gunnysack, carryall, pouch **2** *(infml)* **dismissal**, termination, layoff, discharge, pink slip *(US)* ■ v **1** *(infml)* **dismiss**, lay off, throw out, give somebody notice, give somebody their cards *Opposite*: employ

2 ransack, plunder, destroy, pillage, tear apart

sacking *(infml)* n **dismissal**, discharge, job loss, notice, layoff

sacrament n **rite**, ceremony, ritual, service, mass

sacred adj **holy**, blessed, consecrated, hallowed, revered *Opposite*: secular

sacrifice n **price**, toll, cost, loss, expense ■ v **give up**, forgo, forfeit, let go, surrender

sacrilege n **blasphemy**, desecration, profanity, irreverence, violation *Opposite*: reverence

sacrilegious adj **blasphemous**, profane, irreverent, heretical, impious *Opposite*: pious

sacrosanct adj **1 sacred**, revered, holy, sanctified **2 inviolable**, untouchable, off limits, protected

sad adj **1 unhappy**, miserable, depressed, down, low *Opposite*: happy **2 depressing**, gloomy, miserable, cheerless, distressing *Opposite*: cheerful

sadden v **depress**, distress, upset, dismay, pain *Opposite*: cheer

saddlebag n **basket**, bag, pannier, carrier, holdall

saddle with v **burden**, lumber, encumber, weigh down, land

sadistic adj **cruel**, nasty, callous, heartless, vicious Opposite: kind

sadly adv **1 unhappily**, miserably, gloomily, wretchedly, dejectedly Opposite: happily **2 unfortunately**, unluckily, regrettably, alas Opposite: luckily

sadness n **unhappiness**, misery, depression, dejection, despondency Opposite: happiness

safari n **trek**, expedition, trip, search, quest

safe adj **1 harmless**, benign, innocuous, innocent, nonviolent Opposite: dangerous **2 secure**, protected, sheltered, in safe hands, out of harm's way Opposite: unsafe **3 unharmed**, undamaged, uninjured, unhurt, unscathed **4 reliable**, dependable, trustworthy, careful, cautious Opposite: unsafe ■ n **strongbox**, lockbox, safe-deposit box, vault

safeguard n **protection**, precaution, defence, safety measure, safety device Opposite: hazard ■ v **defend**, protect, preserve, guard, shield Opposite: endanger

---

COMPARE AND CONTRAST CORE MEANING: keep safe from actual or potential damage or attack **safeguard** take steps to prevent somebody or something from being harmed or damaged; **protect** keep somebody or something from any kind of harm or damage; **defend** deter an actual or threatened attack; **guard** work to prevent damage, loss, or attack by being vigilant and taking defensive measures; **shield** prevent harm, damage, or attack by using a physical barrier or by intervening in a protective way.

---

safeguarding n **protection**, preservation, conservation, defence, maintenance Opposite: destruction

safe haven n **refuge**, asylum, haven, sanctuary

safe house n **hideout**, hideaway, retreat, refuge, hidey-hole (infml)

safekeeping n **protection**, care, security, custody, safety

safe place n **refuge**, safe haven, hideaway, haven, sanctuary

safety n **care**, security, protection, shelter, wellbeing Opposite: danger

safety belt n **seat belt**, strap, restraint, harness, safety harness

safety net n **safety device**, safeguard, fail-safe, guard, shield

safety valve n **1 fail-safe**, valve, safety device, safety precaution, overflow **2 release**, channel, outlet

sag v **droop**, wilt, slump, flag, drop ■ n **drop**, slump, dip, fall, depression

saga n **epic**, account, chronicle, tale, legend

sagacious adj **wise**, knowledgeable, learned, erudite, perceptive Opposite: foolish

sagaciousness (fml) see **sagacity**

sagacity n **wisdom**, knowledge, erudition, perceptiveness, intelligence Opposite: stupidity

sagging adj **drooping**, wilting, flaccid, floppy, slumped

saggy see **sagging**

said adj **1 alleged**, supposed, assumed **2 previously mentioned**, above, aforesaid (fml), aforementioned (fml)

sail v **1 set sail**, navigate, cruise, voyage, put out to sea **2 glide**, float, flow, drift, fly

sailing n **boating**, cruising, yachting, navigation

sailor n **seafarer**, mariner, navigator, deckhand, salt (infml)

sail through v **do well**, do with ease, pass with flying colours, breeze through Opposite: fail

saintliness n **virtue**, goodness, piety, holiness, devoutness Opposite: evil

saintly adj **virtuous**, good, holy, pious, devout Opposite: evil

salaam n **greeting**, salutation, bow, nod, acknowledgment ■ v **greet**, bow, salute, nod, acknowledge

salacious adj **risqué**, indecent, crude, improper, obscene

salad days (dated) n **youth**, prime, heyday

salaried adj **remunerated**, on the payroll, on the books, paid, compensated

salary n **income**, pay, wage, payment, remuneration. See COMPARE AND CONTRAST at **wage**.

sale n **1 transaction**, deal, selling, retailing, vending Opposite: purchase **2 auction**, clearance sale, garage sale, jumble sale, car boot sale

saleable adj **vendible**, marketable, commercial, commercially viable

sales assistant n **salesperson**, shop assistant, cashier, floorwalker

salesperson n **1 seller**, trader, marketer, vendor, hawker **2 sales assistant**, shop assistant, cashier, floorwalker

sales representative n **salesperson**, seller, trader, marketer, vendor

salient adj **noticeable**, striking, prominent, outstanding, relevant Opposite: minor

saline adj **salty**, salt, brackish, briny, salted

saliva n **spittle**, spit, drool, dribble, slobber

salivate v **drool**, dribble, slobber, slaver

sallow adj **yellow**, sickly, wan, washed-out, ashen

sally n **1 attack**, sortie, breakout, breakthrough, raid **2 rush**, charge, dash, push ■ v **1 attack**, charge, raid, strike **2 go forth**, go out, venture forth, venture out, set out Opposite: retreat

salon n 1 **soiree**, gathering, rendezvous, meeting, group 2 **beauty salon**, hair salon, hairdresser's, barbershop, barber's

salt away v **hoard**, save, squirrel away, put by, set aside *Opposite*: fritter away

salt water n **brine**, sea water, saline

salty adj **salt**, saline, brackish, salted, briny *Opposite*: sweet

salubrious (fml) adj **healthy**, wholesome, respectable, decent, hygienic *Opposite*: insalubrious (fml)

salutary adj **beneficial**, helpful, useful, valuable, constructive

salutation n **greeting**, acknowledgment, welcome, gesture, salute

salute v **acknowledge**, greet, welcome, gesture, wave ■ n **sign of respect**, salutation, greeting, acknowledgment, signal

salvage v **save**, recover, rescue, retrieve, reclaim

salvation n **redemption**, rescue, recovery, escape, deliverance (fml) *Opposite*: ruination

salve n **lotion**, ointment, balm, balsam, liniment *Opposite*: irritant ■ v **appease**, soothe, comfort, mollify, calm *Opposite*: irritate

salver n **tray**, platter, plate, serving dish, dish

salvo n **barrage**, bombardment, round, torrent, hail

same adj 1 **identical**, alike, matching, similar, equal *Opposite*: different 2 **unchanged**, constant, consistent, uniform, even *Opposite*: changed

sameness n 1 **similarity**, likeness, resemblance, uniformity, equivalence *Opposite*: difference 2 **monotony**, repetitiveness, uniformity, consistency, evenness *Opposite*: variety

samey (infml) adj **repetitive**, unvaried, unchanging, monotonous, similar *Opposite*: varied

samovar n **tea urn**, urn, teapot, jug, kettle

sample n **example**, taster, model, trial, illustration ■ v **test**, try, appraise, try out, check out

sampler n 1 **technician**, tester, analyst, quality control analyst, laboratory technician 2 **selection**, sample, cross section, sampling, representative selection 3 **sample**, tryout, example, taste, illustration 4 **embroidery**, sewing, needlework, handwork

sampling n **sample**, specimen, cross section, selection, test group

sanatorium n **clinic**, hospital, infirmary, hospice, spa

sanctified adj **sacred**, holy, blessed, consecrated, hallowed *Opposite*: desecrated

sanctify v **bless**, consecrate, hallow, dedicate, purify *Opposite*: desecrate

sanctimonious adj **self-righteous**, smug, pious, pompous, self-satisfied *Opposite*: humble

sanctimoniousness n **self-righteousness**, smugness, pomposity, superiority

sanction n 1 **authorization**, permission, approval, agreement, consent *Opposite*: prohibition 2 **support**, approval, encouragement, agreement, affirmation 3 **restriction**, penalty, ban, punishment, injunction ■ v **authorize**, permit, approve, allow, pass *Opposite*: veto

sanctity n **holiness**, blessedness, sacredness, inviolability, purity *Opposite*: profanity

sanctuary n 1 **refuge**, asylum, shelter, safe haven, haven 2 **safety**, protection, refuge, asylum, shelter 3 **reserve**, reservation, national park, nature reserve, preserve (US)

sanctum n 1 **holy of holies**, sanctum sanctorum, temple, altar, shrine 2 **retreat**, den, refuge, study, hideaway

sand n 1 **shingle**, grit, gravel, powder, silt 2 **beach**, strand, shore, dune, shoreline ■ v **rub down**, smooth, sandpaper, polish, rub

sandbank n **sandbar**, dune, mound, bank, hummock

sandbar n **sandbank**, ridge, shallows, shoal

sandpaper v **rub down**, smooth, sand, polish, rub

sandwich n **snack**, roll, sarnie (infml), butty (infml), toasty (infml) ■ v **squeeze in**, squash in, pack in, cram, slot in

WORD BANK
❏ **types of sandwich** club sandwich, double-decker, open sandwich, panini, sub (infml), submarine, wrap

sane adj 1 **well-balanced**, compos mentis, rational, stable, healthy *Opposite*: insane 2 **sensible**, reasonable, rational, sound, wise *Opposite*: irrational

saneness *see* sanity

sang-froid n **self-possession**, calmness, poise, aplomb, self-assurance *Opposite*: anxiety

sanguinary (fml) adj 1 **bloody**, gory, brutal, grim, gruesome 2 **bloodthirsty**, murderous, ruthless, savage, cruel

sanguine adj **confident**, optimistic, cheerful, hopeful, positive *Opposite*: pessimistic

sanitary adj **hygienic**, clean, healthy, wholesome, sterile *Opposite*: insanitary

sanitation n **hygiene**, cleanliness, cleanness, public health, health

sanitize v 1 **purify**, fumigate, disinfect, clean, cleanse *Opposite*: contaminate 2 **censor**, clean up, bowdlerize, water down

sanity n 1 **rationality**, lucidity, reason, stability, saneness *Opposite*: insanity 2 **reasonableness**, sense, rationality, soundness, wisdom *Opposite*: unreasonableness

sap n 1 **juice**, fluid, liquid, latex 2 **energy**, vitality, health, strength, life ■ v 1 **dig down**, burrow, bore, tunnel, mine 2 **weaken**, drain, undermine, deplete, eat away *Opposite*: boost

sapient *adj* **wise**, learned, educated, intelligent, knowing *Opposite*: ignorant

sapling *n* **tree**, seedling, plantlet, sprout, scion

sarcasm *n* **irony**, mockery, cynicism, derision, acerbity

sarcastic *adj* **ironic**, mocking, sardonic, cynical, caustic

---

COMPARE AND CONTRAST CORE MEANING: describes remarks that are designed to hurt or mock

sarcastic contemptuous, scornful, or mocking and intended to hurt or belittle; **ironic** deliberately stating the opposite of the truth, usually with the intention of being amusing; **sardonic** mocking and cynical or disdainful, though not deliberately hurtful; **satirical** using ridicule, especially in a work of art, to criticize somebody's or something's faults, especially in the arts or politics; **caustic** harsh and bitter and intended to mock, offend, or belittle.

---

sarcophagus *n* **coffin**, tomb, casket *(US)*

sardonic *adj* **mocking**, scornful, ironic, sarcastic, derisive. *See* COMPARE AND CONTRAST *at* sarcastic.

sarsen *n* **rock**, boulder, stone, cairn, block

sartorial *adj* **dress**, fashion, clothing

sash *n* **band**, ribbon, belt, cummerbund, tie

sashay *v* **flounce**, sway, strut, prance, swagger

satchel *n* **bag**, shoulder bag, haversack, school bag, briefcase

sate *v* **fill up**, fill, satiate, stuff, gorge

sated *adj* **full**, satiated, gorged, bursting, satisfied *Opposite*: hungry

satellite *n* **1 dependency**, protectorate, colony, overseas territory, subject population **2 satellite television**, satellite TV, satellite broadcasting, digital television, digital TV

satiate *v* **1 glut**, fill, satisfy, sate, fill up **2 gratify**, satisfy, quench, sate, slake

satiated *adj* **1 full**, satisfied, replete, sated, full up *Opposite*: unsatisfied **2 gratified**, satisfied, quenched, sated, slaked

satiety *n* **fullness**, surfeit, glut, repletion

satiny *adj* **lustrous**, luminous, shiny, radiant, glossy *Opposite*: dull

satire *n* **1 mockery**, irony, sarcasm, ridicule, wit **2 parody**, lampoon, burlesque, caricature, travesty

satirical *adj* **mocking**, ironic, sardonic, humorous, sarcastic. *See* COMPARE AND CONTRAST *at* sarcastic.

satirist *n* **humorist**, wit, joker, satirizer, comic

satirize *v* **mock**, ridicule, parody, lampoon, deride

satisfaction *n* **1 contentment**, pleasure, happiness, joy, enjoyment *Opposite*: dissatisfaction **2 gratification**, consummation, fulfilment **3 approval**, liking, taste, contentment, agreement *Opposite*: dissatisfaction **4 redress**, reparation, compensation, settlement, repayment

satisfactory *adj* **acceptable**, reasonable, pleasing, fitting, agreeable *Opposite*: unsatisfactory

satisfied *adj* **content**, pleased, happy, gratified, fulfilled *Opposite*: dissatisfied

satisfy *v* **1 content**, please, gratify, mollify, placate *Opposite*: dissatisfy **2 gratify**, satiate, quench, sate, slake **3 convince**, assure, persuade, reassure, win over **4 fulfil**, comply with, meet, suit, fill

satisfying *adj* **1 pleasing**, gratifying, fulfilling, rewarding, enjoyable *Opposite*: dissatisfying **2 filling**, sustaining, nourishing, substantial, satiating *Opposite*: insufficient

saturate *v* **1 soak**, drench, wet through, douse, steep *Opposite*: dry out **2 oversupply**, overwhelm, overload, flood, inundate

saturated *adj* **1 soaked**, soaking, drenched, wet through, wet *Opposite*: dry **2 packed**, full, brimming, brimful, overfull *Opposite*: empty

saturation *n* **1 wetness**, soaking, drenching, wetting, moistening *Opposite*: dryness **2 fullness**, capacity, overload, satiety, permeation

saturnalia *n* **orgy**, celebration, bacchanalia, revel, party

saturnine *adj* **melancholy**, morose, gloomy, sad, sullen *Opposite*: cheerful

sauce *(infml)* *n* **impudence**, impertinence, rudeness, insolence, nerve

---

WORD BANK

❏ **types of seasonings, sauces, and dips** aioli, apple sauce, barbecue sauce, béarnaise, béchamel, brown sauce, catsup, chilli sauce, coulis, dressing, French dressing, gravy, guacamole, hollandaise, horseradish, hummus, ketchup, marinade, mayonnaise, mint sauce, raita, Russian dressing, salad cream, salsa, satay, soy sauce, stock, tabasco, tahini, taramasalata, tartare sauce, Thousand Island dressing, vinegar, vinaigrette, wasabi, Worcester sauce

---

saucepan *n* **pan**, pot, cooking pot

saucer *n* **plate**, bowl, dish

saucy *adj* **impudent**, smart, rude, impertinent *(fml)*, cheeky

saunter *v* **stroll**, walk, amble, meander, ramble *Opposite*: hurry ■ *n* **walk**, stroll, amble, ramble, meander

sauté *v* **fry**, stir-fry, pan-fry, brown

savage *adj* **1 violent**, unrestrained, vicious, fierce, ferocious *Opposite*: gentle **2 severe**, harsh, drastic, stringent, ruthless *Opposite*: mild **3 undomesticated**, wild, ferocious, fierce, feral *Opposite*: tame ■ *v* **1 attack**, brutalize, mug, maul, mangle **2 criticize**, tear apart, maul, destroy, attack *Opposite*: praise

savagery *n* **cruelty**, violence, barbarity, viciousness, barbarism *Opposite*: gentleness

savanna n grassland, pampas, plains, prairie

savant n guru, philosopher, thinker, pundit, expert

save v 1 rescue, recover, salvage, bail out, revive Opposite: abandon 2 accumulate, bank, salt away, collect Opposite: spend 3 keep back, set aside, put aside, put away, hold back Opposite: use up 4 avoid, prevent, stop, avert, bar ■ prep but, except, apart from, with the exception of, excluding Opposite: including

save for prep but, except, apart from, with the exception of, excluding

saver n investor, collector, hoarder, gatherer, squirrel (infml)

saving n economy, reduction, cutback, discount, cut Opposite: increase

saving grace n merit, advantage, strong point, strong suit, virtue Opposite: failing

savings n investments, reserves, nest egg, funds, hoard Opposite: expenditure

saviour n redeemer, rescuer, knight in shining armour, liberator, deliverer

savoir-faire n confidence, style, flair, poise, sense

savour v enjoy, relish, appreciate, delight in, cherish ■ n taste, smell, flavour, aroma, tang

savourless adj tasteless, insipid, bland, flavourless Opposite: flavourful

savourlessness n tastelessness, insipidness, blandness, flavourlessness Opposite: tastiness

savoury adj 1 salty, salt, spicy, piquant, pungent Opposite: sweet 2 respectable, pleasant, acceptable, nice, wholesome Opposite: unsavoury 3 appetizing, tasty, flavoursome, palatable, delicious Opposite: insipid

savvy (infml) n shrewdness, practicality, knowledge, perception, understanding Opposite: ignorance

saw n saying, proverb, adage, maxim, motto ■ v cut, slice, sever, divide, chop

say v 1 speak, utter, articulate, declare, pronounce 2 convey, indicate, reveal, give away, tell ■ n input, voice, opinion, view, pennyworth ■ adv approximately, roughly, about, around, give or take Opposite: exactly

saying n proverb, adage, maxim, axiom, motto

say-so (infml) n authorization, authority, permission, approval, agreement Opposite: veto

say sorry v apologize, excuse yourself, crawl, grovel, beg forgiveness

say yes v agree, accept, consent, acquiesce, assent Opposite: refuse

say your piece v speak out, speak up, protest, take a stand, make a stand Opposite: hold back

scab n crust, layer, skin, shell, covering

scabbard n sheath, case, covering, cover, casing

scabby adj mangy, scaly, diseased, shabby, dirty Opposite: unblemished

scabrous adj rough, flaky, scaly, mangy, leprous Opposite: smooth

scads (infml) n lots, scores, tons (infml), heaps (infml), buckets (infml) Opposite: none

scaffold n 1 support, framework, frame, platform, shell 2 gallows, gibbet, halter, noose

scaffolding n support, framework, frame, platform, shell

scalawag (dated infml) see scallywag

scald v 1 burn, blister, singe, sear, injure 2 sterilize, boil, steam, autoclave, heat Opposite: contaminate 3 bring to the boil, boil, heat, warm, simmer Opposite: chill

scalding adj 1 boiling, piping hot, baking, burning, blistering Opposite: icy 2 scathing, blistering, critical, fierce, scornful Opposite: complimentary

scale n 1 weighing machine, balance, scales, weighbridge, measure 2 gradation, tier, band, ratio, progression 3 extent, size, range, gamut, degree 4 deposit, crust, fur, covering, plaque 5 plate, flake, skin, scab, scurf ■ v 1 ascend, climb, mount, go up, clamber up 2 peel, pare, skin, exfoliate, flake

scale down v reduce, decrease, lower, cut back, cut down Opposite: scale up

scale up v increase, expand, extend, raise, step up Opposite: scale down

scallop n pinking, edging, scalloping, piping, border

scallywag (dated infml) n mischief-maker, scamp (infml), rascal, monkey (infml), imp

scaly adj flaking, peeling, crusty, encrusted, scabby Opposite: smooth

scamp (infml) n rogue, imp, urchin, rascal, monkey (infml) Opposite: angel

scamper v scurry, scuttle, run, hurry, dash Opposite: dawdle

scan v 1 scrutinize, examine, look into, pore over, inspect 2 skim, skim through, glance at, glance over, browse Opposite: study 3 examine, photograph, visualize, image, X-ray ■ n 1 perusal, skim, examination, inspection, look 2 image, X-ray, CT scan, MRI scan, PET scan

scandal n 1 disgrace, shame, dishonour, humiliation, outrage 2 gossip, tittle-tattle, rumour, talk, rumourmongering

scandalize v horrify, outrage, shock, disgust, dismay Opposite: impress

scandalmonger n gossip, rumourmonger, gossipmonger, newsmonger, snoop (infml)

scandalous adj shocking, outrageous, disgraceful, immoral, shameful Opposite: admirable

scant adj slight, limited, negligible, little, scarce Opposite: extensive

scanty *adj* **1 insufficient**, inadequate, meagre, little, scarce *Opposite*: abundant **2 revealing**, flimsy, light, low-cut, tight

scapegoat *n* **stooge**, victim, accused, culprit, fall guy *(slang)* ■ *v* **blame**, incriminate, condemn, accuse, reproach *Opposite*: exonerate

scar *n* **1 mark**, blemish, mutilation, scratch, wound **2 effect**, wound, trauma, hurt, after-effect ■ *v* **1 damage**, mark, blemish, mutilate, disfigure **2 traumatize**, hurt, affect, damage, mark

scarce *adj* **1 in short supply**, limited, insufficient, inadequate, scant *Opposite*: abundant **2 rare**, uncommon, unusual, infrequent, threatened *Opposite*: common

scarcely *adv* **barely**, hardly, not quite, only just, just *Opposite*: fully

scarceness *see* scarcity

scarcity *n* **1 shortage**, lack, dearth, insufficiency, scarceness *Opposite*: abundance **2 rarity**, uncommonness, infrequency, lack, want *Opposite*: commonness

scare *v* **frighten**, terrify, startle, alarm, panic *Opposite*: reassure ■ *n* **fright**, shock, start, jolt, alarm *Opposite*: reassurance

scarecrow *n* **figure**, effigy, guy, mannequin

scared *adj* **frightened**, afraid, fearful, terrified, nervous *Opposite*: fearless

scaremonger *n* **alarmist**, doomsayer, troublemaker, rumourmonger, newsmonger *Opposite*: optimist

scare off *v* **frighten away**, drive away, chase off, scare away, frighten *Opposite*: welcome

scarf *n* **muffler**, headscarf, bandana, cravat, shawl

scarify *v* **1** *(infml)* **scare**, frighten, alarm, worry, startle *Opposite*: reassure **2 lacerate**, scratch, score, cut, incise

scariness *n* *(infml)* **menace**, creepiness *(infml)*, spookiness *(infml)* *Opposite*: reassurance

scarp *n* **escarpment**, ridge, cliff, bluff, crag

scarred *adj* **1 mutilated**, disfigured, marked, injured, wounded **2 damaged**, defaced, blemished, marked, scratched

scary *(infml)* *adj* **frightening**, chilling, terrifying, petrifying, daunting *Opposite*: reassuring

scat *(infml)* *v* **run away**, run off, escape, flee, abscond

scathing *adj* **scornful**, mocking, derisive, sarcastic, contemptuous *Opposite*: complimentary

scatter *v* **1 throw**, strew, fling, sprinkle, distribute **2 disperse**, collect spread out, spread, flee, take flight *Opposite*: gather

COMPARE AND CONTRAST CORE MEANING: spread around

scatter spread things around physically, especially in a random widespread manner; **broadcast** spread or transmit information, especially by means of radio or television, or scatter seeds over the ground; **distribute** allocate, share, or give out something in a structured or organized way, or spread something over a particular surface or area; **disseminate** spread ideas, information, or attitudes such as goodwill.

scatterbrained *adj* **absent-minded**, vague, forgetful, woolly-headed, careless *Opposite*: focused

scattered *adj* **1 dispersed**, distributed, strewn, sprinkled, disseminated *Opposite*: concentrated **2 infrequent**, isolated, discrete, separate, occasional *Opposite*: frequent

scattering *n* **handful**, sprinkling, trickle, bit, smattering

scattershot *adj* **disorganized**, indiscriminate, random, chaotic, slapdash *Opposite*: focused

scatty *(infml)* *adj* **empty-headed**, forgetful, absent-minded, scatterbrained, dizzy *(infml)* *Opposite*: organized

scavenge *v* **hunt**, forage, search, rummage, sift

scenario *n* **situation**, state of affairs, state, setup, circumstances

scene *n* **1 act**, division, part, section, passage **2 setting**, site, place, background, backdrop **3 sight**, prospect, picture, panorama, view **4 fuss**, commotion, exhibition, incident, spectacle

scenery *n* **1 set**, backdrop, backcloth, background, decor **2 landscape**, panorama, vista, outlook, view

scenic *adj* **picturesque**, beautiful, attractive, lovely, charming *Opposite*: unsightly

scent *n* **1 smell**, odour, aroma, perfume, bouquet **2 trail**, trace, track, spoor **3 perfume**, fragrance, cologne, toilet water, eau de cologne **4 hint**, trace, air, whiff, suggestion ■ *v* **1 predict**, foresee, foretell, sense, feel **2 sniff**, smell, detect, sense, pick up **3 imbue**, perfume, fill, infuse, suffuse. *See* COMPARE AND CONTRAST *at* **smell**.

scented *adj* **perfumed**, fragrant, aromatic, sweet-smelling, fragranced *Opposite*: odourless

sceptic *n* **cynic**, disbeliever, doubter, doubting Thomas, questioner *Opposite*: believer

sceptical *adj* **cynical**, disbelieving, doubtful, doubting, unconvinced *Opposite*: convinced. *See* COMPARE AND CONTRAST *at* **doubtful**.

scepticism *n* **cynicism**, disbelief, doubt, incredulity, uncertainty *Opposite*: conviction

sceptre *n* **staff**, staff of office, mace, rod, insignia

schedule *n* **agenda**, timetable, diary, calendar, list ■ *v* **arrange**, plan, timetable, programme, book *Opposite*: cancel

scheduled *adj* **arranged**, planned, timetabled, programmed, listed *Opposite*: unplanned

schema *n* **plan**, diagram, scheme, schematic, representation

schematize v **systematize**, arrange, structure, organize, draft *Opposite*: disarrange

scheme n **1 plot**, plan, conspiracy, ploy, ruse **2 plan**, method, stratagem, idea, proposal **3 arrangement**, system, structure, outline, organization *Opposite*: chaos **4 diagram**, plan, schematic, graphic, representation ■ v **plot**, conspire, intrigue, connive, plan

schemer n **plotter**, conspirator, conniver, traitor, intriguer

scheming adj **devious**, calculating, conniving, conspiratorial, treacherous *Opposite*: honest

schism n **split**, break, division, rupture, rift *Opposite*: union

schismatic adj **factional**, divisive, clashing, conflicting, controversial *Opposite*: unifying

schlep (*infml*) v **lug**, haul, heave, drag, cart ■ n **trek**, trudge, hike, bore, bind

schmaltz (*infml*) n **sentimentality**, slush, mush, corniness, mawkishness

schmaltzy (*infml*) adj **sentimental**, cloying, sugary, saccharine, slushy

scholar n **academic**, researcher, don, professor, doctor

scholarly adj **learned**, academic, erudite, intellectual, educated *Opposite*: lowbrow

scholarship n **1 grant**, bursary, studentship, subsidy, allowance **2 learning**, erudition, study, knowledge, research *Opposite*: ignorance

scholastic adj **educational**, academic, pedagogic, school, college

school n **group**, set, coterie, brotherhood, sisterhood *Opposite*: individual ■ v **train**, instruct, educate, discipline, teach

WORD BANK

❑ **types of school** academy, boarding school, comprehensive, faith school, grammar school, high school, infant school, junior school, middle school, nursery school, prep school, preschool, primary school, private school, public school, senior high, state school, trade school

schoolchild n **pupil**, student, scholar, schoolboy, schoolgirl

schooling n **education**, teaching, training, instruction, tuition

school of thought n **philosophy**, doctrine, ideology, outlook, attitude

science n **discipline**, knowledge, skill, learning, scholarship

scientific adj **technical**, methodical, systematic, logical, precise *Opposite*: unscientific

scintilla n **jot**, iota, scrap, shred, speck

scintillate v **1 sparkle**, glitter, gleam, flash, glint **2 fascinate**, dazzle, charm, shine, sparkle *Opposite*: bore

scintillating adj **sparkling**, dazzling, brilliant, bright, glittering *Opposite*: dull

scintillation n **sparkling**, glittering, gleaming, flashing, glinting *Opposite*: dullness

scion n **1 cutting**, graft, shoot, implant, implantation **2 offspring**, child, heir, descendant, son *Opposite*: parent

scoff v **1 jeer**, sneer, mock, ridicule, make fun of *Opposite*: praise **2** (*infml*) **eat**, gobble, stuff your face, bolt, wolf *Opposite*: nibble

scoffing adj **mocking**, jeering, sneering, dismissive, contemptuous

scold v **rebuke**, admonish, reprimand, reproach, discipline *Opposite*: praise

scolding n **admonishment**, reprimand, reproach, rebuke, caution *Opposite*: praise

sconce n **light fixture**, bracket, wall lamp, candleholder, light fitting

scoop n **1 ladle**, dipper, serving spoon, server, soup ladle **2** (*infml*) **news story**, story, exclusive, revelation, exposé ■ v **1 dig**, hollow, scrape, shovel, excavate *Opposite*: fill **2 lift**, gather up, pick up, raise, take *Opposite*: drop

scoot (*infml*) v **1 go away**, leave, scat (*infml*), make yourself scarce (*infml*), skedaddle (*slang*) *Opposite*: arrive **2 move quickly**, rush, hurry, scurry, dash *Opposite*: dawdle

scope n **1 possibility**, choice, room, opportunity, space *Opposite*: constraint **2 range**, extent, capacity, span, reach

scorch v **burn**, singe, sear, char, blacken

scorched adj **1 burnt**, singed, seared, charred, blackened **2 dried**, dry as a bone, dry, parched, baked *Opposite*: drenched

scorching (*infml*) adj **boiling**, baking, sweltering, sizzling (*infml*), blazing *Opposite*: freezing

score n **1 total**, tally, mark, result, count **2 notch**, cut, slash, groove, nick ■ v **1 achieve**, chalk up, attain, make, gain **2 keep count**, keep a tally, keep score, count, tot up **3 cut into**, slash, notch, nick, slice **4 scratch**, etch, carve, mark, scrape

scoreboard n **display**, board, panel, notice board

scorecard n **tally**, scoresheet, record, card

scores n **lots**, tons (*infml*), heaps (*infml*), buckets (*infml*), piles (*infml*) *Opposite*: none

scoresheet n **sheet**, scorecard, tally, record

scorn n **contempt**, disdain, disrespect, derision, scornfulness *Opposite*: admiration ■ v **1 show contempt for**, despise, disdain, belittle, deride *Opposite*: admire **2 reject**, spurn, rebuff, turn down, refuse *Opposite*: choose

scorned adj **1 despised**, disdained, belittled, derided, disparaged *Opposite*: admired **2 rejected**, spurned, rebuffed, turned down, refused *Opposite*: chosen

scornful adj **contemptuous**, disdainful, disrespectful, mocking, derisive *Opposite*: admiring

scornfulness n **contempt**, disdain, disrespect, mockery, derision

scotch v **stop**, spoil, foil, scuttle, scupper *Opposite*: initiate

scot-free adv **unpunished**, without punishment, with impunity, lightly, easily

scoundrel n **rogue**, rascal, villain, cheat, crook *(infml)* *Opposite*: hero

scour v **1 scrub**, rub, clean, wash, polish *Opposite*: dirty **2 search**, comb, hunt, go over with a fine-tooth comb, rake through

scourge n **bane**, blight, plague, curse, menace *Opposite*: blessing ▪ v **plague**, curse, afflict, terrorize, torment *Opposite*: bless

scout n **lookout**, spy, watch, undercover agent, detective ▪ v **1 search**, hunt, scout around, look around, cast around *Opposite*: find **2 check out**, reconnoitre, survey, investigate, spy out

scout around v **search**, hunt, scout, look around, cast around

scowl n **glare**, frown, glower, grimace, stare *Opposite*: smile ▪ v **look daggers**, glare, frown, glower, grimace *Opposite*: smile

scrabble v **1 scratch**, dig, scrape, claw, pick **2 grope**, fumble, clutch, rummage, rootle

scragginess n **scrawniness**, boniness, gauntness, skinniness, thinness *Opposite*: plumpness

scraggly adj **messy**, untidy, dishevelled, unkempt, tangled *Opposite*: tidy

scraggy adj **scrawny**, skinny, bony, gaunt, thin *Opposite*: plump. See COMPARE AND CONTRAST at **thin**.

scram *(infml)* v **run off**, run away, get out, get away, bolt

scramble v **1 climb**, clamber, crawl, scrabble, struggle *Opposite*: descend **2 move quickly**, rush, run, scuttle, jostle *Opposite*: plod **3 mix up**, jumble, mix, muddle, confuse *Opposite*: unscramble ▪ n **1 ascent**, climb, clamber, hike *Opposite*: descent **2 rush**, run, stampede, commotion, dash *Opposite*: calm

scrap n **1 piece**, bit, fragment, slip, wisp **2** *(infml)* **fight**, scuffle, tussle, row, clash ▪ v **1 cancel**, abandon, get rid of, do away with, give up *Opposite*: adopt **2 scuffle**, fight, tussle, spar, brawl

scrape v **1 rub**, scratch, scuff, abrade, scour **2 graze**, scratch, scuff, mark, abrade ▪ n **1** *(infml)* **fight**, brawl, clash, fracas, scuffle **2** *(infml)* **predicament**, plight, problem, fix *(infml)*, pickle *(infml)* **3 scratch**, scuff, graze, mark, abrasion

scrape by v **make do**, survive, make ends meet, get by, scratch a living *Opposite*: prosper

scrape out v **hollow out**, scoop out, gouge out, carve out, gouge *Opposite*: fill

scrape together v **collect**, amass, put by, put aside, scrape up *Opposite*: disperse

scrapheap n **rubbish dump**, junkyard, landfill, tip

scrappy adj **1 fragmentary**, fragmented, bitty, patchy, piecemeal *Opposite*: complete **2 disjointed**, inconsistent, disconnected, incoherent, patchy *Opposite*: uniform **3** *(infml)* **plucky**, courageous, determined, spirited, spunky *(infml)* *Opposite*: timid **4** *(infml)* **argumentative**, contrary, confrontational, hotheaded, quarrelsome *Opposite*: docile

scraps n **leftovers**, scrapings, slops, crumbs, leavings

scratch v **1 scrape**, graze, grate, rub, cut **2 itch**, rub, scrape, worry at **3 cancel**, forget, scrap, leave out *Opposite*: keep **4 pull out**, drop out, bow out, withdraw, abandon *Opposite*: continue ▪ n **cut**, scrape, graze, score, nick

scratched adj **scuffed**, scored, scraped, marked, damaged

scratch together v **collect**, amass, put by, put aside, scratch up *Opposite*: disperse

scratchy adj **itchy**, prickly, tickly, irritating, uncomfortable *Opposite*: soft

scrawl v **scribble**, doodle, pencil, write, draw ▪ n **illegible writing**, scribble, doodle, graffiti, squiggle

scrawled adj **indecipherable**, illegible, incomprehensible, scribbled, untidy *Opposite*: neat

scrawniness n **gauntness**, skinniness, boniness, scragginess, thinness *Opposite*: plumpness

scrawny adj **scraggy**, skinny, bony, gaunt, thin *Opposite*: plump. See COMPARE AND CONTRAST at **thin**.

scream n **1 shriek**, yell, cry, yelp, shout *Opposite*: murmur **2** *(infml)* **laugh** *(infml)*, riot *(infml)*, gas *(infml)*, card *(dated infml)*, hoot *(slang)* ▪ v **shout**, shriek, yell, cry, screech *Opposite*: whisper

scree n **rock debris**, talus, rubble, gravel, stones

screech n **scream**, shriek, squeal, cry, yelp *Opposite*: whisper ▪ v **shriek**, scream, squeal, cry, yelp *Opposite*: whisper

screen n **1 partition**, divider, panel, shield, guard **2 shade**, awning, canopy, shelter, curtain **3 monitor**, display, VDU, computer screen, television ▪ v **1 test**, inspect, examine, diagnose, check **2 hide**, conceal, cover, protect, shelter *Opposite*: reveal **3 partition**, separate, divide, mark off, curtain *Opposite*: open out **4 broadcast**, put on, show, transmit, project **5 vet**, select, assess, investigate, test

screening n **1 show**, showing, viewing, programme, projection **2 broadcast**, showing, transmission, run, airing **3 inspection**, testing, examination, diagnosis, checking **4 selection**, vetting, assessment, investigation, inspection

screenplay n **script**, dialogue, scenario, text, writing

screenwriter n **scriptwriter**, writer, dramatist, author, playwright

screw v 1 **twist**, rotate, coil, turn, wind *Opposite*: unscrew 2 **attach**, bolt, fasten, fix, secure 3 **crumple**, twist, distort, contort, crinkle *Opposite*: smooth

screw up v **muster**, gather, summon, call up, pluck up *Opposite*: lose

scribble v 1 **scrawl**, jot, write, dash off *(infml)* 2 **draw**, doodle, scrawl, squiggle ■ n 1 **doodle**, scrawl, jotting, squiggle, design 2 **writing**, handwriting, scrawl, lettering

scribbled adj **scrawled**, jotted, untidy, illegible, indecipherable *Opposite*: neat

scribe n **transcriber**, copyist, clerk, illuminator

scrimmage n **struggle**, tussle, fray, scrum, ruckus ■ v **fight**, battle, skirmish, scuffle, brawl

scrimp v **economize**, save, skimp, draw in your horns, tighten your belt *Opposite*: squander

script n 1 **screenplay**, text, dialogue, words, libretto 2 **writing**, calligraphy, handwriting, hand, cursive

scriptwriter n **writer**, author, playwright, screenwriter, dramatist

scroll n **roll**, parchment, document, certificate, manuscript

scrooge *(infml)* n **miser**, skinflint, niggard, pinchpenny, cheapskate *(infml)*

scrounge *(infml)* v 1 **beg**, borrow, solicit, sponge *(infml)*, cadge *(infml)* *Opposite*: give 2 **scavenge**, rummage, forage, go through, search

scrounger *(infml)* n **beggar**, borrower, cadger *(infml)*, sponger *(infml)*, freeloader *(infml)* *Opposite*: donor

scrub v 1 **clean**, rub, scour, polish, brush *Opposite*: dirty 2 *(infml)* **cancel**, delete, erase, forget about, scratch *Opposite*: schedule ■ n 1 **undergrowth**, brush, bush, brushwood, vegetation 2 **rub**, clean, scour, polish, brush

scruffy adj **untidy**, shabby, tatty, unkempt, dishevelled *Opposite*: tidy

scrum n **tussle**, fray, scuffle, scrimmage, struggle

scrummy *(infml) see* **scrumptious**

scrumptious *(infml)* adj **delicious**, delectable, mouthwatering, tasty, delightful *Opposite*: revolting

scrunch v **crumple**, crush, crunch, crease, wrinkle *Opposite*: smooth

scruple n **misgiving**, doubt, qualm, compunction, hesitation

scrupulous adj 1 **conscientious**, meticulous, thorough, careful, rigorous *Opposite*: sloppy 2 **trustworthy**, reliable, dependable, trusty, upright. *See* COMPARE AND CONTRAST *at* careful.

scrupulousness n 1 **honesty**, reliability, dependability, trustworthiness, decency 2 **conscientiousness**, meticulousness, thoroughness, carefulness, rigour

scrutinize v **examine**, inspect, study, pore over, analyse *Opposite*: skim

scrutiny n **examination**, inspection, study, analysis, search

scud v **speed**, sweep, fly, sail, rush *Opposite*: crawl

scuff v **scrape**, wear away, rub, graze, scratch ■ n **scratch**, scrape, graze, abrasion

scuffle n **fight**, brawl, punch-up, fracas, fray ■ v **wrestle**, fight, come to blows, exchange blows, scrap

scull n **oar**, paddle, blade, sweep ■ v **row**, paddle, propel, canoe

sculpt v **carve**, shape, mould, form, fashion

sculpture n **statue**, statuette, figure, figurine, carving

scum n **froth**, foam, impurities, filth, crust

scupper v **wreck**, stymie, thwart, ruin, spoil

scurf n 1 **dandruff**, dander, dead skin, flakes 2 **encrustation**, scale, crust, deposit, coat

scurrilous adj **scandalous**, slanderous, libellous, defamatory, outrageous *Opposite*: complimentary

scurry v **dash**, scuttle, scamper, dart, rush *Opposite*: saunter

scuttle v 1 **destroy**, stymie, thwart, spoil, ruin 2 **scurry**, scamper, dart, dash, rush *Opposite*: saunter

scythe v **cut**, cut down, hack, slice, sweep

sea n **ocean**, deep, depths, briny *Opposite*: dry land ■ adj **maritime**, aquatic, oceanic, marine, nautical *Opposite*: land

seaboard n **coast**, coastline, shore, seashore, shoreline *Opposite*: interior

sea change n **transformation**, metamorphosis, shift, turnaround, U-turn

seacoast *see* **seaboard**

seafaring adj **maritime**, nautical, oceangoing, seagoing, marine

seafront n **waterfront**, promenade, esplanade, boardwalk, beach

seagoing *see* **seafaring**

seal n 1 **closure**, cover, stopper, lid, cap 2 **stamp**, hallmark, impression, signet, sigil ■ v 1 **close**, fasten, stick, close up, shut *Opposite*: open 2 **guarantee**, settle, finalize, wrap up, confirm

sea lane n **seaway**, shipping lane, sea route, channel, corridor

sealed adj 1 **closed**, stuck down, wrapped, taped up *Opposite*: unsealed 2 **impenetrable**, hermetically sealed, vacuum-packed, airtight, watertight *Opposite*: unsealed

seal off v **close off**, cordon off, fence off, isolate, quarantine *Opposite*: open

seam n 1 **join**, joint, closure, ridge 2 **layer**, stratum, vein, lode

seaman n **sailor**, mariner, seafarer, navigator, deckhand

seamless adj 1 **unified**, all-in-one, one-piece, whole, continuous *Opposite*: joined 2 **smooth**, perfect, faultless, uniform, unified

seamy *adj* **unpleasant**, degenerate, sordid, squalid, seedy *Opposite*: wholesome

seaport *n* **harbour**, port, coastal town, anchorage, dock

sear *v* **burn**, scorch, solder, singe, char

search *v* **examine**, rifle, comb, look for, seek ■ *n* **examination**, hunt, quest, pursuit, exploration

searching *adj* **thorough**, penetrating, incisive, probing, pointed *Opposite*: superficial

searchlight *n* **light**, spotlight, beam, lamp, torch

search out *v* **discover**, uncover, find out, find, research

search party *n* **searchers**, rescue party, rescuers, rescue patrol, emergency workers

search through *v* **sift through**, sort through, rummage, hunt through, ransack

searing *adj* **1 blistering**, sweltering, scorching (*infml*), sizzling (*infml*), roasting (*infml*) *Opposite*: freezing **2 intense**, shooting, stabbing, agonizing, excruciating *Opposite*: mild

seashore *n* **coastline**, shore, shoreline, coast, seacoast

seasick *adj* **sick**, nauseous, queasy, travelsick, ill

seaside *n* **beach**, seafront, seashore, coast, shore

season *n* **period**, term, spell, time, time of year ■ *v* **flavour**, spice, spike, pepper, salt

seasonable *adj* **appropriate**, fitting, timely, opportune, suitable *Opposite*: unseasonable

seasonal *adj* **1 cyclical**, periodic, cyclic, recurrent, spring *Opposite*: year-round **2 limited**, sporadic, intermittent, temporary, casual *Opposite*: permanent

seasoned *adj* **experienced**, veteran, hardened, tested, weathered *Opposite*: inexperienced

seasoning *n* **flavouring**, flavour, zest, zing (*infml*)

seat *n* **1 chair**, bench, couch, pew, stool **2 base**, HQ, control centre, headquarters, centre ■ *v* **1 place**, sit, sit down, set, install **2 accommodate**, hold, sit, contain, take

seating *n* **seats**, chairs, spaces, places, places to sit

WORD BANK
❏ **types of seating** armchair, beach chair, bench, Boston rocker, bucket seat, carver, chair, chaise longue, chesterfield, couch, deck chair, easy chair, highchair, ladder-back, lounger, love seat, pew, recliner, rocking chair, settee, sofa, stall, stool, sunlounger, swivel chair, Windsor chair, wing chair

sea wall *n* **dike**, jetty, breakwater, groyne, embankment

seaway *n* **channel**, sea lane, shipping lane, sea route, canal

secede *v* **withdraw**, break away, break from, disaffiliate, pull out *Opposite*: affiliate

secession *n* **withdrawal**, departure, separation, retreat, retirement

seclude *v* **isolate**, separate, keep away, keep apart, remove

secluded *adj* **private**, sheltered, quiet, isolated, out-of-the-way *Opposite*: public

seclusion *n* **privacy**, shelter, isolation, quiet, solitude

second *adj* **additional**, another, next, subsequent, following ■ *n* **moment**, minute, instant, trice, flash *Opposite*: age ■ *v* **1 support**, agree with, endorse, subscribe, uphold *Opposite*: oppose **2 transfer**, assign, post, attach, send

secondary *adj* **1 subordinate**, minor, inferior, lesser, tributary *Opposite*: primary **2 derived**, derivative, resulting, resultant, consequent *Opposite*: original

second-class *adj* **second-rate**, mediocre, indifferent, middling, second best *Opposite*: first-class

seconder *n* **supporter**, endorser, backer, advocate, assenter

second-guess *v* **predict**, guess, foretell, anticipate, work out

second-hand *adj* **used**, hand-me-down, nearly new *Opposite*: new ■ *adv* **indirectly**, circuitously, through the grapevine *Opposite*: directly

secondly *adv* **then**, furthermore, in addition, what is more, also *Opposite*: firstly

second name *n* **surname**, family name, last name

second-rate *adj* **inadequate**, mediocre, unsatisfactory, poor, below standard *Opposite*: first-rate

second sight *n* **clairvoyance**, foresight, foreknowledge, precognition, intuition

second thoughts *n* **reconsideration**, pangs, doubts, qualms, misgivings

secrecy *n* **concealment**, confidentiality, privacy, mystery, silence *Opposite*: openness

secret *adj* **1 clandestine**, covert, stealthy, surreptitious, furtive *Opposite*: open **2 confidential**, private, classified, top-secret, restricted *Opposite*: public ■ *n* **confidence**, skeleton in the cupboard, mystery, riddle, enigma

COMPARE AND CONTRAST CORE MEANING: conveying a desire or need for concealment
secret intentionally withheld from general knowledge; **clandestine** describes an activity that needs to be concealed, usually because it is illegal or unauthorized; **covert** not intended to be known, seen, or found out, suggesting a lack of honesty or openness; **furtive** cautious and careful in order to escape notice; **stealthy** quiet, slow, and cautious in order to escape notice; **surreptitious** done in a concealed or underhand way to escape notice.

secret agent *n* **spy**, undercover agent, double agent, mole, infiltrator

secretary *n* clerical worker, PA, personal assistant, administrative assistant, office assistant

secretary-general *n* chief executive officer, CEO, head, chief, chair

secrete *v* 1 hide, hide away, conceal, stow, squirrel away *Opposite*: display 2 exude, ooze, emit, produce, squirt *Opposite*: absorb

secretion *n* discharge, excretion, exudation, emission, ooze

secretive *adj* private, mysterious, enigmatic, guarded, reticent *Opposite*: open

secretly *adv* clandestinely, covertly, in secret, surreptitiously, furtively *Opposite*: openly

sect *n* 1 group, clique, faction, camp, party 2 religious group, religious persuasion, denomination, cult, movement

sectarian *adj* 1 religious, denominational, sectional, factional 2 dogmatic, intolerant, bigoted, biased, partisan *Opposite*: tolerant

section *n* part, unit, piece, segment, slice *Opposite*: whole ■ *v* divide, divide up, partition, split, segment *Opposite*: combine

sector *n* 1 part, division, subdivision, segment, portion *Opposite*: whole 2 area, zone, region, quarter, district

secular *adj* earthly, worldly, nonspiritual, profane, lay *Opposite*: spiritual

secure *adj* 1 safe, protected, safe and sound, safe as houses, sheltered *Opposite*: vulnerable 2 confident, assured, self-confident, sure of yourself, self-assured *Opposite*: insecure 3 fixed firmly, closed, fastened, locked *Opposite*: unfastened 4 dependable, reliable, safe, stable, steady *Opposite*: unreliable ■ *v* 1 fix, fasten, make fast, position, attach *Opposite*: loosen 2 make safe, safeguard, fortify, lock, lock up 3 obtain, acquire, get, get hold of, capture *Opposite*: lose 4 guarantee, ensure, give security, indemnify, assure. *See* COMPARE AND CONTRAST *at* get.

securely *adv* firmly, steadily, tightly, strongly, safely

security *n* 1 safety, refuge, sanctuary, haven, safekeeping *Opposite*: danger 2 precautions, safety measures, defence, protection 3 confidence, wellbeing, self-assurance, reassurance, self-confidence *Opposite*: insecurity 4 guarantee, collateral, surety, insurance, indemnity

sedate *adj* 1 dignified, calm, cool, demure, serene *Opposite*: boisterous 2 staid, unexciting, dull, slow-moving, slow *Opposite*: exciting ■ *v* anaesthetize, tranquillize, drug, put under sedation, knock out *Opposite*: revive

sedateness *n* 1 dignity, calmness, coolness, demureness, composedness 2 staidness, dullness, slowness

sedation *n* calm, restfulness, drowsiness, torpor, tranquillity *Opposite*: excitement

sedative *n* tranquillizer, narcotic, barbiturate,

downer *(slang) Opposite*: stimulant ■ *adj* tranquillizing, calming, soothing, relaxing, soporific *Opposite*: stimulating

sedentary *adj* sitting, inactive, deskbound, desk *Opposite*: active

sediment *n* residue, deposit, dregs, remains, grounds

sedition *n* 1 incitement to rebellion, agitation, treason, subversion, rabble-rousing 2 rebellion, mutiny, defiance, unrest, civil disobedience

seditious *adj* rebellious, subversive, treasonable, disloyal, mutinous *Opposite*: loyal

seduce *v* 1 entice, lead astray, lure, allure, tempt 2 persuade, wheedle, inveigle, talk into, coax

see *v* 1 perceive, observe, distinguish, notice, witness 2 understand, realize, perceive, grasp, appreciate *Opposite*: misunderstand 3 meet, visit, pay a visit to, go to see, call on 4 find out, establish, investigate, look into, check 5 imagine, picture, envisage, predict, foresee 6 make sure, see to it, ensure, make certain, guarantee 7 consider it, think about it, weigh it up, give it some thought, think it over 8 date, escort, accompany, go with, go out with 9 look at, refer to, consult, view, regard

see about *v* take care of, look into, investigate, find out about, attend to *Opposite*: leave alone

seed *n* 1 kernel, pip, spore, germ, stone 2 source, beginning, start, starting point, nucleus ■ *v* sow, plant, broadcast, scatter *Opposite*: harvest

seed capital *see* seed money

seediness *n* 1 dinginess, grubbiness, shabbiness, squalor, tattiness *(infml)* 2 sickliness, paleness, roughness *(infml)*

seedling *n* sprout, sapling, plantlet, slip, twig

seed money *n* startup funds, pump priming funds, venture capital, initial investment, working capital

seedy *adj* 1 dingy, sordid, shabby, squalid, sleazy *Opposite*: respectable 2 *(infml)* unwell, ill, sick, poorly *(infml)*, pale *Opposite*: healthy

see eye to eye *v* agree, see things the same way, have the same opinion, be of the same mind *Opposite*: disagree

seeing *conj* considering, bearing in mind, as, since, in view of

see into *v* discern, understand, penetrate, comprehend, figure out

see in your mind's eye *v* imagine, picture, visualize, envision, see

seek *v* 1 search for, try to find, hunt for, pursue, seek out *Opposite*: find 2 strive for, try for, go after, pursue, work towards *Opposite*: achieve 3 ask for, enquire about, request *Opposite*: obtain

seek out v **look for**, seek, search for, try to find, hunt for *Opposite*: find

seek to v **try to**, aspire to, endeavour to, aim to, attempt to *Opposite*: succeed

seem v **appear**, give the impression, seem like, look, look as if

seeming adj **apparent**, outward, ostensible, surface, superficial *Opposite*: real

seemingly adv **1 by all accounts**, on the face of it, to all appearances, rumour has it, or so it seems *Opposite*: actually **2 apparently**, outwardly, ostensibly, superficially, externally *Opposite*: really

seemly adj **appropriate**, decorous, fitting, fit, decent *Opposite*: unseemly

see off v **1 say goodbye to**, bid farewell to, send off, take to the station, take to the airport *Opposite*: welcome **2** (infml) **get rid of**, get shot of (infml), chase off, chase away, force to go *Opposite*: invite **3 defeat**, beat, withstand, fend off, put paid to (infml)

see out v **1 stay**, last, last out, live out, survive **2 show to the door**, show out, say goodbye to, accompany, go with *Opposite*: usher in

seep v **leak**, ooze, trickle, dribble, soak

seepage n **leakage**, leak, outflow, waste, escape

seer n **prophet**, soothsayer, clairvoyant, oracle, fortune-teller

see red (infml) v **lose your temper**, go berserk, be enraged, fly into a rage, rage *Opposite*: calm down

seesaw v **alternate**, go up and down, oscillate, fluctuate, swing *Opposite*: stabilize

seethe v **1 boil**, bubble, froth, foam, churn **2 fume**, rage, be furious, be livid, boil with rage *Opposite*: calm down **3 teem**, swarm, be alive with, be crawling with

seething adj **1 fuming**, furious, livid, beside yourself, enraged *Opposite*: calm **2 boiling**, bubbling, foaming, on the boil, simmering *Opposite*: still **3 bustling**, busy, frantic, heaving, teeming *Opposite*: quiet

see through v **1 understand**, get to the bottom of, be wise to, know inside out, read like a book **2 persevere with**, persist at, stick at, stay with, carry out *Opposite*: quit

see-through adj **transparent**, translucent, sheer, diaphanous, gauzy *Opposite*: opaque

see to v **deal with**, sort out, handle, take care of, manage

see to it v **make sure**, see, ensure, make certain, guarantee

segment n **section**, part, piece, slice, sector *Opposite*: whole ■ v **divide**, split, subdivide, section, portion

segmentation n **division**, subdivision, separation, splitting up, dissection *Opposite*: integration

segregate v **separate**, separate out, isolate, keep apart, set apart *Opposite*: integrate

segregation n **separation**, isolation, exclusion, setting apart, apartheid *Opposite*: integration

seize v **1 take hold of**, grab, grab hold of, get hold of, snatch *Opposite*: relinquish **2 appropriate**, confiscate, take away, sequester, remove *Opposite*: return **3 take control of**, capture, take, take over, annex *Opposite*: lose **4 arrest**, capture, take into custody, apprehend, take hostage *Opposite*: release **5 take advantage of**, grab, jump at, take

seize up v **1 grind to a halt**, jam, fail, stop working, stall **2 stiffen**, stiffen up, freeze up, stick, cramp

seizure n **1 attack**, fit, spasm, convulsion **2 capture**, arrest, abduction, apprehension *Opposite*: release **3 appropriation**, confiscation, commandeering, annexation, capture *Opposite*: return

seldom adv **not often**, hardly ever, rarely, infrequently, occasionally *Opposite*: often

select v **choose**, pick, pick out, decide on, opt for *Opposite*: deselect ■ adj **1 choice**, top quality, first-class, excellent, first-rate *Opposite*: inferior **2 exclusive**, elite, privileged, cliquey, restricted

selected adj **carefully chosen**, designated, nominated, particular, certain *Opposite*: all

selection n **range**, assortment, collection, choice, variety

selective adj **discerning**, discriminating, discriminatory, careful, choosy (infml) *Opposite*: indiscriminate

selectivity n **discrimination**, discernment, choosiness (infml)

selector n **chooser**, picker, committee member, jury member, panel member

self n **personality**, nature, character, psyche, identity

self-abasement n **humbling**, humiliation, mortification, prostration, eating humble pie *Opposite*: self-aggrandizement

self-absorbed adj **full of yourself**, self-regarding, self-centred, narcissistic, egocentric *Opposite*: considerate

self-absorption n **self-preoccupation**, egotism, egoism, egocentricity, self-centredness *Opposite*: generosity

self-acting adj **self-operating**, automatic, automated, mechanized, mechanical

self-aggrandizement n **ambition**, self-promotion, self-importance, self-glorification, self-glory

self-assertive adj **confident**, self-confident, forceful, assured, aggressive *Opposite*: timid

self-assurance n **confidence**, self-confidence, self-possession, poise, assurance *Opposite*: timidity

self-assured adj **confident**, self-confident, poised, assured, self-possessed *Opposite*: timid

self-centred *adj* **selfish**, self-interested, ego-centric, egotistic, egoistic *Opposite*: altruistic

self-centredness *n* **selfishness**, self-interest, egocentricity, egotism, egoism *Opposite*: altruism

self-coloured *adj* **uniform**, plain, single-colour, unpatterned *Opposite*: patterned

self-conceit *n* **smugness**, arrogance, swollen head, boastfulness, conceit *Opposite*: modesty

self-confessed *adj* **admitted**, by your own admission, self-proclaimed, acknowledged, known *Opposite*: closet

self-confidence *n* **confidence**, self-assurance, self-possession, poise, assurance *Opposite*: insecurity

self-confident *adj* **confident**, self-assured, self-possessed, poised, assured *Opposite*: insecure

self-congratulation *n* **self-satisfaction**, smugness, self-praise, self-glorification, self-flattery *Opposite*: self-hatred

self-conscious *adj* **ill at ease**, awkward, uncomfortable, embarrassed, insecure *Opposite*: self-confident

self-contained *adj* **independent**, self-sufficient, self-reliant, autonomous *Opposite*: dependent

self-contradictory *adj* **inconsistent**, self-contradicting, contradictory, illogical, unreasonable *Opposite*: consistent

self-control *n* **self-discipline**, discipline, willpower, restraint, strength of mind *Opposite*: self-indulgence

self-critical *adj* **self-deprecatory**, self-deprecating, self-effacing, reticent, humble

self-defence *n* **self-protection**, self-preservation, defence, resistance

self-denial *n* **abstinence**, abstemiousness, frugality, asceticism, self-discipline *Opposite*: self-indulgence

self-deprecating *adj* **self-critical**, self-deprecatory, self-effacing, modest, humble *Opposite*: boastful

self-deprecation *n* **self-criticism**, self-depreciation, self-effacement, modesty, humility *Opposite*: boasting

self-determination *n* **autonomy**, self-rule, self-government, freedom, independence

self-discipline *n* **self-control**, discipline, willpower, restraint, strength of mind *Opposite*: self-indulgence

self-doubt *n* **uncertainty**, lack of confidence, insecurity, self-loathing, self-hatred *Opposite*: self-confidence

self-effacing *adj* **modest**, quiet, meek, diffident, unassuming *Opposite*: brash

self-employed *adj* **freelance**, your own boss, working for yourself, independent, freelancing *Opposite*: employed

self-esteem *n* **confidence**, self-confidence, self-worth, sense of worth, self-respect *Opposite*: insecurity

self-evident *adj* **obvious**, clear, plain, manifest, undeniable *Opposite*: unclear

self-explanatory *adj* **clear**, easy to understand, easy to follow, understandable, transparent *Opposite*: unclear

self-expression *n* **creativity**, making a statement, assertiveness, individualism, expressing yourself

self-fertilization *n* **self-fertilizing**, self-pollination, self-pollinating, autogamy, hermaphroditism *Opposite*: cross-fertilization

self-flattery *n* **self-congratulation**, self-satisfaction, self-praise, self-glorification, self-aggrandizement *Opposite*: self-abasement

self-glorification *n* **self-promotion**, self-congratulation, self-satisfaction, self-praise, self-flattery *Opposite*: self-deprecation

self-governing *adj* **autonomous**, independent, sovereign, self-determining, self-sufficient *Opposite*: dependent

self-government *n* **autonomy**, independence, self-governance, sovereignty, self-rule *Opposite*: dependence

self-gratification *n* **self-indulgence**, hedonism, pleasure-seeking, high living, selfishness *Opposite*: self-sacrifice

self-hatred *n* **self-contempt**, self-loathing, self-disgust, self-denigration, self-dislike *Opposite*: self-love

self-help *n* **support**, mutual support, group support, help, counselling

self-image *n* **opinion of yourself**, self-perception, self-esteem, self-regard, self-respect

self-immolation *n* **suicide**, self-sacrifice, hara-kiri, suttee, martyrdom

self-importance *n* **arrogance**, pride, egotism, haughtiness, pomposity *Opposite*: humility

self-important *adj* **arrogant**, pompous, conceited, egotistic, bumptious *Opposite*: humble

self-imposed *adj* **chosen**, voluntary, self-inflicted, self-induced, of your own free will *Opposite*: enforced

self-incrimination *n* **self-accusation**, self-implication, confession, admission of guilt, self-blame

self-indulgence *n* **1 decadence**, indulgence, hedonism, pleasure, luxury *Opposite*: restraint **2 self-pity**, childishness, selfishness, self-centredness, self-absorption *Opposite*: restraint

self-indulgent *adj* **1 decadent**, indulgent, hedonistic, epicurean, luxurious *Opposite*: restrained **2 self-pitying**, wallowing, childish, selfish, self-centred *Opposite*: restrained

self-interest *n* **selfishness**, self-centredness, egotism, self-regard, egocentricity *Opposite*: altruism

self-interested *adj* **selfish**, self-centred, self-seeking, egocentric, egoistic *Opposite*: altruistic

selfish *adj* **self-centred**, self-seeking, self-interested, egotistic, egoistic *Opposite*: selfless

selfishness *n* **self-centredness**, self-interest, egotism, egoism, egocentricity *Opposite*: selflessness

selfless *adj* **unselfish**, self-sacrificing, altruistic, generous, noble *Opposite*: selfish

selflessness *n* **unselfishness**, self-sacrifice, altruism, generosity, gallantry *Opposite*: selfishness

self-love *n* **egotism**, selfishness, egocentricity, narcissism, egoism *Opposite*: modesty

self-motivated *adj* **energetic**, dynamic, keen, enthusiastic, driven *Opposite*: unmotivated

self-obsessed *adj* **self-centred**, egocentric, egomaniacal, egotistical, narcissistic

self-opinionated *adj* **1 overconfident**, sure of yourself, cocksure, self-confident, opinionated *Opposite*: diffident **2 conceited**, vain, full of yourself, self-satisfied, bigheaded *(infml) Opposite*: self-deprecating

self-opinioned *see* **self-opinionated**

self-pity *n* **self-indulgence**, misery, unhappiness, defeatism, self-absorption *Opposite*: cheerfulness

self-pitying *adj* **self-absorbed**, wallowing, defeatist, sorry for yourself, miserable *Opposite*: happy-go-lucky

self-possessed *adj* **confident**, self-assured, self-confident, assured, poised *Opposite*: insecure

self-possession *n* **confidence**, self-assurance, self-confidence, assurance, poise *Opposite*: insecurity

self-preservation *n* **self-protection**, self-defence, survival, preservation instinct, survival instinct

self-promotion *n* **self-aggrandizement**, self-importance, self-glorification, self-glory, self-praise *Opposite*: self-deprecation

self-regard *n* **1 self-interest**, self-centredness, selfishness, egotism, egocentricity *Opposite*: altruism **2 self-respect**, self-esteem, self-worth, dignity, pride *Opposite*: self-hatred

self-regarding *adj* **selfish**, self-centred, egocentric, egotistic, self-absorbed *Opposite*: selfless

self-reliance *n* **independence**, self-sufficiency, autonomy, self-confidence, self-assurance *Opposite*: dependence

self-reliant *adj* **independent**, self-sufficient, autonomous, self-confident, self-assured *Opposite*: dependent

self-reproach *n* **self-criticism**, remorse, contrition, shame, guilt *Opposite*: self-congratulation

self-respect *n* **self-esteem**, self-confidence, confidence, dignity, pride *Opposite*: self-hatred

self-restraint *n* **self-control**, self-discipline, discipline, willpower, moderation *Opposite*: abandon

self-righteous *adj* **sanctimonious**, smug, self-satisfied, complacent, pious *Opposite*: humble

self-righteousness *n* **sanctimoniousness**, smugness, complacency, piety, superciliousness *Opposite*: humility

self-rule *n* **self-government**, independence, self-determination, autonomy, self-governance *Opposite*: dependence

self-sacrifice *n* **altruism**, unselfishness, selflessness, self-denial, martyrdom *Opposite*: selfishness

self-sacrificing *adj* **altruistic**, unselfish, selfless, noble, self-denying *Opposite*: selfish

selfsame *adj* **very same**, identical, very, exact, same *Opposite*: different

self-satisfaction *n* **smugness**, complacency, self-righteousness, conceit, arrogance *Opposite*: self-doubt

self-satisfied *adj* **smug**, pleased with yourself, self-righteous, conceited, arrogant

self-seeking *adj* **selfish**, self-centred, self-regarding, egocentric, egoistic *Opposite*: selfless

self-serving *adj* **selfish**, egotistic, self-centred, narcissistic, egocentric *Opposite*: altruistic

self-styled *adj* **self-appointed**, self-proclaimed, so-called, professed, would-be *Opposite*: certified

self-sufficiency *n* **independence**, autonomy, self-reliance, self-support *Opposite*: dependence

self-sufficient *adj* **independent**, autonomous, self-reliant, self-supporting, self-financing *Opposite*: dependent

self-supporting *adj* **self-sufficient**, self-financing, profitable, healthy, successful *Opposite*: struggling

self-will *n* **determination**, obstinacy, stubbornness, pigheadedness, wilfulness *Opposite*: weakness

self-willed *adj* **headstrong**, obstinate, determined, stubborn, pigheaded *Opposite*: weak-willed

self-worth *n* **self-esteem**, self-respect, self-confidence, pride, dignity

sell *v* **1 vend**, wholesale, trade, retail, flog *(infml) Opposite*: buy **2 put up for sale**, market, offer, deal in, auction *Opposite*: buy **3 be bought**, go, be snapped up, be popular, be in demand **4 persuade people to buy**, market, promote, advertise, traffic in

seller *n* **vendor**, retailer, wholesaler, supplier, merchant *Opposite*: buyer

selling *n* **vending**, sales, marketing, trade, retailing *Opposite*: buying

sell out *v* **1 run out**, be out of stock, be snapped up, go, be unavailable *Opposite*: stock up

2 give in, give up, sell your soul, betray your principles, be co-opted

sellout *n* **1 box-office hit**, hit, smash hit, smash, bestseller *Opposite*: flop *(infml)* **2** *(infml)* **betrayal**, treachery, disloyalty, apostasy, co-optation *Opposite*: loyalty

semblance *n* **1 trace**, shred, fragment, measure, modicum **2 appearance**, impression, air, resemblance, façade

semiconscious *adj* **half-conscious**, half-awake, half-asleep, surfacing, dazed

semidarkness *n* **twilight**, half-light, dusk, dimness, gloom

semifinal *n* **round**, heat, leg, match, game

seminal *adj* **influential**, important, formative, pivotal, inspirational *Opposite*: insignificant

seminar *n* **1 meeting**, session, round table, discussion, conference **2 discussion group**, tutorial, class, evening class, talk

seminary *n* **theological college**, divinity school, college, training college, academy

senate *n* **governing body**, legislature, congress, parliament, diet

senator *n* **senate member**, politician, representative, legislator, congresswoman

send *v* **1 direct**, refer, guide, show, lead **2 post**, transmit, dispatch, forward, consign *Opposite*: receive **3 transmit**, project, broadcast, disseminate, give off **4 propel**, hurl, fling, throw, fire *Opposite*: bring

send down *v* **expel**, rusticate, suspend, banish, dismiss

send for *v* **request**, summon, call for, order, assemble *Opposite*: dismiss

send off *v* **dispatch**, send, post, send away, transmit *Opposite*: receive

sendoff *n* **goodbye**, farewell, leaving party, leaving do, valediction *(fml)* *Opposite*: welcome

send on *v* **forward**, redirect, readdress, transfer, pass on *Opposite*: return

send over the edge *v* **derange**, unhinge, unsettle, stress out *(infml)*

send packing *(infml)* *v* **dismiss**, expel, evict, turn out, throw out *Opposite*: welcome

send to Coventry *v* **ostracize**, ignore, freeze out, give the cold shoulder to, exclude

send up *v* **1 raise**, elevate, heighten, boost, bump up *(infml)* *Opposite*: lower **2** *(infml)* **lampoon**, satirize, mock, parody, ridicule

sendup *(infml)* *n* **parody**, lampoon, takeoff, impersonation, caricature

senile *adj* **confused**, disorientated, forgetful, failing, absent-minded

senior *adj* **1 older**, elder, oldest, eldest, first-born *Opposite*: junior **2 high-ranking**, high-grade, superior, higher, leading *Opposite*: junior ■ *n* **1 elder**, first-born, elder sibling, big brother, big sister *Opposite*: junior **2 boss**, superior, chief, manager, leader *Opposite*: junior

senior citizen *n* **pensioner**, OAP, retired person, retiree

seniority *n* **superiority**, supremacy, precedence, priority, position

sensation *n* **1 feeling**, sense, impression, awareness, consciousness *Opposite*: numbness **2 commotion**, stir, fuss, uproar, rumpus *Opposite*: lull **3 phenomenon**, miracle, wonder, marvel, spectacle

sensational *adj* **1 outstanding**, excellent, dramatic, amazing, extraordinary *Opposite*: predictable **2 startling**, shocking, scandalous, melodramatic, lurid *Opposite*: understated **3** *(infml)* **amazing**, astounding, marvellous, exciting, thrilling *Opposite*: boring

sensationalism *n* **exaggeration**, overstatement, luridness, scandal, melodrama *Opposite*: understatement

sensationalist *adj* **startling**, shocking, scandalous, melodramatic, lurid *Opposite*: understated

sense *n* **1 feeling**, sensation, awareness, perception **2 appreciation**, impression, consciousness, awareness, feeling **3 intelligence**, brains, intellect, wisdom, sagacity *Opposite*: folly **4 purpose**, point, reason, function, end **5 opinion**, view, viewpoint, consensus, mood **6 gist**, substance, drift, nub, idea **7 meaning**, denotation, significance, signification, implication ■ *v* **1 detect**, identify, distinguish, recognize, know **2 perceive**, feel, have a feeling, get the impression, discern *Opposite*: observe **3 intuit**, guess, suspect, pick up, feel

senseless *adj* **1 stupid**, silly, foolish, mindless, idiotic *Opposite*: sensible **2 unconscious**, comatose, numb, deadened, knocked out *Opposite*: conscious **3 pointless**, ridiculous, absurd, meaningless, futile *Opposite*: worthwhile

senselessness *n* **1 stupidity**, silliness, foolishness, madness, idiocy *Opposite*: sense **2 pointlessness**, ridiculousness, absurdity, irrationality, meaninglessness

sensibility *n* **responsiveness**, deep feeling, emotional response, receptivity, susceptibility *Opposite*: insensitivity

sensible *adj* **1 level-headed**, sane, rational, reasonable, shrewd *Opposite*: foolish **2 practical**, serviceable, workable, functional, utilitarian *Opposite*: impractical **3** *(fml)* **aware**, conscious, mindful, cognizant *(fml)*. See COMPARE AND CONTRAST at **aware**.

sensibleness *n* **rationality**, level-headedness, reasonableness, shrewdness, wisdom *Opposite*: foolishness

sensitive *adj* **1 responsive**, receptive, susceptible, aware, perceptive *Opposite*: indifferent **2 delicate**, irritable, susceptible, allergic, difficult *Opposite*: robust **3 subtle**, delicate, complex, searching, penetrating *Opposite*: superficial **4 thoughtful**, sympathetic, understanding, perceptive, considerate *Opposite*: unsympathetic **5 thin-skinned**, easily upset, easily hurt, hypersensitive, vulnerable *Opposite*: impervious **6 secret**, confidential, classified, top secret, restricted *Opposite*: public **7 awkward**, tricky, difficult, sticky, delicate *Opposite*: straightforward **8 precise**, exact, delicate, finely tuned, responsive *Opposite*: imprecise

sensitivity *n* **compassion**, sympathy, understanding, kindliness, warmth *Opposite*: indifference

sensitize *v* **1 alert**, make aware, inform, explain, brief *Opposite*: desensitize **2 expose**, make sensitive, irritate, trigger, induce *Opposite*: desensitize

sensor *n* **device**, measuring device, instrument, radar, beam

sensual *adj* **1 sexual**, erotic, voluptuous, fleshly, carnal *Opposite*: ascetic **2 sensory**, carnal, bodily, physical, corporeal *Opposite*: intellectual

sensuous *adj* **sumptuous**, opulent, rich, deep, intense *Opposite*: ascetic

sentence *n* **judgment**, verdict, ruling, decree, condemnation ▪ *v* **pass judgment on**, condemn, punish, send to prison, pronounce judgment on *Opposite*: acquit

sententious *adj* **moralizing**, moralistic, judgmental, critical, censorious *Opposite*: approving

sentient *adj* **1 conscious**, animate, flesh-and-blood, alive, living *Opposite*: inanimate **2 emotional**, responsive, sensitive, perceptive, feeling *Opposite*: intellectual

sentiment *n* **1 feeling**, emotion, response, reaction, attitude **2 sentimentality**, mawkishness, gush, romanticism, corn *(infml)*

sentimental *adj* **mawkish**, romantic, slushy, mushy, maudlin *Opposite*: cynical

sentimentality *n* **mawkishness**, corniness, slushiness, mushiness, romanticism *Opposite*: cynicism

sentimentalize *v* **gush**, emotionalize, romanticize, wax lyrical *(literary)*

sentinel *see* sentry

sentry *n* **guard**, patrol, lookout, watch, sentinel

separable *adj* **divisible**, distinguishable, detachable, removable, discrete *Opposite*: inseparable

separate *adj* **1 unconnected**, disconnected, individual, independent, unattached *Opposite*: connected **2 distinct**, discrete, detached, loose, dispersed *Opposite*: attached ▪ *v* **1 split up**, split, divorce, part, part company **2 divide**, part, disconnect, undo, split *Opposite*: unite **3 break away**, secede, branch out, break free, break *Opposite*: join

separately *adv* **1 independently**, alone, individually, one at a time, singly *Opposite*: together **2 distinctly**, unconnectedly, disjointedly, discretely, severally *Opposite*: together

separateness *n* **distinctness**, disconnectedness, separation, distinctiveness, difference

separate off *v* **divide**, divide off, split off, detach, sever

separate out *v* **strain**, filter, pass through a filter, sieve, extract *Opposite*: cohere *(fml)*

separation *n* **1 parting**, departure, goodbye, farewell, leave-taking *(literary)* *Opposite*: meeting **2 division**, severance, taking apart, partition, disjunction *Opposite*: unification **3 split-up**, split, divorce, estrangement, rift

separatist *n* **dissenter**, secessionist, protester, rebel, freedom fighter

separator *n* **1 divider**, barrier, partition, dividing wall, screen **2 sieve**, strainer, filter, extractor, centrifuge *Opposite*: blender

septic *adj* **poisoned**, infected, festering, gangrenous, diseased *Opposite*: healthy

sepulchral *adj* **funereal**, sombre, sad, dismal, melancholy *Opposite*: cheery

sepulchre *n* **vault**, tomb, grave, crypt, burial chamber

sequel *n* **1 consequence**, development, result, outcome, upshot *Opposite*: prelude **2 follow-on**, continuation, conclusion, follow-up *Opposite*: prequel

sequence *n* **1 series**, succession, run, progression, chain **2 order**, arrangement, classification, categorization, system *Opposite*: disarray

sequential *adj* **1 in sequence**, consecutive, in order, successive, chronological *Opposite*: jumbled **2 consequent**, resulting, resultant, ensuing, following *Opposite*: previous

sequentially *adv* **in sequence**, in succession, successively, in order, consecutively *Opposite*: out of order

sequester *v* **1 confiscate**, requisition, appropriate, impound, seize *Opposite*: restore **2** *(fml)* **isolate**, separate, segregate, cut off, set apart

sequestrate *v* **confiscate**, seize, appropriate, repossess, impound *Opposite*: release

sequestration *n* **confiscation**, appropriation, impounding, seizure, requisitioning *Opposite*: restoration

sequin *n* **spangle**, bead, bauble, star, decoration

serenade *v* **sing**, croon, court, entertain, divert

serendipitous *adj* **fortunate**, lucky, happy, fortuitous, providential. *See* COMPARE AND CONTRAST *at* lucky.

serendipity *n* **fate**, destiny, karma, providence, luck *Opposite*: design

serene *adj* **1 calm**, composed, unruffled, cool, unflustered *Opposite*: agitated **2 tranquil**, calm, peaceful, still, quiet *Opposite*: bustling

serenity *n* **1 composure**, coolness, peace of mind, poise, equanimity *Opposite*: panic **2 tranquillity**, calmness, peacefulness, quietude, quietness *Opposite*: bustle

serial *adj* **sequential**, successive, consecutive, ongoing, in order *Opposite*: random

series *n* **sequence**, succession, run, chain, string

serious *adj* **1 dangerous**, acute, life-threatening, critical, grave *Opposite*: minor **2 important**, momentous, significant, crucial, vital *Opposite*: trivial **3 thought-provoking**, meaningful, intense, deep, profound *Opposite*: lightweight **4 thoughtful**, grave, solemn, sombre, stern *Opposite*: lighthearted **5 earnest**, sincere, genuine, honest, resolute *Opposite*: flippant

seriously *adv* **1 badly**, dangerously, critically, fatally, acutely *Opposite*: slightly **2 earnestly**, truly, sincerely, genuinely, honestly *Opposite*: jokingly **3** (*infml*) **extremely**, very, really, totally, utterly

serious-minded *adj* **earnest**, sensible, sedate, steady, determined *Opposite*: frivolous

seriousness *n* **1 importance**, significance, gravity, weightiness, momentousness *Opposite*: triviality **2 earnestness**, sincerity, genuineness, honesty, resoluteness *Opposite*: flippancy

sermon *n* **1 talk**, address, homily, discourse, oration *Opposite*: conversation **2 lecture**, harangue, homily, talking-to (*infml*), ticking-off (*infml*) *Opposite*: praise

sermonize *v* **preach**, pontificate, moralize, hold forth, lecture *Opposite*: flatter

serpent *n* **traitor**, liar, cheat, sneak, troublemaker *Opposite*: friend

serpentine *adj* **winding**, meandering, twisting, sinuous, bending *Opposite*: straight

serrated *adj* **jagged**, toothed, notched, ragged, saw-toothed *Opposite*: smooth

servant *n* **domestic**, retainer, help *Opposite*: employer

WORD BANK
❑ **types of servant** butler, chambermaid, cleaner, cook, factotum, flunky, footman, lackey, maid, maidservant, major-domo, valet

serve *v* **1 supply**, dish up, serve up, hand out, hand round **2 wait on**, wait at table, wait, attend, tend **3 function**, work, operate, act, perform **4 work for**, help, aid, attend, assist

service *n* **1 help**, assistance, aid, use, benefit *Opposite*: disservice **2 facility**, provision, package, deal, amenity **3 ceremony**, ritual, rite, sacrament, mass **4 overhaul**, examination, check, tune-up, maintenance ■ *v* **repair**, overhaul, examine, tune, check

serviceable *adj* **1 durable**, hard-wearing, strong, stout, tough *Opposite*: flimsy **2 working**, operative, functional, in working order, usable *Opposite*: broken **3 effective**, helpful, practical, useful, practicable *Opposite*: impractical

services *n* **1 service station**, motorway facilities, motorway service station, service area,

filling station **2 service industries**, service sector, service jobs, customer services *Opposite*: manufacturing **3 public amenities**, civic amenities, amenities, public services, council services **4 armed forces**, forces, military, armed services, security forces

servile *adj* **submissive**, abject, fawning, subservient, sycophantic *Opposite*: proud

serving *n* **portion**, helping, plateful, ration, quota

serving dish *n* **platter**, salver, plate, tray, dish

servitude *n* **1 slavery**, bondage, serfdom, enslavement, vassalage *Opposite*: freedom **2 subjection**, subjugation, subordination, dependence, dependency *Opposite*: liberty

session *n* **1 meeting**, sitting, assembly, conference, gathering **2 term**, period, semester, trimester, quarter **3 shift**, stint, go, spell, phase

set *v* **1 put**, place, locate, position, situate *Opposite*: pick up **2 establish**, fix, agree on, appoint, decide *Opposite*: change **3 adjust**, regulate, synchronize, align, programme **4 become hard**, harden, go hard, solidify, congeal *Opposite*: liquefy ■ *n* **1 scenery**, stage set, film set, setting, location **2 collection**, group, arrangement, array, series *Opposite*: individual **3 circle**, group, clique, gang, crowd ■ *adj* **1 established**, usual, customary, traditional, conventional *Opposite*: changing **2 inflexible**, obstinate, determined, resolute, resolved *Opposite*: flexible **3 ready**, prepared, fit, primed, organized *Opposite*: unprepared **4 firm**, congealed, solid, hard, fixed *Opposite*: liquid

set about *v* **begin**, tackle, start, launch into, get down to

set against *v* **1 compare**, contrast, consider, set side by side, oppose **2 pit against**, turn against, set as rivals, set in opposition, alienate *Opposite*: bring together

set alight *v* **kindle**, light, ignite, set light to, set fire to *Opposite*: put out

set apart *v* **1 reserve**, put aside, keep on one side, set aside, separate **2 distinguish**, differentiate, single out, make something stand out, mark out

set aside *v* **1 reserve**, save, keep back, put to one side, lay by *Opposite*: use up **2 reject**, discard, annul, break free from, shake off

set back *v* **delay**, hinder, hold up, impede, slow down *Opposite*: facilitate

setback *n* **hindrance**, holdup, delay, impediment, stumbling block *Opposite*: boost

set down *v* **1 put down**, lay down, place, deposit, put **2 write down**, report, record, chronicle, write out

set eyes on *v* **catch sight of**, observe, notice, sight, spot

set fire to *v* **kindle**, light, ignite, set light to, set alight *Opposite*: put out

set foot in *v* **enter**, go in, come into, show your face, turn up

set forth *(fml)* v state, describe, express, lay down, present

set free v 1 liberate, free, release, discharge, let go *Opposite*: imprison 2 untie, unloose, unshackle, unleash, let loose *Opposite*: tie up

set in v come to stay, be here to stay, take root, become established, become entrenched *Opposite*: pass

set in motion v start, initiate, begin, kick-start, set off *Opposite*: stop

set off v 1 start out, set out, go, depart, leave *Opposite*: arrive 2 detonate, explode, light, ignite, trigger *Opposite*: defuse 3 start, begin, commence, start off, burst out *Opposite*: finish 4 initiate, instigate, launch, inaugurate, begin 5 draw attention to, display, bring out, highlight, enhance

set on v attack, set upon, assault, lay into, terrorize

set on fire v kindle, light, ignite, set alight, set fire to *Opposite*: put out

set out v 1 leave, set off, depart, go, move off *Opposite*: arrive 2 embark on, start, begin, commence, set off *Opposite*: finish 3 plan, aim, intend, determine, design 4 display, lay out, arrange, present, show 5 explain, specify, define, describe, detail

set phrase n expression, phrase, idiom, turn of phrase, saying

set right v correct, rectify, right, put right, put to rights

set store by v deem important, value, esteem, prize, regard highly

sett n paving stone, paving slab, paver, stone, slab

settee n sofa, couch, chaise lounge, divan, futon

setting n location, surroundings, scenery, situation, background

settle v 1 resolve, reconcile, clear up, straighten out, mend 2 stay, inhabit, put down roots, set up house, establish yourself 3 land, perch, alight, roost, come to rest *Opposite*: take off 4 become peaceful, become calm, settle down, calm down, relax *Opposite*: fluster 5 pay, defray, discharge, clear, foot *Opposite*: owe 6 sink, drop, descend, fall, go to the bottom *Opposite*: rise

settled adj established, stable, solid, firm, steady *Opposite*: unsettled

settle down v 1 become less restless, quieten down, relax, calm down, snuggle down *Opposite*: agitate 2 sink, drop, descend, fall, stabilize *Opposite*: rise

settle for v agree to, accept, make do with, take, be happy with *Opposite*: refuse

settle in v 1 adapt, acclimatize, adjust, get used to it, find your feet 2 get comfortable, snuggle down, ensconce yourself, bed down, get comfy

settlement n 1 resolution, conclusion, completion, decision, agreement 2 payment, defrayal, clearance, clearing, reimbursement *Opposite*: receipt 3 community, village, town, township, colony

settle on v choose, pick, select, decide on, agree on *Opposite*: reject

settler n colonizer, colonist, pioneer, pilgrim, immigrant

settle up v pay the bill, pay, pay up, settle the debt, settle your account *Opposite*: quibble

set to v 1 get on with it, put your shoulder to the wheel, make a start, get started, start work 2 come to blows, start fighting, lay into, grapple, tussle

set-to *(infml)* n confrontation, quarrel, altercation, disagreement, row *Opposite*: reconciliation

set up v 1 establish, inaugurate, found, institute, launch 2 erect, raise, build, construct, put up 3 *(infml)* frame, trap, entrap, trick, con

setup n 1 system, arrangement, format, situation, structure 2 *(infml)* frame, trap, trick, deception, con

set upon v attack, assault, lay into, assail, pounce on *Opposite*: defend

seventh heaven n bliss, ecstasy, heaven, nirvana, cloud nine *Opposite*: despair

sever v 1 cut, split, separate, undo, disunite *Opposite*: unite 2 cut off, chop off, lop off, shear off, slice off *Opposite*: attach

several adj some, quite a lot of, a number of, numerous, many

severally adv separately, individually, singly, one at a time, one by one *Opposite*: together

severance n 1 separation, detachment, disconnection, division, taking apart *Opposite*: joining 2 compensation, redundancy pay, redundancy money, severance pay, golden handshake

severe adj 1 harsh, stern, strict, cruel, brutal *Opposite*: gentle 2 acute, grave, critical, mortal, serious *Opposite*: slight 3 plain, simple, spartan, unadorned, unembellished *Opposite*: ornate

severity n 1 harshness, sternness, strictness, cruelty, brutality *Opposite*: gentleness 2 gravity, seriousness, acuteness, dangerousness, awfulness *Opposite*: insignificance 3 plainness, simplicity, starkness, bareness, austerity *Opposite*: opulence

sew v stitch, seam, baste, tack, hem *Opposite*: unpick

sewer n drain, septic tank, cesspit, cesspool, open drain

sewing n stitching, embroidery, tapestry, needlework, needlepoint

sew up v 1 stitch up, sew, stitch, darn, repair *Opposite*: unpick 2 settle, clinch, tie up, finalize, finish

sex n gender, sexual category, masculinity, femininity

sexy *adj* **1 erotic**, sensual, sexual, suggestive, pleasurable **2 voluptuous**, curvaceous, sensuous, alluring, attractive

shabbiness *n* **1 scruffiness**, untidiness, dilapidation, seediness, raggedness *Opposite*: elegance **2 inconsiderateness**, unfairness, meanness, disrespect, negligence *Opposite*: decency

shabby *adj* **1 scruffy**, untidy, ragged, tattered, worn out *Opposite*: elegant **2 inconsiderate**, unjust, mean, dishonourable, contemptible *Opposite*: decent

shack *n* hut, shanty, hovel, lean-to, shed

shackle *v* **1 fetter**, manacle, handcuff, chain, put in irons *Opposite*: free **2 constrain**, restrict, impede, hamper, hinder *Opposite*: facilitate

shackles *n* **fetters**, manacles, chains, restraints, irons

shade *n* **1 shadow**, dark, darkness, gloom, gloominess *Opposite*: light **2 blind**, screen, awning, canopy, cover **3 hue**, tint, tinge, colour, tone **4 hint**, trace, suggestion, touch, dash ■ *v* **1 cover**, shield, protect, screen, veil *Opposite*: expose **2 darken**, eclipse, blot out, shadow, block out *Opposite*: brighten **3 fill in**, hatch, colour, colour in, block in

shades *(infml)* *n* sunglasses, sunspecs *(infml)*, dark glasses, tinted lenses

shadiness *n* **1 dishonesty**, crookedness, underhandedness, shiftiness, suspiciousness *Opposite*: honesty **2 dimness**, dark, darkness, shadowiness, obscurity *Opposite*: brightness

shadow *n* **1 silhouette**, outline, shape, figure, form **2 shade**, dark, darkness, gloom, gloominess *Opposite*: light **3 hint**, trace, suggestion, touch, shade **4 constant companion**, alter ego, sidekick, other self, double **5 private investigator**, private detective, private eye *(infml)*, sleuth *(infml)*, PI *(US)* **6 follower**, stalker, pursuer, tracker, tail *(infml)* **7 ghost**, spectre, spirit, wraith, apparition ■ *v* **1 follow**, trail, track, stalk, observe **2 darken**, eclipse, blot out, shade *Opposite*: brighten. *See* COMPARE AND CONTRAST *at* follow.

shadows *n* shade, dark, darkness, obscurity, dimness *Opposite*: light

shadowy *adj* **1 indistinct**, obscure, vague, indistinguishable, unclear *Opposite*: distinct **2 dim**, dark, murky, gloomy, poorly lit *Opposite*: bright **3 ghostly**, spectral, ethereal, sinister, mysterious *Opposite*: material

shady *adj* **1 out of the sun**, in the shade, shaded, under the trees, cool *Opposite*: sunny **2 dishonest**, underhand, shifty, suspicious, devious *Opposite*: aboveboard

shagginess *n* hairiness, dishevelment, untidiness, bushiness, scruffiness *Opposite*: neatness

shaggy *adj* **hairy**, unkempt, dishevelled, bushy, unshaven *Opposite*: tidy

shake *v* **1 wobble**, judder, jolt, jerk, bounce **2 tremble**, quiver, quake, shudder, shiver **3 agitate**, stir, blend, mix **4 unsettle**, unnerve, disturb, distress, upset *Opposite*: reassure **5 brandish**, flourish, flaunt, wave, wield ■ *n* **1 tremor**, vibration, judder, wobble, lurch **2 shudder**, quiver, quake, tremble, shiver **3 waggle**, wave, flourish, twirl

shake off *v* **1 get rid of**, get away from, lose, elude, leave behind **2 recover from**, recuperate from, get over, get rid of *Opposite*: succumb

shake-out *n* **transformation**, radical change, upheaval, overhaul, reorganization

shake up *v* **1 transform**, overhaul, change drastically, revamp, rethink *Opposite*: leave alone **2 upset**, disturb, distress, shock, alarm *Opposite*: calm down **3 mix**, blend, combine, agitate, shake

shake-up *n* **transformation**, radical change, upheaval, overhaul, reorganization

shakiness *n* **1 tremor**, shaking, trembling, shake, jerkiness *Opposite*: control **2 wobbliness**, instability, flimsiness, fragility, insubstantiality *Opposite*: sturdiness **3 uncertainty**, precariousness, instability, unreliability, weakness *Opposite*: reliability

shaking *n* **vibration**, jolting, juddering, rocking, rattling

shaky *adj* **1 wobbly**, unstable, unsteady, insecure, rickety *Opposite*: steady **2 trembling**, shaking, quivering, quaking, shuddering *Opposite*: composed **3 unsupported**, unsound, questionable, dubious, doubtful *Opposite*: dependable

shallow *adj* **1 low**, thin, light, narrow, surface *Opposite*: deep **2 superficial**, trivial, slight, insubstantial, petty *Opposite*: profound

sham *n* **1 pretence**, deception, charade, con, fraud **2 impostor**, charlatan, con, fake, fraud ■ *adj* **fake**, mock, bogus, imitation, pretended *Opposite*: bona fide ■ *v* **pretend**, fake, put it on, act, play *Opposite*: real

shamble *v* **shuffle**, amble, waddle, drag your feet, walk *Opposite*: stride

shambles *n* **1 fiasco**, disaster, failure, mess, botch *(infml)* *Opposite*: success **2 mess**, muddle, tip, dump, chaos

shambling *adj* **awkward**, ungainly, clumsy, uncoordinated, lumbering *Opposite*: graceful

shambolic *(infml)* *adj* **disorganized**, chaotic, messy, haphazard, confused *Opposite*: orderly

shame *n* **disgrace**, embarrassment, dishonour, humiliation, mortification *Opposite*: pride ■ *v* **embarrass**, discredit, disgrace, humiliate, mortify *Opposite*: honour

shamefaced *adj* **ashamed**, embarrassed, abashed, sheepish, hangdog *Opposite*: proud

shameful *adj* **disgraceful**, reprehensible, dishonourable, discreditable, shocking *Opposite*: honourable

shameless *adj* brazen, barefaced, unabashed, blatant, unashamed *Opposite*: ashamed

shamelessness *n* **lack of remorse**, brazenness, hardheartedness, boldness, impudence *Opposite*: repentance

shank *n* stem, shaft, trunk, rod, bar

shape *n* **1 form**, figure, outline, silhouette, profile **2 character**, nature, form, identity, structure ■ *v* **1 model**, mould, whittle, manipulate, smooth **2 sway**, determine, cause, influence, affect

WORD BANK

❏ **types of angular shape** box, cross, cube, diamond, dodecahedron, dogleg, lozenge, oblong, parallelogram, pentagon, polygon, pyramid, quadrangle, quadrilateral, rectangle, rhomboid, rhombus, square, star, tetragon, tetrahedron, trapezium, trapezoid, triangle

❏ **types of rounded shape** arc, arch, ball, bend, bow, bulb, circle, circlet, coil, cone, crescent, curl, curve, cylinder, dome, figure of eight, globe, heart, helix, hemisphere, hoop, horseshoe, kidney, loop, orb, oval, ring, round, semicircle, sphere, spheroid, spiral, teardrop

shapeless *adj* baggy, loose-fitting, formless, ill-defined, amorphous *Opposite*: defined

shapelessness *n* **amorphousness**, formlessness, bagginess, fluidity *Opposite*: definition

shapely *adj* well-formed, attractive, well-rounded, well-proportioned, pleasing

shape up *v* **1 develop**, progress, improve, come along, come together **2 improve**, pull yourself together, get it together, reform, mend your ways

shard *n* sliver, splinter, spike, shaving, chip

share *v* **1 split**, go halves, divide, divide up, divvy *(infml)* **2 distribute**, allocate, assign, apportion, allot **3 communicate**, let somebody in on, impart, reveal, disclose ■ *n* **part**, portion, segment, cut, stake *Opposite*: whole

shared *adj* common, communal, joint, mutual, collective

share out *v* divide up, give out, parcel out, distribute, allot

sharp *adj* **1 pointed**, razor-sharp, tapered, pointy *Opposite*: blunt **2 quick**, intelligent, razor-sharp, incisive, astute *Opposite*: dull **3 abrupt**, sudden, quick, brusque, urgent *Opposite*: gentle **4 shrill**, piercing, loud, high-pitched, strident *Opposite*: soft **5 harsh**, severe, snappy, sarcastic, snappish *Opposite*: gentle **6 severe**, acute, strong, hard, intense *Opposite*: mild **7 sour**, tangy, acid, acrid, pungent *Opposite*: sweet **8 clear**, well-defined, definite, clear-cut, distinct *Opposite*: imprecise ■ *adv* **exactly**, precisely, on the dot, promptly, punctually

sharpen *v* **1 hone**, whet, grind, file, strop *Opposite*: blunt **2 improve**, hone, perfect, brush up, refine *Opposite*: worsen

sharp-eyed *adj* **1 observant**, watchful, alert, vigilant, attentive *Opposite*: unobservant **2 eagle-eyed**, with good eyesight, with good vision, with eyes like a hawk, hawk-eyed *Opposite*: short-sighted

sharpish *(infml)* *adv* quickly, fast, straightaway, right away, immediately *Opposite*: eventually

sharply *adv* **1 abruptly**, suddenly, all at once, hard, tight *Opposite*: gradually **2 harshly**, severely, cuttingly, unkindly, snappishly *Opposite*: gently **3 alarmingly**, steeply, greatly, dramatically, suddenly *Opposite*: gradually **4 briskly**, abruptly, suddenly, smartly, swiftly *Opposite*: slowly **5 extremely**, clearly, distinctly, acutely, deeply *Opposite*: subtly **6 clearly**, distinctly, strikingly, obviously, eye-catchingly *Opposite*: hazily

sharpness *n* **1 acuity**, perceptiveness, intelligence, quickness, keenness *Opposite*: slowness **2 harshness**, severity, unkindness, snappishness, terseness *Opposite*: gentleness **3 clarity**, definition, distinctness, contrast, intensity *Opposite*: haziness **4 acidity**, sourness, bitterness, tanginess, pungency *Opposite*: sweetness

sharp-sighted *adj* **1 eagle-eyed**, with good eyesight, with good vision, with eyes like a hawk, hawk-eyed **2 observant**, watchful, alert, vigilant, attentive *Opposite*: unobservant

sharp-tongued *adj* sarcastic, caustic, harsh, mean, brusque *Opposite*: gentle

sharp-witted *adj* quick, sharp, quick-witted, acute, bright

shatter *v* **1 smash**, break, smash to smithereens, splinter, fragment **2 destroy**, wreck, crush, blast, demolish *Opposite*: build up

shattered *adj* **1 devastated**, crushed, traumatized, horrified, suffering **2 tired**, exhausted, all in, spent, prostrate *Opposite*: lively

shattering *adj* devastating, crushing, shocking, earthshattering, cataclysmic *Opposite*: wonderful

shatterproof *adj* indestructible, unbreakable, nonbreaking, resistant, strengthened

shave *v* cut off, shear, cut, trim, clip

shaving *n* chip, splinter, flake, shred, sliver *Opposite*: chunk

shawl *n* wrap, stole, scarf, rebozo, cloak

sheaf *n* bundle, cluster, clump, wad, stack

shear *v* cut off, shave, clip, trim, crop

sheath *n* cover, case, casing, covering, scabbard

sheathe *v* **1 put away**, replace, retract, stash *(infml)* *Opposite*: take out **2 envelop**, swathe, cloak, wrap, drape

sheathing *n* casing, covering, outer layer, jacket, shield

shed *v* **1** radiate, emit, disperse, cast, project **2** cast off, slough off, get rid of, moult, lose

shed light on *v* clarify, explain, illuminate, elucidate, clear up

sheen *n* shine, polish, lustre, gloss, gleam

sheep *n* **1** ewe, ram, lamb **2** conformist, follower, traditionalist, lemming, yes man *Opposite*: individualist

sheepish *adj* ashamed, shamefaced, embarrassed, hangdog, guilty *Opposite*: unashamed

sheepishness *n* shame, embarrassment, guilt, awkwardness, self-consciousness

sheer *adj* **1** pure, complete, absolute, utter, unalloyed **2** steep, vertical, perpendicular, precipitous, abrupt *Opposite*: gentle **3** fine, transparent, translucent, thin, diaphanous *Opposite*: thick ■ *adv* vertically, straight up, plumb, precipitously, steeply

sheerness *n* fineness, thinness, translucence, transparency, gauziness *Opposite*: thickness

sheet *n* **1** piece, page, leaf, folio, slip **2** expanse, mass, area, layer

sheet down *v* pour, rain heavily, rain cats and dogs (*infml*), tip down (*infml*), chuck it down (*infml*)

sheik *n* leader, ruler, chief, chieftain, head

shelf *n* **1** ledge, sill, projection, bookshelf, mantelpiece **2** layer, ridge, step, ledge, rock shelf

shell *n* **1** case, casing, covering, shield, crust **2** husk, skeleton, carcass, remains **3** bomb, explosive, missile, mortar, projectile ■ *v* bombard, shoot at, fire at, open fire on, shoot down

shellfish *n* crustacean, mollusc, seafood

WORD BANK
❏ types of shellfish abalone, clam, cockle, crab, crayfish, langoustine, lobster, mussel, oyster, prawn, scallop, shrimp, whelk, winkle

shell out (*infml*) *v* pay out, pay up, pay, spend, give

shelter *n* **1** protection, cover, refuge, retreat, haven **2** housing, accommodation, living quarters, lodging, somewhere to stay ■ *v* **1** protect, shield, cover, defend, harbour **2** take shelter, take refuge, take cover, hide

sheltered *adj* **1** protected, privileged, comfortable, shielded, cosy *Opposite*: harsh **2** secluded, protected, shielded, isolated, insulated *Opposite*: exposed

shelve *v* put on hold, put on ice, defer, abandon, cancel

shenanigans (*infml*) *n* **1** trickery, mischief, trouble, carry-on (*infml*), to-do (*infml*) **2** playfulness, joking around, pranks, tricks, tomfoolery (*infml*)

shepherd *v* marshal, drive, guide, steer, pilot

sherd *see* shard

shield *n* protection, armour, defence, safeguard, buffer ■ *v* protect, guard, defend, shelter, safeguard *Opposite*: expose. *See* COMPARE AND CONTRAST *at* safeguard.

shielded *adj* protected, safeguarded, isolated, defended, sheltered *Opposite*: exposed

shift *v* **1** move, budge, vary, transfer, change **2** (*infml*) remove, get rid of, loosen, lift, clean **3** (*infml*) hurry up, get a move on (*infml*), buck up (*infml dated*), get moving, hurry *Opposite*: slow down ■ *n* **1** move, swing, modification, alteration, change **2** stint, spell, scheduled time, period, turn. *See* COMPARE AND CONTRAST *at* change.

shifting *adj* unstable, ever-changing, fluctuating, fluid, flowing *Opposite*: fixed

shiftless *adj* lazy, idle, good-for-nothing, indolent, slothful *Opposite*: industrious

shifty *adj* suspicious, suspect, dubious, dishonest, untrustworthy *Opposite*: trustworthy

shilly-shally *v* **1** waver, dilly-dally, dither, hesitate, vacillate *Opposite*: decide **2** waste time, hang around, dawdle, delay *Opposite*: forge ahead

shimmer *v* sparkle, glisten, shine, glitter, gleam

shimmering *adj* iridescent, sparkling, shining, gleaming, glistening

shindig (*infml*) *n* party, bash, jamboree, do (*infml*), get-together (*infml*)

shine *v* **1** excel, be good at, stand out, have a gift for, be skilled at *Opposite*: bomb (*infml*) **2** glow, gleam, glimmer, sparkle, glitter **3** polish, burnish, wax, buff, buff up ■ *n* sheen, polish, lustre, gloss, gleam

shining *adj* outstanding, excellent, admirable, brilliant, superb *Opposite*: poor

shiny *adj* glossy, gleaming, glittery, polished, shimmering *Opposite*: dull

ship *n* vessel, craft, boat ■ *v* send, transport, distribute, dispatch, convey

WORD BANK
❏ types of historical vessel clipper, flagship, galleon, galley, Indiaman, longboat, longship, man-of-war, tall ship, windjammer
❏ types of military vessel aircraft carrier, battle cruiser, battleship, cruiser, cutter, destroyer, frigate, gunboat, minesweeper, submarine, warship
❏ types of motor vessel barge, cabin cruiser, canal boat, coaster, container ship, cutter, dredger, factory ship, ferry, ferryboat, freighter, houseboat, hovercraft, hydrofoil, icebreaker, launch, lifeboat, lighter, lightship, motorboat, powerboat, speedboat, steamboat, steamer, tanker, trawler, tug
❏ types of sailing vessel barque, brig, brigantine, catamaran, catboat, dhow, felucca, junk, ketch, sailing boat, schooner, sloop, smack, trimaran, yacht
❏ types of small vessel canoe, dinghy, dory,

dugout, gondola, kayak, life raft, narrow boat, pedalo, pirogue, punt, raft, rowing boat, sampan, scull, skiff

❏ **parts of a sailing vessel** boom, bowsprit, gaff, gaffsail, jib, mainsail, mainstay, mast, mizzen, pennant, sheet, shroud, spanker, spinnaker, topsail

❏ **parts of a ship or boat** bilge, bow, bridge, cabin, capstan, crow's nest, deck, engine room, forecastle, galley, gunwale, helm, hold, hull, keel, outboard motor, outrigger, poop, prow, rowlock, rudder, stateroom, stern, superstructure, tiller

shipment *n* **consignment**, delivery, batch, load, cargo

shipping *n* **delivery**, transportation, distribution, carriage, freight

shipshape *adj* **in order**, neat, tidy, organized, spick-and-span *Opposite*: untidy

shirk *v* **evade**, avoid, dodge, duck, get out of *Opposite*: accept

shirker *n* **lazy person**, slacker, idler, loafer, malingerer *Opposite*: worker

shiver *v* **shake**, tremble, quiver, quake, shudder ■ *n* **quiver**, shudder, tremor, tremble, quake

shoal *n* **sandbar**, sandbank, ridge, shallows

shock *n* **1 surprise**, jolt, blow, bombshell, kick in the teeth **2 distress**, numbness, devastation, disbelief, astonishment ■ *v* **1 stun**, alarm, surprise, frighten, astonish *Opposite*: calm **2 traumatize**, upset, devastate, shake up, alarm *Opposite*: reassure **3 scandalize**, outrage, appal, offend, horrify

shocked *adj* **1 surprised**, stunned, dazed, upset, shaken *Opposite*: indifferent **2 scandalized**, outraged, appalled, offended *Opposite*: indifferent

shocking *adj* **1 outrageous**, scandalous, offensive, disgraceful, reprehensible *Opposite*: acceptable **2 distressing**, startling, upsetting, disturbing, worrying *Opposite*: comforting **3** *(infml)* **dreadful**, awful, bad, appalling, lamentable *Opposite*: pleasant

shockingly *adv* **1 outrageously**, scandalously, disgracefully, reprehensively, unpardonably *Opposite*: acceptably **2 startlingly**, distressingly, upsettingly, disturbingly, worryingly *Opposite*: comfortingly **3 dreadfully**, awfully, appallingly, lamentably, horribly

shock wave *n* **1 repercussion**, reaction, shock, effect **2 tremor**, shudder, shock, trembling, agitation

shoddy *adj* **1 careless**, slapdash, inferior, cheap, substandard *Opposite*: fine **2 inconsiderate**, mean, unkind, dishonest, rotten *Opposite*: considerate

shoelace *n* **cord**, lace, bootlace, tie, fastener

shoo away *v* **chase off**, drive away, frighten away, scare off *Opposite*: invite

shoot *v* **1 fire**, let off, open fire, fire off, fire at **2 kill**, slaughter, shoot down, bring down, gun down *(infml)* **3 spurt**, squirt, burst, jet,

gush **4 film**, photograph, take, snap, capture **5 aim**, point, direct, cast, score **6 start to grow**, produce buds, develop, appear, sprout **7** *(infml)* **dart**, dash, run, race, speed ■ *n* **new growth**, branch, leaf bud, outgrowth, stem

shoot down *v* **1 kill**, slaughter, destroy, murder, bring down **2 attack**, tear to shreds, pick holes in, pillory, criticize

shooting *n* **gunfire**, shelling, bombardment, fire, firing **2 killing**, murder, assassination, execution, slaying

shoot up *v* **appear**, soar, rocket, spring up, mushroom *Opposite*: plummet

shop *n* **1 store**, outlet, showroom, emporium **2 spree**, shopping spree, shopping expedition, walk round the shops, binge **3 workshop**, plant, factory, garage, yard ■ *v* **go shopping**, buy groceries, go window-shopping, go on a spree, go to the shops

WORD BANK

❏ **types of food outlet** bakery, butcher's, chip shop, deli, delicatessen, drive-through, farmers' market, fishmonger's, greengrocer's, grocer's, grocery store, refreshment stand, supermarket, sweetshop, takeaway

❏ **types of retail outlet** bazaar, beauty salon, bookshop, boutique, chain store, charity shop, chemist, corner shop, covered market, department store, discount store, dispensary, duty-free, filling station, flea market, garden centre, hair salon, hairdresser's, hypermarket, kiosk, mall, mart, newsstand, nursery, petrol station, pharmacy, post office, saleroom, service station, superstore, warehouse

shopkeeper *n* **retailer**, seller, salesperson, merchant, trader

shoplift *v* **steal**, rob, pilfer, thieve, pocket

shoplifting *n* **stealing**, theft, thieving, pilfering, pinching *(infml)*

shopper *n* **customer**, consumer, buyer, purchaser, bargain hunter

shopping *n* **errands**, spending, shop, weekly shop, clothes shopping

shopping centre *n* **shopping precinct**, arcade, pedestrian precinct, shopping complex, mall *(US)*

shore *n* **coast**, beach, seashore, coastline, seaboard

shoreline *n* **beach**, shore, seashore, water's edge, coastline

shore up *v* **prop up**, support, hold up, buttress, bolster

shorn of *adj* **deprived of**, stripped of, minus, less, lacking

short *adj* **1 small**, little, petite, tiny, diminutive *Opposite*: tall **2 brief**, quick, rapid, fleeting, passing *Opposite*: lengthy **3 concise**, succinct, condensed, brief, to the point *Opposite*: long **4 curt**, brusque, snappy, abrupt, unfriendly *Opposite*: friendly ■ *adv* **midstream**, abruptly, suddenly, sharply *Oppo-*

site: gradually ■ *n (infml)* **drink**, tot, nip, measure, shot *(infml)*

shortage *n* **lack**, scarcity, deficiency, dearth, famine *Opposite*: excess. *See* COMPARE AND CONTRAST *at* lack.

short break *n* **break**, rest, holiday, weekend away, midweek break

shortcoming *n* **inadequacy**, failing, fault, deficiency, limitation *Opposite*: virtue

short course *n* **crash course**, intensive course, introductory course, refresher course

shorten *v* **cut down**, cut, cut back, curtail, abbreviate *Opposite*: lengthen

shortfall *n* **deficit**, loss, underperformance, gap, lack *Opposite*: excess

short form *n* **abbreviation**, shortening, contraction, acronym, ellipsis

short-handed *adj* **short-staffed**, understaffed, short

short-list *v* **select**, choose, pick out, cream off, narrow down

short-lived *adj* **brief**, fleeting, transitory, passing, short *Opposite*: long-lasting. *See* COMPARE AND CONTRAST *at* temporary.

shortly *adv* 1 **soon**, before long, in a while, in a minute, in a moment *Opposite*: later 2 **curtly**, brusquely, abruptly, briskly, tersely *Opposite*: pleasantly

shortness *n* 1 **smallness**, tininess, squatness, dumpiness *Opposite*: tallness 2 **quickness**, rapidity, speed, transience *Opposite*: length 3 **briefness**, brevity, terseness, conciseness, concision *Opposite*: length 4 **curtness**, brusqueness, abruptness, briskness, terseness *Opposite*: pleasantness

short of *prep* **apart from**, other than, without, bar *Opposite*: including

short-sighted *adj* 1 **myopic**, nearsighted (US) *Opposite*: farsighted 2 **ill-considered**, thoughtless, unthinking, imprudent, ill-advised *Opposite*: farsighted

short-sightedness *n* **thoughtlessness**, imprudence, rashness, hastiness *Opposite*: farsightedness

short-staffed *adj* **short-handed**, understaffed, understrength

short story *n* **novella**, tale, story, fable, parable *Opposite*: epic

short-tempered *adj* **quick-tempered**, irritable, impatient, irascible, touchy

short-term *adj* **temporary**, immediate, instant, short-range, interim *Opposite*: long-term

shot *n* 1 **gunshot**, potshot, round, volley, report 2 **bullet**, cannonball, slug, gunshot, buckshot 3 **picture**, photo, photograph, snapshot, snap 4 **try**, go, attempt, turn, crack *(infml)* 5 *(infml)* **injection**, jab *(infml)*, inoculation, vaccination 6 *(infml)* **measure**, drink, glass, tot, slug *(infml)*

shot in the arm *n* **boost**, fillip, spur, kick-start, stimulus

shot in the dark *n* **guess**, conjecture, speculation, potshot, attempt

should *v* **ought to**, had better, have a duty to, be duty-bound to, must

shoulder *v* **bear**, take on, accept, assume, carry *Opposite*: refuse

shout *v* **yell**, cry, scream, bellow, screech *Opposite*: whisper ■ *n* **cry**, yell, scream, bellow, screech *Opposite*: whisper

shout at *v* **yell at**, scold, reprimand, haul over the coals, berate *Opposite*: praise

shove *v* 1 **push**, thrust, heave, propel, jostle *Opposite*: pull 2 **put**, throw, toss, slap, sling ■ *n* **thrust**, push, heave, jolt

shovel *n* **spade**, scoop, trowel, tool ■ *v* **scoop**, move, dig, spoon, heap

show *v* 1 **present**, display, exhibit, expose, disclose *Opposite*: hide 2 **stand out**, stick out, show up, appear, surface 3 **accompany**, take, guide, direct, point 4 **prove**, illustrate, demonstrate, confirm, indicate *Opposite*: disprove 5 **demonstrate**, illustrate, explain, teach, point out ■ *n* 1 **demonstration**, display, expression, illustration, appearance 2 **performance**, musical, cabaret, play, film 3 **fair**, fête, exhibition, trade show, county show

show business *n* **the stage**, theatre, the boards, films, movies

showcase *n* 1 **glass case**, cabinet, display case, display cabinet, vitrine 2 **platform**, vehicle, setting, stage

showdown *n* **confrontation**, head-to-head, face-off, row, fight

shower *n* 1 **wash**, dip, rinse, spray 2 **cascade**, burst, deluge, hail, spray 3 **cloudburst**, downpour, storm, rainstorm, flurry ■ *v* 1 **wash**, clean up, freshen up, rinse 2 **rain**, rain down, pour, pour down, spit 3 **overwhelm**, inundate, flood, deluge, bombard

showery *adj* **rainy**, wet, changeable, damp, spitting *Opposite*: dry

showground *n* **arena**, ring, enclosure, field, ground

showing *n* **presentation**, performance, viewing, screening, display

showing off *n* **bravado**, boastfulness, boasting, bragging, posturing

show off *v* 1 **boast**, brag, shoot your mouth off, sing your own praises, pose 2 **display**, flaunt, parade, flourish, flash *(infml)* *Opposite*: hide

show-off *(infml)* *n* **boaster**, braggart, bragger, exhibitionist, know-all *(infml)*

showpiece *n* **centrepiece**, pride and joy, focus, attraction, pièce de résistance

showroom *n* **shop**, outlet, store

show up *v* 1 *(infml)* **come**, turn up, arrive, put in an appearance, appear 2 **highlight**, emphasize, point up, bring to light, reveal *Opposite*: hide 3 **stand out**, stick out, show, catch your eye, come to light 4 **embarrass**, humiliate, put somebody to shame, mortify, shame

showy *adj* **1 impressive**, attractive, eye-catching, splendid, magnificent *Opposite*: modest **2 ostentatious**, flashy, gaudy, garish, tasteless *Opposite*: restrained

show your face *v* **turn up**, appear, put in an appearance, come, arrive *Opposite*: hide

shred *n* **scrap**, strip, bit, piece, sliver *Opposite*: whole ■ *v* **slice**, cut up, tear up, rip up, grate

shrewd *adj* **astute**, sharp, smart, perceptive, discerning *Opposite*: naive

shrewdness *n* **astuteness**, sharpness, smartness, perceptiveness, discernment *Opposite*: naivety

shriek *n* **screech**, scream, yell, cry, yelp *Opposite*: whisper

shrill *adj* **piercing**, high-pitched, strident, penetrating, harsh *Opposite*: low

shrine *n* **memorial**, monument, tomb, grave, sanctuary

shrink *v* **1 contract**, shrivel, wither, telescope, shorten *Opposite*: grow **2 fall**, drop, decrease, decline, diminish *Opposite*: rise **3 cower**, cringe, flinch, recoil, draw back *Opposite*: stand your ground. *See* COMPARE AND CONTRAST *at* recoil.

shrinkage *n* **reduction**, decrease, decline, contraction, fall *Opposite*: growth

shrink back *v* **recoil**, cringe, shrink away, shy away, flinch *Opposite*: advance

shrink from *v* **recoil from**, baulk at, avoid, shirk, shun *Opposite*: welcome

shrivel *v* **shrink**, wither, dry up, contract, curl up *Opposite*: expand

shroud *n* **covering**, cover, blanket, layer, cloak

shrub *n* **bush**, plant, tree, flowering shrub

WORD BANK
❏ **types of shrub or bush** azalea, bramble, briar, broom, camellia, elder, forsythia, gardenia, gorse, hawthorn, heather, hydrangea, laurel, lavender, lilac, magnolia, privet, pussy willow, rhododendron, rose, sagebrush, witch hazel

shrubbery *n* **bushes**, undergrowth, border, herbaceous border, hedging

shrug off *v* **dismiss**, pooh-pooh, ignore, treat lightly, make light of

shrunken *adj* **wasted**, emaciated, dried up, withered, shrivelled *Opposite*: bloated

shudder *v* **shake**, tremble, shiver, wince, quake ■ *n* **tremble**, shake, shiver, tremor, judder

shuffle *v* **1 scuffle**, hobble, trundle, shamble, lumber **2 mix up**, jumble up, muddle up, rearrange, reorder

shun *v* **avoid**, turn away from, spurn, reject, eschew *Opposite*: court

shunt *v* **1 push**, shove, move, shift, propel **2** *(infml)* **hit**, collide with, smash into, bump into ■ *n* **1** *(infml)* **collision**, crash, smash, accident, prang *(infml)* **2 shove**, thrust, jolt, push

shush *(infml)* *v* **silence**, hush, quieten, quieten down, shut up *(infml)*

shut *v* **1 close**, close up, push to, fasten, secure *Opposite*: open **2 close down**, close, close up shop, shut down, go out of business *Opposite*: start up

shutdown *n* **closure**, cessation, stoppage, halt, end

shut off *v* **1 switch off**, turn off, close off, close down, shut down *Opposite*: turn on **2 isolate**, cut off, separate, seclude, set apart

shut out *v* **lock out**, keep out, exclude, keep off, debar *Opposite*: let in

shuttle *v* **go back and forth**, travel between, ply between, commute, ferry

shut up *v* **1** *(infml)* **be quiet**, fall silent, quieten down, clam up *(infml)*, pipe down *(infml)* **2 confine**, imprison, cage, shut in, lock in *Opposite*: let loose **3** *(infml)* **silence**, hush, gag, muzzle, cut off **4 close**, close up, lock, lock up, secure *Opposite*: open up

shut up shop *v* **1 stop**, call it a day, turn in, close, shut *Opposite*: start up **2 close down**, shut down, go out of business, go bankrupt, go to the wall *Opposite*: start up

shy *adj* **1 introverted**, retiring, withdrawn, timid, bashful *Opposite*: outgoing **2 cautious**, wary, nervous, afraid, fearful *Opposite*: confident

shy away *v* **retreat**, shrink, recoil, flinch, back off

shyness *n* **introversion**, timidity, bashfulness, inhibition, reticence *Opposite*: boldness

sick *adj* **1 ill**, unwell, bad, under the weather, off-colour *Opposite*: well **2 nauseous**, queasy, bilious, dizzy, green around the gills *(infml)* **3 bored**, up to here, sick to death, sick to the back teeth, sick and tired *(infml)* **4** *(infml)* **tasteless**, in bad taste, gruesome, bizarre, sickening ■ *n* *(infml)* **vomit**, spew, puke *(infml)*, chunder *(infml)*, bile *(literary)*

sickbay *n* **infirmary**, sanatorium, sickroom, hospital

sicken *v* **nauseate**, turn your stomach, repel, disgust, make sick

sickening *adj* **1 disgusting**, nauseating, stomach-churning, shocking, appalling *Opposite*: appealing **2** *(infml)* **annoying**, maddening, irritating, infuriating, disappointing *Opposite*: pleasing

sickly *adj* **1 unhealthy**, weak, ill, unwell, pale *Opposite*: healthy **2 cloying**, overpowering, disgusting, suffocating, nauseating *Opposite*: appealing **3 saccharine**, sentimental, cloying, sickly-sweet, mawkish *Opposite*: tough

sickly-sweet *adj* **saccharine**, cloying, mawkish, sentimental, nauseating

sickness *n* **1 illness**, disease, virus, condition, bad health *Opposite*: health **2 nausea**, vomiting, queasiness, biliousness, throwing up *(infml)*

sick up (infml) v **vomit**, spew, throw up (infml), puke (slang), hurl (slang)

side n **1 surface**, face, elevation, wall, plane **2 part**, area, region, section, segment **3 edge**, boundary, flank, bank, periphery **4 aspect**, facet, feature, quality, characteristic **5 team**, squad, line-up, group, gang

side effect n **unexpected result**, secondary effect, by-product, consequence, knock-on effect

sidekick (infml) n **assistant**, helper, associate, subordinate, partner Opposite: boss

sideline n **hobby**, pastime, offshoot, secondary activity, second job Opposite: career ■ v **1 put aside**, shelve, put off, slow pedal, put on the back burner Opposite: promote **2 relegate**, demote, exclude, downgrade, lay off Opposite: promote

sidelong adj **sideways**, oblique, slanting, indirect, askew Opposite: direct

sidesplitting adj **hilarious**, riotous, uproarious, rollicking, funny Opposite: dull

sidestep v **avoid**, evade, dodge, duck, bypass

side street n **alley**, back street, lane, side road

sidetrack v **distract**, deflect, divert, change the subject, get off the point

side view n **cross section**, profile, section, side, aspect

sideways adj **oblique**, slanting, indirect, sidelong, slanted Opposite: straight ■ adv **to one side**, to the left, to the right, askew, askance Opposite: straight

side with v **back**, support, take somebody's side, be in somebody's camp, take somebody's part Opposite: oppose

sidle v **edge**, creep, slither, snake, inch

siege n **blockade**, cordon, barrier, barricade, obstruction

siesta n **rest**, nap, sleep, catnap, snooze (infml)

sift v **1 sieve**, filter, separate, put through a sieve, strain **2 sort through**, go through, go through with a fine-tooth comb, examine, select

sigh v **1 exhale**, heave a sigh, moan, groan, breathe Opposite: inhale **2 yearn**, long, hanker, pine, want Opposite: dislike ■ n **exhalation**, moan, groan, complaint, lament

sight n **1 vision**, eyesight, ability to see **2 view**, spectacle, prospect, picture, scene ■ v **notice**, catch sight of, spot, see, glimpse Opposite: miss

sighted adj **seeing**, keen-sighted, partially sighted, long-sighted, eagle-eyed Opposite: blind

sights n **tourist attractions**, places of interest, highlights, wonders, marvels

sightseeing n **tourism**, visiting the attractions, going to places of interest, seeing the sights, exploration

sightseer n **tourist**, visitor, holidaymaker, day tripper, tripper (infml) Opposite: resident

sign n **1 symbol**, mark, emblem, insignia, logo **2 signal**, indication, symptom, warning, clue **3 notice**, poster, road sign, hoarding, placard **4 trace**, track, trail, footprint, mark **5 omen**, warning, portent, premonition, indication ■ v **1 autograph**, sign your name, initial, authorize, endorse **2 employ**, contract, hire, engage, take on Opposite: dismiss **3 make signs**, signal, gesture, motion, indicate

signal n **sign**, indication, gesture, indicator, motion ■ v **1 communicate**, indicate, suggest, intimate, hint **2 gesture**, gesticulate, motion, sign, beckon **3 indicate**, mark, herald, portend, announce

signally adv **completely**, notably, totally, absolutely, one hundred per cent

signatory n **party**, participant, guarantor, the undersigned, cosignatory

signature n **name**, autograph, cross, mark, initials

signboard n **sign**, signpost, notice, hoarding, road sign

significance n **1 importance**, impact, substance, weight, magnitude Opposite: meaninglessness **2 meaning**, implication, import, worth, connotation

significant adj **1 meaningful**, knowing, meaning, suggestive, expressive Opposite: blank **2 important**, major, noteworthy, momentous, substantial Opposite: insignificant **3 considerable**, large, major, big, sizable Opposite: paltry

significantly adv **1 considerably**, appreciably, drastically, notably, radically **2 meaningfully**, knowingly, suggestively, pointedly, expressively Opposite: innocently

significant other n **partner**, lover, spouse, other half, better half

signification n **meaning**, sense, gist, significance, denotation

signify v **mean**, indicate, show, imply, suggest

signing n **1 ratification**, validation, adoption, passing, authorization Opposite: rejection **2 new employee**, new player, new arrival, recruit, acquisition

sign on v **enlist**, sign up, enrol, put your name down, register

signpost n **1 signboard**, sign, notice, marker, road sign **2 indication**, suggestion, pointer, marker, sign ■ v **flag**, mark, indicate, label, designate Opposite: conceal

sign up v **1 recruit**, employ, sign, take somebody on, contract Opposite: fire **2 enlist**, join, enrol, become a member, put your name down Opposite: quit

silage n **fodder**, feed, grass, forage

silence n **1 quietness**, quiet, hush, stillness, peace Opposite: noise **2 muteness**, taciturnity, reticence, reserve, uncommunicativeness Opposite: chatter ■ v **1 make quiet**, quieten, hush, muzzle, shut up (infml)

2 stop, put an end to, gag, stifle, suppress *Opposite*: encourage

silent *adj* **1 still**, hushed, soundless, noiseless, quiet *Opposite*: noisy **2 mute**, tongue-tied, uncommunicative, taciturn, reticent *Opposite*: talkative **3 unspoken**, unvoiced, voiceless, tacit, wordless *Opposite*: spoken

COMPARE AND CONTRAST CORE MEANING: not speaking or not saying much

silent not speaking or communicating at any particular time, especially through choice, or not inclined to speak much; **quiet** not inclined to speak much, often because of shyness; **reticent** unwilling to communicate very much, talk freely, or reveal all the facts; **taciturn** habitually reserved in speech and manner; **uncommunicative** not willing to say much, especially not to reveal information, or tending not to say much.

silhouette *n* **outline**, shape, shadow, profile, line

silken *adj* **smooth**, soft, silky, silky-smooth, glossy *Opposite*: coarse

silky *adj* **1 glossy**, smooth, soft, silken, silky-smooth *Opposite*: rough **2 smooth**, honeyed, mellifluous, sweet, unctuous *Opposite*: harsh

sill *n* **ledge**, shelf, ridge, projection, window-sill

silliness *n* **1 stupidity**, ridiculousness, childishness, madness, idiocy *Opposite*: sense **2 triviality**, meaninglessness, mindlessness, puerility, inanity *Opposite*: importance

silly *adj* **1 stupid**, ridiculous, impractical, childish, asinine *Opposite*: sensible **2 trivial**, meaningless, mindless, puerile, senseless *Opposite*: important

silt *n* **deposit**, mud, sediment, sludge, residue

silver-tongued *adj* **eloquent**, smooth-talking, grandiloquent, fluent, flattering *Opposite*: tongue-tied

silvery *adj* **silver**, grey, hoary, shiny

similar *adj* **alike**, like, comparable, parallel, analogous *Opposite*: dissimilar

similarity *n* **resemblance**, comparison, likeness, parallel, correspondence *Opposite*: difference

similarly *adv* **1 alike**, in the same way, comparably, analogously, relatedly *Opposite*: differently **2 likewise**, also, in the same way, correspondingly, equally *Opposite*: on the contrary

similitude *(fml)* *n* **similarity**, resemblance, likeness, sameness, semblance *Opposite*: difference

simmer *v* **1 boil**, bubble, cook **2 seethe**, rumble, bubble, boil, fester

simmer down *v* **cool down**, calm down, settle down, regain your self-control, compose yourself *Opposite*: blow your top *(infml)*

simper *v* **smirk**, grimace, sneer, look smug, look coy *Opposite*: frown ■ *n* **grimace**, smirk,

sneer, smug look, coy look *Opposite*: frown

simple *adj* **1 easy**, straightforward, uncomplicated, trouble-free, effortless *Opposite*: difficult **2 plain**, minimal, unadorned, unfussy, down-to-earth *Opposite*: fancy **3 humble**, modest, unassuming, unpretentious, meek *Opposite*: pretentious **4 guileless**, ingenuous, naive, unsophisticated, green *Opposite*: sophisticated

simple-minded *adj* **1 simplistic**, crude, basic, one-dimensional, unsophisticated *Opposite*: subtle **2 naïve**, childlike, unsophisticated, artless, guileless *Opposite*: sophisticated

simplicity *n* **1 ease**, straightforwardness, effortlessness, easiness, lack of complication *Opposite*: difficulty **2 plainness**, minimalism, cleanness, lack of adornment, austerity **3 humility**, modesty, unpretentiousness, meekness, unassumingness *Opposite*: pride **4 guilelessness**, naivety, ingenuousness, lack of sophistication, artlessness *Opposite*: sophistication

simplified *adj* **cut down**, basic, easy, abridged, shortened *Opposite*: complex

simplify *v* **make simpler**, make easier, make straightforward, abridge, shorten *Opposite*: complicate

simplistic *adj* **naive**, unsophisticated, crude, basic, one-dimensional *Opposite*: sophisticated

simply *adv* **1 just**, only, merely, purely, basically **2 easily**, straightforwardly, in basic terms, in simple terms, in words of one syllable *Opposite*: elaborately **3 plainly**, minimally, cleanly, austerely, unpretentiously *Opposite*: elaborately **4 frankly**, absolutely, obviously, undeniably, unquestionably **5 modestly**, humbly, unassumingly, meekly, unpretentiously *Opposite*: proudly **6 naively**, guilelessly, ingenuously, candidly, innocently *Opposite*: knowingly

simulate *v* **1 replicate**, reproduce, imitate, suggest, copy **2 fake**, pretend, feign, put on, sham **3 mimic**, ape, copy, imitate, parrot

simulated *adj* **1 virtual**, cyber-, computer-generated **2 fake**, imitation, pretend, counterfeit, sham *Opposite*: genuine

simulation *n* **imitation**, reproduction, replication, recreation, mock-up

simulator *n* **simulant**, emulator, trainer

simultaneous *adj* **concurrent**, immediate, instantaneous, real-time, synchronized *Opposite*: separate

sin *n* **1 crime**, misdemeanour, transgression, misdeed, wrongdoing *Opposite*: good deed **2 wickedness**, iniquity, depravity, immorality, debauchery *Opposite*: goodness ■ *v* **transgress**, do wrong, commit a crime, lapse, be led astray

since *conj* **as**, because, given that, seeing as, in view of the fact that ■ *adv* **meanwhile**, in the meantime, subsequently, later, then

sincere adj **1 honest**, open, frank, natural, straight Opposite: disingenuous **2 heartfelt**, genuine, real, true, truthful Opposite: insincere

sincerity n **genuineness**, honesty, earnestness, naturalness, unaffectedness Opposite: insincerity

sinecure n **easy ride**, plum job, soft option, cushy job (infml), cushy number (infml)

sine qua non n **prerequisite**, essential condition, precondition, requirement, necessity

sinewy adj **wiry**, lean, strong, muscly, brawny Opposite: frail

sinful adj **wicked**, bad, evil, corrupt, errant Opposite: virtuous

sing v **1 croon**, chant, hum, warble, carol **2 resonate**, buzz, hum, purr, vibrate

singe v **scorch**, burn, char, sear

singer n **vocalist**, songster, lead singer, soloist, chorister

singing n **vocals**, songs, vocal music, chanting, warbling ■ adj **vocal**, choral, melodic, whistling, humming Opposite: instrumental

single adj **1 solitary**, on its own, lone, sole, solo **2 particular**, distinct, separate, specific, definite Opposite: general **3 unmarried**, unattached, lone, free Opposite: attached ■ n **record**, song, track, release

single-handed adj **unassisted**, unaided, lone, solo, unaccompanied Opposite: assisted ■ adv **by yourself**, on your own, alone, without help, without assistance

single-minded adj **focused**, dedicated, resolute, dogged, driven Opposite: unfocused

single-mindedness n **sense of purpose**, concentration, application, attention, focus Opposite: aimlessness

single out v **pick out**, choose, select, identify, pull out

singly adv **individually**, alone, one by one, one at a time, piecemeal Opposite: together

sing out v **call out**, pipe up, speak up, speak out, shout

sing the praises of v **eulogize**, acclaim, praise, lionize, extol Opposite: criticize

singular adj **remarkable**, extraordinary, particular, outstanding, curious

singularity n **distinctiveness**, individuality, originality, uniqueness, peculiarity

sing your own praises v **boast**, swagger, swank, try to make an impression, brag

sinister adj **menacing**, ominous, threatening, evil, disturbing

sink v **1 go under**, go down, go under the surface, be submerged, go downwards Opposite: float **2 fall**, descend, drop, decline, go down Opposite: rise **3 dig**, drill, mine, bore ■ n **basin**, bowl, hand basin, washbasin

sink in v **go in**, enter, penetrate, diffuse, permeate

sinuous adj **lithe**, supple, twisting, winding, graceful

sip v **taste**, drink, swallow, sup Opposite: gulp ■ n **drink**, swallow, taste, drop, mouthful

siphon v **draw off**, tap, drain off

siren n **alarm**, alert, warning, alarm bell, danger signal

sister n **1 nun**, holy sister, religious, vestal (literary) **2 friend**, supporter, ally, associate ■ adj **fellow**, parallel, associated, corresponding, equivalent

sit v **1 be seated**, sit down, take a seat, take the weight off your feet, take a pew Opposite: stand **2 assemble**, meet, convene, be in session Opposite: disperse **3 be placed**, be positioned, lie, rest, be on top of

sit around v **kill time**, do nothing, lounge around, hang about, hang around

sit down v **be seated**, take a seat, take the weight off your feet, park yourself, take a pew Opposite: stand up

sit-down (infml) n **rest**, break, respite, breather (infml)

site n **place**, location, spot, position ■ v **put**, position, place, situate, locate

sit-in n **protest**, demonstration, rally, vigil, demo (infml)

sitting n **session**, meeting, hearing

situate v **place**, set, put, locate, position

situated (fml) adj **located**, positioned, set, placed, sited

situation n **1 state of affairs**, circumstances, state, condition, status quo **2 location**, position, site, place, setting **3** (fml) **job**, post, position

sixth sense n **intuition**, feeling, hunch, ESP

sizable adj **substantial**, generous, good-sized, ample, large Opposite: small

size n **dimension**, mass, bulk, amount, extent

sizeable see sizable

size up v **assess**, look somebody up and down, take stock of, evaluate, appraise

sizzle v **crackle**, spit, hiss, sputter

sizzling (infml) adj **boiling**, red-hot, baking, blistering, sweltering Opposite: freezing

skate over (infml) v **skim over**, dismiss, pass over, skirt around, fail to deal with Opposite: dwell on

skein n **hank**, ball, bundle, length, coil

skeletal adj **thin**, emaciated, skinny, gaunt, wasted Opposite: obese

skeleton n **1 frame**, bones, carcass **2 plan**, outline, framework, sketch, bare bones (infml) ■ adj **minimum**, basic, essential, minimal Opposite: full

sketch n **draft**, plan, drawing, rough copy, rough ■ v **draw**, outline, draft, delineate, block in

sketchy adj **vague**, unclear, hazy, imprecise, woolly Opposite: detailed

skew v **1 tilt**, slant, twist, angle, slope *Opposite*: straighten **2 distort**, bias, slant, twist, spin

skewed adj **1 tilted**, slanted, twisted, crooked, askew *Opposite*: straight **2 distorted**, biased, slanted, prejudiced, partial *Opposite*: objective

skewer n **spit**, brochette, spike, spear, needle ■ v **impale**, spear, spike, pierce, stab

skewwhiff (*infml*) adj **crooked**, lopsided, tilted, cockeyed, slanted *Opposite*: straight

skid v **slip**, slide, slew, slither, spin out

skilful adj **clever**, adroit, dexterous, skilled, expert *Opposite*: incompetent

skill n **ability**, talent, cleverness, dexterity, expertise. *See* COMPARE AND CONTRAST *at* **ability**.

skilled adj **accomplished**, expert, capable, able, trained *Opposite*: untrained

skim v **1 glide**, fly, float, soar **2 scan**, speed-read, browse, glance at, flick through *Opposite*: peruse

skim off v **cull**, cream off, hive off, handpick, choose

skimp v **stint**, withhold, hold back on, be sparing with, pinch *Opposite*: lavish

skimpy adj **meagre**, insufficient, scanty, inadequate, sparse *Opposite*: generous

skin n **1 hide**, pelt, fur, coat **2 casing**, covering, membrane, crust, coating ■ v **1 peel**, pare, excoriate, desquamate **2 graze**, scrape, flay, scuff

skin-deep adj **superficial**, on the surface, on the outside, shallow, artificial

skinflint n **miser**, pinchpenny, cheapskate (*infml*), penny pincher (*infml*), scrooge (*infml*)

skinniness n **gauntness**, scrawniness, thinness, boniness, leanness *Opposite*: plumpness

skinny adj **thin**, lean, undernourished, emaciated, scrawny *Opposite*: fat. *See* COMPARE AND CONTRAST *at* **thin**.

skin tone n **skin colour**, complexion, skin, facial appearance, flesh colour

skip v **1 hop**, bounce, prance, gambol, caper **2 omit**, leave out, miss out, miss, pass over **3** (*infml*) **avoid**, miss, cut (*infml*), bunk off (*infml*) *Opposite*: attend

skip off (*infml*) v **run away**, make a sharp exit, do a runner, do a moonlight flit, duck out *Opposite*: stay put

skipper (*infml*) n **captain**, boss, chief, head, person in charge

skirmish n **battle**, fight, engagement, scuffle, clash ■ v **clash**, fight, scuffle, tussle, scrap. *See* COMPARE AND CONTRAST *at* **fight**.

skirt v **1 border**, edge, adjoin, abut, neighbour **2 go around**, avoid, evade, bypass, edge past **3 skim over**, pass over, avoid, evade, bypass *Opposite*: tackle

WORD BANK
❏ **types of skirt** dirndl, hobble skirt, kilt, maxi skirt, miniskirt, pencil skirt, sarong, tutu, wraparound

skit n **parody**, satire, spoof, sketch, burlesque

skittish adj **1 wary**, jumpy, edgy, nervous, uneasy **2 playful**, lively, frisky, excited, restless

skiver (*infml*) n **shirker**, layabout, lazybones (*infml*), idler, freeloader (*infml*) *Opposite*: go-getter (*infml*)

skulduggery n **trickery**, tricks, dishonesty, cheating, mischief *Opposite*: honesty

skulk v **lurk**, loiter, creep, prowl, lie in wait

skull (*infml*) n **mind**, brain, head, noggin, noddle (*dated infml*)

sky n **heaven**, blue, atmosphere, firmament (*literary*)

sky-high adj **excessive**, very high, elevated, exorbitant, over-the-top

skyjack v **hijack**, seize, take over, take control of, capture

skyline n **horizon**, distance, prospect, vista

skyrocket (*infml*) v **rise steeply**, go through the ceiling, climb sharply, shoot up, hit the roof (*infml*) *Opposite*: plummet

skyscraper n **multistorey building**, tower, high-rise building

skyward adv **heavenward**, upward, up, above, aloft ■ adj **upward**, heavenward, aloft

skywards *see* **skyward**

slab n **lump**, chunk, block, hunk, piece

slack adj **1 loose**, limp, relaxed, baggy, floppy *Opposite*: taut **2 careless**, inattentive, idle, inefficient, unprofessional *Opposite*: diligent **3 slow-moving**, slow, dull, quiet, sluggish *Opposite*: brisk

slacken v **loosen**, relax, release, slacken off *Opposite*: tighten

slacker n **idler**, loafer, shirker, lazybones (*infml*), skiver (*infml*)

slackness n **1 looseness**, limpness, bagginess, floppiness, droopiness *Opposite*: tautness **2 carelessness**, negligence, laxity, inattention, laziness *Opposite*: meticulousness

slake v **quench**, satisfy, satiate, sate, extinguish *Opposite*: exacerbate

slam (*infml*) v **criticize**, berate, disparage, deride, slate *Opposite*: praise

slander n **1 defamation**, character assassination, disparagement, vilification, calumny (*fml*) **2 slur**, smear, slight, insult, libel ■ v **insult**, malign, slur, smear, disparage *Opposite*: compliment. *See* COMPARE AND CONTRAST *at* **malign**.

slanderous adj **libellous**, defamatory, insulting, malicious, disparaging

slang n **jargon**, vernacular, colloquial speech, dialect, argot

slanging match n argument, shouting match, spat, quarrel, row

slant v incline, lean, skew, slope, tilt ■ n 1 angle, incline, diagonal, pitch, gradient 2 viewpoint, angle, attitude, point of view, perspective

slanted adj biased, prejudiced, one-sided, partial, unfair Opposite: balanced

slanting adj angled, at an angle, sloping, on a slope, oblique Opposite: level

slantways adv diagonally, crossways, crosswise, at an angle, obliquely Opposite: straight

slantwise see slantways

slap n smack, blow, spank, cuff, clout ■ v hit, smack, spank, cuff, swipe

slapdash adj careless, messy, clumsy, hasty, hurried Opposite: meticulous

slaphappy adj slapdash, careless, haphazard, hit-and-miss, irresponsible Opposite: meticulous

slapstick n knockabout, farce, clowning, burlesque, comedy

slash v 1 cut, hack, slice, gash, slit 2 reduce, cut, lower, drop, decrease Opposite: increase ■ n laceration, gash, slit, tear, rip

slat n plank, board, lath

slate (infml) v criticize, censure, disparage, pan (infml), find fault with

slaughter v kill, murder, massacre, butcher, slay (fml or literary) ■ n killing, murder, massacre, carnage, butchery. See COMPARE AND CONTRAST at kill.

slaver v drool, slobber, dribble, salivate

slay (fml or literary) v kill, murder, assassinate, massacre, eliminate

sleaze n corruption, dishonesty, malpractice, scandal, foul play Opposite: probity

sleazy adj 1 seedy, sordid, squalid, grubby, grotty 2 corrupt, immoral, dishonest, shady, slimy Opposite: honest

sleek adj smooth, shiny, glossy, silky, lustrous

sleep n slumber, nap, doze, siesta, catnap ■ v be asleep, slumber, be dead to the world, nap, doze

sleepily adv drowsily, dozily, woozily, wearily, blearily Opposite: alertly

sleep in v oversleep, sleep late, stay in bed, snooze on, ignore the alarm

sleepiness n drowsiness, tiredness, lethargy, somnolence, lassitude Opposite: alertness

sleepless adj 1 wakeful, restless, disturbed, unsleeping, awake 2 alert, active, vigilant, attentive, ready

sleeplessness n 1 insomnia, wakefulness, restlessness 2 alertness, vigilance, readiness, liveliness

sleepy adj 1 drowsy, tired, lethargic, heavy-eyed, sluggish Opposite: alert 2 quiet, dull, slow, inactive, peaceful Opposite: lively

sleet n slush, snow, frozen rain

sleeve n cover, jacket, protective cover, envelope, dust jacket

sleight of hand n dexterity, skill, adroitness, cunning, trickery

slender adj 1 slim, slight, lean, trim, thin Opposite: fat 2 small, slim, meagre, slight, little Opposite: considerable. See COMPARE AND CONTRAST at thin.

slenderness n thinness, slimness, skinniness, fineness, narrowness Opposite: stoutness

sleuth v 1 investigate, look for clues, spy, look into things, check things out 2 track, tail, follow, pursue, stalk ■ n (infml) detective, private detective, Sherlock Holmes, investigator, private eye (infml)

slew v veer, swing, slide, skid, swerve

slice n 1 piece, sliver, wedge, portion, segment 2 share, cut, portion, part, percentage ■ v cut, share, carve, divide, cut up

slick adj 1 polished, professional, efficient, glossy, smooth Opposite: shoddy 2 glib, superficial, untrustworthy, shallow, facile 3 slippery, smooth, glossy, shiny, glassy

slide v 1 glide, slither, slip, skim, skate 2 go down, fall, decrease, diminish, drop Opposite: rise

slight adj 1 small, minor, unimportant, trivial, insignificant Opposite: considerable 2 slim, delicate, thin, feeble, slender Opposite: stocky ■ n snub, insult, slur, smear, rebuff ■ v insult, offend, snub, scorn, affront

slightly adv somewhat, to some extent, a little, a touch, marginally Opposite: considerably

slim adj 1 thin, trim, slender, slight, lean Opposite: fat 2 faint, slender, remote, poor, slight Opposite: considerable ■ v diet, go on a diet, lose weight, watch your weight, reduce (US). See COMPARE AND CONTRAST at thin.

slim down v reduce, streamline, rationalize, cut, cut back Opposite: expand

slime n paste, mucus, gunge (infml), goo (infml), gunk (infml)

slimming adj 1 low-fat, light, diet, low-calorie, healthy Opposite: fattening 2 flattering, becoming, thinning Opposite: unflattering

slimness n 1 narrowness, fineness, slightness, thinness, flatness Opposite: bulkiness 2 slenderness, leanness, svelteness, trimness, thinness Opposite: plumpness

slimy adj 1 greasy, oily, slippery, slick 2 smarmy, oily, grovelling, sycophantic, unctuous

sling v 1 throw, toss, lob, fling, hurl 2 hang, suspend, dangle, drape, hook up

slink v creep, sneak, tiptoe, steal, skulk

slip v 1 trip, fall, lose your balance, lose your footing, tumble 2 slide, glide, slither, skid, skate 3 sneak, steal, creep, flit, slink ■ n blunder, mistake, error, omission, gaffe. See COMPARE AND CONTRAST at mistake.

slip back v revert, relapse, lapse, slide back, return

slippery adj 1 greasy, oily, slick, icy, slimy Opposite: dry 2 sneaky, shifty, crafty, devious, dishonest Opposite: trustworthy

slipshod adj careless, shoddy, slapdash, slack, sloppy (infml) Opposite: thorough

slip up (infml) v make a mistake, go wrong, get it wrong, blunder, trip up

slip-up (infml) n blunder, slip, mistake, error, omission

slit v cut, slash, gash, nick, tear ■ n opening, cut, slash, gash, slot. See COMPARE AND CONTRAST at tear.

slither v slide, glide, slink, slip, skid

sliver n slice, shaving, splinter, flake, shard

slobber v drool, dribble, salivate, slaver

slog v 1 plod, trudge, tramp, trek, hike 2 work, labour, toil, grind, struggle ■ n 1 trek, hike, tramp, trail, marathon 2 drag, effort, strain, grind, struggle

slogan n motto, saying, jingle, catch phrase, watchword

slop v spill, slosh, splatter, splash, swill

slope n gradient, incline, hill, rise, angle ■ v incline, slant, tilt, lean, rise

slope off (infml) v slink, creep, sneak, skulk, steal away

sloppy adj 1 messy, untidy, disordered, chaotic, slovenly Opposite: tidy 2 (infml) slack, shoddy, careless, poor, slipshod Opposite: meticulous 3 (infml) sentimental, slushy, romantic, corny, gushing

slosh v spill, slop, splatter, splash, swill

slot n 1 slit, hole, opening, niche, space 2 time, window, opening, space, period ■ v position, locate, fit, insert, slip

sloth n laziness, idleness, indolence, apathy, sluggishness Opposite: liveliness

slothful adj lazy, idle, sluggish, inactive, indolent Opposite: energetic

slothfulness see sloth

slot in v fit in, squeeze in, accommodate, accept, see

slouch v slump, droop, stoop, sprawl, lounge ■ n (infml) idler, loafer, slacker, shirker, freeloader (infml)

slovenly adj careless, dishevelled, untidy, messy, unkempt

slow adj 1 sluggish, unhurried, measured, deliberate, dawdling Opposite: fast 2 time-consuming, drawn-out, protracted, lengthy, lingering Opposite: quick ■ v slow down, decelerate, brake, reduce, slacken

slow down v 1 decelerate, slow up, slow, brake, reduce speed Opposite: speed up 2 hold up, hold back, delay, slow, retard Opposite: speed up

slowly adv gradually, unhurriedly, bit by bit, little by little, at a snail's pace Opposite: quickly

slowness n leisureliness, sluggishness, deliberateness, gradualness Opposite: fastness

slow up v 1 hold up, hold back, delay, slow, retard Opposite: speed up 2 decelerate, slow down, slow, brake, reduce speed

sludge n mud, slush, mire, muck, slop

slug n 1 bullet, shot, shell, cartridge, pellet 2 (infml) shot, gulp, swallow, mouthful, glassful Opposite: sip 3 blow, hit, thump, punch, whack ■ v 1 (infml) swallow, gulp, down, drink, swill Opposite: sip 2 hit, thump, strike, punch, whack

sluggish adj inactive, lethargic, slow, listless, slothful Opposite: energetic

sluggishness n lethargy, slowness, listlessness, sloth, laziness Opposite: alertness

sluice n channel, conduit, race, drain, gutter ■ v clean, flush, rinse, hose, wash

slum n shanty town, favela, purlieu (fml), colonia (US)

slumber v sleep, drowse, doze, be dead to the world, catnap ■ n 1 sleep, doze, nap, catnap, siesta 2 rest, inactivity, inertia, torpor, laziness

slump v 1 collapse, fall, sink, tumble, lurch 2 slouch, bend, hunch, droop, sprawl 3 decrease, decline, collapse, plummet, crash Opposite: rise ■ n recession, crash, collapse, decline, plummet Opposite: rise

slur v 1 speak, run together, blend, overlap, overrun 2 demean, smear, insult, slight, besmirch ■ n smear, disgrace, insult, slight, stain

slurp v gulp, suck, drink, swallow, down ■ n mouthful, swallow, drink, sip, gulp

slurred adj indistinct, inaudible, unclear, garbled, incoherent Opposite: distinct

slush n sludge, mud, mire, muck, slurry

slushy adj 1 snowy, icy, wet, mushy, sloppy Opposite: dry 2 sentimental, mushy, corny, syrupy, mawkish Opposite: unsentimental

sly adj 1 crafty, cunning, clever, skilful, knowing 2 evasive, wily, devious, furtive, underhand Opposite: honest

slyness n 1 craftiness, cunning, skill, artfulness, cleverness Opposite: clumsiness 2 sneakiness, evasiveness, furtiveness, dishonesty, underhandedness Opposite: openness

smack v 1 hit, clout, slap, cuff, spank 2 suggest, imply, hint at, look like, sound like ■ n 1 slap, blow, clout, cuff, spank 2 taste, flavour, tang, bite, savour

small adj 1 little, minute, tiny, diminutive, miniature Opposite: big 2 unimportant, trivial, slight, lesser, minor Opposite: major

small arms n weapons, guns, firearms, side arms, pistols

smallholding n farm, croft, plot, allotment

smallness n tininess, littleness, minuteness, compactness Opposite: largeness

smalls *(infml)* *n* **underwear**, underclothes, underclothing, undies *(infml)*

small-scale *adj* **1 limited**, modest, moderate, minor, unimportant *Opposite*: large-scale **2 little**, small, miniature, minuscule, tiny *Opposite*: large-scale

small screen *(infml)* *n* **television**, telly *(infml)*, TV *(infml)*, box *(slang)*, goggle-box *(dated infml)*

small talk *n* **chat**, conversation, pleasantries, gossip, chatter

small-time *(infml)* *adj* **petty**, unimportant, local, minor, insignificant *Opposite*: major

smarmy *adj* **sycophantic**, oily, slimy, grovelling, unctuous

smart *adj* **1 elegant**, tidy, stylish, chic, well-dressed *Opposite*: shabby **2 clever**, intelligent, bright, sharp, quick *Opposite*: stupid **3 insolent**, rude, facetious, clever, disrespectful **4 fashionable**, chic, glamorous, stylish, voguish **5 lively**, brisk, vigorous, energetic, quick ■ *v* **sting**, burn, hurt, chafe, tingle. *See* COMPARE AND CONTRAST *at* intelligent.

smart aleck *(infml)* *n* **know-all** *(infml)*, clever Dick *(infml)*, clever clogs *(infml)*, smartypants *(infml)*, wiseacre *(infml)*

smarten *v* **1 spruce up**, clean up, revamp, do up, redecorate *Opposite*: let go **2 speed up**, accelerate, quicken, increase, pick up *Opposite*: slow

smarten up *v* **1 spruce up**, clean up, revamp, do up, redecorate *Opposite*: let go **2 brighten up**, liven up, cheer up, enliven, energize *Opposite*: stagnate

smartly *adv* **1 stylishly**, nattily, neatly, tidily, elegantly *Opposite*: untidily **2 vigorously**, briskly, energetically, quickly, rapidly **3 intelligently**, cleverly, ably, knowledgeably *Opposite*: stupidly

smartness *n* **neatness**, tidiness, elegance, stylishness, chicness *Opposite*: untidiness

smarty-pants *(infml)* *n* **know-all** *(infml)*, clever clogs *(infml)*, clever Dick *(infml)*, smart aleck *(infml)*, wiseacre *(infml)*

smash *v* **shatter**, break, demolish, destroy, crush *Opposite*: repair ■ *n* **1 crash**, bang, crunch **2 blow**, chop, punch, kick, volley **3 accident**, crash, collision, pile-up *(infml)*, wreck *(US)*

smasher *(infml)* *n* **beauty**, cracker *(infml)*, ace *(infml)*, knockout *(infml)*, looker *(infml)*

smashing *(infml)* *adj* **wonderful**, marvellous, great, brilliant *(infml)*, terrific *(infml)* *Opposite*: dreadful

smash up *v* **wreck**, write off, damage, ruin, trash *(infml)*

smash-up *n* **crash**, collision, accident, prang *(infml)*, pile-up *(infml)*

smattering *n* **bit**, modicum, dash, iota, little *Opposite*: lot

smear *v* **1 spread**, coat, daub, cover, wipe **2 sully**, discredit, disgrace, besmirch, tarnish *Opposite*: praise ■ *n* **1 mark**, smudge, blotch, stain, blot **2 slur**, insult, slight, affront, slander

smear campaign *n* **mudslinging**, whispering campaign, muckraking, defamation, slander

smell *v* **1 stink**, reek, pong *(infml)*, whiff *(infml)* **2 sniff**, sense, get a whiff of, suspect, taste ■ *n* **odour**, aroma, perfume, scent, fragrance

COMPARE AND CONTRAST CORE MEANING: the way something smells

smell a neutral, pleasant, or unpleasant quality detected by the nerves of the nose; **odour** a neutral or unpleasant smell; **aroma** a distinctive pleasant smell, especially one related to cooking or food; **bouquet** a characteristic pleasant smell, usually associated with fine wines; **scent** a pleasant, sweet smell, for example the smell of flowers, or the characteristic smell given off by a particular animal; **perfume** a sweet, pleasant, and heady smell, especially the smell of flowers or plants; **fragrance** a sweet pleasant smell, especially a delicate or subtle one; **stink** a strong unpleasant smell; **stench** a strong unpleasant smell, especially one associated with burning or decay; **reek** a strong unpleasant smell.

smelly *adj* **stinking**, reeking, foul, malodorous, putrid *Opposite*: fragrant

smelt *v* **1 melt**, melt down, liquefy, flux **2 found**, cast, produce, manufacture

smidge *(infml)* *see* smidgen

smidgen *(infml)* *n* **dash**, drop, bit, splash, morsel

smile *v* **grin**, beam, smirk, leer, sneer *Opposite*: frown ■ *n* **beam**, grin, smirk, leer *Opposite*: frown

smiley *adj* **smiling**, happy, cheery, sunny, cheerful *Opposite*: miserable ■ *n* **emoticon**, smiley face, symbol, sign-off *(US)*

smirk *n* **grin**, leer, sneer, simper ■ *v* **sneer**, leer, grin, simper

smithereens *(infml)* *n* **pieces**, bits, fragments, shards

smitten *(literary)* *adj* **in love**, besotted, enamoured, head over heels in love, infatuated *Opposite*: indifferent

smog *n* **pollution**, smoke, fog, haze

smoke *n* **fumes**, smog, poisonous gas, firedamp, chokedamp ■ *v* **burn**, be on fire, smoulder

smoke alarm *n* **smoke detector**, fire alarm, sensor

smoke detector *see* smoke alarm

smoke out *v* **1 drive out**, force out, turn out, eject, expel **2 bring in 2 bring to light**, reveal, expose, unearth, discover *Opposite*: conceal

smoker *n* **1 cigarette smoker**, pipe smoker, cigar smoker, chain-smoker, heavy smoker **2 smoking compartment**, smoking car, smoking carriage

smoke screen n **1 cloud of smoke**, wall of smoke, smoke **2 cover-up**, cover, camouflage, screen, mask

smoky adj **misty**, murky, cloudy, foggy, hazy Opposite: clear

smooch (infml) v **kiss**, cuddle, hug, hold each other close, caress ■ n **cuddle**, kiss, hug, caress, embrace

smooth adj **1 flat**, even, level, horizontal, plane Opposite: uneven **2 easy**, flowing, effortless, efficient **3 charming**, suave, persuasive, glib, silver-tongued Opposite: gauche **4 soft**, silky, downy, velvety, shiny Opposite: rough ■ v **flatten**, smooth out, level, iron, press Opposite: crumple

smooth down v **flatten**, iron out, paste down, smooth out, even out Opposite: scrunch

smoothie n **1** (infml) **charmer**, smooth talker, smooth character, fast talker, poser (infml) **2 drink**, fruit juice, milk shake, yogurt drink

smoothly adv **easily**, effortlessly, efficiently, well, slickly Opposite: awkwardly

smoothness n **1 flatness**, evenness, levelness Opposite: unevenness **2 ease**, effortlessness, efficiency Opposite: awkwardness **3 charm**, suaveness, persuasiveness, glibness, slickness **4 softness**, silkiness, velvetiness, sleekness Opposite: roughness

smooth out v **1 flatten**, iron out, paste down, smooth down, even out Opposite: crease **2 ease**, calm, defuse, soothe, smooth over Opposite: stir up

smooth over v **ease**, calm, defuse, soothe, smooth out Opposite: stir up

smooth talk n **flattery**, nonsense, rubbish, garbage, sweet talk (infml) Opposite: sincerity

smooth-tongued adj **smooth-talking**, silver-tongued, eloquent, persuasive, convincing

smoothy see smoothie

smother v **1 suffocate**, stifle, choke, asphyxiate **2 overwhelm**, overpower, oppress, suffocate, stifle **3 suppress**, repress, stifle, hold back, restrain Opposite: express

smoulder v **1 burn**, smoke, glow **2 fume**, seethe, glower, burn, boil **3 lurk**, fester, rumble, linger, persist

smudge n **blotch**, smear, stain, mark, splodge ■ v **smear**, blur, distort, blot, smirch

smug adj **self-satisfied**, superior, self-righteous, arrogant, conceited Opposite: humble

smuggle v **handle contraband**, traffic, run, sneak in, bring in

smugness n **complacency**, arrogance, self-satisfaction, conceit, self-righteousness Opposite: humility

smut n **1 obscenity**, dirt, filth, pornography, erotica **2 soot**, smudge, ash, grime, dirt

smutty adj **1 obscene**, dirty, pornographic, filthy, explicit **2 sooty**, smudged, grimy, dirty, grubby Opposite: pristine **3 crude**, foul-mouthed, indelicate, tasteless, loutish

snaffle (infml) v **steal**, rob, pilfer, pocket, take

snag n **problem**, hitch, difficulty, obstacle, hurdle Opposite: solution ■ v **catch**, rip, tear

snail mail (infml) n **postal service**, post, surface mail, airmail, mail

snake n **sea snake**, water snake, serpent (literary) ■ v **wind**, bend, twist, meander, turn

WORD BANK
❏ **types of non-poisonous snake** anaconda, blacksnake, boa, boa constrictor, garter snake, grass snake, king snake, python, rat snake, water snake, whip snake

❏ **types of poisonous snake** adder, asp, cobra, copperhead, coral snake, diamondback, fer-delance, horned viper, mamba, pit viper, puff adder, rattler, rattlesnake, ringhals, sea snake, sidewinder, taipan, viper, water moccasin

snaky adj **winding**, windy, bendy, twisting, meandering Opposite: straight

snap v **1 break**, crack, shatter, give way, come apart **2 retort**, bark, shout, yell, speak sharply **3 bite**, nip, bite at ■ adj **sudden**, spur-of-the-moment, impulsive, spontaneous, instant Opposite: considered

snappish adj **irritable**, snappy, bad-tempered, short-tempered, sharp Opposite: good-natured

snappy adj **1 irritable**, bad-tempered, short-tempered, sharp, curt Opposite: good-natured **2** (infml) **lively**, brisk, interesting, stimulating, to the point Opposite: dull **3 hasty**, quick, fast, speedy, rapid Opposite: slow **4** (infml) **stylish**, chic, fashionable, smart, elegant Opposite: dowdy

snapshot n **1 photo**, photograph, picture, snap, portrait **2 view**, glimpse, outline, idea, thumbnail sketch

snap up v **grab**, seize, pounce on, take up

snare n **trap**, noose, gin, lasso ■ v **catch**, trap, capture, ensnare, entrap

snarl v **1 growl**, roar, bellow **2 speak angrily**, bark, growl, snap, rasp

snarl up v **jam up**, back up, grind to a halt, come to a standstill, reach gridlock Opposite: free up

snarl-up n **blockage**, holdup, jam, traffic jam, logjam

snatch v **1 grab**, grasp, seize, take **2 steal**, run off with, pinch (infml), filch (infml), nick (slang)

snazzy (infml) adj **flashy**, bright, colourful, loud, ostentatious Opposite: drab

sneak v **1 slip**, steal, creep, slink, tiptoe **2 tell tales**, inform, tell, grass (slang), snitch (slang) ■ n **informer**, telltale, snitch (slang), grass (slang)

sneakiness n **slyness**, furtiveness, stealth, deviousness, cunning Opposite: openness

sneaking adj **niggling**, uneasy, nagging, uncomfortable, worrying

sneak preview n advance showing, premiere, preview, screening, advance screening

sneak thief n pickpocket, shoplifter, burglar, thief, robber

sneak up on v 1 creep up on, steal up on, come up on, come up behind, surprise 2 catch napping, catch unawares, take by surprise, surprise, creep up on

sneaky adj sly, devious, shifty, underhand, mean Opposite: honest

sneer v scorn, scoff, turn your nose up at, mock, deride

sneering adj scornful, contemptuous, disdainful, sarcastic, arrogant Opposite: admiring

sneeze n sniff, sniffle, snuffle, splutter, snort ■ v sniffle, sniff, snuffle, splutter, snort

snicker v whinny, neigh, snort, snuffle, bray

snide adj sarcastic, mean, unpleasant, malicious, spiteful Opposite: pleasant

sniff v 1 snuffle, breathe, inhale Opposite: exhale 2 smell, scent, get a whiff of, catch the scent of ■ n breath, snort, snuffle, lungful, inhalation

sniff at v turn your nose up at, sneer at, hold in contempt, look down on, scorn Opposite: accept

sniffle v 1 sniff, snuffle, snivel, snort, splutter 2 whimper, snivel, cry, weep, sob

sniff out (infml) v discover, find, unearth, track down, detect

sniffy (infml) adj contemptuous, haughty, disdainful, scornful, superior Opposite: humble

snifter (infml) n drink, nightcap, tot, splash, nip

snigger v laugh, smirk, mock, deride, sneer ■ n laugh, sneer, snort, snicker (US)

snip v cut, shear, slice, nick, trim ■ n (infml) bargain, good deal, good buy, steal (infml), giveaway (infml)

sniper n gunman, marksman, assassin, rifleman, shooter

snippet n extract, piece, bit, scrap

snippy (infml) adj irritable, snappy, grumpy, crabby, sharp Opposite: good-tempered

snivel v sob, sniff, cry, weep, whimper

snob n social climber, name-dropper, elitist

snobbery n arrogance, superciliousness, condescension, pretentiousness, conceit Opposite: humility

snobbish adj high and mighty, superior, arrogant, condescending, supercilious Opposite: humble

snobbishness see snobbery

snobby see snobbish

snooker (infml) v thwart, stymie, put paid to (infml), obstruct, hinder Opposite: assist

snoop (infml) v spy, poke around, watch, sneak, pry Opposite: mind your own business ■ n spy, sneak, meddler, intruder, eavesdropper

snooty (infml) adj 1 high and mighty, condescending, hoity-toity, supercilious, snobbish Opposite: humble 2 exclusive, select, posh (infml)

snooze (infml) v doze, sleep, doze off, nap, nod off Opposite: wake up ■ n sleep, doze, nap, catnap, siesta

snore v snort, breathe heavily, snuffle, wheeze

snorkel v swim, dive, scuba dive

snort v grunt, exhale, breathe out, inhale, draw in

snout n nose, muzzle, proboscis, schnozzle (US slang)

snow n sleet, snowflake, slush, hail, ice

snowball v increase, mount, balloon, swell, grow quickly Opposite: decrease

snowbound adj snowed in, snowed up, cut off, isolated, shut in

snowfall n snowstorm, blizzard, whiteout, flurry

snowstorm n blizzard, whiteout, snowfall, flurry

snow under v inundate, swamp, bury, overwhelm, overload

snowy adj snow-white, hoary, white

snub v ignore, coldshoulder, slight, look right through, cut Opposite: acknowledge ■ n rebuff, slight, rejection, rebuke, insult

snub-nosed adj button-nosed, pug-nosed, retroussé

snuff v 1 extinguish, put out, douse, snuff out, blow out Opposite: light 2 (infml) destroy, kill, eliminate, abolish, eradicate Opposite: save

snuffle v sniff, sniffle, snort, snivel, splutter ■ n snort, sniff, sniffle, snivel, splutter

snug adj 1 cosy, warm, comfortable, homely, inviting Opposite: uncomfortable 2 close, well-fitting, neat, close-fitting, tight Opposite: loose

snuggle v nestle, nuzzle, cuddle, burrow, huddle

so adv consequently, as a result, therefore, subsequently, accordingly

soak v 1 immerse, steep, marinate, infuse, saturate 2 drench, douse, saturate, wet, drown Opposite: dry out

soaked adj wet through, saturated, sodden, waterlogged, drenched Opposite: dry

soaking adj drenched, soaked, soaking wet, sopping wet, sopping Opposite: dry

so-and-so (infml) n whatchamacallit (infml), thingamajig (infml), thingummy (infml), thingamabob (infml), whatshisname (infml)

soap n 1 cleanser, detergent, shampoo, soap powder, washing powder 2 (infml) serial, soap opera, series, programme ■ v cleanse, lather, wash, wash down, shampoo

soap opera n serial, series, soap (infml)

soap powder *n* **detergent**, washing powder, soap, soapsuds, cleanser

soapsuds *n* **foam**, lather, suds, froth, bubbles

soar *v* **1 fly**, ascend, climb, wheel, circle *Opposite*: plummet **2 rise**, rocket, climb, mount, go through the roof *Opposite*: plummet

soaring *adj* **rising**, mounting, climbing, spiralling, increasing *Opposite*: plummeting

sob *v* **moan**, cry, weep, snivel, sniffle

sobbing *n* **crying**, weeping, howling, tears, snivelling

sober *adj* **1 abstemious**, clear-headed, temperate, teetotal, moderate **2 serious**, sombre, solemn, thoughtful, calm *Opposite*: frivolous **3 dull**, sombre, drab, dreary, staid *Opposite*: bright **4 rational**, judicious, level-headed, clear-headed, sensible *Opposite*: speculative

soberness *n* **1 seriousness**, solemnity, sombreness, gravity, glumness *Opposite*: frivolity **2 dullness**, sombreness, drabness, plainness, simplicity *Opposite*: brightness **3 rationality**, judiciousness, level-headedness, clear-headedness, lucidity

sobriety *n* **1 abstemiousness**, abstinence, temperance, moderation, soberness **2 seriousness**, sombreness, solemnity, thoughtfulness, calm *Opposite*: flippancy

sobriquet *n* **nickname**, pet name, term of endearment, alias, assumed name

sob story *(infml)* *n* **tale of woe**, hard-luck story, sorry tale, sad story

so-called *adj* **supposed**, alleged, ostensible, purported, self-styled

sociability *n* **1 gregariousness**, companionability, conviviality, hospitality **2 friendliness**, pleasantness, amiability, affability, geniality

sociable *adj* **1 gregarious**, companionable, convivial, good company, hospitable *Opposite*: retiring **2 friendly**, outgoing, amiable, warm, affable *Opposite*: unsociable

social *adj* **communal**, community, common, societal, public ■ *n* **party**, gathering, get-together *(infml)*, do *(infml)*

social climber *n* **hanger-on**, sycophant, toady, snob, socialite

socialism *n* **collectivism**, social democracy, public ownership, communism, communalism

socialist *n* **collectivist**, social democrat, communist, communalist

socialite *n* **trendsetter**, one of the beautiful people, one of the glitterati, member of café society, social climber

socialize *v* **meet people**, go out, get out, mix, mingle

socially *adv* **1 communally**, publicly, within society, generally, collectively **2 in public**, in a social context, with other people, in a crowd **3 as a friend**, outside of work, informally, on a social basis

societal *adj* **social**, group, shared, general, common

society *n* **1 civilization**, culture, humanity, the social order, the world **2 people**, the public, the general public, the populace, the population **3 association**, union, group, guild, league **4 high society**, the upper classes, polite society, the upper crust *(infml)*

sock *(infml)* *n* **hit**, punch, thump, whack, thwack ■ *v* **hit**, punch, thump, whack, thwack

socket *n* **1 hole**, opening, hollow **2 power point**, outlet, plug *(infml)*

sod *n* **turf**, clod, grass, earth

sodden *adj* **saturated**, soaking, soaked, soaking wet, sopping *Opposite*: dry

sofa *n* **settee**, couch, chaise longue, day bed, futon

so far *adv* **up to now**, thus far, hitherto, until now, to date

soft *adj* **1 yielding**, squashy, spongy, pliable, elastic *Opposite*: hard **2 smooth**, silky, supple, velvety *Opposite*: rough **3 low**, mellifluous, melodious, faint, muted *Opposite*: loud **4 gentle**, flowing, delicate, subtle, understated *Opposite*: harsh **5 dim**, diffused, mellow, subtle, gentle *Opposite*: bright **6 lenient**, lax, easy, forgiving, overindulgent *Opposite*: strict **7 tender**, sensitive, gentle, kind, sympathetic *Opposite*: hardhearted **8 wet**, spineless, weak, soppy *(infml)*, pathetic *(infml)*

soft-boiled *adj* **soft-hearted**, soft, sympathetic, sentimental, indulgent *Opposite*: hard-boiled *(infml)*

soften *v* **1 make softer**, relax, make pliable *Opposite*: harden **2 alleviate**, lessen, reduce, diminish, mitigate *Opposite*: exacerbate **3 moderate**, relax, temper, tone down, assuage

soft furnishings *n* **upholstery**, curtains, rugs, cushions, fabrics

soft-hearted *adj* **sympathetic**, kind, caring, warm, good-natured *Opposite*: hardhearted

softie *see* **softy**

softly *adv* **1 tenderly**, delicately, gently, kindly, sympathetically *Opposite*: severely **2 quietly**, gently, mellifluously, melodiously, faintly *Opposite*: harshly **3 dimly**, gently, lightly, subtly, faintly *Opposite*: brightly

softly-softly *adj* **cautious**, discreet, tentative, vigilant, mindful *Opposite*: heavy-handed

softness *n* **1 gentleness**, smoothness, quietness, faintness *Opposite*: harshness **2 pliability**, suppleness, flexibility, elasticity, malleability

soft-pedal *(infml)* *v* **play down**, downplay, make light of, underplay, minimize *Opposite*: emphasize

soft sell *(infml)* *n* **persuasion**, persuasiveness, subtlety, sweet-talking *(infml)*, soft-soaping *(infml)*

soft-soap (infml) v **flatter**, play up to, lay it on thick, sweet-talk (infml), butter up (infml)

soft-spoken adj **quiet**, gentle, calm, tranquil, serene Opposite: loud

soft spot n **weakness**, partiality, affection, weak spot, liking

soft touch n **easy prey**, easy target, pushover (infml), sucker (infml), softy (infml)

softy (infml) n **soft touch**, easy target, easy prey, sucker (infml)

soggy adj **damp**, wet, moist, mushy, squelchy Opposite: dry

soigné adj **well-groomed**, well turned-out, neat, elegant, chic Opposite: dowdy

soil n 1 **earth**, dirt, topsoil, mud, dust 2 **territory**, land, country, ground ■ v **dirty**, get dirty, foul, muddy, stain Opposite: cleanse

soiled adj **dirty**, grubby, muddy, stained, filthy Opposite: clean. See COMPARE AND CONTRAST at dirty.

soiree n **party**, celebration, dinner party, evening, gathering

soirée see **soiree**

sojourn (literary) n **visit**, stay, stop, stopover ■ v **stay**, stop, remain, dwell (literary), abide (archaic)

solace n **comfort**, consolation, support, relief, help Opposite: aggravation

solarium n **conservatory**, sun lounge, suntrap, greenhouse

solder v **join**, fuse, weld, bond, connect

soldier n 1 **fighter**, combatant, warrior, regular, legionnaire Opposite: noncombatant 2 **private**, sapper, gunner, corporal, sergeant 3 **worker**, supporter, campaigner, crusader, workhorse

soldier of fortune n **mercenary**, adventurer, hired gun (slang) Opposite: regular

soldier on v **persevere**, continue, carry on, keep on, keep going Opposite: give up

sole adj 1 **only**, solitary, single, individual, singular 2 **exclusive**, private, unique, special, individual

solecism n **error**, mistake, blunder, slip, gaffe

solely adv **exclusively**, only, merely, just, uniquely

solemn adj 1 **earnest**, sincere, serious, firm, grave Opposite: flippant 2 **sombre**, grave, serious, sober, sad Opposite: cheerful 3 **formal**, official, ceremonial, ritual, sacred

solemnity n **sombreness**, gravity, seriousness, soberness, sadness

solemnize v **celebrate**, honour, make official, formalize, sanctify

solicit v 1 **ask for**, beg, seek, petition for, plead for Opposite: grant 2 **ask**, petition, lobby, plead with, implore (fml)

solicitor n **lawyer**, advocate, legal representative, attorney (US)

solicitous adj **considerate**, caring, attentive, concerned, kind Opposite: uncaring

solicitousness n **concern**, attentiveness, consideration, care, kindness

solicitude n 1 **concern**, attentiveness, consideration, care, kindness Opposite: negligence 2 **anxiety**, concern, worry, unease, apprehension Opposite: serenity

solid adj 1 **hard**, rock-hard, rock-solid, concrete, firm Opposite: soft 2 **dense**, unbroken, continuous, closed, blocked Opposite: hollow 3 **pure**, genuine, unadulterated, one hundred per cent, unmixed 4 **sturdy**, strong, secure, firm, stable Opposite: weak 5 **unanimous**, universal, widespread, popular, general Opposite: patchy 6 **reliable**, dependable, sound, trustworthy, level-headed Opposite: unreliable ■ n 1 **object**, thing, artefact, item, entity 2 **figure**, pyramid, tetrahedron, sphere, icosahedron

solidarity n **unity**, harmony, cohesion, commonality, camaraderie Opposite: discord

solidify v **harden**, go hard, coagulate, congeal, set Opposite: dissolve

solidity n **hardness**, firmness, sturdiness, strength, toughness Opposite: softness

solidness see **solidity**

soliloquy n **monologue**, speech, declamation, oration, dramatic monologue

solitaire n **single stone**, gemstone, jewel, diamond, precious stone

solitary adj 1 **lone**, single, sole, individual, solo Opposite: accompanied 2 **private**, unsociable, unsocial, self-contained, self-sufficient Opposite: sociable 3 **isolated**, desolate, out-of-the-way, secluded, unfrequented

solitary confinement n **isolation**, imprisonment, confinement, detention, custody

solitude n **loneliness**, privacy, isolation, seclusion, separateness

solo adj **single**, unaccompanied, lone Opposite: joint ■ adv **alone**, on your own, singly, by yourself Opposite: together

soloist n **artist**, artiste, musician, singer, vocalist Opposite: accompanist

solubility n **dissolvability**, deliquescence Opposite: insolubility

soluble adj 1 **dissolvable**, deliquescent Opposite: insoluble 2 **solvable**, answerable, fathomable, resolvable, decipherable Opposite: insoluble

solution n 1 **answer**, key, explanation, resolution, way out Opposite: problem 2 **mix**, mixture, liquid, blend, cocktail

solvable adj **soluble**, resolvable, fathomable, answerable, decipherable Opposite: insoluble

solve v **resolve**, crack, answer, explain, get to the bottom of

solvency n **creditworthiness**, affluence, wealth, soundness, comfort Opposite: insolvency

solvent *adj* **in the black**, in credit, in funds, in the money, in clover *Opposite*: insolvent

sombre *adj* **1 depressing**, dull, gloomy, drab, dingy *Opposite*: bright **2 muted**, dark, dull, solemn, funereal *Opposite*: bright **3 depressed**, gloomy, sad, melancholy, funereal *Opposite*: cheerful

some *adv* **approximately**, about, around, roughly, more or less *Opposite*: exactly ■ *adj* **1 a number of**, a quantity of, a little, a few, several *Opposite*: all **2 certain**, particular, selected, specific

somebody *pron* **some person**, someone *Opposite*: nobody ■ *n* **celebrity**, someone, name, superstar, bigwig *(infml) Opposite*: nobody

someday *adv* **one day**, sooner or later, sometime, soon, in the future *Opposite*: never

somehow *adv* **one way or another**, someway, by hook or by crook, come what may, come hell or high water

someone *see* **somebody**

somersault *n* **tumble**, forward roll, flip-flop, cartwheel, flip ■ *v* **turn over**, tumble, flip over, cartwheel, flip

something *adv* **a little**, somewhat, to some degree, rather, slightly *Opposite*: completely

sometime *adv* **at some point**, someday, at some time, in the future, one day *Opposite*: never ■ *adj (fml)* **former**, onetime, previous, earlier, ex *(infml) Opposite*: current

sometimes *adv* **occasionally**, now and then, every now and then, every so often, now and again *Opposite*: always

someway *adv* **somehow**, one way or another, in some way, by some means, by hook or by crook

somewhat *adv* **rather**, fairly, slightly, to some extent, to a certain extent

somewhere *adv* **wherever**, anywhere, anyplace *(US infml)*, someplace *(US infml)*

somnolent *adj* **sleepy**, drowsy, dozy, half asleep, half awake

son *n* **child**, boy, kid *(infml)*

son et lumière *n* **entertainment**, spectacle, light show, tableau, spectacular

song *n* **1 tune**, melody, air, refrain, jingle **2 birdsong**, call, warble, warbling, cry

song and dance *(infml) n* **fuss**, drama, commotion, palaver, hysterics

songbook *n* **anthology**, collection, hymn book, book, hymnal

songster *n* **singer**, vocalist, lead singer, soloist, chanteuse

songwriter *n* **composer**, lyricist, songsmith, librettist

sonic *adj* **auditory**, aural, audible, sound

sonic boom *n* **boom**, shock wave, noise, rumble, roar

sonnet *n* **poem**, verse, rhyme

sonny *(infml) n* **lad**, young man, my boy, my lad, sonny boy *(infml)*

sonny boy *(infml) see* **sonny**

sonority *n* **resonance**, fullness, roundness, richness, reverberation

sonorous *adj* **loud**, deep, resonant, echoing, booming *Opposite*: thin

soon *adv* **almost immediately**, quickly, rapidly, shortly, presently *Opposite*: eventually

sooner *adv* **1 earlier**, faster, more quickly, more rapidly, nearer *Opposite*: later **2 rather**, more readily, more willingly, preferably, as soon *Opposite*: reluctantly

soot *n* **dust**, powder, grime, ashes, dirt

soothe *v* **1 ease**, relieve, alleviate, reduce, palliate *Opposite*: aggravate **2 calm**, pacify, quieten, appease, mollify *Opposite*: excite

soothing *adj* **calming**, comforting, restful, gentle, peaceful *Opposite*: irritating

soothsayer *n* **fortune-teller**, oracle, seer, astrologer, clairvoyant

sooty *adj* **dirty**, grimy, black, filthy, dusty *Opposite*: clean

sop *n* **concession**, offering, bribe, pacifier, gesture

sophisticate *v* **educate**, school, mould, acculturate, tutor ■ *n* **socialite**, trendsetter, connoisseur, aesthete, cognoscente *Opposite*: hoi polloi

sophisticated *adj* **1 urbane**, cultured, chic, erudite, refined *Opposite*: gauche **2 clever**, advanced, high-level, complex, erudite *Opposite*: crude

sophistication *n* **1 refinement**, style, chic, urbanity, elegance *Opposite*: naivety **2 complexity**, cleverness, erudition, difficulty, intricacy *Opposite*: crudeness

sophistry *n* **casuistry**, fallaciousness, illogicality, sophism, dishonesty *Opposite*: logic

soporific *adj* **1 sleep-inducing**, calming, tranquillizing, narcotic, hypnotic *(infml) Opposite*: energizing **2 tedious**, boring, interminable, turgid, endless *Opposite*: stimulating

sopping *adj* **drenched**, soaked, dripping, sodden, saturated *Opposite*: dry

soppy *adj* **1** *(infml)* **sentimental**, mawkish, soft, slushy, corny *Opposite*: unsentimental **2 soaked**, wet, sopping wet, sopping, dripping *Opposite*: dry

soprano *n* **singer**, vocalist, soloist, chanteuse, diva ■ *adj* **high**, high-pitched, shrill, piercing, soaring *Opposite*: bass

sop up *v* **soak up**, mop up, sponge, absorb, wipe

sorbet *n* **water ice**, fruit ice, ice, sherbet *(US)*

sorcerer *n* **wizard**, magician, enchanter, magus, witch

sorceress *n* **witch**, enchantress, sibyl, magician, necromancer *(literary)*

sorcery *n* **witchcraft**, wizardry, magic, black magic, enchantment

sordid *adj* **1 base**, disreputable, sleazy, repugnant, disgusting *Opposite*: uplifting **2 squalid**, distasteful, disgusting, low, dirty *Opposite*: pleasant

sordidness *n* **1 baseness**, sleaze, unpleasantness, repugnance, wretchedness *Opposite*: pleasantness **2 squalor**, grime, filth, squalidness, grubbiness *Opposite*: cleanliness

sore *adj* **1 painful**, uncomfortable, tender, stinging, aching *Opposite*: comfortable **2 annoying**, sensitive, embarrassing, controversial, difficult *Opposite*: uncontroversial **3** (*infml*) **angry**, cross, mad, annoyed, upset *Opposite*: pleased ■ *n* **wound**, abscess, lesion, eruption, blister

sorely (*fml*) *adv* **deeply**, truly, greatly, very much, really *Opposite*: not at all

soreness *n* **tenderness**, pain, discomfort, distress, agony

sorrow *n* **grief**, mourning, sadness, distress, sorrowfulness *Opposite*: joy

sorrowful *adj* **1 distressed**, sad, mournful, grief-stricken, unhappy *Opposite*: joyful **2 distressing**, tragic, sad, solemn, unhappy *Opposite*: happy

sorrowing *adj* **sad**, mournful, grief-stricken, distressed, unhappy *Opposite*: joyful

sorry *adj* **1 apologetic**, regretful, remorseful, repentant, sad *Opposite*: glad **2 pitiful**, miserable, wretched, forlorn, pathetic *Opposite*: fine

sort *n* **1 category**, kind, class, type, genus **2** (*infml*) **personality type**, person, character, type, individual ■ *v* **arrange**, classify, rank, place, sort out *Opposite*: mix up. *See* COMPARE AND CONTRAST *at* **type**.

sorted (*infml*) *adj* **organized**, arranged, in hand, under control, dealt with

sortie *n* **1 attack**, manoeuvre, foray, incursion, inroad *Opposite*: retreat **2 excursion**, trip, outing, journey, jaunt

sort out *v* **1 resolve**, deal with, solve, iron out, fix **2 put in order**, arrange, file, disentangle, tidy up *Opposite*: mix up **3 separate**, distinguish, segregate, sort, divide **4** (*infml*) **punish**, reprimand, scold, deal with, rebuke *Opposite*: reward

SOS *n* **distress signal**, cry for help, call for help, alarm, flare

so-so (*infml*) *adj* **average**, fair, mediocre, unremarkable, indifferent *Opposite*: exceptional

sought-after *adj* **desirable**, coveted, in demand, exclusive, fashionable *Opposite*: unpopular

souk *n* **bazaar**, market, marketplace, flea market, emporium

soul *n* **1 spirit**, consciousness, psyche, will, essence **2 depth**, personality, atmosphere, emotion, passion **3 individual**, person, anyone, someone, example **4 soul music**, gospel, R & B, rhythm and blues, blues

soul-destroying *adj* **demoralizing**, depressing, disheartening, unfulfilling, boring *Opposite*: uplifting

soulful *adj* **expressive**, affecting, sad, moving, poignant *Opposite*: emotionless

soulfulness *n* **expressiveness**, sadness, poignancy, emotion, mournfulness

soulless *adj* **bleak**, utilitarian, characterless, inexpressive, insensitive *Opposite*: soulful

soul mate *n* **friend**, mate, bosom friend, boon companion, confidant

soul-searching *n* **thought**, consideration, contemplation, introspection, assessment

sound *n* **1 noise**, resonance, hum, echo, thud *Opposite*: silence **2 strait**, channel, inlet, fjord ■ *v* **1 seem**, appear, look **2 go off**, ring out, explode, ring, wail **3 announce**, declare, signal, express, ring out ■ *adj* **1 whole**, healthy, unblemished, perfect, normal *Opposite*: infirm **2 sensible**, good, firm, unassailable, reliable *Opposite*: unsound **3 complete**, comprehensive, wide-ranging, all-encompassing, thorough *Opposite*: superficial **4 firm**, rigorous, good, hard, severe *Opposite*: half-hearted

WORD BANK

❏ **types of animal sound** baa, bark, bay, bleat, bray, caterwaul, croak, growl, grunt, howl, mew, miaow, moo, neigh, oink, purr, roar, snarl, squeak, squeal, whinny, woof, yap, yelp

❏ **types of bird sound** caw, cheep, chirp, chirrup, cluck, cock-a-doodle-doo, coo, hoot, peep, quack, screech, squawk, trill, tweet, twitter, warble

❏ **types of human sound** babble, bawl, bellow, boo, catcall, chatter, chortle, chuckle, cry, gasp, giggle, groan, grunt, howl, hum, moan, murmur, mutter, peep, scream, screech, shout, shriek, sigh, slurp, sniffle, snigger, splutter, squeal, titter, wail, wheeze, whimper, whine, whisper, whistle, whoop, yell

❏ **types of continuous sound** beep, bleep, boom, burble, buzz, chug, crackle, creak, drone, gurgle, hiss, honk, hoot, hum, purl (*literary*), purr, rasp, rattle, roar, rumble, rustle, sizzle, sonic boom, swish, swoosh, throb, thunder, toot, whirr, whiz, whoosh

❏ **types of impact sound** bang, beat, bong, bonk (*infml*), bump, clang, clank, clap, clash, clatter, click, clip-clop, clop, clunk, crack, crash, patter, pitter-patter, plop, plunk, pop, ratatat-tat, rattle, slam, smash, splash, splat, squelch, squish, tap, thud, thump, thwack, tick, ticktock, wham

❏ **types of ringing sound** chime, chink, clink, ding, ding-a-ling, ding-dong, honk, hoot, jangle, jingle, knell, peal, ping, pip, ring, ting, tinkle, toll, tootle (*infml*)

sound bite *n* **comment**, announcement, statement, declaration, response

sound effect *n* **sound**, recording, effect, special effect

sounding board *n* **confidant**, confidante, close friend, best friend, intimate

soundings *n* **enquiries**, investigations, research, surveys, market research

soundless *adj* **silent**, noiseless, still, quiet, mute *Opposite*: noisy

soundly *adv* **1 deeply**, well, like a log, peacefully, fast *Opposite*: fitfully **2 thoroughly**, roundly, severely, firmly, decisively

soundness *n* **1 wholeness**, completeness, health, healthiness, fitness *Opposite*: infirmity **2 reliability**, unassailability, security, accuracy, dependability *Opposite*: unreliability **3 completeness**, comprehensiveness, thoroughness, depth, range *Opposite*: superficiality **4 thoroughness**, firmness, severity, rigorousness *Opposite*: half-heartedness

sound off *(infml) v* **hold forth**, go on, have your say, speak up, speak out

sound out *v* **investigate**, test, explore, survey, look into

soundproof *adj* **impenetrable**, insulated, lined, padded, sealed ■ *v* **insulate**, line, seal, pad, protect

sound system *n* **hi-fi**, stereo, music centre, stereo system, audio system

soundtrack *n* **1 recording**, music, dialogue, sound, sound effects **2 music**, album, LP, tape, CD

soupçon *n* **hint**, touch, speck, morsel, modicum *Opposite*: surfeit

soup up *(infml) v* **boost**, enhance, tune up, modify, upgrade

sour *adj* **1 acid**, tart, bitter, acerbic, vinegary *Opposite*: sweet **2 bad**, rancid, off, curdled, fetid *Opposite*: fresh **3 bitter**, disagreeable, unpleasant, bad-tempered, resentful *Opposite*: agreeable ■ *v* **1 curdle**, go sour, go off, ferment, turn **2 taint**, ruin, harm, spoil, embitter *Opposite*: improve

source *n* **1 basis**, foundation, origin, cause, font **2 informant**, spokesperson, informer, supplier, stool pigeon *(slang)* **3 resource**, supply, fund, mine, well **4 natural spring**, upwelling, fount, fountain *Opposite*: estuary ■ *v* **obtain**, find, track down, trace, track. *See* COMPARE AND CONTRAST *at* origin.

sour grapes *n* **resentment**, jealousy, bitterness, ill feeling, envy

sourly *adv* **1 tartly**, bitterly, drily, acridly, acidly *Opposite*: sweetly **2 disagreeably**, unpleasantly, bitterly, resentfully, spitefully *Opposite*: agreeably

sourness *n* **1 acidity**, tartness, bitterness, tang, acridness *Opposite*: sweetness **2 bitterness**, resentment, acrimony, unpleasantness, hostility *Opposite*: pleasantness

sourpuss *(infml) n* **complainer**, grumbler, whiner, grouch *(infml)*, moaner *(infml)*

souse *v* **1 pickle**, marinade, soak, steep, preserve **2 soak**, steep, douse, saturate, immerse

souvenir *n* **memento**, reminder, keepsake, knick-knack, remembrance

sovereign *n* **monarch**, ruler, potentate, king, queen *Opposite*: subject ■ *adj* **1 independent**, autonomous, self-governing, free, self-determining **2 supreme**, dominant, ascendant, predominant, absolute **3 outstanding**, superior, supreme, excellent, matchless

sovereignty *n* **1 dominion**, control, rule, power, authority **2 independence**, autonomy, self-government, freedom, self-determination

sow *v* **spread**, propagate, disseminate, scatter, strew *Opposite*: reap

spa *n* **1 health resort**, thalassotherapy centre, sanatorium, health spa, health farm **2 whirlpool bath**, plunge pool, Turkish bath, sauna, hot tub

space *n* **1 solar system**, galaxy, outer space, deep space, universe **2 interval**, time, period, pause, window **3 area**, place, seat, bay, plot **4** *(infml)* **leeway**, freedom, autonomy, liberty, latitude ■ *v* **spread out**, move apart, space out, set apart

space-age *adj* **hi-tech**, automated, up-to-the-minute, state-of-the-art, new

space capsule *n* **spacecraft**, spaceship, rocket, capsule, vehicle

spacecraft *n* **spaceship**, space rocket, rocket, rocket ship *(US)*

WORD BANK
❑ **types of spacecraft** biosatellite, lander, launch vehicle, lunar module, multistage rocket, orbital space station, orbiter, rocket, rover, satellite, space capsule, spacelab, space probe, space rocket, space shuttle, space station
❑ **parts of a spacecraft** booster rocket, bus, cabin, command module, drogue parachute, footpad, grain, life-support system, nose cone, plasma engine, pod, retropack, rocket engine, shroud, solar cell, stage, thruster

spaceflight *n* **flight**, rocket flight, shuttle flight, space travel, orbiting

space platform *see* **space station**

space probe *n* **rover**, lander, spacecraft, satellite, probe

spacer *n* **insertion**, insert, piece, part, bar

spaceship *n* **1 space capsule**, space shuttle, lunar module, ship, capsule **2 flying saucer**, alien craft, UFO, unidentified flying object

space station *n* **space platform**, orbital space station, spacelab, extraterrestrial base

spacewalk *n* **extravehicular activity**, EVA, moonwalk

spacing *n* **1 space**, arrangement, layout, spaces, gaps **2 arranging**, positioning, placing, ordering, spacing out

spacious *adj* **roomy**, airy, large, open, expansive *Opposite*: cramped

spade *n* **garden spade**, shovel, scoop, snow shovel ■ *v* **dig**, shovel, scoop, excavate, fill in

spadework *n* **groundwork**, research, drudgery, preliminaries, preparatory work

spam *n* junk mail, unsolicited mail, mail, direct mail, junk *(infml)* ■ *v* e-mail, post, block, send, distribute

span *n* 1 distance, width, length, extent, area 2 time, duration, period, limit ■ *v* cross, cover, reach over, extend over, bridge

spangle *n* sequin, bead, bauble, star ■ *v* 1 sprinkle, stud, pepper, dot, spot 2 sparkle, glitter, shine, glisten, twinkle

spank *v* whack, smack, slap, hit, strike

spanking *n* smacking, smack, slap, thrashing, beating ■ *adj* 1 remarkable, excellent, outstanding, wonderful, marvellous *Opposite*: ordinary 2 vigorous, brisk, rapid, fast, lively *Opposite*: weak

spar *n* pole, arm, boom, mast, rod ■ *v* 1 scuffle, fight, box, exchange blows, scrap 2 argue, fence, dispute, squabble, bicker *Opposite*: agree

spare *v* 1 show mercy to, free, release, save, pardon *Opposite*: condemn 2 afford, do without, get by without, manage without, give up *Opposite*: need ■ *adj* 1 replacement, extra, auxiliary, additional, emergency *Opposite*: main 2 sparse, thin, mean, insubstantial, frugal *Opposite*: abundant

spare part *n* reserve, extra, stand-by, part, replacement

spare time *n* free time, leisure time, time off, downtime *(US)*

sparing *adj* 1 frugal, parsimonious, economical, careful, thrifty *Opposite*: generous 2 meagre, sparse, limited, restricted, insufficient *Opposite*: plentiful

spark *n* 1 flash, flicker, sparkle, arc, glint 2 stimulus, catalyst, incentive, spur, trigger ■ *v* 1 sparkle, flicker, glimmer, glint, glow 2 generate, produce, inspire, initiate, set off

sparkle *v* 1 shine, glitter, glisten, flash, flicker 2 fizzle, bubble, fizz, ferment, effervesce 3 excel, scintillate, shine, come into your own, come to life ■ *n* 1 life, vivacity, energy, enthusiasm, gusto *Opposite*: apathy 2 effervescence, carbonation, bubbles, aeration, gassiness

sparkler *(infml)* *n* gem, diamond, gemstone, jewel, precious stone

sparkling *adj* 1 glittering, glistening, twinkling, iridescent, spangled *Opposite*: dull 2 vivacious, witty, brilliant, scintillating, vibrant *Opposite*: dull 3 fizzy, effervescent, carbonated, bubbly, aerated *Opposite*: still

sparkly *see* sparkling

spark off *v* generate, produce, inspire, initiate, set off

sparky *adj* lively, spirited, enthusiastic, bubbly, feisty *(infml)* *Opposite*: lifeless

sparring partner *n* opponent, adversary, sworn enemy, counterpart, opposite number

sparse *adj* thin, spare, scant, light, scarce *Opposite*: dense

sparseness *n* thinness, scarceness, scarcity, meagreness, bareness

spartan *adj* frugal, simple, basic, bare, severe *Opposite*: luxurious

spasm *n* shudder, contraction, seizure, ripple, paroxysm

spasmodic *adj* fitful, irregular, intermittent, occasional, sporadic *Opposite*: continuous

spat *n* quarrel, fight, row, argument, tiff

spate *n* flood, rash, epidemic, wave, sequence

spatial *adj* three-dimensional, 3-D, longitudinal, latitudinal, altitudinal

spatter *v* 1 shower, spray, sprinkle, scatter, splash 2 spray, splatter, shower, mark, splash

spawn *n* 1 roe, frogspawn, fish eggs, eggs, seed 2 brood, issue, offspring, progeny, young ■ *v* 1 lay, deposit, produce 2 reproduce, give birth, procreate, breed, hatch 3 create, generate, produce, initiate, set off

spay *v* neuter, sterilize, castrate, operate on, geld

speak *v* 1 chatter, talk, verbalize, articulate, chat *Opposite*: shut up *(infml)* 2 say, tell, express, state, voice 3 be fluent in, converse in, speak a language 4 address, lecture, preach, give a talk, give a lecture

speaker *n* 1 utterer, chatterer, reciter, talker 2 orator, lecturer, narrator, spokesman, spokeswoman

speak for *v* speak on behalf of, represent, act on behalf of, stand for, argue for

speaking *n* speech, language, communication, discourse, talking

speak out *v* 1 be frank, speak your mind, say your piece, have your say, speak up *Opposite*: equivocate 2 talk loudly, raise your voice, exclaim, shout, speak up *Opposite*: mutter

speak to *v* 1 get in touch with, contact, approach, talk to, address 2 reprimand, discipline, reprove, talk to, have a word with 3 *(fml)* discuss, consider, go into, deal with, address

speak up *v* 1 speak out, exclaim, talk loudly, raise your voice, shout *Opposite*: mutter 2 be frank, speak your mind, say your piece, have your say, protest *Opposite*: equivocate

speak up for *v* support, back, argue for, defend, approve *Opposite*: attack

speak your mind *v* be frank, not beat about the bush, speak up, speak out, make yourself heard *Opposite*: equivocate

spear *n* lance, spike, javelin, assegai, harpoon ■ *v* impale, spike, stab, pierce, gouge

spearhead *n* driving force, forefront, head, lead, leader ■ *v* lead, front, head, organize, direct

special *adj* 1 superior, distinct, different, exceptional, distinctive *Opposite*: ordinary 2 individual, specific, particular, distinct, one *Opposite*: general

special consideration n dispensation, concession, allowance, indulgence, preference

special delivery n express, courier, premium rate, overnight delivery, registered post

special education n special needs education, literacy tuition, numeracy tuition, specialist tuition, specialist support

special effects n effects, FX, computer graphics, lighting, morphing

specialism n 1 specialization, narrowing down, concentration, focusing in, gaining expertise 2 speciality, area of expertise, subject, sphere, forte

specialist n authority, expert, consultant, doyen, whiz (infml)

speciality n specialism, area of expertise, subject, sphere, forte

specialization n 1 narrowing down, concentration, focusing in, gaining expertise, gaining in-depth knowledge Opposite: diversification 2 adaptation, change, mutation, selection, evolution

specialize v concentrate, focus, dedicate yourself to, major in Opposite: diversify

specialized adj particular, dedicated, focused, specific, expert Opposite: generalized

specially adv 1 particularly, in particular, especially, specifically, expressly Opposite: generally 2 personally, individually, to order

species n class, type, kind, sort, genus. See COMPARE AND CONTRAST at type.

specific adj 1 exact, precise, detailed, explicit, definite Opposite: vague 2 particular, peculiar, exclusive, special, restricted Opposite: general 3 distinctive, particular, express, identifiable, certain Opposite: indefinite ■ n detail, particular, aspect, feature, fact Opposite: generality

specification n requirement, condition, plan, order, arrangement

specified adj 1 stated, quantified, definite, spelt out, detailed Opposite: unstated 2 stipulated, required, postulated, restricted, insisted on Opposite: optional

specify v 1 state, identify, spell out, detail, give Opposite: suggest 2 stipulate, agree, lay down, postulate, require

specious adj false, hollow, erroneous, baseless, inaccurate Opposite: valid

speciousness n falsity, hollowness, inaccuracy, falseness, deceptiveness Opposite: validity

speck n 1 dot, fleck, spot, dab, blob 2 particle, fragment, crumb, iota, scrap ■ v dot, fleck, spot, speckle, stipple

speckle n fleck, mark, speck, spot, dot ■ v mark, fleck, dust, stipple, dot

speckled adj spotted, freckled, dotted, stippled, dappled

specs (infml) see spectacles

spectacle n 1 sight, scene, vision, marvel, phenomenon 2 display, show, demonstration, exhibition, event

spectacles n glasses, goggles, specs (infml)

spectacular adj 1 stunning, impressive, amazing, fantastic, fabulous Opposite: humdrum 2 remarkable, huge, great, enormous, mighty Opposite: unimpressive ■ n show, display, performance, extravaganza, special

spectacularly adv extremely, enormously, hugely, monumentally, prodigiously Opposite: mildly

spectate v watch, look on, observe, take in, look Opposite: participate

spectator n viewer, watcher, observer, onlooker, bystander Opposite: participant

spectral adj ghostly, phantom, ethereal, supernatural, ghostlike Opposite: real

spectre n 1 ghost, apparition, phantom, spirit, spook 2 threat, menace, shadow, danger, possibility

spectrum n range, band, field, gamut, variety

speculate v 1 wonder, guess, conjecture, hypothesize, reason 2 consider, contemplate, reflect on, ponder, deliberate Opposite: decide 3 gamble, take risks, hazard, risk, venture

speculation n conjecture, rumour, opinion, gossip, assumption Opposite: fact

speculative adj 1 tentative, approximate, rough, exploratory, provisional Opposite: definite 2 hypothetical, notional, theoretical, academic, abstract Opposite: proven 3 dangerous, risky, unpredictable, uncertain, dicey (infml) Opposite: safe

speculator n risk-taker, investor, entrepreneur, opportunist, adventurer

speech n 1 language, talking, verbal communication, dialogue, words 2 tongue, idiom, dialect, vernacular, native tongue 3 lecture, oration, sermon, talk, homily

speechify (infml) v pontificate, lecture, pronounce, preach, hold forth

speechless adj astonished, astounded, amazed, dumbstruck, wordless

speechmaker n speaker, orator, raconteur, preacher, lecturer

speed n 1 pace, rate, velocity, momentum, tempo 2 haste, hurry, swiftness, speediness, hustle Opposite: slowness ■ v race, fly, zoom, break the speed limit, drive too fast Opposite: crawl

speedily adv quickly, promptly, soon, hastily, hurriedly Opposite: slowly

speediness n 1 quickness, promptness, hastiness, rapidity, speed Opposite: slowness 2 fastness, swiftness, nimbleness, rapidness, fleetness (literary) Opposite: sluggishness

speeding adj fast-moving, hurtling, flying, moving, fast Opposite: slow

speed limit n maximum speed, top speed, permitted speed, limit, restriction

speedometer n speedo, clock, gauge, recorder

speed-read v skim, scan, read

speed trap n radar trap, police trap, traffic control

speed up v accelerate, get faster, get moving, get going, hurry up Opposite: slow down

speedway n track, course, circuit, racetrack

speedy adj 1 quick, immediate, prompt, early, fast Opposite: slow 2 fast-moving, speeding, swift, nimble, fast Opposite: slow

spell v signify, mean, bring, predict, imply ▪ n 1 incantation, curse, enchantment, hex, evil eye 2 influence, fascination, thrall, glamour, enchantment 3 (infml) bout, interlude, stretch, session, time period

spellbinding adj mesmerizing, enthralling, entrancing, fascinating, captivating Opposite: boring

spellbound adj enthralled, fascinated, awestruck, rapt, captivated Opposite: distracted

spell-check v check, check over, check through, correct, proofread

spell out v make obvious, explain in simple terms, make clear, explain, interpret Opposite: obfuscate

spend v 1 use, use up, waste, fritter, squander Opposite: save 2 devote, apply, employ, fill, occupy 3 pay, expend, pay out, splurge, lay out

spending n expenditure, expenses, costs, payments, outgoings Opposite: earnings

spending money n cash, money, ready cash, pin money, pocket money Opposite: savings

spendthrift n wastrel, squanderer, waster, prodigal, profligate Opposite: miser ▪ adj wasteful, extravagant, improvident, prodigal, reckless Opposite: miserly

spent adj 1 exhausted, tired, washed-out, worn-out, shattered Opposite: fresh 2 consumed, used up, expended, paid, paid out Opposite: saved 3 finished, over, done, completed, over and done with Opposite: new

sperm n 1 semen, seed, ejaculate 2 cell, gamete, spermatozoon

spermatozoon n sperm, cell, gamete

spew v 1 disgorge, discharge, vomit, send out, churn out 2 pour out, pour forth, gush, flow, stream Opposite: dribble ▪ n vomit, sick (infml), puke (slang)

sphere n 1 ball, globe, orb, bubble 2 area, speciality, subject, field, area of interest 3 sphere of influence, compass, scope, range, domain

spherical adj sphere-shaped, globular, rotund, circular, round

sphinxlike adj enigmatic, mysterious, cryptic, bemusing, baffling Opposite: transparent

spice n 1 seasoning, flavouring, additive 2 interest, excitement, flavour, colour, a little something Opposite: blandness ▪ v 1 season, flavour, enhance, lace 2 enliven, liven up,

ginger up, lace, add zest to Opposite: tone down

WORD BANK

❏ **types of spice** allspice, aniseed, black pepper, caraway seed, cardamom, cayenne pepper, chilli, cinnamon, clove, coriander, cumin, fenugreek, ginger, ginseng, mace, mustard, nutmeg, paprika, pepper, peppercorn, saffron, turmeric, white pepper

---

spick-and-span adj 1 tidy, clean, neat, immaculate, spotless Opposite: untidy 2 in perfect condition, immaculate, as new, in tiptop condition, in mint condition Opposite: used

spicy adj hot, spiced, curried, piquant, peppery Opposite: mild

spidery adj 1 thin, spindly, angular, squiggly, jerky Opposite: bold 2 gangling, spindly, lanky, skinny, thin Opposite: plump

spiel (infml) n patter, speech, lecture, talk, waffle (infml) ▪ v prattle, pitch, go on, hold forth, jabber

spigot n stopper, plug, bung, cork, peg 2 projection, end, tip, point, spike

spike n point, barb, spear, thorn, spine ▪ v 1 spear, impale, pierce, skewer, run through (literary) 2 (infml) thwart, confound, frustrate, dash, quash Opposite: foster

spiked adj spiky, sharp, pointed, hobnailed, jagged Opposite: smooth

spiky adj prickly, thorny, sharp, bristly, spiny Opposite: smooth

spill v slop, drip, leak, trickle, dribble Opposite: absorb ▪ n 1 leak, spillage, escape, discharge, overflow 2 (infml) tumble, fall, roll, trip, stumble

spillage n 1 spilling, spill, discharge, emission, leak 2 wastage, waste, loss, spill, slick

spill over v 1 overflow, brim over, leak out, run over, spill out 2 spread, extend, overflow, advance, creep

spill the beans (infml) v let the cat out of the bag, give the game away, tell, confess, let on Opposite: keep secret

spin v turn, rotate, revolve, gyrate, whirl ▪ n 1 gyration, rotation, turn, whirl 2 drive, outing, run, trip, jaunt 3 (infml) point of view, viewpoint, slant, angle, bias

spinal adj back, backbone, vertebral

spinal column n spine, back, backbone, vertebrae, vertebral column

spindle n 1 rod, bar, shaft, axle, pole 2 leg, baluster, support, vertical, upright

spindly adj skinny, gangly, lanky, thin, frail Opposite: sturdy

spin doctor (infml) n PR expert, propagandist, publicist, representative, marketing expert

spindrift n spray, sea spray, foam, mist, vapour

spine n spinal column, vertebral column, backbone, back, vertebra

spine-chilling adj **bloodcurdling**, chilling, terrifying, petrifying, frightening Opposite: comforting

spineless adj **gutless**, cowardly, weak, timid, spiritless Opposite: courageous. See COMPARE AND CONTRAST at **cowardly**.

spinelessness n **weakness**, gutlessness, cowardice, feebleness, faint-heartedness Opposite: courage

spine-tingling adj **hair-raising**, thrilling, frightening, gripping, exciting Opposite: soothing

spinner n **rotator**, whirler, whirligig, turner, gyrator

spinney n **wood**, thicket, copse, coppice, grove

spin-off v **derive**, result, develop, grow, follow on ■ n **by-product**, derivative, offshoot, extra, bonus

spin out v **drag out**, prolong, keep going, draw out, eke out Opposite: cut

spiny adj **barbed**, prickly, spiky, bristly, thorny Opposite: smooth

spiral v 1 **escalate**, increase, get worse, run away, rise Opposite: plummet 2 **fly**, rise, ascend, descend, soar

spire n **tip**, spike, pinnacle, point, top Opposite: base

spirit n 1 **soul**, inner self, life force, chi, essence Opposite: body 2 **will**, strength, courage, character, strength of mind 3 **disposition**, temperament, attitude, nature, temper 4 **feeling**, attitude, mood, tendency, atmosphere 5 **ghost**, soul, ghoul, phantom, apparition ■ v **remove**, take away, whisk off, steal, abduct

spirited adj **forceful**, determined, strong-willed, vigorous, energetic Opposite: lacklustre

spiritless adj **spineless**, gutless, cowardly, sad, dejected Opposite: energetic

spirits n **emotional state**, frame of mind, state of mind, mental state, feelings

spiritual adj 1 **religious**, holy, sacred, divine, heavenly Opposite: secular 2 **mental**, emotional, psychological, temperamental, internal Opposite: physical

spiritualist n **medium**, clairvoyant, seer, psychic, mystic

spirituality n **holiness**, sanctity, religiousness, otherworldliness, unworldliness

spit v 1 **expectorate**, splutter, hawk, expel, gob (slang) Opposite: swallow 2 **sputter**, sizzle, pop, spatter, spurt 3 **utter**, splutter, hiss, mutter, say 4 **rain**, shower, drizzle, mizzle, sprinkle (US) 5 **impale**, skewer, spear, spike, run through (literary) ■ n 1 **saliva**, spittle, sputum, dribble 2 **skewer**, rotisserie, brochette, rod, broach

spit and polish (infml) n **meticulousness**, tidiness, cleanliness, orderliness, neatness

spite n **malice**, ill will, ill feeling, vindictiveness, meanness Opposite: goodwill

spiteful adj **malicious**, vindictive, mean, nasty, vicious Opposite: kind

spitefulness see **spite**

spitting image (infml) n **double**, twin, clone, image, spit Opposite: opposite

spittle n **saliva**, spit, sputum, dribble

splash v 1 **plop**, slop, spatter, spray, slap 2 **splatter**, get water on, wet, dash, spray Opposite: dab 3 **wallow**, wade, plop, flap, flop Opposite: glide

splashy adj 1 **gaudy**, garish, bright, bold, colourful Opposite: drab 2 (infml) **showy**, ostentatious, flamboyant, flashy, bold Opposite: restrained

splat n **smack**, splash, plop, slop, slap

splatter v **splash**, spatter, bespatter, dash, spray

splay v 1 **spread**, spread out, spread wide, open, open out Opposite: close up 2 **turn out**, turn outwards, twist, bend, distort ■ adj **outspread**, splayed, splayed-out, spread, spread-out ■ n **slope**, bevel, slant, angle, incline

spleen n **ill temper**, anger, irritation, annoyance, grumpiness Opposite: contentment

splendid adj 1 **magnificent**, grand, superb, impressive, fine Opposite: unimpressive 2 **excellent**, marvellous, wonderful, fabulous, great

splendiferous adj **magnificent**, splendid, superlative, wonderful, superb Opposite: abysmal

splendour n 1 **magnificence**, glory, grandeur, brilliance, impressiveness Opposite: drabness 2 **wonder**, marvel, glory, triumph, miracle

splenetic adj **bad-tempered**, spiteful, irritable, peevish, waspish Opposite: good-tempered

splice v **join**, intertwine, interweave, merge, fix together Opposite: split ■ n **seam**, join, connection, link, joint

spline n 1 **key**, tooth, blade, fin, projection 2 **connecting strip**, connector, connection, joining strip, link

splint v **immobilize**, strap, bind, bandage, secure

splinter n **fragment**, particle, piece, shard, sliver ■ v **fall apart**, crack, disintegrate, come apart, break up Opposite: mend

splinter group n **faction**, sect, offshoot, subset, minority

split v 1 **divide**, rip, tear, crack, come apart Opposite: join 2 **cause a rift in**, breach, divide, partition ■ n 1 **tear**, hole, rip, crack, fissure 2 **difference**, breach, breakup, divergence, rift Opposite: reconciliation 3 **splitting**, ripping, tearing, cracking, rupture 4 **crack**, division, rift, rent, break. See COMPARE AND CONTRAST at **tear**.

split hairs v **quibble**, equivocate, be pedantic, argue, mince matters

split-level *adj* two-tier, twin-tier, twin-level, two-level

split on *(infml) v* inform, tell on, give away, blow the whistle on, betray *Opposite*: protect

split second *n* instant, moment, flash, the twinkling of an eye, second

split-second *adj* instant, instantaneous, immediate, prompt, high-speed *Opposite*: tardy

splitting *adj* excruciating, unbearable, piercing, intense, severe *Opposite*: slight

split up *v part*, break up, split, go your separate ways, end things *Opposite*: unite

split-up *n* breakup, separation, dissolution, ending, divorce *Opposite*: marriage

splodge *see* splotch

splotch *n* spot, stain, mark, blot, blotch ▪ *v* mark, stain, spot, blemish, blot

splurge *v* 1 spend, fritter, waste, squander, run through *Opposite*: save 2 *(infml)* indulge, binge, wallow, spoil, treat ▪ *n* 1 *(infml)* bout, spree, binge, orgy, session 2 *(infml)* display, exhibition, show, parade, demonstration

splutter *v* choke, gasp, cough, spit, stutter

spoil *v* 1 ruin, blemish, blot, blight, impair *Opposite*: improve 2 indulge, pander to, be soft on, pamper, cosset *Opposite*: neglect 3 decay, go rotten, rot, go bad, go off

spoilage *n* 1 decay, rot, decomposition, degeneration, putrefaction 2 waste, wastage, loss, leakage, spillage

spoiled *adj* 1 ruined, damaged, decayed, rotted, rotten *Opposite*: fresh 2 overindulged, ruined, wilful, self-centred, brattish *Opposite*: neglected

spoils *n* 1 plunder, loot, booty, haul, pickings 2 reward, prize, gain, profit, earnings

spoilsport *n* killjoy, stuffed shirt, dog in the manger, curmudgeon, wet blanket *(infml)*

spoilt *see* spoiled

spoke *n* 1 rod, bar, rib, strut, shaft 2 rung, step, foothold, strut, bar

spoken *adj* verbal, vocal, oral, articulated, vocalized *Opposite*: written. *See* COMPARE AND CONTRAST *at* verbal.

spokesperson *n* representative, speaker, voice, spokesman, spokeswoman

sponge *n (infml)* parasite, hanger-on, idler, user, sponger *(infml)* ▪ *v* clean, wipe, wash, rub, mop

sponger *(infml) n* parasite, hanger-on, idler, user, scrounger *(infml) Opposite*: donor

spongy *adj* 1 soft, springy, malleable, elastic, flexible *Opposite*: firm 2 absorbent, porous, osmotic, permeable, penetrable *Opposite*: impermeable 3 soggy, squishy, moist, sodden, waterlogged *Opposite*: dry

sponsor *n* backer, guarantor, patron, promoter, champion ▪ *v* back, support, pay for, subsidize, fund. *See* COMPARE AND CONTRAST *at* backer.

sponsorship *n* backing, support, protection, patronage, funding

spontaneity *n* impulsiveness, naturalness, artlessness, extemporaneity, freedom *Opposite*: constraint

spontaneous *adj* impulsive, unprompted, spur-of-the-moment, natural, artless *Opposite*: planned

spoof *n* 1 hoax, prank, deception, trick, bluff 2 parody, satire, skit, burlesque, caricature ▪ *v* 1 deceive, fool, trick, bluff, hoax 2 satirize, burlesque, parody, caricature, take off *(infml)*

spook *n* 1 spy, mole, double agent, sleuth *(infml)*, snoop *(infml)* 2 *(infml)* ghost, wraith, phantom, spectre, apparition ▪ *v* startle, surprise, shock, alarm, agitate *Opposite*: soothe

spooky *adj* 1 strange, amazing, odd, unnerving, extraordinary *Opposite*: normal 2 *(infml)* frightening, ghostly, unnerving, mysterious, eerie *Opposite*: reassuring

spool *n* reel, coil, pin, bobbin ▪ *v* wind, reel, coil, roll

spoon *v* serve, ladle, spoon over, spoon out, serve up

spoonerism *n* slip of the tongue, mistake, error, Freudian slip, tongue twister

spoon-feed *v* 1 feed, nourish, take care of, look after, care for *Opposite*: neglect 2 mollycoddle, coddle, overindulge, wait on hand and foot, do everything for *Opposite*: neglect

spoonful *n* spoon, portion, serving, teaspoonful, dessertspoonful

spoor *n* trail, track, paw prints, hoof marks, footmarks ▪ *v* track, stalk, follow, trail, hunt

sporadic *adj* irregular, intermittent, infrequent, periodic, erratic *Opposite*: regular. *See* COMPARE AND CONTRAST *at* periodic.

spore *n* reproductive structure, dormant bacterium, bacterium, microorganism

sporran *n* pouch, purse, bag

sport *n* 1 diversion, game, amusement, hobby, pastime *Opposite*: work 2 *(fml)* joking, clowning, teasing, fooling around, fooling about ▪ *v (infml)* wear, don, display, exhibit, show off

WORD BANK

❏ **types of ball game** American football, Australian Rules, baseball, basketball, cricket, football, hockey, hurling, lacrosse, netball, polo, rounders, rugby, Rugby League, Rugby Union, shinty, softball, water polo

❏ **types of combat sport** aikido, boxing, fencing, judo, karate, kendo, kickboxing, kung fu, sumo, tae kwon do, wrestling

❏ **types of court game** badminton, jai alai, pelota, rackets, squash, table tennis, tennis, volleyball

❏ **types of extreme sport** barefoot waterskiing, basejumping, bungee jumping, in-line skating, mountain biking, mountain boarding, skateboarding, skysurfing, sport climbing, street luge, stunt bicycling, wakeboarding

❏ **types of sports equipment** ball, bat, bowl, club,

cue, discus, football, glove, helmet, hockey stick, javelin, lacrosse stick, mallet, mitt, pad, puck, racket, shot, shuttlecock, spikes, tee, wicket ❑ **types of target ball game** billiards, boules, bowling, bowls, croquet, golf, pool, snooker ❑ **types of track and field** cross-country, decathlon, discus, hammer throw, heptathlon, high jump, javelin, long jump, marathon, modern pentathlon, pole vault, relay race, shot put, sprint, steeple-chase, triathlon, triple jump ❑ **types of winter sport** alpine skiing, biathlon, bobsleigh, cross-country skiing, curling, downhill, figure skating, ice dancing, ice hockey, langlauf, Nordic skiing, skiing, ski jump, slalom, snow-boarding, speed skating, toboggan, XC skiing

sporting *adj* fair, generous, honourable, decent, honest *Opposite*: dishonest

sporting chance *n* fair chance, good chance, decent chance, fair shot, reasonable chance

sports *adj* 1 sporting, games, athletic 2 casual, informal, leisure, outdoor, leisurewear

sportscast *n* sports broadcast, sports update, sports programme, televised sports event, televised match

sportscaster *n* sports broadcaster, sports presenter, sports commentator, sports reporter, sports correspondent

sports ground *n* stadium, arena, pitch, field, ground

sportsperson *n* competitor, player, contestant, athlete

sporty *adj* 1 athletic, active, good at sport, fit, muscular *Opposite*: lazy 2 flashy, stylish, jaunty, natty, snazzy *(infml) Opposite*: formal

spot *n* 1 mark, blemish, stain, smudge, speck 2 *(infml)* predicament, mess, difficulty, awkward situation, quandary 3 pimple, pustule, boil, blackhead, whitehead 4 place, location, site, setting, corner 5 bit, soupçon, touch, dash, tad *(infml)* 6 advertisement, commercial, promotion, ad *(infml)*, advert *(infml)* ■ *v* 1 notice, spy, recognize, catch a glimpse of, catch sight of *Opposite*: miss 2 stain, dirty, blemish, smudge, speck *Opposite*: clean

spot check *n* inspection, check, search, examination, visit

spot-check *v* inspect, check, search, examine, double-check

spotless *adj* 1 immaculate, spick-and-span, clean, clean as a new pin, pristine *Opposite*: dirty 2 unblemished, flawless, perfect, faultless, impeccable *Opposite*: flawed

spotlessly *adv* immaculately, extremely, perfectly, absolutely, very

spotlessness *n* 1 cleanliness, cleanness, pristineness, immaculateness, neatness *Opposite*: dirtiness 2 flawlessness, wholesomeness, innocence, stainlessness, irreproachability *Opposite*: imperfection

spotlight *n* attention, limelight, fuss, focus, interest *Opposite*: anonymity ■ *v* highlight, point up, draw attention to, underline, focus on *Opposite*: obscure

spot-on *(infml) adj* 1 exactly right, dead right, bang on *(infml)*, accurate, correct *Opposite*: wrong 2 ideal, just right, perfect, just what we need, just what the doctor ordered *Opposite*: disastrous

spotted *adj* dotted, marked, speckled, dappled, mottled *Opposite*: plain

spotty *adj* 1 mottled, patterned, blotchy, spotted, dotted 2 blemished, pockmarked, covered with spots, pimpled, pimply *Opposite*: unblemished

spouse *n* other half, wife, husband, next of kin, partner

spout *v* 1 spew out, shoot out, discharge, spurt, emit *Opposite*: retain 2 talk, utter, pontificate, ramble on, sermonize ■ *n* 1 jet, fountain, stream, column, spurt 2 tube, pipe, nozzle, outlet, spray

sprain *v* twist, pull, injure, rick, strain

sprawl *v* 1 slump, collapse, lounge, loll, slouch *Opposite*: curl up 2 spread out, cover, extend over, stretch over, trail *Opposite*: shrink ■ *n* stretch, mass, extension, spread, straggle

sprawling *adj* extensive, rambling, expansive, straggling, straggly *Opposite*: contained

spray *n* 1 gush, squirt, mist, jet, fountain 2 atomizer, aerosol, spray can, pump dispenser, sprayer 3 sprig, bouquet, stem, posy, buttonhole ■ *v* 1 scatter, squirt, send out, spew, spurt 2 cover, drench, squirt, mist, dose

spray can *n* aerosol, atomizer, spray, pump dispenser, sprayer

spray gun *n* spray, atomizer, airbrush, sprayer, diffuser

spread *v* 1 open out, unfold, place, lay out, put out *Opposite*: furl 2 increase, extend, multiply, reach, stretch *Opposite*: shrink 3 last, continue, go on, carry on, persist 4 broadcast, disseminate, circulate, publish, propagate 5 apply, put on, smear, daub, butter *Opposite*: remove 6 disperse, distribute, share out, allot, divide *Opposite*: collect ■ *n* 1 range, extent, increase, coverage, span 2 variety, range, selection, array, assortment 3 ranch, estate, farm, plantation, station 4 *(infml)* feast, banquet, binge, meal, supper

spread-eagled *adj* sprawled, sprawling, prone, prostrate, face down *Opposite*: erect

spread out *v* 1 move apart, divide up, split up *Opposite*: amass 2 extend, cover, spread, go as far as, stretch 3 share out, share, divide up, split up

spreadsheet *n* worksheet, database, table

spree *n* 1 binge, extravaganza, fling, orgy, splurge *(infml)* 2 jaunt, outing, trip, excursion, break

sprig *n* spray, twig, stem, branch, shoot

sprightly *adj* energetic, active, spry, lively, agile *Opposite*: lethargic

spring *v* jump, leap, bounce, pounce, launch

yourself ■ n 1 coil, spiral, helix, mainspring, hairspring 2 elasticity, springiness, bounce, give, flexibility 3 leap, bound, jump, bounce, vault 4 springtime, season, seedtime, springtide (literary) 5 source, upwelling, fount, fountain, water source

spring back v ricochet, recoil, shrink

springboard n catalyst, facilitator, spur, trigger, launch pad Opposite: brake

spring-clean v scour, scrub, wash down, dust down, clean out Opposite: dirty

springtime n season, spring, seedtime, springtide (literary)

spring up v appear, emerge, pop up, come into existence, mushroom Opposite: disappear

springy adj bouncy, elastic, supple, pliable, soft Opposite: unyielding

sprinkle v 1 shake over, dust, scatter, cover 2 intersperse, pepper, strew, scatter, litter ■ n sprinkling, shake, dusting, scattering, scatter

sprinkler n 1 sprayer, irrigator, waterer, spray, hose 2 nozzle, rose, showerhead, spray, diffuser

sprinkling n scattering, dash, shake, pinch, bit Opposite: heap

sprint n dash, burst, race, run, cycle race Opposite: marathon ■ v hurry, run, dash, race, gallop Opposite: dawdle

sprinter n runner, racer, competitor

sprite n fairy, nymph, elf, dryad, leprechaun

sprocket n tooth, cog, notch, projection, sprocket wheel

sprout v 1 grow, shoot, develop, bud, spring Opposite: wither 2 spring up, spring, emerge, appear, pop up ■ n shoot, bud, leaf, young branch, new growth

spruce adj smart, neat, dapper, trim, elegant Opposite: scruffy

spruce up v smarten, smarten up, tidy, neaten, improve Opposite: mess up (infml)

spry adj sprightly, lively, active, agile, energetic Opposite: slow

spud (infml) n potato, tater (infml), murphy (dated infml)

spunk (infml) n pluck, spirit, toughness, determination, nerve Opposite: cowardice

spunky (infml) adj plucky, spirited, tough, determined, energetic Opposite: cowardly

spur n 1 incentive, stimulus, incitement, provocation, motive Opposite: disincentive 2 ridge, mountainside, projection, edge, saddle 3 branch, limb, shoot, offshoot, outgrowth 4 spike, point, barb, spine ■ v urge, encourage, incite, prompt, stimulate Opposite: discourage. See COMPARE AND CONTRAST at motive.

spurious adj false, bogus, fake, forged, counterfeit Opposite: genuine

spurn v reject, snub, slight, rebuff, repulse Opposite: accept

spur-of-the-moment adj spontaneous, impulsive, unplanned, impromptu, unpremeditated Opposite: planned

spurt n 1 jet, spray, squirt, gush, spout Opposite: trickle 2 increase, burst, surge, rush, swell ■ v gush, spray, burst, jet, erupt Opposite: trickle

sputter v 1 pop, splutter, spit, sizzle, crackle 2 splutter, gasp, spit, stammer, snort

sputum n mucus, phlegm, saliva, spit, spittle

spy n secret agent, undercover agent, double agent, mole, infiltrator ■ v 1 watch, eavesdrop, listen in, observe, scrutinize 2 work undercover, pry, reconnoitre, snoop (infml), nose around (infml) 3 spot, notice, observe, see 4 discover, search out, detect, find out, observe Opposite: overlook 5 investigate, poke around, explore, search, research

spyhole n peephole, slot, chink, opening, window

spying n undercover work, intelligence work, espionage, eavesdropping, infiltration

spy out v discover, uncover, seek out, sniff out, nose out Opposite: overlook

squabble n quarrel, row, tiff, dispute, argument Opposite: reconciliation ■ v argue, bicker, quarrel, disagree, have words Opposite: make up

squad n group, team, crew, company, gang

squad car n police car, patrol car, panda car, cruiser (US)

squadron n regiment, troop, team, squad, company

squalid adj 1 filthy, dirty, foul, nasty, fetid Opposite: clean 2 seedy, repulsive, sordid, sleazy, low Opposite: charming. See COMPARE AND CONTRAST at dirty.

squall n storm, gust of wind, windstorm, gust, shower

squally adj stormy, gusty, blustery, wild, inclement Opposite: fine

squalor n 1 filth, dirt, dirtiness, foulness, grime Opposite: cleanliness 2 nastiness, sordidness, unpleasantness, degradation, immorality Opposite: charm

squander v waste, spend, throw away, fritter away, dissipate Opposite: save

square n 1 four-sided figure, quadrangle, tetragon, rectangle, parallelogram 2 plaza, open area, marketplace, place, parade ■ adj 1 four-sided, right-angled, rectangular, quadrangular, tetragonal 2 fair, honest, genuine, just, straight Opposite: dishonest ■ v 1 shape, form, file down, sharpen, even up 2 adjust, align, realign, set straight, straighten Opposite: unbalance 3 pay off, settle, clear, pay, balance 4 agree, harmonize, accord, fit, tally Opposite: conflict ■ adv 1 at right angles, directly, straight 2 (infml) fairly, honestly, openly, straightforwardly, straight

squarely adv directly, exactly, evenly, head-on, straight Opposite: indirectly

square meal *n* **nourishment**, hot meal, proper meal, food, sustenance *Opposite*: nibble

square up *v* **1 settle up**, even up, settle your debts, settle the bill, pay up **2 work out**, turn out fine, sort itself out, be arranged, be organized *Opposite*: go wrong **3 face up to**, confront, look something in the eye, tackle, take on *Opposite*: evade **4 put up your fists**, make a stand, put up a fight, stand your ground, take up the gauntlet *Opposite*: run away

squash *v* **1 crush**, flatten, compress, pulp, mash *Opposite*: reshape **2 cram**, squeeze, wedge, force, jam *Opposite*: coax **3 overcome**, stop, conquer, suppress, quash *Opposite*: encourage ■ *n* **squeeze**, crush, congestion, crowd, jam

squashy *adj* **soft**, yielding, spongy, springy, mushy *Opposite*: firm

squat *v* **crouch**, sit on your heels, hunker down, bend *Opposite*: stand ■ *adj* **short**, thickset, thick, stubby, stocky *Opposite*: tall

squatter *n* **unlawful tenant**, unlawful resident, resident, trespasser

squawk *v* **1 screech**, call, cry, squeal, shriek **2** (*infml*) **complain**, protest, whine, wail, grumble ■ *n* (*infml*) **protest**, complaint, whine, wail, grumble

squeak *v* **squeal**, whine, yelp, shrill, pipe

squeak through (*infml*) *v* **scrape through**, scrape by, manage, achieve, do

squeaky *adj* **high-pitched**, shrill, whiny, noisy, creaky

squeaky-clean *adj* **1 virtuous**, righteous, pure, honourable, unimpeachable *Opposite*: corrupt **2 clean**, clean as a new pin, spotless, dirt-free, pristine

squeal *n* **screech**, yelp, shriek, yell, cry ■ *v* **yell**, cry, shriek, yelp, howl

squeamish *adj* **1 nauseous**, queasy, sick, woozy **2 prudish**, delicate, easily upset, easily offended, puritanical *Opposite*: strong **3 fastidious**, particular, scrupulous, fussy, uncompromising *Opposite*: easygoing

squeamishness *n* **1 queasiness**, nauseousness, sickness, qualmishness, seediness (*infml*) **2 delicacy**, prudishness, prudery, shockability, puritanism *Opposite*: toughness

squeeze *v* **1 press**, squash, compress, constrict, pinch **2 find time for**, make time for, make room for, fit in, slot in **3 grip**, hold on, grasp, hug, clutch *Opposite*: release **4 hug**, embrace, cuddle, enfold, clasp *Opposite*: release **5 crush**, squash, cram, crowd, jam *Opposite*: coax **6 extract**, wring, expel, drive out, mangle **7 pressurize**, put pressure on, harass, oppress, lean on (*infml*)

squeeze out *v* **exclude**, express, force out, freeze out, ostracize

squelch *v* **1 squish**, splash, splosh, suck, gurgle **2 crush**, squash, flatten, trample, squish

squelchy *adj* **soggy**, squishy, wet, squidgy, watery *Opposite*: dry

squidgy *adj* **1 soggy**, squelchy, slimy, mushy, marshy *Opposite*: dry **2 squashy**, spongy, springy, pliable, soft *Opposite*: firm

squiggle *n* **scribble**, wavy line, doodle, ornamentation, flourish

squiggly *adj* **wavy**, curvy, wobbly, bumpy, scribbly *Opposite*: straight

squint *v* **narrow your eyes**, peer, peek, look, glance ■ *n* **peep**, peer, quick look, glance, glimpse ■ *adj* (*infml*) **crooked**, lopsided, cross-eyed, off balance, uneven *Opposite*: straight ■ *adv* (*infml*) **lopsidedly**, askew, crookedly, unevenly *Opposite*: straight

squire *n* **1 landowner**, lord, landlord, owner, proprietor *Opposite*: tenant **2 attendant**, retainer, steward, man, servant

squirm *v* **1 wriggle**, writhe, twist, turn, fidget **2 feel shame**, feel embarrassment, feel remorse, feel guilty, feel awkward

squirrel *n* (*infml*) **hoarder**, collector, accumulator, saver, magpie (*infml*) ■ *v* **hoard**, collect, accumulate, store, put aside *Opposite*: throw out

squirt *v* **spurt**, shoot, jet, gush, spray ■ *n* **spurt**, jet, fountain, stream, spray

squish *v* **1 squeeze**, crush, squash, squelch, pinch **2 splash**, squelch, splosh, suck, gurgle

squishy *adj* **squelchy**, soggy, soft, mushy, squidgy *Opposite*: firm

stab *v* **knife**, wound, pierce, cut, spear ■ *n* **1 pang**, twinge, ache, pain, prick **2** (*infml*) **attempt**, go, try, shot, guess

stabbing *n* **knife attack**, assault, wounding, attack ■ *adj* **sharp**, acute, piercing, shooting, intense

stability *n* **constancy**, steadiness, firmness, solidity, permanence *Opposite*: instability

stabilization *n* **steadying**, steadiness, maintenance, balance, equilibrium *Opposite*: change

stabilize *v* **become stable**, even out, become constant, calm, calm down *Opposite*: change

stab in the back (*infml*) *v* **betray**, let down, be disloyal to, sell out, wound ■ *n* **betrayal**, wound, attack, act of disloyalty, act of treachery

stable *adj* **1 steady**, unchanging, even, constant, firm *Opposite*: changeable **2 secure**, fixed, firm, permanent, rigid *Opposite*: unstable **3 calm**, steady, even, settled, level-headed *Opposite*: erratic ■ *n* **1 stall**, shed, stabling **2 team**, gang, string, group, lineup

staccato *adj* **clipped**, disjointed, disconnected, faltering, monosyllabic

stack *n* **1 pile**, heap, mass, mound, mountain **2 chimney**, smokestack, flue ■ *v* **pile**, load, heap, mound, amass

stacked *adj* **loaded**, weighted, set, slanted, fixed

stacks *(infml)* n **lots**, masses, piles *(infml)*, tons *(infml)*, loads *(infml)* Opposite: a few

stadium n **sports ground**, arena, pitch, ground, field

staff n 1 **employees**, personnel, workers, workforce, team 2 **rod**, cane, pole, wand, stick ■ v **operate**, run, work, control, supervise

stage n 1 **phase**, period, step, point, leg 2 **platform**, rostrum, stand, scaffold, podium 3 **theatre**, arena, playhouse, the boards ■ v **put on**, perform, present, show, play

stagecoach n **carriage**, horse-drawn carriage, cart

stage door n **back door**, side door, entrance, way in, exit

stage fright n **first-night nerves**, fear, panic, nerves *(infml)*

stage-manage v **engineer**, contrive, manipulate, devise, set up

stage name n **pseudonym**, alias, assumed name, professional name

stage whisper n **aside**, mutter, murmur Opposite: shout

stagey see **stagy**

stagflation n **slump**, recession, downturn, stagnation, inflation Opposite: growth

stagger v 1 **reel**, lurch, sway, totter, wobble 2 **astound**, amaze, shock, stun, surprise 3 **alternate**, vary, zigzag, rotate, space out Opposite: overlap

staggered adj 1 **stunned**, shocked, amazed, astounded, taken aback Opposite: unaffected 2 **alternated**, spread out, spaced out, zigzagged

staggering adj **astounding**, amazing, confounding, overwhelming, stunning

staging n **performance**, dramatization, production, enactment, presentation

staging post n **stopover**, halt, stop, break, half-way house

stagnant adj 1 **still**, motionless, stationary, standing, immobile Opposite: moving 2 **sluggish**, inactive, inert, torpid, dull Opposite: active

stagnate v 1 **stand still**, come to a halt, grind to a halt, be idle, languish Opposite: progress 2 **fester**, rot, deteriorate, go off, decay 3 **vegetate**, be inactive, idle, be idle, sit around

stagnation n **inactivity**, inaction, inertia, torpor, sluggishness Opposite: movement

stagy adj **theatrical**, dramatic, histrionic, exaggerated, artificial Opposite: unaffected

staid adj **sedate**, serious, grave, sober, dull Opposite: exciting

stain n 1 **mark**, blemish, spot, blot, imperfection 2 **tint**, dye, colour, tinge, pigment 3 **stigma**, slur, disgrace, dishonour, blemish ■ v 1 **blemish**, tarnish, soil, discolour, mark 2 **disgrace**, sully, taint, debase, dishonour Opposite: honour

stained adj **discoloured**, marked, blemished, tainted, tarnished

stair n 1 **step**, tread, rung 2 **staircase**, stairway, flight of steps, set of steps, flight of stairs

stairs n **staircase**, stair, stairway, flight of steps, set of steps

stairwell n **hall**, entrance hall, vestibule, shaft

stake n 1 **bet**, wager, ante, risk, venture 2 **post**, pale, pole, palisade, picket 3 **investment**, claim, share, involvement, concern 4 **prize**, winnings, purse, stakes ■ v **risk**, gamble, bet, venture, hazard

stakeholder n **investor**, shareholder, backer, sponsor, participant

stake out v 1 **mark out**, demarcate, delimit, chalk out, measure out 2 **establish**, clarify, define, limit, restrict 3 *(infml)* **spy on**, watch, keep under surveillance, keep watch on, keep an eye on

stakeout *(infml)* n **close watch**, watch, observation, investigation, examination

stakes n 1 **risk**, risk factor, danger, element of danger 2 **reward**, prize, recompense, incentive, winnings

stale adj 1 **decayed**, sour, old, musty, hard Opposite: fresh 2 **hackneyed**, worn-out, tired, overused, boring Opposite: original

stalemate n **impasse**, deadlock, standoff, logjam, standstill

staleness n 1 **mustiness**, mouldiness, decay, flatness, sourness Opposite: freshness 2 **unoriginality**, overuse, insipidness

stalk n **stem**, shoot, twig, branch, trunk ■ v **follow**, trail, track, pursue, shadow

stalker n **prowler**, pursuer, shadow, tracker, follower

stall n 1 **booth**, stand, arcade, shop, kiosk 2 **compartment**, pen, coop, shed, cubicle ■ v 1 **stop**, cut out, freeze, pause, halt Opposite: keep going 2 **delay**, put off, defer, postpone, suspend Opposite: advance 3 **play for time**, prevaricate, equivocate, hedge, hesitate

stalwart adj 1 **strong**, muscular, athletic, brawny, sturdy Opposite: feeble 2 **resolute**, vigorous, determined, committed, unfaltering Opposite: uncommitted 3 **brave**, courageous, daring, fearless, bold Opposite: cowardly

stamina n **staying power**, endurance, energy, resilience, resistance Opposite: frailty

stammer v **stumble**, stutter, falter, hesitate, pause ■ n **stutter**, hesitant speech, speech impediment

stamp n 1 **mark**, imprint, mould, cast, hallmark 2 **character**, kind, make, sort, type ■ v 1 **trample**, stomp, crush, squash, plod Opposite: tiptoe 2 **imprint**, engrave, inscribe, fix, impress

stampede n **rush**, mad dash, flight, rout, pandemonium ■ v **rush**, hurry, run, dash, sprint

stamping ground *(infml)* n **patch**, haunt, place, home, territory

stamp out v **eradicate**, banish, destroy,

remove, eliminate *Opposite*: cultivate

stance *n* **1 attitude**, position, stand, standpoint, view **2 posture**, deportment, bearing, attitude, carriage *(fml)*

stanch *see* **staunch**

stand *v* **1 rise**, get up, stand up, get to your feet, be on your feet *Opposite*: sit **2 place**, situate, position, set, put **3 erect**, mount, hoist, put up, stick up **4 remain**, halt, stop, continue, exist **5 tolerate**, endure, put up with, abide, bear ■ *n* **1 attitude**, opinion, stance, position, viewpoint **2 stop**, standstill, stay, rest, halt **3 stall**, counter, booth, kiosk, tent **4 platform**, rostrum, stage, place, post **5 rack**, frame, support, holder, shelf

standard *n* **1 criterion**, benchmark, touchstone, paradigm, yardstick **2 norm**, average, mean, par, level **3 flag**, banner, ensign, pennant, streamer ■ *adj* **normal**, typical, average, usual, ordinary *Opposite*: unusual

standard-bearer *n* **leader**, ringleader, prime mover, spearhead, director

standardize *v* **regulate**, homogenize, normalize, even out, regiment *Opposite*: vary

standard of living *n* **level of comfort**, means, level of affluence, wealth, lifestyle

standards *n* **principles**, values, morals, ethics, ideals

stand by *v* **support**, stick by, back, stick up for, side with *Opposite*: abandon

stand-by *n* **1 reserve**, deputy, stand-in, double, understudy **2 substitute**, replacement, spare, backup, reserve ■ *adj* **1 reserve**, fallback, replacement, stand-in, deputy **2 last-minute**, late *Opposite*: reserved

stand down *v* **resign**, step down, quit, bow out, give up

stand firm *v* **persevere**, stand your ground, hold on, hold out, dig in your heels *Opposite*: yield

stand for *v* **1 put up with**, tolerate, abide, withstand, stand **2 mean**, signify, represent, denote, symbolize **3 advocate**, promote, support, champion, endorse

stand in *v* **fill in**, substitute, deputize, take somebody's place, do somebody's work

stand-in *n* **replacement**, understudy, deputy, substitute, reserve

stand in for *v* **take the place of**, deputize for, substitute for, cover for, do the work of

standing *n* **1 rank**, status, position, reputation, station **2 duration**, existence, continuance, age, tenure ■ *adj* **1 established**, settled, fixed, immovable, durable *Opposite*: temporary **2 standup**, vertical, upright, upended, perpendicular *Opposite*: horizontal

standing order *n* **rule**, order, instruction, protocol, procedure

standing stone *n* **obelisk**, menhir, dolmen, megalith, column

standoff *n* **stalemate**, impasse, deadlock, logjam, standstill

standoffish *adj* **distant**, aloof, superior, unapproachable, cold *Opposite*: affable

stand out *v* **1 be obvious**, be prominent, show up, be conspicuous, stick out **2 project**, jut, protrude, jut out, stick out

standpipe *n* **water pipe**, tap, emergency pipe, water supply, hydrant

standpoint *n* **point of view**, position, stance, angle, viewpoint

standstill *n* **halt**, stop, stoppage, full stop, cessation

stand up *v* **1 rise**, stand, get to your feet, get up, arise *(literary)* *Opposite*: sit down **2 endure**, last, survive, continue, hold out

standup *adj* **1 intense**, fierce, furious, blazing, violent *Opposite*: mild **2 erect**, upright, standing, upstanding, vertical *Opposite*: flat **3 solo**, improvised, off-the-cuff, impromptu, ad lib *Opposite*: rehearsed

stand up to *v* **face**, brave, take on, meet head-on, confront *Opposite*: avoid

stand your ground *v* **stand firm**, persist, persevere, reserve, hold out *Opposite*: give in

stanza *n* **verse**, section, stave, couplet, triplet

staple *n* **clip**, fastener, nail, tack, pin ■ *v* **fasten**, affix, clip, attach, secure ■ *adj* **main**, chief, principal, essential, primary *Opposite*: minor

star *n* **celebrity**, superstar, personality, icon ■ *v* **1 feature**, showcase, head the cast, top the bill, play the lead **2 do well**, excel, shine, succeed, stand out

WORD BANK

❏ **types of star** binary star, black hole, brown dwarf, dark star, dwarf star, galaxy, giant star, nebula, nova, pulsar, quasar, red giant, sun, supernova, white dwarf

star billing *n* **top billing**, star status, top of the bill, main attraction, star turn

starboard *adj* **right-hand**, right, right-side *Opposite*: port

starchy *adj* **stiff**, solemn, prudish, prim, austere *Opposite*: relaxed

star-crossed *adj* **ill-fated**, unlucky, ill-starred, doomed, unfortunate *Opposite*: lucky

stardom *n* **fame**, celebrity, prominence, renown, glory *Opposite*: anonymity

stardust *n* **romance**, dreaminess, sentiment, emotion, feeling

stare *v* **gaze**, gape, look intently, ogle, glare *Opposite*: ignore ■ *n* **intent look**, gaze, gape, glare, glower. *See* COMPARE AND CONTRAST *at* gaze.

stare out *v* **outstare**, stare at, look at, gaze at, stare down (US)

star in *v* **play the lead in**, feature in, act in, play in, head the cast

stark *adj* **1 bleak**, bare, barren, desolate, austere *Opposite*: opulent **2 complete**, utter, absolute, sheer, downright *Opposite*: partial **3 plain**, unambiguous, simple, blunt, unadulterated *Opposite*: ambiguous ■ *adv* **completely**, utterly, entirely, wholly, fully *Opposite*: partially

starkness *n* **1** austerity, bleakness, harshness, severity, sparseness *Opposite*: opulence **2 frankness**, unambiguity, blatancy, harshness, bluntness *Opposite*: ambiguity

starlet *n* **actor**, rising young star, new talent, star of tomorrow, star in the making

starlight *n* **glow**, gleam, sheen, twinkle, sparkle

starlit *adj* **starry**, bright, glowing, gleaming, twinkling *Opposite*: dark

starry *adj* **glittery**, shiny, bright, sparkly, brilliant *Opposite*: dull

starry-eyed *adj* **dreamy**, optimistic, idealistic, head-in-the-clouds, happy *Opposite*: cynical

starship *n* **spaceship**, space shuttle, space station, flying saucer

star sign *n* **sign of the zodiac**, birth sign, sun sign, sign, astrological sign

WORD BANK
❏ **types of star sign** Aquarius, Aries, Cancer, Capricorn, Gemini, Leo, Libra, Pisces, Sagittarius, Scorpio, Taurus, Virgo

star-studded *adj* **star-spangled**, all-star, celebrity, big-name, glittering *Opposite*: unknown

star system *n* **constellation**, galaxy, Milky Way, solar system

start *v* **1 begin**, commence, start off, get going, set off *Opposite*: finish **2 create**, found, begin, establish, set up *Opposite*: close **3 set out**, leave, set off, depart, get going *Opposite*: arrive **4 jump**, recoil, flinch, shrink, twitch ■ *n* **1 beginning**, birth, foundation, onset, dawn *Opposite*: end **2 lead**, advantage, edge, boon, gain **3 twitch**, jump, jerk, flinch, jolt **4 shock**, fright, surprise, turn

starter *n* **hors d'oeuvre**, first course, entrée, appetizer, meze

starting point *n* **1 basis**, base, foundation, point of departure, beginning **2 starting line**, starting block, starting grid, starting post, starting gate *Opposite*: finishing line

startle *v* **surprise**, disconcert, shock, alarm, frighten

startled *adj* **surprised**, disconcerted, alarmed, astonished, amazed

startling *adj* **surprising**, astonishing, amazing, astounding, staggering *Opposite*: comforting

start off *v* **1 begin**, commence, get going, start out *Opposite*: finish **2 set off**, start out, be off, get going, start *Opposite*: arrive

start on *v* **1 begin**, tackle, deal with, embark on, get going on *Opposite*: finish **2** (*infml*) **scold**, harass, pester, nag, annoy

start out *v* **1 start off**, start, begin, set off, get going *Opposite*: arrive **2 intend**, mean, plan, propose, expect

start up *v* **1 switch on**, turn on, fire up, power up, ignite *Opposite*: turn off **2 set up**, open, begin, launch, create *Opposite*: close down **3 pipe up**, resound, be heard, begin, start *Opposite*: quieten down **4 leap up**, jump up, stand up, get up, rise *Opposite*: sit down

star turn *n* **main attraction**, star attraction, big name, top of the bill, top act

starvation *n* **hunger**, malnourishment, undernourishment, famishment, famine

starve *v* **have nothing to eat**, go hungry, famish, be malnourished, go short of food *Opposite*: eat

starved *adj* **1 deprived**, bereft, devoid, lacking, without **2** (*infml*) **ravenous**, hungry, famished, starving (*infml*) *Opposite*: replete

starving (*infml*) *adj* **ravenous**, hungry, famished, starved (*infml*) *Opposite*: replete

stash *n* **supply**, hideaway, hoard, mass, pile ■ *v* (*infml*) **hide**, hoard, put away, put by, stockpile

stasis *n* **stability**, motionlessness, status quo, continuity, inertia *Opposite*: change

state *n* **1 condition**, situation, position, status, circumstances **2** (*infml*) **confusion**, turmoil, disarray, disorder, chaos **3 federation**, kingdom, nation, land, territory **4 grandeur**, ceremony, pomp, splendour, glory ■ *adj* **1 public**, government, municipal, state-run, state-owned **2 formal**, official, stately, imperial, royal ■ *v* **utter**, declare, affirm, assert, express

statecraft *n* **government**, management, governance, administration, direction

stateless *adj* **homeless**, nationless, displaced, refugee, outlawed

stateliness *n* **grandeur**, pomp, glory, dignity, majesty

stately *adj* **grand**, splendid, dignified, imperial, majestic *Opposite*: modest

stately home *n* **mansion**, manor, hall, country house, great house

statement *n* **1 declaration**, announcement, report, account, speech **2 record**, account, receipt, invoice

state of affairs *n* **situation**, set of circumstances, condition, setup, position

state of mind *n* **mood**, temper, attitude, feelings, spirits

state-of-the-art *adj* **advanced**, high-tech, cutting-edge, up-to-the-minute, up-to-date *Opposite*: antiquated

state-owned *adj* **public**, public-sector, state, state-run, nationalized *Opposite*: private

stateroom *n* **first-class compartment**, first-class cabin, sleeping compartment, berth, sleeper

state secret *n* **confidential matter**, affair of state, top-secret matter, confidential information, classified material

static *adj* **1 still**, motionless, stationary, inert, standing *Opposite*: moving **2 unchanging**, constant, invariable, unvarying *Opposite*: dynamic

station *n* **1 position**, place, post, location, situation **2 rank**, class, status, position, level ■ *v* **post**, base, position, place, situate

stationary *adj* **motionless**, still, immobile, inactive, fixed *Opposite*: moving

stationery *n* **writing materials**, writing implements, pen and paper, writing paper, notepaper

statistic *n* **number**, figure, digit, piece of data, measurement

statistics *n* **figures**, data, numbers, information

statuary *n* **sculptures**, statues, figures, monuments, busts

statue *n* **figurine**, figure, sculpture, effigy, statuette

statuesque *adj* **stately**, elegant, graceful, majestic, dignified *Opposite*: ungainly

statuette *see* statue

stature *n* **1 build**, height, physique, figure, tallness **2 standing**, importance, prominence, status, rank

status *n* **1 rank**, position, standing, grade, station **2 eminence**, prestige, prominence, importance, significance **3 category**, condition, class, type, stage

status quo *n* **current situation**, existing state of affairs, present circumstances, how things stand

status symbol *n* **asset**, must-have, prize possession

statute *n* **decree**, act, ruling, edict, order

statute book *n* **body of law**, record, legislation, legal code, law book

statute law *n* **written law**, law, constitution, legislation

statutory *adj* **constitutional**, legislative, legal

staunch *v* **stop**, stem, halt, hold back, curb ■ *adj* **loyal**, faithful, steadfast, reliable, dependable *Opposite*: wavering

stave *n* **1 plank**, slat, board, lath, band **2 bar**, rung, tread, step, crosspiece **3 stanza**, verse, section, couplet, triplet

stave off *v* **fend off**, keep at bay, hold off, delay, deflect

stay *v* **1 remain**, wait, hang about, continue, keep on *Opposite*: go **2 reside**, live, inhabit, settle, dwell *(literary)* **3 stop**, halt, delay, defer, put off ■ *n* **1 visit**, break, holiday, stopover, vacation **2 halt**, stop, delay, deferment, adjournment

staying power *n* **stamina**, endurance, determination, doggedness, vigour *Opposite*: frailty

stay on *v* **remain**, stay, stay put, stay behind, stay out *Opposite*: leave

stay out *v* **be out**, not come home, not come back, stop out *(infml)*

stay put *v* **remain**, stay, stay still, tarry, hang on *Opposite*: move

stay up *v* **stop up**, burn the candle at both ends, stay up till all hours, burn the midnight oil, make a night of it

steadfast *adj* **1 unwavering**, unfaltering, resolute, committed, dedicated *Opposite*: wavering **2 loyal**, trusty, dependable, faithful, trustworthy *Opposite*: inconstant *(literary)*

steadfastness *n* **1 resoluteness**, commitment, dedication, persistence, determination *Opposite*: wavering **2 loyalty**, faithfulness, trustworthiness, devotion, dependability *Opposite*: disloyalty

steadily *adv* **progressively**, gradually, increasingly, little by little, bit by bit *Opposite*: suddenly

steadiness *n* **1 control**, stability, firmness, balance, equilibrium *Opposite*: unsteadiness **2 calmness**, composure, equanimity, serenity, reliability *Opposite*: excitability **3 regularity**, uniformity, constancy

steady *adj* **1 stable**, firm, fixed, solid, sturdy *Opposite*: rickety **2 continual**, constant, perpetual, never-ending, ceaseless *Opposite*: intermittent **3 even**, regular, uniform, unchanging, unvarying *Opposite*: irregular **4 calm**, cool, collected, composed, unruffled *Opposite*: excitable ■ *v* **stabilize**, secure, fix, support, strengthen *Opposite*: undermine

steal *v* **1 pilfer**, misappropriate, embezzle, take, pocket **2 creep**, sneak, slip, slink, tiptoe ■ *n* *(infml)* **bargain**, good deal, good buy, giveaway *(infml)*, snip *(infml)* *Opposite*: rip-off *(infml)*

COMPARE AND CONTRAST CORE MEANING: the taking of property unlawfully

steal take something that belongs to somebody else, illegally or without the owner's permission; **pinch** *(infml)* steal something; **nick** *(slang)* steal something; **filch** *(infml)* steal something furtively and opportunistically, usually a small item or something of little value; **purloin** *(fml)* steal something, sometimes used humorously or euphemistically; **pilfer** steal small items of little value, especially habitually; **embezzle** take for personal use money or property that has been given on trust by others, without their knowledge; **misappropriate** take something, especially money, dishonestly or in order to use it for an improper or illegal purpose.

---

stealing *n* **theft**, robbery, burglary, thieving, pilfering

stealth *n* **furtiveness**, surreptitiousness, sneakiness, slyness, craftiness *Opposite*: openness

stealthy *adj* **furtive**, surreptitious, sly, silent, cautious *Opposite*: blatant. *See* COMPARE AND CONTRAST *at* secret.

steam *n* **vapour**, condensation, haze, mist, fog

steamroller *v* **1 compress**, bulldoze, flatten, crush, squash **2 crush**, squash, demolish, destroy, overwhelm **3 force**, compel, coerce, bludgeon, bully

steam up v mist up, fog up, cloud, cloud over, mist over

steamy adj 1 **humid**, muggy, damp, sticky, hot and sticky 2 **misted up**, misty, fogged up, foggy, steamed up Opposite: clear

steel v **strengthen**, toughen, harden, fortify, brace

steely adj 1 **hard**, strong, tough, sturdy, rugged Opposite: soft 2 **determined**, resolute, unyielding, unbending, rigid Opposite: irresolute

steel yourself v **brace yourself**, harden your heart, pluck up your courage, prepare yourself, compose yourself

steep adj 1 **sheer**, vertical, sharp, precipitous, abrupt Opposite: gentle 2 (infml) **unreasonable**, extreme, excessive, expensive, dear Opposite: reasonable ■ v 1 **soak**, immerse, drench, submerge, suffuse 2 **imbue**, permeate, infuse

steeple n **tower**, spire, turret, bell tower, belfry

steeply adv **sharply**, precipitously, abruptly, suddenly Opposite: gently

steepness n **sharpness**, abruptness, gradient, sheerness Opposite: gentleness

steer v 1 **control**, drive, pilot, navigate, manoeuvre 2 **direct**, guide, point, conduct, lead. See COMPARE AND CONTRAST at guide.

steerage n **third class**, bottom deck, tourist class, lower deck

steering committee n **steering group**, board, panel, team, commission

stellar adj 1 **astral**, astronomical, astrophysical, solar, planetary Opposite: earthly 2 **all-star**, star-studded, star-spangled, starry, celebrity Opposite: unknown

stem n **stalk**, shoot, trunk, twig, branch ■ v **stop**, staunch, halt, curtail, restrict Opposite: accelerate

stem from v **arise from**, originate from, come from, derive from, develop from

stench n **stink**, reek, unpleasant smell, foul smell, pong (infml) Opposite: fragrance. See COMPARE AND CONTRAST at smell.

stencil n 1 **template**, cutout, guide, plate, pattern 2 **pattern**, design, lettering, motif, border ■ v 1 **decorate**, adorn, paint, ornament 2 **apply**, paint, work, draw, trace

stentorian adj **loud**, powerful, booming, thunderous, deafening Opposite: quiet

step n 1 **pace**, footstep, stride 2 **move**, movement, action, measure 3 **stage**, phase, period 4 **stair**, rung, tread ■ v **walk**, tread, march, pace, move

step down v 1 **stand down**, resign, retire, bow out, withdraw Opposite: stay on 2 **decrease**, reduce, lower, lessen, restrict Opposite: step up

step in v **intervene**, intercede, interpose, interrupt, get involved

stepladder n **ladder**, steps, portable ladder, folding ladder, stairs

step out v 1 **go out**, step outside, nip out, leave, absent yourself Opposite: stay put 2 **march**, tear along, rush, stride, dash Opposite: crawl

steppe n **prairie**, grassland, plain, savanna, pampas

stepping stone n 1 **stone**, boulder, rock, foothold, bridge 2 **stage**, step, means of access, stage of progress, stage of advancement

step up v **increase**, intensify, improve, maximize, accelerate Opposite: lower

stereophonic adj **stereo**, audio, binaural, hi-fi, high-fidelity

stereotype v **typecast**, label, pigeonhole, categorize, cast

stereotypical adj **conventional**, orthodox, formulaic, banal, hackneyed Opposite: original

sterile adj 1 **germ-free**, disinfected, antiseptic, sterilized, spotlessly clean Opposite: dirty 2 **infertile**, unproductive, barren Opposite: fertile 3 **bare**, fruitless, unfruitful, unproductive, desolate Opposite: verdant 4 **dull**, unimaginative, banal, unstimulating Opposite: creative

sterility n 1 **barrenness**, unfruitfulness, unproductiveness, desolation, bareness Opposite: fruitfulness 2 **infertility**, barrenness, childlessness, unproductiveness, impotence Opposite: fertility 3 **cleanness**, antisepsis, disinfection, decontamination, purity Opposite: contamination 4 **dullness**, unimaginativeness, lack of imagination, lack of creativity, banality Opposite: creativity

sterilization n 1 **purification**, cleansing, disinfection, fumigation, decontamination 2 **neutering**, castration, gelding, spaying

sterilize v 1 **disinfect**, bleach, make germ-free, fumigate, sanitize 2 **neuter**, spay, geld, castrate

sterilizer n **disinfectant**, germicide, antiseptic, bactericide, sanitizer

sterling adj 1 **genuine**, authentic, true, pure, real Opposite: spurious 2 **excellent**, exceptional, matchless, incomparable, worthy Opposite: mediocre

stern adj 1 **strict**, harsh, severe, austere, unsympathetic Opposite: easygoing 2 **grim**, forbidding, formidable, dour, serious Opposite: cheerful

sternness n 1 **severity**, strictness, harshness, firmness, austerity Opposite: leniency 2 **grimness**, seriousness, sombreness, gravity, humourlessness Opposite: cheerfulness

stet v **let it stand**, restore, retain, undo, ignore Opposite: delete

stew n (infml) **difficult situation**, state (infml), flap (infml), tizzy (infml), lather (infml) ■ v 1 **simmer**, boil slowly, braise, casserole, parboil 2 **be upset**, be troubled, be agitated, worry, trouble

stick n **twig**, cane, baton, rod, staff ■ v 1 **spear**, stab, penetrate, pierce, spike **2 attach**, glue, fix, fasten, join *Opposite*: detach **3** *(infml)* **put**, lay, place, set, deposit **4** *(infml)* **push**, put, thrust, shove, poke *Opposite*: withdraw

stick around *(infml)* v **linger**, wait, stay, remain, hang about *(infml)* *Opposite*: leave

stick at v **persist at**, continue with, persist, persevere with, see through *Opposite*: give up

stick by v **remain loyal to**, stay loyal to, remain faithful to, support, adhere to *Opposite*: let down

sticker n **label**, sticky label, sign, marker, bumper sticker

stickiness n **tackiness**, gluiness, gumminess, adhesiveness, pastiness

sticking plaster n **plaster**, dressing, bandage, pad, corn plaster

sticking point n **stumbling block**, bone of contention, impasse, obstacle, deadlock

stick-in-the-mud *(infml)* n **reactionary**, diehard, fogy, fuddy-duddy *(infml)*, stuffed shirt *(infml)* *Opposite*: daredevil

stickler n **pedant**, nitpicker, perfectionist, martinet, hard taskmaster

stick out v **1 extend**, poke out, jut out, push out, thrust out **2 put up with**, endure, bear, weather, see through *Opposite*: give up

stick to v **1 follow**, obey, abide by, stand by, remain faithful to *Opposite*: abandon **2 adhere**, cling, follow, cling to, hold

stick together v **stay close**, remain unified, remain loyal, remain friendly, concur *Opposite*: split up

stick up v **1 protrude**, point upwards, point up, stand up, bristle *Opposite*: hang down **2 point up**, cock, prick up, make vertical, raise up

stick up for v **support**, defend, stand up for, stand by, argue for

stick with v **1 persist with**, continue with, persevere with, see through, stay with *Opposite*: give up **2 stay loyal to**, remain loyal to, remain faithful to, stay close to, stay with *Opposite*: abandon

sticky adj **1 tacky**, gluey, gummy, adhesive, pasty **2** *(infml)* **difficult**, tricky, delicate, awkward, sensitive **3 muggy**, humid, close, clammy, sultry *Opposite*: dry

sticky wicket *(infml)* n **tricky situation**, awkward situation, difficult situation, difficult problem, embarrassing problem

stiff adj **1 rigid**, firm, inflexible, unbending, unbendable *Opposite*: limp **2 severe**, harsh, drastic, stringent, excessive *Opposite*: lenient **3 formal**, stuffy, standoffish, aloof, pompous *Opposite*: relaxed **4 strong**, vigorous, powerful, robust, intense *Opposite*: weak **5 demanding**, exacting, arduous, testing, tough *Opposite*: easy **6 aching**, painful, arthritic, tender, sore

stiffen v **1 harden**, thicken, solidify, congeal,

become rigid *Opposite*: soften **2 strengthen**, make stronger, reinforce, toughen, brace *Opposite*: weaken

stiffly adv **rigidly**, firmly, inflexibly, unbendingly, tautly

stiff-necked adj **obstinate**, arrogant, stubborn, proud, haughty *Opposite*: yielding

stiffness n **1 rigidity**, firmness, inflexibility, tautness, hardness *Opposite*: limpness **2 severity**, harshness, stringency, excessiveness, extremity *Opposite*: leniency **3 formality**, stuffiness, standoffishness, aloofness, pomposity *Opposite*: informality **4 strength**, vigour, power, robustness, intensity *Opposite*: weakness **5 difficulty**, arduousness, laboriousness, rigorousness, toughness *Opposite*: ease

stifle v **1 smother**, asphyxiate, throttle, suffocate, choke **2 suppress**, repress, restrain, curb, hold back *Opposite*: let out

stifling adj **1 hot**, boiling, airless, muggy, close *Opposite*: cool **2 oppressive**, repressive, overpowering, restrictive, inhibiting *Opposite*: liberating

stigma n **shame**, disgrace, dishonour, humiliation

stigmatize v **brand**, slur, defame, mark out, pillory

still adj **1 motionless**, immobile, unmoving, at rest, at a standstill **2 flat**, nonsparkling, uncarbonated ■ v **calm**, allay, dispel, banish, quieten *Opposite*: stir up ■ adv **even now**, in spite of everything, even so, nevertheless, nonetheless

stillborn adj **1 born dead**, dead at birth, miscarried, aborted, dead **2 ineffectual**, useless, ineffective, unsuccessful, abortive *Opposite*: successful

stillness n **motionlessness**, immobility, silence, quietness, tranquillity *Opposite*: movement

stilt n **post**, column, support, pillar, pole

stilted adj **affected**, stiff, wooden, mannered, unnatural *Opposite*: natural

stimulant n **stimulating substance**, tonic, pick-me-up *(infml)*, upper *(slang)*, pep pill *(dated)* *Opposite*: sedative ■ adj **stimulating**, tonic, restorative, intoxicant, energizing *Opposite*: sedative

stimulate v **1 rouse**, arouse, kindle, excite, inspire *Opposite*: dampen **2 quicken**, accelerate, increase, invigorate, promote *Opposite*: slow down

stimulating adj **1 inspiring**, encouraging, motivating, interesting, thought-provoking *Opposite*: boring **2 invigorating**, refreshing, energizing, rousing *Opposite*: relaxing

stimulation n **inspiration**, motivation, encouragement, stimulus, incentive

stimulus n **incentive**, spur, inducement, impetus, provocation

sting v **smart**, prick, tingle, throb, hurt

stinging adj **hurtful**, cutting, harsh, hard, cruel

stingy *(infml) adj* **miserly**, ungenerous, parsimonious, sparing, grudging *Opposite*: generous

stink *v* **smell horrible**, reek, smell, hum *(infml)*, pong *(infml)* ■ *n* **1 stench**, smell, horrible smell, unpleasant odour, reek *Opposite*: perfume **2** *(infml)* **fuss**, scandal, uproar, rumpus, commotion. *See* COMPARE AND CONTRAST *at* **smell**.

stinker *n* **problem**, nightmare, shocker *(infml)*, horror *(infml)*, poser *(infml) Opposite*: delight

stinking *adj* **foul-smelling**, reeking, smelly, stinky, rotten

stink out *v* **make smelly**, permeate, pervade, overpower, fill with a smell *Opposite*: deodorize

stinky *adj* **1 smelly**, stinking, foul-smelling, putrid, rotten *Opposite*: fragrant **2 nasty**, unfair, dishonest, devious, mean-spirited *Opposite*: pleasant

stint *n* **spell**, stretch, time, shift, period

stint on *v* **be sparing with**, be mean with, be parsimonious with, be frugal with, ration

stipend *n* **allowance**, salary, payment, pay, wage. *See* COMPARE AND CONTRAST *at* **wage**.

stipendiary *adj* **paid**, salaried, remunerated ■ *n* **earner**, wage earner, breadwinner, payee, employee

stipple *v* **dab**, paint, dot, speckle, fleck

stippled *adj* **mottled**, dappled, speckled, spotted, flecked

stipulate *v* **specify**, lay down, instruct, order, require

stipulation *n* **condition**, requirement, proviso, demand, specification

stir *v* **1 mix**, blend, swirl, fold, whip **2 rouse**, wake up, move, budge, shift **3 awaken**, arouse, revive, call to mind, bring back **4 motivate**, incite, provoke, excite, inspire **5 agitate**, cause feeling, disturb, trouble, upset ■ *n* **commotion**, disturbance, fuss, uproar, hue and cry

stir-crazy *(infml) adj* **mentally unsettled**, restless, frantic, distraught, agitated

stir-fry *v* **fry**, pan-fry, sauté

stirrer *(infml) n* **troublemaker**, agitator, agent provocateur, firebrand, mischief-maker *Opposite*: peacemaker

stirring *adj* **rousing**, inspiring, moving, emotive, exciting *Opposite*: uninspiring

stirrup *n* **foot support**, strap, loop, ring

stir up *v* **awaken**, reawaken, bring back, kindle, inflame *Opposite*: calm

stitch *v* **1 sew**, sew up, stitch up, darn, baste **2 suture**, sew up, close

stitching *n* **sewing**, stitches, seam, needle-work, embroidery

stock *n* **1 supply**, stockpile, hoard, reserve, accumulation **2 livestock**, farm animals, domestic animals, cattle, sheep ■ *adj* **standard**, typical, routine, run-of-the-mill, ordi-nary ■ *v* **keep**, have a supply of, have available, carry, supply

stockade *n* **1 barrier**, fence, enclosure, palisade, paling **2 enclosure**, fort, pen, fenced area, enclosed area

stockbroker *n* **securities broker**, broker, investment analyst, financial adviser, trader

stock car *n* **racing car**, dragster, hot rod *(slang)*

stock cube *n* **concentrate**, vegetable extract, meat extract, bouillon cube *(US)*

stock exchange *n* **stock market**, trading, bourse, exchange, money market

stockholder *n* **investor**, shareholder, stake-holder, bondholder

stocking filler *n* **Christmas present**, Christmas gift, small present, small gift, extra

stockings *n* **leg coverings**, nylons, hose, tights, leggings

stock-in-trade *n* **1 basic resource**, staple, commodity **2 goods**, equipment, stock, merchandise, wares

stockist *n* **seller**, shop, store, wholesaler, retailer

stock market *n* **financial market**, stock exchange, exchange, market, bourse

stockpile *n* **supply**, hoard, accumulation, store, stock ■ *v* **store up**, stock up on, store, squirrel away, collect. *See* COMPARE AND CONTRAST *at* **collect**.

stockroom *n* **storeroom**, storehouse, store, warehouse

stocks *n* **shares**, bonds, holdings

stock-still *adv* **motionless**, completely still, absolutely still, immobile, without moving *Opposite*: moving

stocktaking *n* **1 evaluation**, assessment, appraisal, reassessment, reappraisal **2 inventory**, listing, itemizing, counting, checking

stock up *v* **stockpile**, hoard, save up, collect, lay in *Opposite*: finish off

stocky *adj* **thickset**, sturdy, solid, stout, squat *Opposite*: slight

stockyard *n* **yard**, enclosure, farmyard, farm, enclosed yard

stodge *(infml) n* **1 heavy food**, solid food, filling food, starchy food, substantial food **2 something dull**, something stuffy, something boring, dull subject, turgidity

stodgy *(infml) adj* **1 heavy**, filling, starchy, indigestible, hard to digest *Opposite*: light **2 dull**, turgid, uninteresting, unexciting, stuffy *Opposite*: lively

stoic *n* **impassive person**, patient person, fatalist, ascetic, unfeeling person ■ *adj* **long-suffering**, impassive, resigned, enduring, tolerant *Opposite*: excitable. *See* COMPARE AND CONTRAST *at* **impassive**.

stoical *see* **stoic**

stoicism *n* **impassiveness**, endurance,

patience, indifference, fortitude *Opposite*: excitability

stoke *v* **1 put fuel on**, add fuel to, fuel, stoke up **2 strengthen**, intensify, stir up, stoke up, encourage

stoke up *see* **stoke**

stole *n* **garment**, shawl, wrap, scarf, pashmina

stolid *adj* **impassive**, unresponsive, dull, emotionless, insensitive *Opposite*: emotional. *See* COMPARE AND CONTRAST *at* **impassive**.

stomachache *n* **stomach pain**, colic, indigestion, cramp, stitch

stomach-churning *see* **stomach-turning**

stomach pump (*infml*) *n* **suction pump**, suction device, aspirator, siphon, syringe

stomach-turning *adj* **sickening**, nauseating, revolting, disgusting, repulsive

stomp *v* **tread heavily**, stamp, tramp, clump, plod

stone-cold *adj* **very cold**, chilly, icy, frozen, freezing *Opposite*: boiling ■ *adv* (*infml*) **completely**, absolutely, utterly, totally, dead

stone-dead *adj* **lifeless**, cold, dead as a dodo, dead as a doornail, deceased (*fml*) *Opposite*: alive

stoneground *adj* **ground**, milled, crushed, powdered

stone's throw *n* **short distance**, stonecast, no distance, short way, hop, skip, and jump

stonewall (*infml*) *v* **1 evade**, obstruct, avoid, refuse, rebuff *Opposite*: cooperate **2 delay**, hold off, hold back, stall

stonewashed *adj* **faded**, worn, distressed, washed-out, acid-washed

stonework *n* **masonry**, brickwork, walls

stony *adj* **1 rocky**, flinty, pebbly, rock-strewn, shingly **2 pitiless**, unfeeling, unsympathetic, unyielding, flinty *Opposite*: compassionate **3** (*infml*) **penniless**, impoverished, impecunious, broke (*infml*), poor *Opposite*: well-off

stony-broke (*infml*) *adj* **penniless**, impoverished, impecunious, poor, bankrupt *Opposite*: well-off

stony-faced *adj* **expressionless**, unemotional, unfriendly, blank, cold *Opposite*: smiling

stony-hearted *adj* **hardhearted**, unfeeling, pitiless, unsympathetic, hard *Opposite*: softhearted

stooge *n* **straight partner**, comic actor, comedian, butt, foil

stool *n* **seat**, chair, footrest, ottoman (*US*)

stoop *v* **1 bend down**, bend forwards, bend over, bend, lean forwards *Opposite*: straighten up **2 lower yourself**, condescend, deign, debase yourself, patronize

stop *v* **1 discontinue**, end, bring to an end, bring to a close, bring to a standstill *Opposite*: begin **2 prevent**, impede, hinder, prohibit, obstruct *Opposite*: permit **3 end**, finish, come to an end, be over, break off *Opposite*: begin

4 pause, interrupt, break off, stop off, take a break *Opposite*: continue **5 block**, block up, block off, obstruct, plug ■ *n* **halt**, break, rest, stopover, stay

stop by *v* **drop in**, call by, call, call in, visit

stopcock *n* **valve**, tap, cock, spigot, stopper

stopgap *n* **temporary solution**, substitute, makeshift, expedient, temporary measure

stop off *v* **call**, call in, stop by, stop, drop in

stop out (*infml*) *v* **stay out**, stay out late, come home late, stay away, sleep over

stopover *n* **break in your journey**, stop, halt, pause, stop-off

stoppage *n* **1 strike**, work stoppage, industrial action, wildcat strike, go-slow **2 blockage**, obstruction, obstacle, barrier

stoppage time *n* **injury time**, timeout, extra time, overtime, extension

stopped *adj* **1 stationary**, still, at a standstill, immobile, motionless *Opposite*: moving **2 clogged**, blocked, congested, backed up, stopped up *Opposite*: open **3 not working**, out of order, out of commission, worn-out, crashed *Opposite*: working

stopper *n* **plug**, bung, cork, top, lid

stop press *n* **late news**, recent news, last-minute news, news flash, postscript

stop up *v* **plug**, plug up, block, block up, block off

stop working *v* **break down**, break, fail, seize up, pack up (*infml*) *Opposite*: function

storage *n* **1 storing**, stowage, stowing, packing, loading **2 storage space**, storage capacity, storage area, stowage, room

WORD BANK

❏ **types of storage space** armoury, arms depot, arsenal, attic, barn, basement, bunker, cellar, depository, depot, dump, garage, gasometer, granary, hangar, hayloft, hold, landfill, larder, loft, luggage compartment, magazine, morgue, mortuary, pantry, rubbish dump, shed, silo, strongroom, treasury, warehouse, water tower, weapon store, woodshed

store *v* **put away**, stow, keep, deposit, put in storage ■ *n* **1 supply**, stockpile, hoard, accumulation, collection **2 shop**, outlet, emporium, showroom **3 warehouse**, depository, depot, stockroom, repository

stores *n* **supplies**, provisions, equipment, goods, food

store up *v* **amass**, hoard, save, accumulate, stockpile

storey *n* **floor**, level, section, division, landing

storm *n* **1 tempest**, squall, gale, hurricane, tornado **2 outburst**, outbreak, explosion, eruption, wave ■ *v* **1 capture**, carry, take by storm, take, overmaster (*literary*) **2 rage**, fume, rant and rave, thunder, bluster **3 stamp**, stomp, stalk, flounce, march

stormbound *adj* **housebound**, confined, isolated, cut off, snowed in

storm cloud *n* **sign of violence**, omen, herald, harbinger, danger signal

storm drain *n* **drain**, storm-water sewer, gutter, channel, drainage system

stormproof *adj* **storm-resistant**, protected, strong, tough, waterproof

storm-tossed *adj* **choppy**, stormy, rough, battered, wild *Opposite*: calm

stormy *adj* **1 squally**, rainy, thundery, blustery, windy *Opposite*: calm **2 tempestuous**, violent, turbulent, unsettled, volatile *Opposite*: placid

story *n* **1 tale**, narrative, account, legend, chronicle **2 account**, report, version, statement, description **3** (*infml*) **lie**, untruth, falsehood, barefaced lie, fib (*infml*) **4 article**, piece, feature, report, item

storybook *adj* **fairy-tale**, fictional, make-believe, mythical, fanciful *Opposite*: real

story line *n* **plot**, narrative, story, theme, scenario

storyteller *n* **1 narrator**, teller of tales, teller, relater, raconteur **2** (*infml*) **liar**, prevaricator, deceiver, fabricator, fibber (*infml*)

stoup *n* **basin**, vessel, bowl, receptacle, chalice

stout *adj* **1 thickset**, heavy, solid, plump, chubby *Opposite*: slender **2 brave**, firm, stalwart, determined, resolute *Opposite*: faint-hearted **3 sturdy**, strong, solid, substantial, tough *Opposite*: flimsy

stouthearted *adj* **courageous**, brave, resolute, bold, valiant *Opposite*: cowardly

stoutness *n* **1 fatness**, heaviness, solidity, plumpness, chubbiness *Opposite*: slenderness **2 sturdiness**, solidity, strength, heftiness, toughness *Opposite*: flimsiness **3 bravery**, firmness, stalwartness, determination, resoluteness

stow *v* **put away**, tidy away, put, pack, store

stowage *n* **stowing**, storage, packing, loading, putting away

stowaway *n* **fare-dodger**, runaway, escapee, escaper, fugitive

straddle *v* **1 be astride**, bestride, sit astride, stand astride **2 span**, include, overlap, link, connect

strafe *v* **bombard**, attack, fire at, shell, blitz ■ *n* **aerial attack**, bombardment, air attack, blitz, shelling

straggle *v* **1 lag**, lag behind, trail, trail behind, fall behind **2 spread untidily**, spread out, sprawl, extend, spread **3 stray**, ramble, maunder, meander, rove *Opposite*: keep up

straggler *n* **dawdler**, laggard, loiterer, lingerer, slowcoach (*infml*) *Opposite*: leader

straggly *adj* **untidy**, unkempt, messy, dishevelled, tousled *Opposite*: tidy

straight *adj* **1 candid**, frank, direct, open, honest *Opposite*: devious **2 level**, upright, horizontal, vertical, perpendicular *Opposite*: askew **3 honest**, straightforward, fair,

law-abiding, aboveboard *Opposite*: dishonest **4 consecutive**, successive, uninterrupted, in a row, running **5 undiluted**, neat, plain, unmixed, unadulterated *Opposite*: diluted **6 tidy**, neat, in order, orderly, organized *Opposite*: untidy ■ *adv* **1 as the crow flies**, in a straight line, directly, from A to B, by the shortest possible route *Opposite*: indirectly **2 directly**, without delay, immediately, at once, instantly *Opposite*: later

straightaway *adv* **immediately**, at once, without delay, right away, promptly *Opposite*: later

straighten *v* **1 make straight**, straighten out, unbend, uncurl, flatten *Opposite*: bend **2 make level**, level, set straight, straighten up, adjust **3 tidy**, tidy up, order, arrange, organize

straighten out *v* **1 make straight**, straighten, unbend, uncurl, flatten *Opposite*: bend **2 put right**, sort out, set right, settle, rectify *Opposite*: confuse

straighten up *v* **align**, justify, straighten, level, make flush

straight-faced *adj* **deadpan**, poker-faced, expressionless, blank, serious *Opposite*: smiling

straightforward *adj* **1 frank**, forthright, candid, direct, honest *Opposite*: devious **2 easy**, simple, facile, uncomplicated, clear-cut *Opposite*: complicated

straightforwardness *n* **1 frankness**, candour, honesty, truthfulness, openness *Opposite*: deviousness **2 ease**, facility, simplicity, clarity, easiness *Opposite*: difficulty

straight-out (*infml*) *adj* **blunt**, unrestrained, direct, frank, honest *Opposite*: restrained

straight-talking *adj* **blunt**, direct, frank, candid, forthright *Opposite*: evasive

strain *v* **1 make a great effort**, try hard, struggle, labour, endeavour **2 damage**, injure, hurt, pull, sprain **3 drain**, sieve, filter, sift, separate **4 tax**, overburden, overload, burden, overtax ■ *n* **1 nervous tension**, tension, stress, worry, anxiety **2 exertion**, effort, tension, struggle, force **3 injury**, sprain, wrench, crick **4 breed**, species, type, form, sort

strained *adj* **1 tense**, forced, artificial, awkward, laboured *Opposite*: natural **2 stressed**, tense, worried, nervous, nervy (*infml*) *Opposite*: calm

strait *n* **passage**, channel, canal, sound

straitened *adj* **impoverished**, severe, distressed, difficult, pinched *Opposite*: comfortable

straitjacket *n* **restriction**, limitation, restraint, shackles, constraint *Opposite*: freedom

strait-laced *adj* **prudish**, puritanical, prim, moralistic, strict *Opposite*: broad-minded

strand *n* **1 thread**, filament, fibre, string, wire **2 lock**, tress, wisp, curl **3 element**, component, constituent, aspect, feature ■ *v* **cut off**, maroon, trap, leave high and dry, abandon *Opposite*: rescue

strange adj 1 odd, bizarre, outlandish, eccentric, weird Opposite: normal 2 unfamiliar, foreign, alien, unknown, mysterious Opposite: familiar 3 inexplicable, surprising, funny, astonishing, perplexing Opposite: unsurprising

strangely adv 1 oddly, bizarrely, outlandishly, eccentrically, weirdly Opposite: normally 2 inexplicably, surprisingly, funnily, astonishingly, perplexingly Opposite: unsurprisingly

strangeness n 1 weirdness, peculiarity, eccentricity, abnormality, incongruity Opposite: normality 2 lack of familiarity, newness, foreignness, mysteriousness

stranger n foreigner, alien, outsider, visitor, guest Opposite: acquaintance

strangle v 1 choke, strangulate, throttle, garrotte, asphyxiate 2 stifle, repress, suppress, inhibit, smother Opposite: express

stranglehold n 1 strong hold, throttlehold, iron grip, grip, lock 2 power, dominion, control, sway, domination

strangulate v strangle, throttle, choke, smother, asphyxiate

strangulation n strangling, throttling, choking, smothering, asphyxiation

strap n band, fastening, belt, strip, leash ■ v fasten, belt, secure, lash, buckle

straphanger (infml) n passenger, traveller, commuter, rider

strapline n subheading, subhead, heading, head, title

strapped (infml) adj needy, wanting, short of money, impecunious, impoverished Opposite: flush (infml)

strapping (infml) adj robust, broad-shouldered, burly, well-built, sturdy Opposite: delicate

stratagem n trick, ruse, ploy, wile, subterfuge

strategic adj planned, tactical, calculated, deliberate, premeditated Opposite: unplanned

strategist n tactician, planner, policymaker, plotter, schemer

strategy n plan, scheme, policy, approach, tactic

stratum (fml) n layer, band, level, division, section

straw n grass, hay, stubble, chaff

straw poll n poll, opinion poll, show of hands, referendum, questionnaire

stray v wander away, wander off, go astray, get lost, drift ■ adj lost, wandering, abandoned, homeless, vagrant

streak n 1 line, band, strip, stripe, vein 2 element, side, trait, characteristic, quality 3 run, stretch, roll ■ v 1 mark, stripe, stain, line, fleck 2 move fast, fly, flash, zoom, whiz

streaky adj stripy, striped, striated, banded, lined

stream n 1 watercourse, river, beck, torrent, rivulet 2 jet, spurt, torrent, cascade Opposite: drip 3 flood, torrent, barrage, onslaught ■ v flow, pour out, flood, gush, spill

streamer n flag, banner, bunting, ribbon, decoration

streamline v rationalize, modernize, update, reorganize, restructure

streamlined adj 1 sleek, smooth, slick, aerodynamic 2 efficient, rationalized, modernized, updated, reorganized Opposite: cumbersome

street credibility n coolness, credibility, sophistication, fashionableness, street cred (infml)

streetwise (infml) adj astute, quick-witted, sharp-witted, smart, sharp Opposite: inexperienced

strength n 1 power, force, might, potency, muscle Opposite: weakness 2 strong point, strong suit, forte, asset, métier Opposite: weakness 3 intensity, concentration, dilution, depth, potency

strengthen v make stronger, reinforce, fortify, brace, toughen Opposite: weaken

strength of mind n resolve, determination, strength, fortitude, willpower Opposite: weakness

strenuous adj 1 taxing, arduous, exhausting, demanding, hard Opposite: light 2 active, energetic, determined, spirited, tireless Opposite: half-hearted. See COMPARE AND CONTRAST at hard.

stress n 1 strain, anxiety, worry, tension, trauma 2 emphasis, importance, weight, accent, urgency ■ v emphasize, lay emphasis on, underline, underscore, accentuate. See COMPARE AND CONTRAST at worry.

stressed adj harassed, worried, strained, tense, anxious Opposite: relaxed

stressed out (infml) see stressed

stressful adj demanding, taxing, worrying, traumatic, tense Opposite: relaxing

stress out (infml) v worry, bother, get to, harass, perturb Opposite: relax

stretch v 1 extend, elongate, enlarge, widen, broaden Opposite: shrink 2 spread out, extend, unfold, spread, unroll 3 be elastic, give, expand, yield ■ n 1 give, bounce, spring, elasticity Opposite: rigidity 2 section, expanse, bit, area, sweep 3 spell, period, stint, time, run

stretch a point v 1 make allowances, bend the rules, turn a blind eye, make an exception 2 exaggerate, overstate, inflate, amplify, embroider Opposite: understate

stretched adj 1 extended, outstretched, elongated, expanded, lengthened Opposite: contracted 2 strained, overextended, pushed, fraught, busy Opposite: relaxed

stretch out v recline, lie back, bask, lounge, sprawl

stretchy *adj* **elastic**, flexible, springy, pliable *Opposite*: rigid

strew *v* **1 scatter**, throw, disperse, distribute, spread *Opposite*: gather **2 litter**, cover, fill, sprinkle, dot

striation *n* **pattern**, marking, corrugation, incision, ridge

stricken *adj* **1 troubled**, tormented, wracked, disturbed, traumatized **2 laid low**, afflicted, suffering, affected, wracked *Opposite*: well **3 injured**, damaged, wounded, hurt, struck

strict *adj* **1 severe**, firm, stern, harsh, stringent *Opposite*: lenient **2 exact**, precise, accurate, narrow, meticulous *Opposite*: inaccurate

strictness *n* **1 severity**, firmness, sternness, harshness, stringency *Opposite*: leniency **2 exactitude**, precision, accuracy, narrowness, meticulousness *Opposite*: inaccuracy

stricture *(fml)* *n* **1 criticism**, attack, rebuke, telling off, censure **2 restriction**, restraint, limit, constraint, limitation

stride *v* **step**, walk, pace, tread, march ■ *n* **1 pace**, step, tread, gait, walk **2 advance**, progress, development, improvement, headway

strident *adj* **1 loud**, harsh, grating, shrill, raucous *Opposite*: soft **2 vociferous**, forceful, persuasive, clamorous, baying *Opposite*: gentle

strife *n* **trouble**, conflict, discord, contention, fighting *Opposite*: harmony

strike *v* **1 hit**, beat, smack, thump, clout **2 collide with**, hit, crash into, smash into, bump into *Opposite*: miss **3 occur to**, come to mind, dawn on, hit, come to **4 attack**, launch an attack, fall on, set on, hit **5 discover**, hit upon, light on, stumble across, chance upon **6 take industrial action**, stop work, come out, down tools, walk out **7 reach**, arrive at, attain, achieve, arrange ■ *n* **1 raid**, attack, assault, foray, air strike **2 industrial action**, go-slow, walkout, work-to-rule, work stoppage

strike down *v* **1 knock down**, floor, fell, bring down, knock out **2 afflict**, lay low, infect, affect, make ill **3 kill**, bring down, murder, assassinate, slaughter

strike it rich *v* **hit the jackpot**, come into money, make your fortune, laugh all the way to the bank, rake it in *(infml)*

strike off *v* **delete**, cross off, remove, withdraw *Opposite*: include

strike out *v* **1 cross out**, delete, score out, strike through, cancel **2 set out**, leave, depart, go, move off *Opposite*: arrive **3 attack**, lash out, set on, assail

striker *n* **1 picket**, picketer, demonstrator, protester **2 forward**, attacker, winger

strike up *v* **start**, begin, commence, initiate, make a start *Opposite*: stop

strike while the iron's hot *v* **take the opportunity**, grab the chance, make the most of it, make hay while the sun shines *(infml)*

striking *adj* **1 conspicuous**, noticeable, marked, remarkable, salient *Opposite*: inconspicuous **2 good-looking**, handsome, attractive, eye-catching, beautiful

striking distance *n* **stone's throw**, short distance, a hairsbreadth, hop, skip, and jump, spitting distance *(infml)*

string *n* **1 cord**, thread, filament, twine, rope **2 sequence**, series, run, chain, succession

string along *(infml)* *v* **1 deceive**, mislead, lead on, lead up the garden path, send on a wild-goose chase **2 tag along**, hang around, go along, go along for the ride, join in **3 agree**, go along with, be of one mind, concur, approve *Opposite*: disagree

stringency *n* **severity**, strictness, rigour, harshness, inflexibility *Opposite*: flexibility

stringent *adj* **severe**, strict, rigorous, stern, harsh *Opposite*: lax

stringer *n* **journalist**, reporter, correspondent, columnist, writer

stringy *adj* **tough**, chewy, sinewy, gristly, fibrous *Opposite*: tender

strip *v* **1 undress**, strip off, doff, shed, peel off *Opposite*: dress **2 deprive**, take away, divest, deny, rid *Opposite*: furnish *(fml)* ■ *n* **band**, sliver, shred, ribbon, slip

stripe *n* **band of colour**, strip, band, line, streak

stripped *adj* **bare**, exposed, unprotected, uncovered, unvarnished *Opposite*: coated

stripped-down *adj* **lean**, spare, sparse, minimalist, utilitarian

strive *v* **struggle**, endeavour, go all out, do your best, do your utmost

stroke *n* **1 hit**, blow, knock, rap, lash **2 rub**, caress, fondle, pat ■ *v* **caress**, fondle, pat, rub

stroll *v* **walk**, amble, saunter, ramble, go for a constitutional ■ *n* **saunter**, walk, amble, turn, wander

strong *adj* **1 powerful**, burly, brawny, muscular, sturdy *Opposite*: weak **2 robust**, sturdy, stout, solid, durable *Opposite*: fragile **3 glaring**, dazzling, bright, stark, brilliant *Opposite*: dim **4 keen**, staunch, dedicated, firm, fanatical *Opposite*: indifferent **5 convincing**, sound, clear, clear-cut, persuasive *Opposite*: weak **6 fervent**, great, intense, deep, deep-seated *Opposite*: weak **7 intense**, concentrated, pungent, piquant, spicy *Opposite*: insipid

strong-arm *(infml)* *adj* **coercive**, forcible, violent, physical, forceful *Opposite*: peaceable ■ *v* **coerce**, compel, force, frighten, bully

strongbox *n* **safe-deposit box**, cash box, safe, coffer, vault

stronghold *n* **fortress**, refuge, bastion, citadel, sanctuary

strong-minded *adj* **1 determined**, dogged, persevering, persistent, resolute *Opposite*: weak-willed **2 confident**, clear-thinking, certain, intelligent, decisive

strong-mindedness *n* **1 determination**, doggedness, perseverance, persistence, resoluteness *Opposite*: vacillation **2 confidence**, strength, strength of character, character, clarity *Opposite*: weakness

strong point *n* strength, forte, asset, métier, strong suit *Opposite*: weakness

strong suit *see* **strong point**

strong-willed *adj* resolute, determined, strong-minded, iron-willed, unbending *Opposite*: weak

strop (*infml*) *n* **bad mood**, bad temper, huff, pet, rage

stroppiness (*infml*) *n* **awkwardness**, uncooperativeness, obstreperousness, difficultness, unhelpfulness

stroppy (*infml*) *adj* **awkward**, uncooperative, obstreperous, difficult, unhelpful *Opposite*: amiable

structural *adj* **1 physical**, mechanical, organizational, operational **2 basic**, important, essential, fundamental, underlying

structure *n* **1 construction**, assembly, building, edifice, erection (*fml*) **2 arrangement**, organization, construction, configuration, makeup ■ *v* arrange, construct, configure, put together, make up

structured *adj* **1 organized**, planned, controlled, designed, arranged *Opposite*: unstructured **2 defined**, coordinated, well-defined, designed, formal *Opposite*: amorphous

struggle *v* **1 strive**, try, strain, fight, work hard *Opposite*: coast **2 fight**, grapple, tussle, wrestle, battle **3 writhe**, wriggle, thrash about, brawl, scuffle ■ *n* **1 tussle**, fight, brawl, scuffle, skirmish **2 effort**, exertion, labour, toil, work

strum *v* play, thrum, improvise, jam, twang

strut *v* swagger, march, parade, prance, walk ■ *n* support, rod, brace, crosspiece, girder

stub *n* stump, end, remains, remnant, counterfoil ■ *v* hit, bump, bang, knock, bash (*infml*)

stubble *n* **1 stalks**, stems, rubbish, debris, refuse **2 whiskers**, five o'clock shadow, growth, beard, moustache

stubborn *adj* **1 persistent**, dogged, tenacious, persevering, determined *Opposite*: half-hearted **2 obstinate**, immovable, inflexible, wilful, mulish *Opposite*: flexible

stubbornness *n* **1 persistence**, tenacity, perseverance, doggedness, stalwartness **2 obstinacy**, inflexibility, obduracy, pigheadedness, mulishness *Opposite*: flexibility

stubby *adj* short, broad, thick, stumpy, squat *Opposite*: slender

stub out *v* extinguish, put out, snuff

stuck *adj* **1 wedged**, fixed, trapped, caught, jammed *Opposite*: loose **2 baffled**, mystified, puzzled, without an answer, at a complete loss

stuck-up (*infml*) *adj* **snobbish**, arrogant, conceited, superior, self-important *Opposite*: unassuming

stud *n* knob, boss, rivet, nail, screw ■ *v* **1 fit with studs**, decorate, fasten, rivet, secure **2 dot**, pepper, sprinkle, scatter, speckle

student *n* scholar, pupil, schoolboy, schoolgirl, schoolchild *Opposite*: teacher

student loan *n* loan, government loan, educational loan, subsidized loan

studied *adj* **deliberate**, intentional, calculated, considered, premeditated *Opposite*: spontaneous

studio *n* **1 workplace**, workshop, workroom, atelier, pottery **2 academy**, conservatory, dance school, ballet school, dance academy

studious *adj* **1 thoughtful**, serious, reflective, bookish, scholarly *Opposite*: frivolous **2 diligent**, painstaking, careful, assiduous, industrious *Opposite*: careless

study *v* **1 learn**, take in, revise, read, swot (*infml*) **2 investigate**, research, experiment, examine, consider ■ *n* **1 learning**, education, training, revision, schoolwork **2 investigation**, examination, survey, review, inquiry **3 report**, findings, conclusions, research paper, analysis

stuff *v* fill, pack, cram, ram, jam ■ *n* **1 material**, substance, matter, raw material **2 things**, objects, paraphernalia, articles, mess **3 possessions**, belongings, things, kit, tackle

stuffed *adj* **1 filled**, lined, packed, jammed, crammed **2** (*infml*) **full**, fit to burst, replete, sated, satiated *Opposite*: hungry

stuffed shirt (*infml*) *n* fogy, old fogy, killjoy, spoilsport, fuddy-duddy (*infml*)

stuffiness *n* **1 airlessness**, staleness, closeness, mugginess, fug *Opposite*: freshness **2 formality**, conventionality, staidness, standoffishness, pomposity *Opposite*: informality

stuff up (*infml*) *v* **make a mess of**, botch (*infml*), mess up (*infml*), foul up (*infml*), blow it (*slang*) *Opposite*: sort out

stuffy *adj* **1 airless**, stale, smelly, hot, warm *Opposite*: fresh **2 strait-laced**, old-fashioned, conventional, formal, pompous *Opposite*: informal **3 congested**, blocked up, stuffed up, clogged up, bunged up (*infml*) *Opposite*: clear

stultify *v* **1 bore**, dull, numb, deaden, put off *Opposite*: stimulate **2 make a fool of**, belittle, ridicule, humiliate, set up (*infml*) **3 cancel out**, block, render useless, pre-empt, vitiate *Opposite*: advance

stumble *v* **1 trip**, trip up, lose your footing, lose your balance, falter **2 stagger**, lurch, sway, blunder, roll **3 hesitate**, stop and start, hem and haw, falter, stammer **4 come across**, find, discover, happen on, chance on ∎ *n* **1 blunder**, trip, stagger, false step, mishap **2 mistake**, hesitation, slip, blunder, slip-up *(infml)*. *See* COMPARE AND CONTRAST *at* **hesitate**.

stumbling block *n* **obstacle**, problem, difficulty, sticking point, obstruction *Opposite*: aid

stump *n* **base**, stub, butt, end, remains ∎ *v* **baffle**, puzzle, perplex, mystify, nonplus *Opposite*: enlighten

stump up *(infml)* *v* **come up with**, pay, provide, put in, contribute *Opposite*: withhold

stumpy *adj* **squat**, stubby, short, thickset, broad *Opposite*: lanky

stun *v* **1 knock out**, paralyse, numb, daze, put out of action *Opposite*: bring round **2 shock**, upset, dumbfound, daze, amaze

stunner *(infml)* *n* **star**, smash, sensation, hit, triumph

stunning *adj* **spectacular**, striking, fabulous, splendid, superb *Opposite*: unimpressive

stunningly *adv* **extremely**, spectacularly, strikingly, fabulously, remarkably *Opposite*: moderately

stunt *v* **inhibit**, restrict, arrest, hold back, impede *Opposite*: assist ∎ *n* **feat**, exploit, act, deed, show

stunted *adj* **underdeveloped**, undersized, small, short, little

stupefaction *n* **confusion**, befuddlement, bemusement, perplexity, bewilderment

stupefied *adj* **1 confused**, fuddled, punch-drunk, stunned, befuddled *Opposite*: clear-headed **2 amazed**, astonished, astounded, stunned, dazed

stupefy *v* **1 amaze**, astonish, astound, surprise, stagger **2 confuse**, befuddle, bewilder, stun, perplex *Opposite*: enlighten

stupendous *adj* **1 astonishing**, astounding, amazing, surprising, stunning *Opposite*: unremarkable **2 fantastic**, wonderful, block, out of this world, marvellous, great *Opposite*: awful **3 huge**, vast, large, colossal, enormous *Opposite*: tiny

stupendously *adv* **tremendously**, impressively, amazingly, exceptionally, remarkably *Opposite*: slightly

stupid *adj* **1 unintelligent**, dull, brainless, obtuse, witless *Opposite*: intelligent **2 foolish**, fatuous, inane, nonsensical, silly *Opposite*: sensible **3 unwise**, senseless, ill-advised, imprudent, injudicious *Opposite*: wise

stupidity *n* **foolishness**, foolhardiness, silliness, inanity, folly *Opposite*: sense

stupor *n* **1 torpor**, lethargy, inertness, limpness, blankness *Opposite*: activeness **2 daze**, dream, trance, shock, numbness *Opposite*: consciousness

sturdiness *n* **strength**, solidity, durability, toughness, hardiness *Opposite*: weakness

sturdy *adj* **1 well-built**, strong, robust, powerful, muscular *Opposite*: frail **2 well-made**, durable, robust, tough, hard-wearing *Opposite*: rickety **3 resolute**, decisive, determined, strenuous, enthusiastic *Opposite*: feeble

stutter *v* **stammer**, trip over your tongue, falter, stumble, hesitate *Opposite*: enunciate ∎ *n* **stammer**, speech disorder, impediment, impairment, speech impediment

sty *n* **cyst**, swelling, lump, boil, sore

style *n* **1 design**, type, sort, form, variety **2 method**, approach, way, manner, fashion **3 flair**, panache, chic, bravura, stylishness *Opposite*: gracelessness **4 luxury**, luxuriousness, extravagance, lavishness, opulence ∎ *v* **1 fashion**, design, shape, cut, adapt **2** *(fml)* **name**, call, nickname, label, term

stylish *adj* **fashionable**, sophisticated, chic, modish, smart *Opposite*: unfashionable

stylishness *n* **style**, flair, chic, panache, smartness *Opposite*: dowdiness

stylistic *adj* **formal**, technical, literary, musical, artistic *Opposite*: spontaneous

stylize *v* **formalize**, abstract, schematize, systematize, outline

stylized *adj* **conventional**, artificial, formalized, formal, unnatural *Opposite*: natural

stymie *v* **hinder**, prevent, block, thwart, confound *Opposite*: enable ∎ *n* **impasse**, dead end, stalemate, standstill, deadlock *Opposite*: breakthrough

suave *adj* **urbane**, smooth, polished, polite, sophisticated *Opposite*: awkward

subcategory *n* **subsection**, subclass, subgroup, subdivision

subconscious *adj* **unconscious**, intuitive, hidden, unintentional, involuntary *Opposite*: deliberate

subcontract *v* **delegate**, farm out, contract out, commission, mandate

subculture *n* **subgroup**, culture, grouping, group, subdivision

subcutaneous *adj* **hypodermic**, hypodermal, intravenous, internal, dermatological

subdirectory *n* **division**, subdivision, directory, file, storage space

subdivide *v* **divide**, section, segment, split, cut *Opposite*: unify

subdivision *n* **1 section**, part, division, sector, tract **2 division**, sectioning, segmenting, separation, splitting up *Opposite*: unification

subdue *v* **1 restrain**, suppress, hold back, control, discipline **2 pacify**, calm, calm down, soothe, mollify **3 subjugate**, conquer, vanquish, defeat, overpower

subdued *adj* **1 passive**, cowed, submissive, quiet, unresponsive *Opposite*: uplifted **2 gentle**, low, restrained, muted, subtle *Opposite*: loud

subeditor *n* **assistant editor**, editorial assistant, assistant, deputy editor, sub *(infml)*

subgroup n **subcategory**, subsection, subclass, subdivision, smaller group

subhuman adj **bestial**, animal, inhuman, inhumane, wicked

subject n **1 topic**, theme, focus, subject matter, area under discussion **2 subordinate**, vassal, liege, dependent, citizen Opposite: sovereign **3 field**, speciality, study, discipline, area

COMPARE AND CONTRAST CORE MEANING: what is under discussion

subject a matter that is under discussion or investigation; **topic** a matter dealt with in a text or discussion; **subject matter** the material dealt with in a film, discussion, or other medium; **matter** the material that is dealt with in speech or writing, as opposed to its presentation; **theme** a distinct, recurring, and unifying idea in music, literature, art, or film; **burden** (literary) the main argument or recurrent theme in music or literature.

subjection n **domination**, subjugation, overpowering, enslavement, oppression

subjective adj **1 slanted**, biased, prejudiced, skewed, one-sided Opposite: objective **2 individual**, particular, idiosyncratic, independent, personal Opposite: general

subjectively adv **personally**, individually, instinctively, intuitively, emotionally Opposite: objectively

subjectivity n **bias**, prejudice, partisanship, partiality Opposite: objectivity

subject matter n **topic**, theme, subject, focus, question. See COMPARE AND CONTRAST at **subject**.

subject to v **cause to experience**, cause to undergo, expose to, put through, make susceptible ■ adj **conditional on**, dependent on, depending on, bound by, answerable to Opposite: unrelated

subjugate v **conquer**, vanquish, subdue, defeat, overpower Opposite: liberate

sublimate v **channel**, redirect, transfer, direct, reroute

sublimation n **redirection**, transferral, direction, rerouting, division

sublime adj **1 inspiring**, inspirational, uplifting, awe-inspiring, moving Opposite: ridiculous **2** (infml) **excellent**, superb, splendid, marvellous, wonderful

subliminal adj **subconscious**, unconscious, hidden, concealed, unintentional Opposite: conscious

submerge v **1 plunge**, immerse, dip, sink, duck **2 suppress**, conceal, hide, stifle Opposite: reveal

submerged adj **underwater**, flooded, inundated, waterlogged, sunken

submission n **1 obedience**, compliance, capitulation, surrender, acquiescence Opposite: resistance **2 proposal**, suggestion, plan, tender, offer

submissive adj **obedient**, passive, compliant, acquiescent, subservient Opposite: assertive

submit v **1 present**, propose, tender, offer, suggest Opposite: withdraw **2 give in**, yield, agree to, acquiesce, resign yourself to Opposite: resist. See COMPARE AND CONTRAST at **yield**.

subnormal adj **substandard**, second-rate, poor, inferior, below average Opposite: superior

subordinate adj **secondary**, lesser, subsidiary, inferior, lower Opposite: main ■ n **assistant**, junior, underling, minion, aide Opposite: boss

subordination n **relegation**, demotion, reduction, subservience

suborn v **incite**, bribe, induce, entice, corrupt

subpoena n **summons**, order, call ■ v **summon**, compel, require, order, command

subscribe v **1 donate to**, give to, pledge, promise, contribute **2 agree with**, approve of, support, condone, hold with Opposite: disagree

subscription n **payment**, donation, contribution

subsequent adj **following**, succeeding, ensuing, successive, consequent Opposite: preceding

subservient adj **obedient**, compliant, acquiescent, docile, deferential Opposite: assertive

subset n **subsection**, subdivision, subgroup, subcategory, subclass

subside v **1 collapse**, cave in, fall down, drop, sink Opposite: rise **2 diminish**, lessen, decrease, dwindle, wane Opposite: build up

subsidence n **subsiding**, sinking, settling, dropping, collapsing

subsidiary adj **1 supplementary**, auxiliary, ancillary, additional, contributory Opposite: main **2 subordinate**, lesser, secondary, junior, lower Opposite: major ■ n **branch**, division, holding, company, firm

subsidize v **finance**, fund, sponsor, back, support

subsidy n **funding**, financial backing, grant, support, aid

subsist v **exist**, survive, live, make ends meet, keep going

subsistence n **survival**, existence, maintenance, sustenance

subspecies n **category**, strain, genus, sort, class

substance n **1 material**, matter, stuff, ingredient, body **2 core**, essence, import, gist, nub **3 affluence**, property, money, means, wealth Opposite: poverty

substandard adj **inferior**, second-rate, poor, subnormal, below average Opposite: superior

substantial adj **considerable**, large, extensive, significant, important Opposite: small

substantially adv **considerably**, significantly, noticeably, markedly, greatly Opposite: insignificantly

substantiate v **validate**, authenticate, verify, corroborate, prove Opposite: disprove

substantiation n **corroboration**, confirmation, validation, authentication, support

substantive adj **1 practical**, applicable, functional, utilitarian Opposite: impractical **2 essential**, fundamental, basic, central, elementary Opposite: secondary **3 independent**, autonomous, separate, individual Opposite: dependent **4 substantial**, decent, considerable, respectable, significant Opposite: insignificant

substantively adv **1 practically**, functionally, applicably **2 essentially**, fundamentally, basically, centrally, elementarily **3 independently**, autonomously, individually, separately **4 substantially**, considerably, significantly, noticeably, markedly Opposite: insignificantly

substitute v **1 replace with**, exchange, use instead, switch, swap (infml) **2 stand in for**, fill in for, take the place of, relieve, deputize for ■ n **alternative**, replacement, stand-in, locum, surrogate

substitution n **replacement**, switch, exchange, changeover, change

subsume v **include**, incorporate, count, list, consider

subterfuge n **trick**, ploy, ruse, stratagem, manoeuvre

subterranean adj **1 underground**, deep, below ground, buried, hidden **2 secret**, clandestine, underground, covert, arcane Opposite: open

subtext n **implication**, hidden agenda, suggestion, connotation, intimation

subtitle n **caption**, legend, surtitle, supertitle

subtle adj **1 slight**, faint, fine, thin, imperceptible Opposite: coarse **2 understated**, delicate, indirect, elusive, refined Opposite: blunt **3 intelligent**, experienced, sensitive, shrewd, perceptive Opposite: obtuse **4 cunning**, sly, crafty, devious, tricky Opposite: ingenuous

subtleness n **1 delicacy**, subtlety, refinement, intricacy, elusiveness Opposite: bluntness **2 intelligence**, experience, sensitivity, shrewdness, perceptiveness **3 cunning**, deviousness, slyness, craftiness, trickiness Opposite: ingenuousness **4 slightness**, faintness, fineness

subtlety n **1 delicacy**, subtleness, refinement, intricacy, elusiveness Opposite: blatancy **2 detail**, nicety, fine point, nuance **3 sensitivity**, delicacy, tact, discernment, finesse

subtract v **take away**, take from, take off, deduct, withdraw Opposite: add

subtraction n **deduction**, removal, withdrawal, debit, deletion Opposite: addition

suburb n **conurbation**, district, environs, commuter belt, development Opposite: centre

suburban adj **outlying**, peripheral, out-of-town, outer, residential Opposite: central

suburbia n **suburbs**, commuter belt, conurbation, environs, outskirts Opposite: centre

subvention (fml) n **1 grant**, subsidy, payment, donation, endowment **2 aid**, support, backing, sponsorship, funding

subversion n **rebellion**, sedition, treason, mutiny, insurrection Opposite: compliance

subversive adj **dissident**, rebellious, revolutionary, insubordinate, seditious Opposite: law-abiding ■ n **traitor**, collaborator, mutineer, revolutionary, insubordinate Opposite: patriot

subvert v **undermine**, overthrow, destabilize, sabotage, disrupt Opposite: support

subway n **underpass**, tunnel, passageway

subzero adj **freezing**, bitter, icy, ice-cold, glacial Opposite: tropical

succeed v **1 achieve**, accomplish, hit the target, turn out well, be successful Opposite: fail **2 do well**, get ahead, prosper, be successful, thrive Opposite: fail **3 follow**, come after, replace, supersede, supplant Opposite: precede

succeeding adj **following**, subsequent, ensuing, next, successive Opposite: preceding

success n **1 achievement**, accomplishment, victory, triumph, feat Opposite: failure **2 hit**, winner, sensation, star, triumph Opposite: failure

successful adj **1 fruitful**, positive, effective, efficacious (fml) Opposite: unsuccessful **2 prosperous**, up-and-coming, well-off, wealthy, rich Opposite: poor **3 flourishing**, thriving, booming, profitable, lucrative Opposite: ailing

succession n **series**, sequence, chain, run, string Opposite: individual

successive adj **consecutive**, succeeding, following, sequential, uninterrupted Opposite: single

successor n **heir**, inheritor, replacement, beneficiary Opposite: predecessor

success story n **success**, winner, sensation, hit, triumph

succinct adj **concise**, pithy, brief, to the point, laconic Opposite: long-winded

succinctness n **concision**, pithiness, conciseness, brevity, briefness Opposite: verbosity

succulence n **juiciness**, lusciousness, tenderness, moistness, tastiness Opposite: dryness

succulent adj **juicy**, moist, tender, luscious, delicious Opposite: dry

succumb v **1 give way**, yield, give in, submit, surrender Opposite: withstand **2 die**, pass away, perish, depart, expire (fml). See COMPARE AND CONTRAST at **yield**.

such as *adv* for example, like, namely, viz, as

suck *v* 1 draw, pull on, lap, slurp, drink 2 extract, draw, pull, force, sweep, bear ■ *n* slurp, draw, pull, drink, taste

sucker *n* 1 gull, dupe, pushover *(infml)*, mug *(slang)*, mark *(slang)* ■ *v* trick, con, fool, gull, dupe

suck in *v* 1 involve, implicate, entangle, embroil, draw in *Opposite*: exclude 2 breathe in, inhale, draw in, take in, pull in

suck up *v* 1 absorb, soak up, take up, sop up *Opposite*: exude 2 *(infml)* ingratiate yourself, flatter, grovel, toady, crawl *(infml)*

suction *n* force, pressure, pull, draw, drag

sudden *adj* unexpected, abrupt, rapid, swift, hasty *Opposite*: gradual

suddenly *adv* unexpectedly, abruptly, rapidly, swiftly, all of a sudden *Opposite*: gradually

suddenness *n* unexpectedness, quickness, abruptness, rapidity, swiftness

suds *n* lather, bubbles, foam, froth, spume *(literary)*

sue *v* 1 *(fml)* petition, beg, plead, appeal, implore *(fml)* 2 litigate, prosecute, indict, file a suit, charge

suffer *v* 1 feel pain, hurt, agonize, ache, smart 2 undergo, experience, bear, endure, go through 3 tolerate, endure, bear, put up with, stand 4 deteriorate, fall off, be impaired, drop off *(infml)*

sufferance *n* 1 tolerance, toleration, acquiescence, allowance, permission *Opposite*: prohibition 2 endurance, stamina, staying power, stoicism, fortitude

sufferer *n* invalid, victim, patient, case, martyr

suffering *n* 1 pain, distress, agony, torment, affliction 2 sorrow, grief, misery, woe, anguish

suffice *(fml)* *v* be sufficient, do, serve, suit

sufficiency *n* right amount, adequacy, abundance, plenty *Opposite*: insufficiency

sufficient *adj* adequate, enough, satisfactory, necessary, appropriate *Opposite*: inadequate

suffocate *v* smother, choke, stifle, throttle, asphyxiate

suffuse *v* spread through, pervade, fill, saturate, flood

sugar *n* *(infml)* honey, sweetheart, darling, dearest, precious ■ *v* sweeten, dress up, disguise, titivate, improve

sugary *adj* 1 sweet, syrupy, sickly, sugared, sweetened *Opposite*: bitter 2 sentimental, mawkish, gushy, mushy, syrupy *Opposite*: dry

suggest *v* 1 propose, put forward, advise, recommend, advocate *Opposite*: veto 2 imply, insinuate, intimate, indicate, hint 3 remind, bring to mind, call to mind, evoke, conjure up. *See* COMPARE AND CONTRAST *at* recommend.

suggestibility *n* susceptibility, openness, vulnerability, credulousness, credulity *Opposite*: strong-mindedness

suggestible *adj* susceptible, impressionable, gullible, credulous, malleable *Opposite*: strong-minded

suggestion *n* 1 proposal, proposition, submission, recommendation, idea *Opposite*: order 2 implication, hint, insinuation, intimation, indication *Opposite*: statement 3 evocation, air, aura, hint, trace

suggestive *adj* 1 evocative, redolent, reminiscent, indicative, expressive 2 improper, indelicate, indecent, lewd, risqué

suicidal *adj* 1 *(infml)* desperate, cheerless, hopeless, unhappy, miserable 2 dangerous, treacherous, perilous, reckless, madcap *Opposite*: sensible

suicide *n* 1 death, self-destruction, self-immolation 2 recklessness, rashness, perversity, irresponsibility, madness

suit *n* costume, ensemble, dress suit, trouser suit, uniform ■ *v* 1 go with, match, fit, be fitting, agree with *Opposite*: clash 2 flatter, become, show up, enhance

WORD BANK

❏ types of suit all-in-one, black tie, boiler suit, business suit, catsuit, dress suit, jumpsuit, overalls, pinstripe suit, trouser suit, white tie, zoot suit

suitability *n* appropriateness, aptness, fittingness, fitness, correctness *Opposite*: unsuitability

suitable *adj* appropriate, apposite, fit, apt, right *Opposite*: inappropriate

suitcase *n* case, luggage, baggage, bag, valise

suite *n* set, collection, group, complement

suited *adj* right, matched, well-matched, appropriate, apposite *Opposite*: wrong

sulk *v* mope, be in a mood, feel sorry for yourself, be in a huff, pout *Opposite*: rejoice *(literary)* ■ *n* bad temper, mood, temper, huff, bad mood

sulkiness *n* moodiness, resentfulness, temper, bad temper, moroseness *Opposite*: joviality

sulky *adj* morose, angry, resentful, sullen, unsociable *Opposite*: jovial

sullen *adj* surly, morose, hostile, bad-tempered, dour *Opposite*: friendly

sullenness *n* surliness, hostility, bad temper, moodiness, moroseness *Opposite*: friendliness

sullied *adj* tainted, dishonoured, discredited, corrupt, disgraced

sully *v* tarnish, taint, smear, denigrate, spoil *Opposite*: praise

sulphurous *adj* acrid, reeking, stinking, foul, bitter

sultry *adj* hot, humid, muggy, stifling, oppressive *Opposite*: fresh

sum *n* 1 figure, amount, quantity, entirety, totality 2 **calculation**, addition, computation, summation

summarily *adv* **instantly**, immediately, instantaneously, abruptly, suddenly *Opposite*: eventually

summarize *v* sum up, précis, abridge, recap, go over *Opposite*: elaborate

summary *n* précis, synopsis, digest, sum-up, outline *Opposite*: exposition ■ *adj* 1 **swift**, rapid, instant, immediate, instantaneous *Opposite*: considered 2 **short**, brief, concise, abridged, succinct

summation *n* 1 **addition**, calculation, computation, sum 2 **sum total**, total, sum, final total, grand total 3 **summary**, summing up, synopsis, outline, précis

summer *n* 1 **summertime**, dog days, midsummer, solstice *Opposite*: winter 2 **warm weather**, sun, sunshine, warmth, heat 3 **prime**, best time, summertime, best years, golden age

summerhouse *n* gazebo, pagoda, hut, shed, shelter

summertime *see* summer

summery *adj* warm, balmy, sunny, hot *Opposite*: wintry

summit *n* 1 **peak**, top, pinnacle, apex, acme *Opposite*: base 2 **conference**, meeting, summit meeting, talks

summon *v* 1 **call**, send for, call for, call upon, beckon *Opposite*: dismiss 2 **convene**, call together, get together, gather, assemble *Opposite*: dismiss 3 **muster**, rouse, find, activate, rally *Opposite*: demobilize

summons *n* order, writ, directive, command, subpoena

sumptuous *adj* **costly**, lavish, splendid, opulent, spectacular *Opposite*: meagre

sumptuousness *n* **luxuriousness**, luxury, lavishness, splendour, opulence

sums *(infml)* *n* **mathematics**, arithmetic, maths, calculation

sum total *n* whole, totality, entirety, aggregate, summation

sum up *v* summarize, recap, synopsize, encapsulate, abridge *Opposite*: elaborate

sunbaked *adj* hardened, dried, sun-dried, heated, cracked

sunbathe *v* sun yourself, bask, tan, catch some rays *(slang)*

sunbeam *n* ray, beam, shaft, sunlight, sunshine *Opposite*: moonbeam

Sunday best *n* **best clothes**, finery, formal wear, best bib and tucker *(infml)*

sundown *n* sunset, nightfall, twilight, dusk, evening *Opposite*: sunrise

sun-dried *adj* dried, preserved, dried up, dehydrated, jerked *Opposite*: fresh

sundries *n* miscellany, miscellanea, hotchpotch, assortment, odds and ends

sundry *adj* **various**, miscellaneous, assorted, varied, different *Opposite*: uniform

sunglasses *n* dark glasses, sunspecs *(infml)*, shades *(infml)*

sunk *adj* 1 **ruined**, dashed, in trouble, defeated, destroyed *Opposite*: successful 2 **depressed**, downcast, downhearted, dejected, in the dumps *Opposite*: happy

sunken *adj* 1 **submerged**, underwater, immersed 2 **hollow**, gaunt, deep-set, cadaverous, pinched 3 **recessed**, lower, settled, dipped, depressed *Opposite*: raised

sunless *adj* **dark**, cloudy, overcast, murky, gloomy *Opposite*: sunny

sunlight *n* sunshine, daylight, light, rays, sunbeams

sunlit *adj* sunny, bright, light, sundrenched, bathed in light *Opposite*: dark

sunnily *adv* **cheerfully**, cheerily, happily, genially, gaily *Opposite*: gloomily

sunny *adj* 1 **sunlit**, bright, luminous, brilliant, cloudless *Opposite*: dark 2 **cheerful**, cheery, bright, bright and breezy, positive *Opposite*: gloomy

sunrise *n* **dawn**, daybreak, break of day, first light, daylight *Opposite*: sunset

sunscreen *see* suntan lotion

sunset *n* sundown, dusk, evening, night, nightfall *Opposite*: sunrise

sunshade *n* parasol, umbrella, garden umbrella, beach umbrella, awning

sunshine *n* sunlight, light, rays, sunbeams, brightness *Opposite*: rainfall

sunspecs *see* sunglasses

sunspot *(infml)* *n* resort, tourist spot, holiday resort, beach resort

suntan cream *see* suntan lotion

suntan lotion *n* sun lotion, sun cream, suntan cream, sunscreen, sunblock

suntanned *adj* brown, tanned, bronzed, sunburnt *Opposite*: pale

suntan oil *see* suntan lotion

sup *v* spoon, sip, drink, partake of, lap *Opposite*: gulp ■ *n* mouthful, sip, swallow, drink, draught *Opposite*: gulp

super *adj* 1 *(infml)* **wonderful**, fantastic, great, marvellous, fabulous *Opposite*: awful 2 **superior**, better, enhanced, improved, outstanding *Opposite*: inferior

superabundant *adj* **overabundant**, in excess, excessive, extra, abounding *Opposite*: insufficient

superannuated *adj* 1 **retired**, pensioned off, discharged, elderly, aged *Opposite*: working 2 **out-of-date**, antiquated, out of fashion, outmoded, passé *Opposite*: fashionable 3 **worn out**, worn, unusable, used up, useless *Opposite*: new

superb *adj* **excellent**, outstanding, wonderful, splendid, fabulous *Opposite*: abysmal

superbug n **supergerm**, germ, microorganism, pathogen, bug (infml)

supercharge v **1 boost**, modify, charge, power up, amplify Opposite: downgrade **2 charge**, overdo, load, overload, hype Opposite: understate

supercilious adj **arrogant**, contemptuous, disdainful, pompous, superior Opposite: humble

superciliousness n **arrogance**, contemptuousness, contempt, condescension, haughtiness Opposite: humility

supercool (infml) adj **cool**, modern, contemporary, fashionable, trendy (infml) Opposite: passé

super-duper (infml) adj **excellent**, marvellous, colossal, impressive, pleasing Opposite: inferior

superego n **conscience**, integrity, scruples, sense of propriety, sense of judgment

superficial adj **1 shallow**, trivial, trifling, unimportant, paltry Opposite: profound **2 surface**, shallow, external, exterior, on the surface Opposite: deep **3 insincere**, shallow, artificial, phoney, apparent Opposite: sincere **4 cursory**, sketchy, rapid, hasty, quick Opposite: thorough

superficiality n **shallowness**, triviality, frivolity, levity, paltriness Opposite: profundity

superficially adv **1 apparently**, seemingly, supposedly, outwardly, ostensibly Opposite: wholly **2 cursorily**, sketchily, rapidly, hastily, casually Opposite: thoroughly

superfine adj **1 delicate**, fine, light, sheer, fragile Opposite: coarse **2 superior**, first-class, first-rate, high-quality, best Opposite: inferior

superfluity n **1 oversupply**, excess, overabundance, surfeit, surplus Opposite: insufficiency **2 luxury**, extra, frill, trifle, indulgence Opposite: necessity

superfluous adj **extra**, surplus, redundant, unnecessary, unessential Opposite: basic

supergrass (infml) n **informer**, informant, grass (slang), squealer (slang), rat (slang)

superhero n **champion**, crusader, rescuer, fighter, protector

superhuman adj **phenomenal**, prodigious, staggering, heroic, exceptional Opposite: normal

superimpose v **place over**, overlay, lay over, apply to, cover

superintend v **supervise**, manage, oversee, administer, control Opposite: ignore

superintendent n **manager**, supervisor, administrator, officer, controller Opposite: underling

superior adj **1 better**, better-quality, advanced, improved, enhanced Opposite: inferior **2 excellent**, high-class, top-quality, exclusive, first-class Opposite: second-rate **3 higher**, upper, over, above Opposite: lower **4 condescending**, arrogant, disdainful, supercilious, aloof Opposite: humble **5 larger**, greater, bigger, higher, more Opposite: smaller ■ n **boss**, manager, chief, elder, better Opposite: inferior

superiority n **1 advantage**, dominance, lead, pre-eminence, power Opposite: inferiority **2 condescension**, arrogance, haughtiness, disdain, aloofness Opposite: humility

superiority complex n **superiority**, inflated ego, self-importance, disdain, superciliousness Opposite: inferiority complex

superlative adj **excellent**, unmatched, unbeatable, untouchable, best Opposite: unremarkable

supernatural adj **paranormal**, mystic, mystical, ghostly, ghostlike Opposite: natural

---

WORD BANK

❑ **types of supernatural being** banshee, brownie, elf, fairy, fairy godmother, fay (literary), genie, imp, jinni, pixie, poltergeist, sprite

---

supernumerary adj **1 extra**, excessive, superfluous, spare, surplus Opposite: necessary **2 substitute**, extra, auxiliary, ancillary, standby Opposite: permanent

superpower n **world power**, giant, power bloc, global force, global influence

supersaver n **discount**, special offer, concession

supersede v **succeed**, take over, overtake, supplant, replace Opposite: precede

superstar n **star**, megastar, celebrity, icon, luminary Opposite: nobody

superstition n **fallacy**, false notion, delusion, misconception, fantasy

superstitious adj **credulous**, gullible, illogical, irrational, delusory Opposite: rational

superstructure n **1 structure**, construction, elevation, frame, framework Opposite: foundation **2 idea**, concept, system, structure, argument Opposite: premise

supertitle n **surtitle**, caption, legend

supervene (fml) v **1 interrupt**, charge in, butt in, appear, turn up **2 ensue**, follow, supersede, succeed, pursue

supervise v **oversee**, manage, administer, control, run Opposite: neglect

supervision n **1 management**, direction, administration, regulation, command Opposite: neglect **2 care**, custody, guardianship, protection, guidance

supervision order n **charge**, order, authorization, mandate, appointment

supervisor n **manager**, administrator, superintendent, controller, overseer Opposite: underling

supervisory adj **managerial**, administrative, superintendent, managing, controlling Opposite: subordinate

supine *adj* 1 **flat**, horizontal, flat on one's back, prostrate, prone *Opposite*: standing 2 **lethargic**, passive, inactive, apathetic, listless *Opposite*: vigorous

supplant *v* **oust**, displace, succeed, replace, unseat *Opposite*: install

supple *adj* 1 **lithe**, agile, mobile, double-jointed, sinuous *Opposite*: stiff 2 **bendable**, elastic, plastic, pliant, pliable *Opposite*: rigid

supplement *n* 1 **addition**, extra, complement, enhancement, increase *Opposite*: deduction 2 **section**, insert, appendix, attachment, rider ■ *v* **add**, complement, accompany, enhance, improve *Opposite*: deduct

supplemental *see* supplementary

supplementary *adj* **extra**, additional, added, add-on, top-up *Opposite*: deducted

suppleness *n* **litheness**, agility, mobility, flexibility, limberness *Opposite*: stiffness

suppliant *(fml) adj* **prayerful**, petitionary, begging, pleading, supplicant *(fml) Opposite*: beneficent ■ *n* **petitioner**, applicant, aspirant, suitor, beggar *Opposite*: benefactor

supplicant *(fml) n* **petitioner**, applicant, suitor, aspirant, beggar *Opposite*: donor

supplicate *(fml) v* **appeal**, petition, request, beg, entreat *Opposite*: grant

supplication *(fml) n* **appeal**, request, entreaty, petition, plea *Opposite*: concession

supplier *n* **provider**, trader, seller, dealer, contractor *Opposite*: consumer

supplies *n* **provisions**, materials, goods, food, stores

supply *v* **provide**, give, make available, sell, bring *Opposite*: receive ■ *n* **amount**, quantity, fund, reserve, stock *Opposite*: dearth

support *v* 1 **hold up**, reinforce, prop up, maintain, shore up *Opposite*: weaken 2 **sustain**, provide for, keep, take care of, look after *Opposite*: neglect 3 **help**, encourage, back up, aid, be there for *Opposite*: abandon 4 **favour**, champion, back, follow, espouse *Opposite*: oppose 5 **corroborate**, confirm, verify, bear witness, prove *Opposite*: deny 6 *(literary)* **bear**, hold, carry, sustain, take ■ *n* 1 **prop**, foundation, scaffold, brace, stanchion 2 **sustenance**, provision, care, funding, funds *Opposite*: abandonment 3 **corroboration**, confirmation, verification, authentication, substantiation *Opposite*: denial 4 **assistance**, encouragement, backing, help, aid

supporter *n* **follower**, fan, enthusiast, devotee, ally *Opposite*: detractor

support group *n* **encounter group**, forum, self-help group, therapy group, circle

supporting *adj* **secondary**, backup, subsidiary, supportive, auxiliary *Opposite*: primary

supportive *adj* **helpful**, caring, sympathetic, compassionate, reassuring *Opposite*: unhelpful

support system *n* **friends**, network, helpers, group, support

suppose *v* 1 **presume**, assume, understand, believe, expect 2 **imagine**, pretend, consider, theorize, hypothesize

supposed *adj* 1 **hypothetical**, theoretical, imaginary, fictional, made-up *Opposite*: actual 2 **thought**, believed, assumed, alleged, understood *Opposite*: known

supposedly *adv* **allegedly**, evidently, apparently, theoretically, hypothetically *Opposite*: actually

supposing *conj* **assuming**, suppose, let's say, let's assume, say

supposition *n* 1 **belief**, guess, idea, theory, possibility *Opposite*: fact 2 **guesswork**, inference, hypothesis, speculation, conjecture *Opposite*: knowledge

suppress *v* 1 **hold back**, repress, stifle, restrain, contain *Opposite*: express 2 **overpower**, overwhelm, overturn, conquer, defeat *Opposite*: submit 3 **muffle**, withhold, censor, smother, quash *Opposite*: publicize

suppression *n* 1 **repression**, containment, control, restraint, inhibition *Opposite*: expression 2 **conquest**, defeat, destruction, overthrow, clampdown 3 **withholding**, cover-up, concealment, censorship, veil of secrecy *Opposite*: revelation

suppurate *v* **discharge pus**, fester, weep, ooze, seep

supranational *adj* **multinational**, international, cosmopolitan, worldwide, universal *Opposite*: local

supremacist *n* **chauvinist**, racist, xenophobe, bigot, sexist

supremacy *n* 1 **pre-eminence**, ascendancy, primacy, superiority, domination *Opposite*: inferiority 2 **reign**, sovereignty, rule, authority, power

supreme *adj* 1 **highest**, best, ultimate, superlative, utmost *Opposite*: worst 2 **sovereign**, dominant, uppermost, first, highest

supremely *adv* **extremely**, completely, enormously, absolutely, superlatively

supremo *(infml) n* **leader**, head, chief, authority, expert

surcharge *v* **charge extra**, charge again, charge more, tack on, levy again ■ *n* **extra charge**, supplement, extra, price, hidden extra

sure *adj* 1 **unquestionable**, undisputable, certain, definite, guaranteed *Opposite*: uncertain 2 **certain**, in no doubt, convinced, positive, confident *Opposite*: uncertain 3 **dependable**, reliable, effective, trustworthy, trusty *Opposite*: unreliable

sure-fire *(infml) adj* **guaranteed**, dependable, safe, assured, foolproof *Opposite*: doubtful

sure-footed *adj* 1 **agile**, skilled, confident, skilful, nimble *Opposite*: clumsy 2 **confident**, competent, unerring, capable, infallible

surely *adv* 1 **certainly**, definitely, of course,

without doubt, unquestionably *Opposite*: doubtfully **2 confidently**, assuredly, with conviction, with confidence, with assurance *Opposite*: insecurely

sureness *n* **certainty**, certitude, confidence, assurance, firm belief *Opposite*: uncertainty

sure thing *(infml)* *n* **certainty**, safe bet, odds-on chance, winner, cert *(infml)*

surety *n* **security**, indemnity, guarantee, warranty, bond

surf *n* **waves**, breakers, rollers, whitecaps, spray

surface *n* **outside**, top, exterior, façade, side *Opposite*: inside ■ *adj* **superficial**, shallow, external, exterior, outward *Opposite*: inner ■ *v* **1 rise**, float up, come up, go up, emerge *Opposite*: sink **2 appear**, reappear, turn up, show up, pop up **3 become known**, come to light, come out, come out in the open, emerge **4 coat**, cover, skim, overlay, resurface

surface mail *n* **overland mail**, regular mail, first-class mail, second-class mail, registered mail *Opposite*: airmail

surfeit *n* **excess**, surplus, glut, flood, oversupply *Opposite*: deficit

surge *v* **rush**, rush forward, flow, pour, gush ■ *n* **flow**, outpouring, gush, rush, heave

surgeon *n* **doctor**, physician, medical practitioner, specialist, neurosurgeon

surgical *adj* **1 medical**, clinical, operating, invasive **2 precise**, exact, accurate, definite, meticulous *Opposite*: imprecise

surly *adj* **gruff**, brusque, abrupt, short, curt *Opposite*: friendly

surmise *v* **guess**, deduce, infer, construe, gather *Opposite*: know ■ *n* **guesswork**, deduction, inference, conclusion, assumption *Opposite*: knowledge

surmount *v* **1 overcome**, prevail, conquer, triumph, get through *Opposite*: fail **2** *(fml)* **scale**, climb, top, clear, ascend *Opposite*: descend

surmountable *adj* **manageable**, conquerable, resolvable, controllable, winnable *Opposite*: intractable

surname *n* **last name**, family name, cognomen *Opposite*: first name

surpass *v* **exceed**, better, outdo, outshine, improve on *Opposite*: trail

surplus *n* **excess**, extra, spare, leftovers, remainder *Opposite*: shortfall ■ *adj* **extra**, excess, spare, remaining, additional *Opposite*: essential

surprise *v* **1 startle**, alarm, astonish, astound, amaze **2 catch unawares**, catch napping, take by surprise, burst in on, intrude on ■ *n* **1 shock**, revelation, bolt from the blue, disclosure, bombshell *(infml)* **2 astonishment**, amazement, wonder, disbelief, shock

surprised *adj* **astonished**, astounded, amazed, taken aback, staggered

surprising *adj* **astonishing**, astounding, amazing, shocking, startling *Opposite*: expected

surprisingly *adv* **1 astonishingly**, astoundingly, amazingly, unexpectedly, unpredictably **2 to my surprise**, to my amazement, out of the blue, without warning, without prior notice

surreal *adj* **strange**, weird, odd, unreal, dreamlike *Opposite*: ordinary

surrender *v* **1 give in**, give up, admit defeat, lay down your arms, yield *Opposite*: hold out **2 relinquish**, give up, hand over, part with, forfeit *Opposite*: retain ■ *n* **admission of defeat**, submission, laying down of arms, capitulation, renunciation *Opposite*: perseverance. *See* COMPARE AND CONTRAST *at* **yield**.

surreptitious *adj* **furtive**, secret, sneaky, sly, covert *Opposite*: open. *See* COMPARE AND CONTRAST *at* **secret**.

surreptitiousness *n* **secrecy**, covertness, discretion, concealment, stealth *Opposite*: openness

surrogacy *n* **substitution**, proxy, standing in, surrogateship, replacement

surrogate *n* **substitute**, replacement, proxy, stand-in, deputy

surround *v* **1 enclose**, encircle, encase, enfold, envelop **2 besiege**, lay siege to, encircle, hem in ■ *n* **border**, mount, edge, edging, frame

surrounding *adj* **nearby**, close, adjacent, neighbouring, immediate *Opposite*: distant

surroundings *n* **environs**, surrounds, setting, environment, background

surtax *n* **surcharge**, tax, levy, extra, supplement *Opposite*: relief

surtitle *n* **supertitle**, caption, legend

surveillance *n* **observation**, investigation, scrutiny, reconnaissance, shadowing

survey *n* **1 analysis**, appraisal, scrutiny, evaluation, assessment **2 inspection**, examination, investigation, review, inquiry ■ *v* **1 look at**, consider, peruse, regard, think about **2 examine**, study, inspect, assess, analyse **3 plot**, chart, map out, measure, graph *Opposite*: sketch

surveyor *n* **inspector**, assessor, examiner, reviewer, evaluator

survival *n* **existence**, endurance, being, subsistence, persistence *Opposite*: death

survive *v* **1 live**, live on, endure, carry on, go on *Opposite*: perish **2 outlive**, outlast, live through *Opposite*: die

surviving *adj* **living**, alive, enduring, persisting, remaining *Opposite*: gone

survivor *n* **fighter**, stayer, sticker, toughie *(infml)*

susceptibility *n* **1 vulnerability**, defencelessness, weakness, exposure, predisposition *Opposite*: imperviousness **2 sensitivity**, receptiveness, openness, touchiness, impressionableness *Opposite*: hardness

susceptible *adj* **1 sensitive**, receptive, open, impressionable, swayable *Opposite*: impervious **2 vulnerable**, at risk, liable, prone, disposed *Opposite*: invulnerable

suspect *v* **1 think**, believe, suppose, imagine, guess **2 doubt**, distrust, mistrust, have doubts, disbelieve *Opposite*: trust ■ *n* **accused**, defendant, respondent ■ *adj* **suspicious**, doubtful, dubious, unsure, questionable *Opposite*: trustworthy

suspend *v* **1 hang**, hang up, dangle, swing, string up **2 interrupt**, check, break off, adjourn, hold *Opposite*: resume **3 postpone**, put on hold, defer, delay, stay *Opposite*: bring forward

suspended *adj* **1 hanging**, floating, hovering, dangling, strung up **2 postponed**, put off, deferred, adjourned, held over *Opposite*: advanced **3 barred**, banned, proscribed, excluded *Opposite*: allowed

suspended sentence *n* **deferred sentence**, deferment, sentence, punishment, judgment

suspense *n* **1 anticipation**, expectation, expectancy, excitement, tension *Opposite*: flatness **2 uncertainty**, unsureness, doubt, insecurity, confusion *Opposite*: knowledge **3 anxiety**, apprehension, tension, fear, nervousness *Opposite*: calm

suspension *n* **interruption**, holdup, check, postponement, delay *Opposite*: resumption

suspicion *n* **1 doubt**, question, inkling, misgiving, feeling *Opposite*: certainty **2 mistrust**, apprehension, distrust, disbelief, wariness *Opposite*: trust **3 hint**, suggestion, trace, touch, tinge

suspicious *adj* **1 suspect**, dubious, shady, shifty, untrustworthy *Opposite*: trustworthy **2 doubtful**, distrustful, mistrustful, apprehensive, wary *Opposite*: sure

suss *(infml)* *v* **solve**, figure out, work out, crack, decipher

sustain *v* **1 withstand**, bear, tolerate, endure, weather *Opposite*: buckle **2 experience**, undergo, suffer, incur, contract **3 maintain**, continue, carry on, keep up, keep going *Opposite*: quit **4 nourish**, keep going, feed, nurture *Opposite*: deplete **5 support**, hold up, prop up, keep up, maintain

sustainable *adj* **1 maintainable**, bearable, justifiable, workable, defensible **2 ecological**, environmental, green, natural, balanced *Opposite*: unsustainable

sustained *adj* **continued**, constant, continual, continuous, nonstop *Opposite*: temporary

sustenance *n* **nourishment**, food, nutrition, provisions, rations *Opposite*: deprivation

susurrate *v* **rustle**, whisper, murmur, breathe

suture *n* **seam**, join, junction, joint, closure ■ *v* **sew**, sew up, stitch, stitch up, close *Opposite*: cut

suzerain *n* **superpower**, colonial power, ruling nation

svelte *adj* **lithe**, graceful, slender, willowy, sylphlike *Opposite*: stocky

Svengali *n* **manipulator**, controller, guru, charmer, guide

swab *n* **gauze**, lint, cloth, wipe, pad ■ *v* **wipe**, clean, cleanse, moisten, wash

swaddle *v* **wrap**, bandage, wrap up, swathe, envelop *Opposite*: unwrap

swag *n* **1 curtain**, drape, hanging, drapery **2 festoon**, garland, chain

swagger *v* **strut**, parade, flounce, prance, sweep *Opposite*: creep ■ *n* **boastfulness**, arrogance, bluster, conceit, boasting *Opposite*: timidity

swaggering *adj* **1 boastful**, boasting, blustering, bragging, vaunting *Opposite*: modest **2 self-important**, self-satisfied, strutting, smug, arrogant *Opposite*: self-effacing

swallow *v* **1 ingest**, consume, take in, down, eat *Opposite*: vomit **2 gulp**, sip, gulp down, gobble up *Opposite*: regurgitate **3 destroy**, engulf, swallow up, take over, gobble up **4 suppress**, repress, choke back, hold back, hide *Opposite*: express **5 retract**, take back, back down, recant, eat your words **6** *(infml)* **believe**, accept, fall for, credit, buy *(US infml)* *Opposite*: reject ■ *n* **gulp**, sip, nip, mouthful, swig *(infml)*

swamp *n* **wetland**, marsh, bog, mire, fen ■ *v* **1 flood**, inundate, deluge, engulf, drown *Opposite*: drain **2 overwhelm**, snow under, overload, inundate, flood

swampland *n* **swamps**, marshes, marshland, bog, wetland

swampy *adj* **marshy**, boggy, muddy, slushy, squelchy *Opposite*: dry

swan *(infml)* *v* **wander**, drift, float, laze, idle

swank *(infml)* *n* **1 bragger**, swaggerer, exhibitionist, boaster, show-off *(infml)* **2 ostentation**, show, display, affectation, exhibitionism ■ *v* **show off**, swagger, strut, parade, boast

swanky *(infml)* *adj* **upmarket**, glamorous, high-class, stylish, elegant *Opposite*: downmarket

swan song *n* **farewell**, final act, last act, curtain, finale *Opposite*: debut

swap *(infml)* *v* **exchange**, trade, barter, do a deal, change ■ *n* **changeover**, substitution, exchange, switch, interchange

swap over *v* **switch**, change over, change round, interchange, change places

sward *n* **turf**, grass, grassland, green, lawn

swarm *n* **1 group**, cloud, flight **2 horde**, crowd, throng, flock, bevy ■ *v* **1 crowd**, throng, mass, flock, pile **2 teem**, be overrun, bristle, be alive with, be full **3 group**, hover, circle, fly, rise

swarming *adj* **crawling**, teeming, brimming, overrun, crowded *Opposite*: empty

swarthy *adj* **dark**, weather-beaten, dark-complexioned, leathery, tanned *Opposite*: pale

swashbuckler n 1 adventurer, daredevil, swash, buccaneer, pirate 2 **action movie**, pirate film, period film, action film, adventure movie

swashbuckling adj 1 **daring**, adventurous, heroic, exciting, cavalier Opposite: timid 2 **strutting**, swaggering, boasting, blustery, blustering Opposite: modest

swat v **swipe**, slap, hit, smack, thwack

swatch n **sample**, batch, strip, snip, piece

swathe v 1 **wrap**, cover, bandage, bind, entwine Opposite: unwrap 2 **enfold**, envelop, drape, cloak, shroud Opposite: expose ■ n **strip**, ribbon, band, wrapping, bandage

sway v 1 **swing**, waver, oscillate, move to and fro, rock 2 **bend**, lean, veer, slant, tilt 3 **influence**, bias, affect, control, persuade ■ n **power**, influence, control, authority, command Opposite: subjection

swear v 1 **affirm**, assert, declare, claim, maintain 2 **vow**, pledge, promise, give your word, attest 3 **curse**, blaspheme, damn, utter profanities, execrate (literary or fml) Opposite: bless

swear by v **trust**, rely on, depend on, have faith in, put your faith in Opposite: doubt

swear in v **inaugurate**, install, initiate, induct, administer an oath to Opposite: discharge

swear off v **give up**, renounce, abstain from, desist from, stop

swearword n **expletive**, four-letter word, curse, oath, bad language

sweat v 1 (infml) **worry**, fret, panic, be anxious, be concerned Opposite: relax 2 **perspire**, swelter, wilt, drip

sweat out v **wait out**, see through, endure, see out, stick out Opposite: give up on

sweaty adj 1 **perspiring**, covered with sweat, clammy, damp, sticky Opposite: dry 2 **hot**, boiling, warm, sticky, sultry Opposite: cool

sweep v 1 **brush**, clean up, tidy up, clear away, brush off 2 **speed**, zoom, race, fly, dash Opposite: creep 3 **carry**, move, seize, grab, take 4 **arc**, arch, bend, bow, curve ■ n 1 (infml) **sweepstake**, lottery, draw, raffle, game of chance 2 **arc**, arch, bend, bow, swing 3 **scope**, range, extent, stretch, span

sweep aside v **dismiss**, ignore, brush aside, have done with, reject Opposite: consider

sweep away v 1 **bowl over**, astonish, carry away, astound, overwhelm 2 **brush**, sweep up, clean up, clear up, remove

sweeping adj 1 **far-reaching**, comprehensive, all-encompassing, extensive, across-the-board Opposite: restricted 2 **indiscriminate**, generalized, general, broad, blanket Opposite: specific

sweep somebody off his/her feet v **attract**, enchant, charm, allure, beguile Opposite: turn off (infml)

sweepstake n **lottery**, draw, raffle, game of chance, prize draw

sweep up v **brush**, tidy up, clean, pick up, clean up

sweet adj 1 **sugary**, syrupy, saccharine, sweetened, honeyed Opposite: bitter 2 **fresh**, pure, wholesome Opposite: foul 3 **sweet-smelling**, fragrant, perfumed, scented, odorous (literary) Opposite: smelly 4 **melodious**, melodic, harmonious, musical, tuneful Opposite: harsh 5 **satisfying**, gratifying, enjoyable, rewarding, pleasing Opposite: unrewarding 6 **kind**, thoughtful, considerate, pleasant, amiable Opposite: inconsiderate 7 **lovable**, charming, engaging, appealing, attractive Opposite: unappealing ■ n 1 **bonbon**, chew, mint, confection, confectionery 2 **dessert**, pudding, afters (infml)

sweeten v 1 **make sweeter**, add sugar to, sugarcoat, sugar, honey 2 **enhance**, improve, better, intensify, heighten 3 **pacify**, mollify, appease, soothe, soften up Opposite: aggravate

sweetener n 1 **sweet substance**, sugar, saccharine, aspartame 2 **bribe**, inducement, carrot, honey, molasses

sweetening n **sweet substance**, sweetener, sugar, saccharine, aspartame

sweetheart n **darling**, dear, dearest, beloved, pet

sweetie (infml) see **sweetheart**

sweetie pie (infml) see **sweetheart**

sweetness n 1 **sugariness**, syrupiness, saccharinity Opposite: sourness 2 **charm**, cuteness, appeal, attractiveness, delightfulness 3 **kindness**, thoughtfulness, consideration, pleasantness, amiability Opposite: unkindness 4 **freshness**, pureness, purity, wholesomeness 5 **melodiousness**, harmony, pleasantness, mellifluousness Opposite: harshness 6 **fragrance**, sweet smell, perfume 7 **lovableness**, charm, appeal, attraction

sweetness and light n **pleasantness**, harmony, peace, friendliness, concord Opposite: unpleasantness

sweet nothings n **romantic words**, romantic phrases, loving words, endearments, pillow talk

sweet-smelling adj **aromatic**, perfumed, fragrant, sweet-scented, fresh Opposite: smelly

sweet talk (infml) n **flattery**, smooth talk, cajolery, flannel (infml), blarney (infml)

sweet-talk (infml) v **charm**, flatter, smooth-talk, persuade, cajole Opposite: bully

sweet tooth n **craving**, taste, fondness, liking, relish

swell v 1 **puff up**, puff out, swell up, bulge, bloat Opposite: deflate 2 **increase**, grow, enlarge, inflate, expand Opposite: decrease 3 **add to**, increase, enhance, improve, expand Opposite: diminish ■ n 1 **wave**, undulation, billow, breaker, surge 2 (dated infml) **fop**, fashion plate, clotheshorse (infml), dandy (dated), beau (archaic)

swelling n **bulge**, bump, puffiness, inflammation, distension

swelter v **feel hot**, sweat, perspire, overheat, burn Opposite: shiver

sweltering adj **boiling**, baking, burning up, red-hot, blistering Opposite: freezing

swerve v **veer**, veer off, turn sharply, swing over, change direction

swift adj **quick**, speedy, fast, rapid, prompt

swiftness n **rapidity**, quickness, fastness, pace, speed Opposite: slowness

swig (infml) v **drink**, swill, toss off, take a drop, guzzle (infml) ■ n **mouthful**, draught, nip, drink

swill v 1 **rinse**, sluice, wash out, wash down, swab 2 **gulp down**, swig (infml), guzzle (infml), knock back (infml), quaff (literary) ■ n **pig food**, slops, pigswill, mash, scraps

swim v 1 **bathe**, go for a dip, go swimming 2 **spin**, whirl, reel, sway

swimming baths (dated) see **swimming pool**

swimmingly adv **successfully**, well, smoothly, easily, like a house on fire Opposite: laboriously

swimming pool n **pool**, plunge pool, baths, lido, swimming baths (dated)

swindle v **cheat**, con, dupe, trick, double-cross ■ n **fraud**, hoax, embezzlement, confidence trick, con

swindler n **cheat**, trickster, charlatan, fraud, embezzler

swine n **hog**, boar, pig

swing v 1 **dangle**, hang, hang down, be suspended, sway 2 **swerve**, veer, reel, pivot, rotate 3 **rock**, fluctuate, move back and forth, sway, move backwards and forwards 4 (infml) **manage**, succeed in, accomplish, arrange, bring off ■ n **swipe**, smack, slap, thump, blow

swing at v **hit**, hit out at, lash out, strike, thump

swingeing adj **severe**, harmful, punishing, harsh, draconian Opposite: mild

swing round v **wheel round**, spin round, wheel around, turn round, swivel round

swipe v 1 (infml) **steal**, pilfer, make off with, walk off with, run off with 2 **hit**, swing at, lash out, hit out at, strike ■ n 1 **blow**, hit, swing, slap, smack 2 (infml) **critical remark**, cutting remark, dig, putdown (infml) Opposite: compliment

swipe card n **plastic card**, magnetic card, smart card, key card, credit card

swirl v **whirl**, twirl, spin, eddy, churn ■ n **twirl**, whirl, spin, eddy

swish v **hiss**, whoosh, whistle, whisper, rustle ■ adj (infml) **smart**, upmarket, fashionable, posh (infml), classy (infml) Opposite: downmarket

switch n 1 **control**, lever, button, knob, key 2 **change**, shift, adjustment, difference, modification 3 **exchange**, substitution, changeover, replacement, trade 4 **whip**, lash, crop, cat-o'-nine-tails

switchback n **bend**, twist, zigzag, hairpin, turn

switch off v 1 **shut down**, stop, deactivate, disconnect, cut Opposite: switch on 2 (infml) **relax**, unwind, stop worrying, stop paying attention, chill out (infml)

switch on v **turn on**, start, start up, activate, connect Opposite: switch off

swivel v **spin**, rotate, revolve, pivot, turn round

swollen adj **distended**, inflamed, engorged, puffy, puffed-up

swollen head n **conceit**, self-conceit, pride, vanity, arrogance Opposite: modesty

swollen-headed adj **conceited**, full of yourself, vain, self-important, puffed up Opposite: modest

swoon v **pass out**, faint, black out, lose consciousness, faint away ■ n **faint**, blackout, loss of consciousness, unconsciousness

swoop v **pounce**, jump, leap, dive, fly down

swoosh v **rustle**, swish, rush, swirl, whiz

swordplay n **sword fighting**, fencing, duelling, foil fencing, combat

sworn adj **confirmed**, affirmed, avowed (fml)

swot (infml) v **study**, revise, cram (infml), mug up (infml), bone up (infml)

sybarite n **voluptuary**, sensualist, hedonist, epicurean, pleasure-lover Opposite: spartan

sycophancy n **servility**, obsequiousness, flattery, fawning, toadying

sycophant n **toady**, flatterer, minion, yes man, bootlicker (infml)

sycophantic adj **ingratiating**, flattering, kowtowing, obsequious, apple-polishing (US slang)

syllabus n **course outline**, curriculum, programme, programme of study, prospectus

sylph n **nymph**, sprite, fairy, dryad, naiad

sylphlike adj **slender**, willowy, lithe, slim, graceful Opposite: hefty

symbiosis n **cooperation**, interdependence, relationship, association, synergy Opposite: independence

symbiotic adj **mutually beneficial**, interdependent, synergetic, cooperative, reciprocal Opposite: independent

symbol n 1 **sign**, representation, character, figure, mark 2 **emblem**, image, badge, logo

symbolic adj **representative**, figurative, emblematic, representational

symbolism n **imagery**, allegory, representation

symbolize v **represent**, be a symbol of, be a sign of, signify, stand for

symmetrical adj **balanced**, even, equal, proportioned, regular Opposite: asymmetric

symmetry n **regularity**, balance, equilibrium,

evenness, proportion *Opposite*: asymmetry

sympathetic *adj* **1 understanding**, concerned, kind, kindly, compassionate *Opposite*: unfeeling **2 approving**, in agreement, in accord, supportive, well-disposed *Opposite*: against **3 agreeable**, congenial, likable, friendly, amiable *Opposite*: disagreeable

sympathize *v* **empathize**, feel sorry for, commiserate, express sympathy, understand

sympathizer *n* **partisan**, backer, follower, adherent, well-wisher *Opposite*: opponent

sympathy *n* **1 understanding**, compassion, kindness, consideration, empathy *Opposite*: incomprehension **2 pity**, commiseration, condolences **3 approval**, agreement, support, backing

symphonic *adj* **musical**, orchestral, instrumental, classical, philharmonic

symposium *n* **conference**, seminar, meeting, convention

symptom *n* **indication**, sign, warning sign, indicator

symptomatic *adj* **indicative**, suggestive, characteristic

synchronize *v* **harmonize**, coordinate, orchestrate, bring into line, match

synchronized *adj* **coordinated**, harmonized, corresponding, matched, in time

syncopate *v* **modify**, play, shift, swing, stress

syncopation *n* **shift of accent**, modification, accent, stress, rhythm

syndicate *n* **association**, collective, consortium, organization, group

syndrome *n* **condition**, disease, pattern, set of symptoms, disorder

synergy *n* **working together**, interaction, cooperation, combined effect, collaboration

synonym *n* **alternative word**, alternative expression, other word, substitute, replacement

synonymous *adj* **identical**, the same, one and the same, equal, tantamount *Opposite*: different

synopsis *n* **outline**, rundown, précis, summing up, summary

syntax *n* **grammar**, sentence structure, language rules, composition, word order

synthesis *n* **1 mixture**, amalgamation, combination, blend, fusion *Opposite*: separation **2 production**, creation, making, manufacture

synthesize *v* **1 manufacture**, create, make, produce **2 fuse**, blend, combine, amalgamate, integrate *Opposite*: separate

synthetic *adj* **1 artificial**, fake, mock, imitation, faux *Opposite*: real **2 insincere**, sham, bogus, put on, phoney *Opposite*: genuine

syrup *n* **golden syrup**, treacle, molasses, sauce, maple syrup

syrupy *adj* **1 sugary**, thick, treacly, sweet **2 sentimental**, sickly, mawkish, cloying, schmaltzy *(infml)*

system *n* **1 scheme**, arrangement, classification, structure, organism **2 method**, technique, procedure, routine, approach **3 orderliness**, regularity, method, logic *Opposite*: disorder

systematic *adj* **methodical**, orderly, organized, efficient, logical *Opposite*: disorganized

systematize *v* **arrange**, order, regulate, sort, classify

systemic *adj* **universal**, complete, general

T

tab *n* **tag**, flap, label, ticket, stub

tabernacle *n* **chest**, cabinet, container, case, box

table *n* **1 bench**, board, desk, counter, stand **2 food**, fare, diet, provision, menu **3 chart**, graph, diagram, spreadsheet, record ■ *v* **propose**, put forward, submit, suggest, enter *Opposite*: withdraw

WORD BANK

❏ **types of table** bedside table, card table, coffee table, console, davenport, desk, dining table, dressing table, end table, escritoire, gateleg table, occasional table, Pembroke table, picnic table, roll-top desk, tea table, trestle table, vanity table, worktable, writing desk

tableau *n* **display**, picture, montage, scene, representation

tablecloth *n* **cover**, cloth, covering

tableland *n* **plain**, flatland, prairie, plateau, upland *Opposite*: lowland

table mat *n* **place mat**, coaster, mat, pad, trivet

tablet *n* **1 pill**, capsule, lozenge **2 slab**, block, bar, cake, lump

tableware *n* **crockery**, plates, dishes, dinner service, tea service

tabloid *n* **paper**, newspaper, red-top *(infml)*, rag *(infml)* ■ *adj* **sensationalist**, shocking, lurid, scandalous, yellow

taboo *adj* **1 offensive**, unmentionable, unthinkable, distasteful, off-limits **2 forbidden**, banned, prohibited, barred, proscribed *Opposite*: acceptable ■ *n* **ban**, prohibition, bar, restriction, interdict ■ *v* **forbid**, ban, prohibit, bar, proscribe *Opposite*: allow

tabular *adj* **flat**, level, smooth, even, horizontal

tabulate *v* **tabularize**, chart, arrange, organize, present

tabulation *n* **tabularization**, arrangement, organization, presentation, formulation

tacit *adj* **unspoken**, implicit, inferred, implied, understood *Opposite*: explicit

taciturn *adj* **reserved**, uncommunicative, reticent, silent, quiet *Opposite*: garrulous. *See* COMPARE AND CONTRAST *at* silent.

taciturnity *n* **reserve**, uncommunicativeness, reticence, silence, quietness *Opposite*: garrulousness

tack *n* 1 **nail**, pin, screw, staple, clip 2 **approach**, tactic, line, method, policy 3 **direction**, path, bearing, course, way ■ *v* 1 **pin**, nail, fasten, attach, affix *Opposite*: unfasten 2 **append**, add on, tag on, stick on, attach *Opposite*: remove

tackiness *(infml)* *n* **tastelessness**, bad taste, vulgarity, cheapness, nastiness *Opposite*: tastefulness

tackle *n* 1 **challenge**, attack, block, confrontation, throw 2 **equipment**, apparatus, kit, outfit, tools ■ *v* 1 **undertake**, begin, embark upon, attempt, engage in 2 **confront**, challenge, face, speak to, collar 3 **block**, stop, throw, seize, grab

tacky *adj* 1 **sticky**, messy, gluey, gummy, adhesive *Opposite*: dry 2 *(infml)* **tasteless**, in bad taste, vulgar, cheap, nasty *Opposite*: tasteful

tact *n* **diplomacy**, discretion, sensitivity, delicacy, thoughtfulness *Opposite*: tactlessness

tactful *adj* **diplomatic**, discreet, sensitive, delicate, thoughtful *Opposite*: tactless

tactic *n* **method**, approach, course, ploy, policy

tactical *adj* **strategic**, planned, premeditated, pre-emptive, psychological *Opposite*: accidental

tactician *n* **strategist**, negotiator, planner, schemer, diplomat

tactics *n* **strategy**, planning, campaign, manoeuvres, devices

tactile *adj* 1 **tangible**, palpable, perceptible, physical, concrete *Opposite*: intangible 2 **demonstrative**, physical, affectionate, touchy-feely *(infml)* *Opposite*: reserved

tactless *adj* **insensitive**, undiplomatic, indiscreet, indelicate, thoughtless *Opposite*: tactful

tactlessness *n* **insensitivity**, indiscretion, indelicacy, thoughtlessness, inconsiderateness *Opposite*: tact

tad *(infml)* *n* **bit**, little, touch, mite, dash *Opposite*: lot

tag *n* **label**, ticket, tab, docket, identifier ■ *v* 1 **mark**, label, ticket, docket, identify 2 **append**, tack on, add on, attach, stick on *Opposite*: remove

tag along *v* **link up**, join in, follow, accompany, go with

tail *(infml)* *n* **follower**, shadow, stalker, pursuer, tracker ■ *v* **follow**, trail, track, shadow, stalk

tailback *n* **traffic jam**, queue, line, gridlock, logjam

tail end *n* **end**, close, ending, conclusion, finish *Opposite*: start

tailgate *v* **dog**, hound, be hard on the heels of, follow, pursue

tail light *n* **rear light**, tail lamp, brake light, stoplight *(US)* *Opposite*: headlight

tail off *v* **fade**, peter out, dwindle, decrease, fall away *Opposite*: build up

tailor *v* 1 **make**, make to measure, cut, fashion, mould 2 **adapt**, customize, custom-build, modify, fit

tailored *adj* 1 **custom-made**, bespoke, made-to-measure, tailor-made, handmade *Opposite*: off-the-peg 2 **fitted**, shaped, well-cut, figure-hugging, close-fitting *Opposite*: casual 3 **adapted**, customized, custom-built, modified, altered

tailor-made *adj* 1 **perfect**, ideal, right, suitable, appropriate *Opposite*: wrong 2 **made-to-measure**, bespoke, custom-made, tailored, handmade *Opposite*: off-the-peg

tailpiece *n* **end**, end piece, finale, finial, coda

tailspin *n* 1 **nosedive**, dive, spin, spiral, descent 2 *(infml)* **panic**, flap, turmoil, flat spin, whirl

taint *v* **contaminate**, pollute, stain, spoil, infect *Opposite*: enhance ■ *n* **stain**, blemish, blot, defect, fault

tainted *adj* **contaminated**, polluted, stained, spoiled, soiled *Opposite*: pure

take *v* 1 **remove**, appropriate, acquire, grab, seize *Opposite*: give 2 **carry**, transfer, fetch, bring, transport *Opposite*: leave 3 **conquer**, capture, win, seize, secure *Opposite*: lose 4 **grasp**, grab, seize, catch, catch on to *Opposite*: drop 5 **choose**, select, procure, receive, buy *Opposite*: leave 6 **accompany**, bring, escort, guide, lead 7 **undertake**, adopt, accept, take on, assume *Opposite*: refuse 8 **bear**, stand, endure, tolerate, suffer *Opposite*: reject 9 **support**, hold up, hold, bear, manage 10 **contain**, hold, accept, accommodate, house 11 **study**, learn, read, do, take up *Opposite*: teach 12 **consider**, look at, discuss, examine, think about *Opposite*: disregard 13 **require**, need, demand, use, accept *Opposite*: reject 14 **derive**, draw, experience, feel, extract 15 **presume**, assume, believe, consider, perceive 16 **succeed**, work, stick, root, come off *(infml)* *Opposite*: fail 17 **subtract**, deduct, take away, take off, remove *Opposite*: add ■ *n* 1 **receipts**, takings, earnings, income, revenue *Opposite*: expenditure 2 **shot**, sequence, scene 3 **impression**, interpretation, opinion, view, point of view

take aback *v* **surprise**, stun, shock, nonplus, knock for six *(infml)*

take a back seat *v* **hold back**, restrain yourself, rein back, stay out of it

take a break v rest, relax, take time out, come up for air, pause *Opposite*: press on

take a breather *(infml) see* **take a break**

take account of v allow for, take into consideration, bear in mind, make allowances for, keep in mind *Opposite*: ignore

take a chance v gamble, venture, risk it, chance it, stick your neck out *Opposite*: play safe

take action v act, do something, take the plunge, take the bull by the horns, get stuck in

take a dim view of v disapprove of, not think much of, frown on, object to, dislike *Opposite*: approve

take advantage of somebody v exploit, use, mistreat, abuse, take for a ride

take advantage of something v make the most of, cash in on, profit from, exploit, make use of

take a fancy to v like, approve of, take a liking to, be fond of, love *Opposite*: dislike

take after v resemble, act like, imitate, look like, bear a resemblance to *Opposite*: differ

take a gamble v gamble, venture, risk it, chance it, stick your neck out *Opposite*: play safe

take amiss v take the wrong way, take exception, take umbrage, take offence, be put out *Opposite*: understand

take an oath v promise, swear, pledge, vow, give your word

take apart v 1 dismantle, take to bits, take to pieces, break up, pull apart *Opposite*: assemble 2 *(infml)* criticize, censure, condemn, lash, pan *(infml)* *Opposite*: praise

take as read v accept, believe, take at face value, take for granted, assume *Opposite*: challenge

take at face value v believe, accept, take as read, take for granted, rely on *Opposite*: question

take a turn for the worse v go from bad to worse, deteriorate, decline, slip, relapse *Opposite*: improve

take away v 1 remove, cart off, carry off, carry away, take off *Opposite*: bring 2 subtract, deduct, take, take off *Opposite*: add

takeaway adj ready-made, precooked, prepared, to go, carryout ■ n ready-made meal, fast food, carryout, takeout *(US)*, ready meal

take back v 1 withdraw, retract, recant, renounce, disclaim *Opposite*: stick to 2 regain, recapture, retake, recover, retrieve *Opposite*: give back 3 return, exchange, refund, redeem, trade in *Opposite*: keep 4 reinstate, reaccept, bring back, welcome back, have back *Opposite*: dismiss 5 remind, transport, jog your memory, put you in mind of, make you think of

take by storm v 1 capture, overwhelm, storm, seize, conquer 2 captivate, enthral, bowl over, impress, charm

take by surprise v surprise, burst in on, catch napping, take unawares, catch unawares

take care v 1 be careful, pay attention, mind out, look out, watch out 2 make sure, ensure, make certain, confirm, check *Opposite*: neglect

take care of v 1 look after, care for, nurse, tend, support *Opposite*: neglect 2 deal with, see to, handle, manage, do *Opposite*: neglect

take charge v assume responsibility, take over, hold the fort, take the reins, take up the baton *Opposite*: step down

take control *see* **take charge**

take cover v hide, take shelter, shelter, take refuge, conceal yourself *Opposite*: emerge

take down v 1 note, jot down, write down, make a note of, record 2 dismantle, demolish, knock down, pull down, take apart *Opposite*: put up 3 humiliate, humble, deflate, embarrass, mortify *Opposite*: puff up

take effect v happen, function, work, operate, succeed

take exception v take offence, take umbrage, be put out, object, disapprove *Opposite*: welcome

take five *(infml)* v take a break, take time out, take a rest, rest, relax *Opposite*: keep on

take flight v run away, run off, flee, take off, decamp *Opposite*: stay put

take for a ride v cheat, deceive, swindle, trick, con

take for granted v 1 assume, presume, take as read, expect, count on 2 undervalue, underrate, hold cheap, hold in contempt, disregard *Opposite*: appreciate

take heart v cheer up, perk up, brighten up, take comfort, snap out of it *Opposite*: lose heart

take home v make, be paid, net, earn, get

take-home pay n net income, net salary, net wages, net pay, net income after deductions

take in v 1 absorb, understand, comprehend, grasp, assimilate *Opposite*: ignore 2 include, contain, comprise, encompass, cover *Opposite*: exclude 3 deceive, dupe, fool, mislead, trick 4 let in, receive, admit, entertain, accommodate *Opposite*: bar 5 reduce, alter, shrink, shorten, draw in *Opposite*: let out

take in hand v deal with, cope with, tackle, get to grips with, take on

take into consideration v allow for, take into account, bear in mind, make allowances for, keep in mind *Opposite*: ignore

take into custody v arrest, detain, imprison, confine, hold *Opposite*: release

take in your stride v deal with, cope with, accept, take on board, manage

take issue with v disagree, differ, beg to differ, oppose, challenge *Opposite*: agree

take it easy v **1 relax**, unwind, put your feet up, laze about, laze around *Opposite*: toil **2 calm down**, relax, simmer down, keep your shirt on, lighten up *(infml) Opposite*: explode

take legal action v go to court, sue, press charges, prosecute, litigate

taken adj **occupied**, in use, engaged, spoken for, busy *Opposite*: free

take no notice of v **ignore**, disregard, pay no attention, pay no heed, close your eyes *Opposite*: notice

take off v **1 remove**, discard, strip off, slip out of, peel off *Opposite*: put on **2 deduct**, subtract, take away, take, remove *Opposite*: add **3** *(infml)* **parody**, imitate, mimic, impersonate, satirize **4 cancel**, suspend, discontinue, abolish, do away with *Opposite*: reinstate **5 launch**, depart, leave, lift off, fly off *Opposite*: land **6** *(infml)* **leave**, go, depart, disappear, set out *Opposite*: stay **7** *(infml)* **succeed**, flourish, bloom, boom, prosper *Opposite*: flop *(infml). See* COMPARE AND CONTRAST *at* imitate.

takeoff n **1 departure**, ascent, launch, lift off, start *Opposite*: touchdown **2** *(infml)* **imitation**, impersonation, impression, parody, skit

take offence v **take exception**, take umbrage, take amiss, take the wrong way, be put out

take on v **1 undertake**, assume, deal with, accept, adopt *Opposite*: refuse **2 employ**, hire, engage, sign, bring on board *Opposite*: fire **3 adopt**, acquire, gain, display, show *Opposite*: lose **4 face**, confront, oppose, fight, vie with *Opposite*: avoid

take on board v **1 understand**, grasp, comprehend, realize, absorb *Opposite*: deny **2 accept**, include, accommodate, implement, allow for *Opposite*: reject

take out v **1 remove**, extract, pull out, bring out, fish out *Opposite*: insert **2 arrange**, organize, set up, obtain, acquire *Opposite*: cancel **3 ask out**, invite out, accompany, treat, take *Opposite*: stand up **4 vent**, direct, aim, express, relieve

take over v **1 take possession of**, annex, capture, hijack, seize *Opposite*: cede *(fml)* **2 take control**, take charge, take the reins, step in, assume responsibility *Opposite*: step down

takeover n **coup**, overthrow, seizure, appropriation, occupation *Opposite*: secession

take part v **join in**, participate, play, play a part, cooperate *Opposite*: opt out *(infml)*

take place v **happen**, occur, have effect, go on, come about

take pleasure in v **delight in**, enjoy, be taken with, love, take great delight in *Opposite*: hate

take possession of v **take over**, take control of, sequester, impound, occupy *Opposite*: abandon

take precedence v **have priority**, outweigh, come first, come before, predominate

take prisoner v **capture**, take captive, take hostage, seize, imprison *Opposite*: release

taker n **customer**, client, patron, purchaser, buyer

take root v **set in**, develop, start, grow, settle in *Opposite*: die off

take shape v **form**, develop, crystallize, take form, shape up *Opposite*: dissolve

take steps v **make a start**, proceed, start, take action, do something

take stock v **reflect**, weigh up, sum up, think over, count your blessings

take the blame v **take responsibility**, face the music, own up, get it in the neck *(infml)*, carry the can *(infml) Opposite*: get away with

take the bull by the horns v **take the plunge**, bite the bullet, grasp the nettle, take the initiative, jump in *Opposite*: hold back

take the edge off v **dampen**, blunt, dilute, relieve, mitigate *Opposite*: heighten

take the lead v **blaze a trail**, set a trend, originate, break new ground, break through *Opposite*: fall behind

take the mickey *(infml)* v **tease**, make fun of, laugh at, bait, kid

take the place of v **replace**, succeed, displace, supersede, take over from

take the plunge v **dive in**, jump in, throw caution to the wind, take the bull by the horns, bite the bullet *Opposite*: hold back

take the rough with the smooth v **take the bad with the good**, make the best of things, make the best of a bad job, look on the bright side, keep your chin up *Opposite*: crack up *(infml)*

take to v **1 warm to**, take a fancy to, take a liking to, fall for, get on with *Opposite*: dislike **2 begin**, start, commence, take up, go in for *Opposite*: stop

take to court v **prosecute**, sue, take legal action, press charges, file a suit

take to pieces v **take apart**, take to bits, dismantle, disassemble, strip down *Opposite*: put together

take to task v **reprimand**, scold, rebuke, reprove, haul over the coals *Opposite*: praise

take to your heels v **run away**, run off, flee, run, show a clean pair of heels *Opposite*: stay put

take unawares v **surprise**, catch on the hop, catch out, catch off guard, take by surprise

take up v **1 start**, go in for, adopt, engage in, assume *Opposite*: give up **2 continue**, resume, go on, pick up, carry on *Opposite*: leave off **3 raise**, lift, pick up, gather up, hoist *Opposite*: put down **4 shorten**, raise, lift, pin up, gather up *Opposite*: let down **5 occupy**, fill, cover, absorb, consume

take-up n **acceptance**, reception, use, participation, response

take up the baton v **take control**, take charge,

take over, take the reins, step in *Opposite*: step down

take up the gauntlet *v* **accept a challenge**, take on, confront, stand up to *Opposite*: run away

taking *adj* **captivating**, attractive, enchanting, pleasing, winning *Opposite*: unattractive

takings *n* **earnings**, income, proceeds, profits, receipts *Opposite*: expenditure

tale *n* 1 **account**, fiction, romance, anecdote, legend 2 **lie**, untruth, rumour, falsehood, story *Opposite*: truth

talent *n* **aptitude**, flair, gift, bent, knack

COMPARE AND CONTRAST CORE MEANING: the natural ability to do something well

talent a natural ability to do something well that can be developed by training; **gift** a natural ability, especially an artistic ability, or a social skill; **aptitude** a natural ability to do or learn something, especially one that is not yet fully developed; **flair** a natural ability to do something well, especially creative or artistic ability; **bent** a natural ability, inclination, or liking for something; **knack** an intuitive ability to do something well, especially one that might not be developed by training; **genius** exceptional intellectual or creative ability.

talented *adj* **gifted**, accomplished, able, brilliant, artistic

taleteller *n* **informer**, turncoat, snitch *(slang)*, stool pigeon *(slang)*, rat *(slang)*

talisman *n* **stone**, jewel, amulet, charm, trinket

talk *v* 1 **communicate**, speak, chat, gossip, chatter 2 **converse**, debate, compare notes, have a word, have a discussion 3 **confess**, betray, turn over, inform, crack ■ *n* 1 **conversation**, exchange, dialogue, tête-à-tête, heart-to-heart 2 **lecture**, speech, address, discourse, oration 3 **gossip**, conversation, rumour, chatter, speculation 4 **language**, words, vocabulary, jargon, speech

talkative *adj* **chatty**, verbose, garrulous, voluble, loquacious *Opposite*: reticent

COMPARE AND CONTRAST CORE MEANING: talking a lot

talkative willing to talk readily and at length; **chatty** talking freely about unimportant things in a friendly way; **gossipy** talking with relish about other people and their lives, often unkindly or maliciously; **garrulous** excessively or pointlessly talkative; **loquacious** tending to talk a great deal.

talkativeness *n* **chattiness**, verbosity, garrulousness, volubility, fluency *Opposite*: reticence

talk back *v* **argue**, answer back, defy, retort, quibble

talker *n* **communicator**, conversationalist, speaker, gossip, chatterer

talking *n* 1 **speaking**, conversation, chat, chatting, gossip 2 **debate**, words, discussion, negotiation, conference

talking point *n* **topic of conversation**, debating point, issue, question, hot topic

talking-to *(infml)* *n* **dressing-down**, reprimand, lecture, tongue-lashing, scolding

talk into *v* **persuade**, coax, induce, convince, move *Opposite*: talk out of

talk out of *v* **dissuade**, sway, put off, discourage, deter *Opposite*: talk into

talk over *v* **discuss**, negotiate, debate, review, go into

talks *n* **negotiations**, discussions, summit, dialogue, conference

tall *adj* 1 **high**, big, giant, lofty, lanky *Opposite*: short 2 **difficult**, hard, complicated, demanding, trying *Opposite*: easy 3 **incredible**, unbelievable, unlikely, far-fetched, exaggerated *Opposite*: likely

tallness *n* **height**, loftiness, size, lankiness, stature *Opposite*: shortness

tall story *see* **tall tale**

tall tale *n* **cock-and-bull story**, unlikely story, tale, tall story, fairy tale

tally *v* 1 **match**, correspond, agree, check, equate *Opposite*: clash 2 **compute**, count, reckon, score, total ■ *n* **score**, count, total, reckoning, calculation

talon *n* **claw**, nail, fingernail, hook, spur

tame *adj* 1 **domestic**, domesticated, broken, trained, disciplined *Opposite*: wild 2 **docile**, meek, compliant, subdued, unresisting *Opposite*: rebellious 3 **bland**, dull, insipid, boring, unexciting *Opposite*: exciting ■ *v* 1 **domesticate**, break in, train, discipline, pacify 2 **repress**, suppress, overcome, subjugate, subdue

tameness *n* 1 **docility**, meekness, compliance, submissiveness, obedience *Opposite*: rebelliousness 2 **blandness**, dullness, insipidness, flatness, tedium *Opposite*: excitement

tamp *v* **fill**, pack, stuff, cram, compress

tamper *v* 1 **interfere**, meddle, monkey with, fool with, tinker 2 **corrupt**, rig, influence, manipulate, bribe

tampon *n* **plug**, pad, wad, swab, compress

tan *n* **suntan**, sunburn, colour, bronze, brownness ■ *v* 1 **bronze**, go brown, brown, toast, burn 2 **treat**, preserve, process, dye, wash

tang *n* **trace**, hint, smack, suggestion, flavour

tangent *n* **line**, curve, angle, refraction, curvature

tangential *adj* **peripheral**, lateral, oblique, divergent, indirect *Opposite*: central

tangibility *n* 1 **palpability**, perceptibility, physicality, reality, solidity *Opposite*: intangibility 2 **actuality**, reality, clarity, plainness, obviousness *Opposite*: intangibility

tangible *adj* 1 **palpable**, touchable, perceptible, concrete, physical *Opposite*: intangible 2 **actual**, substantial, real, certain, evident *Opposite*: intangible

tangle *v* 1 **knot**, twist, snarl, interweave, intertwine *Opposite*: untangle 2 **snag**, catch, snarl, snare, hook *Opposite*: undo 3 **trap**, catch, ensnare, entangle, enmesh *Opposite*: release **4 come up against**, confront, mess with, square up, oppose *Opposite*: avoid ■ *n* **1 mass**, jumble, knot, mesh, web **2 mess**, jam, difficulty, mix-up, complication

tangled *adj* **1 knotted**, twisted, snarled, interwoven, intertwined *Opposite*: straight **2 complicated**, confused, knotty, complex, messy *Opposite*: straightforward

tangy *adj* pungent, sharp, strong, piquant, tasty *Opposite*: bland

tank *n* cistern, boiler, reservoir, container, chamber

tankard *n* mug, beer mug, jug, stein, toby jug

tanker *n* transporter, freighter, lorry, truck

tanned *adj* brown, bronzed, suntanned, dark, sunburnt *Opposite*: pale

tantalize *v* tease, entice, torment, torture, tempt *Opposite*: turn off *(infml)*

tantalizing *adj* teasing, enticing, tormenting, tempting, provocative *Opposite*: boring

tantamount *adj* equal, equivalent, the same as, synonymous, as good as *Opposite*: different

tantrum *n* outburst, fit of temper, fit, frenzy, fret

tap *n* **1 blow**, rap, knock, bang, beat **2 stopper**, plug, bung, cork **3 valve**, stopcock, spout, spigot, faucet *(US)* ■ *v* **1 rap**, knock, bang, beat, strike **2 draw off**, draw out, extract, run off, release *Opposite*: block up **3 bug**, listen in on, record, monitor, intercept **4** *(infml)* **use**, utilize, draw on, draw off, exploit

tape *n* **1 ribbon**, strip, string, tie, band **2 adhesive tape**, sticky tape, insulating tape, masking tape, packing tape **3 cassette**, cassette tape, video, videotape, video cassette **4 tape measure**, measuring tape, measure, tapeline ■ *v* **1 record**, tape-record, copy, save, video *Opposite*: erase **2 stick**, fasten, attach, secure, bind *Opposite*: detach

tape measure *n* tape, measuring tape, measure, rule, ruler

taper *v* **1 narrow**, come to a point, thin down, dwindle, elongate *Opposite*: widen **2 reduce**, phase out, taper off, tail off, diminish *Opposite*: increase ■ *n* **1 candle**, torch, light, flame **2 narrowing**, point, thinning down, dwindling, elongation

tape-record *v* tape, record, copy, save, video

tapered *adj* **1 tapering**, narrowing, pointed, elongated, shaped *Opposite*: flared **2 gradually reduced**, phased out, tailed off, diminished, decreased

tapering *adj* tapered, narrowing, pointed, elongated, shaped *Opposite*: widening

tapestry *n* wall hanging, drapery, arras

tar *n* asphalt, Tarmac, pitch, macadam, blacktop *(US)*

tardiness *n* lateness, delay, belatedness, unpunctuality *Opposite*: punctuality

tardy *adj* late, delayed, overdue, belated, unpunctual *Opposite*: punctual

target *n* **1 board**, mark, bull's eye, bull, goal **2 aim**, objective, object, focus, end **3 butt**, victim, scapegoat, foil, recipient ■ *v* **1 aim at**, aim for, focus on, home in on, seek out **2 direct**, aim, point, level, train

tariff *n* **1 tax**, duty, due, excise, levy **2 price**, price list, rate, charge, cost

Tarmac *n* tar, asphalt, pitch, macadam, bitumen

tarn *n* lake, pool, pond, loch, lagoon

tarnish *v* **1 dull**, discolour, stain, smear, smudge *Opposite*: clean **2 sully**, damage, stain, taint, blot *Opposite*: enhance

tarnished *adj* **1 dull**, discoloured, stained, smeared, smudged *Opposite*: shiny **2 sullied**, damaged, stained, tainted, blotted *Opposite*: enhanced

tarpaulin *n* canvas, cover, sheet, sheeting, tarp *(infml)*

tarry *v* **1 remain**, stay, stay put, visit, sojourn *(literary)* **2 linger**, loiter, dawdle, hang around, hesitate

tart *adj* **1 sharp**, acid, acidic, sour, bitter *Opposite*: sweet **2 acerbic**, biting, sharp, sour, acid *Opposite*: kind ■ *n* **pie**, tartlet, pastry, quiche, flan

tartan *n* pattern, plaid, check

tartar *n* plaque, deposit, residue, coating, scale

tartness *n* **1 sharpness**, acidity, sourness, bitterness *Opposite*: sweetness **2 acerbity**, sharpness, sourness, acidity, bitterness *Opposite*: kindness

tart up *(infml)* *v* smarten up, tidy up, decorate, do up, make up

task *n* job, chore, duty, mission, commission

task force *n* team, unit, squad, detail, crew

tassel *n* bobble, tuft, fringe, braid, edging

taste *n* **1 sense of taste**, palate, discrimination, sensitivity, perception **2 flavour**, tang, savour, hint, smack **3 try**, sample, test, bite, nibble **4 liking**, preference, leaning, penchant, fondness *Opposite*: dislike **5 discrimination**, discernment, judgment, tastefulness, good taste ■ *v* **1 discern**, pick up, recognize, get, feel **2 sample**, try, test, eat, bite *Opposite*: devour **3 experience**, sample, preview, get a taste of, get a hint of

tasteful *adj* discerning, discriminating, sophisticated, refined, stylish *Opposite*: tasteless

tastefulness *n* discernment, discrimination, judgment, taste, sophistication *Opposite*: tastelessness

tasteless *adj* **1 bland**, flavourless, flat, insipid, weak *Opposite*: tasty **2 in bad taste**, in poor taste, cheap, flashy, loud *Opposite*: tasteful **3 vulgar**, crude, foul-mouthed, boorish, gross

tastelessness *n* **1 blandness**, flavourlessness, flatness, insipidness, weakness *Opposite*: tastiness **2 bad taste**, poor taste, cheapness, flashiness, loudness *Opposite*: tastefulness

taster n 1 **analyst**, sampler, buyer, specialist, connoisseur 2 **preview**, foretaste, appetizer, sample, excerpt

tastiness n **deliciousness**, flavour, yumminess, juiciness, succulence Opposite: tastelessness

tasty adj **delicious**, flavoursome, mouth-watering, appetizing, succulent Opposite: tasteless

tat (infml) n **rubbish**, junk (infml), jumble, scrap, seconds

tater (infml) n **potato**, spud (infml), murphy (dated infml)

tattered adj **torn**, ragged, tatty, dilapidated, frayed Opposite: smart

tatters n **rags**, shreds, bits, pieces, strips

tattiness n **shabbiness**, scruffiness, raggedness, dilapidation, untidiness Opposite: smartness

tattle v gossip, tittle-tattle, prattle, chat, chatter Opposite: keep secret (infml) ■ n 1 **gossip**, tattler, telltale, informer, informant 2 **tittle-tattle**, gossip, prattle, chat, chatter Opposite: fact

tattler n **gossip**, tattle, sneak, telltale, informer

tattoo n 1 **design**, pattern, picture, decoration, mark 2 **signal**, summons, call, recall, order 3 **parade**, display, tournament, show, pageant

tatty adj **shabby**, worn, scruffy, dog-eared, down-at-heel Opposite: smart

taunt v **mock**, tease, jeer, sneer, goad Opposite: compliment ■ n **insult**, gibe, sneer, affront, criticism Opposite: compliment

taunting adj **mocking**, provocative, provoking, teasing, spiteful Opposite: kind

taut adj 1 **tight**, stretched, rigid, stiff, tense Opposite: slack 2 **worried**, anxious, stressed, tense, nervous Opposite: calm

tauten v **tighten**, stretch, stiffen, pull tight, tense Opposite: slacken

tautness n **tightness**, tension, pull, stretch, rigidity Opposite: slackness

tautological adj **repetitious**, repetitive, inelegant, reiterative, redundant

tautology n **repetition**, reiteration, duplication, redundancy, superfluity

tavern (archaic) n **inn**, pub, local, bar, watering hole (infml)

tawdriness n **cheapness**, gaudiness, flashiness, showiness, tastelessness Opposite: tastefulness

tawdry adj **cheap**, gaudy, flashy, showy, tasteless Opposite: tasteful

tax n **duty**, levy, toll, excise, tariff ■ v 1 **charge**, hit, burden, cream off, deduct Opposite: exempt 2 **strain**, overtax, overstretch, stretch, overload Opposite: relieve 3 **accuse**, reproach, blame, confront, present

taxable adj **chargeable**, assessable, dutiable, rateable, payable Opposite: tax-exempt

taxation n 1 **fiscal policy**, tax policy, tax system, revenue system, taxes 2 **duty**, levy, toll, dues, excise

tax-exempt adj **exempt from taxation**, exempt, untaxed, tax-free, duty-free Opposite: taxable

taxing adj **demanding**, tough, difficult, strenuous, challenging Opposite: effortless

taxonomy n **classification**, nomenclature, taxonomic system, catalogue, categorization

tea n **drink**, infusion, tisane, brew, decoction

tea break n **break**, coffee break, rest, refreshment break, elevenses

teach v 1 **impart**, communicate, show, explain, clarify Opposite: learn 2 **educate**, tutor, train, instruct, coach Opposite: learn

COMPARE AND CONTRAST CORE MEANING: impart knowledge or skill in something
teach impart knowledge or skill to somebody by instruction or example; **educate** increase the knowledge or develop the abilities of somebody by formal teaching or training, especially in a school or college context; **train** teach the skills necessary for a particular task or job by means of instruction, observation, and practice; **instruct** teach somebody a subject, methodology, or skill, not necessarily in a school or college context; **coach** give special tuition to one person or a small group of people, especially in preparation for an exam, or teach sports, artistic, or life skills; **tutor** give somebody individual tuition in a particular subject or skill; **school** train somebody in a particular skill or area of expertise in a thorough and detailed way; **drill** teach something by means of repeated exercises and practice.

teacher n **educator**, tutor, instructor, coach, trainer Opposite: student

teaching n 1 **education**, lessons, instruction, coaching, training Opposite: learning 2 **philosophy**, ideas, principles, beliefs, thinking

team n 1 **side**, squad, players, lineup, crew 2 **group**, band, crew, gang, panel

team-mate n **colleague**, co-player, partner, fellow player

teamster n **driver**, carter, charioteer, handler, trainer

team up v **join forces**, collaborate, cooperate, work together, get together Opposite: split up

teamwork n **cooperation**, collaboration, joint effort, solidarity, communication

tear v 1 **rip**, rend, split, gash, slash Opposite: join 2 **sprain**, rip, pull, injure, damage 3 **snatch**, rip, grab, wrench, pluck Opposite: coax 4 **dash**, rush, hurry, rip, streak Opposite: saunter ■ n 1 **slit**, rip, split, slash, gash Opposite: join 2 **teardrop**, drop, droplet, drip, bead

COMPARE AND CONTRAST CORE MEANING: pull apart forcibly

tear pull something apart, either by accident or on purpose, leaving jagged edges; **rend** pull something apart violently; **rip** tear something with a sudden rough splitting action, accompanied by a distinctive noise, especially accidentally; **split** divide something into two parts with a single movement, usually by force.

tear apart v 1 destroy, fragment, wreck, separate, dismantle *Opposite*: reunite 2 **distress**, disturb, devastate, pain, hurt *Opposite*: reassure

tear away v drag away, pull away, haul away, depart, leave *Opposite*: linger

tearaway n **delinquent**, troublemaker, hoodlum, hooligan (*infml*), yob (*infml*)

tear down v demolish, rip down, pull down, destroy, remove *Opposite*: construct

teardrop n tear, drop, droplet, drip, bead

tearful adj 1 in tears, crying, weeping, sobbing, howling 2 **sad**, emotional, unhappy, mournful, melancholy *Opposite*: cheerful

tear into v lay into, attack, go for, round on, set on *Opposite*: praise

tear-jerker (*infml*) n **sentimental story**, drama, tragedy, sad story, weepie (*infml*) *Opposite*: comedy

tear up v rip up, shred, destroy, rip to pieces, rip to shreds

tease v 1 joke, laugh, mock, kid, taunt 2 **torment**, harass, pester, bother, annoy *Opposite*: pet 3 **tantalize**, arouse, lead somebody on, encourage, excite *Opposite*: satisfy ■ n joker, clown, mocker, teaser, tormentor

teaser n 1 puzzle, puzzler, brainteaser, tough one, mystery 2 **tease**, joker, clown, mocker, leg-puller (*infml*)

tea service n **tea set**, cups and saucers, china, porcelain, crockery

tea set see **tea service**

teasing adj 1 **playful**, mocking, tongue-in-cheek, mischievous, jokey *Opposite*: serious 2 **provocative**, coy, flirtatious, suggestive, tempting *Opposite*: straightforward ■ n **playfulness**, banter, repartee, raillery, leg-pulling (*infml*) *Opposite*: seriousness

tea-time n **dinnertime**, suppertime, mealtime, time for tea, time for dinner

technical adj 1 **technological**, scientific, industrial, mechanical 2 **practical**, mechanical, procedural, methodological, methodical 3 **nominal**, official, strict, narrow, literal *Opposite*: loose 4 **specialized**, precise, official, professional, specialist *Opposite*: general

technicality n detail, small point, trifle

technician n **specialist**, expert, operator, mechanic, engineer

technique n **method**, system, practice, modus operandi, procedure

technological adj **technical**, scientific, industrial, high-tech

technologist n **scientist**, engineer, technician, boffin (*infml*), maven (*US*)

technology n 1 **equipment**, machinery, tools 2 **skill**, knowledge, expertise, know-how (*infml*)

tedious adj **boring**, dull, dreary, monotonous, mind-numbing *Opposite*: interesting

tediousness n **boredom**, dullness, dreariness, monotony, tedium *Opposite*: excitement

tedium see **tediousness**

teem v 1 swarm, crowd, abound, be full, be stuffed 2 **pour**, pelt, stream, rain, rain cats and dogs (*infml*) *Opposite*: drizzle

teeming adj **swarming**, packed, crowded, heaving, crawling *Opposite*: empty

teen (*infml*) adj **teenage**, adolescent, youth, young, juvenile ■ n teenager, adolescent, young person, youth, youngster

teenage adj **adolescent**, young, youth, juvenile, teen (*infml*)

teenager n **adolescent**, young person, youth, youngster, young adult. See COMPARE AND CONTRAST at **youth**.

teens n **adolescence**, youth, young adulthood

teeny (*infml*) adj **tiny**, small, little, minute, wee *Opposite*: enormous

tee off v drive off, start, begin, commence, initiate

teeter v totter, stagger, wobble, shake, dodder

teething troubles n **problems**, glitches, difficulties, snags, hitches

teetotal adj **dry**, nondrinking, abstemious, abstinent, sober

telecaster n **broadcaster**, presenter, announcer, commentator, newsreader

telecommuter n **homeworker**, teleworker, freelancer, outworker

telecommuting n **working from home**, freelancing, outworking

telegram n **wire**, cable, message, telegraph, telex

telegraph v **send by wire**, send a message, cable, wire, transmit

telegraphic adj **concise**, abbreviated, condensed, truncated, succinct *Opposite*: verbose

telemarketing see **telesales**

telepathic adj **clairvoyant**, psychic, telekinetic, extrasensory, subconscious

telepathy n **thought transference**, ESP, extrasensory perception, mind-reading, sixth sense

telephone v **phone**, call, give somebody a call, ring, buzz (*infml*)

telephone call n **call**, ring, phone call, bell (*infml*), buzz (*infml*)

telesales *n* **telephone sales**, marketing, sales, telemarketing

telescopic *adj* 1 **magnifying**, enlarging, telephoto, zoom 2 **collapsible**, retractable, foldaway, foldup, compactible

telethon *n* **fundraiser**, phone-in, charity appeal, broadcast appeal, solicitation

televise *v* **broadcast**, emit, relay, put out, put on

television *n* **telly**, TV *(infml)*, small screen *(infml)*, box *(slang)*, goggle-box *(dated infml)*

teleworker *n* **telecommuter**, homeworker, freelancer, outworker

teleworking *n* **telecommuting**, freelancing, outworking, homeworking

tell *v* 1 **inform**, let know, say, advise, notify *Opposite*: keep in the dark 2 **relate**, narrate, recount, describe, report 3 **express**, say, voice, communicate, state 4 **instruct**, order, direct, command, charge 5 **distinguish**, recognize, differentiate, identify, discriminate *Opposite*: confuse 6 **divulge**, disclose, expose, reveal, inform *Opposite*: keep secret

tell against *v* **count against**, go against, work against, weigh against

tell apart *v* **distinguish**, differentiate, tell one from another, identify, tell the difference between

teller *n* **cashier**, banker, bank clerk

telling *adj* 1 **revealing**, informative, significant, telltale, indicative *Opposite*: uninformative 2 **effective**, expressive, important, significant, influential *Opposite*: ineffective

telling-off *(infml)* *n* **reprimand**, scolding, dressing-down, lecture, tongue-lashing *Opposite*: praise

tell lies *v* **lie**, tell untruths, tell stories, dissemble, perjure yourself *Opposite*: tell the truth

tell off *(infml)* *v* **reprimand**, scold, rebuke, give a talking-to, haul over the coals *Opposite*: commend

tell stories *v* **tell lies**, lie, tell untruths, prevaricate, fabricate

telltale *adj* **revealing**, informative, betraying, significant, divulging *Opposite*: uninformative ■ *n* **informer**, sneak, gossip, blabbermouth *(infml)*, snitch *(slang)*

tell the truth *v* **be honest**, give your word, be straight with, be open, be truthful *Opposite*: lie

temerity *n* **nerve**, audacity, gall, boldness, impudence *Opposite*: reticence

temp *n* **temporary worker**, office temporary, fill-in, stand-in, temporary secretary ■ *v* **do temporary work**, fill in, stand in

temper *n* 1 **anger**, rage, bad mood, bad humour, mood 2 **disposition**, temperament, state of mind, frame of mind, humour ■ *v* **moderate**, mitigate, alleviate, soften, lighten *Opposite*: intensify

temperament *n* **nature**, character, personality, disposition, temper

temperamental *adj* **unpredictable**, erratic, unreliable, undependable, up and down *Opposite*: consistent

temperance *n* 1 **teetotalism**, sobriety, abstinence, abstemiousness, soberness *Opposite*: intemperance 2 **self-control**, restraint, self-restraint, moderation, self-denial *Opposite*: indulgence

temperate *adj* 1 **restrained**, self-controlled, controlled, measured, reasonable *Opposite*: intemperate 2 **moderate**, mild, clement, pleasant, comfortable *Opposite*: extreme

tempered *adj* **hardened**, toughened, hard, annealed, strengthened

tempest *n* 1 *(literary)* **storm**, gale, thunderstorm, hurricane, cyclone *Opposite*: calm 2 **uproar**, commotion, tumult, upheaval, disturbance

tempestuous *adj* 1 **stormy**, rough, turbulent, intemperate, inclement *Opposite*: calm 2 **emotional**, passionate, intense, hysterical, violent *Opposite*: relaxed

template *n* **pattern**, master, stencil, model, prototype

tempo *n* **beat**, speed, pulse, rhythm, measure

temporal *adj* 1 **chronological**, time-based, sequential, progressive, historical *Opposite*: spatial 2 **worldly**, earthly, secular, lay, profane *Opposite*: spiritual

temporary *adj* **passing**, transitory, short-lived, fleeting, ephemeral *Opposite*: permanent

---

COMPARE AND CONTRAST CORE MEANING: lasting only a short time

temporary lasting or designed to last for a short time; **fleeting** very brief or rapid; **passing** superficial and not long-lasting; **transitory** existing only for a short time; **ephemeral** lasting for a short time and leaving no permanent trace; **evanescent** *(literary)* disappearing after a short time and soon forgotten; **short-lived** lasting only for a short time.

---

temporize *v* **delay**, defer, procrastinate, take your time, hesitate *Opposite*: set to

tempt *v* 1 **lure**, allure, entice, attract, excite *Opposite*: repel 2 **invite**, attract, appeal, draw, move *Opposite*: put off

temptation *n* 1 **desire**, craving, urge, impulse, compulsion *Opposite*: repulsion 2 **persuasion**, coaxing, inducement, enticement, invitation *Opposite*: repulsion 3 **lure**, enticement, attraction, offer, invitation

tempted *adj* **of a mind to**, attracted, interested, curious, drawn *Opposite*: uninterested

tempting *adj* **alluring**, enticing, attractive, appealing, inviting *Opposite*: unappealing

tenable *adj* **reasonable**, acceptable, defensible, plausible, rational *Opposite*: untenable

tenacious *adj* **stubborn**, obstinate, resolute, firm, persistent *Opposite*: irresolute

tenacity *n* **stubbornness**, obstinacy, resolve,

firmness, persistence *Opposite*: irresolution

tenancy *n* **occupancy**, rental, contract, lease, tenure *Opposite*: ownership

tenant *n* **renter**, occupier, occupant, resident, lodger *Opposite*: landlord

tend *v* **1 have a habit of**, have a tendency to, incline, lean towards, be disposed **2 incline**, veer, lean, bend, verge **3 look after**, care for, take care of, cultivate, attend to *Opposite*: neglect **4 be in charge of**, manage, keep an eye on, watch over, watch

tendency *n* **1 propensity**, bent, leaning, inclination, predisposition **2 trend**, drift, movement, bias, current

tendentious *adj* **provocative**, opinionated, biased, partisan, subjective *Opposite*: impartial

tender *adj* **1 sensitive**, delicate, sore, raw, painful **2 loving**, caring, affectionate, fond, kind *Opposite*: rough **3 young**, youthful, immature, inexperienced, impressionable *Opposite*: seasoned ■ *n* **proposal**, proposition, bid, offer, submission ■ *v* **offer**, proffer, present, give, hand in *Opposite*: withdraw

tenderfoot *(infml)* *n* **novice**, recruit, raw recruit, newcomer, beginner *Opposite*: old hand

tenderhearted *adj* **soft-hearted**, compassionate, sympathetic, kind, soft *Opposite*: hardhearted

tenderheartedness *n* **soft-heartedness**, compassion, sympathy, tenderness, kindness *Opposite*: hardheartedness

tenderize *v* **beat**, smash, hit, soak, steep

tenderness *n* **1 sympathy**, gentleness, kindness, kind-heartedness, fondness *Opposite*: unkindness **2 sensitivity**, soreness, rawness, painfulness, inflammation

tendril *n* **1 stem**, vine, shoot, frond, branch **2** *(literary)* **twist**, coil, wisp, lock, curl

tenement *n* **block of flats**, apartment block, high-rise, housing project *(US)*

tenet *n* **principle**, theory, idea, assumption, belief

tenor *n* **mood**, tone, gist, drift, meaning

tense *adj* **1 anxious**, nervous, stressed, worried, edgy *Opposite*: relaxed **2 taut**, tight, rigid, stiff, strained *Opposite*: loose

tensile *adj* **ductile**, stretchy, stretchable, workable, malleable *Opposite*: rigid

tension *n* **1 worry**, nervousness, anxiety, stress, strain *Opposite*: relaxation **2 conflict**, ill feeling, friction, hostility, mistrust *Opposite*: ease **3 tautness**, tightness, stiffness, strain, pressure *Opposite*: relaxation

tent *n* **shelter**, marquee, bivouac, camp, pavilion

tentacle *n* **limb**, organ, appendage, feeler, antenna

tentative *adj* **1 hesitant**, cautious, faltering, unsure, timid *Opposite*: sure **2 provisional**, exploratory, speculative, unconfirmed, indefinite *Opposite*: definite

tenuous *adj* **weak**, shaky, unsubstantiated, questionable, feeble *Opposite*: convincing

tenure *n* **1 tenancy**, freehold, occupancy, occupation, lease *Opposite*: ownership **2** *(fml)* **term**, duration, span, period, time

tepid *adj* **1 lukewarm**, hand hot, blood hot, warmish, warm *Opposite*: icy **2 unenthusiastic**, half-hearted, lukewarm, indifferent, apathetic *Opposite*: enthusiastic

tercentenary *n* **300th anniversary**, anniversary, commemoration, celebration, festival

term *n* **1 word**, expression, phrase, name, idiom **2** *(fml)* **period**, time, stretch, tenure, span ■ *v* **call**, name, label, dub, designate

terminal *adj* **fatal**, incurable, deadly, mortal, lethal *Opposite*: curable ■ *n* **1 station**, airport, rail terminal, passenger terminal, terminus **2 workstation**, visual display unit, VDU, computer, monitor. *See* COMPARE AND CONTRAST at **deadly**.

terminally *adv* **fatally**, incurably, mortally, lethally, critically

terminate *v* **end**, finish, come to an end, conclude, stop *Opposite*: start

termination *(fml)* *n* **end**, finish, close, expiry, conclusion *Opposite*: start

terminology *n* **terms**, language, expressions, vocabulary, jargon

terminus *n* **last stop**, station, end of the line, depot, garage

terms *n* **1 footing**, rapport, relations, relationship, standing **2 conditions**, stipulations, provisos, provisions, requisites **3 language**, expressions, vocabulary, terminology, jargon

terrace *n* **walkway**, promenade, patio, veranda, porch *(US)*

terraced *adj* **1 in terraces**, stepped, ridged, tiered, split-level **2 adjoining**, attached, joined *Opposite*: detached

terrain *n* **land**, topography, territory, ground, landscape

terrestrial *adj* **1 earthly**, worldly, global, telluric *Opposite*: extraterrestrial **2 land-dwelling**, surface-dwelling, land, earthbound

terrible *adj* **1 extreme**, severe, serious, grave, intense *Opposite*: mild **2 horrible**, horrifying, horrific, horrendous, frightful *Opposite*: pleasant **3 awful**, dreadful, rotten, appalling, poor *Opposite*: wonderful

terribly *adv* **1 very**, extremely, tremendously, exceedingly, incredibly *Opposite*: slightly **2 awfully**, appallingly, offensively, intolerably, horribly *Opposite*: pleasantly

terrific *adj* **1 enormous**, great, huge, massive, tremendous *Opposite*: insignificant **2** *(infml)* **wonderful**, marvellous, excellent, remarkable, superb *Opposite*: awful

terrifically *adv* **very**, extremely, tremendously, exceedingly, incredibly *Opposite*: slightly

terrified *adj* **frightened**, horrified, scared, scared stiff, petrified *Opposite*: unafraid

terrify *v* **frighten**, horrify, scare, petrify, shock *Opposite*: comfort

terrifying *adj* **frightening**, petrifying, chilling, startling, alarming *Opposite*: reassuring

territorial *adj* **1 regional**, local, land, provincial, national **2 defensive**, protective, possessive, assertive, jealous

territory *n* **1 land**, terrain, ground, area, region **2 country**, land, state, province, region **3 field**, subject, speciality, area, terrain **4 patch**, beat, domain, pitch, property

terror *n* **1 fear**, horror, dread, fright, alarm *Opposite*: security **2** (*infml*) **nuisance**, troublemaker, imp, pest (*infml*), horror (*infml*)

terrorism *n* **intimidation**, terror, resistance, guerrilla warfare, sabotage

terrorist *n* **guerrilla**, partisan, freedom fighter, saboteur, nonstate actor

terrorize *v* **terrify**, frighten, scare, threaten, intimidate *Opposite*: reassure

terror-stricken *adj* **terrified**, petrified, scared to death, scared stiff, frightened out of your wits *Opposite*: calm

terse *adj* **1 abrupt**, curt, short, brusque, clipped *Opposite*: expansive **2 concise**, brief, succinct, pithy, short and sweet *Opposite*: wordy

terseness *n* **1 abruptness**, curtness, shortness, brusqueness, snappishness *Opposite*: expansiveness **2 concision**, brevity, succinctness, pithiness, economy *Opposite*: verbosity

test *n* **1 examination**, exam, quiz, trial, assessment **2 trial run**, trial, test drive, run-through, practice **3 proof**, evidence, sign, criterion, yardstick **4 ordeal**, hardship, tribulation, torment, difficulty ∎ *v* **try**, try out, put to the test, examine, quiz

testament *n* **evidence**, witness, testimony, proof, demonstration

test drive *n* **trial run**, trial, drive, run, spin

test-drive *v* **try out**, try, take for a spin, put something through its paces, drive

tested *adj* **verified**, tried, confirmed, established, experienced *Opposite*: untried

tester *n* **sample**, trial size, free sample, free gift

testify *v* **1 give evidence**, bear witness, appear, swear, state **2** (*fml*) **prove**, show, confirm, bear out, indicate *Opposite*: disprove

testimonial *n* **1 recommendation**, reference, endorsement, confirmation, statement **2 tribute**, honour, reward, celebration, acknowledgedary

testimony *n* **1 evidence**, statement, declaration, deposition, affidavit **2 indication**, demonstration, testament, evidence, witness

testiness (*infml*) *n* **irritability**, grumpiness, impatience, touchiness, crabbiness

testing *adj* **challenging**, difficult, taxing, tough, trying *Opposite*: easy

test match *n* **international**, match, game, cricket match, rugby match

testy (*infml*) *adj* **irritable**, grumpy, impatient, touchy, crabby *Opposite*: even-tempered

tetchiness (*infml*) *see* **testiness**

tetchy (*infml*) *see* **testy**

tether *n* **rope**, chain, lead, rein, tie ∎ *v* **tie up**, tie, hitch, fasten, secure *Opposite*: release

text *n* **1 manuscript**, transcript, typescript, writing, script **2 passage**, piece, article, extract, content **3 textbook**, schoolbook, reader, primer, manual ∎ *v* **communicate**, contact, correspond, send a text message, write

textbook *n* **text**, schoolbook, reader, primer, manual ∎ *adj* **model**, classic, typical, prime, definitive *Opposite*: atypical

textile *n* **fabric**, cloth, material, piece goods, yard goods

textual *adj* **written**, word-based, documented, documentary, stylistic

texture *n* **feel**, touch, surface, consistency, quality

textured *adj* **surfaced**, raised, rough, coarse, bumpy *Opposite*: smooth

thank *v* **express thanks**, show gratitude, express gratitude, show appreciation, be grateful

thankful *adj* **1 grateful**, appreciative, gratified, obliged, beholden *Opposite*: ungrateful **2 pleased**, glad, relieved, happy, satisfied *Opposite*: dissatisfied

thankfully *adv* **1 gratefully**, appreciatively, with gratitude, with thanks *Opposite*: ungratefully **2** (*infml*) **luckily**, happily, mercifully, fortunately, as luck would have it

thankfulness *n* **gratitude**, thanks, appreciation, appreciativeness, recognition *Opposite*: ingratitude

thankless *adj* **unappreciated**, unrewarding, unacknowledged, taken for granted, difficult *Opposite*: rewarding

thanks *n* **gratitude**, appreciation, thankfulness, appreciativeness, recognition *Opposite*: ingratitude

thanks to *prep* **because of**, on account of, due to, owing to, as a result of

thatch *n* **1 roofing**, roof, straw, rushes, reeds **2 thick hair**, hair, shock, mop, tresses

thaw *v* **melt**, defrost, soften, liquefy, warm up *Opposite*: freeze

theatre *n* **1 playhouse**, auditorium, theatre-in-the-round, cinema, hall **2 drama**, plays, dramatic art, the stage, acting **3 sphere**, focus, realm, scene, site

theatregoer *n* **playgoer**, drama-lover, thespian, spectator, literati (*fml*)

theatrical adj **1 dramatic**, acting, stage, dramaturgical **2 melodramatic**, dramatic, histrionic, exaggerated, affected *Opposite*: restrained

theft n **robbery**, stealing, burglary, shoplifting, holdup

theism n **faith**, belief, religion, piety *Opposite*: atheism

theme n **1 subject**, topic, idea, subject matter, matter **2 melody**, music, refrain, leitmotif, theme tune. *See* COMPARE AND CONTRAST *at* **subject**.

then adv **1 at that time**, at that moment, at that point, at that juncture, then and there *Opposite*: now **2 next**, afterwards, subsequently, later, and **3 in that case**, so, therefore **4 on the other hand**, but then, then again, but then again, nonetheless **5 and**, in addition, too, also, besides

theological adj **religious**, scriptural, doctrinal, dogmatic, spiritual

theology n **divinity**, religion, religious studies, doctrine, dogmatics

theorem n **proposition**, formula, deduction, statement, proposal

theoretical adj **theoretic**, hypothetical, academic, notional, imaginary *Opposite*: concrete

theorist n **philosopher**, thinker, theoretician, theorizer, academic

theorize v **hypothesize**, conjecture, imagine, conceive, put forward

theory n **1 philosophy**, model, concept, system, scheme **2 hypothesis**, premise, presumption, conjecture, supposition

therapeutic adj **1 curative**, remedial, corrective, restorative, medicinal *Opposite*: preventive **2 healing**, relaxing, calming, satisfying, helpful *Opposite*: stressful

therapist n **psychoanalyst**, psychotherapist, analyst, psychiatrist, counsellor

therapy n **treatment**, rehabilitation, healing, help, remedy

thereabouts adv **around there**, around then, near there, in that area, or so

thereafter adv **after that**, from that time on, afterwards, subsequently, then *Opposite*: previously

the real McCoy (infml) n **the real thing**, the genuine article, the very thing, the real deal (US)

thereby adv **so**, in that way, by this means, in so doing, in this manner

therefore adv **consequently**, so, and so, then, as a result

thereupon (fml) adv **immediately**, directly, consequently, subsequently, accordingly

thermal adj **warm**, hot, tepid, volcanic *Opposite*: cool ■ n **warm air**, current, updraught

thermostat n **regulator**, control, device, bimetallic strip, sensor

thesaurus n **vocabulary list**, word list, lexicon

thesis n **1 dissertation**, paper, essay, composition, treatise **2 proposition**, theory, notion, hypothesis, idea *Opposite*: antithesis

thespian n **actor**, actress, player, artiste, personality

thick adj **1 deep**, broad, fat, wide, chunky *Opposite*: thin **2 viscous**, syrupy, gooey, glutinous, heavy *Opposite*: runny **3 dense**, profuse, bushy, impenetrable, copious *Opposite*: thin **4 filled**, full, covered, crowded, teeming *Opposite*: empty **5 pronounced**, impenetrable, distinct, extreme, marked *Opposite*: slight **6 indistinct**, slurred, muffled, hoarse, gruff *Opposite*: clear

thicken v **congeal**, stiffen, set, solidify, clot *Opposite*: thin

thicket n **copse**, coppice, grove, covert, undergrowth *Opposite*: clearing

thickness n **1 viscosity**, stiffness, body, texture, stodginess *Opposite*: fluidity **2 width**, breadth, depth, wideness, chunkiness *Opposite*: thinness

thickset adj **stocky**, heavy, hefty, bulky, solid *Opposite*: slight

thick-skinned adj **1 unsympathetic**, insensitive, callous, unfeeling, tactless *Opposite*: sensitive **2 impervious**, unconcerned, unmoved, tough, hardened *Opposite*: thin-skinned

thief n **robber**, burglar, shoplifter, pickpocket, bandit

thieve v **steal**, rob, shoplift, raid, burgle *Opposite*: return

thimble n **cover**, cap, protector

thin adj **1 narrow**, fine, slim, threadlike, slender *Opposite*: thick **2 skinny**, slim, slender, bony, lean *Opposite*: fat **3 watery**, weak, dilute, diluted, runny *Opposite*: thick **4 sheer**, gauzy, diaphanous, light, fine *Opposite*: thick **5 reedy**, high, tinny, shrill, squeaky *Opposite*: resonant ■ v **water down**, dilute, thin out, weaken, disperse *Opposite*: condense

---

COMPARE AND CONTRAST CORE MEANING: without much flesh, the opposite of fat

thin having little body fat; **lean** muscular and fit-looking, without excess fat; **slim** pleasingly thin and well-proportioned; **slender** gracefully and attractively thin; **emaciated** unhealthily thin, usually because of illness or starvation; **scraggy** or **scrawny** unpleasantly or unhealthily thin and bony; **skinny** extremely thin.

---

thing n **1 object**, article, item, entity, gadget **2 occurrence**, event, incident, phenomenon, matter **3 detail**, point, idea, issue, feature **4** (infml) **obsession**, fixation, mania, craze, preoccupation

thingamabob (infml) n **thing**, whatsit (infml), thingamajig (infml), thingummy (infml), thingy (infml)

thingamajig (infml) see **thingamabob**

things n **belongings**, clothes, possessions, equipment, stuff

519 **threadbare**

thingumabob (*infml*) *see* **thingamabob**
thingumajig (*infml*) *see* **thingamabob**
thingummy (*infml*) *see* **thingamabob**
thingy (*infml*) *see* **thingamabob**
think v **1 reason**, contemplate, reflect, ponder, deliberate *Opposite*: act **2 believe**, feel, consider, judge, agree *Opposite*: doubt
thinker n **philosopher**, theorist, intellectual, academic, scholar *Opposite*: doer
thinking adj **rational**, thoughtful, intelligent, discerning, intellectual *Opposite*: unthinking ■ n **thoughts**, philosophy, idea, theory, accepted wisdom
think over v **reflect**, deliberate, ponder, weigh up, chew over *Opposite*: forget
think-tank n **committee**, body, advisory board, group of experts, commission
think the world of v **have a high regard for**, think highly of, like, have a high opinion of, look up to
think through v **consider**, contemplate, ponder, mull over, weigh up
think twice v **think carefully**, be careful, be wary, take heed, consider
think up v **invent**, devise, come up with, create, dream up
thinner n **solvent**, diluent, diluter, stripper, cleaner
thinness n **1 narrowness**, fineness, slenderness, slimness, shallowness *Opposite*: thickness **2 skinniness**, emaciation, leanness, boniness, lankiness *Opposite*: fatness
thin-skinned adj **sensitive**, hypersensitive, easily upset, emotional, touchy *Opposite*: thick-skinned
third party n **intermediary**, go-between, arbitrator
third-rate adj **poor quality**, inferior, mediocre, poor, shoddy *Opposite*: first-class
thirst n **1 dehydration**, dryness, thirstiness, thirsting **2 craving**, desire, longing, hunger, eagerness *Opposite*: apathy ■ v **desire**, crave, want, ache, pine
thirsty adj **1 dehydrated**, dry, parched, thirsting, gasping **2 desiring**, craving, eager, keen, hungry *Opposite*: apathetic
thong n **string**, cord, band, strap, belt
thorn n **prickle**, barb, spike, spine, point
thorny adj **1 tricky**, problematic, awkward, controversial, knotty *Opposite*: uncontroversial **2 prickly**, barbed, spiky, spiny, pointed
thorough adj **1 methodical**, careful, systematic, painstaking, meticulous *Opposite*: careless **2 full**, detailed, exhaustive, in-depth *Opposite*: careless **3 absolute**, complete, total, out-and-out, utter *Opposite*: partial. *See* COMPARE AND CONTRAST *at* **careful**.
thoroughbred adj **pedigree**, purebred, pure
thoroughfare n **main road**, through road,

street, road, way *Opposite*: backstreet
thoroughgoing adj **1 full**, detailed, systematic, exhaustive, in-depth *Opposite*: careless **2 complete**, thorough, absolute, total, out-and-out *Opposite*: partial
thoroughly adv **1 methodically**, carefully, systematically, painstakingly, meticulously *Opposite*: carelessly **2 completely**, absolutely, totally, utterly, from top to bottom *Opposite*: partially
thoroughness n **care**, attention to detail, meticulousness, scrupulousness, diligence *Opposite*: carelessness
though conj **although**, while, even if, even though, despite the fact that ■ adv **however**, and yet, yet, nevertheless, nonetheless
thought n **1 consideration**, contemplation, thinking, attention, reflection **2 idea**, notion, brain wave, inspiration, concept **3 ideas**, philosophy, thinking, notions, accepted wisdom
thoughtful adj **1 considerate**, kind, caring, unselfish, selfless *Opposite*: thoughtless **2 pensive**, meditative, contemplative, brooding, reflective **3 careful**, meticulous, painstaking, thorough, deep *Opposite*: superficial
thoughtfulness n **1 consideration**, kindness, care, unselfishness, selflessness *Opposite*: thoughtlessness **2 pensiveness**, meditation, contemplation, reflection, thought **3 care**, attention to detail, attention, thought, carefulness *Opposite*: superficiality
thoughtless adj **1 inconsiderate**, unkind, uncaring, selfish, insensitive *Opposite*: thoughtful **2 careless**, heedless, reckless, negligent, unthinking *Opposite*: prudent
thoughtlessness n **1 inconsideration**, unkindness, selfishness, insensitivity, tactlessness *Opposite*: thoughtfulness **2 carelessness**, heedlessness, recklessness, negligence, inattention *Opposite*: prudence
thought-provoking adj **stimulating**, challenging, provocative, interesting, inspiring *Opposite*: dull
thoughts n **opinion**, view, point of view, feelings, judgment
thrash v **1 beat**, whip, give a hiding, spank, smack **2 defeat**, beat, trounce, whip, paste *Opposite*: lose **3 toss**, writhe, flail, squirm, roll
thrashing n **1 beating**, whipping, spanking, battering, lashing **2 defeat**, rout, downfall, conquest, beating *Opposite*: victory
thrash out v **hammer out**, resolve, solve, discuss, debate
thread n **1 cotton**, cord, yarn, strand, fibre **2 idea**, drift, gist, sequence, story line ■ v **1 string**, wind, loop, lace, pass through **2 make your way**, pick your way, edge through, squeeze through, negotiate
threadbare adj **1 worn**, worn-out, shabby, ragged, thin *Opposite*: new **2 well-worn**, trite,

hackneyed, clichéd, banal *Opposite*: original

threat *n* **1 warning**, menace, intimidation **2 danger**, risk, hazard, menace, peril *Opposite*: promise

threaten *v* **1 intimidate**, bully, menace, warn, terrorize *Opposite*: reassure **2 endanger**, jeopardize, menace, compromise, cloud *Opposite*: guard **3 loom**, lurk, hover, portend, creep up

threatened *adj* **endangered**, at risk, in peril, vulnerable, dying out *Opposite*: safe

threatening *adj* **1 intimidating**, bullying, menacing, hostile, aggressive *Opposite*: reassuring **2 ominous**, menacing, foreboding, inauspicious, sinister *Opposite*: reassuring

three-dimensional *adj* **1 three-D**, solid, deep *Opposite*: two-dimensional **2 believable**, realistic, convincing, lifelike, true-to-life *Opposite*: two-dimensional

thresh *v* winnow, flail, separate, beat, rub

threshold *n* **1 doorway**, door, doorstep, entrance, entry **2 starting point**, verge, brink, edge, dawn *Opposite*: end **3 level**, limit, maximum, ceiling, outside

thrift *n* **frugality**, economy, carefulness, caution, prudence *Opposite*: extravagance

thrifty *adj* **frugal**, economical, careful, cautious, prudent *Opposite*: extravagant

thrill *v* **excite**, electrify, exhilarate, delight, inspire *Opposite*: bore ■ *n* **adventure**, delight, joy, pleasure, quiver *Opposite*: bore

thrilled *adj* **excited**, electrified, exhilarated, ecstatic, elated *Opposite*: disappointed

thriller *n* **whodunit**, murder mystery, crime novel, detective story, page-turner

thrilling *adj* **exciting**, electrifying, exhilarating, delightful, inspiring *Opposite*: boring

thrive *v* **1 be healthy**, grow well, flourish, bloom, blossom *Opposite*: decline **2 be successful**, flourish, prosper, boom, bloom *Opposite*: fail

thriving *adj* **flourishing**, prosperous, booming, blooming, blossoming *Opposite*: failing

throaty *adj* **husky**, hoarse, croaky, gruff, guttural *Opposite*: piping

throb *v* **pound**, thump, pulsate, pulse, thud ■ *n* **pounding**, thump, pulsation, pulse, rhythm

thrombosis *n* **coagulation**, clotting, blockage, occlusion

throne *n* **1 seat**, chair, cathedra **2 power**, authority, sovereignty, command, rule

throng *n* **multitude**, mass, crowd, horde, swarm *Opposite*: few ■ *v* **crowd**, pack, jam, cram, inundate *Opposite*: disperse

throttle *v* **1 regulate**, control, adjust, correct, check **2 strangle**, choke, garrotte, strangulate, suffocate **3 silence**, gag, muzzle, stifle, subdue

through *prep* **1 across**, past, throughout, within, round **2 during**, throughout, during the course of, in **3 via**, out of, by way of, by

means of **4 because of**, owing to, due to, as a result of

through and through *adv* **completely**, totally, entirely, utterly, at heart *Opposite*: partially

throughout *prep* **through**, during, all over, during the course of, in

throughput *n* **amount**, quantity, data, material, output

throw *v* **1 fling**, toss, hurl, pitch, lob *Opposite*: catch **2 drop**, leave, put, cast, toss **3 project**, cast, direct, send out, beam **4 move**, flick, switch, connect, disconnect **5 organize**, arrange, host, give, hold **6** (*infml*) **confuse**, puzzle, bewilder, perplex, baffle ■ *n* **1 toss**, lob, heave, pitch, fling **2 rug**, cover, blanket, shawl, coverlet

COMPARE AND CONTRAST CORE MEANING: send something through the air

throw cause something to go through the air using a physical movement; **chuck** (*infml*) throw something in a reckless or aimless way; **fling** throw something fast using a lot of force; **heave** (*infml*) throw something large or heavy with effort in a particular direction; **hurl** throw something with great force; **toss** throw something small or light in a casual or careless way; **cast** throw something to a particular place or into a particular thing, or throw a fishing line or net.

throw away *v* **1 discard**, throw out, get rid of, dispose of, dump *Opposite*: keep **2 waste**, squander, fritter away, ruin, spoil *Opposite*: make the most of

throwaway *adj* **1 disposable**, paper, plastic **2 wasteful**, profligate, extravagant, careless, improvident *Opposite*: frugal **3 off-the-cuff**, casual, offhand, passing, spontaneous *Opposite*: intended

throwback *n* **reversion**, regression, resemblance, relic, retrogression

throw in *v* **1 add**, drop in, include, mention, refer to **2 include**, add, give, tack on, add on

throw in the towel (*infml*) *v* **give in**, surrender, give up, admit defeat, concede *Opposite*: stand firm

throw off *v* **1 shake off**, shed, shrug off, get rid of, discard *Opposite*: keep **2 elude**, evade, escape, give somebody the slip, shake off

throw out *v* **1 discard**, throw away, get rid of, dispose of, dump *Opposite*: keep **2 expel**, eject, show the door, dismiss, kick out (*infml*) *Opposite*: welcome **3 dismiss**, reject, disallow, turn down, refuse *Opposite*: pass

throw up *v* **1 cause**, create, produce, bring to light, pose *Opposite*: conceal **2** (*infml*) **abandon**, give up, relinquish, resign, throw away *Opposite*: keep **3** (*infml*) **vomit**, be sick, gag, retch, spew

throw yourself into *v* **engross yourself in**, immerse yourself in, bury yourself in, devote yourself to, commit to

thrum *v* **strum**, pluck, twang, play, brush

thrust v 1 push, shove, force, propel, prod 2 stretch, extend, stretch out, reach, reach out ■ n 1 shove, push, prod, lunge, drive 2 attack, assault, offensive, push, drive 3 point, gist, meaning, focus, direction 4 power, force, propulsion, momentum, impetus

thug n brute, criminal, mugger, hoodlum, gangster

thumb v flick through, flip through, leaf through, skim, browse through Opposite: pore over

thumbs-down (infml) n disapproval, rejection, denial, no, veto Opposite: thumbs-up (infml)

thumbs-up (infml) n approval, acceptance, agreement, endorsement, ratification Opposite: thumbs-down (infml)

thump v punch, hit, whack, pummel

thumping (infml) adj large, huge, enormous, impressive ■ adv very, exceptionally, extremely, inordinately, really

thunder n din, boom, rumble, roar, clap ■ v 1 boom, roar, resound, rumble, clap 2 shout, bellow, boom, roar, yell Opposite: whisper

thunderbolt n 1 thunderclap, clap of thunder, thunder, crash of thunder 2 shock, surprise, bolt from the blue, eye opener, kick in the face

thunderclap see thunderbolt

thundering (dated infml) adj great, impressive, large, extreme, big ■ adv very, extremely, enormously, hugely, inordinately

thunderous adj deafening, loud, roaring, booming, crashing

thunderstorm n storm, downpour, deluge, rainstorm, cloudburst

thunderstruck adj incredulous, amazed, taken aback, stunned, shocked

thus (fml) adv 1 therefore, consequently, as a result, so, accordingly 2 like this, in this way, in this manner, as follows, like so

thus far adv up till now, up to now, yet, so far, hitherto

thwack n smack, clap, knock, rap, whack ■ v hit, strike, whack, smack, slap

thwart v frustrate, spoil, prevent, foil, ruin Opposite: aid

tic n twitch, spasm, convulsion, fit, paroxysm

tick (infml) n moment, second, minute, instant, trice

ticket n 1 permit, travel document, voucher, receipt, coupon 2 label, tag, tab, marker, sticker

ticking-off (infml) n reprimand, rebuke, scolding, dressing-down, telling-off (infml) Opposite: commendation

tickle v 1 prickle, irritate, scratch, itch 2 amuse, entertain, delight, please, make somebody laugh

tickler (infml) n puzzle, riddle, problem, enigma, poser

ticklish adj tricky, delicate, thorny, awkward, problematic Opposite: straightforward

tickly adj prickly, itchy, irritating, scratchy

tick off (infml) v rebuke, scold, reprimand, reprove, haul over the coals

tidal wave n 1 tsunami, bore, eagre 2 surge, wave, swell, deluge

tiddly (infml) adj minute, small, teeny (infml), weeny (infml), titchy (infml) Opposite: ginormous (infml)

tide n current, flow, surge, wave, drift

tidiness n neatness, trimness, orderliness, order, regulation

tidy adj 1 neat, orderly, shipshape, in order, organized Opposite: untidy 2 smart, immaculate, well-groomed, well-turned-out, dapper Opposite: untidy 3 large, fair, considerable, sizable, reasonable Opposite: small ■ v neaten, tidy up, clear up, straighten, arrange

tie v 1 bind, fasten, secure, attach, lash Opposite: untie 2 be equal, draw, finish equal, finish even, be neck and neck (infml) ■ n 1 bond, link, connection, relation, join 2 draw, dead heat, equal finish, stalemate

tiebreaker n deciding game, tie-break, decider

tie in v connect, associate, relate, link, join Opposite: disconnect

tie-in n link, relationship, connection, linkup, association

tie in knots v confuse, muddle, mix up, baffle, bewilder

tier n row, level, layer, stage, rank

tie the knot (infml) v get married, marry, wed, walk down the aisle, get hitched (infml)

tie up v 1 lash, truss, fasten, lace, tie Opposite: untie 2 complete, clinch, finalize, resolve, end

tie-up n link, connection, linkup, association, relationship

tiff n quarrel, argument, row, falling-out, squabble

tight adj 1 taut, stretched, tense, firm, stiff Opposite: loose 2 close-fitting, body-hugging, skintight, snug, fitted Opposite: baggy 3 firm, fixed, strong, unyielding, tough Opposite: weak 4 strict, stringent, harsh, firm, tough Opposite: lax 5 mean, tightfisted, parsimonious, niggardly, stingy (infml) Opposite: generous 6 difficult, problematic, awkward, tricky, tough Opposite: easy

tighten v make tighter, tauten, constrict, stiffen, squeeze Opposite: loosen

tighten your belt v cut back, economize, retrench, draw in your horns, scrimp and save

tightfisted adj miserly, mean, tight, grasping, parsimonious Opposite: generous

tightfistedness n scrimping, meanness, stinginess, tightness, miserliness Opposite: generosity

tight-fitting *adj* tight, close-fitting, snug, figure-hugging, skintight *Opposite*: baggy

tightknit *adj* closely connected, integrated, united, interwoven, intertwined

tight-lipped *adj* silent, uncommunicative, reticent, withdrawn, taciturn *Opposite*: loquacious

tightness *n* tension, tautness, stiffness, rigidity *Opposite*: looseness

tight spot *n* tight corner, difficult position, tricky situation, predicament, quandary

till *n* cash register, cash box, box, drawer, tray ▪ *v* plough, dig, cultivate, turn over, rake

tilt *v* tip, slope, slant, lean, list *Opposite*: straighten up ▪ *n* slope, slant, angle, gradient, incline

tilted *adj* slanted, slanting, sloping, sloped, lopsided *Opposite*: level

timber *n* wood, logs, planks, lumber *(US)*

timbre *n* tone, pitch, resonance, sound, quality

time *n* 1 period, while, spell, stretch, stint 2 occasion, instance, moment, point, instant 3 era, age, epoch, period, season 4 tempo, rhythm, beat, speed, measure ▪ *v* 1 count, measure, clock, calculate, record 2 schedule, programme, timetable, plan, arrange

WORD BANK
❏ types of time period calendar month, fortnight, leap year, lunar month, midweek, month, quarter, semester, trimester, week, weekend, year

time bomb *n* tinderbox, volcano, accident waiting to happen, flashpoint

time-consuming *adj* laborious, slow, inefficient, long, onerous *Opposite*: timesaving

time-honoured *adj* traditional, customary, habitual, age-old, respected *Opposite*: recent

time lag *n* lapse, interlude, gap, interval, pause

timeless *adj* eternal, ageless, enduring, undying, everlasting *Opposite*: ephemeral

timelessness *n* agelessness, endurance, endlessness, changelessness, immutability *Opposite*: transience

timely *adj* opportune, well-timed, appropriate, apt, judicious *Opposite*: untimely

time off *n* leisure, free time, spare time, leave, holiday

timepiece *n* chronometer, timer, clock

timesaving *adj* quick, streamlined, efficient, effective, improved *Opposite*: time-consuming

timescale *n* timetable, schedule, programme, time, period

timeserver *n* opportunist, weathercock, waverer, equivocator, vacillator *Opposite*: stalwart

time span *n* duration, period, extent, length, span

timetable *n* schedule, agenda, plan, programme, calendar ▪ *v* schedule, arrange, plan, organize, programme

timeworn *adj* 1 shabby, tattered, threadbare, worn, well-worn *Opposite*: brand-new 2 hackneyed, overworked, stale, trite, stock *Opposite*: original

timid *adj* nervous, shy, fearful, timorous, diffident *Opposite*: bold

timidity *n* nervousness, shyness, fearfulness, timorousness, diffidence *Opposite*: boldness

timing *n* judgment, technique, skill, effectiveness, control

timorous *adj* nervous, fearful, timid, frightened, scared *Opposite*: brave

timorousness *n* nervousness, fearfulness, timidity, shyness, fear *Opposite*: bravery

tin *n* 1 can, tin can, canister, container, cylinder 2 box, container, caddy, biscuit tin, cake tin

tincture *n* 1 solution, essence, distillate, extract, distillation 2 tinge, tint, hint, nuance, tone

tinder *n* kindling, firewood, brushwood, sticks, twigs

tinderbox *n* flashpoint, crucible, volcano, no-go area, accident waiting to happen

ting *v* ding, ding-a-ling, ring, ping, tinkle

tinge *n* hint, touch, dash, drop, trace ▪ *v* tint, colour, stain, shade, mix

tingle *v* prickle, sting, itch, tickle, prick ▪ *n* sting, prickle, itch, tickle, prick

tingling *adj* prickly, itchy, scratchy, burning, stinging

tinker *v* 1 fiddle, tamper, interfere, fool around, play 2 repair, mend, fix, put right

tinkle *v* ring, jingle, clink, chink, ding ▪ *n* *(infml)* call, ring, phone, phone call, telephone call

tinny *adj* 1 thin, high, metallic, shrill, ringing *Opposite*: resonant 2 shoddy, cheap, worthless, inferior, poor

tinsel *n* 1 metallic thread, glitter, streamer, spangle, decoration 2 showiness, glitz, flashiness, pretentiousness, glitter

tint *n* 1 shade, colour, hue, touch, trace 2 rinse, dye, colourant, streak, highlight ▪ *v* dye, colour, shade, streak, rinse

tiny *adj* minute, miniature, minuscule, small, little *Opposite*: enormous

tip *v* 1 tilt, slope, slant, lean, list *Opposite*: straighten up 2 knock over, pour, empty, spill, knock 3 give, slip, reward, pay, bribe ▪ *n* 1 slope, slant, angle, gradient, incline 2 rubbish dump, civic amenity point, landfill, garbage dump *(US)* 3 *(infml)* hovel, pigsty, dump *(infml)*, hole *(infml)*, pigpen *(US)* 4 gratuity, gift, reward, bonus, extra 5 warning, clue, pointer, prompt, hint 6 hint, suggestion, idea, pointer

tip off *v* warn, inform, advise, forewarn, tip the wink *(infml)*

tip-off *(infml) n* warning, clue, hint, pointer, prompt

tipster n **adviser**, consultant, analyst, informant, informer

tiptoe v **creep**, sneak, steal, skulk, glide Opposite: stamp

tiptop (infml) adj **first-rate**, excellent, superb, first-class, superlative Opposite: dreadful

tirade n **outburst**, rant, diatribe, harangue, lecture

tire v **exhaust**, wear out, drain, fatigue, enervate

tired adj **1 weary**, sleepy, drowsy, fatigued, exhausted Opposite: energetic **2 bored**, weary, sick, jaded, dissatisfied **3 overused**, trite, hackneyed, clichéd, old Opposite: fresh

tiredness n **weariness**, sleepiness, fatigue, drowsiness, exhaustion Opposite: energy

tireless adj **untiring**, diligent, determined, unstinting, assiduous Opposite: weary

tirelessness n **diligence**, determination, assiduousness, indefatigability, industriousness Opposite: weariness

tiresome adj **annoying**, irritating, tedious, wearisome, dull

tiring adj **exhausting**, strenuous, arduous, wearing, demanding

tissue n **1 soft tissue**, fleshy tissue, flesh, matter, material **2 web**, net, network, mass, series

titan n **giant**, superman, superwoman, genius Opposite: nobody

titanic adj **colossal**, monumental, immense, gigantic, massive Opposite: insignificant

titbit n **1 morsel**, taste, bite, dainty, delicacy **2 gossip**, snippet, scrap, scandal, news

titch (infml) n **little person**, pip squeak (infml), shorty (infml), tiddler (infml) Opposite: bruiser (infml)

titchy (infml) adj **tiny**, minute, weeny (infml), teeny (infml), teeny-weeny (infml) Opposite: massive

tit for tat n **retaliation**, blow for blow, revenge, reprisal, vengeance

tithe n **church tax**, tax, duty, contribution, portion

titivate v **do up**, dress up, adorn, decorate, beautify

titivation n **adornment**, embellishment, beautification, prettification, enhancement

title n **1 name**, heading, label, designation **2 championship**, trophy, cup, award **3 ownership**, entitlement, deed, right, claim ■ v **call**, name, label, designate, refer to

titled adj **noble**, aristocratic, patrician, blue-blooded, upper-class

title deed n **title**, deed, document, proof of ownership, ownership

titleholder n **1 champion**, winner, reigning champion, cupholder **2 owner**, proprietor, possessor, vendor, holder

title page n **front page**, title, opening page, frontispiece

tittle-tattle n **gossip**, scandal, hearsay, tale, word of mouth ■ v **gossip**, chatter, prattle, yak (infml), chinwag (infml)

titular adj **nominal**, in name only, supposed, ostensible, so-called Opposite: actual

tizzy (infml) n **panic**, dither, flap (infml), lather (infml), state (infml)

T-junction n **junction**, intersection, fork, road junction

toady n **flatterer**, sycophant, groveller, creep (infml), crawler (infml) ■ v **grovel**, fawn, flatter, kowtow, crawl (infml)

toadying n **obsequiousness**, sycophancy, servility, flattery, fawning ■ adj **obsequious**, sycophantic, servile, flattering, fawning

to all intents and purposes adv **practically**, in practice, virtually, as good as, pretty much (infml)

toast n **1 salute**, tribute, pledge, health **2 darling**, favourite, delight, sweetheart ■ v **1 grill**, brown, crisp, heat, cook **2 drink to**, pledge, salute, drink the health of

toasty adj **warm**, snug, cosy, pleasant Opposite: chilly

toboggan n **sleigh**, sledge, bobsleigh, luge, sled (US) ■ v **1 sleigh**, sledge, luge, sled (US) **2 slip**, slide, hurtle, tumble

tocsin n **alarm**, warning, bell, siren, signal

today adv **nowadays**, these days, currently, now, at the moment Opposite: yesteryear

toddle v **1 totter**, patter, pad, waddle **2** (infml) **walk**, stroll, amble

toddler n **child**, baby, tot (infml), kid (infml)

to-do (infml) n **fuss**, commotion, bother, scene, kerfuffle (infml)

toehold n **start**, advantage, jumping-off point, beginning, entry

toff (infml) n **aristocrat**, aristo (infml), nob (infml), swell (dated infml), dandy (dated)

together adv **1 jointly**, as one, mutually, in concert, collectively Opposite: alone **2 simultaneously**, at once, at the same time, concurrently, all together Opposite: separately ■ adj (infml) **composed**, calm, collected, organized, cool Opposite: flustered

togetherness n **closeness**, intimacy, devotedness, friendship, inseparability Opposite: estrangement

together with prep **as well as**, accompanied by, with, alongside, in addition to

toggle n **1 fastener**, peg, button, buckle, clasp **2 switch**, key, command, button, lever ■ v **change**, change over, switch, move, transfer

togs (infml) n **clothes**, outfit, dress, clothing, kit

toil n **work**, labour, drudgery, slog, hard work Opposite: relaxation ■ v **labour**, strive, work, slog, slave Opposite: take it easy

toilet n **1 lavatory**, chamber pot, urinal, latrine, water closet **2 public convenience**, powder room, ladies, gents, WC **3** *(fml)* **washing**, dressing, grooming, bathing, toilette

toiletry *n* **beauty product**, skincare product, cosmetic product

WORD BANK

❏ **types of toiletry** aftershave, bath salts, body scrub, body milk, body wash, bubble bath, cleanser, cleansing cream, cologne, conditioner, cotton wool, dental floss, deodorant, eau de cologne, eau de toilette, face cream, face scrub, facial mask, foam bath, hair gel, hair mousse, hair spray, hand cream, moisturizer, mouthwash, night cream, perfume, shampoo, shaving cream, shower gel, soap, talcum powder, toilet water, toner, toothpaste

toilette *(literary) n* **dressing**, grooming, bathing, getting dressed, preparations

toilet water *n* **cologne**, eau de cologne, eau de toilette, scent, aftershave

token *n* **1 mark**, demonstration, sign, symbol, indication **2 voucher**, coupon, slip, coin **3 keepsake**, remembrance, souvenir, reminder, memento ■ *adj* **symbolic**, nominal, perfunctory, empty

tolerable *adj* **1 bearable**, acceptable, endurable, supportable *(literary)* Opposite: unbearable **2 reasonable**, average, passable, fair, adequate Opposite: intolerable

tolerance *n* **broad-mindedness**, acceptance, open-mindedness, lenience, charity Opposite: intolerance

tolerant *adj* **accepting**, easygoing, lenient, broad-minded, open-minded Opposite: intolerant

tolerate *v* **stand**, bear, abide, put up with, endure Opposite: forbid

toleration *n* **allowance**, acceptance, open-mindedness, broad-mindedness, liberality Opposite: prejudice

toll *n* **1 fee**, tax, levy, payment, duty **2 peal**, ring, ding-dong, clang, ding-a-ling

tollbooth *n* **barrier**, gate, kiosk, booth, ticket office

tollgate *n* **barrier**, gate, entrance, exit

tomb *n* **burial chamber**, catacomb, grave, burial place, crypt

tombola *n* **lottery**, draw, raffle, game of chance

tomboyish *adj* **boyish**, unladylike, mannish, boisterous, unruly

tombstone *n* **headstone**, gravestone, monument

tome *n* **book**, volume, digest, work

tomfoolery *(infml) n* **silliness**, horseplay, mischief, clowning, fooling around Opposite: sensibleness

ton *(infml) n* **mass**, mountain, lot, ocean, stack *(infml)*

tonality *n* **tone**, timbre, pitch, sound, sound quality Opposite: atonality

tone *n* **1 sound**, pitch, quality, timbre **2 quality**, manner, character, attitude, tendency **3 character**, atmosphere, feel, ambience **4 colour**, hue, tint, tinge, shade

tone down *v* **dilute**, moderate, soften, restrain, modulate Opposite: intensify

toneless *adj* **colourless**, expressionless, monotonous, neutral, monochrome Opposite: vibrant

tone up *v* **firm up**, strengthen, get in shape, exercise

tongue *n* **language**, patois, dialect, speech, idiom. *See* COMPARE AND CONTRAST *at* **language**.

tongue-in-cheek *adj* **lighthearted**, ironic, insincere, flippant, whimsical Opposite: serious

tongue-tied *adj* **speechless**, shy, awkward, silent, inarticulate Opposite: talkative

tonic *n* **boost**, fillip, stimulant, shot in the arm, livener

tonnage *n* **weight**, heaviness, capacity, size

tons *adv* **a lot**, a great deal, lots, loads *(infml)*, heaps *(infml)* ■ *n (infml)* **lots**, plenty, oodles *(infml)*, loads *(infml)*, piles *(infml)*

too *adv* **1 also**, as well, in addition, besides, moreover **2 excessively**, overly, extremely, exceedingly, overmuch Opposite: insufficiently

tool *n* **instrument**, implement, device, means, utensil

WORD BANK

❏ **types of carpentry tool** awl, bradawl, drill, hammer, jigsaw, mallet, plane, sander, saw, vice
❏ **types of cosmetic tool** comb, curling tongs, emery board, hair dryer, hairbrush, nail clippers, nail file, nail scissors, nailbrush, razor, shaving brush, tweezers
❏ **types of general tool** bellows, blowtorch, crowbar, file, grease gun, jack, jemmy, lathe, machine tool, pincers, pliers, plumb line, plunger, poker, pump, punch, rasp, screwdriver, socket spanner, socket wrench, soldering iron, spade, spanner, tongs, trowel
❏ **types of medical instrument** forceps, lancet, probe, scalpel, speculum, stethoscope, syringe

tooth *n* **1 fang**, tusk, chopper *(slang)* **2 indentation**, projection, tine, cog, prong

WORD BANK

❏ **types of tooth** baby tooth, bucktooth *(infml)*, canine, chopper, cuspid, denture, eyetooth, fang, incisor, milk tooth, molar, premolar, wisdom tooth

toothless *adj* **powerless**, useless, impotent, ineffective, ineffectual Opposite: effective

toothsome *adj* **delicious**, palatable, tasty, appetizing, mouthwatering Opposite: unappetizing

tootle *(infml) v* **1 drive slowly**, go slowly, pootle, meander, wend your way Opposite: dash **2 hoot**, toot, sound, honk, beep ■ *n* **drive**, pootle, meander, crawl Opposite: dash

top *n* **1 pinnacle**, summit, peak, apex, crown

Opposite: bottom **2 cork**, lid, cap, cover, stopper ■ *adj* **1 highest**, topmost, maximum, uppermost *Opposite*: bottom **2 best**, first, chief, principal, important ■ *v* **outdo**, surpass, better, improve on, cap

WORD BANK
❑ **types of sweater or cardigan** cardigan, crew neck, jersey, jumper, polo neck, pullover, sweater, turtleneck, twinset, V neck
❑ **types of top** basque, blouse, bodice, body warmer, bolero, boob tube *(slang)*, bustier, gilet, halter, jerkin, polo shirt, shirt, smock, surplice, sweatshirt, T-shirt, tabard, tank top, tee, tunic, vestment, waistcoat

top-class *adj* **best**, world-class, first-class, first-rate, top-flight

top drawer *n* **1 cream**, crème de la crème, elite, pick, best **2 aristocracy**, nobility, high society, gentry, upper class

top-drawer *adj* **1 top-flight**, best, first-rate, first-class, premium **2 upper class**, high class, noble, titled, aristocratic

top-flight *adj* **top-drawer**, best, first-rate, first-class, premium

top-heavy *adj* **unbalanced**, unstable, uneven, disproportionate, lopsided

topic *n* **theme**, subject, matter, issue, subject matter. *See* COMPARE AND CONTRAST *at* **subject**.

topical *adj* **up-to-date**, interesting, current, newsworthy, contemporary

topicality *n* **interest**, relevance, newsworthiness, current interest, contemporaneity

top-level *adj* **highest**, most senior, most important, most powerful

topmost *adj* **highest**, uppermost, top, peak *Opposite*: bottommost

topnotch *(infml) adj* **top-class**, first-rate, superior, first-class, excellent *Opposite*: inferior

top-of-the-range *adj* **best**, most expensive, exclusive, premium, premier *Opposite*: basic

topographical *adj* **geographical**, structural, natural, landscape, environmental

topography *n* **features**, landscape, geography, structure, countryside

topping *n* **top layer**, coating, glaze, garnish, frosting *Opposite*: filling

topple *v* **1 fall over**, tip over, collapse, fall, tumble **2 bring down**, overthrow, depose, oust, remove

top-quality *adj* **choice**, select, fine, rare

top-ranking *adj* **high-ranking**, senior, important, powerful, high-level

top-rated *adj* **favourite**, popular, well-liked, top, top ten *Opposite*: inferior

tops *(infml) adv* **at most**, as a maximum, at the most, max *(slang)*

top-secret *adj* **undercover**, covert, secret, clandestine, restricted

topsoil *n* **soil**, earth, loam, dirt, peat

topspin *n* **forward spin**, spin, momentum, force, impetus

topsy-turvy *adj* **confused**, disordered, chaotic, in disarray, upside down *Opposite*: orderly

top up *v* **1 refill**, replenish, refuel, freshen **2 make up**, augment, complete, chip in *(infml)*

top-up *n* **1 supplement**, increase, increment, extra, addition **2 refill**, fill-up, replenishment, extra serving, extra measure

tor *n* **peak**, crag, outcrop, rock face

torch *n* **penlight**, light, lamp, lantern, flash *(US infml)* ■ *v (infml)* **burn down**, set on fire, set light to, put a match to, set fire to

torchlight *n* **beam**, light, illumination, lamplight

torment *v* **annoy**, tease, plague, persecute, taunt *Opposite*: comfort ■ *n* **1 anguish**, suffering, agony, distress, pain *Opposite*: pleasure **2 nuisance**, bane, plague, annoyance, irritation *Opposite*: delight

tormented *adj* **anguished**, tortured, distressed, grief-stricken, plagued

tormenter *see* **tormentor**

tormentor *n* **oppressor**, tyrant, persecutor, bully, teaser

torn *adj* **1 ripped**, frayed, ragged, tattered, shabby **2 undecided**, uncertain, in a quandary, in a dilemma, unable to decide *Opposite*: decided

tornado *n* **hurricane**, whirlwind, cyclone, storm, windstorm

torpedo *(infml) v* **ruin**, destroy, wreck, spoil, thwart

torpid *adj* **lazy**, languorous, listless, sluggish, apathetic *Opposite*: energetic

torpor *n* **inactivity**, inertia, indolence, languor, lethargy *Opposite*: excitement

torque *n* **rotating force**, rotation, twisting, turning, turning force

torrent *n* **1 rush**, flood, flow, deluge, gush *Opposite*: trickle **2 outburst**, flood, flow, tide, stream

torrential *adj* **heavy**, pouring, driving, lashing, drenching *Opposite*: light

torrid *adj* **1 hot**, stifling, sweltering, boiling, burning *Opposite*: cool **2 passionate**, amorous, impassioned, erotic, steamy *(infml)*

torsion *n* **twisting**, turning, turning force, rotation, spin

tort *n* **wrongful act**, unlawful act, illegal act, offence, misdemeanour

tortuous *adj* **1 twisting**, winding, convoluted, circuitous, indirect *Opposite*: direct **2 complex**, complicated, intricate, difficult, involved *Opposite*: simple **3 devious**, deceitful, crafty, sly, artful *Opposite*: straightforward

torture *v* **torment**, afflict, persecute, brutalize, punish ■ *n* **agony**, torment, anguish, pain, suffering

torturer n intimidator, bully, pesterer, harasser, teaser

tosh (*infml*) n rubbish, nonsense, stuff and nonsense, twaddle (*infml*), bunkum (*infml*)

toss v 1 throw, pitch, fling, lob, hurl 2 mix, stir, blend, mix up ▪ n lob, throw, pitch, heave, fling. See COMPARE AND CONTRAST at throw.

toss-up n even chance, chance, risk, fifty-fifty, luck of the draw

tot n 1 dram, finger, thimbleful, snifter (*infml*) 2 (*infml*) toddler, child, baby, small child, kid (*infml*)

total n sum, whole, entirety, full amount, totality ▪ adj 1 entire, whole, full, complete, aggregate Opposite: partial 2 absolute, unmitigated, complete, unreserved, out-and-out ▪ v 1 add up, count up, tot up, calculate, sum 2 amount to, add up to, come to, equal, make

totalitarian adj authoritarian, tyrannous, one-party, oppressive, autocratic Opposite: democratic

totalitarianism n despotism, absolutism, tyranny, autocracy, authoritarianism

totality n entirety, whole, total, sum, full amount Opposite: part

totally adv completely, entirely, absolutely, wholly, fully Opposite: partly

tote (*infml*) v 1 carry, cart, lug, haul, heave 2 brandish, carry, hold, wield, bear

totem n 1 ritual object, sacred symbol, icon, charm, talisman 2 symbol, representation, emblem, image, icon

totemic adj symbolic, emblematic, iconic, representative

totter v walk unsteadily, stagger, wobble, teeter, stumble

tot up v add up, add together, count up, total, calculate

touch n 1 pat, tap, stroke, fondle, feel 2 trace, bit, dash, drop, hint 3 style, facility, gift, knack, ability ▪ v 1 handle, feel, finger, tap, stroke 2 converge, meet, come into contact, join, contact Opposite: separate 3 move, affect, upset, stir, touch a chord 4 match, come close to, meet, rival, equal

touch-and-go adj uncertain, unpredictable, doubtful, unknown, risky Opposite: certain

touch down v land, alight, come down, set down, arrive Opposite: take off

touchdown n 1 landing, descent, arrival Opposite: blastoff 2 score, try, point

touched adj affected, moved, warmed, heartened, impressed Opposite: unmoved

touchiness n irritability, impatience, grumpiness, cantankerousness, moodiness Opposite: composure

touching adj moving, poignant, stirring, tender, pitiful. See COMPARE AND CONTRAST at moving.

touch on v deal with, refer to, mention, treat, allude to

touchstone n criterion, standard, benchmark, yardstick, hallmark

touch up v retouch, restore, freshen, freshen up, refurbish

touchy adj 1 sensitive, quick-tempered, impatient, petulant, cantankerous Opposite: even-tempered 2 delicate, sensitive, tricky, awkward, ticklish

touchy-feely (*infml*) adj demonstrative, expressive, effusive, unreserved, emotional Opposite: undemonstrative

tough adj 1 durable, strong, sturdy, robust, hardy Opposite: weak 2 hard, chewy, stringy, stiff, leathery Opposite: tender 3 threatening, rough, hard, harsh, dangerous Opposite: pleasant 4 difficult, hard, demanding, exacting, arduous Opposite: easy 5 severe, strict, rigid, inflexible, stern Opposite: lenient. See COMPARE AND CONTRAST at hard.

toughen v strengthen, harden, build up, reinforce, fortify Opposite: weaken

toughened adj hardened, reinforced, strengthened, fortified, unbreakable

tough-minded adj realistic, determined, tough, single-minded, resilient Opposite: weak-willed

toughness n 1 durability, hardiness, robustness, roughness, stoutness Opposite: flimsiness 2 hardness, chewiness, stringiness, stiffness Opposite: tenderness 3 roughness, harshness, hardness, danger Opposite: pleasantness 4 difficulty, arduousness, strenuousness, challenge, trickiness Opposite: ease 5 severity, strictness, rigidity, inflexibility, firmness Opposite: leniency

toupee n wig, hairpiece, hair extension

tour n trip, excursion, expedition, outing, journey ▪ v sightsee, explore, visit, travel around, go around

tourism n travel, holiday business, leisure industry, service sector, travel industry

tourist n traveller, sightseer, visitor, holidaymaker, day tripper

touristy adj crowded, busy, much-frequented, popular, overvisited Opposite: quiet

tournament n contest, competition, event, tourney, game

tourniquet n band, strap, bandage

tousle v tangle, ruffle, rumple, dishevel, disorder Opposite: tidy

tousled adj dishevelled, messy, tangled, ruffled, windswept Opposite: tidy

tout v advertise, hype, flaunt, push, publicize Opposite: understate ▪ n seller, hawker, peddler, vendor

tow v pull, drag, draw, haul, lug. See COMPARE AND CONTRAST at pull.

towards prep 1 in the direction of, to, near, just before 2 regarding, concerning, for, about, on

towel n cloth, bath towel, bath sheet, hand

towel, guest towel ∎ *v* **dry**, rub down, rub, wipe, dab

tower *v* 1 **loom**, overlook, be head and shoulders above, soar, rise 2 **surpass**, exceed, excel, top, transcend

towering *adj* **high**, tall, soaring, lofty, immense *Opposite*: short

tower of strength *(infml)* *n* **rock**, mainstay, anchor, helper, advocate

town *n* **municipality**, city, settlement, township, metropolis. *See* COMPARE AND CONTRAST *at* **city**.

townie *(infml)* *n* **town dweller**, city dweller, urbanite, city slicker

townsfolk *n* **townspeople**, populace, residents, inhabitants

township *n* **small town**, urban area, settlement, town, hamlet

townspeople *n* **townsfolk**, populace, residents, inhabitants

towpath *n* **path**, footpath, bridleway, canal path, track

towrope *n* **towline**, rope, line, cable, cord

toxic *adj* **poisonous**, deadly, lethal, noxious, contaminated *Opposite*: harmless

toxicity *n* **poisonousness**, venomousness, deadliness, noxiousness, harmfulness *Opposite*: harmlessness

toxin *n* **poison**, pollutant, contaminant, venom

toy with *v* 1 **flirt with**, tease, philander 2 **play with**, fiddle with, fidget with, handle, finger 3 **think about**, consider, ponder, contemplate, entertain *Opposite*: dismiss

trace *v* 1 **draw**, outline, copy, mark out, sketch 2 **find**, locate, discover, hunt down, track down ∎ *n* 1 **sign**, indication, evidence, remnant, residue 2 **suggestion**, hint, dash, drop, touch

tracery *n* **decoration**, pattern, design, interlacing, ornamentation

track *n* 1 **trail**, footprints, footsteps, path, trace 2 **path**, pathway, road, way, trail ∎ *v* **follow**, hunt down, chase, pursue, stalk

track down *v* **find**, hunt down, catch, capture, discover

tracker *n* **trailer**, follower, chaser, hunter, shadow

tract *n* 1 **area**, territory, zone, region, expanse 2 **pamphlet**, article, treatise, leaflet

tractability *n* 1 **docility**, controllability, manageability, obedience, manipulability *Opposite*: intractability 2 **malleability**, pliability, workability, ductility, elasticity *Opposite*: intractability

tractable *adj* 1 **docile**, controllable, manageable, obedient, manipulable *Opposite*: intractable 2 **malleable**, pliable, workable, ductile, elastic *Opposite*: intractable

traction *n* 1 **adhesive friction**, grip, purchase, adhesion 2 **power**, tractive force, pull, tow, tug

trade *n* 1 **commerce**, business, industry, market, dealings 2 **occupation**, job, employment, line of work, profession 3 **customers**, public, patrons, custom, clientele ∎ *v* 1 **deal**, buy and sell, do business, operate, traffic 2 **exchange**, barter, negotiate, swap *(infml)*, dicker *(infml)*

trade fair *n* **exhibition**, exposition, fair, display, show

trade in *v* **exchange**, redeem, give in part payment, barter, swap *(infml)*

trade-in *n* **part exchange**, exchange, deal, transaction, swap *(infml)*

trademark *n* 1 **symbol**, logo, emblem, brand 2 **characteristic**, feature, trait, attribute, facet

trade name *n* **brand name**, brand, trademark, name, registered trademark

trade-off *n* **compromise**, balance, adjustment, interchange, transaction

trader *n* **dealer**, buyer, seller, broker, agent

tradition *n* **custom**, institution, ritual, habit, convention *Opposite*: innovation. *See* COMPARE AND CONTRAST *at* **habit**.

traditional *adj* **usual**, conventional, customary, established, fixed *Opposite*: progressive

traditionalism *n* **conventionalism**, conservatism, conformity, orthodoxy, fundamentalism *Opposite*: progressivism

traditionalist *n* **conservative**, purist, fundamentalist, conformist *Opposite*: progressive ∎ *adj* **traditional**, conservative, purist, old-school, orthodox *Opposite*: progressive

traduce *v* **criticize**, disparage, malign, run down, defame *Opposite*: praise

traffic *n* 1 **road traffic**, traffic flow, circulation, stream of traffic, rush-hour traffic 2 **transportation**, movement, passage, toing and froing, travel 3 **trade**, commerce, business, dealings, transactions ∎ *v* 1 **have dealings**, deal in, trade, trade in, transfer 2 **smuggle**, run, handle

traffic jam *n* **tailback**, bottleneck, gridlock, holdup

tragedy *n* **disaster**, calamity, catastrophe, misfortune, heartbreak *Opposite*: joy

tragic *adj* **sad**, disastrous, catastrophic, heartbreaking, heartrending *Opposite*: joyous

tragicomic *adj* **bittersweet**, poignant, affecting, moving

trail *v* 1 **tug**, drag, pull, draw, tow *Opposite*: push 2 **follow**, track, tail, shadow, trace 3 **drop back**, lag behind, fall behind, straggle, follow on *Opposite*: lead ∎ *n* 1 **path**, track, way, road, footpath 2 **track**, footprints, footsteps, paw marks, paw prints

trail away *v* **fade**, disappear, grow faint, die away, diminish *Opposite*: intensify

trailblazer *n* **pioneer**, leader, innovator, entrepreneur, architect

trailer n clip, preview, ad (infml), promo (infml), advert (infml)

train n 1 **procession**, file, convoy, line 2 **sequence**, chain, succession, string, series ■ v 1 **teach**, coach, educate, instruct, tutor 2 **exercise**, work out, keep fit, keep in shape 3 **aim**, direct, focus, point, line up. See COMPARE AND CONTRAST at **teach**.

trained adj **skilled**, qualified, proficient, accomplished, competent

trainee n **apprentice**, learner, novice, beginner Opposite: trainer

trainer n **coach**, teacher, guide, instructor, mentor Opposite: trainee

training n 1 **tuition**, education, schooling, teaching, guidance 2 **exercise**, working out, keep fit, physical activity, drill

traipse (infml) v **trudge**, tramp, plod, slog, trek

trait n **mannerism**, peculiarity, attribute, characteristic, feature

traitor n **conspirator**, collaborator, turncoat, defector, deserter Opposite: loyalist

traitorous adj **disloyal**, faithless, duplicitous, deceitful, treacherous Opposite: loyal

trajectory n **route**, course, flight, path, line

trammel n **restriction**, limitation, hindrance, curb, constraint ■ v 1 **confine**, limit, restrain, restrict, hinder 2 **ensnare**, snare, catch, net, entangle

tramp n 1 **vagrant**, homeless person, beggar, vagabond, hobo 2 **traipse**, march, trek, hike, trudge ■ v **trudge**, trek, hike, traipse, march

trample v **crush**, flatten, walk on, stamp on, step on

trance n **dream**, daze, spell, stupor, reverie Opposite: alertness

tranquil adj 1 **calm**, serene, peaceful, still, relaxing Opposite: noisy 2 **composed**, calm, cool, unruffled, unperturbed Opposite: agitated

tranquillity n 1 **calm**, serenity, stillness, peacefulness, hush Opposite: turmoil 2 **composure**, equanimity, calmness, coolness, self-possession Opposite: panic

tranquillize v **sedate**, calm, put out, put under, knock out

transact v **carry out**, conduct, manage, handle, perform

transaction n **deal**, business, contract, matter, operation

transatlantic adj **transoceanic**, inter-continental, long-haul

transcend v **rise above**, go beyond, exceed, go above, excel

transcendence n 1 **divine existence**, other-worldliness, state of grace, perfection, wholeness Opposite: mundaneness 2 **superiority**, greatness, excellence, pre-eminence, loftiness Opposite: inferiority

transcendent adj 1 **superior**, excellent, supreme, great, unequalled Opposite: inferior 2 **divine**, perfect, heavenly, supernatural, otherworldly Opposite: earthy 3 **mystical**, awe-inspiring, uplifting, inspirational, inspiring

transcendental adj 1 **mystical**, awe-inspiring, uplifting, inspirational, inspiring 2 **divine**, perfect, heavenly, supernatural, otherworldly

transcontinental adj **pancontinental**, coast-to-coast, continent-wide

transcribe v **copy out**, write out, copy, set down, write down

transcript n **record**, copy, text, transcription

transcription see transcript

transect v **divide**, bisect, cut, split, cut across

transfer v 1 **move**, transport, relocate, remove, shift 2 **transmit**, convey, hand on, hand over, turn over ■ n 1 **transmission**, handover, assignment, allocation, transference 2 **relocation**, removal, move, resettlement, displacement

transference n **transfer**, conversion, devolution, conveyance, transmission

transfiguration n **metamorphosis**, transformation, makeover, change, conversion

transfigure v **change**, metamorphose, transform, convert, transmute

transfix v 1 **fascinate**, mesmerize, engross, spellbind, hypnotize 2 **stab**, spike, gore, run through, pierce

transform v **alter**, convert, change, transmute, renovate. See COMPARE AND CONTRAST at **change**.

transformation n **alteration**, conversion, revolution, renovation, makeover

transgress v **misbehave**, disobey, go astray, lapse, sin Opposite: behave

transgression n **wrongdoing**, misbehaviour, disobedience, lapse, sin

transgressor n **wrongdoer**, lawbreaker, sinner, offender, criminal

transience n **briefness**, brevity, impermanence, transitoriness, shortness Opposite: permanence

transient adj **fleeting**, brief, passing, transitory, temporary Opposite: permanent

transit n **transportation**, transfer, transport, travel, shipment

transition n **changeover**, shift, change, alteration, move

transitional adj **intermediate**, in-between, interim, provisional, temporary Opposite: permanent

transitory adj **fleeting**, passing, brief, temporary, momentary Opposite: permanent. See COMPARE AND CONTRAST at **temporary**.

translate v 1 **interpret**, decode, decipher, explain, render (fml) 2 **convert**, transform, transmute, turn, change

translation n **conversion**, paraphrase, version, rendition, interpretation

translator *n* interpreter, decoder, decipherer, converter

transliterate *v* transcribe, convert, translate, transmute, transform

transliteration *n* transcription, conversion, translation, transformation, rendering

translucence *n* **1 transparency**, sheerness, filminess, limpidity, translucency *Opposite*: opacity **2 glow**, luminosity, brightness, luminescence, luminousness *Opposite*: dullness

translucent *adj* **1 transparent**, semitransparent, see-through, lucid, clear *Opposite*: opaque **2 glowing**, luminous, radiant, shining, lustrous *Opposite*: dull

transmigrate *v* wander, migrate, travel, shift, drift *Opposite*: settle

transmigration *n* migration, wandering, travelling, movement, shifting

transmissible *adj* communicable, infectious, contagious, catching

transmission *n* **1 spread**, communication, diffusion, conduction **2 programme**, show, broadcast

transmit *v* **1 convey**, hand on, spread, communicate, diffuse **2 put on the air**, send out, put out, broadcast

transmittable *adj* communicable, infectious, catching, contagious

transmittance *n* transmission, diffusion, conduction, transfer, transferral

transmutation *n* transfiguration, transmogrification, change, transformation, alteration

transmute *v* transfigure, transmogrify, transform, alter, change. *See* COMPARE AND CONTRAST at **change**.

transnational *adj* international, multinational, transcontinental, intercontinental, global ■ *n* **multinational**, conglomerate, corporation

transparency *n* **1 clearness**, limpidity, translucence, filminess, sheerness *Opposite*: opacity **2 slide**, photograph, photo, shot *Opposite*: print **3 clarity**, plainness, obviousness, directness, unambiguousness *Opposite*: ambiguousness

transparent *adj* **1 see-through**, clear, translucent, crystal clear *Opposite*: opaque **2 obvious**, clear, apparent, plain, evident *Opposite*: unclear

transpire *v* happen, occur, take place, come about, go on

transplant *v* remove, relocate, move, transfer, shift

transplantation *n* relocation, movement, transfer, replacement, uprooting

transport *v* convey, move, bring, carry, transfer ■ *n* **1 conveyance**, carriage, transportation, transference, passage **2 vehicle**, transportation, conveyance, means of transport

transportable *adj* mobile, portable, movable, travel, transferable

transportation *n* transport, conveyance, carriage, transference, passage

transporter *n* carrier, haulier, courier, shipper, delivery service

transpose *v* **1 invert**, switch, reverse, exchange, swap *(infml)* **2 move**, transfer, rearrange, alter, reorder

transposition *n* **1 reversal**, inversion, switch, exchange, substitution **2 rearrangement**, reordering, recasting, relocation, shuffle

transubstantiation *(fml)* *n* conversion, transformation, metamorphosis, mutation, alteration

transverse *adj* crosswise, at right angles, sloping, oblique, slanting

trap *n* ruse, trick, snare, deception, con ■ *v* **1 catch**, ensnare, entrap, ambush, corner *Opposite*: release **2 trick**, deceive, dupe, con, ensnare

trap door *n* hatch, flap, small door, entrance, doorway

trapped *adj* **1 shut in**, locked in, stuck, surrounded, hemmed in *Opposite*: released **2 stuck**, caught, jammed, stuck fast, wedged *Opposite*: free

trappings *n* accessories, accoutrements, paraphernalia, trimmings, frills

trash *n* nonsense, rubbish, drivel, gibberish, double talk ■ *v* *(infml)* **wreck**, destroy, ruin, damage, smash

trashy *adj* cheap, worthless, tasteless, shabby, rubbishy *Opposite*: quality

trauma *n* shock, upset, disturbance, ordeal, suffering

traumatic *adj* shocking, disturbing, upsetting, distressing, harrowing

traumatize *v* shock, upset, distress, devastate, disturb

traumatized *adj* disturbed, shocked, upset, troubled, distressed *Opposite*: unaffected

travail *n* hard work, toil, effort, exertion, labour

travel *v* journey, tour, take a trip, voyage, trek ■ *adj* **portable**, lightweight, foldaway, collapsible, transportable

traveller *n* **1 itinerant**, New Age traveller, nomad, rover, wanderer **2 explorer**, voyager, tourist, holidaymaker, trekker

travelogue *n* travel piece, talk, lecture, travel programme

travels *n* voyage, journey, trip, exploration, trekking

travel-sick *adj* queasy, nauseous, unwell, ill, seasick

traverse *v* cross, pass through, negotiate, navigate, go across

travesty *n* charade, caricature, sham, parody, mockery

trawl *v* **1 fish**, catch fish, go fishing **2 hunt**, search, rummage around, sift, look through ■ *n* **search**, investigation, hunt, rummage, scan

tray n **1** salver, platter, serving dish, plate, baking tray **2** receptacle, container, in-tray, out-tray, in-box (US)

treacherous adj **1** unfaithful, traitorous, disloyal, deceitful, false Opposite: loyal **2** dangerous, hazardous, precarious, unsafe, perilous Opposite: safe

treachery n deceit, treason, deceitfulness, sedition, disloyalty Opposite: loyalty

treacly adj **1** sticky, glutinous, gooey, gluey, syrupy **2** sentimental, mawkish, romanticized, romantic, slushy

tread v **1** trample, crush, squash, flatten, stomp **2** walk, step, stride, tramp, pace ▪ n step, footstep, footfall, tramp, stamp

treadle n foot pedal, lever, control

treadmill n daily grind, routine, drudgery, toil, slog

treason n sedition, treachery, disloyalty, subversion, betrayal Opposite: allegiance

treasonable adj traitorous, treacherous, subversive, disloyal, rebellious

treasure n **1** wealth, riches, money, valuables, cache **2** star, paragon, pearl, prize, gem (infml) ▪ v cherish, value, prize, adore, hold dear Opposite: neglect

treasured adj dear, precious, loved, cherished, beloved

treasurer n banker, bursar, bookkeeper, accountant, financial officer

treat v **1** regard, consider, think of, behave towards, act towards **2** care for, take care of, doctor, cure, nurse **3** pay for, pick up the check, pick up the tab, pay the bill, give **4** indulge, spoil, pamper, make a fuss of **5** deal with, go into, discuss, handle, touch on ▪ n luxury, extravagance, indulgence, delight, pleasure Opposite: necessity

treatise n dissertation, discourse, essay, thesis, paper

treatment n **1** cure, healing, care, therapy, medicine Opposite: placebo **2** handling, behaviour, conduct, dealing, management

treaty n agreement, accord, contract, pact, truce

treble adj **1** triple, three times, thrice, threefold **2** high-pitched, high, shrill, piping ▪ v increase, triple, increase threefold, increase by three, multiply

tree n **1** sapling, bush, shrub **2** diagram, tree diagram, family tree, hierarchy, pyramid

treetop n crown, canopy, foliage

trek v hike, walk, ramble, march, tramp ▪ n walk, hike, ramble, journey, march

trellis n lattice, grille, fence, fencing, frame

tremble v shiver, shake, shudder, quiver, judder ▪ n shake, shiver, shudder, quake, quiver

trembling n shaking, vibrating, quivering, shuddering, wobbling ▪ adj **1** unsteady, vibrating, quivering, shuddering, quaking Opposite: still **2** timorous, tremulous, nervous, terrified, fearful Opposite: confident

tremendous adj **1** great, incredible, fabulous, terrific, marvellous Opposite: awful **2** huge, great, enormous, vast, immense Opposite: tiny

tremendously adv very, extremely, greatly, enormously, vastly Opposite: slightly

tremor n **1** shake, tremble, vibration, quiver, shiver **2** earthquake, shock, quake (infml)

tremulous adj **1** unsteady, quivering, trembling, quavering, shaky Opposite: steady **2** timid, timorous, trembling, shy, fearful Opposite: confident

trench n ditch, channel, drain, dugout, trough

trenchancy n incisiveness, forcefulness, acerbity, brutality, directness Opposite: gentleness

trenchant adj incisive, cutting, sharp, biting, acerbic Opposite: mild

trend n **1** tendency, drift, leaning, inclination, movement **2** fashion, style, look, craze, vogue

trendsetter n innovator, pacesetter, modernizer, leader, leading light Opposite: imitator

trendsetting adj influential, innovative, cutting-edge, leading, new Opposite: conventional

trendy (infml) adj fashionable, in, up-to-the-minute, cool, stylish Opposite: unfashionable

trepidation n fear, anxiety, unease, nervousness, apprehension Opposite: equanimity

trespass v intrude, infringe, encroach, invade, interlope

trespasser n intruder, squatter, interloper, snooper (infml) Opposite: guest

tress n lock, strand, curl, tuft, wisp

tresses n locks (literary), hair, curls, ringlets

trestle n support, bracket, stand, frame, framework

triad n trio, threesome, triangle, troika, triumvirate

trial n **1** test, examination, experiment, tryout, audition **2** hearing, court case, court-martial, prosecution, legal proceedings **3** ordeal, hardship, suffering, trouble, misery ▪ adj experimental, probationary, pilot, provisional, test

triangle n threesome, trio, three-way relationship, triad, trinity

triangular adj three-sided, trilateral, three-cornered, wedge-shaped, deltoid

tribal adj ethnic, family, ancestral, familial, group

tribe n **1** people, ethnic group, community, society, population **2** (infml) family, clan, people (infml)

tribulation n **misfortune**, trial, suffering, ordeal, distress

tribunal n **1 court**, court of law, law court **2 board**, panel, committee, body

tributary n **branch**, arm, offshoot, river, stream

tribute n **1 compliment**, mark of respect, honour, praise, acknowledgment **2 tax**, duty, excise, toll, payment

trice n **instant**, flash, moment, twinkling, no time

trick n **1 deception**, ploy, ruse, hoax, dodge **2 joke**, prank, stunt, caper **3 knack**, technique, skill, secret **4 habit**, mannerism, trait, characteristic, way ■ v **deceive**, cheat, mislead, trap, fool ■ adj **fake**, false, artificial, bogus, hoax Opposite: real

trickery n **1 deception**, deceit, fraud, scam (slang), sting (slang) **2 dishonesty**, deception, deceit, fraudulence, chicanery

trickiness n **1 difficulty**, complication, delicacy, awkwardness, intricacy Opposite: simplicity **2 craftiness**, slipperiness, deviousness, slyness, duplicity Opposite: honesty

trickle v **drip**, drop, seep, dribble, ooze Opposite: flood ■ n **dribble**, drop, drip Opposite: flood

trickster n **cheat**, swindler, charlatan, fraud, slippery customer

tricky adj **1 complicated**, delicate, awkward, thorny, problematic Opposite: simple **2 devious**, sly, deceitful, crafty, cunning Opposite: straight

trier n **1 tester**, experimenter, taster, volunteer, guinea pig **2 sticker**, fighter, striver, struggler, stayer Opposite: defeatist

trifle n **1 nothing**, frippery, triviality **2 smidgen**, bit, little, drop, touch

trifling adj **trivial**, petty, small, tiny, silly Opposite: significant

trigger v **activate**, set off, cause, generate, start Opposite: halt

trigger-happy (infml) adj **rash**, violent, dangerous, wild, unpredictable

trigger off v **activate**, set off, cause, generate, start Opposite: halt

trill v **warble**, quaver, shrill, tweet, vibrate

trillion (infml) n **lots**, tons (infml), loads (infml), masses (infml), stacks (infml)

trilogy n **series**, sequence, set, cycle, trio

trim v **1 clip**, cut, shear, pare, prune Opposite: lengthen **2 cut back**, prune, decrease, lower, shave Opposite: augment (fml) **3 decorate**, adorn, embroider, embellish, edge ■ adj **1 tidy**, orderly, smart, spruce, dapper Opposite: messy **2 slim**, fit, shapely, sleek, slender Opposite: bulky ■ n **decoration**, adornment, frill, edge, border

trimming n **decoration**, adornment, frill, garnish, extra

trimmings n **1 side dishes**, extras, accompaniments **2 extras**, accompaniments, additions, accessories, embellishments **3 clippings**, parings, bits, pieces, nail clippings

trimness n **1 neatness**, tidiness, smartness, spruceness, orderliness **2 slenderness**, slimness, compactness, sleekness, thinness

trinity n **threesome**, trio, triad, troika, triplet

trinket n **ornament**, charm, knick-knack, bauble, gewgaw

trio n **threesome**, triad, troika, trinity, triangle

trip n **1 journey**, tour, excursion, expedition, outing **2 slip**, stumble, tumble, fall ■ v **1 stumble**, trip up, slip, tumble, falter **2 skip**, hop, prance, caper, dance

tripartite adj **three-way**, three-party, multilateral, triple

tripe (infml) n **rubbish**, nonsense, garbage, drivel, trash Opposite: fact

triple adj **1 tripartite**, three-way, three-layered, triple-decker Opposite: single **2 treble**, threefold, multiple Opposite: single ■ v **treble**, triplicate, multiply by three, increase, boost Opposite: reduce

triplet n **trio**, triad, threesome, troika

tripper (infml) n **tourist**, day tripper, holidaymaker, visitor, excursionist (dated)

trip up v **1 stumble**, trip, slip, tumble, fall **2 trap**, trick, confuse, disconcert, unsettle

trite adj **commonplace**, stale, tired, pedestrian, worn Opposite: original

triteness n **dullness**, tiredness, staleness, corniness, banality Opposite: originality

triumph n **1 victory**, achievement, conquest, accomplishment, coup Opposite: failure **2 rejoicing**, pride, elation, delight, satisfaction Opposite: sorrow ■ v **succeed**, prevail, win, overcome, be victorious Opposite: lose

triumphal adj **ceremonial**, commemorative, victory, heroic, celebratory

triumphant adj **1 winning**, victorious, glorious, dominant, proud **2 exultant**, celebratory, jubilant, elated, delighted Opposite: sorrowful

triumph over v **overcome**, defeat, beat, prevail over, get the better of

triumvirate n **trio**, threesome, triad, troika, triplet

trivet n **stand**, support, rest, tripod

trivia n **minutiae**, trivialities, froth, nonsense, trifles Opposite: essentials

trivial adj **unimportant**, small, inconsequential, slight, trifling Opposite: crucial

triviality n **1 unimportance**, inconsequence, worthlessness, insignificance, pettiness Opposite: importance **2 trifle**, nothing, frippery

trivialize v **play down**, belittle, underestimate, make light of, tone down Opposite: highlight

troika n **trio**, triumvirate, threesome, triad, triplet

troll v 1 fish, angle, trail, spin, lure 2 amble, wander, saunter, drift, walk ■ n giant, ogre, hobgoblin, goblin, monster

troop n crowd, horde, throng, multitude, herd ■ v 1 move, gather, rally, come together, get together 2 march, parade, stream, trudge, traipse

trophy n cup, award, medal, crown, title

tropical adj hot, steamy, humid, sultry, stifling Opposite: temperate

trot v jog, run, hurry, scurry, scamper Opposite: saunter

troubadour n minstrel, musician, poet, wandering minstrel, bard (literary)

trouble n 1 problem, difficulty, dilemma, nuisance, snag Opposite: ease 2 worry, concern, distress, anxiety, care 3 complaint, ailment, disease, illness, malady Opposite: good health 4 effort, bother, inconvenience, work, thought 5 strife, unrest, disorder, disturbance, discontent Opposite: accord ■ v 1 concern, worry, distress, agitate, harass 2 bother, put out, inconvenience, disturb, burden 3 make an effort, take pains, exert yourself, bother Opposite: hang back. See COMPARE AND CONTRAST at bother.

troubled adj 1 anxious, concerned, bothered, worried, disturbed Opposite: calm 2 problematic, tricky, awkward, difficult Opposite: easy

trouble-free adj easy, simple, painless, straightforward, uncomplicated Opposite: troublesome

troublemaker n mischief-maker, menace, agitator, firebrand, rabble-rouser Opposite: conciliator

troubleshooter n 1 technician, engineer, mechanic, problem solver, expert 2 mediator, consultant, ombudsman, adviser, counsellor

troublesome adj 1 worrying, upsetting, bothersome, wearisome, difficult Opposite: trouble-free 2 disorderly, rowdy, unruly, uncooperative, undisciplined Opposite: well-behaved

trough n 1 manger, crib, rack, holder 2 channel, furrow, trench, gutter, ditch 3 depression, low, low pressure area Opposite: ridge

trounce v beat, thrash, rout, crush, overwhelm. See COMPARE AND CONTRAST at defeat.

trouncing n routing, thrashing, crushing, drubbing, beating

troupe n company, cast, band, ensemble, group

trousseau n bridal goods, bottom drawer, hope chest (US)

truancy n absence, nonattendance, absenteeism, malingering, skiving (infml) Opposite: attendance

truant n absentee, malingerer, shirker, skiver (infml) ■ v shirk, go AWOL, malinger, skive (infml), bunk off (infml)

truce n ceasefire, armistice, treaty, peace, respite

truculence n defiance, belligerence, sullenness, insolence, impertinence Opposite: enthusiasm

truculent adj hostile, belligerent, defiant, quarrelsome, argumentative Opposite: easygoing

trudge v tramp, traipse, slog, plod, trek ■ n slog, trek, hike, march, haul

true adj 1 factual, accurate, right, correct, proper Opposite: false 2 real, genuine, actual, valid, authentic Opposite: fake 3 faithful, dedicated, constant, loyal, sincere Opposite: unfaithful

true-blue adj right-wing, traditional, conservative, diehard, old-school

true-life adj genuine, realistic, real-life, real, true

true to life adj realistic, convincing, accurate, authentic, lifelike Opposite: unrealistic

truism n axiom, cliché, maxim, adage, saying

truly adv 1 really, in fact, beyond doubt, actually, indeed 2 sincerely, faithfully, honestly, in all honesty, genuinely Opposite: insincerely 3 very, greatly, really, indeed, exceptionally

trump v outdo, go one better, call somebody's bluff, undermine, outmanoeuvre

trumped-up adj false, fake, invented, made-up, fabricated Opposite: genuine

truncate v shorten, abbreviate, trim, cut, prune Opposite: lengthen

trundle v 1 roll, roll along, rattle, labour, wheel 2 traipse, trail, saunter, lumber, wander

trunk n stem, bole, stalk

trunks n swimming trunks, bathing trunks, shorts

truss v bind, tie up, tie, tether, string

trust n 1 faith, belief, hope, conviction, confidence Opposite: distrust 2 custody, care, protection, responsibility, guard ■ v 1 have faith in, believe, rely on, depend on, confide in Opposite: distrust 2 hope, believe, expect, assume, suppose Opposite: despair 3 entrust, confide, assign, consign, commit

trustee n 1 fund manager, fund administrator, director 2 representative, deputy, agent, executor, guardian

trustfulness n unwariness, credulity, innocence, lack of caution, trustingness Opposite: wariness

trusting adj gullible, credulous, unquestioning, believing, naive Opposite: suspicious

trustworthiness n honesty, dependability, reliability, fidelity, constancy Opposite: dishonesty

trustworthy adj dependable, reliable, responsible, truthful, honest Opposite: corrupt

trusty adj faithful, dependable, reliable, constant, loyal Opposite: unreliable

truth *n* **1 fact**, certainty, reality, actuality, veracity *Opposite*: untruth **2 honesty**, integrity, fidelity, sincerity

truthful *adj* **1 honest**, straight, frank, open, straightforward *Opposite*: dishonest **2 correct**, true, reliable, accurate, exact *Opposite*: false

truthfulness *n* **1 honesty**, truth, candour, frankness, openness *Opposite*: dishonesty **2 accuracy**, reliability, correctness, exactitude, faithfulness *Opposite*: inaccuracy

try *v* **1 attempt**, endeavour, strive, aim, seek **2 test**, sample, taste, appraise, evaluate **3 strain**, vex, tax, exasperate, annoy *Opposite*: soothe **4 judge**, put on trial, hear, take to court ■ *n* **attempt**, effort, go, stab (*infml*), crack (*infml*)

trying *adj* **annoying**, tiresome, irritating, wearisome, frustrating *Opposite*: soothing

try out *v* **test**, sample, check out, experiment with, appraise

tryout *n* **trial**, test, evaluation, audition, assessment

tryst *n* **assignation**, rendezvous, meeting, date, encounter

try your hand *v* **experiment**, try out, have a shot, make an attempt, have a go (*infml*)

tub *n* **1 container**, carton, pot, drum, barrel **2 bath**, hip bath, hot tub, plunge bath, bathtub

tubby (*infml*) *adj* **plump**, podgy, chubby, portly, overweight *Opposite*: skinny

tube *n* **pipe**, cylinder, hose, conduit, duct

tuber *n* **storage organ**, rhizome, root, underground stem

tubing *n* **tubes**, pipes, plumbing

tubular *adj* **tube-shaped**, cylindrical, tube-like, hollow

tuck *v* **1 insert**, put, push, slip, place *Opposite*: remove **2 pleat**, fold, dart, gather, pucker ■ *n* **1 pleat**, fold, dart, gather, pucker **2 food**, nosh (*infml*), grub (*infml*), tucker (*infml*)

tucker (*infml*) *n* **food**, tuck, nosh (*infml*), grub (*infml*), chow (*slang*)

tuft *n* **clump**, tussock, cluster, bunch, truss

tug *v* **pull**, tow, haul, heave, jerk *Opposite*: push ■ *n* **yank**, heave, pull, jerk, haul *Opposite*: push. *See* COMPARE AND CONTRAST *at* pull.

tug of war *n* **tussle**, power struggle, struggle, battle, wrangle *Opposite*: agreement

tuition *n* **instruction**, teaching, schooling, training, education

tumble *v* **1 fall over**, fall down, stumble, trip up, topple *Opposite*: stand up **2 plummet**, drop, nose-dive, plunge, dive *Opposite*: rise

tumbledown *adj* **ramshackle**, rickety, rundown, derelict, dilapidated

tumbler *n* **1 glass**, tall glass, beaker, whisky glass, highball glass (*US*) **2 acrobat**, gymnast, aerialist, trapeze artist, entertainer

tummy (*infml*) *n* **stomach**, abdomen, paunch, pot, gut

tumour *n* **growth**, lump, cancer, polyp

tumult *n* **uproar**, commotion, clamour, hubbub, hullabaloo *Opposite*: peace

tumultuous *adj* **1 unrestrained**, unbridled, riotous, boisterous, rowdy *Opposite*: restrained **2 turbulent**, confused, chaotic, agitated *Opposite*: calm

tune *n* **melody**, song, air, jingle, harmony ■ *v* **adjust**, fine-tune, change, alter, modify

tuneful *adj* **melodic**, melodious, harmonious, musical, pleasant *Opposite*: discordant

tuneless *adj* **unmusical**, droning, monotone, atonal, monotonous *Opposite*: tuneful

tune-up *n* **service**, overhaul, fine-tune, check, maintenance

tunnel *n* **1 channel**, passageway, subway, shaft, underpass *Opposite*: bridge **2 burrow**, hole, warren, earth, sett ■ *v* **excavate**, burrow, dig, mine, channel

turbid *adj* **1 muddy**, cloudy, opaque, dirty, murky *Opposite*: clear **2 confused**, muddled, disorganized, scrambled, chaotic *Opposite*: clear

turbulence *n* **1 commotion**, confusion, turmoil, disorder, unrest *Opposite*: calm **2 violence**, rowdiness, unruliness, riotousness, restlessness **3 storminess**, tempestuousness, choppiness, blusteriness

turbulent *adj* **1 confused**, unstable, chaotic, tumultuous, in turmoil *Opposite*: orderly **2 violent**, rowdy, unruly, riotous, quarrelsome *Opposite*: peaceful **3 stormy**, tempestuous, raging, choppy, blustery *Opposite*: settled

tureen *n* **bowl**, serving dish, dish, casserole

turf *n* **1 lawn**, grass, pasture, meadow, verdure **2** (*infml*) **area of expertise**, sphere of influence, field, territory, orbit **3** (*infml*) **territory**, patch, beat, neighbourhood, home turf

turgid *adj* **pompous**, boring, dull, hard going, stilted *Opposite*: amusing

turmoil *n* **chaos**, disorder, confusion, uproar, tumult *Opposite*: order

turn *v* **1 twist**, revolve, rotate, go around, spin **2 direct**, aim, point, focus, set **3 bend**, change direction, bear, veer, meander **4 go**, become, alter, convert, transform **5 curdle**, go sour, sour, spoil, go off ■ *n* **1 bend**, corner, junction, fork, curve **2 rotation**, revolution, twist, spin, twirl **3 fright**, scare, shock, start, jolt **4 fit**, seizure, attack, funny turn, spasm **5 ride**, spin, jaunt, trip, outing **6 errand**, favour, good turn, service, good deed **7 performance**, act, skit, sketch, party piece **8 go**, try, chance, opportunity, shot (*infml*)

turn a blind eye to *v* **overlook**, ignore, take no notice of, disregard, excuse *Opposite*: condemn

turnabout *n* **reversal**, sea change, U-turn, turnround, change

turn against v turn on, reject, rebuff, spurn, exclude

turn away v dismiss, reject, repel, rebuff, refuse *Opposite*: welcome

turn away from v reject, give up, abandon, abjure, relinquish *Opposite*: take up

turn back v 1 go back, retrace your steps, return *Opposite*: continue 2 fold back, fold down, fold over, turn down, turn over

turncoat n traitor, deserter, defector, collaborator, double agent

turn down v 1 refuse, decline, reject, disallow, veto *Opposite*: accept 2 lessen, lower, decrease, reduce, muffle *Opposite*: turn up

turned-out adj groomed, dressed, presented, clad, got up *(infml)*

turn in v 1 hand in, hand over, give in, remit, submit 2 inform on, blow the whistle on, betray, report, hand over 3 *(infml)* go to bed, go to sleep, hit the sack *(infml)*, hit the hay *(infml) Opposite*: rise

turning n turn-off, junction, exit, minor road, ramp *Opposite*: entrance 2 joinery, carpentry, woodwork, carving, cabinetmaking

turning point n crossroads, defining moment, decisive moment, crisis, watershed

turn off v 1 switch off, deactivate, shut down, disable, stop *Opposite*: turn on 2 relax, unwind, switch off, wind down, take it easy *Opposite*: gear up 3 *(infml)* disgust, irritate, bore, deter, displease *Opposite*: attract

turn-off n turning, exit, junction, minor road, turn

turn of phrase n way with words, way of putting things, way of speaking, style, manner

turn on v 1 switch on, start, activate, get going, set in motion *Opposite*: turn off 2 depend on, rest on, hinge on, centre on, hang on 3 attack, go for, round on, lay into, set upon *Opposite*: defend 4 *(infml)* arouse, excite, interest, enthuse, stimulate *Opposite*: turn off

turn out v 1 turn off, switch off, deactivate, shut down, disable *Opposite*: turn on 2 attend, turn up, show up, appear, put in an appearance 3 evict, throw out, empty, eject, expel *Opposite*: welcome 4 end up, work out, come out, transpire, result 5 produce, make, manufacture, churn out, assemble

turnout n crowd, audience, attendance, gathering

turn over v 1 capsize, flip over, overturn, upturn, turn turtle 2 mull over, think about, go over, consider, reflect on 3 hand over, hand in, give in, remit, submit *Opposite*: hold onto

turnover n 1 incomings, income, gross revenue, business, revenue *Opposite*: costs 2 throughput, sales, trade, business, buying and selling 3 staff renewal rate, hiring and firing rate, staff resignation rate, staff resignations, staff turnover

turn round v 1 complete, finish, accomplish,

process 2 improve, boost, increase, bump up *(infml)*

turnround n 1 dispatch, processing, completion 2 reversal, sea change, U-turn, turnabout, change

turnstile n gate, barrier, entrance, park entrance, kissing gate

turn the corner v get better, start to improve, look up, be on the turn, be out of danger

turn to v consult, refer to, fall back on, resort to, rely on

turn turtle v capsize, flip over, turn over, overturn, upturn

turn up v 1 increase, amplify, intensify, boost, step up *Opposite*: turn down 2 come to light, surface, appear, reappear, materialize *Opposite*: disappear 3 find, uncover, unearth, dig up, discover *Opposite*: conceal 4 arrive, appear, attend, put in an appearance, come

turn your back on v ignore, abandon, leave behind, put behind you, forsake *Opposite*: take care of

turn your nose up at v scorn, disdain, sneer at, sniff at, reject *Opposite*: accept

turn your stomach v sicken, disgust, repel, revolt, nauseate *Opposite*: attract

turpitude *(fml)* n immorality, wickedness, depravity, baseness, improbity

turret n tower, battlement, steeple, bartizan

tussle v fight, brawl, scuffle, clash, struggle ■ n brawl, fight, struggle, scuffle, clash

tutelage n instruction, guidance, teaching, coaching, expert hand

tutor n teacher, instructor, don, professor, lecturer ■ v teach, educate, instruct, school, coach. *See* COMPARE AND CONTRAST *at* teach.

tutorial n class, lesson, seminar, lecture, discussion group

TV *(infml)* n television, telly, small screen *(infml)*, box *(slang)*, goggle-box *(dated infml)*

twaddle *(infml)* n nonsense, balderdash, rubbish, drivel, garbage *Opposite*: sense

twang n accent, drawl, intonation, inflection, resonance ■ v reverberate, vibrate, ping, plunk

tweak v 1 pinch, nip, jerk, twist, tug 2 *(infml)* fine-tune, correct, adjust, modify, regulate ■ n nip, pinch, twist, jerk, tug

twee adj cutesy, bijou, quaint, dainty, sweet

tweedy adj casual, informal, sporty, horsey, outdoor

tweet v chirp, peep, chirrup, twitter, cheep

twenty-four/seven adv around the clock, all the time, constantly, always

twice adv two times, double, twofold

twiddle v fidget, fiddle, play, toy, handle

twig n branch, shoot, stem, stick ■ v *(infml)* understand, grasp, comprehend, realize, discern

twilight n dusk, nightfall, evening, sunset, sundown *Opposite*: dawn

twilit *adj* **dusky**, shady, shadowy, moonlit, crepuscular *(literary) Opposite*: sunlit

twin *n* **double**, doppelgänger, clone, identical twin, Siamese twin ■ *adj* **1 identical**, matching, alike, indistinguishable, like *Opposite*: different **2 dual**, double, twofold, paired *Opposite*: single ■ *v* **pair**, link, join, match, associate

twine *n* **string**, thread, cord, yarn ■ *v* **coil**, twist, wind, loop, snake

twinge *n* **pang**, pain, stitch, ache, wrench

twinkle *v* **shine**, sparkle, glimmer, gleam, flicker ■ *n* **sparkle**, gleam, glimmer, flicker, shine

twinkling *n* **flash**, second, moment, split second, instant

twirl *v* **1 wind**, coil, twist, curl, bend **2 spin**, rotate, whirl, turn, revolve ■ *n* **1 coil**, spiral, twist, loop **2 whirl**, spin, revolution, rotation, turn

twist *v* **1 wind**, coil, curl, bend, twirl **2 rotate**, turn, screw, unscrew, wind **3 sprain**, pull, hurt, injure, turn **4 distort**, misrepresent, alter, manipulate, warp *Opposite*: clarify **5 meander**, snake, wind, curve, bend **6 contort**, screw up, grimace, crumple, writhe ■ *n* **1 rotation**, screw, wind, turn **2 spiral**, coil, kink, curl, bend **3 development**, change, turn, incident, event

twisted *adj* **1 warped**, perverse, sick, perverted, abnormal *Opposite*: wholesome **2 misshapen**, distorted, warped, bent, deformed *Opposite*: straight

twisting *adj* **winding**, meandering, bendy, twisty, windy

twist somebody's arm *v* **compel**, force, pressure, coerce, persuade

twisty *adj* **winding**, tortuous, meandering, bendy, snaking *Opposite*: straight

twit *(dated) n* **fool**, buffoon, dupe, sucker *(infml)*, boob *(infml)*

twitch *v* **jerk**, jolt, shudder, yank, convulse ■ *n* **tic**, spasm, jerk, jolt, convulsion

twitcher *(infml) n* **birdwatcher**, ornithologist, birder *(US)*

twitchiness *n* **jitteriness**, jumpiness, restlessness, uneasiness, nervousness

twitchy *(infml) adj* **nervous**, fidgety, on edge, agitated, jumpy *Opposite*: still

two-dimensional *adj* **1 flat**, flattened, plane, smooth, level *Opposite*: three-dimensional **2 superficial**, shallow, oversimplified, formulaic, cardboard *Opposite*: complex

two-faced *adj* **hypocritical**, false, insincere, deceitful, double dealing *Opposite*: genuine

twofold *adj* **double**, dual, twin

twosome *n* **pair**, duo, couple, two of a kind

two-time *v* **1 betray**, mislead, deceive, double-cross, take in **2 be unfaithful**, cheat, deceive, play away *(infml)*, cuckold *(archaic)*

two-tone *adj* **stripy**, striped, light-and-dark, two-toned *Opposite*: plain

two-way *adj* **reciprocal**, cooperative, shared, mutual, collaborative

tycoon *n* **magnate**, mogul, business person, industrialist

tyke *n* **child**, imp, urchin, tearaway, monkey *(infml)*

type *n* **1 kind**, sort, category, class, genre **2 font**, typeface, lettering, print, style ■ *v* **key**, input, enter, key in ■ *n (infml)* **character**, individual, person, sort

COMPARE AND CONTRAST CORE MEANING: a group having a common quality or qualities

type a group of individuals or items with strongly marked and readily defined similarities; **kind** a group of individuals or items connected by shared characteristics; **sort** a general word used in the same way as *kind*; **category** a set of things that are classified together because of common characteristics; **class** used in the same way as *category*; **species** a specific group of animals, plants, insects, or other organisms, used in formal taxonomic classification; **genre** a particular style of painting, writing, dance, or other art form.

typecast *v* **stereotype**, pigeonhole, categorize, limit, restrict

typeface *n* **script**, type, font, lettering, print

typhoon *n* **storm**, cyclone, tornado, hurricane, tropical storm

typical *adj* **1 characteristic**, archetypal, distinctive, representative, emblematic *Opposite*: uncharacteristic **2 usual**, normal, standard, mainstream, average *Opposite*: unusual

typify *v* **characterize**, epitomize, symbolize, exemplify, personify

typo *(infml) n* **misprint**, typographical error, keyboarding error, error, mistake *Opposite*: correction

typography *n* **1 design**, typesetting, formatting, layout, composition **2 print style**, font, type, lettering, script

tyrannical *adj* **oppressive**, dictatorial, autocratic, despotic, authoritarian

tyrannize *v* **oppress**, dictate, bully, domineer, intimidate

tyranny *n* **oppression**, dictatorship, autocracy, domination, despotism

tyrant *n* **oppressor**, dictator, bully, autocrat, despot

tyro *n* **novice**, beginner, learner, newcomer, trainee *Opposite*: veteran. *See* COMPARE AND CONTRAST *at* **beginner**.

U

ubiquitous adj **omnipresent**, universal, pervasive, global, abundant

UFO n **flying saucer**, spaceship, spacecraft

ugliness n **1 unattractiveness**, unsightliness, hideousness, repulsiveness Opposite: attractiveness **2 violence**, hostility, cruelty, viciousness, malice Opposite: friendliness **3 unpleasantness**, dreadfulness, horridness, obnoxiousness, foulness

ugly adj **1 unattractive**, hideous, unsightly, revolting, repulsive Opposite: attractive **2 nasty**, threatening, dangerous, intimidating, menacing Opposite: friendly **3 unpleasant**, horrible, dreadful, horrid, obnoxious Opposite: nice. See COMPARE AND CONTRAST at **unattractive**.

ulcer n **boil**, abscess, pustule, carbuncle, sore

ulterior adj **hidden**, concealed, secret, underhand, unknown Opposite: transparent

ulterior motive n **hidden agenda**, hidden intention, design, scheme

ultimate adj **1 final**, last, eventual, decisive, definitive Opposite: first **2 fundamental**, basic, essential, supreme, extreme Opposite: superficial

ultimately adv **in the end**, eventually, in due course, finally, at last Opposite: initially

ultimatum n **challenge**, demand, requirement, petition, stipulation

ultra adj **extreme**, radical, revolutionary, excessive, extremist Opposite: mainstream

ultramodern adj **avant-garde**, progressive, modernistic, radical, futuristic Opposite: old-fashioned

umbrage n **offence**, exception, resentment, affront, slight

umbrella n **1 parasol**, sunshade, brolly (infml) **2 aegis**, auspices, authority, protection, support

umpire n **referee**, adjudicator, arbitrator, arbiter, mediator ■ v **adjudicate**, referee, arbitrate, judge, mediate

umpteen (infml) adj **countless**, numerous, innumerable, millions of, myriad

unabashed adj **unashamed**, unembarrassed, shameless, bold, brazen Opposite: abashed

unabated adj **persistent**, undiminished, relentless, unrelieved, unrelenting Opposite: reduced

unable adj **powerless**, incapable, impotent, inept, incompetent Opposite: able

unabridged adj **full-length**, complete, whole, entire, uncut Opposite: abridged

unacceptable adj **intolerable**, insupportable, undesirable, objectionable, deplorable Opposite: acceptable

unaccommodating adj **unhelpful**, awkward, uncooperative, difficult, disobliging Opposite: helpful

unaccompanied adj **alone**, by yourself, on your own, lone, solitary

unaccomplished adj **1 unfinished**, incomplete, uncompleted, unfulfilled, undone Opposite: accomplished **2 unskilful**, amateurish, unpolished, inexpert, untalented Opposite: accomplished

unaccountable adj **inexplicable**, puzzling, strange, unfathomable, baffling Opposite: explicable

unaccounted-for adj **missing**, lost, absent, gone, disappeared

unaccustomed adj **1 unused**, not used, inexperienced, unfamiliar, unacquainted Opposite: accustomed **2 unfamiliar**, unusual, different, new, strange Opposite: accustomed

unachievable adj **unattainable**, impracticable, impossible, unfeasible, inaccessible Opposite: achievable

unacquainted adj **ignorant**, unaccustomed, unaware, uninformed, unknowledgeable Opposite: knowledgeable

unadorned adj **plain**, bare, austere, simple, unembellished Opposite: ornate

unadulterated adj **pure**, untouched, untainted, complete, unmodified Opposite: tainted

unadventurous adj **cautious**, conservative, careful, timid, shy Opposite: daredevil

unaffected adj **1 unchanged**, unaltered, unmoved, impervious, impassive Opposite: different **2 genuine**, natural, unpretentious, sincere, modest Opposite: pretentious

unafraid adj **fearless**, bold, confident, brave, courageous Opposite: afraid

unaided adv **unassisted**, independently, by yourself, of your own accord, on your own Opposite: jointly

unalleviated adj **constant**, unrelieved, unremitting, unmitigated, inexorable Opposite: intermittent

unalloyed adj **pure**, sheer, absolute, total, utter Opposite: partial

unalterable adj **unchangeable**, fixed, irreversible, final, set Opposite: impermanent

unambiguous adj **unmistakable**, clear-cut,

explicit, definite, decided *Opposite*: vague

unambitious *adj* **apathetic**, unaspiring, unenterprising, unassertive, lazy *Opposite*: ambitious

unanimous *adj* **common**, agreed, undisputed, undivided, united *Opposite*: undecided

unannounced *adj* **unexpected**, impromptu, spontaneous, surprise *Opposite*: arranged

unanswerable *adj* **unfathomable**, insoluble, unresolvable, unsolvable, inexplicable

unanticipated *adj* **surprising**, unexpected, unlooked-for, unforeseen, unsuspected *Opposite*: expected

unapologetic *adj* **impenitent**, unrepentant, unreformed, unremorseful, without regret *Opposite*: penitent

unappealing *adj* **unattractive**, unpleasant, disagreeable, uninviting, unlikable *Opposite*: appealing. *See* COMPARE AND CONTRAST *at* **unattractive.**

unappetizing *adj* **unattractive**, unpleasant, unenticing, uninviting, unpalatable *Opposite*: appetizing

unapproachable *adj* **distant**, unfriendly, aloof, cold, standoffish *Opposite*: approachable

unarguable *adj* **beyond doubt**, incontestable, incontrovertible, indisputable, beyond question *Opposite*: arguable

unarmed *adj* **unprotected**, defenceless, exposed, vulnerable, weaponless *Opposite*: armed

unashamed *adj* **unembarrassed**, unapologetic, blatant, brazen, barefaced *Opposite*: ashamed

unasked *adj* **1 unsolicited**, uninvited, unsought, unexpected, unimaginable *Opposite*: expected **2 uninvited**, unwelcome, excluded, unexpected, left out

unassailable *adj* **1 incontrovertible**, unquestionable, impregnable, irrefutable, indisputable *Opposite*: tenuous **2 invincible**, unbeatable, impregnable, indomitable, invulnerable *Opposite*: vulnerable

unassisted *adj* **unaided**, single-handed, solo, lone *Opposite*: assisted

unassuming *adj* **modest**, humble, self-effacing, unassertive, meek *Opposite*: arrogant

unattached *adj* **free**, uncommitted, single, unmarried, separated *Opposite*: attached

unattainable *adj* **unachievable**, impossible, unfeasible, inaccessible, unreachable *Opposite*: attainable

unattractive *adj* **unappealing**, ugly, nasty, unpleasant, distasteful *Opposite*: attractive

---

COMPARE AND CONTRAST CORE MEANING: not pleasant to look at

unattractive not pleasant in appearance; **unsightly** spoiling an appearance which would otherwise be quite attractive; **ugly** very unpleasant to look at; **hideous** extremely unpleasant to look at; **homely** (*mainly US*) describes somebody who is not attractive; **plain** describes somebody, especially a woman, who is not attractive.

---

unattractiveness *n* **ugliness**, unpleasantness, unsightliness, distastefulness, repulsiveness *Opposite*: attractiveness

unauthorized *adj* **illegal**, unlawful, unofficial, unsanctioned, unlicensed *Opposite*: legitimate

unavailability *n* **unobtainability**, inaccessibility, unattainability, unreachability, absence *Opposite*: availability

unavailable *adj* **1 unobtainable**, inaccessible, unattainable, unreachable, absent *Opposite*: available **2 engaged**, busy, occupied, unobtainable *Opposite*: available

unavailing *adj* **vain**, unsuccessful, futile, failed, ineffective *Opposite*: successful

unavoidability *n* **inevitability**, inescapability, certainty, necessity, obligation

unavoidable *adj* **inevitable**, inescapable, obvious, manifest, obligatory *Opposite*: avoidable

unaware *adj* **ignorant**, uninformed, oblivious, unconscious, unmindful *Opposite*: conscious

unawares *adv* **by surprise**, off guard, unexpectedly, on the hop *(infml)*

unbalance *v* **disturb**, unhinge, derange, distort, destabilize *Opposite*: stabilize

unbalanced *adj* **1 uneven**, lopsided, unequal, crooked, top-heavy *Opposite*: even **2 unstable**, disturbed, unhinged, deranged *Opposite*: well-balanced **3 biased**, one-sided, inequitable, prejudiced, unfair *Opposite*: impartial

unbearable *adj* **intolerable**, agonizing, excruciating, awful, insufferable *Opposite*: tolerable

unbeatable *adj* **invincible**, supreme, unassailable, unconquerable, peerless *Opposite*: vulnerable

unbeaten *adj* **undefeated**, unsurpassed, successful, triumphant, victorious

unbecoming *adj* **improper**, inappropriate, incorrect, unsuitable, unflattering *Opposite*: fitting

unbelief *n* **nonbelief**, scepticism, incredulity, agnosticism, atheism *Opposite*: faith

unbelievable *adj* **1 implausible**, incredible, far-fetched, fantastic, unlikely *Opposite*: plausible **2 incredible**, amazing, extraordinary, astonishing, great *Opposite*: ordinary

unbelievably *adv* **extraordinarily**, incredibly, extremely, very, exceptionally *Opposite*: unremarkably

unbeliever *n* **nonbeliever**, sceptic, atheist, agnostic, freethinker *Opposite*: believer

unbelieving *adj* **incredulous**, sceptical, doubting, suspicious, questioning *Opposite*: credulous

unbend *v* **straighten**, release, free, relax, loosen *Opposite*: bend

unbending *adj* **inflexible**, fixed, rigid,

adamant, obdurate *Opposite*: flexible

unbiased *adj* **impartial**, balanced, dispassionate, neutral, unprejudiced *Opposite*: partial

unbind *v* **untie**, release, free, undo, liberate *Opposite*: bind

unblemished *adj* **flawless**, perfect, untarnished, pure, blameless *Opposite*: flawed

unblock *v* **clear**, unclog, free, clear out, clean out *Opposite*: block

unbolt *v* **unfasten**, unlock, open, unscrew, release *Opposite*: lock

unbounded *adj* **limitless**, unrestrained, abundant, boundless, uncontrolled *Opposite*: limited

unbowed *adj* **undefeated**, defiant, stubborn, determined, relentless *Opposite*: defeated

unbreakable *adj* **indestructible**, strong, permanent, indissoluble, firm *Opposite*: fragile

unbridled *adj* **unrestrained**, uncontrolled, uninhibited, unconcealed, unchecked *Opposite*: contained

unbroken *adj* **continuous**, constant, uninterrupted, steady, complete *Opposite*: intermittent

unburden *(fml)* *v* **relieve**, divest, free, release, let go *Opposite*: brood

unbutton *v* **undo**, open, unfasten *Opposite*: fasten

uncalled-for *adj* **unjustified**, unwarranted, undeserved, unprovoked, gratuitous *Opposite*: justifiable

uncanny *adj* **eerie**, weird, strange, mysterious, supernatural

uncared-for *adj* **neglected**, unloved, untended, unkempt, unattended *Opposite*: cherished

uncaring *adj* **hardhearted**, unfeeling, heartless, indifferent, cold *Opposite*: caring

unceasing *adj* **constant**, continuous, interminable, never-ending, perpetual *Opposite*: sporadic

unceremonious *adj* **abrupt**, hasty, rushed, terse, rude *Opposite*: gracious

uncertain *adj* **1 unsure**, vague, doubtful, hesitant, undecided *Opposite*: sure **2 indeterminate**, inexact, undefined, indefinite, ambiguous *Opposite*: exact. *See* COMPARE AND CONTRAST *at* **doubtful**.

uncertainty *n* **doubt**, indecision, hesitation, vagueness, ambiguity *Opposite*: confidence

unchain *v* **release**, unlock, unfetter, unshackle, liberate *Opposite*: chain

unchangeable *adj* **fixed**, unalterable, unvarying, constant, unchanged *Opposite*: changeable

unchanged *adj* **unaffected**, unmoved, untouched *Opposite*: affected

unchanging *adj* **static**, fixed, invariable, unchangeable, rigid *Opposite*: flexible

uncharacteristic *adj* **unusual**, atypical, abnormal, out of character, unexpected *Opposite*: typical

uncharitable *adj* **mean**, unkind, hurtful, spiteful, cruel *Opposite*: generous

uncharted *adj* **unexplored**, new, unfamiliar, unmapped, unknown *Opposite*: familiar

unchecked *adj* **unimpeded**, unrestrained, unhindered, unrestricted, unconstrained *Opposite*: restricted

uncivil *adj* **rude**, discourteous, impolite, insulting, bad-mannered *Opposite*: courteous

uncivilized *adj* **1 primitive**, barbaric, uncultured, unsophisticated, crude *Opposite*: civilized **2 remote**, distant, far-off, isolated, unreachable *Opposite*: reachable **3 coarse**, impolite, discourteous, unrefined, vulgar *Opposite*: polite

unclasp *v* **unfasten**, undo, open, unbuckle, untie *Opposite*: fasten

unclassified *adj* **1 random**, unsystematic, disorganized, unorganized, uncategorized *Opposite*: organized **2 open**, public, released, unconcealed, accessible *Opposite*: secret

unclean *adj* **1 impure**, dirty, contaminated, polluted, infected *Opposite*: pure **2 unchaste**, sinful, impure, unworthy, immoral *Opposite*: chaste. *See* COMPARE AND CONTRAST *at* **dirty**.

uncleanness *n* **1 dirtiness**, filthiness, impurity, griminess, squalor *Opposite*: cleanness **2 unchasteness**, sinfulness, impurity, unworthiness, immorality *Opposite*: chasteness

unclear *adj* **1 indistinct**, hazy, indeterminate, blurred, indistinguishable *Opposite*: clear **2 uncertain**, doubtful, undecided, unsure, in doubt *Opposite*: definite. *See* COMPARE AND CONTRAST *at* **obscure**.

unclench *v* **relax**, release, open, let go, slacken *Opposite*: tighten

unclog *v* **unblock**, clear, free, release, clean out *Opposite*: block

unclothe *v* **undress**, strip, uncover, disrobe *(fml)* *Opposite*: dress

unclothed *adj* **bare**, naked, uncovered, undressed, nude *Opposite*: dressed

uncoil *v* **unravel**, unwind, undo, untwist, release *Opposite*: twist

uncomfortable *adj* **1 painful**, tight, rough, scratchy, itchy *Opposite*: comfortable **2 embarrassing**, awkward, difficult, tricky, unpleasant *Opposite*: enjoyable **3 uneasy**, awkward, ill at ease, embarrassed, tense *Opposite*: relaxed

uncommitted *adj* **casual**, uninterested, indifferent, unattached, free *Opposite*: committed

uncommon *adj* **rare**, unusual, infrequent, scarce, special *Opposite*: common

uncommunicative *adj* **reserved**, reticent, taciturn, silent, withdrawn *Opposite*: talkative. *See* COMPARE AND CONTRAST *at* **silent**.

uncomplaining *adj* **accepting**, tolerant, long-suffering, patient, accommodating *Opposite*: intolerant

uncomplicated *adj* **simple**, straightforward, unfussy, basic, unsophisticated *Opposite*: complex

uncomplimentary *adj* disparaging, derogatory, unflattering, negative, rude *Opposite*: complimentary

uncompromising *adj* **inflexible**, rigid, adamant, unbending, obdurate *Opposite*: flexible

unconcealed *adj* **obvious**, open, evident, apparent, blatant *Opposite*: hidden

unconcern *n* **indifference**, apathy, disregard, nonchalance, disinterest *Opposite*: anxiety

unconcerned *adj* **indifferent**, unworried, nonchalant, undaunted, undisturbed *Opposite*: anxious

unconditional *adj* **unqualified**, total, categorical, absolute, unrestricted *Opposite*: qualified

unconditioned *adj* **unrestricted**, limitless, undefined, unlimited, open-ended *Opposite*: restricted

unconfident *adj* **insecure**, unsure, nervous, apprehensive, self-doubting *Opposite*: self-assured

unconfined *adj* **free**, liberated, released, loose, at large *Opposite*: restricted

unconfirmed *adj* **unverified**, unsubstantiated, unproven, unofficial, unsupported *Opposite*: verified

uncongenial *adj* **disagreeable**, unfriendly, unwelcoming, unpleasant, inhospitable *Opposite*: friendly

unconnected *adj* **separate**, unrelated, independent, distinct, isolated *Opposite*: linked

unconquerable *adj* **unbeatable**, unassailable, unattainable, insurmountable, indomitable *Opposite*: vulnerable

unconscionable *adj* **1 unacceptable**, shocking, horrifying, immoral, reprehensible *Opposite*: acceptable **2 unreasonable**, beyond the pale, irrational, ridiculous, illogical *Opposite*: reasonable

unconscious *adj* **1 comatose**, insentient, insensible, out cold, cataleptic *Opposite*: awake **2 unaware**, oblivious, ignorant, unwitting, insensible *Opposite*: aware **3 unintentional**, automatic, mechanical, instinctive, involuntary *Opposite*: deliberate ■ *n* id, superego, ego, self, psyche

unconsciousness *n* **oblivion**, sleep, nothingness, insentience, catalepsy *Opposite*: consciousness

unconsidered *adj* **hasty**, unthinking, impulsive, reactive, imprudent *Opposite*: considered

unconstitutional *adj* **illegal**, unauthorized, unlawful, undemocratic, unofficial *Opposite*: lawful

unconstrained *adj* **unimpeded**, free, unrestrained, unrestricted, unhindered *Opposite*: restricted

unconstructive *adj* **unhelpful**, negative, unenthusiastic, uncooperative, ineffectual *Opposite*: constructive

uncontaminated *adj* **pure**, clean, unadulterated, antiseptic, sterilized *Opposite*: contaminated

uncontrollable *adj* **1 irrepressible**, uncontainable, overpowering, wild, overwhelming **2 unruly**, disobedient, out of control, unmanageable, disorderly *Opposite*: well-behaved

uncontrolled *adj* **unrestrained**, abandoned, wild, hysterical, uninhibited *Opposite*: restrained

uncontroversial *adj* **undisputed**, uncontentious, uncontended, unquestionable, indisputable *Opposite*: controversial

unconventional *adj* **eccentric**, unusual, alternative, avant-garde, strange *Opposite*: conventional

unconventionality *n* **eccentricity**, originality, nonconformity, oddness, quirkiness *Opposite*: conventionality

unconvinced *adj* **sceptical**, incredulous, disbelieving, unimpressed, unmoved *Opposite*: convinced

unconvincing *adj* **implausible**, unimpressive, weak, feeble, unsuccessful *Opposite*: persuasive

uncooked *adj* **raw**, rare, fresh, unprepared *Opposite*: cooked

uncooperative *adj* **unhelpful**, disobliging, awkward, obstinate, contrary *Opposite*: amenable

uncoordinated *adj* **clumsy**, ungainly, awkward, ungraceful, inept *Opposite*: graceful

uncork *v* **1 open**, break open, unplug, break into, pop open *Opposite*: plug **2 unleash**, release, give vent to, pour out, set free *Opposite*: hold in

uncorrupted *adj* **unadulterated**, unspoiled, uncontaminated, chaste, pure *Opposite*: corrupted

uncounted *adj* **innumerable**, countless, numerous, myriad, incalculable *Opposite*: few

uncouple *v* **undo**, disengage, separate, detach, unyoke *Opposite*: join

uncouth *adj* **rude**, uncivilized, bad-mannered, ill-mannered, foul-mouthed *Opposite*: polite

uncouthness *n* **rudeness**, vulgarity, bad manners, crudeness, coarseness *Opposite*: politeness

uncover *v* **expose**, discover, reveal, unearth, find out *Opposite*: conceal

uncovered adj **exposed**, bare, open, naked, revealed *Opposite*: concealed

uncovering n **exposure**, discovery, disclosure, revelation *Opposite*: concealment

uncritical adj **indiscriminating**, accepting, credulous, naive, gullible *Opposite*: discriminating

unction n **1 balm**, ointment, salve, oil, lotion **2 earnestness**, fervour, zeal, passion, enthusiasm

unctuous adj **1 ingratiating**, sycophantic, slimy, smarmy, obsequious *Opposite*: arrogant **2 oily**, greasy, fatty, slippery, slimy

uncultivated adj **1 unrefined**, unsophisticated, coarse, uncultured, unpolished *Opposite*: refined **2 fallow**, untilled, unplanted, unfarmed *Opposite*: cultivated

uncultured adj **unrefined**, philistine, boorish, unsophisticated, uncultivated *Opposite*: refined

uncurl v **straighten**, straighten out, uncoil, flatten, unwind *Opposite*: curl

uncut adj **unabridged**, complete, full-length, unedited, uncensored *Opposite*: abridged

undamaged adj **unspoiled**, untouched, unharmed, unhurt, intact *Opposite*: spoiled

undaunted adj **fearless**, unconcerned, unworried, carefree, undisturbed *Opposite*: scared

undeceive v **inform**, tell, notify, enlighten, disabuse *Opposite*: deceive

undecided adj **1 in two minds**, in doubt, dithering, vacillating, uncertain *Opposite*: decided **2 unresolved**, open, unclear, vague, ambivalent *Opposite*: certain

undecipherable adj **illegible**, unreadable, inexplicable, mysterious, unfathomable *Opposite*: clear

undecorated adj **plain**, simple, unornamented, austere, spartan *Opposite*: ornate

undefeated adj **unbeaten**, reigning, unvanquished, unconquered, unbowed *Opposite*: defeated

undefended adj **unguarded**, unprotected, unfortified, deserted, defenceless *Opposite*: defended

undefiled adj **unsullied**, pure, unpolluted, unblemished, unstained *Opposite*: defiled *(fml)*

undefined adj **indeterminate**, vague, approximate, open-ended, indefinite *Opposite*: defined

undemanding adj **easy**, straightforward, light, simple, unchallenging *Opposite*: demanding

undemocratic adj **inequitable**, unfair, autocratic, high-handed, dictatorial *Opposite*: democratic

undemonstrative adj **unemotional**, restrained, phlegmatic, stoical, impassive *Opposite*: demonstrative

undeniable adj **irrefutable**, indisputable, incontestable, incontrovertible, unquestionable *Opposite*: questionable

undependable adj **unreliable**, unpredictable, variable, erratic, fickle *Opposite*: dependable

under prep **1 below**, in, underneath, beneath *(fml)* *Opposite*: above **2 below**, less than *Opposite*: over

underachieve v **disappoint**, flounder, drift, drop out, underperform *Opposite*: excel

underage adj **juvenile**, immature, youthful, young, callow

underclothes n **underwear**, underclothing, underthings, undies *(infml)*

underclothing see **underclothes**

undercover adj **secret**, hidden, covert, disguised, clandestine *Opposite*: open

undercurrent n **1 current**, tide, undertow, pull, stream **2 feeling**, hint, undertow, suggestion, connotation

undercut v **undermine**, destabilize, detract, weaken, damage *Opposite*: strengthen

underdeveloped adj **immature**, small, undersized, weak, unused

underdog n **loser**, small fry, runner up, second best, little guy

underdone adj **rare**, bloody, pink, undercooked *Opposite*: overdone

underemphasize v **play down**, understate, underplay, minimize, underrate *Opposite*: overemphasize

underestimate v **undervalue**, underrate, misjudge, miscalculate *Opposite*: overestimate

underfed adj **malnourished**, starving, frail, weak, undernourished *Opposite*: well-fed

undergo v **experience**, feel, suffer, endure, undertake *Opposite*: avoid

underground adj **1 subterranean**, below ground, covered, buried, deep **2 subversive**, secretive, dissident, alternative, covert *Opposite*: open

undergrowth n **bushes**, scrub, brushwood, vegetation, understorey

underhand adj **deceitful**, dishonest, sneaky, mean, sly *Opposite*: open ■ adv **deceitfully**, dishonestly, sneakily, slyly, craftily *Opposite*: openly

underhanded see **underhand**

underlie v **lie beneath**, lie behind, motivate, cause, inspire

underline v **underscore**, emphasize, highlight, feature, stress *Opposite*: ignore

underling n **minion**, inferior, subject, junior, subordinate *Opposite*: superior

underlying adj **fundamental**, original, causal, primary, basic

undermine v **weaken**, dent, chip away at, challenge, destabilize *Opposite*: bolster

underneath prep **under**, below, beneath *(fml)* *Opposite*: on top of ■ n **base**, bottom, underside, footing, foundation *Opposite*: top

undernourished adj **malnourished**, underfed,

starved, hungry, famished *Opposite*: well-fed

undernourishment *n* **malnutrition**, starvation, hunger, famine

underperform *v* **fail**, underachieve, disappoint, flounder, drift *Opposite*: excel

underpin *v* **1 shore up**, prop up, reinforce, support, buttress *Opposite*: undermine **2 support**, underlie, lie beneath, give support to, bolster *Opposite*: weaken

underpinning *n* **foundation**, reinforcement, groundwork, keystone, bedrock

underplay *v* **make light of**, minimize, understate, play down, talk down *Opposite*: overplay

underprice *v* **cheapen**, undersell, underrepresent, understate *Opposite*: overprice

underprivileged *adj* **disadvantaged**, deprived, poor, needy, neglected *Opposite*: well-off

underprop *v* **underpin**, shore up, prop up, jack up, reinforce *Opposite*: undermine

underrate *v* **undervalue**, underestimate, think little of, devalue, misjudge *Opposite*: overrate

underrated *adj* **undervalued**, underestimated, unappreciated, unrecognized, misunderstood *Opposite*: overrated

underrepresent *v* **understate**, undersell, lessen, play down, make light of *Opposite*: overemphasize

underscore *v* **underline**, highlight, emphasize, accentuate, call attention to *Opposite*: ignore

undersea *adj* **submarine**, underwater, bathyal, bathypelagic

undersell *v* **understate**, play down, make light of, denigrate, cheapen *Opposite*: oversell

undershrub *n* **subshrub**, bush, plant

underside *n* **base**, bottom, underneath, basement, foundation

undersized *adj* **puny**, underdeveloped, small, short, stunted *Opposite*: extra-large

understand *v* **1 comprehend**, appreciate, know, recognize, realize **2 sympathize**, empathize, identify, appreciate

understandable *adj* **comprehensible**, clear, logical, reasonable, fathomable *Opposite*: incomprehensible

understanding *adj* **sympathetic**, empathetic, considerate, thoughtful, kind *Opposite*: unsympathetic ■ *n* **1 agreement**, arrangement, deal, contract, settlement **2 sympathy**, empathy, identification, consideration, kindness *Opposite*: indifference **3 grasp**, perception, intellect, mind, wit *Opposite*: ignorance **4 interpretation**, construction, personal feeling, estimation, perception

understate *v* **play down**, minimize, devalue, belittle, make little of *Opposite*: exaggerate

understated *adj* **modest**, inconspicuous, discreet, unfussy, minimalist *Opposite*: exaggerated

understatement *n* **irony**, dryness, sarcasm, underestimation *Opposite*: exaggeration

understood *adj* **unspoken**, tacit, silent, unstated, unwritten *Opposite*: explicit

understorey *n* **forest floor**, bushes, underwood, brush, scrub

understrength *adj* **1 understaffed**, short-handed, short-staffed, short, down **2 dilute**, weak, thin, diluted, watered down

understudy *n* **substitute**, cover, stand-by, stand-in, replacement

undertake *v* **take on**, assume, start, commence, embark on *Opposite*: relinquish

undertaker *n* **funeral director**, embalmer, mortician *(US)*

undertaking *n* **responsibility**, task, job, enterprise, commission

under-the-counter *adj* **illegal**, unofficial, illicit, wrongful, criminal *Opposite*: aboveboard

under-the-table *adj* **underhand**, unofficial, secret, surreptitious, sneaky *Opposite*: aboveboard

underthings *n* **underwear**, underclothes, underclothing, undies *(infml)*

undertone *n* **hint**, suggestion, trace, tinge, undercurrent *Opposite*: overtone

undertow *n* **current**, undercurrent, tide, pull, stream

undervalue *v* **underrate**, underestimate, play down, devalue, belittle *Opposite*: overrate

underwater *adj* **1 submerged**, sunken, flooded, subaquatic, subsurface *Opposite*: dry **2 undersea**, submarine, sunken, submerged, marine

underway *adj* **happening**, in progress, ongoing, on the go, proceeding

underwear *n* **underclothes**, underclothing, underthings, undies *(infml)*

WORD BANK
❑ **types of lower-body underwear** bloomers *(dated)*, boxer shorts, briefs, camiknickers, corset, crinoline, drawers, foundation garment, garter, girdle, G-string, jockstrap, knee-highs, knickers, leg-warmer, long johns, nylons, panties, pants, petticoat, slip, sock, stockings, support stockings, thigh-highs, thong, tights, underpants, underskirt
❑ **types of upper body underwear** basque, body, body stocking, bodysuit, bra, camisole, chemise, string vest, teddy, undershirt, vest

underweight *adj* **skinny**, skin-and-bone, scrawny, half-starved, underfed *Opposite*: overweight

underworld *n* **gangland**, criminal world, nether world ■ *adj* **criminal**, gangland, illicit, illegal, unlawful *Opposite*: legal

underwrite *v* **guarantee**, countersign, back, endorse, fund

underwriter *n* **sponsor**, backer, supporter, guarantor, financier

undeserved *adj* **unwarranted**, unmerited, unearned, unfair, unjustifiable *Opposite*: deserved

undesirable *adj* **unwanted**, unwelcome, uninvited, objectionable, disagreeable *Opposite*: desirable

undetectable *adj* **untraceable**, indiscernible, unnoticeable, imperceptible, invisible *Opposite*: obvious

undetermined *adj* **1 hesitating**, undecided, irresolute, unsettled, vacillating *Opposite*: decided **2 unresolved**, indeterminate, indefinite, undecided, incalculable *Opposite*: definite **3 unknown**, undiscovered, unidentified, unheard of, unfamiliar *Opposite*: known

undeveloped *adj* **immature**, young, embryonic, unripe, emergent *Opposite*: mature

undeviating *adj* **unswerving**, firm, solid, absolute, total *Opposite*: shaky

undies *(infml)* *n* **underwear**, underclothes, underclothing, underthings

undignified *adj* **unseemly**, unbecoming, indecorous, improper, humiliating *Opposite*: dignified

undiluted *adj* **straight**, neat, unadulterated, unmixed, full-strength *Opposite*: diluted

undiplomatic *adj* **tactless**, crass, thoughtless, indiscreet, inconsiderate *Opposite*: diplomatic

undirected *adj* **purposeless**, aimless, directionless, pointless, wandering *Opposite*: purposeful

undisciplined *adj* **unmanageable**, out of control, wild, unruly, disobedient *Opposite*: well-behaved

undisclosed *adj* **secret**, unnamed, hidden, unrevealed, unidentified *Opposite*: known

undisguised *adj* **unconcealed**, plain, straightforward, open, public *Opposite*: concealed

undisposed *adj* **unwilling**, loath, reluctant, unprepared, hesitant *Opposite*: disposed

undisputed *adj* **acknowledged**, undoubted, certain, undeniable, unquestionable *Opposite*: questionable

undistinguished *adj* **ordinary**, everyday, run-of-the-mill, commonplace, nothing special *Opposite*: unusual

undistorted *adj* **factual**, truthful, exact, accurate, straight *Opposite*: inaccurate

undisturbed *adj* **1 uninterrupted**, in peace, unbroken, unobstructed *Opposite*: interrupted **2 untouched**, intact, whole, flawless, undamaged *Opposite*: damaged **3 peaceful**, serene, composed, at peace, at ease *Opposite*: anxious

undivided *adj* **complete**, entire, whole, total, full *Opposite*: partial

undo *v* **1 unfasten**, untie, unbutton, loosen, disengage *Opposite*: fasten **2 cancel out**, cancel, nullify, invalidate, render null and void

undoing *n* **downfall**, ruin, ruination, collapse, destruction *Opposite*: making

undone *adj* **1 uncompleted**, unfinished, incomplete, half-done, unconcluded *Opposite*: done **2 unfastened**, open, gaping, unzipped, unbuttoned **3 ruined**, in trouble, lost, in deep water, destroyed *Opposite*: fine

undoubted *adj* **certain**, sure, absolute, definite, indubitable *Opposite*: doubtful

undreamed-of *adj* **unexpected**, unhoped-for, unimaginable, unanticipated, unlooked-for *Opposite*: anticipated

undress *v* **strip off**, strip, unclothe, remove your clothes, bare *Opposite*: dress

undressed *adj* **naked**, bare, nude, stripped, with nothing on *Opposite*: dressed. See COMPARE AND CONTRAST *at* **naked.**

undue *adj* **unwarranted**, excessive, unnecessary, unjustified, unjustifiable *Opposite*: justified

undulant *(fml)* *see* **undulating**

undulate *v* **roll**, ripple, rise and fall, swell, heave

undulating *adj* **rolling**, rising and falling, swelling, heaving, surging

undulation *n* **wave**, ripple, furrow, crinkle, wrinkle

unduly *adv* **excessively**, overly, disproportionately, unjustifiably, undeservedly *Opposite*: justifiably

undying *adj* **unending**, never-ending, endless, perpetual, eternal *Opposite*: inconstant

unearned *adj* **undeserved**, unwarranted, unmerited, unjustified, uncalled-for

unearth *v* **1 dig up**, exhume, disinter, excavate, extract *Opposite*: bury **2 disclose**, reveal, expose, publicize, bring to light *Opposite*: cover up

unearthly *adj* **1 eerie**, weird, bizarre, strange, macabre *Opposite*: normal **2 unreasonable**, inappropriate, outrageous, ridiculous, absurd *Opposite*: acceptable

unease *n* **anxiety**, nervousness, restlessness, awkwardness, uneasiness *Opposite*: calm. See COMPARE AND CONTRAST *at* **worry.**

uneasiness *n* **anxiety**, nervousness, restlessness, awkwardness, unease *Opposite*: calmness

uneasy *adj* **anxious**, nervous, troubled, uncomfortable, ill at ease *Opposite*: calm

uneconomic *adj* **1 unprofitable**, not viable, lossmaking, profitless *Opposite*: profitable **2 inefficient**, wasteful, uneconomical, improvident, extravagant *Opposite*: efficient

uneconomical *adj* **inefficient**, wasteful, extravagant, uneconomic, profligate *Opposite*: efficient

unedited *adj* **complete**, unabridged, unexpurgated, uncut, full-length *Opposite*: edited

uneducated *adj* **unschooled**, untaught, igno-

rant, illiterate, uninformed *Opposite*: educated

unembellished *adj* **1 unadorned**, plain, without ornamentation, simple, straightforward *Opposite*: fancy **2 factual**, unembroidered, undistorted, truthful, straightforward *Opposite*: fictional

unembroidered *adj* **factual**, unembellished, undistorted, truthful, unvarnished *Opposite*: florid

unemotional *adj* **impassive**, dispassionate, undemonstrative, unresponsive, detached *Opposite*: emotional

unemployed *adj* **jobless**, out of work, out of a job, unwaged, laid off *Opposite*: employed

unemployment *n* **joblessness**, job loss, redundancy, idleness *Opposite*: employment

unending *adj* **endless**, never-ending, eternal, everlasting, interminable *Opposite*: finite

unendurable *adj* **insufferable**, unbearable, intolerable, insupportable, excruciating *Opposite*: bearable

unenlightened *adj* **1 prejudiced**, ignorant, narrow, narrow-minded, closed-minded *Opposite*: enlightened **2 unaware**, uninformed, ignorant, oblivious, unacquainted *Opposite*: informed

unenthusiastic *adj* **apathetic**, indifferent, unresponsive, lukewarm, half-hearted *Opposite*: enthusiastic

unenviable *adj* **undesirable**, disagreeable, unpleasant, uninviting, objectionable *Opposite*: enviable

unequal *adj* **1 uneven**, unbalanced, lopsided, asymmetrical, disproportionate *Opposite*: equal **2 unfair**, inequitable, one-sided, mismatched, unbalanced *Opposite*: fair **3 unsatisfactory**, unfit, unable, incapable, inadequate

unequalled *adj* **unrivalled**, matchless, unsurpassed, incomparable, unique *Opposite*: ordinary

unequivocal *adj* **clear**, plain, unambiguous, unmistakable, explicit

unerring *adj* **certain**, sure, absolute, positive, definite *Opposite*: faulty

unessential *adj* **dispensable**, superfluous, unnecessary, inessential, replaceable *Opposite*: essential

unethical *adj* **unprincipled**, immoral, wrong, bad, unscrupulous *Opposite*: ethical

uneven *adj* **1 rough**, jagged, bumpy, patchy, irregular *Opposite*: level **2 unequal**, unbalanced, lopsided, asymmetrical, disproportionate *Opposite*: equal **3 mismatched**, one-sided, unfair, unbalanced, disproportionate *Opposite*: fair

unevenness *n* **1 roughness**, jaggedness, bumpiness, patchiness *Opposite*: evenness **2 inequality**, one-sidedness, disparity *Opposite*: equality **3 asymmetry**, disproportion, irregularity *Opposite*: symmetry

uneventful *adj* **boring**, monotonous, ordinary, humdrum, dull *Opposite*: exciting

unexceptionable *adj* **inoffensive**, unobjectionable, faultless, irreproachable, acceptable *Opposite*: exceptionable *(fml)*

unexceptional *adj* **undistinguished**, nondescript, anonymous, modest, indifferent *Opposite*: extraordinary

unexcited *adj* **calm**, restrained, subdued, unresponsive, impassive *Opposite*: excited

unexciting *adj* **dull**, boring, tedious, monotonous, humdrum *Opposite*: exciting

unexpected *adj* **unforeseen**, unanticipated, unpredicted, surprising, startling *Opposite*: expected

unexplained *adj* **mysterious**, unsolved, inexplicable, impenetrable, arcane *Opposite*: apparent

unexpressed *adj* **unstated**, unspoken, unsaid, unknown *Opposite*: articulated

unfailing *adj* **reliable**, certain, dependable, trustworthy, constant *Opposite*: erratic

unfair *adj* **1 unjust**, inequitable, iniquitous, unwarranted, unmerited *Opposite*: fair **2 unethical**, dishonest, dishonourable, deceitful, underhand *Opposite*: honest **3 partial**, one-sided, biased, prejudicial, discriminating *Opposite*: fair

unfairness *n* **1 injustice**, wrongness, wrong, iniquitousness, unreasonableness *Opposite*: fairness **2 underhandedness**, dishonesty, dishonourableness, deceitfulness, fraudulence *Opposite*: honesty **3 partiality**, one-sidedness, bias, prejudice, discrimination *Opposite*: fairness

unfaithful *adj* **disloyal**, false, untrue, adulterous, treacherous *Opposite*: faithful

unfaithfulness *n* **disloyalty**, infidelity, falseness, adultery, treachery *Opposite*: faithfulness

unfaltering *adj* **untiring**, indefatigable, tireless, unflagging, persistent *Opposite*: faltering

unfamiliar *adj* **1 unknown**, new, untried, strange, alien *Opposite*: familiar **2 unacquainted**, unaccustomed, unaware, unversed, unskilled *Opposite*: familiar

unfamiliarity *n* **1 newness**, strangeness, unusualness, foreignness, exoticism *Opposite*: familiarity **2 unaccustomedness**, inexperience, ignorance, unawareness, lack of experience *Opposite*: familiarity

unfashionable *adj* **out-of-date**, outmoded, dated, old-fashioned, behind the times *Opposite*: trendy *(infml)*

unfasten *v* **undo**, unhook, unlock, disengage, detach *Opposite*: fasten

unfastened *adj* **undone**, loosened, untied, unbuttoned, unzipped *Opposite*: fastened

unfathomable *adj* **1 deep**, profound, bottomless, unsounded, unplumbed *Opposite*: shallow **2 incomprehensible**, impenetrable, inscrutable, unknowable, indecipherable *Opposite*: straightforward

unfavourable *adj* **1 disapproving**, negative, uncomplimentary, opposed, hostile *Opposite*: approving **2 harmful**, adverse, bad, detrimental, disadvantageous *Opposite*: beneficial

unfeasible *adj* **impracticable**, impractical, unworkable, unachievable, out of the question *Opposite*: feasible

unfeeling *adj* **unsympathetic**, hardhearted, callous, cruel, heartless *Opposite*: sympathetic

unfetter *v* **release**, liberate, free, unchain, unshackle *Opposite*: fetter

unfettered *adj* **freed**, unencumbered, unconstrained, unregulated, autonomous *Opposite*: constrained

unfilled *adj* **empty**, vacant, void, unoccupied, untaken *Opposite*: full

unfinished *adj* **incomplete**, uncompleted, fragmentary, partial, ongoing *Opposite*: finished

unfit *adj* **1 unsuitable**, inappropriate, unsuited, inapt, unacceptable *Opposite*: suitable **2 unqualified**, incompetent, inept, useless, incapable *Opposite*: competent **3 out of shape**, out of condition, unhealthy, weak, puny *Opposite*: fit

unfitted *adj* **unsuited**, unequipped, unprepared, unsuitable, unqualified *Opposite*: fitted

unfitting *adj* **unsuitable**, inappropriate, unbecoming, out of place, unseemly *Opposite*: fitting

unfix *v* **detach**, loosen, disengage, separate, undo *Opposite*: attach

unflagging *adj* **untiring**, indefatigable, tireless, unfaltering, persistent *Opposite*: weak

unflappability *n* **calmness**, coolness, patience, composure, control *Opposite*: excitability

unflappable *adj* **composed**, calm, unflustered, collected, imperturbable *Opposite*: anxious

unflattering *adj* **1 unbecoming**, unattractive, unappealing, ugly *Opposite*: becoming **2 critical**, uncomplimentary, faultfinding, unfavourable *Opposite*: complimentary

unfledged *adj* **inexperienced**, naive, innocent, fresh, immature *Opposite*: experienced

unflinching *adj* **unwavering**, constant, steady, undaunted, persistent *Opposite*: wavering

unflustered *adj* **composed**, calm, unflappable, collected, imperturbable *Opposite*: agitated

unfocused *adj* **1 blurred**, unclear, fuzzy, indistinct, bleary *Opposite*: clear **2 ill-defined**, nonspecific, imprecise, woolly, vague *Opposite*: focused

unfold *v* **1 open out**, open up, unfurl, spread out, display *Opposite*: fold up **2 explain**, clarify, make known, disclose, reveal *Opposite*: conceal **3 develop**, evolve, grow, progress, advance *Opposite*: deteriorate

unforced *adj* **voluntary**, natural, spontaneous, unwitting, unprompted *Opposite*: forced

unforeseeable *adj* **unexpected**, unanticipated, undreamed-of, unpredictable, surprise *Opposite*: predictable

unforeseen *adj* **unexpected**, unanticipated, unpredicted, surprising, startling *Opposite*: expected

unforgettable *adj* **memorable**, remarkable, treasured, cherished, haunting *Opposite*: unremarkable

unforgivable *adj* **unpardonable**, inexcusable, indefensible, unjustifiable, intolerable *Opposite*: understandable

unforgiving *adj* **1 intolerant**, merciless, pitiless, remorseless, vindictive *Opposite*: tolerant **2 demanding**, exacting, taxing, challenging, hard *Opposite*: easy

unformed *adj* **1 shapeless**, formless, indistinct, imprecise, amorphous *Opposite*: distinct **2 undeveloped**, immature, green, callow, underdeveloped *Opposite*: mature

unformulated *adj* **vague**, indistinct, unclear, hazy, nebulous *Opposite*: clear

unforthcoming *adj* **uncommunicative**, reticent, taciturn, standoffish, distant *Opposite*: voluble

unfortunate *adj* **1 unlucky**, luckless, unsuccessful, unhappy, ill-fated *Opposite*: lucky **2 disastrous**, calamitous, doomed, hopeless, fateful *Opposite*: fortunate **3 inappropriate**, inopportune, ill-timed, tactless, untimely *Opposite*: timely ■ *n* **wretch**, underdog, loser, lame duck, weakling

unfortunately *adv* **1 unluckily**, unhappily, regrettably, sadly, alas *Opposite*: fortunately **2 inappropriately**, inopportunely, tactlessly, ill-advisedly, regrettably *Opposite*: appropriately

unfounded *adj* **groundless**, unsupported, baseless, unsubstantiated, speculative *Opposite*: proven

unfreeze *v* **relax**, rescind, repeal, release, liberate *Opposite*: freeze

unfrequented *adj* **lonely**, neglected, isolated, quiet, desolate *Opposite*: busy

unfriendliness *n* **aloofness**, surliness, coldness, coolness, frostiness *Opposite*: friendliness

unfriendly *adj* **1 aloof**, distant, surly, cold, frosty *Opposite*: friendly **2 unfavourable**, ill-disposed, inimical, hostile, auspicious *Opposite*: well-disposed

unfruitful *adj* **1 unsuccessful**, unprofitable, unproductive, unrewarding, fruitless *Opposite*: profitable **2 infertile**, sterile, barren, bare, fruitless *Opposite*: fertile

unfurl *v* **open out**, open up, unfold, spread out, expand *Opposite*: fold up

unfurnished *adj* **bare**, empty, unequipped, unfitted *Opposite*: furnished

unfussy *adj* **understated**, simple, uncomplicated, modest, plain *Opposite*: fussy

ungainliness *n* **1 gracelessness**, awkwardness, clumsiness, inelegance, gaucheness *Opposite*: gracefulness **2 awkwardness**, unwieldiness, cumbersomeness, heaviness, clumsiness *Opposite*: convenience

ungainly *adj* **1 graceless**, awkward, clumsy, inelegant, ungraceful *Opposite*: graceful **2 awkward**, unwieldy, cumbersome, inconvenient, heavy *Opposite*: convenient

ungenerous *adj* **1 miserly**, tightfisted, parsimonious, mean, grudging *Opposite*: generous **2 mean-spirited**, nasty, mean, unkind, cruel *Opposite*: kind

unglued *adj* **1 separated**, detached, parted, disconnected, divided *Opposite*: whole **2** (*infml*) **upset**, angry, disconcerted, hysterical, unnerved *Opposite*: calm

ungodly *adj* **1 impious**, irreligious, irreverent, blasphemous, profane *Opposite*: pious **2 wicked**, sinful, immoral, corrupt, depraved *Opposite*: virtuous **3** (*infml*) **unreasonable**, unearthly, late, unsocial, ridiculous *Opposite*: reasonable

ungovernable *adj* **uncontrollable**, out of control, unmanageable, unruly, anarchic *Opposite*: controllable

ungraceful *adj* **1 clumsy**, ungainly, graceless, uncoordinated, lumbering *Opposite*: elegant **2 rude**, impolite, discourteous, gruff, brusque *Opposite*: polite

ungracious *adj* **ill-mannered**, discourteous, rude, impolite, bad-mannered *Opposite*: gracious

ungrateful *adj* **1 unappreciative**, thankless, churlish, unmindful, ungracious *Opposite*: grateful **2 unpleasant**, unrewarding, thankless, unsatisfying *Opposite*: rewarding

ungratefully *adv* **unappreciatively**, churlishly, thanklessly, ungraciously *Opposite*: gratefully

ungratefulness *n* **unappreciativeness**, ingratitude, churlishness, thanklessness, ungraciousness *Opposite*: gratitude

unguarded *adj* **1 unprotected**, undefended, unshielded, unfortified, defenceless *Opposite*: guarded **2 unwary**, careless, indiscreet, thoughtless, imprudent *Opposite*: guarded

unguent *n* **ointment**, salve, balm, oil, unction

unhampered *adj* **unrestricted**, unimpeded, unhindered, unconstrained, free *Opposite*: restricted

unhappily *adv* **1 sadly**, miserably, discontentedly, despondently, dejectedly *Opposite*: happily **2 unfortunately**, unluckily, regrettably, alas, sadly *Opposite*: luckily

unhappiness *n* **sadness**, sorrow, grief, misery, discontent *Opposite*: happiness

unhappy *adj* **1 sad**, miserable, discontented, despondent, dejected *Opposite*: happy **2 unfortunate**, ill-fated, hopeless, doomed, fateful *Opposite*: fortunate **3 inappropriate**,

ill-chosen, infelicitous, tactless, unfortunate *Opposite*: well-chosen **4 displeased**, annoyed, upset, angry, disappointed *Opposite*: pleased

unharmed *adj* **uninjured**, unhurt, unscathed, undamaged, unscratched *Opposite*: harmed

unhealthy *adj* **1 sick**, unfit, out of condition, out of shape, sickly *Opposite*: well **2 harmful**, detrimental, injurious, damaging, unwholesome *Opposite*: healthy **3 corrupt**, unwholesome, morbid, unnatural, ghoulish *Opposite*: wholesome

unheard *adj* **unheeded**, disregarded, ignored, overlooked, unnoticed

unheard-of *adj* **1 unknown**, unfamiliar, new, obscure, undiscovered *Opposite*: well-known **2 unprecedented**, exceptional, extraordinary, novel, unusual *Opposite*: ordinary **3 offensive**, rude, disgusting, repulsive, shocking *Opposite*: inoffensive

unhelpful *adj* **1 uncooperative**, contrary, awkward, unaccommodating, obstructive *Opposite*: helpful **2 useless**, unconstructive, impractical, unnecessary, negative *Opposite*: useful

unhelpfulness *n* **1 uncooperativeness**, unsupportiveness, contrariness, impracticality *Opposite*: helpfulness **2 uselessness**, negativity, pointlessness, needlessness, worthlessness *Opposite*: usefulness

unhesitating *adj* **prompt**, unreserved, wholehearted, confident, forthright *Opposite*: tentative

unhindered *adj* **unimpeded**, unconstrained, unrestricted, unobstructed, unchecked

unhinge *v* **unbalance**, derange, madden, drive insane, disturb

unhinged *adj* **unbalanced**, deranged, disturbed, irrational, crackers (*infml*) *Opposite*: sane

unhitch *v* **unfasten**, untie, undo, uncouple, detach *Opposite*: fasten

unholy *adj* **1 unconsecrated**, unhallowed, unblessed, profane, secular *Opposite*: consecrated **2 ungodly**, blasphemous, secular, immoral, evil *Opposite*: holy **3 outrageous**, ungodly, disgraceful, scandalous, shocking

unhook *v* **undo**, release, uncouple, detach, disengage *Opposite*: hook

unhoped-for *adj* **unexpected**, unanticipated, surprising, undreamed-of, unforeseen *Opposite*: expected

unhopeful *adj* **doubtful**, despondent, gloomy, dejected, pessimistic *Opposite*: hopeful

unhurried *adj* **slow**, easygoing, dawdling, calm, deliberate *Opposite*: hurried

unhurt *adj* **uninjured**, unharmed, undamaged, unscathed, safe *Opposite*: hurt

unhygienic *adj* **insanitary**, unclean, polluted, unhealthy, foul *Opposite*: hygienic

unidentified *adj* **nameless**, anonymous, faceless, unnamed, unknown *Opposite*: known

unidentified flying object *see* UFO

unification *n* **amalgamation**, union, merger, alliance, association *Opposite*: split

unified *adj* **united**, combined, amalgamated, incorporated, integrated *Opposite*: disjointed

uniform *n* **livery**, dress, costume, garb, attire *(fml) Opposite*: mufti ■ *adj* **1 unchanging**, unvarying, even, unbroken, undeviating *Opposite*: uneven **2 consistent**, standardized, homogeneous, harmonized, regular *Opposite*: inconsistent **3 identical**, like, alike, similar, equal *Opposite*: different

uniformity *n* **consistency**, regularity, standardization, homogeneity, evenness *Opposite*: inconsistency

unify *v* **unite**, join, amalgamate, merge, combine *Opposite*: separate

unilateral *adj* **one-sided**, independent, autonomous, autarchic, individual *Opposite*: joint

unimaginable *adj* **inconceivable**, unbelievable, incredible, unthinkable, indescribable *Opposite*: conceivable

unimaginative *adj* **dull**, boring, insipid, bland, uninspired *Opposite*: imaginative

unimpaired *adj* **undamaged**, unaffected, unhindered, perfect, operational *Opposite*: impaired

unimpassioned *adj* **unemotional**, cool, detached, sober, calm *Opposite*: impassioned

unimpeachable *adj* **faultless**, flawless, impeccable, irreproachable, blameless *Opposite*: blameworthy

unimpeded *adj* **without hindrance**, unhindered, unhampered, unchecked, unconstrained *Opposite*: hindered

unimportance *n* **insignificance**, inconsequentiality, irrelevance, slightness, triviality *Opposite*: importance

unimportant *adj* **inconsequential**, slight, insignificant, trivial, trifling *Opposite*: important

unimpressed *adj* **unenthusiastic**, uninspired, unconvinced, unmoved, indifferent *Opposite*: enthusiastic

unimpressive *adj* **uninspiring**, indifferent, mediocre, unimposing, insignificant *Opposite*: impressive

unimproved *adj* **unchanged**, unaltered, natural, original, unworked *Opposite*: improved

unincorporated *adj* **independent**, separate, distinct, stand-alone, autonomous *Opposite*: incorporated

unindustrialized *adj* **undeveloped**, farming, agricultural, rural *Opposite*: industrialized

uninformative *adj* **unhelpful**, vague, uncommunicative, unproductive, useless *Opposite*: informative

uninformed *adj* **ignorant**, uneducated, unaware, unacquainted, unfamiliar *Opposite*: informed

uninhabitable *adj* **derelict**, dilapidated, ramshackle, tumbledown, run-down *Opposite*: habitable

uninhabited *adj* **unoccupied**, unpopulated, deserted, abandoned, unpeopled *Opposite*: inhabited

uninhibited *adj* **1 unrestrained**, outgoing, unconstrained, candid, open *Opposite*: shy **2 wanton**, abandoned, dissolute, licentious, immodest *Opposite*: restrained

uninitiated *adj* **inexperienced**, unskilled, unversed, unqualified, untrained *Opposite*: experienced

uninjured *adj* **unhurt**, unharmed, undamaged, intact, safe *Opposite*: hurt

uninspired *adj* **bland**, insipid, boring, dull, unimaginative *Opposite*: inspired

uninspiring *adj* **dull**, lacklustre, lifeless, boring, tame *Opposite*: inspiring

uninstructed *adj* **untaught**, unschooled, uneducated, uninformed, untutored *Opposite*: educated

unintelligent *adj* **stupid**, foolish, silly, inane, daft *(infml) Opposite*: clever

unintelligible *adj* **incomprehensible**, inarticulate, incoherent, garbled, jumbled *Opposite*: intelligible

unintended *see* unintentional

unintentional *adj* **accidental**, inadvertent, unplanned, chance, involuntary *Opposite*: intentional

uninterested *adj* **indifferent**, apathetic, blasé, impassive, unconcerned *Opposite*: concerned

uninteresting *adj* **boring**, dull, unexciting, tedious, monotonous *Opposite*: interesting

uninterrupted *adj* **continuous**, continual, nonstop, incessant, never-ending *Opposite*: sporadic

uninvited *adj* **unwelcome**, unwanted, undesirable, unsought, unsolicited *Opposite*: welcome

uninviting *adj* **unappealing**, unattractive, bleak, unpalatable, disgusting *Opposite*: attractive

uninvolved *adj* **1 detached**, removed, aloof, unconcerned, indifferent *Opposite*: involved **2 uncomplicated**, straightforward, easy, simple, plain *Opposite*: convoluted **3 single**, footloose and fancy free, unmarried, unattached, free *Opposite*: attached *(infml)*

union *n* **1 amalgamation**, combination, blending, coming together, joining together *Opposite*: separation **2 coalition**, alliance, association, confederacy, confederation **3 agreement**, harmony, accord, unity, unison *Opposite*: discord **4 marriage**, matrimony, wedlock, bond, wedding *Opposite*: divorce

unique *adj* **sole**, single, one-off, exclusive, exceptional *Opposite*: common

uniqueness *n* **individuality**, exclusivity, exceptionality, inimitability, distinctiveness *Opposite*: commonness

unison *n* **agreement**, harmony, accord, unity, union *Opposite*: discord

unit *n* **1 component**, element, part, piece, item **2 corps**, detachment, group, company, troop

unite *v* **1 join**, fuse, mix, bond, come together *Opposite*: separate **2 marry**, wed, hitch, bond, tie

united *adj* **joint**, combined, amalgamated, unified, cohesive *Opposite*: separated

unitize *v* **1 bring together**, unite, combine, centralize, condense *Opposite*: separate **2 separate**, take apart, break up, divide up, disassemble *Opposite*: join

unity *n* **agreement**, harmony, accord, unison, union *Opposite*: disarray

universal *adj* **worldwide**, widespread, general, common, collective *Opposite*: local. *See* COMPARE AND CONTRAST *at* widespread.

universalism *n* **breadth**, amplitude, diversity, gamut, spectrum

universe *n* **cosmos**, world, creation, life, space

university *n* **institution of higher education**, college, academia, academy, academe *(fml)*

unjust *adj* **unfair**, undue, undeserved, unmerited, unwarranted *Opposite*: just

unjustifiable *adj* **indefensible**, unwarrantable, inexcusable, unforgivable, unpardonable *Opposite*: justifiable

unjustified *adj* **unfounded**, baseless, unfair, unwarranted, unpardonable *Opposite*: justified

unjustly *adv* **unfairly**, unreasonably, partially, one-sidedly, discriminatorily *Opposite*: fairly

unkempt *adj* **dishevelled**, untidy, rumpled, tousled, messy *Opposite*: tidy

unkind *adj* **nasty**, mean, cruel, callous, heartless *Opposite*: kind

unkindness *n* **nastiness**, meanness, cruelty, callousness, heartlessness *Opposite*: kindness

unknot *v* **untie**, undo, unpick, disentangle, unstitch *Opposite*: knot

unknowable *adj* **incomprehensible**, enigmatic, mysterious, indecipherable, arcane *Opposite*: comprehensible

unknowing *adj* **1 unwitting**, ingenuous, naive, innocent, ignorant *Opposite*: knowing **2 unintentional**, accidental, inadvertent, unintended, unplanned *Opposite*: deliberate

unknown *adj* **1 unidentified**, indefinite, mysterious, unheard of, nameless *Opposite*: known **2 unfamiliar**, strange, foreign, alien, undiscovered *Opposite*: familiar ■ *n* **nonentity**, nobody, newcomer, beginner, stranger *Opposite*: celebrity

unlaboured *adj* **effortless**, easy, painless, trouble-free, carefree *Opposite*: laboured

unlace *v* **undo**, unfasten, unthread, unknot, untie *Opposite*: lace

unlatch *v* **open**, undo, unfasten, unlock, unbolt *Opposite*: latch

unlawful *adj* **illegal**, illicit, illegitimate, wrongful, nonlegal *Opposite*: lawful

COMPARE AND CONTRAST CORE MEANING: not in accordance with laws or rules
unlawful not permitted by the law or by the rules of an organization or religion, or not recognized as valid by those laws or rules; **illegal** contravening a specific written statute, rule, or law, especially a criminal law; **illicit** not permitted by the law, suggesting especially that something is considered morally wrong or unacceptable; **wrongful** (often used in civil lawsuits) unjust, unfair, or against conscience, but not punishable by criminal law; **nonlegal** not established or affected under common law or legislation.

unlearned *adj* **uneducated**, illiterate, unschooled, unlettered, untutored *Opposite*: educated

unleash *v* **set free**, give a free rein to, allow to run free, allow to run riot, uncheck *Opposite*: control

unless *prep* **if not**, if, except, save, but for

unlettered *adj* **uneducated**, illiterate, unschooled, untaught, untutored *Opposite*: educated

unlicensed *adj* **uninhibited**, unrestricted, unrestrained, abandoned, immoral *Opposite*: inhibited

unlike *adj* **different**, dissimilar, nothing like, distinct, contrasting *Opposite*: like

unlikelihood *n* **improbability**, doubtfulness, implausibility, dubiousness, questionability *Opposite*: likelihood

unlikely *adj* **1 improbable**, doubtful, dubious, questionable *Opposite*: likely **2 implausible**, dubious, doubtful, suspect, incongruous *Opposite*: credible

unlimited *adj* **limitless**, infinite, unrestricted, unrestrained, boundless *Opposite*: limited

unlisted *adj* **private**, ex-directory, unpublished, confidential, secret *Opposite*: listed

unlit *adj* **dark**, darkened, dim, pitch-black, murky *Opposite*: bright

unload *v* **unpack**, drop off, drop, deliver, empty *Opposite*: load

unlock *v* **1 undo**, release, unchain, open, unbolt *Opposite*: lock **2 solve**, reveal, answer, expose, get to the bottom of

unlooked-for *adj* **unexpected**, undreamed-of, unanticipated, uninvited, unsolicited *Opposite*: expected

unloose *v* **set free**, release, let out, unleash, let off the lead *Opposite*: tie up

unlovely *adj* **unattractive**, objectionable, obnoxious, nasty, ugly *Opposite*: attractive

unluckiness *n* **bad luck**, misfortune, ill luck, mishap *Opposite*: luck

unlucky *adj* **1 unsuccessful**, wretched, hapless,

unfortunate, tragic *Opposite*: lucky **2 inauspicious**, fateful, ill-fated, doomed, star-crossed *Opposite*: fortunate

unmake *v* **1 undo**, take apart, reverse, deconstruct, dismantle *Opposite*: put back **2 demote**, fire, sack, replace, expel

unmanageable *adj* **uncontrollable**, unruly, riotous, out of control, out of hand *Opposite*: manageable

unmanliness *n* **weakness**, cowardliness, timidity, fearfulness, apprehension *Opposite*: manliness

unmanly *adj* **weak**, cowardly, timid, fearful, apprehensive *Opposite*: manly

unmannered *adj* **1 rude**, boorish, impolite, crude, coarse *Opposite*: well-mannered **2 unaffected**, easy, natural, genuine, simple *Opposite*: affected

unmannerly *adj* **rude**, impolite, ill-mannered, bad-mannered, disrespectful *Opposite*: polite

unmarked *adj* **spotless**, unblemished, pristine, immaculate, perfect *Opposite*: marked

unmarried *adj* **single**, unattached, bachelor, spinster, free *Opposite*: married

unmask *v* **expose**, blow the whistle on, reveal, unveil, debunk *Opposite*: conceal

unmatched *adj* **supreme**, matchless, unrivalled, consummate, unparalleled

unmeant *adj* **unintended**, accidental, inadvertent, unplanned, unintentional *Opposite*: deliberate

unmentionable *adj* **taboo**, offensive, prohibited, forbidden, restricted *Opposite*: respectable ■ *n* **taboo**, no-go area, anathema, no-no *(infml)*

unmerciful *adj* **1 cruel**, severe, harsh, hard, unsparing *Opposite*: merciful **2 excessive**, unrelenting, extreme, remorseless, unremitting

unmerited *adj* **undeserved**, unwarranted, unjustified, unearned, unjust *Opposite*: fair

unmindful *adj* **unaware**, oblivious, unconscious, careless, heedless *Opposite*: mindful

unmistakable *adj* **obvious**, definite, distinctive, unambiguous, unique *Opposite*: ambiguous

unmitigated *adj* **sheer**, pure, absolute, unadulterated, unalloyed

unmodified *adj* **original**, unchanged, basic, untouched *Opposite*: modified

unmotivated *adj* **apathetic**, unenthusiastic, indifferent, shiftless, uninterested *Opposite*: keen

unmovable *adj* **inflexible**, rigid, stubborn, obstinate, obdurate *Opposite*: flexible

unmoved *adj* **indifferent**, unaffected, unresponsive, insensitive, impassive *Opposite*: touched. *See* COMPARE AND CONTRAST *at* **impassive**

unmoving *adj* **still**, motionless, inactive, lifeless, inert *Opposite*: moving

unmusical *adj* **unmelodic**, dissonant, discordant, jarring, harsh *Opposite*: musical

unnamed *adj* **unidentified**, anonymous, unspecified, nameless, unknown *Opposite*: named

unnatural *adj* **1 abnormal**, aberrant, atypical, unusual, perverted *Opposite*: normal **2 strange**, odd, peculiar, atypical, irregular *Opposite*: typical **3 supernatural**, weird, bizarre, paranormal, uncanny *Opposite*: ordinary **4 artificial**, contrived, affected, insincere, pretend *Opposite*: natural

unnecessary *adj* **needless**, pointless, redundant, superfluous, gratuitous *Opposite*: necessary

unneeded *adj* **extra**, superfluous, unnecessary, surplus, unwanted *Opposite*: necessary

unnerve *v* **alarm**, frighten, scare, upset, nonplus *Opposite*: calm

unnerved *adj* **frightened**, scared, alarmed, unsettled, anxious *Opposite*: calm

unnerving *adj* **frightening**, unsettling, demoralizing, intimidating, upsetting *Opposite*: comforting

unnoticeable *adj* **invisible**, imperceptible, unremarkable, inconspicuous, hidden *Opposite*: conspicuous

unnoticed *adj* **unobserved**, overlooked, ignored, unseen, disregarded

unnumbered *adj* **1 numberless**, numerous, myriad, countless, many *Opposite*: few **2 unidentified**, unmarked, untagged, uncounted

unobjectionable *adj* **inoffensive**, agreeable, pleasant, innocuous, harmless *Opposite*: unpleasant

unobservant *adj* **inattentive**, unperceptive, incurious, negligent, careless *Opposite*: observant

unobserved *adj* **unnoticed**, ignored, overlooked, unseen, disregarded *Opposite*: evident

unobstructed *adj* **clear**, free, unhindered, passable, open *Opposite*: barred

unobtainable *adj* **unavailable**, unattainable, inaccessible, out of stock *Opposite*: available

unobtrusive *adj* **inconspicuous**, unremarkable, modest, bland, discreet *Opposite*: conspicuous

unoccupied *adj* **1 inactive**, at a loose end, idle, unemployed, out of work *Opposite*: busy **2 vacant**, free, untenanted, empty, disused *Opposite*: occupied. *See* COMPARE AND CONTRAST *at* **vacant**.

unofficial *adj* **unauthorized**, unsanctioned, informal, unendorsed, private *Opposite*: official

unopposed *adj* **unchallenged**, unobstructed, unrestricted, unhampered, unimpeded *Opposite*: challenged

unorganized *adj* **1 chaotic**, disorganized,

muddled, messy, disorderly *Opposite*: well-organized **2 careless**, disorganized, unprepared, sloppy, slapdash *Opposite*: methodical

unoriginal *adj* **derivative**, copied, imitative, clichéd, banal *Opposite*: original

unoriginality *n* **derivativeness**, triteness, staleness, imitativeness, banality *Opposite*: originality

unorthodox *adj* **unconventional**, nonconformist, untraditional, unusual, eccentric *Opposite*: orthodox

unpack *v* **unload**, take out, empty, undo, empty out *Opposite*: pack up

unpaid *adj* **1 unsettled**, outstanding, overdue, due, owed *Opposite*: paid **2 voluntary**, amateur, honorary, free *Opposite*: paid

unpalatable *adj* **1 inedible**, indigestible, disgusting, revolting, foul-tasting *Opposite*: tasty **2 unacceptable**, unpleasant, painful, disagreeable, harsh *Opposite*: acceptable

unparalleled *adj* **unmatched**, supreme, matchless, beyond compare, unequalled *Opposite*: mediocre

unpardonable *adj* **unforgivable**, indefensible, inexcusable, deplorable, reprehensible *Opposite*: understandable

unpeg *v* **undo**, unfasten, untie, detach, release *Opposite*: fasten

unperceptive *adj* **undiscerning**, unobservant, insensitive, obtuse, indiscriminate *Opposite*: perceptive

unperturbed *adj* **calm**, at peace, tranquil, collected, composed *Opposite*: anxious

unpick *v* **unravel**, untangle, untie, undo, disentangle

unplanned *adj* **1 unintended**, accidental, unintentional, unexpected, inadvertent *Opposite*: planned **2 spontaneous**, impromptu, ad hoc, unprepared, spur-of-the-moment *Opposite*: planned

unpleasant *adj* **1 disagreeable**, nasty, unlikable, horrible, horrid *Opposite*: pleasant **2 unfriendly**, hostile, cold, unkind, spiteful *Opposite*: friendly

unpleasantness *n* **1 disagreeableness**, nastiness, horribleness, horridness, distastefulness *Opposite*: pleasantness **2 ill feeling**, trouble, fuss, bother, upset *Opposite*: harmony **3 unfriendliness**, spitefulness, nastiness, unkindness, offensiveness *Opposite*: friendliness **4 disagreement**, conflict, argument, quarrel, dispute *Opposite*: agreement

unplug *v* **1 unblock**, clear, free, clean, release **2 disconnect**, switch off, undo, take out, remove *Opposite*: plug in

unplumbed *adj* **mysterious**, unfathomable, enigmatic, unexplored, unknowable *Opposite*: known

unpolluted *adj* **clean**, pure, uncontaminated, untainted, fresh *Opposite*: contaminated

unpopular *adj* **disliked**, hated, out of favour, shunned, detested *Opposite*: popular

unpopulated *adj* **abandoned**, deserted, depopulated, uninhabited, empty *Opposite*: overcrowded

unpractised *adj* **inexperienced**, unrehearsed, unschooled, untrained, unfamiliar *Opposite*: practised

unprecedented *adj* **unparalleled**, extraordinary, record, first-time, unique *Opposite*: ordinary

unpredictability *n* **randomness**, impulsiveness, volatility, fickleness, changeableness *Opposite*: predictability

unpredictable *adj* **random**, erratic, changeable, impulsive, volatile *Opposite*: predictable

unpredicted *adj* **surprising**, unexpected, shocking, astonishing, unforeseen *Opposite*: predicted

unprejudiced *adj* **fair**, neutral, tolerant, unbiased, evenhanded *Opposite*: biased

unpremeditated *adj* **unplanned**, unintended, impulsive, spur-of-the-moment, sudden *Opposite*: premeditated

unprepared *adj* **1 unready**, unsuspecting, ill-equipped, unqualified, untrained *Opposite*: prepared **2 improvised**, unrehearsed, ad hoc, impromptu, spontaneous *Opposite*: rehearsed

unprepossessing *adj* **ugly**, unattractive, plain, unpleasant, uninviting *Opposite*: attractive

unpretentious *adj* **modest**, unassuming, unaffected, natural, self-effacing *Opposite*: pretentious

unpretentiousness *n* **modesty**, humility, humbleness, simplicity, artlessness *Opposite*: grandiosity

unprincipled *adj* **dishonest**, corrupt, amoral, immoral, devious *Opposite*: honest

unprintable *adj* **rude**, foul, offensive, shocking, coarse *Opposite*: inoffensive

unproblematic *adj* **easy**, smooth, straightforward, trouble-free, simple *Opposite*: tricky

unprocessed *adj* **natural**, whole, unrefined, untreated, crude

unproductive *adj* **1 fruitless**, infertile, barren, sterile, blocked *Opposite*: fertile **2 idle**, lazy, slow, wasteful, inefficient *Opposite*: productive

unprofessional *adj* **1 unethical**, unprincipled, immoral, dishonourable, wrong *Opposite*: ethical **2 amateurish**, amateur, slack, inexpert, shoddy *Opposite*: expert

unprofitable *adj* **1 lossmaking**, unsuccessful, running at a loss, nonpaying, insolvent *Opposite*: profitable **2 unhelpful**, useless, pointless, futile, fruitless *Opposite*: helpful

unpromising *adj* **gloomy**, bleak, discouraging, doubtful, off-putting *Opposite*: encouraging

unprompted *adj* **spontaneous**, unforced, impulsive, off your own bat *(infml)*, willing *Opposite*: forced

unpronounceable adj unsayable, difficult, impossible

unpronounced adj silent, mute, unvoiced, unspoken, unsaid Opposite: voiced

unprotected adj defenceless, undefended, open to attack, insecure, vulnerable Opposite: secure

unproven adj/unverified, unconfirmed, untried, untested, undocumented Opposite: proven

unprovoked adj gratuitous, wanton, senseless, motiveless, uncalled-for Opposite: provoked

unqualified adj 1 untrained, unprofessional, ill-equipped, inexpert, untaught Opposite: trained 2 definite, unreserved, absolute, complete, utter Opposite: qualified

unquantifiable adj immeasurable, uncountable, unidentifiable, indefinable, indeterminate Opposite: quantifiable

unquestionable adj indisputable, incontestable, absolute, undeniable, categorical Opposite: arguable

unquestioned adj undisputed, accepted, unchallenged, automatic, logical Opposite: questionable

unquestioning adj unthinking, wholehearted, obedient, absolute, automatic Opposite: reluctant

unquiet adj 1 noisy, turbulent, loud, rowdy, boisterous Opposite: quiet 2 anxious, unsettled, restless, agitated, fidgety Opposite: calm

unravel v 1 undo, untie, unknot, loosen, disentangle Opposite: tie 2 solve, clear up, resolve, sort out, get to the bottom of 3 fail, go wrong, fall apart, collapse, crumble Opposite: come together

unreadable adj 1 illegible, incomprehensible, indecipherable, scrawled, scribbled Opposite: legible 2 impenetrable, dense, tedious, turgid, boring Opposite: readable 3 blank, expressionless, impassive, poker-faced, inscrutable

unreal adj 1 false, artificial, imitation, fake, pretend Opposite: genuine 2 imaginary, dreamlike, illusory, fantastic, weird Opposite: real

unrealistic adj impractical, idealistic, impracticable, improbable, unlikely Opposite: practical

unreality n 1 strangeness, incongruity, oddness, weirdness, abnormality Opposite: reality 2 fantasy, delusion, fancy, self-delusion, illusion Opposite: reality

unreasonable adj 1 irrational, perverse, arbitrary, unreasoning, awkward Opposite: rational 2 excessive, exorbitant, immoderate, extravagant, extreme Opposite: reasonable

unreasonableness n 1 irrationality, arbitrariness, awkwardness, perverseness, difficultness Opposite: rationality 2 excessiveness, injustice, exorbitance, extravagance, unfairness Opposite: reasonableness

unreceptive adj disinclined, ill-disposed, unwilling, resistant, unteachable Opposite: receptive

unreconstructed adj 1 old-fashioned, unchanging, unrepentant, dyed-in-the-wool, traditional 2 unchanged, unaltered, unvaried, unmodified, original

unrefined adj 1 unprocessed, untreated, raw, crude, untouched Opposite: refined 2 vulgar, unsophisticated, uncultured, crude, coarse Opposite: sophisticated

unreformed adj unapologetic, unrepentant, dyed-in-the-wool, inveterate, diehard Opposite: reformed

unrehearsed adj unprepared, impromptu, off-the-cuff, spontaneous, impulsive Opposite: prepared

unrelated adj 1 unconnected, separate, distinct, dissimilar, disparate Opposite: linked 2 irrelevant, beside the point, extraneous, unconnected, impertinent (fml) Opposite: relevant

unrelenting adj remorseless, relentless, insistent, merciless, pitiless Opposite: yielding

unreliability n 1 undependability, untrustworthiness, unpredictability, changeableness, irregularity Opposite: dependability 2 inaccuracy, fallibility, untrustworthiness, flimsiness, dubiousness Opposite: reliability

unreliable adj 1 undependable, fly-by-night, variable, unpredictable, changeable Opposite: dependable 2 inaccurate, fallacious, flimsy, threadbare, untrue Opposite: reliable

unrelieved adj constant, unbroken, chronic, unmitigated, unalleviated Opposite: intermittent

unremarkable adj ordinary, everyday, commonplace, average, typical Opposite: remarkable

unremitting adj constant, incessant, continuous, chronic, unrelenting Opposite: intermittent

unremorseful adj unrepentant, unapologetic, impenitent, unashamed, shameless Opposite: apologetic

unrepentant adj impenitent, unapologetic, unashamed, shameless, unremorseful Opposite: remorseful

unreserved adj 1 unqualified, total, complete, utter, absolute Opposite: qualified 2 open, demonstrative, candid, frank, extrovert Opposite: reserved

unresolved adj unsettled, unanswered, uncertain, vague, pending Opposite: settled

unresponsive adj unfeeling, insensitive, indifferent, impassive, uncaring Opposite: responsive

unresponsiveness n unfeelingness, insensitivity, indifference, impassiveness, coldness Opposite: responsiveness

unrest n 1 **discontent**, turbulence, strife, conflict, disturbance Opposite: calm 2 **anxiousness**, anxiety, disquiet, worry, uneasiness Opposite: peace

unrestrained adj **uncontrolled**, wild, unrestricted, abandoned, uninhibited Opposite: restrained

unrestricted adj **open**, unobstructed, unhindered, unlimited, unhampered Opposite: restricted

unrevealed adj **secret**, hidden, unknown, mysterious, clandestine Opposite: known

unrewarding adj **thankless**, fruitless, unfulfilling, unsatisfactory, difficult Opposite: satisfying

unrighteous adj 1 **sinful**, wicked, evil, irreligious, unholy Opposite: righteous 2 **unjust**, unfair, ill-deserved, unkind, wrong Opposite: just

unripe adj **immature**, green, young, fresh, undeveloped Opposite: ripe

unrivalled adj **unequalled**, unique, singular, unsurpassed, extraordinary Opposite: ordinary

unroll v **open**, unfurl, stretch out, spread out, unfold Opposite: roll up

unruffled adj **calm**, tranquil, unmoved, in control, at ease Opposite: flustered

unruliness n **boisterousness**, disruptiveness, disorderliness, rowdiness, recalcitrance Opposite: orderliness

unruly adj **boisterous**, disruptive, disorderly, rowdy, wild Opposite: orderly

COMPARE AND CONTRAST CORE MEANING: not submitting to control
unruly boisterous, disruptive, and difficult to control or discipline; **intractable** (fml) strongwilled and rebellious, refusing to be controlled or to submit to discipline; **recalcitrant** obstinate and defiant in refusing to submit to discipline or control; **obstreperous** noisy, difficult to control, and uncooperative; **wilful** stubbornly disregarding the opinions or advice of others; **wild** showing a general lack of control or restraint; **wayward** disobedient and uncontrollable.

unrushed adj **unhurried**, slow, leisurely, calm, gentle Opposite: hurried

unsafe adj **dangerous**, insecure, hazardous, risky, perilous Opposite: secure

unsaid adj **tacit**, unspoken, implicit, silent, unstated Opposite: spoken

unsatisfactory adj **inadequate**, unacceptable, substandard, disappointing, insufficient Opposite: acceptable

unsatisfied adj **displeased**, discontented, unhappy, unfulfilled, disgruntled Opposite: pleased

unsavoury adj 1 **unpleasant**, disagreeable, revolting, disgusting, repellent Opposite: pleasant 2 **immoral**, unpleasant, villainous, shady, unacceptable Opposite: wholesome

unscathed adj **unharmed**, intact, unhurt, untouched, safe Opposite: injured

unschooled adj **uneducated**, untaught, untutored, untrained, illiterate Opposite: educated

unscientific adj **intuitive**, instinctive, irrational, unempirical, seat-of-the-pants (infml) Opposite: systematic

unscramble v **decode**, sort out, decipher, work out, make out Opposite: encode

unscrew v **take off**, remove, detach, loosen, undo Opposite: tighten

unscripted adj **unplanned**, unexpected, impromptu, impulsive, unscheduled

unscrupulous adj **dishonest**, unprincipled, corrupt, immoral, deceitful Opposite: honest

unscrupulousness n **dishonesty**, corruptness, crookedness, immorality, deviousness Opposite: honesty

unseal v **open**, uncap, unstop, break open, unscrew Opposite: seal

unseasonable adj 1 **unusual**, abnormal, unexpected, odd, strange Opposite: seasonable 2 **untimely**, inopportune, ill-timed, inconvenient, unwelcome Opposite: seasonable

unseat v **depose**, oust, overthrow, dethrone, remove Opposite: enthrone (fml)

unseemliness n **impropriety**, tastelessness, uncouthness, loutishness, rudeness Opposite: propriety

unseemly adj **inappropriate**, rude, uncouth, improper, indecorous Opposite: proper

unseen adj **hidden**, unnoticed, unobserved, invisible, concealed Opposite: noticeable

unselective adj **indiscriminating**, undiscerning, blanket, haphazard, random Opposite: discerning

unselfish adj **selfless**, generous, noble, magnanimous, liberal Opposite: selfish

unselfishness n **selflessness**, generosity, magnanimity, kindness, consideration Opposite: selfishness

unsentimental adj **unemotional**, impassive, unfeeling, hard-bitten, tough Opposite: sentimental

unsettle v **worry**, disturb, upset, disconcert, unnerve Opposite: soothe

unsettled adj 1 **anxious**, worried, disturbed, upset, disconcerted Opposite: calm 2 **changeable**, variable, unpredictable, uncertain, changing Opposite: settled 3 **undecided**, unresolved, undetermined, open-ended, arguable Opposite: decided

unsettling adj **upsetting**, worrying, disturbing, disconcerting, disquieting Opposite: soothing

unshackle v **release**, unchain, let loose, set free, liberate Opposite: chain

unshakable adj **steadfast**, resolute, constant, unwavering, entrenched Opposite: wavering

unshaped *adj* unformed, formless, shapeless, amorphous, indistinct *Opposite*: shaped

unsheathe *v* draw, pull, remove, extract, uncover

unsightliness *n* ugliness, hideousness, horridness, unpleasantness, nastiness *Opposite*: attractiveness

unsightly *adj* unattractive, ugly, hideous, unpleasant, unprepossessing *Opposite*: attractive. *See* COMPARE AND CONTRAST *at* unattractive.

unskilful *adj* inept, unskilled, untrained, untalented, incompetent *Opposite*: skilful

unskilled *adj* inexpert, amateurish, untrained, uneducated, unqualified *Opposite*: trained

unsmiling *adj* stern, severe, serious, dour, grim-faced *Opposite*: cordial

unsnag *v* disentangle, clear, free, untangle, release *Opposite*: snag

unsnarl *v* disentangle, clear, free, untangle, unblock *Opposite*: tangle

unsociable *adj* unfriendly, antisocial, aloof, shy, standoffish *Opposite*: friendly

unsolicited *adj* unwelcome, unwanted, uninvited, unsought, spontaneous *Opposite*: requested

unsolvable *adj* impenetrable, unknowable, impossible, unfathomable, insoluble *Opposite*: soluble

unsolved *adj* unexplained, unresolved, mysterious, baffling *Opposite*: resolved

unsophisticated *adj* 1 unworldly, naive, inexperienced, ingenuous, simple *Opposite*: sophisticated 2 crude, simple, unrefined, basic, primitive *Opposite*: advanced

unsought *adj* unsolicited, spontaneous, uninvited, uncalled-for, unwanted

unsound *adj* 1 ill, frail, unwell, unhealthy, sick *Opposite*: well 2 unsafe, unstable, rickety, in poor condition, ramshackle *Opposite*: secure 3 illogical, specious, flawed, fallacious, erroneous *Opposite*: logical

unsparing *adj* 1 merciless, harsh, cruel, unforgiving, severe *Opposite*: merciful 2 generous, munificent, openhanded, liberal, charitable *Opposite*: frugal

unspeakable *adj* 1 indescribable, inexpressible, unutterable, undefinable, overwhelming 2 awful, disgusting, appalling, foul, revolting

unspeakably *adv* 1 indescribably, inexpressibly, unutterably, undefinably, unbelievably 2 terribly, awfully, appallingly, horribly, horrendously

unspeaking *adj* silent, mute, wordless, still, speechless *Opposite*: verbose

unspecified *adj* unnamed, indefinite, vague, indeterminate, undetermined *Opposite*: specific

unspiritual *adj* earthly, worldly, mundane, material, irreligious *Opposite*: spiritual

unspoilt *adj* 1 pristine, pure, perfect, untouched, unharmed *Opposite*: marred 2 uncorrupted, natural, innocent, pure, wholesome *Opposite*: spoiled

unspoken *adj* tacit, understood, silent, implicit, undeclared *Opposite*: explicit

unsporting *adj* dishonest, unfair, dishonourable, disreputable, mean-spirited *Opposite*: sporting

unsportsmanlike *adj* dirty, dishonest, nasty, foul, unethical *Opposite*: exemplary

unspotted *adj* 1 unstained, clean, spotless, unblemished, pristine *Opposite*: spotted 2 pure, moral, unblemished, faultless, righteous *Opposite*: impure 3 unobserved, unseen, unnoticed, unperceived, undiscovered *Opposite*: seen

unstable *adj* 1 unbalanced, uneven, wobbly, rickety, ramshackle *Opposite*: steady 2 volatile, unpredictable, unsteady, erratic, unhinged *Opposite*: stable

unstated *adj* unspecified, unspoken, tacit, understood, implicit *Opposite*: specified

unsteadiness *n* 1 tremulousness, instability, shakiness, precariousness, treacherousness *Opposite*: stability 2 changeability, erraticism, variability, unreliability, irregularity *Opposite*: constancy

unsteady *adj* 1 wobbly, shaky, unstable, uneven, rickety *Opposite*: stable 2 changeable, erratic, variable, unreliable, irregular *Opposite*: constant

unstick *v* release, free, take off, take down, take apart *Opposite*: stick

unstinting *adj* generous, charitable, openhanded, liberal, unsparing *Opposite*: stingy (*infml*)

unstipulated *adj* unspecified, unstated, unmentioned, undeclared *Opposite*: specified

unstop *v* unblock, free, clear, unplug, open up *Opposite*: stop

unstoppable *adj* irresistible, overwhelming, overpowering, persistent, unrelenting *Opposite*: avoidable

unstrained *adj* cloudy, milky, opaque, murky *Opposite*: clear

unstrap *v* undo, remove, unbuckle, unshackle, unleash *Opposite*: tie up

unstressed *adj* relaxed, carefree, at ease, cool, calm *Opposite*: stressed

unstructured *adj* formless, shapeless, amorphous, free *Opposite*: structured

unstudied *adj* unaffected, natural, genuine, sincere, relaxed *Opposite*: affected

unsubstantiated *adj* unconfirmed, unproven, unsupported, uncorroborated *Opposite*: proven

unsuccessful *adj* ineffective, failed, vain, unproductive, abortive *Opposite*: successful

unsuitability *n* inappropriateness, inaptness,

unbecomingness, incongruity, incompatibility *Opposite*: appropriateness

unsuitable *adj* inappropriate, unbecoming, unfitting, inapt, unbefitting *Opposite*: appropriate

unsullied *adj* pure, clean, unblemished, faultless, untarnished *Opposite*: tarnished

unsung *adj* unacknowledged, silent, unrecognized, anonymous, nameless *Opposite*: renowned

unsupported *adj* uncorroborated, unconfirmed, unsubstantiated, unverified, unfounded *Opposite*: supported

unsure *adj* 1 uncertain, doubtful, unconvinced, dubious, suspicious *Opposite*: certain 2 unconfident, hesitant, shy, insecure, irresolute *Opposite*: confident. *See* COMPARE AND CONTRAST *at* doubtful.

unsurpassed *adj* unrivalled, unmatched, supreme, incomparable, unequalled *Opposite*: ordinary

unsurprising *adj* predictable, foreseeable, expected, anticipated, foreseen *Opposite*: surprising

unsurprisingly *adv* of course, naturally, obviously, expectedly, predictably *Opposite*: surprisingly

unsuspected *adj* unanticipated, unpredicted, unknown, unimagined, surprise *Opposite*: known

unsuspecting *adj* unwary, gullible, credulous, innocent, unsuspicious *Opposite*: wary

unsustainable *adj* unjustifiable, unmaintainable, unverifiable, untenable, indefensible *Opposite*: sustainable

unswerving *adj* unwavering, staunch, reliable, trusty, solid *Opposite*: wavering

unsymmetrical *adj* asymmetrical, uneven, irregular, lopsided *Opposite*: symmetrical

unsympathetic *adj* unfeeling, uncaring, insensitive, cold, indifferent *Opposite*: caring

unsystematic *adj* haphazard, random, chaotic, disorganized, disorderly *Opposite*: organized

untainted *adj* unpolluted, undamaged, unblemished, unspoiled, pure *Opposite*: tainted

untaken *adj* available, unclaimed, unoccupied, free, spare *Opposite*: taken

untangle *v* unravel, disentangle, untie, unpick, straighten out *Opposite*: tangle

untapped *adj* unused, unexploited, untouched, available, intact *Opposite*: used

untarnished *adj* unblemished, clean, spotless, shining, unsullied *Opposite*: blemished

untaught *adj* untutored, uneducated, untrained, natural, born *Opposite*: trained

untenable *adj* indefensible, unsustainable, weak, unsound, shaky *Opposite*: watertight

untested *adj* 1 inexperienced, unproven, inexpert, new, raw *Opposite*: experienced 2 experimental, untried, unapproved, unverified, unproven *Opposite*: reliable

untether *v* release, untie, unstrap, unchain, free *Opposite*: tie up

unthinkable *adj* 1 absurd, ridiculous, unlikely, impossible, improbable *Opposite*: likely 2 unimaginable, impossible, fantastic, unbelievable, incredible *Opposite*: conceivable

unthinking *adj* 1 careless, thoughtless, tactless, undiplomatic, inconsiderate *Opposite*: thoughtful 2 instinctive, automatic, mechanical, intuitive, impulsive *Opposite*: calculated

unthreatened *adj* secure, safe, safe and sound, protected, impregnable *Opposite*: threatened

untidiness *n* 1 mess, disorder, muddle, disarray, jumble *Opposite*: order 2 shabbiness, scruffiness, raggedness *Opposite*: smartness

untidy *adj* 1 messy, in a mess, disorderly, muddled, jumbled *Opposite*: neat 2 unkempt, ragged, shabby, scruffy, bedraggled *Opposite*: smart

untie *v* 1 unknot, unfasten, loosen, undo, unravel *Opposite*: fasten 2 release, free, set free, unleash, let loose *Opposite*: tie up

until *prep* up until, while waiting for, pending, till, up to

untimely *adj* 1 ill-timed, inconvenient, inappropriate, unfortunate, inopportune *Opposite*: timely 2 premature, early, precocious, advance *Opposite*: late

untiring *adj* tireless, determined, dogged, indefatigable, constant *Opposite*: faltering

untold *adj* 1 indescribable, inexpressible, indefinable, ineffable *(fml)* 2 uncountable, countless, innumerable, myriad, numberless *Opposite*: few

untouchable *adj* unattainable, matchless, superlative, superior, unrivalled *Opposite*: ordinary

untouched *adj* 1 unhurt, intact, unharmed, undamaged, safe and sound *Opposite*: injured 2 unaffected, indifferent, unmoved, unimpressed, unconcerned *Opposite*: affected

untoward *adj* 1 annoying, unpleasant, inconvenient, troublesome, awkward *Opposite*: pleasant 2 inappropriate, unfitting, unseemly, improper, unbecoming *Opposite*: appropriate

untrained *adj* untaught, inexpert, untutored, unqualified, inexperienced *Opposite*: trained

untrammelled *adj* unrestricted, free, unhindered, unimpeded, liberated *Opposite*: restrained

untreated *adj* unprocessed, unrefined, natural, raw, crude *Opposite*: treated

untried *adj* untested, inexperienced, unproven, new, novel *Opposite*: tested

untroubled adj peaceful, calm, tranquil, undisturbed, unflustered Opposite: troubled

untrue adj 1 false, incorrect, wrong, fallacious, untruthful Opposite: true 2 cheating, unfaithful, disloyal, treacherous, two-faced Opposite: faithful

untrustworthiness n unreliability, dishonesty, deceitfulness, disloyalty, treachery Opposite: dependability

untrustworthy adj unreliable, dishonest, deceitful, disloyal, treacherous Opposite: dependable

untruth n lie, falsehood, fiction, fabrication, deceit Opposite: truth. See COMPARE AND CONTRAST at lie.

untruthful adj lying, mendacious, dishonest, deceitful, false Opposite: truthful

untruthfulness n dishonesty, deceit, lies, falsehood, fabrication Opposite: truthfulness

untutored adj untaught, uneducated, untrained, unschooled, unqualified Opposite: educated

unusable adj useless, out of commission, unworkable, inoperative, broken Opposite: usable

unused adj 1 new, brand-new, fresh, pristine Opposite: used 2 idle, vacant, unemployed, unexploited, fallow 3 unaccustomed, unfamiliar, unacquainted, inexperienced Opposite: familiar

unusual adj 1 uncommon, rare, infrequent, scarce, unfamiliar Opposite: common 2 strange, odd, curious, extraordinary, abnormal Opposite: ordinary

unutterable adj unspeakable, indescribable, inexpressible, indefinable, ineffable (fml)

unvarying adj unwavering, constant, unchanging, consistent, inflexible Opposite: varying

unveil v 1 uncover, unwrap, bare, expose Opposite: cover 2 reveal, expose, make public, divulge, show Opposite: conceal

unveiling n 1 opening, launch, presentation, inauguration, debut Opposite: closure 2 revelation, disclosure, exposure, uncovering, release Opposite: cover-up

unventilated adj airless, stuffy, unaired, close, stale Opposite: airy

unverified adj unconfirmed, unsupported, unsubstantiated, uncorroborated, unproven Opposite: verified

unvoiced adj unspoken, silent, secret, hidden, mute Opposite: spoken

unwaged adj unemployed, jobless, out of work, redundant, on the dole (infml) Opposite: employed

unwanted adj 1 surplus, superfluous, unnecessary, discarded, redundant Opposite: necessary 2 unwelcome, unsolicited, annoying, undesirable, uninvited Opposite: welcome

unwariness n incautiousness, unguardedness, rashness, carelessness, gullibility Opposite: wariness

unwarrantable adj uncalled-for, indefensible, unjustifiable, unforgivable, inexcusable

unwarranted adj unjustified, undeserved, unnecessary, gratuitous, needless Opposite: justified

unwary adj imprudent, unguarded, rash, careless, unsuspecting Opposite: wary

unwashed adj dirty, grubby, grimy, sordid, squalid Opposite: clean

unwavering adj firm, staunch, solid, steadfast, untiring Opposite: irresolute

unwearied adj unflagging, tireless, indefatigable, uncomplaining, unceasing

unwelcome adj unwanted, undesirable, annoying, unsolicited, uninvited Opposite: welcome

unwelcoming adj hostile, unfriendly, standoffish, unreceptive, inhospitable Opposite: friendly

unwell adj ill, sick, under the weather, out of sorts Opposite: well, poorly (infml)

unwholesome adj unpleasant, distasteful, objectionable, nasty, disagreeable Opposite: pleasant

unwholesomeness n 1 foulness, insalubriousness, noxiousness, unhealthiness, harmfulness Opposite: wholesomeness 2 coarseness, indecency, vulgarity, foulness, profanity Opposite: wholesomeness

unwieldy adj awkward, heavy, bulky, cumbersome, clumsy Opposite: manageable

unwilling adj reluctant, disinclined, grudging, loath, unenthusiastic Opposite: willing

COMPARE AND CONTRAST CORE MEANING: lacking the desire to do something
unwilling not prepared to do something; **reluctant** showing no enthusiasm for doing something and only doing it if forced; **disinclined** showing a lack of enthusiasm for something rather than a strong objection to it; **averse** (fml) strongly opposed to or disliking something; **hesitant** not keen to do something because of uncertainty or lack of confidence; **loath** having reservations about doing something.

unwillingness n reluctance, disinclination, refusal, indisposition, aversion Opposite: willingness

unwind v 1 undo, loosen, unravel, untwist, disentangle Opposite: wind 2 relax, wind down, slow down, calm down, kick back Opposite: work up

unwise adj foolish, imprudent, rash, ill-advised, injudicious Opposite: prudent

unwitting adj 1 unaware, unsuspecting, ignorant, innocent, unconscious Opposite: knowing 2 accidental, involuntary, unin-

unwonted *adj* **unusual**, atypical, uncharacteristic, singular, unexpected *Opposite*: customary

unworkable *adj* **impracticable**, unusable, unfeasible, ineffectual, impractical *Opposite*: viable

unworldliness *n* **innocence**, naivety, simplicity, ingenuousness, callowness *Opposite*: worldliness

unworldly *adj* **inexperienced**, callow, green, ingenuous, artless *Opposite*: experienced

unworried *adj* **calm**, untroubled, at ease, unruffled, unflustered *Opposite*: perturbed

unworthiness *n* 1 **worthlessness**, contemptibility, pitifulness, unfitness 2 **shamefulness**, dishonour, discredit, shame, disgrace

unworthy *adj* 1 **undeserving**, worthless, contemptible, pitiful, unfit *Opposite*: deserving 2 **shameful**, degrading, dishonourable, disgraceful, disreputable *Opposite*: reputable

unwrap *v* **undo**, unpack, remove, open, tear open *Opposite*: wrap

unwritten *adj* 1 **spoken**, oral, unrecorded, vocal, unprinted *Opposite*: written 2 **understood**, accepted, traditional, tacit, known

unyielding *adj* 1 **firm**, unbending, obstinate, steadfast, obdurate *Opposite*: acquiescent 2 **inflexible**, rigid, stiff, unbending, solid *Opposite*: flexible

unyoke *v* **untie**, separate, disjoin, unhook, loose *Opposite*: join

unzip *v* 1 **undo**, unfasten, open, disengage, free 2 **open**, expand, access, decompress *Opposite*: compress

up *adj* 1 **awake**, out of bed, up and about, active, up and doing *Opposite*: asleep 2 **happy**, positive, optimistic, hopeful, cheerful *Opposite*: down 3 **winning**, in the lead, ahead, leading *Opposite*: behind

up-and-coming *adj* **emerging**, rising, budding, promising, talented *Opposite*: over-the-hill

up-and-down *adj* 1 **moody**, temperamental, changeable, tempestuous, turbulent *Opposite*: equable 2 **rising and falling**, bobbing, bouncing

upbeat *(infml) adj* **optimistic**, cheerful, positive, buoyant, bubbly *Opposite*: downbeat *(infml)*

upbraid *v* **scold**, reproach, tear a strip off, chastise, reprimand *Opposite*: praise

upbringing *n* **education**, childhood, background, rearing, nurture

update *v* 1 **inform**, bring up-to-date, keep informed, keep posted, fill in 2 **modernize**, revise, renew, bring up-to-date, renovate

upend *v* **turn over**, tip up, tip over, upset, topple *Opposite*: right

up-front *(infml) adj* **straightforward**, honest, frank, plain-spoken, open *Opposite*: coy

upgrade *v* 1 **promote**, advance, elevate, raise, move up *Opposite*: demote 2 **improve**, update, renew, modernize, renovate *Opposite*: downgrade ■ *n* 1 **promotion**, advancement, elevation, exaltation *Opposite*: demotion 2 **improvement**, upgrading, renovation, modernization, enhancement

upgrading *n* 1 **promotion**, advancement, step up, advance, progression *Opposite*: demotion 2 **improvement**, renovation, modernization, transformation, enhancement

upheaval *n* **disturbance**, turmoil, disorder, confusion, cataclysm *Opposite*: peace

upheave *v* **lift up**, raise, thrust up, elevate, lift *Opposite*: drop

uphill *adj* 1 **climbing**, ascending, rising, mounting *Opposite*: downhill 2 **difficult**, hard, arduous, demanding, tough *Opposite*: easy

uphold *v* **support**, sustain, maintain, defend, endorse

upholster *v* **cover**, pad, stuff, fill, decorate

upholstery *n* **fabric**, furnishings, covers, furniture, material

upkeep *n* **maintenance**, repairs, keep, conservation, preservation

upland *n* **moorland**, high ground, highland, plateau, tableland *Opposite*: lowland

uplift *v* 1 **elevate**, raise, hoist, lift *Opposite*: drop 2 **inspire**, enrich, improve, move, hearten *Opposite*: depress

uplifting *adj* **inspiring**, elevating, improving, enriching, heartening *Opposite*: depressing

uplighter *n* **standard lamp**, lamp, floor lamp *(US)*

upmarket *adj* **expensive**, high-class, smart, chic, exclusive *Opposite*: downmarket

upper *adj* **higher**, greater, better, superior *Opposite*: lower

upper circle *n* **gallery**, loggia, balcony, circle, dress circle

upper class *n* **aristocracy**, nobility, noblesse, gentry, elite *Opposite*: lower class

upper-class *adj* **aristocratic**, noble, blue-blooded, highborn *(literary) Opposite*: lower-class

upper crust *see* upper class

uppercut *n* **blow**, punch, hit, haymaker *(slang)*

upper hand *n* **advantage**, initiative, ascendancy, edge, control *Opposite*: disadvantage

uppermost *adj* 1 **highest**, top, topmost, upmost *Opposite*: bottom 2 **primary**, main, principal, chief, greatest *Opposite*: last

uppity *adj* 1 *(infml)* **presumptuous**, pretentious, snobbish, haughty, bumptious *Opposite*: humble 2 *(dated infml)* **stubborn**, difficult, cantankerous, irritable, tetchy *(infml) Opposite*: flexible

uprate *v* **increase**, raise, upgrade, up, adjust *Opposite*: decrease

upright *adj* **1 standing**, straight, vertical, erect *Opposite*: horizontal **2 righteous**, moral, honourable, decent, honest *Opposite*: immoral

uprightness *n* **righteousness**, morality, honourableness, decency, honesty *Opposite*: immorality

uprising *n* **rebellion**, revolution, revolt, rising, unrest

uproar *n* **disturbance**, noise, chaos, pandemonium, upheaval *Opposite*: quiet

uproarious *adj* **hilarious**, funny, riotous, raucous, boisterous

uproot *v* **1 pull up**, deracinate, dig up, rip up *Opposite*: plant **2 displace**, evacuate, move on, relocate, deracinate *Opposite*: settle

uprush *n* **rush**, surge, updraught, draught, blast

upset *v* **1 spill**, knock over, tip over, overturn, upend *Opposite*: right **2 disturb**, disrupt, reorder, reverse, mix up *Opposite*: order **3 distress**, hurt, disturb, sadden, trouble *Opposite*: please ■ *n* **1 defeat**, disappointment, affront, letdown, shock **2 surprise**, shock, confusion, disarray, disruption ■ *adj* **sad**, disturbed, unhappy, hurt, disappointed *Opposite*: composed

upset stomach *n* **indigestion**, stomachache, heartburn, bellyache *(infml)*, tummy ache *(infml)*

upsetting *adj* **distressing**, disturbing, hurtful, offensive, disappointing *Opposite*: pleasing

upshot *n* **result**, outcome, consequence, effect, end

upside *n* **advantage**, benefit, plus *(infml)*, positive *(infml)* *Opposite*: disadvantage

upside-down *adj* **1 upturned**, wrong way up, wrong side up, overturned, on its head *Opposite*: upright **2 in a mess**, in a state *(infml)*, messy, untidy, topsy-turvy *Opposite*: orderly

upstage *v* **outdo**, outmanoeuvre, put somebody's nose out of joint, outshine, surpass

upstanding *adj* **virtuous**, honest, decent, respectable, honourable *Opposite*: degenerate

upstart *n* **nobody**, unknown, parvenu, arriviste, nonentity *Opposite*: grandee

upstretched *adj* **raised**, upraised, upturned, outstretched, extended *Opposite*: hanging down

upsurge *n* **increase**, rise, surge, gain, expansion *Opposite*: decrease

upswing *n* **increase**, improvement, upturn, turnround, upsurge *Opposite*: downswing

uptake *n* **1 acceptance**, approval, interest, commitment, agreement *Opposite*: refusal **2 understanding**, comprehension, perception, appreciation, apprehension *Opposite*: incomprehension

up-tempo *adj* **exciting**, lively, fast, rapid, frenetic *Opposite*: dull

uptight *(infml) adj* **tense**, bothered, anxious, wound up, neurotic *Opposite*: calm

up-to-date *adj* **1 informed**, in touch, conversant, in the know, au fait **2 current**, latest, new, brand-new, modern *Opposite*: old-fashioned **3 fashionable**, cool, chic, trendy *(infml)*, à la mode *(dated) Opposite*: passé

up-to-the-minute *adj* **latest**, current, contemporary, state-of-the-art, contemporaneous *Opposite*: out-of-date

upturn *v* **overturn**, capsize, tip over, upset, turn turtle *Opposite*: right ■ *n* **improvement**, recovery, revival, growth, expansion *Opposite*: slump

upward *adj* **1 ascendant**, mounting, skyward, uphill, ascending *Opposite*: downward **2 rising**, improving, increasing, growing, expanding *Opposite*: downward

upwards *adv* **up**, uphill, higher, skyward, in the air

upwelling *n* **upsurge**, surge, burst, outburst, outpouring

upwind *adj* **windward**, exposed, open, bare, windy *Opposite*: leeward

up with *adj* **abreast**, up-to-date, familiar, conversant, au fait

urban *adj* **city**, town, built-up, municipal, inner-city *Opposite*: rural

urbane *adj* **sophisticated**, refined, courteous, suave, polished *Opposite*: unsophisticated

urbanite *n* **metropolitan**, cosmopolitan, citizen, resident, townie *(infml) Opposite*: rustic

urbanity *n* **sophistication**, refinement, courteousness, courtesy, suaveness *Opposite*: uncouthness

urbanization *n* **development**, suburbanization, expansion, sprawl, spread

urban myth *n* **myth**, folktale, tale, tall story, fable

urban sprawl *n* **urbanization**, development, suburbia, sprawl, expansion

urchin *n* **imp**, rascal, tyke, brat, tearaway

urge *v* **1 advise**, recommend, exhort, prevail on, press *Opposite*: dissuade **2 advocate**, commend, promote, back, support *Opposite*: downplay **3 encourage**, drive, push, force, impel *Opposite*: discourage ■ *n* **need**, wish, impulse, desire, inclination *Opposite*: disinclination

urgency *n* **1 need**, exigency, importance, necessity, hurry *Opposite*: unimportance **2 earnestness**, insistence, perseverance, firmness, resolve *Opposite*: vacillation

urgent *adj* **1 vital**, crucial, pressing, imperative, burning *Opposite*: trivial **2 earnest**, insistent, persuasive, pleading, demanding *Opposite*: half-hearted

urgently *adv* **immediately**, straightaway, instantly, at once, directly *Opposite*: whenever

urn *n* **vase**, container, vessel, pot, jug

usable *adj* **functional**, practical, serviceable, working, functioning *Opposite*: unusable

usage *n* **1 treatment**, handling, control, management, running **2 practice**, procedure, custom, norm, tradition

use *v* **1 employ**, make use of, utilize, exercise, bring into play *Opposite*: forgo **2 consume**, expend, spend, exhaust, use up *Opposite*: conserve **3 manipulate**, exploit, take advantage of, mistreat, abuse **4 behave toward**, handle, treat, manipulate, manage **5 benefit from**, make use of, enjoy, avail yourself of, tap ■ *n* **1 expenditure**, consumption, wear and tear, wastage, depletion *Opposite*: saving **2 treatment**, handling, manipulation, exploitation, management **3 employment**, application, utilization, exploitation, consumption *Opposite*: disuse **4 purpose**, function, application, service, role **5 usefulness**, help, assistance, benefit, aid *Opposite*: harm

COMPARE AND CONTRAST CORE MEANING: put something to use
use put something into action or service; **employ** make use of something such as a tool or a resource in a particular way; **make use of** use what is readily available, especially in a sensible or economical way; **utilize** find a practical or unintended use for something.

used *adj* **1 second-hand**, castoff, hand-me-down, recycled *Opposite*: new **2 expended**, old, worn, worn out, consumed *Opposite*: remaining **3 exploited**, taken advantage of, misused, manipulated, abused

used to *adj* **1 accustomed**, hardened, inured, schooled, conditioned *Opposite*: unaccustomed **2 familiar**, at home, au fait, at ease, easy *Opposite*: unfamiliar

useful *adj* **1 practical**, helpful, serviceable, of use, constructive *Opposite*: useless **2 convenient**, valuable, beneficial, advantageous, expedient *Opposite*: disadvantageous

usefulness *n* **1 practicality**, helpfulness, worth, utility, convenience *Opposite*: uselessness **2 valuableness**, convenience, advantageousness, expediency, suitability

useless *adj* **1 unusable**, impractical, unserviceable, inoperable, unworkable *Opposite*: useful **2 unsuccessful**, futile, ineffectual, unavailing, worthless *Opposite*: successful **3** (*infml*) **inept**, hopeless, incompetent, inefficient, ineffectual *Opposite*: effective

uselessness *n* **1 impracticality**, unusableness, inoperability, unworkability, inadequacy *Opposite*: usefulness **2 unsuccessfulness**, pointlessness, futility, ineffectualness, ineffectiveness *Opposite*: worth **3** (*infml*) **ineptness**, hopelessness, ineffectiveness, incompetence, inefficiency *Opposite*: effectiveness

user *n* **operator**, worker, employer, manipulator, handler

user-friendliness *n* **accessibility**, manageability, handiness, manipulability, convenience *Opposite*: inaccessibility

user-friendly *adj* **accessible**, comprehensible, intelligible, manipulable, manageable *Opposite*: inaccessible

use up *v* **expend**, consume, exhaust, wear out, deplete *Opposite*: conserve

usher *n* **attendant**, escort, guide, leader, conductor ■ *v* **escort**, conduct, guide, steer, pilot

usher in *v* **herald**, introduce, lead to, announce, signal *Opposite*: see out

usual *adj* **1 normal**, typical, common, standard, natural *Opposite*: exceptional **2 habitual**, routine, everyday, customary, familiar *Opposite*: irregular

COMPARE AND CONTRAST CORE MEANING: often done, used, bought, or consumed
usual normal, common, or typical; **customary** conforming to regular or typical practice; **habitual** done so often or repeatedly that the behaviour or practice has become ingrained; **routine** normal, regular, and usual in every way, even predictable, repetitive, and monotonous; **wonted** (*fml*) usual or typical.

usually *adv* **normally**, typically, customarily, generally, by and large *Opposite*: exceptionally

usurp *v* **seize**, appropriate, take over, assume, commandeer *Opposite*: surrender

usury *n* **moneylending**, overcharging, extortion, daylight robbery (*infml*), highway robbery (*US infml*)

utensil *n* **tool**, instrument, implement, appliance, device

WORD BANK
❑ **types of utensil** beater, bottle opener, can opener, corkscrew, drainer, garlic press, grater, juice extractor, lemon squeezer, liquidizer, mill, mincer, mortar, nutcracker, opener, peeler, pestle, sieve, soup ladle, spatula, strainer, tin-opener, whisk

utilitarian *adj* **practical**, useful, serviceable, functional, down-to-earth *Opposite*: useless

utility *n* **1 usefulness**, practicality, efficiency, handiness, helpfulness *Opposite*: uselessness **2 convenience**, service, benefit, worth, advantage *Opposite*: worthlessness

utilization *n* **use**, application, employment, deployment, operation

utilize *v* **use**, apply, employ, operate, develop *Opposite*: forgo. *See* COMPARE AND CONTRAST *at* use.

utmost *adj* **1 greatest**, highest, extreme, chief, supreme *Opposite*: least **2 farthest**, extreme, most distant, farthermost, remotest

utopia *n* **ideal**, paradise, never-never land, heaven, Shangri-la

utopian *adj* **1 ideal**, perfect, ultimate, best, model **2 idealistic**, naive, impracticable, impractical, unworkable *Opposite*: pragmatic ■ *n* **idealist**, romantic, visionary, dreamer, purist *Opposite*: pragmatist

utter *v* **say**, speak, pronounce, express, state ■ *adj* **absolute**, total, complete, sheer, downright *Opposite*: partial

utterance *n* **1 word**, sound, note, noise, exclamation *Opposite*: silence **2 statement**, speech, remark, declaration, announcement

U-turn *n* **1 turn**, rotation, revolution, about-turn, volte-face **2 change**, reversal, climbdown, volte face, about-turn

vacancy *n* **job**, post, situation *(fml)*, position, opening

vacant *adj* **1 empty**, available, unoccupied, not in use, void *Opposite*: occupied **2 blank**, empty, expressionless, indifferent, vacuous *Opposite*: alert

COMPARE AND CONTRAST CORE MEANING: lacking contents or occupants

vacant without occupants or contents, often temporarily; **unoccupied** not lived in by anybody, or currently without occupants; **empty** not containing or holding anything, or without occupants; **void** having no contents, or having no incumbent, occupant, or holder.

vacate *v* **1 empty**, evacuate, clear out, free, divest *Opposite*: fill **2 leave**, relinquish, check out, give up, depart *Opposite*: occupy

vacation *n* **holiday**, break, trip, rest, retreat

vaccinate *v* **inoculate**, immunize, protect, jab *Opposite*: expose

vaccination *n* **inoculation**, injection, immunization, jab *(infml)*, shot *(infml)*

vaccine *n* **inoculation**, injection, serum, preparation, shot *(infml)*

vacillate *v* **waver**, hesitate, chop and change, dither, think twice *Opposite*: decide. *See* COMPARE AND CONTRAST *at* **hesitate**.

vacillating *adj* **irresolute**, indecisive, hesitant, dithering, fickle *Opposite*: resolute

vacillation *n* **indecisiveness**, irresoluteness, indecision, irresolution, hesitancy *Opposite*: resolution

vacuity *(fml)* *n* **mindlessness**, blankness, vacantness, inaneness, stupidity *Opposite*: intelligence

vacuous *adj* **stupid**, unintelligent, inane, vacant, mindless *Opposite*: intelligent

vacuum *n* **void**, space, emptiness, nothingness, blankness

vagabond *n* **vagrant**, tramp, beggar, drifter, traveller *Opposite*: resident

vagary *n* **whim**, fancy, notion, mood, quirk *Opposite*: choice

vagrancy *n* **homelessness**, penury, destitution, rootlessness, begging *Opposite*: residence

vagrant *n* **vagabond**, tramp, beggar, drifter, hobo *Opposite*: resident ■ *adj* **nomadic**, itinerant, wandering, roaming, roving *Opposite*: settled

vague *adj* **1 unclear**, imprecise, indefinite, ambiguous, equivocal *Opposite*: definite **2 indistinct**, unclear, indistinguishable, hazy, fuzzy *Opposite*: clear **3 absent-minded**, abstracted, distracted, distant, unclear *Opposite*: alert

vagueness *n* **1 nebulousness**, imprecision, indistinctness, ambiguity, elusiveness *Opposite*: precision **2 abstraction**, absent-mindedness, pensiveness, dreaminess *Opposite*: attentiveness **3 haziness**, fuzziness, formlessness, imprecision, blurredness *Opposite*: clarity

vain *adj* **1 proud**, conceited, narcissistic, arrogant, self-important *Opposite*: humble **2 useless**, ineffective, otiose, unsuccessful, hopeless *Opposite*: successful **3 empty**, hollow, idle, pointless, futile *Opposite*: reliable

COMPARE AND CONTRAST CORE MEANING: without substance or unlikely to be carried though

vain failing to have or unlikely to have the intended or desired result; **empty** lacking substance, sincerity, or truthfulness; **hollow** not sincere or genuine; **idle** unlikely to be carried out or impossible to put into effect.

valediction *(fml)* *n* **farewell**, goodbye, sendoff, adieu *(literary)*, leave-taking *(literary)*

valedictory *(fml)* *n* **farewell**, goodbye, parting, leave-taking *(literary)* *Opposite*: welcome ■ *adj* **parting**, farewell, goodbye, final, last *Opposite*: welcoming

valet *v* **clean**, clean out, vacuum, tidy, polish

valetudinarian *n* **1 convalescent**, patient, invalid, valetudinary **2 hypochondriac**, neurotic, valetudinary ■ *adj* **sickly**, feeble, unhealthy, frail, weak *Opposite*: healthy

valiant *adj* **brave**, courageous, heroic, fearless, noble *Opposite*: cowardly

valid *adj* **1 reasonable**, sound, rational, justifiable, legitimate *Opposite*: unjustifiable **2 lawful**, legal, binding, effective, in force *Opposite*: illegal **3 usable**, acceptable, authorized, endorsed, official *Opposite*: unusable **4 convincing**, compelling, sound, persuasive, cogent *Opposite*: unconvincing

COMPARE AND CONTRAST CORE MEANING: worthy of acceptance or credence
valid having a solid foundation or justification; **cogent** forceful and convincing to the intellect and reason; **convincing** likely to overcome doubts and win the support of those who hear it; **reasonable** acceptable and according to common sense; **sound** based on good sense and acceptable reasoning and worthy of approval.

validate *v* **1 prove**, substantiate, confirm, authenticate, corroborate *Opposite*: disprove **2 authorize**, certify, endorse, ratify, legalize *Opposite*: invalidate

validation *n* **1 authentication**, proof, endorsement, confirmation, corroboration **2 authorization**, endorsement, ratification, certification, legalization *Opposite*: invalidation

validity *n* **1 legality**, authority, legitimacy, authenticity, lawfulness **2 cogency**, rationality, legitimacy, soundness, strength *Opposite*: weakness

valley *n* **gorge**, dale, basin, vale *(literary)*, dell *(literary) Opposite*: hill

valorous *adj* **noble**, brave, courageous, heroic, fearless *Opposite*: cowardly

valour *n* **boldness**, courage, bravery, heroism, fearlessness *Opposite*: cowardice

valuable *adj* **1 costly**, expensive, priceless, dear, important *Opposite*: inexpensive **2 invaluable**, helpful, important, valued, useful *Opposite*: worthless **3 cherished**, valued, appreciated, respected, treasured

valuation *n* **estimate**, assessment, evaluation, appraisal, survey

value *n* **1 worth**, price, cost, rate, charge **2 benefit**, importance, worth, significance, usefulness *Opposite*: insignificance ■ *v* **1 rate**, assess, estimate, evaluate, appraise **2 prize**, appreciate, respect, esteem, treasure *Opposite*: scorn

valued *adj* **appreciated**, respected, esteemed, treasured, cherished

valueless *adj* **inconsequential**, worthless, insignificant, paltry, miserable *Opposite*: valuable

values *n* **principles**, standards, morals, ethics, ideals

valve *n* **regulator**, controller, stopcock, tap, spigot

vampire *n* **parasite**, hanger-on, predator, sponge, freeloader *(infml)*

vamp up *v* **repair**, rework, revamp, do up, modernize

van *n* **forefront**, front, lead, head, vanguard

vandal *n* **criminal**, trespasser, delinquent, thug, hooligan *(infml)*

vandalism *n* **damage**, destruction, defacement, wreckage, sabotage

vandalize *v* **destroy**, damage, deface, wreck, break

vane *n* **blade**, slat, fin, plate, strip

vanguard *n* **1 front line**, front, advance guard *Opposite*: rearguard **2 forefront**, front, lead, head, cutting edge

vanish *v* **1 disappear**, evaporate, go missing, fade away, peter out *Opposite*: appear **2 become extinct**, die out, disappear, cease to exist, be exterminated

vanished *adj* **disappeared**, missing, died out, gone, extinct *Opposite*: present

vanity *n* **1 pride**, narcissism, self-importance, conceit, arrogance *Opposite*: humility **2 futility**, emptiness, uselessness, pointlessness, worthlessness *Opposite*: value

vanquish *v* **defeat**, conquer, subjugate, crush, subdue *Opposite*: surrender. *See* COMPARE AND CONTRAST *at* **defeat**.

vantage point *n* **1 viewpoint**, viewing platform, belvedere, lookout, crow's nest **2 standpoint**, viewpoint, angle, point of view, perspective

vapid *adj* **1 lifeless**, uninteresting, unexciting, vacuous, tame *Opposite*: lively **2 flavourless**, insipid, tasteless, weak, tame *Opposite*: tasty

vaporize *v* **1 turn to vapour**, evaporate, boil away, boil, heat *Opposite*: condense **2 vanish**, disappear, evaporate, fade away, go away **3 destroy**, annihilate, burn, incinerate, burn away *Opposite*: preserve

vaporizer *n* **nebulizer**, atomizer, aerosol, spray, inhaler

vaporous *adj* **1 gaseous**, smoky, misty, steamy, foggy **2 volatile**, unstable, unpredictable, explosive, flammable *Opposite*: stable **3 insubstantial**, ephemeral, impermanent, evanescent, nebulous *Opposite*: solid **4 fanciful**, ridiculous, implausible, fantastic, unreal *Opposite*: real **5 murky**, hazy, cloudy, obscure, dim *Opposite*: clear

vapour *n* **1 gas**, air, ether **2 clouds**, fumes, smoke, water vapour, miasma **3 aerosol**, spray, mist

variability *n* **1 erraticism**, inconsistency, capriciousness, changeability, unpredictability *Opposite*: predictability **2 unevenness**, patchiness, irregularity, inconsistency *Opposite*: consistency **3 flexibility**, adaptability, fickleness, inconstancy, mutability *Opposite*: fixedness

variable *adj* **1 varying**, changing, fluctuating, changeable, erratic *Opposite*: constant **2 uneven**, patchy, up-and-down, irregular, inconsistent *Opposite*: consistent **3 mutable**, adjustable, flexible, capricious, inconstant *Opposite*: fixed

variance *n* **1 alteration**, modification, adjustment, change **2 divergence**, disparity, difference, discrepancy, inconsistency *Opposite*: consistency **3 conflict**, clash, dissent, dispute, difference of opinion *Opposite*: agreement

variant adj irregular, different, optional, modified, abnormal ■ n **variation**, alternative, deviation, modification, departure

variation n 1 variant, adaptation, reworking, departure, alteration 2 **difference**, disparity, dissimilarity, distinction, discrepancy Opposite: similarity

varied adj **heterogeneous**, diverse, wide-ranging, mixed, different Opposite: homogeneous

variegated adj **spotted**, mottled, pied, dappled, speckled Opposite: uniform

variety n 1 **diversity**, change, variability, variation Opposite: monotony 2 **type**, kind, form, sort, category 3 **collection**, diversity, assortment, selection, multiplicity

variety show n show, revue, cabaret, entertainment, performance

various adj 1 **numerous**, many, a number of, several, countless Opposite: few 2 **a variety of**, a range of, an assortment of, a mixture of, different Opposite: same

varnish n lacquer, paint, finish, glaze, coating ■ v paint, glaze, finish, polish, lacquer

vary v 1 **change**, alter, fluctuate, adjust, adapt Opposite: standardize 2 **diverge**, differ, be different, contrast, fluctuate Opposite: conform. See COMPARE AND CONTRAST at **change**.

vase n rose bowl, urn, jug, pot, container

vast adj **massive**, huge, enormous, gigantic, immense Opposite: small

vastly adv **much**, greatly, infinitely, immensely, immeasurably Opposite: slightly

vastness n **massiveness**, incalculability, limitlessness, immensity, hugeness

vat n container, cask, barrel, tank, drum

vault n 1 **arch**, dome, cupola 2 **crypt**, cellar, mausoleum, undercroft, burial chamber 3 **strongroom**, treasury, safe, treasure house ■ v jump, leap, spring, hurdle, bound

vaulted adj **curved**, domed, arched

vaunt v **puff**, boast, brag, show off, hype Opposite: play down

vaunted adj **hyped**, praised, promoted, advertised, flaunted Opposite: downplayed

vector n course, trajectory, path, flight path, route

veer v **change course**, turn, swing, swerve, bend

vegan n fruitarian, vegetarian, veggie (infml)

vegetable adj **plant**, herbal, vegetal

WORD BANK
❑ types of **root vegetable** beet, beetroot, carrot, cassava, celeriac, mangel-wurzel, new potato, pak choi, parsnip, potato, rutabaga, sugar beet, swede, sweet potato, turnip, yam
❑ types of **vegetable** artichoke, asparagus, aubergine, brassica, broccoli, Brussels sprout, cabbage, cauliflower, corn on the cob, courgette, fennel, garlic, greens, kale, leek, marrow, okra, onion, pumpkin, spinach, squash, sweetcorn, Swiss chard

vegetarian n **fruitarian**, vegan, lacto-vegetarian, ovolactovegetarian, veggie (infml)

vegetate v sit around, stagnate, twiddle your thumbs, kill time, loaf

vegetation n **plants**, plant life, flora, ground cover, bedding

veggie (infml) n lactovegetarian, fruitarian, vegetarian, ovolactovegetarian, vegan

vehemence n **forcefulness**, intensity, fervour, passion, violence Opposite: indifference

vehement adj **fervent**, passionate, heated, violent, intense Opposite: apathetic

vehicle n 1 **means of transport**, transport, conveyance 2 **medium**, means of expression, channel, means, mouthpiece

WORDBANK
❑ types of **commercial or industrial vehicle** articulated lorry, backhoe, black cab, breakdown lorry, bulldozer, cab, combine, combine harvester, crane, digger, dumper truck, earthmover, hackney cab, hackney carriage, hearse, juggernaut, lorry, minicab, pick-up, removal van, roadroller, snowplough, steamroller, tanker, taxi, tractor, transporter, truck, van
❑ types of **leisure vehicle** all-terrain vehicle, bobsleigh, cablecar, camper, campervan, caravan, chair lift, dogsled, dune buggy, go-cart, golf cart, land yacht, luge, mobile home, motor home, sledge, sleigh, snowmobile, toboggan, trailer
❑ types of **military vehicle** amphibian, armoured car, jeep, tank
❑ types of **public service vehicle** ambulance, bus, charabanc, coach, dustcart, fire engine, minibus, panda car (infml), police car, shuttle, squad car
❑ types of **control** accelerator, brake, choke, clutch, gas gauge, gear lever, horn, pedal, rev counter, speedometer, steering wheel, wheel
❑ types of **internal feature** air bag, back seat, booster seat, cab, child seat, cup holder, dashboard, driving seat, glove compartment, headrest, passenger seat, rearview mirror, seat belt, sound system, sun visor
❑ types of **external feature** brake light, bumper, exhaust pipe, fog light, hazard light, headlight, high beam, hubcap, indicator, kick-start, mud flap, mudguard, number plate, plate, roof rack, sidelight, silencer, tail light, turn signal, tyre, wheel, windscreen wiper, wing mirror
❑ parts of an **external structure** aerofoil, axle, bodywork, bonnet, boot, chassis, coachwork, fin, grille, hull, side mirror, spoiler, sunroof, tailgate, windscreen, wing

veil n mask, blanket, shroud, covering, curtain ■ v cover, conceal, hide, mask, cloak Opposite: reveal

veiled adj 1 **indirect**, oblique, obscure, covert, roundabout Opposite: overt 2 **masked**, cloaked, shrouded, covered, hooded *Opposite*: uncovered

vein *n* **1 layer**, seam, lode, stratum, deposit **2 mood**, frame of mind, manner, strain, attitude **3 streak**, strip, stripe, line

veined *adj* **patterned**, marbled, lined, streaked

veld *n* **grassland**, savanna, prairie, plain

veldt *see* veld

velocity *n* **speed**, rate, rapidity, swiftness, pace

velvety *adj* **soft**, smooth, silky, downy, furry *Opposite*: rough

venal *adj* **1 corruptible**, mercenary, bribable, bent, unprincipled *Opposite*: honest **2 corrupt**, degenerate, decadent, lawless, amoral *Opposite*: aboveboard

vend *v* **sell**, trade, deal in, hawk, flog *(infml)*

vendetta *n* **1 feud**, blood feud, quarrel, dispute, grudge **2 campaign**, crusade, war, battle, hate campaign

vending machine *n* **slot machine**, dispenser, snack machine, coin-operated machine

vendor *n* **seller**, retailer, dealer, supplier, merchant

veneer *n* **1 covering**, facing, finish, surface, layer **2 appearance**, semblance, pretence, guise, show ■ *v* **cover**, finish, conceal, plate

venerable *adj* **respected**, esteemed, honoured, revered, admired *Opposite*: disreputable

venerate *v* **revere**, worship, adore, idolize, esteem *Opposite*: disrespect

veneration *n* **worship**, adoration, reverence, honour, respect *Opposite*: disdain. *See* COMPARE AND CONTRAST *at* regard.

vengeance *n* **revenge**, retribution, reprisal, retaliation, punishment

vengeful *adj* **vindictive**, implacable, unforgiving, revengeful, resentful *Opposite*: merciful

venial *adj* **forgivable**, excusable, pardonable, understandable, minor *Opposite*: unforgivable

venom *n* **1 poison**, toxin, bane *Opposite*: antidote **2 malice**, spite, rancour, spleen, acrimony *Opposite*: affection

venomous *adj* **1 poisonous**, deadly, toxic, noxious, lethal *Opposite*: harmless **2 malicious**, spiteful, virulent, bitter, rancorous

vent *n* **opening**, outlet, aperture, escape, exhaust ■ *v* **express**, give vent to, find expression for, voice, release *Opposite*: suppress

ventilate *v* **1 air**, aerate, air out, freshen **2 publicize**, make public, make known, air, express

ventilation *n* **air circulation**, airing, aeration

ventilator *n* **1 fan**, vent, opening, flue, aperture **2 life support machine**, respirator, breathing apparatus, iron lung

venture *n* **1 undertaking**, course, endeavour, project, mission **2 business enterprise**, undertaking, scheme, project, endeavour ■ *v* **1 hazard**, dare, undertake, brave, try **2 offer**, put forward, volunteer, express, say **3 presume**, dare, be so bold, take the liberty, have the audacity

venturesome *(fml)* *adj* **1 daring**, adventurous, enterprising, bold, brave *Opposite*: cautious **2 hazardous**, chancy, dangerous, risky, perilous *Opposite*: safe

venue *n* **site**, place, location, scene, setting

veracious *adj* **honest**, truthful, genuine, principled, dependable *Opposite*: dishonest

veracity *n* **1 truth**, accuracy, reliability, genuineness, authenticity *Opposite*: falsity **2 truthfulness**, honesty, integrity, uprightness, reliability *Opposite*: dishonesty

veranda *n* **terrace**, balcony, porch, loggia, gallery

verbal *adj* **spoken**, oral, vocal, unwritten, voiced *Opposite*: unspoken

---

COMPARE AND CONTRAST CORE MEANING: expressed in words

verbal using words, especially spoken words, rather than pictures or physical action; **spoken** expressed with the voice; **oral** expressed in spoken form rather than in writing.

---

verbalization *n* **articulation**, expression, speech, voicing

verbalize *v* **express**, articulate, voice, put into words, speak

verbatim *adj* **exact**, word for word, precise, literal, word-perfect *Opposite*: imprecise ■ *adv* **word for word**, exactly, precisely, to the letter, literally *Opposite*: approximately

verbiage *n* **empty words**, claptrap *(infml)*, waffle *(infml)*, gobbledegook *(infml)*

verbose *adj* **wordy**, prolix, long-winded, talkative, bombastic *Opposite*: taciturn. *See* COMPARE AND CONTRAST *at* wordy.

verbosity *n* **long-windedness**, garrulousness, wordiness, prolixity, loquaciousness *Opposite*: succinctness

verdant *adj* **green**, lush, luxuriant, fertile, leafy

verdict *n* **decision**, judgment, finding, result, outcome

verdigris *n* **patina**, tarnish, corrosion, greenness, coloration

verdure *n* **greenery**, lushness, vegetation, flora, plant life

verge *n* **edge**, border, threshold, approach, limit ■ *v* **be near to**, approach, border on, come close to, near

verge on *see* verge

verifiable *adj* **demonstrable**, provable, confirmable, certifiable, showable *Opposite*: moot

verification *n* **confirmation**, corroboration, proof, substantiation, authentication *Opposite*: contradiction

verified *adj* **confirmed**, proved, shown, tested, substantiated *Opposite*: unconfirmed

verify v **confirm**, bear out, prove, authenticate, validate *Opposite*: disprove

verisimilitude *(fml)* n **truth**, credibility, authenticity, reliability, plausibility *Opposite*: falsity

veritable adj **absolute**, real, genuine, out-and-out, authentic *Opposite*: false

verity *(fml)* n **truth**, fact, principle, reality, sincerity

verminous adj **infested**, pest-ridden, louse-ridden, rat-infested, crawling

vernacular n **dialect**, language, patois, argot, colloquial speech

versatile adj **1 adaptable**, flexible, resourceful, multitalented, all-round *Opposite*: inflexible **2 multipurpose**, adaptable, handy, useful, nifty *(infml)* *Opposite*: inflexible

versatility n **1 adaptability**, flexibility, resourcefulness *Opposite*: inflexibility **2 usefulness**, handiness, niftiness *(infml)*

verse n **1 stanza**, canto, section, unit **2 poetry**, rhyme, blank verse, free verse, doggerel *Opposite*: prose

versed adj **experienced**, competent, conversant, proficient, knowledgeable *Opposite*: inexperienced

version n **1 account**, description, report, side, story **2 form**, type, variety, kind, sort **3 adaptation**, edition, translation, rendering

versus prep **1 against**, contra, in competition with **2 as opposed to**, contrasted with, set against, against, as against

vertebrate n **animal**, mammal, bird, reptile, amphibian *Opposite*: invertebrate

vertex n **apex**, summit, height, pinnacle, apogee *Opposite*: base

vertical adj **perpendicular**, upright, erect, straight up, straight down *Opposite*: horizontal

vertiginous adj **high**, dizzying, tall, lofty, exposed

vertigo n **dizziness**, giddiness, unsteadiness, faintness, lightheadedness

verve n **vitality**, energy, dynamism, vigour, dash *Opposite*: lethargy

very adv **extremely**, incredibly, awfully, exceptionally, exceedingly *Opposite*: a bit *(infml)* ■ adj **actual**, self-same, same, identical, exact

vessel n **1 container**, pot, bowl, jug, pitcher **2 boat**, ship, craft

vest v **devolve**, consign, entrust, assign, lodge

vested interest n **1 special interest**, interest, concern, stake, investment **2 stakeholder**, supporter, shareholder

vestibule n **entrance hall**, foyer, lobby, antechamber, atrium

vestige n **trace**, sign, mark, indication, hint

vestigial adj **1 residual**, remaining, imperceptible, token **2 nonfunctioning**, functionless, stunted, degenerate, atrophic *Opposite*: functional

vestment n **1 robe**, garment, dress, habit, uniform **2 surplice**, chasuble, cope, vesture *(archaic)*

vet v **examine**, check, scrutinize, research, inspect

veteran n **expert**, old hand, past master, trouper, old-timer *Opposite*: novice

veto n **1 rejection**, refusal, bar, disallowance, prevention *Opposite*: approval **2 prohibition**, ban, sanction, embargo, order *Opposite*: release ■ v **1 reject**, turn down, bar, disallow, refuse *Opposite*: approve **2 prohibit**, ban, forbid, outlaw, proscribe *Opposite*: permit

vex v **1 annoy**, displease, irk, irritate, anger *Opposite*: pacify **2 agitate**, distress, trouble, bother, torment *Opposite*: placate **3 confound**, confuse, perplex, puzzle, tease *Opposite*: enlighten

vexation n **annoyance**, upset, displeasure, bother, irritation *Opposite*: satisfaction

vexatious adj **annoying**, upsetting, irritating, troublesome, bothersome *Opposite*: placatory

vexed adj **1 irritated**, provoked, annoyed, upset, angry *Opposite*: calm **2 debated**, controversial, contentious, fractious, problematic *Opposite*: uncomplicated

vexing adj **annoying**, puzzling, frustrating, worrying, worrisome *Opposite*: easy

via prep **by way of**, through, by

viability n **practicability**, feasibility, practicality, capability, sustainability *Opposite*: impracticality

viable adj **practicable**, worthwhile, feasible, practical, sustainable *Opposite*: impossible

vial n **ampoule**, vessel, container, flask, bottle

vibrancy n **vitality**, vivacity, animation, enthusiasm, effervescence *Opposite*: lethargy

vibrant adj **1 pulsating**, energetic, vibrating, effervescent, alive *Opposite*: listless **2 bright**, dazzling, vivid, brilliant, flamboyant *Opposite*: dull

vibrate v **shake**, quiver, tremble, shudder, judder

vibration n **shaking**, quivering, trembling, shuddering, juddering *Opposite*: stillness

vicarage n **rectory**, manse, church house, parsonage, residence

vicarious adj **1 displaced**, indirect, remote, removed, distanced *Opposite*: direct **2 empathetic**, sympathetic, assumed, imagined, adopted **3 delegated**, surrogate, substitute, proxy, deputized

vice n **1 depravity**, iniquity, evil, wickedness, immorality *Opposite*: goodness **2 defect**, failing, flaw, imperfection, fault *Opposite*: strength

vicinal adj **1 neighbouring**, adjacent, nearby, close, proximate *Opposite*: distant **2 local**, district, municipal, regional, provincial *Opposite*: international

vicinity n **neighbourhood**, environs, locality, district, area

vicious adj 1 **ferocious**, savage, wild, brutish, fierce Opposite: gentle 2 **spiteful**, malicious, mean, rancorous, backbiting Opposite: kind

vicious circle n **catch-22**, no-win situation, impasse, stalemate

viciousness n 1 **ferociousness**, savagery, wildness, brutishness, ferocity Opposite: gentleness 2 **maliciousness**, meanness, spitefulness, rancorousness, venomousness Opposite: kindness

vicissitudes n **changes**, variations, vagaries, ups and downs, fluctuations

victim n 1 **fatality**, casualty, sufferer, injured party 2 **dupe**, butt, target, object, prey

victimization n **persecution**, discrimination, oppression, ill-treatment, harassment Opposite: favouritism

victimize v **persecute**, discriminate against, harass, oppress, pick on Opposite: favour

victor n **winner**, champion, conqueror, medallist, prizewinner Opposite: loser

victorious adj **winning**, triumphant, champion, prizewinning, successful Opposite: losing

victory n **conquest**, triumph, win, success Opposite: defeat

victuals n **food**, provisions, supplies, foodstuffs, food and drink

video v **videotape**, record, tape, film, capture

WORD BANK
❑ **types of video equipment** camcorder, DVD, palmcorder, video camera, video cassette, video cassette recorder, videodisk, video recorder, videotape

---

video display terminal n **screen**, monitor, interface, terminal, viewer

videotape v **record**, video, tape, film, capture

vie v **compete**, contend, contest, strive, fight Opposite: collaborate

view n 1 **sight**, vision, observation, examination, scrutiny 2 **scene**, picture, spectacle, prospect, vista 3 **opinion**, interpretation, assessment, understanding ■ v 1 **look at**, see, regard, observe, notice 2 **inspect**, examine, look over, look at, observe 3 **consider**, regard, think of, perceive, look on

viewable adj 1 **available**, on view, on display, accessible 2 **fit**, presentable, acceptable, all right, appropriate Opposite: inappropriate

viewer n **watcher**, spectator, onlooker, ogler, observer

viewing n 1 **watching**, inspecting, seeing, observing, looking 2 **programming**, broadcasts, programmes, broadcasting, showing

viewpoint n 1 **point of view**, view, perspective, standpoint, position 2 **vantage point**, viewing platform, belvedere, lookout, crow's nest

vigil n **night watch**, watch, wake

vigilance n **watchfulness**, attentiveness, observance, care, caution Opposite: inattentiveness

vigilant adj **watchful**, alert, attentive, on your guard, wary Opposite: inattentive. See COMPARE AND CONTRAST at **cautious**.

vignette n 1 **design**, decoration, illustration, frontispiece, picture 2 **essay**, article, piece, monograph 3 **picture**, painting, drawing, photograph, print 4 **scene**, extract, clip, fragment, snippet

vigorous adj **robust**, active, strong, energetic, dynamic Opposite: feeble

vigour n 1 **vitality**, energy, robustness, strength, heartiness Opposite: lethargy 2 **intensity**, forcefulness, force, ferocity, gusto Opposite: feebleness 3 **potency**, strength, life, robustness, stamina Opposite: weakness

vile adj 1 **disgusting**, loathsome, revolting, repulsive, repellent Opposite: admirable 2 **evil**, wicked, shameful, depraved, base Opposite: good 3 **unpleasant**, horrid, horrible, dreadful, awful Opposite: pleasant. See COMPARE AND CONTRAST at **mean**.

vileness n 1 **evil**, depravity, wickedness, lowness, degradation Opposite: goodness 2 **unpleasantness**, dreadfulness, awfulness, horridness, horribleness Opposite: pleasantness 3 **repulsiveness**, loathsomeness, hatefulness, despicableness

vilification n **maliciousness**, abuse, disparagement, criticism, backbiting Opposite: acclaim

vilify v **malign**, abuse, denigrate, belittle, disparage Opposite: compliment. See COMPARE AND CONTRAST at **malign**.

village n **hamlet**, rural community, settlement

villager n **country dweller**, rustic, country cousin (dated)

villain n **scoundrel**, rogue, desperado, heavy, baddie (infml) Opposite: hero

villainous adj 1 **wicked**, criminal, heinous, depraved, iniquitous Opposite: good 2 **unpleasant**, undesirable, obnoxious, offensive, unreliable Opposite: pleasant

villainy n **wickedness**, wrongdoing, evil, foul play, badness Opposite: goodness

vim (infml) n **vitality**, energy, exuberance, verve, vigour Opposite: lethargy

vindicate v 1 **justify**, maintain, claim, support, defend 2 **clear**, exonerate, absolve, acquit, exculpate (fml) Opposite: implicate

vindication n 1 **exoneration**, absolution, acquittal, exculpation (fml) Opposite: implication 2 **justification**, evidence, proof, assertion

vindictive adj 1 **vengeful**, unforgiving, revengeful, rancorous, implacable Opposite: forgiving 2 **spiteful**, malicious, mean, cruel, hurtful Opposite: kind

vindictiveness n 1 **spite**, malice, cruelty, nastiness, unkindness Opposite: kindness 2 **vengefulness**, bitterness, rancour, resentment

vine n climber, creeper, liana

vinegary adj 1 sour, astringent, acidic, acid, tart Opposite: sweet 2 irritable, sour, bitter, embittered, unpleasant Opposite: pleasant

vintage n era, time, age, epoch, period ■ adj 1 classic, typical, traditional, essential, prime Opposite: atypical 2 out-of-date, dated, antique, old, outmoded Opposite: new

vinyl n LPs, records, discs, singles, albums

violate v 1 disregard, infringe, defy, breach, disobey Opposite: obey 2 disrupt, disturb, interrupt, encroach upon, intrude upon Opposite: respect 3 defile, desecrate, spoil, destroy, ruin Opposite: venerate

violation n 1 infringement, breach, contravention, defiance, disobedience Opposite: obedience 2 disruption, intrusion, encroachment, disturbance, interruption Opposite: respect 3 defilement, desecration, destruction, ruin, abuse Opposite: veneration

violence n 1 physical force, pugnaciousness, pugnacity, aggression, fighting Opposite: passivity 2 ferocity, strength, force, fierceness, viciousness Opposite: gentleness

violent adj 1 pugnacious, aggressive, brutal, cruel, sadistic Opposite: peaceful 2 fierce, ferocious, vehement, vicious, forceful Opposite: gentle

VIP n dignitary, name, luminary, star, celebrity

viperish adj malicious, spiteful, nasty, unkind, malevolent Opposite: kind

virtual adj 1 near, practical, effective, fundamental, essential Opposite: actual 2 computer-generated, simulated, cybernetic

virtually adv 1 in effect, effectively, essentially, fundamentally, to all intents and purposes 2 almost, nearly, near, nigh on, close to

virtual reality n computer modelling, simulated reality, computer simulation, simulation, VR

virtue n 1 goodness, righteousness, integrity, honesty, morality Opposite: wickedness 2 asset, feature, quality, advantage, benefit Opposite: disadvantage

virtuosity n skill, technique, brilliance, flair, talent

virtuoso n 1 musician, bravura player, artist, maestro 2 wunderkind, genius, prodigy, ace (infml), wizard (infml)

virtuous adj good, righteous, worthy, honourable, moral Opposite: bad

virulent adj 1 infectious, contagious, poisonous, lethal, strong Opposite: weak 2 malicious, bitter, vituperative, venomous, fierce Opposite: kind

virus n 1 illness, infection, sickness, disease 2 computer virus, Trojan horse, worm

visa n endorsement, pass, entry permit, documents, papers

visage n look, appearance, aspect, form, mien (fml)

vis-à-vis prep 1 regarding, in relation to, in respect of, re, with reference to 2 versus, compared with, contrasted with, in comparison with, opposite to

viscera n internal organs, intestines, entrails, guts, bowels

visceral adj instinctual, instinctive, intuitive, gut, primitive Opposite: reasoned

viscid adj thick, sticky, gooey, gluey, treacly Opposite: runny

viscosity n viscidness, thickness, stickiness, gluiness, gooeyness Opposite: fluidity

viscous adj viscid, thick, sticky, glutinous, gelatinous Opposite: runny

visibility n 1 discernibility, perceptibility, conspicuousness, luminosity Opposite: invisibility 2 prominence, familiarity, profile, image, high profile

visible adj 1 noticeable, observable, perceptible, evident, in evidence Opposite: invisible 2 prominent, high-profile, familiar, ubiquitous

vision n 1 eyesight, sight, ability to see 2 concept, mental picture, idea, image, visualization 3 revelation, prophecy, dream, hallucination, apparition 4 foresight, imagination, forethought, prescience, farsightedness

visionary adj 1 inventive, creative, farseeing, prescient, original Opposite: unimaginative 2 unrealistic, impracticable, quixotic, fanciful, unworkable Opposite: practicable ■ n prophet, dreamer, thinker, seer

visit v 1 call on, call in on, drop in on, go to see, pay a visit 2 go to, stay in, stay at, stop with, stop at ■ n 1 social call, official visit, call, duty call 2 stay, stopover, holiday, break, trip

visitation n 1 visit, examination, inspection, check, checkup 2 punishment, curse, calamity, blight, catastrophe

visitor n caller, guest, tourist, sightseer

visitor centre n tourist centre, information office, inquiry office, information point, help point

visor n screen, blind, eyeshade

vista n view, panorama, outlook, scene, landscape

visual adj 1 graphic, pictorial, filmic, painterly, photographic 2 concrete, visible, discernible, observable, evident 3 optical, chromatic, ophthalmic, ocular ■ n graphic, visual aid, illustration, picture, photograph

visual aid n model, film, video, chart, illustration

visualization n 1 imagining, conjuring up, picturing, conception 2 mental image, mental picture, vision, hallucination, image 3 positive thinking, therapy, cognitive therapy, meditation, image creation

visualize v imagine, envisage, picture, see in your mind's eye, dream of

vital *adj* **1 important**, crucial, fundamental, critical, necessary *Opposite*: unimportant **2 energetic**, vigorous, vivacious, dynamic, vibrant *Opposite*: lifeless. *See* COMPARE AND CONTRAST *at* **necessary**.

vitality *n* **liveliness**, energy, vivacity, vigour, life *Opposite*: lethargy

vitalize *v* **animate**, energize, buoy up, bolster, hearten *Opposite*: deaden

vitally *adv* **extremely**, indispensably, enormously, absolutely, really

vitreous *adj* **enamel**, vitric, vitriform, glasslike, glassy

vitriol *n* **hatred**, bitterness, venom, spleen, sarcasm *Opposite*: love

vitriolic *adj* **spiteful**, venomous, hurtful, acerbic, bitter *Opposite*: kind

vituperation *n* **1 outburst**, attack, criticism, censuring, condemnation **2 abuse**, venom, vitriol, savaging, mauling

vituperative *adj* **insulting**, abusive, offensive, malicious, slanderous

vivacious *adj* **vibrant**, lively, bubbly, cheerful, spirited *Opposite*: languid

vivacity *n* **high-spiritedness**, liveliness, animation, verve, vivaciousness *Opposite*: lethargy

vivid *adj* **1 intense**, rich, gaudy, bright, glowing *Opposite*: dull **2 fresh**, distinct, clear, crystal clear, lucid *Opposite*: vague **3 striking**, powerful, strong, clear, intense *Opposite*: understated **4 active**, lively, creative, ingenious, original *Opposite*: prosaic

vividness *n* **1 richness**, gaudiness, colourfulness, brightness, vibrancy *Opposite*: dullness **2 freshness**, distinctness, clarity, lucidity, clearness *Opposite*: vagueness **3 power**, strength, clarity, intensity **4 liveliness**, creativity, ingeniousness, flamboyance, intensity *Opposite*: banality

vocabulary *n* **1 language**, words, terms, expressions, terminology **2 dictionary**, glossary, lexicon, word list. *See* COMPARE AND CONTRAST *at* **language**.

vocal *adj* **1 uttered**, verbal, voiced, spoken, unwritten *Opposite*: silent **2 outspoken**, frank, insistent, vociferous, voluble *Opposite*: quiet

vocalist *n* **singer**, lead vocalist, backing vocalist, lead singer, backing singer

vocalize *v* **express**, voice, articulate, give voice to, put into words

vocals *n* **lyrics**, words, singing, chorus

vocation *n* **1 career**, profession, job, occupation, work **2 aptitude**, inclination, talent, bent, urge

vocational *adj* **occupational**, professional, job-related, career, work

vociferous *adj* **clamorous**, vocal, loud, voluble, raucous *Opposite*: quiet

vogue *n* **fashion**, trend, craze, rage, mode

voguish *adj* **1 fashionable**, elegant, chic, stylish, modish *Opposite*: unfashionable **2 passing**, in vogue, in, up-to-the-minute, popular *Opposite*: unpopular

voice *n* **1 speech**, singing, vocal sound, power of speech **2 opinion**, say, right of speech, expression, declaration ▪ *v* **1 express**, assert, declare, proclaim, opine *(fml)* **2 pronounce**, articulate, utter, declare, intone *(fml)*

voiced *adj* **stated**, enunciated, spoken, uttered, expressed

voiceless *adj* **1 silent**, unspeaking, mute, taciturn, wordless *Opposite*: speaking **2 unrepresented**, disenfranchised, invisible, ignored, forgotten *Opposite*: represented

voiceover *n* **narration**, commentary, narrative

void *adj* **1 annulled**, cancelled, invalid, null and void, negated *(fml)* *Opposite*: valid **2 empty**, vacant, unoccupied, not in use, occupied ▪ *n* **empty space**, emptiness, vacuum, hollowness, abyss ▪ *v* **cancel**, annul, render null and void, vacate, reject. *See* COMPARE AND CONTRAST *at* **vacant**.

volatile *adj* **1 unstable**, precarious, changeable, dangerous, hazardous *Opposite*: stable **2 unpredictable**, explosive, hot-blooded, impulsive, fickle *Opposite*: placid

volatility *n* **1 instability**, precariousness, changeability, explosiveness *Opposite*: stability **2 unpredictability**, explosiveness, hot-bloodedness, impulsiveness, fickleness *Opposite*: placidity

volition *n* **wish**, will, decision, choice, desire *Opposite*: coercion

volley *n* **torrent**, shower, stream, cascade, barrage ▪ *v* **lob**, hit, strike, kick

volte-face *n* **about-turn**, U-turn, reversal, change of direction, change of heart

voluble *adj* **talkative**, fluent, articulate, verbose, loquacious *Opposite*: taciturn

volume *n* **1 quantity**, amount, degree, size, level **2 capacity**, size, dimensions, measurements, bulk **3 book**, tome, work **4 part**, section, edition

voluminous *adj* **big**, huge, large, capacious, roomy *Opposite*: small

voluntarily *adv* **willingly**, of your own accord, happily, gladly, freely *Opposite*: reluctantly

voluntary *adj* **1 unpaid**, charitable, volunteer *Opposite*: professional **2 intended**, intentional, controlled, deliberate, chosen *Opposite*: involuntary

volunteer *n* **helper**, unpaid worker, candy striper *(US)* ▪ *v* **1 offer**, come forward, agree, step up, undertake **2 give**, offer, tell, advise, inform

vomit *v* **1 be sick**, be nauseous, be nauseated, gag, retch **2 expel**, spew out, spew forth, eject, send out ▪ *n* **sick**, vomitus, barf *(infml)*, chunder *(infml)*, puke *(slang)*

voracious *adj* **insatiable**, avid, hungry, ravenous, gluttonous *Opposite*: sated

voraciousness see voracity

voracity n greed, greediness, gluttony, hunger, rapaciousness

vortex n 1 whirlpool, whirlwind, waterspout, tornado, cyclone 2 quagmire, morass, maelstrom, turbulence, whirlwind

vote n ballot, election, division, secret ballot, show of hands ■ v choose, cast your vote, elect, opt for, support Opposite: abstain

voter n elector, constituent, supporter, backer

votive adj 1 ritual, prayerful, supplicatory (fml), precatory (fml) 2 promised, pledged, vowed, contractual, agreed

voucher n coupon, ticket, receipt, chit (dated), check (US)

vouch for v speak for, support, guarantee, back up, stand up for

vouchsafe v 1 give, grant, offer, bestow (fml) 2 (fml) promise, agree, allow, permit, consent

vow n promise, oath, pledge, guarantee, declaration ■ v swear, promise, guarantee, undertake, declare

voyage n journey, trip, expedition, passage, crossing ■ v journey, sail, cruise, travel

voyager n traveller, explorer, adventurer, tourist, vacationer (US)

vulgar adj 1 rude, offensive, crude, bad, earthy Opposite: decent 2 tasteless, brash, common, kitsch, ostentatious Opposite: tasteful 3 bad-mannered, uncouth, discourteous, unrefined, rude Opposite: polite

vulgarism n 1 obscenity, swear word, four-letter word, expletive, rude word 2 colloquialism, popular expression, idiom, common term

vulgarity n 1 rudeness, offensiveness, crudeness, crudity, earthiness Opposite: decency 2 bad manners, uncouthness, rudeness, loutishness, boorishness Opposite: politeness 3 tastelessness, brashness, ostentatiousness, commonness, kitsch Opposite: tastefulness 4 swearword, curse, bad language, four-letter word, rude word

vulnerability n susceptibility, weakness, defencelessness, helplessness, exposure Opposite: invincibility

vulnerable adj susceptible, weak, defenceless, helpless, exposed Opposite: invincible

vulturine adj opportunistic, exploitative, greedy, avaricious, grasping

W

wackiness (infml) n zaniness, silliness, wildness, eccentricity, oddness Opposite: conventionality

wacky (infml) adj silly, zany, madcap, way out, off the wall Opposite: conventional

wad n 1 bundle, roll, sheaf, stack, pile 2 lump, mass, cushion, clump, chunk 3 twist, chew, portion, gob (slang) ■ v 1 plug, lag, stuff, fill, pad 2 compress, scrunch, squeeze, compact, screw

wadding n padding, lining, insulation, lagging, filling

waddle v toddle, sway, shuffle, wobble

wade v paddle, stride, walk, splash

wade through v plough through, struggle through, battle through, tackle, deal with

wafer-thin adj thin, paper-thin, slim

waffle (infml) v go on, ramble, make small talk, blabber, babble ■ n nonsense, rubbish, drivel, balderdash, gobbledegook (infml)

waft v drift, float, glide, sail, fan ■ n puff, breath, gust, breeze, draught

wag v wave to and fro, move from side to side, flap, wiggle, waggle ■ n 1 wiggle, waggle, shake, twitch, wave 2 (dated) wit, humorist, comedian, comic, joker

wage n salary, pay, earnings, income, take-home pay ■ v carry on, conduct, pursue, engage in, fight

COMPARE AND CONTRAST CORE MEANING: money given for work done

wage a fixed regular payment made on an hourly, weekly, or daily basis, especially to manual workers; **salary** a fixed regular annual sum, usually paid on a monthly basis, especially to clerical or professional workers; **pay** a wage or salary; **fee** a payment made to a professional person by a client; **remuneration** payment for work, goods, or services; **emolument** (fml) any payment for work; **honorarium** money given in exchange for services for which there is normally no fixed charge; **stipend** a regular payment or allowance for living expenses, especially one made to a member of the clergy or a student.

wage earner n breadwinner, provider, earner, worker, supporter

wage packet n wage, salary, pay packet, wages, earnings

wager n bet, gamble, stake, ante, flutter (infml) ■ v bet, gamble, stake, risk, venture

wages n salary, pay, earnings, income, take-home pay

wage war on v oppose, combat, resist, fight, do battle

waggish *(dated)* adj **humorous**, witty, mischievous, droll, jocular

waggishness *(dated)* n **humorousness**, wit, mischievousness, mischief, drollness

waggle v **wiggle**, wag, shake, wave to and fro, move from side to side

waif n **stray**, soul, urchin, orphan, ragamuffin *(dated)*

wail v 1 **howl**, moan, weep, yowl, keen 2 **complain**, fuss, whine, kick up a fuss *(infml)*, kick up a storm *(infml)* ■ n 1 **howl**, moan, yowl, scream, cry 2 **complaint**, protest, whine, fuss

wainscot n **panelling**, wainscoting, cladding, lining

waistline n **waist**, middle, midriff

wait v 1 **stay**, remain, hang around, linger, stop 2 **delay**, pause, hold your fire, postpone, hang on 3 **expect**, anticipate, await, wait on ■ n **delay**, pause, interval, postponement, gap

waiter n **server**, attendant, maître d', head waiter, maître d'hôtel

waiting area n **concourse**, foyer, meeting point, waiting room, reception

wait on v 1 **care for**, serve, mother, nurse, take care of 2 *(infml)* **expect**, anticipate, await, wait for

waive v **surrender**, give up, relinquish, put aside, ignore *Opposite*: retain

waiver n 1 **disclaimer**, relinquishment, renunciation, abdication, abandonment 2 **contract**, agreement, bond

wake v 1 **wake up**, awaken, stir, come round, come to 2 **arouse**, stir, awaken, rouse, kindle *Opposite*: stifle

wakeful adj 1 **restless**, disturbed, sleepless, unable to sleep, insomniac *Opposite*: drowsy 2 **alert**, vigilant, on guard, attentive, aware *Opposite*: inattentive

wakefulness n 1 **restlessness**, sleeplessness, insomnia, tossing and turning, restiveness *Opposite*: drowsiness 2 **alertness**, vigilance, attentiveness, awareness, watchfulness *Opposite*: inattentiveness

waken *see* **wake up**

wake up v 1 **wake**, awaken, stir, come round, come to *Opposite*: go to sleep 2 **liven up**, come to life, come alive, revive, animate

walk v **go on foot**, stroll, amble, saunter, march ■ n 1 **stroll**, saunter, march, amble, promenade *(fml)* 2 **gait**, pace, tread, stride, way of walking

walkabout *(infml)* n **walk**, stroll, saunter, amble, tour

walk a tightrope v **tread dangerously**, invite trouble, ask for trouble, ask for it, skate on thin ice

walk away v 1 **abandon**, leave, withdraw, abdicate, back down from 2 **win**, triumph, sail through, succeed, walk it *(infml)*

walk down the aisle v **get married**, marry, tie the knot *(infml)*, get hitched *(infml)*, get spliced *(slang)*

walker n **hiker**, rambler, stroller

walking adj **outdoor**, hiking, rambling, cross-country, heavy-duty

walking stick n **cane**, stick, bamboo, staff

walk in on v **barge in**, march in, interrupt, intrude, butt in

walk off v **turn your back**, walk away, leave, go, quit *Opposite*: remain

walk off with v **steal**, embezzle, pocket, appropriate, take

walk-on n **bit part**, cameo, minor part, extra, nonspeaking part

walk out v 1 **leave**, storm out, go off in a huff, flounce out, take yourself off *(infml)* 2 **go on strike**, down tools, take industrial action, stop work

walkout n **strike**, stoppage, protest, industrial action

walk out on *(infml)* v **leave**, abandon, leave in the lurch, go, desert

walk over *(infml)* v **defeat**, beat, overpower, trounce, thrash

walkover *(infml)* n **easy victory**, child's play, runaway, runaway victory, pushover *(infml)* *Opposite*: challenge

walk through v **rehearse**, practise, run through

walkway n 1 **path**, footpath, pathway, pavement, alley 2 **aisle**, corridor, passage, passageway

wall n **partition**, divider, screen, panel, bulkhead

wallet n **folder**, file, case, holder

wallop *(infml)* v 1 **thump**, smack, thwack, strike, hit 2 **defeat**, beat, trounce, whip, destroy ■ n 1 **blow**, thump, bash, smack, thwack 2 **fizz**, punch, clout, pizazz *(infml)*, buzz *(infml)*

walloping *(infml)* n 1 **beating**, thrashing, hiding *(infml)* 2 **defeat**, drubbing, rout, hiding *(infml)* ■ adj **huge**, enormous, gigantic, stupendous, massive ■ adv **extremely**, very, tremendously, inordinately, stupendously

wallow v **flounder**, stumble, lurch, stagger, welter

wallow in v **enjoy**, bask in, revel in, relish, make the most of

wallpaper n **wall covering**, paper, lining paper

wall-to-wall *(infml)* adj **omnipresent**, all-pervasive, nonstop, ceaseless, never-ending

waltz n *(infml)* **cinch** *(infml)*, piece of cake *(infml)*, breeze *(infml)*, pushover *(infml)*, walkover *(infml)* ■ v 1 **walk**, stroll, swan, breeze, saunter 2 **romp**, sail, steam, whizz, cruise

wan adj 1 **pallid**, ashen, ashy, drawn, washed-out 2 **listless**, feeble, weak, down, depressed *Opposite*: strong

wand n **baton**, stick, rod, pointer

wander v **1 stroll**, meander, walk, ramble, roam **2 drift**, stray, digress, lose the point, lose the thread ■ n **walk**, stroll, ramble, mosey (infml), mooch (slang)

wanderer n **nomad**, vagrant, itinerant, traveller, rover

wandering adj **itinerant**, nomadic, peripatetic, travelling, drifting Opposite: settled

wanderlust n **desire to travel**, itchy feet, travel bug

wane v **diminish**, decrease, decline, get smaller, fade Opposite: wax (literary)

wangle (infml) v **engineer**, contrive, obtain, get, fix (infml)

waning adj **fading**, declining, weakening, diminishing, disappearing Opposite: increasing

wannabe (infml) n **hopeful**, aspirant, imitator, clone, camp follower ■ adj **aspiring**, aspirational, would-be, hopeful, budding

want v **1 desire**, wish for, long for, crave, covet **2 need**, require, lack, be short of, miss ■ n **1 lack**, absence, shortage, scarcity, dearth **2 poverty**, famine, hunger, need, neediness

COMPARE AND CONTRAST CORE MEANING: seek to have, do, or achieve something

want feel a need or desire for something; **desire** want something very strongly; **wish** have a strong, sometimes unrealistic, desire to have or to do something; **long** have a strong desire for somebody or something, especially something difficult to achieve; **yearn** want something very much, especially with a feeling of sadness when it seems unlikely that it can ever be obtained; **covet** have a strong desire to possess something that belongs to somebody else, or (fml) want something very much; **crave** want something very much, especially when this desire is physical.

wanted adj **required**, sought, sought after, hunted, desired

wanting adj **deficient**, inadequate, imperfect, not good enough, not up to standard Opposite: adequate ■ prep **without**, lacking, in need of, short of, minus

wanton adj **1 gratuitous**, motiveless, meaningless, reckless, needless Opposite: justifiable **2 immoral**, immodest, abandoned, licentious, lustful Opposite: restrained **3 malevolent**, malicious, cruel, vicious, nasty Opposite: benign **4 excessive**, extravagant, unrestrained, heedless, unreasonable Opposite: restrained

wantonness n **depravity**, debauchery, immorality, shamelessness, impiety Opposite: restraint

wants n **needs**, requirements, desires, requests, wishes

war n **1 warfare**, hostilities, fighting, combat, action Opposite: peace **2 campaign**, battle, struggle, fight, conflict **3 competition**, rivalry, feud, battle, struggle. See COMPARE AND CONTRAST at fight.

warble v **sing**, trill, pipe up, chirrup, sing out

war cry n **battle cry**, rallying call, call to arms

warden n **custodian**, curator, keeper, steward, superintendent

warder n **prison officer**, jailer, custodian, guard, screw (slang)

ward off v **defend against**, protect against, deflect, hold off, keep at bay

wardrobe n **clothes**, clothing, apparel, gear (infml), attire (fml)

wares n **goods**, merchandise, produce, products, commodities

warfare n **1 fighting**, conflict, combat, action, hostilities **2 rivalry**, feud, competition, contest, struggle

warhorse n **campaigner**, warrior, stalwart, old hand, master

wariness n **caution**, suspicion, care, circumspection, guardedness Opposite: carelessness

warlike adj **1 belligerent**, aggressive, bellicose, confrontational, hostile Opposite: friendly **2 martial**, military, militaristic, warring, war

warlock n **sorcerer**, wizard, enchanter, witch, necromancer (literary)

warlord n **military leader**, general, chieftain, guerrilla leader, commander

warm adj **1 temperate**, tepid, balmy, hot, lukewarm Opposite: cool **2 kind**, kindly, warmhearted, kind-hearted, friendly Opposite: unfriendly **3 cosy**, inviting, restful, cheerful, cheery Opposite: unwelcoming **4 lively**, passionate, ardent, fiery, enthusiastic Opposite: cool **5 sincere**, heartfelt, deep, earnest, wholehearted ■ v **1 heat**, heat up, reheat, warm up, melt Opposite: cool **2 take to**, become fond of, take a liking to, take a fancy to, get on with Opposite: cool off **3 become enthusiastic about**, get going on, get fired up about, get excited, become enthused ■ n **warmth**, warmness, heat Opposite: cold

warm-blooded adj **passionate**, impetuous, enthusiastic, ardent, emotional Opposite: cold-blooded

warm-hearted adj **kindly**, tender, kind, sympathetic, affectionate Opposite: cold-hearted

warm-heartedness n **tenderness**, kindness, sympathy, affection, love Opposite: coldheartedness

warmness see warmth

warmonger n **hawk**, belligerent, jingo, jingoist, aggressor Opposite: peacemaker

warmongering n **sabre rattling**, belligerence, aggression, jingoism, hawkishness Opposite: peacemaking

warmth n **1 warmness**, heat, hotness Opposite: cold **2 balminess**, temperateness, high temperature, warmness Opposite: coldness **3 friendliness**, cordiality, warm-heartedness, kind-heartedness, warmness Opposite: coldheartedness **4 enthusiasm**, eagerness, earnestness, ardour, fervour *Opposite*: apathy

warm up *v* 1 limber up, loosen up, get loose, stretch *Opposite*: cool of 2 **warm**, heat, heat up, reheat, warm through *Opposite*: cool off

warm-up *n* exercises, limbering up, loosening up, preparation

warn *v* 1 caution, advise, inform, notify, tell 2 alert, forewarn, advise, tell, notify

warning *n* 1 threat, indication, portent, wake-up call, forewarning 2 notice, caution, caveat, word of warning, advice ■ *adj* cautionary, threatening, cautioning

warn off *v* deter, discourage, dissuade, put off, scare off

war of words *n* argument, row, slanging match, disagreement, fight

warp *v* 1 distort, twist, deform, bend, buckle *Opposite*: straighten 2 **change**, pervert, damage, distort, misrepresent ■ *n* twist, bend, distortion, deviation, alteration

warped *adj* 1 misshapen, distorted, deformed, twisted, bent 2 **changed**, damaged, distorted, misrepresented, confused 3 partial, biased, one-sided, prejudiced, skewed *Opposite*: impartial

warrant *n* authorization, permit, licence, authority, certification ■ *v* 1 merit, deserve, necessitate, call for, demand 2 guarantee, affirm, certify, secure, assure

warranty *n* guarantee, contract, pledge, assurance

warren *n* 1 hole, earth, habitat, burrow, lair 2 maze, labyrinth, catacomb

warring *adj* belligerent, combatant, fighting, sparring, opposing *Opposite*: friendly

warrior *n* soldier, fighter, combatant, trooper

wart *n* lump, growth, verruca

war-torn *adj* war-ravaged, frontline, battle-weary, war-scarred, battle-scarred *Opposite*: peaceful

wary *adj* watchful, cautious, suspicious, distrustful, mistrustful *Opposite*: careless. *See* COMPARE AND CONTRAST *at* **cautious**.

wash *v* 1 clean, bathe, rinse, sponge down, wash down 2 bathe, bath, clean up, wash up (US) 3 flow over, splash, lap, swish, pound 4 erode, wash away, carry away, bear away, sweep away ■ *n* 1 shower, shampoo, sponge, rinse, wash-down 2 layer, film, coat, overlay, coating 3 stain, tint, rinse, suffusion, colouring

washable *adj* colourfast, easy-care, noniron, preshrunk, unfading

washbasin *n* hand basin, basin, bowl, sink, washbowl

washbowl *see* **washbasin**

wash down *v* clean, rinse, sluice, sponge down, hose down

washed-out *adj* 1 wan, pallid, ashen, ashy, drawn 2 exhausted, tired out, used up, drained, all in *Opposite*: energetic

washed-up *(infml)* *adj* unsuccessful, finished, defeated, through, failed *Opposite*: successful

washer *n* seal, gasket, liner, ring, lining

washing *n* 1 laundry, dirty linen, dirty clothes, wash 2 wash, weekly wash, clothes wash 3 coat, coating, film, layer, overlay

wash out *v* wash, rinse, flush, swill, hose

washout *(infml)* *n* failure, dead loss, disaster, disappointment, flop *(infml)* *Opposite*: success

wash over *v* flow over, engulf, sweep over, overwhelm, come over

wash your hands of *v* disown, abandon, refuse to have anything to do with, absolve yourself, ignore

waspish *adj* 1 irritable, touchy, irascible, cantankerous, peevish *Opposite*: affable 2 malignant, spiteful, malicious, nasty, vindictive *Opposite*: friendly

waspishness *n* 1 irritability, touchiness, irascibility, cantankerousness, peevishness *Opposite*: affability 2 spitefulness, spite, malice, maliciousness, nastiness *Opposite*: friendliness

waspy *see* **waspish**

wastage *n* waste, surplus, excess, leftovers

waste *v* 1 squander, fritter away, misuse, dissipate, throw away *Opposite*: save 2 ravage, devastate, ruin, spoil, despoil 3 atrophy, wither, become emaciated, waste away, weaken *Opposite*: strengthen ■ *n* litter, rubbish, grey water, garbage *(US)*, trash *(US)* ■ *adj* 1 excess, surplus, unwanted, discarded, remaining 2 uncultivated, barren, bare, fallow *Opposite*: cultivated

waste away *v* wither, waste, atrophy, become emaciated, weaken *Opposite*: strengthen

wasted *adj* 1 missed, misused, lost, unexploited, unused 2 ravaged, withered, shrunken, atrophied, emaciated *Opposite*: healthy 3 futile, fruitless, unproductive, worthless, useless *Opposite*: worthwhile

wasteful *adj* extravagant, careless, uneconomical, profligate, lavish *Opposite*: frugal

wastefulness *n* extravagance, carelessness, profligacy, improvidence, lavishness *Opposite*: frugality

wasteland *n* wilds, wilderness, desert, badlands, wastes

wastes *see* **wasteland**

watch *v* 1 observe, look at, stare at, gaze at, survey *Opposite*: ignore 2 pay attention to, beware, mind, be cautious about, consider 3 spy on, stalk, keep under observation, keep an eye on, keep under surveillance 4 look after, keep an eye on, mind, guard, watch over *Opposite*: neglect ■ *n* guard, lookout, sentry, sentinel

watchdog *n* ombudsman, supervisory body, regulator, overseer

watcher n **observer**, onlooker, spectator, viewer, witness

watchful adj **observant**, attentive, alert, vigilant, on the alert *Opposite*: inattentive

watchfulness n **alertness**, attention, vigilance, caution, care *Opposite*: inattentiveness

watchman n **night watchman**, guard, security guard, custodian, caretaker

watch out v **1 be careful**, look out, be alert, be wary, take care **2 look out**, look, wait, watch, be on the lookout

watch over v **supervise**, look after, keep an eye on, guard, mind *Opposite*: neglect

watchtower n **lookout tower**, lookout post, observation tower, crow's nest

watchword n **motto**, slogan, maxim, byword, catch phrase

watch your step v **be careful**, take care, watch out, look out, pay attention

watch your weight v **be on a diet**, diet, slim, watch what you eat, cut down

water n **liquid**, rainwater, seawater, mineral water, tap water ■ v **1 soak**, spray, irrigate, drench, sprinkle **2 fill with tears**, stream, run, fill up, well

water bird n **waterfowl**, freshwater bird, duck

waterborne adj **1 aquatic**, floating, marine, riverine **2 transmissible**, contagious, catching

watercourse n **1 ditch**, conduit, drain, culvert **2 waterway**, channel, stream, river, rivulet

water down v **1 dilute**, thin down, weaken, attenuate *Opposite*: thicken **2 soften**, reduce, moderate, mitigate, regulate *Opposite*: beef up *(infml)*

watered-down adj **1 diluted**, dilute, thin, weak, insipid *Opposite*: concentrated **2 moderated**, weakened, vapid, qualified, toned-down *Opposite*: unqualified

waterfall n **cascade**, cataract, falls, weir, force

waterfowl n **water bird**, freshwater bird, duck

waterfront n **harbour**, lakefront, seafront, oceanfront, water's edge

water hole n **oasis**, pool, pond, water source, spring

watering hole n **1 oasis**, pool, pond, water hole, wallow **2** *(infml)* **bar**, pub, club

waterless adj **dry**, arid, parched, dehydrated

water line n **1 load line**, Plimsoll line, Plimsoll mark, watermark **2 tidemark**, watermark, high watermark, floodmark, tideline

waterlogged adj **sodden**, sopping, drenched, wet, soaking *Opposite*: dry

watermark n **1 mark**, imprint, logo, emblem **2 water line**, load line, Plimsoll line, Plimsoll mark **3 tidemark**, water line, high watermark, floodmark, tideline

waterproof adj **water-resistant**, rainproof, watertight, impermeable *Opposite*: permeable

watershed n **turning point**, defining moment, breaking point, seminal moment, crisis

waterside n **riverbank**, shore, bank, water's edge, waterfront ■ adj **waterfront**, beachfront, seaside, lakeside, riverside

watertight adj **1 sealed**, waterproof, impermeable, rainproof *Opposite*: permeable **2 incontrovertible**, unassailable, sound, firm, irrefutable *Opposite*: weak

waterway n **watercourse**, canal, river, channel, stream

waterworks n **tears**, crying, weeping, sobbing, blubbering *(infml)*

watery adj **1 wet**, soggy, squelchy, boggy, moist *Opposite*: dry **2 watered-down**, thin, weak, runny, diluted *Opposite*: thick **3 feeble**, faint, weak, wan, hazy *Opposite*: forceful **4 bland**, tasteless, insipid, weak, diluted *Opposite*: strong

wave v **1 gesticulate**, gesture, signal, beckon **2 brandish**, flourish, wield, wag, shake **3 flutter**, flap, sway, undulate, move to and fro ■ n **1 breaker**, roller, dumper, ripple, surge **2 upsurge**, groundswell, tendency, trend, movement **3 gesture**, signal, sign **4 rash**, spate, outbreak, epidemic, series **5 current**, surge, impulse, oscillation, undulation **6 curl**, kink, undulation, ringlet

waver v **1 dither**, hesitate, be indecisive, be irresolute, vacillate **2 tremble**, shake, flutter, flicker, shudder. *See* COMPARE AND CONTRAST *at* hesitate.

wavering n **fluctuation**, vacillation, indecisiveness, irresolution, uncertainty *Opposite*: resolution ■ adj **1 indecisive**, uncertain, undecided, vacillating, uncommitted *Opposite*: decisive **2 flickering**, shaky, trembling, quivering, unsteady

waviness n **curliness**, unevenness, undulation, corrugation, sinuosity

wavy adj **curly**, curvy, crimped, undulating *Opposite*: straight

wax n **beeswax**, candle wax, tallow ■ v **1 polish**, shine, buff, put a shine on, buff up **2** *(literary)* **become**, turn, grow, start to be **3** *(literary)* **expand**, increase, enlarge, get bigger, grow *Opposite*: wane

waxen adj **pale**, pallid, ashen, ashy, wan

waxiness n **greasiness**, fattiness, slipperiness, shininess, slickness

waxwork n **figure**, manikin, model, effigy, replica

way n **1 method**, means, technique, mode, system **2 custom**, style, practice, tradition, discipline **3 route**, road, direction, path **4 street**, avenue, lane, path, pathway

waylay v **accost**, intercept, surprise, ambush, lie in wait for

way of life n **lifestyle**, customs, habits, traditions

way of thinking n **ideas**, beliefs, opinion, philosophy, position

way-out adj **1** *(infml)* **unusual**, peculiar, odd,

strange, weird *Opposite*: conventional **2** *(dated infml)* **excellent**, wonderful, terrific, fantastic, great

ways *n* **habits**, conduct, customs, behaviour, traditions

ways and means *n* **methods**, approaches, means, devices, systems

wayside *n* **roadside**, verge, kerb, edge, hard shoulder

wayward *adj* **wilful**, naughty, unruly, errant, disobedient *Opposite*: well-behaved. *See* COMPARE AND CONTRAST *at* unruly.

waywardness *n* **wilfulness**, naughtiness, disobedience, unruliness, rebelliousness *Opposite*: obedience

weak *adj* **1 feeble**, frail, infirm, debilitated, puny *Opposite*: robust **2 tired**, faint, enervated, exhausted, drained *Opposite*: strong **3 delicate**, insubstantial, flimsy, wispy, fragile *Opposite*: sturdy **4 vulnerable**, defenceless, helpless, unprotected, unguarded *Opposite*: invulnerable **5 powerless**, ineffectual, toothless, inadequate, feeble *Opposite*: powerful **6 cowardly**, spineless, faint-hearted, timid, weak-willed *Opposite*: bold **7 faint**, feeble, low, dim, soft *Opposite*: strong **8 watery**, diluted, insipid, bland, tasteless *Opposite*: strong **9 unconvincing**, half-hearted, ineffectual, feeble, implausible *Opposite*: convincing

---

COMPARE AND CONTRAST CORE MEANING: lacking physical strength or energy

weak not physically fit or mentally strong; **feeble** lacking physical or mental strength or health; **frail** in a physically weak state as a result of illness or advanced years; **infirm** lacking strength as a result of long illness or advanced years; **debilitated** with strength and energy temporarily diminished as a result of illness or physical exertion; **decrepit** *(infml)* made weak by advanced years; **enervated** made weak and tired by physical or mental exertion.

---

weaken *v* **1 grow weaker**, deteriorate, fail, decline, wane *Opposite*: strengthen **2 give in**, cave in, give way, yield, vacillate *Opposite*: stand firm **3 damage**, destabilize, detract from, shake, undermine *Opposite*: bolster **4 dilute**, water down, thin, adulterate *Opposite*: strengthen **5 enfeeble**, exhaust, enervate, debilitate, sap *Opposite*: fortify

weakened *adj* **debilitated**, enfeebled, deteriorated, declining, faded

weakening *n* **deterioration**, decline, damage, destabilization, undermining *Opposite*: strengthening

weak-kneed *adj* **spineless**, cowardly, weak, feeble, submissive *Opposite*: courageous

weakness *n* **1 flaw**, fault, Achilles' heel, weak spot, weak point *Opposite*: strength **2 frailty**, feebleness, flimsiness, fragility, debility *Opposite*: robustness **3 powerlessness**, vulnerability, defencelessness, helplessness,

impotence *Opposite*: strength **4 fondness**, liking, taste, soft spot, penchant *Opposite*: dislike **5 faintness**, softness, dimness, paleness, feebleness *Opposite*: strength **6 wateriness**, blandness, lack of flavour, insipidity *Opposite*: strong flavour

weak point *see* **weak spot**

weak spot *n* **weakness**, Achilles heel, failing, fault, limitation

weak-willed *adj* **irresolute**, spineless, vacillating, easily led, spiritless *Opposite*: resolute

weal *n* **swelling**, welt, wound, mark, contusion *(fml)*

wealth *n* **1 riches**, prosperity, affluence, means, assets *Opposite*: poverty **2 large quantity**, abundance, cornucopia, variety, choice *Opposite*: dearth

wealthy *adj* **rich**, well-off, well-to-do, affluent, prosperous *Opposite*: poor

weapon *n* **1 armament**, firearm, missile, gun **2 defence**, deterrent, big stick

weaponry *n* **arms**, armaments, arsenal, weapons, ordnance

weapon store *n* **arsenal**, armoury, storeroom, store, cache

wear *v* **1 be dressed in**, dress in, show off, have on, put on **2 display**, bear, carry, hold, show **3 rub**, fray, scuff, grind, wear out ■ *n* **1 deterioration**, wear and tear, friction, abrasion, scuffing **2 dress**, clothing, clothes, garments, uniform

wear and tear *n* **deterioration**, wear, attrition, abrasion, erosion

wear away *v* **erode**, wear down, wear out, eat at, eat away at

wear down *v* **overcome**, weaken, erode, wear away, wear out

weariness *n* **1 tiredness**, exhaustion, fatigue, lethargy, inertia *Opposite*: energy **2 apathy**, disillusionment, jadedness, disenchantment *Opposite*: enthusiasm

wearing *adj* **tiring**, exhausting, trying, tiresome, wearisome *Opposite*: refreshing

wearisome *adj* **tiresome**, boring, tedious, trying, thankless *Opposite*: stimulating

wear off *v* **weaken**, fade, lessen, diminish, disappear *Opposite*: increase

wear out *v* **1 exhaust**, tire out, fatigue, sap, drain *Opposite*: invigorate **2 use up**, run down, fray, deplete, trash *(infml)* *Opposite*: renovate

weary *adj* **1 tired**, tired out, all in, worn out, exhausted *Opposite*: fresh **2 disillusioned**, disenchanted, jaded, worn down, fed up *(infml)* *Opposite*: enthusiastic ■ *v* **drain**, sap, exhaust, tire, lose patience

wearying *adj* **tiresome**, wearisome, tiring, exhausting, wearing

wear yourself out *v* **tire yourself out**, exhaust yourself, run yourself into the ground, overdo it, burn the candle at both ends

weather n **climate**, meteorological conditions, climatic conditions, elements ∎ v **1 endure**, withstand, sit out, ride out, last out *Opposite*: succumb **2 erode**, corrode, season, toughen, harden

weather-beaten adj **worn**, battered, windswept, weathered, gnarled

weather-bound adj **delayed**, held up, fogbound, snowbound, postponed

weathercock *see* weather vane

weathered adj **worn**, battered, windswept, weather-beaten, gnarled

weatherproof adj **watertight**, waterproof, rainproof, stormproof, windproof

weather vane n **wind indicator**, wind gauge, weathercock, anemometer, windsock

weave v **1 interlace**, lace, intertwine, plait, knit *Opposite*: unpick **2 invent**, create, compose, construct, fabricate **3 zigzag**, stagger, wind, twist, crisscross ∎ n **pile**, texture, nap

web n **network**, mesh, net, tissue, grid

webbing n **lattice**, trellis, netting, network, strap work

wed v **1 get married**, walk down the aisle, say "I do", get hitched *(infml)*, tie the knot *(infml)* *Opposite*: split up **2 join in matrimony**, marry, join in wedlock, unite **3 join**, link, unite, marry, merge *Opposite*: separate **4** *(fml or literary)* **marry**, take in marriage, espouse *(archaic)* *Opposite*: divorce

wedded adj **1 marital**, conjugal, married, matrimonial, connubial *(literary)* **2 committed**, devoted, linked, connected, attached *Opposite*: unattached

wedding n **marriage**, wedding ceremony, marriage ceremony, nuptials *(fml)*

wedge n **segment**, block, chock, sliver, hunk ∎ v **1 lodge**, hold, fix, jam, block *Opposite*: dislodge **2 cram**, pack, jam, ram, stuff

wedlock n **matrimony**, marriage, married state

wee adj **small**, minute, petite, little, tiny *Opposite*: big

weed v **hoe**, tidy, pick over, clear

WORD BANK
❑ **types of weed** bindweed, burdock, chickweed, dandelion, dock, goosegrass, ground elder, nettle, ragwort, shepherd's purse, stinging nettle, thistle

weed out v **remove**, extract, discard, get rid of, eliminate *Opposite*: select

weedy adj **weak**, puny, thin, scraggy, feeble *Opposite*: strong

weekend v **stay**, holiday, take a break, visit, vacation *(US)*

weekender n **tourist**, holidaymaker, visitor, sightseer, vacationer *(US)*

weensy *(infml) see* weeny

weeny *(infml)* adj **tiny**, little, small, wee, minute *Opposite*: huge

weep v **1 cry**, sob, wail, snivel, boohoo **2 leak**, suppurate, seep, exude, ooze

weepie *(infml)* n **movie**, film, melodrama, tearjerker *(infml)*

weepy adj **1 oversentimental**, slushy, mushy, syrupy, overemotional **2 (infml) tearful**, emotional, sad, miserable, sensitive

weigh v **consider**, ponder, weigh up, think about, evaluate

weigh against v **count against**, tell against, militate against, countervail

weigh down v **1 worry**, depress, get down, trouble, burden *Opposite*: hearten **2 overload**, load down, burden, charge, encumber

weight n **1 heaviness**, mass, bulk, weightiness, heft *(US)* **2 burden**, load, encumbrance **3 influence**, power, substance, significance, import

weighted adj **biased**, prejudiced, slanted, subjective, one-sided *Opposite*: impartial

weightiness n **1 weight**, heaviness, mass, bulk, heft *(US)* **2 gravity**, seriousness, importance, heaviness, import

weighting n **allowance**, premium, increment

weightless adj **light**, feathery, insubstantial, ethereal, airy *Opposite*: heavy

weighty adj **1 heavy**, big, substantial, hefty, bulky *Opposite*: insubstantial **2 important**, serious, grave, solemn, momentous *Opposite*: frivolous

weigh up v **assess**, evaluate, consider, examine, size up

weir n **dam**, barrage, dike, barrier, wall

weird adj **strange**, odd, bizarre, peculiar, unusual *Opposite*: normal

welcome adj **1 at home**, comfortable, at ease, relaxed, comfy *(infml)* *Opposite*: unwelcome **2 longed-for**, long-awaited, timely, opportune, heaven-sent *Opposite*: untimely **3 appreciated**, pleasurable, delightful, pleasing, pleasant *Opposite*: unwelcome ∎ n **greeting**, reception, salutation, salute, hospitality *Opposite*: farewell ∎ v **1 greet**, receive, hail, meet, salute **2 accept**, appreciate, approve, jump at, be grateful for *Opposite*: reject

welcoming adj **friendly**, warm, hospitable, convivial, openhearted *Opposite*: unwelcoming

weld v **fuse**, join, repair, solder, link *Opposite*: separate ∎ n **repair**, join, link, joint, bond

welfare n **wellbeing**, interests, happiness, good, safety *Opposite*: harm

well n **1 shaft**, bore, borehole, pit **2 spring**, fountain, artesian well, source, water supply ∎ v **1 spring up**, brim, surge, rise, gush *Opposite*: subside **2 grow**, rise, swell, intensify, increase *Opposite*: subside ∎ adv **1 pleasingly**, splendidly, perfectly, pleasantly, nicely *Opposite*: badly **2 properly**, ethically, acceptably, correctly, suitably *Opposite*: improperly **3 competently**, ably, skilfully, capably, satisfactorily *Opposite*: badly **4** justly, appropriately, fairly, fittingly, justifiably *Opposite*: unfairly **5 comfortably**, easily, agreeably **6 favourably**, highly, admiringly, kindly, positively *Opposite*: unfavourably **7 thoroughly**, fully, carefully, completely, meticulously *Opposite*: partially **8 clearly**, precisely, in detail, distinctly, perfectly *Opposite*: poorly **9 familiarly**, intimately, closely, personally, deeply *Opposite*: slightly **10 anyway**, anyhow, in any case, to cut a long story short, now then **11 good-naturedly**, good-humouredly, cheerfully, jovially, genially ■ *adj* **1 healthy**, glowing, fit, fighting fit, on form *Opposite*: unwell **2 satisfactory**, all right, good, lucky, fortunate *Opposite*: unsatisfactory

well-adjusted *adj* **stable**, normal, level-headed, well-balanced, sane *Opposite*: maladjusted

well-advised *adj* **sensible**, prudent, wise, judicious, shrewd *Opposite*: ill-advised

well-appointed *adj* **well-equipped**, well-resourced, fully furnished, well-furnished, luxurious

well-argued *adj* **clear**, clearly stated, cogent, sensible, lucid *Opposite*: illogical

well-balanced *adj* **1 sensible**, rational, stable, judicious, well-adjusted *Opposite*: unstable **2 harmonious**, balanced, well-proportioned, proportionate, coordinated *Opposite*: unbalanced

well-behaved *adj* **good**, obedient, dutiful, well-mannered, polite *Opposite*: disobedient

wellbeing *n* **happiness**, comfort, security, good, welfare

well-beloved *adj* **1 loved**, cherished, desired, beloved, adored *Opposite*: hated **2 respected**, honoured, venerated, revered, esteemed *Opposite*: disgraced

wellborn *adj* **aristocratic**, blue-blooded, noble, patrician, highborn (*literary*) *Opposite*: lowly

well-bred *adj* **polite**, well-mannered, mannerly, courteous, refined *Opposite*: common

well-built *adj* **sturdy**, strong, muscular, muscly, burly *Opposite*: puny

well-chosen *adj* **choice**, appropriate, apposite, apt, relevant *Opposite*: inappropriate

well-defined *adj* **distinct**, sharp, definite, clear, precise *Opposite*: vague

well-designed *adj* **1 elegant**, stylish, well-made, chic, classy (*infml*) **2 handy**, ingenious, clever, useful, neat

well-developed *adj* **1 well-built**, strong, toned, finely honed, muscular *Opposite*: puny **2 sophisticated**, well-rounded, strong, mature, acute *Opposite*: underdeveloped

well-disposed *adj* **approving**, friendly, kindly, sympathetic, benevolent *Opposite*: hostile

well-dressed *adj* **smart**, chic, stylish, elegant, well turned-out *Opposite*: scruffy

well-educated *adj* **cultured**, erudite, knowledgeable, well-read, learned *Opposite*: ignorant

well-endowed *adj* **1 affluent**, wealthy, well-to-do, rich, moneyed *Opposite*: poor **2 gifted**, skilled, talented, able, skilful

well-equipped *adj* **well-appointed**, well-resourced, well-furnished, luxurious, lavish *Opposite*: spartan

well-established *adj* **firm**, deep-rooted, unshakable, fixed, ingrained *Opposite*: shaky

well-expressed *adj* **eloquent**, persuasive, fluent, expressive, articulate *Opposite*: inarticulate

well-fed *adj* **1 healthy**, well-nourished, thriving, flourishing **2 overweight**, fat, obese, bulky, stout *Opposite*: thin

well-founded *adj* **logical**, understandable, justifiable, substantiated, sound *Opposite*: illogical

well-groomed *adj* **well-turned-out**, well-dressed, smart, dapper, spruce *Opposite*: unkempt

well-grounded *adj* **1 knowledgeable**, well-informed, au fait, conversant, well-acquainted *Opposite*: ignorant **2 well-founded**, logical, understandable, justifiable, substantiated *Opposite*: illogical

well-heeled (*infml*) *adj* **wealthy**, well-off, comfortable, rich, affluent *Opposite*: poor

well-informed *adj* **knowledgeable**, informed, in the know, up-to-date, educated *Opposite*: uneducated

well-intentioned *adj* **well-meant**, well-meaning, kindly, goodhearted, benevolent *Opposite*: malicious

well-kept *adj* **1 neat**, tidy, well-maintained, orderly, ordered *Opposite*: untidy **2 preserved**, safe, cherished, treasured, confidential

well-known *adj* **famous**, renowned, eminent, familiar, recognized *Opposite*: unknown

well-mannered *adj* **polite**, mannerly, decent, decorous, courteous *Opposite*: impolite

well-matched *adj* **compatible**, suited, complementary, well-suited, suitable *Opposite*: incompatible

well-meaning *adj* **well-intentioned**, kind, kindly, goodhearted, benevolent *Opposite*: malicious

well-meant *adj* **well-intentioned**, kind, kindly, kind-hearted, goodhearted *Opposite*: malicious

well-nigh *adv* **nearly**, almost, nigh on, practically, just about *Opposite*: totally

well-off *adj* **1 wealthy**, rich, comfortable, affluent, prosperous *Opposite*: poor **2 lucky**, fortunate, in luck, privileged, blessed *Opposite*: unfortunate

well-oiled *adj* **efficient**, smooth-running, well-organized, effective, well-ordered *Opposite*: inefficient

well-ordered *adj* **tidy**, regimented, disciplined, efficient, well-organized *Opposite*: inefficient

well-organized *adj* **efficient**, disciplined, well-ordered, regimented, ordered *Opposite*: inefficient

well-paid *adj* **lucrative**, profitable, productive, rewarding, remunerative

well-preserved *adj* **youthful**, fresh-looking, young-looking, girlish, boyish *Opposite*: wizened

well-read *adj* **knowledgeable**, educated, cultured, erudite, well-educated *Opposite*: uninformed

well-rounded *adj* **1 experienced**, seasoned, accomplished, well-versed, mature *Opposite*: inexperienced **2 comprehensive**, varied, wide, balanced, broad *Opposite*: narrow **3 shapely**, pleasing, well-formed, attractive, curvaceous *Opposite*: unattractive

well-spoken *adj* **articulate**, eloquent, refined, fluent, coherent *Opposite*: inarticulate

well-suited *adj* **compatible**, well-matched, complementary, of a kind, suited *Opposite*: incompatible

well-thought-of *adj* **respected**, esteemed, highly regarded, reputable, admired *Opposite*: despised

well-thought-out *adj* **well-planned**, well-organized, clever, ingenious, elegant *Opposite*: disorganized

well-timed *adj* **timely**, opportune, propitious, felicitous, appropriate *Opposite*: untimely

well-to-do *adj* **wealthy**, rich, well-off, affluent, prosperous *Opposite*: poor

well-tried *adj* **tried and tested**, established, well-founded, acknowledged, well-known *Opposite*: untried

well-turned *adj* **1 shapely**, graceful, elegant, well-formed, pretty *Opposite*: inelegant **2 eloquent**, well-crafted, well-expressed, articulate, witty *Opposite*: clumsy

well-turned-out *adj* **neat**, smart, spruce, dapper, well-dressed *Opposite*: unkempt

well up *v* **surge**, gush forth, spring up, spill over, emanate *Opposite*: subside

well-versed *adj* **knowledgeable**, familiar, experienced, informed, well-read *Opposite*: ignorant

well-wisher *n* **supporter**, sympathizer, friend, guardian angel *(infml) Opposite*: detractor

well-worn *adj* **1 worn**, worn out, ragged, threadbare, frayed *Opposite*: brand-new **2 hackneyed**, timeworn, unoriginal, banal, overworked *Opposite*: original

welt *n* **weal**, swelling, ridge, wound, mark

welter *n* **flurry**, jumble, mass, confusion, muddle ■ *v* **wallow**, roll, pitch and toss

wend *v* **proceed**, go, travel, move, journey *Opposite*: stay put

western *n* **cowboy film**, spaghetti western, horse opera

wet *adj* **1 damp**, soaked, soaking, drenched, sodden *Opposite*: dry **2 rainy**, showery, drizzly, damp, misty *Opposite*: dry ■ *n* **1 moisture**, wetness, liquid, damp, dampness *Opposite*: dry **2 wet weather**, rain, drizzle, damp, dampness *Opposite*: dry ■ *v* **make wet**, dampen, moisten, soak, saturate *Opposite*: dry

wet blanket *(infml) n* **spoilsport**, killjoy, party pooper *(infml)*, stick-in-the-mud *(infml)*, stuffed shirt *(infml)*

wetland *n* **marsh**, swamp, fen, bog, marshes *Opposite*: desert

wetness *n* **dampness**, damp, humidity, condensation, moisture *Opposite*: dryness

whack *v* **hit**, thump, slap, strike, clout ■ *n* **thump**, blow, slap, thwack, clout

whacked *(infml) adj* **tired**, tired out, shattered, exhausted, worn-out *Opposite*: fresh

whacking *(infml) adj* **huge**, enormous, massive, gigantic, mammoth *Opposite*: piddling *(infml)*

wharf *n* **quay**, quayside, jetty, pier, dock

whatchamacallit *(infml) n* **whatnot**, thingamabob *(infml)*, thingumajig *(infml)*, thingy *(infml)*, thingummy *(infml)*

whatever *pron* **anything**, everything, all, no matter what, whatsoever ■ *adv* **at all**, whatsoever, of any kind

whatsoever *adj* **at all**, whatever, of any kind

wheedle *v* **1 coax**, cajole, inveigle, charm, persuade *Opposite*: bully **2 coax out**, winkle out, get out, draw out, obtain

wheel *v* **1 roll**, trundle, manoeuvre, move **2 turn**, veer, swing, circle, swivel

wheel around *v* **swivel around**, swing around, turn round, spin around, turn full circle

wheel clamp *n* **clamp**, lock, immobilizer, Denver boot *(US)*

wheel-clamp *v* **clamp**, immobilize, secure, lock

wheeler-dealer *(infml) n* **fixer**, negotiator, dealer, trader

wheeze *v* **1 breathe heavily**, gasp, rasp, pant, rattle **2 speak hoarsely**, whisper, hiss, rasp, pant

wheeziness *n* **breathlessness**, hoarseness, gasping, puffing, panting

wheezy *adj* **breathless**, hoarse, short of breath, out of breath, husky

whelp *n* **cub**, pup, puppy, baby, offspring ■ *v* **give birth**, bear young, pup, cub, litter

whenever *conj* **every time**, each time, each and every time, on every occasion, when

whereabouts *n* **location**, situation, position, site, place

whereas *conj* **while**, where, but, however, although

whereupon *(fml) conj* **at which point**, at which, as a result of which, so, and so

wherewithal *n* **means**, ability, resources, money, finances

whet *v* **1 sharpen**, hone, grind, file *Opposite*: blunt **2 stimulate**, arouse, augment, rouse, kindle *Opposite*: quell

whiff *n* **1 smell**, aroma, scent, odour, reek **2 trace**, vestige, sign, hint, suggestion ■ *v (infml)* **reek**, pong *(infml)*, smell, stink, hum *(infml)*

whiffy *(infml) adj* **smelly**, stinking, foul-smelling, fetid, pongy *(infml) Opposite*: fragrant

while *conj* **1 as**, at the same time as, even as, during which **2 but**, however, in contrast, whereas **3 even though**, though, although, despite the fact, whereas ■ *n* **time**, period, interval, little, bit

while away *v* **pass**, spend, idle, fritter away, kill

whim *n* **impulse**, urge, notion, quirk, caprice

whimper *v* **cry**, whine, sob, snivel, moan

whimsical *adj* **1 fanciful**, quirky, unusual, imaginative, original *Opposite*: practical **2 amusing**, playful, humorous, witty, quaint *Opposite*: serious **3 erratic**, unpredictable, random, impulsive, capricious *Opposite*: dependable

whimsy *n* **1 quaintness**, oddity, oddness, eccentricity, quirkiness *Opposite*: seriousness **2 fancy**, flight of fancy, whim, caprice, fantasy

whine *v* **1 whimper**, cry, wail, moan, bleat **2 grumble**, complain, gripe *(infml)*, moan *(infml)*, bellyache *(infml) Opposite*: accept **3 wail**, moan, howl, drone, hum ■ *n* **complaint**, wail, whimper, cry, moan *(infml)*. See COMPARE AND CONTRAST *at* **complain**.

whiner *n* **grumbler**, complainer, whinger *(infml)*, moaner *(infml)*, grouch *(infml)*

whinge *(infml) v* **whine**, complain, bleat *(infml)*, moan *(infml)*, bellyache *(infml) Opposite*: accept

whinger *(infml) n* **complainer**, grumbler, whiner, malcontent, moaner *(infml)*

whinny *v* **neigh**, whicker, nicker

whip *v* **1 flog**, thrash, beat, lash, flagellate **2 whisk**, beat, cream, aerate, stir **3** *(infml)* **steal**, take, rob, thieve, pinch *(infml)* ■ *n* **lash**, crop, cat-o'-nine-tails, switch

whiplash *n* **blow**, stroke, lash, hit, impact

whip-round *(infml) n* **collection**, appeal, kitty, fund

whip up *v* **1 stir up**, drum up, incite, provoke, arouse *Opposite*: pacify **2** *(infml)* **rattle off**, prepare, concoct, cook, produce

whirl *v* **1 spin**, twirl, reel, rotate, turn ■ *n* **1 rotation**, spin, twirl, turn, flick **2 flurry**, bustle, hustle, commotion, tumult

whirlpool *n* **eddy**, vortex, swirl, current, waterspout

whirlwind *n* **tornado**, hurricane, cyclone, waterspout, vortex ■ *adj* **rapid**, short-lived, tumultuous, brief, swift *Opposite*: leisurely

whirr *v* **hum**, purr, buzz, whine, drone

whisk *v* **1 beat**, whip, cream, aerate, stir **2 take**, bundle, bustle, hustle, whip *Opposite*: drag

whisker *n* **fraction**, inch, millimetre, hair's-breadth

whiskers *n* **facial hair**, sideburns, moustache, muttonchops, stubble

whisper *v* **murmur**, sigh, mutter, breathe, utter *Opposite*: shout ■ *n* **rumour**, word, gossip, tale, hint *Opposite*: fact

whistle *v* **screech**, shrill, shriek, hoot, toot

whistle-blower *n* **informer**, mole, telltale, snitch *(slang)*, grass *(slang)*

whistle-stop *adj* **barnstorming**, whirlwind, lightning, rapid, speedy *Opposite*: relaxed

whit *(dated) n* **iota**, bit, jot, grain, speck

white *adj* **1 snowy**, silver, silvery, bleached, grey *Opposite*: black **2 pale**, pallid, ashen, wan, washed-out *Opposite*: flushed **3 frosty**, snowy, hoary, icy, frozen

---

WORD BANK

❑ **types of white** cream, eggshell, ivory, magnolia, off-white, oyster, pearl, platinum, silver, snow white

---

whitecap *n* **crest**, surf, breaker, white horses, wave

white-collar *adj* **professional**, managerial, management, salaried, office *Opposite*: blue-collar

white-hot *adj* **1 incandescent**, glowing, white, luminescent, hot *Opposite*: ice-cold **2 intense**, fevered, frenetic, frenzied, excited *Opposite*: lethargic

white-knuckle *adj* **exhilarating**, frightening, terrifying, exciting, roller-coaster *Opposite*: safe

whiten *v* **blanch**, whitewash, bleach, fade, pale *Opposite*: darken

whiteness *n* **paleness**, milkiness, lightness, pallor, wanness *Opposite*: ruddiness

whiteout *n* **blizzard**, snowstorm, storm

whitewash *n* **1 distemper**, lime, whitening, paint **2 cover-up**, deception, conspiracy, plot, concealment *Opposite*: exposure **3** *(infml)* **defeat**, rout, one-horse race, trouncing, beating *Opposite*: triumph ■ *v* **1 paint**, decorate, distemper, cover, smear **2 misrepresent**, cover up, conceal, explain away, gloss over *Opposite*: expose **3 trounce**, defeat, beat, rout, outclass *Opposite*: succumb

white water *n* **1 rapids**, torrents, foam, spray, current **2 shallows**, shoals, sandbanks, sandbar

whittle *v* **carve**, shape, fashion, shave, sculpt

whittle away *v* **eat into**, erode, eat away at, reduce, consume *Opposite*: build up

whittle down v cut down, trim, pare down, reduce, diminish *Opposite*: increase

whiz v 1 whirr, hum, hiss, buzz, rattle 2 dash, go, nip *(infml)*, pop *(infml)*, zip *(infml)* *Opposite*: dawdle ■ n *(infml)* **expert**, prodigy, genius, whiz kid *(infml)*, bright spark *(infml)*

whiz kid *(infml)* n **prodigy**, expert, genius, wizard *(infml)*, whiz *(infml)*

whodunit n **mystery**, thriller, cliffhanger

whole adj 1 **entire**, complete, full, in one piece, total *Opposite*: partial 2 **intact**, in one piece, unbroken, undivided, unspoiled *Opposite*: broken 3 **unimpaired**, healthy, sound, fit, well *Opposite*: unhealthy 4 **healed**, cured, healthy, restored, rehabilitated *Opposite*: ill ■ n 1 **sum total**, aggregate, total, unit, entity 2 **entirety**, totality, unity, everything, all *Opposite*: part

wholehearted adj **enthusiastic**, passionate, unreserved, total, unstinting *Opposite*: grudging

wholeness n **completeness**, entirety, totality, unity, fullness

wholesale adj **extensive**, comprehensive, across-the-board, indiscriminate, blanket *Opposite*: partial ■ adv **indiscriminately**, extensively, comprehensively, generally, broadly *Opposite*: partially

wholesaler n **trader**, retailer, supplier, dealer, vendor

wholesome adj 1 **healthy**, healthful, nutritious, good, nourishing *Opposite*: unwholesome 2 **decent**, moral, clean, honest, clean-living *Opposite*: unwholesome 3 **sensible**, open, honest, commonsensical, practical *Opposite*: unhelpful 4 **fit**, healthy, fresh-faced, clean-cut, ruddy *Opposite*: unhealthy

wholesomeness n 1 **freshness**, healthiness, healthfulness, naturalness, goodness *Opposite*: unwholesomeness 2 **morality**, uprightness, decency, integrity, virtuousness *Opposite*: immorality 3 **common sense**, sense, practicality, good sense, openness *Opposite*: impracticality 4 **healthiness**, fitness, glow, ruddiness, haleness *Opposite*: unwholesomeness

wholly adv 1 **completely**, entirely, totally, altogether, utterly *Opposite*: partially 2 **solely**, exclusively, only, just, absolutely *Opposite*: generally

whoop v cry out, shout, scream, howl, hoot

whoosh n dash, zoom, rush, spurt, surge ■ v 1 **rush**, zoom, burst, whistle, whiz *Opposite*: dawdle 2 **zoom**, whistle, swish, hiss, roar

whopper *(infml)* n 1 **monster**, giant, elephant, Goliath, leviathan 2 **lie**, untruth, tale, fabrication, falsehood *Opposite*: truth

whopping *(infml)* n **thrashing**, defeat, drubbing, pasting *(infml)*, licking *(infml)* ■ adj **enormous**, gigantic, monstrous, huge, big *Opposite*: tiny

whorl n spiral, coil, curl, twist, swirl

whys and wherefores n **reasons**, ins and outs, details, the full picture, motives

wicked adj 1 **evil**, bad, wrong, depraved, immoral *Opposite*: good 2 **mischievous**, naughty, roguish, impish, teasing *Opposite*: respectful 3 **mean**, cutting, acerbic, sharp, malicious *Opposite*: gentle 4 *(infml)* **distressing**, dreadful, awful, atrocious, severe *Opposite*: excellent

wickedness n 1 **evil**, badness, iniquity, sin, impiety *Opposite*: goodness 2 **impishness**, cheekiness, naughtiness, mischievousness

wicker n cane, rattan, wickerwork, bamboo

wicket n **gate**, door, opening, aperture, entrance

wide adj 1 **broad**, ample, large, thick, spacious *Opposite*: narrow 2 **extensive**, varied, widespread, inclusive, eclectic *Opposite*: narrow 3 **baggy**, roomy, loose, loose-fitting, capacious *Opposite*: tight ■ adv off course, off target, off the mark, wide of the mark, out

wide-awake *(infml)* adj **fully awake**, alert, bright-eyed and bushy-tailed, perky, watchful *Opposite*: asleep

wide-eyed adj 1 **amazed**, astonished, open-mouthed, dumbfounded, flabbergasted *(infml)* *Opposite*: impassive 2 **naive**, innocent, inexperienced, green, credulous *Opposite*: knowing

widely adv **extensively**, broadly, generally, far and wide, commonly *Opposite*: narrowly

widen v **broaden**, extend, expand, enlarge, make wider *Opposite*: narrow

wide-open adj 1 **open wide**, gaping, yawning, cavernous, agape *(literary)* 2 **unpredictable**, undecided, anybody's guess, unsettled, in the balance *Opposite*: settled 3 **vulnerable**, unprotected, exposed, unguarded, at risk *Opposite*: protected

wide-ranging adj **extensive**, widespread, comprehensive, across-the-board, inclusive *Opposite*: narrow

widespread adj **extensive**, prevalent, general, common, rife *Opposite*: limited

COMPARE AND CONTRAST CORE MEANING: occurring over a wide area

widespread existing or happening in many places, or affecting many people; **prevalent** occurring commonly or widely as a dominant feature; **rife** full of or severely affected by something undesirable that occurs frequently or in great numbers over a wide area, especially when it appears to be uncontrollable; **epidemic** spreading more quickly and more extensively than expected; **universal** affecting the whole world or everyone in the world.

width n breadth, thickness, girth, size, measurement

wield v 1 **exercise**, exert, use, have, employ 2 **brandish**, manipulate, handle, ply, carry *Opposite*: conceal

wife n **spouse**, partner, mate, consort *Opposite*: husband

wig v *(dated infml)* **berate**, lambaste, lecture, take to task, dress down ■ n **toupee**, hairpiece, periwig, extension, rug *(infml)*

wiggle v **wriggle**, waggle, twist, jiggle, squirm ■ n **jiggle**, shake, wriggle, twist, waggle

wiggly adj **undulating**, wavy, curved, curvy, curving *Opposite*: straight

wigwam n **tepee**, tent, yurt, hut, lodge

wild adj 1 **untamed**, undomesticated, uncultivated, natural, feral *Opposite*: tame 2 **rough**, desolate, barren, remote, uninhabited *Opposite*: gentle 3 **stormy**, blustery, squally, tempestuous, windswept *Opposite*: calm 4 **enthusiastic**, eager, mad, excited, thrilled *Opposite*: unenthusiastic 5 **rowdy**, undisciplined, riotous, unruly, rough *Opposite*: orderly 6 **overwhelmed**, overcome, overpowered, devastated, destroyed 7 **untidy**, dishevelled, unkempt, tousled, messy *Opposite*: tidy 8 *(infml)* **outrageous**, madcap, foolish, unconventional, irrational *Opposite*: sensible. *See* COMPARE AND CONTRAST *at* **unruly**.

wilderness n **wilds**, rough country, wasteland, desert, outback

wildlife n **flora and fauna**, nature, natural world, environment, biota

wildness n 1 **roughness**, remoteness, desolation, barrenness, harshness 2 **rowdiness**, lack of control, lack of discipline, unruliness, roughness *Opposite*: orderliness 3 **dishevelment**, messiness, scruffiness, untidiness, unruliness *Opposite*: tidiness 4 *(infml)* **recklessness**, madness, foolishness, passion, waywardness

wiles n **tricks**, trickery, guile, deceit, artifice *(fml)*

wilful adj 1 **deliberate**, determined, intentional, conscious, malicious *Opposite*: unwitting 2 **stubborn**, obstinate, headstrong, perverse, obstreperous *Opposite*: compliant. *See* COMPARE AND CONTRAST *at* **unruly**.

wilfulness n 1 **premeditation**, consciousness, deliberateness, maliciousness, malevolence 2 **stubbornness**, obstinacy, perverseness, perversity, obstreperousness *Opposite*: compliance

wiliness n **cunning**, wiles, craftiness, guile, craft *Opposite*: ingenuousness

will n 1 **mind**, brain, consciousness, thoughts, thought processes 2 **determination**, resolve, willpower, motivation, spirit 3 **desire**, inclination, wish, longing, determination 4 *(fml)* **bidding**, command, dictate, wish, desire ■ v **want**, wish, yearn, desire, long

willies *(infml)* n **shakes**, goose pimples, jitters *(infml)*, creeps *(infml)*, shivers *(infml)*

willing adj 1 **prepared**, ready, set, agreeable, disposed *Opposite*: unwilling 2 **eager**, keen, enthusiastic, game, helpful *Opposite*: reluctant

willingly adv 1 **freely**, readily, gladly, happily, cheerfully *Opposite*: unwillingly 2 **eagerly**, enthusiastically, keenly, cooperatively, readily *Opposite*: reluctantly

willingness n 1 **readiness**, inclination, will, preparedness, disposition *Opposite*: unwillingness 2 **enthusiasm**, alacrity, motivation, eagerness, keenness *Opposite*: reluctance

willowy adj 1 **graceful**, slim, elegant, lissom, svelte *Opposite*: stocky 2 **flexible**, bendable, malleable, springy, supple *Opposite*: stiff

willpower n **determination**, resolve, resolution, iron will, strength of will *Opposite*: weakness

willy-nilly adv **regardless**, anyway, in any case, like it or not, unceremoniously ■ adj **haphazard**, random, unsystematic, arbitrary, unselective *Opposite*: methodical

wilt v **droop**, shrivel, wither, fade, wane *Opposite*: flourish

wily adj **crafty**, cunning, guileful, sly, devious *Opposite*: ingenuous

win v 1 **come first**, succeed, triumph, be victorious, be successful *Opposite*: lose 2 **gain**, earn, secure, attain, collect *Opposite*: lose ■ n **victory**, success, triumph, landslide, conquest *Opposite*: defeat

wince n 1 **grimace**, scowl, flinch, gasp, cringe *Opposite*: smile 2 **recoil**, flinch, cringe, jump, start ■ v 1 **grimace**, scowl, shudder, flinch, gasp *Opposite*: smile 2 **recoil**, flinch, jump, cringe, shrink. *See* COMPARE AND CONTRAST *at* **recoil**.

winch n **hoist**, windlass, pulley, crane, capstan ■ v **raise**, hoist, lift, lift up, pull

wind n **current of air**, breeze, gale, squall, gust ■ v 1 **coil**, twist, encircle, roll, wrap around *Opposite*: unwind 2 **snake**, meander, bend, curve, twist

WORD BANK
❑ **types of wind** antitrade, bise, chinook, cyclone, foehn, harmattan, hurricane, khamsin, levanter, mistral, monsoon, northeaster, northwester, Santa Ana, simoom, sirocco, southeaster, southwester, tornado, trade wind, tramontana, typhoon, westerly

windbreak n **shelter**, panel, barrier, screen, fence

wind down v **relax**, unwind, rest, loosen up, hang loose *(infml)*

winded adj **breathless**, out of breath, short of breath, panting, gasping

windfall n **bonus**, handout, bonanza, payout, dividend

winding adj **zigzagging**, snaky, snaking, twisting, curving *Opposite*: straight

windlass n **winch**, hoist, crane, capstan, pulley

window n 1 **pane**, windowpane, glass, glazing 2 **gap**, space, opening, hole 3 **opportunity**, period, chance, slot, window of opportunity 4 **dialogue box**, box, frame, display, interface

---

WORD BANK

❑ **types of window** bay window, casement, dormer window, fanlight, French window, lancet window, picture window, porthole, rose window, sash window, skylight

❑ **parts of a window** ledge, pane, sill, window ledge, windowpane, windowsill

---

windowpane *n* pane, window, glass, glazing

windowsill *n* ledge, window ledge, sill, shelf

windstorm *n* storm, wind, gale, hurricane, cyclone

windswept *adj* desolate, windy, barren, inhospitable, exposed *Opposite*: sheltered

wind up *v* 1 end, conclude, bring to an end, complete, finish *Opposite*: start off 2 **liquidate**, close down, close, shut down, terminate *(fml)* 3 *(infml)* **tease**, have somebody on, kid, fool, pull somebody's leg *(infml)* 4 *(infml)* **infuriate**, enrage, madden, annoy, irritate *Opposite*: amuse

wind-up *n (infml)* **joke**, trick, prank, practical joke, tease ■ *adj* **clockwork**, mechanical, spring-operated, manual

windy *adj* 1 **blustery**, breezy, stormy, gusty, squally *Opposite*: still 2 *(infml)* **wordy**, voluble, verbose, pompous, bombastic *Opposite*: meek

wing *n* 1 **annexe**, extension, part, arm, section 2 **division**, subdivision, arm, section, department ■ *v* 1 **fly**, head, speed, race, whiz 2 **injure**, wound, hurt, maim, shoot

wink *v* flash, twinkle, sparkle, glitter, glint

winkle out *v* extract, worm, draw out, prise, wheedle

winner *n* 1 **victor**, champion, conqueror, leader, frontrunner *(infml)* *Opposite*: loser 2 **success**, hit, sensation, triumph, sure thing *(infml)* *Opposite*: failure

winning *adj* 1 **successful**, triumphant, victorious, best, champion 2 **charming**, captivating, endearing, persuasive, engaging *Opposite*: unprepossessing

winnings *n* prize money, prize, money, earnings, receipts

winnow *v* examine, go through, sort through, pick over, inspect

win over *v* convince, persuade, convert, win round, bring round

winsome *adj* charming, fetching, sweet, lovely, attractive

winter *n* 1 **wintertime**, midwinter, depth of winter *Opposite*: summer 2 **end**, twilight, close, closing, ending

wintriness *n* chilliness, coldness, bitterness, iciness, bleakness *Opposite*: warmth

wintry *adj* chilly, cold, bracing, freezing, nippy *Opposite*: summery

wipe *v* 1 **rub**, polish, mop, swab, clean 2 **erase**, remove, delete, obliterate, destroy 3 **smear**, spread, rub, distribute, streak

wipe out *(infml)* *v* annihilate, destroy, eradicate, obliterate, exterminate *Opposite*: protect

wipe the floor with *(infml)* *v* defeat, beat hollow, thrash, trounce, outclass

wipe the slate clean *(infml)* *v* make a fresh start, start afresh, forgive and forget, bury the hatchet, let bygones be bygones

wire *n* flex, cable, lead, line, filament ■ *v* connect, hook up, install, equip

wired *adj* 1 **strengthened**, supported, reinforced, held together, bound 2 *(infml)* **online**, on the Net, on the Web, connected 3 *(infml)* **energetic**, excited, wound up, hyperactive

wiretap *v* tap, bug, monitor, listen in on, eavesdrop ■ *n* tap, monitor, bug *(infml)*

wiriness *n* 1 **leanness**, slimness, thinness, muscularity, strength *Opposite*: fatness 2 **coarseness**, stiffness, bristliness, roughness, scratchiness *Opposite*: softness

wiry *adj* 1 **lean**, slim, thin, muscular, sinewy *Opposite*: fat 2 **coarse**, stiff, bristly, rough, scratchy *Opposite*: soft

wisdom *n* understanding, sense, knowledge, insight, perception *Opposite*: foolishness

wise *adj* 1 **astute**, intelligent, clever, prudent, sensible *Opposite*: foolish 2 **knowledgeable**, learned, informed, erudite, aware *Opposite*: ignorant 3 **shrewd**, cunning, crafty, devious, wily

wisecrack *(infml)* *n* witticism, quip, riposte, gibe, retort ■ *v* joke, quip, gibe, retort, gag

wish *v* 1 **want**, desire, crave, require, covet 2 **demand**, ask, request, ask for, bid ■ *n* 1 **desire**, aspiration, hope, yearning, longing *Opposite*: disinclination 2 **request**, demand, bidding, command, requirement. *See* COMPARE AND CONTRAST *at* want.

wishful thinking *n* delusion, fantasy, self-delusion, self-deception, idealism *Opposite*: reality

wishy-washy *(infml)* *adj* 1 **indecisive**, irresolute, weak, feeble, spineless *Opposite*: decisive 2 **watery**, insipid, bland, tasteless, weak *Opposite*: strong

wisp *n* strand, scrap, tendril, thread, lock

wispy *adj* flimsy, fine, thin, light, slight *Opposite*: substantial

wistful *adj* pensive, melancholy, thoughtful, reflective, contemplative *Opposite*: satisfied

wistfulness *n* melancholy, pensiveness, reminiscence, nostalgia, dreaminess *Opposite*: contentment

wit *n* 1 **wittiness**, jocularity, facetiousness, fun, humour *Opposite*: seriousness 2 **comedian**, humorist, comic, joker, satirist 3 **intelligence**, smartness, cleverness, intellect, keenness *Opposite*: stupidity

witch *n* enchantress, sorceress, magician, occultist, necromancer *(literary)*

witch doctor *n* shaman, healer, soothsayer, medium, druid

with *prep* **1 together with**, along with, in conjunction with, beside, alongside *Opposite*: without **2 in addition to**, plus, including, as well as, and *Opposite*: without

withdraw *v* **1 remove**, take out, extract, pull out, draw *Opposite*: insert **2 retract**, renounce, disavow, revoke, take back *Opposite*: confirm **3 leave**, depart, retire, pull out, retreat *Opposite*: remain

withdrawal *n* **1 removal**, extraction, drawing, taking out, taking away *Opposite*: insertion **2 retraction**, renunciation, revocation, disclaimer, abjuration *Opposite*: confirmation **3 retreat**, departure, leaving, abandonment, retirement *Opposite*: arrival **4 alienation**, depression, isolation, detachment

withdrawn *adj* **reserved**, inhibited, solitary, introverted, introvert *Opposite*: outgoing

wither *v* **1 shrivel**, wilt, dry up, shrink, droop *Opposite*: bloom **2 weaken**, waste away, decline, fade, wane *Opposite*: strengthen **3 crush**, mortify, humiliate, abash, put down

withering *adj* **contemptuous**, scornful, sarcastic, sneering, arrogant *Opposite*: complimentary

with hindsight *adv* **in retrospect**, retrospectively, looking back, from experience

withhold *v* **hold back**, keep back, refuse, deny, suppress *Opposite*: give

within *adv* **inside**, in, indoors, in the interior *Opposite*: outside

within an ace of *prep* **within reach of**, a hair's-breadth from, a stone's throw from, on the verge of

with-it *(dated infml) adj* **cool**, fashionable, up-to-date, modern, modish

with one accord *(fml) adv* **simultaneously**, as one, in unison, together, unanimously

with one voice *see* **with one accord**

without *prep* **devoid of**, lacking, minus, in default of, sans *(literary) Opposite*: with

without fail *adv* **for certain**, reliably, like clockwork, unfailingly, dependably

without further ado *adv* **immediately**, at once, straightaway, forthwith, without delay

with reason *adv* **rightly**, with good cause, justifiably, justly, properly *Opposite*: unjustifiably

with reference to *see* **with regard to**

with regard to *prep* **regarding**, as regards, relating to, in connection with, concerning

with respect to *see* **with regard to**

withstand *v* **endure**, survive, resist, bear, weather *Opposite*: succumb

witless *adj* **foolish**, stupid, mindless, unintelligent, silly *Opposite*: sensible

witness *n* **observer**, spectator, bystander, onlooker, watcher ■ *v* **1 see**, observe, view, perceive, watch **2 countersign**, endorse, sign, attest, authenticate

wits *n* **reason**, shrewdness, acumen, faculties, mind

witter *(infml) v* **prattle**, gabble, go on, rattle on, chatter

wittering *(infml) n* **chatter**, babble, prattle, gabble, blather *(infml)*

witticism *n* **quip**, joke, riposte, gibe, one-liner

wittiness *n* **cleverness**, sharpness, keenness, comedy, sense of humour *Opposite*: dullness

wittingly *adv* **knowingly**, consciously, purposely, on purpose, intentionally *Opposite*: unwittingly

witty *adj* **amusing**, droll, humorous, funny, entertaining *Opposite*: dull

wiz *(infml) n* **expert**, prodigy, genius, wizard *(infml)*, ace *(infml)*

wizard *n* **1 sorcerer**, warlock, magician, shaman, witch doctor **2** *(infml)* **expert**, prodigy, genius, virtuoso, boffin *(infml)*

wizardry *n* **1 sorcery**, magic, divination, shamanism, spells **2 skill**, expertise, genius, brilliance, accomplishment

wizened *adj* **wrinkled**, lined, wrinkly, withered, crinkly *Opposite*: smooth

wobble *v* **1 shake**, vibrate, tremble, bob, quiver **2 quaver**, wave, shake, vary, oscillate **3 dither**, waver, vacillate, shilly-shally, hesitate *Opposite*: take the plunge

wobbliness *n* **1 shakiness**, unsteadiness, instability, ricketiness, rockiness *Opposite*: steadiness **2** *(infml)* **weakness**, unsteadiness, shakiness, trembling, reeling *Opposite*: steadiness

wobbly *adj* **1 unstable**, unsteady, rickety, rocky, shaky *Opposite*: steady **2** *(infml)* **weak**, trembling, woozy, dizzy, unsteady *Opposite*: fit

wodge *(infml) n* **lump**, chunk, pile, heap, handful *Opposite*: fragment

woe *n* **1 affliction**, misfortune, calamity, disaster, trouble *Opposite*: joy **2 grief**, distress, anguish, affliction, sadness *Opposite*: happiness

woebegone *adj* **miserable**, anguished, despairing, sad, wretched *Opposite*: cheerful

woeful *adj* **1 unhappy**, doleful, sad, sorrowful, mournful *Opposite*: cheerful **2 distressing**, traumatic, harrowing, tragic, unpleasant **3 pathetic**, pitiful, regrettable, bad, inadequate *Opposite*: wonderful

wok *n* **pan**, frying pan, skillet

wolf *n* *(infml)* **Casanova**, Don Juan, Romeo, womanizer, Lothario *(literary)* ■ *v* **gobble**, bolt, gulp down, devour, gorge *Opposite*: nibble

woman *n* **female**, lady, matron *Opposite*: man

womanhood *n* **1 adulthood**, maturity, independence *Opposite*: manhood **2 women**, womankind, females, womenfolk *Opposite*: mankind

womankind *n* **women**, womanhood, females, womenfolk *Opposite*: mankind

womanly *adj* **female**, feminine *Opposite*: manly

wonder n 1 **surprise**, astonishment, awe, amazement, admiration 2 **miracle**, phenomenon, marvel, sensation, curiosity ∎ v 1 **speculate**, doubt, question, conjecture, ponder 2 **marvel**, admire, gaze at, be amazed

wonderful adj 1 **magnificent**, superb, amazing, astonishing, fantastic Opposite: awful 2 **delightful**, pleasing, great, brilliant, perfect

wonderland n **utopia**, paradise, heaven, never-never land, nirvana

wonderment n **amazement**, astonishment, awe, surprise, bewilderment

wonky (infml) adj 1 **unreliable**, unsteady, insecure, wobbly, shaky Opposite: steady 2 **askew**, wrong, uneven, bent, off-centre Opposite: level

wont (fml) adj **accustomed**, used, in the habit of, inclined, liable Opposite: unaccustomed ∎ n **habit**, custom, tendency, preference, practice. See COMPARE AND CONTRAST at **habit**.

woo (literary) v **court**, persuade, encourage, entice, pursue Opposite: discourage

wood n 1 **timber**, firewood, logs, planks, kindling 2 **forest**, woodland, copse, covert, coppice

woodcarving n 1 **carving**, sculpture, woodwork, art, craft 2 **sculpture**, figure, embellishment, adornment, feature

woodcut n 1 **block**, carving, design, matrix 2 **print**, engraving, picture, illustration, portrait

wooded adj **forested**, woody, timbered, arboreal, sylvan (literary)

wooden adj 1 **wood**, timber, woody, ligneous 2 **stilted**, inexpressive, stiff, emotionless, deadpan Opposite: expressive 3 **dull**, toneless, flat Opposite: resonant

woodland n **forest**, wood, woods, timberland

woods n **wood**, forest, woodland, copse, covert

woodshed n **shed**, outbuilding, outhouse, garden shed, lean-to

woodwork n 1 **carpentry**, joinery, cabinetmaking, turning 2 **fittings**, doors, window frames, skirting boards, skirting 3 (infml) **goalpost**, crossbar, upright, goal, post

WORD BANK
❑ **types of woodwork** cabinetmaking, carpentry, carving, joinery, marquetry, woodcarving

woody adj **forested**, wooded, timbered, woodland, arboreal

woof v **bark**, yap, yelp

woolgather v **daydream**, dream, be miles away, fantasize, be lost in thought

woollen adj **knitted**, woven, wool, woolly, crocheted

woollens n **clothing**, sweaters, jumpers, cardigans

woolliness n **vagueness**, vagueness, haziness, haziness, obscurity

woolly adj 1 **woollen**, knitted, woven, wool, crocheted 2 **vague**, confused, unfocused, unclear, ill-defined Opposite: clear

woozy adj **dizzy**, faint, lightheaded, unsteady, nauseous Opposite: clear-headed

word n 1 **term**, expression, name 2 **chat**, conversation, talk, discussion, announcement 3 **information**, news, communication, gen (infml), info (infml) 4 **rumour**, report, whisper, gossip, tittle-tattle 5 **promise**, assurance, guarantee, oath, pledge 6 **command**, order, authorization, say-so (infml), go-ahead (infml) 7 **password**, code word, magic word, key word ∎ v **express**, phrase, couch, utter, articulate

word for word adv **verbatim**, in the same words, faithfully, exactly, precisely Opposite: loosely

word-for-word adj **verbatim**, faithful, exact, precise, accurate Opposite: loose

wordiness n **long-windedness**, verbosity, loquaciousness, prolixity Opposite: succinctness

wording n **phrasing**, words, language, phraseology, diction

wordless adj **silent**, mute, nonverbal, mimed, gestured

word list n **vocabulary**, glossary, dictionary, thesaurus, lexicon

word-perfect adj 1 **verbatim**, word for word, perfect, impeccable, consummate Opposite: unprepared 2 **correct**, accurate, exact, precise, literal

wordplay n **punning**, puns, repartee, wit, banter

WORD BANK
❑ **types of wordplay** acrostic, anagram, logogram, malapropism, palindrome, pun, spoonerism, telestich

words n 1 **argument**, disagreement, difference of opinion, dispute, confrontation 2 **lyrics**, verses, chorus, libretto, text

wordy adj **verbose**, long-winded, rambling, loquacious, prolix Opposite: concise

COMPARE AND CONTRAST CORE MEANING: too long or not concisely expressed
wordy using an excessive number of words in writing or speech; **verbose** expressed in language that is wordy and not precise; **long-winded** tediously wordy in speech or writing; **rambling** excessively long with many changes of subject, making it difficult to follow; **prolix** tiresomely wordy; **diffuse** lacking organization and conciseness.

work n 1 **labour**, employment, job, vocation, occupation Opposite: unemployment 2 **effort**, exertion, labour, toil, slog Opposite: leisure 3 **composition**, design, creation, opus, masterpiece ∎ v 1 **toil**, labour, slog, drudge 2 **perform**, bring about, produce, effect (fml) 3 **succeed**, be successful, thrive, work out, come off *(infml)* **4 operate**, control, drive, run, function

workable *adj* **practical**, practicable, feasible, doable *Opposite*: impracticable

workaday *adj* **everyday**, ordinary, plain, homespun, commonplace *Opposite*: extraordinary

work against *v* **counteract**, cancel out, oppose, run counter to, interfere with *Opposite*: support

workaholic *n* **overachiever**, type A, workhorse *(infml) Opposite*: idler

workbench *n* **bench**, worktop, work surface, worktable

workbook *n* **exercise book**, schoolbook, notebook, jotter, notepad

worked up *(infml) adj* **agitated**, upset, excited, worried, hot and bothered *Opposite*: calm

worker *n* **employee**, member of staff, hand, operative, wage earner

work force *n* **personnel**, staff, employees, workers, human resources

workhorse *(infml) n* **hard worker**, good worker, rock, mainstay, pillar

working *adj* **1 operational**, functioning, effective, running *Opposite*: broken **2 employed**, occupied, at work, in work, salaried *Opposite*: unemployed

working class *n* **manual workers**, hoi polloi, the masses, proletariat, wage-earners *Opposite*: aristocracy

working group *n* **task force**, team, working party, committee, unit

working out *n* **exercising**, physical exercise, exercise, training, physical training

working party *see* **working group**

workings *n* **mechanism**, machinery, works, moving parts

workload *n* **amount of work**, assignment, job, load, capacity

workmate *n* **colleague**, coworker, fellow worker

work of art *n* **1 objet d'art**, creation, painting, sculpture, picture **2 masterpiece**, beauty, tour de force, pièce de résistance, work of genius *Opposite*: disaster *(infml)*

work on *v* **1 develop**, hone, build up, work up, perfect **2 influence**, sway, persuade, pressurize, pressure

work out *v* **1 exercise**, train, drill **2 solve**, figure out, decipher, resolve, deduce **3 understand**, comprehend, make sense of, fathom, conceive **4 plan**, devise, outline, sketch, arrange. *See* COMPARE AND CONTRAST *at* **deduce**.

workout *n* **1 exercise session**, exercises, training, aerobics, callisthenics **2 test**, road test, trial, run

workplace *n* **place of work**, workshop, workstation, work, office

workroom *n* **room**, workshop, study, office, studio

works *n* **1 factory**, plant, installation, industrial unit, manufacturing plant **2 mechanism**, workings, machinery, moving parts **3 *(infml)* everything**, the whole thing, the lot, all of it, the whole kit and caboodle *(infml)*

worksheet *n* **1 homework sheet**, handout, test, quiz, question sheet **2 schedule**, job sheet, log, record

workshy *adj* **lazy**, idle, indolent, slothful, apathetic

workspace *n* **working area**, workstation, workplace, booth, cubicle

workstation *n* **workplace**, workspace, computer terminal

work surface *n* **surface**, worktop, workbench, workspace, work unit

worktop *n* **counter**, bench, work surface

work to rule *v* **go slow**, take industrial action, slow down

work-to-rule *n* **go-slow**, industrial action, slowdown *(US)*

work up *v* **1 develop**, work on, hone, improve, refine **2 agitate**, upset, disturb, provoke, irritate *Opposite*: calm

workup *n* **diagnosis**, examination, checkup, medical

world *n* **1 Earth**, planet, globe **2 biosphere**, ecosphere, creation, all God's creatures, flora and fauna **3 humankind**, humanity, the human race **4 domain**, realm, sphere, circle, area

world-beater *n* **champion**, superstar, one in a million, star, classic

world-class *adj* **first-rate**, first-class, superlative, outstanding, topnotch *(infml)*

world-famous *adj* **famous**, renowned, popular, acclaimed, notorious *Opposite*: unknown

worldliness *n* **1 materialism**, consumerism, acquisitiveness, greed, secularism **2 experience**, knowledge, sophistication, worldly wisdom

worldly *adj* **1 material**, temporal, earthly, materialistic, human **2 experienced**, sophisticated, mature, knowing, worldly wise *Opposite*: naive

worldly goods *n* **possessions**, belongings, assets, property

worldly-wise *adj* **sophisticated**, experienced, mature, knowing, worldly *Opposite*: naive

world-weariness *n* **discontent**, melancholy, boredom, ennui

world-weary *adj* **jaded**, discontented, bored, melancholic

worldwide *adj* **universal**, international, all-inclusive, wide-reaching, global *Opposite*: local

worm-eaten *adj* **1 wormy**, worm-infested, holey, rotten, decaying **2 dilapidated**, ramshackle, tumbledown, rickety

worm out *v* **elicit**, find out, coax out, ferret out, inveigle

worn *adj* **damaged**, shabby, tatty, dog-eared, dilapidated

worried *adj* **concerned**, anxious, apprehensive, nervous, bothered *Opposite*: unconcerned

worrier *n* **pessimist**, neurotic, fidget, worry-guts *(infml)*, fusspot *(infml)*

worrisome *adj* **troublesome**, worrying, annoying, irritating, bothersome

worry *v* **1 be anxious**, fret, be troubled, be concerned, be bothered **2 annoy**, pester, bother, trouble, disturb **3 touch**, pick, interfere with, claw at, tear at ■ *n* **anxiety**, unease, disquiet, discomfort, care

COMPARE AND CONTRAST CORE MEANING: a troubled mind

worry a troubled state of mind resulting from concern about current or potential difficulties; **unease** a feeling of anxiousness or lack of satisfaction with a situation; **care** a state of troubled anxiety; **anxiety** nervous apprehension about a future event or a general fear of possible misfortune; **angst** nonspecific chronic anxiety about the human condition or the state of the world; **stress** the worry and nervous apprehension related to a particular situation or event, for example a job or the process of moving house.

worrying *adj* **perturbing**, disturbing, upsetting, disquieting, nerve-racking *Opposite*: reassuring

worse *adj* **not as good as**, inferior, of inferior quality, poorer, of poorer quality *Opposite*: better

worsen *v* **1 get worse**, deteriorate, degenerate, go downhill, degrade *Opposite*: improve **2 make something worse**, exacerbate, aggravate, impair, inflame *Opposite*: improve

worsening *n* **deterioration**, aggravation, degeneration, decline *Opposite*: improvement

worship *v* **adore**, love, revere, adulate, deify ■ *n* **adoration**, love, reverence, respect, devotion

worshipful *adj* **reverential**, respectful, reverent, deferential, adoring

worshipper *n* **celebrant**, adorer, venerator, participant, believer

worst *adj* **nastiest**, vilest, poorest, wickedest, foulest *Opposite*: best

worth *n* **1 value**, price, cost, rate **2 merit**, appeal, significance, attraction, importance **3 wealth**, means, assets, value, substance

worthiness *n* **1 merit**, value, worth, praiseworthiness **2 dullness**, earnestness, boringness

worthless *adj* **1 valueless**, of no value, of little worth, insignificant, useless *Opposite*: valuable **2 empty**, hollow, meaningless, futile, pointless

worthlessness *n* **1 insignificance**, unimportance, irrelevance, triviality *Opposite*: value **2 pointlessness**, meaninglessness, futility, emptiness, hollowness

worthwhile *adj* **valuable**, useful, meaningful, sensible, advisable *Opposite*: worthless

worthy *adj* **1 commendable**, praiseworthy, laudable, admirable, valuable **2 well-intentioned**, well-meaning, earnest, pedestrian, dull

would-be *adj* **hopeful**, aspiring, prospective, budding, potential

wound *n* **injury**, lesion, cut, gash, sore ■ *v* **1 injure**, hurt, harm, damage, mutilate **2 offend**, upset, hurt, injure, distress

wounded *adj* **1 injured**, hurt, suffering **2 offended**, hurt, upset, distressed, aggrieved

wounding *adj* **hurtful**, cutting, acerbic, sharp *Opposite*: kind

wow *(infml)* *n* **winner**, smash, triumph, sensation, knockout *(infml)* *Opposite*: flop *(infml)*

wraith *n* **ghost**, phantom, apparition, spirit, spectre

wrangle *v* **argue**, dispute, quarrel, bicker, squabble ■ *n* **dispute**, argument, quarrel, squabble, disagreement

wrap *v* **1 enfold**, drape, swathe, cover, envelop **2 wrap up**, gift wrap, package *Opposite*: unwrap ■ *n* **1 shawl**, cloak, stole, cape **2 wrapping**, packaging, casing, covering

wrapper *n* **covering**, wrapping, wrap, cover, packaging

wrapping *n* **packaging**, covering, casing, wrap, cover

wrap up *v* **1 wrap**, gift wrap, parcel, package *Opposite*: unwrap **2 dress warmly**, muffle up, bundle up *(infml)* **3 conclude**, complete, finish, finish off, end *Opposite*: begin

wrath *n* **anger**, rage, fury, madness, ire *(fml)*. *See* COMPARE AND CONTRAST *at* anger.

wrathful *adj* **furious**, angry, irate, enraged, fuming

wreak *v* **cause**, do, inflict, create, bring about

wreath *n* **garland**, circlet, headdress, laurel

wreathe *v* **1 adorn**, cover, garland, swathe, festoon **2 twist**, writhe, coil, wind

wreck *v* **destroy**, ruin, demolish, break, shatter ■ *n* **ruin**, remains, wreckage, shell, hulk

wreckage *n* **ruins**, remains, debris, wreck, rubble

wrecked *adj* **1 broken**, smashed, damaged, ruined, cracked **2** *(infml)* **exhausted**, worn-out, bushed *(infml)*, done in *(infml)*

wrench *v* **1 strain**, injure, hurt, pull, sprain **2 pull**, tug, haul, heave, jerk ■ *n* **1 injury**, sprain, strain, crick **2 pull**, tug, haul, heave, jerk

wrest *v* **1 gain**, take, seize, grasp **2 grab**, snatch, tug, pull

wrestle *v* **struggle**, fight, grapple, tussle, brawl

wretch *n* **1 unfortunate**, victim, languisher, sufferer, poor thing **2 rogue**, rascal, imp, horror *(infml)*, scallywag *(dated infml)* **3** *(fml)* **scoundrel**, rascal, rogue, villain, blackguard

wretched adj **1 miserable**, desolate, heart-broken, pitiful, dejected Opposite: happy **2 harsh**, hard, deprived, inferior Opposite: comfortable **3 worthless**, base, despicable, inadequate, inferior Opposite: noble **4 irritating**, annoying, infuriating, frustrating, exasperating

wriggle v **wiggle**, writhe, turn, squirm, twist

wring v **squeeze**, twist, mangle, press, compress

wrinkle n **crease**, crinkle, line, fold, furrow ■ v **screw**, crumple, crinkle, crease, fold Opposite: smooth

wrinkled adj **1 crumpled**, creased, crinkly, rucked, rumpled Opposite: smooth **2 wrinkly**, wizened, weathered, lined, furrowed Opposite: smooth

wrinkly see **wrinkled**

writ n **summons**, court order, injunction, restraining order

write v **1 inscribe**, put pen to paper, transcribe, engrave, carve **2 write down**, put in writing, note down, enter, record **3 compose**, create, script, author, devise **4 send a letter to**, drop a line to, correspond with, contact, get in touch with

write down v **record**, note down, jot down, set down, put in writing

write off v **1** (infml) **cancel**, forget, disregard, set aside, abandon **2 wreck**, ruin, destroy, demolish, total (US slang)

writer n **author**, novelist, playwright, poet, journalist

write-up n **report**, article, piece, review, critique

writhe v **squirm**, wriggle, twist, struggle, thrash

writing n **1 script**, symbols, inscription, marks, characters **2 text**, literature, prose, journalism, copy

written adj **on paper**, printed, in black and white, in print

wrong adj **1 incorrect**, mistaken, erroneous, off beam, wide of the mark Opposite: right **2 immoral**, wicked, dishonest, illegal, sinful Opposite: right **3 amiss**, not right, unsuitable, improper, inappropriate Opposite: suitable ■ n **sin**, crime, injury, harm, damage ■ v **insult**, injure, wound, harm, ill-treat

wrongdoer n **criminal**, offender, sinner, reprobate, outlaw

wrongdoing n **bad behaviour**, unlawful activity, crime, offence, misconduct

wrong-foot v **catch out**, surprise, take unawares, take by surprise, trip up

wrongful adj **illegal**, unlawful, unfair, unjust, criminal Opposite: rightful. See COMPARE AND CONTRAST at **unlawful**.

wrong-headed adj **1 unreasonable**, obstinate, stubborn, perverse **2 irrational**, unreasoning, unthinking, ill-considered, ill-conceived

wrought-up adj **tense**, nervous, agitated, excited, on edge

wry adj **ironic**, cynical, sardonic, dry, droll

wryness n **humour**, irony, satire, dryness, drollness

XYZ

xenophobia n **chauvinism**, racial intolerance, dislike of foreigners, nationalism, prejudice Opposite: tolerance

xenophobic adj **chauvinistic**, intolerant, nationalistic, prejudiced, racist Opposite: tolerant

yak (infml) v **chatter**, chat, talk, gossip, natter

yammer (infml) v **chatter**, chat, talk, gossip, natter

yank v **pull**, tug, jerk, wrench, snatch ■ n **tug**, pull, jerk, wrench, heave. See COMPARE AND CONTRAST at **pull**.

yap v **1 bark**, yelp, bay, woof **2** (infml) **chatter**, chat, talk, gossip

yard n **1 patio**, courtyard, terrace, back yard **2 enclosure**, work area, storage area

yardstick n **measure**, index, gauge, benchmark, standard

yarn n **1 thread**, fibre, wool **2** (infml) **story**, tale, tall story, shaggy dog story, anecdote

yawn v **1 stretch**, stretch yourself, rub your eyes, sigh, nod **2 gape**, split, fly open, gap, crack Opposite: close up ■ n **bore**, nonevent, waste of time, mind-numbing experience, drag (infml) Opposite: laugh

yawning adj **deep**, cavernous, gaping, wide, open Opposite: narrow

yearbook n **annual**, annual report, almanac

yearly adj **annual**, twelve-monthly, year on year ■ adv **annually**, every year, once a year

yearn v **desire**, long, crave, ache, hanker. See COMPARE AND CONTRAST at **want**.

yearning n **desire**, longing, yen, hunger, thirst

year-round adj **constant**, continual, continuous, perennial Opposite: seasonal

years n **an age**, an inordinate length of time, aeons, ages (infml), centuries (infml)

yell v **shout**, scream, shriek, roar, bellow ■ n **shriek**, shout, scream, roar, bellow

yell at v **scold**, shout at, tear off a strip, rebuke, lash

yelp v **bark**, yap, cry, squeal, squeak

yen n **urge**, desire, wish, longing, yearning

yes adv **affirmative**, sure, certainly, absolutely, of course Opposite: no ■ n **affirmative**, positive response, nod, aye, thumbs-up (infml) Opposite: no

yesteryear n **past**, long ago, former times, days gone by, olden days Opposite: today

yet adv **1 up till now**, so far, thus far, hitherto, until now **2 however**, nevertheless, nonetheless, still, in spite of that

yield v **1 produce**, bear, generate, bring in, return **2 give in**, submit, surrender, succumb, capitulate Opposite: resist **3 give up**, concede, grant, relinquish, resign Opposite: keep ■ n **1 harvest**, crop, produce, vintage **2 profit**, earnings, income, revenue, return

COMPARE AND CONTRAST CORE MEANING: give way

yield give way to something such as force, pressure, entreaty, or persuasion; **capitulate** cease to resist a superior force, especially one that seems invincible, sometimes without having offered strong opposition; **submit** accept somebody else's authority or will, especially reluctantly or under pressure; **succumb** give in to something due to weakness or the failure to offer effective opposition; **surrender** give way to the power of another person and stop offering resistance, usually after active opposition.

yielding adj **1 soft**, elastic, springy, squashy, resilient Opposite: firm **2 compliant**, acquiescent, docile, accommodating, tractable Opposite: stubborn

yob (infml) n **thug**, vandal, hoodlum, yobbo (infml), hooligan (infml)

yoke n **repression**, oppression, burden, bondage, encumbrance

yomp (infml) v **trudge**, march, clump, stomp, clomp

young adj **1 youthful**, little, juvenile, adolescent, immature Opposite: old **2 new**, early, undeveloped, fledgling, beginning Opposite: established ■ n **offspring**, children, babies, litter, brood

WORD BANK
❑ types of young animal **bullock, calf, colt, cub, fawn, foal, heifer, joey, kid, kitten, lamb, leveret, piglet, pup, puppy, whelp, yearling**
❑ types of young bird **chick, cygnet, duckling, eaglet, eyas, fledgling, gosling, nestling, owlet, pullet, squab**

younger generation n **young people**, youth, teenagers, adolescents, youngsters

young person n **teenager**, adolescent, youngster, juvenile, child Opposite: adult

youngster n **child**, young person, teenager, youth, adolescent Opposite: adult. See COMPARE AND CONTRAST at **youth**.

youth n **1 childhood**, adolescence, formative years, infancy, early life Opposite: adulthood **2 child**, teenager, youngster, minor, young person Opposite: adult

COMPARE AND CONTRAST CORE MEANING: somebody who is young

youth a man or boy who is in his teens or early twenties; **child** a young person between birth and the onset of puberty; **kid** (infml) a child or young person; **teenager** somebody between the ages of thirteen and nineteen; **youngster** somebody who is young, or somebody younger than others mentioned or present.

youthful adj **1 young**, childlike, childish, boyish, girlish Opposite: old **2 vigorous**, energetic, lively, enthusiastic, active Opposite: sluggish

youthfulness n **1 youth**, freshness, newness, childishness, first flush of youth Opposite: age **2 enthusiasm**, energy, radiance, vigour, liveliness Opposite: sluggishness

yowl v **howl**, squall, squeal, wail, caterwaul

yucky (infml) adj **nasty**, revolting, horrid, unpleasant, disgusting Opposite: yummy (infml)

yummy (infml) adj **delicious**, tasty, mouthwatering, delectable, luscious Opposite: yucky (infml)

zany adj **unconventional**, madcap, crazy (infml), wacky (infml)

zap (infml) v **1 destroy**, kill, annihilate, exterminate, delete **2 change channels**, switch channels, flick through, cruise, surf **3 whiz**, zoom, tear, rip, shoot Opposite: dawdle

zappy (infml) adj **lively**, forceful, striking, eye-catching, energetic

zeal n **enthusiasm**, passion, fanaticism, fervour, ardour Opposite: apathy

zealot n **extremist**, fanatic, bigot, evangelist, dogmatist Opposite: moderate

zealous adj **enthusiastic**, keen, passionate, fervent, ardent Opposite: apathetic

zenith n **peak**, summit, pinnacle, top, acme Opposite: nadir

zeppelin n **airship**, dirigible, blimp, aircraft, balloon

zero n **nothing**, nil, nought, zilch (infml)

zest n **1 enthusiasm**, keenness, gusto, relish, appetite Opposite: apathy **2 taste**, tang, piquancy, bite, spice

zestful adj **enthusiastic**, keen, passionate, dynamic, energetic Opposite: apathetic

zigzag v **wind**, meander, crisscross, weave, snake

zilch (infml) n **nothing**, zero, nil, nought

zillion (infml) n **squillion**, million, billion, shed-load, truckload